Production/ Operations Management

Quality, Performance, and Value

Fifth Edition

James R. Evans

University of Cincinnati

West Publishing Company

Minneapolis/Saint Paul
New York
Los Angeles
San Francisco

Dedication

To Beverly, Kristin, and Lauren

British Library Cataloguing-in-Publication Data.
A catalogue record for this book is available from the
British Library.

Library of Congress Cataloging-in-Publication Data
Evans, James R. (James Robert), 1950-
    Production/operations management:
        quality, performance, and value
  James R. Evans. — 5th ed.
        p.   cm.
    Includes bibliographical references and index.
    ISBN 0-314-06247-5 (hard : alk. paper)
    1. Production management.   2. Factory
management.   I. Title.
TS155.E82   1997   96-1000
658.5—dc20   CIP

Production Credits

Text Design: David J. Farr, ImageSmythe
Composition: Carlisle Communications, Ltd.
Copyediting: Maggie Jarpey
Editorial Services: Emily McNamara
Indexing: Sandi Schroeder, Schroeder Indexing Service

Cover Images: **Top left** Photo courtesy of The Document
Company, Xerox; **Top right** Used with permission of
Eastman Chemical Company; **Bottom left** Chevron
Corporation; **Bottom right** Photo courtesy of Wainwright
Industries, Inc.; **Background image** Chevron
Corporation.

West's Commitment to the Environment

 TEXT IS PRINTED ON 10% POST CONSUMER RECYCLED PAPER

 Printed with **Printwise**
Environmentally Advanced Water Washable Ink

Contents in Brief

Contents

PART II Strategic Issues in Operations 173

Supplemental Chapters

Appendixes

Preface

The purpose of *Production/Operations Management: Quality, Performance, and Value,* Fifth Edition, is to provide students of business administration with a sound understanding of the concepts, techniques, and applications of contemporary production and operations management (P/OM). As we approach the next century, our country's need for improvements in quality and productivity has never been so great. Our international competitiveness and survival in the global marketplace depend upon our ability to make these improvements—and that requires that students in all functional areas of business acquire a body of basic knowledge and appreciations that can be applied in their future jobs. This philosophy is the basis of this book.

Production/Operations Management combines the managerial issues of P/OM with technical tools and quantitative applications. Practical applications in actual manufacturing and service organizations are described throughout the book and in the innovative end-of-chapter "P/OM in Practice" feature.

Changes in Fifth Edition

In preparing this edition, the author was influenced greatly by recent experience as an examiner for the Malcolm Baldrige National Quality Award. The Baldrige criteria represent a philosophy of managing operations built upon the foundation of total quality principles. The 1995 revised criteria, in particular, make it clear that the pursuit of quality, performance, and value is a basic business philosophy. This belief underlies the definition of P/OM given in Chapter 1: *The purpose of operations management is to deliver ever improving value for customers through the continuous improvement of overall company performance and capabilities.* The core concepts underlying the Baldrige criteria provide a natural framework for viewing the field of production and operations management, and thus are integrated strongly throughout this edition, though without an explicit focus on the Baldrige award itself. As a result of this new orientation, several major changes have been made in the organization and content of this edition, which are reflected in the new title. All chapters have been streamlined, updated, and revised where appropriate with new explanatory material, new "P/OM in Practice" cases, and new real-world examples, designated as "Applied P/OM" features. Several new chapter have been written as well. In addition, a pizza restaurant scenario has been added throughout the book to illustrate and explain P/OM concepts in a simple setting that would be very familiar to students.

Organization

The book's content is logically organization into five parts and a set of supplementary quantitative-methods chapters:

Part I: Foundation of P/OM. The first five chapters provide foundation material on basic concepts and issues in P/OM: the concept of customer value, managing for quality and high performance, the role of P/OM in strategic planning, the importance of measurement of operations' processes and results, and the operations manager's role in human resources.

Part II: Strategic Issues in Operations. Chapters 6 through 8 focus on strategic product design and development, forecasting and capacity planning, and facility location and distribution system design.

Part III: Designing and Managing Production Processes. Chapters 9 through 12 deal with the issues of process technology and design, workplace design and layout, process management, and statistical quality control.

Part IV: Managing Materials. This section includes an introduction to materials and inventory management, quantitative decision models for inventory management, and lean production—emphasizing JIT and constraint management.

Part V: Planning and Scheduling. This part consists primarily of operational activities: aggregate planning and master scheduling, material requirements planning, operations scheduling, production-activity control, and project planning and management.

Supplementary Chapters. Discussions of quantitative methods appear in the five supplementary chapters at the back of the book. This gives the instructor flexibility in selecting and sequencing quantitative material in the course design.

In addition, tables useful in many quantitative computations, a comprehensive glossary of key terms, and solutions to selected problems are found at the end of the book.

Content

To reflect the new emphasis of this edition, several new chapters have been written and others have been reorganized or substantially revised. When appropriate, each chapter has been updated to reflect new and current trends in P/OM. Also, each chapter with quantitative material now has a section of "Solved Problems" to help the student better understand these techniques. End-of-chapter questions are broken into two sections: (1) "Review Questions" test the student's basic understanding of concepts introduced in the chapter, and (2) "Discussion Questions" invite the student to apply the concepts to his or her own experiences or pose thought-provoking issues that have no stock answers. These provide a rich source of classroom discussion.

The key changes in individual chapters are described below.

••• *Chapter 1: Introduction to Production and Operations Management.* This chapter lays a new foundation for the importance of P/OM in today's global competitive environment, focusing on the major themes that have characterized P/OM in the past half-century. Collectively, these form the basis for what may be called "total quality management": a focus on customer value through lean and efficient production efforts. Management-science methods are introduced in the appendix to this chapter.

••• *Chapter 2: Managing for Quality and High Performance.* This chapter, which focuses on productivity/quality management principles, has been substantially revised to include more contemporary views of quality management, particularly those that form the basis for the Malcolm Baldrige National Quality Award. Also included is a description of ISO 9000 and a comparison of it with the Baldrige criteria.

••• *Chapter 3: P/OM and Strategic Planning.* This chapter has been substantially revised to focus on key issues of strategy that relate to competitive advantage and the role that quality and manufacturing play in strategic planning. Also included is a new section on strategy formulation and deployment as practiced by today's leading companies.

••• *Chapter 4: Measuring Operations Performance.* This is a new chapter that addresses the scope of performance measurement in operations, including suppliers, product and service quality, business support services, and company operational results. Productivity and cost-of-quality measurement are integrated into this discussion. A section on managing quality and performance data focuses on reliability, accessibility, and analysis of data.

••• *Chapter 5: Work Design and Human Resource Management.* This chapter consolidates and expands upon materials found in other chapters in the previous edition. It focuses on human resource management issues that are relevant to operations managers, particularly concepts of empowerment and teamwork, and the design of high-performance work systems.

••• *Chapter 6: Product Design and Development.* This chapter includes a heavier focus on quality within the product-design function. New or expanded topics include quality-function deployment, robust design, teamwork, and service/product design.

••• *Chapter 7: Forecasting and Capacity Planning.* Forecasting is now tied more closely to capacity planning. This chapter provides an introduction to forecasting needs and approaches; the appendix (formerly a supplementary chapter) discusses quantitative forecasting techniques in depth.

••• *Chapter 8: Facility Location and Distribution System Design.* A new section on push and pull distribution systems has been included in this chapter.

••• *Chapter 9: Process Technology and Design.* Several chapters from the previous edition dealing with process technology, design, and work methods have been reorganized to provide a better focus and foundation for process management. In addition, the role of automation has been toned down. This chapter introduces process technology and automation, its strategic importance, and key issues in designing production processes.

••• *Chapter 10: Workplace Design and Facility Layout.* Layout and workplace design have been brought together in this new chapter, establishing better ties between macro- and micro- design issues.

••• *Chapter 11: Process Management.* This a new chapter that addresses fundamental issues of quality control and process improvement. It logically follows issues of process and workplace design, introducing techniques for defect prevention, total productive maintenance, and continuous improvement.

••• *Chapter 12: Statistical Quality Control.* This chapter, which was at the end of the previous edition, has been moved up to reflect the growing importance of quality as well as to support the principles of process management introduced in Chapter 11. A new section on c- and u- charts has been included and acceptance sampling has been de-emphasized.

••• *Chapter 13: Materials and Inventory Management.* New discussions on supplier partnerships and the use of information technology for materials management have been added. The production lot-size model has been moved to Chapter 14, and service levels and demand uncertainty have been included in this chapter to better integrate EOQ (economic order quantity) models and applications.

••• *Chapter 14: Decision Models for Inventory Management.* This chapter now follows "Materials and Inventory Management," providing a more logical organization of topics than before.

••• *Chapter 15: Lean Production: Just-in-Time and Synchronous Manufacturing.* This chapter has been substantially revised to provide a more contemporary focus on JIT and its essential elements and a new treatment of constraint management. Both JIT and constraint management are cast within the context of lean production.

••• *Chapter 16: Aggregate Production Planning and Master Scheduling.* The transportation model for aggregate planning, which was dropped from the previous edition, has been returned to accommodate the wishes of several reviewers.

••• *Chapter 17: Material Requirements Planning.* The MRP time-phasing matrix now includes a row for "planned order receipts" and the discussion of the contrasts among JIT, MRP, and constraint management has been simplified.

••• *Chapter 18: Operations Scheduling and Production-Activity Control.* This chapter has been reorganized around principles of finite capacity scheduling to better reflect current practice. A section on constraint-based scheduling (drum-buffer-rope) has been added.

••• *Chapter 19: Project Planning and Management.* Sections on cost estimating and budgeting and budget control have been added.

••• *Supplementary Chapters.* A section describing the simplex method for linear programming has been added to the linear programming supplement.

Spreadsheets

Recognizing the growing use of spreadsheets in business, Microsoft Excel applications are used wherever appropriate. All named spreadsheet files can be made available to professors and students. Problems that refer directly to these templates are designated with the symbol: ▐█ .

Flexibility

Production/Operations Management, provides the instructor with substantial flexibility in selecting topics to meet specific course needs. For example, instructors who wish to focus on the broad managerial issues of P/OM (particularly if their students have had prior exposure to management-science techniques) with less emphasis on quantitative approaches might use this one-quarter course outline:

••• Introduction to P/OM (Chapter 1)

••• Managing for Quality and High Performance (Chapter 2)

••• P/OM and Strategic Planning (Chapter 3)

••• Measuring Operations Performance (Chapter 4)

••• Work Design and Human Resource Management (Chapter 5)

••• Product Design and Development (Chapter 6)

- Technology and design issues (selected sections from Chapters 9 and 10)
- Process Management (Chapter 11)
- Materials and Inventory Management (Chapter 12)
- Lean Production and Synchronous Manufacturing (Chapter 15)

On the other hand, instructors who desire more emphasis on quantitative techniques and management-science applications in P/OM might use this one-quarter course outline:

- Introduction to P/OM (Chapter 1)
- Managing for Quality and High Performance (Chapter 2)
- Measuring Operations Performance (Chapter 4)
- Selected supplementary chapters on management science
- Forecasting and Capacity Planning (Chapter 7)
- Facility Location and Distribution System Design (Chapter 8)
- Technology and design issues (selected sections from Chapters 9 and 12)
- Inventory-management issues and models (selected sections from Chapters 13 and 14)

Selected sections from:

- Aggregate Production Planning and Master Scheduling (Chapter 16)
- Material Requirements Planning (Chapter 17)
- Operations Scheduling and Production-Activity Control (Chapter 18)
- Project Planning, Scheduling, and Control (Chapter 19)

One-semester courses can expand in either direction, depending on the instructor's orientation and the students' knowledge and experience. It is probably impossible to cover adequately all material in the book in one semester.

Acknowledgements

I express my appreciation to all those colleagues who have reviewed the manuscript for this and previous editions and provided many valuable comments. I have made every effort to respond to the "customer needs" they have voiced and to continuously improve the book. The reviewers who have provided significant input for this edition include:

Benjamin L. Abramowitz
University of Central Florida

Harold P. Benson
University of Florida

Dinesh S. Dave
Appalachian State University

Donald R. Edwards
Baylor University

Lawrence D. Fredendall
Clemson University

F. Theodore Helmer
Northern Arizona University

Tim C. Ireland
Oklahoma State University

Sanjay Lillaney
Rutgers University-Newark

Barbara A. Osyk
University of Akron

Diane H. Parente
SUNY College-Fredonia

Richard A. Reid
The University of New Mexico

Roger C. Schoenfeldt
Murray State University

Girish Shambu
Canisius College

Mandyam M. Srinivasan
The University of Tennessee-Knoxville

Sam G. Taylor
University of Wyoming

Special appreciation goes to Tim Shannon, manager of Mio's Pizzeria—Mt. Washington, in Cincinnati, from whom many of the ideas for the "MamaMia's" scenarios throughout the book were developed. I also thank my editors, Mary Schiller, Esther Craig, and Amy Gabriel, and other at West Publishing Company for their continued excellent support.

James R. Evans
Cincinnati, Ohio

In Part I we introduce some fundamental issues of production and operations management (P/OM). Chapter 1 introduces the concept of a production system and traces the evolution of P/OM from a focus on output and efficiency to today's focus on quality, customer satisfaction, and value. Included are an overview of the various decision areas and questions that operations managers must address in designing and operating effective production systems. The chapter appendix introduces techniques of management science in P/OM.

Chapter 2 focuses on principles of quality and productivity management. The needs to improve productivity and to enhance quality are major considerations in operations management decisions, and such improvements can have a significant impact on cost and profitability. The Malcolm Baldrige National Quality Award framework has influenced greatly the way in which today's businesses are managed. The core principles that underlie the Baldrige criteria, and can be seen throughout the book, are introduced here.

Chapter 3 casts P/OM planning and decisions within the overall framework of strategic business planning. Today, planning to meet high-level financial and marketing objectives is intimately tied with planning to achieve quality and operational performance goals. These are important elements of achieving competitive advantage.

Chapter 4 describes the scope and role of performance measurement in operations—ways in which operations managers can assess how well they are doing and identify areas for improvement. The ways include measuring the performance of suppliers, product and service quality, business support services, and company operational results.

Chapter 5 concludes Part I by discussing the role of work design and human resource management in achieving quality and productivity objectives. Important human resource issues that affect operations managers include empowerment, teamwork, and approaches to designing high-performance work systems.

Part I
Foundations
of P/OM

Chapter One
Introduction to Production and Operations Management

Chapter Outline

Appendix: Management Science Models in P/OM

MamaMia's Pizza is a small, family-oriented restaurant. It has seating capacity for about 30 customers and also provides delivery within a limited local area. As a student, you have most likely patronized a similar business. Like any business, MamaMia's has three major management concerns: (1) acquiring the capital to start and continue to run the business—the *finance* function; (2) attracting customers, selling, and distributing the products—the *marketing* function; and (3) making products and delivering services—the *production* or *operations* function. From that perspective, managing a pizza parlor is not much different from managing a manufacturing plant, hotel, hospital, or bank. All require good financial management, marketing expertise, and skills in managing operations.

We typically use the term **production** to denote the process of converting or transforming resources—materials, machines, employees, time—into goods or services. The goods and services might be automobiles, computers, health care, or financial transactions. Many people equate the term *production* with manufacturing; however, it applies equally to the creation of services and to "quasi-manufacturing" activities such as the development of computer software. The term **operations** broadly describes the set of all activities associated with the production of goods and services. Operations involves not only production, but also *transportation,* whereby the location of something or someone is changed; *supply,* whereby the ownership or possession of goods is changed; and *service,* the principal characteristic of which is the treatment or accommodation of something or someone. MamaMia's restaurant is a good example of each of those activities. The basic tasks of preparing, cooking, and packaging pizzas are essentially production functions. Delivering pizzas to customers' homes involves transportation, supply, and service. Providing food for pickup or dining in involves both supply and service.

Managing the resources needed to produce goods and services is called **production/operations management (P/OM),** or simply **operations management.** (In this book we use those terms interchangeably.) This chapter explains the concept, scope, and purpose of P/OM in manufacturing and service organizations. Specifically, it addresses:

••• The importance of operations management in creating customer value.

••• The types of activities in which operations managers engage, and the hierarchical nature of planning and decision making.

••• The structure of production systems in manufacturing and service.

••• How P/OM has evolved during the twentieth century and the challenges operations managers face today and may face in the future.

Operations Management for Competitive Success

Why is P/OM necessary? Recent history provides the answer to that question. Many industries, especially in the manufacturing sector, struggled just to survive during the 1980s. The U.S. share of the world auto market dropped substantially, and nearly all consumer electronics products now come from Japan and other Asian nations. Many other industries as well, including machine tools, computers, steel, and cameras, have been devastated by foreign competitors. In 1987 *Business Week* posed a stern warning: "Unless the United States gets its manufacturing operations back in shape—and fast—it could lose any hope of maintaining the foundation on which tomorrow's prosperity rests."[1] Even in the service industry, foreign competition has stiffened. Most of the largest banks in the world, for example, are Japanese.

Companies tried various financial and marketing approaches to alleviate the situation during the 1980s. Billions of dollars were poured into new domestic facilities and equipment—more than $40 billion was invested in the auto industry alone—and yet the United States continued to lose ground.[2] At the same time, manufacturing productivity and the quality of goods produced continued to improve at a faster rate in foreign countries than in the United States. Marketing campaigns emphasizing quality commitment and nationalistic appeals such as "Buy American" were unsuccessful in countering the foreign challenge, as American consumers were much too sophisticated and knowledgeable about product and service quality to be swayed by slogans alone.

Since neither finance nor marketing could provide a solution, what remained was operations. In the late 1980s, a major study conducted by the MIT Commission on Industrial Productivity cited several reasons why the United States had lost its ability to compete, including:

••• An over-emphasis on marketing and finance at the expense of manufacturing.

••• Underinvestment in research and development, facilities, and employee development.

••• Lack of cost-effective manufacturing systems to produce high-quality products to meet changing consumer demands.

••• Organizational barriers separating design, manufacturing, and marketing.

The commission's findings pointed to *poor management practices* as the key factor in our decline of competitiveness and suggested that effective P/OM with an emphasis on improving quality and operational performance would be the key to competitive success. Considerable evidence supports that claim. We have seen Japanese and other foreign investors purchase failing American companies, build new factories in the United States, and make them successful because of the way they manage operations. A highly celebrated example is New United Motor Manufacturing (NUMMI).

Applied P/OM

New United Motor Manufacturing (NUMMI)

Better management, not technology investment, transforms an ineffi-cient GM auto plant.

New United Motor Manufacturing, Inc. (NUMMI) is a joint venture between General Motors (GM) and Toyota. In setting up the company, Toyota transformed an antiquated California assembly plant into GM's most efficient factory. Before GM closed the plant in 1982, it was a battleground between inflexible managers and a work force whose rate of absenteeism was 20 percent. Toyota quickly turned it around by hiring the best of the former work force and replacing GM's 100 job classifications with teams of multiskilled workers. Absenteeism dropped to less than 2 percent.

Productivity in the plant grew to twice the average level in GM plants. There is no special technology; the difference is in the way Toyota managers organize and operate the plant. New products are designed for easy assembly and easy modification; production layout is organized by product needs, not by function; production flow is managed so carefully that inventories are almost nonexistent; all workers share responsibility for quality; and employees participate in nearly all decisions. Even without much automation, each worker was producing 63 cars a year by 1989, more than in any other U.S. plant and 40 percent above average.

Other examples abound. At Honda of America Manufacturing Co. and Nissan Motor Mfg. USA, results have been similar to NUMMI's.[3] Sony claims that its production lines in its San Diego plant have the same rate of productivity as its Japanese factories; workers are different, but operations management standards are the same. U.S. managers and unions have taken notice. As a result, many companies such as Xerox, Caterpillar, Deere & Co., 3M, General Electric, and Ford have adopted and are implementing new approaches to managing operations. The results have been impressive. As *Fortune* noted in 1994, "Now American companies are pushing Japanese rivals back in such key industries as motor vehicles, semiconductors, and computers. Critical made-in-U.S.A. products that were on the endangered list—machine tools, for example, and high-tech devices for making semiconductors—are vibrantly alive."[4]

The New Management Paradigm

Business today is exceedingly complex as a result of many changes that have taken place over the last 50 years. Today's consumers demand innovative products, high quality, quick response, impeccable service, and low prices; in short, they want *value* (discussed in more detail later) in every purchase. Moreover, companies, large and small, must operate in global markets and compete against sophisticated international competitors. Computers and other forms of advanced technology now dominate manufacturing and service. Managing in this environment—which changes continually—is difficult. P/OM provides both the principles and tools for helping today's managers meet the challenge.

The traditional management paradigm revolves around four basic functions—planning, organizing, directing, and controlling. *Planning* provides the basis for future activities by developing goals and objectives, and establishing guidelines, actions, and schedules for meeting them. *Organizing* is the process of bringing together the resources—personnel, materials, equipment, and capital—necessary to perform planned activities. *Directing* is the process of turning plans into realities by assigning specific tasks and responsibilities to employees, motivating them, and coordinating their efforts. Finally, *controlling*—the evaluation of performance and the application of corrective measures—is necessary to ensure that plans are achieved.

Viewing management in this traditional way tends to compartmentalize a business organization into narrow functions. As a result, managers will tend to suboptimize the individual components, sometimes to the detriment of the system as a whole. The new management paradigm views a business enterprise as a *total system,* in which activities are to be coordinated not only vertically throughout the organization, but also horizontally across multiple functions. P/OM provides the natural framework for accomplishing such coordination.

The lack of integration of business functions has, over the years, limited the effectiveness of business organizations in meeting their fundamental purpose: serving customers, employees, stockholders, and the community. Operations management is actually the only function by which managers can directly affect the value provided to all stakeholders. Good operations management can provide the high-quality goods and services that customers demand by motivating and developing the skills of the people who actually design, produce, and deliver goods and services, while maintaining efficient operations to ensure an adequate return on investment and at the same time protecting the environment. Contemporary operations management activities include

- Understanding the needs of customers, measuring customer satisfaction, and using that information to develop new and improved products and services.
- Exploiting technology to respond rapidly and flexibly to customer requirements and to improve productivity.
- Continually improving products, processes, and systems to reduce errors, defects, and waste and improve responsiveness and business performance.
- Using customer, product and service performance, operations, supplier, employee-related, and cost/financial information to support evaluation and decision making.
- Developing the skills of employees and motivating them through education, training, rewards, recognition, teamwork, and other effective human resource practices.
- Seeing the "big picture" across hierarchical, organizational, and functional boundaries; continually learning from co-workers, competitors, and customers; and adapting to change in the organization.

Quality guru W. Edwards Deming stated simply that people work in the system, and managers work on the system to improve it continuously with their help. Thus, **the purpose of operations management is to deliver ever-improving value for customers through the continuous improvement of overall company performance and capabilities.** That view of operations management defines the theme of our book. We next introduce some basic concepts and terminology that are important to gain a better understanding of the scope of P/OM.

Scope of P/OM

P/OM is a broad discipline that involves many different activities. The key activities and examples of issues that might relate to managing operations at MamaMia's, the restaurant discussed earlier, follow.

1. *Quality management.* How can MamaMia's continually improve the quality of its goods and services? What steps can be taken to ensure consistency and good taste of every pizza?

2. *Strategic business planning.* What are the mission and vision of MamaMia's? To serve local clientele with high quality, unique offerings? To expand into a national franchise as a low-cost producer?

3. *Performance measurement.* What information and data are needed to make sure quality and performance goals are being met? How should MamaMia's measure customer satisfaction?

4. *Human resources management.* How should employees be trained, compensated, and motivated to meet the objectives of the business?

5. *Designing and developing products and services.* What types of food products should the restaurant offer? What effects would the introduction of spaghetti and lasagna dinners have on operations? Should telefax service be offered?

6. *Forecasting and capacity planning.* What is the projected growth rate of demand? How many cooks are required? How much oven capacity and how many dining room tables are needed? How many drivers are necessary? Should the restaurant expand?

7. *Location and distribution.* If the company decides to expand to other areas of the community, where should it build? How large should the local delivery area be?

8. *Technology and automation.* Should orders be written by hand or sent directly to the kitchen by computer? Is it feasible to develop "traveling kitchens" in vans so that drivers can prepare pizzas without returning to the restaurant?

9. *Process design and facility layout.* What is the best process for pizza preparation and assembly? How should the kitchen facilities be configured to make the process efficient? Does the work environment meet federal safety regulations?

10. *Inventory and materials management.* How much cheese, sauce, toppings, and so on should be kept on hand? When should new materials be ordered?

11. *Production planning and scheduling.* How many pre-baked crusts should be prepared in anticipation of the dinner crowd? When should they be prepared?

12. *Operations scheduling.* How should employees be scheduled to meet varying demands over the week? What are the best delivery routes?

13. *Project management.* If a new facility is constructed, how should all activities be scheduled to ensure that the project is completed on time?

Of course, specific issues would be different for a machine tool manufacturing manager, a hotel manager, or a hospital administrator. Also, managers in large organizations might have the responsibility for only one or a few of the activities. That is reflected in the wide variety of jobs in the operations management field, some of which are production supervisor, inventory manager, warehouse manager, customer service manager, quality assurance supervisor, and project manager. In a small company, the president or plant manager might perform most of the activities. But invariably, everyone in business performs many of them at one time or another, no matter what his or her actual job title is. Thus, studying operations management is sure to be important to your future business career.

P/OM principles are not complicated. On the contrary, they are very simple, but they do require discipline and vision to implement. In the following description of a DuPont plant's experience, we see that application of simple P/OM principles—seeking the causes of problems, modifying the design and operation of the system, measurement, and education and training—can lead to dramatic results.

Applied P/OM
DuPont

DuPont's textile plant improves manufacturing performance with P/OM principles.[5]

DuPont's May Plant in Camden, South Carolina, employs approximately 125 people and produces roughly 69 million pounds of textile fiber each year. The textile area includes production, shipping, inspection, and testing. Textile fibers are produced in a continuous spinning operation. After fiber is wound on a spool, it is placed on a special buggy that holds many spools. The buggies are wheeled to a test-and-inspection station. Finally, the product is grouped, packaged, and shipped.

Spinning machines cannot be shut down without incurring tremendous startup costs. Even slowing production will adversely affect product consistency and quality. Those facts complicated the job of the plant managers, who faced many problematic issues. The quality of work life for operators, supervisors, and area managers was poor, with many safety problems. There were constant telephone calls from customers about delivery schedules, calls that were often unpleasant and at times confrontational. Customers' orders were not being met in a timely way. Other problems were product shortages, excessive backlogs, high inventories, and lost or misplaced yarn. Product-quality variation and production yields were unacceptable. There was ongoing pressure from the marketing group, as well as from plant executives, to stem the flow of customer complaints.

Employees, supervisors, and managers were eager for change. One area supervisor had been exposed to world-class P/OM principles and prompted the journey toward successfully and permanently resolving the problems. One step was to lock up many of the buggies except when needed for an emergency. With fewer buggies in operation, bottlenecks became acutely visible, and the sources of problems were more quickly identified and corrected. The result was a smoother flow of product through the facility. Jobs were simplified, and a visual control system was adopted. In the new system, buggies were placed only in small marked-off spaces, which limited the amount of inventory and flagged problems. Even forklifts had specific parking places to enable easy identification of the ones that were leaking fluid and posed a safety problem. Employees measured the time it took products to move through the facility and backlogs at each work station, plotting the results so that deviations could be identified quickly and corrected. Extensive on-the-job education and training, supplemented by meetings and individual coaching and counseling, helped to involve all employees in the improvement efforts.

As a result of those initiatives, work-in-process inventory was reduced an astounding 96 percent, working capital declined by $2 million, employee suggestions increased 300 percent, and product quality improved 10 percent. Most of the results were achieved within the first three months after implementation of the changes.

Classifying P/OM Activities

One way of putting the operations management function into a useful framework is to classify P/OM activities into a hierarchy: strategic, tactical, and operational. That classification corresponds roughly to the roles of top managers, middle managers, and workers/supervisors. *Strategic planning and decision making* is broad in scope and involves corporate policies and long-term resource-acquisition decisions—responsibilities of top managers. It might include defining the organization's mission and purpose, choosing product lines and distribution and marketing channels, and designing the performance appraisal and compensation system. Strategic planning involves a long time horizon, such as three to five years, and a high degree of uncertainty and risk.

Top managers specify the goals middle managers must accomplish, as well as the constraints within which they must operate. Thus, the sphere of middle managers' responsibility, *tactical planning and decision making,* is narrower in scope and involves resource allocation and utilization rather than resource acquisition. In manufacturing organizations, tactical planning normally occurs at the plant level and involves a medium-term time horizon and a moderate degree of uncertainty and risk. Tactical issues include acquiring the resources needed to produce a product, designing production facilities, determining work-force and production levels, implementing human resource policies, and improving quality.

Finally, *operational planning and decision making,* the responsibility of supervisors, factory workers, and front-line service workers, involves a short time horizon and very little uncertainty and risk. Duties might include adjusting daily production schedules, managing materials and work-in-process, controlling product quality, and managing customer relations.

The three categories of planning and decision making are *hierarchical.* That is, strategic plans and decisions made at upper levels in the organization are fed downward and provide the guidelines within which tactical plans and decisions are made. Those, in turn, are fed downward and provide guidelines for operational plans and decisions. The results of plans and decisions are fed upward in a similar way. Within a properly coordinated system, several benefits can accrue to the organization: The system as a whole will work together cohesively to achieve its goals and objectives; departments and managers will make plans and decisions that support each other; and objectives, policies, and operational constraints will be understood by all involved.

Production Systems

The collection of all interrelated activities and operations involved in producing goods and services is called a **production system.** This book is concerned with production systems for both manufacturing and service organizations. Manufactured goods are tangible items that can be transferred from one place to another and can be stored for purchase by a consumer at a later time. For example, goods such as automobiles, home appliances, and packaged foods are usually produced in one location and purchased in another. **Service** is a "social act which takes place in direct contact between the customer and representatives of the service company."[6] Services include all nonmanufacturing organizations except those in such industries as agriculture, mining, and construction. Examples include hotels, health and legal services, educational institutions, financial institutions, transportation organizations, and public utilities.

In many organizations the production of goods and the production of services go hand in hand. Consider, for example, MamaMia's restaurant, where various food items are converted into consumable products (pizzas), but where the speed and quality of customer service are just as important. We tend to classify such businesses as service organizations rather than as manufacturing organizations because they compete more on the basis of the services provided than the products sold. Moreover, many organizations we consider primarily as manufacturing also provide services as well as goods. An example is a manufacturer such as Xerox that produces copiers and provides extensive maintenance and repair services.

Components of a Production System

Figure 1.1, a schematic diagram of a production system, shows that any production system consists of six principal components: inputs, outputs, suppliers, customers, processes, and managers. Decisions and feedback influence the process.

Inputs and Outputs. *Inputs* to a production system consist of the resources—materials, capital, equipment, personnel, information, and energy—that are used to produce the desired *outputs,* namely, finished goods and services. Examples of inputs and outputs are crude oils that are converted into gasoline, a set of plastic parts purchased overseas that are assembled into a toy, various equipment and skilled firefighters that extinguish fires and save lives, and foodstuffs, chefs, waiters, and waitresses that produce meals and a pleasant dining experience.

Suppliers and Customers. Suppliers provide the inputs to a production system. Usually they are external to the firm. For example, a tire manufacturer supplies tires to an automobile assembly plant, a chemical firm supplies chemicals to a pharmaceutical manufacturer, or a grocery distributor supplies meats, cheeses, and vegetables to MamaMia's. In the past, the suppliers' role in the production system was accorded less importance than it is today, even though their ability to produce and deliver quality materials and parts in a timely way clearly

Figure 1.1 Components of Production Systems

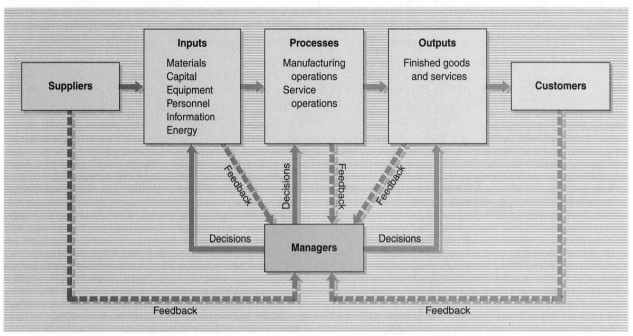

affects all subsequent activities of the organizations that depend on them. Modern managers regard suppliers as *partners* in the production system, and attempt to develop long-term cooperative relationships based on mutual trust.

Suppliers can also be internal to the firm. For example, the machining department supplies product to the assembly department, a secretarial pool supplies finished documents to managers, upper managers supply budgets and other resources to lower-level managers, and the pizza kitchen is a supplier to the delivery worker.

Outputs are provided to customers. There are different types of customers. Those who ultimately purchase a firm's final goods and services are usually called **consumers.** The role consumers play in a production system has changed in recent years. Previously, companies developed products that they thought customers wanted without making the extensive effort in market research that characterizes today's approach. Consumer input was not used in designing the product, nor sought to determine how well the product was liked. If the product did not sell, it was scrapped, and the company tried something else. Today, companies recognize that customer input and feedback are essential in designing and redesigning products to provide satisfaction, and every opportunity is taken to obtain such information. For example, MamaMia's might ask customers to fill out a simple satisfaction survey with every purchase.

Before reaching consumers, a product may flow through a chain of many firms or departments, each of which add some value to it. For example, an automobile engine plant may purchase steel from a steel company and produce engines that are transported to an assembly plant. The steel company is a supplier to the engine plant; the engine plant is a supplier to the assembly plant. Likewise, the engine plant is a customer of the steel company, and the assembly plant is a customer of the engine plant. Such customers are usually called **exter-**

nal customers. MamaMia's might produce partially baked pizzas for local grocery stores. In that case, the grocery stores are external customers.

The recipients of goods and services from internal suppliers are called **internal customers.** Thus, the assembly department is an internal customer of the machining department, managers are internal customers of the secretarial pool, and the pizza chef is the internal customer of the order taker. Most companies consist of many such "chains of customers." The job of every employee is to meet the needs of his or her internal customers so as to satisfy the ultimate customer, the consumer. For example, an illegible or incomplete order can result in the wrong pizza being delivered to the customer. The concept of the internal customer is a profound change in P/OM thinking. It is a concept that helps employees to see how they fit into the system and how their work contributes to the final product, and it enables managers to view the organization as a system.

Processes.   One of the most important ideas in P/OM is the concept of a **process,** a sequence of activities that is intended to produce a certain result for a customer, such as a physical product, a service, or information. A typical manufacturing system, for example, consists of several key processes: receiving, conversion, subassembly, final assembly, packaging, and shipping. *Receiving* includes unloading inbound goods from transportation vehicles, verifying that proper quantities are received in good condition and satisfy quality requirements, and preparing the goods for production or storage. *Conversion* is changing the shape or composition of raw materials or components, such as by drilling, grinding, or crushing. (In metalworking industries, the term *fabrication* is used to denote the process of modifying the physical characteristics of materials by forming, machining, joining, and so on.) *Subassembly* is joining components together to form a part of the final product. *Final assembly* is combining all materials, components, and subassemblies into the finished product. *Packaging* is the process of preparing the product for shipping to the customer, and *shipping* is the process of physically moving the product to the customer either directly or through distribution channels such as wholesalers and retailers.

Service processes, unlike manufacturing processes, do not produce a tangible product, but rather create satisfaction by meeting the needs of customers. A major urban hospital in Cincinnati, for example, defines three key service processes: diagnosis, treatment, and transition management. Each consists of various subprocesses. For instance, lab testing and fitness assessment are important diagnostic processes; treatment processes include surgery, therapy, and medication; and transition management processes include rehabilitation and home care.

Some processes at MamaMia's are order entry, pizza assembly, baking, packaging, and delivery. Note that they are a mix of manufacturing and service processes.

Managers and Feedback.   Managers coordinate the production system by acquiring the inputs, controlling and improving the processes, and ensuring that outputs are available at the proper time and place to satisfy demand. They make *decisions* that affect such key business factors as productivity, quality, cost, schedules, and employee well-being. In services, managers must often focus their attention on their employees' "people" skills rather than on technical issues.

Finally, *feedback* from suppliers and customers, and information about inputs, outputs, and production-system performance, help managers plan effectively or take corrective action when necessary. At MamaMia's, employees might measure the length of time between ordering and serving or track complaints by category. Feedback about order cycle time may lead to adjustments in staffing or increased oven capacity. Managers might react to complaints by increasing employee training or improving the consistency of pizza-topping quantities. Good feedback enables an organization to improve the products and services offered and better meet the demands of the marketplace. Table 1.1 summarizes the elements of the production system for various manufacturing and service organizations.

Environment of a Production System

The production system is greatly affected by its environment—that is, other functional areas of the firm, such as finance or marketing, and various external influences on the company, such as economic conditions, government regulations, competing organizations, and evolving technology. The relationships for a typical firm are illustrated in Figure 1.2.

The external environment influences the overall policies and objectives of the company, and hence indirectly the production system. Within the firm, though, other functional areas have a more direct impact on production:

1. *Financial decisions* affect the choice of manufacturing equipment, use of overtime, cost-control policies, and price-volume decisions.
2. *Accounting* provides data on costs and prices that help managers evaluate performance.

Table 1.1 Examples of Production Systems in Manufacturing and Service

System	Inputs	Conversion Process	Outputs	Managers	Feedback
Auto assembly plant	Labor Energy Robots Auto parts	Welding Manual assembly Painting	Automobiles	Supervisors Plant managers	Labor cost Production quantities Quality
Oil refinery	Crude oil Energy Equipment Labor	Chemical reaction Separation	Gasoline Kerosine Other chemical products	Plant manager Chemists	Chemical composition Volume
Hospital	Patients Staff Beds Drugs Medical equipment	Operations Drug administration Health-status monitoring	Healthy individuals Lab results	Chief of staff Head nurse	Patient response to medication Surgical complications
Post office	Labor Sorting equipment Trucks	Transporting letters and packages	Mail delivery	Postmasters Shift supervisors	Average delivery times Parcels damaged

Figure 1.2
The Production System and
Its Environment

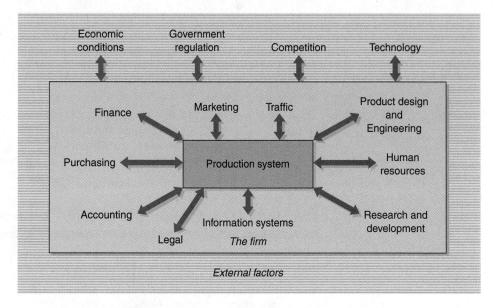

3. *Marketing* is responsible for understanding customer needs, generating and maintaining demand for the firm's products, ensuring customer satisfaction, and developing new markets and product potential.

4. *Product design and engineering* determines product specifications to meet customer needs and the production methods necessary to make the products.

5. *Human resources* recruits and trains employees and is responsible for employee development, motivation, and union relationships.

6. *Research and development* investigates new ideas and their potential uses as consumer products.

7. *Purchasing* is responsible for acquiring the materials and supplies necessary for production. (Entire production lines have been shut down because of the shortage of a five-cent part.)

8. *Traffic* is responsible for distributing the finished goods to customers. (Customers may be lost if products are not shipped and delivered as promptly as promised.)

9. *Legal services* ensure that laws and regulations for product labeling, performance, safety, packaging, transportation, and other contractual requirements are met.

10. *Information systems* provide the means for capturing, analyzing, and coordinating the information needs of each of the preceding areas.

Note that each of the functions is in turn itself affected by the production system.

The corporate functions are not independent of each other. For example, financial considerations affect decisions made in all other functional areas, and engineering specifications on materials assist purchasing in identifying qualified suppliers. It is important to realize that all of the functions are interrelated in one system. Our purpose here, however, is not to examine the firm as a complete entity, but rather to focus attention on the firm's production and operations activities.

Figure 1.3
Evolution of P/OM

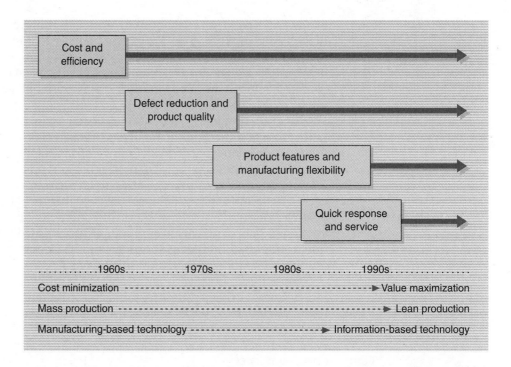

In the last century, P/OM has undergone more changes than any other functional area of business and is the most important factor in competitiveness. That is one of the reasons why every business student needs a basic understanding of the field. To better understand the challenges facing modern business and the role of P/OM in meeting them, let us first briefly trace the history and evolution of the field.

Figure 1.3 is a chronology of major themes that have changed the scope of P/OM in the twentieth century and the focal points on which businesses have competed in the market. First, an internal P/OM focus on cost and efficiency has changed to an external focus on providing value to customers through improved quality, better products, faster response, and lower prices. Second, manufacturing has changed from a system of mass production characterized by independent functions to a streamlined system of interdependent functions known as *lean production*. Finally, an emphasis on customer satisfaction through quick response and service has shifted the focus from manufacturing technology to information technology as a principal means of meeting business objectives.

Growth of Manufacturing

Contemporary P/OM has its roots in the Industrial Revolution that occurred during the late eighteenth and early nineteenth centuries in England. Until that time, goods had been produced in small shops by artisans and their apprentices without the aid of mechanical equipment. The "production system" was not complex. Workers were autonomous and self-employed, with deep knowledge of their work and broad skills enabling them to do a job from start to finish. During the Industrial Revolution, however, many new inventions came into being that allowed goods to be manufactured with greater ease and speed. The inventions reduced the need for individual artisans and led to the development of modern factories.

Factories developed into complex systems of interrelated processes that required different methods of managing. Managers drew upon British economist Adam Smith's concept of the *division of labor*—that is, having different workers perform different tasks rather than having one worker acquire the skills necessary to perform the entire job—and similar ideas by Charles Babbage in the early nineteenth century. Babbage believed that the total cost of a product could be lowered by hiring workers with different skills and paying them according to their expertise. In addition, he investigated managerial and organizational structures, human relations, new-product development, and price-volume-profit relationships in the marketplace.

Those ideas, along with the concept of *interchangeable parts* introduced by Eli Whitney in 1798, paved the way for modern manufacturing. Henry Ford put them into practice by introducing the modern assembly line in the early 1900s. That development greatly reduced the costs of manufacturing, paving the way for mass production and making a wide variety of products affordable to the average consumer.

The era of *scientific management,* emphasizing the refinement of mass production, was led by Frederick W. Taylor, often called the "father of scientific management." Taylor had progressed from a laborer to chief engineer. That experience enabled him to study production at the most detailed level, focusing on workers, the methods of work, and the wages paid for productivity. He believed that the responsibilities for production should differ between management and labor; managers should be responsible for planning, directing, and organizing work, whereas workers should be concerned only with carrying out their assigned tasks. Taylor also believed in fostering a spirit of cooperation between management and labor and in selecting the best worker for the job. His "science of management" was based on observation, measurement and analysis of work, improvement in work methods, and economic incentives. It changed the nature of work dramatically, as workers were assigned to small, highly repetitive tasks that required only narrow skills.

Many of Taylor's contemporaries extended and enriched his thinking. Henry Gantt recognized the use of rewards other than wages to promote morale; he developed the now famous *Gantt chart* for scheduling and monitoring work. Frank and Lillian Gilbreth investigated work planning and employee training. Some of their more important contributions were the development of motion study and job-improvement methods.

In the 1930s Elton Mayo conducted a series of studies at Western Electric's Hawthorne Works. Mayo, influenced by Taylor, sought to determine whether a set of working conditions could be created within a factory environment that would maximize worker productivity. One experiment involved changing light intensity and measuring the effect on worker productivity. Mayo found that an increase in light intensity led to higher productivity. However, in trying to replicate the experiments, he discovered that even when light intensity was reduced to previous settings, worker productivity continued to increase. It seemed that the extra attention the workers received by being part of the experiment was what led to their increased productivity. Unfortunately, the implications of the Hawthorne studies and some of Taylor's ideas on fostering cooperation between managers and workers were not fully integrated into management practices until much later, and for many years managers continued to focus solely on cost and efficiency.

During World War II a new discipline arose that has had a significant influence on business and industry. Known as *operations research,* or *management science,* it recognized that many physical situations can be represented adequately by a mathematical model. Among the first applications of that approach to operations management was the determination of the optimum size of convoys for transporting military supplies to Europe. Management science techniques enabled business and industry to reduce costs and improve efficiency for very complex operational problems. As computing technology grew, management science evolved into a powerful tool for addressing complex P/OM problems. Examples of how management science tools can be applied in P/OM are provided throughout the book.

During the years following World War II, the United States was in a dominant position in manufacturing. The world was hungry for American products, and managers of manufacturing firms had only one goal: keep the production lines running and reap more profits. Operations managers, grounded in the principles of Taylor, concentrated primarily on efficiency and quantity of production, which led to a higher level of specialization and refinement in job tasks. The operations manager's goal was to keep the production line running and to keep efficiency high. Job specialization led to boring, repetitive tasks. The management of manufacturing operations evolved into an atmosphere of control and spawned a vicious cycle of adversarial relations with unions.

As international trade grew in the 1960s, the emphasis on cost reduction and operations efficiency increased. Many companies moved their factories to low-wage countries. Managers became enamored with technology as a result of the space program, computers, and new electronic developments. Advanced technology revolutionized production, and continues to do so today. However, unlike today, in the 1960s and 1970s technology was viewed primarily as a method of reducing costs; it distracted managers from the important goal of improving the quality of products and the processes that produce them. American business was soon to face a rude awakening.

The Quality Revolution

As Japan was rebuilding from the devastation of World War II, two U.S. consultants, W. Edwards Deming and Joseph Juran, were sought extensively by Japanese industry. Both had ties to the Bell Telephone System and Western Electric dating back to the 1930s and had worked with several quality control pioneers who developed new statistical theories and methods of inspection to improve product quality. Those methods proved to be of enormous benefit during World War II, enabling the United States to develop highly reliable products to support the war effort. Unfortunately, their use diminished after the war, as managers in the United States again focused their attention on cost and efficiency.

Deming and Juran told Japanese executives that continual improvement of quality would open world markets and improve their economy. The Japanese eagerly embraced that message. They embarked on a massive effort to train the work force, using statistical tools developed at Western Electric and other innovative management tools to identify causes of quality problems and fix them. They made steady progress in reducing defects and paid careful attention to what consumers wanted. Those efforts continued at a relentless pace until, by the mid 1970s, the world discovered that Japanese goods had fewer defects, were more reliable, and better met consumer needs than American goods. As a result, Japanese firms captured major shares of world markets in many different industries.

Facing a crisis, U.S. business began to take notice. The "quality revolution" began in the United States in 1980 when NBC televised a program entitled "If Japan Can . . . Why Can't We?" featuring W. Edwards Deming and his role in transforming Japanese industry. As a result of that program, Ford Motor Company, and then many other companies, sought to understand Deming's message and transform their management by emphasizing quality. Quality has now become an obsession with top managers of nearly every major company. In 1987 the U.S. government established the Malcolm Baldrige National Quality Award to focus national attention on quality. Because of the critical importance of quality, it is a dominant theme in this book; nearly every chapter discusses the relationship of quality within the context of the chapter material.

Rise of "Lean Production" and "Soft Manufacturing"

As the goals of low cost and high product quality became "givens," companies began placing increasing emphasis on innovative designs and product features to gain a competitive edge. One of Deming's key messages to Japanese managers was the need to study consumer needs continually and use that intelligence to develop better products and production processes. That viewpoint changed the focus of production from cost and efficiency to better satisfying the needs of customers through continual improvement of products and production systems. It changed the concept of quality to mean much more than simply defect reduction—quality meant offering consumers new and innovative products that not only met their expectations, but surprised and delighted them.

Inflexible mass-production methods that produced high volumes of standardized products using unskilled or semiskilled workers and expensive single-purpose machines, though very efficient and cost effective, were inadequate for the new goals of increased product variety and continual product improvement. The production system had to change. New approaches for managing manufacturing systems—called **lean production**—emerged in Japan that enabled companies to manufacture products better, cheaper, and faster than their competitors, while facilitating innovation and increased product variety. (Interestingly, lean production was embodied in Henry Ford's early operations; only 81 hours elapsed between mining iron ore and driving a new car off the assembly line. Ford made that possible by fully integrating manufacturing, transportation, and mining operations.) Today's lean production systems employ multiskilled workers, cross-functional teams, integrated communications, supplier partnerships, and highly flexible, increasingly automated machines to produce wide varieties of products. They focus on effective use of resources, elimination of waste, and continuous improvement, thereby reducing costs and defects. Such systems combine the best features of old-style craft production and early twentieth-century mass production: the ability to produce a wide variety of customized products delivered with short lead times. Incorporating product innovation with price, quality, and flexibility requires a coordinated effort among all facets of an organization, particularly marketing, finance, and operations.

In recent years, information technology has driven manufacturing capability to new heights. *Soft manufacturing,* also called *agile manufacturing,* blends automation and computing technology, allowing companies to customize and produce single quantities of products at mass-production speeds. For instance, at an IBM plant in North Carolina, a 40-worker team builds 12 different products—ranging from bar-code scanners, to fiber-optic connectors for mainframe computers, to satellite communication devices for truck drivers—simultaneously. Each worker has a computer screen that displays a checklist of parts to install and guides the worker through the assembly steps if help is needed.[7]

Soft manufacturing grew out of *flexible manufacturing systems (FMSs):* complex, highly automated, computer-controlled systems that produce a large variety of parts without human intervention. Manufacturers discovered that FMSs were inherently vulnerable to failure, and that robots' lack of intelligence led to many problems in some cases. Soft manufacturing systems therefore break large FMSs into manageable cells of machines, using robots to perform simple tasks at which they excel, such as spot-welding, and leaving the intelligent decisions to workers supported by information technology. Other characteristics of soft manufacturing are multiskilled employees, self-directed work teams, and extensive partnering of all customers and suppliers. Soft manufacturing helped the United States to surpass Japan and Germany and regain the top spot in manufactured exports by the mid 1990s.

Quick Response and Customer Service

Quick response is an outcome of lean production, and an important source of competitive advantage. Companies that do not respond quickly to changing customer needs will lose out to competitors that do. Furthermore, speed to market not only increases sales, but can also increase profits through lower costs. Companies therefore focus on **total cycle time,** the time needed to meet a customer's requirement. If a firm is to minimize total cycle time, it cannot tolerate inefficiencies or poor quality. Consequently, the firm must stress both quality improvement and operational performance, thus bringing down costs of production while providing a high-quality product that increases sales.

Quick response is achieved by continually improving and *reengineering* processes, that is, fundamentally rethinking and redesigning processes to achieve dramatic improvements in cost, quality, speed, and service. That task includes developing products faster than competitors, speeding ordering and delivering processes, rapidly responding to changes in customers' needs, and improving the flow of paperwork. An example of quick response is the production of the custom-designed Motorola pager, which is completed within 80 minutes and often can be delivered to the customer the same day.

Applied P/OM

Motorola

Cycle-time reduction is key to Motorola's focus on total customer satisfaction.

Motorola is one of the 150 largest U.S. industrial corporations. Its principal product lines are communication systems and semiconductors, and its goals are to increase its global market share and to become the best in class in all aspects—people, marketing, technology, product, manufacturing, and service. The company began its quest for quality and recognition as a world-class manufacturer in 1979 when it established as its basic objective *total customer satisfaction.*

A major factor in meeting many of the company's goals is the reduction of total cycle time, which begins when a customer expresses a need and ends when the customer happily pays the company. Cycle-time reduction applies to all processes in the company, including design, order entry, manufacturing, marketing, and even administrative functions such as auditing. Motorola has succeeded in reducing the time to

- Produce certain products—from weeks to less than an hour.
- Fill an order for portable radios—from 55 days to 15.
- Close the financial books—from one month to four days.
- Write and file a patent claim—from two to three years to two months.

Products are *what* we produce; service is *how* we provide them. Consumers today are more sensitive to the how than the what. Product quality is taken for granted; everyone has become better at developing products. But since nearly every company is also in the service business , particularly when one considers ordering, technical support, delivery, and field service, companies can differentiate themselves in that area.

Service is an important consideration for companies that produce a product, but it is the sole consideration of many other companies. Since 1970 there has been little growth in the number of manufacturing jobs in the United States, but there has been tremendous job growth in the service sector. Services now dominate the American economy, generating nearly three-fourths of the gross domestic product and accounting for almost 80 percent of all jobs. In fact, *Fortune* noted that all net job creation through the year 2005 will come from services.[8]

With the increasing importance of services, the emphasis of P/OM is changing. Service requires new types of workers—flexible, creative people who are able to work with minimal supervision. Customer service is playing a more prominent role, and information technology is a dramatic new force in all kinds of industries and businesses. Many of the scientific and behavioral management approaches originally developed for manufacturing operations are being widely applied in services.

Focus on Customer Satisfaction and Value

Today's consumers have high expectations. They demand an increasing variety of products with new and improved features that meet their changing needs. They expect products that are defect-free, have high performance, are reliable and durable, and are easy to repair. They also expect rapid and excellent service for the products they buy. For the services they buy, customers expect short waiting and processing times, availability when needed, courteous treatment from employees, consistency, accessibility and convenience, accuracy, and responsiveness to unexpected problems.

Companies must now compete on all those dimensions. Today, the concept of quality includes every possible factor that helps to meet or exceed customer expectations. Customers of MamaMia's, for instance, might expect a hot pizza with fresh ingredients and an ample supply of toppings that is consistent every time and ready when promised, as well as quick delivery, courteous service, and adequate parking. Purchasers of automobiles, computer software, or banking services have similarly comprehensive expectations. If a firm can consistently discover customers' expectations and meet them, it will achieve a competitive advantage that is difficult to overcome. Note that meeting and exceeding customer expectations is an externally focused definition of quality.[9]

Quality coupled with price defines the notion of **value.** The decision to purchase a product or service is based on an assessement of the perceived quality in relation to the price. If the ratio is high, the product or service has high value, and is more likely to be successful. In recent years, many major companies such as Procter & Gamble have seen their market share erode because of private-label goods that provide better perceived value. As a result, they have instituted *value pricing*—permanently lower prices that provide significant advantages to their external customers as well as consumers. Many retail chains such as Wal-Mart and Toys "R" Us thrive on everyday low prices.

The focus on value has also forced many companies to rethink service. If product quality cannot be economically improved and prices cannot be lowered, services may offer an opportunity for improvement, as in the case of Hewlett-Packard.

Applied P/OM

Hewlett-Packard

Hewlett-Packard delights customers through increased value.[10]

The Instrument Systems Division of Hewlett-Packard (HP) faced a problem when a key competitor announced a price decrease for voltmeters. Should HP do nothing and risk losing sales, or should it lower its price to retain volume but lose revenues? A third alternative was chosen instead: to hold the price steady, but increase the warranty from one to three years. The product's reliability was quite high, so the additional cost for the extra warranty would be much less than the profit increase. Also, rather than having customers wait for a failing unit to be repaired, HP changed its warranty policy to include shipment of a new unit within 24 hours. The perceived value of those additional services actually increased market share and profitability.

Modern Challenges to P/OM

Shifts from cost and efficiency to value, from mass production to lean production, from manufacturing technology to information technology, and from a national economy to a world economy have made operations management critically important in modern business. Workers are different; they demand increasing levels of empowerment and more meaningful work. Customers are different; their demands and expectations are much higher. Technology is different; computers and automation have dramatically changed the nature of work, requiring constant learning and more abstract thinking. Finally, the environment is different; we live in a global business environment without boundaries. Such changes in business are occurring at an increasingly rapid pace, and we can expect them to continue in the future. Operations managers clearly face important challenges in preparing for the twenty-first century.

World-Class Management in a Global Economy

Business today is truly international. We have passed from the era of huge regional factories with large labor forces and tight community ties. With advances in communications and transportation, we have entered the era of the "borderless marketplace." No longer are "American" or "Japanese" products manufactured exclusively in America or Japan. The Mazda Miata, for example, was designed in California, financed in Tokyo and New York, tested in England, assembled in Michigan and Mexico, and built with components designed in New Jersey and produced in Japan. Nations such as Korea, Taiwan, Singapore, Mexico, Brazil, and India are rapidly becoming industrialized and competitive in major markets.

The global manager's job is to exploit technologies as effectively as possible. He or she must meet the varying needs of worldwide customers and make such decisions as determining where to locate production and whether to outsource components or build them in-house. In addition, the global manager must understand and implement new ideas developed elsewhere, and work within the cultural constraints of different countries. Even Japanese companies, which have historically maintained a provincial attitude toward business, are establishing manufacturing facilities in the United States and Europe and investing in research and development laboratories outside Japan.

Global integration, the coordination and balancing of global resources, is vital for international competition. Companies can no longer operate centrally within regional boundaries or they will lose access to essential markets. Similarly, they cannot develop a disconnected system of geographically scattered operations or they will face losing precious economies of scale. Xerox Corporation is one of many organizations that have discovered the need for global integration.

Applied P/OM

Xerox Corporation

Xerox pursues a strategy of global integration[11]

In the 1970s Xerox Corporation was a typical international firm. It made products in the United States for U.S. markets, and subsidiaries such as Fuji Xerox developed products for other markets. Each company controlled its own suppliers, assembly plants, and distribution channels independently. The managers of the plants were not concerned with how each fit into the overall production plans of Xerox Corporation and rarely communicated with one another.

By 1981 Xerox executives had begun to rethink the company's structure, examining ways to cut costs, reduce excessive inventory, and improve product delivery. As competitors such as Canon globalized copier production and achieved significant market penetration, Xerox recognized the need to pursue a strategy of global integration. Among the key decisions made by the company were

- The creation of a central purchasing group incorporating representatives from multinational operating companies. Xerox reduced its global supplier base from about 5,000 suppliers to slightly more than 400.
- The establishment of a "Leadership through Quality" program to improve product quality, streamline manufacturing processes, and reduce costs.
- The design of functionally and geographically integrated teams for new product delivery to all major markets.
- The creation of a multinational task force on global integration. All plants were required to adopt global standards for basic processes that apply to all operations, maintain common business processes tailored to local needs where necessary, and set site-specific processes for systems that had to conform to local regulations.
- The formation of a Central Logistics and Asset Management organization to base individual plant production levels on customer orders and reduce excess inventory.

The innovations resulted in savings of millions of dollars as well as significant improvements in new product introduction and market delivery.

Leaders in the global marketplace will be **world-class** firms that can meet consumer demands in price, quality, and time at low cost. In short, world-class companies achieve manufacturing excellence and set the standards that other companies try to meet or beat. World-class companies make full use of *total quality management* approaches. They train, involve, and empower all employees to make continuous improvements, using cross-functional teams to break down barriers among designers, marketers, and manufacturing personnel. They seek to minimize cycle times, often reducing them from months to days, and use state-of-the-art technology and low-cost production methods.

In achieving world-class status, an organization's operations managers play a critical role. Their job is to

••• Find methods to reduce manufacturing costs while simultaneously improving quality.

••• Integrate the roles of marketing and manufacturing to ensure that customer expectations are met throughout the production process.

••• Reduce the time needed to develop, manufacture, and deliver new products as customer demands and expectations increase.

••• Create an environment that motivates every employee.

••• Make suppliers and customers part of the "quality team."

Those tasks are not easy to achieve; they require commitment, cooperation, and hard work. But they are crucial to the survival of modern businesses.

P/OM in Practice

At the end of each chapter, we include a "P/OM in Practice" section to present case studies of how operations management principles have been skillfully applied to real problems or situations. As you read these cases, consider the technical details of the methods as well as *why* the organization used them and *how* they were implemented. Several questions follow each case to stimulate thought and discussion.

The Ritz-Carlton Hotel Company: Service Through People[12]

The Ritz-Carlton Hotel Company is one example of an outstanding service company. In 1992 it became the first hospitality organization to receive the Malcolm Baldrige National Quality Award (described fully in the next chapter). The hotel industry is very competitive, one in which customers place high emphasis on reliability, timely delivery, and price value. The Ritz-Carlton® focuses on the principal concerns of its main customers and strives to provide highly personalized, genuinely caring service. Attention to its employees, processes, and use of information technology are three of the

many strengths of The Ritz-Carlton that helped it receive national recognition.

The Ritz-Carlton's company philosophy is "Ladies and Gentlemen Serving Ladies and Gentlemen." Its credo states, "The genuine care and comfort of our guests is our highest mission." The company's "three steps of service" are (1) a warm greeting in which employees use the guest's name, (2) anticipation of and compliance with the guest's needs, and (3) a warm farewell, again using the guest's name if possible. A Ritz-Carlton employee will not point a guest in a desired direction ; he or she will lead the guest to the desired destination. In attending to complaints, employees must respond within 10 minutes and follow up with a phone call within 20 minutes to make sure the customer is satisfied. The employees have the responsibility to solve problems, and they are given considerable latitude and authority in doing so to ensure total customer satisfaction. Any failure, such as not having a room ready on time, requires complimentary cocktails, an amenity sent to the room, and a letter of apology.

Employees are empowered to "move heaven and earth to satisfy a customer," to contact other employees

to help resolve a problem swiftly, to spend up to $2,000 to satisfy a guest, to decide the business terms of a sale, to become involved in setting plans for their work area, and to speak with anyone in the management hierarchy about any problem.

The company's objectives are to improve the quality of its products and services, reduce cycle time, and improve price value and customer retention. At each level of the company, teams are charged with setting objectives and devising action plans, which are reviewed by the corporate steering committee. Such an approach ensures that (1) all teams are aligned around a common vision and agreed-upon objectives, (2) all employees are encouraged to think beyond the demands of daily activities, and (3) continual communication is maintained among the diverse functions that make up the company.

To provide the personalized service demanded by the company's customers, the human resource function works in close coordination with all other functions. All hotels have a director of human resources and a training manager, both of whom are assisted by the hotel's quality leader. Each work area has a departmental trainer who is charged with the training and certification of new employees in that unit. The Ritz-Carlton uses a highly predictive "character trait recruiting" instrument to determine a candidate's capability to meet the requirements of each of 120 job positions. New employees receive two days' orientation by senior executives to demonstrate methods and instill the Ritz-Carlton values. Three weeks later managers monitor the effectiveness of the instruction and make necessary changes in a follow-up session. Later, new employees must pass written and skill-demonstration tests to become certified in their work areas.

Every employee receives instruction designed to make him or her a certified quality engineer capable of identifying wasteful complexity within his or her work. In all, employees receive more than 100 hours of quality education to foster premium service commitment, solve problems, set strategic quality plans, and generate new ideas. And every day, in every work area, during every shift, a quality lineup meeting of employees occurs for a briefing session.

Customized hotel products and services, such as meetings and banquet events, receive the full attention of cross-functional teams. In the process of designing and delivering customized services, all internal and external suppliers become involved as early as possible, production and delivery capabilities are verified prior to each event, samples are prepared and critiqued by event planners, and "after-event" assessments are conducted for continuous improvement.

The Ritz-Carlton applies information technology to capture and use customer-satisfaction data and other important data in real time. Its information systems enable every employee to collect and use data on a daily basis, including on-line guest-preference information, quantity of er-

ror-free products and services, and complaints indicating opportunities for improvement. A guest-profiling system that registers the individual preferences of 240,000 guests who have stayed at least three times at any of the hotels gives front-desk employees immediate access to such information as whether a guest smokes, whether he or she prefers wine or a rose in the evening, and even what kind of pillow is preferred.

Those are only a few of the key operations management activities practiced at The Ritz-Carlton. The results are impressive. Customer satisfaction is upward of 95 percent. Employee turnover is only 48 percent, versus an annual industry average of more than 100 percent. One-hundred percent of key group accounts were retained in 1991. The number of employees needed per guest room during pre-opening activities of a new hotel was reduced 12 percent. Within a three-year period, The Ritz-Carlton reduced the number of hours worked per guest room by 8 percent. Housekeeping cost per occupied room was reduced from $7.90 at the end of 1991 to $7.30 at the beginning of 1992. The average time required to clean a room has decreased from 30 to 28.5 minutes. Even elevator waiting time has been reduced by 33 percent. Departmental profits per available guest room are nearly five times the industry average. One lesson the hotel has learned is to never underestimate the value of even one idea or improvement effort.

Questions for Discussion

1. How does The Ritz-Carlton deliver value to its customers?
2. How do human resources and information technology help achieve the objectives of the company?
3. What productivity improvements are cited? Do you believe quality im-

provement efforts have had a direct effect on productivity? Why?

Saturn Corporation Is Built on Value and Satisfaction[13]

General Motors' Saturn project has become a test of whether U.S. industry can adapt and beat the Japanese automakers at what they do best. Saturn was born in June 1982, when GM started a top-secret project aimed at revolutionizing carmaking in the United States. It was named *Saturn* after the rocket that helped the United States overcome the Soviets' lead in space exploration. About two and one-half years later, GM's chairman Roger Smith called Saturn the "key to GM's long term competitiveness, survival, and success." The Saturn Corporation was formed as a wholly owned subsidiary of General Motors in January 1985.

Here is a chronology of the events in the production of the Saturn:

- *November 1983.* Roger Smith officially unveils the project: a 60-mpg, $6000 subcompact.
- *September 1984.* The first Saturn vehicle is assembled for testing.
- *January 1985.* GM announces that it will invest $5 billion in Saturn, employ 6,000 people to build it, and produce 500,000 cars per year.
- *July 1985.* GM and the United Automobile Workers (UAW) announce a unique agreement for Japanese-style production of Saturn cars at Spring Hill, Tennessee.
- *October 1986.* Hurt by delays and management changes, GM cuts the original production plans in half—investing $3 billion, employing 3,000 workers, and producing 250,000 cars per year.
- *January 1988.* GM starts recruiting Saturn employees.

- *Spring 1990.* First group of Saturns are assembled for testing of mass-manufacturing systems.
- *Summer 1990.* Production of cars for dealers begins.
- *October 1990.* Saturns are scheduled to go on sale as 1991 models.

In the small-car market in which Saturn vehicles are competing, quality is essential. Meeting and exceeding customers' requirements and expectations on a consistent basis is one of the key strategies contributing to the success of Saturn. To accomplish that objective, the Saturn project began with a clean slate. Nothing in GM's manufacturing past was required for building the Saturn; all design and engineering approaches were new. The Saturn manufacturing complex is self-sufficient, having its own stamping plants, power-train assembly, and foundries. Saturn was originally intended to be a high-tech factory full of automated equipment and robots. However, GM's joint venture with Toyota proved that labor-management relations could do more for quality and productivity than automation. Workers are chosen more for their interpersonal skills than for technical skills.

Saturn fabricates and assembles both manual and automatic transmissions on the same line, in any sequence, a first for an American manufacturer. Cars move along the line on wooden pallets, and workers travel with them, which is easier on workers' legs than walking down the line on concrete to install parts. GM even overhauled the administrative systems. As each finished car exits the plant, Saturn's computers automatically authorize payment to suppliers. The company has only one database for all its financial operations, including purchasing, payroll, and dealer billing.

Saturn does not have a formal "quality department." There is no one "director of quality." Instead, a series of Quality Councils set quality goals and provide general direction. The councils are composed of both UAW union and management-team members who meet on a periodic basis. The highest Quality Council is chaired by the president of the local UAW union and the president of Saturn Corporation. In addition to Quality Councils, Saturn has Specific Quality Resource Areas to aid and support the team member assembling the vehicles on the factory floor. The Quality Resource Areas are also responsible for the development and audit of Quality Procedures, Quality Methods, and Quality Systems.

Saturn's corporate philosophy reads as follows.

We, the Saturn Team, in concert with the UAW and General Motors, believe that meeting the needs of Customers, Saturn Members, Suppliers, Dealers and Neighbors is fundamental to fulfilling our mission.

To meet our customers' needs:

- Our products and services must be world leaders in value and satisfaction.

To meet our members' needs:

- We will create a sense of belonging in an environment of mutual trust, respect and dignity.
- We believe that all people want to be involved in decisions that affect them, care about their jobs and each other, take pride in themselves and in their contributions and want to share in the success of their efforts.
- We will develop the tools, training and education for each member, recognizing individual skills and knowledge.

- We believe that creative, motivated, responsible team members who understand that change is critical to success are Saturn's most important asset.

To meet our suppliers' and dealers' needs:

- We will strive to create real partnerships with them.
- We will be open and fair in our dealings, reflecting trust, respect and their importance to Saturn.
- We want dealers and suppliers to feel ownership in Saturn's mission and philosophy as their own.

To meet the needs of our neighbors, the communities in which we live and operate:

- We will be good citizens, protect the environment and conserve natural resources.
- We will seek to cooperate with government at all levels and strive to be sensitive, open and candid in all our public statements.

By continuously operating according to this philosophy, we will fulfill our mission.

That statement represents a fundamental commitment not to be compromised or undermined by decisions that could be attractive in the short term but would lead the organization to a very different direction in the long run. Every decision must fit Saturn's philosophy.

Saturn's culture can be summed up in one word: *partnership.* Starting from ground level, Saturn defined the new values necessary to compete effectively and set out to attract the kind of GM managers and UAW workers who would be willing to assume the challenges and risks associated with those values. The key to creating such an environment was a close partnership between GM and the UAW in most strategic, tactical, and operational decisions. Such sharing of decision making and building of mutual trust was unique in the American auto industry. Educational initiatives directed at improving union leaders' business knowledge and managers' "people" knowledge to strengthen communication were important elements of the partnership.

One of the major innovations is GM's agreement with the UAW. Teams of workers have broad decision-making powers and responsibilities. They receive hundreds of hours of training and must understand the economics behind each car. Major differences from previous contracts are noteworthy.

- The contract has no specific expiration date. Exactly one year from the date the first car came off the line, management and labor could begin modifying the contract, if necessary, on a day-to-day basis.
- Saturn workers have a hand in the design of the vehicle and the factory.
- Job classifications, which number in the dozens in traditional automobile factories, have been cut to only a few. As a result, a production worker can do a simple repair without halting production to wait for an electrician or other specialist.
- Saturn workers are on salary and receive 80 percent of the wages other UAW members receive, but are eligible for bonuses depending on the car's success.

Worker involvement is unprecedented. Intensive training and elimination of barriers between management and labor characterize Saturn. Teams of line workers do more than just assemble parts; they "hire" workers, approve parts from suppliers, choose their own equipment, and handle administrative matters such as their budgets. Workers and union representatives have much input on business issues. In 1991, when managers increased production and wound up raising the number of defects, line workers staged a slowdown during the visit of GM's chairman. The president of the UAW stated, "We are not going to sacrifice quality to get productivity." Managers eventually eased off their production goals.

The heart of the organizational structure of Saturn is a *work unit*, a team of about 15 people who make decisions by consensus. Work units evolve, starting as conventional teams with external union and management advisors, then later assuming the responsibilities traditionally assigned to a supervisor or foreman. The team hires other members, teaches them Saturn's mission, philosophy, and values, and ensures that they develop the skills necessary to perform the team's tasks. As group interaction increases, the team moves toward becoming completely self-directed. Team members, most of whom have worked from 5 to 25 years in the auto industry, receive from 250 to 750 hours of intensive education and training just to prepare for their jobs. The education emphasizes behavioral subjects, leadership, and team development, and even includes learning to read a balance sheet. Saturn opens its books internally and expects employees to know how much their operations are adding to the cost of the car.

Partnerships extend to suppliers and dealers. Saturn's goal is to establish a long-term partnership with only one supplier for each input based on mutual trust, high quality standards, just-in-time delivery, and continuous improvement. Because situations in which dealers feel threatened by competition from one another have proven to be counterproductive in the automobile industry, Saturn dealers have designated market areas and help their counterparts in other regions as needed.

Day-to-day monitoring of product quality is accomplished through the use of statistical methods, adherence to Saturn Quality Systems and Procedures, the appropriate use of various problem-solving tools, quality-related education in a team environment, and inherent team motivation and enthusiasm. Work-unit members receive customer feedback from the field within 24 hours to allow for rapid analysis and appropriate corrective action.

In 1994 Saturn captured 3.18 percent of the U.S. car market, with 73 percent of the buyers classified as "plus business" to General Motors. Had Saturn not been available, those buyers would not have purchased a GM product. Ongoing surveys show that 97 percent of Saturn owners say they would "enthusiastically recommend the purchase of a Saturn car" to a friend, relative or neighbor.

Questions for Discussion

1. How do the issues discussed in this case relate to concepts introduced in this chapter?

2. GM had hoped to reduce the time needed to bring a new car to market with Saturn. The Japanese were able to do it in three years or less, but Saturn took eight years. Why do you think the project took so long?

3. Write a research report on the status of Saturn to date. Questions you may consider include: How has the car sold relative to imports? How do dealers focus on the customer? What do the GM annual reports say?

Summary of Key Points

••• Production is the process of converting or transforming resources into goods or services. Operations include all activities associated with production and may involve manufacturing, transportation, supply, and service. Production/operations management (P/OM), therefore, refers to the management of all resources needed to produce goods and services. The true purpose of P/OM is to deliver customer value through continuous improvement of overall company performance and capabilities.

••• A hierarchical classification of planning and decision making provides a useful framework with which to view P/OM. Such classification categorizes plans and decisions as strategic, tactical, or operational and encompasses a wide spectrum of areas including strategic business planning, product and process design, materials management, and planning, scheduling, and quality control.

••• A production system is the collection of all interrelated activities and operations involved in producing goods and services. Production systems consist of suppliers, inputs, processes, outputs, customers (both external and internal), and management. This framework applies equally to manufacturing and service systems.

••• A process is a sequence of activities that is intended to produce a certain result for a customer. Typical processes in a manufacturing system include receiving, conversion, assembly, packaging, and shipping.

••• The production system is influenced by various environmental factors including economic factors, government regulations, competition, and technology. All other functional areas within the firm also influence production.

••• The Industrial Revolution laid the foundation for the development and growth of P/OM. Most of the twentieth century was focused on the development of tools and techniques for improving cost effectiveness and operations efficiency. In the last two decades, however, quality, product variety, manufacturing flexibility, quick response, service, and value have emerged as important issues.

••• Operations managers must focus on ensuring the production of high-quality goods and services, providing them in the proper quantities at the proper time, managing human resources, and adapting to organizational change.

••• Business is now recognizing that competitive success cannot be achieved solely through exceptional finance and marketing efforts. P/OM is a critical element of business strategy and must be understood by all managers, regardless of their functional discipline.

Key Terms

Production
Operations
Production/Operations Management (P/OM)
Operations management
Production system
Service
Consumers
External customers
Internal customers
Process
Lean production
Total cycle time
Value
Global integration
World-class

Review Questions

1. Define *production.*

2. To which activities does the term *operations* refer? Briefly explain each of those activities, and provide examples of real companies that perform such operations.

3. Describe the major planning and decision-making areas that are important to managing operations. What are some of the generic issues addressed in each area?

4. Explain the hierarchical classification of planning and decision making.

5. Define *production system?* Define its major components, and provide examples of each for both a manufacturing and a service system.

6. Explain the difference between external and internal customers and suppliers. Provide several examples of each.

7. Define *process.* Describe the typical processes in a manufacturing system.

8. Discuss the major environmental influences on the production system. Which are external and which are internal to the firm?

9. Discuss the major changes and trends in P/OM that have occurred during this century.

10. Explain the major differences between craft production and mass production.

11. What were the key reasons for Japan's emergence as a global industrial competitor?

12. What impacts did lean production have on manufacturing systems?

13. Define *total cycle time.* Why is it an important concern to business?

14. What does the term *quality* mean today? How does it differ from the older concept of "defect-free products"?

15. Explain the concept of *value.* How does value tie together all the evolutionary trends in P/OM?

16. What implications did the MIT Commission on Industrial Productivity study have for P/OM?

17. Explain the role of operations managers in delivering customer value through the continuous improvement of overall company performance and capabilities.

18. Define *global integration,* and explain why it is important to modern operations management.

19. Define *world-class.*

20. Discuss some of the challenges facing modern operations managers.

Discussion Questions

1. Explain how the various functions of P/OM might apply in these situations (in a manner similar to the discussion of MamaMia's).

    a. Police services

    b. Street maintenance

    c. University education

2. Would these decisions be classified as strategic, tactical, or operational?

    a. Adding more grocery clerks to checkout counters when lines become long.

    b. Deciding to install a drive-through window in a fast-food restaurant.

    c. Scheduling X-ray equipment for the next day.

    d. Leasing 100,000 square feet of warehouse space for the next month.

    e. Planning a storefront display for the Christmas holiday season.

3. Would you expect a first-line supervisor to be involved in strategic planning? If not, with what level of planning would you expect such a person be involved, and why?

4. Provide three examples of manufacturing systems in the same fashion as in Table 1.1.

5. Provide three examples of service systems in the same fashion as in Table 1.1.

6. A three-way classification system for organizations could categorize by manufactured product versus service, profit versus nonprofit, and public versus private. List the categories for each of these organizations:

    a. Water works   f. Bakery

    b. Bank   g. Blood bank

    c. Library   h. State license plate

    d. Post office   production

    e. Local bar   i. Church

    j. Drugstore   l. Federal reserve

    k. School

7. Explain the role of feedback in service industries such as fire departments, state legislatures, post offices, charities, and ambulance services.

8. Do you believe the "Taylor system" of scientific management might have contributed to the competitive woes of U.S. businesses in recent years? On what do you base your opinion?

9. Find some articles about recent winners of the Malcolm Baldrige National Quality Award. Explain how those companies' operations management practices have contributed to improvement in the quality of their product or service.

10. Write a report on the growth of Japanese automobile plants in the United States. How are they managed? How do their management practices differ from those of traditional U.S. automakers?

11. Interview an operations manager of a local company. Why did he or she choose that career path? What rewards and opportunities does this person find in the job?

12. List at least five activities that each of these managers would perform in managing people and in managing work.

    a. Manager of an automobile assembly plant

    b. Manager of a hamburger franchise

    c. Head chef

    d. Branch manager of a local bank

    e. Warehouse manager

13. The director of material management for a large manufacturing company stated: "All significant problems impacting manufacturing effectiveness result from one very common problem—incomplete and inaccurate planning, monitoring, and controlling regarding all aspects and phases of the business and manufacturing operations." Do you agree or disagree with that statement? Explain.

Notes

1. *Business Week,* April 20, 1987, p. 56.

2. Elizabeth A. Haas, "Breakthrough Manufacturing," *Harvard Business Review,* March–April 1987, pp. 75–81. Copyright 1987 by the President and Fellows of Harvard College; all rights reserved.

3. "The Difference Japanese Management Makes," *Business Week,* July 14, 1986, pp. 47–50.

4. "Competitiveness—How U.S. Companies Stack Up Now," *Fortune,* April 18, 1994, pp. 52–64. See also Alex Taylor III, "U.S. Cars Come Back," *Fortune,* November 16, 1992, pp. 52–85.

5. Adapted from Thomas J. Billesbach, "Applying Lean Production Principles to a Process Facility," *Production*

and Inventory Management Journal 35, no. 3 (third quarter 1994), pp. 40–44.

6. Richard Norman, *Service Management: Strategy and Leadership* (New York: John Wiley & Sons, 1984).

7. Gene Bylinsky, "The Digital Factory," *Fortune,* November 14, 1994, pp. 92–110.

8. Ronald Henkoff, "Service Is Everybody's Business," *Fortune,* June 27, 1994, pp. 48–60.

9. Carol A. Reeves and David A. Bednar, "Defining Quality: Alternatives and Implications," *Academy of Management Review* 19, no. 3 (1994), pp. 419–445.

10. Thomas F. Wallace, "The Value Proposition, The Total Product and Customer Delight," *APICS—The Performance Advantage,* February 1994, pp. 46–47.

11. Michael E. McGrath and Richard W. Hoole, "Manufacturing's New Economies of Scale," *Harvard Business Review,* May–June 1992, pp. 94–102. Copyright 1992 by the President and Fellows of Harvard College; all rights reserved.

12. Cheri Henderson, "Putting on the Ritz," *The TQM Magazine* 2, no. 5 (November–December 1992), pp. 292–296; and The Ritz-Carlton Hotel Company Application Summary, 1992 Winner, Malcolm Baldrige National Quality Award.© 1994, The Ritz-Carlton Hotel Company, All rights reserved. RITZ-CARLTON is a federally registered trademark of The Ritz-Carlton Hotel Company, L.L.C.

13. Based on a variety of materials provided by the Saturn Assistance Center, Saturn Corporation, Spring Hill, Tennessee, and used with permission; and Frederick Standish, "As Saturn's Debut Nears, Skepticism Still Abounds," *The Cincinnati Enquirer,* July 7, 1990, p. F-2; "Here Comes GM's Saturn," *Business Week,* April 9, 1990, pp. 56–62; "Saturn Workers Say 'No' to Speed Up," *APICS—The Performance Advantage,* February 1992, p. 11; and "Saturn," *Business Week,* August 17, 1992, pp. 86–91.

Chapter Appendix
Management Science Models in P/OM

In Chapter 1 we identified the types of issues addressed by operations managers. The best decision-making approach for a particular situation depends on the type of problem. Routine, repetitive problems can usually be programmed and solved at lower levels of an organization. Problems that are novel and unstructured usually cannot be programmed and must be solved at higher levels of the organization. For example, the weekly scheduling of jobs in a factory is a highly repetitive task for which a computerized system using quantitative decision techniques is likely to be used. In contrast, the decision to invest in a new, advanced manufacturing system would require the expert judgment of experienced managers.

Many P/OM decisions can be facilitated through the use of quantitative methods. The role of quantitative analysis in the managerial decision-making process is summarized by the flowchart in Figure 1A.1. The process is initiated when a problem becomes apparent. The manager responsible for making a decision or selecting a course of action will probably make an analysis of the problem that includes

••• A statement of the specific goals or objectives.
••• An identification of all constraints.
••• An evaluation of alternative decisions.
••• A selection of the apparent "best" decision for solving the problem.

The manager's analysis may take two basic forms: qualitative and quantitative. The *qualitative* analysis will be based primarily on the manager's judgment and experience. Such analysis includes the manager's intuitive "feel" for the problem and is more an art than a science. If the manager has had experience with similar problems or if the problem is relatively simple, a qualitative analysis is appropriate. However, if the manager has had little experience with similar problems or if the problem is sufficiently important and complex, a *quantitative* analysis is needed, in which the facts or data associated with the problem

Figure 1A.1
Role of Quantitative Analysis in the Decision-Making Process

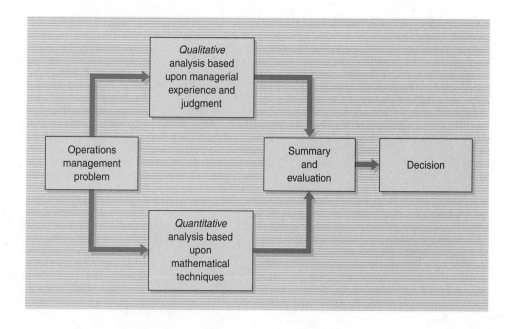

are used to develop mathematical expressions that describe objectives, constraints, and relationships. Then, by using one or more such techniques, the analyst provides a decision recommendation based on the quantitative aspects of the problem.

Both qualitative and quantitative analyses of a problem provide important information for the decision maker. In many cases, an operations manager may draw upon both sources and, through comparing and evaluating all of the information, arrive at a final decision.

Many quantitative tools are available to assist operations managers in solving decision problems. The tools fit into two categories. Some are *problem-specific techniques,* such as methods for finding the best location for a central facility, balancing an assembly line, or sequencing machines in a production facility. Others are *general tools* useful in solving a variety of problems whose objectives and structures are similar. They include statistical methods and related problem-analysis aids and techniques of management science such as linear programming, simulation, and waiting-line theory. These general tools of management science have broad applicability. For instance, simulation can be used to analyze proposed designs for production or service facilities and can also be used to evaluate scheduling rules for production sequencing.

In this appendix we introduce management science models for analyzing and solving P/OM problems. Details of the mechanics of these models are presented in Supplementary Chapters A through E at the end of the book. The emphasis in this appendix is not on the techniques per se, but rather on the *use* of the techniques to contribute to better decision making. In addition, examples of specific applications of the methods in P/OM decision making appear throughout the book. Many of the techniques can be implemented on a spreadsheet, and spreadsheets are used throughout this book whenever appropriate. You are encouraged to use a spreadsheet to solve end-of-chapter problems.

Management Science/Operations Research Techniques

Of the variety of names used for the body of knowledge and methodology involving quantitative approaches to decision making, two of the most widely known and accepted are **management science (MS)** and **operations research (OR).** Operations research is usually associated with mathematically based problem-solving approaches. Management science is a broad discipline that includes all rational approaches to decision making based on applications of scientific methodology. The management science function considers organizational objectives and resources and, by using a scientific problem-solving approach, attempts to establish long- and/or short-range policies and decisions that are in the best interest of the organization. A management science problem may be as specific as improving the efficiency of a production line or as broad as establishing a long-range corporate strategy involving a combination of financial, marketing, and manufacturing considerations. Thus management science techniques can be useful at all levels of decision making.

Often, the terms *management science* and *operations research* are used interchangeably or together (MS/OR). Actually, MS/OR may be more broadly defined to include a multidisciplinary scientific approach to decision making. In practice, MS/OR studies are frequently conducted by an MS/OR team, which might consist of a quantitative specialist, an engineer, an accountant, a behavioral scientist, and a manager from the particular problem area being studied (for example, marketing, finance, or manufacturing). While the analysis of a problem situation almost always includes some qualitative considerations, significant portions of most MS/OR studies are based on quantitative decision-making techniques.

A central theme in the MS/OR approach to decision making is a problem orientation. Nearly all MS/OR projects begin with the recognition of a problem that does not have an obvious solution. Quantitative analysts may then be asked to assist in identifying the "best" decision or solution for the problem. Reasons for using an MS/OR approach in the decision-making process might be that

1. The problem is complex, and the manager cannot develop a good solution without the aid of quantitative specialists.
2. The problem is very important (for example, a large amount of money is involved), and the manager desires a thorough analysis before attempting a decision.
3. The problem is new, and the manager has no previous experience on which to draw in making a decision.
4. The problem is repetitive, and the manager saves time and effort by relying on quantitative procedures to make the routine decision recommendations.

For example, the scheduling of many jobs in a manufacturing facility can potentially involve millions of solutions. Finding a schedule that meets the objectives is a very difficult task because of the vast number of possibilities. Locating a new factory is an irreversible decision that involves large amounts of capital. Planning for production of an entirely new product involves activities never before performed. And if inventories must be continually reordered on a routine basis, an MS/OR program can keep costs low and free the manager for more important tasks.

The power of management science has been enhanced in recent years by improvements in information systems, particularly in the development of bigger and faster computers, database technology, and expert systems. *Expert systems* are computer programs that store human knowledge and process that knowledge as a human expert would. They are particularly suited for relatively unstructured problems with inexact data that require qualitative reasoning.

A study by Ford and others examined the use of MS/OR techniques in production among the 500 largest industrial firms.[1] The findings were that MS/OR use is frequent in scheduling, forecasting, advertising, and sales research. Those applications involve highly repetitive decisions that occur with high frequency and thus are well suited to quantitative techniques. Regression analysis, linear programming, and simulation are the most utilized methods in a variety of P/OM application areas.

Mathematical Models

Most applications of management science in P/OM are based on a mathematical model. A **model** is any representation of a real object or situation. Some models are physical replicas of an object, such as an architect's scale model of a new manufacturing plant. They are called *iconic models.* Others are physical in form but do not have the same physical appearance as the object being modeled. They are called *analog models.* For example, the layout of machines on a plant floor can be represented by paper cutouts of different colors and sizes.

Still other models—the primary type we study—represent a real situation with a system of symbols and mathematical relationships and expressions. They are referred to as **mathematical models.** For instance, operations managers often make use of break-even analysis to determine how much must be produced and sold before a product becomes profitable. Break-even analysis is based on mathematical models for cost, revenue, and profit. An example of the use of break-even analysis appears later in this subsection.

The value of a model is that it enables us to draw conclusions about real situations by studying and analyzing it. For example, an airplane designer might test an iconic model of a new airplane in a wind tunnel to learn about the potential flying characteristics of the full-size airplane. Similarly, a mathematical model may be used to draw conclusions about how much profit will be earned if a specified quantity of a particular product is sold. With each example, an analyst would be able to test and experiment with the model to learn about the real situation.

In general, experimenting with models requires less time and is less expensive than experimenting with the real object or situation. Certainly a model airplane is quicker and less expensive to build and study than the full-size airplane. Similarly, a mathematical model of profit allows a quick identification of profit expectations without requiring the manager to wait and see what the profit is after actually producing and selling a certain number of units. In addition, models have the advantage of reducing the risk associated with the real situation. For example, bad designs or bad decisions that cause the model airplane to crash or a mathematical model to project a $10,000 loss can be avoided in the real situation. Of course, the accuracy of the conclusions and decisions based on a model depend on how well the model represents the real situation.

Data preparation is an important step in applying management science. In many cases, data can be obtained from company records, accounting personnel, and so on. A good computerized information system often assists a manager in obtaining the data necessary to solve a decision problem. In other cases, data may have to be collected by time-study observation or a statistical sampling procedure. Data preparation is often a costly and time-consuming part of the decision process.

Once the model development and data preparation steps have been completed, the model can be solved. In this step, the analyst attempts to identify the values of the decision variables that provide the "best" output for the model. The specific decision-variable value or values providing the best output are referred to as the *optimal solution* for the model. Rarely can that solution be found without the aid of a computer. However, throughout this book, simple examples are used to illustrate the essential concepts. You should be aware that real models are usually much larger and more complex than the examples presented here.

It is important to realize that model development and model solution are not completely separable. While an analyst wants to develop an accurate model or representation of the actual problem situation, he or she also wants to be able to find a solution to the problem. If the only goal were to develop the most accurate and realistic mathematical model possible, the model may end up so large and complex that obtaining a solution with it is impossible. A model that works is preferable to one that does not , even if it provides only a rough approximation of the best decision. As you learn more about the quantitative solution procedures available, you will have a better idea of the types of mathematical models that can be developed and solved.

After a model solution has been obtained, both the quantitative analyst and the manager will want to know how good the solution really is. While the analyst has undoubtedly taken many precautions to develop a realistic model, often the goodness or accuracy of the model cannot be assessed until model solutions are generated. Model testing and validation are frequently conducted with relatively small "test" problems that have known or at least expected solutions. If the model generates the expected solutions and if other output information appears correct, the go-ahead may be given for using the model on the full-scale problem. Otherwise, corrective action such as model modification and/or collection of more accurate input data is probably needed.

To illustrate the use of a mathematical model, a break-even analysis for analyzing a production problem follows.

Example

Computing the Break-Even Point for a Product

Eberle Electronics is considering expanding its production facility to manufacture an electrical component. David Rogers, an operations manager, has been asked to determine how many units would have to be produced and sold in order to break even. The cost for new equipment and installation is $100,000. Each unit produced would have a variable cost of $12 per unit and sell for $20.

The equation for total cost is

$$\text{total cost} = \text{fixed cost} + \text{variable cost}.$$

The fixed cost is that portion of total cost that does not vary with the amount produced. If 10,000 units were produced and sold, the total cost would be

$$\text{total cost} = 100{,}000 + 12(10{,}000)$$

$$= \$220{,}000.$$

The revenue received from selling 10,000 units would be $20(10,000) = \$200,000$, so at this production level, the firm would incur a loss of $220,000 - \$200,000 = \$20,000$. However, if 13,000 units were produced and sold, the projected profit would be

$$20(13{,}000) - 100{,}000 - 12(13{,}000) = \$4{,}000.$$

The amount of sales at which the net profit is zero—or equivalently, the point where total cost equals total revenue—is called the **break-even point.** Figure 1A.2 is a simple spreadsheet designed to find the break-even point by varying the sales quantity. We can find the break-even point mathematically by letting x be the sales volume at the break-even point and setting the total revenue equal to total cost. For this example,

Figure 1A.2 Spreadsheet for Break-Even Analysis (EBERLE.XLS)*

	A	B	C	D	E	F	G	H
1	Eberle Electronics							
2								
3	Fixed cost	$ 100,000						
4	Variable cost	$ 12						
5	Selling price	$ 20						
6								
7	Sales quantity	Total revenue	Total cost	Total profit				
8	10000	$ 200,000	$ 220,000	$ (20,000)				
9	10500	$ 210,000	$ 226,000	$ (16,000)				
10	11000	$ 220,000	$ 232,000	$ (12,000)				
11	11500	$ 230,000	$ 238,000	$ (8,000)				
12	12000	$ 240,000	$ 244,000	$ (4,000)				
13	12500	$ 250,000	$ 250,000	$ -				
14	13000	$ 260,000	$ 256,000	$ 4,000				
15	13500	$ 270,000	$ 262,000	$ 8,000				
16	14000	$ 280,000	$ 268,000	$ 12,000				
17	14500	$ 290,000	$ 274,000	$ 16,000				
18								

$$\text{total cost} = 100,000 + 12x$$

$$\text{total revenue} = 20x.$$

Thus,

$$20x = 100,000 + 12x$$

and hence

$$x = 12,500.$$

If sales are less than 12,500 units, the firm will incur a loss; if sales are more than 12,500, a profit will be realized. This is illustrated in Figure 1A.3. Such information, when combined with sales forecasts, can assist the manager in deciding whether or not to pursue the expansion.

We caution the reader that *any* mathematical model can be dangerous when misused or used carelessly. Most models have a number of implicit assumptions. For example, an assumption in break-even analysis is that time is not a critical variable. At the very least, revenues and costs are assumed to occur simultaneously. In reality, costs are incurred well in advance of their associated revenues. Not having sufficient working capital to maintain a firm until it earns

---

*All named spreadsheets (.XLS) throughout the book are available as Excel files on the ancillary disks which accompany the main text.

Figure 1A.3
Break-Even Analysis for
Facility Expansion Decision

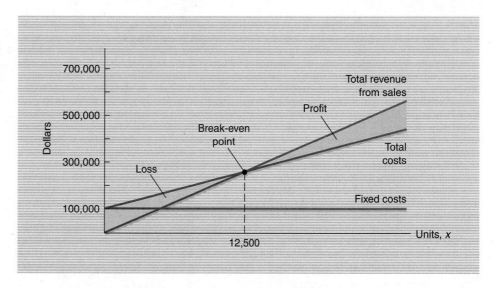

a steady flow of revenues is a very common cause of failure for new businesses. The model also assumes that costs and prices are constant over time. That is rarely true. Not only may the costs of inputs and the price of the product change over time, but they may change by disproportionate amounts so that the cost/price relationships are altered.

Another assumption is that neither unit variable costs nor unit prices vary with the quantity produced or sold. Quantity discounts are common in all industries, and the price may be adjusted for many other buyer concessions such as rapid payment or delayed delivery. Likewise, fixed costs may not be truly fixed over the entire range of output. If the output is low, the firm will trim as many of its fixed charges as possible.

The model assumes that facilities and equipment have infinite capacity. Actually, as the output increases, the production system's capacity is reached and additional facilities are needed. They produce sudden increases in fixed costs. Finally, the assumption of constant variable and fixed costs per unit implies that a single technology is used over the entire range of output. As output increases or decreases, the typical firm may be forced to change to a different technology. In such cases, both fixed and variable costs are changed.

We see that even in a very simple model such as break-even analysis, a decision maker must draw upon considerable experience and judgment in interpreting the answers and incorporating factors that cannot be quantified. Thus, caution must be exercised in using quantitative decision tools. Nevertheless, such methods can be extremely useful when they are properly applied.

Management Science: Success and Failure

Since management science is a relatively new discipline, it has not yet been fully integrated into managerial decision making in all levels and all organizations. Many companies cannot afford to maintain a professional staff of management scientists or hire consultants whenever a potential project arises. In many companies, industrial engineers, market research analysts, and other personnel trained in management science perform quantitative analyses. Thus there have been numerous successful applications of management science, particularly at the operational level. Many of the examples presented in this book are typical of ongoing projects in the P/OM area. With the growing use and declining cost of computers and microprocessors, the use of management science in P/OM is continually growing.

Management science is not a magic cure for P/OM problems. There are many reasons why quantitative methods "fail" or are not accepted by managers. Some common reasons include

1. *Expectations of the manager and analyst.* Managers may expect the mathematical techniques to provide answers beyond what they are capable of providing. Also, management scientists may expect managers to be able to understand models that are too complex for them.

2. *Limitations of model building.* Decision problems in operations management usually have multiple, conflicting objectives. Many models cannot capture their realism and can deal with only a single objective.

3. *Time constraints.* Models often require substantial data preparation. They may not be able to provide a solution in time for a manager to use it.

4. *Dynamic environment.* Whereas the operations manager lives in a changing, dynamic world, the solution to a model often solves only a static problem. If the solution is not carefully implemented, poor results may occur as conditions change.

5. *Resistance to change.* Many traditional managers are reluctant to accept solutions provided by mathematical methods and computers. Although that attitude is changing, such skepticism persists.

6. *Preconceived solutions.* Managers may have preferred alternatives prior to any analysis, quantitative or otherwise. Even though the results of a model may indicate a better solution, it may be rejected.

Throughout the decision-making process, managers and management scientists must work together closely to overcome these types of problems.

Key Terms

Management science (MS)
Operations research (OR)
Model
Mathematical model
Break-even point

Notes

1. F. Nelson Ford, David A. Bradbard, William N. Ledbetter, and James F. Cox, "The Use of Operations Research in Production Management," *Production and Inventory Management* 28, no. 3 (1987), pp. 59–62.

Problems

1. Suppose the variable cost for the Eberle Electronics example increases to $14. Use the spreadsheet model to find the new break-even point. Verify your answer mathematically.

2. Clifton Electrical Equipment, Inc. , is considering manufacturing electrical switches. Preliminary cost estimates follow.

Fixed costs	$10,000.00 per year
Unit revenue	$0.45 per switch
Direct material	$0.15 per switch
Direct labor	$0.10 per switch
Overhead	$0.05 per switch

a. What is the break-even volume?

b. If the fixed costs and direct labor are both underestimated by 10 percent, what is the break-even volume?

3. A nonprofit organization receives a subsidy of $100,000 per year from the city. The unit revenue for the services it provides is $0.75. The unit variable cost is $1.00, and the annual fixed costs are $50,000.

a. Up to what level will the operations be economical? Use break-even analysis.

b. If the city is willing to increase its subsidy by 25 percent, how much additional service can the organization provide if unit revenue is lowered to $0.65?

4. Generally, higher product prices result in decreased demand, whereas lower product prices result in increased demand. Let

$$D = \text{annual demand for a product in units and}$$

$$p = \text{price per unit.}$$

Assume a firm accepts the following price-demand relationship as realistic.

$$D = 1,000 - 20p$$

where the price (p) must be between $15 and $40.

a. How many units can the firm sell at the $15 per unit price? At the $40 per unit price?

b. Show the mathematical model for the total revenue (TR), which is the annual demand multiplied by the unit price.

c. On the basis of other considerations, the firm's managers will consider only the price alternatives of $20, $25, and $30. Use your model from part (b) to determine the price alternative that will maximize the TR.

d. What is the expected annual demand and TR with your recommended price?

5. A firm is considering expanding its production operation so that it can introduce a new product into the market. The estimated cost for equipment purchases and installation is $100,000. The $100,000 will be incurred by the company as a one-time start-up cost. The variable cost for each unit produced is $12.

a. Letting x indicate the number of units produced, develop a total cost model.

b. If the product sells for $20 per unit, develop a total profit model expressed in terms of x, the number of units produced.

c. If the sales forecast is 10,000 units of the new product, should the firm proceed with the production expansion project?

Chapter Two
Managing for Quality and High Performance

Chapter Outline

Applied P/OM

Schlitz Brewing Company
Ford Motor Company
Nissan Motor Corporation
AT&T
Scandinavian Airlines System

P/OM in Practice

Zytec, Inc. Builds on the Deming Philosophy
Total Quality Management at AT&T

I n Chapter 1 we defined the notion of customer value—the relationship between the quality of products and services that a company offers to the price. The *Customer Value Policy* of MamaMia's Pizza is prominently displayed in the restaurant:

••• We shall produce products and provide services at all times which meet or exceed the expectations of our customers.

••• We shall continually strive to improve the performance of all our operations.

••• We shall not be content to be "as good" as our competitors; our commitment is to be increasingly superior in all that we do.

••• Contribution to improving quality and operational performance is a responsibility shared by everyone at MamaMia's.

MamaMia's goals are as appropriate for a large company as for a small one, and the principles for meeting them are the same for either. Companies can enhance value either by improving product and service quality relative to price or by lowering price while maintaining quality. Improving quality requires a commitment to understanding and meeting customer needs; lowering prices requires better operational performance. In describing these principles, this chapter will address

••• The importance, scope, and fundamental elements of total quality management (TQM) as an operations strategy for competitive advantage.

••• Similarities and differences in the quality management philosophies of Deming, Juran, and Crosby.

••• The nature of the Malcolm Baldrige National Quality Award, particularly the use of the Baldrige criteria as a model and assessment tool for total quality management.

••• The scope of the worldwide ISO 9000 quality system standards and how they differ from the Baldrige Award criteria.

••• Factors that contribute to successful implementation of TQM within an organization, as well as the pitfalls and barriers to implementation.

Productivity and Quality

Productivity—the ratio of the output of a production process to the inputs used, reveals the extent to which the resources of an organization are being managed effectively in transforming inputs to outputs. Productivity measurement is explained fully in Chapter 4, but as a simple example consider the fact that at MamaMia's productivity might be measured as the number of pizzas produced per labor hour.

American industry has had a long-standing love affair with productivity, particularly since the introduction of the "Taylor system" of production described in Chapter 1. As General Electric CEO Jack Welch stated, "For a company and for a nation, productivity is a matter of survival."[1] A low rate of productivity growth spawns a vicious cycle in which (1) fewer units produced means higher unit costs of labor, machinery, and energy; (2) higher unit costs lead to higher prices for goods and services; (3) higher prices lead to declines in sales volume; (4) lower sales volumes result in decreased revenues; (5) decreased revenues lead to idle plant capacity, lower employment, and reduced spending on research and development; and (6) those reductions in turn cause further declines in productivity, higher costs, increased unemployment, and a decline in the standard of living. Clearly, any nation that wants to be competitive in an international marketplace cannot allow that cycle to begin. Although the United States still ranks first among nations in the productivity of its manufacturing and services industries, improvement has slowed and competitors such as Japan and Germany are gaining, so the national emphasis on productivity is appropriate. However, an overemphasis on productivity often leads to a neglect of quality, as occurred in the case of the Schlitz Brewing Company.

Applied P/OM
Schlitz Brewing Company

A focus on cost at the expense of quality led to the demise of Schlitz.[2]

In the early 1970s Schlitz, the second largest brewer in the United States, began a cost-cutting campaign that included reducing the quality of beer ingredients by switching to corn syrup and hop pellets and shortening the brewing cycle by 50 percent. In the short term, Schlitz achieved higher returns on sales and assets than Anheuser-Busch. *Forbes* magazine asked, "Does it pay to build quality into a product if most customers don't notice? Schlitz seems to have a more successful answer." Soon after, however, market share and profits fell rapidly. By 1980 Schlitz's sales had declined 40 percent, the stock price fell from $69 to $5, and the company was eventually sold.

In general, American industry has been persuaded of the folly of sacrificing quality to increase productivity. Both are important, and quality improvements, if implemented correctly, may lead to higher productivity and lower costs by reducing rework, scrap, and after-sale service. We often use the term **hidden factory** to refer to the portion of plant capacity that exists to rework unsatisfactory parts, retest and reinspect rejected units, and so on. The hidden factory can account for 15 to 40 percent of a plant's capacity, and it exists solely because of poor quality.

Although some operations managers, especially those whose performance is evaluated on cost and quantity of output, still erroneously believe that quality improvements must inevitably lower productivity, most have discovered the fallacy of such thinking. Many major American companies, such as Motorola, Xerox, and U.S. automobile makers, learned about the importance of quality the hard way through serious competitive crises in the early 1980s. They saw that high productivity alone could not ensure business success. Moreover, they discovered that quality meant more than just controlling product defects, but included determining, meeting, and if possible exceeding customer expectations. With the help of leading quality experts, particularly W. Edwards Deming,

Joseph Juran, and Philip Crosby, top managers began to recognize quality as an essential element of competitive success, and it quickly became the focus of management strategy and decision making. Ford Motor Company's operating philosophy exemplifies that focus.

Applied P/OM
Ford Motor Company

The Ford operating philosophy is built around the quality theme.

The operating philosophy of Ford Motor Company is to meet customer needs and expectations by establishing and maintaining an environment that encourages all employees to pursue never-ending improvement in productivity and the quality of products and services throughout the corporation, its supply base, and its dealer organizations. To support that philosophy, Ford developed a set of "Guiding Principles" to achieve its mission:[3]

1. Quality comes first.
2. Customers are the focus of everything we do.
3. Continuous improvement is essential to our success.
4. Employee involvement is our way of life.
5. Dealers and suppliers are our partners.
6. Integrity is never compromised.

The term **total quality management (TQM)** conveys a total, companywide effort to achieve customer satisfaction through full involvement of the entire workforce as well as customers and suppliers, with a focus on continuous improvement (as reflected in Ford's "Guiding Principles"). TQM is both a comprehensive managerial philosophy and a collection of tools and approaches for its implementation. The key principles of TQM are to (1) satisfy the needs of customers, (2) prevent poor quality rather than correcting problems after the fact, (3) develop in everyone an attitude of continuous improvement, (4) understand the value of measuring performance to identify opportunities and maintain improvements, and (5) eliminate chronic sources of inefficiencies and costs. At MamaMia's, for example, that means providing good-tasting pizzas, complete with the desired crusts and toppings, along with the dining and delivery services that customers want. It means getting orders correct the first time and delivering them promptly. It also means seeking ideas for improvement from chefs, servers, and deliverers, as well as recording and analyzing customer complaints to identify areas needing improvement. Finally, it means streamlining food preparation through more effective kitchen layouts and perhaps shortening order-cycle time through computer technology.

It is unfortunate that a three-letter acronym is used to represent the philosophy embodied by TQM. Such acronyms tend to suggest the latest business fad that will eventually fade. Although the term may eventually disappear, TQM principles will remain. TQM is more than simply quality management; it is a *business management* framework for firms that aspire to be world class. Many believe it is now the *minimum requirement* for competing in the global market, and should form a natural framework for operations management. Over the last two decades, the principles of TQM have become engrained in the culture of America's leading companies and embraced by their leaders.

Economic Value of High Productivity and Quality

Shetty and Buehler point out, "Making companies productive and competitive is the ultimate responsibility of the manager."[4] Adding to the obvious economic value of productivity is the now accepted economic value of quality, which is what makes a company competitive in today's global market. For profit-making enterprises the combination of high quality and productivity translates into increased profitability, and for nonprofit organizations it means providing better services at lower cost. Thus, TQM—which encompasses both quality and productivity—benefits all organizations by

- Improving customer satisfaction through better and more reliable goods and services.
- Reducing waste and inventory.
- Increasing flexibility in meeting market demands.
- Reducing work in process.
- Improving delivery times.
- Better utilizing human resources.

The economic value of quality is further indicated by the following study results from Technical Assistance Research Programs, Inc.:

- The average company never hears from 96 percent of its unhappy customers. For every complaint received, the company has 26 customers with problems, 6 of which are serious.
- Of the customers who make complaints, more than half will do business with that organization again if their complaint is resolved. If the customer feels that the complaint was resolved quickly, this figure jumps to 95 percent.
- The average customer who has had a problem will tell 9 or 10 others about it. Customers who have had complaints resolved satisfactorily will tell only about 5 others.

Obviously, the ability to satisfy customers and maintain their loyalty translates directly to the bottom line.

Let us investigate how both quality and productivity increase *profitability,* which is a function of revenue and cost. *Revenue* depends on the selling price and the sales volume; *cost* is the value of the inputs or resources used to produce the outputs. Since operations managers are responsible for transforming inputs into outputs, productivity and quality decisions made by operations managers directly affect revenue, cost, and profitability.

To better understand the relationship between inputs, the transformation process, outputs, productivity, and quality, consider the basic definition of profit.

$$\text{Profit} = \text{revenue} - \text{cost}$$

Clearly, profit is positive if revenue is greater than cost. A change in any of the following factors can change profitability:

1. Selling price of the product or service.
2. Quantity of product or service sold.
3. Unit cost of a resource.
4. Quantity of a resource used per unit of output.

Suppose the cost of materials or other resources increases. A firm can attempt to offset such an increase in cost by increasing the selling price of the product or service in hopes of increasing the revenue. However, in the presence of competition, an increase in price may be accompanied by a decrease in sales and hence may not achieve the desired increase in revenue. Therefore, to maintain profitability, the firm may try to offset the increased cost of resources by attempting to increase the output per unit of resource used. Doing so provides an improvement in productivity. An alternative approach to maintaining or increasing profits is to improve the quality of the product so as to command a higher price or greater market share. Thus, profitability is sensitive to changes in both productivity and quality. Improved production quality, resulting in reduced scrap and rework, will reduce manufacturing and service costs, also leading to higher profits. This discussion is summarized in Figure 2.1.

Scope of Quality Management

Quality management is the responsibility of everyone in a company. Marketing and design, manufacturing, and service people all bear some portion of that responsibility. First, marketing people must identify customer expectations. Next, designers must ensure that those expectations are understood and translated into appropriate specifications for goods and services. **Specifications** are design characteristics that are defined by targets and tolerances. *Targets* are ideal values for which production is expected to strive; *tolerances* are acceptable deviations from these ideal values, established in recognition that it is impossible to meet the targets all the time. For example, MamaMia's might specify that a small pizza will contain 8.0 ± 0.5 ounces of cheese. The value 8.0 is the target, and ± 0.5 is the tolerance. Thus, a pizza may have between 7.5 and 8.5 ounces of cheese and still be acceptable. Similar specifications are used for services; for example, MamaMia's might specify that an express pizza will be served within five minutes after being ordered.

Once specifications are developed, it is up to the manufacturing or service-delivery function to ensure that they are met. Clearly, a five-minute pizza is not possible if it must be prepared and cooked from scratch. Thus, marketing and design people cannot simply throw a design "over the wall" to operations and

Figure 2.1
Economic Impacts of
Productivity and Quality

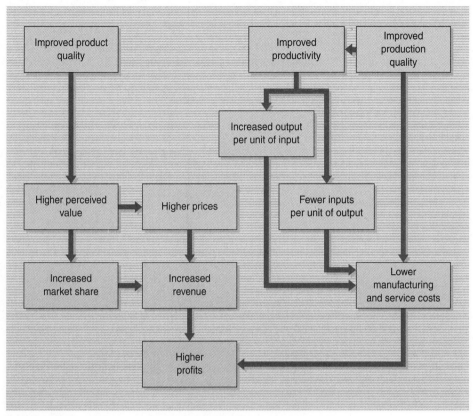

Note: The arrows can be interpreted as meaning "leads to."

expect production. Rather, they must work closely with operations managers to make sure their ideas can be carried out with the available equipment and personnel. A prime cause of poor quality is poor communication between marketing and operations. Figure 2.2 summarizes a *customer-driven quality cycle.*

Definitions of Quality

From this framework we see that there are two principal ways of viewing quality. One is from the customer's perspective: a quality product or service must meet (or exceed) customer requirements and expectations. That characteristic is often called *fitness for use.* As Nissan Motor Corporation discovered, the "fitness" is determined not by the company but by the customer.

Applied P/OM

Nissan Motor Corporation

"Fitness for use" depends on understanding customer needs.[5]

Nissan tested the U.S. market for Datsun in 1960. Although the car was economical, it was slow, hard to drive, low-powered, and not very comfortable. In essence, it lacked most of the qualities that American drivers expected. The company's U.S. representative, Mr. Katayama, kept asking questions and sending answers back to Tokyo. For some time, the company refused to believe that American tastes were different from their own. After many years of nagging, Mr. Katayama finally got a product that Americans liked—the 240Z.

Figure 2.2
Customer-Driven Quality
Cycle

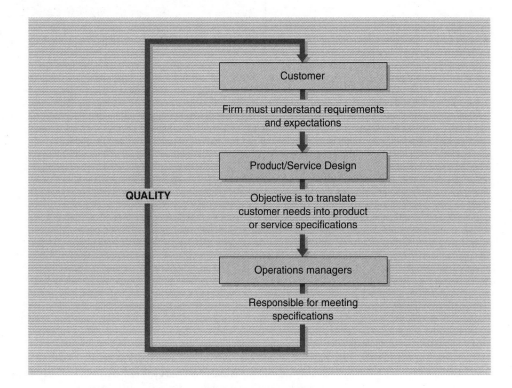

The second way of viewing quality is from the producer's perspective: a quality product or service must *conform to specifications*. Thus, if the cheese specification for a pizza is 8.0 ± .05 ounces, any value within that specification is considered conforming (acceptable) but values above 8.5 or below 7.5 ounces are considered nonconforming (unacceptable), as illustrated in Figure 2.3.

That view of quality has come under much scrutiny in recent years because of the work of Japanese engineer Genichi Taguchi. Taguchi suggests that *any* deviation from a target causes some loss, either to the manufacturer or to the con-

Figure 2.3
Conformance to
Specifications

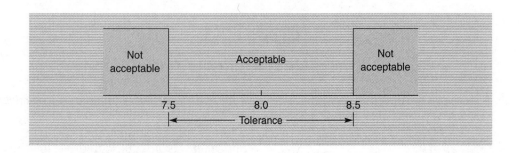

sumer. When targets are met, products are more consistent and losses are minimized. Considerable evidence supports that theory. In one case, managers at Ford's Batavia, Ohio, plant, which produces transmissions for both Ford and Mazda automobiles, discovered that Ford-built units were failing more and costing more in warranty claims than identical units built by Mazda in Japan. After tearing down both types, engineers found that all parts on the Ford-built units met blueprint specifications, although there was some variation. However, when measuring dimensions on the Mazda-built parts, the engineer thought that the measuring gage was broken; the readings were all the same—right on target! Taguchi's lesson was clearly illustrated!

Quality Organization

Traditional organizations are designed vertically, along hierarchical lines of authority. For example, many companies have "quality assurance departments" similar to finance and marketing departments. Typically, such departments are part of a traditional line-and-staff organization and are viewed by others as responsible for quality. TQM, in contrast, suggests that every manager and every employee is a quality manager of his or her own work processes. When companies accept this *process view,* they structure the quality organization around functional or cross-functional teams. The resultant organization chart usually looks something like that in Figure 2.4. In such an organizational structure, mid-level "lead" teams and worker-level quality improvement (QI) teams have the major responsibility to implement quality. Thus the ownership and the accountability for quality are spread throughout the organization. In such a structure, operations managers serve on a variety of quality teams. The specialists in the "quality department" serve only as advisors to the rest of the company—they may perform special statistical studies, train employees, or help managers interpret quality data, but they are not responsible for quality. And all employees

Figure 2.4
Team-Based Quality
Organization

SOURCE: Thomas H. Berry, *Managing the Total Quality Transformation.* (New York: McGraw-Hill, 1991). Reproduced with permission of McGraw-Hill, Inc.

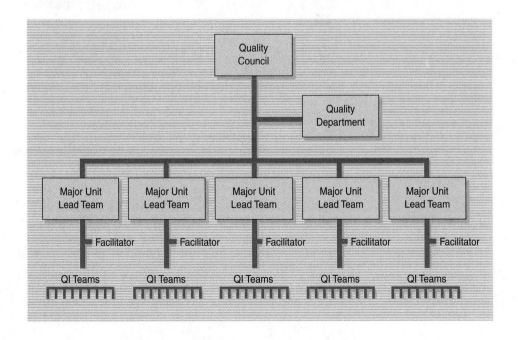

report to a top-level **quality council,** a steering committee of senior managers. Quality councils assume many responsibilities, such as incorporating TQM into the company's strategic planning process and coordinating the overall effort.

Applied P/OM
AT&T

The AT&T Quality Council assumes a variety of responsibilities.[6]

The elements of the AT&T Quality Council include

1. *Leadership*—promoting and articulating the quality vision, communicating responsibilities and expectations for management action, aligning the business management process with the quality approach, maintaining high visibility for commitment and involvement, and ensuring that businesswide support is available in the form of education, consulting, methods, and tools.

2. *Planning*—planning strategic quality goals, understanding basic customer needs and business capabilities, developing long-term goals and near-term priorities, planning human resource goals and policies, understanding employees' perceptions about quality and work, ensuring that all employees have the opportunity and skills to participate, and aligning reward and recognition systems to support the quality approach.

3. *Implementation*—forming key business process teams, chartering teams to manage and improve the processes, reviewing improvement plans, providing resources for improvement, enlisting all managers in the process, reviewing quality plans of major organizational units, and enlisting suppliers and business partners for joint quality planning.

4. *Review*—tracking progress through customer satisfaction and internal measures of quality, monitoring progress in attaining improvement objectives, celebrating successes, improving the quality system through auditing and identifying improvement opportunities, planning improvements, and validating the impact of improvements.

Quality in Service Organizations

Modern quality management matured in the manufacturing sector. As the importance of services continues to grow, more attention is being paid to service quality. However, services differ from manufacturing in many ways, and the differences have important implications for quality management. For example:

1. *The output of many service systems is intangible, whereas manufacturing produces tangible and visible products.* In manufacturing, we can assess quality against firm design specifications (for example, the depth of cut should be .125″), but in services, quality can be assessed only against nebulous expectations and experiences (What is a good sales experience?). Manufactured goods

can be recalled or replaced, but poor service can be rectified only by apologies and reparations.

2. *Services are produced and consumed simultaneously, whereas in manufacturing production precedes consumption.* Work must often be performed at the convenience of the customer, and at times or in places where supervisory personnel are not present. Hence, services cannot be inventoried as can manufactured goods. As there is no opportunity to inspect the "finished product" for quality, much more attention must be paid to training service personnel and building quality into a service.

3. *Services are generally labor-intensive, whereas manufacturing is more capital-intensive.* For example, patient care in hospitals depends heavily on the performance of nurses, doctors, and other medical staff. Banks have found that the friendliness of tellers is a key factor in retaining depositors. Hence, the behavior and morale of service employees is critical in delivering a quality service experience.

4. *Customers often are involved in the service process, whereas manufacturing is performed away from the customer.* Customers in a quick-service restaurant place orders, carry their food to the table, and even clear the table when finished. Information technology, such as automatic teller machines, has reduced the labor intensity in many service processes and placed more work on the customer. Argueably, customer satisfaction may decrease with reductions in personal interaction.

5. *Customer needs and performance standards are often difficult to identify and measure, primarily because the customer defines them, and each customer is different.* In addition, the production of services may require a higher degree of customization than that of manufactured goods. A doctor, lawyer, insurance salesman, and even a food-service employee must tailor the service provided to the individual customer. In manufacturing, the goal is uniformity.

6. *Service organizations may handle larger volumes of transactions than manufacturing organizations.* For example, on any given day, the Royal Bank of Canada handles more than 5.5 million transactions for 7.5 million customers through 1,600 branches and more than 3,500 banking machines. Federal Express handles 1.5 million shipments at 1,650 sites in 127 countries. Such large volumes increase the opportunity for error.

Those differences create distinct challenges for service quality assurance. Many firms, such as Walt Disney Co. and Marriott Hotels, have developed excellent quality systems that combine behavioral and technical sciences.

Quality Management Philosophies

Three individuals, W. Edwards Deming, Joseph M. Juran, and Philip B. Crosby, have had profound influence in transforming management practices. Although their philosophies center on quality, they differ in many respects. Deming, for example, proposed sweeping cultural change. Juran and Crosby, in contrast, seek to implement quality management within the system to which American managers are accustomed. This section briefly describes their philosophies and provides some comparisons and contrasts.

W. Edwards Deming

The term *quality* has become nearly synonymous with the name of W. Edwards Deming, who died in 1993. Deming was invited to Japan after World War II to help the Japanese in their efforts to improve quality. In recognition of his contributions, the Japanese instituted a prestigious international award, the Deming Prize, to honor companies that achieve superior levels of quality. Deming's philosophy is not so much about quality per se as it is about management practices that lead to superior quality. Therefore, it provides some important ideas for operations management.

Deming focused on the improvement of product and service conformance to specification by reducing uncertainty and variability in the design and manufacturing process. In mechanical assemblies, for example, variation in part dimensions from their specifications leads to inconsistent performance and premature wear and failure. Likewise, inconsistency in services frustrates customers and hurts the reputation of the company. To achieve reduction of variation, Deming advocated a continuous cycle of product design, manufacture, testing, and sales followed by market surveys and then redesign, and so forth. He claimed that higher quality leads to higher productivity, which in turn leads to long-term competitive strength. The Deming "Chain Reaction" (Figure 2.5) summarizes that idea. Improvements in quality lead to lower costs because of less rework, fewer mistakes, fewer delays and snags, and better use of time and materials. Lower costs, in turn, lead to productivity improvements. With better quality and lower prices, the firm can achieve a larger market share and thus stay in business, providing more and more jobs. Deming stressed that top management has the overriding responsibility for quality improvement.

Figure 2.5
The Deming Chain Reaction

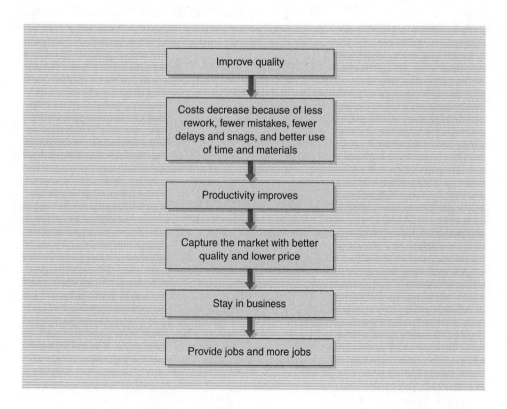

Deming identified two sources of improvement in any process:

1. Reducing "common causes" of variation inherent in the production system.
2. Eliminating isolated "special causes" of variation identifiable with a specific individual, machine, or batch of materials.

Common causes of variation are due to the system—as managers have designed it . For instance, suppose a piece of wood is to be cut to a precise length of 25.35 inches. If the worker is provided with only a hand saw, table, and yardstick, consistently cutting lengths of such precision will be virtually impossible. Improvements in conformance can be achieved only if managers provide more accurate equipment and training in proper work methods. Moreover, if the saw blade is worn or chipped, the quality will deteriorate. Such special causes can be identified by the worker and corrected. Statistical methods provide a means for identifying special and common causes of variation in processes.

Deming's 14 Points for Management

Deming emphatically stated that managerial practices are in need of a radical overhaul, as summarized in his "14 points" (see Table 2.1). Some of the points are quite controversial and are often misunderstood. According to Deming, none of the 14 points should be viewed in isolation, and companies cannot be selective in the ones they want to implement. Each of the points is discussed here.

1. *Management commitment.* Businesses must take a long-term view and invest in innovation, training, and research rather than emphasizing short-term profits.
2. *Learn the new philosophy.* Achieving competitive success in today's global economy requires a customer-driven approach based on mutual cooperation between labor and management and a never-ending cycle of improvement rather than on numbers-driven production, quotas, and adversarial work relationships.
3. *Understand inspection.* Quality by inspection encourages defects, because "someone else" catches and fixes problems. It increases costs and decreases productivity. Inspection should be used as a tool for improvement.
4. *End price tag decisions.* Purchasing decisions have traditionally been driven by cost, not quality. Inferior materials and components increase costs in later stages of production. Deming urged businesses to establish long-term relationships with a few suppliers that will lead to loyalty and enhanced opportunities for improvement.
5. *Improve constantly.* Western managers have typically viewed improvement in the context of large, expensive innovations such as robotics and computer-integrated manufacturing. The success of Japanese manufacturers, however, is due primarily to continuous, small, incremental improvements.
6. *Institute training.* Employees need the proper tools and knowledge to do a good job, and it is management's responsibility to provide them. Training not only improves quality and productivity, but also enhances workers' morale by showing them that the company is dedicated to helping them and is investing in their future.

Table 2.1 Dr. Deming's 14 Points

1. Create and publish to all employees a statement of the aims and purposes of the company or other organization. The management must demonstrate constantly their commitment to this statement.
2. Learn the new philosophy, top management, and everybody.
3. Understand the purpose of inspection, for improvement of processes and reduction of cost.
4. End the practice of awarding business on the basis of price tag alone.
5. Improve constantly and forever the system of production and service.
6. Institute training.
7. Teach and institute leadership.
8. Drive out fear. Create trust. Create a climate for innovation.
9. Optimize toward the aims and purposes of the company the efforts of teams, groups, staff areas.
10. Eliminate exhortations for the work force.
11. (a) Eliminate numerical quotas for production. Instead, learn and institute methods for improvement.
    (b) Eliminate M.B.O. Instead, learn the capabilities of processes, and how to improve them.
12. Remove barriers that rob people of pride of workmanship.
13. Encourage education and self-improvement for everyone.
14. Take action to accomplish the transformation.

Source: Reprinted from *Out of the Crisis* by W. Edwards Deming by permission of MIT and W. Edwards Deming. Published by MIT, Center for Advanced Engineering Study, Cambridge, MA 02139. Copyright 1986 by W. Edwards Deming.

7. *Institute leadership.* The job of managers is leadership, not supervision, and providing guidance, not simply directing work. Supervisors should be coaches, not policemen. Leadership can help to eliminate fear and thus encourage teamwork.

8. *Drive out fear.* Many workers are in constant fear of punishment or reprisals for failing to meet quotas and of being blamed for problems that are beyond their control. Managers compete against each other to protect their own jobs. Fear encourages short-term thinking, not long-term improvement.

9. *Optimize team efforts.* Barriers between individuals and departments lead to poor quality, because "customers" do not receive what they need from their "suppliers." Teamwork is an important means of achieving a company's goals of meeting customer needs and improving processes.

10. *Eliminate exhortations.* Slogans and exhortations calling for improved quality assume that poor quality results from a lack of motivation. On the contrary, workers become frustrated when they cannot improve because the system that managers have established limits their performance. Motivation can be better achieved through trust and leadership than with slogans.

11. *Eliminate quotas and MBO (management by objectives).* Numerical quotas reflect short-term perspectives and thus do not encourage long-term improvement. The typical American MBO system focuses on results, not processes, and encourages short-term behavior.

12. *Remove barriers to pride in workmanship.* The Taylor system has promulgated the view of workers as a "commodity." Managers assume they are smarter than workers and do not use the workers' knowledge and experience to the fullest extent.

13. *Institute education.* Training in Point 6 refers to job skills; education refers to self-development. Firms have a responsibility to develop the value and self-worth of the individual. That is a powerful motivation method.

14. *Take action.* Deming's philosophy is a major cultural change, and many firms find it difficult. Top managers must institute the process and include everyone in it.

One company that has embraced the Deming philosophy is Zytec, Inc. We discuss its experience in a P/OM in Practice case at the end of the chapter.

Joseph M. Juran

Joseph M. Juran joined Western Electric in the 1920s during its pioneering days in the development of statistical methods for quality and spent much of his time as a corporate industrial engineer. Juran taught quality principles to the Japanese in the 1950s just after Deming and was a principal force in their quality reorganization. Like Deming, he approached the crisis in quality with new thinking.

Juran's approaches are designed to fit into a company's current strategic business planning with minimal risk of rejection. Juran contends that employees at different levels of an organization speak in different "languages." (Deming advocated statistics as a common language.) Top managers speak in the language of dollars, workers speak in the language of things, and middle managers must be able to speak both languages and translate between dollars and things. To get top managers' attention, quality issues must be cast in the language they understand—dollars. Hence, Juran advocates the accounting and analysis of quality costs to direct attention to quality problems. At the operational level, Juran's focus is on increasing conformance to specifications through elimination of defects, with extensive support by statistical tools for analysis. Thus, his philosophy fits well into existing management systems.

Juran defines quality as *fitness for use.* Like Deming, he advocates a never-ending spiral of activities including market research, product development, design, planning for manufacture, purchasing, production process control, inspection and testing, and sales, followed by customer feedback. Because of the interdependency of those functions, competent companywide quality management is crucial. Senior managers must play an active and enthusiastic leadership role in the quality management process.

Juran's prescriptions center on three major quality processes, called the **Quality Trilogy** (a registered trademark of the Juran Institute):

1. *Quality planning*—the process for preparing to meet quality goals.
2. *Quality control*—the process for meeting quality goals during operations.
3. *Quality improvement*—the process for breaking through to unprecedented levels of performance.

Japanese efforts at quality improvement were supported by massive training programs and top management leadership. Training in managerial quality-oriented concepts as well as training in the tools for quality improvement, cost reduction, data collection, and analysis is one of the most important components of Juran's philosophy. The Japanese experience, he feels, leaves little doubt as to the significance of the return to quality training in competitive advantage, reduced failure costs, higher productivity, smaller inventories, and better delivery performance. Accordingly, his Juran Institute provides substantial training in the form of seminars, videotapes, and other materials.

Philip B. Crosby

Philip B. Crosby was corporate vice-president for quality at International Telephone and Telegraph (ITT) for 14 years after working his way up from line inspector. After leaving ITT, he established Philip Crosby Associates in 1979 to develop and offer training programs. The essence of Crosby's quality philosophy is embodied in what he calls the Absolutes of Quality Management and the Basic Elements of Improvement. His Absolutes of Quality Management follow.

1. *Quality means conformance to requirements, not elegance.* Crosby believes requirements must be clearly stated so that they cannot be misunderstood and so that measurements can be taken to determine conformance to them. Any nonconformance detected represents absence of quality. Setting requirements is the responsibility of managers.

2. *Quality problems are the responsibility of those who cause them.* Hence, there are accounting quality problems, manufacturing quality problems, design quality problems, front-desk quality problems, and so on. The quality department measures conformance, reports, results, and leads the drive to develop a positive attitude toward quality improvement, but it does not shoulder the responsibility for quality problems. This point is similar to the message in Deming's Point 3.

3. *There is no such thing as the economics of quality; it is always cheaper to do the job right the first time.* Crosby supports the premise that "economics of quality" has no meaning. Quality is free. What costs money are all actions that involve not doing jobs right the first time. The Deming Chain Reaction sends a similar message.

4. *The only performance measurement is the cost of quality.* The cost of quality is the expense of nonconformance. Many companies spend 15 to 20 percent of their sales dollars on quality costs, whereas a company with a well-run quality management program can achieve a cost of quality that is less than 2.5 percent of sales. Crosby's program calls for measuring and publicizing the cost of poor quality to call problems to managers' attention, to select opportunities for corrective action, and to track quality improvement over time.

5. *The only performance standard is zero defects.* As Crosby describes it,

> Zero Defects is a performance standard. It is the standard of the craftsperson regardless of his or her assignment. . . . The theme of ZD is *do it right the first time.* That means concentrating on preventing defects rather than just finding and fixing them.[7]

Crosby's Basic Elements of Improvement are determination, education, and implementation. By *determination*, Crosby means that top managers must be serious about quality improvement. The Absolutes should be understood by everyone; that can be accomplished only through *education*. Finally, every member of the management team must understand the *implementation* process.

Unlike Juran and Deming, Crosby advocates a primarily behavioral program. He places more emphasis on management and organizational processes for changing corporate culture and attitudes than on the use of statistical techniques. Like Juran's and unlike Deming's, his approach fits well within existing organizational structures.

Crosby's approach, however, provides relatively few details about how firms should address the finer points of quality management. The focus is on managerial thinking rather than on organizational systems. By allowing managers to determine the best methods to apply in their own firm's situations, his approach tends to avoid some of the implementation problems experienced by firms that have tried to adopt the Deming philosophy.

Elements of Total Quality Management

TQM pulls many of the ideas of Deming, Juran, and Crosby into a set of core principles for integrating customer and company performance requirements into an effective management system built around quality. (Those core values are embodied in the Malcolm Baldrige National Quality Award Criteria, discussed in the next section.)

Strategic Planning

High quality is not achieved instantaneously. It is the result of long-term strategic planning that reflects commitments to customers, employees, stockholders, suppliers, the public, and the community. Of course, different resources, systems, and constituent relationships require different strategies. MamaMia's, for example, may decide to focus on high-quality dine-in service or primarily on fast home delivery. Then it must design systems to support that focus. Its strategy will differ according to its focus—but any strategy should integrate quality into all aspects of business planning. Strategic planning is discussed in Chapter 3.

Fact-Based Management

Fact-based management is built on a framework of measurement, information, and analysis. The type of *measurements* used depends on the company's strategy. Thus, if MamaMia's strategic focus is on home delivery, its key measurements might be delivery time and pizza temperature upon delivery. All key processes and the outputs and results of those processes should be measured.

Information needed for performance assessment and improvement should be gathered on customers, product and service performance, operations, market, competitive comparisons, suppliers, employees, and cost and financial data. *Analysis* refers to extracting larger meaning from such data to support evaluation and decision making at all levels of the company—thus supporting company planning, performance review, operations improvement, and comparisons with competitors or "best practices." Use of information as a basis for operations management decisions is discussed in Chapter 4.

Leadership and Human Resources Management

Leadership is the responsibility of all managers. It entails creating and communicating a customer orientation, clear and visible values, and high expectations. All managers in effect serve as role models to nonmanagerial employees, and top managers serve as role models to other, subordinate managers. Such role modeling works best in a teamwork setting. For example, MamaMia's manager might work side by side with new employees in the kitchen. The team approach has proven successful in engaging employee participation and enhancing motivation. Senior managers should recognize and reward both team and individual accomplishments. Helpful to the team approach are well-designed suggestion systems, with training, financial, and technical support provided to employees to develop their ideas. (At MamaMia's a team consisting of the manager, order taker, chef, and deliverer might study ways of improving the total cycle time for delivering pizzas).

The person in any organization who best understands his or her job and how it can be improved is the one performing it. Thus, employees must be empowered to make decisions that affect quality and performance. This viewpoint represents a major shift in the philosophy of management, as the traditional philosophy is that the work force should be "managed" to conform to existing business systems. Human resources issues in operations are discussed in Chapter 5.

Customer-Driven Design

Quality is judged by the customer, and the customer's judgment may be influenced by many factors involved in purchase, ownership, and service experiences. Customer-driven quality demands constant sensitivity to those many factors—as well as to emerging customer and market requirements. Although defect and error reduction is important, it is not enough; a company must also be aware of the opportunity to introduce new products to meet changing customer and market needs. An organization such as MamaMia's might use focus groups or customer-satisfaction surveys to gather information about such needs.

Customer-driven quality requires a "prevention" orientation so that anticipated problems are prevented by building quality into products and services. In general, the costs of preventive measures at the design stage are much lower than the costs of correcting problems that occur downstream. Another requirement of customer-driven design is to minimize design-to-introduction cycle time by coordinating marketing, design, manufacturing, and other functions in the organization—a necessity for meeting the demands of rapidly changing markets. Customer-driven design and its relationship with operations are examined in Chapter 6. Following is an example describing how Scandinavian Airlines System (SAS) met its design goals.

Applied P/OM

Scandinavian Airlines System

Scandinavian Airlines improves the design of its service system[8]

Improving the design of its service system transformed Scandinavian Airlines System (SAS) in Sweden. When president and CEO Jan Carlzon took over SAS in 1980, the company was suffering from the effects of an oil shock, two years of financial losses, and high labor costs. As a result, it could not afford to compete on the basis of price alone with U.S. and Asian airlines. Carlzon set about creating a quality image by reconfiguring airplanes to give more comfort and amenities to business-class passengers; training and empowering employees to handle problems swiftly, competently, and without excessive "red tape"; improving ground service; and offering (as a special service) low standby fares for passengers under the age of 27. Ground service was improved by providing better express check-in service, new business facilities such as computers and fax machines, and automatic delivery of luggage to hotels owned by or linked to SAS's full-service travel agency. In discussing how the company attained its quality objectives, Carlzon stressed the need to determine what kind of behavioral change should take place at the "moment of truth" when the employee comes into contact with the customer during the process of delivering the company's service.

Continuous Improvement

Continuous improvement means improvement both incremental and "breakthrough" as a part of daily operations and of all work units of a company. It is the essence of total quality management (TQM). Problems should be eliminated at their source, and opportunities to do better should be sought. Improvements may be of several types:

••• Enhancing value to the customer through new and improved products and services (at MamaMia's this might mean new pizza toppings or new services such as a five-minute lunch).

••• Reducing errors, defects, and waste (at MamaMia's, ensuring the right toppings before cooking).

••• Improving responsiveness and cycle-time performance (MamaMia's might use a team-based approach to service rather than assigning servers to individual tables).

••• Improving productivity and effectiveness in the use of all resources (MamaMia's might reduce paper orders through direct computer entry).

Thus, continuous improvement can be achieved, not only by providing better products and services, but also by being more responsive and efficient. Continuous improvement in operations is discussed in Chapter 11.

The goal of continuous improvement, which is the heart of TQM, requires a management approach much different from the traditional one in which departments, functions, or collections of individuals are managed independently of one another. TQM views an organization as a system of interdependent processes, linked horizontally through a network of (internal and external) suppliers and customers. Thus, every person is a process manager, having some ownership of the production process. A manager's job is to provide the leadership for efforts at continual improvement by everyone, working together.

Malcolm Baldrige National Quality Award

Japan has promoted TQM since the early 1950s, when its industrial leaders welcomed the teachings of Deming and Juran. But, as we saw in Chapter 1, it took almost 30 years for the TQM principles to take root in America. Once they did, the "quality" movement burgeoned, helped along by the Malcolm Baldrige National Quality Award, which was instituted by an act of Congress to recognize American companies with exemplary quality management practices. The idea is for such companies to provide role models to others in the nation. Named after the secretary of commerce who was killed in an accident shortly before the Senate acted on the legislation, the Baldrige award was signed into law on August 20, 1987.

In other words, the award aims to improve the competitiveness of U.S. industry by recognizing world-class quality management practices and then—most importantly—having the recognized companies share their knowledge with others. The award has stimulated study and education in TQM practices, and has provided a common vocabulary that facilitates communication among firms in all sectors of the economy. Furthermore, it has created a sense of excitement about quality among top executives throughout the nation. Its principles are an important part of this book.

The Baldrige award's examination is based on a set of seven criteria, the dynamics of which are illustrated in Figure 2.6. The criteria create a framework of four basic elements:

1. Senior executive leadership sets directions, creates values, goals, and systems, and guides the pursuit of customer value and company performance improvement.
2. The system consists of a set of well-defined and well-designed processes for meeting the company's customer and performance requirements.
3. Measures of progress provide a results-oriented basis for channeling actions to delivering ever-improving customer value and company performance.
4. The basic goal of the system is the delivery of ever-improving value to customers and success in the marketplace.

Following is a description of each of the seven Baldrige criteria:

1. *Leadership*—senior executives' personal leadership and involvement in creating and sustaining a customer focus, clear values and expectations, and a

Figure 2.6
Malcolm Baldrige National
Quality Award Framework
of Dynamic Relationships

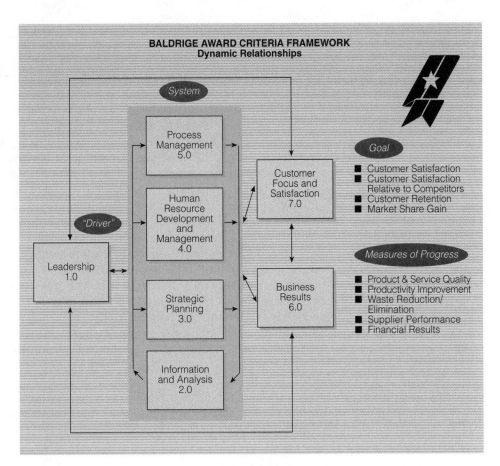

leadership system that promotes performance excellence, as well as public
responsibility and corporate citizenship.

2. *Information and analysis*—the management and effectiveness of the use of
data and information to support customer-driven performance excellence
and marketplace success.

3. *Strategic planning*—how the company sets strategic directions, and how it
determines key plan requirements and translates them into an effective performance management system.

4. *Human resources development and management*—how the work force is enabled to build and maintain an environment conducive to performance excellence, full participation, and personal and organizational growth.

5. *Process management*—including customer-focused design, product and service delivery processes, support services, and supply management involving
all work units, as well as research and development. This criterion includes
how key processes are designed, effectively managed, and improved to
achieve higher performance.

6. *Business results*—the company's performance and improvement in key business areas—product and service quality, productivity and operational effectiveness, supply quality, and financial performance indicators linked to those
areas.

7. *Customer focus and satisfaction*—the company's systems for customer learning and for building and maintaining customer relationships, and results for key measures of business success—that is, customer satisfaction and retention, market share, and satisfaction relative to competitors.

Each major category is assigned a maximum number of points that can be earned during the evaluation process. A scoring system for examination items is based on three evaluation dimensions: approach, deployment, and results. *Approach* refers to the methods the company uses to achieve the purposes addressed in each category. *Deployment* refers to the extent to which the approaches are applied to all relevant areas and activities addressed and implied in each category. *Results* refers to the outcomes and effects in achieving the purposes addressed and implied in the criteria. A team of national experts evaluates applications according to these dimensions.

An *Application Guidelines* booklet published each year describes in detail the information that must be documented. Like quality itself, the specific award criteria are continually improved each year to better reflect the changing scope and process of TQM. The current booklet can be obtained by contacting the U.S. Department of Commerce. (A single free copy can be obtained by contacting the Malcolm Baldrige National Quality Award, National Institute of Standards and Technology, Route 270 and Quince Orchard Road, Administration Building Room A537, Gaithersburg, MD 20899. Telephone: (301) 975-2036. FAX: (301) 948-3716.)

According to the award guidelines, up to two companies can win a Baldrige award in each category of manufacturing, small business, and service. Table 2.2 lists the winners through 1995.

Table 2.2   Malcolm Baldrige National Quality Award Winners

Year	Manufacturing	Small Business	Service
1988	Motorola, Inc. Westinghouse Commercial Nuclear Fuel Division	Globe Metallurgical, Inc.	
1989	Xerox Corp. Business Products and Systems Milliken & Co.		
1990	Cadillac Motor Car Division IBM Rochester	Wallace Co., Inc.	Federal Express
1991	Solectron Corp. Zytec Corp.	Marlow Industries	
1992	AT&T Network Systems Texas Instruments Defense Systems & Electronics Group	Granite Rock Co.	AT&T Universal Card Services The Ritz-Carlton Hotel Co.
1993	Eastman Chemical Co.	Ames Rubber Corp.	
1994		Wainwright Industries, Inc.	AT&T Consumer Communication Services GTE Directories Corp.
1995	Armstrong World Industries' Building Products Operation Corning Telecommunications Products Division		

In evaluating applications for the award, examiners have noted several common strengths and weaknesses. Most companies that apply for the award have strong senior management leadership and are driven by the needs of customers and the marketplace. They have aggressive goals and high expectations. Most companies have invested heavily in human resources development, and, as a result, employee involvement is continuing and expanding. Those that score well usually have strong information systems, helping to link external customer-satisfaction measurements with internal measurements such as process quality and employee satisfaction.

Common weaknesses among firms that do not score well include

••• Weak information systems.

••• Delegation of quality responsibility to lower levels of the company.

••• A partial quality system; for example, one that is strong in manufacturing but weak in support services.

••• Unclear definition of what quality means in the organization.

••• Lack of alignment among diverse functions within the firm; that is, all processes are not driven by common goals and nor do all use the same approaches.

••• Failure to use all listening posts to gather information that is critical to decision making.

Among the more disappointing results found by Baldrige administrators is that (1) relatively few organizations actually practice *total quality,* (2) many lack a quality vision or do not effectively translate the vision into a business strategy, (3) many still emphasize the negative side of quality—defect reduction rather than customer focus—and (4) the gap between the best and the average companies is quite large.

Impacts of the Baldrige Award

The Baldrige award has generated an incredible amount of interest in quality, both within the United States and internationally. Winning companies have made tens of thousands of presentations describing their quality management approaches and practices. Many states have instituted awards similar to the Baldrige and based on the Baldrige criteria. The criteria have been used to train hundreds of thousands of people and have served as a self-assessment tool within organizations.

A U.S. government General Accounting Office (GAO) study commissioned by Congressman Donald Ritter looked for the impact of TQM practices on the performance of 22 companies that had received Baldrige-award site visits during 1988 and 1989. Four broad areas were analyzed: (1) employee relations, (2) operating procedures, (3) customer satisfaction, and (4) financial performance. The study showed that companies that had adopted the TQM practices advocated by the Baldrige award experienced an overall improvement in corporate performance. In nearly all cases, companies that used TQM practices achieved better employee relations, higher productivity, greater customer satisfaction, increased market share, and improved productivity. *Business Week* reported that if a person had invested $1,000 in each publicly traded winning company from

Figure 2.7 GAO Total Quality Management Model

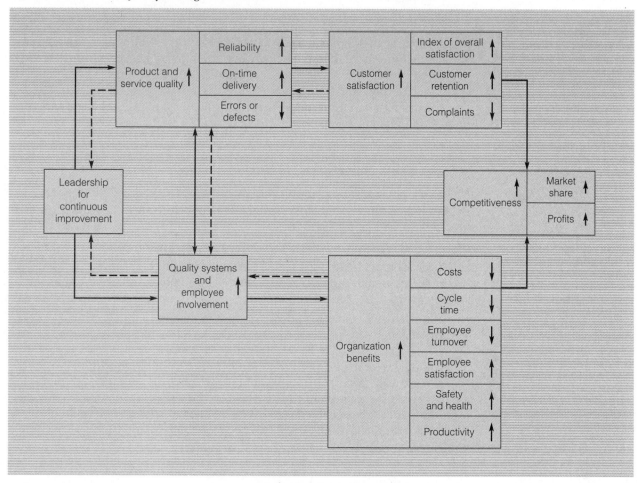

the time the award was announced through September 30, 1993, that person would have gained a cumulative return of 89.2 percent, excluding dividends, compared to a 33.1 percent return on the Standard & Poor's 500.[9]

Each of the companies studied developed its practices in an environment unique to itself, with its own opportunities and problems. However, there were common features in the TQM systems they used that were major contributing factors to improved performance, as summarized in Figure 2.7. Note that none of the companies reaped the benefits of TQM immediately. Allowing sufficient time for results to be achieved was as important as initiating the program.

ISO 9000 Standards

As quality has become a major focus of businesses throughout the world, various organizations have developed standards and guidelines. Terms such as "quality management," "quality control," "quality system," and "quality assurance" have acquired different and sometimes conflicting meanings from country to country, within a country, and even within an industry.[10] As the European Community moved toward the European free trade agreement, which went into effect at the end of 1992, quality management became a key strategic objective, making it imperative to resolve the differences in terminology and standardize quality requirements for European countries within the common market, as well as those wanting to do business with those countries. Accordingly, a specialized agency for standardization, the International Organization for Standardization, founded in 1946 and consisting of representatives from the national-standards bodies of 91 nations, adopted a series of written quality standards in 1987. The standards have been adopted in the United States by the American National Standards Institute (ANSI) with the endorsement and cooperation of the American Society for Quality Control (ASQC). The original U.S. standards were called the ANSI/ASQC Q90-1987 series and were revised in 1994. The standards are recognized by about 100 countries, including Japan. In some foreign markets, companies will not buy from noncertified suppliers. Thus, meeting those standards is becoming a requirement for international competitiveness.

The ISO 9000 series of standards are *quality system standards,* and are intended to ensure that a company conforms to specified requirements in the areas of design/development, production, installation, and service. They are based on the premise that certain generic characteristics of management practices can be standardized, and that a well-designed, well-implemented, and carefully managed quality system provides confidence that the outputs will meet customer expectations and requirements.

Structure of the ISO 9000 Standards

The ISO 9000 standards define three levels of quality assurance:

••• Level 1 (ISO 9001) applies to firms that design, develop, produce, install, and service products.

••• Level 2 (ISO 9002) applies to firms engaged only in production and installation.

••• Level 3 (ISO 9003) applies to firms engaged only in final inspection and testing of products.

Two other standards, ISO 9000 and ISO 9004, define the basic elements of a comprehensive quality assurance system and provide guidance on applying the appropriate level.

The standards focus on 20 key requirements:

1. *Management responsibility*—for establishing, documenting, and publicizing the company's policy, objectives, and commitment to quality and customer satisfaction.

2. *Quality system*—involving a quality manual that meets the criteria of the applicable standard (9001, 9002, or 9003) to ensure conformance to requirements.

3. *Contract review*—to ensure that requirements are adequately defined and that the capability exists to meet requirements.

4. *Design control*—to ensure that requirements are being met and that procedures are in place for design planning and design changes.

5. *Document control*—through procedures for approval, distribution, change, and modification.

6. *Purchasing*—procedures to ensure that purchased products conform to requirements.

7. *Purchaser-supplied products*—procedures to verify, store, and maintain purchased items.

8. *Product identification and traceability*—procedures to identify and trace products during all stages of production, delivery, and installation.

9. *Process control*—to ensure that production processes are carried out under controlled conditions. The processes must be documented and monitored, and workers must use approved equipment and have specified criteria for workmanship.

10. *Inspection and testing*—to ensure that all products are inspected and tested.

11. *Inspection, measuring, and test equipment*—involving maintenance of records at all stages of inspection and testing.

12. *Inspection and test status*—involving labeling of products throughout all stages of production.

13. *Control of nonconforming product*—procedures to ensure that the company avoids inadvertent use of nonconforming product.

14. *Corrective action*—to solve problems of nonconformance and prevent others in the future.

15. *Handling, storage, packaging, and delivery*—procedures to properly handle, store, and deliver products.

16. *Quality records*—to identify, collect, index, file, and store all records relating to the quality system.

17. *Internal quality audits*—to determine whether company activities comply with requirements.

18. *Training*—to identify needs and provide training of employees.

19. *Servicing*—as required by company contracts with customers.

20. *Statistical control*—to control processes, products, and services.

To illustrate the scope of those requirements, let us look more closely at the first one, management responsibility. The requirements are that managers must (a) establish, document, and publicize their policy, objectives, and commitment to quality and customer satisfaction; (b) designate a representative with authority and responsibility for implementing and maintaining the requirements of the standard; (c) define the responsibility, authority, and relationships for all employees whose work affects quality; and (d) conduct in-house verification and review of the quality system.

To illustrate how ISO 9000 standards might apply to MamaMia's, let us consider the purchasing element.[11] The standards specify that MamaMia's must have procedures to ensure that purchased products conform to its requirements. MamaMia's quality manual might include the following policies and procedures:

The quality and freshness of the food items used to produce the pizza are crucial to the quality control of the final product. At least two reputable suppliers shall be identified for each food product that goes into the pizza. Those suppliers shall be selected on their ability to provide quality products on a timely basis.

Each individual food item shall be listed and the appropriate characteristics (including freshness, texture, color, packaging, etc.) described on a *perishable food item* sheet. Those sheets shall be part of the ISO documentation package.

Each supplier qualified to supply a particular food item shall be required to review and sign a copy of the food specification for that particular item. The signed specification shall be kept on file by the store manager as a part of its ISO documentation. One or more suppliers will be selected to supply sundry items to support the pizza (boxes, napkins, etc.). Suppliers will coordinate with MamaMia's to ensure timely delivery of those non-perishable items.

The standards do not specify how MamaMia's should design or operate the purchasing function; they state only that procedures must be developed and used consistently.

Compliance is ensured through a registration process. The ISO 9000 standards originally were intended to be advisory and to be used for two-party contractual situations (between a customer and supplier) and for internal auditing. However, they quickly evolved into a basis for companies to have their quality management systems "certified" or to achieve "registration" through a third-party auditor, usually a laboratory or some other accreditation agency (called a *registrar*). That process began in the United Kingdom. Rather than a supplier being audited for compliance with the standards by each customer, the registrar certifies the company, and that certification is accepted by all of the supplier's customers. Recertification is required every three years. Individual sites—not entire companies—must achieve registration individually. All costs are borne by the applicant, so the process can be quite expensive.

Perspectives on ISO 9000

Many misconceptions exist about what ISO 9000 actually is. The standards do not specify any measure of quality performance; specific product-quality levels are set by the company. Rather, the standards are based on the principle that quality should be defined by the product or service's *fitness for purpose,* and that the customer is the one who decides on that definition. The company is then required to have a verifiable process in place to ensure that it consistently produces what it says it will produce, thus deserving the confidence of the customers who have deemed the product satisfactory. The standards emphasize documenting conformance of quality systems to the company's quality manual and established quality system requirements. Having an ISO 9000–certified supplier assures the customer that the level of quality received once will be delivered consistently the next time and the next. A supplier can comply with the standards and still produce a poor-quality product—as long as it is done consistently!

ISO 9000 standards are not concerned with activities such as leadership, strategic planning, or customer-relationship management. Nevertheless, they provide a set of good general practices for quality assurance systems, and are an excellent starting point for companies that have no formal quality assurance program. Many companies find that their current quality systems already comply with most of the standards. For companies in the early stages of formal quality programs, the standards enforce the discipline of control that is necessary to pursue continuous improvement. The requirement of periodic audits ensures that the stated quality system will continue and become ingrained in the company.

Moreover, the rigorous documentation required by ISO 9000 standards helps companies uncover problems and improve their processes. At DuPont, for example, ISO 9000 has been credited with helping to increase on-time delivery from 70 to 90 percent, decrease cycle time from 15 days to 1.5 days, increase first-pass yields from 72 to 92 percent, and reduce the number of test procedures by one-third.

The standards are intended to apply to all types of businesses, including electronics and chemicals, and to services such as health care, banking, and transportation. As of early 1993, only about 550 company sites in the United States were certified. In contrast, some 15,000 to 20,000 companies were certified in the United Kingdom. During the first nine months of 1993 registrations worldwide grew by 70 percent to about 45,000—evidence of the growing global interest in the standards, driven primarily by marketplace demands. By June of 1994, the United States had almost 4,000 registrations, and the United Kingdom had over 36,000.

QS 9000

Late in 1994 the Big Three automobile manufacturers—Ford, Chrysler, and General Motors—released *QS 9000,* an interpretation and extension of ISO 9000 for automotive suppliers. QS 9000 represents a collaborative effort of those firms to bring together their individual quality requirements and global ISO standards. Truck manufacturers Mack Trucks, Freightliner, Navistar International, PACCAR Inc, and Volvo GM also participated in the process. The goal was to develop fundamental quality systems that provide for continuous improvement, emphasizing defect prevention and the reduction of variation and waste in the supply chain. QS 9000 applies to all internal and external suppliers of production and service parts and materials. Chrysler, Ford, GM, and truck manufacturers will require all suppliers to establish, document, and implement quality systems based on the standards according to individual customers' timing.

QS 9000 is based on ISO 9000 and includes all ISO requirements. However, QS 9000 goes well beyond ISO 9000 standards with additional requirements for continuous improvement, manufacturing capability, and production-part approval processes. Many of the concepts in the Malcolm Baldrige National Quality Award criteria are reflected in QS 9000. For example, under "Management Responsibility" (the first element in the ISO standards), there is a requirement that suppliers document trends in quality, operational performance (productivity, efficiency, effectiveness), and current quality levels for key product and service features, and compare them with those of competitors and/or appropriate benchmarks. Suppliers are also required to have a documented process for determining customer satisfaction, one that specifies the frequency of determination and how objectivity and validity are assured. Trends in customer satisfaction and key indicators of customer dissatisfaction must be documented and supported by objective information, compared to those of competitors or to benchmarks, and reviewed by senior managers. The wording is almost identical to that in the Baldrige criteria.

In addition, registration with QS 9000 requires demonstration of effectiveness in meeting the *intent* of the standards, rather than simply meeting the "do it as you document it" standard. For instance, while ISO 9000 requires "suitable maintenance of equipment to ensure continuing process capability" under "Process Control," QS 9000 requires suppliers to identify key process equipment, provide appropriate resources for maintenance, and develop an effective, planned total preventive maintenance system. What is more, the system should include a procedure that describes the planned maintenance, scheduled maintenance, and predictive maintenance methods. Also, extensive requirements for documenting process monitoring and operator instructions, as well as process capability and performance requirements, are built into the standards. Finally, there are additional requirements that pertain specifically to Ford, Chrysler, and GM suppliers. Thus, registration with QS 9000 will also achieve ISO 9000 registration, but ISO-certified companies do not automatically meet the additional QS 9000 requirements.

Contrasts between ISO 9000 and Baldrige Award Criteria[12]

Despite the publicity surrounding the Malcolm Baldrige National Quality Award and ISO 9000, there is considerable confusion about them. Two common misconceptions are that the Baldrige award and ISO 9000 registration cover similar requirements and that both address improvement and results, and thus are both forms of achievement recognition. In reality, the two are distinctly different instruments that can reinforce one another when properly used. Many companies are using the criteria for the Baldrige award and for ISO 9000 certification compatibly, sometimes sequentially and sometimes simultaneously. Table 2.3 describes the key differences between the two sets of criteria.

Implementing Total Quality Management

Clearly, TQM represents a significant change in organizational culture. That change is not without costs—costs involving time, commitment, and discomfort as a result of change. TQM requires new styles of managing and an entirely new set of skills,[13] which include thinking in terms of systems, defining customer requirements and planning improvements; team building and group participation; encouraging openness, delegating and coaching, and creating climates of trust; problem solving with data; and implementing change and developing a lifelong learning style.

While TQM has received unprecedented attention from American business, the report card has not always been good. A comprehensive study conducted by Ernst & Young and the American Quality Foundation in 1991 shows that many companies are stumbling in their efforts. Only a small percentage involve employees in suggestion programs, use customer complaints in identifying

Table 2.3 Contrasts between Baldrige Award and ISO 9000

	Baldrige Award Program	**ISO 9000 Registration**
Focus	Competitiveness: customer value and operational performance.	Conformity to practices specified in the registrant's own quality assurance system.
Purpose	Educational: to share competitiveness learning.	To provide a common basis for assuring buyers that specific practices conform with the providers' stated quality systems.
Quality definition	Customer-driven.	Conformity of specified operations to documented requirements.
Improvement/results	Heavy dependence on results and improvement.	Does not assess outcome-oriented results or improvement trends.
Role in the marketplace	A form of recognition, but not intended to be a product endorsement or certification.	Provides customers with assurances that a registered supplier has a documented quality system and follows it.
Nature of assessment	Four-stage review process.	Evaluation of quality manual and working documents and site audits to ensure conformance to stated practices.
Feedback	Diagnostic feedback on approach, deployment, and results.	Audit feedback on discrepancies and findings related to practices and documentation.
Criteria improvement	Annual revision of criteria.	Revisions of 1987 document issued in 1994, focusing on clarification.
Responsibility for information sharing	Winners required to share quality assurance and improvement strategies.	No obligation to share information.
Service quality	Service excellence a principal concern.	Standards focused on repetitive processes, without a focus on critical service-quality issues such as customer-relationship management and human resources development.
Scope of coverage	All operations and processes of all work units. All ISO 9001 requirements are within the scope of the Baldrige award.	Covers only design/development, production, installation, and servicing. Requirements address less than 10 percent of the Baldrige criteria.
Documentation requirement	Criteria do not spell out documentation requirements.	Documentation is a central audit requirement.
Self-assessment	Principal use of criteria is in self-assessment of improvement practices.	Standards are used primarily in "contractual situations" or other external audits.

new products or services, or use quality performance in determining the pay of senior executives. U.S. efforts seem far behind those of Japan and Germany. A similar study by Arthur D. Little of 500 U.S. companies revealed that only one-third felt their TQM programs were having a significant impact on their competitiveness.

One of the reasons for failure is that many businesses view TQM as a "program" rather than as a way to meet business objectives. As such, efforts at improving and maintaining quality tend to be isolated from day-to-day business operations. To be effective, quality practices must become a routine part of doing business. It is a common mistake for managers to confuse TQM activities with results. That is, they fail to see that simply creating improvement teams or measuring the amount of training is not an indicator of success. Many consultants recommend that a company start with small improvements and short-term goals, and generate some early success stories that can provide the incentive to continue and demonstrate the link between the activities and the results. Although TQM efforts are designed to produce long-term results, short-term successes help to sustain a company along the way.

Studies of highly successful companies have suggested that certain key factors in their organizational culture have contributed to their success:[14]

1. **A sharp focus on quality through strategic planning.** Successful companies have a guiding vision, and have developed detailed, well-communicated strategic plans. Strategies are long-term and focus on investment in research and development, training, process design, and continuous improvement—factors important to long-run effectiveness , not just short-term efficiency. For example, Motorola has a two major goals: defect prevention (its goal is two defects per billion by the year 2000) and cycle-time reduction reductions in all processes.

2. **Commitment and involvement of top management.** Without exception, top management commitment and leadership is the key "driver" in the successful implementation of TQM. Top managers, ideally starting with the CEO, must become the organization's TQM leaders and provide the vision, encouragement, and recognition necessary to overcome old habits. Speeches and rhetoric are not enough; senior managers must be actively involved in setting the organization's mission and vision, and then "walk the talk."

3. **Integration of customer-satisfaction goals across functions.** Customer-satisfaction goals drive the quality effort in successful firms. Everyone inside the organization is viewed as a customer of an internal or external supplier, and the final customer is seen as the final arbiter of quality. Specific tasks and responsibilities for achieving customer satisfaction are assigned to all departments and individuals. That approach requires a *systems view*, rather than the traditional functional focus, and improved communications across organizational levels, functions, product lines, and locations.

4. **Employee participation and training.** TQM is most effective when all employees participate in the improvement efforts. Therefore employees must be empowered to make decisions that affect quality. Their participation in developing and implementing new and better systems may be encouraged by recognizing team and individual accomplishments, promoting risk-taking by removing the fear of failure, instituting effective suggestion systems, and providing financial and technical support to develop their ideas. Training in TQM philosophies and techniques should be steady and continuous, and involve everyone in the company, from entry-level workers to the CEO.

5. **Customized efforts.** Impatient for immediate success, managers often adopt off-the-shelf quality programs and practices that imitate Japanese approaches without making the necessary adjustments for U.S. culture. Managers should develop approaches that maximize their own cultural strengths, perhaps borrowing from Japanese approaches, but not blindly imitating them. Companies that take the time to create such customized plans report the best results.

6. **Linkage to financial returns.** A successful quality initiative does not guarantee financial success—although many argue that without it, a company eventually will be doomed to failure. However, quality often requires a substantial investment, so wise managers pay close attention to the financial returns on quality investments. Quality, like any business decision, should add value to the organization.

P/OM in Practice

Zytec, Inc. Builds on the Deming Philosophy[15]

Zytec is a small company in Minnesota that designs and manufactures electronic power supplies and repairs power supplies and CRT monitors. Most customers are large multinational companies, and Zytec competes for business with Far Eastern and European companies as well as with approximately 400 U.S. companies. Founded in 1984, Zytec is the fastest growing U.S. electronic power supply company, and the largest power supply repair company in North America. In 1991 it won the Malcolm Baldrige National Quality Award.

Since its start, Zytec has used quality and reliability of its products and services as the key strategy to differentiate it from competitors. The company's mission statement is

Zytec is a company that competes on value, provides technical excellence in its products and services, and believes in the importance of execution. We believe in a simple form and lean staff, the importance of people as individuals, and the development of productive employees through training and capital investment. We focus on what we know best, thereby making a fair profit on current operations to meet our obligations and perpetuate our continued growth.

To carry out that mission, Zytec's senior executives decided to embrace Deming's 14 points as the cornerstone of the company's quality improvement culture. They established the Deming Steering Committee to guide the process and champion individual Deming points while acting as advisors to the three Deming Implementation Teams. Meetings were held with every Zytec employee to increase knowledge of Deming's points, and many employees attended Deming seminars. Thus, Deming's 14 points guide Zytec's actions, from long-range strategic planning to employee empowerment to leadership.

The Deming approach to setting goals and developing plans for quality leadership requires that planning be based on data. Zytec collects data by soliciting customer feedback, conducting market research, and studying its customers, suppliers, competitors, and industry leaders. Cross-functional teams use the data to set long-range strategic planning goals. Departmental planning teams then develop detailed action plans to implement those goals.

Human resources planning is guided by Deming's 14 points and the strategic plan. For example, Point 7 demands that companies institute leadership. Zytec's long-range strategic plan includes the implementation of "self-managed work groups in which employees make most day-to-day decisions while management focuses on coaching and process improvement." A long-range strategic objective that derives from the plan is, "Managers will be trained to become better coaches/facilitators." A short-range human resources objective is, "Managers will become facilitators of self-managed work groups."

Employees in the self-managed work groups, in cross-functional teams, and as individuals are granted broad authority to achieve their team and personal goals. For example, any employee can spend up to $1,000 to resolve a customer complaint without prior authority, hourly workers can make process changes with the agreement of only one other person, and sales people are authorized to travel whenever they feel it is necessary for customer service.

Zytec encourages employees to contribute to continuous improvement by providing opportunities to grow and participate, and through extensive quality-oriented training. As of February 1991, the average employee had received 72 hours of internal quality-related training. New skills are reinforced by giving employees the authority and opportunity to use them. Ongoing assistance is available through in-line trainers in each production line, the training department, and managers at all levels and in all departments.

Zytec believes that all employees should be viewed as customer-contact personnel. In 1990 over half had direct customer contact. All employees therefore receive customer-relationship training. Specialized training is provided for sales representatives and account managers. Zytec improves its role in customer relationships by listening to customers, surveying customers, and comparing its sales and service practices against those of 11 world-class organizations. Complaints are formally measured, monitored, and resolved through Zytec's Customer Action Request process. Root causes of complaints are determined, and the processes are improved to eliminate the cause.

The result of training, involvement, and empowerment is that Zytec's employees believe Deming's 14 points are more than vague guidelines. Since 1984 Zytec has surveyed employees each year to gauge how effectively the company has implemented Deming's points. Figure 2.8 shows how employee's perception scores improved through 1990.

Zytec has three principal quality goals for its suppliers: 3.4 defectives per million opportunities, 96 percent on-time delivery to the day, and a 25-day lead time. Those requirements are underscored in all communications with suppliers and supported by technical assistance and training. Zytec is committed to open communication and development of true partnerships with its suppliers and often involves them in the early stages of a development program to benefit from their knowledge.

The results of Zytec's attention to Deming's philosophy are impressive. Product quality improved from 99 percent in 1988 to 99.7 percent in 1990. Product reliability—measured as mean time between failures in hours—improved by a magnitude of 10 in just five years and ranks among the world's highest. In a two-year period, warranty costs fell by 48 percent, repair cycle time was reduced by 31 percent, product costs were cut by 30 to 40 percent, internal yields improved by 51 percent, manufacturing cycle time fell by 26 percent, and scrap rate was cut in half. In an independent survey of power supply manufacturers, Zytec ranked number one against its competitors and exceeded the industry average in 21 of 22 attributes deemed important to its customers.

Figure 2.8 Survey Results on Employee Implementation of Deming's 14 Points at Zytec

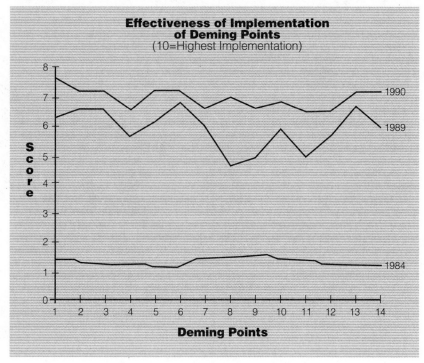

Questions for Discussion

1. Explain how Zytec views its production system.

2. From the limited information presented in this case, describe which of Deming's 14 points are addressed by Zytec, and how the company supports the underlying philosophy of that point.

Total Quality Management at AT&T[16]

AT&T has been one of the pioneers of quality, revolutionizing industrial practices and helping to make AT&T products among the best in the world. In 1988 the company took major steps to change its management practices and focus on total quality. It put customers at the top of the organization, began a process of structural and operational change aimed at making it the best in the world at delivering the

benefits of information technology, and reshaped the company structure into business units aligned directly with customers. In 1992 two divisions—the Network Transmission Systems and Universal Card Services—won the Malcolm Baldrige National Quality Award; a third won in 1994.

The fundamental principles that guide AT&T are

- The customer comes first.
- Quality happens through people.
- All work is part of a process.
- Suppliers are an integral part of our business.
- Prevention is achieved through planning.
- Quality improvement never ends.

AT&T's Total Quality Approach, shown in Figure 2.9, is built on those principles. It consists of four elements:

Figure 2.9 AT&T Total Quality Approach

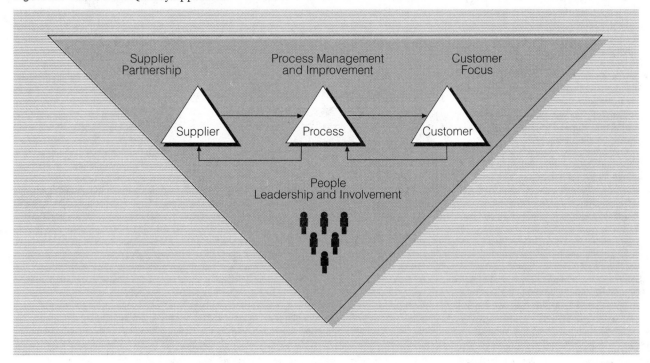

customer focus, management and improvement, supplier partnership, and the leadership and involvement (of AT&T employees). It has the power to direct change, aligning and focusing employee efforts to ensure that results meet the needs of customers, other employees, stockholders, suppliers, and communities. The Total Quality Approach has two dimensions. The horizontal dimension represents how the company manages work to add value for customers. The vertical dimension represents a new way for employees to work together, requiring full involvement of people and a new role for leadership.

AT&T defines quality as consistently meeting customer expectations. It challenges the company to identify customers, anticipate and understand what they need and expect, and ensure that all they do contributes to their ability to deliver. One example of that customer

focus occurred when a cardholder called AT&T Universal Card Services in hope that the office might have a record of a recent purchase by his wife, a victim of Alzheimer's disease who had disappeared on vacation. The AT&T associate who received the call verified the story and investigated. Each day he checked the account regularly. On the fifth day he received a call from a merchant whose description fit the missing woman, and notified the husband and police. A medical team was dispatched and the woman was returned safely to her family.

AT&T aligns its work processes to satisfy its customers. It aligns both large, cross-functional processes that deliver products and services to outside customers as well as the many internal processes whose suppliers and customers are inside the company. Throughout AT&T, cross-functional teams manage and improve

processes, following the company's "Process Quality Management and Improvement Methodology":

1. Establish process-management responsibilities.
2. Baseline the current process and identify customer requirements.
3. Define and establish measures.
4. Assess conformance to customer requirements.
5. Investigate to find improvement opportunities.
6. Rank the opportunities and set objectives.
7. Continuously improve the process.

The AT&T Supplier Quality Policy states clearly the company's commitment to work in partnership with suppliers toward a common goal—customer satisfaction:

Figure 2.10   AT&T's Shared Values

Our Common Bond
We commit to these values to guide our decisions and behavior:

Respect for Individuals
We treat each other with respect and dignity, valuing individual and cultural differences. We communicate frequently and with candor, listening to each other regardless of level or position. Recognizing that exceptional quality begins with people, we give individuals the authority to use their capabilities to the fullest to satisfy their customers. Our environment supports personal growth and continuous learning for all AT&T people.

Dedication to Helping Customers
We truly care for each customer. We build enduring relationships by understanding and anticipating our customers' needs and by serving them better each time than the time before. AT&T customers can count on us to consistently deliver superior products and services that help them achieve their personal and business goals.

Highest Standards of Integrity
We are honest and ethical in all our business dealings, starting with how we treat each other. We keep our promises and admit our mistakes. Our personal conduct ensures that AT&T's name is always worthy of trust.

Innovation
We believe innovation is the engine that will keep us vital and growing. Our culture embraces creativity, seeks different perspectives, and risks pursuing new opportunities. We create and rapidly convert technology into products and services, constantly searching for new ways to make technology more useful to customers.

Teamwork
We encourage and reward both individual and team achievements. We freely join with colleagues across organizational boundaries to advance the interests of customers and shareowners. Our team spirit extends to being responsible and caring partners in the communities where we live and work.

By living these values, AT&T aspires to set a standard of excellence world wide that will reward our shareowners, our customers, and all AT&T people.

We view our suppliers as an integral part of our business. Relationships with our suppliers are driven by our customers and built on Total Quality Principles and Practices. We commit to a Supplier Management Process that continuously improves our ability to add value for AT&T customers.

One example of supplier partnerships involves local telephone companies that provide AT&T access to their customers. Following divestiture, AT&T established a Financial Assurance Organization to check the accuracy of access charges and to correct errors. By 1989 AT&T employed 1,100 people working to duplicate the sup-

plier's access-billing system, anticipate charges, and resolve problems. In 1990 AT&T began a joint effort with Pacific Bell to design a single-access billing verification process—involving both supplier and customer—that shifted focus from correction to prevention, moved accountability for accuracy to the supplier, and replaced post-bill resolution with pre-bill certification. As a result, the validation process was reduced from three months to 24 hours, accuracy is up, and costs are down.

The new role of leadership is represented by the inverted pyramid in Figure 2.9. Customers are at the top of the organization; leaders provide direction, empowerment, and support

for the people who create value for those customers. AT&T's shared values—respect for the individual, dedication to helping customers, highest standards of integrity, innovation, and teamwork—influence decisions and define how employees work together (see Figure 2.10). A Management Executive Committee, serving as the AT&T Quality Council, sets policy and strategy. The Corporate Quality Office supports the council and helps develop and deploy methods, guidelines, and tools to advance efforts throughout the company. A Quality Steering Committee, made up of quality managers from all units, fosters communication and guides company-wide improvement efforts.

The Total Quality Approach calls for full involvement of all employees. Employees are involved beyond their natural work groups on quality councils, on cross-functional process-management teams, on quality improvement teams in daily work, on quality-of-work-life teams, and through suggestion systems. Teamwork is a critical factor in achievement and improvement at AT&T. Throughout the company, teams are applying the Total Quality Approach to improve their ability to serve customers. The contributions of teams range from dramatic reductions in costs and time intervals to small process changes that add up to increased customer satisfaction. For example, unreliable test and measurement equipment was causing quality problems at the Reading Works. A team recommended a new calibration system built on a partnership between calibration engineers and the production line. The new system has cut calibration costs in half, and the quality of test and measurement equipment now exceeds industry standards. The new process has been recognized as "best in industry worldwide" by a Motorola Quality Assurance audit team.

Questions for Discussion

1. Explain how AT&T's Total Quality Approach supports the principles of TQM discussed in this chapter.
2. Discuss some of the key practices, techniques, and infrastructure that support AT&T's quality focus.

Summary of Key Points

••• Productivity and quality are two key performance dimensions for managing manufacturing and service organizations. Productivity, the ratio of outputs to inputs, is important to the competitive survival of nations in today's global environment. However, overemphasizing productivity may lead to poor quality and hence to customer dissatisfaction. As improved quality usually leads to improved productivity, quality management has emerged as the central focus of management strategy.

••• Total quality management is a companywide effort to achieve customer satisfaction through the full involvement of the entire work force, as well as customers and suppliers, in the attempt at continuous improvement. Improved product and production quality usually leads to increased profitability.

••• Quality can be defined from several perspectives. Two definitions are *fitness for use* (the customer perspective) and *conformance to specifications* (the producer's perspective). A key objective of quality management is to reduce variation in the production process.

••• Modern organizations organize quality around cross-functional teams that report to a top-level Quality Council. Quality assurance specialists serve as advisors and perform statistical studies, train employees, and help managers interpret quality-related data.

••• Service differs considerably from manufacturing, and the difference has important implications for quality management. In contrast to manufacturing, service involves vague expectations and specifications, simultaneous production and consumption, high labor intensity, customer involvement, customization, and extremely high volumes of transactions.

••• The philosophy of W. Edwards Deming focuses on continuous improvement through the reduction of variability by eliminating special causes of variation and reducing common causes of variation. His 14 points prescribe a radical change in management philosophy, although the basic concepts of leadership, cooperation, learning, process management, continuous improvement, employee fulfillment, and customer satisfaction should be part of any management system.

••• The philosophies of Juran and Crosby focus on integrating quality into more traditional management practices. They encompass planning, control, and improvement with emphasis on quality cost management, education, problem-solving tools, and behavioral change.

••• The core principles of TQM are strategic planning, fact-based management, leadership and human resources management, customer-driven product and service design, and continuous improvement and learning. Those principles are embodied in the Malcolm Baldrige National Quality Award criteria, which have become a universal framework for planning and assessing quality systems in both manufacturing and service organizations.

••• ISO 9000 is a series of quality system standards to ensure that a company conforms to stated requirements in design/development, production, installation, and service. ISO 9000 is much narrower in scope than the Baldrige criteria, but it has become critical in meeting contractual and trade regulations and in marketing products internationally. Recently U.S. automobile manufacturers released QS 9000, an extension of the ISO standards for the automotive industry.

••• Successful implementation of TQM requires good strategic planning, top management involvement and commitment, integration of customer-satisfaction goals throughout the organization, employee participation and training, customized efforts, and linkage to financial returns.

Key Terms

Productivity
Hidden factory
Total quality management (TQM)
Specifications
Quality council
Quality Trilogy

Review Questions

1. Define *productivity.* Why is it important to a nation as a whole?

2. What are some of the consequences of low productivity growth and poor quality?

3. Define *hidden factory.*

4. Define *total quality management.* What benefits can it provide to an organization? Why is TQM now viewed as a framework for business management?

5. Explain how improved quality and productivity can lead to higher profits.

6. Explain the concept of targets and tolerances. Provide some examples different from those in the text.

7. Explain the distinguishing features of the main definitional views of quality: fitness for use and conformance to specifications. How can they be applied operationally in an organization?

8. Describe the customer-driven quality cycle. What parts of the organization are responsible for each step?

9. What implications does the Taguchi loss function have for quality management?

10. How is quality organized in many modern organizations?

11. How does quality differ in manufacturing and service organizations?

12. Summarize Deming's philosophy. Explain how it differs from traditional management practices and why.

13. Explain the Deming Chain Reaction.

14. How do the philosophies of Juran and Crosby differ from that of Deming?

15. Explain Juran's *Quality Trilogy.*

16. Summarize the key elements of total quality management.

17. Why was the Malcolm Baldrige National Quality Award instituted? Explain the impact the award has had on American business.

18. List and explain the seven categories of the Baldrige award and the scoring guidelines.

19. What is ISO 9000? How does it differ from the Baldrige award?

20. Discuss the important issues an organization must face when implementing total quality management. What approaches will enhance the chances for successful implementation?

Discussion Questions

1. If you were to develop a "Customer Value Policy" for your operations management class, how would you define it?

2. Interview a production manager at a local company to determine the company's "hidden factory." Does the company know the elements of its hidden factory and the costs?

3. Cite an example in which you experienced poor quality in a product or service. Did you complain to the company? Did you tell others about it? Has that experience changed your purchasing practices?

4. Select some service in which you are involved (for instance, with your fraternity or a student organization). How might you apply the customer-driven quality cycle in Figure 2.2 to develop and deliver that service?

5. Select a service with which you are familiar. Discuss some of the implications of managing quality in this service relative to the differences between service and manufacturing that were discussed in this chapter.

6. Discuss the rationale behind the Deming Chain Reaction. Will it always be true?

7. Which of Deming's 14 points do you think are the most controversial? Why? Interview some managers to solicit their feelings on Deming's views.

8. How might Deming's 14 points be applied in running a college or university? How about an individual classroom?

9. Which philosophy—Deming's, Juran's, or Crosby's—are you most comfortable with? Why?

10. Are the basic elements of TQM really any different from the practices that every manager should perform? Why do many managers find them difficult to accept?

11. Obtain a copy of the current year's Malcolm Baldrige National Quality Award criteria. Develop a short questionnaire that a company might use to assess its management practices based on the criteria.

12. Select a past winner of the Baldrige award, and find some articles describing that company's quality system (many articles are published about the winners). Write a P/OM in Practice case similar to that of Zytec, Inc., in this chapter.

13. Develop other portions of a quality manual for MamaMia's Pizza based on the ISO 9000 standards similar to those stated for purchasing in this chapter.

14. Interview managers of a local company that has achieved or is pursuing ISO 9000 or QS 9000 registration. What problems does it face or did it encounter in achieving registration?

15. Discuss where specific elements of ISO 9000 are incorporated (either implicitly or explicitly) in the latest version of the Baldrige criteria.

16. If you were managing MamaMia's, what would you do to implement total quality management? What barriers might you face?

17. Consider the following scenarios.[17] Discuss the productivity/quality interaction in these situations and suggest steps that managers might take to improve the situations.

a. An organization inspects incoming resources when they are received, again at key partial product-completion stages, and again at the final product level. Unacceptable output at each stage is rejected and dealt with accordingly or appropriately. Rework is possible, and defects are identified and corrected.

b. A group of five spray painters on an assembly line operate with basic job training but with little feedback as to the actual outcomes resulting from their efforts. Inspectors down the line, isolated from the line personnel, evaluate the output from the painting department based on specific quality attributes (runs, too-wide or too-narrow shading stripes, and so on).

c. A firm is committed to achieving high quality in the goods and services it produces. The quality-control department has convinced management that in order to accomplish that, all goods and services produced must be inspected. A significant amount of effort and other resources has been devoted to building and developing a large quality control organization that emphasizes inspection, correction, and zero defects.

Notes

1. Thomas A. Stewart, "U.S. Productivity: First but Fading," *Fortune,* October 19, 1992, pp. 54–57.

2. Bradley T. Gale, "Quality Comes First When Hatching Power Brands," *Planning Review,* July–August 1992, pp. 4–9, 48.

3. Ford Motor Company 1984 Annual Report.

4. Y. K. Shetty and V. M. Buehler, *Productivity and Quality through Science and Technology* (New York: Quorum Books, 1988).

5. Gregory M. Seal, "1990s—Years of Promise, Years of Peril for U.S. Manufacturers," *Industrial Engineering,* January 1990, pp. 18–21.

6. AT&T Quality Steering Committee, *Leading the Quality Initiative,* AT&T Bell Laboratories Technical Publications Center, 1991, pp. 13–14.

7. Philip B. Crosby, *Quality Is Free* (New York: McGraw-Hill, 1979), pp. 200–201.

8. Kenneth Labich, "An Airline That Soars on Service," *Fortune,* December 31, 1990, pp. 94–96.

9. "Betting to Win on the Baldie Winners," *Business Week,* October 18, 1993, p. 8.

10. Michael J. Timbers, "ISO 9000 and Europe's Attempts to Mandate Quality," *The Journal of European Business,* March–April 1992, pp. 14–25.

11. Adapted from Jeffrey G. Waring, "An ISO 9000 Certified Pizza Isn't All That Far-Fetched," *Journal for Quality and Participation* 16, no. 6 (1993), pp. 20–23.

12. Curt W. Reimann and Harry S. Hertz, "The Malcolm Baldrige National Quality Award and ISO 9000 Registration," *ASTM Standardization News,* November 1993, pp. 42–53.

13. Thomas H. Tappen, Jr., "Beyond Systems—The Politics of Managing in a TQM Environment," *National Productivity Review,* Winter 1991–1992, pp. 9–19.

14. George H. Labovitz and Yu Sang Chang, "Learn from the Best," *Quality Progress,* May 1990, pp. 81–85; J. M. Juran, "Strategies for World Class Quality," *Quality Progress,* March 1991, pp. 81–85; Thomas H. Berry, *Managing the Total Quality Transformation* (New York: McGraw-Hill, 1991), chapter 9; and Rahul Jacob, "TQM—More Than a Dying Fad?" *Fortune,* October 18, 1993, pp. 66–72.

15. Adapted from Zytec Malcolm Baldrige National Quality Award Application Summary. Used with permission.

16. Adapted from *AT&T's Total Quality Approach,* Issue 1.1, December 1992. Used with permission of AT&T © 1992. All rights reserved.

17. Adapted from "Productivity and Quality: What Is the Connection" by D. Scott Sink and J. Bert Keats in *Proceedings of the 1982 Fall Industrial Engineering Conference,* Norcross, Georgia (Institute of Industrial Engineers), pp. 227–283.

Chapter Outline

Chapter Three
P/OM and Strategic Planning

Applied P/OM

P/OM in Practice

Every business is concerned with its competitiveness and long-term growth, which are determined by **corporate strategy**—the strategy of the organization as a whole, set by top management (though, ideally, with input from other organizational levels). **Strategic planning** is the process of determining long-term goals, policies, and plans for an organization.

The concept of *strategy* has different meanings to different people. James Brian Quinn characterizes it thus:

> [Strategy is] a pattern or plan that integrates an organization's major goals, policies, and action sequences into a cohesive whole. A well-formulated strategy helps to marshal and allocate an organization's resources into a unique and viable posture based on its relative internal competencies and shortcomings, anticipated changes in the environment, and contingent moves by intelligent opponents.[1]

Basically, then, a strategy is the approach by which an organization seeks to develop the capabilities required for achieving its *competitive advantage* (discussed later). Effective strategies develop around a few key concepts and thrusts—such as customer satisfaction—which provide a focus for the entire organization. The objective of strategic planning is to build a posture that is so strong in selected ways that the organization can achieve its goals despite unforeseeable external forces that may arise.

The three basic components of corporate strategy are the marketing and sales strategy, the design strategy, and the operations strategy. The *marketing and sales strategy* defines the markets in which a firm will compete, identifies consumer needs in those markets, and determines the timing and extent of new product introductions. For example, should MamaMia's focus on gourmet, dine-in pizza service, or should it compete primarily in a responsive home delivery market?

The *design strategy* determines how the firm will match its technological capability with market needs to develop specifications for competitively priced goods and services. As a small, family-owned business, MamaMia's would have difficulty competing with home-delivery giants such as Domino's and Pizza Hut because it lacks capability in the form of wide distribution networks.

Finally, the *operations strategy* (discussed in detail later) sets parameters for how the firm's resources will be converted into goods and services that meet the design specifications. For example, hiring part-time college students and having a lot of employee turnover would probably be a poor match for a strategy based on high-quality, personal service. All three strategies—marketing/sales, design, and operations—must be consistent and support the overall corporate strategy.

Because corporate strategy has traditionally emphasized marketing and financial considerations, the operations strategy has received the least amount of high-level attention. In fact, in some organizations, operations has not even been considered a factor of the corporate strategy. Consequently, operations managers have often been placed in the position of having to react to strategic plans that were developed from primarily financial and marketing perspectives. In many cases, the result has been low productivity and quality. Recently, however, top managers have recognized that operations strategy is vitally important to an organization's long-term success, and that employees at all organizational levels must be involved in the strategic planning process.

The purpose of this chapter is to explore the scope of strategic planning in general, and operations strategy in particular. As we study individual P/OM topics in succeeding chapters, we shall relate them to the strategic issues discussed in this chapter. Specifically addressed are

••• Major components of operations strategy as they affect both manufacturing and service.

••• Generic strategies for achieving competitive advantage.

••• Role of quality in modern strategic business planning.

••• Elements of typical strategic planning processes.

••• Contemporary quality-based approaches to implementing strategy.

Scope of Strategic Planning

Since strategy is the result of a series of hierarchical decisions about goals, directions, and resources, most large organizations have three levels of strategy: corporate, business, and functional. Figure 3.1 illustrates those strategies and their hierarchical relationships.

Figure 3.1   Hierarchy of Strategic Planning in a Corporation

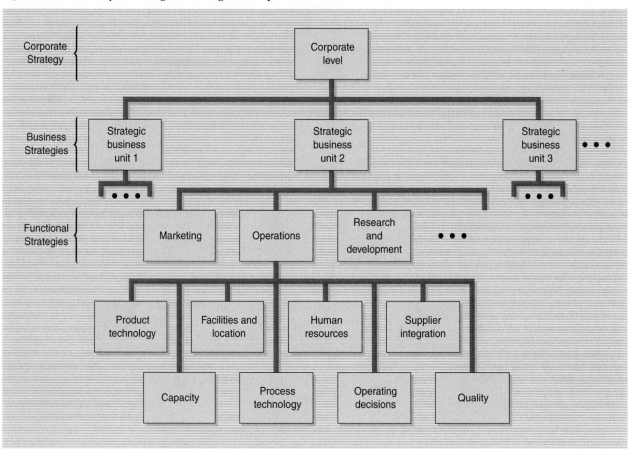

A corporate strategy is necessary to define the businesses in which the corporation will participate and develop plans for the acquisition and allocation of resources among those businesses. A corporate strategy includes all the components shown in Figure 3.1. It requires consideration of environmental factors such as customer demand, labor supply, material sources, capital sources, the company's strengths and weaknesses, and the competitors' strengths and weaknesses. Corporate strategic planning addresses such questions as: What must we do particularly well? What are our greatest challenges? How will we measure performance?

The businesses in which the firm will participate are often called **strategic business units (SBUs),** and they are usually defined as families of products having similar characteristics or methods of production. SBUs might be organized along broad material or process lines, such as steel, glass, plastics, or machine tools, or by consumer-product segments, such as health-care products, foods, and so on. Strategic plans differ among SBUs, but must be consistent with the overall corporate strategy. The major decisions involve which products and markets to pursue and how best to compete in those markets. Should emphasis be on price, quality, speed of delivery, or service? Should distribution be centralized or decentralized? Answers to such questions depend on the nature of the business, and they define the business strategy.

The core elements of *business strategy* typically are finance, marketing, and operations. Each area must work within particular constraints, and those constraints affect its strategy. For instance, finance may have certain requirements of return on capital investment, profit, or budgetary limits. Marketing is constrained by the customer base and the competitors. Operations may be constrained by location, capacity, processes, and supporting services. Changes in the business environment make strategic thinking and planning essential— changes brought about by shareholders, markets, customer needs, competition, new laws and regulations, new technologies, and so on. The constraints and needs drive the strategy.

Business strategy has traditionally been dominated by either finance or marketing considerations. Conflicts with operations often result. For example, marketing managers want a wide line of products and short delivery times; those preferences necessitate short production runs and fast product changeover, both of which can degrade productivity and result in higher production costs. Hence, if operations managers are evaluated on short-run performance measures such as quarterly costs or productivity, conflicts arise. For the firm to be successful, the expertise and the concerns of all three elements—finance, marketing, and operations—must be integrated into a cohesive business strategy. An operations strategy that supports corporate business objectives is crucial for evaluating trade-offs, discovering opportunities, setting priorities, and providing the resources necessary to meet objectives.

The third level of the strategic planning hierarchy is the *functional strategy.* Within the boundaries set by the business strategy, each functional area—marketing, manufacturing, research and development, and so on—develops strategies that support its particular business focus. Figure 3.1 illustrates key elements of operations strategy, each of which is discussed later in this chapter. Other functional areas have different elements, of course, but our focus is clearly on manufacturing and service operations.

Strategy and Competitive Advantage

The term **competitive advantage** denotes a firm's ability to achieve market superiority over its competitors by offering better customer value. Competitive advantage can be achieved in many ways, such as outperforming competitors on price or quality, identifying new market opportunities to create customer value before competitors do, or responding quickly to changing customer needs. Consequently, a business can choose to focus its efforts along several dimensions to achieve competitive advantage. The question to be decided is which dimensions should receive the most emphasis. A study of strategy practices of U.S. and Japanese machine tool manufacturers revealed major differences in firms' emphasis between the two countries.[2] U.S. companies tend to emphasize superior design and design customization, whereas Japanese firms emphasize research and development effort aimed at creating new products and achieving low-cost production. Apparently the Japanese choices have been better, since their manufacturers have consistently gained market share in the industry at the expense of U.S. manufacturers.

Successful strategies exploit a company's **distinctive competencies**—the strengths unique to that company. Such strengths might be a particularly skilled or creative work force, strong distribution networks, or the ability to rapidly develop new products or change production-output rates. A distinctive competency for MamaMia's might be a proprietary family recipe! The operations function, and manufacturing in particular, can contribute strongly to creating a competitive advantage. Sadly, most U.S. firms do not recognize that fact and have thus fallen prey to foreign competitors that do.

The literature on competitive strategy suggests that a firm can have two basic types: low-cost and differentiation.[3] In making decisions, operations managers must understand which type of advantage the company is seeking.

Low-Cost Strategy

Many firms gain competitive advantage by establishing themselves as the low-cost leader in an industry. Such firms generally produce high volumes of mature products (products in the mature stage of the product life cycle) and can therefore afford to offer lower prices than firms producing smaller volumes of newer products. Low cost can result from high productivity and high capacity utilization. Usually that means long production runs of a narrow model range with little customization and infrequent design changes. For example, should MamaMia's decide to focus on cost leadership in home delivery, it would probably have to restrict the variety of pizza options.

Low-cost leaders often enter markets that have already been established by other firms. Pizza Hut, for instance, entered the home delivery market after Domino's. It places considerable emphasis on achieving economies of scale and finding cost advantages from all sources.

As pointed out in the last chapter, lower costs often result from quality improvements. Innovations in product design and process technology can reduce the costs of production, and efficiencies gained through meticulous attention to operations lead to lower costs. Many Japanese firms have adopted and adapted product innovations and process technologies that were developed in the United States, thus producing high-quality products at lower costs and gaining greater market shares.

Cost leadership in high-volume products is possible through a variety of approaches:[4]

••• Early manufacturing involvement in the design of the product, both for make-versus-buy decisions and to verify that the production processes can achieve required tolerances.

••• Product design to take advantage of automated equipment by minimizing the number of parts, eliminating fasteners, making parts symmetric whenever possible, avoiding rigid and stiff parts, and using one-sided assembly designs.

••• Limited product models and customization in distribution centers rather than in the factory.

••• A manufacturing system designed for a fixed sequence of operations in which every effort is made to ensure zero defects at the time of shipment. Work-in-process inventory is reduced as much as possible this way, and multiskilled, focused teams of employees are used.

Cost leadership is impossible with an inferior product. The product must be perceived as comparable with competitors, or the firm will be forced to discount prices so far below competitors' prices to gain sales that the product becomes unprofitable.

Differentiation Strategy

To use a differentiation strategy successfully, a firm must be unique in its industry along some dimension that is widely valued by customers. An example is a power tool manufacturer that improves its product reliability well beyond that of competitors and thus was able to secure a premium price.[5] MamaMia's might differentiate itself from competitors by offering a line of gourmet pizzas with smoked oysters and artichokes, Italian pancetta and sweet onion, and other unusual toppings.

As customers become more demanding, many mass markets are becoming more fragmented. As a result, many companies find it necessary to meet individual customer needs or narrowly segment their markets, using differentiation strategies to target those markets. They adopt operations strategies that offer flexibility. For example, Harley-Davidson's annual output is relatively small (around 40,000 bikes per year). However, it offers numerous models, accessories, and customized features that make almost every bike unique. It can do so because its manufacturing operations are built around programmable robots and other forms of flexible automation.[6]

A firm that uses differentation as its source of competitive advantage cannot ignore cost, however. It must achieve a cost position on a par with its competitors', and reduce costs in all areas that do not affect differentiation.

Low-Cost and Differentiation Strategies Compared

A contrast between the low-cost and differentiation strategies is provided by two very different companies, Hewlett-Packard and Texas Instruments.

Applied P/OM
Hewlett-Packard and Texas Instruments

HP and TI pursue significantly different strategies.[7]

Texas Instruments (TI) prefers to pursue competitive advantages based on larger, more standard markets and a long-term, low-cost position. Hewlett-Packard (HP) seeks competitive advantages in selected smaller markets based on unique, high-value, functional performance. TI enters markets early, expands and consolidates its position, and achieves a dominant market share when the product matures. HP creates new markets and then exits or introduces other new products as cost-conscious competitors enter the market. TI emphasizes cost reduction to build volume, while HP adds features to hold prices longer, thus achieving higher profit margins and earlier returns on investment.

Those corporate strategies are reflected in the operations decisions that each company makes. For example, TI uses capital-intensive and cost-effective production processes such as assembly lines staffed with less-skilled assemblers. HP uses more flexible processes, employing higher-skilled assemblers and producing in lower volumes. TI uses more industrial engineers to improve productivity, while HP uses more product engineers to develop new performance features for its products. TI makes more of its own components, while HP purchases more. Clearly, TI's operations strategy would not work as well for HP, and vice versa. What is important is that the operations strategy chosen by each firm supports the overall corporate strategy.

Those issues apply to services as well. For example, Marriott's Fairfield Inn is designed to appeal to business travelers who want clean, comfortable rooms at moderate prices. Its strategy is therefore focused on cost leadership. The Ritz-Carlton hotels, on the other hand, focus on differentiation. They provide exceptional personal attention, twice-a-day housekeeping service, and amenities such as bathrobes and rooms with bay windows, and can command premium prices based on those special and superior offerings.

Competitive Advantage through Quality and Value

True competitive advantage is gained from meeting or exceeding customer expectations—the fundamental definition of quality. A business may concentrate on any of several quality-related dimensions:

••• Superior product design.
••• Outstanding service.
••• High flexibility and variety.
••• Continuous innovation.
••• Rapid response.

Rarely can a firm achieve superiority in all those dimensions, so it must make trade-offs according to its specific "market-driven" strategies for achieving its desired goals. The choices affect the way in which operations are managed.

Traditionally, management strategists advocated focusing on a single dimension of quality. However, as consumers become more demanding, many firms are finding they can no longer compete along only one dimension. A periodic survey of U.S. manufacturing firms conducted at Boston University shows that manufacturers believe the most important competitive priorities are conformance quality, on-time delivery, product reliability, low price, and fast delivery.[8] Those findings support the notion that creating customer value leads to competitive success. As the report states, "The basic requirements do not change [over repeated surveys since 1990], and if a firm cannot deliver these basics, it cannot stay in business."

We see a similar focus in services. Avis, Inc., for instance, identifies four primary drivers of customer satisfaction as

1. *Product*—the cars provided.
2. *Environment*—the arena of service delivery.
3. *Speed*—the pace of service delivery.
4. *Price*—fair, competitive price for a service offering good value.

This is where a strategy of total quality management fits in. It boosts a firm's performance in all the aforementioned areas. Let us look at each one.

Competing on Superior Product Design. Among the most important strategic decisions a firm makes are those involving the selection and development of new products and services. Those decisions determine the growth, profitability, and future direction of the firm. Products of superior design that are appealing, reliable, easy to operate, and economical to service give a perception of quality to the consumer. New Balance Athletic Shoe, Inc., for example, is unique in its industry by offering "true width" sizing in all of its models to ensure a customized fit. Engineers design advanced materials into New Balance shoes for cushioning and support. A "suspension system" features a "roll bar" that resists back-and-forth foot motion; it consists of a midsole cushioning pad that disperses shock and a contrabalance heal design that acts like an inverted trampoline.[9]

Competing on Service. At one time, manufacturing companies viewed service as much less important than the product itself. Now, though, service is widely recognized as perhaps the greatest opportunity for competitive advantage. As the average level of product quality has increased overall among competitors, consumers are turning toward service as the primary means of differentiating among firms. Companies that have capitalized on this consumer trend have generally done the following:[10]

1. Established service goals that support business and product-line objectives.
2. Identified and defined customer expectations for service quality and responsiveness.
3. Translated customer expectations into clear, deliverable service features.
4. Set up efficient, responsive, and integrated service delivery systems and organizations.
5. Monitored and controlled service quality and performance.
6. Provided quick but cost-effective response to customers' needs.

To compete effectively on the basis of services associated with its product, a company must examine its operations and identify those that bear most directly on such services. Often it must restructure responsibilities and redraw organization charts. And sometimes it must break management molds and think about service in new ways!

Competing on Flexibility and Variety.   Many firms use flexibility and/or variety as a competitive weapon. **Flexibility** is the capacity of a production system to adapt successfully to changing environmental conditions and process requirements. **Variety** refers to its ability to produce a wide range of products and options.

Companies that can change product lines more rapidly in the face of changing consumer demands can thus exploit new technologies and gain a competitive advantage in certain markets. Some firms provide custom service on complex systems for low-volume customers and markets. They must be excellent at product design and responsiveness to customers. Other firms do little innovation themselves, but take product designs from customers and produce custom products on a low-volume basis. Both types of firms must have considerable flexibility in their production operations to produce low volumes and customized products. High quality is a must, as is delivery on schedule.

A lack of flexibility has hurt the U.S. auto industry. GM's Oshawa, Ontario, plant shut down for three months to gear up for the 1995 Chevrolet Lumina, and after starting built only 288 cars in the first six weeks. Ford took more than two months to switch its Kansas City, Missouri, plant to produce new 1995 models of the Ford Contour and Mercury Mystique. In contrast, Honda's Maryville, Ohio, plant produced its last 1993 Accord on Friday, August 27, 1993, and began producing an all-new 1994 model the next Monday, reaching full speed of 48 cars per hour in six weeks. While the quality gap between U.S. and Japanese products narrows, many Japanese firms are focusing their strategies on flexibility and variety—more and better product features, factories that can change product lines quickly, expanded customer service, and continually improving new products. Toshiba and Nissan are two examples.

Applied P/OM
Toshiba and Nissan

Toshiba and Nissan design factories for high flexibility.[11]

Toshiba's computer factory assembles nine different word processors on the same production line, and 20 varieties of laptop computers on another. The flexible lines guard against running short of a hot model or overproducing one whose sales have slowed. Nissan is another company with high flexibility. It describes its strategy as "five anys": to make anything in any volume anywhere at any time by anybody. Nissan's high-tech Intelligent Body Assembly System can weld and inspect body parts for any kind of car, all in 46 seconds. As U.S. automakers think about dropping entire car lines, Nissan is gearing up to fill market niches with more models.

Competing on Innovation.   Firms on the leading edge of product technology usually focus on research and development as a core component of their strategy. Their ability to innovate and introduce new products is a critical success factor. Product performance, not price, is the major selling feature in these cases. When competitors enter the market and profit margins fall, such companies often drop out of the market while continuing to introduce innovative products. Their strategies emphasize outstanding product research, design, and development; high product quality; and the ability to modify production facilities so as to produce new products frequently. Hewlett-Packard is an example of this type of company.

Today, leading companies do not wait for customers' needs and desires to change; they use innovation to create new ones. At 3M, for example, every division is expected to get 25 percent of its sales each year from products that did not exist five years earlier. Thus managers are forced to think seriously about innovation. Such a perspective not only results in new products, but helps managers to create better processes that improve quality.

Competing on Time.   In today's fast-paced society, people hate to wait. Time has come to be recognized as one of the most important sources of competitive advantage in recent years. The total time required by a company to deliver a finished product that satisfies customers' needs is referred to as the company's **product lead time.** It includes time spent on design, engineering, purchasing, manufacturing, testing, packaging, and shipping.

Short product lead times enable companies to introduce new products and penetrate new markets more rapidly. Being the first to market a new product enables a firm to charge a higher price, at least until competitive products are offered. For example, when first introduced, Motorola's pocket-sized cellular telephone was 50 percent smaller than any competing Japanese product and sold for twice the price.

Another advantage of short product lead times is that every month saved in development time can save a large company millions of dollars in expenses. Still another is that short lead times reduce the need to forecast long-term sales, allowing more accurate production plans to be developed and reducing inventory. In other words, short lead times increase a company's flexibility in responding to changing customer needs.

Integrating Quality with Strategic Business Planning

Strategic business planning has traditionally revolved around financial and marketing goals. Until the 1980s it was viewed as separate and distinct from issues of customer-driven quality and operational-performance improvement, which were typically performed at low levels of the organization and focused entirely on manufacturing and technology.

However, the role of quality in business strategy has taken two significant steps since 1980. First, many firms have come to recognize that a strategy driven by quality can lead to significant market advantages. Second, the lines between quality planning and generic business planning have become increasingly blurred. Customer-driven quality and operational performance excellence are now considered key strategic business issues, integral to overall business planning. Quality improvement objectives such as increasing customer satisfaction, reducing defects, and reducing process cycle times are generally now given as much attention as financial and marketing objectives by leading companies. The current trend is to integrate quality planning within normal business planning. Thus, *strategic quality planning* is synonymous with *strategic business planning*. In fact, one category in the Malcolm Baldrige National Quality Award criteria was changed from "Strategic Quality Planning" to "Strategic Planning" in 1995 to emphasize this point.

In most companies, complete integration of TQM into strategic business planning occurs only when decreasing profits demand it. At first quality takes a back seat to meeting financial targets, increasing sales, expanding capacity, or boosting production. However, in the face of market crises, such as those that arose in the 1970s and 1980s, top managers begin to realize the importance of quality as a basis for strategic planning. Xerox is one of many companies that have come to that realization, as its "Leadership through Quality" strategy signifies.

Applied P/OM

Xerox

"Leadership through Quality" is the business strategy for Xerox.[12]

The Xerox "Leadership through Quality" strategy is built on three elements: quality principles, management actions and behaviors, and quality tools.

Quality principles are

••• Quality is the basic business principle for Xerox to continue to be a leadership company.

••• We will understand our customers' existing and latent requirements.

Part One

- We will provide all our external and internal customers with products and services that meet their requirements.
- Employee involvement, through participative problem solving, is essential to improve quality.
- Error-free work is the most cost-effective way to improve quality.

Management actions and behaviors are

- We will assure strategic clarity and consistency.
- We will provide visible supportive management practices, commitment, and leadership.
- We will set quality objectives and measurement standards.
- We will establish and reinforce a management style of openness, trust, respect, patience, and discipline.
- We will establish an environment in which each person can be responsible for quality.

Quality tools are

- The Xerox quality policy.
- Competitive benchmarking and goal setting.
- Systematic defect- and error-prevention processes.
- Training for leadership through quality.
- Communication and recognition programs that reinforce leadership through quality.
- A measure for the cost of quality (or its lack).

After the formation of this strategy, senior executives at Xerox defined the goals they would strive to achieve and the activities necessary to implement those goals over the next five years.

Operations Strategy

From Figure 3.1 we saw that **operations strategy** consists of eight major components: product technology, capacity, facilities and location, process technology, human resources, operating decisions, integration of suppliers, and quality. Let us consider each in turn.

Product Technology

Products range from those that are custom-made to those that are manufactured in large volume. Custom products are unique, and cost is generally not an important issue. On-time delivery, quality, and the capability to design and manufacture different products can determine success. On the other hand, companies that manufacture high-volume types of products usually benefit most from standardization in design, low manufacturing cost, and high availability of the product through inventories and distribution channels. Thus it is important that product designers understand the nature of the manufacturing process and its implications for cost, flexibility, quality, and innovativeness.

Some products, such as soft drinks and pizzas, have long product life cycles; others, such as sophisticated electronics products (for example, personal-computer printers) have very short life cycles. Marketing strategies to renew or extend product life cycles often depend on introducing technological improvements in the product. Such strategies must be coordinated with manufacturing for success. Product design issues are further discussed in Chapter 6.

Capacity

Capacity, a measure of the amount of output that can be produced over a period of time, is an important resource that a firm can control. A firm must make many strategic decisions about capacity, such as the amount of capacity to have, the timing of capacity changes, and the type of capacity. For example, what is the economic effect of expanding MamaMia's restaurant versus building a new facility or of having one large facility versus several small ones? Are capacity decisions different for well-established products and new products? How does a firm make capacity decisions to cope with cyclic variations in demand? How does a firm best take advantage of economies of scale in planning capacity? Consequences of capacity decisions normally influence cost, flexibility, and dependability. Capacity decisions are discussed thoroughly in Chapter 7.

Facilities and Location

Facilities and their locations are closely related to capacity decisions. Managers must trade off economies associated with centralized production facilities with distribution costs and customer service. For instance, oil companies often locate processing plants near supplies of crude oil to achieve economies of scale. Individual distribution outlets are located much closer to customers. Decisions on how to structure product groups within plants, what types of processes to develop, and what volume to produce are important, especially in rapidly changing industries. For instance, in the semiconductor industry, small, low-volume plants are built for new products with considerable risk, whereas high-volume plants are used for stable and mature products. Chapter 8 addresses those issues.

Process Technology

A process-oriented system employing general-purpose equipment allows for flexibility in manufacturing different products. A product-oriented system, with special-purpose equipment dedicated to the production of one or a few products, provides high volume and low unit costs.

Automation is making process decisions quite difficult, primarily because highly automated plants are very expensive. For example, Deere and Company spent $500 million on its automated Waterloo, Iowa, plant, and General Electric spent over $300 million in automation improvements alone in its Erie, Pennsylvania, facility. Moreover, automation changes the manufacturing cost structure, labor requirements, and the ability to deliver products. For instance, robotics affords greater product variety and the flexibility to change products and adjust to volume changes without additional capital expenditures. Robotics also generally results in lower costs for materials, scrap, labor, and supervision and yields improved quality. Thus, process decisions directly influence cost, flexibility, quality, and innovativeness. Process technology and automation are the subjects of Chapter 9.

Human Resources

The management of the work force has important long-term implications for manufacturing strategy. Long-term commitments to labor unions to solve short-term problems have come back to haunt many companies. For instance, wage concessions made in the U.S. steel industry contributed to many of the problems now facing that industry. In addition, union protection of multiple job classifications has reduced work-force flexibility and made it difficult to increase productivity and introduce automation in the United States.

     The relationship between people and machines presents special challenges for organizations facing increased automation. Automation increases the need for skilled technicians; consequently, the design of work systems, training, motivation, and compensation become important manufacturing considerations. Questions that must be addressed include: Should jobs be created for generalists or specialists? What degree of supervision is appropriate? Should emphasis be placed on work measurement and standards? Those are difficult questions to answer in today's technological age, and they affect every dimension of competitive advantage. Chapter 5 addresses many of those issues.

Operating Decisions

How operations are planned and controlled affects cost, quality, and dependability. While actual decisions are more of a tactical and operational nature, the policies used for making such decisions have long-term effects. New philosophies and techniques for manufacturing planning and control have been developed in recent years. The Japanese have popularized the notion of zero inventories and just-in-time purchasing and production; W. Edwards Deming has advocated increased worker control over quality, and the Japanese have proven the value of that idea. Today's managers must carefully consider such philosophies and techniques in view of their strategic implications. Chapters 13 through 15 focus on these topics.

Integration of Suppliers

One aspect of strategy involves the level of materials control between suppliers and manufacturers. Should we make components or purchase them from external suppliers? Should we acquire suppliers or merge with them? Should we use one or several suppliers? Issues of cost, quality, dependability, and flexibility enter into such decisions.

Increased integration of suppliers, or "partnership strategy," requires more complex control by operations managers. Rather than working in a competitive purchasing environment as in the United States, Japanese firms approach supplier relations much differently. They often work with only one or a few suppliers in an atmosphere of mutual dependence and trust. They help to train their suppliers in methods of quality control. In return, they expect 100 percent delivery of materials and components when needed. That approach supports their operational policy of just-in-time production (discussed in Chapter 15).

Quality

The multiple dimensions of quality—performance, features, reliability, durability, serviceability, and aesthetics—imply that goods and services can be differentiated in many ways. Note, however, that a company should not necessarily attempt to excel in each of those dimensions. In fact, some products or services can be improved on one dimension only by sacrifices on another; for example, speed versus fuel economy in automobiles. Such trade-offs make quality an important dimension of a manufacturing strategy.

To illustrate that point, Garvin describes the differences between Steinway & Sons and Yamaha, two of the leading manufacturers of pianos.[13] Steinway & Sons has been the industry leader because of the even voicing, sweetness of register, duration of tone, long lives, and fine cabinetwork of its pianos, each of which is handcrafted and unique in sound and style. Yamaha, in contrast, has developed a reputation for manufacturing quality pianos in a very short time. That was done by emphasizing reliability and conformance (low on Steinway's list of priorities), rather than artistry and uniqueness. Unlike Steinway & Sons, Yamaha produces its pianos on an assembly line. Whatever dimensions of quality a company chooses to emphasize should reflect customer needs and expectations. Yamaha and Steinway have successfully fulfilled two different sets of such needs and expectations, both valid.

Operations Strategy Applied to Service Organizations

The major elements of operations strategy just discussed are also relevant to service organizations, although their relative importance varies. Following are some typical questions that service organizations must address in regard to operations strategy. By examining these areas in conjunction with overall corporate objectives, effective service strategies can be developed. (Service strategy will be examined after a discussion of manufacturing strategy.)

1. *Product technology.* In a fast-food restaurant, should sandwiches be made to customers' orders (as at Wendy's) or made to one or more specifications and stored (as at McDonald's)? Likewise, a grocery store must decide whether or not to use scanners as opposed to manual reading of prices.

2. *Capacity.* Is capacity the right kind? An airline might consider changing from large jets (which provide economies of scale) to smaller jets and more frequent flights (which provide a greater degree of customer service). Because

no inventories are available to buffer demand, capacity defines the service organization's ability to meet demand. Too high a capacity requires a high fixed-cost structure, while too low a capacity can result in inadequate service delivery, resulting in the loss of (dissatisfied) customers.

3. *Facilities and location.* In many service organizations, such as restaurants and hotels, location is a critical strategic decision. For instance, should a hotel locate in a downtown area or along an expressway? The number of units of a multisite business and their relative location to competitors is also an important decision.

4. *Process technology.* In designing the service delivery, what level of technology, mechanization, and automation should be used? Many service processes are moving toward increased levels of self-service, often computer-based, to replace traditional human interaction. For example, a bank customer has the choice of using automatic tellers or human tellers.

5. *Human resources.* Because of varying levels in demand, many service organizations are forced to use part-time employees and staff that are cross-trained in a variety of skills. Personnel with more customer contact must understand customer interactions and have better "people skills" than task-oriented personnel who work behind the scenes.

6. *Operating decisions.* Perhaps the most critical issue in customer satisfaction in many service businesses is that of waiting lines. Operating decisions that affect customer perceptions of waiting and service quality are critical for long-term success. For instance, many managers of grocery and discount-department stores are able to shift employees from such ancillary activities as stocking shelves to staffing checkout lines as demand increases.

7. *Supplier integration.* The ability to meet demand requires timely and efficient delivery of supplies. Supermarket chains operate their own distribution centers to better control the logistics of supply. A fast-food corporation may decide it should raise its own cattle rather than rely on external suppliers.

8. *Quality.* Consistency in service delivery is key to service quality. Customers' perceptions of service quality are affected by each of the other components of strategy.

Manufacturing Strategy

In manufacturing organizations, operations strategy is usually referred to as **manufacturing strategy,** meaning the way the capabilities of the manufacturing function are developed to support the desired competitive advantage of the business unit and to complement the efforts of other functions.[14] The subject of a manufacturing strategy, then, is not the product or service, but the capabilities that provide it.

Developing a manufacturing strategy involves a variety of choices and trade-offs. For example, in choosing a facility location, should we locate closer to suppliers or to customers? Should we use primarily manual labor or invest in automation and other advanced technology? The choices made will depend on the type of business. On one hand, research and development–driven firms on the leading edge of product technology need high quality, high flexibility, and product variety. At the other extreme, the cost minimizers require low cost, high product availability, and high-volume production. Following is an example of the latter from IBM.

Applied P/OM

IBM

Manufacturing strategy characteristics for a high-volume, low-cost IBM product revolve around efficiency.[15]

In IBM's manufacturing strategy for a high-volume low-cost product (summarized below), notice the planned involvement of manufacturing in design, development of production processes, and quality-assurance systems. Note also how all the components of the strategy relate to the ultimate objectives of high volume and low cost. For instance, automated production helps to achieve a high volume of production; customizing in distribution centers eliminates the need for great product variety in the manufacturing function itself and reduces the cost of maintaining large manufacturing inventories.

1. *Early manufacturing involvement in* design, process verification, and sourcing (make/buy) decisions.
2. *Design for automation by* minimizing the number of parts, eliminating fasteners, providing for self-alignment with no adjustments, making parts symmetrical where possible, avoiding parts that interfere with automation, making parts rigid and stiff, providing close tolerances, and making assembly one-sided.
3. *Limited models and features to ensure* stable product design, group engineering changes for the "model year," and customization of the product in distribution centers.
4. *Building to plan for* finished goods owned by sales, continuous-flow manufacturing, supplier integration, zero defects, reduction of work-in-process inventory, and multiskilled, focused team.
5. *Defect-free at shipment.*

Service Strategy

In service organizations, as explained earlier, operations strategy is referred to as *service strategy.* Since most services are produced and marketed at the same place and time—and often by the same person—a service strategy usually integrates both marketing and operations. The term **strategic service vision** has been coined to define such a service strategy.[16] A strategic service vision focuses on four elements:

1. Identification of a target market segment.
2. Development of a service concept to address targeted customers' needs.
3. Design of an operating strategy to support the service concept.
4. Design of a service delivery system to support the operating strategy.

Identification of a *target market segment* necessitates understanding the characteristics of various market segments, their importance, the needs of customers in those segments, and how well those needs are currently being served. The *service concept* specifies which elements of the service are to be provided for customers, how those elements are perceived by the customers, and how they should be designed, delivered, or marketed. The *operating strategy* identifies which components—operations, financing, marketing, human resources, and so on—are the most important and the component on which the most effort will be concentrated. It also specifies how quality and cost will be controlled and the expected results. Finally, the design of the *service delivery system* defines the role of people, technology, capacity, equipment, and procedures in the strategy; in addition, it specifies the extent to which the service design helps ensure quality standards and differentiates the service from the competition.

Chase has suggested that it is the extent of customer contact that distinguishes service industries from manufacturing industries.[17] **Customer contact** refers to the physical presence of the customer in the system. The extent of contact is the percentage of time the customer must be in the system relative to the total time it takes to serve him or her. Systems in which the percentage is high are called *high-contact systems;* those in which it is low are called *low-contact systems.* Many low-contact systems, such as check processing at a bank, can be treated as quasi-manufacturing systems, since most of the principles and concepts used in manufacturing apply. Service systems with high customer contact are more difficult to control and design than those with low customer contact. Table 3.1 lists areas of service strategy that have important implications in the design of the service delivery system in high-contact systems versus low-contact systems.

Let us examine the implications of high-contact and low-contact systems on the four major performance criteria for operations: efficiency, quality, flexibility, and dependability. *Efficiency* is of more concern to low-contact systems because of the importance of equipment and technology. In high-contact systems, *quality* control is more important, and cost reduction through economies of scale is more difficult to achieve. Low-contact systems are more amenable to statistical methods of process-quality control similar to those used in manufacturing. The presence of the customer makes quality control more difficult for high-contact systems. Training and motivation of employees are the principal means of quality assurance.

Flexibility is important in high-contact systems. The use of computer technology, for example, can greatly increase the flexibility of a service operation by providing more time for people to work with customers, hence providing the capability to respond faster and more flexibly to a wider range of customer demands. *Dependability* is achieved through careful scheduling and inventory control. For high-contact systems, scheduling emphasis is on personnel, while for low-contact systems the emphasis is on scheduling tasks and jobs. Scheduling personnel to be available for providing service is more difficult because of uncertainties in customer demand. Personnel must be available when the customer is present. To some extent, "customer inventory" can be controlled in high-contact systems through appointments and reservation scheduling, which improve the dependability of service delivery. Proper scheduling of jobs in low-contact systems can improve dependability.

In developing a service strategy, Chase suggests answering several questions:

Table 3.1   Major design considerations for high- and low-contact systems.

Decision	High-Contact System	Low-Contact System
Facility location	Operations must be near the customer.	Operations may be placed near supply, transportation, or labor.
Facility layout	Facility should accommodate the customer's physical and psychological needs and expectations.	Facility should enhance production.
Product design	Environment as well as the physical product define the nature of the service.	Customer is not in the service environment, so the product can be defined by fewer attributes.
Process design	Stages of production process have a direct immediate effect on the customer.	Customer is not involved in the majority of processing steps.
Scheduling	Customer is in the production schedule and must be accommodated.	Customer is concerned mainly with completion dates.
Production planning	Orders cannot be stored, so smoothing production flow will result in loss of business.	Both backlogging and production smoothing are possible.
Worker skills	Direct work force comprises a major part of the service product and so must be able to interact well with the public.	Direct work force need only have technical skills.
Quality control	Quality standards are often in the eye of the beholder and hence variable.	Quality standards are generally measurable and hence fixed.
Time standards	Service time depends on customer needs, and therefore time standards are inherently loose.	Work is performed on customer surrogates (e.g., forms), and time standards can be tight.
Wage payment	Variable output requires time-based wage systems.	"Fixable" output permits output-based wage systems.
Capacity planning	To avoid lost sales, capacity must be set to match peak demand.	Storable output permits setting capacity at some average demand level.
Forecasting	Forecasts are short-term, time-oriented.	Forecasts are long-term, output-oriented.

Source: Reprinted by permission of the *Harvard Business Review.* An exhibit from "Where Does the Customer Fit in a Service Operation?" by Richard B. Chase (November–December 1978). Copyright © 1978 by the President and Fellows of Harvard College; all rights reserved.

1. What kind of operating system do you have? That is, what is the extent of customer contact? Time-study and work-measurement techniques are often useful in making this assessment and obtaining some quantitative measures.

2. Are your operating procedures geared to your present structure? For example, is employee compensation matched to the nature of the system—high-contact systems based on time and low-contact systems based on output?

3. Can you realign your operations to reduce unnecessary direct-customer service? Can some tasks be taken away from high-contact employees? Can the work force be organized into high- and low-contact groups?

4. Can you take advantage of the efficiencies offered by low-contact operations? Can scheduling or forecasting techniques that have proven useful in manufacturing settings be employed?

5. Can you enhance the customer contact you do provide? This can be accomplished, for instance, by adding workers at peak times, keeping longer business hours, or adding those little "personal touches" to the service.

6. Can you relocate parts of your service operations to lower your facility costs? For example, Fotomat uses small drop-off points, whereas actual film processing is done in larger facilities to take advantage of economies of scale.

Haywood-Farmer extends this concept along two other dimensions, which results in a segmentation of service organizations with important strategic implications.[18] In addition to customer contact, we can differentiate among service organizations by the degree of *service customization* and the degree of *labor intensity* as shown in the three-dimensional classification scheme in Figure 3.2. Examples of service organizations in each octant are

1. Utilities, transportation of goods.
2. Lecture teaching, postal services.
3. Stock brokering, courier services.
4. Repair services, wholesaling, retailing.
5. Computerized teaching, public transit.
6. Fast food, live entertainment.
7. Charter services, hospitals.
8. Design services, advisory services.

This classification scheme provides additional guidance in setting a service strategy. Services low in all three dimensions are similar to factories. Strategy should be based on aspects such as facilities, process technology, and supplier integration. The focus should be on efficiency and quality. As customer contact increases, one must consider the impact of labor intensity. For services with low

Figure 3.2
Three-Dimensional Classification of Service Systems

SOURCE: John Haywood-Farmer, "A Conceptual Model of Service Quality," *International Journal of Operations and Production Management* 8, no. 6 (1988), pp. 19–29. Reprinted by permission of MCB University Press Limited.

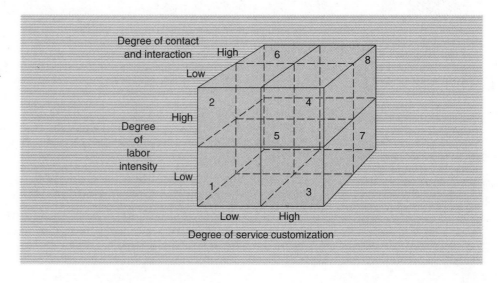

labor intensity, the customer's impression of physical facilities and process technology are important. For high levels of labor intensity, more attention must be paid to human resources. As customization increases, the service product and process must be designed to fit the customer. Thus, issues of product and process technology become the principal strategic focus relative to the levels of labor intensity and customer contact.

Strategy Formulation and Implementation

Effective organizations share several common approaches in their strategic planning efforts. First, the planning process is not restricted to top managers. All employees are viewed as an important resource in the planning, valued for their knowledge of customers and processes. Such employee involvement greatly enhances the effectiveness of implementation.

Second, customer needs and desires drive the strategy. Strategic planning processes are aligned with the organization's primary focus on customer satisfaction. Third, effective organizations involve suppliers, and often customers, in the strategic planning process. And fourth, they have well-established feedback systems for continuous measurement and reevaluation of the planning process, thus ensuring that planning remains effective despite changes in customer requirements and in the competitive environment.

Strategic Planning Process

Most companies follow some well-defined process for strategic planning. A generic example is shown in Figure 3.3. Note that the organization's leaders first must decide on a mission, a vision, and a set of guiding principles for the organization as the foundation for the strategic plan. The next step is assess the gap between where the organization is now and where it wants to be as described in

Figure 3.3
Strategic Planning Process

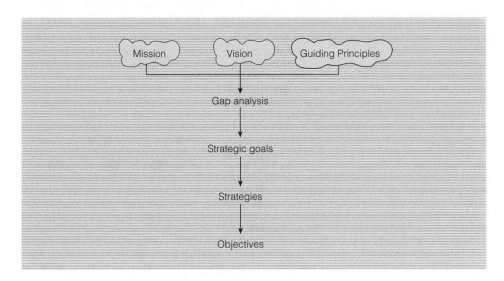

its mission statement and vision. Then, from that assessment, goals, strategies, and objectives are developed that will enable the organization to bridge the gap.

The **mission** of a firm defines its reason for existence; it asks the question, "Why are we in business?" A mission statement usually describes the products and services the organization provides, the technologies used to provide those products and services, the types of markets, important customer needs, and distinctive competencies. For example, the mission for MamaMia's Pizza might be "to create satisfied customers by producing and serving the best tasting pizzas for dine-in and limited local delivery, using old-fashioned hand tossing and preparation, and Mama's original recipe." Thus, a firm's mission defines its purpose and the value it intends to contribute to its customers or society. The mission also serves to guide the development of strategies by establishing the context within which daily operating decisions are made. In addition, it helps in making trade-offs among the various performance measures and between short- and long-term goals. Finally, it can inspire employees to focus their efforts toward achieving the overall purpose of the organization.

The **vision** describes where the organization is headed—that is, what it intends to be in the future. It should state the basic goals and characteristics that will shape the organization's strategy for reaching the desired future state. A vision should be clear and exciting to an organization's employees. It should be linked to customers' needs, convey a general strategy, and be consistent with the culture and values of the organization. The vision of MamaMia's might be "to be recognized as providing the best pizza in town, continually exceeding the expectations of our customers and employees."

Guiding principles define attitudes and policies that need to be followed by all employees at all levels of the organization in order for the vision to be realized. Guiding principles for MamaMia's might include the following:

1. *Quality.* We are committed to a philosophy of quality in everything we do. We support a customer focus, continuous improvement, personal fulfillment, and the pursuit of excellence in our food, service, and people.
2. *Integrity.* We are committed to integrity in all our promises and actions.
3. *Teamwork.* We are committed to the principles of teamwork, respect for individuals, open communication, and cultural diversity.

An example of how a company's mission, vision, and guiding principles form the foundation for its strategic plan is provided by Federal Express.

Applied P/OM

Federal Express

FedEx has consistently applied its mission, vision, and guiding principles in its business decisions.

The *mission* of Federal Express is to "produce outstanding financial returns by providing totally reliable, competitively superior global air-ground transportation of high priority goods and documents that require rapid, time-sensitive delivery." The *vision* of the company is reflected in its motto: "People, Service, Profits." The motto is succinct and easy for anyone to understand. It reflects the needs of the company's three major customer groups: employees (people), consumers who use FedEx (service), and shareholders (profits). Moreover, all decisions are evaluated by how they affect people, service, and profits—*in that order*. Finally, *guiding principles* for FedEx are reflected in the statement, "We will be helpful, courteous, and professional to each other and the public. We will strive to have a completely satisfied customer at the end of each transaction."

The mission, vision, and guiding principles must be supported by top managers and others who lead, especially the CEO. They have to be transmitted, practiced, and reinforced through symbolic and real action before they become "real" to the employees and the people, groups, and organizations in the external environment that do business with the firm.

After the *gap analysis,* in which managers compare the present status of the organization with its desired future status, they formulate goals, strategies, and objectives for changing that present status. *Goals* are broad statements that set the general direction of what the organization wants to achieve. *Strategies* are key actions that will help to achieve the goals. *Objectives* are specific, measurable actions that support the strategies.

For example, goals for MamaMia's might be

1. To embrace and implement our motto, "Customers First."
2. To provide facilities, equipment, systems, and training that contribute to the accomplishment of our mission.

One strategy for achieving the first goal might be "to educate and train all employees in total quality management (TQM) principles." Objectives supporting that strategy might include

1. Provide introductory training to all new employees.
2. Develop and implement a continuous TQM education and training program.

The specific process by which strategic planning is performed varies among companies. Figure 3.4 shows the strategic quality planning process for Eastman Chemical Company, a 1993 winner of the Malcolm Baldrige National Quality Award. This is only one example of many possible approaches to strategic quality planning. What is important is not how it is done, but whether a systematic process is used to do it.

Strategy Deployment

Top managers need a method to ensure that their plans and strategies are executed successfully within the organization. Managers must determine specific responsibilities for meeting objectives at lower levels of the organization, and provide the necessary resources. The traditional approach to deploying strategy is top-down by management directive. However, from a TQM perspective, subordinates are both customers *and* suppliers. Therefore, their input is essential. An iterative process in which senior managers ask what lower levels of the

Part One

Figure 3.4
Strategic Quality Planning at Eastman Chemical Company (Used with permission of Eastman Chemical Company)

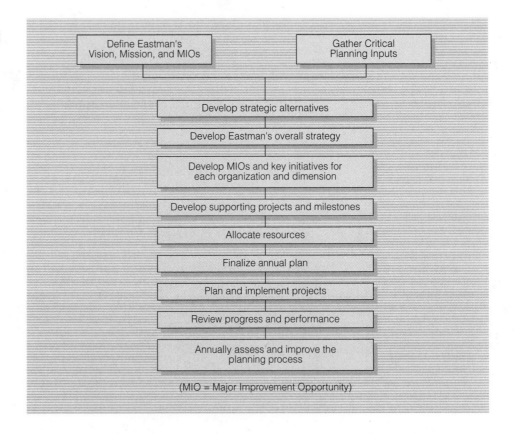

organization can do, what they need, and what conflicts may arise can avoid many of the implementation problems that managers typically face.

The Japanese deploy strategy through a process known as *hoshin kanri,* often referred to in the United States as *policy deployment* or *management by planning.* Many companies, most notably Florida Power and Light, Hewlett-Packard, and AT&T, have adopted that process. The literal Japanese translation of *hoshin kanri* is "pointing direction."[19] The idea is to point, or align, the entire organization in a common direction. Hewlett-Packard calls policy deployment "a process for annual planning and implementation which focuses on areas needing significant improvement." AT&T's definition is "an organization-wide and customer-focused management approach aimed at planning and executing breakthrough improvements in business performance." Regardless of the particular definition, policy deployment emphasizes organization-wide planning and priority setting to provide resources to meet objectives and measure performance as a basis for improvement. Policy deployment is essentially a TQM approach based on the following principles:[20]

••• Top managers are responsible for developing and communicating a vision, then building organization-wide commitment to its achievement.

••• The vision is deployed through the development and execution of annual policy statements (plans).

••• All levels of employees actively participate in generating a strategy and action plans to attain the vision.

••• At each level, progressively more detailed and concrete means to accomplish the annual plans are determined. The plans are hierarchical, cascading downward from top managers' plans. There should be a clear link to common goals and activities throughout the organizational hierarchy.

••• Each organizational level sets priorities to focus on areas needing significant improvement, and to concentrate on activities that are the most highly related to the vision.

••• Implementation responsibilities, timetables, and progress measures are determined.

••• Frequent evaluation and modification based on feedback from regularly scheduled audits of the process are provided.

••• Plans and actions are based on analysis of the root causes of a problem rather than only its symptoms.

••• Planning has a high degree of detail, including the anticipation of possible problems during implementation.

••• Emphasis is on improving the planning process as opposed to simply focusing on outcomes.

Figure 3.5 provides a simplified description of the policy deployment process, in which top managers develop and communicate a vision, then build organization-wide commitment to its achievement. The long-term strategic plan forms the basis for shorter-term planning. The vision is deployed through the development and execution of annual objectives and plans. All levels of employees actively participate in generating a strategy and action plans to attain the vision. At each level, progressively more detailed and concrete means to accomplish the objectives are determined.

Objectives for policy deployment should be challenging, but people should feel that they are attainable. To this end, middle managers negotiate with senior managers about what objectives will achieve the strategies and what process changes and resources might consequently be required. Middle managers then negotiate with the implementation teams the final short-term objectives and the performance measures that will be used to indicate progress toward accomplishing the objectives. Those performance measures are specific checkpoints to ensure the effectiveness of individual elements of the strategy. The implementation teams are empowered to manage the actions and schedule their activities. Periodic reviews (monthly or quarterly) track progress and diagnose problems. Managers may modify objectives on the basis of the reviews, as indicated by the feedback loop in Figure 3.5. Top managers are responsible for conducting annual reviews to evaluate results as well as the deployment process itself, and those reviews serve as a basis for formulating the next planning cycle.

The negotiation process is called *catchball* (represented by the baseball symbol in Figure 3.5). Leaders communicate midterm objectives and measures to middle managers, who develop short-term objectives and recommend necessary resources, targets, and roles or responsibilities. These are discussed and debated until agreement is reached. The objectives are then given to lower levels of the organization to be used in developing short-term plans. Catchball is an up, down, and sideways communication process as opposed to an autocratic, top-down management style. In the spirit of Deming, it focuses on optimizing the system rather than on individual employees' or departments' goals

Figure 3.5
Policy Deployment Process

SOURCE: Adapted from Kersi F. Munshi, "Policy Deployment: A Key to Long-Term TQM Success," *ASQC Quality Congress Transactions,* Boston, 1993, pp. 236–244. The American Society for Quality Control, Inc., 1993. Reprinted with Permission.

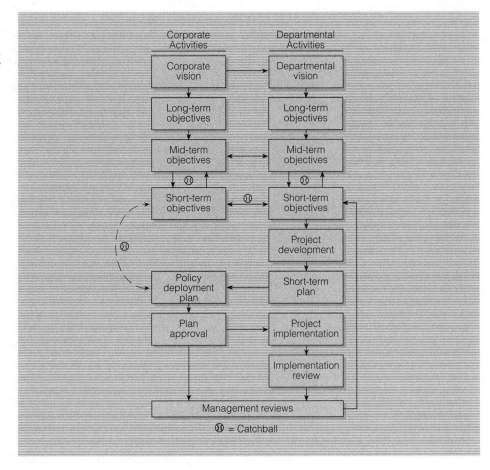

and objectives. Clearly, the process can occur only in a TQM culture that fosters open communication.

P/OM in Practice

Strategy Formulation for a Computer Equipment Manufacturer[21]

With annual sales of over $8 billion and 82,000 employees worldwide, a highly decentralized computer equipment firm uses a hierarchical approach in formulating manufacturing strategy at several levels within the firm as depicted in Figure 3.6. Corporate strategy represents the starting point for manufacturing strategy and for the business plans of the operating units. However, the corporate business plan precedes the corporate strategy. The corporate strategy is reviewed and revised constantly, and thus is highly responsive to changes in both the internal and external environments. At the corporate level, broad corporate strategic objectives are formulated to provide a set of expectations for lower-level manufacturing strategies.

The corporate strategy and the corporate business plan provide the basis for group-level manufacturing strategy.

The responsibility for formulating the group-level manufacturing strategy rests on the manufacturing systems group, a collection of the manufacturing departments of the various divisions in the group. A fundamental goal in formulating the group manufacturing strategy is to identify and relate all strategic elements formed at the group level to the other plans and strategies developed at higher levels in the hierarchy. Thus, in addition to the corporate strategy and business plan, the group must respond to its

Figure 3.6 Manufacturing Strategy Process for the Computer Equipment Manufacturer

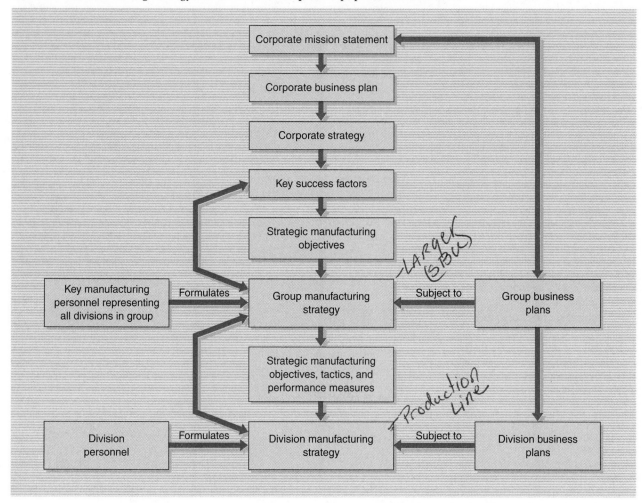

own business plan, the plans of the Corporate Manufacturing Council (in which each group participates), and any ongoing *major* research and development program activities that will involve the group. Initial efforts at manufacturing strategy focus on how the group's manufacturing resources can contribute to the higher-level plans, and in particular how they can provide a competitive advantage.

After potential competitive contributions are defined, each division within the group is polled to determine what manufacturing strategy is currently being followed. The approach involves prioritizing the major bases of competition (i.e., quality, cost, availability, and design) for each division. That procedure was validated within the firm by conducting two separate surveys. Each respondent was first asked to rank the competitive variables in importance to the customer, and at a later time the respondent was asked how the variables would be ranked on their perceived importance in day-to-day

operations. The discrepancies in the results provided the basis for evaluating how patterns of decisions were being made. The group looked at categories of resources to decide what was currently being done in manufacturing and what opportunities for change were possible. Specific strategies are formulated for each of the categories of resources in the manufacturing strategy, and in addition, performance measures and tactics for accomplishing the strategy are decided upon.

At lower levels, the process is further refined. A division manufacturing strategy is formulated by establishing strategic objectives that are consistent with the group manufacturing strategy. At the same time, there is an effort to provide an appropriate level of detail to focus the strategy to a particular strategic objective. The process involves defining the strategic objective, creating a specific tactical plan for each strategic objective, and then defining specific performance measures for each tactical objective. The process is further refined by identifying appropriate departmental tactical objectives for each department within the division. With the support of the tactical plans, performance measures, activity plans for implementation of the tactical plans, and supporting organizational plans, implementation can be easily monitored and strategies can be executed.

The firm has been able to exercise considerable flexibility in revising strategy on an ongoing basis. In their hierarchical approach, top managers develop strategic directions and objectives, while both middle- and lower-level managers indicate what can realistically be accomplished given current resource levels. That information is fed back to top managers, who, after consideration, may reformulate the strategic objectives. The process can be reactivated any time business conditions dictate the need for a change.

Questions for Discussion

1. Discuss the relationship between the division manufacturing strategy and the group manufacturing strategy. In what ways does one affect the other?
2. Why are the divisions polled? How do the results of the polling affect the manufacturing strategy?

Strategic Planning at AT&T Consumer Communications Services[22]

AT&T Consumer Communications Services (CCS) provides local toll, interstate, and international long-distance services that enable more than 80 million consumers to stay in touch with the important people in their lives. At the heart of the business is the AT&T Worldwide Intelligent Network, which handles about 175 millions calls on a typical business day, with more than 99 percent connected on the first try.

Research shows that customers rely on CCS for call completion, network features, call transmission quality, network reliability, ordering services, information and assistance, sales inquiries, and billing questions and adjustments. Key objectives to meet those needs include unsurpassed call clarity; crisp, crystal-clear long-distance connections; dedicated customer-service representatives available 24 hours a day, seven days a week; accurate, itemized billing; personalized savings options; and affordable prices.

CCS designs long- and short-term plans to meet financial and quality commitments to AT&T and its shareholders while sustaining its "best-in-class" status for customer and employee satisfaction. The unifying forces behind the plans are the company's vision, mission, and values. The mission of CCS is stated simply: "We are dedicated to being the world's best at bringing people together—giving them easy access to each other and to the information and services they want and need—anytime, anywhere, through networking services."

The planning process integrates the needs of CCS with the various strategic business units (SBUs). Key company plans are

1. Growth in traditional long-distance service to gain market share and retain old and acquire new customers.
2. Growth in nontraditional long-distance service in new markets and wireless communication services.
3. Achievement of financial objectives of reducing unit costs and sustaining growth.
4. Global expansion.

Two main groups manage the CCS strategic planning process. The Strategic Planning Council (SPC) meets every other week, and the Business Unit Planning Team meets monthly. The teams consist of representatives from the SBUs and production/delivery and business-support processes. The SPC is the primary body, making decisions and giving priorities to business-unit strategies and initiatives. The planning approach has four major elements:

- Reviewing and understanding current and future needs of customer segments.
- Assessing CCS strengths and weaknesses versus the competition.
- Identifying strategic short- and long-term threats and opportunities.
- Establishing goals and reworking processes to achieve those goals.

The approach aligns the planning of SBUs with other planning for communications products and services, production/delivery processes that serve customers, business-support processes that guide the SBUs in producing and delivering products and services, and processes that benchmark and track evolving technology in the industry. CCS goals are conveyed through all processes to ensure alignment of each employee's individual work goals with CCS's strategic initiatives. Members of the planning teams communicate through conferences, staff meetings, publications, quarterly and annual reports, town meetings, and videos.

CCS recognizes that planning processes must be evaluated and improved constantly. The SPC and Business Unit Planning team have responsibility for that "continual improvement." The team reviews indicators relating to the planning process: "best practices," data on how well employees understand strategic initia-

tives, information and feedback from the AT&T Chairman's Quality Award assessment, and direct measures of quality related to cycle time and performance. Once the data are analyzed, the team identifies improvement opportunities, which are assigned for implementation by the SPC. The Business Unit Planning team also evaluates the deployment, that is, how well the plans have been communicated and understood. The process includes employee input through annual surveys.

Questions for Discussion

1. Discuss the elements of the CCS strategic planning process that support effective strategic planning as described in this chapter.
2. Does strategic planning at CCS appear to be one and the same with strategic *quality* planning? Why?
3. Discuss the importance of evaluating and improving the planning process itself. How do each of CCS's approaches contribute to better planning?

Summary of Key Points

- ••• Strategic planning determines an organization's long-term goals, policies, and plans. Key elements of strategy are marketing and sales, design, and operations. Operations strategy is becoming recognized as an important factor in increasing a firm's competitiveness.

- ••• Competitive advantage denotes a firm's ability to achieve market superiority over its competitors. It can be achieved in two ways: through low cost or price, or through differentiation based on various quality dimensions.

- ••• Strategy is driven by a company's philosophy, and it is hierarchical. Corporate strategy directs the strategic business units (SBUs). Organizations can be classified by their corporate strategies, which in turn, depend on functional strategies. Operations strategy must be integrated into the overall corporate business strategy.

- ••• Key dimensions for differentiation strategies are superior product design, outstanding service, high flexibility and variety, continuous innovation, and rapid response.

- ••• Today, strategic quality planning is considered synonomous with strategic business planning. Leading companies integrate customer-driven quality and operational-performance improvement with their traditional financial and marketing plans.

- ••• The key components of manufacturing strategy are product technology, capacity, facilities and location, process technology, human resources, operat-

ing decisions, integration of suppliers, and quality. Those components are also important to service organizations.

- ••• In service organizations the degree of customer contact, service customization, and labor intensity necessitates different strategies. Successful service strategies are based on careful research of what customers want, so that well-designed products and services will meet and exceed customer expectations. Service elements within manufacturing organizations require the same careful attention to meet strategic corporate objectives.

- ••• Strategic planning begins with an organization's mission, vision, and guiding principles. By conducting an analysis of gaps, a company can develop goals, strategies, and objectives to achieve its mission and vision.

- ••• Policy deployment is a process for deriving and implementing key strategic objectives based on continuous improvement. It involves active participation of employees at all levels and frequent evaluation and possible modification of plans and actions.

Key Terms

Corporate strategy
Strategic planning
Strategic business units (SBUs)
Competitive advantage
Distinctive competencies

Flexibility
Variety
Product lead time
Operations strategy
Manufacturing strategy
Strategic service vision
Customer contact
Mission
Vision
Guiding principles

Review Questions

1. Briefly explain the three components of corporate strategy.

2. Define *strategic business units.*

3. Define *competitive advantage.* What are the major dimensions of competitive advantage?

4. Explain *distinctive competencies.* Provide some examples for well-known companies.

5. Explain cost and differentiation strategies. What types of capabilities must firms have to pursue each of those strategies?

6. Explain the importance of various quality-related dimensions in differentiation strategies. Provide some different examples of companies that pursue those strategies.

7. Why is quality planning a necessary component of strategic business planning? Why do leading companies purposely refuse to distinguish between the two?

8. Discuss how corporate strategy at Hewlett-Packard differs from that at Texas Instruments.

9. Define *operations strategy.*

10. What are the major components of operations strategy? Why is each important?

11. Match each business strategy with the most appropriate manufacturing mission:

Business Strategy
a. Market dominance
b. Specialty market niche
c. Delivery response
d. Market coverage response
e. Custom product response
f. Product innovation
g. Technical innovation

Manufacturing Mission
1. Introduce a variety of products
2. Support new-product technology
3. Lowest unit cost
4. Produce to changing schedules
5. Manufacture to specification
6. Manufacture all new products
7. Produce to small batch runs

12. How do operations strategies in service and manufacturing organizations differ?

13. What is a strategic service vision?

14. Discuss the importance of customer contact in service organizations. What is the difference between high-contact and low-contact systems?

15. What implications do high-contact and low-contact systems have for efficiency, quality, flexibility, and dependability?

16. Describe Haywood-Farmer's classification of services. Add at least one new example to each octant of Figure 3.2.

17. How does the Xerox "Leadership through Quality" strategy support TQM?

18. Define the terms *mission, vision,* and *guiding principles.* Why must organizations begin their strategic planning process by formulating those definitions?

19. Explain how the elements of Eastman Chemical Company's strategic planning process support effective planning.

20. Explain the principles of policy deployment.

Discussion Questions

1. Study several major corporations' annual reports. What do they say about their competitive advantage? How does their strategy support their focus? Write a paper, quoting liberally from the annual reports.

2. Find, report, and discuss current examples of how companies are using quality, dependability, flexibility, innovativeness, and time for competitive advantage.

3. In your role as a student, develop your own statements of mission, vision, and guiding principles. How would you create a strategy to achieve your mission and vision?

4. Research some of the background of recent Baldrige winners. Discuss different approaches those firms use to integrate quality into their business strategies.

5. How can TQM improve the process of strategic planning?

6. Interview managers at some local companies to determine whether their businesses have a well-defined mission, vision, and guiding principles. If they do, how are those translated into strategy? If not, what steps should be taken?

7. Does your university or college have a mission and strategy? How might policy deployment be used in a university setting?

8. Contrast the following vision statements in terms of their usefulness to an organization.

a. To become the industry leader and achieve superior growth and market share.

b. To become the best-managed electric utility in the United States and an excellent company overall and to be recognized as such.

c. To be the best at everything we do, exceeding customer expectations; growing our business to increase its value to customers, employees, shareowners, and communities in which we work.

9. How might the strategic planning concepts discussed in this chapter be applied to a business school or an individual academic department? Formulate a set of questions for interviewing your department head or dean.

10. Select some service at your school (e.g., class scheduling, financial aid, bookstore) and apply the concept of the strategic service vision to it. Prepare a report that describes your strategy.

Notes

1. James Brian Quinn, *Strategies for Change: Logical Incrementalism* (Homewood IL: Richard D. Irwin, 1980).

2. Suresh Kotha and Paul M. Swamidass, "Business and Manufacturing Strategy Practices in the U.S. and Japanese Machine Tool Industries," Report #MCT 94-01, The Thomas Walter Center for Technology Management, Auburn University, February 1994.

3. Michael E. Porter, *Competitive Advantage: Creating and Sustaining Superior Perfo rmance* (New York: The Free Press, 1985).

4. H. Lee Hales, "Time Has Come for Long-Range Planning of Facilities Strategies in Electronic Industries," *Industrial Engineering*, April 1985.

5. J. M. Juran, *Juran on Quality by Design* (New York: The Free Press, 1992), p. 181.

6. Robert M. Grant, R. Krishnan, Abraham B. Shani, and Ron Baer, "Appropriate Manufacturing Technology: A Strategic Approach," *Sloan Management Review 33*, no. 1 (Fall 1991), pp. 43–54.

7. Adapted from Steven C. Wheelwright, "Strategy, Management, and Strategic Planning Approaches," *Interfaces 14*, no. 1 (January–February 1984), pp. 19–33.

8. Jay S. Kim, "Beyond the Factory Walls: Overcoming Competitive Gridlock," Manufacturing Roundtable Research Report Series, Boston University School of Management, September 1994.

9. Jay Finegan, "Surviving in the Nike/Reebok Jungle," *Inc.*, May 1993, pp. 98–108.

10. Jeffrey Margolies, "When Good Service Isn't Good Enough," *The Price Waterhouse Review 32*, no. 3 (1988), pp. 22–31.

11. Thomas A. Stewart, "Brace for Japan's Hot New Strategy," *Fortune*, September 21, 1992, pp. 62–73.

12. Courtesy Xerox Corporation

13. David A. Garvin, *Managing Quality: The Strategic and Competitive Edge* (New York: The Free Press, 1988).

14. S. C. Wheelwright, "Competing through Manufacturing," in Ray Wild (ed.), *International Handbook of Production and Operations Management* (London: Cassell Educational, Ltd., 1989), pp. 15–32.

15. Adapted from H. Lee Hales, "Time Has Come for Long-Range Planning of Facilities Strategies in Electronic Industries," *Industrial Engineering*, April 1985. Copyright Institute of Industrial Engineers, 25 Technology Park/Atlanta, GA 30092.

16. James L. Heskett, "Lessons in the Service Sector," *Harvard Business Review*, March–April 1987, pp. 118–126. Copyright 1987 by the President and Fellows of Harvard College; all rights reserved.

17. Richard B. Chase, "Where Does the Customer Fit in a Service Operation?" *Harvard Business Review*, November–December 1978, pp. 137–142. Copyright 1978 by the President and Fellows of Harvard College; all rights reserved.

18. John Haywood-Farmer, "A Conceptual Model of Service Quality," *International Journal of Operations and Production Management* 8, no. 6 (1988), pp. 19–29.

19. Bob King, *Hoshin Planning: The Developmental Approach* (Methuen, MA: GOAL/QPC, 1989).

20. The Ernst & Young Quality Improvement Consulting Group, *Total Quality: An Executive's Guide for the 1990s* (Homewood, IL: Dow Jones–Irwin, 1990).

21. Adapted from Ann S. Marucheck and Ronald T. Pannesi, "The Manufacturing Strategy Process: Principles and Practice," Graduate School of Business Administration, University of North Carolina, Chapel Hill, NC 27599.

22. AT&T/CCS 1994 Malcolm Baldrige National Quality Award Application Summary. © 1994. Adapted with permission of AT&T. All rights reserved.

Chapter Four
Measuring
Operations
Performance

Operations managers make the decisions that are supposed to help an organization meet or exceed customer expectations and make productive use of its resources. To know whether their decisions are effective, they need a means of measuring organizational performance so they can see where problems are occurring and where corrective action is needed. Then they can set realistic improvement priorities. Moreover, measurements provide a scorecard of business performance and make accomplishments visible to the work force. Knowing that one is doing a good job—or a better job than before—is a powerful motivator!

Measurements enable managers to make decisions on the basis of facts, not opinions. MamaMia's managers might take measurements to answer such questions as: What do customers think of our food and service? How efficiently are we using our resources? Could we reduce costs or improve productivity? How much is poor quality costing us? Are we receiving the best quality and service from our suppliers? Every business asks similar questions; however, some do better than others in collecting appropriate data and analyzing it properly. The wrong kind of measurement can be dangerous. The popular phrase, "How you are measured is how you perform," expresses a warning. For example, Analog Devices, a successful Massachusetts analog and digital equipment manufacturer, embraced TQM but found its stock price steadily declining. One of the company's key measures (on which managers were rewarded) was new-product introduction time. The objective was to reduce it from 36 to 6 months. The product-development team focused on that objective—and as a result, engineers turned away from riskier new products and designed mundane derivatives of old products that no longer met customers' needs. (The company subsequently scrapped that goal.)[1] Thus, it is vitally important that the right measures be selected and used.

In this chapter we will review the major categories of performance measurement that should command a manager's attention, and discuss specific approaches for such measurement. Specific subjects addressed are

- Key measures of quality and operational performance used by leading organizations.
- Procedure for developing good performance indicators.
- Important issues related to measuring customer satisfaction, productivity, and quality costs.
- Key factors in the management of quality and performance data.

Scope of Performance Measurement

Most businesses have traditionally used organizational performance data that are based on financial considerations, such as return on investment or earnings per share; or on productivity, such as labor efficiency or machine utilization. With the increasing emphasis on customer satisfaction as a strategic dimension of performance, though, customer-related quality measures such as defect rates and response time are becoming increasingly important.

The model of a production system in Figure 1.2 (in Chapter 1) provides a convenient structure for addressing the subject of performance measurement. There are four key elements in the system: suppliers and inputs, outputs and customers, processes (both core and support), and the overall system itself. Thus, measurement should focus on

1. *Supplier performance*—the inputs to the production system.
2. *Product and service quality*—the outputs of the system and the core processes that create products and services.
3. *Business and support services*—functions and processes that support a company's core manufacturing or service capabilities.
4. *Company operational performance*—customer-related measures, productivity, cycle time, and financial data.

Supplier Performance

The term **suppliers** (or **vendors**) refers to providers of goods and services that may be used at any stage in the production, delivery, and use of a company's own products and services. Thus, suppliers include distributors, dealers, warranty repair services, and contractors, as well as manufacturers of materials and components.

Obviously, such businesses are critically important to the success of the organizations they serve. If the quality of purchased materials and parts is poor, the quality of the end product will be poor. Also, if suppliers cannot provide their customer organizations with accurate and timely delivery, it will be difficult for the customers to meet their own schedules. Therefore, to achieve its own quality objectives, an organization needs to obtain product-quality and service-performance data on its possible suppliers. Typical data that companies collect on suppliers relate to materials and parts, pricing, and delivery performance. For example, MamaMia's might collect data on the freshness of ingredients, fat content in meat, and menu and advertisement print copy quality.

Today, many companies not only evaluate suppliers' products and services, but also evaluate their internal quality systems by using auditing techniques. Many companies establish formal programs to rate suppliers' performance and "certify" ones that show the capability to supply good-quality products in a timely manner and at a fair price. Using certified suppliers makes inspections unnecessary, reduces the number of suppliers used, and gives the suppliers an incentive for continuously improving quality and service to their customer organizations to attract more business. A survey by *Purchasing* magazine reported that almost two-thirds of major manufacturing firms in the United States have supplier rating and/or certification programs.[2] Florida Power and Light is one such firm.

☰ Applied P/OM

Florida Power and Light (Part a)

Florida Power and Light has a three-tier vendor certification program.[3]

Suppliers to Florida Power and Light (FP&L) can be certified as a "Quality Vendor," "Certified Vendor," and "Excellent Vendor." To become a

Quality Vendor, a supplier must offer products or services that meet basic requirements of quality, cost, delivery, and safety. In addition, the supplier must have a quality improvement process in place and must demonstrate that it has achieved significant improvements. It must have an audit system to certify the process and the results. To become a Certified Vendor, the supplier must also demonstrate the use of statistical process control and prove that its processes can meet FP&L's specification requirements. It must be able to document its capability and have a plan for continuous quality improvement. To achieve Excellent Vendor status, a supplier must demonstrate the ability to exceed FP&L's specification requirements, employ reliability-assurance techniques, and show that quality improvement is a central part of its management system.

Product and Service Quality

Customers demand defect-free products and responsive services. Product- and service-quality indicators tell a company whether its customers are receiving those kinds of products and services—without involving the customers. American Airlines provides an example in its ground-operations indicators.

Applied P/OM
American Airlines

American Airlines monitors key process measures.[4]

The ground-operations area of American Airlines is concerned primarily with the service passengers receive at airports. It routinely measures several factors that customers have told it are important, such as ticket-counter waiting time, cabin-door opening time, bag-delivery time, bag-delivery announcements, and cabin cleanliness. The data are collected by monthly self-audits at each site and by a Field Support Team of trained observers who visit airports to check those performance characteristics as well as other factors such as safety. Results are reviewed by various managers, including the executive vice-president of operations. Trends are analyzed, and corrective measures, if warranted, are put in place.

A common indicator of manufacturing quality is the *number of nonconformities per unit*. Historically, the term **defect** was used instead of **nonconformity.** Because of the negative connotation of *defect* and its potential implications in liability suits, *nonconformity* has become widely accepted. However, we occasionally use those terms interchangeably to be consistent with current literature and practice.

Many companies classify defects into three categories:[5]

1. *Critical defect*—one that judgment and experience indicate will surely result in hazardous or unsafe conditions for individuals using, maintaining, or depending on the product and will prevent performance of the function of the

product. For MamaMia's, this might be meat that is not cooked properly. Every effort should be made to identify and prevent critical defects.

2. *Major defect*—one that is not critical but is likely to materially reduce the usability of the unit for its intended purpose. For MamaMia's, this might be delivering the wrong size pizza or serving one with a burnt crust. Obviously, such defects should be avoided whenever possible.

3. *Minor defect*—one that is not likely to materially reduce the usability of the item for its intended purpose or to have any bearing on the effective use or operation of the unit. An example at MamaMia's might be a pizza that is poorly sliced. Although such defects do not affect fitness for use, they may draw major negative responses from customers.

In services, a measure of quality analogous to defects per unit is *errors per opportunity.* Each customer transaction provides an opportunity for many different types of errors. Service indicators should be linked closely to customer satisfaction so that they form the basis for improvement efforts. For example, MamaMia's manager might keep track of the number and type of wrong orders or measure the time from order to delivery. Federal Express uses 10 different factors to measure its service quality.

Applied P/OM
Federal Express

Federal Express has an extensive service-quality measurement system.

Federal Express developed a composite measure called the service quality indicator (SQI) that is a weighted sum of 10 factors reflecting customers' expectations of company performance. The weights reflect the relative importance of each failure. Losing a package, for instance, is more serious than delivering it a few minutes late. The index is reported weekly and summarized on a monthly basis.

Federal Express Service-Quality Indicator Factors

Error Type	Description	Weight
1. *Complaints Reopened*—customer complaints [on traces, invoices, missed pickups, etc.] reopened after an unsatisfactory resolution.		3
2. *Damaged packages*—packages with visible or concealed damage or spoilage due to weather or water damage, missed pickup, or late delivery.		10
3. *International*—a composite score of performance measures of international operations.		1
4. *Invoice adjustments*—customer requests for credit or refunds for real or perceived failures.		1
5. *Late pick-up stops*—packages that were picked up later than the stated pick-up time.		3
6. *Lost packages*—claims for missing packages or with contents missing.		10
7. *Missed proof of delivery*—invoices which lack written proof of delivery information.		1

Error Type	Description	Weight
8. *Right Day Late*—delivery past promised time on the right day.		1
9. *Traces*—Package status and proof of delivery requests not in the COSMOS IIB computer system (the FedEx "real time" tracking system).		3
10. *Wrong Day Late*—delivery on the wrong day.		5

Source: Service Quality Indicators at Federal Express (internal company document). Used with permission.

Research has shown that consumers use five key dimensions to assess service quality:[6]

1. **Tangibles**—physical facilities, equipment, and appearance of employees.
2. **Reliability**—ability to perform the promised service dependably and accurately.
3. **Responsiveness**—willingness to help customers and provide prompt service.
4. **Assurance**—knowledge and courtesy of employees, and their ability to inspire trust and confidence in customers.
5. **Empathy**—caring, individualized attention the firm provides to its customers.

Those dimensions should form the basis for quality measurement in service organizations. Note that all but the first pertain to behavioral characteristics, which are more difficult to measure than technical dimensions.

In addition to product indicators, firms collect extensive data about the processes that create the products and services. Process data can reflect defect and error rates of intermediate operations, and also internal efficiency measures such as cost, time, and environmental impact. Examples of process measurements are (1) time to prepare and send a bill, (2) filing errors per week, (3) time required to make an engineering change, and (4) keypunch errors per day. MamaMia's manager might weigh pizza crusts before assembly and cooking, or use "mystery customers" to provide information on the courtesy of employees.

It is essential that internal measures be driven by quality characteristics that are important to customers. For example, American Express analysts monitor telephone conversations for politeness, tone of voice, accuracy of the transaction, and so on. They also compare the judgments of the analysts to the judgments of customers in post-transaction interviews to assess the relevance of their internal measurements. When differences are found between customer satisfaction and internal measures of performance,—when internal measures seem good, yet customer satisfaction is low—the company may be measuring the wrong things. It is therefore important to compare external data with internal data.

Business and Support Services

Business and support services include units and operations involving finance and accounting, software services, sales, marketing, public relations, information services, purchasing, personnel, legal services, plant and facilities management, basic research and development, and secretarial and other administrative services. At AT&T Universal Card Services, for instance, key support services include collections, constituency management, customer acquisition, human resource management, information management, and financial management. Such processes contribute to the quality of a company's core products and services, and companies need to measure processing times, error rates, and other relevant aspects of performance. As noted in Chapter 2, quality management is everyone's responsibility; measurement of *all* processes in an organization reinforces that concept.

Company Operational Results

Data on products and processes are valuable to middle and supervisory managers, but top managers need different information indicating the effectiveness of the overall system. Measures of customer satisfaction, of productivity, and of efficiency are important to top managers. Examples include generic indicators such as use of labor, materials, energy, capital, and assets. Specific indicators might include productivity or cost indexes, waste reduction, energy efficiency, cycle time, and attitudes and opinions of employees.

Top managers makes most decisions with an eye toward the bottom line, so good financial data are extremely important. A key financial performance indicator is the *cost of quality,* which enables managers to prioritize improvement projects and gauge the effectiveness of total quality efforts. Customer satisfaction, productivity, and cost-of-quality measurement are discussed later in this chapter.

Types of Measurements

Measurements can be classified into two categories, attributes and variables. An **attribute** is a characteristic of quality that is either present or absent in the unit or product under consideration. Hence, attributes take one of two values—for instance, conforming or not conforming, within tolerance or out of tolerance, complete or incomplete. Attribute measurements might show, for example, whether the color of an item from a printing process is acceptable, whether the diameter of a shaft is within specification limits of $1.60 \pm 0.01''$, or whether the correct pizza is served. Common attribute measurements are fraction or percent defective, number of errors per opportunity, and defects per unit.

Variables, the second type of measurement, are appraised in terms of values on a continuous scale—for instance, length or weight. They indicate the *degree* of conformance to specifications. Rather than showing whether the diameter of a shaft meets a specification of $1.60 \pm 0.01''$, a variable measurement would give the actual *value* of the diameter. The weight of cheese on a pizza and the time from order to delivery are also variable measurements. Table 4.1 provides additional examples of both attribute and variable measurements.

Inspection by attributes is usually simpler than inspection by variables because it can be done more quickly and easily. Less information needs to be recorded. In a statistical sense, however, attribute inspection is less efficient than variable inspection and requires a larger sample to obtain the same amount of statistical information. That difference can become time-consuming and/or expensive. Most quality and performance characteristics in services are attributes, which is perhaps one reason why service organizations have been slow to adopt formal measurement approaches.

Table 4.1 Examples of Attribute and Variable Measurements

Attributes	Percent accurate invoices
	Number of lost parcels
	Number of complaints
	Mistakes per week
	Percent shipments on time
	Errors per thousand lines of code
	Percent absenteeism
Variables	Time waiting for service
	Number of hours per week correcting documents
	Time to process travel expense accounts
	Days from order receipt to shipment
	Cost of engineering changes per month
	Time between system crashes
	Cost of rush shipments

Developing Performance Indicators

As the manager of MamaMia's, what quality and performance indicators would you use to monitor your business? After a little thought, you can probably come up with several dozen or more. However, you probably would not have the time and resources to measure or observe all of them. How should you select the most meaningful quality performance indicators?

Companies can make two fundamental mistakes in measurement: (1) not measuring key characteristics that are critical to company performance or customer satisfaction and (2) taking irrelevant or inappropriate measurements. In the first case, the company may lose competitive advantage. In the second, it may waste time and resources.

The number of performance indicators seems to grow with time, and some may have become obsolete. IDS Financial Services, a subsidiary of American Express, used to measure more than 4,000 individual tasks—functions such as phone calls, mail coding, and application acceptance. In redesigning its information management system, IDS decided that only 80 measurements were relevant.

Generally, performance indicators should be strongly related to customer satisfaction and provide the kind of information that enables a company to anticipate potential problems. In other words, data should be preventive!

Good indicators should also be easy to understand and interpret, provide factual assistance for decision making, be a basis for comparative analysis, and be economical to apply. Consider MamaMia's. Suppose market research determines that two of the key customer expectations are a tasty pizza and a pleasant eating environment. As discussed in the last chapter, customer expectations must be translated into product characteristics. Suppose a product characteristic for a "tasty pizza" is fresh ingredients. A possible measure for "fresh ingredients" is elapsed time since purchase. Similarly, a product characteristic for "pleasant eating environment" is a clean dining area. Possible measures might be the number of times customers must wait for a table to be cleaned, number of clean tables available at 15-minute intervals, and frequency of washing the floor. Each indicator should be evaluated as to whether improvement in its performance results in more satisfied customers. If there is no apparent relationship, perhaps the indicator should be scrapped.

Indicators should also be driven by other factors important to the success of the business. Those **key business factors** are elements of a business that affect strategic planning, design and management of process quality, human resources development and management, and data collection and analysis. They include the nature of a company's products and services, principal customers and their requirements, competitive environment, facilities and technologies, and suppliers. If managers can define the key factors that make the business successful, they can define the appropriate measurements and data requirements. For example, if a large portion of MamaMia's business were the delivery of bulk orders to fraternities and parties around a college campus, it would require a different set of measurements than if it catered to walk-in dining in an upscale suburban residential neighborhood.

To assess the value of a company's performance indicators, a matrix diagram such as the one in Figure 4.1 can be used. The rows correspond to customer requirements and key operational performance factors, and the columns correspond to existing indicators. With such a matrix, it is easy to see whether some requirements are not being measured or whether some indicators do not relate to key requirements and can be eliminated.

A systematic process for generating useful performance measures follows.[7]

1. *Identify all customers of the system and determine their requirements and expectations.* Ask, who are my customers, and what do they expect? Tools such as customer surveys, focus groups, and user panels help to address those questions. Customer expectations change over time, so feedback must be obtained regularly.

2. *Define the work process that provides the product or service.* Ask, what do I do that affects customer needs, and what is my process?

3. *Define the value-adding activities and outputs that comprise the process.* Identify each step in the system where value is added and an intermediate output is produced. This step should identify internal customers and lead to weeding out activities that fail to add value to the process and that contribute to waste and inefficiency.

4. *Develop performance measures or indicators.* Each key process step identified in Step 3 represents a critical point where value is added to the output for

Figure 4.1
Matrix Diagram for
Evaluating Measurements
and Customer
Requirements

Customer Requirement	Time between seating and ordering	Time between ordering and delivery	Amount of toppings	•••
Hot pizza		✓		
Tasty			✓	
Good Service	✓			
Good value				
Correct order				
⋮				

the next (internal) customer until the final output is produced. Ask, what should I look at to determine how well the process is producing to customer requirements? Also, what deviations can occur, and what are the sources of variability?

5. *Evaluate the usefulness of each performance measure.* Ask the following questions about each measure: Is it at a critical point where value-adding activities occur? Is it controllable? Is obtaining the data needed for the measure feasible?

To illustrate that approach, consider the process of placing and filling a pizza order. Customer expectations for such a process might be a quick response and a fair price. The process that provides this service is shown in Figure 4.2. At the start of this process, the order taker is an (internal) customer of the caller (who provides the pizza order). Later, the caller is a customer of the deliverer (either at the pickup window or the caller's home). Also, the cook is a customer of the order taker (who prepares the documentation for the pizza that has been ordered).

Some possible performance measures are

••• Number of pizzas, by type per hour. If the number is high, perhaps cooking time and/or preparation is being short-cut or delivery times are being reduced.

••• Number of pizzas rejected per number prepared. A high number can indicate a lack of proper training of cooks that results in poor products and customer complaints.

••• Time to delivery. A long time might indicate a problem within the restaurant or inadequate training of the driver.

••• Number of errors in collections. Numerous errors can result in lost profits and higher prices.

Figure 4.2
Example of a Pizza-Ordering and Filling-Process (Home Delivery)

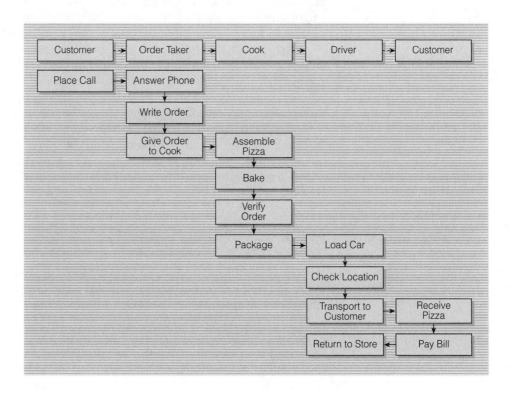

••• Raw materials (dough, etc.) or finished pizzas inventory. A high inventory might result in spoilage and excess costs. Low inventory might result in lost orders or excessive customer waiting time.

Notice that these measures are related to the customer expectations. Can you think of any others?

Measuring Customer Satisfaction

Through customer feedback, a company learns how satisfied its customers are with its products and services, and sometimes learns about competitors' products and services. Measures of customer satisfaction reveal areas that need improvement, and show whether changes actually result in improvement. An effective customer-satisfaction measurement system provides the company with customer ratings of specific product and service features and indicates the relationship between those ratings and the customer's likely future market behavior. It tracks trends and reveals patterns of customer behavior from which the company can predict customer needs and wants.

Customer-satisfaction measures may include product attributes such as product quality, product performance, and maintainability; service attributes such as attitude, on-time delivery, exception handling, and technical support; image attributes such as reliability and price; and overall satisfaction measures. At Federal Express, for example, customers are asked to rate everything from billing to the performance of couriers, package condition, tracking and tracing capabilities, complaint handling, and helpfulness of employees. MamaMia's might rate food appearance, taste, temperature, and portions, as well as cleanliness, staff friendliness, attentiveness, and perception of value.

Customer data should include comparisons with key competitors, but that is not possible if a company surveys only its own customers. Consequently, companies often rely on third parties to conduct blind surveys to determine who key competitors are and how their products and services compare. Such information may reveal key quality characteristics that are being overlooked.

Questionnaires must be designed scientifically to reveal differences in satisfaction levels and significant relationships between variables. Data should be collected on a frequent and systematic basis. Modern technology, such as computer databases in conjunction with a variety of statistical analysis tools, can assist in that task.

Analyzing and Using Customer Feedback

It is critical that somebody in a company have the responsibility and accountability for developing improvement plans based on customer-satisfaction results. Many companies tie managers' annual bonuses to those results.

Customer-satisfaction measurement should also distinguish between processes that have high impact on satisfaction and those that do not. One way to do so is to collect information on both the *importance* and the *performance* of key quality characteristics. Such data can be evaluated using by means of the

Figure 4.3
Performance-Importance
Comparison

	Performance	
Importance	**Low**	**High**
Low	Who Cares?	Overkill
High	Vulnerable	Strengths

grid shown in Figure 4.3. A firm would like to have high performance on important characteristics—ones that enhance competitiveness—and not waste resources on less important characteristics. Xerox Corporation has an effective
system of customer-satisfaction measurement.

Applied P/OM

Xerox Corporation

*Xerox integrates customer feedback into its continuous improvement
activities.*[8]

Since the early 1980s Xerox has been surveying tens of thousands of
customers annually and tracking the results through its Customer
Satisfaction Measurement System (CSMS). The data guide continuous improvements in the corporation. For instance, the CSMS uncovered the fact
that customers wanted one-call, one-person problem resolution. As a result, Xerox created six Customer Care Centers, staffed by specially trained
customer-care representatives who handle some 1.2 million telephone
calls and about a million written inquiries each year. Employees are cross-
trained and empowered to adjust bills, correct forms, or take other steps to
solve problems singlehandedly. Any problems that cannot be instantly resolved are given a 10-day-resolution deadline. The files remain open until
customers confirm that they are totally satisfied with Xerox's actions.
CSMS data also showed that customer satisfaction is linked to cycle time—
the elapsed time between the reporting phone call and the solution of the
problem. Further, the data revealed that simply knowing when a technician will arrive has a positive effect on satisfaction. Xerox modified the system to call customers shortly after problems are reported and give them
an estimated time of arrival.

Productivity Measurement

Productivity has often been confused with efficiency—the ratio of the time
needed to perform a task to some predetermined "standard" time. However,
people now realize that doing unnecessary work efficiently is not productive.
Productivity is interpreted as effectiveness (doing the *right* things efficiently),
which is outcome, not output, oriented.

Formally, we define **productivity** as the ratio of output of a production process to the input.

$$\text{productivity} = \frac{\text{output}}{\text{input}} \tag{4.1}$$

As output increases for a constant level of input, or as the amount of input decreases for a constant level of output, productivity increases. Thus, a productivity measure describes how well the resources of an organization are being used to produce output.

The ways in which output and input are measured can provide very different measures of productivity. Outputs are tangibles such as the number of pizzas produced or the number of lines of computer code written. Because quality should be included in productivity measurement, more appropriate definitions of outputs might be the number of pizzas *that meet customer requirements* or the number of *error-free* lines of code written.

Productivity is usually expressed in one of three forms: as total productivity, multifactor productivity, or partial factor productivity. **Total productivity** is the ratio of total output to total input,

$$\text{total productivity} = \frac{\text{total output}}{\text{total input}} \tag{4.2}$$

Total input consists of all resources used in the production of goods and services; for example, total input includes labor, capital, raw materials, and energy. Those resources are often converted to dollars so that a single figure can be used as an aggregate measure of total input. Examples of total productivity ratios are tons of steel produced per dollar of input and dollar value of wheat produced per dollar of input. The resources making up total output must be expressed in the same units, and the resources making up total input must be expressed in the same units. However, the total output and total input need not be in the same units. For example, total output could be expressed as the number of units produced and total input could be expressed in dollars.

Total productivity ratios reflect *simultaneous* changes in inputs and outputs. As such, they provide the most inclusive type of index for measuring productivity. However, total productivity ratios do not show the interaction between each input and output separately and thus are too broad to be used as a tool for improving specific areas of operations.

Multifactor productivity is the ratio of total output to a subset of inputs.

$$\text{multifactor productivity} = \frac{\text{total output}}{\text{subset of inputs}} \tag{4.3}$$

For example, a subset of inputs might consist of only labor and materials, or only labor and capital. The use of a multifactor measure as an index of productivity, however, may ignore important inputs and thus may not accurately reflect overall productivity.

Finally, **partial-factor productivity** is the ratio of total output to a single input.

$$\text{partial-factor productivity} = \frac{\text{total output}}{\text{single input}} \tag{4.4}$$

Table 4.2 Examples of Partial Productivity Measures

Labor Productivity	**Capital Productivity**
Units of output per labor-hour	Units of output per dollar input
Value added per labor-hour	Dollar output per dollar input
Dollar output per labor-hour	Inventory turnover ratio (dollar sales per
Production value per labor-hour	dollar inventory)
Shipments per labor cost	
Machine Productivity	**Energy Productivity**
Units of output per machine-hour	Units of output per kilowatt-hour
Tons of output per machine-hour	Units of output per energy cost
	Production value per barrel of fuel

The U.S. Bureau of Labor Statistics uses "total economic output per total worker-hours expended" as a measure of national productivity; in doing so, the bureau is computing a partial-factor productivity measure.

Operations managers generally utilize partial productivity measures—particularly labor-based measures—because the data are readily available. In addition, since total or multifactor measures provide an aggregate view, partial-factor productivity measures are easier to relate to specific processes. However, labor-based measures do not include mechanization and automation in the input; thus, when mechanization replaces labor, misinterpretation may occur.

Table 4.2 shows several other commonly used partial productivity measures that can be used in both manufacturing and service organizations. For example, "units of output per labor-hour" might represent the number of radios produced per labor-hour in a factory or the number of transactions per teller hour in a bank.

Example

Computing Productivity Measures: Miller Chemicals (Part a)

A division of Miller Chemicals produces water purification crystals for swimming pools. The major inputs used in the production process are labor, raw materials, and energy. The spreadsheet in Figure 4.4 shows the amount of output produced and input used for 1994 and 1995. By dividing the pounds of crystals produced by each input individually, we obtain the partial productivity measures shown in columns D through F.

An example of a multifactor productivity measure is output per nonlabor dollar. For 1994 we have

$$\frac{100,000}{\$5,000 + \$30,000} = 2.857 \text{ lb / nonlabor dollar.}$$

For 1995 we have

$$\frac{150,000}{\$6,000 + \$40,000} = 3.261 \text{ lb / nonlabor dollar.}$$

Thus we see that the output per nonlabor dollar was higher in 1995. A total productivity measure can be computed by dividing the total output by the total cost. For 1994 we have

Figure 4.4 Spreadsheet for Computing Productivity Measures (MILLER_1.XLS)

	A	B	C	D	E	F
1	Miller Chemicals					
2		1994	1995		1994	1995
3	*Outputs*					
4	Pounds of crystals	100,000	150,000			
5						
6	*Inputs*			*Productivity measure*		
7	Direct labor hours	20,000	28,000	Output/direct labor-hour	5.000	5.357
8	Direct labor cost	$ 180,000	$ 350,000	Output/direct labor-dollar	0.556	0.429
9	Energy used (kWh)	350,000	400,000	Output/kilowatt-hour	0.286	0.375
10	Energy cost	$ 5,000	$ 6,000	Output/energy-dollar	20.000	25.000
11	Raw materials used (lb)	120,000	185,000	Output/lb. of raw material	0.833	0.811
12	Raw material cost	$ 30,000	$ 40,000	Output/raw material dollar	3.333	3.750
13						

$$\text{total productivity} = \frac{100,000}{\$180,000 + \$5,000 + \$30,000} = 0.465 \text{ lb / dollar.}$$

For 1995 we have

$$\text{total productivity} = \frac{150,000}{\$350,000 + \$6,000 + \$40,000} = 0.379 \text{ lb / dollar.}$$

Using Productivity Measures

Productivity measures give the operations manager an indication of how to improve productivity: either increase the numerator of the productivity measure, decrease the denominator, or do both. For example, consider the labor-productivity measure given by the number of units produced per labor-hour. If, for a fixed number of labor-hours, the output can be increased, or if, for a fixed number of units of output, labor can be reduced, productivity will be improved. That might be accomplished through increased automation, improving quality, new work methods, or wage-incentive programs.

Within a single time period, productivity measures can be used to compare similar operations within the same firm, to compare the firm's performance against industrywide data, and/or to compare its performance with that of similar firms. For example, a fast-food franchisor can use productivity data to compare different franchised outlets and/or to compare its productivity with that of its competitors.

Productivity Indexes

Since productivity is a relative measure, it must be compared to something to be meaningful. It can be compared to values for similar businesses or to the firm's own productivity data. This allows measurement of the impact of certain decisions, such as the introduction of new processes, equipment, worker motivation techniques, and so forth.

Figure 4.5 Spreadsheet for Computing Productivity Indexes (MILLER_2.XLS)

	A	B	C	D	E	F	G
1	Miller Chemicals						
2		1994	1995		1994	1995	1995
3	Outputs						Index
4	Pounds of crystals	100,000	150,000				
5							
6	Inputs			Productivity measure			
7	Direct labor hours	20,000	28,000	Output/direct labor-hour	5.000	5.357	1.071
8	Direct labor cost	$180,000	$350,000	Output/direct labor-dollar	0.556	0.429	0.771
9	Energy used (kWh)	350,000	400,000	Output/kilowatt-hour	0.286	0.375	1.313
10	Energy cost	$ 5,000	$ 6,000	Output/energy-dollar	20.000	25.000	1.250
11	Raw materials used (lb)	120,000	185,000	Output/lb. of raw material	0.833	0.811	0.973
12	Raw material cost	$ 30,000	$ 40,000	Output/raw material dollar	3.333	3.750	1.125
13							

A **productivity index** is the ratio of productivity measured in some time period to the productivity in a base period. For instance, if the base-period productivity is computed to be 1.25 and the next period's productivity is 1.18, the ratio 1.18/1.25 = .944 indicates that productivity has decreased to 94.4 percent of the base period value. By tracking such indexes over time, managers can evaluate the success (or lack of success) of various projects and decisions.

Example

Computing Productivity Indexes: Miller Chemicals (Part b)

Let us consider the Miller Chemicals Company example discussed in the preceding example. If we use 1994 as a base period, we can compute a productivity index for 1995 by dividing each productivity measure for 1995 by its 1994 value. For example, the 1995 productivity index for output/direct labor-hour is 5.357 ÷ 5.000 = 1.071, which indicates that productivity has increased by 7.1 percent. The productivity indexes are summarized in column G of Figure 4.5 (the remainder of the spreadsheet is identical to Figure 4.4). How would you interpret the indexes?

Total or multifactor productivity measures are generally preferable to partial measures. The reason is that focusing on productivity improvement in a narrow portion of an organization may actually decrease overall productivity. A simple example illustrates this point. Suppose productivity is measured by

$$\frac{\text{total units produced}}{\text{total labor cost} + \text{total equipment cost}}.$$

Assume 10,000 units are being produced currently, with annual labor and equipment costs of $50,000 and $25,000, respectively. Thus from equation 4.5, the measure of productivity is

$$\frac{10,000}{\$50,000 + \$25,000} = .133 \text{ units of output per dollar input.}$$

Labor productivity, however, is measured for this example as

$$\frac{10,000}{\$50,000} = .20 \text{ units of output per labor-dollar.}$$

Suppose a $10,000 reduction in labor can be achieved by investing in a more advanced machine. Labor productivity will increase to

$$\frac{10,000}{\$40,000} = .25 \text{ units of output per labor-dollar.}$$

Thus, from a partial-productivity perspective, this investment appears to be attractive. If the annual cost with the new equipment increases to $40,000, however, (4.5) would be

$$\frac{10,000}{\$40,000 + \$40,000} = .125 \text{ units of output per dollar input}$$

and hence overall productivity would actually decrease. It is therefore necessary to examine the simultaneous effects of all changes on productivity.

Productivity measures are statistics; as with all statistics, it is easy to misuse them or to mask information unintentionally. Consider, for example, an employee earning $18,000 per year who produces 1,000 units of output per year. A trainee of lesser skill is hired at $10,000 to assist this employee, and together they produce 1,700 units per year. A partial measure of labor productivity is

$$\frac{\text{number of units produced per year}}{\text{labor years}} = \frac{1,700}{2}$$

$$= 850 \text{ units of output per labor-year.}$$

Because the current (one-person) system has a labor productivity value of 1,000, we conclude that productivity has decreased in terms of average output per worker. However, suppose labor productivity is measured as number of units produced per dollar input. For the one-person system, the labor productivity is equal to

$$\frac{\text{number of units}}{\text{dollar input}} = \frac{1,000}{\$18,000} = 0.56 \text{ units per labor-dollar.}$$

Computing the same measure with the trainee, we find that the labor productivity is $1,700 \div \$28,000 = .061$. On that basis, hiring the trainee resulted in about a 9 percent improvement in productivity. In such situations, it is better to use the units per dollar input productivity measure since it takes into account the *relative* value of the inputs; that is, the difference in wages implies a difference in skill level. The first measure, on the other hand, implicitly assumes that each labor-year is equivalent. The point of these illustrations is that we must be very careful when using partial productivity measures.

Productivity in Service Organizations

Many employees in service organizations perform the same tasks as employees in manufacturing organizations. For instance, in many manufacturing firms, employees work on an assembly line; their counterparts in a service organization provide services by performing tasks in mail rooms, cafeterias, insurance offices, and so on. In both manufacturing and service organizations, productivity is an important issue.

In many service organizations, productivity measures such as the number of letters sorted per employee, number of meals prepared per cook, or number of miles of roads treated with salt per dollar expended can be developed in the same way as their counterparts in manufacturing organizations. In other service organizations, especially those engaged in knowledge work with high customer contact such as consulting, legal services, or health care, productivity is generally more difficult to measure. Inputs and outputs may not be as easy to identify as in manufacturing contexts. For example, a common definition of nursing productivity in the health care field is "hours per patient day." It ignores indirect nursing care, ancillary costs, and overhead. A better way of defining nursing productivity is the ratio of the total revenues generated by patients admitted to the unit to all resources consumed in treating the patient.[9] The following example shows how productivity can be measured in a health care organization.

Example

Computing Productivity Measures: Nursing Units

Costs and other relevant information for two nursing units that admit and treat similar patients during a six-month period is shown in Figure 4.6. Total inputs in dollars are calculated by multiplying total patient days by the number of nursing hours per patient day and the total direct nursing care cost per hour, and adding the remaining costs per patient day multiplied by the number of patient days and the fixed overhead cost. Thus, for Unit A, total inputs are

$$(5000)(4.7)(\$14.70) + (\$17.90)(5000) + (\$37.60)(5000)$$
$$+ (\$31.50)(5000) + \$102,311 = \$882,761.$$

Figure 4.6 Spreadsheet for Computing Productivity Measures for Nursing Units (NURSING.XLS)

	A	B	C	D	E	
1	Nursing Unit Productivity Measures					
2						
3		Unit A	Unit B			
4	Total patient days	5000	6120			
5	Nursing hours/patient day	4.7	4.6			
6	Total direct nrusing care cost/hour	$ 14.70	$ 13.85			
7	Total indirect nursing care cost/patient day	$ 17.90	$ 17.20			
8	Average room and bed cost/patient day	$ 37.60	$ 36.00			
9	Variable overhead cost/patient day	$ 31.50	$ 31.10			
10	Fixed overhead cost/nursing unit	$ 102,311.00	$ 110,425.00			
11	Revenues generated per unit	$ 1,394,500.00	$1,887,000.00			
12						
13	Total inputs	$882,761.00	$1,016,246.20			
14						
15	Total productivity	1.58	1.86			
16						

Total productivity, as given in cells B15 and C15 in Figure 4.6, is found by dividing total revenues by the total inputs. We see that Unit B is more productive than Unit A. The productivity ratios might be adjusted by quality scores that can be developed by instruments measuring the degree to which a nursing unit complies with accrediting standards. Partial-productivity measures, such as direct-nursing-care productivity, might also be computed. That is one of the problems at the end of the chapter.

Cost of Quality

All organizations measure and report costs as a basis for control and improvement. In the 1950s the concept of the **cost of quality** emerged, which refers specifically to the cost of *poor* quality—the costs associated with avoiding poor quality or those incurred as a result of poor quality.

Quality problems expressed as the number of defects have little impact on top managers, who are generally concerned with financial performance, until they are translated into the appropriate financial language. Then they can help managers evaluate the relative importance of quality problems and also identify major opportunities for cost reduction.

Quality-Cost Classification

Quality costs can be organized into four major categories: prevention costs, appraisal costs, internal-failure costs, and external-failure costs. **Prevention costs** are those expended to keep nonconforming products from being made and reaching the customer. They include

1. *Quality planning costs*—such as salaries of individuals associated with quality planning and problem-solving teams, the development of new procedures, new equipment design, and reliability studies.
2. *Process-control costs*—which include costs spent on analyzing production processes and implementing process control plans.
3. *Information-systems costs*—which are expended to develop data requirements and measurements.
4. *Training and general management costs*—which include internal and external training programs, clerical staff expenses, and miscellaneous supplies.

An example of a prevention cost for MamaMia's would be processing customer-satisfaction survey results.

Appraisal costs are those expended on ascertaining quality levels through measurement and analysis of data to detect and correct problems. They include

1. *Test and inspection costs*—those associated with incoming materials, work-in-process, and finished goods, including equipment costs and salaries.
2. *Instrument maintenance costs*—those associated with the calibration and repair of measuring instruments.

3. *Process-measurement and process-control costs*—which involve the time spent by workers to gather and analyze quality measurements.

Appraisal costs at MamaMia's might be measuring the weight of dough or cheese before pizza assembly to ensure the correct amount.

Internal-failure costs are costs incurred as a result of unsatisfactory quality that is found before the delivery of a product to the customer. Examples include

1. *Scrap and rework costs*—including material, labor, and overhead.
2. *Costs of corrective action*—arising from time spent determining the causes of failure and correcting production problems.
3. *Downgrading costs*—such as revenue lost by selling a product at a lower price because it does not meet specifications.
4. *Process failures*—such as unplanned machine downtime or unplanned equipment repair.

A burned pizza that is discarded would be an internal failure at MamaMia's.

External-failure costs are incurred after poor-quality products reach the customer. They include

1. *Costs due to customer complaints and returns*—including rework on returned items, cancelled orders, and freight premiums.
2. *Product-recall costs and warranty claims*—including the cost or repair or replacement as well as associated administrative costs.
3. *Product-liability costs*—resulting from legal actions and settlements.

The cost of pizzas sent back by customers or discounts offered because of late delivery would be examples of external-failure costs at MamaMia's.

Standard accounting systems are generally able to provide quality-cost data for direct labor, overhead, scrap, warranty expenses, product-liability costs, and maintenance, repair, and calibration efforts on test equipment. However, they are not structured to capture many other types of important cost-of-quality information. Costs related to service effort, product design, remedial engineering effort, rework, in-process inspection, and engineering-change losses must usually be estimated or collected through special efforts. Some costs due to external failure such as customer dissatisfaction and future lost revenues are impossible to estimate accurately. While prevention costs are the most important, it is usually easiest to determine appraisal, internal-failure, external-failure, and prevention costs, in that order.

Like productivity measures, quality costs are often reported as an index—that is, the ratio of the current value to a base-period value. Some common quality-cost indexes are quality cost per direct labor hour, quality cost per manufacturing cost dollar, quality cost per sales dollar, and quality costs per unit of production. All of those indexes, while extensively used in practice, have a fundamental problem. A change in the denominator can appear to be a change in the level of quality or productivity alone. For instance, if direct labor is decreased through managerial improvements, the direct-labor-based index will increase even if there is no change in quality. Also, the common inclusion of overhead in manufacturing cost is certain to distort results. Nevertheless, such indexes can help in comparing quality costs over time. Generally, sales bases are the most popular, followed by cost, labor, and unit bases.[10]

Quality-cost data can be broken down by product line, process, department, work-center, time, or cost category to make data analysis more convenient and useful to managers.

Example

Computing Quality Cost Indexes

A company collects quality costs by cost category and product for each time period, say one month, as shown in the upper portion of the spreadsheet in Figure 4.7.

It may compute a total quality-cost index as

$$\text{quality cost} = \frac{\text{total quality costs}}{\text{direct labor costs}}.$$

Alternatively, it may compute individual indexes by category, product, and time period, as are summarized in the lower portion of Figure 4.7.

Such information can be used to identify areas that require improvement. Of course, it is up to managers and engineers to discover the precise nature of the improvement needed. For example, a steady rise in internal-failure costs and decline in appraisal costs might indicate a problem in assembly, maintenance of testing equipment, or control of purchased parts.

A useful analysis tool for quality-cost data is called **Pareto analysis,** a technique devised by Joseph Juran in the 1950s. Juran named it after Vilfredo Pareto

Figure 4.7 Spreadsheet for Computing Quality Cost Indexes (COSTINDX.XLS)

	A	B	C	D	E	F	G	H	
1	Quality Cost Indexes								
2		January			February				
3	Cost Category	Product A	Product B		Product A	Product B			
4									
5	Prevention	$2,000	$4,000		$2,000	$4,000			
6	Appraisal	$10,000	$20,000		$13,000	$21,000			
7	Internal failure	$19,000	$106,000		$16,000	$107,000			
8	External failure	$54,000	$146,000		$52,000	$156,000			
9	Total	$85,000	$276,000		$83,000	$288,000			
10	Standard direct labor costs	$35,000	$90,000		$28,000	$86,000			
11									
12	Quality cost index								
13									
14	Prevention	0.057	0.044		0.071	0.047			
15	Appraisal	0.286	0.222		0.464	0.244			
16	Internal failure	0.543	1.178		0.571	1.244			
17	External failure	1.543	1.622		1.857	1.814			
18	Total	2.429	3.067		2.964	3.349			

(1848–1923), an Italian economist who determined that 85 percent of the wealth in Milan was owned by only 15 percent of the people. Similarly, Juran observed that the vast majority of quality problems generally result from only a few causes. Pareto analysis consists of ordering cost categories from largest to smallest. For example, chances are that 70 or 80 percent of all internal-failure costs are due to only one or two manufacturing problems. Identifying those "vital few," as they are called, will assure that corrective action will have a high return for a low dollar input.

For most companies embarking on a quality-cost program, the highest costs typically are in the external-failure category, followed by internal-failure, appraisal, and prevention, in that order. Clearly, the order should be reversed; that is, most quality costs should be in prevention, some in appraisal, perhaps a few in internal failure, and virtually none in external failure. Thus, companies should first attempt to drive external failure costs to zero by investing in appraisal activities to discover the sources of failure and take corrective action. As quality improves, failure costs will decrease, and the amount of appraisal can be reduced as the emphasis shifts to prevention activities.

Quality Costs in Service Organizations

Quality costs in service organizations differ from those in manufacturing organizations. In manufacturing, they are primarily product-oriented; in services, they are labor-dependent. Since quality in service organizations depends on employee-customer interaction, appraisal costs tend to account for a higher percentage of total quality costs than they do in manufacturing. In addition, internal-failure costs tend to be much lower for high-contact service organizations, where there is little opportunity to correct an error before it reaches the customer—at which point it represents an external failure.

Since a much greater proportion of operating cost is attributed to people, a reduction in total quality costs often means a reduction in time worked and hence in personnel. That is particularly true if a large proportion of time is built into the system for rework and other failure activities. Unless a positive strategy is developed to make alternative use of human talents, the threat of job losses will surely result in a lack of cooperation in developing and using a quality-cost program.

External-failure costs can become an extremely significant out-of-pocket expense to consumers of services. Consider the costs of interrupted service, such as telephone, electricity, or other utilities; delays in waiting to obtain service or excessive time in performing the service; errors made in billing, delivery, or installation; or unnecessary service. For example, a family moving from one city to another may have to pay additional costs for lodging and meals if the moving van does not arrive on the day promised; if a doctor's prescription needs to be changed because of faulty diagnosis, the patient pays for unnecessary drugs; if a computer makes a billing error, several phone calls, letters, and copies of cancelled checks may be needed to correct the mistake.

Managing Quality and Performance Data

Good information management is critical to business success. First, companies must ensure that quality and performance data are reliable and accessible to all who need them. Second, they must use appropriate tools to analyze the data.

Data Reliability and Accessibility

The familiar computer cliche, "Garbage in, garbage out," applies equally well to any kind of data, including quality and performance data. Any measurement is subject to error. **Measurement reliability** means how well the measuring instrument (which may be manual instruments, automated equipment, or surveys and questionnaires) consistently measures the "true value" of the characteristic being measured. Measurement reliability in manufacturing is assured by properly calibrating and periodically checking measuring instruments. In services, a useful approach to ensuring data reliability is periodic auditing of the data collection processes by internal cross-functional teams or external auditors. Standardized forms, clear instructions, and adequate training help to ensure that data collection is performed consistently.

It makes no sense to collect data if they are not available to the right employees when they need them. Thus good information management depends on data accessibility as much as data reliability. In most companies, data are accessible to top managers and others on a need-to-know basis. In TQM-focused companies, quality and performance data are accessible to everyone. A customer-service representative need not tell a customer to wait for a call-back while needed information is obtained. At Milliken, a Baldrige-award-winning textile company, all databases, including product specifications, process, data, supplier data, customer requirements, and environmental data, are immediately available to every associate throughout the computer network. Electronic charts showing key quality measures and trends are displayed throughout the plant and in business-support departments. Such data accessibility empowers employees and helps them participate in quality improvement efforts.

Analysis and Use of Quality and Performance Data

Data related to quality and operational performance need to be aggregated into useful measures that top managers can understand and apply in strategic planning and decision making. Some companies develop an aggregate customer satisfaction index (CSI) by weighting satisfaction results, market share, and gains or losses of customers. We have previously examined how Federal Express aggregates different quality components into a single index. However, simple aggregation of data is not enough. Managers must also understand the linkages between quality and key measures of business performance. For example, a company should understand how product- and service-quality improvement correlates with such business indicators as customer satisfaction, retention, market share, operating costs, revenues, and value-added per employee; how employee satisfaction relates to customer satisfaction; and how problem resolution affects costs and revenues. Federal Express correlates its 10 quality components with customer satisfaction through extensive market research. Additionally, it conducts focus groups and other surveys to validate the relationships.

The quantitative modeling of cause-and-effect relationships between external and internal performance criteria is called **interlinking.**[11] With interlinking models, managers can objectively determine the effects of adding resources or changing the system to reduce waiting time. This is *management by fact.* Florida Power and Light uses interlinking to good effect.

Applied P/OM

Florida Power and Light (Part b)

A simple interlinking model is used by Florida Power and Light.[12]

In studying the telephone operation of its customer-service centers, Florida Power and Light (FP&L) sampled customers to rate their level of satisfaction with waiting times on the telephone. Satisfaction began to fall significantly at about two minutes (see Figure 4.8). FP&L also found that customer satisfaction is directly related to how callers perceive the quality of the phone representatives. Research showed that excessive waiting times established a bias in the ratings. Eliminating that bias would contribute substantially to accurate measurement of customer satisfaction with the phone-contact experience. To improve customer satisfaction, FP&L developed a system to notify customers of the anticipated wait and give them a choice of holding or deferring the call to a later time. Customers were actually willing to wait longer without being dissatisfied if they knew the length of wait ahead of time; thus, customer satisfaction was improved even when call traffic was heavy.

Figure 4.8
Interlinking Model of
Customer Satisfaction and
Time on Hold

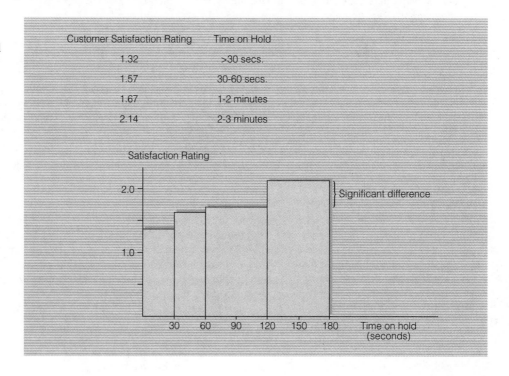

Customer Satisfaction Rating	Time on Hold
1.32	>30 secs.
1.57	30-60 secs.
1.67	1-2 minutes
2.14	2-3 minutes

P/OM in Practice

Productivity Improvement at Southwest Tube[13]

Beginning in the late 1970s, Southwest Tube faced major competitive threats in its main product line of small-diameter carbon steel tubing. The market was not expanding, and the company's manufacturing capacity was significantly greater than market demand required. As a result of competition, prices were dropping. In addition, manufacturing costs were rising for both labor and raw materials.

Commitments for raw materials were made six months to a year in advance, so very little could be done to reduce the raw material cost of finished goods. Managers concluded that if the company was going to survive, labor productivity would have to be improved. Four areas needing improvement were identified: manufacturing supervision, absenteeism and turnover, measurement and reporting, and work force scheduling.

One of the key early improvements in manufacturing supervision involved defining improved staffing levels at manufacturing work centers. That was done in a two-step process: first, using past actual performance, and second, using the results from work-measurement studies. For example, initial crew size estimates for the weld mill operation indicated that six people should be assigned to operate the mill. Work-measurement studies indicated that five people could run the mill if improved work methods were utilized. At the end of three years of continuing improvements in work methods, it was found that three people were able to run a weld mill. Another improvement in manufacturing supervision involved publishing goals for each production center and then reporting on progress toward meeting those goals. That process provided feedback to workers and helped them understand the need to compare performance to production goals.

In a number of operations, full work crews are needed to run the mill, staff a finishing floor, or move raw materials in the yard. When some workers in a crew are absent, other ones must be found to temporarily make up a full crew; that often leads to reduced productivity, since on-the-job training must be conducted for the new crew members. High turnover of employees has caused similar problems. In an attempt to solve the turnover problem, the environment was changed. First, since the plant was old and had a history of poor maintenance and inadequate housekeeping, it was cleaned and painted and the scrap was hauled away. A by-product of those actions was an improved safety record. Uniforms were provided for manufacturing employees, a job analysis was conducted, and pay scales were altered to establish fair wages and clarify the compensation program. Those improvements enabled Southwest Tube to attract a higher-quality work force, which in turn led to a 75 percent reduction in turnover.

Measurement and reporting of manufacturing performance were improved by creating an earned hour per production report. The report gave Southwest Tube managers and workers the ability to objectively compare output and productivity against performance targets. Methods improvements were identified and implemented throughout the plant. For example, new methods were developed for handling material in the plant to reduce waiting time between work centers.

Production at Southwest Tube usually required a three-shift operation six or seven days a week. The old rotating shift schedule had several negative features: days off were irregular from week to week; shifts rotated every week; and support crews (maintenance, tool room, warehouse, and others) worked different schedules that often resulted in significant gaps in coverage. A new scheduling plan was developed to solve those problems and meet production and labor cost goals. The new schedule called for four 12-hour days followed by three days off. Some of the benefits were: workers got double-time pay for the last eight hours of work each week; one shift supervisor was eliminated; the number of manufacturing employees was reduced; shifts could be stabilized and not require rotation; and a full day for maintenance was available.

One of the questions that arose was whether workers could remain productive through 48 hours of work in physically demanding jobs over a four-day period. The answer was an unqualified yes, based on results over a four-year period. Table 4.3 shows some of the changes in output versus labor input. The accident rate was reduced by a factor of 2 during the same period.

This case shows how attention to people and equipment problems and needs can result in significant productivity gains. None of the improvements were easy to implement; in fact, it took more than six months to convince the work force that productivity enhancement was in their best interest. The founder and president of Southwest Tube, F. William Weber, has acclaimed the success of the program and stated publicly that it literally saved the company from bankruptcy.

Questions for Discussion

1. How can absenteeism and turnover affect productivity?
2. What did Southwest Tube do to reduce absenteeism and turnover?

Table 4.3 Production Results for Southwest Tube

Fiscal Year	Cold Draw Department		Weld Mill Department	
	Labor (1,000 hr)	Output (1,000 ft)	Labor (1,000 hr)	Output (1,000 ft)
1980	228	18,269	132	22,434
1981	234	19,576	157	34,777
1982	183	17,633	102	26,715
1983	150	18,870	77	25,277

3. Did scheduling of employees have an effect on productivity at Southwest Tube? Explain.

4. Compute the labor productivity indexes for each year and each department using the data in Table 4.3. How much did productivity increase in this time period?

Measurement and Data Management at Xerox[14]

Measurement and data analysis are the cornerstones of Xerox's total quality effort. In 1989 Xerox had more than 375 major information systems supporting the business, of which 175 related specifically to the management, evaluation, and planning of quality. Figure 4.9 illustrates the scope and depth of the data used to support a prevention-based approach to quality improvement. The 175 sources of quality data are used in more than 300 specific applications in the management, evaluation, and planning of quality.

The Xerox quality measurement system extends from suppliers to customers. Metrics are specified at key measurement points of the Xerox Delivery Process. The answer to the question, "What information can help us meet both internal and external customer requirements?" determines which information the company includes in its quality-related information

systems. Each major operation, such as the U.S. Marketing Group or Development and Manufacturing, is assigned to a System Review Board consisting of senior managers whose responsibility is to validate customer requirements and oversee the process by which those requirements are turned into detailed specifications. As requirements develop, line and MIS (management information system) groups work closely together to ensure that needs are met within the information/data system.

The Xerox data management system ensures data accuracy, validity, timeliness, consistency, standardization, and easy access. Procedures are in place for the collection, retention, and security of data. Users—internal customers—work closely with the data management organizations to define requirements for the timely use, dissemination, and presentation of data and information. Validity, accuracy, and timeliness are ensured by the Data Systems Quality Assurance Steps shown in Figure 4.10 during the design, construction, and major upgrade of each data system. Accessibility is enhanced by one of the most extensive computer networks in the world, linking hundreds of Xerox sites on four continents to provide information 24 hours a day, seven days a week.

Xerox has several major systems for collecting, tracking, analyzing, in-

tegrating, and focusing data on specific decisions for actions. One, the Automated Installation Quality Report system, contains data on the installation and initial performance of every machine at a customer location anywhere in the United States. This database can be entered from anywhere, and is accessed for quality analysis and action from the customer interface back to design. A second system, called Technology Readiness, is a conceptual framework for bringing together all the information about technology that is needed to develop a new product. It prescribes data and data-analysis requirements for failure modes, critical parameters, subsystem interactions, achievable manufacturing variances, and system performance against goals that reflect both internal and external customer-satisfaction requirements.

The primary measure of product quality is defects per machine. A defect is defined as any variance from customer requirements. In the early 1980s, Xerox tracked only defects attributable to internal operations. After the total quality effort began, defects arising from all causes were given equal focus. Product teams use statistical tools and cost-of-quality analysis to track improvements. Beginning in 1985, Xerox manufacturing-quality measurements became a mirror image of customer requirements. After a new

Figure 4.9 Scope and Depth of Xerox Quality-Related Data

134 Data Uses to EVALUATE the Quality of All Xerox Work Processes

SCOPE ▶ / ▼ DEPTH	CUSTOMER 17	SUPPLIER 13	INTERNAL OPS 23	PRODUCT/ SERVICES 20	EMPLOYEES 17	COMPETITION 10	BENCHMARK 15	SAFETY 18	ENVIRON-MENTAL 1
PLANNING 15	• Cust. Sat. Data	• Local Cont Validation	• L-T-Q Assess • PDP Phase	• Reliability Data	• Employee Attitude	• Prod Assess • Dealer Dist	• TQC Benchmark-	• Occup Illness Data	

Left depth labels (outer table): PLANNING 15, DESIGN 26, MANUFACTURING 34, SALES 12, SERVICE 18, ADMIN 14, SUPPORT 15

79 Data Uses to Enable MANAGEMENT Decisions for Continuous Improvement

SCOPE ▶ / ▼ DEPTH	CUSTOMER 7	SUPPLIER 9	INTERNAL OPS 28	PRODUCT/ SERVICES 17	EMPLOYEES 10	COMPETITION 3	BENCHMARK 3	SAFETY 2
PLANNING 10	• Cust. Sat. Data	• Site and sourcing data	• L-T-Q Assess • Team Tracking	• Xerox Dev Process	• Mgmt. Styles Scores	• Competitive News Flash	• Org Plng Consultant	• UL Data

Left depth labels (middle table): PLANNING 10, DESIGN 18, MANUFACTURING 16, SALES 10, SERVICE 9, ADMIN 8, SUPPORT 8

92 Data Uses to PLAN for Continuous Quality Improvement

SCOPE ▶ / ▼ DEPTH	CUSTOMER 12	SUPPLIER 17	INTERNAL OPS 14	PRODUCT/ SERVICES 17	EMPLOYEES 14	COMPETITION 9	BENCHMARK 9
PLANNING 27	• Customer Requirements • Focus Group Findings • Market Research	• Supplier Base • Technical Plans • Product Array Data • Quality History Data	• Team Excellence Reports • Leadership Through Quality Assessments	• Product - Quality - Reliability - Operability - Productivity - Planning • BRMS	• Training Stats • Human Resource Data	• Trade Assoc. Reports • Trade Show Reports • Competitive Scenarios	• Benc Nws • Benc Ref • Benc Data
DESIGN 15	• Customer Visits Data • Problem ID Data	• Commodity Mix • Build Site(s) • Technology Data	• Cost of Quality Data • PDP Test Data	• Reliability • FMEA • Product Life Data • Config. Data	• Mgmt. Styles Scores • Employee Attitude Survey	• Competitive Support Practices Data	• Benc Prac Data
MANUFACTURING 12	• Customer Visits Data	• Commodity Team Surveys • Proc. Capability Data • Source Verif. Data	• Suggestion System • Production Line Quality Data	• Product Quality Data • In-Line Quality Data	• Mgmt. Styles Scores • Employee Attitude Survey	• Competitive Support Practices Data	• Benc Prac Data
SALES 10	• Customer Sat. Data • Problem ID Data	N/A	• Establishment Plng Info Sys • Int. Mktg Sys • Copy Vol Sys	• Demo Skills Profile	• Mgmt. Styles Scores • Employee Attitude Survey	• Competitive Support Practices Data	• Benc Prac Data
SERVICE 11	• Customer Sat. Data	• Spares Demand Data	• Field Service Suggestions • Cancels Data	• Serv Call Data • Field Rel • Field Perf Data	• Mgmt. Styles Scores • Employee Attitude Survey	• Competitive Support Practices Data	• Benc Prac Data
ADMIN 9	• Customer Sat. Data • Order-To-Invoice Data • Billing Quality Data	N/A	• Audit Results	• Performance Data	• Mgmt. Styles Scores • Employee Attitude Survey Scores	• Competitive Support Practices Data	• Benc Prac Data
SUPPORT 8	N/A	• Education - Total Quality Control - Stat Process Control	• Quality Team Results • Cost of Quality Data	• Grievance System Reports	• Xerox Employee Assist Prog. • Reward & Recog. Data	• Competitive Support Practices Data	• Benc Prac Data

machine is installed, quality results for product reliability are monitored via customer reports. To verify internal results, early unscheduled maintenance calls are used as a key indicator. Other measures the company tracks include product development and delivery lead times, repair response time and efficiency, operability and productivity, total cost of ownership, billing accuracy, delivery of supplies, order entry, professionalism, sales-representative attention, and administrative competence.

Questions for Discussion

1. Discuss how data captured by Xerox span the entire scope of company performance.

2. The description of Xerox's data and information approaches was writ-

Figure 4.10 Data Systems Quality Assurance Steps

No.	Data Systems Quality Assurance Steps	VALIDITY	
		Data Accuracy	Data Timeliness
1	Is the specific data definition consistent with today's need?	Requirement Check	
2	Is the process flow from data input of ultimate use defined and disciplined?	Process Check	Timing Check
3	Is the data integrity maintained under all possible test conditions?	Accuracy Standard Check	
4	Is there a mechanism for introducing change in the process flow without disrupting the system?		Improvement Check
5	Is there a process for users to correct errors in the data?	Error Correction Check	
6	Is there a process for evaluating data errors for root cause and correction?	Root Cause Check	
7	Is a set of integrated performance standards and measurements in place for data input, processing and output?	Performance Check	Performance Check
8	Is there a system in place to improve the validity of, or eliminate the need for, this data?	Continuous Improvement Check	Continuous Improvement Check

ten before the concept of interlinking became popular. What types of interlinking information might Xerox now employ based on the information presented here?

3. "Operability" means expanded features that are simple and easy to use, such as auto jam clearance, document handling, and easy-load paper and toner cartridges. How might you measure operability?

Summary of Key Points

••• Measurements enable managers to make decisions on the basis of facts, identify problems, take corrective action when necessary, and set improvement priorities. Four key areas of performance measurement are (1) suppliers, (2) product and service quality, (3) business and support services, and (4) company operational results. Data are of either the attribute (present or absent) or variable (measured on a continuous scale) type.

••• Suppliers are providers of goods and services. Quality levels, pricing, and delivery performance are key measures of supplier performance. Many companies have formal supplier rating and certification programs.

••• Product- and service-quality indicators focus on the outcomes of internal manufacturing and service processes. Common indicators include nonconformities per unit and errors per opportunity. Service-quality measures often gauge behavioral characteristics such as reliability, responsiveness, assurance, and empathy, in addition to tangibles. All business and support processes in a company should be measured. Top management requires information on customer satisfaction, productivity, and cost.

••• Performance indicators should represent the factors that predict customer satisfaction and are driven by key business factors. Good performance indicators can be established by closely examining the processes that create products and services.

••• Customer-satisfaction measures enable managers to understand customer perceptions, discover areas for improvement, and track trends. Satisfaction surveys should include competitor comparisons and be designed scientifically to allow useful statistical analysis. Measures of both the importance and performance of quality attributes should be collected and compared.

••• Productivity is the ratio of output to input. It is usually expressed as total productivity, multifactor productivity, or partial-factor productivity. Productivity measures are useful for controlling performance, and they provide a basis for comparison with other entities in the firm.

••• Quality-cost programs allow quality problems to be translated into the language of upper managers—money. Quality-cost information enables managers to identify opportunities for quality improvement, aids in budgeting and cost control, and serves as a scoreboard to evaluate an organization's success.

••• Quality costs generally are broken down into prevention, appraisal, internal-failure, and external-failure costs. Such costs are often expressed as indexes with labor, manufacturing cost, sales, or unit measurement bases. Pareto analysis helps to identify quality problems that account for a large percentage of costs and, if solved, will result in high returns on investment.

••• Effective data management should take into account data reliability and accessibility.

••• Interlinking is the quantitative modeling of cause-and-effect relationships between external and internal performance criteria. Interlinking enables managers to determine the effects of internal variables under their control objectively with external measures and hence to make better managerial decisions.

Key Terms

Suppliers (vendors)
Defect
Nonconformity
Tangibles
Reliability
Responsiveness
Assurance
Empathy
Attribute
Variable
Key business factors
Productivity
Total productivity
Multifactor productivity
Partial-factor productivity
Productivity index
Cost of quality
Prevention costs

Appraisal costs
Internal-failure costs
External-failure costs
Pareto analysis
Measurement reliability
Interlinking

Review Questions

1. What are the uses and benefits of good performance measurement?

2. List the key elements of performance measurement in production systems, and provide some examples of each.

3. What are the key measures of supplier performance? What is the purpose of supplier-certification programs?

4. Why is the term *nonconformity* often used instead of *defect*?

5. Describe the five key dimensions of service quality.

6. What are the major types of data that top managers require?

7. Explain the difference between attribute and variable measurement and provide some examples.

8. Describe the process of defining useful performance indicators.

9. Of what value are customer-satisfaction measures to managers?

10. Explain some of the key issues involved in developing customer-satisfaction measurements.

11. What is importance-performance analysis, and how can it be used to make effective decisions?

12. Explain the differences between total, multifactor, and partial-factor productivity measurements. Why are total or multifactor measures preferable to partial productivity measures?

13. How does productivity measurement differ in manufacturing and service organizations?

14. Why are quality-cost programs valuable to managers?

15. List and explain the four major categories of quality costs, giving examples of each.

16. How are quality costs measured and collected in an organization?

17. Discuss how index numbers are often used to analyze quality-cost data.

18. How do quality costs differ between service and manufacturing organizations?

19. What is Pareto analysis, and how is it used in analyzing quality cost data?

20. What do we mean by measurement reliability?

21. Why is accessibility of data important? How does information technology help?

22. What is interlinking? What benefits do interlinking models provide?

Discussion Questions

1. Identify specific quality and performance measures that would be useful in each of the following operations:
   a. Hotel
   b. Post office
   c. Department store
   d. Bus system
   e. Emergency room

2. How can measurement help in the daily operations of your college or university?

3. Discuss how quality and performance measurements can be used in a fraternity or student organization.

4. Consider the following measurements for an airline. Would they be attribute or variable measurements? Explain your answers.
   a. Passengers bumped per flight
   b. Delay times of departures
   c. Time spent at check-in counter
   d. Customers with lost baggage
   e. Delivery time for baggage

5. In a bank, the following measures are taken. Are they attributes or variables? Explain your answers.
   a. Time spent waiting for a teller
   b. Errors made in check handling
   c. Customer inquiries
   d. Turnaround time for mail transactions
   e. Computer breakdowns

6. Interview managers at a local company to identify the key business factors for that company. What quality indicators does that company measure? Are they consistent with the key business factors?

7. Many "course and instructor evaluation" systems consist of inappropriate or ineffective measurements. Discuss how the principles in this chapter can be used to develop an effective measurement system for instructor performance.

8. Many restaurants and hotels use "tabletop" customer-satisfaction surveys. Find several of them at local businesses and evaluate the types of questions and items included in the surveys. What internal performance indicators might be appropriate? How might such customer-related information be linked to internal-performance indicators?

9. Design a customer-satisfaction survey for some organization or process in which you are involved. Explain how you derived the questions in your survey.

10. Explain how productivity measures can be very misleading if quality is not taken into account.

11. Ask some local business people if their companies conduct cost-of-quality evaluations. If they do not, why don't they? If they do, how do they use the information?

12. What types of quality costs might be relevant to your college and university? Can they be measured?

13. Many quality experts, such as Joseph Juran and Philip Crosby, are firm advocates of cost-of-quality evaluations. Deming, however, states that "the most important figures are unknown and unknowable." How do you resolve those conflicting opinions?

14. If you are familiar with spreadsheet software, discuss how such programs can be used by managers to analyze quality-cost data. Design a spreadsheet that would be appropriate for that task.

15. In the making of cheese, companies test milk for somatic cell count to ensure prevention of diseases and test it for bacteria to determine how clean it is. They also perform a freezing-point test to see that the milk has not been diluted with water (if diluted, it will freeze at a lower temperature and increase production costs, since all excess water must be extracted). Final cheese products are subjected to tests for weight, foreign elements, chemicals, and taste and smell. What customer-related measures might interlink with those internal measures?

Notes

1. Jeremy Main, *Quality Wars* (New York: The Free Press, 1994), p. 130.

2. Tom Stundza, "Suppliers on the Hot Seat," *Purchasing,* January 17, 1991, pp. 92–98.

3. John J. Hudiburg, *Winning with Quality: The FPL Story* (White Plains, NY: Quality Resources, 1991).

4. Private communication from Stephen D. Webb, manager of quality control, ground operations, American Airlines.

5. Glenn E. Hayes and Harry G. Romig, *Modern Quality Control* (Encino, CA: Benziger, Bruce & Glencoe, Inc., 1977).

6. A. Parasuraman, V. A. Zeithaml, and L. L. Berry, "SERVQUAL: A Multiple-Item Scale for Measuring Consumer Perceptions of Service Quality," *Journal of Retailing* 64, no. 1 (Spring 1988), pp. 12–40.

7. U.S. Office of Management and Budget, "How to Develop Quality Measures That Are Useful in Day-to-Day Measurement," U.S. Department of Commerce, National Technical Information Service, January 1989.

8. "Quality '93: Empowering People with Technology," *Fortune,* October 1993, advertisement.

9. Vincent K. Omachonu, *Total Quality and Productivity Management in Health Care Organizations* (Milwaukee, WI: American Society for Quality Control, and Norcross, GA: Industrial Engineering and Management Press, 1991), p. 176.

10. Edward Sullivan and Debra A. Owens, "Catching a Glimpse of Quality Costs Today," *Quality Progress* 16, no. 12 (December 1983), pp. 21–24.

11. David A. Collier, *The Service/Quality Solution* (Milwaukee, WI: ASQC Quality Press, and Burr Ridge, IL: Richard D. Irwin, 1994).

Part One

12. Bob Graessel and Pete Zeidler, "Using Quality Function Deployment to Improve Customer Service," *Quality Progress* 26, no. 11 (November 1993), pp. 59–63.
13. Adapted from James M. Shirley and Thomas M. Box, "Productivity Gains at Southwest Tube," *Production and Inventory Management* 28, no. 4 (1987), pp. 57–60.

14. Adapted with permission of Xerox Corporation from Xerox 1989 Malcolm Baldrige National Quality Award Application.

Solved Problems

1. The Slaggert printing company produces a variety of brochures, reports, and other printed material for business customers. The plant manager has tracked quality-related costs over the past year. What do the data in Table 4.4 suggest?

Table 4.4 Data for Solved Problem 1

Cost Element	Amount ($)
Proofreading	710,000
Quality planning	10,000
Press downtime	405,000
Bindery waste	75,000
Checking and inspection	60,000
Customer complaint remakes	40,000
Printing plate revisions	40,000
Quality improvement projects	20,000
Other waste	55,000
Correction of typographic errors	300,000

Solution
The first step is to assign each quality-cost element to the appropriate category—prevention, appraisal, internal failure, or external failure:

```
PREVENTION
   QUALITY PLANNING                              $10,000
   QUALITY IMPROVEMENT PROJECTS                   20,000
                                    TOTAL         30,000

APPRAISAL
   PROOFREADING                                  710,000
   CHECKING AND INSPECTION                        60,000
                                    TOTAL        770,000

INTERNAL FAILURE
   PRESS DOWNTIME                                405,000
   BINDERY WASTE                                  75,000
   PRINTING PLATE REVISIONS                       40,000
   OTHER WASTE                                    55,000
   CORRECTION OF TYPOGRAPHICAL ERRORS            300,000
                                    TOTAL        875,000

EXTERNAL FAILURE:
   CUSTOMER-COMPLAINT REMAKES                     40,000
                                    TOTAL         40,000
```

Internal-failure costs account for 51 percent of the total, and appraisal costs account for about 45 percent. Hence, although the company is spending a lot of money in appraisal activities, it still has a significant amount of internal failure. Apparently, much more effort needs to be expended on quality improvement projects, particularly to reduce press downtime and typographical errors.

2. A department consists of three types of employees: laborers earning $5 per hour, machine operators earning $10 per hour, and machinists earning $16 per hour. For a certain job, over two periods, the data in Table 4.5 were collected:

Table 4.5 Data for Solved Problem 2

	Labor Hours	
Type of Employee	*Period 1*	*Period 2*
Laborer	20	16
Machine operator	12	16
Machinist	6	9

Output increased by 20 percent in period 2. How has productivity changed?

Solution

Since labor costs are given, we will use a total labor-cost productivity measure. With no knowledge of actual output figures, we index output for period 1 as 100 and for period 2 as 120 (or 1.0 and 1.2, for example). Then we divide the output index for each period by the sum of the input costs to obtain the productivity measure. The total labor costs for each period are shown below.

```
                         PERIOD 1     PERIOD 2
        LABORER            $100         $80
        MACHINE OPERATOR    120         160
        MACHINIST            96         144
                          ------       ------
                          $316         $384
```

The productivity index for period 1 is 100/316 = .3165; for period 2 it is 120/384 = .3125. The relative change in productivity in period 2 is (.3125 − .3165)/.3165 = −.0126, or a decline of 1.26 percent.

3. A steel company produces long, thin sheets of steel called *coils* that each weigh 10 to 15 tons. The slitting operation involves cutting the coils into smaller widths. An average of 5,000 tons per month is sold. The scrap rate from this operation is 3 percent. Material costs are $600 per ton. It takes .75 hours of labor at a rate of $20 per hour to produce one ton sold.

a. How many tons per month must be produced to meet the sales demand?
b. What annual savings would result from decreasing the scrap rate from 3 percent to 2 percent?

Solution

a. The required production to make 5,000 tons of good product with a 3 percent scrap rate is 5,000/(1 − .03) = 5,155 tons (*not* 5,000 times 1.03!).
b. The required production to make 5,000 tons of good product with a 2 percent scrap rate is 5,000/.98 = 5,102 tons. If the scrap rate is 3 percent, the additional 155 tons per month requires $93,000 in material and (.75)(20)(155) = $2325 in labor, for a total of $95,325. If the scrap rate is 2 percent, the additional 102 tons costs $61,200 in material

and $1,530 in labor, for a total of $62,730. The difference incurred by reducing the scrap rate from 3 to 2 percent is $32,595 per month, or $391,140 annually.

Problems

1. Quick Delivery (QD) is a local package-delivery service. QD has "benchmarked" Federal Express and adopted that company's service-quality index. Over a four-week period, QD incurred the distribution of errors shown in Table 4.6.

Table 4.6 Data for Problem 1

Error Type	Week 1	2	3	4
1	16	5	8	10
2	1	0	2	1
3	0	0	1	0
4	21	17	12	16
5	8	5	2	2
6	3	0	1	1
7	12	5	8	3
8	4	2	0	1
9	2	1	0	3
10	42	31	56	25

a. Compute a composite score for each week.
b. Conduct Pareto analysis on the results for each error category. What suggestions might you make about a quality improvement program based on these results?

2. A computer retail store routinely measures customer satisfaction. Customers are asked to rate each attribute on the following scales.

Importance
1 - very important
2 - important
3 - of less importance

Performance
1 - strongly agree
2 - agree
3 - no opinion
4 - disagree
5 - strongly disagree

A sample of 100 customers yielded the results listed in Table 4.7.

Table 4.7 Data for Problem 2

	Importance 1	2	3	Performance 1	2	3	4	5
The store was clean.	85	12	3	96	4	0	0	0
The products were easy to find.	92	8	0	0	3	32	61	4
Salespeople were readily available.	73	15	12	92	3	5	0	0
Salespeople were polite and friendly.	91	9	0	2	18	46	30	4
Salespeople were knowledgeable.	64	21	15	82	15	3	0	0
Sales people suggested the items I needed.	22	17	61	41	46	13	0	0
Checkout was reasonably quick.	80	12	8	85	10	4	1	0
My sales receipt was complete and accurate.	98	2	0	95	5	0	0	0
I felt my purchase was a good value.	93	7	0	16	73	11	0	0
I felt welcome at the store.	53	38	9	5	12	82	1	0

Analyze these data. What do they suggest to the managers of the store?

3. For the Miller Chemicals example, suppose that for 1995 output was only 140,000 lb while direct labor hours and costs are 10% higher. How do the productivity measures and indexes change?

4. Productivity measures for a manufacturing plant over a six-month period follow:

Month	Jan.	Feb.	Mar.	Apr.	May	June
Productivity	1.46	1.42	1.49	1.50	1.30	1.25

Using January as the base period, compute a productivity index for February to June, and comment on what those productivity indexes tell about the productivity trend.

5. The data in Table 4.8 are available for the first two quarters of the current year. Using total-dollar measures of input and output, compare the total profit and productivity achieved for the two quarters. How does second-quarter productivity compare with the first-quarter productivity? Use partial-factor productivity to identify what might be done to improve productivity and profitability during the third quarter.

Table 4.8 Data for Problem 5

	First Quarter	Second Quarter
Unit selling price	$20.00	$21.00
Total units sold	10,000	8,500
Labor hours	9,000	7,750
Labor cost/hour	$10.00	$10.00
Material usage (lb)	5,000	4,500
Material cost/pound	$15.00	$15.50
Other costs	$20,000	$18,000

6. A manufacturing firm uses two measures of productivity:
  a. Total sales/Total inputs
  b. Total sales/Total labor inputs

Given the data for the last three years (Table 4.9), calculate the productivity ratios. How would you interpret the results? All figures are in dollars.

Table 4.9 Data for Problem 6

	Year 1	Year 2	Year 3
Sales	110	129	124
Materials	62	73	71
Labor	28	33	28
Overhead	8	12	10

7. Total productivity is often expressed as

$$\frac{\text{total output}}{\text{total input}} = \underbrace{\frac{\text{total output}}{\text{labor}}}_{\substack{\text{labor}\\\text{productivity}}} \cdot \underbrace{\frac{\text{labor}}{\text{total input}}}_{\substack{\text{labor}\\\text{intensity}}}$$

Compute total productivity for the data in Table 4.10.

Table 4.10 Data for Problem 7

Year	Labor Productivity	Labor Intensity
1989	2.0	.6
1990	2.2	.6
1991	2.7	.5
1992	3.4	.4
1993	3.8	.4
1994	3.7	.4
1995	4.0	.3

How would you analyze this information?

8. A hamburger factory produces 50,000 hamburgers each week. The equipment used costs $5,000 and will remain productive for three years. The labor cost per year is $8,000.

a. What is the productivity measure of "units of output per dollar of input" averaged over the three-year period?

b. We have the option of $10,000 equipment, with an operating life of five years. It would reduce labor costs to $4,000 per year. Should we consider purchasing this equipment (using productivity arguments alone)?

9. A major airline is attempting to evaluate the effect of recent changes it has made in scheduling flights between New York City and Los Angeles. Data available are given in Table 4.11.

Table 4.11 Data for Problem 9

	Number of Flights	Number of Passengers
Month prior to schedule change	20	8,335
Month after schedule change	24	10,608

a. Using passengers per flight as a productivity indicator, comment on the apparent effect of the schedule change.

b. Suggest another measure of productivity that the airline may want to consider.

10. A fast-food restaurant has a drive-through window and during peak lunch times can handle a maximum of 80 cars per hour with one person taking orders, assembling them, and acting as cashier. The average sale per order is $3.50. A proposal has been made to add two workers and divide the tasks among the three. One will take orders, the second will assemble them, and the third will act as cashier. With this system it is estimated that 120 cars per hour can be serviced. All workers earn the minimum wage. Use productivity arguments to recommend whether or not to change the current system.

11. A computer software firm provides a 20' × 30' office for its six systems analysts and plans to hire two additional analysts. To maintain a 100-square-foot working space per analyst, the firm's owner-manager is considering expansion. The cost of expansion is $40 per square foot with annual maintenance costs of $4 per square foot. The useful life of floor space is 20 years. By how much should employee productivity increase to justify the additional expenditure? The current salary of the systems analysts is $25,000.

12. Refer to the nursing-unit productivity example in this chapter and compute partial productivity measures for

a. Direct nursing care

b. Indirect nursing care

c. Combined direct and indirect nursing care

How do these partial productivity measures compare to the total productivity measures?

13. For the situation described in Solved Problem 3, compute the improvement in productivity that results from decreasing the scrap rate from 3 to 2 percent. How much additional savings and productivity improvement will result if the scrap rate is decreased further, to just 1 percent?

 14. Modify the spreadsheet in Figure 4.7 to determine quality-cost indexes for March, given the assumptions in Table 4.12.

Table 4.12 Data for Problem 14

	Product A	Product B
Prevention	+10%	+10%
Appraisal	−20%	−15%
Internal failure	−30%	−5%
External failure	+5%	−12%
Direct labor	−2%	−10%

15. Analyze the cost data in Table 4.13. What implications do these data suggest to managers?

Table 4.13 Data for Problem 15

	Product		
	A	*B*	*C*
Total sales	$537,280	$233,600	$397,120
External failure	42%	20%	20%
Internal failure	45%	25%	45%
Appraisal	12%	52%	30%
Prevention	1%	3%	5%

Note: Figures represent percentages of quality costs by product.

16. Compute a sales-dollar index base to analyze the quality-cost information in Table 4.14, and prepare a memo to management.

Table 4.14 Data for Problem 16

	Quarter			
	1	*2*	*3*	*4*
Total sales	$4,120	$4,206	$4,454	$4,106
External failure	40.8%	42.2%	42.8%	28.6%
Internal failure	168.2%	172.4%	184.4%	66.4%
Appraisal	64.2%	67.0%	74.4%	166.2%
Prevention	28.4%	29.2%	30.2%	40.2%

17. Given the cost elements in Table 4.15, determine the total percentage in each of the four major quality-cost categories.

Table 4.15 Data for Problem 17

Cost Element	Amount Cost
Incoming test and inspection	7,500
Scrap	35,000
Quality training	0
Inspection	25,000
Test	5,000
Adjustment cost of complaints	21,250
Quality audits	2,500
Maintenance of tools and dies	9,200
Quality control administration	5,000
Laboratory testing	1,250
Design of quality assurance equipment	1,250
Material testing and inspection	1,250
Rework	70,000
Quality problem solving by product engineers	11,250
Inspection equipment calibration	2,500
Writing procedures and instructions	2,500
Laboratory services	2,500
Rework due to vendor faults	17,500
Correcting imperfections	6,250
Setup for test and inspection	10,750
Formal complaints to vendors	10,000

18. Use Pareto analysis to investigate the quality losses in a paper mill (Table 4.16). What conclusions do you reach?

Table 4.16 Data for Problem 18

Category	Annual Loss
Downtime	38,000
Testing costs	20,000
Rejected paper	560,000
Odd lot	79,000
Excess inspection	28,000
Customer complaints	125,000
High material costs	67,000

Chapter Outline

Applied P/OM

P/OM in Practice

Chapter Five
Work Design and Human Resource Management

amaMia's Pizza is a small business—one manager, some kitchen staff to prepare and cook the pizzas, an order taker/cashier, and some delivery employees. There are no robots or complex machines. The quality of the food and services that customers receive depends on the skills, dedication, and efforts of the people working there. As in most organizations, the front-line workers—those who have the highest contact with the customers—are probably the lowest paid in the business. Providing the leadership to make work meaningful and to motivate employees so that they can satisfy and delight customers and work toward improving quality and productivity is one of the biggest challenges for operations managers. Businesses are beginning to learn that to satisfy customers, they must first satisfy employees. That requires attention to the design of the work environment and the daily management of people.

Work design and human resource practices should enable and encourage all employees to contribute effectively to achieve high-performance. The term **high-performance work systems** denotes job and organization designs that lead not only to high levels of performance, but also to greater flexibility and more rapid response to changing customer requirements. Such systems may include various types of teams and job-enrichment activities and usually entail greater employee responsibility and motivation based on performance-linked compensation and recognition. They must be supported by education and training.

In this chapter, we explore the key issues in the management and design of high-performance work systems—the issues critical to understanding the role of operations management in modern manufacturing and service organizations. Specifically, we address

••• How the changing nature of work has caused fundamental changes in the management of operations.

••• The role of leadership and empowerment in modern operations management.

••• The important elements in the design of high-performance work systems and how those practices are applied in leading companies.

Human Resource Management and the Operations Function

All businesses have three principal resources: financial, physical, and human. The human resource is the only one that competitors cannot copy, and it is the only one that can *synergize*—that is, produce output whose value is greater than the sum of its parts. Many global competitors, such as Japan, Taiwan, Singapore, and Switzerland, have developed their competitive advantage primarily through the human resource.

Proper attention to the human resource can result in great rewards, as Presmet Corporation proved.

Applied P/OM

Presmet Corporation

Presmet Corporation found that listening to workers can result in higher motivation and significant benefits.[1]

In 1985 Presmet Corporation, a unionized, inner-city producer of structural powder-metal parts in Worcester, Massachusetts, faced a bleak future. It had just undergone a series of layoffs, had no capital, and was producing parts for a maturing market. Three years later, however, it was producing 35 percent more product than in the previous year, and costs were less than they had been in 1984. The turnaround was due to better utilization of the human resource. In 1985 managers had begun asking workers for ideas and, more importantly, listening to them. That approach gave workers motivation to improve, and they became happier in their jobs. The results included a 25 percent increase in setups, a 50 percent reduction in inspection, 30 percent reduction in finished goods inventory, 40 percent reduction in work-in-process inventory, a 38 percent increase in production, and a 36 percent reduction in supervision.

The Changing Nature of Work

Utilization of the human resource in work has changed over the centuries and in recent years. Before the Industrial Revolution, skilled craftspeople applied all of their resources to producing their products, because their families' livelihood depended directly on the sale of those products. In the early 1900s Frederick W. Taylor proposed that a factory should be managed scientifically. He advocated work methods design, work standards, worker selection and training, and piecework incentives. Taylor separated the planning function from execution, because many foremen and workers lacked the skills and education needed for planning their work. Increased mechanization and specialization of job tasks resulted.

The Taylor system dramatically improved productivity. As pressures for productivity increased, however, quality declined and adversarial relationships between labor and management developed. Further, extreme division of labor was resulting in employee boredom, fatigue, and dissatisfaction.

The Taylor system failed to make use of an organization's most important asset—the knowledge and creativity of its work force. Essentially, the Taylor system philosophy assumes that

1. People are part of work processes.
2. Processes must be controlled externally to be productive.
3. Managers must carefully control what people do.

Recently, managers have begun to realize that this philosophy no longer works very well. The new thinking is that

1. People design and improve processes.
2. Processes must be controlled by the workers who run them.
3. Managers must obtain the commitment of people to design, control, and improve processes so that they can remain productive.

This view results in higher quality, lower costs, improved productivity, and higher job satisfaction. It supports the goal of enhancing customer value and satisfaction, but it requires that employees be given the training and responsibilities to achieve that goal, and to feel that they indeed make a difference. Coors Brewing Company has followed this philosophy with great success.

Applied P/OM

Coors Brewing Company

Coors' philosophy is that job satisfaction leads to customer satisfaction.[2]

The Customer Satisfaction Improvement Program at Coors is designed to give employees the skills needed to fulfill one major responsibility: to satisfy and, it is hoped, delight their customers, especially internal customers. Coors engaged in a massive training program to learn TQM principles, and structured its organization systems (compensation, evaluation, and so on) to support the new effort. Pete Coors, CEO, explained it simply: "We're moving from an environment where the supervisor says, 'This is the way it is going to be done and if you don't like it go someplace else,' to an environment where the supervisor can grow with the changes, get his troops together, and say, 'Look, you guys are operating the equipment, what do *you* think we ought to do?' "[3] Coors has successfully developed in its employees a passion for their jobs and pride in their work that translates into measurable improvements in productivity, a remarkably low turnover rate, and the delivery of high-quality product and service throughout the system.

With the new thinking, operations managers face such new responsibilities as investing extra effort in employee development, coping with higher levels of ambiguity and uncertainty, and dealing with obsolete skills and careers that are casualties of change. At Xerox, for example, managers will not be considered for promotion unless they visibly demonstrate support for the company's quality strategy, personally use quality processes and tools, use customer-satisfaction measures in business decisions, encourage feedback from peers, superiors, and customers, recognize and reward subordinates who practice quality improvement, and provide coaching and guidance to those requiring help.

Workers too must cope with changing attitudes, new skill requirements, and increased responsibility. Whereas some welcome the challenges of an "enriched" job, others resent them. But there is no going back. Direct manufacturing jobs have become so mechanized that just a few workers can control an entire automated plant; thus, it is critical that the work force be reliable, dedicated, and competent. Many tasks that cannot be mechanized are being performed outside the country, where labor costs are lower.

The current trend toward more automation creates more "monitoring" jobs than "doing" jobs. Indeed, some observers have recently suggested that the notion of "job" itself is disappearing.[4] The modern concept of a job emerged early in the nineteenth century to describe the work required in newly developed factories. Before people had "jobs," they worked just as hard, but on ever-changing tasks, in a variety of locations, without rigid schedules. Now the mass production and complex organizational structures that created nineteenth-century style factory jobs are disappearing, and we may be returning to the less structured approach to work. Certainly General Electric's plant in Lynn, Massachusetts, is much different from the typical assembly-line setup.

Applied P/OM
General Electric

Competition has forced GE to change the ways people work.[5]

In Lynn, Massachusetts, the birthplace of General Electric, many factories have been closed. The one that remains makes engines for small jet aircraft and has less than half the employees it had in the mid 1980s. At that plant, however, changes have been dramatic. People are working harder, smarter, more flexibly, and more cooperatively. One worker, who for years operated automatic lathes in a rather boring, repetitive job, is trained to master many machines and can make aircraft engine parts from start to finish. Operations managers have moved from carpeted offices to cinderblock cubicles on the factory floor. Foremen no longer command and discipline workers; instead, they lead and coach them. Neckties are gone, and hourly workers can park within the factory gates, a privilege once reserved for salaried workers. Teams of machine maintenance workers work without a foreman and decide their own schedule and work assignments.

Managing High-Performance Work Systems

Operations managers can do many things to foster high-performance work systems. At the the planning stage, they should ensure that human resources plans are consistent with strategic business plans and fully address the needs and development of the entire work force. For example, a manufacturer of high-technology consumer electronics products that has as key strategies product innovation and development of advanced technologies might include in its human resources plans the goal of increasing the knowledge and skills of product design engineers and diagnostic technicians. At MamaMia's, a strategy of providing outstanding customer service would require a continuing focus on employee attitudes and communication skills, and perhaps teamwork within the kitchen and dining staff to improve responsiveness.

Employee participation can be fostered through suggestion systems and teams, which are discussed later in this chapter. Operations managers can also use employee surveys and measure key indicators of employee satisfaction to help identify problem areas. For example, AT&T conducts an opinion survey every two years to measure employee attitudes and the effect of improvement efforts. Results are compared internally and against benchmarks of other high-performance companies.

All managers are now taking on roles as coaches, teachers, and facilitators, rather than directors and controllers. They need to learn to work as partners with hourly employees and with other managers in cross-functional efforts to achieve business objectives. Such practices suggest that the traditional notion of *management* is evolving toward *leadership*.

Leadership

Leadership is the right to exercise authority and the ability to achieve results from people and systems under one's authority. Strong leadership, especially from the senior managers of the organization, is absolutely necessary to develop and sustain a high-performance work organization. Leaders motivate and encourage employees, build consensus among diverse groups or individuals, and force decisions to the lowest possible level. Leaders may try to provide a motivating climate for employees and develop enthusiasm with rhetoric, but actions often speak louder than words. In June 1994, Chrysler CEO Robert Eaton canceled a scheduled test-drive session for his managers and held a quality improvement meeting instead. That action was prompted by Chrysler's poor scores in recent J.D Power and Associates automobile quality surveys.[6]

Leaders set high expectations. Motorola set aggressive goals of reducing defects per unit of output in every operation by a hundredfold in four years and reducing cycle time by 50 percent each year. One of Hewlett-Packard's goals is to reduce the interval between product concept and investment payback by one-half in five years. To promote such "stretch goals," leaders provide the resources and support to meet them, especially training. They facilitate, coach, and build teams that support the organization's mission.

Leaders provide an environment with few bureaucratic rules and procedures, in which subordinates can experiment and take risks, employees talk openly about problems, teamwork is encouraged and supported, and employees understand their responsibilities for quality and productivity improvement. Solectron Corporation, a Malcolm Baldrige National Quality Award winner, gives workers responsibility for meeting quality goals and has its managers foster teamwork to enable the workers to do so. It has created a strong "family" atmosphere, promotes clear and effective communications, and recognizes and rewards groups for exceptional performance.

Empowerment

Empowerment means giving employees authority to make decisions, gain greater control over their work, and thus more easily satisfy customers. For example, MamaMia's servers and drivers might be empowered to replace a pizza or provide it free if they perceive any dissatisfaction from a customer.

More companies talk about empowerment than truly practice it. Neverthe-less, examples of empowerment abound:

••• Workers in Coors' container operation give each other performance evalua-tions, and even screen, interview, and hire new people for the line.

••• At AT&T, design engineers have the authority to stop a design, and line oper-ators can stop the production line if they detect a quality problem.

••• At Ritz-Carlton Hotels, each employee can "move heaven and earth" and spend up to $2,000 to satisfy a customer. Employees are also trained to specifically contact others in the organization to help resolve a problem.

••• Hourly employees at GM's Antilock Brake System plant in Dayton, Ohio, can call in suppliers to help solve problems, and manage scrap, machine down-time, absences, and rework.

The need to empower the entire work force in order for quality efforts to succeed has long been recognized, even though such empowerment has only recently been put into practice. Juran wrote that "ideally, quality control should be delegated to the workforce to the maximum extent possible."[7] Five of Deming's 14 points relate directly to the notion of empowerment:[8]

Point 6: Institute training.

Point 7: Teach and institute leadership.

Point 8: Drive out fear. Create trust. Create a climate for innovation.

Point 10: Eliminate exhortations for the work force.

Point 13: Encourage education and self-improvement for everyone.

Those points, in essence, recommend involving employees more directly in de-cision-making processes, giving them the security and confidence to make de-cisions, and providing them with the necessary tools and training.

Successful empowerment of employees requires that:[9]

••• Employees be provided education, resources, and encouragement.

••• Policies and procedures be examined for needless restrictions on employees' ability to serve customers.

••• There be an atmosphere of trust rather than resentment and punishment for failure.

••• Information be shared freely rather than closely guarded as a source of con-trol and power.

••• Workers feel their efforts are desired and needed for the success of the organization

••• Managers be given the support and training to adopt a "hands-off" leader-ship style.

••• Employees be trained in the amount of latitude they are allowed. Formulating decision rules and providing role-playing scenarios are excellent ways of teaching employees.

Empowerment may threaten some managers. It involves developing lead-ership at lower levels of the organization by spreading power downward and outward, which means that managers must relinquish some of their power. Not only do many people resent giving up power, but there is a fear that workers will abuse their new privileges. However, experience shows that front-line workers generally are more conservative than managers. For example, companies that have empowered employee groups to evaluate performance and grant pay raises to their peers have found that such groups are much tougher than managers.

Empowerment gives managers new responsibilities. They must hire and develop people capable of handling empowerment, encourage risk-taking, and recognize achievements. Giving employees information on company finances and the financial implications of empowered decisions is also important. To help employees make decisions on issues affecting production, a department manager at Texas Eastman Chemicals Plant, a division of Kodak, gave operators a daily financial report that showed how their decisions affected the bottom line. Subsequently, department profits doubled in four months and quality improved by 50 percent as employees began suggesting cost-saving improvements.[10]

Empowerment can be viewed as vertical teamwork between managerial and nonmanagerial personnel. It builds confidence in workers by showing them that the company trusts their ability to make decisions on their own. It generates commitment and pride. It also gives employees better experience, with which they may advance their careers. It benefits customers who buy the company's products and services in that empowered employees often can reduce bureaucratic red tape, such as having to seek a supervisor's signature, and thus make transactions speedier and more pleasant.

Designing High-Performance Work Systems

A critical issue facing operations managers is the design of jobs for individual workers. A **job** is the set of tasks an individual performs. **Job design** involves determining the specific job tasks and responsibilities, the work environment, and the methods by which the tasks will be carried out to meet the goals of production. Two broad objectives must be satisfied in job design. One is to meet the goals of productivity and quality in production; the other is to make the job safe, satisfying, and motivating for the worker. Thus, an effective job design enables a worker to perform his or her task well, which results in higher levels of productivity and quality and lower costs for the firm.

Resolving conflicts between the need for technical and economic efficiency and the need for employee satisfaction is the challenge that faces managers in designing jobs. Clearly, efficiency improvements are needed to keep a firm competitive. However, it is also clear that any organization with a large percentage of dissatisfied employees cannot be competitive.

We will examine the design of the physical workplace in another chapter; here we consider the social and psychological work environment. That environment should give workers motivation to perform their jobs in a quality fashion and a sense of satisfaction. As demonstrated by Maslow, workers cannot be motivated by pride in their work unless their basic human needs are satisfied first. Workers must have a sense of job security and be compensated fairly. They must have some comprehension of what is expected and of how the job fits into

Figure 5.1
The Sociotechnical
Approach to Job Design

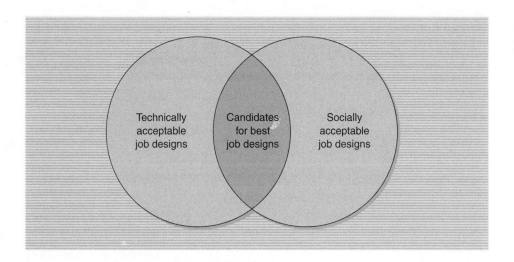

the overall scheme of things. Only then will team concepts and broader responsibilities become important. Workers can be given challenges and opportunities
for personal growth in their jobs. Every effort must be made to involve workers
in the outcome of their work and in changes that affect their work. In addition,
there must be appropriate incentives and rewards for achieving goals and objectives, not just for the output produced. The work environment has a social
structure, with official and unofficial activities, beliefs, and interactions. Job design must address both the official and the unofficial structures.

Consideration of both the technology of production and the social aspects
of the work environment—called the **sociotechnical approach** to job design—
has been prevalent since the 1950s. What is sought is a job design that provides
for high levels of performance and at the same time a satisfying job and work
environment. The overlap region of Figure 5.1 depicts the design sought by the
sociotechnical approach: it represents an integration of the social consequences of work with the traditional cost and quality considerations of production. The costs of employee turnover, training, and absenteeism, which result
from lack of job satisfaction, may lead managers to sacrifice cost savings in production efficiency to improve job satisfaction and thereby achieve greater cost
savings as a result of better job performance.

At MamaMia's, for instance, a purely technical approach to high efficiency
would be to create an "assembly line" atmosphere in which one individual
makes dough, another puts on toppings, and another cooks the pizzas.
However, more job satisfaction might result from each person making pizzas
from start to finish, and perhaps rotating jobs between the kitchen and dining
area.

Motivation and Work Design

Motivation can be defined as an individual's response to a felt need. Thousands
of studies have been performed over the years on human and animal subjects
in attempts to understand and refine the concept of motivation. It is an extremely complex phenomenon that is not fully understood, but its importance
in job design is quite clear.

Figure 5.2
Hackman and Oldham's
Complete Job
Characteristics Model

SOURCE: J. Hackman/G. Oldham,
Work Redesign, © 1980, by Addison-
Wesley Publishing Co., Inc.
Reprinted with permission of the
publisher.

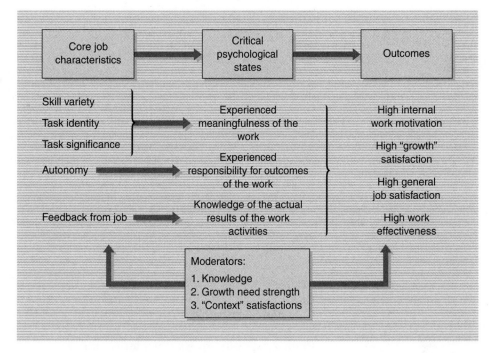

Many theories of work motivation have been developed by behavioral scientists over the past 75 years. They can be classified as either content models or process models. *Content models* describe how and why people are motivated to work. Two of the best known are the hierarchy-of-needs theory developed by Abraham Maslow and the two-factor theory developed by Frederick Herzberg. You may have studied them in previous management courses or psychology courses.

Process models explain the dynamic process whereby individuals make choices in an effort to obtain desired rewards. Included in this category are the expectancy concepts of Kurt Lewin and E. C. Tolman, B. F. Skinner's reinforcement model, Victor Vroom's valence/expectancy model, and the performance/satisfaction approach of Porter and Lawler. Reviews of those theories can be found in many other books. Here we focus very specifically on the motivational aspects of job design.

The Hackman and Oldham model shown in Figure 5.2 attempts to explain the motivational properties of job design by tying together the technical and human components of a job. This model is an effective operationalization of earlier motivation theories and research studies. It draws heavily on the work of Herzberg and others and has been validated in numerous organizational settings. The model contains four major parts:

1. Critical psychological states.
2. Core job characteristics.
3. Moderating variables.
4. Outcomes.

Three critical psychological states drive the model. *Experienced meaningfulness* is the psychological need of workers to feel that their work is a significant contribution to the organization and society. *Experienced responsibility* indicates the need of workers to be accountable for the quality and quantity of their work. *Knowledge of results* implies that all workers feel a need to know how their work is evaluated and what the results of the evaluation are. Affecting the critical psychological states are five core job characteristics:

1. *Task significance*—the degree to which the job gives the participant the feeling that it has a substantial impact on the organization, or the world.
2. *Task identity*—the degree to which the worker can perceive the task as a whole, identifiable piece of work from start to finish.
3. *Skill variety*—the degree to which the job requires the worker to have and to use a variety of skills and talents.
4. *Autonomy*—The degree to which the task permits freedom, independence, and personal control to be exercised over the work.
5. *Feedback from the job*—The degree to which clear, timely information about the effectiveness of individual performance is available.

An example that illustrates characteristics of the Hackman and Oldham model is the case of a small Delaware firm that produces space suits for astronauts. The work requires hand crafting with conventional sewing machinery as well as use of high technology in testing the suits for proper functioning. Task significance and task identity are evident in the workers' ability to see the job as being of extreme importance and as fitting into a complete unit. Skill variety and autonomy are somewhat limited, since conventional sewing techniques must be used and rigid specifications must be followed precisely. However, other motivating aspects of the job may compensate for the lack of those characteristics. Feedback on results is timely and individualized.

Job Enlargement and Enrichment

High-performance work environments provide opportunities for continual learning and personal growth for all employees. During the scientific management era, when operations managers sought to improve productivity through division of labor and increased specialization, an assembly-line worker might simply tighten bolts all day. The reverse situation is the goal today—one in which workers' abilities are challenged and developed, workers are granted more responsibility, and they are allowed to see the results of their efforts. Such jobs reflect "enlargement" and "enrichment."

Job enlargement is the reverse of specialization. It is horizontal expansion of the job to give the worker more variety—although not more responsibility. Job enlargement might be accomplished, for example, by giving a production-line worker the task of building an entire product rather than a small subassembly, or by job rotation, such as rotating nurses among hospital wards or flight crews on different airline routes. It is theorized that the loss of specialization's efficiency will be made up in the long run by better motivation, reduced turnover, and lower costs, thus increasing the *effectiveness* of the firm.

Job enrichment is vertical expansion of job duties to give the worker more responsibility. For instance, an assembly worker may be given the added responsibility of testing a completed assembly, so that he or she acts also as a quality inspector. A prime example of job enrichment is the "quality-circle" concept discussed later in this chapter. By giving a group of workers the responsibility for solving problems of production and quality control, management increases the variety of skills and abilities that they use, makes their jobs more meaningful, and gives them more involvement in decision making and feedback.

Employee Involvement

Tom Peters suggests involving everyone in everything—in quality and productivity improvement, measuring and monitoring results, budget development, new-technology assessment, recruiting and hiring, making customer calls, and in customer visits.[11] Many approaches can be used to encourage employee involvement. For example, some companies have found that having production workers visit customers helps them understand their role in customer satisfaction. Federal Express has call-in opportunities on the corporate television network to enable employees to interact with managers. Having employees rate the quality of suppliers' items (both external and internal) is another way of involving them in quality improvement. Leading companies do whatever they can to encourage upward communication throughout the company, such as having roundtable meetings with managers and open-door policies. At MamaMia's, employees might take note of food that is not eaten or special customer requests and meet together to discuss ways of better serving customers.

Perhaps the most specific way to encourage individual participation in operations management activities is to institute a **suggestion system.** Usually employees are rewarded for implemented suggestions. A suggestion system can inspire employees to think about ways to save costs, increase quality, or improve other elements of work such as safety while they are working. Thinking makes even routine work more enjoyable. Writing the suggestions down improves workers' reasoning ability and writing skills. Satisfaction results from seeing ideas implemented and the job made easier, safer, or better. Motivation is provided by the possibility of peer recognition and even monetary rewards. Also, just by thinking about ways to improve their work processes, workers gain an increased understanding of those processes that may lead to promotions and better interpersonal relationships in the workplace.

Suggestion systems, like most successful quality improvement methods, originated in the West but were refined in Japan. Most large Japanese firms and about half of the small and medium-size firms there have suggestion systems. At Toyota, for instance, nearly 3 million ideas a year are generated—an average of 60 per employee—and 85 percent are implemented by management. Some U.S. companies also are benefiting from suggestion systems. General Motors established a suggestion system over 50 years ago, and the Cadillac Division believes it is one of the secrets to its quality success. Cadillac asked teams of employees to tear apart the Seville and put it back together; the teams returned with 330 suggestions on how to improve the car. Cadillac commits to answering all suggestions within 24 hours; 70 percent of the suggestions received involve quality issues.

Nevertheless, suggestion systems seem to have relatively poor rates of participation in the United States in comparison with Japan. The overall participation rate in Japan exceeds 65 percent, and many companies such as Toyota have participation rates above 90 percent, but the typical rate in U.S. firms is only about 8 percent.[12] Experts estimate that the average number of suggestions per year made by employees in the U.S. automobile industry is only about 0.1. One of the reasons is that most U.S. suggestion systems are focused on obtaining ideas for significant cost savings and innovative procedures or products. They may not give fair consideration of suggestions that promise modest savings or gradual quality or productivity improvements over a longer period. Ideas that will save impressive sums of money are rare. Also, many U.S. managers typically take a passive approach to a suggestion system, waiting for employees to make the first move rather than prompting them and reminding them to be alert to new ideas. Moreover, typically many employees are restricted from making suggestions in their own work stations and are unable to find time outside their regular work schedules to develop ideas. In contrast, the Japanese have modified U.S. suggestion systems to fit their own culture, stressing participation and employee motivation over economic benefits. Japanese employees are encouraged to look for ways to accomplish on small, gradual, but continuous improvements. Also, management support in the United States is generally less than enthusiastic, in direct contrast to that in Japan, and American unions have not supported suggestion programs, especially when jobs might be at risk. In Japan, unions are company-based; thus, any activity that is good for the company is good for the union and its employees. Finally, the group-centered culture in Japan encourages cooperation rather than individual competition.

Teams

A **team** is a small number of people with complementary skills who are committed to a common purpose, set of performance goals, and approach for which they hold themselves mutually accountable.[13] Although organizations have traditionally been formed around task or work groups, the concept of teams and teamwork—which provide an integration of work groups—has taken the spotlight in TQM environments. Teams may perform a variety of problem-solving activities, such as determining customer needs, developing a flowchart to study a process, brainstorming to discover improvement opportunities, selecting projects, recommending corrective actions, and tracking the effectiveness of solutions. Problem solving is more effective in groups, because groups tend to facilitate more creative solutions. Teams also enhance esprit de corps among employees, thereby improving their attitudes and overall job satisfaction, as well as increasing their concern for productivity and quality. Teams may even assume many traditional managerial functions. For example, an assembly team at GM's Saturn plant interviews and hires its own workers, approves parts from suppliers, chooses its equipment, and handles its own budget.

The central role of teams, and the need for such team skills as cooperation, interpersonal communications, cross-training, and group decision making, represents a fundamental shift in how the work of public and private organizations is performed in the United States and most countries in the Western world. Results from an ASQC/Gallup telephone survey in 1993 of 1293 randomly selected full-time employed adults showed the prevalence and impact of teamwork.[14] Eight of 10 employees reported that some type of team activities were taking place at work, and two of three reported participating in team activities. Forty percent of those surveyed said that quality was the major goal of the teamwork; 22 percent said that efficiency and productivity were the major goals; 18 percent indicated that profitability or cost reduction was the goal; and 25 percent reported other goals or "don't know." Employees who participated in team activities or who worked in organizations with formal quality improvement programs were found to feel more empowered, were more satisfied with the rate of improvement in quality in their companies, and were much more likely to have received training on both job-related and problem-solving/team-building skills than other employees.

Among the most common types of teams are[15]

1. *Quality circles*—which meet regularly to address workplace problems involving quality and productivity (they are discussed in detail later).
2. *Problem-solving teams*—which are formed to solve a specific problem after which they disband.
3. *Management teams*—which consist mainly of managers from various functions such as sales and production that coordinate work among teams.
4. *Work teams*—which perform entire jobs, rather than specialized, assembly-line work. When work teams are empowered, they are called *self-managed teams* (discussed later in detail).
5. *Virtual teams*—the members of which communicate by computer, take turns as leaders, and join and leave the team as necessary.

Work teams and quality circles typically are intraorganizational; that is, members usually come from the same department or function (such as a kitchen team or server team at MamaMia's). Management teams, problem-solving teams, and virtual teams are cross-functional; they work on specific tasks or processes that cut across boundaries of several different departments regardless of their organizational home. Self-managed teams are the most advanced concept in teamwork. They are complex and vary greatly in how they are structured and how they function.

Leading companies, large and small, use all types of teams to improve quality and productivity. Federal Express has more than 4,000 "Quality Action Teams." More than 60 percent of Cadillac employees are members of some team. Granite Rock, with less than 400 people, has about 100 functioning teams, including 10 "Corporate Quality Teams," project teams, purchasing teams, task forces, and function teams composed of people who do the same job at different locations. Special efforts keep the teams relevant and make sure that no teams exist just for the sake of having them. Eastman Chemical Company involves its teams in developing objectives and measures that are integrated with company and organizational goals defined by the company's strategic planning process. Each supervisor belongs to at least two teams: the one made up of his or her direct subordinates and the team led by his or her immediate supervisor. Besides these "interlocking" teams, Eastman uses cross-functional process-improvement teams, process-management teams, internal customer/supplier partnership teams, focus groups, safety meetings, and employee surveys to promote involvement.

Problem solving drives the team concept. Teams identify, analyze, and solve quality and productivity problems. Problem-solving techniques are taught to members by team leaders with the assistance of a facilitator, who is a full-time or part-time resource person. New York Life has put the problem-solving function of teams to good use.

Applied P/OM:

New York Life

"Gravediggers" exemplify the power of teamwork in reducing costs at New York Life.[16]

Throughout the New York Life organization, teams with such unlikely names as Hot Pursuit, Watch Dogs, Just the Fax, French Connection, and Raiders of the Lost Transactions are streamlining operations. One of the most successful efforts is the work of an 18-person team formed to determine why 7,000 letters a week—primarily premium notices—were being returned by the post office as "undeliverable." Called the Gravediggers because of their focus on digging up addresses, the team, composed of employees from around the country, met weekly via teleconferences. Using problem-solving approaches, they discovered root causes such as policyholders moving and forgetting to notify the company, addresses that did not fit into the mailing envelope windows, addresses on applications that were difficult to read, and inadequate procedures for locating more accurate addresses. After a variety of corrective measures were implemented, the volume of returned mail was reduced by more than 20 percent, saving over $600,000 through bar coding and sorting.

The team concept in quality was developed and refined through quality circles in Japan and evolved to the powerful self-managed teams in evidence at many U.S. companies today. In the next two sections we examine these two types of team approaches.

Quality (Control) Circles.   The term *quality control circles (QCCs)* was coined in Japan in the early 1960s and brought to the United States in the early 1970s, where it took five years for the concept to begin to blossom. The term *quality control circles* was shortened some years ago to **quality circles** (QCs), which is in common use in the United States. These small groups of employees from the same work area meet regularly and voluntarily to identify, solve, and implement solutions to work-related problems. Quality circles typically range from four to 15 members whose supervisor usually, though not always, is the leader of the circle. The leader moderates discussion and promotes consensus while the circle members make their own decisions. Circle members receive training in group problem solving, running meetings, and making presentations. They choose their own problems, collect information, analyze the problems, and develop solutions that are presented to managers who make decisions on the recommendations.

Quality circles grew out of training the Japanese received in the 1950s from W. Edwards Deming and Joseph Juran. Essentially, the Japanese took American concepts of quality control and changed the organizational implementation according to the Japanese philosophy of relying on production workers for much of the necessary planning and creativity in production.

Circles employ brainstorming techniques for generating alternative solutions, look for causes of problems rather than just symptoms, make extensive use of statistical tools, and use visual aids to present their recommendations to managers. Organizationally, communications problems are reduced and resistance to change is minimized by quality circles. In addition, they foster a cooperative atmosphere, improve worker self-confidence, and encourage the development of leadership abilities. The ultimate result is improvement in quality and productivity.

When quality circles were introduced in the United States, many efforts failed and so the concept itself was criticized. Many managers had regarded quality circles as a panacea; thinking all they needed to do was to start them up and allow the workers to solve all organizational problems. The true cause of failure was the lack of management support, characterized by inadequate funding, lack of proper training, middle-management resistance, and lack of attention to implementation. Under such circumstances, circle workers quickly lost interest and initiative. To echo the philosophies of Deming and Juran, workers alone cannot solve problems that are management's responsibility.

Quality circles are still strong in Japan. Main reported that a 1988 survey in Japan found a nationwide total of 743,000 circles.[17] Toyota uses the problem-solving skills of circles and engineers to its advantage. When Toyota found that 50 percent of its warranty losses were caused by 120 large problems and 4,000 were due to small problems, it assigned the large problems to its engineers and the small ones to its quality circles.[18]

Self-Managed Teams.   Today many companies are moving beyond the traditional team approaches to problem solving and decision making and adopting the **self-managed team** (SMT), or self-directed work-team concept. In that participative-management approach, employees are encouraged to take on many of the roles formerly held only by managers. For employees in SMTs, the focus on quality and improvement shifts from a passive, management-initiated one to a highly active, independent one. The SMT has been defined as "a highly trained group of employees, from 6 to 18, on average, fully responsible for turning out a well-defined segment of finished work. The segment could be a final product, like a refrigerator or ball bearing; or a service, like a fully processed insurance claim. It could also be a complete but intermediate product or service, like a finished refrigerator motor, an aircraft fuselage, or the circuit plans for a television set."[19]

The SMT concept was developed in Britain and Sweden in the 1950s. One of the early companies to adopt SMTs was Volvo, the Swedish auto manufacturer. Pioneering efforts in SMT development were made by Procter & Gamble in 1962 and by General Motors in 1975. Those U.S. developments were concurrent with the Japanese quality-team developments, which in many cases could not be classified as true SMTs because of their limited autonomy. SMTs began to gain popularity in the United States in the late 1980s.

Among the features of SMTs are that they[20]

••• Share various management and leadership functions.

••• Plan, control, and improve their own work processes.

••• Set their own goals and inspect their own work.

••• Often create their own schedules and review their performance as a group.

••• Often prepare their own budgets and coordinate their work with other departments.

••• Usually order materials, keep inventories, and deal with suppliers.

••• Often are responsible for acquiring any new training they might need.

••• Often hire their own replacements or assume responsibility for disciplining their own members.

••• Take responsibility for the quality of their products and services.

Good results have been obtained from SMTs at AT&T.

Applied P/OM:
AT&T Credit Corporation

SMTs enrich jobs and improve results at AT&T.[21]

In most financial companies, the jobs in the back offices consist of processing applications, claims, and customer accounts. Such jobs are similar to manufacturing assembly lines: dull and repetitive. They represent the division of labor into small tasks and the organization of work by function that is characteristic of many service organizations. At AT&T Credit Corporation, which was established in 1985 to provide financing for customers who lease equipment, one department handled applications and checked the customer's credit standing, a second drew up contracts, and a third collected payments. No one person had responsibility for providing full service to a customer.

The company president decided to hire suitable employees and give them ownership of and accountability for the process. Although his first concern was to increase efficiency, his approach provided more rewarding jobs as an additional benefit. In 1986 the company set up 11 teams of 10 to 15 newly hired workers in a high-volume division serving small business. The three major lease-processing functions were combined in each team. The company also divided its national staff of field agents into seven regions and assigned two or three teams to handle business from each region. In that way, the same teams always worked with the same sales staff, establishing a personal relationship with them and their customers. Above all, team members took responsibility for solving customers' problems. Their slogan became, "Whoever gets the call owns the problem."

Members make most decisions on how to deal with customers, schedule their own time off, reassign work when people are absent, and interview prospective new employees. The teams process up to 800 lease applications daily, more than twice the number processed under the old system, and have reduced the time for final credit approvals from several days to within 24 to 48 hours.

Teams, especially self-managed teams, are changing traditional organizational structures dramatically. One example is General Electric's plant in Bayamon, Puerto Rico,[22] which makes surge protectors for electric power stations and transmission lines. It employs 172 hourly workers, 15 salaried "advisors," and one manager—a three-level hierarchy. The true organizational structure is process-focused. Every hourly worker is on a team that meets weekly.

Each team owns part of the work, such as assembly or shipping and receiving. Team members come from all areas of the plant, so the entire spectrum of operations is represented. Advisors speak up only when teams need help. To facilitate team development, workers change jobs every six months through four main work areas (getting pay raises with each rotation). They receive other raises and bonuses for skill improvements and meeting performance goals. In its first year, the plant became 20 percent more productive than its nearest equivalent on the mainland.

SMTs have many benefits, but implementation is not always easy. Significant barriers include insufficient training, supervisor resistance, incompatible organizational systems, and lack of planning or management support.

Recognition and Rewards

Many employees charged with additional quality-related responsibilities eventually ask, "What's in it for me?" Recognition and rewards answer that question. Rewards can be monetary or nonmonetary, formal or informal, individual or group. They tell employees that the organization values their efforts and they provide motivation to improve. Most important, they should lead to behaviors that increase customer satisfaction.

Intrinsic and extrinsic rewards are the key to sustained individual efforts. Intrinsic rewards are those supplied by the work itself. A well-designed job makes work intrinsically rewarding. On the other hand, a well-designed pay, benefit, and recognition system provides extrinsic motivation to employees. At the IRS, for example, employees are recognized for their accomplishments through newsletters, certificates and pins, awards breakfasts, and annual picnics. They are also given financial awards for suggestions and innovative ideas. Money is usually the most effective extrinsic reward, but it can have an intrinsic effect, too, since wages are an important determinant of individuals' psychological perception of their work. Employees who perceive their wages as inadequate tend to have low morale.

Wage incentives have been found to improve productivity without great capital investment, to reduce costs, to increase morale, and to improve supervisory effectiveness. Such incentives should reward employees for above-normal performance. One of the earliest and most widely used types of wage-incentive plans provides a salary increase or some type of cash bonus. Examples are commission and piece-rate incentive plans. Individual incentive or bonus plans attempt to tie pay directly to individual performance and are generally considered more effective than pay raises or salary increases in motivating employees.

A typical plan might be for a worker to earn an additional 1 percent for every 1 percent above the standard rate. For example, if an employee works at a rate of 117 percent during a week, she or he will be paid an additional 17 percent above the normal rate. Other plans, called *group incentive plans,* base incentive earnings on the average efficiency of a group of workers. This type of plan encourages cooperation among workers and it appears to be gaining wider acceptance by both employees and employers.

Many individuals believe that financial rewards are not effective motivators for changing behavior in work situations. However, they have been used extensively in business and industry, and their effectiveness is evident at Lincoln Electric Company.

Applied P/OM:

Lincoln Electric Company

Some companies find financial incentives improve productivity and increase employee morale.

Lincoln Electric Company in Cleveland, Ohio, a world leader in arc-welding equipment, initiated a bonus plan in 1934 based on the concepts that

1. Each employee's job security is fully protected.
2. Employees must see increased productivity reflected in increased take-home pay and job security.
3. Increased productivity and reduced costs are passed on to customers.
4. Management will continue to use earnings to develop the company and its market position.

Since 1934, the company has paid more in annual bonuses than in regular wages, and its employees are among the most productive and highest paid in the world.

Traditional incentive plans conflict with current philosophies such as TQM and just-in-time production. A popular alternative to traditional piecework incentives is **gainsharing,** whereby both employees and the company share in financial gains resulting from improved productivity and profitability. These programs are designed to motivate employees to improve their productivity through more effective use of labor, capital, and raw materials. Typically the current level of productivity is weighed against an established base level. Credit and compensation for improvements are shared equally between factory workers and managers. The emphasis is on group productivity as opposed to individual incentives, and the programs normally supplement rather than replace existing pay systems. Gainsharing systems are popular with factory workers because they provide for greater employee involvement. Their advantages include

- Improved productivity and quality.
- Improved quality of work life.
- Increases in the number of cost-saving ideas generated.
- Higher levels of teamwork and cooperation.
- Improved communication between labor and management.
- Increased employee-manager cooperation for improvement.
- Increased employee motivation.

In the absence of performance appraisal, compensation must be based on new criteria. Many TQM-focused companies now base their compensation on the market rate for an individual with proven capabilities and then increase the employee's wages and responsibilities as his or her capabilities increase. One company that exemplifies the new trends in compensation is Nucor Corporation.

Applied P/OM:

Nucor Corporation

Employees at Nucor Corporation earn significant bonuses for productivity and quality improvement.[23]

In 1988 workers at Nucor's nonunionized steel mills were earning base hourly rates of $5.80 to $9.02 per hour, less than half the average rate for unionized steel workers. Yet, because of productivity and quality bonuses, the average Nucor worker earned about $2,000 more per year than the average industry worker. Nucor was producing a ton of steel with less than four hours of labor, while comparable Japanese and other U.S. mills were requiring about five and six hours per ton, respectively. During downturns, Nucor managers' bonuses are often cut, although hourly workers continue to receive their productivity and quality bonuses, and Nucor has not had a layoff in current history. In 1983 when the United Steel Workers agreed to cuts in pay and benefits to improve the competitiveness of the U.S. steel industry, Nucor announced a 5 percent wage increase.

Some of the key practices for employee recognition and rewards include

1. *Giving both individual and team awards.* At the Ritz-Carlton Hotel Co., for example, individual awards include verbal and written praise and the most desirable job assignments. Team awards include bonus pools and sharing in the gratuity system.

2. *Involving everyone.* Recognition programs involve both front-line employees and senior managers. Solectron, for instance, rewards groups by buying lunch for entire divisions and bringing in ice cream for the entire plant.

3. *Tying rewards to quality based on measurable objectives.* Leading companies recognize and reward behavior, not just results. Many companies reward employees for participating in the suggestion program by providing cash awards for each implemented suggestion even before the suggestion brings results. Many rewards are linked to customer-satisfaction measures.

4. *Allowing peers and customers to nominate and recognize superior performance.* Texas Instruments, for example, has a Site Quality Award to recognize the top 2 percent of employees on the basis of peer nomination.

5. *Publicizing extensively.* At the IRS, team and individual recognition is publicized in a newsletter, certificates and pins are awarded for cooperative effort, and the Processing Division conducts an awards breakfast and end-of-year picnic at which contributors and teams are recognized.

6. *Making recognition fun.* Domino's Pizza stages a national "Olympics," in which teams from the company's three regions compete in 15 events based on 15 job categories, such as doughmaking, driving, answering the telephone, and delivery. The finals are broadcast live to commissaries around

the country, and winners attend three days of discussion with upper managers to explore what's good about the company, what needs improvement, and how improvements can be made.[24]

Training and Education

Training, particularly training related to quality improvement, is one of the largest initial costs in any company and, not surprisingly, one that many companies are reluctant to incur. However, training and education have become an important responsibility for companies that support employee empowerment, which entails acquisition of new knowledge and skills. Subjects addressed might include quality awareness, leadership, project management, communications, teamwork, problem solving, interpreting and using data, meeting customer requirements, process analysis, process simplification, waste reduction, cycle-time reduction, error-proofing, and other issues that affects employee effectiveness, efficiency, and safety. In many cases, training and education programs might include job-enrichment skills and job rotation that enhance employees' career opportunities. They might also cover basic skills such as reading, writing, language, and basic mathematics needed for quality and operational performance improvement.

Customer needs should drive training strategies. For example, customer-contact personnel might need a higher level of training in behavioral topics whereas manufacturing engineers need advanced statistical methods. At IBM Rochester managers tell the education department what they need, and programs are designed to meet those needs. By treating the training function as an internal supplier, the company reduced the time to deliver training programs from five days to two.

Companies committed to TQM invest more heavily in training than others. Motorola and Texas Instruments, for example, provide at least 40 hours of training to every employee. Cadillac sent more than 1,400 employees to a four-day Deming seminar at a cost of nearly $1 million. Leading companies have formal training departments that have evolved along with their overall quality systems. Training needs are identified jointly by employees and their supervisors.

P/OM in Practice

Job Enlargement and Job Enrichment at Toyota Motor Company[25]

Toyota Motor Company has long attempted to reduce cost, labor hours, and number of defects by increasing the number of suggestions from workers, promoting quality-control circles, and developing worker motivation. In the 1970s Toyota surveyed workers' desires and other factors affecting motivation at its Tsutsumi plant. Major workers desires identified were

••• To improve oneself through the present job.

••• To work optimistically in the shop, unconcerned with company objectives and aims.

••• To overcome various frustrations in the present job such as those caused by excessive direction from a supervisor and needless company regulations.

Three factors found to strongly influence motivation were rest time, job rotation, and the number of workers per group. The company also surveyed and analyzed job characteristics and working conditions in the plant. In response to the findings, an interesting production system focusing on behavioral characteristics was implemented in 1975.

Because of fluctuating demand for different models of cars, the work load in the various departments of the plant changes. When the work load of a particular department is low, it is desirable to transfer workers from that department to one with an increased work load. Thus, workers must be versatile and trained for many different operations. Toyota designed its production system to harmonize those company needs with workers desires.

For example, to enhance the workers' desire to improve themselves and

to overcome frustrations, the new system was designed to

• Enlarge the opportunity for workers to exhibit their abilities.

• Offer workers the opportunity to learn a wide variety of jobs without restriction.

• Allow workers to take breaks freely during working hours.

• Vary the number of workers in a group from 8 to 15, according to shop characteristics.

In the shop, whenever Worker A wants to take a break or perform another job, he signals the group leader or relief person by tapping him on the shoulder or calling to him. The group leader or relief person then moves to Worker A's workstation and does Worker A's job. While the leader is working, Worker A may rest or smoke a cigarette. After this break, he goes to another worker, B, and taps him on the shoulder or he calls for another worker who wants to take a break. If Worker B wants to rest, he follows the same procedure. Worker B moves from his workstation, and worker A does worker B's job. If worker B does not want to take a break, worker A goes to another worker, C, and signals to him with a tap on the shoulder. Worker C then moves from his workstation, and A takes his place. If Worker X wants a break, he calls to worker C, who then goes to X's workstation after his break. In that way, all workers change places until the last workers taps the leader or relief person on the shoulder, and the group leader or relief person then returns to his original position.

Experiments indicate that the rotation time for each group varies from one to one and one-half hours, depending on the size of the group. Thus, each worker learns several jobs,

and all workers are better able to rotate in their jobs freely.

Introducing this system required the effort of both the company and workers. For example, the company offered all workers who desired it the opportunity to master different jobs. Workers had to master a large number of jobs so that their group could accomplish its tasks.

After implementation of the system, productivity and quality increased, while at the same time workers' desires were satisfied. For instance, from 1974 to 1980, the percentage of operators with the ability to handle several different jobs increased from 40 to 95, the number of suggestions per year per worker increased from 14 to 50, defects were reduced almost by half, and the time needed to produce a car fell from 10.9 to 7.6 labor hours.

Questions for Discussion

1. In what ways did Toyota provide opportunities for workers to learn a variety of jobs?

2. Explain how workers can take breaks freely during working hours without disrupting operations.

3. How does the number of workers in a group affect the rotation time?

Taking Care of People at Federal Express[26]

"Take care of our people; they, in turn will deliver the impeccable service demanded by our customers, who will reward us with the profitability necessary to secure our future"— *Federal Express Manager's Guide.*. "People" is the first component of the Federal Express corporate philosophy: People—Service—Profit. Federal Express is dedicated to the principle that its employees are its "most important resource." Because the company believes in team effort and insists on an open atmosphere, it developed and refined a fair and equitable process for handling grievances, the Guaranteed Fair Treatment Procedure (GFTP). That process affirms an employee's right to appeal any eligible issue through a systematic review of progressively higher levels of management (see Figure 5.3), and provides an atmosphere for employees to discuss their complaints with managers without fear of retaliation. Employees can have their concerns addressed all the way up the management chain to the CEO, Frederick W. Smith, if necessary. In fact, Mr. Smith sits down every week with the executive vice-president, chief personnel officer, and two other senior VPs to review GFTP cases that have progressed to the final stage. Employees

are not assured of a judgement in their favor; however, the right to participate within the guidelines of the process is guaranteed.

One of the company's most effective quality tools is the Survey/Feedback/Action (SFA) program, which measures continuous leadership improvement. The program has been a part of the company's human resources commitment since 1980 and provides employee feedback about managers' effectiveness and overall satisfaction about the company. Once a year, every member within every workgroup anonymously participates in the survey. The first 10 questions assess the immediate manager's leadership abilities as perceived by their customers—the people in their workgroup. Some examples are

- • • My manager asks for my ideas about work.
- • • I can tell my manager what I think.
- • • My manager tells me when I do a good job.

Individual responses are kept confidential, but overall survey results are passed on to the managers, who must then schedule a feedback session with their employees. Managers are encouraged to use quality improvement techniques to develop solutions to the problems identified in the survey. An action plan is prepared and serves as an ongoing quality improvement guide for the issues identified during the feedback session. The results of the survey are then tallied into an overall corporate leadership score, which subsequently is used to diagnose corporate-wide

Figure 5.3
Federal Express Guaranteed
Fair Treatment Procedure
(GFTP)

Step 1   Management Review

- Employee has seven days in which to submit a GFT complaint. Management has 10 days to respond. An employee who doesn't agree with the decision has seven days to appeal.

  Over half of the GFTs filed are resolved in this first step.

Step 2   Officer Review

- May uphold the decision, overturn it, modify management's decision or initiate a Board of Review. Management has 10 days to render a decision. An employee who doesn't agree with the decision has seven days to appeal.

Step 3   Executive Review

- Five member Appeals Board
  Frederick W. Smith, CEO;
  William J. Razzouk, Executive Vice President;
  James A. Perkins, CPO; and
  Two officers assigned on a rotating basis.

- May uphold, overturn, or initiate a Board of Review. Decision must be rendered within 14 days. Employee receives written response within 3 calendar days of the decision.

leadership problems and as a benchmark for setting the following year's corporate "People" goal.

The Open Door Policy encourages employees to communicate their ideas and concerns directly to managers, even when the subject is controversial. However, unlike the GFTP, it has no time restrictions on filing and no limit to the number of Open Door issues an employee may file. If a manager receives an Open Door question, a response to the employee's inquiry must be handled as a top priority in accordance with the company's "People First" philosophy. The manager responding must also explain the reasoning behind his or her response.

Federal Express's widely dispersed work force needs timely information. One of the most effective methods of providing it is the company's satellite-linked television network, called FXTV. The special broadcasts, initiated to improve communication between senior managers and the employee population, provide front-line feedback vital to the quality improvement process. Employees are encouraged to call in during question-and-answer periods, which usually accompany all programs.

Federal Express uses a variety of formal reward and recognition programs to encourage excellence in both individual and team performance.

1. *Bravo Zulu Award.* The name is U.S. Navy jargon for "well done." Any manager can bestow this award on employees who have clearly gone above and beyond their job responsibilities.
2. *Golden Falcon Award.* This is the highest honor given to nonmanagement employees for outstanding customer service. Employees are recognized for demonstrating "exceptional performance achievements or unselfish acts that enhance customer service."
3. *Service Circle of Excellence Award.* On a monthly basis, Federal Express's highest-performing stations are reviewed for selection as winners of this award.
4. *Star/Superstar Program.* Individual employees with consistently high job performance can be recognized through the Star/Superstar Program, which provides a percentage of salary as a lump-sum cash award.

Training is a fundamental element of Federal Express's quality process. More than $225 million is spent annually on skills and recurrent training. All customer-contact people receive extensive training before they assume their jobs. For example, call-center agents participate in six weeks of training that includes lectures on fea-

tures of service, interactive videos, and role-playing sessions. Sales professionals receive extensive training emphasizing customer satisfaction. Finally, the Leadership Institute provides leadership training and development for managers.

The Quality Academy, established under the auspices of the Human Resources Development Department, assists in the continuing use of quality principles by educating participants about the processes and practical tools available to management and quality professionals. Courses include quality action teams, benchmarking, cycle-time reduction, facilitation skills, statistical process control, and an interactive video study. Generally, all employees can participate in these courses.

Questions for Discussion

1. Explain how human resources activities at Federal Express will help to achieve the "Service" and "Profit" components of the company's philosophy.
2. How do Federal Express's human resources management processes support the fundamental principles of TQM: customer focus, participation and teamwork, and continuous improvement?

Summary of Key Points

- The Taylor system of division of labor and job specialization has contributed to many of the problems that Western management faces today. Operations managers now face new challenges in designing jobs and managing the human resource to counteract these problems.
- The changing nature of jobs that has resulted from increased automation requires a highly trained and em-

powered work force and managers who function as coaches, teachers, and facilitators. Operations managers play a critical role in high-performance work systems by planning human resources strategies that are consistent with business goals, promoting individual and group participation, measuring employee satisfaction, and generally becoming better leaders.

- Leadership is the right to exercise authority and the ability to achieve results from inspiring and motivating people and groups of people under that authority.

Leaders set high expectations for others, motivate them to achieve goals, and build consensus within and among groups.

- Empowerment means giving someone the authority and power to make decisions so they can better satisfy customers without going through the delay of bureaucratic rules and procedures. Empowerment may threaten many managers who fear losing power and/or control, and it requires new responsibilities of them and of the workers under their purview. However, it builds worker confidence and can produce outstanding results.

- Job design involves determining the specific job tasks and responsibilities, the work environment, and the methods by which tasks will be carried out to meet production goals and make the job safe, satisfying, and motivating to the worker.

- The sociotechnical approach to job design considers both production technology and the work environment's physical and social aspects.

- Motivation theories suggest that effective job design ensures meaningful work, task identity, skill variety, autonomy, and feedback. Those job characteristics can be enhanced through job enlargement and enrichment, employee involvement, teamwork, training, and recognition and rewards.

- Teams can enhance quality and productivity. Types include quality circles, problem-solving teams, management teams, work teams, and virtual teams. Most companies use teams to tap into workers' knowledge and creativity for improving performance. Self-managed teams are growing in popularity, particularly as organizational structures "flatten" and workers assume increased responsibilities.

- Monetary and nonmonetary rewards along with fair compensation systems can motivate employees and reinforce individual and team efforts. Training and education are also highly motivating and are proven long-term investments in an organization's most important resource, people.

Key Terms

High-performance work systems
Leadership
Empowerment
Job
Job design
Sociotechnical approach
Job enlargement

Job enrichment
Suggestion system
Team
Quality circle
Self-managed team
Gainsharing

Review Questions

1. Explain why the Taylor system of scientific management has led to many of the problems the United States now faces in international competitiveness.
2. Explain the differences between the Taylor philosophy and modern thinking.
3. Summarize the changes taking place in the work environment and their implications for operations managers.
4. What can operations managers do to foster high-performance work systems?
5. Define *leadership*. Why is it an important attribute for operations managers?
6. Define *empowerment*, and discuss some of the issues that arise in operations management as empowerment becomes more important.
7. Define *job design*. How has management viewed job design since the Industrial Revolution?
8. Why is job design important in P/OM?
9. What aspects of the physical, social, and psychological environments are important in job design?
10. Describe Hackman and Oldham's model of motivation. What are its implications for job design?
11. Distinguish between job enlargement and job enrichment. Provide at least three examples of each.
12. How can participative approaches to problem solving improve productivity and quality?
13. Discuss the differences between U.S. and Japanese suggestion systems. What can managers do to make such systems successful?
14. Define *team*. How do teams help to improve productivity and quality?
15. Define the major types of teams that are common today.
16. Define *quality circles*. What are their benefits?
17. Why did quality circles initially fail in the United States? Relate your explanation to Deming's ideas discussed in Chapter 2.
18. Define *self-managed teams*. What benefits can SMTs provide an organization?
19. Describe individual and group wage-incentive plans. In your opinion, how important are wage incentives for increasing productivity and quality?
20. Describe some of the key practices relating to employee recognition and rewards.

21. Why are training and education important? What are some common P/OM topics taught in leading companies?

Discussion Questions

1. What types of activities might MamaMia's manager pursue to improve work design and the management of its people?

2. Interview some managers or research local companies to provide some examples of how the changing competitive environment is causing operations managers to change work systems.

3. Have any work-related changes occurred in your college or university recently? What prompted them? How do they differ from past practice?

4. Do you agree that the traditional notion of "job" is disappearing? What are the implications for our society?

5. What types of questions might employee-satisfaction surveys include? Design one for MamaMia's.

6. Provide some examples of leadership that you have experienced. How does leadership differ from management?

7. Give some examples of outstanding customer service you received from empowered employees. Were you surprised?

8. How might the concept of empowerment be applied in a classroom?

9. What is the job of a student? How might job-design concepts improve it?

10. Is fear a good motivator? Despite the fact that it is inconsistent with Deming's philosophy, can you think of any situations in which it might be appropriate?

11. How might job-enlargement and job-enrichment concepts apply to MamaMia's?

12. Study teamwork practices at a local company or nonprofit organization. What types of teams does it use? What difficulties has it encountered in implementing or operating those teams?

13. How important would nonmonetary recognition be to you? Would it make a difference in your motivation or performance? Why or why not?

Notes

1. James King, "Inner-City Manufacturer Proving It Can Be Made Better in America—for Less—Thanks to Its Workers," *Target*, Spring 1988, p. 25.

2. Alan Wolf, "Coors' Customer Focus," *Beverage World*, March 1991.

3. Alan Wolf, "Golden Opportunities," *Beverage World*, February 1991.

4. William Bridges, "The End of the Job," *Fortune*, September 19, 1994, pp. 62–74.

5. Peter T. Kilborn, "General Electric's Birthplace Reborn," *The Cincinnati Enquirer*, September 12, 1993, p. E1.

6. James R. Healey, "Eaton Shifts Chrysler Meeting to Focus on Quality," *USA Today*, June 28, 1994, p. 1B.

7. J.M. Juran, *Juran on Leadership for Quality: An Executive Handbook* (New York: The Free Press, 1989) p. 264.

8. Phillip A. Smith, William D. Anderson, and Stanley A. Brooking, "Employee Empowerment: A Case Study," *Production and Inventory Management* 34, no. 3 (Third Quarter, 1993), pp. 45–50.

9. AT&T Quality Steering Committee, *Great Performances*, AT&T Bell Laboratories, 1991, p. 39; and William Smitley and David Scott, "Empowerment: Unlocking the Potential of Your Work Force, *Quality Digest* 14, no. 8 (August 1994), pp. 40–46.

10. Robert S. Kaplan, "Texas Eastman Company," Harvard Business School Case, No. 9 190-039.

11. Tom J. Peters, *Thriving on Chaos: Handbook for a Management Revolution* (New York: Alfred A. Knopf, 1988).

12. Karen L. Muse and Mark P. Finster, "A Comparison of Employee Suggestion Systems in Japan and the USA," *University of Wisconsin Working Paper*, 1989.

13. Jon R. Katzenback and Douglas K. Smith, "The Discipline of Teams," *Harvard Business Review*, March–April 1993, pp. 111–120.

14. John Ryan, "Employees Speak on Quality in ASQC/ Gallup Survey," *Quality Progress*, December 1993, pp. 51–53.

15. Brian Dumaine, "The Trouble with Teams," *Fortune*, September 5, 1994, pp. 86–92.

16. "Gravedigging at New York Life," *Fortune*, September 21, 1992, advertisement.

17. Jeremy Main, *Quality Wars* (New York: The Free Press, 1994), p. 62.

18. Ibid.

19. Jack D. Orsburn, Linda Moran, Ed Musselwhite, and John H. Zenger, *Self-Directed Work Teams* (Homewood, IL: Business One–Irwin, 1990), p. 8.

20. Richard S. Wellins, William C. Byham, and Jeanne M. Wilson, *Empowered Teams* (San Francisco: Jossey-Bass, 1991).

21. Adapted from "Benefits for the Back Office, Too," *Business Week*, July 10, 1989, p. 59.

22. "The Search for the Organization of Tomorrow," *Fortune*, May 18, 1993, pp. 91–98.

23. Nancy J. Perry, "Here Comes Richer, Riskier Pay Plans," *Fortune*, December 19, 1988, pp. 50–58.

24. "Domino's Pizza, Inc.," in *Profiles in Quality* (Boston: Allyn and Bacon, 1991), pp. 90–93.

25. Adapted from R. Muramatsu, H. Miyazaki, and K. Ishii, "A Successful Application of Job Enlargement/Enrichment at Toyota." *IIE Transactions* 19, no. 4 (1987), pp. 451–459. Copyright Institute of Industrial Engineers, 25 Technology Park/Atlanta, Norcross, GA 30092.

26. Adapted from *Federal Express Corporation Quality Profile*, Federal Express Corporation, 2005 Corporate Avenue, Memphis, TN 38132. Used with permission.

Strategic issues are ones that affect an organization for a long period of time. Three major strategic issues for operations managers are developing new products, planning operations capacity, and configuring distribution systems. Chapter 6 discusses approaches to product design and development, focusing on their impact on operations. The impact of product design on quality and operations performance is a major theme of the chapter.

Chapter 7 describes the planning necessary to ensure that an organization has the resources it needs for accomplishing its production goals. Such planning depends heavily on accurate forecasting, a topic introduced in this chapter. The chapter appendix presents a variety of quantitative approaches for forecasting.

Chapter 8 discusses facility location and the design of distribution systems. It explains how location decisions can help an organization achieve its production and strategic objectives.

Part II
Strategic Issues in Operations

Chapter Six
Product Design and Development

Perhaps the most important strategic decisions for a firm involve the selection and development of new products and services. In fact, decisions about what products and services to offer and how to position them in the marketplace determine the growth, profitability, and future direction of the firm. A business such as MamaMia's Pizza operates in a highly competitive environment. Competitors have introduced giant-size party pizzas; gourmet pizzas such as Mexican, seafood, and Cajun; new items such as spicy chicken wings; and guaranteed fast delivery. MamaMia's managers must pay constant attention to consumer needs and expectations to continually introduce new products or services that delight its customers. A firm can achieve a significant competitive advantage by having products that are more appealing, reliable, easy to operate, or economical to service than others.

A superior product, however, is not the sole criterion for product design. Products also must be manufactured efficiently and economically. This is where operations management can make substantial contributions to the product-design process. It can bring superior products to market faster and reduce their cost. For products in which parts alone are 65 to 80 percent of the manufacturing cost, design may account for 90 percent or more of the total manufacturing cost. The cost of replacing a poorly designed component in the field can be a thousand times greater than that of changing specifications during the design process.

The operations function is responsible for designing and implementing the production/delivery process for the product. Thus, operations managers must be closely involved in the entire design process. A simple design generally results in ease of assembly, which reduces the assembly time and requires smaller inventories. Key strategic criteria—productivity, quality, and flexibility—all improve while costs are reduced.

This chapter specifically addresses

••• The importance of design from a strategic perspective and the product-development process.

••• Approaches for incorporating customer needs and expectations into the design process.

••• Techniques for ensuring high quality and reliability.

••• Methods for improving the manufacturability of products and reducing product-development time.

••• Approaches to designing services.

Product Decisions and Business Strategy

The decision to develop new products is an important strategic decision that can make or break a firm in a highly competitive market. The Schwinn Bicycle Company case illustrates the implications of a poor product-development strategy.

Applied P/OM

Schwinn Bicycle Company

Schwinn misses an opportunity in product design.[1]

The name Schwinn has been synonymous with bicycles for most of this century. Through its network of independent dealers, Schwinn sold one of every four bicycles in 1950; by 1975 it sold only one in ten. By the late 1970s, Schwinn's market share had dropped below 8 percent. The Schwinn-trademark bicycles, with their distinctive balloon tires, coaster brakes, and black and gold fenders, were displaced by lighter, faster, sleeker, or cheaper bikes made by foreign and domestic competitors. Analysts suggest that the firm lost its competitive advantage in the late 1970s and early 1980s when it resisted changing its traditionally heavier bike line to lighter bicycles and mountain bikes, which made up about 70 percent of sales in 1992. In other words, the company failed to respond to an emerging customer need (or desire).

In late 1992 Schwinn, a privately held company, filed for protection under Chapter 11 of the federal bankruptcy code. Since then, the company has changed its product line to lighter, sleeker-looking bicycles and is employing new technologies in manufacturing. In addition, it is upgrading its health and physical-fitness products line, which accounts for about 25 percent of its business.

P/OM Issues in Product Strategy

Basically, a firm can produce three types of products: custom products, option-oriented products, and standard products.[2] *Custom products,* generally made in small quantities, are designed to meet customers' specifications. The production cost is relatively high, and quality assurance requires careful attention at every step in the manufacturing process. Since custom products are produced only on demand, the customer must wait for the product to be made. Customers probably would not request custom food items at a restaurant like MamaMia's. However, in organizations that cater to customers' personal desires, such as cruise ships or at a Ritz-Carlton hotel, it would not be unusual for the chefs to prepare specific food items on request.

Option-oriented products are unique configurations of subassemblies that are designed to fit together. The customer participates in choosing the options to be assembled. The subassemblies are made in relatively large quantities; therefore costs are reduced and quality is easier to achieve because of repetition. Since the manufacturer cannot anticipate all of the configurations a customer may desire, though, the customer must wait while the product is assembled to the desired configuration. Individual pizza orders can be considered option-oriented products; the "subassemblies"—dough, toppings, and so on— can be prepared ahead of time.

Standard products are made in larger quantities. The customer has no options from which to choose, and quality is easiest to achieve with these products because they are made the same way every time. Salads and chicken wings are examples of standard products that might be found at MamaMia's. Since the manufacturer makes standard products in anticipation of customer demand, the customer will have to wait for the product only if it is out of stock.

Standard products offer many advantages. They can be mass-produced on assembly lines very efficiently. With fewer different parts to purchase, make, and assemble, quality is generally higher. In addition, standard products simplify purchasing and customer service. For example, orders of components will be more consistent in terms of what is ordered, and shipments can be scheduled more frequently, resulting in lower inventories. The disadvantage of standard products is that they offer little flexibility in meeting changing customer needs.

In the fast-food industry, these strategic choices are exemplified in the competition between McDonald's, which produces a standard product and achieves an advantage in terms of service delivery, and Burger King and Wendy's, which produce option-oriented products requiring longer food-preparation time that reduces service speed. Neither the standard nor the option-oriented approach is necessarily better; each firm must decide what strategic trade-offs are best.

Many products begin as custom products and over time become standard products. The ability to guide products along this progression can determine a company's success. Henry Ford, for example, was one of the first to standardize production of the automobile. Later, however, consumers demanded more variety of options, and the American automobile evolved into the classic option-oriented product. Customers can now choose from dozens of colors, seat types, engines, transmissions, tires, and other options. The number of possible configurations can easily grow into the hundreds of thousands. A proliferation of options results in higher inventories, increased difficulty of scheduling, and other operations management problems. Automobile manufacturers therefore are seeking to streamline their designs and reduce the number of options offered to customers. For instance, General Motors once installed 65 different turn-signal levers in its cars. It reduced the number of levers to 26 by 1994 and now has a target of no more than eight.

Some automobile manufacturers, particularly in the low-end and luxury markets, have not only drastically reduced options, but have arranged for some of them to be installed by the dealer rather than in the manufacturing plant. Flexibility is achieved by offering several model variations of the same car and frequent design changes. The Japanese can produce up to seven models on a single production line. Most U.S. manufacturers' production lines are dedicated to a single model. General Motors, however, has embarked on a "common parts/common systems" strategy that seeks to reduce the number of basic U.S. car designs from 12 to five by the end of the century. Likewise, Toyota and other Japanese manufacturers are seeking to reduce the number of different parts in their cars.[3]

Product-Development Process

When W. Edwards Deming lectured to Japanese managers, he contrasted the "old way" of product development—(1) design it, (2) make it, and (3) try to sell it—with a "new way":[4]

1. Design the product (with appropriate tests).
2. Make it, and test it in the production line and in the laboratory.
3. Put in on the market.
4. Test it in service through market research. Find out what the user thinks of it, and why the nonuser has not bought it.
5. Redesign the product in light of consumer reactions to quality and price.

Modern product-development processes capture that basic philosophy by their heavy emphasis on consumer research and product testing and refinement. Figure 6.1 shows the typical **product-development process,** consisting of idea generation, concept development, product/process development, full-scale production, and finally product introduction and evaluation. The figure shows the process for a manufactured product, but similar steps are followed in developing new services.

Following such a process is certainly no guarantee of success, since products may fail because of external influences such as competition or economic factors. However, most failures are the result of ineffective planning, a problem the product-development process is designed to solve. Let us examine each step in detail.

Idea Generation

Ideas for new products can arise from a variety of sources internal and external to the firm. Many ideas come from customers or from employees. More often than not, however, new-product ideas are developed through systematic research within the firm.

Such research begins with listening to the **voice of the customer**—what customers say they want. Obviously, consumers want products that are affordable, easy to install and operate, perform to expectations, reliable and durable, have well-documented instructions, and are easy to fix and maintain. But in addition they want products to have some very specific features. For example, they might want a pizza to be "tasty," or a portable stereo to have "good sound quality." An important part of the product-development process—and a central

Figure 6.1
Structured Product-
Development Process

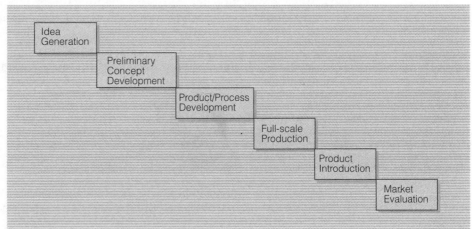

theme of the Deming quality philosophy—is market evaluation of customer perceptions to discern these customer desires, which should lead to continuous improvements in products as well as new-product ideas. Perdue Farms has pursued that philosophy to good effect.

Applied P/OM

Perdue Farms

Understanding customer needs and using that information to improve competitiveness is important to Frank Perdue's chicken business.[5]

Frank Perdue set out to discover customers' key purchase criteria for chicken. They included a yellow bird, high meat-to-bone ratio, no pinfeathers, freshness, availability, and brand image. He also determined the relative importance of each criterion, and how well the company and its competitors were meeting each of them. By systematically improving his ability to meet customers' criteria relative to the competition, Perdue gained market share even though his chickens were premium-priced. Among Perdue's innovations was the purchase of a used jet engine to dry the chickens so that all pinfeathers could be singed off!

Just listening to the voice of the customer is not enough, however. A Japanese professor, Noriaki Kano, identifies three classes of customer needs or wants:

1. *Dissatisfiers*—features that are expected in a product or service and therefore produce dissatisfaction if they are absent. In an automobile, a radio, a heater, and the required safety features are examples. They are assumed to be givens, and customers do not feel it necessary to specifically request them.

2. *Satisfiers*—features that customers specifically request for full satisfaction. Air-conditioning and a compact-disc player are examples for an automobile.

3. *Exciters/delighters*—innovative features that customers would not expect, and might not even know exist, but that they like. Airbags and antilock brakes were examples when first introduced. Computerized navigation systems, which Avis began testing in 1994, might become a true exciter/delighter.

The importance of these classifications is that, while "satisfiers" are relatively easy to determine through routine marketing research, it takes special effort to anticipate customer perceptions about "dissatisfiers" and "exciters/delighters." Over time, exciters/delighters become satisfiers as customers become used to them, and eventually satisfiers become dissatisfiers. Automobile airbags, for example, have become satisfiers, if not dissatisfiers, for most people. Thus, companies must continually study customer wants to ensure they are providing all three classifications of features.

The development and application of new technology to meet customer needs is the role of **research and development (R&D).** R&D efforts are focused on creating a new product, extending product and/or process life by improvements, and ensuring safety of the product or process for employees, users, and

Table 6.1 Fundamental Questions for Screening New-Product Ideas

Criteria	Fundamental Questions
Product development	Is the product new or simply an imitation? Can we produce it with existing facilities? Is it technically feasible? Will there be an patent or other legal problems?
Market	What is the current market for this product? Is it expected to grow? What is the competition? How will this product affect our existing product line?
Financial	What will the return on investment be? How will this product contribute to our overall profitability? How will development and production affect our cash flow?

the environment. R&D is costly because it requires expensive equipment and highly qualified personnel. In addition, high risk is involved. For each successful R&D project, there are many failures. Nonetheless, the average payoff from the small number of successes can far outweigh the investment loss from the unsuccessful projects.

Concept Development

New ideas must be studied for feasibility; that is done in the concept-development phase. Companies perform initial screenings and economic analyses to determine the market potential and financial impacts of new ideas and eliminate ones that do not appear to have a high potential for success, thus avoiding excessive development costs. Many ideas are rejected immediately because of marketing factors, because they are technically infeasible, or because they are impractical to produce. Others are eliminated because of budgetary considerations or because they do not meet corporate goals and objectives. Product ideas that survive an initial screening may be eliminated later during a formal economic analysis or even during later product-development stages because of new technological discoveries or production problems that cannot be economically corrected.

Table 6.1 lists the fundamental questions considered for each of the major criteria used in initial screening. To develop a quantitative assessment of product success based on those criteria, a **scoring model** is often used. Each criterion is broken down into a set of attributes. Several levels for each attribute are determined, and a value or score is assigned to each. The score assigned each level reflects the relative benefits of that level. The actual scores chosen are usually the result of analyses by operations managers.

Example : ## Using a Scoring Model for New-Product Justification

Power Fitness, Inc. is thinking of introducing a new aerobic exercise machine. A scoring model for this product idea is shown in Table 6.2. Knowledgeable experts within the organization choose specific values for each level. Summing the maximum and minimum scores for all attributes within each criterion yields the results shown in Table 6.3.

These rather rough estimates show that the new-product idea ranks high on product-development criteria, average on market criteria, and high on financial criteria.

Table 6.2 Scoring Model Example

Criterion	Level	Score	
Product Development			
1. Development time	Less than 6 months	√	+2
	6 months to 1 year	____	+1
	1–2 years	____	−1
	More than 2 years	____	−2
2. Experience	Considerable	____	+2
	Some	____	+1
	Little	√	−1
	None	____	−2
3. Length of product life	More than 8 years	√	+2
	5–8 years	____	+1
	3–5 years	____	−1
	3 or less	____	−2
4. Materials	Available inside firm	____	+2
	Available outside	√	+1
	Limited availability inside	____	−1
	Limited availability outside	____	−2
5. Equipment	Present equipment usable	____	+2
	Some new equipment	√	+1
	Mostly new equipment	____	−1
	New production facility	____	−2
Market			
6. Marketability	Current customers	____	+2
	Mostly current customers	√	+1
	Some current customers	____	−1
	All new customers	____	−2
7. Stability	Highly stable	√	+2
	Fairly stable	____	+1
	Unsteady	____	−1
	Highly volatile	____	−2
8. Trend	New market	____	+2
	Growing	√	+1
	Stationary	____	−1
	Decreasing	____	−2
9. Advertising	Little required	____	+2
	Moderate requirements	____	+1
	High requirements	____	−1
	Extensive	√	−2
10. Competition	None	____	+2
	One or two competitors	____	+1
	Several competitors	√	−1
	Many competitors	____	−2

(continued)

Table 6.2 Scoring Model Example (continued)

Criterion	Level		Score
11. Demand	Stable	_____	+2
	Subject to business cycle	_____	+1
	Seasonal	✓	−1
	Seasonal and subject to business cycle	_____	−2
Financial			
12. Return on investment	30% or more	✓	+2
	25%–30%	_____	+1
	20%–25%	_____	−1
	Less than 20%	_____	−2
13. Capital Outlay	Low	_____	+2
	Moderate	✓	+1
	High	_____	−1
	Extensive	_____	−2

Table 6.3 Results of Scoring Model Example

Criterion	Maximum Possible Score	Minimum Possible Score	Total Score
Product Development	+10	−10	+5
Market	+12	−12	0
Financial	+ 4	− 4	+3
			+8

In this example, all attributes of all criteria are assumed to have equal importance. That assumption can easily be modified by weighing the values. For example, if return on investment is believed to be twice as important as capital outlay, the scores for return on investment could be multiplied by 2 in Table 6.2.

Scoring models provide a rough, quantitative measurement of product potential. The purpose of *economic analysis* is to determine more specific quantitative measures of profitability and return on investment as a basis for deciding whether or not to commit further resources toward development of an idea. Such an analysis requires an accurate estimate of demand, usually obtained through forecasting. Market-research personnel have considerable experience in sales estimation and can usually provide this information. Forecasting is discussed further in the next chapter.

In addition to demand forecasts, estimates of production costs must be obtained and the selling price of the product must be estimated. Break-even analysis is a useful tool for estimating the economic impact of a new product.

Example

Break-Even Analysis for New-Product Justification

Let us illustrate the use of break-even analysis for Power Fitness, Inc. Suppose the marketing department estimates that 4,000 units can be sold on an annual basis. The estimate is based on current trends in the industry and sales projections. The engineering and accounting departments have estimated that production costs would be as follows.

Variable costs per unit	
Manufacturing	$55
Selling and administrative	5
Total variable costs	$60
Fixed costs	
Manufacturing	$350,000
Selling and administrative	100,000
Total fixed costs	$450,000

Competitive products are priced from $100 to $250. To capture the projected share of the market, the company would like to keep the selling price at $150. If we let S represent total sales, the total cost (TC) is estimated to be

$$TC = 450,000 + 60S.$$

At a selling price of $150, the total revenue ($TR$) would be

$$TR = 150S,$$

yielding the break-even point:

$$450,000 + 60S = 150S$$
$$90S = 450,000$$
$$S = 5,000.$$

Figure 6.2 is a spreadsheet for this analysis. Since annual sales are estimated to be 4,000 units, the break-even point of 5,000 units will be reached after the product is on the market 15 months. Because the life cycle of this product is relatively long, this analysis indicates a sound investment.

Figure 6.2
Spreadsheet for Break-Even Analysis (POWERFIT.XLS)

	A	B	C	D	E	F	G	H
1	Power Fitness, Inc.							
2								
3	Fixed cost	$ 450,000						
4	Variable cost	$ 60						
5	Selling price	$ 150						
6								
7	Sales quantity	Total revenue	Total cost	Total profit				
8	4000	$ 600,000	$ 690,000	$ (90,000)				
9	4250	$ 637,500	$ 705,000	$ (67,500)				
10	4500	$ 675,000	$ 720,000	$ (45,000)				
11	4750	$ 712,500	$ 735,000	$ (22,500)				
12	5000	$ 750,000	$ 750,000	$ -				
13	5250	$ 787,500	$ 765,000	$ 22,500				
14	5500	$ 825,000	$ 780,000	$ 45,000				
15	5750	$ 862,500	$ 795,000	$ 67,500				
16	6000	$ 900,000	$ 810,000	$ 90,000				
17								

Product Design

For manufactured goods, the design process begins by determining specifications for all materials, components, and parts. Specifications consist of nominal (or target) values and tolerances. The **nominal specifications,** sometimes called *product parameters,* determine the functional ability and performance characteristics of the product. **Tolerances** specify the precision required to achieve the desired performance. Tolerances are necessary because of natural variation in the outputs of any production process. For a MamaMia's pizza, specifications might indicate the weight of cheese and meat on each pizza. The amount of cheese on a small pizza might be specified as 10 ±0.5 ounces.

In determining design specifications, designers must take into account both technical requirements and economics. Materials, for example, must be chosen to satisfy the functional requirements of the product. Certain materials can be machined to much closer tolerances than others; different materials may require different manufacturing methods.

Designers also have to consider the costs of manufacturing and distributing the product so that it can be priced competitively. Products are targeted toward specific markets. Mercedes-Benz automobiles, for example, are marketed to individuals with high income, while many other models of automobiles are marketed to individuals with average income. It would make little sense for a company to design a product for mass consumer appeal if the costs of manufacturing and distributing the product are very high.

Testing and Refinement

Product development includes *prototype testing,* in which a model (real or simulated) is constructed to test the product's physical properties or use under actual operating conditions. Such testing might include performance tests, stress tests, environmental tests, wear-out tests, and other reliability tests. Road-testing an automobile or using a consumer panel to test a new pizza are some examples. Such testing is important in uncovering any problems and correcting them prior to full-scale production. In addition, companies must test the processes used in manufacturing. As Deming and Juran both advocate, the testing process should continue even after the product is introduced to the marketplace. Market evaluations and customer feedback should be used to initiate continuous improvements.

Customer-Driven Design

The voice of the customer should drive the design process. Extensive research and analysis about customer needs and expectations is essential. In the past, product specifications were identified by engineers and managers according to what they thought customers wanted, and often their perceptions of consumer desires were inaccurate. Figure 6.3 summarizes the process of using information on what customers want as the basis for producing the desired product or service. Technical specifications for design quality represent managers' percep-

Figure 6.3
The Customer-Perceived-
Quality Focus of Product
Design

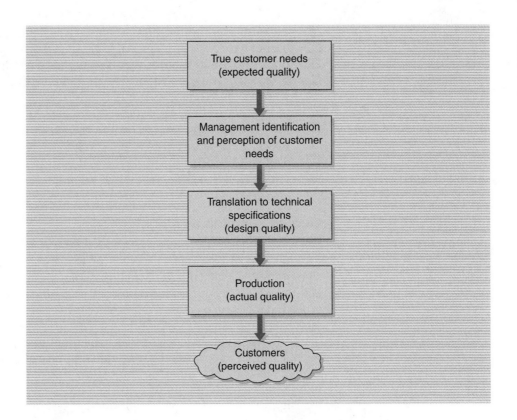

tion of customer requirements and may not always be translated into the actual
quality achieved by production. Moreover, customers' perceptions of a product's quality may not match the actual quality because of biases developed by
brand image, advertising, and experience with competing products.

Perceived quality is the difference between *expected quality* and *actual
quality.* If actual quality is higher than expected quality, customers will be pleas-
antly surprised. If actual quality is lower than expected quality, they will be dissatisfied. Therefore, it is essential to find out what customer expectations are.
Ames Rubber Company does so by involving customers in the product-development process.

Applied P/OM

Ames Rubber Company

*Product-development personnel at Ames maintain close communica-
tion with the customer.[6]*

Ames Rubber Company, a producer of rubber rollers for office machines and a Malcolm Baldrige National Quality Award winner, uses a four-
step approach to product development. Typically, a new product is initiated through a series of meetings with the customer and Sales/Marketing
or Technical Services Group. From those meetings, a product brief is prepared listing all technical, material, and operational requirements. It is

forwarded to internal departments, such as Engineering, Quality, and Manufacturing. The technical staff then selects materials, processes, and procedures, and submits them to the customer. Upon the customer's approval, a prototype is made. The prototype is delivered to the customer, who evaluates and tests it, and reports results to Ames. Ames makes any modifications that are requested, and the prototype is returned to the customer for further testing. The process continues until the customer is completely satisfied. Next, a limited pre-production run is made, and data collected during the run are analyzed and shared with the customer. Upon approval, full-scale production is initiated.

Quality Function Deployment

Another effective approach for ensuring that customer needs are met in the design process is called **quality function deployment (QFD).** Developed by the Japanese, QFD is both a philosophy and a set of planning and communication tools that focus on customer requirements in coordinating the design, manufacturing, and marketing of goods.

QFD represents a departure from the traditional product-planning process in which product concepts are originated by design teams or R&D groups and then are tested and refined, produced, and marketed. Such a process typically relies little on customer input, and often much effort and time must be spent redesigning the product and its production systems to "get it right." QFD alleviates those problems.

A major benefit of QFD is improved communication and teamwork among all constituencies in the production process—such as between marketing and design, design and manufacturing, and purchasing and suppliers—which prevents misinterpretation of product objectives during the production process. Also, QFD helps to determine the causes of customer dissatisfaction, and it is a useful tool for competitive analysis of product quality by top managers. Productivity as well as quality improvements result. Most significantly, the time for new product development is reduced. QFD allows companies to simulate the effects of new design ideas and concepts, thus enabling companies to gain competitive advantage by bringing new products into the market sooner.

The basis of QFD is the translation of customer requirements (the "whats") into the appropriate technical requirements (the "hows") for each stage of product development and production. The process is initiated with a matrix, which because of its structure (shown in Figure 6.4) is often called the **House of Quality.**

The process begins by identifying the voice of the customer and technical features of the design. For the voice of the customer to be effective, it is important to use the customer's own words; designers and engineers may misquote them. The technical features, however, must be expressed in the language of the designer and engineer and form the basis for subsequent design, manufacturing, and service process activities.

The roof of the House of Quality shows the interrelationships between any pair of technical features. Various symbols are used to denote the strength of the relationships, as shown in Figure 6.5, and the relationships help in answering questions such as, "How does a change in one product characteristics affect others?" and in assessing tradeoffs between characteristics. Features can be examined collectively rather than individually.

Figure 6.4
The House of Quality

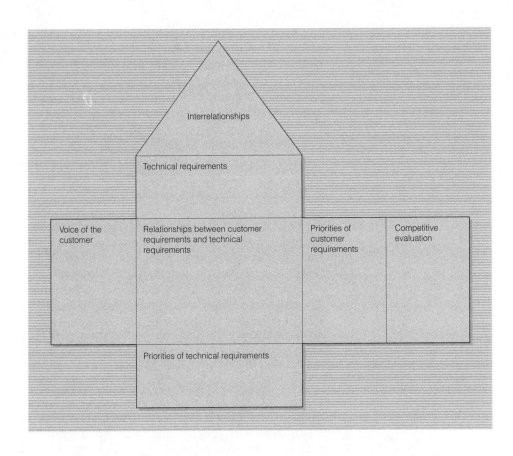

Figure 6.5
House of Quality Example
for MamaMia's Restaurant

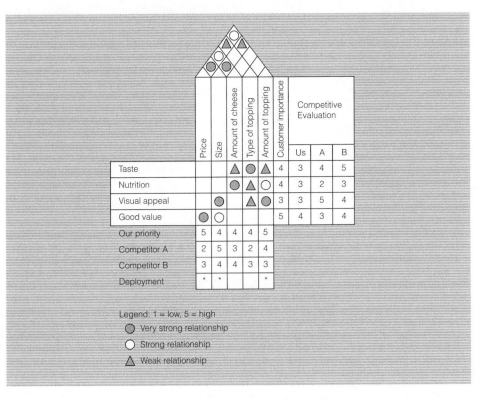

Next, a relationship matrix between the customer requirements and the technical features is developed (see Figure 6.5), which shows whether the final technical features adequately address the customer attributes, an assessment that may be based on expert experience, customer responses, or controlled experiments. The lack of a strong relationship between a customer attribute and any of the technical features would suggest that the final product will have difficulty in meeting customer needs. Similarly, if a technical feature does not affect any customer attribute, it may be redundant.

The next step is to add market evaluation and key selling points. It includes rating the importance of each customer attribute and evaluating existing products on each of the attributes to highlight the absolute strengths and weaknesses of competing products. This step links QFD to a company's strategic vision and allows priorities to be set in the design process. For example, if an attribute receives a low evaluation on all competitors' products, focusing on that attribute can help to gain a competitive advantage. Such attributes become key selling points and help in establishing promotion strategies.

Next, technical features of competitive products are evaluated and targets are developed. These evaluations are compared with the competitive evaluation of customer attributes to spot any inconsistency between customer evaluations and technical evaluations. On the basis of customer-importance ratings and existing product strengths and weaknesses, targets for each technical feature are set.

The final step is to select technical features that have a strong relationship to customer needs, have poor competitive performance, or are strong selling points. Those characteristics will need to be "deployed," or translated into the language of each function in the design and production process, so that proper actions and controls are taken to ensure that the voice of the customer is maintained. Characteristics that are not identified as critical do not need such rigorous attention.

The example of a house of quality in Figure 6.5 is for MamaMia's attempt to develop a "signature" pizza. The voice of the customer in this case consists of four attributes. The pizza should be tasty, be healthy, be visually appealing, and should provide good value.

The "technical features" that can be designed into this particular product are price, size, amount of cheese, type of additional toppings, and amount of additional toppings. The symbols in the matrix in Figure 6.5 show the relationships between each customer requirement and technical feature. For example, taste bears a moderate relationship with amount of cheese and a strong relationship with type of additional toppings. In the roof, price and size area seen to be strongly related (as size increases, the price must increase). The competitive evaluation shows that competitors are currently weak on nutrition and value, so those attributes can become key selling points in a marketing plan if the restaurant can capitalize on them. Finally, at the bottom of the house are targets for the technical features based on an analysis of customer importance ratings and competitive ratings. The features with asterisks are the ones to be "deployed," or emphasized in subsequent design and production activities.

The House of Quality gives marketing an important tool to understand customer needs and gives top managers strategic direction. However, it is only the first step in the QFD process. Three other houses of quality are used to carry the voice of the customer to component-parts characteristics, process planning, and production planning decisions. Advanced books on QFD should be consulted for more information.

Design for Quality and Reliability

During the 1980s the quality revolution awakened companies to the importance of designing quality into products and services rather than simply trying to weed out defects or recover from service errors. Now the complexity of modern products has heightened the importance of quality in design. "Traditional" products such as bicycles, hand tools, and hydraulic pumps have far simpler designs and manufacturing processes than the "modern" products of recent technology that incorporate sophisticated electronics. For instance, a single state-of-the-art integrated circuit may involve more than 200 manufacturing steps.

Many aspects of product design can adversely affect both quality and productivity.[7] Parts are sometimes designed with features that are difficult to fabricate repeatedly or with tolerances that are unnecessarily tight. Some parts lack details for self-alignment or features that prevent insertion in the wrong orientation. In other cases, parts are so fragile or so susceptible to corrosion or contamination that some of them are damaged in shipping or by internal handling. Sometimes, because of lack of refinement, a design simply has more parts than are really needed to perform the desired functions, so the chance of assembly error is increased. Thus, problems of poor design can show up as errors, poor yield, damage, or functional failure in fabrication, assembly, test, transport, and end use. Table 6.4 illustrates design guidelines for improving quality, yield, and cost.

Robust Design

A product's performance is affected by manufacturing imperfections, environmental factors, and human variations in operating the product. Product design should take those issues into account. A high-quality product performs near its performance target consistently throughout its life span and under all operating conditions. Good design should identify the settings of product or process parameters that minimize the sensitivity of designs to sources of variation in the factory and in use. Products that are insensitive to external sources of variation are called **robust.** An example of a robust design is the "gear effect" designed into modern golf clubs, which brings the ball back on line even if it is hit off the "sweet spot" of the club.

Quite recently, an approach to design developed by Japan's Genichi Taguchi has received considerable attention. Taguchi's premise is simple: Instead of constantly directing effort toward controlling a production process to assure consistent quality, design the product to achieve high quality despite the variations that will occur on the production line. Taguchi's approach is based on the use of statistically designed experiments to optimize the design and manufacturing process. His methods are being incorporated into computer-aided design systems (discussed later in this chapter). ITT Corporation's implementation of Taguchi's technique cut defects by more than half, saving $60 million in the first two years.[8] AT&T has also used this approach.

Table 6.4 Design Guidelines for Improving Productivity and Quality

Guideline and Effects		Improvement
Minimize number of parts		
• Fewer part and assembly drawings	→	Fewer drawings and instructions to control
• Less-complicated assemblies	→	Lower assembly error rate
• Fewer parts to hold to required quality characteristics	→	Higher consistency of part quality
• Fewer parts to fail	→	Higher reliability
Minimize number of part numbers		
• Fewer variations of like parts	→	Lower assembly error rate
Design for robustness (Taguchi method)		
• Low sensitivity to component variability	→	Higher first-pass yield
	→	Less degradation of performance with time
Eliminate adjustments		
• No assembly adjustment errors	→	Higher first-pass yield
• Eliminates adjustable components with high failure rates	→	Lower failure rate
Make assembly easy and foolproof		
• Parts cannot be assembled wrong	→	Lower assembly error rate
• Obvious when parts are missing	→	Lower assembly error rate
• Assembly tooling designed into part	→	Lower assembly error rate
• Parts are self-securing	→	Lower assembly error rate
• No "force fitting" of parts	→	Less damage to parts, better serviceability
Use repeatable, well-understood processes		
• Part quality easy to control	→	Higher part yield
• Assembly quality easy to control	→	Higher assembly yield
Choose parts that can survive process operations		
• Less damage to parts	→	Higher yield
• Less degradation of parts	→	Higher reliability
Design for efficient and adequate testing		
• Less mistaking "good" for "bad" product and vice versa	→	Truer assessment of quality, less unnecessary work
Lay out parts for reliable process completion		
• Less damage to parts during handling and assembly	→	Higher yield, higher reliability
Eliminate engineering changes on released products		
• Fewer errors due to changeovers and multiple revisions/versions	→	Lower assembly error rate

Source: Douglas Daetz, "The Effect of Product Design on Product Quality and Product Cost," *Quality Progress,* June 1987. Copyright © 1987 Hewlett-Packard Company. All rights Reserved. Reprinted with Permission.

Applied P/OM
AT&T

AT&T realizes the importance of robust design.[9]

Consider the situation AT&T faced when it developed an integrated circuit for amplifying voice signals. As originally designed, the circuit had to be manufactured very precisely to avoid variations in the strength of the signal. Such a circuit would have been costly to make because of the stringent quality controls needed during the manufacturing process. But AT&T's engineers, after testing and analyzing the design, realized that if the resistance of the circuit were reduced—a minor change with no associated costs—the circuit would be much less sensitive to manufacturing variations. The result was a 40 percent improvement in quality.

Techniques of Quality Engineering

The term **quality engineering** refers to a process of designing quality into a product based on a prediction of potential quality problems prior to production. Among the many tools of quality engineering are value engineering/value analysis and design reviews.

Value Engineering/Value Analysis.   The object of **value engineering** and **value analysis** is to analyze the function of every component of a product, system, or service to determine how that function can be accomplished most economically, without degrading the quality of the product or service. *Value engineering* refers to cost avoidance or cost prevention before production, whereas *value analysis* refers to cost reduction during production. Typical questions that are asked during value engineering/value analysis studies include

••• What are the functions of a particular component? Are they necessary? Can they be accomplished in a different way?

••• What materials are used? Can a less costly material be substituted? For example, can off-the-shelf items be used in place of custom-specified components?

••• How much material is wasted during manufacturing? Can waste be reduced by changing the design?

Some examples are provided by Vincent Reuter.[10] One company originally made an exhaust manifold in an air compressor from cast iron, which required several machining steps. By switching to a powder metal process, it reduced four machine steps to one. The savings amounted to $50,000 per year. Another company formerly packed bottles of shampoo in plain chipboard cartons for distributors. By changing to a plastic six-pack holder similar to that used in the beverage industry, it saved more than $100,000 in the first year. Even simple ideas such as reusing packing material from incoming shipments to pack outgoing shipments have resulted in savings of more than $600,000 for many companies.

In addition to lower costs and higher profits, value engineering and value analysis result in better products, improved product performance and reliability, higher quality, faster delivery through reduced lead times, and increased standardization that leads to improved maintenance and lower repair costs.

Design Reviews.   To ensure that all important design objectives are taken into account during the design process, many companies have instituted formal **design reviews.** The purpose of a design review is to stimulate discussion and raise questions to generate new ideas and solutions to problems. Design reviews can facilitate standardization and reduce the costs associated with frequent design changes by helping designers anticipate problems before they occur. Hence, design reviews are nothing more than good planning.

Generally, there are three major design reviews: preliminary, intermediate, and final. The *preliminary review* establishes early communication among marketing, engineering, manufacturing, and purchasing personnel and provides better coordination of their activities. It usually involves higher levels of management than subsequent reviews and concentrates on strategic issues in design that relate to customer requirements—and thus the ultimate quality of the product—such as completeness of specifications, value and appearance, make-or-buy decisions, reliability requirements, and liability issues.

After the design is well established, an *intermediate review* takes place so that the design can be studied in more detail to identify potential problems and suggest corrective action. Finally, just before release to production, a *final review* is held. Materials lists, drawings, and other detailed design information are studied with the purpose of preventing costly changes after production startup.

A design-review process usually includes a **failure-mode-and-effects analysis (FMEA),** in which each component of a product is listed along with the way it may fail, the cause of failure, the effect or consequence of failure, and how it can be corrected by improving the design. For instance, one of the components of a table lamp is the socket; a typical FMEA for that component might be

Failure: cracked socket.

Causes: excessive heat, forcing bulb, bumping.

Effects: may cause shock.

Correction: use improved materials.

An FMEA can uncover serious design problems prior to manufacturing and improve the quality and reliability of a product considerably.

Reliability Engineering and Management

Formally, **reliability** is defined as the probability that a product, piece of equipment, or system performs its intended function for a stated period of time under specified operating conditions. This definition has four important elements: probability, time, performance, and operating conditions.

First, reliability is defined as a *probability,* that is, a value between 0 and 1. For example, a probability of 0.97 indicates that, on average, 97 of 100 items will perform their function for a given period of time under specified operating conditions. Often reliability is expressed as a percentage simply to be more descriptive.

The second element of the definition is *time.* Clearly, a device having a reliability of 0.97 for 1,000 hours of operation is inferior to one that has the same reliability for 5,000 hours of operation, if the objective of the device is long life.

Performance refers to the objective for which the product or system was made. The term *failure* is used when performance of the intended function is not met. There are two types of failures: **functional failure,** which occurs early in a product's life due to manufacturing or material defects such as a missing connection or a faulty component, and **reliability failure,** which occurs after some period of use.

The final component of the reliability definition is *operating conditions,* which refers to the type and amount of use and the environment in which the product is used. For example, the operating conditions of an ordinary dress watch are not the same as those of a sport watch that one might wear while swimming.

By defining a product's intended environment, performance characteristics, and lifetime, tests can be designed and conducted to measure the probability of survival (or failure). The analysis of such tests enables manufacturers to better predict reliability and to improve product and process designs accordingly.

Reliability engineering consists of a variety of techniques to build reliability into products and test their performance. Reliability engineers determine failure rates of individual components to predict the reliability of complex systems. They use standardized components with proven track records and backup (redundant) components to guard against failure of main components. *Life testing,* that is, running devices until they fail, enables engineers to measure the failure characteristics to better understand and eliminate their causes. Other tests are designed to check products' ability to withstand environmental factors such as temperature, humidity, vibration, and shock.

Reliability management is the total process of establishing, achieving, and maintaining reliability objectives. It is similar in principle to TQM in that it centers on defining customer performance requirements and their economic impacts, selecting components, designs, and suppliers that meet reliability and cost criteria, determining reliability requirements for machines and equipment, and analyzing field data as a means of improving reliability.

Reliability can be improved by using better components or by adding redundant components. In either case, costs increase; thus, trade-offs must be made. The effects can often be computed easily, as the following section shows.

System Reliability

A *system* is a related group of components that work together to accomplish a task. The reliability of a system is the probability that the system will perform satisfactorily over a specified period of time.

Many products consist of several components that are in series but function independently of one another, as illustrated in Figure 6.6. If one component fails, the entire system fails. If we know the individual reliability, p_j, for each component, j, we can compute the total reliability of an n-component series system, R. We note that the joint probability of n independent events can be computed as the product of the individual probabilities. Thus, if the individual reliabilities are denoted by $p_1, p_2, \ldots, p_n$ and the system reliability is denoted by R, then

$$R = p_1 p_2 \ldots p_{n.} \tag{6.1}$$

Other systems consist of several parallel components that function independently of each other, as illustrated in Figure 6.7. The entire system will fail only if

Figure 6.6
Series System

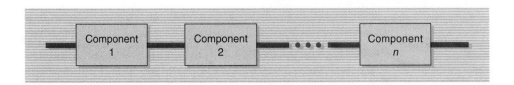

Figure 6.7
Parallel System

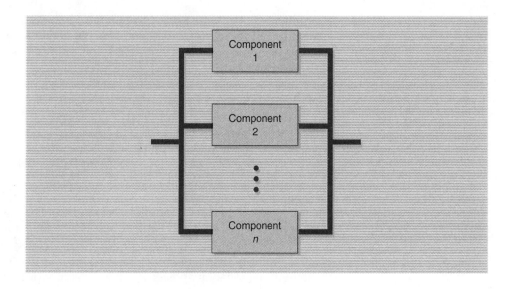

all components fail; this is an example of **redundancy.** The system reliability is computed as

$$R = 1 - (1 - p_1)(1 - p_2) \ldots (1 - p_n) \qquad (6.2)$$

Many other systems are combinations of series and parallel components. To compute the reliability of such systems, first compute the reliability of the parallel components using Equation 6.2 and treat the result as a single series component; then use Equation 6.1 to compute the total series reliability. A solved problem at the end of this chapter illustrates this computation.

Design for Disassembly

Environmental concerns are placing unprecedented government and consumer pressures on product and process designs. There is a clamor for "socially responsible" designs. States and municipalities are running out of landfill space. The concept of "design for disassembly" addresses these concerns in two ways: recyclability and repairability.[11]

One aspect of designing for disassembly is that products can be taken apart for their components to be repaired, refurbished, melted down, or otherwise salvaged for reuse. General Electric's plastics division, which serves the durable-goods market, uses only thermoplastics for its products.[12] Unlike many other varieties of plastics, thermoplastics can be melted down and recast into other shapes and products. GE's "refrigerator of the future" is composed of a series of plastic insulating boxes that can be taken apart quickly, with all mechanical equipment contained in a module that runs up the back of the box like a spine. That configuration makes the refrigerator not only easier to take apart, but also easier to service.

Recyclability creates new challenges for designers and consumers. Designers must strive to use fewer types of materials, and the materials must have certain characteristics (such as thermal properties of plastics) that allow them to be reused. They must also refrain from using certain methods of fastening, such as glues and screws, in favor of quick-connect/disconnect bolts and the like. Obviously, these mandated changes in design have an impact on tolerances, durability, and product quality, and thus, on production processes.

Repairable products are not a new idea, but the concept went out of fashion in the 1960s and 1970s in the United States during the time of the "throwaway society." Now designing for disassembly promises to bring back easy, affordable product repair. For example, Whirlpool Corporation is developing an appliance that is specifically designed for repairability, with its parts sorted for easy coding. The repairability feature has the potential for great consumer appeal.

Design for Manufacture and Assembly

Design for manufacture (DFM) ensures that product designs can be efficiently executed on the production floor. Even product designs that use simple components sometimes result in complex or difficult assembly operations, and inexpensive product designs sometimes result in products that are difficult or expensive to service or support. DFM is meant to prevent such complications. One example of DFM in action involved a team of designers at Thermos, who were designing an electric grill with tapered legs. The manufacturing team member noted that tapered legs would have to be custom made and persuaded designers to make them straight.[13]

Computer-aided design (CAD) facilitates DFM by enabling a designer to interact with the computer in the design process and to eliminate time-consuming activities such as drawing blueprints and constructing prototypes. A typical CAD system includes an interactive computer graphics system and databases of documentation and stored images of parts and assemblies. One or more video terminals are connected to the digital computer. A CAD system allows replication of portions of images to use in other areas of the design when the product has repetitive features. It can also move or copy portions of the screen from one location to another and zoom in on portions of the screen. The system can manipulate or analyze the image in a variety of ways. For example, it can rotate or turn a three-dimensional representation of an object and dynamically show vibration and stress as force is applied.

Among the major advantages of using CAD are the flexibility in visualization afforded to the designer and the capability of testing the design for engineering feasibility without building a prototype. The computer prototype provides the same information that a physical model would. However, changes can be made much faster and more cheaply. For example, a common design activity at General Motors is reducing the weight of a chassis cross member. It used to involve a long wait while prototypes were constructed and tested. If the design was found to be infeasible, the process had to be repeated, sometimes two or three times. Up to 40 to 50 percent of the time involved in design activity can be saved through CAD.

More sophisticated CAD systems go beyond the design and drafting stages. They electronically transfer information about the physical dimensions of the product and the manufacturing steps required to produce it to computer-aided manufacturing equipment. Some systems have simulation and animation capabilities whereby the operation of the product can be visualized. Thus, CAD technology not only increases the designers' productivity, but also improves the quality of the design and manufacturing process.

Product Simplification

Product simplification is an important aspect of DFM. Simple designs enable manufacturers to reduce assembly lead times and thus improve productivity, quality, flexibility, and customer response. For example, the redesign of the Cadillac Seville rear-bumper assembly reduced the number of parts by half and cut assembly time by 57 percent, to less than 8 minutes, saving the company over $450,000 annually in labor costs.[14] Since many of the eliminated parts were squeak- and rattle-causing fasteners, nuts, bolts, and screws, the change also improved the quality of the car.

Product simplification encourages the use of standard parts and components that are widely available and are less expensive because vendors can produce them on a mass basis. Also, because they do not have to be designed in-house, the development time is decreased.

One method of product simplification is **modular design,** which allows manufactured parts and services to be combined in a large number of ways. For example, many of the options available on automobiles can be used on a variety of models in a manufacturer's line; it is simply a matter of assembling the proper components for the customer's order. Printed circuitboards are built in modules for television sets; computing equipment is modular in the sense that different central processing units, disk drives, keyboards, and so on, can be combined.

Modular design enables manufacturers to accommodate varying consumer preferences and still take advantage of the low costs of mass production. Daniel Whitney relates an example of successful modular design.[15] A company wanted to be able to respond within 24 hours to worldwide orders for its electronic products line. Orders were small and required a large variety of different features. Engineers decided to redesign the products in modules, with different combinations of features in each module. All versions of each module were made identical on the outside so that assembly machines could handle all of them. The company can now make up an order for any set of features by selecting the respective modules and assembling them, without human intervention, from electronic order receipt to packaging.

Teamwork in Product Design and Development

All departments play crucial roles in the design process. Whereas the designer's objective is to meet functional requirements, the manufacturing engineer's objective is to produce the designed product efficiently. The salesperson wants the product to have features and a price that make it easy to sell, and finance personnel want to make a profit on it. Purchasing must ensure that purchased parts meet quality requirements. Packaging and distribution personnel must ensure that the product reaches the customer in good operating condition. Clearly, all business functions have a stake in the product; therefore, all must work together. Whitney relates an example of what happens when there is a lack of understanding and cooperation in the design process.[16]

Proper operation of a particular household appliance depended on very close tolerances. The manufacturer's styling department, however, demanded designs of a particular shape and appearance that prevented such tolerances and they would not listen to manufacturing's concerns. Built from single parts on one long production line, the product could not be tested until it was complete. When testing did occur, it established that the finished product had to be adjusted in order to work, or taken apart to find out why it did not work. No one who understood the problem had sufficient authority to solve it, and no one with sufficient authority understood the problem. The company is no longer in business.

Unfortunately, the product-development process is often performed in an uncooperative way in many large firms that remain in business but sacrifice quality and cost savings by their serial development process. In the early stages of development, design engineers dominate the process. Later, the prototype is transferred to manufacturing for production. Finally, marketing and sales personnel are brought into the process. That approach entails a long and costly product-development time—up to 90 percent of manufacturing costs may be committed before manufacturing engineers have any input to the design. At that late stage, design changes can be a problem, and the final product may not even be the best one for market conditions when it is introduced. Ford Motor Company avoided this problematic serial approach in its product development of Taurus/Sable automobiles.

Applied P/OM

Ford Motor Company

Ford took a radical new approach to product development in designing the Ford Taurus/Mercury Sable line of automobiles.[17]

Recognizing that the company was not competitive on quality in the international marketplace, Ford threw out its traditional product-development organizational structure. "Team Taurus" took a program-management approach, in which representatives from all the various units—planning, design, engineering, and manufacturing—worked together as a group. Communication was dramatically improved, and many problems were resolved much earlier in the process. For instance, manufacturing suggested changes in design that resulted in higher productivity and better quality.

Other changes included "reverse engineering," in which Ford engineers disassembled other companies' cars to learn how they were designed. Comprehensive market surveys were conducted to determine customers' wants and preferences. Ford even asked assembly-line workers for their advice before the car was designed. Workers complained that they had trouble installing doors because the body panels were made up of too many pieces. Designers reduced the number of panels from eight to two. One worker suggested that all bolts should have the same head size so that workers would not have to change wrenches constantly. These examples clearly illustrate the importance of operations in product design and development and their impacts on both quality and productivity.

The Taurus/Sable has been one of Ford's biggest success stories since the Mustang and has established new levels of quality both in the United States and abroad. Chrysler and General Motors have moved toward similar program-management styles of product development.

The cooperative approach to product development is called **concurrent engineering** or **simultaneous engineering.** Basically, it entails the continuing product-development involvement and responsibility of all major functions that contribute to getting a product to market, from ideation through sales. Multifunctional teams, usually consisting of four to 20 members and including every specialty in the company, are responsible for all aspects of product development, including product design, production process design, design for manufacturability and assembly, and supplier issues.

Globalization has important implications for product development.[18] Integrated design for the global market can eliminate costly redesigns each time that the company wants to enter a new market. A "core" product can be designed that can be tailored to meet the needs of local markets. In some cases, companies have developed specific kits for individual countries that contain preprogrammed memory chips, documentation, and special power cords.

The use of international design teams can turn a multinational firm's scattered operations into a competitive advantage. If the members of a product design team are located throughout the world rather than at a central site, each team member can monitor local tastes, technical standards, and changing government regulations. They can also stay abreast of new technology and gain quicker access to competitors' products. Such an approach requires good communication systems. Digital Equipment Corporation, for example, created an electronic-mail network linking 100,000 employees around the world. It estimates that the network has contributed to reducing product-development time by half in just four years.

Designing Services

Researchers have suggested that services have three basic components: (1) physical facilities, processes, and procedures; (2) employees' behavior, and (3) employees' professional judgment.[19] Thus, designing a service essentially involves determining an effective balance of those components. MamaMia's Pizza, for instance, must consider not only the menu, but the decor and atmosphere, the processes by which customers are seated and served, what employees say and how they say it, and how they react to problems and complaints. The goal is to provide a service whose elements are internally consistent and focused to meet the needs of a specific target-market segment. Too much or too little emphasis on one component will lead to problems and poor customer perceptions. For example, too much emphasis on procedures might result in timely and efficient service, but might also suggest insensitivity and apathy toward the customer. Too much emphasis on behavior might provide a friendly and personable environment, but slow, inconsistent, or chaotic service. Too much emphasis on professional judgment might lead to good solutions to customer problems but also to slow, inconsistent, or insensitive service.

Services differ in their degree of customer contact and interaction, labor intensity, and customization. For example, a railroad is low on all three dimensions, whereas an interior design service is high on all three. A fast-food restaurant is high on customer contact and labor intensity, but low on customization. Such classification is useful in approaching service design.

Services low on all three dimensions are very similar to manufacturing organizations. The emphasis on quality should be focused on the physical facilities and procedures; behavior and professional judgment are relatively unimportant. For services low in labor intensity, the customer's impression of physical facilities, processes, and procedures is important, and special care must be taken to make sure equipment is reliable and easy to use.

As customer contact and interaction increase, more attention must be paid to making sure the staff behave appropriately. As labor intensity increases, variations between individuals become more important; however, the elements of personal behavior and professional judgment will remain relatively unimportant as long as the degree of customization and of customer contact and interaction remains low. As customization increases, professional judgment becomes more important in the customer's perception of service quality. Of course, some services are high on all three dimensions.

Service-Quality Standards

In services, quality standards take the place of the dimensions and tolerances applicable in manufacturing. Examples of such standards for one of the airline industry leaders, Swissair, include

- Ninety percent of calls are answered within 30 seconds.
- Ninety percent of passengers are checked in within 3 minutes of arrival.
- Baggage claim time is only 10 minutes between the first and last customer.

Many service standards are much more difficult to define and measure than manufacturing specifications. They require extensive research into customer needs and attitudes about timeliness, consistency, accuracy, and other service attributes discussed in preceding chapters. Whereas many specifications developed for manufactured products are defined by a target and allowable tolerance, service specifications typically are "smaller is better." Thus, the true service standard is zero defects, and any other standards (such as the preceding examples for Swissair) should be construed as interim standards and targets only.

Charles Zimmerman and John Enell suggest some questions that should be considered in planning for quality in services:[20] What service standards are already in place? Which of those standards have been clearly communicated to all service personnel? Have they been communicated to the public? Which of them require refinement? What is the final result of the service provided? What should it ideally be?

Some important questions related to time include: What is the maximum access time that a patron will tolerate without feeling inconvenienced? How long should it take to perform the service itself? What is the maximum time for completion of service before the customer's view of the service is negatively affected? When does the service begin and what is used as an indicator of completion of the service? How many different people must deal with the consumer in completing the service?

In relation to completeness and consistency, a service organization should ask these questions: What components of the service are essential? Desirable? Superfluous? What components or aspects of service must be controlled to deliver a service encounter of equal quality each time it occurs? Which components can differ from encounter to encounter while still leading to a total service encounter that meets standards? What products that affect its service performance does a service organization obtain from other sources?

Answers to such questions, while difficult to develop, provide the information necessary for the effective use of techniques such as quality function deployment in service-quality planning.

Service-Process Design

A core service product is a *process*—that is, a method of doing things. Preparing an invoice, taking a telephone order, processing a credit card, preparing food, checking out of a hotel, and teaching a class are all examples of service processes. Service-process designers must focus on doing things right the first time, minimizing process complexities, and making the process immune to inadvertent human errors, particularly when employees are interacting with customers. A complicating factor is that service processes often involve both internal and external activities. For example, in a bank, poor service can result from the way tellers treat customers and also from poor quality of computers and communications equipment that is beyond the tellers' control. Internal activities must be concerned primarily with efficiency (quality of conformance), whereas external activities—with direct customer interaction— must focus on effectiveness (quality of design). All too often, persons involved in internal operations do not know how their work affects the customer whom they do not see. They need to understand how they add value to the customer.

A good way to start designing a service is to answer the following questions: What is the purpose of the process? How does the process create customer satisfaction? What are the essential inputs and outputs of the process? The service design specifies in detail the sequence of steps—value-adding activities and specific tasks—involved in delivering the service and is usually depicted as a **flowchart.** Such a graphical representation provides an excellent communication device for visualizing and understanding the service operation. Flowcharts can become the basis for job descriptions, employee-training programs, and performance measurement. They help managers to estimate human resource, information systems, equipment, and facilities requirements. As design tools, they enable managers to study and analyze services prior to implementation in order to improve quality and operational performance. Figure 6.8 is a flowchart for the customer-complaint resolution process at GTE Directories, a leading Yellow Pages publisher and 1994 winner of the Malcolm Baldrige National Quality Award.

Once a process is designed, we may ask several fundamental questions about it:

Figure 6.8 GTE Directories Customer-Complaint Resolution Process

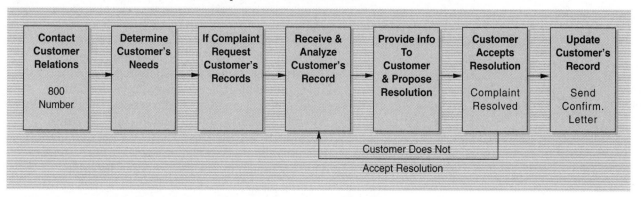

Reprinted by permission of GTE Directories Corporation 1995

1. Are the steps in the process arranged in logical sequence?

2. Do all steps add value? Can some steps be eliminated and should others be added to improve quality or operational performance? Can some be combined? Should some be reordered?

3. Are capacities of each step in balance; that is, are there bottlenecks that increase customer waiting time?

4. What skills, equipment, and tools are required at each step of the process? Should some steps be automated?

5. At which points in the system might errors occur that would result in customer dissatisfaction, and how might those errors be corrected?

6. At which point or points should quality be measured?

7. Where interaction with the customer occurs, what procedures and guidelines should employees follow that will present a positive image?

Dealing with symptoms of errors in internal operations and introducing extra inspection steps rather than seeking the root cause of errors and correcting them leads to inefficiencies and unnecessary costs.

Error-Proofing Services

Error-proofing services[21] simply means designing procedures to prevent errors from occurring. Service error-proofing must account for the customers' activities as well as those of the producer, and fail-safe methods must be set up for interactions conducted directly or by phone, mail, or other technologies such as ATM. Error-proofing procedures can be classified by the type of error they are designed to prevent: server errors or customer errors.

Server errors result from the task, treatment, or tangibles of the service. *Task errors* include doing work incorrectly, work not requested, work in the wrong order, or too slowly. Some examples of fail-safe devices for task errors are computer prompts, color-coded cash register keys, measuring tools such as McDonald's french-fry scoop, and signaling devices. *Treatment errors* occur in the contact between the server and the customer. Lack of courteous behavior and failure to acknowledge, listen, or react appropriately to the customer are examples of such errors. A certain bank ensures eye contact between employees and customers by requiring tellers to record the customer's eye color on a checklist as they start the transaction. To promote friendliness at a certain fast-food restaurant, trainers provide four specific cues for when to smile: when greeting the customer, when taking the order, when telling about the dessert special, and when giving the customer change. They encourage employees to observe whether the customer smiled back, a natural reinforcer for smiling. *Tangible errors* are those in the physical elements of the service, such as unclean facilities, dirty uniforms, poor temperature control, and document errors. Hotels wrap paper strips around towels to help the housekeeping staff identify clean linen and show which items should be replaced. Spell-checkers in word-processing software eliminate document misspellings (if they are used!)

Customer errors occur during preparation, the service encounter, or resolution. Customer errors in *preparation* include the failure to bring necessary materials to the encounter, understand their role in the service transaction, and engage the correct service. Digital Equipment Corporation provides a flowchart to specify how to place a service call. By guiding customers through three yes-or-no questions, it ensures that they have the necessary information before calling. Customer errors during an *encounter* can be due to inattention, misunderstanding, or simply a memory lapse. They include failure to remember steps in the process or follow instructions. Fail-safe examples include beepers that signal customers to remove cards from ATM machines, and locks on airplane lavatory doors that must be closed to turn on the lights. Customers may also make errors at the *resolution* stage of a service encounter. Errors include failure to signal service failures, learn from experience, adjust expectations, and execute appropriate post-encounter actions. Hotels might enclose a small gift certificate to encourage guests to provide feedback. Strategically placed tray-return stands and trash receptacles remind customers to return trays in fast-food facilities.

Automation in Service Design

The service sector has traditionally been highly labor-intensive. Automation is clearly changing the way services are offered. In most service industries, this means that fewer jobs are available and new skills are required. These facts cause some serious concern to both labor and management. Examples of the role of automation in different types of services follow.[22]

Food-Service Industry. Arby's, Inc., tested a system that will slice, weigh, and move portions of roast beef to a sandwich-making station. Arby's has also installed touch-sensitive screens with which customers place their orders, much like automated teller machines. The device asks whether the customer intends to dine in or take out, asks the customer to make menu selections, keeps a running tally of the cost, and even performs some salesmanship—if a customer orders only a sandwich and fries, the machine suggests a soft drink. Order times are reduced by almost 50 percent and accuracy is improved.

At many restaurants, waiters and waitresses use hand-held order-entry computer terminals to speed the ordering process. An order is transmitted instantaneously to the kitchen or bar, where it is displayed and the bill is printed.

The system is designed to save time and improve accuracy by standardizing the order-taking procedure and eliminating handwritten orders.

Retail Sales. Grocery stores have been using bar-code scanners for many years at checkout counters, and most major retail stores have adopted this technology. Not only does the use of bar-coding save time for customers, but the computer system can automatically adjust the store's inventory records each time an item is sold. Some retailers use similar systems to reorder products automatically when inventories reach predetermined levels. Credit authorizations, which once took several minutes by telephone, are now accomplished in seconds through computerized authorization systems.

Retail stores are experimenting with other innovative forms of automation. Florsheim shoe stores have electronic kiosks in which a customer can search an electronic catalog of all styles and colors of shoes and place an order. Some automobile dealerships use videodisc systems to allow customers to select and view a car from thousands of possible options.

Financial Services. Automation in financial services began in the 1930s with mechanical machines that sorted checks into a series of pockets, each containing checks for a particular bank. Today, automatic teller machines (ATMs) provide improved customer service and reduce the costs associated with conventional teller transactions. Electronic fund-transfer systems have made possible direct payroll deposit and MasterCard and VISA debit cards, for example. Trust administrators, cash managers, and portfolio managers all routinely use computer hardware and software to make complex financial decisions.

Public and Government Services. The U.S. Postal Service expects to deliver 250 billion pieces of mail per year by the year 2000. Mail carriers spend about 50 percent of their time placing mail in the proper order for delivery. In 1985, 19 percent of the postal service's $29 billion budget was used for manual sorting. Now it is spending approximately $35 million to find ways of exploiting robotics, vision systems, and other forms of advanced technology for mail handling. Optical character-recognition systems can read and sort 5,000 pieces of mail per hour. That compares to 800 pieces of mail per hour for a human sorter and 1,650 per hour for a mechanical sorter.

The postal service also has developed a self-service, computerized change-of-address station. With a keyboard and touch screen, users enter their change-of-address information and the names and addresses of businesses that need to receive it. Then the user "pays the machine," and it prints out stamped postcards with the old and new addresses on them. Currently about 70 percent of address-change notifications are submitted to the postal service on or after the moving date, which results in the need to forward more than 2.3 billion pieces of mail each year. The system could save $200 million annually.

Health-Care Services. Health care has quickly adopted automation. Automation can be found in nearly every type of medical technology. Examples include

CAT scanners, fetal monitors, laboratory diagnosis machines, pacemakers, and medical information systems. Computerized "expert systems" act as advisors to physicians in making diagnoses and prescribing treatments.

Education Services.   Computers are becoming as basic to the classroom as chalk and blackboards. Computer-assisted instruction (CAI) is changing the way many students learn; they can learn at their own pace, and the teacher is freed of many time-consuming and repetitive tasks. Library research improved dramatically with the introduction of computerized bibliographic databases in the late 1970s.

Hotel and Motel Services.   The operations function of hotels and motels uses electronic reservation systems, message and wake-up systems, and key and lock systems. Many other activities that are not apparent to guests are automation-based, such as automatic ironing machines and automated cleanup, vacuum, wash, and wax machines. Such technologies improve the quality and timeliness of service and reduce operating costs.

P/OM in Practice

A Tale of Failure in Product Development[23]

In 1981 the market share and profits for General Electric's appliance division were falling. The company's technology was antiquated in comparison with that of foreign competitors. For example, making refrigerator compressors required 65 minutes of labor in comparison with just 25 minutes by competitors in Japan and Italy, both of which had lower labor costs. The alternatives were obvious to GE: it should either purchase compressors from Japan or Italy, or design and build a better model. By 1983 the company had decided to build a new rotary compressor in-house and committed $120 million for a new factory. GE was not a novice in rotary compressor technology; it had invented it and had been using it in air-conditioners for many years. A rotary compressor weighs less, has one-third fewer parts, and is more energy-efficient than the reciprocating compressors the company was currently using.

Also, it takes up less space, which provides more room inside the refrigerators and thus better serves customer requirements.

Nonetheless, some engineers had argued against the rotary compressor, claiming it ran hotter than reciprocating compressors. In most air-conditioners that is not a problem, since the coolant cools the compressor. In a refrigerator, however, the coolant flows only one-tenth as fast, and the unit runs about four times longer in one year than in an air-conditioner. GE had had problems with the early rotary compressors in air-conditioners. Although the bugs had been eliminated in smaller units, GE quit using rotaries in larger units after frequent breakdowns in hot climates.

GE managers and design engineers were concerned about other issues. Rotary compressors make a high-pitched whine, and managers were afraid that it would adversely affect consumer acceptance. Many hours were spent by managers and consumer test panels on this issue. The

new design also required key parts to work together with a tolerance of only 50 millionths of an inch. Nothing had been mass-produced with such precision before, but manufacturing engineers felt certain they could achieve it.

The compressor they finally designed was identical to the one used in air-conditioners with one exception: two small parts inside the compressor were made of powdered metal rather than hardened steel and cast iron as in the air-conditioners. That material was chosen because it could be machined to much closer tolerances and it reduced machining costs. The fact that it had been tried a decade earlier on air-conditioners and did not work was told to the design engineers who were new to designing compressors, but they did not pay attention.

A consultant suggested that GE consider a joint venture with a Japanese company that had a rotary refrigerator compressor already on the market. Management rejected that idea. The original designer of the air-conditioner rotary compressor, who had left GE, offered his services as a consultant, but GE declined the offer, writing him that they had sufficient technical expertise.

About 600 compressors were tested in 1983 without a single failure. They were run continuously for two months under elevated temperatures and pressures intended to simulate five years' operation. GE normally conducts extensive field testing of new products; its original plan to test models in the field for two years was reduced to nine months to meet time pressures to complete the project. The technician who disassembled and inspected the parts thought they did not look right. Parts of the motor were discolored, indicating excessive heat. Bearings were worn, and it appeared that high heat was breaking down the lubricating oil. The technician's supervisors discounted those findings and did not relay them to upper levels of management. Another consultant who evaluated the test results believed that something was wrong because only one failure was found in two years. The consultant recommended that test conditions be intensified. That, too, was rejected by management.

In 1986, only two and one-half years after board approval, the new factory was producing compressors at a rate of 10 per minute. By the end of the year, over 1 million had been produced. Market share rose and the new refrigerator appeared to be a success. In July 1987 the first compressor failed. Soon after, reports of other failures in Puerto Rico arrived. By September, the appliance division knew it had a major problem. By December, the plant stopped making the compressor. It was not until 1988 that the problem was diagnosed as excessive wear in the two powdered-metal parts, which caused the oil to burn up. The cost of replacing the compressors in 1989 alone was $450 million. By mid 1990, GE had voluntarily replaced nearly 1.1 million of the compressors with ones it purchased from six suppliers, five of them foreign.

Questions for Discussion

1. What elements of the product-development process caused this disaster? What individuals were responsible?
2. Discuss how quality-engineering techniques might have improved the product-development process.
3. What lessons do you think GE learned from this experience?

Testing Audio Components at Shure Bros., Inc.[24]

The philosophy at Shure Bros., Inc., is reliability oriented. Microphones are tested for reliability well beyond the warranty period, with the goal of providing the customer long-term service and satisfaction. Microphones are found in environments as diverse as churches, schools, bars, stores, and the outdoors. All those places represent potential challenges to the integrity of the microphone, which can be damaged by handling, mishandling, or long-term abuse. Random drops from a height of several feet are not uncommon.

In vehicles, extremes of heat and cold, vibration, shock, and repeated switch actuation and cable flexing must be considered. Sand and dust are likely to be present. Reliability is critical, as there will probably be no backup available in an emergency on the road.

Sound professionals require reliability and cannot tolerate a noisy or dead microphone in the middle of a live performance or recording session. Yet repeated setup and tear-down during concert tours pose many problems.

Many standardized destructive tests developed by the military, the Electronic Industry Association, and the American Society for Testing and Materials are employed to gain knowledge of product failure. In addi-

tion, the following specialized environmental tests are conducted:

- *Microphone drop test.* This is an unpackaged test consisting of a random free-fall onto the floor. The test height is six feet, designed to simulate a fall from a tall shelf or an accidental drop by a very tall person at shoulder height. Ten drops must be sustained without significant loss of performance.

- *Barrel tumble.* A specially constructed barrel is used to tumble small, unpackaged microphones. This test is designed to simulate and exceed the roughest treatment expected in handling or transporting microphones loose in a case.

- *Stair-tumble test.* A shipping carton is packed with a dozen units, sealed with tape, and tumbled down 17 steel steps onto a concrete floor. Ten tumbles must be sustained without loss of function or severe loss of appearance of the packaging. This test allows for evaluation of possible damage during shipping.

- *Outside weathering test.* This test exposes test units to actual outside weather. It aids in evaluating finishes and the performance of products that might actually be used outside such as microphones and sound-reinforcement equipment.

The preceding are some examples of in-house reliability testing designed to simulate actual operating conditions. They help to ensure the company's goal of marketing products with a long life of useful service.

Questions for Discussion

1. What reliability requirements do each of the tests described here address?
2. Since CDs have become the most popular form of audio music, propose some tests that a manufacturer of CDs might perform.

Summary of Key Points

- Product design influences the cost of manufacturing and the strategic criteria of efficiency, quality, dependability, and flexibility. Thus, it is an important issue for operations managers.

- In selecting products, businesses can choose custom, option-oriented, or standard products. Standard products are easier to produce and control, yet they limit flexibility in meeting changing customer demands and dealing with shorter product life cycles.

- The product-development process consists of idea generation, concept development, product/process development, full-scale production, and market introduction and evaluation.

- The actual design process consists of determining product parameters and tolerances. These should be driven by the voice of the customer and should exceed the customer's expectations.

- Quality function deployment (QFD) is a process for ensuring that customer requirements are captured in the design of products and in production delivery processes. A principal component of QFD is the "house of quality," which serves as a basic design, competitive-evaluation, and planning tool.

- Design has a great influence on quality. Today's products are more complex than ever before and hence are more difficult to manufacture. Design activities must be coordinated with manufacturing.

- Quality engineering is the process of designing quality into a product and predicting potential quality problems prior to production. Two important techniques of quality engineering are value analysis/value engineering and design review.

- Reliability is the probability that a product, piece of equipment, or system will perform its intended function for a specified period of time under specified operating conditions.

- Reliability engineering is concerned with designing and manufacturing products with high reliability and testing them for that feature.

- Reliability management is similar to quality management in that it should be driven by customer requirements and involve all areas of the production system from design through field service.

- Design for manufacture (DFM) ensures that product designs can be produced efficiently on the factory floor. DFM is supported by computer-aided design (CAD) and product-simplification approaches.

- Concurrent, or simultaneous, engineering is an approach to effectively manage product development through teamwork while reducing product-development time and creating higher-quality designs.

- Designing services requires balanced attention to physical facilities, employee behavior, and employee professional judgment. Services can be represented by process flowcharts that enable one to study the service design, eliminate inefficiencies and potential errors, and determine error-proofing needs. Automation plays a significant role in many services in improving quality and productivity.

Key Terms

Product-development process
Voice of the customer
Research and development (R&D)
Scoring model
Nominal specifications
Tolerances
Quality function deployment
House of Quality
Robust
Quality engineering
Value engineering
Value analysis
Design reviews
Failure-mode-and-effects analysis (FMEA)
Reliability
Functional failure
Reliability failure
Reliability engineering
Reliability management
Redundancy
Design for manufacture (DFM)
Computer-aided design (CAD)
Product simplification
Modular design
Concurrent engineering
Simultaneous engineering
Flowchart

Review Questions

1. Why is the selection and development of new products an important strategic decision?

2. Explain the difference between custom, option-oriented, and standard products. Of what significance to P/OM is this distinction?

3. Discuss the general steps in the product-development process. How do they differ for manufactured products versus services?

4. List the major sources of idea generation in product development.

5. Discuss the differences between pure and applied research. What types of organizations would be likely to engage in each type of research?

6. Explain the concepts of nominal specifications and tolerances. Provide at least two examples.

7. What is meant by the *voice of the customer?* Of what value is the voice of the customer in product design?

8. Explain the significance of Kano's classification of customer needs as dissatisfiers, satisfiers, and exciters/delighters.

9. How can customer's perceptions of product quality be affected by the design process? What implications does this have for operations managers?

10. Explain the philosophy behind quality function deployment (QFD).

11. How does product design affect quality? What can be done to improve quality through product design?

12. Define *robust* as it applies to design.

13. Define *quality engineering.* What benefits can it provide?

14. Explain the concept of failure-mode-and-effects analysis (FMEA).

15. Define *reliability.* Explain the definition thoroughly.

16. What is the difference between functional failure and reliability failure?

17. Explain how to compute the reliability of series, parallel, and series-parallel (combinations of series and parallel components) systems.

18. Define *reliability engineering.*

19. How is reliability management similar to total quality management?

20. Why is design for disassembly important in today's society?

21. Explain the concept behind design for manufacture (DFM).

22. What is CAD? How can it help to improve productivity and quality in product design?

23. What benefits does modular design have for the product development process?

24. What is product simplification?

25. Define *concurrent engineering.* Explain how it is normally approached and the benefits it can provide.

26. Explain the use of flowcharts in designing services. What questions should be asked in examining the flowcharts?

Discussion Questions

1. Discuss the differences between "traditional" and "modern" products. Why are these differences significant?

2. Why was Deming's "new way" of product development such a great departure from the "old way"? How was this exemplified in the Ford Taurus/Sable experience?

3. Discuss how you might apply a scoring model in selecting a job or purchasing an automobile or new appliance.

4. Using whatever market-research techniques you feel are appropriate, define a set of customer attributes for

   a. An "excellent" cup of coffee.
   b. A college registration process.

How might QFD be used to improve those processes? Define a set of "hows" and try to construct the relationship matrix for the house of quality for each of these examples.

5. Most organizations have well-defined mission statements that include a set of goals for the firm and actions that the firm can take. How might QFD be used to ensure that the actions are consistent with the goals? Find some company's mission statement to illustrate this use of QFD.

6. Choose some product or service with which you are familiar. Develop some typical value-analysis questions for this product or service.

7. Explain why some products are purposely designed to be lower in overall quality than similar or competing products. That is, why might a firm choose to manufacture a particular product at less than the product's maximum possible quality level?

8. Choose some manufactured product and perform an FMEA on it.

9. How do all areas of the firm affect the reliability of the products it manufactures?

10. The College of Business at the University of Clifton is considering developing a new program in TQM. Discuss how the product-development process can be applied to this situation. (You may want to interview some professors to obtain a better understanding of new-program development at a university.)

11. Discuss the similarities and differences in process-design activities for manufacturing and service organizations.

12. Refer to the flowchart of a car rental check-in and check-out process in Figure 6.9. Using the fundamental questions posed in the "Designing Services" section, analyze the process and suggest improvements.

13. Use your past experiences as a guide to construct a flowchart detailing the sequence of steps involved in each of these service operations.

   a. Cashing a check at a bank
   b. Renewing license plates
   c. Obtaining a new driver's license
   d. Filling a prescription at a pharmacy

Using the questions posed in the "Designing Services" section, discuss how these operations might be analyzed or improved upon.

14. A bank is trying to decide on the best waiting-line system for its customers. Currently customers wait in individual lines (see Figure 6.10a), whereas the proposed method would have customers wait in one line for the next available teller (see Figure 6.10b). What operational differences are there between these systems? How might they affect customer perceptions or teller productivity? Can simulation be used to analyze these systems? What data would the bank have to collect? Why might simulation be preferable to actually trying the proposed method?

Figure 6.9
Figure for Discussion
Question 13

Source: W. Earl Sasser, R. Paul Olsen,
and D. Daryl Wyckoff, *Management
of Service Operations: Text, Cases,
and Readings* p. 74. Copyright ©
1978. Reprinted by permission of
Prentice-Hall, Englewood Cliffs, NJ.

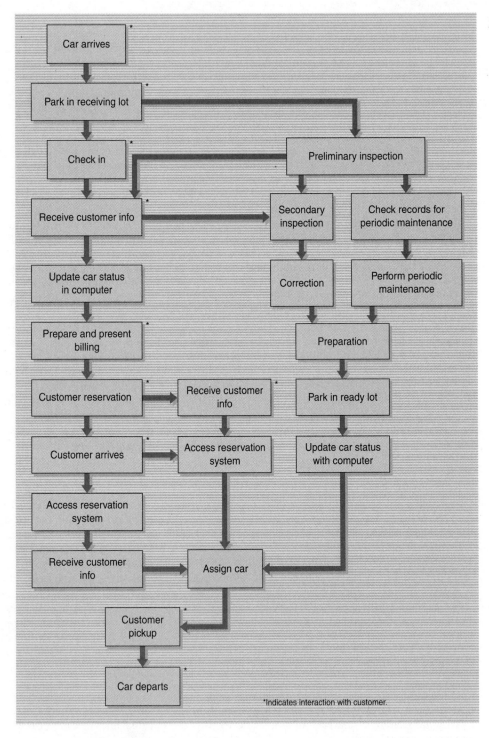

*Indicates interaction with customer.

Figure 6.10
Figure for Discussion
Question 15

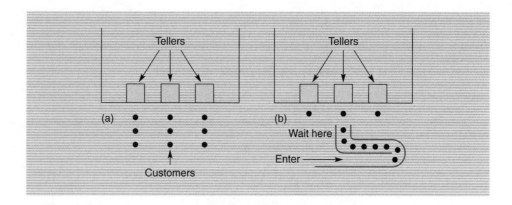

16. Describe examples of automation that you have seen recently in service operations. How do they contribute to achieving customer satisfaction or in error-proofing the services?

Notes

1. Stanley Ziemba, "A Tottering Schwinn Puts Kickstand Down," *Chicago Tribune*, October 9, 1992, pp. 1, 20; and Jeff McKinney, "Bike Dealers Chart Decline of Schwinn," *Cincinnati Enquirer*, October 10, 1992, p. B-4.

2. This discussion is adapted from Charles A. Horne, "Product Strategy and the Competitive Advantage," *P&IM Review with APICS News*, 7, no. 12 (December 1987), pp. 38–41. Reprinted with permission from The American Production and Inventory Control Society, Inc.

3. Brad Stratton, "Editorial Comment: Expanding on Deming's Fourth Point," *Quality Progress* 27, no. 1 (January 1994), p. 5.

4. Peter J. Kolesar, "What Deming Told the Japanese in 1950," *Quality Management Journal* 2, no. 1 (Fall 1994), pp. 9–24.

5. Robert D. Buzzell and Bradley T. Gale, *The PIMS Principles. Linking Strategy to Performance* (New York: The Free Press, 1987).

6. Ames Rubber Corporation, *Application Summary for the 1993 Malcolm Baldrige National Quality Award.*

7. Adapted from Douglas Daetz, "The Effect of Product Design on Product Quality and Product Cost," *Quality Progress*, June 1987, pp. 63–67. Copyright © 1987, Hewlett-Packard Co. All rights reserved. Reprinted with permission.

8. "How to Make It Right the First Time," *Business Week*, June 8, 1987, p. 142.

9. John Mayo, "Process Design as Important as Product Design," *The Wall Street Journal*, October 29, 1984, p. 29.

10. Vincent G. Reuter, "What Good Are Value Analysis Programs?" *Business Horizons* 29 (March–April 1986), pp. 73–79.

11. Bruce Nussbaum and John Templeton, "Built to Last—Until It's Time to Take It Apart," *Business Week*, September 17, 1990, pp. 102–106.

12. Ibid.

13. Brian Dumaine, "Payoff from the New Management," *Fortune*, December 13, 1993, pp. 103–110.

14. *Business Week: Quality 1991* (special issue), October 25, 1991, p. 73.

15. Daniel E. Whitney, "Manufacturing by Design," *Harvard Business Review*, July–August 1988, pp. 83–91.

16. Ibid.

17. "How Ford Hit the Bull's-Eye with Taurus," *Business Week*, June 30, 1986, pp. 69–70.

18. Michael E. McGrath and Richard W. Hoole, "Manufacturing's New Economies of Scale," *Harvard Business Review*, May–June 1992, pp. 94–102. Copyright 1992 by the President and Fellows of Harvard College; all rights reserved.

19. John Haywood-Farmer, "A Conceptual Model of Service Quality," *International Journal of Operations and Production Management* 8, no. 6 (1988), pp. 19–29.

20. Charles D. Zimmerman III and John W. Enell, "Service Industries," section 33 in J. M. Juran, ed., *Juran's Quality Control Handbook*, 4th ed. (New York: McGraw-Hill, 1988).

21. Richard B. Chase and Douglas M. Stewart, "Make Your Service Fail-Safe," *Sloan Management Review* 35, no. 3 (Spring 1994), pp. 35–44.

22. Adapted in part from David A. Collier: "The Service Sector Revolution: The Automation of Services," *Long Range Planning* 16, no. 6, with kind permission from Pergamon Press Ltd., Oxford, UK.

23. Thomas F. O'Boyle, "GE Refrigerator Woes Illustrate the Hazards in Changing a Product," *The Wall Street Journal*, May 7, 1990, pp. A1, A6. Reprinted by permission of *The Wall Street Journal*, © 1990 Dow Jones & Company, Inc. All rights reserved worldwide.

24. Adapted from Roger Franz, "Audio Component Reliability," *Quality*, June 1983, pp. 50–51. Reprinted with permission from Hitchcock Publishing, a Capital Cities/ABC Inc., Company.

Solved Problems

1. A firm is faced with the choice of three new product designs. It uses the scoring model in Table 6.5.

Table 6.5 Data for Solved Problem 1

Criterion	Max. Score	Min. Score	Product 1	Product 2	Product 3
Product development					
Time	+ 5	− 5	+3	−2	0
Material availability	+ 5	− 5	+4	+3	+ 5
Market					
Competition	+10	−10	+7	+6	+ 2
Demand	+10	−10	+7	+5	+ 1
Financial					
Risk	+10	−10	+3	−5	− 9
Returns	+10	−10	+4	+5	+10

a. What is the proportion of weight assigned to product development as compared to marketing and financial criteria?
b. Which product would be chosen using these data?
c. If all three factors were given equal weight, what would the scores be?

Solution
a. It can be seen from the maximum and minimum scores that product development is only half as important as financial and marketing criteria.
b. The scores for each product are:

> Product 1: 28
> Product 2: 12
> Product 3: 9

Product 1 would be selected.
c. The minimum and maximum scores for product development also should be made +10 and −10 for each of the subcriteria. Thus, scores for the subcriteria would be doubled. Product 1 would still be selected.

2. An electronic product consists of three components in series. To prevent failure, the designer is considering adding a redundant component so that if one fails, the product will still work. This is illustrated in Figure 6.11.
The reliabilities of each component are

Component	A	B	C
Reliability	.60	.75	.70

a. Analyze the system reliability, assuming there is only *one* component of each type.
b. How much is the reliability improved by having two parallel components at each operation?

Figure 6.11
Figure for Solved Problem 2

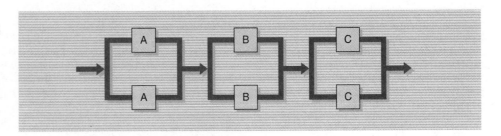

Figure 6.12
Figure for Solved Problem 2
Solution

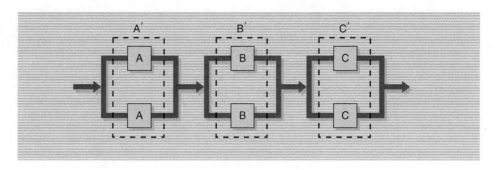

Solution

a. With only one component assumed, we use Equation 6.1:

$$R = (.6)(.75)(.70) = .315$$

b. First compute the reliabilities for each pair of parallel components as shown in Figure 6.12, using Equation 6.2.

$$R_{A'} = 1 - (.4)^2 = .84$$
$$R_{B'} = 1 - (.25)^2 = .9375$$
$$R_{C'} = 1 - (.30)^2 = .91$$

Next, compute the reliability of these parallel systems in series using Equation 6.1:

$$R = (.84)(.9375)(.91) = .717$$

Problems

1. Modify the POWERFIT.XLS spreadsheet to show cash flow over a 5-year horizon, assuming that all fixed costs occur in year 1. How do a 10% and a 20% reduction in the selling price affect profitability?

2. A manufacturing firm is considering developing a new product for commercial use. During the economic-analysis phase of the product-development process, analysts developed two alternatives for manufacturing the product:

Alternative A. Expand current manufacturing facilities and make the product at one of the firm's manufacturing plants. Fixed cost of the expansion is estimated at $200,000. Variable manufacturing costs are projected to be $15 per unit.

Alternative B. Purchase the primary component of the product from a supplier and assemble the product at one of the firm's manufacturing plants. Since this alternative would not require facilities expansion, its fixed manufacturing, selling, and administrative expenses are estimated at only $48,000. The purchased primary component would cost $13 per unit, and there would be an additional $5 variable cost per unit to assemble the final product.

a. Conduct a break-even analysis for the new product under both alternatives for a selling price of $20 per unit.

b. If the projected volume for the new product were 30,000 units, which production alternative, if any, would you recommend?

c. What would the projected volume need to be before the alternative *not* recommended in part b would be the preferred alternative?

3. The O'Neill Shoe Company will produce a special style of shoe if the order size is large enough to provide a reasonable profit. For each special style order, the company incurs a

fixed cost of $2,500 for the production setup. The variable cost is $40 per pair, and each pair sells for $70.

a. Let x indicate the number of pairs of shoes produced. Develop a mathematical model for the total cost of producing x pairs of shoes.

b. Let P indicate the total profit. Develop a mathematical model for the total profit realized from an order for x pairs of shoes.

c. How large must the shoe order be before O'Neill will break even?

4. Myers Products is considering introducing three new products. Existing production facilities will not be able to handle the additional volume at the current time; thus management needs to choose one product to introduce now. The information in Table 6.6 has been determined:

Table 6.6 Data for Problem 4

Criteria	Min. Score	Max. Score	Product I	II	III
Product development	− 5	+ 5	4	0	−4
Market	−10	+10	2	9	8
Financial	−20	+20	16	14	17
			22	23	21

a. What is the relative importance of the three criteria? How might the actual scores reflect risk?

b. Should the total score be used to choose the product? If not, how should Myers assess this information?

c. Suppose the additional information in Table 6.7 is available.

Table 6.7 Additional Data for Problem 4

Criteria	Product I	II	III
Expected annual sales	6,000	9,000	12,000
Contribution to profit per unit	$8	$10	$9
Fixed costs of development	$125,000	$100,000	$180,000
Product lifetime (years)	10	5	12

How might this information affect the decision?

5. A producer of electronic games is evaluating a new product that will have a variable cost of $18 and is expected to sell for $49. The fixed cost allocated to production will be $50,000. What is the break-even point?

6. The game manufacturer in Problem 5 is considering three different games for the upcoming season. Production capacity allows the company to choose only one. All have the same approximate profitability. Using the scoring model in Table 6.8, which game would be the best decision?

Table 6.8 Scoring Model for Problem 6

Criteria	Min. Score	Max. Score	Product A	Product B	Product C
Market risk	−10	10	0	6	3
Design time	−5	5	2	2	3
Financial risk	−10	10	5	−1	2
Design costs	−6	6	4	2	5

7. A system is composed of three components in series.
a. What is the reliability of this system if the probability of failure of each component is as shown in Figure 6.13?

Figure 6.13
Figure for Problem 7

b. If Component B is backed up with another component whose probability of failure is 0.15, what is the overall reliability?
8. A piece of electronic equipment used for aviation has the three elements whose reliabilities are shown in Figure 6.14.

Figure 6.14
Figure for Problem 8

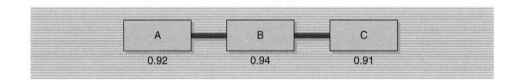

a. What is the reliability of this system?
b. If each of the elements is provided with standby elements of equal reliability, by how much is the overall reliability improved?
c. If the three standby elements can function only as a total standby system, what is the overall reliability?
9. This problem refers to the break-even analysis example in this chapter and can be approached using techniques of decision analysis (see Supplementary Chapter B). Because of the difficulty of accurately estimating sales due to intense industry competition and an uncertain economy, the company has taken a position that it will move forward in developing the aerobic exerciser only if the first-year profits are positive. Thus, the company faces this decision: d_1, develop the product, d_2, stop now before incurring any capital expenses. To simplify the analysis, three states of nature have been identified:

$$s_1 = \text{low demand, 3,000 units per year.}$$

$$s_2 = \text{moderate demand, 5,000 units per year.}$$

$$s_3 = \text{high demand, 8,000 units per year.}$$

a. Construct a payoff table for this decision situation.
b. What decision should be made under
   (1) Optimistic criteria?
   (2) Conservative criteria?
   (3) Minimax regret?
c. Suppose the probabilities of the states of nature are estimated to be $P(s_1) = .3$, $P(s_2) = .4$, and $P(s_3) = .3$. What is the best decision? What is the expected value of perfect information? How can managers interpret this information?
d. A marketing study would result in three indicators:

$$I_1 = \text{low demand expected.}$$

$$I_2 = \text{moderate demand expected.}$$

$$I_3 = \text{high demand expected.}$$

Conditional probabilities of the indicators given the true states of nature follow.

	$P(I_k\|S_j)$		
	s_1	s_2	s_3
I_1	.80	.05	.10
I_2	.10	.90	.20
I_3	.10	.05	.70

What is the optimal decision strategy? What is the expected value of sample information? What does this mean? (Note: This part of the question can be solved by using *The Operations Manager* software available for use with this book.)

Chapter Outline

Chapter Seven
Forecasting and Capacity Planning

In a general sense, **capacity** is what a manufacturing or service system can produce in a particular time period—for example, the number of pizzas that can be produced on a weekend night at MamaMia's Pizza. Capacity, then, is determined by the resources available to an organization—facilities, equipment, and labor. At MamaMia's Pizza, capacity is determined by food-preparation space, oven size, and number of employees.

Strategic capacity planning is the process of determining the types and amounts of resources and production capacity necessary to implement an organization's strategic plan. The objective is to specify the proper mix of facilities, equipment, and labor required to meet both current and future product demand. Because of its strategic nature, long-range capacity planning involves a joint effort among the operations, marketing, and finance functions of an organization. Important issues to be considered include

1. How is the market for existing products changing, and how will current and future technological innovations affect operations?
2. Can existing facilities accommodate new products and adapt to changing demand for existing products?
3. Should new facilities be built? Should existing ones be modified, expanded, or closed? What are the financial implications of such decisions?
4. How large should facilities be, and where should they be located? Should there be a few large facilities near suppliers, or numerous smaller facilities near customers?
5. When should facility changes take place?
6. How much equipment and labor will be required for future operations?

Answers to these questions require **forecasting,** an important tool in P/OM for capacity planning, the subject of this chapter, as well as for other strategic, tactical, and operational decisions. (The appendix to this chapter introduces various quantitative methods for forecasting, and forecasting issues are raised in many other chapters.) Specifically, this chapter addresses

••• The role of forecasting in P/OM decisions, and the strengths and weaknesses of various forecasting techniques.
••• Key issues in strategic capacity planning and the role of the product life cycle.
••• Ways of defining and measuring capacity, and effective strategies for capacity planning.
••• Approaches to planning facilities, equipment, and labor needs.
••• The use of the learning curve to estimate certain capacity needs.

Forecasting in P/OM

Forecasts of future demand are needed at all levels of organizational decision making. Operations managers need estimates of the demand for goods and services for time horizons ranging from one day to several years. *Long-range* sales forecasts are necessary to plan for the expansion of production and distribution facilities and to determine future needs for equipment and labor. *Intermediate-range* sales forecasts over a 3- to 12-month period are needed to plan work-force levels, allocate budgets among product divisions, and establish purchasing policies. For example, a purchasing department may negotiate a substantial discount by contracting to order a large amount of a particular material or component over the next year. Intermediate-range forecasts also help human resources departments plan for future hiring, employee training, and so on. *Short-range* sales forecasts are used by operations managers to plan production schedules and assign workers to jobs, to determine short-term capacity requirements, and to aid shipping departments in planning transportation needs and establishing delivery schedules.

Many different types of forecasts are made in an organization. Consider a consumer products company, such as Procter & Gamble or Colgate-Palmolive, that makes many different products in various sizes. Long-range forecasts might be expressed in total sales dollars for use in financial planning by top managers. At lower organizational levels, however, managers of the various product groups need aggregate forecasts of sales volume for their products in units that are more meaningful to them—for example, pounds of a certain type of soap—to establish production plans. Finally, managers of individual manufacturing facilities need forecasts by brand and size—for instance, the number of 64-ounce boxes of Tide—to plan material usage and production schedules. The forecasts must be consistent across organizational levels to be effective planning aids. In addition, special forecasts—such as forecasts of material and production costs, prices, and so on—may be required for new products and promotional items. Clearly, forecasts are of many different types and in different units of measurement, depending on their purpose.

Forecasting demand for services is just as important as forecasting demand for manufactured products, especially when heavy capital investment is needed to provide the service. For example, airlines need forecasts of demand for air travel to plan their purchases of airplanes. Operations managers in the travel and tourism industry make seasonal forecasts of demand; university administrators require enrollment forecasts; city planners need forecasts of population trends to plan highways and mass transit systems; and restaurants need forecasts to be able to plan for food purchases.

Service organizations have some unique characteristics that affect forecasting. For instance, demand in many service industries, such as the airline and hotel industries, is highly seasonal. Demand for services may also vary with the day of the week or the time of day. Grocery stores, banks, and similar organizations need very short-term forecasts to plan work-shift scheduling and vehicle routing and make other operating decisions to accommodate variations in demand.

Many firms that provide customized services find it easy to forecast the number of customers that will demand service in a particular time period, but quite difficult to forecast the mix of services that will be required or the time it will take to provide those services. Hence, such firms need special forecasts of service mix.

Classification of Forecasting Techniques

Various mathematical and judgmental forecasting techniques are available to address the many different situations described here. Which technique should

Figure 7.1
A Classification of
Forecasting Methods

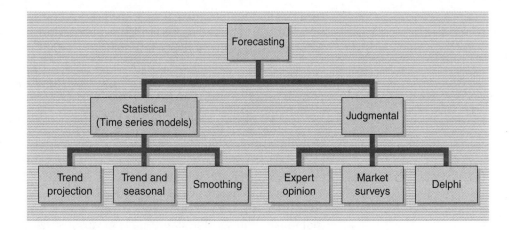

be used depends on the variable being forecast and the time horizon. If we are forecasting weekly sales of a product, for instance, it is reasonable to assume that recent trends will probably continue into the future, so a quantitative technique that uses historical data to make a forecast will probably be useful. Suppose however, that we are asked to forecast the length of time before a current technology becomes obsolete. Certainly past data are no help here. Such forecasts must be based to a large extent on the opinions and expertise of people who are knowledgeable about changing technology.

The two examples of forecasting weekly sales versus product obsolescence exemplify a basic distinction between forecasting approaches. As Figure 7.1 shows, forecasting methods can be classified as either *statistical* or *judgmental.* Statistical forecasting is based on the assumption that the future will be an extrapolation of the past. Its most common methods, called **time-series models,** are trend projection, trend projection adjusted for seasonal influences, and smoothing methods. Those quantitative techniques are described in the appendix to this chapter.

Judgmental Forecasting

When no historical data are available, only judgmental forecasting is possible. But even when historical data are available and appropriate, they cannot be the sole basis for prediction. The demand for products and services is affected by a variety of factors such as interest rates, inflation, and other economic conditions. Competitors' actions and government regulations also have an impact. Thus, some element of judgmental forecasting is always necessary. One interesting example of the role of judgmental forecasting occurred during the recession of the mid 1970s. All economic indicators pointed toward a future period of low demand for manufacturers of machine tools. However, the forecasters of one such company recognized that recent government regulations for automobile pollution control would require the auto industry to update its current technology by purchasing new tools. As a result, this machine-tool company was prepared for the new business.

Techniques commonly used in judgmental forecasts are expert opinion, market surveys, and the Delphi method. Forecasting by *expert opinion* simply consists of gathering judgments and opinions of key personnel based on their

Figure 7.2
The Forecasting System

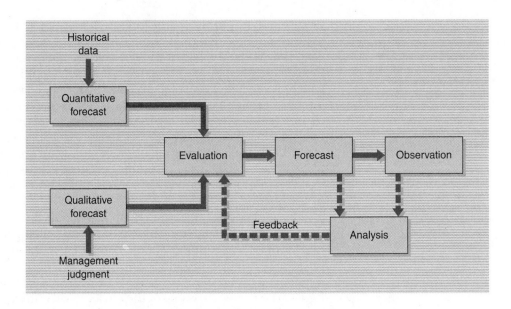

experience and knowledge of the situation. Though such forecasts are sometimes very inaccurate, the advantage of using expert judgment is its low cost in comparison to other methods. *Market surveys* use questionnaires, telephone contacts, or personal interviews as a means of gathering data. The cost of such surveys is high due to labor costs, postage, low response rates, and post-survey processing. Moreover, these surveys are highly subject to bias. In the *Delphi method,* several experts are questioned individually about their perceptions of future events. The experts are not consulted as a group to avoid consensus being reached because of dominant personality factors. Instead, the responses and supporting arguments of each individual are summarized by an outside party and returned to the experts along with further questions. The process iterates until a consensus is reached by the group, which usually takes only a few rounds. The Delphi method is useful for long-range forecasting and for predicting technological changes. An example of its use is discussed later in this chapter.

Forecasting in Practice

Surveys of practicing managers reveal that they rely much more on judgmental methods of forecasting than on quantitative methods, despite the fact that they are very familiar with many quantitative approaches.[1] Companies most often rely on managers' opinions for short-range forecasts and on group opinions for longer-range forecasts. However, manufacturing firms use quantitative techniques more frequently than service firms.

The major reasons given for using judgmental methods rather than quantitative methods are (1) greater accuracy and (2) the difficulty of obtaining the data necessary for quantitative techniques. Also, judgmental methods seem to create a feeling of "ownership" and add a commonsense dimension. Quantitative forecasts often are adjusted judgmentally as managers incorporate environmental knowledge that is not captured in quantitative models.

Both quantitative and judgmental aspects are incorporated in a practical forecasting system. Figure 7.2 illustrates the basic approach. The first step is to understand the purpose of the forecast. For instance, if financial personnel need a sales forecast to determine capital investment strategies, a long (two- to five-year) time horizon is necessary. For such forecasts, using aggregate groups of items is usually more accurate than using individual-item forecasts added together. These forecasts would probably be measured in dollars. In contrast, production personnel may need short-term forecasts for individual items as a basis for procurement of materials and scheduling. In this case, dollar values would not be appropriate; rather, forecasts should be made in terms of units of production.

If historical data are available, they should be first plotted over time. The plot can be used to answer such questions as: Is there an upward or downward trend? Is there significant variation about the trend line? Is there any evidence of seasonality?

The choice of a forecasting method depends on several criteria. Among them are the time span for which the forecast is being made, the needed frequency of forecast updating, data requirements, the level of accuracy desired, the level of aggregation, and the quantitative skills needed. Table 7.1 summarizes the relative differences among the principal forecasting methods used in P/OM. The *time span* is one of the most critical criteria. Different techniques are applicable for long-range, intermediate-range, and short-range forecasts. Also important is the frequency of updating that will be necessary. For example, the Delphi method takes considerable time to implement and thus would not be appropriate for forecasts that must be updated frequently.

Obviously, all forecasters desire as much accuracy as possible, but they may decide to sacrifice some accuracy to satisfy other criteria. For example, the highest level of accuracy may demand forecasting techniques that are too costly or take too long to complete.

The level of aggregation often dictates the appropriate method. Forecasting the total amount of soap to produce over the next planning period is certainly different from forecasting the amount of each individual product to produce. Aggregate forecasts are generally much easier to develop, whereas detailed forecasts require more time and resources.

Table 7.1 Comparison of Forecasting Techniques

	Forecasting Technique					
Criterion	**Expert Opinion**	**Market Surveys**	**Delphi Method**	**Trend**	**Trend and Seasonal**	**Smoothing**
Time span	Short/ medium	Medium	Medium/ long	Short/ medium/long	Short/ medium	Short/ medium
Ease of updating	Rather easy	Somewhat difficult	Difficult	Easy	Easy	Easy
Data required	Very little	Little	None	Detailed	Detailed	Detailed
Accuracy	Usually good	Good	Good for long term	Good	Good	Good
Aggregation level	Aggregate forecasts	Aggregate forecasts	Limited detail	Detailed	Detailed	Detailed
Technical skills	Minimal	Moderate	Minimal	High	High	Medium

Finally, different forecasting methods require different levels of technical ability and understanding of mathematical principles and assumptions. One of the most dangerous things a manager can do is to use a method that she or he does not understand.

Strategic Issues in Capacity Planning

Capacity planning is a crucial element of the operations strategy because it has major cost implications. The capacity decision must be made in the face of considerable uncertainty about future product demand. Consider the fact that in the 1960s and early 1970s, when U.S. firms were able to sell all they could produce, manufacturing capacity was increased as fast as possible; in the late 1970s and through the 1980s, however, the impacts of foreign competition and higher interest rates resulted in a substantial decrease in factory expansion. Overcapacity in many industries resulted in layoffs and plant closures.

Capacity decisions depend on the growth (or decline) of demand for products and services as characterized by the *product life cycle,* which is discussed next.

Product Life Cycle

Figure 7.3 is a graph of sales volume versus time for a typical new product. Such a graph is referred to as a **life-cycle curve.** As this curve shows, immediately after a product is *introduced,* sales grow slowly. Then there is a period of rapid *growth* as the product gains acceptance and markets for it develop (assuming, of course, the product survives the initial phase). This phase is followed by a period of *maturity,* in which demand levels off and no new distribution channels are available. The product design become standardized, which causes competitors to focus marketing strategies more on offering the best price for a similar product than on offering a significantly better product for a similar price. Finally, the product may begin to lose appeal as substitute products are introduced and become more popular. During this *decline* phase, the product is either discontinued or replaced by a modified or entirely new product.

Many essential consumer goods—such as soaps, cleaners, and canned foods—have long and almost never-ending maturity phases. For such products, advertising and minor product improvements play key roles in maintaining

Figure 7.3
Product Life-Cycle Curve

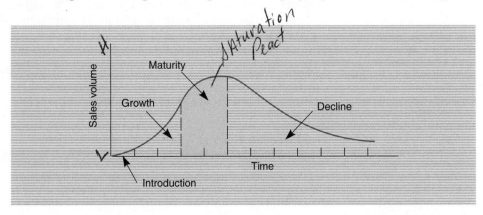

sales volume, particularly in the face of new competition, thus preventing the product from entering the decline phase of the life cycle.

A product's life cycle has important strategic implications, not only for capacity planning, but for other strategic decisions as well. The best time to increase market share is in the introduction phase. Design changes are frequent when a product is first introduced, typically to make the product more innovative. Operations managers must maintain a high degree of flexibility to be responsive to the design changes, and the work force must be highly skilled to adapt quickly to changing production requirements. Production runs are short and unit costs are high during this phase; consequently, operations managers must cope with changing schedules and overcapacity. High capital investment in production facilities is usually not necessary. Quality is of utmost importance, and any design or manufacturing defects must be quickly identified and eliminated.

As the product moves into the growth stage, sales volume increases and marketing's role in the corporate strategy is enhanced. Forecasting is critical: manufacturing must have the capacity to meet the growing demand. Operations is driven by the market, and the focus is on process innovation. Both the product and the process must achieve high reliability to eliminate "latent defects"—ones that do not appear during manufacturing but crop up after some period of use. Production volume increases, and capacity growth and utilization become critical.

As products mature, costs become critical. Manufacturing must focus on improving productivity and minimizing costs. Less production flexibility is needed as the product becomes more standardized, although some product innovation is possible and often desirable to maintain market share. The firm must invest in efficient and high-volume production facilities for supporting long production runs.

Finally, as demand declines and a product is phased out of the marketplace, the firm must maintain control over cost. Capacity needs are reduced, and overcapacity typifies the decline phase.

Because of the product life cycle, resource needs change over time. Capacity planning must therefore account for the forecasted product mix and the aggregate effect of different life cycles on resource requirements. A large capital investment and a long time horizon usually are involved in adding resources such as facilities and equipment, and once the decisions are made, they cannot be easily reversed.

The strategic variables discussed in Chapter 3—quality, product-development time, and flexibility—all affect capacity decisions. Insufficient capacity can easily result in poor quality if pressures for output increase. Rapid product development and high production flexibility might make increasing capacity appear to be a good plan, yet facilities, equipment, and labor are expensive. Also, capacity is not solely a function of capital equipment; it is also heavily influenced by operating procedures. Engineers create capacity through their designs; managers allocate capacity through their decisions; schedules specify the use of capacity to satisfy orders. Capacity should be used for continuous improvement of these strategic variables.

Strategic Capacity Planning

Capacity decisions are aimed at using a corporation's resources to maximize long-term profit while meeting cash-flow requirements. The cost of potential

Figure 7.4
Strategic Capacity-Planning Process

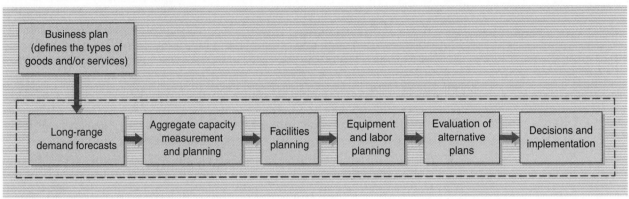

excess capacity must be balanced against the cost of potential lost sales due to too little capacity. Excess capacity costs money, especially for capital-intensive firms such as paper mills and steel mills. In contrast, in industries such as aircraft production, which operate with a continual backlog of orders, higher capacity will allow faster delivery times. Too little capacity can result in the inability to meet customer demand, particularly in service industries. However, tight capacity allows for higher equipment utilization and a better return on investment. What really complicates the decision is that the capacity plan must be based on long-term forecasts, which are usually uncertain. Other factors to consider include interest rates, technology improvements, construction costs, competition, and government regulations.

Figure 7.4 provides an overview of the strategic capacity-planning process. The business plan sets the direction of the organization by specifying the types of goods or services that are offered. As a first step in determining the resources required to produce each good or service, the organization must develop a long-range forecast of demand. The forecast should take into account such factors as industry trends, the rate and direction of technological innovation, the likely behavior of competitors, and the impact of international markets and sources of supply. American Hoist and Derrick provides an example of the importance of forecasting in capacity planning.

Applied P/OM
American Hoist and Derrick

Accurate forecasting is a crucial element of American Hoist and Derrick's capacity-planning process.[2]

American Hoist and Derrick is a manufacturer of construction equipment, with annual sales of several million dollars. Its sales forecast is an actual planning figure and is used to develop the master production schedule, cash flow projections, and work-force plans. One of the important components of the forecasting process is the use of the Delphi method of judgmental forecasting.

Top managers wanted an accurate five-year forecast of sales to plan for expansion of production capacity. The Delphi method was used in conjunction with regression models and exponential smoothing to generate a forecast. A panel of 23 key personnel was established, consisting of persons who had been making subjective forecasts, those who had been using or were affected by the forecasts, and those who had a strong knowledge of the market and corporate sales. Three rounds of the Delphi method were performed, each requesting estimates of gross national product, construction equipment industry shipments, American Hoist and Derrick construction-equipment group shipments, and American Hoist and Derrick corporate value of shipments. As the Delphi technique progressed, responses for each round were collected, analyzed, summarized, and reported back to the panel. In the third-round questionnaire, not only were the responses of the first two rounds included, but additional related facts, figures, and views of external experts were sent.

As a result of the Delphi experiment, the sales forecast error was less than .33 percent; in the following year the error was under 4 percent. Those levels represented considerable improvement over previous forecast errors of plus or minus 20 percent. In fact, the Delphi forecasts were more accurate than regression models or exponential smoothing, which had forecast errors of 10 to 15 percent. An additional result of the exercise was educational. Managers developed a uniform outlook on business conditions and corporate sales volume and thus had a common base for decision making.

Forecasts of demand for goods and services must then be translated into a measure of capacity needed. For instance, from the forecast of product demand, a manufacturing firm concluded that 2,400 machine hours would be needed in the milling department next year; anticipated growth in machine hours needed was expected to be 5 percent a year over the following five years. In another instance, an airline translated a demand forecast for flight services into an estimate of the number of flight attendants needed to meet the projected level of demand.

Capacity measurements must be translated into facility, equipment, and labor plans. *Facility needs* can be met by expanding or contracting existing facilities, constructing new facilities, or closing old ones. The firm needs to ask whether it should have one large facility or several smaller ones; where plants, warehouses, and so on should be located; and what the focus of each facility should be. (The subject of location is an important issue in itself and is discussed in detail in the next chapter.) *Equipment needs* might be met by purchasing additional machines or by replacing old machines with newer and faster technology. *Labor needs* might be met by hiring new workers or retraining present employees. Automation issues have an impact on both equipment and labor needs.

Both equipment and labor plans must be consistent with the capacity and facility plans. Also, although they are not discussed here, the financial issues associated with meeting capacity requirements naturally influence the selection of a capacity plan, as the example of Pfizer, Inc., shows.

Applied P/OM

Pfizer, Inc.

Pfizer, Inc., uses computer modeling to develop long-range capacity plans.[3]

At the Easton, Pennsylvania, plant of Pfizer, Inc., a producer of industrial materials used in paints, plastics, foods, cosmetics, and other products, the long-term planning for plant facilities is done on a divisional basis. A computer model converts forecasted product demand over a 10-year horizon into capacity needs by type of production process. Those needs are matched against current plant capacities so that capacity additions and cash requirements can be planned. The end result is a pro forma cash flow and profit/loss statement. Changes in the timing of capital additions are tested iteratively, as are different assumptions about the marketplace. The analysis is performed annually, and the result is the long-range capacity plan.

Capacity Definition and Measurement

Capacity is defined and measured in a variety of ways.[4] Two useful definitions are theoretical capacity and demonstrated capacity. **Theoretical capacity** is the maximum output capability possible, allowing no adjustments for preventive maintenance, unplanned downtime, shutdowns, and so on. **Demonstrated capacity** is the proven capacity calculated from actual output performance data. Demonstrated capacity is generally less than theoretical capacity when production losses due to scrap, machine breakdowns, rework, sick time, and so on, are taken into account. A simple example illustrates the differences.

Suppose a small machine shop that is designed to operate one shift per day five days per week can produce 500 units per shift with its current equipment, product mix, and workforce. The theoretical capacity of the shop is

$$(500 \text{ units/shift})(1 \text{ shift/day})(5 \text{ days/week}) = 2,500 \text{ units/week}.$$

If 10 percent of the productive time is used for preventive maintenance and product changeover setups, we would expect an output of .90(2,500) = 2,250 units/week. However, because of unanticipated machine breakdowns, defective output, material shortages, and other unplanned delays, the actual output might be only 2,000 units/week. That would be the shop's demonstrated capacity.

Theoretical capacity cannot be increased unless facilities or labor force are expanded (possibly through the use of overtime) or modified. Demonstrated capacity can often be increased by operational improvements such as improving work methods to reduce setup times or purchasing machines with lower maintenance requirements.

Figure 7.5
Production Process for a
Household Cleaner

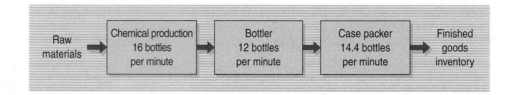

Setup time is an important factor in demonstrated capacity. Short setup times clearly increase capacity. In addition, they increase flexibility by allowing rapid product changeovers. Long setup times are the reason for some manufacturers' long production runs, which create excess inventory and increase the time for product delivery. With short production runs, both product delivery time and inventory are reduced. Fast setup times are necessary if short production runs are to be feasible. The Japanese have pioneered techniques for reducing setup time. A method called "Single-Minute Exchange of Die (SMED)" developed by Shigeo Shingo has often reduced setup times from hours to minutes.[5] (A die is a fixture that attaches to a machine for forming parts.) Many companies worldwide have adopted this technique and achieved substantial improvements in productivity.

When several different operations are performed in sequence, the capacity of the system is determined by the slowest operation, the *bottleneck,* in the system. Suppose the bottling operation is an intermediate step in the production of a household cleaner. The complete process is shown in Figure 7.5. Suppose the chemical process can produce at a rate of 2 gallons per minute and that each bottle holds 16 ounces. The bottling department can produce 12 bottles per minute, and the case packer packages 12 bottles per case at a rate of 1.2 cases per minute. If we translate each production rate into bottles per minute, we see that the production rate of the *chemical* process is

(2 gallons/minute)(8 bottles/gallon) = 16 bottles/minute.

The production rate of the *bottling* department is 12 bottles/minute, and the production rate of the *case packer* is

(1.2 cases/minute)(12 bottles/case) = 14.4 bottles/minute.

Since the bottling rate is the slowest (12 bottles per minute), the capacity of the entire system is 12 bottles per minute. Hence, the bottling process limits system production and is the bottleneck (no pun intended!) in the system. Capacity improvements and investment decisions should be focused on bottleneck operations.

Capacity can be measured in one of two ways. One measure of capacity is the *rate of output per unit of time.* In the household-cleaner example, capacity was measured in this way. The unit of measure selected should be that of the product produced; tons per month and parts per minute are examples. If a plant produces only one type of product, capacity is usually easy to define. In a sugar refinery, for example, a logical measure of capacity is tons of sugar per month (or per day, per week, and so on). However, if more than one product is produced, an output-rate capacity measure may be misleading. To illustrate, let us consider a small winery. A good measure of capacity is the number of gallons

Table 7.2 Capacity Measures

Organization	Measure of Capacity
	Output Measures
Automobile plant	Automobiles/hour
Law firm	Billable hours/week
Oil refinery	Barrels of oil/day
Electric company	Megawatts of electricity/hour
Paper producer	Tons of paper/week
	Input Measures
Jet engine plant	Machine-hours/month
	Labor-hours/month
Airline	Number of seats/flight
Hotel	Number of rooms, number of beds
Grocery store	Number of checkout lines
Warehouse	Cubic feet of space
Tennis club	Number of courts
Department store	Number of square feet

or barrels of wine produced per month. However, red wine takes longer to age than white wine. If the winery is producing half red wine and half white wine and then changes to a 30 and 70 percent mix, the capacity as an output measure would clearly increase, even though the physical facilities and labor do not change. Hence the product mix of a firm will affect capacity if it is measured this way. That need not always be the case, however. For example, the capping department of the winery may have a capacity of 6,000 bottles per day, which obviously does not depend on the type of wine produced.

The second principal method of measuring capacity is in terms of *units of input*. In manufacturing, many capacity measures are expressed in hours of available time. For example, demonstrated capacity is often expressed as the average number of items produced multiplied by the standard hours per item. (The standard time is the length of time that should ideally be required to run one item through an operation.) In service organizations, units of input is a more meaningful measure of capacity than rate of output, since the ability to meet demand depends primarily on the resources available. An example of an input measure of capacity is the number of beds available in a hospital. This partially determines the amount of service demand that can be accommodated (along with equipment and labor).

Other capacity measures are given in Table 7.2. Both input and output measures are useful in resource-requirements planning. The appropriate measure to use depends on the type of organization and the nature of the product.

Example : ## Capacity Measurement for a Quick-Service Restaurant

Fast Burger, Inc., is building a new restaurant near a busy shopping mall. The restaurant will be open 15 hours per day 360 days per year. Managers have analyzed demand patterns at similar Fast Burger outlets and concluded that the restaurant should have the capacity to handle a peak hourly demand of 1,000 customers. Consequently, they would like to determine how many grills, deep fryers, and soft drink spouts are needed.

The average customer purchase is

1 burger (4-ounce hamburger or cheeseburger)
1 bag of french fries (4 ounces)
1 soft drink (12 ounces)

A 36 × 36-inch grill can cook 450 ounces of burgers every 10 minutes, and a single-basket deep fryer can cook 4 pounds of french fries in 6 minutes, or 40 pounds per hour. Finally, one soft drink spout can dispense 50 ounces of soft drink per minute, or 3000 ounces per hour.

To determine the equipment needed to meet peak hourly demand, Fast Burger must translate expected demand in terms of customers per hour into needs for grills, deep fryers, and soft drink spouts. First note that the peak hourly needs for burgers, french fries, and soft drinks are as follows.

Product	Peak Hourly Need (ounces)
Burgers	4,000
French fries	4,000
Soft drinks	12,000

Since the hourly capacity of a grill is $(450)(6) = 2700$ ounces, the number of grills needed to satisfy a peak hourly demand of 4000 ounces of burgers is

$$\text{number of grills} = \frac{4000}{2700} = 1.48 \text{ grills}$$

To determine the number of single-basket deep fryers needed to meet a peak hourly demand of 4000 ounces of french fries, we must first compute the hourly capacity of the deep fryer.

$$\text{capacity of the deep fryer} = \frac{4000 \text{ oz / hr}}{16 \text{ oz / lb}} = 250 \text{ lb / hr}$$

Hence, the number of single-basket deep fryers needed is $250/40 = 6.25$.

Finally, the number of soft drink spouts needed to satisfy peak demand of 12,000 ounces is

$$\text{number of soft drink spouts needed} = \frac{12,000}{3000} = 4$$

After reviewing this analysis, the managers decided to purchase one 36 × 36-inch grill and a smaller, 30 × 30-inch grill. A deep-fryer capacity of seven baskets was planned, and a five-spout soft drink system was installed. Although their analysis showed a need for only four spouts, the managers wanted to provide some margin for error, primarily because they felt the peak hourly demand for soft drinks might have been underestimated.

Strategies for Capacity Planning

Capacity-planning strategies involve an assessment of existing capacity, forecasts of future capacity requirements, choice of alternative ways to build capacity, and financial evaluation. Forecasts of aggregate demand can be obtained by combining demand estimates over product life cycles as shown in Figure 7.6.

In developing a long-range capacity plan, a firm must make a basic economic trade-off between the cost of capacity and the opportunity cost of not having adequate capacity. Capacity costs include both the initial investment in facilities and the annual cost of operating and maintaining the facilities. The cost of not having sufficient capacity is the opportunity loss incurred from lost sales and reduced market share. Opportunity costs are very difficult to quantify. Conceptually, at least, the level of capacity should minimize the present value of the total cost, as shown in Figure 7.7.

This model assumes one level of capacity over a specified period, as opposed to incremental capacity increases. The advantage of such an approach is that the fixed costs of building and construction need to be incurred only once, and thus the firm can take advantage of any economies of scale.

Figure 7.6
Determining Aggregate
Demand from Life-Cycle
Curves

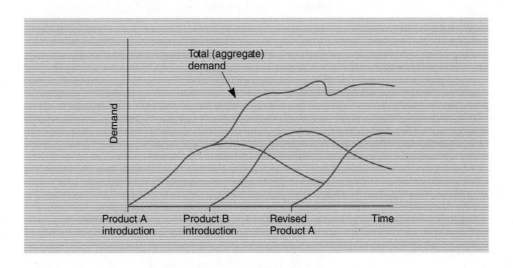

Figure 7.7
Model of Capacity/Cost
Trade-Offs

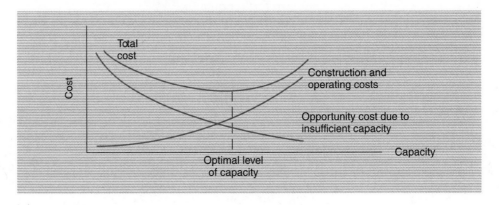

Figure 7.8 The Three Strategies: (a) Matching Capacity with Demand, (b) Excess Capacity Policy, (c) Capacity Shortage Policy

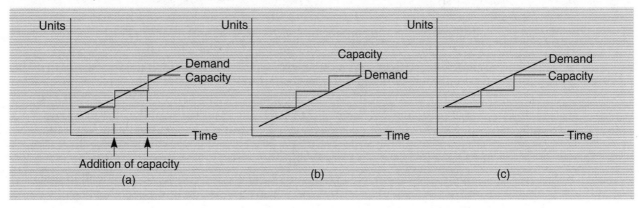

Several disadvantages are associated with this approach, however. The firm may not be able to acquire the considerable financial resources required for a major capacity expansion, and substantial risks are involved if forecasts are incorrect. Note also that if aggregate demand exhibits steady growth, the facility will be underutilized for a long period of time, since the level of capacity is planned for the end of the time horizon. Other disadvantages relate to the fact that new and unforeseen products and technology, government regulations, and other factors affecting capacity needs may alter capacity requirements. The alternative is to view capacity expansion incrementally. Such an approach requires determining the *amount, timing,* and *form* of capacity changes.

To illustrate capacity expansion decisions, let us make two assumptions: (1) capacity is added in "chunks," or discrete increments, such as five units per change, and (2) demand is steadily increasing. There are three basic options for matching capacity with demand.

Figure 7.8(a) illustrates the strategy of matching capacity additions with demand as closely as possible. When the capacity curve is above the demand curve, the firm has excess capacity; when it is below, there is insufficient capacity to meet demand. During periods of capacity shortage, there are several alternatives. The firm can incur lost sales and possibly lose market position, or it can make short-term capacity expansions through subcontracting, overtime, additional shifts, and so forth. (In Chapter 17 we discuss short-term capacity decisions in further detail.)

Figure 7.8(b) shows a capacity-expansion policy with the goal of maintaining sufficient capacity to minimize the chances of not meeting demand. Since there is always excess capacity, a "cushion" against unexpected demand from large orders or new customers is provided. This cushion also enables the firm to give good customer service, since backorders will rarely occur.

Finally, Figure 7.8(c) illustrates a policy of capacity expansion that lags behind demand and results in constant capacity shortage. Such a strategy requires less investment and provides for high capacity utilization and thus a higher rate of return on investment. However, it can also reduce long-term profitability through overtime and productivity losses that occur as the firm scrambles to satisfy demand. In the long run, such a policy can lead to a permanent loss of market position.

Figure 7.9
Alternative Size/Timing
Capacity Strategies

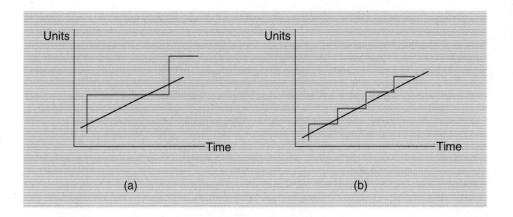

With all of these strategies, the firm has the option of making frequent small capacity increments or fewer large increments. These options are shown in Figure 7.9. The choice should be based on careful economic analysis of the cost and risks associated with excess capacity and capacity shortages. The ability and desire of the firm to make short-term capacity adjustments must also be taken into account. With proprietary technology, for example, subcontracting would not be feasible.

Decision-Analysis Techniques

Decision-analysis techniques can assist decision makers in selecting from among several capacity alternatives with uncertain future outcomes. Decision analysis techniques are discussed in detail in Supplementary Chapter B. This section presents a simple example in which decision trees are used to analyze a capacity-expansion decision.

Example

Application of Decision Analysis to a Capacity-Expansion Problem

Southland Corporation's decision to produce a new line of recreational products has resulted in the need to construct a new plant. The decision as to plant size depends on projections of marketplace reaction to the new product line. To conduct an analysis, marketing managers defined three levels of possible long-run demand. The following payoff table shows the projected profit in millions of dollars for the three levels of demand.

	Long-Run Demand		
Decision	*Low*	*Medium*	*High*
Small plant	150	200	200
Large plant	50	200	500

Figure 7.10
Decision Tree for Southland Corporation's Capacity-Expansion Problem

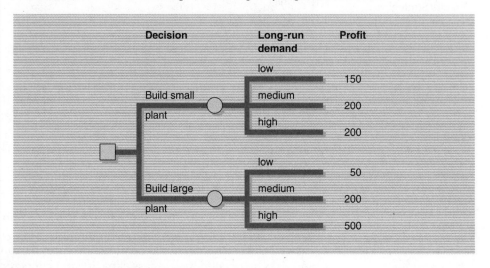

Assume that the best estimate of the probability of low long-run demand is 0.20, of medium long-run demand is 0.15, and of high long-run demand is 0.65. What is the recommended decision?

Figure 7.10 shows the decision tree for this situation. If Southland chooses to build a small plant, the expected profit is computed as

$$.2(150) + .15(200) + .65(200) = \$190 \text{ million}.$$

If the company chooses to build a large plant, the expected profit is

$$.2(50) + .15(200) + .65(500) = \$365 \text{ million}.$$

Thus, on the basis of expected value, the best decision is to build a large plant. In Discussion Question 8 you will be asked to comment on the assumptions behind this reasoning.

Capacity Planning for Service Organizations

Capacity planning presents a different problem for the production of services than for the production of manufactured goods. If demand is cyclical in manufacturing, shortages can usually be avoided by building up inventory during slow periods or arranging to subcontract production with another firm. In a service organization like MamaMia's Pizza, it would be unwise to make more pizzas on Thursday in anticipation of large demand on Friday evening! However, capacity can be adjusted to some extent by scheduling more kitchen staff and drivers on weekends and holidays when demand is high. Such short-term capacity decisions are discussed in subsequent chapters. At MamaMia's, a major constraint is the oven capacity. It cannot be adjusted in the short run, and thus must be built into the facility to meet peak periods of demand.

As in manufacturing organizations, it is important to balance capacity at various stages of a service process to avoid bottlenecks. Balancing is probably even more important for service organizations, in fact, since manufactured goods do not complain about waiting, but people do!

In deciding to change capacity, service and manufacturing organizations must make similar decisions. They must be concerned with the amount, timing, and form of capacity additions. It is easy to add the wrong kind of capacity for producing services. For instance, to increase passenger capacity, some airlines purchased jumbo jets. That turned out to be a poor strategic decision when competitors increased capacity by flying more frequently with smaller jets. While their total capacity was the same in terms of seats per day, the more frequent flight schedules provided better customer service and gained increased market share for the airline providing the service.

Another strategic error a service organization can make is to increase only a portion of its service capacity. For example, if a hotel adds more rooms, it must also increase capacity in its restaurants, meeting rooms, and recreational facilities to accommodate a larger number of guests.

Detailed Capacity Planning

Detailed capacity planning involves determining specific facility, equipment, and labor requirements for supporting the aggregate capacity needs identified through long-range forecasts.

Facility Planning

Additional capacity can be created in a variety of ways. Old facilities can be expanded and modernized, or new facilities can be built. In planning additional facilities, one must consider several issues, the first of which is the number and/or the size of the facilities to be added. Arguments based on **economies of scale** are often used to justify large facilities. In general, the per-unit manufacturing costs increase at a slower rate than the production volume. For example, if we let F equal the total fixed cost, V equal the variable cost per unit, and Q equal the production quantity, then

$$\text{total cost per unit} = \frac{\text{fixed cost} + \text{variable cost}}{\text{total production}} = \frac{F + VQ}{Q}$$

$$= \frac{F}{Q} + V.$$

The per-unit variable cost, V, is constant (the same for all production levels). As Q increases, F/Q decreases; that is, fixed costs are spread over more units and hence total cost per unit decreases. When capacity is added, the initial increase in the production quantity, Q, is usually not large enough to offset the additional fixed costs, and thus higher total costs per unit are incurred. However, as production volume increases and more of the additional capacity is utilized, benefits from economies of scale begin to accrue.

There are also disadvantages to large facilities, or **diseconomies of scale.** A larger work force requires more supervisors and managers, leading to a higher level of bureaucracy. Large facilities can reduce the focus of the plant and lead to inefficiencies and loss of strategic position. For example, in the electronics industry the three major areas of production focus are development and proto-type manufacturing, component manufacturing, and assembly and test. By concentrating each within a single small facility, the firm can achieve many strategic advantages. For instance, development and prototype manufacturing requires high technology and high flexibility in product changeover; component manufacturing needs high volume and limited flexibility; assembly and test should have more specialized and dedicated equipment and high-volume throughput capability. In addition, with one large plant there is increased vulnerability to natural disasters, strikes, and future reductions in demand. With smaller facilities, a firm can sell off plants much more easily if cash is needed or a change in strategic direction occurs.

One must also consider the costs of transporting raw materials to the plants and finished products to warehouses or customers. Such costs will very likely offset all or a significant part of the manufacturing cost advantage of a single large plant. These issues are treated more fully in the next chapter.

Another issue that must be addressed is the daily utilization of the facility. Should it operate on a single shift or around the clock? The high capital costs of equipment tend to favor continuous operation. Routine start-up and shutdown of equipment can lead to excessive maintenance costs. On the other hand, there may be labor cost differentials for evening and night shifts, and the quality of the labor force available during those times might be lower. Typically, capital-intensive industries operate on a three-shift basis and labor-intensive industries operate with a single shift.

Equipment and Labor Planning

Determining equipment needs for manufactured products begins with an analysis of the items to be produced and the equipment needed to manufacture them. That requires a detailed specification of individual parts and components that make up a product, the method of manufacture, and the sequence of production and assembly steps. From this information, it is possible to determine the processing time, p (usually in minute per piece), for each operation and the efficiency, e, of the operation. *Efficiency* is a dimensionless quantity defined as the fraction of time that the equipment is operating. The analysis takes into account such factors as setup time on the machine, maintenance, and unexpected failures. The details of this analysis are within the scope of *process analysis and design* and *work measurement* and are discussed in Chapters 9 and 10.

If the required production is R units per day and H hours are available each day, the number of machines required (N) can be calculated by the formula,

$$N = \frac{pR}{60He}.$$

That is,

$$N = \text{number of machines required}$$

$$= \frac{(p \text{ minutes } / \text{ unit})(R \text{ units } / \text{ day})}{(60 \text{ minutes } / \text{ hour})(H \text{ hours } / \text{ day } / \text{ machine})(e)}.$$

This is a very approximate measure of equipment requirements, since it does not include such factors as scrap and rework, changes in product mix, or delays from previous production operations. However, it is useful as a planning tool to determine general equipment requirements.

To illustrate the use of equation 7.1, consider the bottling department of a consumer goods plant that manufactures liquid household cleaners. Each bottling machine can fill 6 bottles per minute at an efficiency of .85. The department works one shift per day (8 hours), and the required production is 5,000 bottles per day. The number of bottling machines needed to meet this demand is

$$N = \frac{(1/6)(5000)}{60(8)(.85)} = 2.04.$$

The required production can be approximately satisfied with two machines.

Equation 7.1 can also be used to estimate labor requirements. For example, suppose a company is interested in determining the number of technicians needed for the final test of a product. If each technician can work at a rate of p minutes per unit at an efficiency e (taking into account fatigue, personal time, and so forth), then Equation 7.1 can be used to determine the number of technicians needed to meet a required output rate R.

In service organizations, labor planning is a very important aspect of capacity planning. Examples include nurse staffing in hospitals and operator staffing at a telephone company. Equation 7.1 usually must be modified for service organizations, since service employees perform a variety of tasks at different times. Also, activities are usually longer in duration, so it is generally better to measure activities in hours rather than in minutes.

In general,

$$N = \frac{\sum_{i=1}^{k} p_i R_i}{Te}$$

where

N = labor requirements,
k = the number of different activities performed,
p_i = time for activity i,
R_i = workload per unit of time for activity i,
T = total time available, and
e = efficiency factor.

Example | **Labor Planning for a Service Organization**

A social worker performs two major activities. Activity 1 requires 4 hours and activity 2 requires 1.5 hours. Each person is available 40 hours per week, and an allowance for personal time and nonroutine activities is 20 percent. Thus, the efficiency factor is $1 - .20 = .80$. The estimated work load is 40 cases per week of type 1 and 60 cases per week of type 2. Let

p_1 = time for activity 1 = 4 hours,
p_2 = time for activity 2 = 1.5 hours,
R_1 = number of cases per week of type 1 = 40,

R_2 = number of cases per week of type 2 = 60, and
T = 40 hours per week (this replaces the term $60H$ in equation 7.1).

Then the staff size required for this agency is calculated as follows:

$$N = \frac{p_1R_1 + p_2R_2}{Te}$$

$$= \frac{4(40) + 1.5(60)}{40(.8)}$$

$$= 7.8125$$

Thus eight workers are needed to meet the forecasted demand.

Learning Curve

If you have ever learned to type or play a musical instrument, you know that the longer and more often you work at it, the better you become. The same is true in production and assembly operations, as was recognized in the 1920s at Wright-Patterson Air Force Base in the assembly of aircraft. Studies showed that the number of labor hours required to produce the fourth plane was about 80 percent of the amount of time spent on the second; the eighth plane took only 80 percent as much time as the fourth; the sixteenth plane 80 percent of the time of the eighth, and so on. The decrease in production time as the number produced increases is illustrated in Figure 7.11. As production doubles from x units to $2x$ units, the time per unit of the $2x$th unit is 80 percent of the time of the xth unit. This is called an 80 percent **learning curve.** Such a curve exhibits a steep initial decline and then levels off as workers become more proficient in their tasks.

Defense industries (e.g., the aircraft and electronics industries), which introduce many new and complex products, use learning curves to estimate labor

Figure 7.11
An 80 Percent Learning
Curve

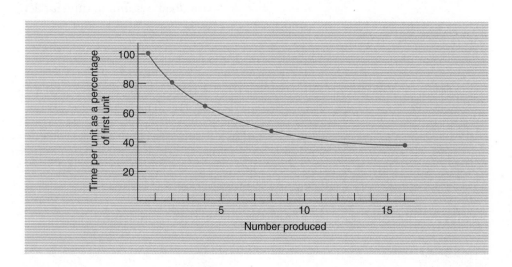

requirements and capacity, determine costs and budget requirements, and plan and schedule production. Eighty-percent learning curves are generally accepted as a standard, although the ratio of machine work to manual assembly affects the curve percentage. Obviously, no learning takes place if all assembly is done by machine. As a rule of thumb, if the ratio of manual to machine work is 3 to 1 (three-fourths manual), then 80 percent is a good value; if the ratio is 1 to 3, then 90 percent is often used. An even split of manual and machine work would suggest the use of an 85 percent learning curve. The learning factor may also be estimated from past histories of similar parts or products.

Mathematically, the learning curve is represented by the function

$$y = ax^{-b}$$

where
  x = number of units produced,
  a = hours required to produce the first unit,
  y = time to produce the xth unit, and
  b = constant equal to $\dfrac{-\ln p}{\ln 2}$ for a $100p$ percent learning curve.

Thus, for an 80 percent learning curve, $p = .8$ and

$$b = \frac{-\ln .8}{\ln 2} = \frac{-(-.223)}{.693} = .322.$$

For a 90 percent curve, $p = .9$ and

$$b = \frac{-\ln .9}{\ln 2} = \frac{-(-.105)}{.693} = .152.$$

Example

Using the Learning Curve for Labor Planning

Suppose a manufacturing firm is introducing a new product and has determined that a 90 percent learning curve is applicable. Estimates of demand for the next three years are 50, 75, and 100 units. The time to produce the first unit is estimated to be 3,500 hours. Therefore, the learning-curve function is

$$y = 3,500x^{-.152}.$$

Consequently, the time to manufacture the second unit will be

$$3,500\,(2)^{-.152} = 3,150 \text{ hours.}$$

Table 7.3 gives the cumulative number of hours required to produce the three-year demand in increments of 25 units. Thus, to produce the 50 units in the first year, the firm will require 112,497 hours. If we assume that each employee works 160 hours per month, or 1,920 hours per year, we find that for the first year the firm will need

$$\frac{112,497}{1,920} = 59 \text{ employees}$$

Table 7.3 Cumulative Time Required under Learning-Curve Function

Cumulative Units	Cumulative Hours Required
25	61,996
50	112,497
75	159,164
100	203,494
125	246,160
150	287,545
175	327,894
200	367,374
225	406,112

to produce this product. In the second year, the total number of hours required will be the difference between the cumulative requirements for the first two years' production (246,160 hours) and the first year's production (112,497 hours), or

$$246{,}160 - 112{,}497 = 133{,}663 \text{ hours.}$$

So the labor requirements for the second year are

$$\frac{133{,}663}{1920} = 70 \text{ employees.}$$

Similarly, for the third year, the labor requirements are

$$\frac{406{,}112 - 246{,}160}{1920} = 83 \text{ employees.}$$

These are aggregate numbers; at a more detailed planning level, they will vary according to how production is actually scheduled over the year.

Values for learning-curve functions can be computed easily through the use of tables. Tables 7.4 and 7.5 present unit values and cumulative values, respectively, for learning curves from 60 percent through 95 percent. To find the time to produce a specific unit, multiply the time for the first unit by the appropriate factor in Table 7.4. For the 90 percent learning curve example presented earlier, the time for the second unit is 3,500(.9000) = 3,150. The time for the third unit is 3,500(.8462) = 2961.7, and so on.

To find the time for a cumulative number of units, we can use Table 7.5. Thus, for a 90 percent learning curve, if the time for the first unit is 3,500, the time for the first 25 units is 3,500(17.7132) = 61,996. Similarly, the time for the first 100 units is 3,500(58.1410) = 203,494. The values in Table 7.3 were found using this table.

Managerial Issues

While the theory implies that improvement will continue forever, in actual practice the learning curve flattens out. As management interest in the initial production of a new item decreases, operators may reach a level of production that

Table 7.4 Table of Unit Values for Learning Curves

nth unit

p	.60	.65	.70	.75	.80	.85	.90	.95
x b	.737	.621	.515	.415	.322	.234	.152	.074
1	1.0000	1.0000	1.0000	1.0000	1.0000	1.0000	1.0000	1.0000
2	0.6000	0.6500	0.7000	0.7500	0.8000	0.8500	0.9000	0.9500
3	0.4450	0.5052	0.5682	0.6338	0.7021	0.7729	0.8462	0.9219
4	0.3600	0.4225	0.4900	0.5625	0.6400	0.7225	0.8100	0.9025
5	0.3054	0.3678	0.4368	0.5127	0.5956	0.6857	0.7830	0.8877
6	0.2670	0.3284	0.3977	0.4754	0.5617	0.6570	0.7616	0.8758
7	0.2383	0.2984	0.3674	0.4459	0.5345	0.6337	0.7439	0.8659
8	0.2160	0.2746	0.3430	0.4219	0.5120	0.6141	0.7290	0.8574
9	0.1980	0.2552	0.3228	0.4017	0.4929	0.5974	0.7161	0.8499
10	0.1832	0.2391	0.3058	0.3846	0.4765	0.5828	0.7047	0.8433
11	0.1708	0.2253	0.2912	0.3696	0.4621	0.5699	0.6946	0.8374
12	0.1602	0.2135	0.2784	0.3565	0.4493	0.5584	0.6854	0.8320
13	0.1510	0.2031	0.2672	0.3449	0.4379	0.5480	0.6771	0.8271
14	0.1430	0.1940	0.2572	0.3344	0.4276	0.5386	0.6696	0.8226
15	0.1359	0.1858	0.2482	0.3250	0.4182	0.5300	0.6626	0.8184
16	0.1296	0.1785	0.2401	0.3164	0.4096	0.5220	0.6561	0.8145
17	0.1239	0.1719	0.2327	0.3085	0.4017	0.5146	0.6501	0.8109
18	0.1188	0.1659	0.2260	0.3013	0.3944	0.5078	0.6445	0.8074
19	0.1142	0.1604	0.2198	0.2946	0.3876	0.5014	0.6392	0.8042
20	0.1099	0.1554	0.2141	0.2884	0.3812	0.4954	0.6342	0.8012
21	0.1061	0.1507	0.2087	0.2826	0.3753	0.4898	0.6295	0.7983
22	0.1025	0.1465	0.2038	0.2772	0.3697	0.4844	0.6251	0.7955
23	0.0992	0.1425	0.1992	0.2722	0.3644	0.4794	0.6209	0.7929
24	0.0961	0.1387	0.1949	0.2674	0.3595	0.4747	0.6169	0.7904
25	0.0933	0.1353	0.1908	0.2629	0.3548	0.4701	0.6131	0.7880
30	0.0815	0.1208	0.1737	0.2437	0.3346	0.4505	0.5963	0.7775
35	0.0728	0.1097	0.1605	0.2286	0.3184	0.4345	0.5825	0.7687
40	0.0660	0.1010	0.1498	0.2163	0.3050	0.4211	0.5708	0.7611
45	0.0605	0.0939	0.1410	0.2060	0.2936	0.4096	0.5607	0.7545
50	0.0560	0.0879	0.1336	0.1972	0.2838	0.3996	0.5518	0.7486
55	0.0522	0.0829	0.1272	0.1895	0.2753	0.3908	0.5438	0.7434
60	0.0489	0.0785	0.1216	0.1828	0.2676	0.3829	0.5367	0.7386
65	0.0461	0.0747	0.1167	0.1768	0.2608	0.3758	0.5302	0.7342
70	0.0437	0.0713	0.1123	0.1715	0.2547	0.3693	0.5243	0.7302
75	0.0415	0.0683	0.1084	0.1666	0.2491	0.3634	0.5188	0.7265
80	0.0396	0.0657	0.1049	0.1622	0.2440	0.3579	0.5137	0.7231
85	0.0379	0.0632	0.1017	0.1582	0.2393	0.3529	0.5090	0.7198
90	0.0363	0.0610	0.0987	0.1545	0.2349	0.3482	0.5046	0.7168
95	0.0349	0.0590	0.0960	0.1511	0.2308	0.3438	0.5005	0.7139
100	0.0336	0.0572	0.0935	0.1479	0.2271	0.3397	0.4966	0.7112
125	0.0285	0.0498	0.0834	0.1348	0.2113	0.3224	0.4800	0.6996
150	0.0249	0.0444	0.0759	0.1250	0.1993	0.3089	0.4669	0.6902
175	0.0222	0.0404	0.0701	0.1172	0.1896	0.2979	0.4561	0.6824
200	0.0201	0.0371	0.0655	0.1109	0.1816	0.2887	0.4469	0.6757
225	0.0185	0.0345	0.0616	0.1056	0.1749	0.2809	0.4390	0.6698
250	0.0171	0.0323	0.0584	0.1011	0.1691	0.2740	0.4320	0.6646
275	0.0159	0.0305	0.0556	0.0972	0.1639	0.2680	0.4258	0.6599
300	0.0149	0.0289	0.0531	0.0937	0.1594	0.2625	0.4202	0.6557
350	0.0133	0.0262	0.0491	0.0879	0.1517	0.2532	0.4105	0.6482
400	0.0121	0.0241	0.0458	0.0832	0.1453	0.2454	0.4022	0.6419

Table 7.4 Table of Unit Values for Learning Curves (continued)

p	.60	.65	.70	.75	.80	.85	.90	.95
x b	.737	.621	.515	.415	.322	.234	.152	.074
450	0.0111	0.0224	0.0431	0.0792	0.1399	0.2387	0.3951	0.6363
500	0.0103	0.0210	0.0408	0.0758	0.1352	0.2329	0.3888	0.6314
550	0.0096	0.0198	0.0389	0.0729	0.1312	0.2278	0.3832	0.6269
600	0.0090	0.0188	0.0372	0.0703	0.1275	0.2232	0.3782	0.6229
650	0.0085	0.0179	0.0357	0.0680	0.1243	0.2190	0.3736	0.6192
700	0.0080	0.0171	0.0344	0.0659	0.1214	0.2152	0.3694	0.6158
750	0.0076	0.0163	0.0332	0.0641	0.1187	0.2118	0.3656	0.6127
800	0.0073	0.0157	0.0321	0.0624	0.1163	0.2086	0.3620	0.6098
850	0.0069	0.0151	0.0311	0.0608	0.1140	0.2057	0.3587	0.6070
900	0.0067	0.0146	0.0302	0.0594	0.1119	0.2029	0.3556	0.6045

Table 7.5 Table of Cumulative Values for Learning Curves

x	$p = .60$	$p = .65$	$p = .70$	$p = .75$	$p = .80$	$p = .85$	$p = .90$	$p = .95$
1	1.0000	1.0000	1.0000	1.0000	1.0000	1.0000	1.0000	1.0000
2	1.6000	1.6500	1.7000	1.7500	1.8000	1.8500	1.9000	1.9500
3	2.0450	2.1552	2.2682	2.3838	2.5021	2.6229	2.7462	2.8719
4	2.4050	2.5777	2.7582	2.9463	3.1421	3.3454	3.5562	3.7744
5	2.7104	2.9455	3.1950	3.4591	3.7377	4.0311	4.3392	4.6621
6	2.9774	3.2739	3.5928	3.9345	4.2994	4.6881	5.1008	5.5380
7	3.2158	3.5723	3.9601	4.3804	4.8339	5.3217	5.8447	6.4039
8	3.4318	3.8469	4.3031	4.8022	5.3459	5.9358	6.5737	7.2612
9	3.6298	4.1021	4.6260	5.2040	5.8389	6.5332	7.2898	8.1112
10	3.8131	4.3412	4.9318	5.5886	6.3154	7.1161	7.9945 ·	8.9545
11	3.9839	4.5665	5.2229	5.9582	6.7775	7.6860	8.6890	9.7919
12	4.1441	4.7800	5.5013	6.3147	7.2268	8.2444	9.3745	10.6239
13	4.2951	4.9831	5.7685	6.6596	7.6647	8.7925	10.0516	11.4511
14	4.4381	5.1770	6.0257	6.9940	8.0923	9.3311	10.7212	12.2736
15	4.5740	5.3628	6.2739	7.3190	8.5105	9.8611	11.3837	13.0921
16	4.7036	5.5413	6.5140	7.6355	8.9201	10.3831	12.0398	13.9066
17	4.8276	5.7132	6.7467	7.9440	9.3218	10.8977	12.6899	14.7174
18	4.9464	5.8791	6.9727	8.2453	9.7162	11.4055	13.3344	15.5249
19	5.0606	6.0396	7.1925	8.5399	10.1037	11.9069	13.9735	16.3291
20	5.1705	6.1950	7.4065	8.8284	10.4849	12.4023	14.6078	17.1302
21	5.2766	6.3457	7.6153	9.1110	10.8602	12.8920	15.2373	17.9285
22	5.3791	6.4922	7.8191	9.3882	11.2299	13.3765	15.8624	18.7241
23	5.4783	6.6346	8.0183	9.6604	11.5943	13.8559	16.4833	19.5170
24	5.5744	6.7734	8.2132	9.9278	11.9538	14.3306	17.1002	20.3074
25	5.6677	6.9086	8.4040	10.1907	12.3086	14.8007	17.7132	21.0955
30	6.0974	7.5398	9.3050	11.4458	14.0199	17.0907	20.7269	25.0032
35	6.4779	8.1095	10.1328	12.6179	15.6428	19.2938	23.6660	28.8636
40	6.8208	8.6312	10.9024	13.7232	17.1935	21.4252	26.5427	32.6838
45	7.1337	9.1143	11.6245	14.7731	18.6835	23.4955	29.3658	36.4692
50	7.4222	9.5654	12.3069	15.7761	20.1217	25.5131	32.1420	40.2239

is expected of them and hold that rate. In some cases, even if the work can be produced faster, the material required for that rate may not be available in sufficient quantities.

Learning curves can apply to individual operators or, in an aggregate sense, to the entire process for a new product. The terms *improvement curve, experience curve,* and *manufacturing progress function* are often used to describe the learning phenomenon in the aggregate context. Those curves can be used for cost estimating and pricing, short-term work scheduling, setting manufacturing performance goals, and determining incentive payments for piecework employees. From a strategic perspective, a firm may use the learning curve concept to establish a pricing schedule that does not initially cover cost in order to gain increased market share.

Managers should realize that improvement along a learning curve does not take place automatically. Learning-curve theory is most applicable to new products or processes that have a high potential for improvement and when the benefits will be realized only when appropriate incentives and effective motivational tools are used. Organizational changes may also have significant effects

Table 7.5 Table of Cumulative Values for Learning Curves (*continued*)

x	p = .60	p = .65	p = .70	p = .75	p = .80	p = .85	p = .90	p = .95
55	7.6904	9.9896	12.9553	16.7386	21.5147	27.4843	34.8766	43.9511
60	7.9413	10.3906	13.5742	17.6658	22.8678	29.4143	37.5740	47.6535
65	8.1774	10.7715	14.1674	18.5617	24.1853	31.3071	40.2377	51.3333
70	8.4006	11.1347	14.7376	19.4296	25.4708	33.1664	42.8706	54.9924
75	8.6123	11.4823	15.2874	20.2722	26.7273	34.9949	45.4753	58.6323
80	8.8140	11.8158	15.8188	21.0921	27.9572	36.7953	48.0539	62.2544
85	9.0067	12.1367	16.3335	21.8910	29.1628	38.5696	50.6082	65.8599
90	9.1912	12.4461	16.8329	22.6708	30.3459	40.3198	53.1399	69.4498
95	9.3683	12.7451	17.3182	23.4329	31.5081	42.0474	55.6504	73.0250
100	9.5388	13.0345	17.7907	24.1786	32.6508	43.7539	58.1410	76.5864
125	10.3079	14.3614	19.9894	27.6971	38.1131	52.0109	70.3315	94.2095
150	10.9712	15.5326	21.9722	30.9342	43.2335	59.8883	82.1558	111.5730
175	11.5576	16.5883	23.7917	33.9545	48.0859	67.4633	93.6839	128.7232
200	12.0853	17.5541	25.4820	36.8007	52.7000	74.7885	104.9641	145.6931
225	12.5665	18.4477	27.0669	39.5029	57.1712	81.9021	116.0319	162.5066
250	13.0098	19.2816	28.5638	42.0833	61.4659	88.8328	126.9144	179.1824
275	13.4216	20.0653	29.9855	44.5588	65.6246	95.6028	137.6327	195.7354
300	13.8068	20.8059	31.3423	46.9427	69.6634	102.2301	148.2040	212.1774
350	14.5112	22.1796	33.8916	51.4760	77.4311	115.1123	168.9596	244.7667
400	15.1451	233.4362	36.2596	55.7477	84.8487	127.5691	189.2677	277.0124
450	15.7230	24.5987	38.4799	59.8030	91.9733	139.6656	209.1935	308.9609
500	16.2555	25.6835	40.5766	63.6753	98.8473	151.4506	228.7851	340.6475
550	16.7500	26.7028	42.5680	67.3900	105.5032	162.9622	248.0809	372.1002
600	17.2125	27.6662	44.4684	70.9671	111.9671	174.2309	267.1118	403.3421
650	17.6474	28.5808	46.2889	74.4225	118.2598	185.2815	285.9030	434.3918
700	18.0583	29.4528	48.0387	77.7693	124.3985	196.1346	304.4757	465.2653
750	18.4482	30.2869	49.7254	81.0183	130.3976	206.8073	322.8479	495.9759
800	18.8193	31.0871	51.3552	84.1786	136.2693	217.3144	341.0347	526.5353
850	19.1737	31.8568	52.9333	87.2580	142.0242	227.6687	359.0497	556.9538
900	19.5131	32.5989	54.4644	90.2631	147.6709	237.8811	376.9043	587.2402

on learning. Changes in technology or work methods will affect the learning curve, as will the institution of productivity and quality-improvement programs.

The following factors can affect the applicability of the learning curve and/or the amount of learning that occurs.

1. The learning curve does not usually apply to supervisory personnel, skilled craftspeople, or jobs that have nonrepetitive job tasks.

2. A change in the ratio of indirect labor or supervisory talent to direct labor can alter the rate of learning.

3. The institution of incentive systems, bonus plans, quality initiatives, and the like may increase learning.

4. Changes in product design, raw material usage, and/or the production process may significantly alter the learning curve.

5. A contract phaseout may result in a lengthening of production times for the last units produced, since employees want to prolong their income period.

6. The lack of proper maintenance of tools and equipment, the nonreplacement of tools, or the aging of equipment can have a negative impact on learning.

7. The transfer of employees may result in an interruption or a regression to an earlier stage of the learning curve, or may necessitate a new learning curve.

P/OM in Practice

Production-Capacity Analysis at Champion International[6]

Champion International Corporation is one of the largest forest-products companies in the world. It employs more than 41,000 people in the United States, Canada, and Brazil, and managers over 3 million acres of timberland in the United States. Its objective is to maximize the return of the timber base by converting trees into three basic product groups: (1) building materials, such as lumber and plywood; (2) white paper products, including printing and writing grades of white paper; (3) brown paper products, such as liner-board and corrugated containers. Given the highly competitive markets within the forest products industry, survival dictates that Champion maintain its position as a low-cost producer of quality products.

That requires an ambitious capital program to improve the timber base and to build additional modern, cost-effective timber conversion facilities.

An integrated pulp and paper mill is a facility in which wood chips and chemicals are processed to produce paper products or dried pulp. First, wood chips are cooked and bleached in the pulp mill; the resulting pulp is piped directly into storage tanks, as shown in Figure 7.12. From the storage tanks the pulp is sent to either the paper mill or a dryer. In the paper mill, the pulp is routed to one or more paper machines, which produce the finished paper products. Alternatively, the pulp is sent to a dryer, and the dried pulp is then sold to paper mills that do not have the capability of producing their own pulp. The total system, referred to as an *integrated pulp and paper mill*, is a large facility costing several hundred million dollars.

One of Champion's major pulp and paper facilities consists of a pulp mill, three paper machines, and a dryer. As the facility developed, the pulp mill was found to produce more pulp than the combination of paper machines and the dryer could use. A study was undertaken to determine whether it would be worthwhile to invest in improvements to increase the capacity of the dryer. One of the first questions to be answered in the study was how much additional pulp could be produced and dried, given each possible capacity increase on the dryer.

A simple approach to this question is to look at average flows. For example, the pulp mill has a capacity of 940 tons per day (TPD), the three paper machines together average 650 TPD of pulp use, and the dryer can handle 200 TPD. Based on average flows, for each ton of increased dryer

Figure 7.12 The Champion Integrated Pulp and Paper Mill

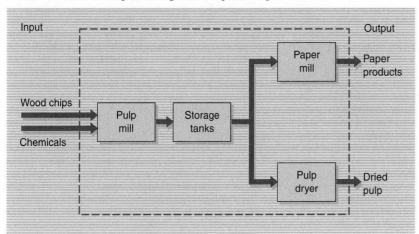

capacity one more ton of pulp can be produced in the pulp mill. Note, however, that this is true only until the capacity of the dryer reaches 290 TPD, after which further improvements to the dryer will have no benefit.

The above analysis is inadequate because it ignores the day-to-day deviations from the average. That is, all of the equipment in the mill is subject to downtime and to variations in efficiency. For example, suppose that on one day the pulp mill is inoperable for more than the average length of time and the paper machines are having less than the usual downtime. In this case very little pulp would be available for the dryer, regardless of its capacity. The lack of pulp would not "average out" on days when the opposite conditions occur, as much more pulp would be available than the pulp dryer can handle. Consequently, the pulp storage tanks would become full, and the pulp mill would have to shut down.

From this analysis, we can conclude that in order not to reduce the production on the paper machines, the ratio of additional pulp production to the increase in dryer capacity is less than 1. Since the benefits of any investment in

the dryer are directly proportional to this ratio, a computer simulation study was undertaken to estimate the ratio as precisely as possible.

The simulation model had four components: the pulp mill, the paper machines, the pulp dryer, and the storage tanks. The capacities of these components were determined as described next.

Pulp Mill

The pulp mill was assumed to have an average production rate of 1044 TPD when operating, with an average of 10 percent downtime. The actual downtime used in the model in each time period simulated was drawn randomly from a sample of actual downtimes at the pulp mill over several months. Thus, one day the pulp mill might be down 2 percent of the time, the next day 20 percent, and so on.

Paper Machines

The rate of pulp flow to the paper machines in a time period is a function of the type of paper being made and the amount of downtime on the paper machines. In the simulation, the rate of

pulp flow was based on a typical schedule of types of paper to be made. Each machine's downtime was drawn from a sample of actual downtimes.

Pulp Dryer

In each run of the model, the dryer downtime was drawn from a sample of actual downtimes. The capacity of the dryer was set at different levels in different runs.

Storage Tanks

The connecting link between the pulp mill, the paper machines, and the dryer is the pulp storage tanks. In the model, all pulp produced by the pulp mill is added to the inventory in the tanks. All pulp drawn by the dryer and paper machines is subtracted from the inventory. If the storage tanks are empty, the model must shut down the paper machines. If the tanks are full, the pulp mill must be shut down. The actual rate at which the dryer is operated at any moment must be set by the model (as it is in reality) to try to keep the storage tanks from becoming "too empty" or "too full."

A computer program was developed to simulate the process. The simulation program was run at various levels of dryer capacity. The results showed that for every TPD of additional pulp capacity, approximately 0.8 TPD of additional pulp could be dried without reducing the production on the paper machines. That number was then used by managers in comparing the costs and benefits of the capital investment necessary to increase the dryer's capacity. Note that if the "average basis" analysis had been used, the benefits of the project would have been overstated by 25 percent.

Questions for Discussion

1. Briefly describe the function of an integrated pulp and paper facility.

2. What is the primary reason Champion conducted a study of its integrated pulp and paper facility?

3. Why is an analysis of average flows inadequate in comparing the costs and benefits of expanding the pulp dryer capacity?

Capacity Planning in a Nonprofit Service Organization[7]

Recording for the Blind is a national nonprofit service organization that provides recorded educational books at no charge to blind and physically and perceptually handicapped students and professionals. Because the capacity of its New York location was limited and insufficient for future expansion, the organization moved in 1983 to a new modern-design, one-level facility in Princeton, New Jersey. The move led to the design and implementation of an updated, integrated production system utilizing high-technology automated material handling.

A capacity-planning study was undertaken to examine present and future client needs, resources, availability of technology, labor requirements, and capital and operational costs. With demand increasing at 8 to 9 percent per year and only 16 percent of the budget coming from federal funds, cost savings was a primary goal. A second goal was to reduce the lead time for duplicating a book and processing an order.

Figure 7.13 shows that the demand pattern for books is seasonal, with peaks in January, June, and September. Low-demand months can be utilized to balance yearly production capacity needs. A standby library was created to store multiple copies of preduplicated best-sellers. However, only a limited inventory is possible. Five percent of the titles constitute 50 percent of the demand, whereas 95

Figure 7.13 Demand Pattern: 5 Years' Average Demand per Month

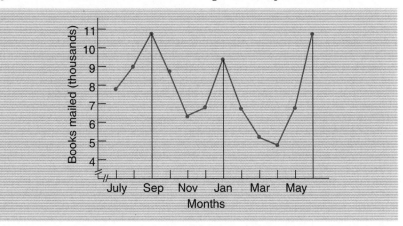

Figure 7.14 Demand Projections to 1990

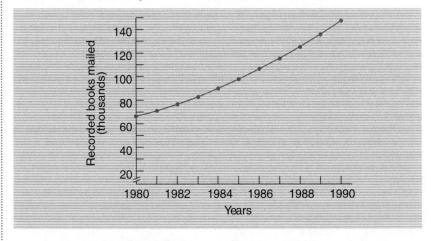

percent are in a bracket of highly random demand pattern.

To define total capacity requirements for calculating the work-station loads and labor needs, a three-year (1980–1982) demand pattern was analyzed. A production-capacity requirement of 450 books per day was established for 1984–1985. With a given 95 percent productivity, that yields an average of 427 books per day. The calculations were based on a demand trend of 88 percent growth per year (see Figure 7.14). The actual

performance before the move was standing at 74 percent productivity (333 books per day in 1982) with 39 production-line employees. The new system had to provide, at the same cost per book or less, an increase of 28 percent in the daily production average.

New automated equipment and system integration were the key elements in achieving the organizations objectives. For example, an automated storage and retrieval system was designed for rapid access to the

20,000 most active titles; conveyors were designed to connect all work stations; tape-duplicating machines were modified to double their speed; and automated sorting equipment with laser scanners was proposed for use in restocking returned items.

After two years' experience with the new system, Recording for the Blind had a 21 percent productivity improvement, enabling it to provide 27 percent more books in 1985 than in 1983. Unit costs were reduced by 16 percent, and 97 percent of orders were mailed within five working days from receipt. These statistics and expected trends are summarized in Figure 7.15.

Questions for Discussion

1. Explain how Recording for the Blind determined the production capacity necessary for 1984–1985.

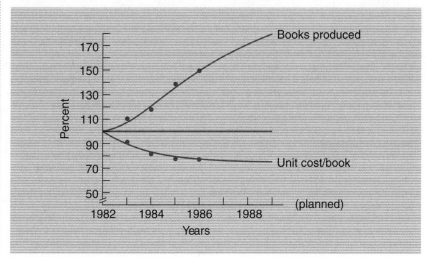

Figure 7.15 Books Produced and Cost per Book

2. What actions did Recording for the Blind take that led to a 21 percent productivity increase by 1985? How is productivity measured?

Summary of Key Points

● Forecasting involves predicting the future. Operations managers need forecasts for long-, medium, and short-range decisions. Demand forecasts serve as a basis for strategic capacity plans.

● Forecasting techniques can be broken down into statistical techniques (time-series models), including trend projection, trend projection adjusted for seasonality, and smoothing methods; and judgmental techniques, which include expert opinion, market surveys, and the Delphi method. Effective forecasting systems combine both statistical and judgmental forecasts.

● Capacity is what a manufacturing or service system can produce in a particular time period. Strategic capacity planning is the process of determining the types and amounts of resources that are required to implement an organization's strategic plan. It consists of translating long-range demand forecasts into facility, equipment, and labor needs. A firm must balance the cost of having excess capacity against the potential cost of losing sales due to too little capacity.

● Theoretical capacity is the maximum output capability that can be achieved; demonstrated capacity is the proven capability resulting from actual output performance. Capacity is measured either as the rate of output per unit of time or in terms of units of input.

● An understanding of the product life cycle can help in forecasting aggregate demand as a basis for capacity decisions. Capacity-expansion decisions require determinations of the amount, timing, and form of capacity changes.

● In planning facilities, one must consider the number and size of facilities, economies and diseconomies of scale, distribution costs, and daily operating issues. At the operational level, capacity plans are expressed in terms of detailed needs for equipment and labor.

● The learning curve is often used to estimate capacity needs for producing new products over time. The learning curve is also useful for cost estimating and pricing, short-term work scheduling, setting performance goals, and determining incentive payments.

Key Terms

Capacity
Strategic capacity planning
Forecasting
Time-series model
Life-cycle curve
Theoretical capacity
Demonstrated capacity
Economies of scale
Diseconomies of scale
Learning curve

Review Questions

1. Provide a general definition of *capacity*.
2. What is strategic capacity planning?
3. Explain the product life cycle. What implication does it have for operations strategy?
4. Why is forecasting an important technique in P/OM?
5. Explain the uses of forecasting in long-range, intermediate-range, and short-range decision making. What forecasting techniques are often used for each of those time horizons?
6. Briefly summarize the classification scheme of forecasting methods presented in this chapter.
7. Discuss the difference between statistical and judgmental forecasting methods. What circumstances warrant one over the other?
8. Discuss some of the fundamental issues that should be considered in strategic capacity planning.
9. Why are capacity decisions an important element of operations strategy?
10. Outline the strategic capacity planning process, focusing on its hierarchical nature.
11. Explain the difference between theoretical capacity and demonstrated capacity.
12. Why is setup time an important factor in determining capacity?
13. What is a "bottleneck" in a production process?
14. Discuss the differences between input measures of capacity and output measures of capacity. Provide some examples of each that are different from those in Table 7.2.
15. How can the product life cycle be used for capacity planning?
16. What issues are involved in planning capacity changes? Discuss the common strategies used for capacity expansion.
17. How does capacity planning differ in manufacturing and service organizations?
18. Discuss the capacity issues involved in facility planning.

19. Explain the principle behind the learning curve. What are some applications of the learning curve?
20. What factors may affect the applicability of the learning curve or the amount of learning that takes place?

Discussion Questions

1. Discuss the various forecasting issues that might affect an organization like MamaMia's Pizza. What specific types of forecasts are needed to run the business effectively? Should they be developed by statistical or judgmental techniques?
2. Discuss some forecasting issues that you encounter in your daily life. How do you make your forecasts?
3. Discuss why many managers seem to use judgmental techniques even though they might have received training in statistical methods.
4. Illustrate, by examples of typical applications, the various types of judgmental forecasting techniques.
5. Explain the various types of capacity issues that MamaMia's Pizza might face. For each, describe the types of information needed to make effective decisions.
6. Describe the product life cycles for
  a. A top 40 compact disk.
  b. Jell-O.
  c. A computer microprocessor.
7. Define capacity measures for a
  a. Brewery.
  b. Police precinct.
  c. Movie theater.
  d. Restaurant.
8. In decision analysis for facility expansion (see the example in the "Decision-Analysis Techniques" section), the expected-monetary-value criterion assumes that decisions are made repeatedly. In practice, facility expansion is a one-time decision. Comment on the interpretation of decision-analysis information in light of these observations.
9. A new employee is hired at MamaMia's Pizza to prepare pizzas in the kitchen. What factors might suggest that a learning curve is applicable to that activity? What learning-curve rate might be appropriate?

Notes

1. Nada R. Sanders and Karl B. Manrodt, "Forecasting Practices in U.S. Corporations: Survey Results," *Interfaces* 24, no. 2 (March–April 1994), pp. 92–100.
2. Adapted from Shankar Basu and Roger Schroeder, "Incorporating Judgments in Sales Forecasts: Applying the Delphi Method at American Hoist and Derrick,"

Interfaces 7, no. 3 (June 1977), pp. 18–27. Reprinted by permission of The Institute of Management Sciences, 290 Westminster Street, Providence, RI 02903, USA. Copyright 1977.

3. W. L. Berry, T. E. Vollmann, and D. C. Whybark, *Master Production Scheduling: Principles and Practice* (Falls Church, VA: American Production and Inventory Control Society, 1979).

4. James F. Cox III, John H. Blackstone, Jr., and Michael S. Spencer (eds.), 7th ed. *APICS Dictionary,* (Falls Church, VA: American Production and Inventory Control Society, 1992).

5. Shigeo Shingo, *A Revolution in Manufacturing: The SMED System* (Cambridge, MA: Productivity Press, 1985).

6. The author expresses his appreciation to Bill Griggs and Walter Foody of Champion International for providing this application.

7. Joseph G. Jarkon and Ravinder Nanda, "Resource Requirement Planning Achieves Production Goals for Non-Profit Organization." Reprinted from *Industrial Engineering* magazine, October 1985. Copyright Institute of Industrial Engineers, 25 Technology Park/Atlanta, Norcross, GA 30092.

Solved Problems

1. An automobile transmission-assembly plant normally operates one shift per day five days per week. During each shift, 400 transmissions can be completed. Over the next four weeks, the plant has planned shipments according to the following schedule.

Week	1	2	3	4
Shipments	1,800	1,700	2,000	2,100

a. What is the theoretical capacity?
b. At what percentage of capacity is the plant actually operating?

Solution

a. Theoretical capacity = (1 shift/day)(5 days/week)(400 transmissions/shift)(4 weeks)
$$= 8{,}000 \text{ transmissions}$$

b. Total shipment = 7,600. Thus,

$$7{,}600/8{,}000 = .95$$

or 95 percent of the theoretical capacity over the four-week period. Note that planned shipments are 105 percent of capacity in week 4.

2. Xtech, Inc., makes and sells electronic testing equipment in the industrial market. Two products, called *Microtester* and *Macrotester,* are assembled from two components: C1 and C2. Each Microtester is assembled from two C1s and one C2; each Macrotester is assembled from two C1s and three C2s. Three machines are used in the production of components C1 and C2. Component C1 requires one and one-half hours on machine 1, two hours on machine 2, and one hour on machine 3. Component C2 requires one hour on machine 1, one and one-half hours on machine 2, and three hours on machine 3. Xtech is projecting annual demand of 2,900 units of the Microtester and 2,100 units of the Macrotester. Planning is now underway for additional equipment. In particular, managers want to know how many of each of the machines are needed. Experience with the three machines suggests utilization rates of .97, .95, and .92 for machines 1, 2, and 3, respectively. The firm is planning a single-shift operation, which provides 2,000 working hours per year. How many machines of each type are required?

Solution

$$\text{Demand for C1} = 2(2{,}900) + 2(2{,}100) = 10{,}000$$

$$\text{Demand for C2} = 1(2{,}900) + 3(2{,}100) = 9{,}200$$

Machine hour requirements:

Component	No. Needed	Machine 1	Machine 2	Machine 3
C1	10,000	15,000	20,000	10,000
C2	9,200	9,200	13,800	27,600
Total Machine Hrs		24,200	33,800	37,600

At 100 percent utilization,

Number of machine type 1 needed = 24,200/2,000 = 12.1

Number of machine type 2 needed = 33,800/2,000 = 16.9

Number of machine type 3 needed = 37,600/2,000 = 18.8

To account for utilization rates:

Machine 1 needs = 12.1/.97 = 12.40 or 13

Machine 2 needs = 16.9/.95 = 17.79 or 18

Machine 3 needs = 18.8/.92 = 20.43 or 21

3. Mary Johnson, the tax assessor for Yates County, has estimated that her office must perform 200 property reevaluations per day. Each staff member assigned to the reevaluation will work an eight-hour day. If it takes a staff member 10 minutes to do a reevaluation, and the efficiency of any staff member is .75, how many staff members must be assigned to this project?

Solution
Using equation 7.1, we have

$$N = \frac{(10 \text{ minutes / unit})(200 \text{ units})}{(60 \text{ min / hour})(8 \text{ hours / day / person})(.75)} = 5.56$$

or about six staff members.

4. A sporting goods firm has been commissioned to build five sailboats for a Florida resort. The first boat took 6,000 labor-hours to build. How many labor-hours will it take to complete the order, assuming that a 90 percent learning curve is applicable? Draw graphs of time per boat and cumulative production time as a function of the number of boats produced.

Solution
Using Table 7.4 with a 90 percent learning curve, we have the times listed in Table 7.6.

Table 7.6 Solved Problem 4 Solution

Unit	Time required
1	6,000
2	5,400
3	5,077
4	4,860
5	4,698
	26,035

Or, using Table 7.5,

$$6,000(4.3392) = 26,035.$$

Problems

1. The roller coaster at Treasure Island Amusement Park consists of 15 cars, each of which can carry up to three passengers. If each run takes 1.5 minutes and the time to unload and load riders is 3.5 minutes, what is the maximum capacity of the system in number of passengers per hour? Would the actual capacity equal that value? Explain.

2. The basic pizza-making process at MamaMia's consists of (1) preparing the pizza, (2) baking it, and (2) cutting and boxing (or transferring to a platter for dine-in service). It takes five minutes to prepare a pizza, eight minutes to bake it, and one minute to cut and box or transfer. If the restaurant has only one preparer, what is the theoretical capacity of the pizza-making operation? What if two preparers are available. Will this change the bottleneck?

3. A grocery store has five regular checkout lines and one express line (12 items or less). Based on a sampling study, it takes 11 minutes on the average for a customer to go through the regular line and 4 minutes to go through the express line. The store is open from 9 A.M. to 9 P.M. daily.

a. What is the store's maximum capacity?

b. What is the capacity if the regular checkout lines operate according to the schedule in Table 7.7? (The express line is always open.)

Table 7.7 Data for Problem 3

Hours/Day	Mon	Tue	Wed	Thur	Fri	Sat	Sun
9–12	1	1	1	1	3	5	2
12–4	2	2	2	2	3	5	4
4–6	3	3	3	3	5	3	2
6–9	4	4	4	4	5	3	1

4. The quad chair lift at Whiteface Mountain Ski Resort carries four skiers in each chair to the top of the intermediate slope in 4 minutes. The time between loading skiers on successive chairs is 15 seconds.

a. What is the normal capacity of the system in number of skiers per hour?

b. If only one skier gets on the chair being loaded approximately 10 percent of the time, will the capacity of the system be affected? Explain.

c. Frequently it is necessary to stop the chair lift temporarily to assist beginning skiers in safely getting on and off. How could the resort's operations manager assess the effect of this practice on the lift capacity?

5. A small manufacturer estimates the following demand for a product (in thousands of units) over the next five years.

Year	1	2	3	4	5
Demand	114	129	131	134	133

Currently the manufacturer has eight machines that operate on a two-shift basis. Twenty days are available for scheduled maintenance of equipment. Each item takes 26 minutes to produce.

a. What is the theoretical capacity?

b. At what levels will the firm be operating over the next five years?

c. If demand above 20 percent of normal capacity for two consecutive years warrants purchase of new machines, how many should the firm acquire?

6. A company manufactures four products on three machines. Table 7.8 is the production schedule for the next six months.

Table **7.8** Data for Problem 6 (production schedule)

Product	Jan	Feb	Mar	Apr	May	Jun
1	200	0	200	0	200	0
2	100	100	100	100	100	100
3	50	50	50	50	50	50
4	100	0	100	0	100	0

Table 7.9 gives the number of hours each product requires on each machine.

Table **7.9** Data for Problem 6 (hours/product/machine)

Machine	Product 1	2	3	4
1	0.25	0.15	0.15	0.25
2	0.33	0.20	0.30	0.50
3	0.20	0.30	0.25	0.10

Setup times are roughly 20 percent of the operation times. Table 7.10 gives the machine hours available during the six months.

Table **7.10** Data for Problem 6 (machine hours)

Machine	Jan	Feb	Mar	Apr	May	Jun
1	120	60	60	60	60	60
2	180	60	180	60	180	60
3	120	60	120	60	120	60

Determine whether there is enough capacity to meet the product demand.

7. Womer Industries is planning a new production facility to make two products. The labor-hour requirements for the products in the three production departments are given in Table 7.11.

Table **7.11** Data for Problem 7

Department	Product 1	2
A	1.50	3.00
B	2.00	1.00
C	.25	.25

Forecasted demand for products 1 and 2 is 5,000 and 8,000 units per year, respectively. The plant will operate one shift (40 hours/week), 50 weeks per year. How many employees will be needed in each department? What if employees work at an average efficiency of 0.90?

8. A plant manufactures three products, A, B, and C. A drill press is required to perform one operation for each product. Machine operators work at 75 percent efficiency and the machines have 95 percent efficiency. The plant operates one shift five days per week. The operation times for each product follow.

Product	A	B	C
Operation Time (minutes)	5.0	1.85	7.0

Determine the amount of equipment and number of machine operators needed to produce 10,000 units per month.

9. The Myatt House Restaurant has a capacity for 100 patrons. Business at lunch is fair, but business for dinner Tuesday through Saturday is excellent. The owner of the restaurant is considering adding another dining room with a seating capacity of 50 to use for dinner. The building's owner has agreed to build the addition for an extra $1,600 rent per month. The cost of new decorations and fixtures, amortized over their lifetime, and associated interest expense would amount to $7,000 per year. Maintenance and utility costs would rise by $3,000 per year. Additional personnel required to support the expansion would include a new chef, extra waitresses, and a hostess, and wages for these employees would be $35,000.

The average dinner bill per person is $12 for food and $4 for alcoholic beverages, for a total average bill of $16.00. The food cost is 40 percent and the beverage cost is 25 percent of the average dinner bill. Other, miscellaneous expenses vary with sales and are estimated at 10 percent of the total bill.

Over a period of several weeks a survey was made of the number of people who left because of long waiting times (no reservations are accepted). Table 7.12 gives those statistics, along with the maximum waiting time that was observed.

Table 7.12 Data for Problem 9

Day	Average Number of Turnaways	Maximum Waiting Time (minutes)
Tuesday	10	30
Wednesday	10	30
Thursday	15	40
Friday	40	80
Saturday	45	90
	120	

Compute the break-even point for the number of additional customers that can be served. Should the Myatt House expand? Why or why not?

10. JR's Income Tax Service is determining its staffing requirements for the next income tax season. Income tax preparers work 50 hours per week from January 15 through April 15. There are two major tasks: preparation of short forms and preparation of long forms. The time normally needed to prepare a short form is 15 minutes; long forms takes 50 minutes if all records are in order. Fifteen percent of customers using the long form have complicated problems that require approximately one-half hour of additional work. The usual mix of customers requiring long versus short forms is 40 to 60 percent. A personal allowance of 15 percent is given over the three-month period. JR expects 1,000, 3,500 and

5,000 customers for each of the three months, respectively. How many preparers are needed each month to meet that demand?

11. The process for renewing a driver's license at the Archer County Courthouse is as follows. First, the clerk fills out the application, then the clerk takes the driver's picture, and finally the typist types and processes the new license. It takes an average of five minutes to fill out an application, one minute to take a picture, and seven minutes to type and process the new license.

a. If there are two clerks and three typists, where will the bottleneck in the system be? How many drivers can be processed in one hour if the clerks and typists work at 80 percent efficiency?

b. If 40 drivers are to be processed each hour, how many clerks and typists should be hired?

12. The consumer loan division of a major bank wants to determine the size of the staff it would need to process up to 200 loan applications per day. It estimated that each loan officer can process a loan application in approximately 20 minutes. If the efficiency of a loan officer is .8 and each loan officer works seven hours each day, how many loan officers would be needed to handle that volume of business?

13. A state department of transportation district is responsible for 300 miles of highway. During a winter storm, salt trucks spread an average of 400 pounds of salt per mile and travel at an average speed of 25 mph. Because of nonproductive travel time, the average efficiency of the trucks (that is, the productive time spent salting the roads) is 60 percent. How many seven-ton trucks will be needed to complete the process of salting all roads within two hours?

14. Linda Bryant recently started a small home-construction company. In a effort to foster high quality, rather than subcontracting individual work, she has formed teams of employees who are responsible for the entire job. She has contracted with a developer to build 20 homes of similar size. She has four teams of workers. The first homes were built in an average of 145 days. How long will it take to complete the contract if an 85 percent learning curve applies?

15. Suppose a manufacturer of copiers has concluded that a 75 percent learning curve applies to the time a beginning service technician takes to install copy machines. If the time required to install the first copy machine is estimated to be four hours, what is an estimate of the time required by a new technician to install the second and third copiers?

16. A manufacturer has committed to supply 16 units of a particular product in four months (i.e., 16 weeks) at a price of $30,000 each. The first unit took 1,000 hours to produce. Even though the second unit took only 750 hours to produce, the manufacturer is anxious to know:

a. If the delivery commitment of 16 weeks will be met.

b. Whether enough labor is available (currently 500 hours is available per week).

c. Whether or not the venture is profitable.

Apply learning-curve theory to each of those issues. Assume the material cost per unit equals $22,000, labor equals $10 per labor-hour, and overhead = $2,000 per week.

17. Operating at an 80 percent learning rate, the first unit took 72 hours to produce. How long will the 32nd unit take?

18. Given the following data:

Fixed costs for one shift	= $60,000
Unit variable cost	= $7
Selling price	= $12
Number of machines	= 5
Number of working days in year	= 340
Processing time per unit	= 60 minutes

a. What is the capacity with a single shift?

b. What is the capacity with two shifts? The additional fixed cost for a second shift is $40,000.
c. What is the break-even volume with a single-shift operation?
d. What is the maximum revenue with a single shift?
e. What is the break-even volume with a two-shift operation?
f. Draw the break-even chart.

19. The Gray Corporation is considering constructing a new plant to handle a new product line of synthetic drugs. A large plant and a small plant are being considered. The decision will depend on the long-run average demand. The probability of high demand is estimated to be .65; moderate demand, .15; and low demand, .20. The payoff (in thousands of dollars per year over a 10-year horizon) is projected as shown in Table 7.13.

Table 7.13 Data for Problem 19

	Long-Run Average Demand		
Decision	*High*	*Medium*	*Low*
Build large	250	100	25
Build small	100	100	75

Construct a decision tree for this problem and determine the optimal strategy.

20. For the Gray Corporation in problem 19, suppose the facility decision can be time-phased; that is, if a small plant is built, the company will consider expanding it in three years if initial demand is high. If the initial demand is moderate or low, then no further decisions will be considered. Revise the decision tree to account for this. (*Hint:* There will be two decision nodes.)

21. For the situation described in problem 20, suppose the payoffs for building a small plant initially and then expanding are as shown in Table 7.14. Further, suppose that the probabilities of initial demand being high, moderate, and low are .60, .20, and .20, respectively. Also, if the initial demand is high, then the probabilities of long-run average demand being high, moderate, and low are .85, .10, and .05, respectively. Will Gray's decision strategy differ in this case?

Table 7.14 Data for Problem 21

Long-Run Average Demand		
High	*Medium*	*Low*
200	90	10

Chapter Appendix
Techniques of Forecasting and Time-Series Analysis

Appendix Outline

This appendix presents quantitative techniques of forecasting: trend projection for long-range forecasting, the multiplicative time-series model for intermediate-range forecasting, and smoothing methods for short-range forecasting.

Time-Series Models

Statistical methods of forecasting are based on the analysis of historical data, called a **time series,** in which a set of observations is measured at successive *points* in time or over successive *periods* of time. For example, if we are asked to provide quarterly estimates of sales volume, we are working with time-period data.

To explain the pattern of behavior of the data in a time series it is often helpful to think of the time series as consisting of four components: trend, cyclical, seasonal, and irregular components.

Trend Component

In time-series analysis the measurements may be taken every hour, day, week, month, or year or at any other regular interval.* Although time-series data generally exhibit random fluctuations, the time series may still show gradual shifts or movements to relatively higher or lower values over a longer period of time. This gradual shifting of the time series—usually due to such long-term factors as changes in population, demographic characteristics, technology, consumer preferences, and the like—is referred to as the **trend.**

For example, a manufacturer of photographic equipment may see substantial month-to-month variability in the number of cameras sold. Reviewing the sales over the past 10 to 15 years, however, this manufacturer may find a steady increase in the annual sales volume. While actual month-to-month sales volumes may vary substantially, the gradual growth in sales over time shows an upward trend for the time series. Figure 7A.1 shows a straight line that may be a good approximation of a steady trend in the sales data.

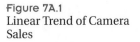
Figure 7A.1
Linear Trend of Camera Sales

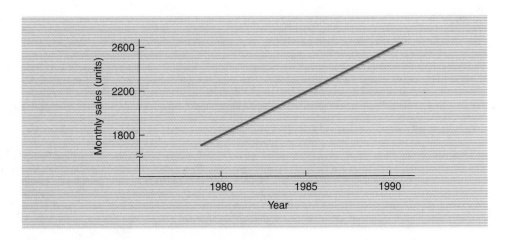

*Attention is restricted here to time series for which values are recorded at equal intervals. Treatment of series for which observations are not made at equal intervals is beyond the scope of this book.

Figure 7A.2
Examples of Time-Series
Trend Patterns

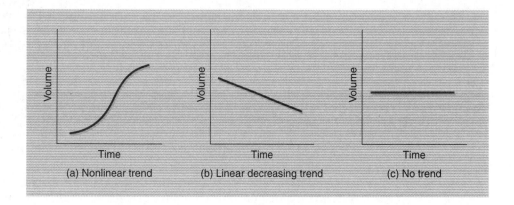

     (a) Nonlinear trend   (b) Linear decreasing trend   (c) No trend

Figure 7A.2 shows some other time-series trend patterns. The nonlinear trend describes a time series in which there is very little growth initially, followed by a period of rapid growth, and then a leveling off. This might be a good representation of sales for a product from introduction through a growth period and into a period of market saturation. The linear decreasing trend displays a steady decrease over time. The horizontal line (part c) indicates the lack of any consistent increase or decrease over time; it is the case of no trend.

Cyclical Component

Although a time series may exhibit a gradual shifting or trend pattern over long periods of time, future values of the time series cannot be expected to be *on* the trend line. Time series often show alternating sequences of points below and above the trend line over long periods of time. Any regular pattern or sequence of points above and below the trend line is attributable to the **cyclical component** of the particular time series as shown in Figure 7A.3. Cyclical behavior often reflects multiyear cyclical movements in the economy triggered by, for example, periods of moderate inflation followed by periods of rapid inflation.

Figure 7A.3
Trend and Cyclical
Components of a Time
Series (Data points are one
year apart.)

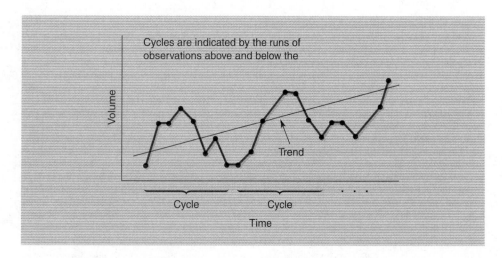

Seasonal Component

Many time series show a regular pattern of variability within short periods. For example, a manufacturer of swimming pools expects low sales activity in the fall and winter months, with peak sales occurring in the spring and summer months. Manufacturers of snow-removal equipment and heavy clothing, however, expect the opposite yearly pattern. The component of the time series that represents the variability in the data due to seasonal influences is called the **seasonal component.**

We generally think of seasonal movement in a time series as occurring within one year, but the seasonal component can also be used to represent any repeating pattern that is less than one year in duration. For example, daily traffic-volume data show within-the-day "seasonal" behavior, with peak levels during rush hours, moderate flow during the rest of the day and early evening, and light flow from midnight to early morning.

Irregular Component

The **irregular component** of the time series is the residual or "catch-all" factor that accounts for the deviation of the actual time-series value from what we would expect given the effects of the trend, cyclical, and seasonal components. It accounts for the random variability in the time series caused by short-term, unanticipated, and nonrecurring factors that affect the time series. Thus this component is unpredictable.

Because of the irregular component, *forecasts are never 100 percent accurate.* That is crucial for operations managers to remember when using forecasts in decision making. The best that can be hoped for is to identify a pattern that is helpful in making an estimate based on many factors, statistical and judgmental.

Forecasting methods for time series may involve the

1. Trend component (trend-projection model).
2. Trend and seasonal components (multiplicative time-series model).
3. Irregular component (moving-averages and exponential-smoothing models).

Forecast Accuracy

Because of the inherent inability of any model to forecast accurately, quantitative measures of forecast accuracy are useful for evaluating the accuracy of alternative forecasting methods. Clearly, we want forecast errors to be small. Suppose a forecasting method provided the forecast values in Table 7A.1 for a time series.

Forecast error is the difference between the observed value of the time series and the forecast. Thus, the forecast error in week 1 is $21 - 20 = 1$ and in week 10 it is $23 - 25 = -2$.

As a means of measuring forecast accuracy, you might simply add the forecast errors over time. However, if the errors are random (as they should be if the choice of forecasting method is appropriate), some errors will be positive and

Table 7A.1 Forecast Value of Time-Series Data

Week	Time-Series Value	Forecast Value
1	21	20
2	26	24
3	32	35
4	29	28
5	22	25
6	28	26
7	17	24
8	25	19
9	26	26
10	23	25

Table 7A.2 Forecast Error of Time-Series Data

Week	Time-Series Value	Forecast Value	Forecast Error	(Error)^2
1	21	20	1	1
2	26	24	2	4
3	32	35	−3	9
4	29	28	1	1
5	22	25	−3	9
6	28	26	2	4
7	17	24	−7	49
8	25	19	6	36
9	26	26	0	0
10	23	25	−2	4

some will be negative, resulting in a sum near zero regardless of the size of the individual errors. That problem is avoided by squaring the individual forecast errors. For the example data, the forecast errors and squared errors are as shown in Table 7A.2.

The sum of the squared errors is 117, and the average of the squared errors is $117/10 = 11.7$. The average of the squared errors is commonly referred to as the **mean square error (MSE).** MSE is an often-used measure of the accuracy of a forecasting method and is one we will use in this appendix.

Long-Range Forecasting Using Trend Projection

In this section we explain how to forecast the values of a time series that has a long-term linear trend. Specifically, let us consider a particular manufacturer's time-series data for bicycle sales over the past 10 years, as shown in Table 7A.3 and Figure 7A.4. Note that 21,600 bicycles were sold in the first year, 22,900 were sold in the second, and so on; in Year 10, the most recent year, 31,400 bicycles were sold. Although the graph in Figure 7A.4 shows some up-and-down move-

Table 7A.3 Bicycle Sales Time-Series Data

Year (t)	Sales in Thousands (Y_t)	Year (t)	Sales in Thousands (Y_t)
1	21.6	6	27.5
2	22.9	7	31.5
3	25.5	8	29.7
4	21.9	9	28.6
5	23.9	10	31.4

ment over the past 10 years, the time series shows an overall increasing, or upward, trend in the number of bicycles sold.

After we view the time-series data in Table 7A.3 and the graph in Figure 7A.4, we might agree that a linear trend, as shown in Figure 7A.5, provides a reasonable description of the long-run movement in the series. Thus we can now concentrate on finding the linear function that best approximates the trend.

For a linear trend, the estimated sales volume expressed as a function of time can be written as

$$T_t = b_0 + b_1 t \tag{7A.1}$$

where T_t = trend value for bicycle sales in period t,
b_0 = intercept of the trend line,
b_1 = slope of the trend line, and
t = time in years.

In the linear-trend relationship in Equation 7A.1 we will let $t = 1$ for the time of the first observation in the time series, $t = 2$ for the time of the second observation, and so on.

Figure 7A.4
Graph of the Bicycle Sales
Time-Series Data

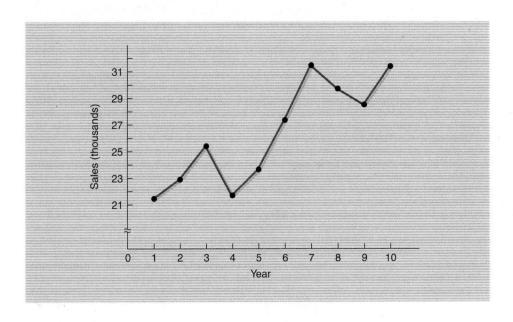

Figure 7A.5
Trend of a Linear Function
for Bicycle Sales

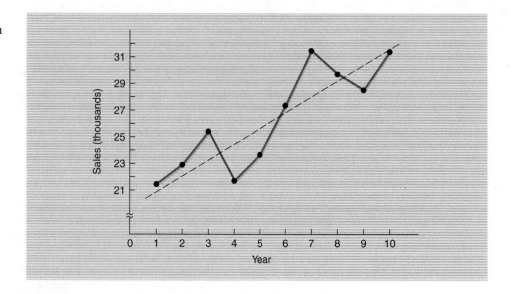

The approach most often used to determine the linear function that best approximates the trend is based on the *least-squares method*, which identifies the values of b_0 and b_1 that minimize the sum of squared forecast errors. That is,

$$\sum_{t=1}^{n} (Y_t - T_t)^2 \tag{7A.2}$$

where Y_t = actual value of the time series in period t,
    T_t = forecast or trend value of the time series in period t, and
    n = number of periods.

The least-squares method, which is also used for the statistical technique known as *regression analysis,* is described in most elementary statistics books. These formulas can be used to compute the value of b_0 and the value of b_1 using this approach:

$$b_1 = \frac{\sum tY_t - (\sum t \sum Y_t)/n}{\sum t^2 - (\sum t)^2/n} \tag{7A.3}$$

$$b_0 = \overline{Y} - b_1 \overline{t} \tag{7A.4}$$

where $\overline{Y}$ = average value of the time series; that is,

$$\overline{Y} = \frac{\sum Y_t}{n}$$

and $\overline{t}$ = average value of t; that is, $\overline{t} = \dfrac{\sum t}{n}$.

The summations in these formulas are for values of t from one through n.

Example

Computing a Linear Trend

Using Equations 7A.3 and 7A.4 for b_1 and b_0 and the bicycle-sales data of Table 7A.3, we have the following calculations.

t	Y_t	tY_t	t^2
1	21.6	21.6	1
2	22.9	45.8	4
3	25.5	76.5	9
4	21.9	87.6	16
5	23.9	119.5	25
6	27.5	165.0	36
7	31.5	220.5	49
8	29.7	237.6	64
9	28.6	257.4	81
10	31.4	314.0	100
Totals 55	264.5	1,545.5	385

$$\bar{t} = \frac{55}{10} = 5.5 \text{ years}$$

$$\bar{Y} = \frac{264.5}{10} = 26.45 \text{ thousands}$$

$$b_1 = \frac{1{,}545.5 - (55)(264.5)/10}{385 - (55)^2/10} = \frac{90.75}{82.5} = 1.1$$

$$b_0 = 26.45 - 1.10(5.5) = 20.4$$

Therefore,

$$T_t = 20.4 + 1.1t \tag{7A.5}$$

is the expression for the linear-trend component of the bicycle sales time series.

Trend Projections

The slope of 1.1 (in Equation 7A.5) indicates that over the past 10 years the firm has had an average growth in sales of around 1,100 units per year. If we assume that this 10-year trend in sales is a good indicator of the future, then Equation 7A.5 can be used to project the trend component of the time series. For example, substituting $t = 11$ into the equation yields next year's trend projection, T_{11}, or

$$T_{11} = 20.4 + 1.1(11) = 32.5.$$

On the basis of the trend component, we would forecast sales of 32,500 bicycles next year.

Figure 7A.6
Some Possible Functional
Forms for Nonlinear-Trend
Patterns

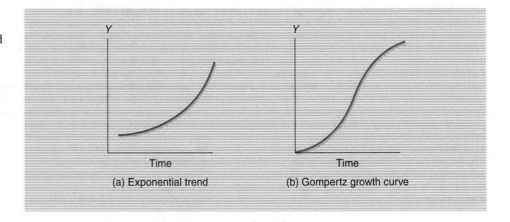

(a) Exponential trend   (b) Gompertz growth curve

The use of a linear function to model the trend is common. However, as we discussed earlier, time series sometimes exhibit a nonlinear trend. Figure 7A.6 shows two common nonlinear trend functions. More advanced textbooks discuss in detail how to solve for the trend component when a nonlinear function is used and how to decide when to use such a function. For our purposes it is sufficient to note that the analyst should select the function that provides the best fit to the time-series data.

Intermediate-Range Forecasting: Multiplicative Time-Series Model

In this section we expand our discussion by showing how to forecast a time series that has both trend and seasonal components. The approach we will take is first to remove the seasonal component from the time series to obtain a **deseasonalized time series.** As a result, we can use the least-squares method described in the previous section to identify the trend component. Then, using a trend-projection calculation, we will be able to forecast the trend component of the time series in future periods. The final step in developing the forecast will be to incorporate the seasonal component by using a seasonal factor to adjust the trend projection.

In addition to a trend component (T) and a seasonal component (S), we will assume that the time series also has an irregular component (I). The irregular component accounts for any random effects in the time series that cannot be explained by the trend or seasonal component. We will assume that the actual time-series value, denoted by Y_t, is described by the *multiplicative time-series model:*

$$Y_t = T_t \times S_t \times I_t. \tag{7A.6}$$

In this model T_t is the trend measured in units of the item being forecast. However, the S_t and I_t components are measured in relative terms: values above 1.00 indicate effects above the normal or average level, and values below 1.00 indicate below-average levels for each component. To illustrate the use of Equation 7A.6 to model a time series, suppose we have a trend projection of 540

Table 7A.4 Quarterly Data for Sales of Television Sets

Year	Quarter	Sales (1,000s)
1	1	4.8
	2	4.1
	3	6.0
	4	6.5
2	1	5.8
	2	5.2
	3	6.8
	4	7.4
3	1	6.0
	2	5.6
	3	7.5
	4	7.8
4	1	6.3
	2	5.9
	3	8.0
	4	8.4

units. In addition, suppose that $S_t = 1.10$ shows a seasonal effect 10 percent above average, and $I_t = 0.98$ shows an irregular effect 2 percent below average. With those values in Equation 7A.6, the time-series value would be $Y_t = 540(1.10)(0.98) = 582$.

In this section we illustrate the use of the multiplicative model with trend, seasonal, and irregular components by working with the quarterly data presented in Table 7A.4 and Figure 7A.7. These data show the television-set sales (in thousands of units) for a particular manufacturer over the past four years. We begin by showing how to identify the seasonal component of the time series.

Figure 7A.7
Graph of Quarterly
Television-Set-Sales Time
Series

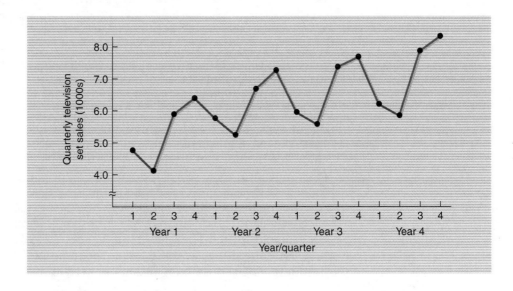

Example

Calculating the Seasonal Indexes

By referring to Figure 7A.7, we can begin to identify a seasonal pattern for the sales of television sets. Specifically, we observe that sales are lowest in the second quarter of each year, followed by higher sales levels in quarters 3 and 4. The computational procedure used to identify each quarter's seasonal influence requires the identification of the seasonal components, S_t, for each season of the time series.

The computation of seasonal indexes begins with the computation of **moving averages** for the time series. Since we are working with quarterly sales data (four time periods, or quarters, per year), we will use four data values in each of the moving averages. For example, the first moving average is simply the average quarterly sales over the first year. Using television-set sales for quarters 1, 2, 3, and 4, the calculation of the first moving average is

$$\frac{4.8 + 4.1 + 6.0 + 6.5}{4} = \frac{21.4}{4} = 5.35.$$

Continuing the moving-average calculation, we next add the 5.8 value for the first quarter of year 2 and drop the oldest value, 4.8, for the first quarter of year 1. Thus the second moving average, based on time periods 2, 3, 4, and 5, is

$$\frac{4.1 + 6.0 + 6.5 + 5.8}{4} = \frac{22.4}{4} = 5.60.$$

As we look back at the calculation of the first moving average, 5.35, it may make sense to associate this value with the "middle" quarter of the moving-average group. However, since there is an even number of quarters in the calculation, there is no middle quarter.

Hence, the moving-average values we have computed do not correspond directly to the original quarters of the time series. We can resolve this difficulty by using the midpoints between successive moving-average values. Thus, by averaging 5.35 and 5.60, we have $(5.35 + 5.60)/2 = 5.475$ as the value for quarter 3. Similarly, we associate a moving-average value of $(5.60 + 5.875)/2 = 5.738$ with quarter 4. What results is called a *centered moving average*. A complete summary of the centered-moving-average calculations for the television-set sales data is shown in Table 7A.5.

A plot of the actual time-series values and the corresponding centered moving average is shown in Figure 7A.8. Note particularly how the centered-moving-average values tend to "smooth out" the fluctuations in the time series. Since the moving-average values are for four quarters of data, they do not include fluctuations that are due to seasonal influences. Each point in the centered moving average represents what the value of the time series would be if there were no seasonal or irregular influence.

We can identify the seasonal-irregular effect in the time series by dividing each time-series observation by the corresponding centered moving average. For example, the third quarter of year 1 shows $6.0/5.475 = 1.096$ as the combined seasonal-irregular component. The resulting seasonal-irregular values for the entire time-series values are summarized in Table 7A.6.

Table 7A.5 Centered Moving Averages for Television-Set-Sales Time Series

Year	Quarter	Sales	Four-Quarter Moving Average	Centered Moving Average
1	1	4.8		
	2	4.1		
	3	6.0	5.350	5.475
	4	6.5	5.600	5.738
2	1	5.8	5.875	5.975
	2	5.2	6.075	6.188
	3	6.8	6.300	6.325
	4	7.4	6.350	6.400
3	1	6.0	6.450	6.538
	2	5.6	6.625	6.675
	3	7.5	6.725	6.763
	4	7.8	6.800	6.838
4	1	6.3	6.875	6.938
	2	5.9	7.000	7.075
	3	8.0	7.150	
	4	8.4		

Consider the third quarter. The results from years 1, 2, and 3 show third-quarter values of 1.096, 1.075, and 1.109, respectively. Thus in all cases the seasonal-irregular component appears to have an above-average influence in the third quarter. Since the year-to-year fluctuations in the seasonal-irregular component can be attributed primarily to the irregular component, we can average the computed values to eliminate the irregular influence and obtain an estimate of the third-quarter seasonal influence as follows.

$$\frac{1.096 + 1.075 + 1.109}{3} = 1.09$$

Figure 7A.8
Graph of Time Series and Centered Moving Average for Quarterly Television-Set Sales

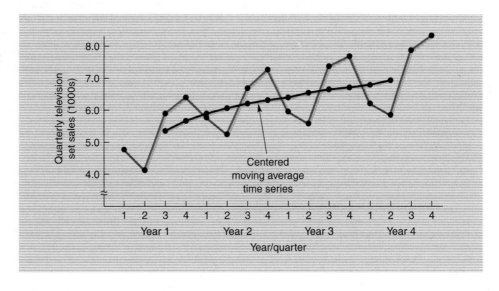

Table 7A.6 Seasonal-Irregular Factors for Television-Set-Sales Time Series

Year	Quarter	Sales (1,000s)	Centered Moving Average	Seasonal-Irregular Component
1	1	4.8		
	2	4.1		
	3	6.0	5.475	1.096
	4	6.5	5.738	1.133
2	1	5.8	5.975	0.971
	2	5.2	6.188	0.840
	3	6.8	6.325	1.075
	4	7.4	6.400	1.156
3	1	6.0	6.538	0.918
	2	5.6	6.675	0.839
	3	7.5	6.763	1.109
	4	7.8	6.838	1.141
4	1	6.3	6.938	0.908
	2	5.9	7.075	0.834
	3	8.0		
	4	8.4		

We refer to 1.09 as the *seasonal index* for the third quarter. In Table 7A.7 we summarize the calculations involved in computing the seasonal indexes for the television-set-sales time series. Thus, we see that the seasonal index is 0.93 for quarter 1, 0.84 for quarter 2, 1.09 for quarter 3, and 1.14 for quarter 4.

The values in Table 7A.7 provide some information about the seasonal component in television-set sales. The best sales quarter is the fourth, with sales averaging 14 percent above the average quarterly level. The worst, or slowest, sales quarter is the second; its seasonal index of 0.84 shows that sales average 16 percent below the average quarterly sales.

One final adjustment is sometimes necessary in computing the seasonal index. The multiplicative model requires that the average seasonal index equal 1.00; that is, the sum of the four seasonal indexes in Table 7A.7 should equal 4.00. This is necessary if the seasonal effects are to even out over the year, as they must. The average of the seasonal indexes in our example is equal to 1.00, and hence this type of adjustment is not necessary. In other cases a slight adjustment may be necessary. The adjustment can be made by simply multiplying each seasonal index by the number of seasons *divided by* the sum of the unadjusted seasonal indexes. For quarterly data, for example, we would multiply

Table 7A.7 Seasonal Index Calculations for Television-Set-Sales Time Series

Quarter	Seasonal-Irregular Component Values $(S_t I_t)$	Seasonal Index (S_t)
1	0.971, 0.918, 0.908	0.93
2	0.840, 0.839, 0.834	0.84
3	1.096, 1.075, 1.109	1.09
4	1.133, 1.156, 1.141	1.14

each seasonal index by 4 (sum of the unadjusted seasonal indexes). Some of the problems at the end of this appendix require this adjustment in order to obtain the appropriate seasonal indexes.

Deseasonalizing the Time Series

In many cases the purpose of finding seasonal indexes is to remove the seasonal effects from a time series—to *deseasonalize* it. Using the notation of the multiplicative model, we have

$$Y_t = T_t \times S_t \times I_t.$$

By dividing each time-series observation by the corresponding seasonal index, we remove the effect of seasonality from the time series. The deseasonalized time series for television-set sales is summarized in Table 7A.8. Figure 7A.9 is a graph of the deseasonalized television-set-sales time series.

Looking at Figure 7A.9, we see that despite some up-and-down movement in the past 16 quarters, the time series seems to have an upward linear trend. To identify that trend we can use the same procedure we introduced for identifying trends when forecasting with annual data. In this case, since we have deseasonalized the data, quarterly sales values can be used. Thus for a linear trend, the estimated sales volume expressed as a function of time can be written:

$$T_t = b_0 + b_1 t$$

where T_t = trend value for television-set sales in period t,
           b_0 = intercept of the trend line, and
           b_1 = slope of the trend line.

Table 7A.8 Deseasonalized Time Series for Television-Set Sales

Year	Quarter	Sales (1,000s) (Y_t)	Seasonal Index (S_t)	Deseasonalized Sales ($Y_t/S_t = T_t I_t$)
1	1	4.8	0.93	5.16
	2	4.1	0.84	4.88
	3	6.0	1.09	5.50
	4	6.5	1.14	5.70
2	1	5.8	0.93	6.24
	2	5.2	0.84	6.19
	3	6.8	1.09	6.24
	4	7.4	1.14	6.49
3	1	6.0	0.93	6.45
	2	5.6	0.84	6.67
	3	7.5	1.09	6.88
	4	7.8	1.14	6.84
4	1	6.3	0.93	6.77
	2	5.9	0.84	7.02
	3	8.0	1.09	7.34
	4	8.4	1.14	7.37

Figure 7A.9
Graph of Deseasonalized
Time Series for Television-
Set Sales

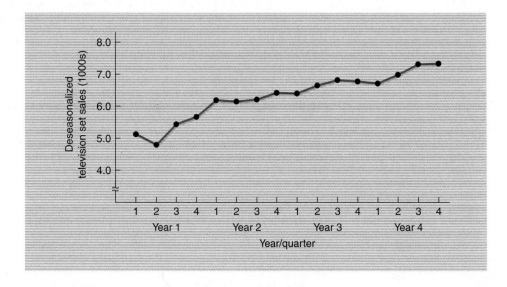

As before, we will let $t = 1$ for the time of the first observation in the time series, $t = 2$ for the time of the second observation, and so on. Thus, for the deseasonalized television-set sales time series, $t = 1$ corresponds to the first deseasonalized quarterly sales value, and $t = 16$ corresponds to the most recent deseasonalized quarterly sales value. The formulas for computing the value of b_0 and the value of b_1 are again

$$b_1 = \frac{\sum tY_t - (\sum t \sum Y_t)/n}{\sum t^2 - (\sum t)^2/n}$$

$$b_0 = \bar{Y} - b_1\bar{t}.$$

Note, however, that Y_t now refers to the deseasonalized time-series value at time t, not to the actual value of the time series.

Example

Using the Deseasonalized Time Series to Identify Trend

Using the given relationships for b_0 and b_1 and the deseasonalized sales data of Table 7A.8, we have the following calculations.

t	Y_t (deseasonalized)	tY_t	t^2
1	5.16	5.16	1
2	4.88	9.76	4
3	5.50	16.50	9
4	5.70	22.80	16
5	6.24	31.20	25
6	6.19	37.14	36
7	6.24	43.68	49

(continued)

t	Y_t (deseasonalized)	tY_t	t^2
8	6.49	51.92	64
9	6.45	58.05	81
10	6.67	66.70	100
11	6.88	75.68	121
12	6.84	82.08	144
13	6.77	88.01	169
14	7.02	98.28	196
15	7.34	110.10	225
16	7.37	117.92	256
Totals 136	101.74	914.98	1,496

From these calculations, we have

$$\bar{t} = \frac{136}{16} = 8.5$$

$$\bar{Y} = \frac{101.74}{16} = 6.359$$

$$b_1 = \frac{914.98 - (136)(101.74)/16}{1496 - (136)^2/16} = \frac{50.19}{340} = 0.148$$

$$b_0 = 6.359 - 0.148(8.5) = 5.101.$$

Therefore,

$$T_t = 5.101 + 0.148t$$

is the expression for the linear-trend component of the time series.

The slope of 0.148 indicates that over the past 16 quarters, the firm has had an average deseasonalized growth in sales of about 148 sets per quarter. If we assume that the past 16-quarter trend in sales data is a reasonably good indicator of the future, then this equation can be used to project the trend component of the time series for future quarters. For example, substituting $t = 17$ into the equation yields next quarter's trend projection, T_{17}.

$$T_{17} = 5.101 + 0.148(17) = 7.617$$

Using the trend component only, we would forecast sales of 7,617 television sets for the next quarter. Similarly, if we were to use the trend component only, we would forecast sales of 7,765, 7,913, and 8,061 television sets in quarters 18, 19, and 20, respectively.

Now that we have a forecast of sales for each of the next four quarters based on trend, we must adjust the forecasts to account for the effect of season.

Seasonal Adjustments

Since the seasonal index for the first quarter is 0.93, for example, the forecast for the first quarter of year 5 can be obtained by multiplying the forecast based on trend ($T_{17} = 7{,}617$) times the seasonal index (0.93). Thus, the forecast for the next quarter is $7{,}617(0.93) = 7{,}084$. Table 7A.9 shows the quarterly forecast for quarters 17, 18, 19, and 20. The quarterly forecasts show the high-volume fourth quarter with a 9,190-unit forecast, while the low-volume second quarter has a 6,523-unit forecast.

Table 7A.9 Quarter-by-Quarter Short-Range Forecasts for Television-Set Sales Time Series

Year	Quarter	Trend Forecast	Seasonal Index (see Table 7A.7)	Quarterly Forecast
5	1	7,617	0.93	$(7{,}617)(0.93) = 7{,}084$
	2	7,765	0.84	$(7{,}765)(0.84) = 6{,}523$
	3	7,913	1.09	$(7{,}913)(1.09) = 8{,}625$
	4	8,061	1.14	$(8{,}061)(1.14) = 9{,}190$

Models Based on Monthly Data

The television-set sales example provided in this section has used quarterly data to illustrate the computation of seasonal indexes with relatively few computations. Many businesses use monthly rather than quarterly forecasts. In such cases the procedures introduced in this section can be applied with minor modifications. First, a 12-month moving average replaces the four-quarter moving average; second, 12 monthly seasonal indexes, rather than four quarterly seasonal indexes, need to be computed. Other than those changes, the computational and forecasting procedures are identical. Problem 8 at the end of the appendix asks you to develop monthly seasonal indexes for a situation requiring monthly forecasts.

Short-Range Forecasting Using Smoothing Methods

Over a short time period, trend, seasonal, or cyclical components are not very important. In this section we discuss forecasting techniques that are appropriate for a fairly stable time series, one that exhibits no significant trend, cyclical, or seasonal effects. In such situations the objective of the forecasting method is to "smooth out" the irregular component of the time series through some type of averaging process.

Moving Averages

In the preceding section, we introduced the method of moving averages as a step in the computation of seasonal indexes for a time series. The **moving aver-**

age associated with any time period is simply an average of the most recent n data values in the time series. Mathematically, the moving-average calculation is

$$\frac{\sum (\text{most recent } n \text{ data values})}{n}.$$

In short-range forecasting, the moving average for one period is used as the forecast for the next period.

Example

Forecasting with Moving Averages

To illustrate the moving-averages method, consider the 12 weeks of data presented in Table 7A.10 and Figure 7A.10. These data show the number of gallons of gasoline sold by a gasoline distributor in Bennington, Vermont, over the past 12 weeks.

To use moving averages to forecast the gasoline sales time series, we must first select the number of data values to be included in the moving average. As an example, let us compute forecasts based on a three-week moving average. The moving-average calculation for the first three weeks of the gasoline-sales time series is

$$\frac{17 + 21 + 19}{3} = 19.$$

Table 7A.10 Gasoline-Sales Time Series

Week	Sales (1,000s of gallons)	Week	Sales (1,000s of gallons)
1	17	7	20
2	21	8	18
3	19	9	22
4	23	10	20
5	18	11	15
6	16	12	22

Figure 7A.10 Graph of Gasoline-Sales Time Series

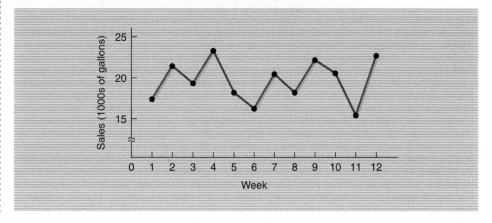

Table 7A.11 Summary of the Three-Week Moving-Average Calculations

Week	Time-Series Value	Moving-Average Forecast	Forecast Error	(Error)^2
1	17			
2	21			
3	19			
4	23	19	4	16
5	18	21	−3	9
6	16	20	−4	16
7	20	19	1	1
8	18	18	0	0
9	22	18	4	16
10	20	20	0	0
11	15	20	−5	25
12	22	19	3	9
		Totals	0	92

This moving-average value is then used as the forecast for week 4. Since the actual value observed in week 4 is 23, we see that the *forecast error* in week 4 is 23 − 19 = 4.

The calculation for the second three-week moving average is

$$\frac{21 + 19 + 23}{3} = 21.$$

This provides a forecast for week 5 of 21. The error associated with this forecast is 18 − 21 = −3. Thus we see that the forecast error can be positive or negative, depending on whether the forecast is too low or too high.

A complete summary of the three-week moving-average calculations for the gasoline-sales time series is shown in Table 7A.11 and Figure 7A.11. The mean square error for these forecasts is 92/9 = 10.22.

Figure 7A.11 Graph of Gasoline-Sales Time Series and Three-Week Moving-Average Forecasts

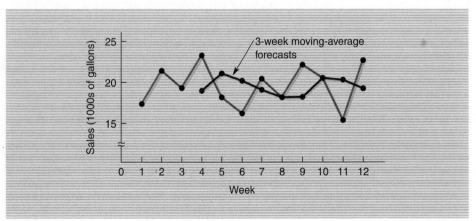

The number of data values to be included in the moving average is arbitrary. Thus, it should not be surprising that for a particular time series, different numbers of data values differ in their ability to forecast the time series accurately. One way to find the best number is to use trial and error to identify the number that minimizes the MSE measure of forecast accuracy. Then, if we are willing to assume that the number that is best for the past will also be best for the future, we would forecast the next value in the time series using the number of data values that minimized the MSE for the historical time series. Problem 14 at the end of this appendix asks you to consider four-week and five-week moving averages for the gasoline-sales data. A comparison of the MSE for each will indicate the number of weeks of data you may want to include in the moving-average calculation.

Exponential Smoothing

Exponential smoothing is a forecasting technique that uses a weighted average of past time-series values to forecast the value of the time series in the next period. The basic exponential-smoothing model is

$$F_{t+1} = \alpha Y_t + (1 - \alpha)F_t \qquad (7A.9)$$

where F_{t+1} = forecast of the time series for period $t + 1$,
    Y_t = actual value of the time series in period t,
    F_t = forecast of the time series for period t, and
    α = **smoothing constant** $(0 \le \alpha \le 1)$.

To see that the forecast for any period is a weighted average of *all the previous actual values* for the time series, suppose we have a time series consisting of three periods of data: Y_1, Y_2, and Y_3. To get the exponential-smoothing calculations started, we let F_1 equal the actual value of the time series in period 1; that is, $F_1 = Y_1$. Hence the forecast for period 2 would be written as

$$F_2 = \alpha Y_1 + (1 - \alpha)F_1$$

$$= \alpha Y_1 + (1 - \alpha)Y_1$$

$$= Y_1.$$

In general, then, the exponential-smoothing forecast for period 2 is equal to the actual value of the time series in period 1.

To obtain the forecast for period 3, we substitute $F_2 = Y_1$ in the expression for F_3; the result is

$$F_3 = \alpha Y_2 + (1 - \alpha)Y_1.$$

Finally, substituting this expression for F_3 in the expression for F_4, we obtain

$$F_4 = \alpha Y_3 + (1 - \alpha)[\alpha Y_2 + (1 - \alpha)Y_1]$$

$$= \alpha Y_3 + \alpha(1 - \alpha)Y_2 + (1 - \alpha)^2 Y_1.$$

Hence we see that F_4 is a weighted average of the first three time-series values. The sum of the coefficients, or weights, for Y_1, Y_2, and Y_3 will always equal 1. A similar argument can be made to show that any forecast F_{t+1} is a weighted average of the previous t time-series values.

An advantage of exponential smoothing is that it is a simple procedure and requires very little historical data. Once the smoothing constant, α, has been selected, only two pieces of information are needed to compute the forecast for the next period. Referring to Equation 7A.9, we see that with a given α, we can compute the forecast for period $t + 1$ simply by knowing the actual and forecast time-series values for period t, that is, Y_t and F_t.

Example

Forecasting with Exponential Smoothing

To illustrate the exponential-smoothing approach to forecasting, consider the gasoline-sales time series presented in Table 7A.10 and Figure 7A.10. As we have said, the exponential-smoothing forecast for period 2 is equal to the actual value of the time series in period 1. Thus, with $Y_1 = 17$, we will set $F_2 = 17$ to get the computations started. Referring to the time-series data in Table 7A.10, we find an actual time-series value in period 2 of $Y_2 = 21$. Thus period 2 has a forecast error of $21 - 17 = 4$.

Continuing with the exponential-smoothing computations provides the following forecast for Period 3.

$$F_3 = 0.2Y_2 + 0.8F_2 = 0.2(21) + 0.8(17) = 17.8$$

Once the actual time-series value in period 3, $Y_3 = 19$, is known, we can generate the forecast for period 4 as

$$F_4 = 0.2Y_3 + 0.8F_3 = 0.2(19) + 0.8(17.8) = 18.04.$$

By continuing these calculations, we are able to determine the weekly forecast values and the corresponding weekly forecast errors shown in Table 7A.12. Note that we have not shown an exponential-smoothing forecast or the forecast error for period 1, because F_1 was set equal to Y_1 to begin the smoothing computations. For week 12, we have $Y_{12} = 22$ and $F_{12} = 18.48$. Could you use this information to generate a forecast for week 13? Using the exponential-smoothing model, we have

$$F_{13} = 0.2Y_{12} + 0.8F_{12}$$

$$= 0.2(22) + 0.8(18.48) = 19.18.$$

Thus, the exponential-smoothing forecast of the sales amount in week 13 is 19.18, or 19,180 gallons of gasoline. With this forecast the firm can make plans and decisions accordingly. Although the accuracy of the forecast will not be known until the firm conducts its business through week 13, the exponential-smoothing model provides a good forecast for the unknown 13th-week gasoline-sales volume. Figure 7A.12 is the plot of the actual and the forecast time-series values. Note in particular how the forecasts "smooth out" the irregular fluctuations in the time series.

Table 7A.12 Summary of Exponential-Smoothing Forecasts and Forecast Errors for Gasoline Sales with Smoothing Constant $\alpha = 0.2$

Week (t)	Time-Series Value (Y_t)	Exponential-Smoothing Forecast (F_t)	Forecast Error ($Y_t - F_t$)
1	17		
2	21	17.00	4.00
3	19	17.80	1.20
4	23	18.04	4.96
5	18	19.03	−1.03
6	16	18.83	−2.83
7	20	18.26	1.74
8	18	18.61	−0.61
9	22	18.49	3.51
10	20	19.19	0.81
11	15	19.35	−4.35
12	22	18.48	3.52

In the preceding smoothing calculations we used a smoothing constant of $\alpha = 0.2$, although any value of α between 0 and 1 is acceptable. Some values yield better forecasts than others, however. Some insight into choosing a good value for α can be obtained by rewriting the exponential-smoothing model as follows.

$$F_{t+1} = \alpha Y_t + (1 - \alpha)F_t$$

$$F_{t+1} = \alpha Y_t + F_t - \alpha F_t$$

$$F_{t+1} = \underbrace{F_t}_{\substack{\text{Forecast} \\ \text{in period } t}} + \underbrace{\alpha(Y_t - F_t)}_{\substack{\text{Forecast error} \\ \text{in period } t}} \tag{7A.10}$$

So we see that the new forecast, F_{t+1}, is equal to the previous forecast, F_t, plus an adjustment, which is α *times* the most recent forecast error, $Y_t - F_t$. That is, the forecast in period $t + 1$ is obtained by adjusting the forecast in period t by a

Figure 7A.12
Graph of Actual and Forecast Gasoline-Sales Time Series with Smoothing Constant, $\alpha = 0.2$

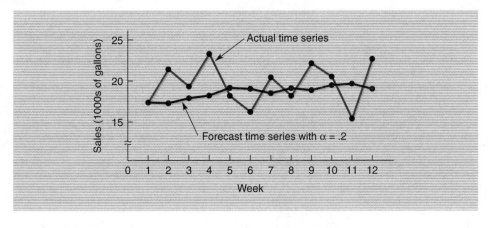

fraction of the forecast error. If the time series is very volatile and contains substantial random variability, a small value of the smoothing constant is preferred. The reason for this choice is that since much of the forecast error is due to random variability, we do not want to overreact and adjust the forecasts too quickly. For a fairly stable time series with relatively little random variability, larger values of the smoothing constant have the advantage of quickly adjusting the forecasts when forecasting errors occur and therefore allowing the forecast to react faster to changing conditions.

The criterion we will use to determine a desirable value for the smoothing constant, α, is the same as the criterion we proposed earlier for determining the number of periods of data to include in the moving-averages calculation. That is, we choose the value of α that minimizes the mean square error (MSE).

Figure 7A.13 is a spreadsheet that calculates exponential smoothing forecasts and forecast errors for three different smoothing constants: 0.2, 0.3, and 0.1. We see that, among those values, MSE is smallest for $\alpha = 0.2$, indicating that it results in a more accurate forecast. Using trial-and-error, we could easily experiment with other smoothing constants to try to find better values. It is good practice to analyze new data to see whether the smoothing constant should be revised to provide better forecasts.

Forecasting with Spreadsheets

It is quite straightforward to implement the formulas for forecasting that are introduced in this appendix on a spreadsheet (as we did for exponential smoothing), and a problem at the end of this appendix will ask you to do so. In addition, Microsoft EXCEL has built-in capability for performing regression analysis for linear trend, moving average, and exponential smoothing forecasting. Those techniques can be found by selecting the *Tools* option from the main menu, followed by *Data Analysis* in the submenu. After selection of the particular technique, a dialog box appears requesting the input data range, a range to place the output, some output options, and settings for any relevant parameters. Figure 7A.14 is an example for computing moving averages for the gasoline

Figure 7A.13
Spreadsheet for
Exponential Smoothing
Calculations
(EXSMOOTH.XLS)

	A	B	C	D	E	F	G	H	I	J	K
1	Exponential Smoothing Model										
2	Smoothing constant:		0.2			0.3			0.1		
3				Forecast	Squared		Forecast	Squared		Forecast	Squared
4	Week	Value	Forecast	Error	Error	Forecast	Error	Error	Forecast	Error	Error
5	1	17	17.00			17.00			17.00		
6	2	21	17.00	4.00	16.00	17.00	4.00	16.00	17.00	4.00	16.00
7	3	19	17.80	1.20	1.44	18.20	0.80	0.64	17.40	1.60	2.56
8	4	23	18.04	4.96	24.60	18.44	4.56	20.79	17.56	5.44	29.59
9	5	18	19.03	-1.03	1.07	19.81	-1.81	3.27	18.10	-0.10	0.01
10	6	16	18.83	-2.83	7.98	19.27	-3.27	10.66	18.09	-2.09	4.38
11	7	20	18.26	1.74	3.03	18.29	1.71	2.94	17.88	2.12	4.48
12	8	18	18.61	-0.61	0.37	18.80	-0.80	0.64	18.10	-0.10	0.01
13	9	22	18.49	3.51	12.34	18.56	3.44	11.83	18.09	3.91	15.32
14	10	20	19.19	0.81	0.66	19.59	0.41	0.17	18.48	1.52	2.32
15	11	15	19.35	-4.35	18.94	19.71	-4.71	22.23	18.63	-3.63	13.18
16	12	22	18.48	3.52	12.38	18.30	3.70	13.69	18.27	3.73	13.94
17				Total	98.80		Total	102.86		Total	101.78
18				MSE	8.98		MSE	9.35		MSE	9.25

Figure 7A.14
Moving Average Forecasting
with Microsoft Excel
(GASOLINE.XLS)

	A	B	C	D	E	F	G	H	I	
1	Gasoline	Sales Forecasting								
2										
3	Week	Sales								
4	1	17								
5	2	21								
6	3	19								
7	4	23								
8	5	18								
9	6	16								
10	7	20								
11	8	18								
12	9	22								
13	10	20								
14	11	15								
15	12	22								
16										

Figure 7A.14 is an example for computing moving averages for the gasoline sales data discussed earlier in this appendix.

Mean Absolute Deviation and Tracking Signals

Another commonly used measure of forecast accuracy is the **mean absolute deviation (MAD).** This measure is simply the average of the sum of the absolute deviations for all the forecast errors. Using the errors in Figure 7A.13, we obtain

$$MAD = \frac{\sum |Y_t - F_t|}{11}$$

$$= \frac{4.00 + 1.20 + \cdots + 4.35 + 3.52}{11}$$

$$= \frac{28.56}{11} = 2.596.$$

A major difference between MSE and MAD is that the MSE measure is influenced much more by large forecast errors than by small errors (since the errors are squared for the MSE measure). The selection of the best measure of forecasting accuracy is not a simple matter. Indeed, forecasting experts often disagree on which measure should be used.

MAD, however, is useful in *tracking* a forecast; that is, in monitoring the forecast to determine whether the forecasting technique being used remains adequate. The tracking method most often used is to compute a moving sum of forecast errors *divided* by the MAD; that is,

$$\frac{\sum (Y_t - F_t)}{MAD}$$

where the sums of both forecast errors and MAD are computed over the last *n* periods.

Example : ## Computing a Tracking Signal

Let us illustrate this for $n = 6$ using the data in Figure 7A.13. The first tracking signal that we can compute is after week 7. Summing the forecast errors for weeks 2 through 7 yields 8.04. The MAD for this period is $15.76/6 = 2.63$. Therefore, the tracking signal in period 7 is $8.04/2.63 = 3.06$. Continuing in this way for weeks 8 through 12, we find the following tracking signals.

Week (t)	$\Sigma(Y_t - F_t)$	MAD	Tracking Signal
8	3.43	$12.37/6 = 2.06$	1.67
9	5.74	$14.68/6 = 2.45$	2.34
10	1.59	$10.53/6 = 1.76$	.90
11	-1.73	$13.85/6 = 2.31$	$-.75$
12	4.62	$14.54/6 = 2.42$	1.91

Generally, if the tracking signal is within limits such as -3 to 3, or -5 to 5 (defined subjectively), the forecast is considered good. If, however, the tracking signal exceeds one limit, the forecaster should examine the demand pattern and forecasting technique chosen. Tracking in this manner is appropriate for all forecasting, not just for exponential smoothing.

Key Terms

Time series
Trend
Cyclical component
Seasonal component
Irregular component
Forecast error
Mean square error (MSE)
Deseasonalized time series
Moving averages
Exponential smoothing
Smoothing constant
Mean absolute deviation (MAD)

Review Questions

1. Define *time series*.
2. Briefly explain each component of a time series.
3. Why are forecasts never completely accurate? What does this mean for operations managers?
4. Describe the process of long-range forecasting using trend projection.
5. Define *multiplicative time series*.
6. Define *moving average*.
7. Define *deseasonalized time series*.
8. Explain the philosophy behind exponential smoothing.
9. Explain the two basic ways to measure forecast accuracy.
10. Define *tracking signal*.

Solved Problems

1. Average attendance figures at a major university's home football games have the seven-year pattern shown in Table 7A.13.

Table 7A.13 Data for Solved Problem 1

Year	Attendance	Year	Attendance
1	28,000	5	30,500
2	30,000	6	32,200
3	31,500	7	30,800
4	40,000		

Develop the linear-trend expression for this time series. Use the trend expression to forecast attendance for year 8.

Solution

The trend equation is given by Equation 7A.1. To find b_1 and b_0 we use Equations 7A.3 and 7A.4. The terms in Equation 7A.3 are as follows.

$$\sum t = 28 \qquad \sum t^2 = 140 \qquad \sum Y_t = 213,400$$

$$\sum tY_t = 865,400 \qquad n = 7$$

Then

$$b_1 = \frac{\sum tY_t - (\sum t \sum Y_t)/n}{\sum t^2 - (\sum t)^2/n}$$

$$= \frac{865,400 - (28)(213,400)/7}{140 - (28)^2/7}$$

$$= \frac{11,800}{28} = 421.429$$

and

$$b_0 = \bar{Y} - b_1\bar{t} = 30,485.714 - 421.429(4) = 28,800$$

Thus, the trend expression is as follows:

$$T_t = 28,800 + 421.429t$$

When $t = 8$, we have $T_8 = 32,171.432$.

2. The quarterly sales data for a college textbook over the past three years are listed in Table 7A.14.

Table 7A.14 Data for Solved Problem 2

	Year 1	Year 2	Year 3
Quarter 1	1,690	1,800	1,850
Quarter 2	940	900	1,100
Quarter 3	2,625	2,900	2,930
Quarter 4	2,500	2,360	2,615

a. Show the four-quarter moving-average values for this time series.
b. Compute seasonal indexes for the four quarters.
c. When does the textbook publisher experience the largest seasonal effect? Does this appear reasonable? Explain.

Solution

a. The moving averages are given in Table 7A.15.

Table 7A.15 Solved Problem 2 Solution, part (a)

Year	Quarter	Sales	Moving Average
1	1	1,690	—
	2	940	—
	3	2,625	—
	4	2,500	1938.75
2	1	1,800	1966.25
	2	900	1956.25
	3	2,900	2025.00
	4	2,360	1990.00
3	1	1,850	2002.50
	2	1,100	2052.50
	3	2,930	2060.00
4	2,615	2123.75	

b. Seasonal indexes are shown in Table 7A.16.

Table 7A.16 Solved Problem 2 Solution, part (b)

Quarter	Seasonal-Irregular Component Values		Seasonal Index	Adjusted Seasonal Index
1	.904,	.900	0.9020	0.900
2	.448,	.526	0.4870	0.486
3	1.344,	1.453	1.3985	1.396
4	1.275,	1.164	1.2195	1.217
		Total	4.0070	

Note: adjustment for seasonal index $= \dfrac{4.000}{4.007} = 0.9983$

c. The publisher experiences the largest seasonal index in quarter 2. This appears reasonable since the April, May, June sales period would correspond to sales for summer sessions, which generally have the smallest enrollment.

3. A retail store records the number of units of customer demand during each sales period. Use the demand data in Table 7A.17 to develop three-period and four-period moving-average forecasts. Compute the MSE for each. Which number of periods provides the better moving-average forecast?

Table 7A.17 Data for Solved Problem 3

Period	Demand	Period	Demand
1	86	7	91
2	93	8	93
3	88	9	96
4	89	10	97
5	92	11	93
6	94	12	95

Figure 7A.15
Spreadsheet for Solved
Problem 3 Solution

	A	B	C	D	E	F	G	H	I	J
1			n = 3		Error	n = 4		Error		
2	Period	Demand	Forecast	Error	Squared	Forecast	Error	Squared		
3	1	86								
4	2	93								
5	3	88								
6	4	89	89.00	0.00	0.00					
7	5	92	90.00	2.00	4.00	89.00	3.00	9.00		
8	6	94	89.67	4.33	18.78	90.50	3.50	12.25		
9	7	91	91.67	-0.67	0.44	90.75	0.25	0.06		
10	8	93	92.33	0.67	0.44	91.50	1.50	2.25		
11	9	96	92.67	3.33	11.11	92.50	3.50	12.25		
12	10	97	93.33	3.67	13.44	93.50	3.50	12.25		
13	11	93	95.33	-2.33	5.44	94.25	-1.25	1.56		
14	12	95	95.33	-0.33	0.11	94.75	0.25	0.06		
15				Total	53.78			49.69		
16				MSE	5.98			6.21		
17										

Solution
Figure 7A.15 is a spreadsheet for solving this problem. In regard to MSE, the three-period moving-average forecasts perform better.

4. The number of pizzas sold at MamaMia's on Friday nights was as shown in Table 7A.18.

Table 7A.18 Data for Solved Problem 4

Week	Demand	Week	Demand
1	22	6	24
2	18	7	20
3	23	8	19
4	21	9	18
5	17	10	21

Use exponential smoothing with $\alpha = 0.2$ to develop a forecast for week 11.

Solution.
Figure 7A.16 is a spreadsheet for this problem. The forecast for week 11 is

$$F_{11} = 0.2(21) + 0.8(20.08) = 20.26.$$

Figure 7A.16
Spreadsheet for Solved
Problem 4 Solution

	A	B	C	D	E	F	G	H	I	J	K
1	Exponential Smoothing Model										
2	Smoothing constant:		0.2								
3				Forecast	Squared						
4	Week	Value	Forecast	Error	Error						
5	1	22	22.00								
6	2	18	22.00	-4.00	16.00						
7	3	23	21.20	1.80	3.24						
8	4	21	21.56	-0.56	0.31						
9	5	17	21.45	-4.45	19.78						
10	6	24	20.56	3.44	11.84						
11	7	20	21.25	-1.25	1.55						
12	8	19	21.00	-2.00	3.99						
13	9	18	20.60	-2.60	6.75						
14	10	21	20.08	0.92	0.85						
15				Total	64.33						
16				MSE	7.15						
17											

Part Two

Problems

1. Develop spreadsheets for performing linear trend and moving average forecast calculations. Apply them to the examples in this appendix.

2. The monthly sales of a new business software package at a local discount software store were as follow.

Week	1	2	3	4	5	6
Sales	360	415	432	460	488	512

a. Develop the linear-trend equation.

b. Using the result from part a, determine the forecast for the seventh and ninth months.

3. The president of a small manufacturing firm is concerned about the continual growth in manufacturing costs in the past several years. The time series of the cost per unit for the firm's leading product over the past eight years is given in Table 7A.19.

Table 7A.19 Data for Problem 3

Year	Cost/Unit ($)	Year	Cost/Unit ($)
1	20.00	5	26.60
2	24.50	6	30.00
3	28.20	7	31.00
4	27.50	8	36.00

a. Make a graph of this time series. Does a linear trend appear to exist?

b. Develop a linear-trend expression for the time series. What average cost increase has the firm been realizing per year?

4. Table 7A.20 gives enrollment data for a state college for the past six years.

Table 7A.20 Data for Problem 4

Year	Enrollment	Year	Enrollment
1	20,500	4	19,000
2	20,200	5	19,100
3	19,500	6	18,800

Develop a linear-trend expression, and comment on what is happening to enrollment at this institution. Use the trend expression to forecast enrollment for year 7.

5. Canton Supplies, Inc., is a service firm that employs approximately 100. Because of the necessity of meeting monthly cash obligations, management wants to develop a forecast of monthly cash requirements. Because of a recent change in operating policy, only the past seven months of data are considered relevant. Develop a linear-trend expression for the historical data in Table 7A.21. Use the trend expression to forecast cash requirements for each of the next two months.

Table 7A.21 Data for Problem 5

Month	Cash Required ($1,000)	Month	Cash Required ($1,000)
1	205	5	230
2	212	6	240
3	218	7	246
4	224		

6. The Costello Music Company has been in business five years. During that time its sales of electric organs has grown from 12 units to 76 units per year. Fred Costello, the firm's owner, wants to forecast next year's organ sales. The historical data follow.

Year	1	2	3	4	5
Sales	12	28	34	50	76

a. Make a graph of this time series. Does a linear trend appear to exist?
b. Develop a linear-trend expression for the time series. What is the average increase in sales that the firm has been realizing per year?
7. Hudson Marine has been an authorized dealer for C&D marine radios for seven years. The number of radios it has sold each year is reported below.

Year	1	2	3	4	5	6	7
Number Sold	35	50	75	90	105	110	130

a. Make a graph of this time series. Does a linear trend appear to exist?
b. Develop a linear trend for the time series.
c. Using the linear trend developed in part b, forecast next year's sales.
8. The sales of treadmills at Tom's Sporting Goods show a linear trend described by the equation,

$$T_t = 15 + 1.5t$$

where t is the number of quarters since the item was introduced and T_t is not adjusted for seasonality. Quarterly data for the last three years are given in Table 7A.22.

Table 7A.22 Data for Problem 8

Quarter	Year 1	Year 2	Year 3
1	28	35	44
2	17	23	29
3	21	25	33
4	29	39	40

Compute the seasonality factors, and generate forecasts for the next four quarters.

9. Using a 12-month moving-average calculation, identify the monthly seasonal indexes for three years of expenses (Table 7A.23) for a six-unit apartment building in southern Florida.

Table 7A.23 Data for Problem 9

| | Year | | |
Month	1	2	3
January	170	180	195
February	180	205	210
March	205	215	230
April	230	245	280
May	240	265	290
June	315	330	390
July	360	400	420
August	290	335	330
September	240	260	290
October	240	270	295
November	230	255	280
December	195	220	250

10. Refer to the Hudson Marine example in Problem 7. Suppose the quarterly sales values for the seven years of historical data are as given in Table 7A.24.

Table 7A.24 Data for Problem 10

| | Quarter | | | | Total |
Year	1	2	3	4	Sales
1	6	15	10	4	35
2	10	18	15	7	50
3	14	26	23	12	75
4	19	28	25	18	90
5	22	34	28	21	105
6	24	36	30	20	110
7	28	40	35	27	130

a. Show the four-quarter moving-average values for this time series. Plot both the original time series and the moving-average series on the same graph.
b. Compute the seasonal indexes for the four quarters.
c. When does Hudson Marine experience the largest seasonal effect? Does this seem reasonable? Explain.
11. Consider the Costello Music Company example in Problem 6. Quarterly sales data are given in Table 7A.25

Table 7A.25 Data for Problem 11

Year	Quarter				Total Sales
	1	*2*	*3*	*4*	
1	4	2	1	5	12
2	6	4	4	14	28
3	10	3	5	16	34
4	12	9	7	22	50
5	18	10	13	35	76

a. Compute the seasonal indexes for the four quarters.

b. When does Costello Music experience the largest seasonal effect? Does this appear reasonable? Explain.

12. Refer to the Hudson Marine data presented in Problem 10.

a. Deseasonalize the data, and use the deseasonalized time series to identify the trend.

b. Use the results of part a to develop a quarterly forecast for next year.

c. Use the seasonal indexes developed in Problem 10 to adjust the forecasts developed in part b to account for the effect of season.

13. Consider the Costello Music Company time series presented in Problem 11.

a. Deseasonalize the data, and use the deseasonalized time series to identify the trend.

b. Use the results of part a to develop a quarterly forecast for next year.

c. Use the seasonal indexes developed in Problem 11 to adjust the forecasts developed in part b to account for the effect of season.

14. Refer to the gasoline-sales time series data in Table 7A.10.

a. Compute four- and five-week moving averages for the time series.

b. Compute the mean square error (MSE) for the four- and five-week moving-average forecasts.

c. What appears to be the best number of weeks of past data to use in computing the moving average? Remember that the MSE for the three-week moving average is 10.22.

15. Forecasts and actual sales of portable CD players at Just Say Music! are given in Table 7A.26.

Table 7A.26 Data for Problem 15

Month	Forecast	Sales
March	150	170
April	220	229
May	205	192
June	256	271
July	250	238

a. What is the mean absolute deviation (MAD)?

b. What is the forecast for August, using a three-period moving average?

c. If the actual demand for August is 268, what would the forecast be for September?

16. Use the gasoline-sales time-series data from Table 7A.10 to compute exponential-smoothing forecasts using $\alpha = 0.1$. Using the MSE criterion, would you prefer a smoothing constant of $\alpha = 0.1$ or $\alpha = 0.2$ here?

17. With a smoothing constant of $\alpha = 0.2$, equation 7A.9 shows that the forecast for the 13th week of the gasoline-sales data from Table 7A.10 is given by $F_{13} = 0.2Y_{12} + 0.8F_{12}$. However, the forecast for week 12 is given by $F_{12} = 0.2Y_{11} + 0.8F_{11}$. Thus we could combine these two results to show that the forecast for the 13th week can be written

$$F_{13} = 0.2Y_{12} + 0.8(0.2Y_{11} + 0.8F_{11})$$
$$= 0.2Y_{12} + 0.16Y_{11} + 0.64F_{11}.$$

a. Making use of the fact that $F_{11} = 0.2Y_{10} + 0.8F_{10}$ (and similar expressions for F_{10} and F_9), continue to expand the expression for F_{13} until it is written in terms of the past data values, $Y_{12}, Y_{11}, Y_{10}, Y_9, Y_8$, and the forecast for period 8.

b. Refer to the coefficients or weights for the past data $Y_{12}, Y_{11}, Y_{10}, Y_9$, and Y_8. What observation do you make about how exponential smoothing weights past-data values in arriving at new forecasts? Compare this weighting pattern with the weighting pattern of the moving-averages method.

18. Use $\alpha = 0.3$ to compute the exponential-smoothing values for the time series of the sales of a particular product over the past 12 months (Table 7A.27).

Table 7A.27 Data for Problem 18

Month	Sales	Month	Sales
1	105	7	145
2	135	8	140
3	120	9	100
4	105	10	80
5	90	11	100
6	120	12	110

19. Modify the spreadsheet in Figure 7A.13 to analyze the forecasting errors for the time series in Problem 18 by using smoothing constants of 0.1 and 0.5. Which smoothing constant appears to provide the better forecasts?

20. The number of component parts used in a production process each of the last 10 weeks is reported in Table 7A.28.

Table 7A.28 Data for Problem 20

Week	Parts	Week	Parts
1	200	6	210
2	350	7	280
3	250	8	350
4	360	9	290
5	250	10	320

Use a smoothing constant of 0.25 to develop the exponential-smoothing values for this time series. Indicate your forecast for next week.

21. A chain of grocery stores had the following weekly demand (cases) for a particular brand of laundry soap.

Week	1	2	3	4	5	6	7	8	9	10
Demand	31	22	33	26	21	29	25	22	20	26

a. Develop three- and four-period moving average forecasts, and compute MSE for each. Which provides the better forecast? What would be your forecast for week 11?

b. Develop exponential-smoothing forecasts with smoothing constants of $\alpha = 0.1$ and 0.3. Using the MSE criterion, which provides a better forecast?

c. What would your forecast for week 11 be?

22. United Dairies, Inc., supplies milk to independent grocers in Dade County, Florida. Managers of United Dairies want to develop a forecast of the number of half-gallons of milk sold per week. Sales data for the past 12 weeks are given in Table 7A.29

Table 7A.29 Data for Problem 22

Week	Sales (units)	Week	Sales (units)
1	2750	7	3300
2	3100	8	3100
3	3250	9	2950
4	2800	10	3000
5	2900	11	3200
6	3050	12	3150

Use these 12 weeks of data and exponential smoothing with $\alpha = 0.4$ to develop a forecast of demand for the 13th week.

23. Consider these six-period demand data:

Period	1	2	3	4	5	6
Demand	121	133	146	157	169	183

a. Develop the linear-trend model.

b. Develop exponential-smoothing forecasts with $\alpha = 0.3$ and $\alpha = 0.4$.

c. Which model provides the best forecasts? Discuss.

d. What is the forecast for period 7?

24. Use the gasoline-sales data and exponential-smoothing forecasts shown in Figure 7A.13 ($\alpha = 0.3$).

a. Compute the mean-absolute-deviation (MAD) measure of forecast accuracy.

b. Exponential-smoothing forecasts for $\alpha = 0.2$ and $\alpha = 0.3$ provide the following MSE measures of forecast accuracy.

α	MSE
0.2	8.98
0.3	9.35

The MAD measure for $\alpha = 0.2$ is 2.596. Using the results of part a, does the MAD criterion also support the use of $\alpha = 0.2$ as the better smoothing constant?

c. Using the data in Figure 7A.13, compute the tracking signal for weeks 7 through 12 using $n = 6$.

25. Use the demand data in Solved Problem 3 with the three-period and four-period moving-average forecasts you developed.

a. Compute the MAD for the three-period and four-period forecasts. Which method is better using the MAD criterion?

b. Using $n = 6$, compute the tracking signal for periods 7 to 12. Compare the tracking-signal results for three-period and four-period moving-average forecasts.

Chapter Eight
Facility Location and Distribution System Design

Through forecasting and capacity planning, a firm can determine whether additional long-range production and/or storage capacity is required. As suggested in the preceding chapter, one alternative for meeting additional capacity requirements is to expand existing facilities. For instance, the popularity of MamaMia's pizzas might warrant additional dining space or a bigger kitchen to support increased demand for delivery. That approach may not always be possible; for example, there may be insufficient land for expansion. It may not even be desirable; a firm may want to build one or more other facilities close to targeted customers in order to keep delivery times short. Thus, determining appropriate locations for new facilities such as plants, warehouses, retail stores, hospitals, and restaurants is an important part of strategy. Related to the location decision is the distribution decision: how goods are to be transported to customers to meet customer-service objectives while minimizing costs. This chapter presents basic concepts and procedures for facility-location and distribution-system decisions for manufacturing and service organizations. Specifically addressed are

••• The importance of location and distribution to operations.

••• Key issues in planning location and distribution strategies.

••• Application of scoring models and various quantitative approaches to facility-location and distribution-system design.

••• Application of computer-based modeling to location/distribution analysis and decision making.

••• Important factors and common approaches related to locating service facilities.

Location/Distribution Strategy

Location decisions can have a profound effect on a firm's competitive advantage. For example, a firm might choose to locate a plant in a new geographic region not only to reduce distribution costs, but also to create cultural ties between the firm and the local community. The relationships established may attract new business and improve the firm's market position in relation to distant competitors. But location decisions can also be a source of problems, as Honda discovered.

Applied P/OM

Honda of America Manufacturing, Inc.

Honda was faced with transportation problems in locating in a rural area.[1]

Honda of America Manufacturing, Inc., located a new automobile plant near Marysville, Ohio. An important factor in that decision was the state's agreement to build a four-lane highway linking the site to the interstate highway system. Subsequently, the state announced a delay of at least six years in completing the highway. The lack of a good transportation system can cause problems in recruiting labor and delays in delivery of supplies, which may adversely affect manufacturing, so Honda suffered from its location decision in this particular case.

"Bottom-line" criteria in location decisions, such as low costs, low taxes, and low wages, are not always the most important factors in such decisions—anything that relates to overall operations strategy must be considered. New facilities require large amounts of capital investment and, once built, cannot easily be moved.

Location decisions also affect the management of operations at lower levels of the organization. For instance, if a manufacturing facility is located far from sources of raw materials, it may take a considerable amount of time to deliver an order, and there will be more uncertainty as to the actual time of delivery. To guard against shortages, larger inventories must be carried, thus increasing costs. Likewise, if a plant or warehouse is located far from market centers, higher transportation costs are incurred in delivering finished goods to customers. The availability of labor and utilities, state and local politics, climate, and other factors all affect the productivity and quality of the production system.

Since the early 1970s, the annual growth in free-world trade has been double the annual growth of the gross national product.[2] Thus, many companies must cope with the issues of global distribution, such as time zones, foreign languages, international funds transfer, customs, tariffs and other trade restrictions, packaging, and foreign cultural practices. They need an adaptive and integrated distribution system based on customer requirements that effectively utilizes information technology and human resources.

Business Logistics

To understand the importance of location in meeting strategic objectives, you need to understand **business logistics**—the management of all activities that facilitate product flow to the point of final consumption as well as the information flows that are necessary to provide adequate levels of customer service at reasonable costs.[3] The key elements of a logistics system, or the production/distribution system, are transportation, inventory, and order processing (Figure 8.1). Raw materials and components are ordered from suppliers and must be transported to manufacturing facilities for production into finished goods. Finished goods are generally shipped to regional warehouses (often called *distribution centers*) and finally to retail stores, where they are made available to customers. At each plant, warehouse, and retail store, inventory is maintained to meet demand in a reasonable amount of time. As inventory levels diminish, orders are sent to the next-higher level for replenishing stock. Customer demand sets the entire process in motion.

The principal goal of a logistics system is to provide customers with an accurate and quick response to their orders at the lowest possible cost. Thus, the prime objective of location decisions is to position each element of the production/distribution system effectively with respect to the overall system. A manufacturing facility, for example, must be strategically positioned between its suppliers and its customers (which may be distribution centers or retail outlets). Larger firms have more complex location decisions; they must position both plants and warehouses advantageously with respect to suppliers, retail outlets, and each other. Rarely are

Figure 8.1
Production/Distribution
System

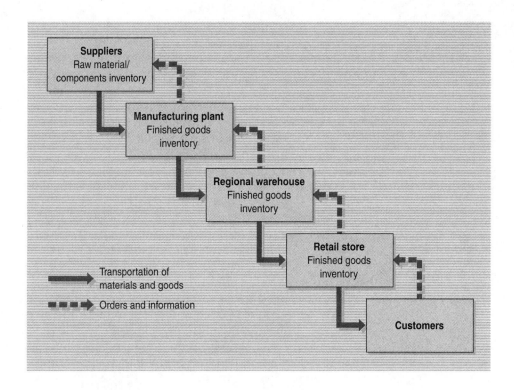

both these decisions made simultaneously, however. Typically, the plant is located with respect to suppliers and a fixed set of warehouses, whereas warehouses are located with respect to manufacturing plants and markets. We will focus on the location decision for a single facility (such as a plant), the location of warehouses in the distribution system, transportation planning, and the special cases of locating retail, public service, and emergency facilities.

Push versus Pull Distribution Systems

Forecasting plays an important role in logistics planning.[4] Demand variation necessitates maintaining sufficient product to maximize customer service. However, distribution centers are not designed to handle peak requirements, except when sales are relatively flat. During peak periods, then, the product is either backed up at the plant or stored at a temporary location. Those factors greatly affect the strategic choice of a distribution system.

There are two basic approaches for addressing this issue. One approach is to "push" all products from the plants to the distribution centers on the basis of projected sales. An inaccurate sales forecast in a push system leads to increased inventory, larger distribution centers, and higher stock-transfer costs. Each distribution center must have enough inventory to cover systemwide forecast inaccuracies and individual regional sales fluctuations. Transportation costs increase as products are shipped between distribution centers to accommodate customer demands. Material handling increases as products are unloaded and stored, then later removed from storage and loaded for shipment. However, a push system has several benefits, including small plant warehouses, good customer service, and full-truckload shipments (which are less costly) to the distribution centers.

An alternative is a system that "pulls" products from plants on the basis of actual demand. An inaccurate sales forecast has less impact here, since only production is based on the forecast. The distribution center facilitates **cross-docking**—a process by which products are unloaded from plant shipments, staged on the docks (but not sent to storage), and quickly reloaded for shipment to individual customers. In an ideal pull system, a customer order generates an order from the distribution center to the plant, and the plant produces the product when the order is received and immediately ships it. Realistically, the plant must maintain sufficient buffer inventory from which to pull orders. A pull system therefore requires larger plant warehouses, has slower order-response time, and increases less-than-full-truckload shipments. However, stock transfers between distribution centers are eliminated, distribution centers can carry lower stock levels, and there are opportunities for shipping directly from plants to customers. Pull systems are related to the concept of "just-in-time," which is discussed in Chapter 15.

Push systems work best when sales patterns are consistent and when there is a small number of distribution centers and products. Pull systems are more effective when there are many production facilities, many points of distribution, and a large number of products. To determine the best overall distribution strategy, a firm must consider transportation costs and methods, inventory costs, storage requirements, sales trends and projected growth, production capacity, customer demand, and other factors dictated by corporate policy.

Location Planning and Analysis

Location decisions are based on both economic and noneconomic factors. Table 8.1 is a list of important location factors for site selection. Economic factors include *facility costs* such as construction, utilities, insurance, taxes, depreciation, and maintenance; *operating costs,* including fuel, direct labor, and administrative personnel (which may vary considerably by location); and *transportation costs,* the costs associated with moving goods from their origins to the final destinations. Economic factors, especially construction costs, taxes, and wage rates, vary by location. Low wage rates are a major reason many companies move factories to other countries. Many states offer tax incentives to entice companies to build plants there. Transportation costs can be a large proportion of the total delivered cost of a product, however, and locating a plant far from sources of supply or customers can commit a company to significant transportation costs. Thus, the plant location decision must attempt to minimize combined production and transportation costs.

Noneconomic factors include the availability of labor, transportation services, and utilities; climate, community environment, and quality of life; and state and local politics. There must be a sufficient supply of labor to meet planned production levels; in addition, workers must have the appropriate skills. Labor-intensive firms may want to locate where wage rates and costs of training are low. Some companies may require trucking service, while other firms may require rail service. Other firms need to be close to water transportation or major airports. All production activities require such services as electric-

Table 8.1 Location Factors for Site Selection

Labor Factors	Transportation Factors	Utilities Factors	Climate, Community Environment, and Quality of Life Factors	State and Local Political Factors
Labor supply	Closeness to sources of supply	Water supply	Climate and living conditions	Taxation policies
Labor-management relations	Closeness to markets	Waste disposal	Schools (elementary and high school)	Tax structure
Ability to retain labor force	Adequacy of transportation modes	Power supply	Universities and research facilities	Opportunity for highway advertising
Availability of technical and executive personnel	Costs of transportation	Fuel availability and cost	Community attitudes	
Labor rates		Communications	Religious factors	
			Property costs	

ity, water, and waste removal. For example, chemical-processing, paper, and nuclear-power companies require large amounts of water for cooling and therefore would consider only locations near an abundant water supply. A favorable climate is good for employee well-being and morale. Taxes, the cost of living, and educational and cultural facilities are all important to employees, particularly if they are relocating. Community attitudes should also be evaluated. For example, industries that handle high-risk chemicals or radioactive substances are particularly susceptible to unfavorable public reaction and legislation and are less likely to locate in urban areas. Finally, the political attitudes of the state can be either favorable or unfavorable to locating there. Activities such as industrial development programs, revenue-bond financing, state industrial loans, and tax inducements are often important factors in choices to locate in one state instead of another.

Location planning is typically conducted hierarchically. Three basic decisions must be made: the regional decision, the community decision, and the site decision. The *regional* decision involves choosing a general region of the country—the Northeast, the Midwest, the Southwest, and so on. In this era of globalization, various regions of the world might also be considered, such as Mexico, South America, or the Pacific Rim. Factors that affect the regional decision include the locations of major customers and sources of materials and supply; labor availability and costs; degree of unionization; land, construction, and utility costs; and climate. The *community* decision involves selecting a specific city or community in which to locate. In addition to the factors cited for the regional decision, a company would consider managers' preferences, community services and taxes (as well as tax incentives), available transportation systems, banking services, and environmental impacts. Finally, the *site* decision involves the selection of a particular location within the chosen community. Site costs, proximity to transportation systems, utilities, and zoning restrictions are among the factors to be considered.

Scoring Models for Facility Location

The most common method for evaluating noneconomic factors in a facility-location study is to use a *scoring model* such as that discussed in Chapter 6 for product-selection decisions. Applied to facility location, a scoring model consists of a list of major location criteria, each of which is partitioned into several levels. A score is assigned to each level that reflects its relative importance. For example, consider these qualitative factors:

••• Climate.
••• Water availability.
••• Schools.
••• Housing.
••• Community attitude.
••• Labor laws.

An illustrative scoring model is shown in Table 8.2. In this table, the levels for each factor range from 0, representing the least desirable, to either 4 or 5, representing ideal conditions. Notice that the maximum number of points assigned differs among the factors. This implies that higher-rated factors are more important than those with lower ratings.

For instance, from Table 8.2, it appears that water availability and housing, each with 10 points for the maximum score, are of equal importance and are less important than the other criteria. Community attitude carries the most weight, a maximum of 60 points, and is thus the most important criterion in this example. The weighting of the factors is rather subjective and is best done after careful analysis by a group of experienced personnel.

Example

Using a Scoring Model for Facility Location

The Halvorsen Supply Company has identified two sites for a new facility. Using the scoring model in Table 8.2, managers have evaluated each site as follows.

Criterion	Site A		Site B	
Climate	Wide variation	18	Ideal	30
Water	Sufficient quantity	8	Sufficient; treated	6
Schools	High-quality public	12	Low-quality public	8
Housing	Wide range	10	Acceptable	6
Community	Cooperative	45	Cooperative	45
Labor laws	No hardship	16	Few; not troublesome	24
Total		109		119

Site B appears to have a slight advantage overall for these criteria. However, Site B is better than Site A only in climate and labor laws; it is less desirable than Site A in water, schools, and housing. Those factors might be important in attracting

Table 8.2 Facility-Location Scoring Model

Level		Score
	1. Climate	
(0)	Unlivable or prohibitive to planned manufacture; corrective measures cannot change conditions.	0
(1)	Extreme variation in climate conditions; susceptible to violent, destructive storms, floods, and so on.	6
(2)	Wide climate variation; infrequent destructive climatic forces.	12
(3)	Wide climate variation; little likelihood of destructive climatic forces.	18
(4)	Moderate climatic variation; very livable; corrective measures are needed for limited periods of the year.	24
(5)	Ideal for both living and manufacturing. Limited climatic variation.	30
	2. Water Availability	
(0)	Unavailable.	0
(1)	Available in small quantities; premium prices; of dubious purity for manufacturing process.	2
(2)	Available in sufficient quantities for households, but not for manufacturing processes.	4
(3)	Available in sufficient quantities for manufacturing, but highly treated.	6
(4)	Available in sufficient quantities and pure enough for proposed manufacturing process.	8
(5)	An abundance for proposed usage; very pure.	10
	3. Schools	
(0)	No schools.	0
(1)	Only low-quality public schools through high-school level.	4
(2)	Only low-quality public schools through high-school level, but good private schools.	8
(3)	High-quality public schools through high-school level.	12
(4)	High-quality public schools through high-school level; excellent private, vocational, and junior colleges; colleges or universities are very near.	16
(5)	High-quality public schools through high-school level; excellent private, vocational, and junior colleges; colleges or universities are very near; comprehensive adult education program.	20
	4. Housing	
(0)	Nonexistent.	0
(1)	Largely unavailable and of poor quality.	2
(2)	Largely available, but of poor quality.	4
(3)	Available; acceptable quality; reasonable rates.	6
(4)	Excellent quality; limited range of types; reasonable rates.	8
(5)	Excellent quality; wide range of types; reasonable rates.	10
	5. Community Attitude	
(0)	Hostile, bitter, noncooperative.	0
(1)	Parasitic in nature.	15
(2)	Noncooperative.	30
(3)	Cooperative.	45
(4)	Friendly and more than cooperative.	60

(Continued)

Table 8.2 Facility-Location Scoring Model *(continued)*

Level		Score
	6. Labor Laws	
(0)	Strict and rigidly enforced.	0
(1)	Strict, but not rigidly enforced.	8
(2)	Work no hardship on employment policy.	16
(3)	Very few and not troublesome.	24
(4)	Nonexistent or of such a nature as to be conducive to good relations.	32

Source: Adapted from R. Reed, *Plant Layout: Factors, Principles, and Techniques* (Homewood, IL: Irwin, 1961). Used with permission.

a skilled labor force and in getting managerial personnel to relocate. Other factors such as construction, labor, transportation, and utility costs also must be considered. The final approval, however, rests with top managers.

Distribution-System Design

Warehousing plays a crucial role in total distribution design. Consider, for example, a large national grocery chain that manufactures many products under its own name, maintains regional distribution centers, and owns hundreds of retail stores. Such a firm would have a distribution structure similar to that in Figure 8.1. Note that the firm has control over the location of all intermediate components in the logistics system.

Suppose this firm does not own any warehouses, and that shipments of finished goods must be made directly from its plants to its retail stores. If the factory is located far from its supplies of raw materials, premiums must be paid for transporting the materials to the plant (inbound transportation costs). Also, longer delivery times increase the chances of material shortages for production. On the other hand, if the plant is located far from clusters of retail stores, transportation costs incurred in shipping from the plant to the retail stores (outbound transportation costs) are higher. As before, it takes longer to deliver an order to a retail store. That could result in out-of-stock situations, which reduce the level of customer service. However, the use of warehouses placed close to the markets could provide quick, efficient delivery to retail stores, while still allowing factories to be near suppliers.

Warehouses and distribution centers play an important intermediary role between plants and retail stores. They allow a company to store finished goods for efficient distribution to points of use. For example, suppose MamaMia's expanded nationally and opened franchises in major cities. Rather than shipping small quantities of supplies from various distributors to each of its restaurants, MamaMia's might use a warehouse to *consolidate* orders, as shown in Figure 8.2. **Consolidation** increases productivity since transport vehicles are used more efficiently, and reduces unit costs. Western Electric and The Greater New York Blood Program illustrate the use of consolidation in a manufacturing and in a service organization.

Figure 8.2
Product Consolidation

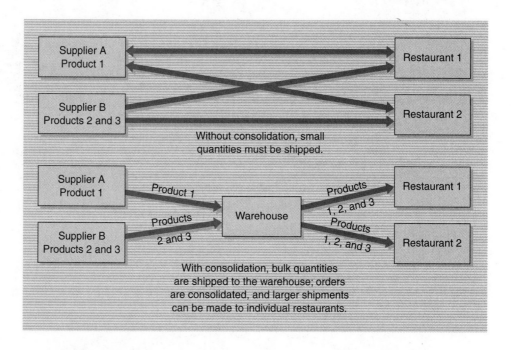

Applied P/OM
Western Electric

Western Electric streamlined its distribution system through consolidation.[5]

Western Electric was faced with spiraling costs of distribution as well as cumbersome inventory control and order processing for 50,000 items used by its field installations. Under the old system, products were warehoused at separate factories and shipped in odd lots to 26 service centers as needed. To reduce costs and improve productivity, Western Electric designed seven regionalized material management centers (MMC). Factory orders are now shipped in truckload lots directly to the MMCs, where orders are processed and consolidated for shipment to individual service centers.

Applied P/OM
The Greater New York Blood Program

Consolidation of blood distribution reduced cost and improved service.[6]

The Greater New York Blood Program established a regional blood center with responsibility for collecting and distributing blood to individual hospital blood banks. A prototype system implemented in Long Island improved utilization, which resulted in an 80 percent waste reduction,

Figure 8.3 Examples of Consolidation in Manufacturing and Service Organizations

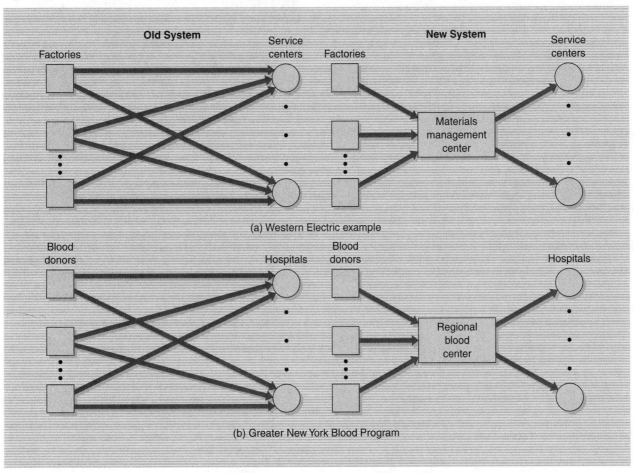

with annual savings of $500,000. In addition, it increased the availability of blood to patients and decreased the number of elective surgeries that must be postponed because of lack of the right products.

Here we see a direct analogy between production and service operations in that surgeries (production) depend greatly on the management and distribution of blood (raw materials). Figure 8.3 illustrates the system analogies between these two examples.

Cost and Service Trade-Offs

As the number of distribution centers increases, total transportation costs generally decline, since facilities are closer to customers. On the other hand, inventory and order-processing costs rise, since more inventory is carried and there is a corresponding increase in paperwork and other administrative costs. These trade-offs are illustrated in Figure 8.4. The optimum number of distribution centers will balance transportation costs with inventory and order-processing costs.

Figure 8.4
Cost Trade-Offs in
Distribution-System Design

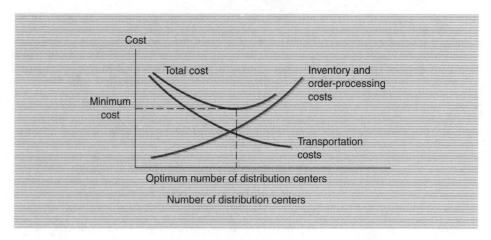

The level of customer service also varies with the number of distribution centers. Customer service is often measured by the average order-processing time—that is, the time between receipt of an order at the warehouse and its shipment, the percentage of shipments delivered within *x* days of order receipt, or the percentage of orders accurately filled. The first two measures depend on the number and location of warehouses; the third depends on internal control. The closer warehouses are to retail stores, the shorter is the average time to process and deliver an order. Thus, increasing the number of warehouses provides better service, since the average distance to retail stores is shorter. This relationship is shown in Figure 8.5. Comparing it with Figure 8.4, we see that low cost and a high level of customer service are conflicting criteria. Therefore, the optimum number of warehouses in Figure 8.4 may correspond to an unacceptable level of service. The managers responsible for location decisions must make some difficult decisions in balancing those criteria. The optimal decision depends on the overall goals and objectives of the firm and the firm's customer-service policies.

Warehouse Location: Center-of-Gravity Method

A method for determining the location for a single consolidation warehouse is called the **center-of-gravity method.** Although it does not explicitly address

Figure 8.5
Relationship between
Distribution-System Design
and Customer Service

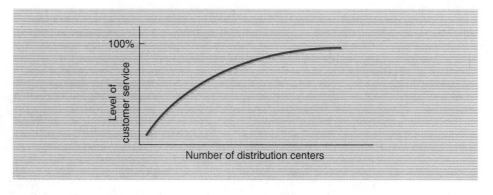

customer-service objectives, it can be used to assist managers in balancing cost and service objectives.

The center-of-gravity method takes into account the locations of plants and markets, the volume of goods moved, and transportation costs in arriving at the best location for a single intermediate warehouse. It would seem reasonable to find some "central" location between the plants and customers at which to locate the warehouse. But distance alone should not be the principal criterion, since the volume shipped from one location to another also affects the costs. To incorporate both distance and volume, the *center of gravity* is defined as the location that minimizes the weighted distance between the warehouse and its supply and distribution points, with the distance weighted by the volume supplied or consumed. The first step in this procedure is to place the locations of existing supply and distribution points on a coordinate system. The origin of the coordinate system and scale used are arbitrary, as long as the relative distances are correctly represented. That can be easily done by placing a grid over an ordinary map. The center of gravity is determined by equations 8.1 and 8.2, and can easily be implemented on a spreadsheet.

$$C_x = \frac{\sum_i x_i W_i}{\sum_i W_i} \tag{8.1}$$

$$C_y = \frac{\sum_i y_i W_i}{\sum_i W_i} \tag{8.2}$$

where

C_x = x-coordinate of the center of gravity,
C_y = y-coordinate of the center of gravity,
x_i = x-coordinate of location i,
y_i = y-coordinate of location i, and
W_i = volume of goods moved to or from location i.

The following example illustrates the application of the center-of-gravity method.

Example

Using the Center-of-Gravity Method

Taylor Paper Products is a producer of paper stock used in newspapers and magazines. Taylor's demand is relatively constant and thus can be forecast rather accurately. The company's two plants are located in Hamilton, Ohio, and Kingsport, Tennessee. They distribute paper stock to four major markets: Chicago, Pittsburgh, New York, and Atlanta. The board of directors has authorized the construction of an intermediate warehouse to service those markets.

Coordinates for the plants and markets are shown in Figure 8.6. For example, we see that location 1, Hamilton, is at the coordinate (58, 96); therefore, $x_1 = 58$ and $y_1 = 96$. Hamilton and Kingsport produce 400 and 300 tons per month, respectively. Demand at Chicago, Pittsburgh, New York, and Atlanta is 200, 100, 300, and 100 tons per month, respectively. With that information, the center of gravity coordinates are computed as follows:

Figure 8.6   Coordinate Locations of Plants and Customers

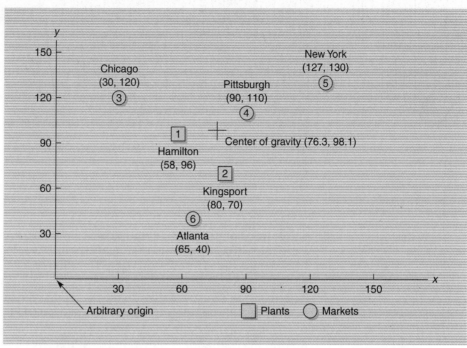

$$C_x = \frac{(58)(400) + (80)(300) + (30)(200) + (90)(100) + (127)(300) + (65)(100)}{400 + 300 + 200 + 100 + 300 + 100}$$

$$= 76.3$$

$$C_y = \frac{(96)(400) + (70)(300) + (120)(200) + (110)(100) + (130)(300) + (40)(100)}{400 + 300 + 200 + 100 + 300 + 100}$$

$$= 98.1$$

This location (76.3, 98.1) is shown by the cross on Figure 8.6. By overlaying a map on this figure, we see that the location is near the border of southern Ohio and West Virginia. Managers now can search that area for an appropriate site.

Figure 8.7 is a spreadsheet designed to calculate the center of gravity by using the =SUMPRODUCT function in Microsoft Excel. The formula for cell B12 is = SUMPRODUCT(B4:B9,D4:D9)/SUM(D4:D9) and the formula for cell B13 is

Figure 8.7   Spreadsheet for calculating the center of gravity (TAYLOR.XLS)

	A	B	C	D	E	F	G	H
1	Taylor Paper Products							
2								
3	Location	x-coordinate	y-coordinate	Tons/month				
4	Hamilton	58	96	400				
5	Kingsport	80	70	300				
6	Chicago	30	120	200				
7	Pittsburgh	90	110	100				
8	New York	127	130	300				
9	Atlanta	65	40	100				
10								
11	Center of gravity							
12	x-coordinate	76.3						
13	y-coordinate	98.1						
14								

Figure 8.8   Modified Spreadsheet for Taylor Paper Products

	A	B	C	D	E	F	G	H
1	Taylor Paper Products							
2								
3	Location	x-coordinate	y-coordinate	Tons/month				
4	Hamilton	58	96	200				
5	Kingsport	80	70	200				
6								
7	Pittsburgh	90	110	100				
8	New York	127	130	300				
9								
10								
11	Center of gravity							
12	x-coordinate	93.4						
13	y-coordinate	104.0						
14								

=SUMPRODUCT(C4:C9,D4:D9)/SUM(D4:D9). Further examination of Figure 8.6 shows that unnecessary movement would be required to ship from the warehouse to Chicago and Atlanta. Perhaps it would be better to ship directly from Kingsport to Atlanta and from Hamilton to Chicago, using a central warehouse to service Pittsburgh and New York. By removing Atlanta and Chicago (by deleting rows 6 and 9 of the spreadsheet) and adjusting the plant capacities we would have the solution shown in the spreadsheet in Figure 8.8.

This is slightly southeast of Pittsburgh. Taylor Products can use this information in conjunction with actual cost data, estimated service times, and other intangible factors to arrive at a decision, or perhaps to investigate other alternatives.

The center-of-gravity method is based on the assumption that transportation rates to and from the warehouse are equal. In locating a warehouse for which inbound transportation costs differ from outbound costs as is the case in many practical problems, equations 8.1 and 8.2 must be modified by placing proportionately more weight on the more costly routes.

Distribution Planning and Analysis

Planning is essential to determine the optimal distribution network for providing customers with the right quantity of goods, at the right places, at the right time and minimizing total delivered cost of the product at its final destination. (The *delivered cost* is the cost of manufacturing, warehousing, and transportation.) In designing a distribution network, companies must ask: How many total manufacturing sites are needed? Where should they be located? Which products should be produced at the sites? What is the best distribution network to support the manufacturing sites? Comprehensive modeling approaches consider location, product assignment, and transportation simultaneously. However, such models involve integer linear programming and consequently are often very large and difficult to use. For large companies like Shell Oil, which supplies five products from three refineries to over 100 plants and then distributes those products to over 20,000 customers, such problems are staggering.[7]

Transportation Problem

If plant and/or warehouse locations are fixed, a minimum-cost distribution plan can be found by solving a **transportation problem.** This is a special type of linear program that arises in planning the distribution of goods and services from several supply points to several demand locations. Usually the quantity of goods available at each supply location (origin) is limited, and a specified quantity of goods is needed at each demand location (destination). With a variety of shipping routes and differing transportation costs for the routes, the objective is to determine how many units should be shipped from each origin to each destination so that all destination demands are satisfied with a minimum total transportation cost. The problem can be modeled formally as a linear program (see Supplementary Chapter D).

$$\min \quad \sum_{i=1}^{m} \sum_{j=1}^{n} c_{ij} x_{ij} \qquad (8.3)$$

subject to

$$\sum_{j=1}^{n} x_{ij} \leq a_i, \text{ for all } i \qquad (8.4)$$

$$\sum_{i=1}^{m} x_{ij} = b_j, \text{ for all } j \qquad (8.5)$$

$$x_{ij} \geq 0, \text{ for all } i, j \qquad (8.6)$$

where x_{ij} is the amount shipped from origin i to destination j at unit cost c_{ij}, a_i is the amount available at origin i, and b_j is the amount demanded at destination j. A very efficient procedure is presented in Supplementary Chapter E, which also describes how to model and solve transportation problems using Microsoft Excel Solver. In the following example, we illustrate the use of the transportation problem in finding a minimum-cost distribution plan.

Example

Finding a Minimum-Cost Distribution Plan

Arnoff Enterprises manufactures the central processing unit (CPU) for a line of personal computers. The CPUs are manufactured in Seattle, Columbus, and New York and shipped to warehouses in Pittsburgh, Mobile, Denver, Los Angeles, and Washington, DC, for further distribution. Table 8.3 shows the unit transportation costs, the supply at each plant, and the demand at each warehouse. The company seeks to determine a minimum-cost distribution plan that satisfies all demands at the warehouses. In addition, the company is considering closing the Denver warehouse and shifting its demand to Los Angeles. It needs to know how that would affect the total cost.

Using Microsoft Excel Solver described in Supplementary Chapter E, we find that the minimum total transportation cost is $150,000. This is obtained by shipping

4,000 units from Seattle to Denver,

5,000 units from Seattle to Los Angeles,

Table 8.3 Transportation Data for Arnoff Enterprises

| Plant | Warehouse | | | | | Origin Supply |
	Pittsburgh	Mobile	Denver	Los Angeles	Washington	
Seattle	10*	20	5	9	1	9,000
Columbus	2	10	8	30	6	4,000
New York	9	20	7	10	4	8,000
Units Required	3,000	5,000	4,000	6,000	3,000	21,000

*Unit transportation costs are shown in each box.

> 4,000 units from Columbus to Mobile,
>
> 3,000 units from New York to Pittsburgh,
>
> 1,000 units from New York to Mobile,
>
> 1,000 units from New York to Los Angeles, and
>
> 3,000 units from New York to Washington, DC.

When the Denver warehouse is closed and its demand is shifted to Los Angeles, the total cost increases by $16,000. The only difference in the solution is that Seattle now ships all 9,000 units directly to Los Angeles. Managers can now use this information to determine if the increase in transportation cost can be offset by savings from closing the Denver warehouse. A problem at the end of this chapter will ask you to solve these problems to verify the results.

Computer-Based Modeling

Two drawbacks in using the transportation model alone are that it assumes that facility locations are fixed and does not consider location and transportation simultaneously. The transportation model can be used in a naive fashion to address this situation. For example, suppose three potential locations are available for constructing warehouses to serve several markets. Each warehouse has a different fixed cost associated with its construction and operations. A series of transportation problems can be solved using all combinations of one, two, or three warehouses. By adding the appropriate fixed costs to the minimum transportation cost for each alternative, the best combination of warehouses can be determined. You will be asked to do this in Problem 11 at the end of the chapter.

It is easy to see that the number of problems that must be solved grows very large as the number of potential warehouses increases. In practice, comprehensive computerized logistics-planning systems are available to assist managers in studying strategic logistics problems. Computerized systems enable managers to determine answers to such questions as

How many warehouses should we have, and where should they be located?

What size should they be?

How should customers be assigned to various warehouses?

How much of each product should be sent to each warehouse from each plant?

What modes of transportation are most economical?

How much savings will result from system improvements?

One of the most useful applications of computerized distribution-planning systems is investigating the effects of environmental changes and business policies on the distribution system.[8] This is referred to as asking "what-if" questions. A computerized system that enables a manager to study potential changes, whether controllable or otherwise, provides a great amount of information for decision making. Some typical uses of such a system are investigating the effects of

1. Changes in demand structure.
2. Changes in fuel costs for transportation.
3. Transportation strikes, natural disasters, and energy shortages.
4. Plant-capacity expansion proposals.
5. New product lines.
6. Deletion of product lines.
7. Prices changes.
8. New markets.
9. Transportation using common carriers versus private fleets.
10. Adding new distribution centers.

Distribution planning need not always involve complex models. A practical alternative approach is to allow managers to choose plant locations, assign products to plants, and evaluate the impact on total delivered cost by solving transportation problems for each product to find the optimal distribution plan. In that way managers can experiment and include factors that cannot be modeled mathematically. Many companies such as Procter & Gamble are successfully using such systems—based on linear programming models or computer simulation—to plan, design, and evaluate facility location and product-distribution strategies.

Applied P/OM

Procter & Gamble[9]

Procter & Gamble (P&G) produces and markets a variety of consumer products such as detergents, diapers, coffee, pharmaceuticals, soaps, and paper products worldwide. In 1994, P&G embarked on a major strategic planning initiative called the North American Product Sourcing Study.

P&G was interested in consolidating its product sources and optimizing its distribution system design throughout North America. An interactive computer-based decision support system based on a variant of the transportation problem was used to develop product sourcing and distribution options involving more than 50 product categories, 60 plants, 10 distribution centers, hundreds of suppliers, and 1,000 customer warehouses/destinations. Issues the team investigated included the impact of closing certain plants and consolidating production in others on costs and customer service. Use of the computer-based model provided rapid evaluation of a variety of strategic options. Solutions were displayed on a map of North America by means of a geographic information system. That enabled strategic planners to review immediately the impact of their decisions across North America. Annual savings amounted to approximately $200 million.

Computer-based distribution and location planning is receiving a boost from recent developments in *geographic information system (GIS)* technology. By combining data on demographics and traffic patterns, PepsiCo Inc. uses GIS to help find the best locations for new Pizza Hut and Taco Bell outlets. Federal Express uses it to place its drop boxes and estimate the number of trucks and planes it needs during peak periods.[10]

Service-Facility Location

Up to this point the emphasis of this chapter has been on decisions involving manufacturing-facility locations, which differ significantly from those involving service-facility locations. In a manufacturing operation, the location analysis considers distribution costs and customer service. Service facilities, in contrast, do not have the traditional product-distribution channel structure shown in Figure 8.1. Service facilities are the terminal points in the system, the points where demand takes place. Either the customer travels to the service facility (as in the case of a hospital), or the service facility travels to the customer (as in the case of a mobile library unit). Since service facilities generally serve a small geographic area, the principal trade-off is between the number of facilities to have and the travel cost between the customers and facilities. Hence, service-facility location problems often involve multiple sites.

For profit-seeking service organizations, perhaps the most important criterion is road access or the availability of public transportation. The visibility of the site from highways, traffic volume around the site, parking, and location of competitors are also critical factors. For emergency services such as fire protection and police, response time and reliability are the principal criteria. In this section we discuss location decisions for retail outlets, public-service facilities, and emergency facilities.

Retail-Facility Location

The major criterion used in locating a retail facility is the volume of demand. It might be measured by dollar sales revenue for a grocery store or restaurant, or by the number of visitors each year for an amusement park. In any case, esti-

by the number of visitors each year for an amusement park. In any case, estimates of demand must be obtained for potential locations.

Consider the situation of a bank that needs to determine future locations for automatic teller machines (ATMs). The success of an ATM site is measured by the number of transactions that occur there each month, so some way of predicting that volume is required. The statistical technique of *regression analysis* can be used by specifying a set of independent variables that are related to the number of transactions. This can be established through meetings with the bank executives and branch managers in charge of existing sites. The following variables are typical.

1. Population in a given census tract (census tracts might be chosen as site locations because of their size and the availability of demographic data for them).
2. Median income per census tract.
3. Median age per census tract.
4. Median educational level per census tract.
5. Location of the ATM at a bank branch or not.
6. Number of ATM cards in a given ZIP code (from bank records).
7. Commercial or residential nature of the ATM site.
8. Dollar sales per retail establishment.
9. Traffic counts at the site (obtained from the regional planning agency).
10. Number of employed persons.
11. Number of occupied households.
12. Number of persons between the ages of 20 and 30.
13. Number of years existing ATM has been in use.

With data for census tracts corresponding to existing ATM locations, a regression equation that relates the most important independent variables to the volume of transactions can be developed. The regression model can be used by bank executives to predict the volume of transactions and thus determine good future locations for automatic tellers.

In locating facilities that are oriented toward sales, the principal factors are market-related and the important data are demographic. Other intangible factors that influence retail location are competition, zoning laws, traffic patterns and accessibility, and aesthetic qualities of the location. As in industrial location analysis, a scoring model can be used to rank potential sites.

Public-Service-Facility Location

Public-service facilities include post offices, schools, highways, parks, and so on. A major problem in locating such facilities is the lack of easily quantifiable data. How does one define "social cost" or "social benefit"? Some of the typical criteria used in public-service location decisions include the average distance or time traveled by the users of the facilities and the maximum distance or travel time between the facility and its intended population. Another factor not present in industrial location problems is that public facilities create demand; one would like to locate facilities to serve the largest segment of the population.

In this sense, the problem is similar to locating a bank or grocery store, except that profit is not a motivating factor. Cost/benefit analysis is often used to determine public-facility location.

Emergency-Facility Location

Emergency facilities such as fire stations, ambulance stations, and police substations should be located so as to minimize response time between the notification of an emergency and the delivery of service. The problem is complicated by the random nature of demand, but we will ignore that issue to simplify the following example of locating a fire station in a small township.

Example | ## Locating a Fire Station

Marymount is a small township on the outskirts of a large city. Currently the township is serviced by the city fire department just outside the township limits. However, costs of purchasing that service have been escalating, and the township trustees have decided to organize their own fire department. The township is divided into several zones based on the geographic structure of the community. The center of each zone, the distance between zones, and the travel time in minutes along the major roads are shown in Figure 8.9.

Where should the fire station be located? We first must define an objective to use in evaluating potential sites. Suppose the goal is to locate the station so that the maximum response time to any other zone is the shortest possible. We assume that the route taken corresponds to the shortest time between zones. For instance, suppose the station is located in zone 1. We must determine how long it would take to travel to each of the other zones in the shortest possible time. For our purposes, we do this by inspecting Figure 8.9 and verifying that the shortest travel times from zone 1 to all others are as follows.

To Zone	2	3	4	5	6	7	8
Shortest Time	2	6	4	4	5	7	7

Figure 8.9   Zone Connections for Marymount Township

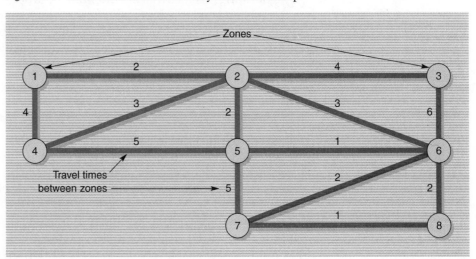

For example, the shortest route from zone 1 to zone 7 is through zones 2, 5, and 6. The maximum response time from zone 1 to any other zone is 7 minutes. Next, suppose we locate in zone 2. The shortest times from zone 2 to all other zones are as follows.

To Zone	1	3	4	5	6	7	8
Shortest Time	2	4	3	2	3	5	5

The longest time is 5 minutes. Therefore, zone 2 is a better location than zone 1 according to this criterion. If we compute the shortest travel times from each zone to every other zone, we obtain the following.

From	To								Longest time (min)
	1	2	3	4	5	6	7	8	
1	—	2	6	4	4	5	7	7	7
2	2	—	4	3	2	3	5	5	5
3	6	4	—	7	6	6	8	8	8
4	4	3	7	—	5	6	8	8	8
5	4	2	6	5	—	1	3	3	6
6	5	3	6	6	1	—	2	2	6
7	7	5	8	8	3	2	—	1	8
8	7	5	8	8	3	2	1	—	8

To minimize the longest response time, the fire station should be located in Zone 2.

Several quantitative techniques are more efficient for large problems than inspecting each possible site individually. Such techniques are beyond the scope of this book, however.

The center-of-gravity method is often used to locate service facilities. Retail outlets, power-generating stations, sewage-treatment plants, and waste-disposal facilities are but a few examples. To illustrate, suppose MamaMia's is attempting to determine a good location for a new outlet. Customers are drawn from several population centers. The center-of-gravity method can be used, where W_i represents the population of center i. Table 8.4 illustrates examples of weights for other applications.

Table 8.4 Applications of Center-of-Gravity Method in Service-Facility Location

Organization	Weights
Power-generating station	Demand for power at each customer location
Sewage-treatment plant	Volume of sewage arising from each region of a city or county
Waste-disposal facility	Average amount of waste transported from residential neighborhoods and industrial sites

P/OM in Practice

Better Distribution through Better Marketing[11]

In a common business practice called *trade loading*, wholesale and retail customers (known as the "trade") are induced—by discounts and other promotions—to "load" by buying more product than they can promptly resell. As a result, particularly in packaged-goods businesses, products stack up in warehouses, trucks, and railcars. A typical grocery item takes 84 days to travel from the factory floor to the retail-store shelf. The scenario can be described as follows.

1. The manufacturer stockpiles ingredients and packaging supplies to meet peak production levels.
2. Plants prepare huge runs. Scheduling is chaotic, with more overtime and temporary workers.
3. Freight companies charge premium rates for the manufacturer's periodic blow-out shipments.
4. Distributors overstock as they binge on short-term discounts. Cartons sit for weeks inside warehouses.
5. At distribution centers the goods are overhandled, and damaged items go back to the manufacturer.
6. Twelve weeks after the items leave the production line, they may not be fresh for the consumer.

Trade loading begins when manufacturers want higher market share or need to meet quarterly profit targets. It often requires deep discounts and deals that strain the logistics system, resulting in higher costs and inventories. Consumers end up paying for the inefficiency in higher costs and lower quality. Contrast the preceding scenario to the following one.

1. Without trade loading, no more panic purchases are necessary.

The company cuts down on inventories, improving its cash flow.
2. Factories run on normal shifts. The company cuts down on overtime pay and additional workers.
3. The manufacturer eliminates peaks and valleys in its demand for distribution services, saving as much as 5 percent in shipping costs.
4. Wholesaler's inventories are reduced substantially, improving storage and handling costs by as much as 17 percent.
5. Retailers receive undamaged products. Their perception of the manufacturer's quality improves.
6. The consumer gets the goods 25 days earlier and at a 6 percent lower price.

Clearly, the latter scenario is a win-win situation for all stakeholders.

Procter and Gamble (P&G) is one company that faced such a situation. The company was making 55 daily price changes on some 80 brands, necessitating rework on every third order. Often, special packaging and handling were required. Orders peaked during the promotions, resulting in excessive overtime in factories followed by periods of underutilization. Plants ran at 55 to 60 percent of rated capacity, with huge swings in output. Warehouses overloaded during slow periods and the transportation systems were overworked during peak times. P&G recognized the problems and took drastic steps to deliver products to the consumer at lower costs while simultaneously improving efficiencies in its logistic systems. As Chairman Edwin L. Artzt stated, "Consumers won't pay for a company's inefficiency."

P&G's solution was *value pricing*—pricing products at a reasonable "everyday low price," somewhere between the normal retail price and the sale prices frequently offered. With

value pricing, demand rates are much smoother. Retailers automatically order products as they sell them. When 100 cases of Cheer detergent leave a retailer's warehouse, a computer orders 100 more. Both P&G and retailers save money. Plant efficiency rates increased to more than 80 percent across the company, and North American inventories dropped 10 percent. One grocery store chain saved $500,000 by ordering toilet paper, tissues, and towels in this way; another saw sales of Pampers and Luvs diapers increase 10 percent as the ordering system kept its shelves fully stocked.

P&G also discovered that up-and-down pricing was eroding the brands' value as perceived by consumers. That is, consumers began to think that P&G's brands were worth only their discount prices. When prices were discounted, consumers stocked up, but they were substituting competitors' products when P&G's were not on sale. Value pricing helps to establish brand loyalty. For example, Dawn dishwashing liquid used to sell anywhere from 99 cents to $1.99. With value pricing, its retail price is in the range from 1.29 to $1.49, its U.S. market share has risen more than two percentage points, and consumer surveys show Dawn's image as "good value" has strengthened.

Questions for Discussion

1. Describe the chain of events that would occur under trade loading in the logistics system. Try to draw a diagram showing how inventory levels at each point in the logistics system might fluctuate over time (and in relation with one another) when prices increase and decrease.

2. Explain how elimination of trade loading and a switch to value pricing relate to the Deming philosophy (Chapter 2). What dimensions of quality improve?

Locating a Blood Bank in Quebec City[12]

The Red Cross Blood Donor Clinic and Transfusion Center has been located in downtown Quebec for 20 years. Increases in the population served and improvements in service provided have resulted in needs for additional staff and equipment. Those needs were not planned for in the original building design, and the present site had no room for expansion; consequently, administrators of the center sought to relocate.

Three main activities influenced the location decision. First, donors travel to the center by public or private transportation. Second, the center delivers blood and blood products throughout the Quebec urban community and eastern Quebec Province. Finally, the center holds mobile blood donor clinics over that same extensive territory.

Early in the study, the following site-selection criteria were identified.

1. Access to the road network for the mobile clinics and for the blood delivery vehicles so as to increase efficiency and minimize delays, operating costs, and deterioration of blood products in transit.
2. The ability to attract a larger group of donors through better visibility or ease of access.
3. Convenience to both public and private transportation.
4. Little sensitivity to changes in the population distribution or in the road network.
5. Ease of travel to and from work for center employees.
6. Minimum internal space and lot size.
7. Acceptability of the site to the management committees and governmental authorities.

A variety of data were collected, including population data, donor data, public-transport trip data, and delivery data. Several different center-of-gravity models were used to analyze the data, each with differently weighted criteria to identify a recommended location. One model used the population of all donors who attended the center; another used locations where deliveries were made. In all, 10 different models were used. The sites proposed by the models were evaluated by using other qualitative factors. Several alternative locations based on other factors were proposed. Five sites were selected as final candidates for the center location.

Each of the final sites were evaluated according to four criteria.

1. Accessibility to the road network.
2. Accessibility to the public transit network.
3. Proximity to the centers of gravity.
4. Availability of a lot or suitable building.

Table 8.5 shows the rankings of the five sites on the four criteria. The rankings were converted to "preference weights" by a simple method. The method applied to road access is shown in Table 8.6. A "1" indicates that the row site is preferred to the column site. The weight is the sum of the row entries divided by the sum of all entries. That method was applied for each of the criteria. Table 8.7 shows the final weightings obtained.

The purpose of the modeling process was not to determine a single optimal solution, but rather to provide good solution alternatives that might be considered by the decision makers. The modeling process also provided justifications for turning down any unsuitable sites that might be

Table 8.5 Ranking of Five Sites on Four Criteria

Site	Road Access	Bus Access	Proximity to Centers of Gravity	Availability of a Lot or Building
A	1	5	1	1
B	3	3	2	1
C	2	2	3	4
D	5	1	4	4
E	4	4	5	1

Table 8.6 Preference Weights for Road Access

Site	1	2	3	4	5	Weight
A	—	1	1	1	1	0.4
B	0	—	0	1	1	0.2
C	0	1	—	1	1	0.3
D	0	0	0	—	0	0.0
E	0	0	0	1	—	0.1

Table 8.7 Final Weights and Overall Ranking

Site	Road Access	Bus Access	Proximity to Centers of Gravity	Availability of a Lot or Building	Overall Rank
A	0.4	0.0	0.4	0.67	1
B	0.2	0.2	0.3	0.67	2
C	0.3	0.3	0.2	0.00	4
D	0.0	0.4	0.1	0.00	5
E	0.1	0.1	0.0	0.67	3

suggested during the complex negotiation process.

Questions for Discussion

1. Discuss the issues that had the major impact on the location decision for the blood bank.

2. Comment on differences in location criteria for manufacturing and service-sector applications that are evident from this example.

Summary of Key Points

••• Location decisions are capital-intensive, long-term decisions that are an integral part of operations strategy. Location affects both financial and service aspects of a company's operations.

••• Business logistics refers to the management of all activities that facilitate product flow to the point of final consumption and the information flows that provide adequate levels of customer service at reasonable cost.

••• "Push" distribution systems move products from plants to distribution centers on the basis of forecasted sales; "pull" systems draw product from plants on the basis of actual demand. Each system has advantages and disadvantages. The choice should be driven by the firm's overall strategy and various economic and noneconomic factors.

••• Location studies consist of initial planning, geographic screening, data analysis, and evaluation and selection, and they incorporate careful analysis of economic and noneconomic factors. Hierarchical decisions about the choice of region, community, and specific site must be made.

••• Techniques for assisting managers in location and distribution planning include scoring models, the center-of-gravity method, and the transportation model. Sophisticated computerized systems allow simultaneous analysis of location and transportation decisions.

••• In locating service facilities, the principal tradeoff is between the number of facilities and the travel cost between customers and facilities. Service applications include retail-facility location, public-service-facility location, and emergency-facility location.

Key Terms

Business logistics
Cross-docking
Consolidation
Center-of-gravity method
Transportation problem

Review Questions

1. Explain the importance of location decisions to overall business strategy.

2. Define *business logistics*. What are its key elements?

3. Summarize the differences, advantages, and disadvantages of push versus pull distribution systems.

4. Describe the stages of a typical location project.

5. Briefly discuss the major economic and noneconomic factors that influence location decisions.

6. Discuss the hierarchical decisions that must be made in location planning.

7. What are some of the advantages and disadvantages of using scoring models for location analysis?

8. How does consolidation affect cost and service in a distribution system?

9. What are the implications of increasing the number of warehouses in a distribution system?

10. Explain the assumptions behind the center-of-gravity method. Why does it work?

11. Explain the role of the transportation model in distribution planning.

12. What role do computerized distribution-planning systems play in strategic decision making?

13. Discuss the process of developing a strategic distribution plan. How can quantitative analysis and qualitative analysis be used in this process?

14. Discuss the major differences between manufacturing and service organizations with respect to facility-location decisions.

15. How do the objectives differ in location decisions for retail, public-service, and emergency facilities?

16. Discuss how the center-of-gravity method can be used in making decisions on service-facility location.

Discussion Questions

1. What specific issues might MamaMia's owners consider in deciding whether to open a second restaurant? How would they obtain the necessary information?

2. How might cultural practices affect global distribution practices and policies?

3. Describe the logistics system that would support an operation like MamaMia's. Should it be a push or a pull system? Why?

4. What would be the characteristics of a logistics system that incorporates both the push and pull philosophies? What benefits would such a system have over a pure form of either system?

5. Explain where key information for location decisions can be found.

6. Design criteria and a scoring model for deciding on a location for a new MamaMia's Pizza restaurant.

7. If MamaMia's expands to several locations throughout a city, what changes should take place in its distribution-system strategy?

8. Suppose a major corporation has dozens of plants and distribution centers and wants to improve the effectiveness of its distribution system. One approach is to design an ideal system from a "clean sheet" analysis (that is, with no constraints) based on projected demographics and demand forecasts that extend 20 years into the future. How might such an analysis be used to reconfigure the system for the long term?

9. Discuss some of the possible reasons a grocery chain might close one store and open another.

10. What considerations would be important to a bank in selecting a branch location? What information would be needed for making the decision?

Notes

1. "Honda Encounters Some Surprises on the Road to Marysville, Ohio," *The Wall Street Journal*, March 22, 1983.

2. James A. Tompkins, "Distribution Today and Tomorrow," *APICS—The Performance Advantage* 4, no. 4, (April 1994).

3. Ronald H. Ballou, *Basic Business Logistics* (Englewood Cliffs, NJ: Prentice-Hall, 1978), p. 9.

4. This discussion is adapted from Brian Hudock, "Distribution Strategies in the 90s," *The Competitive Edge* newsletter, vol. 7, no. 2, published by Tompkins Associates, Inc.

5. "Regionalized Material Management for Best Use of Equipment, Space, and Manpower." Reprinted with permission from *Industrial Engineering* magazine, October 1977. Copyright Institute of Industrial Engineers, 25 Technology Park/Atlanta, Norcross, GA 30092.

6. Reprinted by permission of E. Brodheim and G. P. Prastacos, "The Long Island Blood Distribution System as a Prototype for Regional Blood Management," *Interfaces* 9, no. 5 (October 1979), 3–19. Copyright 1979, The Institute of Management Sciences, 290 Westminster Street, Providence, RI 02908.

7. Thomas K. Zierer, "Applications of Linear and Mixed Integer Programming to Shell's Distribution Network," TIMS/ORSA National Meeting, San Francisco, 1977.

8. A. M. Geoffrion and R. F. Powers, "Facility Location Analysis Is Just the Beginning," *Interfaces* 10, no. 2 (April 1980), pp. 22–30.

9. Adapted from David R. Anderson, Dennis J. Sweeney, and Thomas A. Williams, *Quantitative Methods for Business*, 6th ed., West Publishing Co., 1995, and information provided by Tom Chorman and Franz Dill of Procter & Gamble.

10. "Computer Maps Pop Up All Over the Map," *Business Week*, July 26, 1993, pp. 75–76.

11. Adapted from Patricia Sellers, "The Dumbest Marketing Ploy," *Fortune*, October 5, 1992, pp. 88–94; Patricia Gallagher, "Value Pricing for Profits," *The Cincinnati Enquirer*, December 21, 1992, pp. D-1, D-6; "Procter & Gamble Hits Back," *Business Week*, July 19, 1993, pp. 20–22; and Bill Sapority, "Behind the Tumult at P&G," *Fortune*, March 7, 1994, pp. 75–82.

12. Adapted from W. L. Price and M. Turcotte, "Locating a Blood Bank," *Interfaces* 16, no. 5 (September–October 1986), pp. 17–26 and tables 7, 8, and 9, by permission. Copyright (1986) The Institute of Management Sciences, 290 Westminster Street, Providence, RI 02908.

Solved Problems

1. MamaMia's wants to build a satellite kitchen, from which only home deliveries will be made, in a nearby suburb. The suburb is partitioned into four customer zones. Table 8.8 shows population figures and travel times between the zones and three potential sites. Which site would be the best?

Table 8.8 Data for Solved Problem 1

Customer Zone	Population	Average Travel Times (min.)		
		Site A	Site B	Site C
1	800	4	9	13
2	1,200	5	4	8
3	1,500	9	6	3
4	500	8	5	12

Solution
Because the sites are fixed, we need only evaluate the total weighted time from each site to each customer zone. The zone population is assumed to be a good predictor of the number of customers. The total weighted times follow.

Site A: $4(800) + 5(1,200) + 9(1,500) + 8(500) = 26,700$

Site B: $9(800) + 4(1,200) + 6(1,500) + 5(500) = 23,500$

Site C: $13(800) + 8(1,200) + 3(1,500) + 12(500) = 30,500$

Thus, Site B appears to be the best location.

2. Jim Dean is opening four "Dean's Club" bulk-discount grocery hypermarkets in a large midwestern city after purchasing the buildings from a bankrupt department store. Jim needs to open a consolidation warehouse to distribute the goods. Table 8.9 shows the coordinate locations of each store, and the expected weekly volume of goods that must be shipped to each store. Where should Jim begin to search for a warehouse site?

Table 8.9 Data for Solved Problem 2

Store	x-coordinate	y-coordinate	Volume
1	20	4	2,000
2	10	15	2,500
3	6	12	1,700
4	4	20	1,000

Solution
The center of gravity will provide the best location. The coordinates of the center of gravity are

$$C_x = \frac{20(2,000) + 10(2,500) + 6(1,700) + 4(1,000)}{2,000 + 2,500 + 1,700 + 1,000} = 11$$

$$C_y = \frac{4(2,000) + 15(2,500) + 12(1,700) + 20(1,000)}{2,000 + 2,500 + 1,700 + 1,000} = 11.93.$$

3. Milford Lumber Company ships construction materials from three wood-processing plants to three retail stores. The shipping cost, monthly production capacities, and monthly demand for framing lumber are given in Table 8.10. Formulate a transportation problem for finding the minimum-cost distribution plan.

Table 8.10 Data for Solved Problem 3

Plant	Store A	Store B	Store C	Capacity
1	4.5	3.1	2.0	280
2	5.1	2.6	3.8	460
3	4.1	2.9	4.0	300
Demand	250	600	150	

Solution
Let x_{ij} represent the amount shipped from plant i to store j. The transportation problem can be modeled as

$$\min 4.5x_{1A} + 3.1x_{1B} + 2.0x_{1C} + 5.1x_{2A} + 2.6x_{2B} + 3.8x_{2C} + 4.1x_{3A} + 2.9x_{3B} + 4.0x_{3C}$$

subject to capacity restrictions

$$x_{1A} + x_{1B} + x_{1C} \le 280$$
$$x_{2A} + x_{2B} + x_{2C} \le 460$$
$$x_{3A} + x_{3B} + x_{3C} \le 300$$

and demand requirements

$$x_{1A} + x_{2A} + x_{3A} = 250$$
$$x_{1B} + x_{2B} + x_{3B} = 600$$
$$x_{1C} + x_{2C} + x_{3C} = 150$$

and nonnegativity constraints

$$x_{ij} \ge 0 \text{ for all } i,j.$$

Problems

1. Crawford Sports Equipment requires additional capacity to meet increasing demand for its new line of golf clubs. The company can expand the capacity at its existing plant or build a new one at another location. Projected costs for expansion and building are given in Table 8.11. Determine the best decision for forecasted demand for 10,000 to 50,000 units.

Table 8.11 Data for Problem 1

Cost Category	Expansion	Build Site A	Build Site B
Fixed costs	$400,000	$1,050,000	$800,000
Direct labor cost/unit	80	64	78
Direct material cost/unit	190	200	190

(Continued)

Table 8.11 Data for Problem 1 (continued)

Cost Category	Expansion	Build Site A	Build Site B
Overhead cost/unit	40	30	45
Transportation cost/unit	2.80	1.30	2.10

2. The data in Table 8.12 relate to the operating costs of three possible locations for a manufacturing plant.

Table 8.12 Data for Problem 2

	Location 1	Location 2	Location 3
Fixed costs	$110,000	$125,000	$150,000
Direct material cost per unit	8.5	8.4	8.6
Direct labor cost per unit	4.2	3.9	3.7
Overhead per unit	1.2	1.1	1.0
Transportation costs per 1000 units	800	1,100	950

    a. Which location would minimize the total costs given an annual production of 50,000 units?

    b. For what levels of manufacture and distribution would each location be best?

3. An industrialist faced with choosing among four possible locations uses the scoring model shown in Table 8.13. Which location would be the best?

Table 8.13 Data for Problem 3

		Location			
Criteria	Weight	1	2	3	4
Raw material availability	0.2	G	P	OK	VG
Infrastructure	0.1	OK	OK	OK	OK
Transportation costs	0.5	VG	OK	P	OK
Labor relations	0.1	G	VG	P	OK
Quality of life	0.1	G	VG	P	OK

Points   VG = Very good: 5 points
G = Good: 4 points
OK = Acceptable: 3 points
P = Poor: 1 point

4. Goslin Chemicals has decided to build a new plant in the Sunbelt to take advantage of new solar-powered heating units. Three sites have been proposed: Phoenix, Arizona; El Paso, Texas; and Mountain Home, Arkansas.

    a. Construct a scoring model using the criteria in Table 8.2 in which the factors have the following priorities:

        (1) Climate.

        (2) Water availability.

        (3) Labor laws and community attitude.

(4) Schools and housing.
(Factors having the same priority should have the same rating scale.)
b. Suppose the three sites have ratings as shown in Table 8.14. Under the system constructed in part a to this problem, which seems to be most preferable?

Table 8.14 Data for Problem 4

	Level Assigned		
Factor	*Phoenix*	*El Paso*	*Mountain Home*
Climate	5	4	3
Water	3	5	4
Labor	4	2	1
Attitude	4	5	4
Schools	5	3	2
Housing	4	2	3

5. Given the locational information and volume of material movements from a supply point to several retail outlets (Table 8.15), find the optimal location for the supply point using the center-of-gravity method.

Table 8.15 Data for Problem 5

	Location Coordinates		Material
Retail Outlet	*x*	*y*	**Movements**
1	20	5	1,200
2	18	15	2,500
3	3	16	1,600
4	3	4	1,100
5	10	20	2,000

6. Broderick's Burgers wants to determine the best location for drawing customers from three population centers. The map coordinates of the three centers follow.

Population Center 1: $x_1 = 2$, $y_1 = 12$

Population Center 2: $x_2 = 9$, $y_2 = 6$

Population Center 3: $x_3 = 1$, $y_3 = 1$

a. What location will minimize the total distance from the three centers?
b. Population Center 1 is four times as large as Center 3, and Center 2 is twice as large as Center 3. The firm feels that the importance of locating near a population center is proportional to its population. Find the best location under these assumptions.
7. A large metropolitan campus needs to erect a parking garage for students, faculty, and visitors. The garage has a planned capacity of 1,000 cars. From a survey, it is estimated that 30 percent of the arrivals to campus go to the Business School and adjacent buildings; 40 percent go to the engineering complex; 20 percent go to the University Center

Figure 8.10
Campus Map for Problem 7

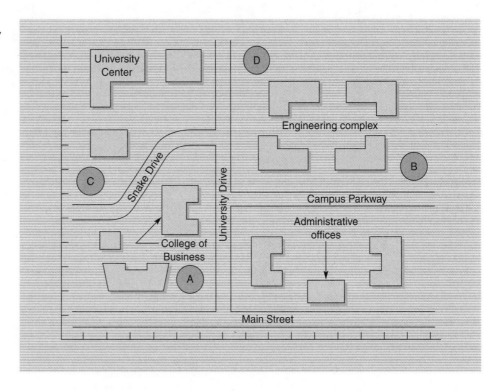

area; and 10 percent go to the administrative offices (see campus map, Figure 8.10). Four potential sites (A, B, C, and D) are being considered. Which one would be best for the new garage?

8. A national drugstore chain prefers to operate one outlet in a town that has four major market segments. The number of potential customers in each segment along with the coordinates are given in Table 8.16.

Table 8.16 Data for Problem 8

	Location Coordinates		
Market Segment	x	y	**Number of Customers**
1	2	18	1,000
2	15	17	600
3	2	2	1,500
4	14	2	2,400

a. Which would be the best location by the center-of-gravity method?

b. If after five years half the customers from Segment 4 are expected to move to Segment 2, where should the drugstore shift, assuming the same criteria are adopted?

9. Microserve provides computer repair service on a contract basis to customers in five sections of the city. The five sections, the number of service contracts in each section, and the x, y coordinates of each section are as shown in Table 8.17.

Table 8.17 Data for Problem 9

Section	No. of Contracts	Coordinates	
		x	y
Parkview	90	8.0	10.5
Mt. Airy	220	6.7	5.9
Valley	50	12.0	5.2
Norwood	300	15.0	6.3
Southgate	170	11.7	8.3

Use the center-of-gravity method to determine an ideal location for a service center.

10. Muscle Motor Parts produces components for motorcycle engines. It has plants in Amarillo, Texas, and Charlotte, North Carolina, and supply factories in Detroit and Atlanta. Production and cost data for a major component are shown in Table 8.18. Formulate a transportation model to determine the best distribution plan.

Table 8.18 Data for Problem 10

Plant	Freight Costs		Capacity	Unit Cost
	Detroit	Atlanta		
Amarillo	$12	$8	1,200	$125
Charlotte	$9	$3	3,000	$140
Demand	2,000	900		

11. The R. K. Martin Company is in the process of planning for new production facilities and developing a more efficient distribution system design. At present it has one plant at St. Louis with a capacity of 30,000 units. Because of increased demand, management is considering four potential new plant sites: Detroit, Denver, Toledo, and Kansas City. Figure 8.11 summarizes the projected plant capacities, the cost per unit of shipping from each plant to each destination, and the demand forecasts over a one-year planning horizon. Assume the following fixed costs of constructing the new plant.

Detroit	$175,000
Toledo	$300,000
Denver	$375,000
Kansas City	$500,000

The company wants to minimize the total cost of plant construction and distribution.

    a. Explain how the transportation model can be used to make this decision.

    b. Suppose only one additional plant is to be constructed. Determine the best choice.

12. Apply Microsoft Excel Solver to verify the solutions to the Arnoff Enterprises example in this chapter.

13. Klein Chemicals, Inc., produces a special oil-base material that is currently in short supply. Four of Klein's customers have already placed orders that in total exceed the combined capacity of Klein's two plants. Klein's managers face the problem of deciding how many units it should supply to each customer. Since the four customers are in different industries, the pricing structure allows different prices to be charged to different

Figure 8.11
Distribution Data for
Problem 11

Origin	Destination			Capacity
	Boston	Atlanta	Houston	
Detroit	5	2	3	30,000
Toledo	4	3	4	20,000
Denver	9	7	5	30,000
Kansas City	10	4	2	40,000
St. Louis	8	4	3	30,000
Destination Demand	30,000	20,000	20,000	

customers. However, slightly different production costs at the two plants and varying transportation costs between the plants and customers make a "sell to the highest bidder" strategy unacceptable. After considering price, production costs, and transportation costs, Klein has established the profit per unit for each plant/customer alternative as shown in Table 8.19.

Table 8.19 Unit Project Data for Problem 13

Plant	Customer			
	D_1	D_2	D_3	D_4
Clifton Springs	$32	$37	$30	$40
Danville	$36	$30	$25	$37

The plant capacities and customer orders are as given in Table 8.20.

Table 8.20 Plant and Customer Data for Problem 13

Plant	Capacity (units)	Customer	Orders (units)
Clifton Springs	5,000	D_1	2,000
		D_2	5,000
Danville	3,000	D_3	3,000
		D_4	2,000

How many units should each plant produce for each customer to *maximize* the total profit? Which customer demands will not be met?

14. Sound Electronics, Inc., produces a battery-operated tape recorder at plants in Martinsville, North Carolina; Plymouth, New York; and Franklin, Missouri. The unit transportation costs for shipments from the three plants to distribution centers in Chicago, Dallas, and New York are given in Table 8.21.

Table 8.21 Unit Transportation Costs Data for Problem 14

From	To		
	Chicago	*Dallas*	*New York*
Martinsville	1.45	1.60	1.40
Plymouth	1.10	2.25	0.60
Franklin	1.20	1.20	1.80

After considering transportation costs, managers decide not to use the Plymouth-Dallas route. The plant capacities and distributor orders for the next month are listed in Table 8.22.

Table 8.22 Capacities and Demands Data for Problem 14

Plant	Capacity (units)	Distributor	Order (units)
Martinsville	400	Chicago	400
Plymouth	600	Dallas	400
Franklin	300	New York	400

Because of different wage scales at the three plants, the unit production costs varies from plant to plant. Given costs of $29.50 per unit at Martinsville, $31.20 per unit at Plymouth, and $30.35 per unit at Franklin, find the production and distribution plan that minimizes the total production and transportation costs.

15. Ace Manufacturing Company has orders for three similar products.

Product	A	B	C
Order (units)	2,000	500	1,200

Three machines are available for the manufacturing operations, all of which produce all the products at the same production rate. However, because of varying defect percentages of each product on each machine, the unit costs of the products vary depending on the machine used. Machine capacities for the next week, and the unit costs, are listed in Tables 8.23 and 8.24.

Table 8.23 Machine Capacities Data for Problem 15

Machine	Capacity (units)
I	1,500
II	1,500
III	1,000

Table 8.24 Unit Production Costs Data for Problem 15

Machine	Product		
	A	*B*	*C*
I	$1.00	$1.20	$0.90
II	$1.30	$1.40	$1.20
III	$1.10	$1.00	$1.20

Figure 8.12
Problem 16

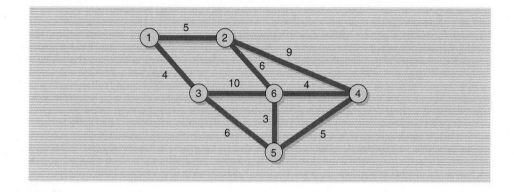

a. Use the transportation model to develop the minimum-cost production schedule for the products and machines.

b. Find an alternate optimal production schedule.

16. In locating an emergency facility to serve six communities, the criterion adopted is minimizing the maximum response time. The travel times between the six communities are indicated in Figure 8.12. Where should the facility be located?

17. If the objective in Problem 16 is to choose a location based on *average* response time, which is the best location?

18. Grave City is considering relocating a number of police substations to obtain better enforcement in high-crime areas. The locations being considered and the areas each could cover are listed in Table 8.25.

Table 8.25 Data for Problem 18

Potential Location for Substation	Areas Covered
A	1, 5, 7
B	1, 2, 5, 7
C	1, 3, 5
D	2, 4, 5
E	3, 4, 6
F	4, 5, 6
G	1, 5, 6, 7

Find the minimum number of locations necessary to provide coverage to all areas. Where should the police substations be located?

19. The Farmington City Council is attempting to choose one of three sites as the location for its life squad facility. The city manager has developed a matrix showing the distance (in miles) from each of the sites to the five areas that must be served. (Table 8.26).

Table 8.26 Data for Problem 19

	Area Served				
Site	*1*	*2*	*3*	*4*	*5*
A	1.2	1.4	1.4	2.6	1.5
B	1.4	2.2	1.3	2.1	.7
C	2.7	3.2	.8	.9	.7

The number of emergency runs to each of these areas over the past three months is: Area 1, 100; Area 2, 20; Area 3, 100; Area 4, 170; Area 5, 200.

a. If the council decides to choose the site on the basis of minimizing the longest response time, which site should be selected?

b. If the council decides to minimize the annual cost (in terms of miles traveled) of operating the facility, which site should be selected?

20. Izzy Rizzy's Trick Shop specializes in gag gifts, costumes, and novelties. Izzy owns a store on the south side of Chicago and is considering opening a second store on the north side. A sample of 10 customers yielded these data.

Amount of Sale ($)	17	15	40	20	15	25	20	30	30	35
Age	20	17	32	40	35	21	18	25	36	31

Izzy believes age is the most important factor for his customers. He is considering three possible locations: one is in the high-rise, near-north side, where many singles in the 25–35 age group reside; the second is near a residential area in which the majority of the population is over 35; the third is near a college campus. From these data, where should Izzy locate?

21. The city of Binghamton is attempting to determine the best location for an ambulance facility that will serve the entire city. The network of zones within the city is shown in Figure 8.13. Where should Binghamton locate the service facility to minimize the maximum distance to any zone?

Figure 8.13
Data for Problem 21

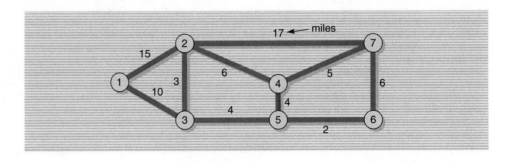

Part III
Designing and Managing Production Processes

This part of the book examines how physical facilities and production processes are designed and managed for high quality and performance. Manufacturing a quality product or delivering a quality service is impossible without adequate technological resources. Chapter 9 introduces process technology and automation, their strategic importance, and key issues in designing production processes—all from a broad perspective. Chapter 10 narrows the scope of process design by focusing on the details of facility layout and workplace design.

High performance is achieved through careful attention to defect prevention, equipment maintenance, and a continual effort to find better ways of doing a job. Chapter 11 addresses two important issues that operations managers face daily: controlling production processes to maintain high levels of performance, and improving them to achieve even higher levels of performance. The control of processes to achieve consistently high quality is supported through various quantitative tools, particularly statistical process control (SPC). Techniques of SPC are introduced in Chapter 12.

Chapter Outline

Chapter Nine
Process Technology and Design

Applied P/OM

P/OM in Practice

A **process** is a specific combination of machines, operators, work methods, materials, tools, and environmental factors that together convert inputs to outputs. At MamaMia's Pizza, the pizza production process is quite simple:

1. A customer places an order.
2. The pizza is assembled.
3. The pizza is placed in an oven to bake.
4. The pizza is inspected for quality and order correctness.
5. The pizza is either boxed and delivered to the customer's home or delivered to the customer's table.

Many other production processes are much more complex. For example, the process for the production of soft drinks, shown in Figure 9.1, includes various chemical processes, filling and can assembly, inspections, and case formation before the cans are distributed to retail stores.

A national report on competitiveness in the United States noted:

> U.S. industrial performance has suffered not only from a failure to coordinate the design and manufacturing functions effectively but also from a lack of attention to the manufacturing process itself. . . . U.S. firms are still devoting only a third of their R&D expenditure to the improvement of process technology; the other two-thirds is allocated to the development of new and improved products. In Japan these proportions are reversed. . . . Many factors have contributed to the decline of the U.S. machine-tool industry, but among the most important was a widespread neglect of production technology by users of machine tools throughout American industry.[1]

The choice of technology affects a firm's ability to manufacture products that meet the customers' requirements and the firm's strategic goals of quality, flexibility, dependability, and cost. Because operations managers must be able to evaluate a process in terms of its ability to meet the organization's strategic objectives, they must understand both the technical and the managerial implications of process technology.

It is not only the large companies that face important strategic decisions about process technology. A small business like MamaMia's faces similar decisions. They might include whether to use a manual, handwritten order-entry and tracking system versus one that is computerized, or whether to use a conventional oven that requires close attention to baking time versus a conveyor-paced oven that provides uniform baking times without human attention.

This chapter addresses important issues of process technology and design, specifically

••• Classification of production systems and processes.
••• Strategic importance of process decisions and their linkage to product decisions.
••• Role of automation in modern production.
••• Approaches and tools for process planning and design.
••• Role of work measurement in modern production.

Figure 9.1 Typical Soft-Drink Production Process

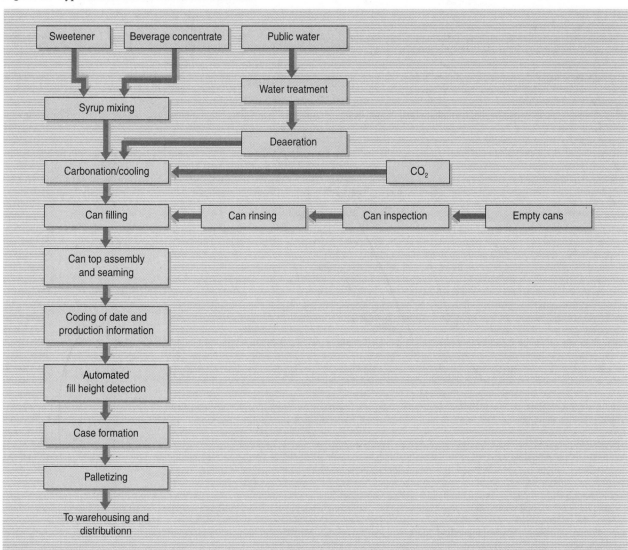

Process Technology

When we think of **process technology**, we generally think of the methods and equipment used to manufacture a product or deliver a service. **Hard technology** involves the application of computers, sensors, robots, and other mechanical and electronic aids. Robotic welding and painting, automated sorting and assembly, and computer-integrated manufacturing are revolutionizing many industries and significantly improving productivity. **Soft technology** refers to the application of computer software and other techniques that support manufacturing and service organizations. Examples include office-automation software such as word processing packages, database management systems, and manufacturing resource-management software.

Part Three

Table 9.1 Common Manufacturing Process

A. Forming processes

1. *Casting.* Forming objects by putting liquid or viscous material into a prepared mold or form.
2. *Bending.* The process by which bars, rods, wire, tubing, and sheet metal are bent into shapes in dies.
3. *Rolling.* The process by which metal is squeezed between two revolving rolls.
4. *Extrusion.* Forcing metal (often aluminum) or plastics out through specially formed discs.
5. *Forging.* Forming of metal (usually hot) by individual and intermittent applications of pressure, instead of by applying continuous pressure as in rolling.
6. *Powder metallurgy.* Forming objects by compressing powdered metal or alloy with or without other materials and heating without thoroughly melting. This is often used for materials with high melting points.
7. *Spinning.* Forming a metal part from a flat, rotating disk by applying controlled pressure to one side and causing the metal to flow against a rotating form that is held against the opposite side.
8. *Stamping.* Forcing a hardened steel punch against a flat metal surface.
9. *Wire drawing.* Pulling a rod through several dies of decreasing diameter until the desired diameter is obtained.

B. Machining processes

1. *Boring.* Enlarging of a hole that has previously been drilled.
2. *Broaching.* Metal removal by means of an elongated tool having a number of successive teeth of increasing size that cut in a fixed path.
3. *Counterboring.* Enlarging one end of a drilled hole.
4. *Drilling.* Producing a hole by forcing a rotating drill against it.
5. *Grinding.* Removal of metal by means of a rotating, abrasive wheel.
6. *Milling.* Progressive removal of small increments of metal from the workpiece as it is fed slowly to a cutter rotating at high speed.
7. *Reaming.* Bringing a hole to more exact size and better finish by slightly enlarging it.
8. *Shearing.* Cutting of metals in sheet or plate form without the formation of chips or by burning.
9. *Turning.* Producing an external cylindrical or conical surface through the relative action between a rotating workpiece and a longitudinally fed, single-point cutting tool.

C. Joining processes

1. *Mechanical joining.* Use of bolts or rivets to join two pieces.
2. *Soldering.* Joining by means of a molten metal or alloy.
3. *Welding.* Joining metals by concentrating heat, pressure, or both at the joint in order to coalesce the adjoining areas.
4. *Adhesive.* Use of glues or other adhesives to join materials.
5. *Snap-in assembly.*

D. Heat-treating processes

1. *Hardening.* Heat followed by rapid cooling.

E. Surface-treating processes

1. *Buffing.* Providing a shiny or high luster.
2. *Galvanizing.* A rust-prevention process.
3. *Miscellaneous processes:* painting, planing, sandblasting, degreasing, waxing.

Adapted from Don T. Phillips and Rodney J. Heisterberg, "Development of a Generalized Manufacturing Simulator (GEMS)," Report No. GEMS-5-77. Prepared for National Science Foundation, Department of Industrial Engineering, Texas A&M University, December 1, 1977.

Table 9.1 is a summary of the more common types of manufacturing processes. (Knowing the terminology is helpful in communicating with manufacturing engineers and production workers.) This list is by no means exhaustive, though. For example, special processes are used for plastic-injection molding, silicon-chip formation, in food and textile processing, and in the chemical industry.

Process technology is an essential component of an organization's operations strategy. Although the VCR was invented in America and the CD player in Holland, the Japanese have dominated those industries because of their mastery of process technology. Thus, an operations manager needs to understand the impact of process technology on a firm's ability to achieve its strategic goals of customer satisfaction and operational performance.

Hayes and Wheelwright[2] suggest that a narrow general-management perspective on process technology may be the source of many strategic problems that have surfaced in U.S. manufacturing firms. Table 9.2 summarizes that view and Table 9.3 lists characteristics of the broader viewpoint they recommend.

Table 9.2 Narrow Corporate View of Process Technology

1. Technology is *narrowly defined* and is the responsibility of the technical specialist and lower-level operating manager.
2. Process technology is *separable,* and individual projects can be examined and evaluated in isolation.
3. Manufacturing-technology decisions related to *specific products;* the fact that equipment remains in use over several product generations is ignored.
4. All important issues and decisions can be addressed within the framework of the *capital budgeting process.*
5. Significant competitive moves come from *major breakthroughs,* not from small incremental changes that are largely invisible to top managers.
6. Technical knowledge is in the domain of the *specialist* and is neither required nor useful to general managers, who believe they must deal with "the big picture."

Source: Adapted from Hayes and Wheelwright, pp. 189–191. Copyright © 1984. Reprinted by permission of John Wiley & Sons, Inc.

Table 9.3 Broad Corporate View of Process Technology

1. Process technology is defined in terms of information and materials flows, linkages, controls, and potential for improvement and is viewed as a *total system.*
2. Manufacturing technology is an *integrated activity* that cuts across functional boundaries and is continuous over time.
3. Technology is a set of *general capabilities* that meet the firm's current needs as well as future product market strategies.
4. Technology is a product of *holistic decision making* that includes a variety of subjective elements, nonfinancial and financial and long-term as well as short-term.
5. Improvement comes from *incremental efforts* that are difficult for competitors to imitate.
6. Technical competence is essential for *general managers* as well as technical specialists.

Source: Adapted from Hayes and Wheelwright, pp. 192–194.

Taking a broad view of process technology results in top managers having greater familiarity with the technology being used, which leads to upper-level decisions that support an organization's operations strategy. As a result, upper managers can better prepare the firm for changes in market conditions.

Classification of Production Systems and Processes

Firms produce either *in response to* customer orders or *in anticipation of* them. Thus, production systems can usually be classified into one of two general categories: *make-to-order* and *make-to-stock*. Since manufacturers of jet engines produce only in response to orders from aircraft builders, their production systems would be classified as make-to-order. Manufacturers of radios and other small appliances, however, build inventories for future sale, so their systems are make-to-stock. Restaurants and self-service cafeterias also exemplify make-to-order and make-to-stock systems, respectively.

The two systems differ with respect to the *variety* and *quantity* of products made. Make-to-order production systems typically produce a larger variety of products in smaller quantities than do make-to-stock production systems. Therefore, different production processes are appropriate for the two systems. Types of production processes are

••• Continuous-flow.
••• Mass, or assembly-line.
••• Batch, or intermittent.
••• Job shop.
••• Project.

Table 9.4 provides manufacturing and service examples for each type. As we move down the list from continuous-flow to project production processes, variety increases and volume decreases.

Continuous-flow production processes are characterized by high production volume and a high degree of product standardization. Such processes use highly specialized and dedicated equipment and often a high degree of automation. Since the equipment is highly specialized, there is little need to

Table 9.4 Examples of Production Processes

Type of Process	Manufacturing	Service
Continuous-flow	Chemicals; paper	Electricity generation; license-plate renewal
Mass/Assembly-line	Automobile; appliances	Package sorting/distribution; dry cleaning
Batch	Books; clothing	Fast food; course-packet duplication services
Job-shop	Machine tools; printing	Legal services; hotels and restaurants
Project	Cruise ships; aircraft	Architectural plans; tax-return preparation

change machine setups for different products or for a highly skilled work force. Because of the high volume, unit costs are generally low.

Mass, or *assembly-line,* production processes are used for high-volume production of discrete parts. Usually only a small variety of different products are produced, although there may be many minor model variations. As with continuous-flow production processes, specialized equipment and automation are common. Machine setups are infrequent, labor skill requirements are low, and as a result, unit costs also are low.

Batch, or *intermittent,* production processes are used for producing small lots of similar products. The products are made in batches with short production runs, and the same sequence of operations is generally followed. Such processes usually differ from mass production in the materials used, machine setups, and layout. More labor skills are necessary to set up machines and perform a wider variety of tasks during production. These differences increase unit costs.

Job-shop production processes produce a wide variety and small quantity of specialized products. Products are generally customized; they may be produced by entirely different sequences of operations. Job shops are essentially make-to-order systems, whereas continuous flow, mass, and batch production processes are generally make-to-stock processes. More general-purpose equipment is used, and there is less opportunity for specialized, automated equipment. The labor force must be highly skilled and able to perform a wide variety of tasks on different jobs. Unit production costs are higher than for other production processes.

A *project* production process is one in which a unique and usually large and complex item is produced. The construction industry utilizes the project production process. The products are assembled at a fixed location, and components and subassemblies must be brought to that location. Labor skills and costs are generally high.

For each of these types of production systems, a firm has the option of three types of process technology: manual, mechanized, and automated. *Manual* technology uses no machinery to perform manufacturing or assembly tasks; *mechanized* technology utilizes machines that are under human control; and *automated* technology uses computers to control the process. Although there are now a number of highly automated technology processes, many U.S. factories depend primarily on mechanized technology.

Strategic Implications of Product and Process Decisions

Table 9.5 summarizes the basic differences among the five types of production processes. One can see that in selecting the appropriate production process, a firm must make various trade-offs. Each production process provides certain strategic advantages. As production volume increases, for example, a company can exploit automation and specialized equipment with less reliance on human labor, thus lowering unit costs through economies of scale and less frequent machine setups. Clearly, process technology should change as a product moves through the various stages of its life cycle (see Chapter 7).

The relationship between process technology and the products a firm manufactures has important implications for operations strategy. Managers must

Table 9.5 Characteristics of Production Processes

Type of Production Process	Product and Process Characteristics					
	Product Volume	Product Variety	Automation and Specialized Equipment	Labor Skills	Frequency of Machine Setup and Change	Unit Cost
Continuous-flow	High	Low	High	Low	Low	Low
Mass/ assembly-line	Medium	Medium	High	Low	Low	Low
Batch	Medium	Medium	Medium	Medium	Medium	Medium
Job-shop	Low	High	Low	High	High	High
Project	Low	High	Low	High	N/A	High

match process technology to products to achieve a competitive advantage. In a classic article, Hayes and Wheelwright suggest representing the interaction of product and process structure in the **product-process matrix** portrayed in Figure 9.2.[3] The diagonal of the matrix represents typical matchings of products and processes. For instance, in a commercial printing firm, each job is unique, so a job-shop process is usually most effective in meeting its needs. Manufacturers of heavy equipment that offer several basic models with a variety of options use a batch process in which volumes of a given model are produced intermittently. High-volume operations that produce only a few models, such as the assembly of automobiles or appliances, use mass-production and/or assembly-line processes. Finally, for high-volume, commodity-type products, such as oil, paper, or sugar, highly specialized, inflexible, and capital-intensive equipment is used in a continuous-flow setting.

Moving down the diagonal of the product-process matrix, the emphasis in both product and process structure shifts from high flexibility to low cost. Thus, product and process structure must be jointly reviewed to properly focus operations strategy. As products move through their life cycle, processes must be adjusted accordingly.

By positioning a business off the diagonal of the product-process matrix, a company can differentiate itself from its competitors. If that is done intentionally, it can help to achieve a competitive edge. For example, Rolls-Royce produces a small line of automobiles using a process similar to a job shop rather than the traditional mass-production methods of other automobile manufacturers. Each car requires about 900 hours of labor. The stainless-steel radiator takes 12 hours of metal bending and hand-soldering. Most automobile manufacturers assemble an entire car in that amount of time. For Rolls Royce this strategy has worked. However, if a firm drifts off the diagonal unintentionally, numerous problems can result. Movement to the right of the diagonal makes it increasingly difficult to coordinate production and marketing. For example, increased volume demands can cause a job-shop operation to lose the economies of scale afforded by batch and mass-production processes. Production control becomes more complex, and the continual need for product changeovers makes it difficult to maintain high volumes. With movement to the left of the diagonal, profitability may suffer, since volume remains small but equipment costs increase. Any potential savings in production efficiency from more streamlined processes might be lost, because the firm would have decreased flexibility to meet market demands.

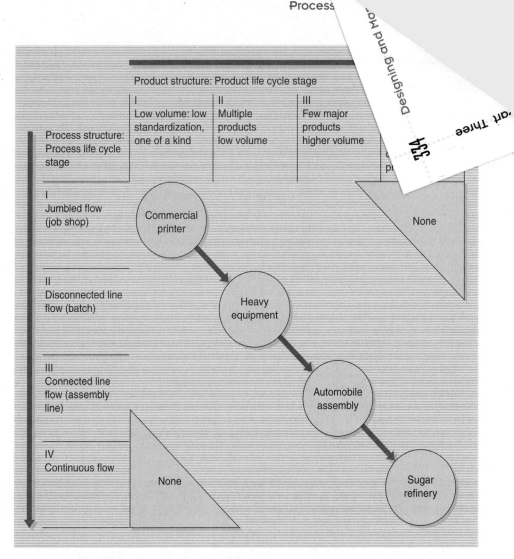

Figure 9.2
Product–Process Matrix

The product-process matrix suggests that companies face a choice between strategy of providing high volumes of standardized products at low costs or smaller volumes of highly differentiated products at higher costs. Higher volumes generally restrict a firm's flexibility, especially if the firm relies heavily on specialized equipment. That was a problem once faced by Ford.

Applied P/OM

Ford Motor Company

Automation at Ford inhibited flexibility [4]

Many years ago, every major piece of equipment in Ford Motor Company's most automated factory was designed to accommodate a narrow range of processing operations. The machines were so tightly wedded to the production of eight-cylinder engines that a shift to six-cylinder engines would have necessitated changes throughout the plant. When market conditions forced Ford to opt for the smaller engines, the company

≡ had to close the plant because it could not convert its specialized equipment to a different set of tasks.

By limiting the number of products and processes, a firm might increase its productivity (through specialization and learning) and achieve a competitive advantage. However, today's factories are faced with increasingly diverse consumer demands. In many industries, consumers are finely segmented and require an array of products that differ in many characteristics. In the food industry, for example, consumer needs vary by container size (individual versus family), culture (Italian versus Mexican), convenience (microwave versus bulk), and price (generic versus premium).[5] Manufacturers are moving toward "mass customization" to be able to produce high volumes of increasingly large numbers of products. Sony, for instance, obtains information from actual sales of various Walkman models and then quickly adjusts its product mix to conform to those sales patterns. That approach requires the ability to quickly change product lines and processes as consumer needs change—a deliberate shift upward in the product-process matrix. Even Rolls-Royce is shifting its position in the matrix. In a complete overhaul of its factory, Rolls created 16 zones of 60 to 100 workers each and then subdivided them into 10 zones. They work in a customer-supplier relationship with neighboring zones. As a result, cars spend only 32 days in the factory instead of 76, and the company lowered its break-even point from 2,700 cars annually to 1,300.[6]

Understanding the product-process matrix can help a firm focus more appropriately on what it does well so it can work to achieve "distinctive competence" in that area of production.

Automation and Advanced Technology

Before the Industrial Revolution, manufacturing tasks such as weaving cloth or forging and bending metal, were performed primarily by the same people who provided both the power and the control for the production process. As the Industrial Revolution progressed, machines such as lathes and drill presses provided more of the power for manufacturing, but workers retained much of the control of the process. Today, **automation**—the use of machines to provide both power and control over the production process—is making a significant impact in improving both productivity and quality. Automation is making the work environment more comfortable for workers and freeing them from onerous and dangerous jobs, such as sanding and painting automobile bodies. It also enables firms to improve productivity and quality, and increase the flexibility needed to respond rapidly to changing demands. This section reviews key elements of modern automation—the building blocks for modern, integrated factory automation systems that integrate machines, hardware, and information.

Numerical Control

Automation and advanced technology began in the 1950s with the development of **numerically controlled (NC)** machine tools, which enable the machinist's skills to be duplicated by a computer program that is stored on a computer medium such as punched paper tape. The computer program controls the movements of a tool used to make complex shapes.

NC systems were probably the earliest version of *computer-aided manufacturing (CAM)* (discussed later). Today many systems use **computer numerical control (CNC),** in which the machine is controlled by a small computer. Computer systems will even prepare detailed instructions automatically if the part shape, tools required, and machining information are provided.

For example, a part might require several holes of various sizes to be drilled. An N/C drill press with an automatic tool changer would automatically position the part so that each hole is drilled in the proper order. While the part is being repositioned the tool is automatically changed when necessary. Upon completion, the part is removed by an operator and the machine sets up to begin a new part. The sequence of drilling is programmed so that a minimum time is required to perform all operations. The operator has only to load and unload parts and push a button to begin processing, and thus can tend several NC machines at one work center.

Robotics

A **robot** is a programmable machine designed to handle materials or tools in the performance of a variety of tasks. Industrial robots were first introduced in 1954; in 1969 General Motors installed the first robot for spot-welding automobiles.

Figure 9.3 is an illustration of an industrial robot consisting of two major components: a manipulator, much like a human arm and wrist that carries a tool to perform work, and a control system that provides the guidance to direct the manipulator to follow a prescribed sequence of operations. The manipulator usually

Figure 9.3
Cincinnati Milacron Robot System

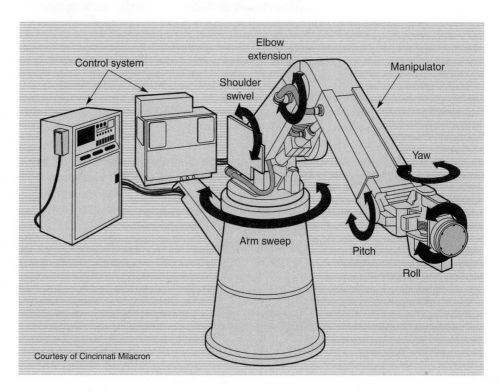

Courtesy of Cincinnati Milacron

has six basic motions, as illustrated in Figure 9.3, allowing for horizontal, vertical, rotational, and radial movement. Not all robots are capable of performing all six motions; some may perform only a subset of them. Robots can be "taught" a large number of sequences of motions and operations and even to make certain logical decisions. Also, a robot can be reprogrammed and transported from one application to another, leading to reduced labor requirements, improvements in quality, increased capacity, and more flexibility of low-volume production equipment.

At General Motors, for example, over 90 percent of the welds are performed by robots. Robots are also used to deliver parts and materials from one area of an automotive plant to another. Robots have even been developed to operate an automatic transmission and to drive on an actual road by computer control. Other typical applications are spray painting, machining operations such as drilling and assembly, inspection, and material handling. Robots are especially useful for working with hazardous materials or heavy objects; for instance, in nuclear power plants robots are used to do work in highly radioactive areas. In services, robots help doctors complete tedious brain surgery by drilling very precise holes into the skull.

Robots are not necessarily the perfect solution to every problem. Approximately 30,000 Ford Aerostar minivans were recalled because robots had failed to make certain key welds. At the Campbell Soup Company, every time a certain defect was found in a case of soup, the robot would drop the case. After analysis, Campbell decided to replace the robot with three human employees. Despite occasional problems, however, robot technology is continually advancing and will undoubtedly provide competitive advantages for the organizations that understand how to use it.

Vision Systems

Machine vision systems automatically receive and interpret an image of a real scene to obtain information and/or control machines or processes. Vision systems consist of a camera and video analyzer, a microcomputer, and a display screen. Among their numerous applications in production are:[7]

1. *Sorting*—of parts, assemblies, products, and containers by quantity, size, shape, color, or other characteristics. For example, vision systems are used to sort fruit and other food products by size and volume.

2. *Guidance and tracking*—for example, inspecting logs for knots and grain direction in the wood-products industry. Other applications include locating parts for pickup or assembly from a moving conveyor.

3. *Character recognition*—that is, reading or verifying printed text or serial numbers. Vision systems are used to verify the date and lot code on many products, especially in the pharmaceutical industry.

4. *Quality control*—by finding defects in welding, drilling, assembly, and so on and determining whether containers are properly filled. The automotive industry was an early user of machine vision systems. They are used in conjunction with robots to weld body seams of varying widths, tighten imprecisely located bolts, mark identification numbers on engines and transmissions using lasers, and arrange car hoods on racks that have unevenly spaced slots. General Motors is one of many automotive manufacturers that use vision systems.

Applied P/OM

General Motors

Vision systems at General Motors improve quality.[8]

At a General Motors plant in Lansing, Michigan, a vision-equipped robot system finds the exact location of a dozen lower-suspension-rail bolts and then uses a pneumatic nut-runner attachment to tighten the bolts to precise torque specifications. The system works by visually locating two gauge holes on the underbody of the car. From those two known points, the robot's control computer can calculate the exact locations of the 12 bolts and guide wrench sockets to the bolt heads. The vision feature is needed because the cars can be located as much as three inches fore or aft in the overhead conveyor cradles; a robot not equipped with vision would be unable to find the bolts! The system has resulted in more accurate bolt torquing and less manual rework downstream on the assembly line.

Information-Based Technology

The most significant changes in technology over the past two decades, especially in the service sector, involve information technology. To speed order entry at MamaMia's Pizza, for instance, a touch-sensitive computer screen can be linked to a customer database. When a repeat customer calls, the employee need only ask for the customer's phone number to bring up the customer's name, address, and delivery directions (for a new customer, the information need only be entered once). The employee would be able to address the customer immediately by name, enhancing the perception of service quality, and then enter the specific combination of toppings quickly on the touch-sensitive screen to print the order for pizza preparation, eliminating errors due to misreading of handwritten orders.

Bar-code technology (discussed further in Chapter 13) eliminates the need for people to keyboard information into a computer, greatly speeding processing and reducing errors. Frank's Nursery and Crafts, a chain of almost 300 plant and crafts stores, uses hand-held scanners to read product bar codes. If an item is out of stock, orders can be placed immediately. Considerable paperwork was eliminated by this system, and the time spent replenishing inventories was cut by 75 percent. A satellite system linked to Visa USA, Inc. has reduced credit-card approval time from 45 to 7 seconds, greatly reducing customer waiting time and long checkout lines.

Banks and insurance and financial institutions are using technology to streamline their operations. Automatic teller machines have been commonplace for many years. At Society National Bank in Cleveland, 70 percent of phone calls are handled through a voice-mail system, freeing customer service representatives to help customers who have more important issues. United Services Automobile Association (USAA) has spent $130 million since 1969 on computer and imaging technologies to improve customer service and lower costs. Its information system can track details such as what auto parts are being fixed most often, using the information to communicate with parts suppliers for improvement.[9]

Many companies have replaced paper instructions on the shop floor with computers that enable production workers to retrieve assembly instructions, current drawings, and other information whenever necessary. One example is seen at Hewlett-Packard.

Applied P/OM

Hewlett-Packard

Information technology supports mass customization efforts[10]

At Hewlett-Packard's personal computer business, virtually every computer is customized to the buyer's specifications. Computers are only partially assembled when they arrive at HP's Roseville, California, distribution center. Workers on the final assembly line, who cannot possibly be trained to assemble the myriad combinations of modems, CPUs, and other components, use bar-code scanners as each computer comes down the assembly line. Scanning brings up detailed directions and diagrams for assembling the particular unit on a video screen in front of the worker.

Sensors capture quality information and feed it directly into computers for immediate analysis. **Electronic data interchange (EDI)** enables companies to communicate design information among engineers, customers, and suppliers around the world. Wal-Mart, for instance, uses EDI to send purchase orders and invoices to suppliers. Electronic mail and local area network (LAN) "groupware" such as *Lotus Notes* also allow widespread sharing of information. For example, when a customer calls a company about a product problem, the typical process is for a service representative to identify the problem and write a report that gets passed around to various managers and engineers until some action is taken. With groupware, the problem can be posted on a network bulletin board. Other service representatives who might have encountered a similar problem can respond, as can individuals from engineering, design, and other areas in the company. That approach leads to a team effort in addressing the problem.[11]

According to *Business Week*, information technology is changing business by helping to break down old corporate barriers, allowing information to be shared instantly across departments and down to production workers; reducing cycle times, defects, and waste; streamling ordering and customer-supplier communications; helping to create "virtual offices" from workers in varied locations; and allowing customer-service representatives to access companywide databases to solve customer problems instantly.

Automated Manufacturing Systems

The combination of computers and sophisticated multipurpose machine tools provides highly flexible production systems. Computers are also being used extensively in design and engineering, referred to as **computer-aided design/computer-aided engineering (CAD/CAE).** Similarly, the knowledge base on which production planning and control decisions are made has improved significantly. From the combination of such knowledge bases with physical process control, **computer-assisted manufacturing (CAM)** was born.

Systems that perform multiple functions under computer control are called **flexible manufacturing systems (FMS).** They consist of numerical-control (N/C) machines linked by automated material-handing devices or robots. The union of CAD/CAE and CAM with FMS represents the latest development in manufacturing, which is known as **computer-integrated manufacturing (CIM)**. This section discusses those technologies and their strategic implications for operations management.

Computer-Aided Design/Computer-Aided Engineering (CAD/CAE)

Early CAD/CAE systems were basically computer-controlled plotting systems; today's systems are much more sophisticated. CAD/CAE enables engineers to design, analyze, test, and "manufacture" products before they physically exist, thus ensuring that a product can be manufactured to specifications when it is released to the shop floor. In addition, CAD/CAE systems allow the storage and retrieval of designs for easy updating and automatic creation of bills of materials and process information for production-planning and scheduling systems.

The systems can also create the correct programs for CNC (computer numerical control) machines. Quality thus improves significantly, since the chances of machine operators entering the incorrect program are virtually eliminated. If necessary, a terminal can be placed at the workplace for the operator to view the plans on the screen, eliminating paper drawings that can become obsolete or lost. Specific parts can be enlarged on the screen to facilitate reading and use by the operator.

Computer-Aided Manufacturing (CAM)

Computer-aided manufacturing (CAM) involves computer control of the manufacturing process, such as determining tool movements and cutting speeds. CAM has advantages over conventional manufacturing approaches under many conditions, such as when

- Several different parts with variable or cyclic demands are produced.
- Frequent design changes are made.
- The manufacturing process is complex.
- There are multiple machining operations on one part.
- Expert operator skills and close control are required.

Each machine in a CAM system has the ability to select and manipulate a number of tools according to programmed instructions; thus, CAM provides a high degree of flexibility in performing and controlling manufacturing processes.

Caterpillar Corporation, for instance, uses CAM to make components for tractor-engine drive assemblies. About a dozen machines stand on both sides of a railroad-like track, along which a transfer device shuttles parts among the work stations where 30 to 40 machining operations are performed. Operators at entry and exist points clamp the parts on and off the transfer mechanism; the rest of the process is computer-driven.[12]

Flexible Manufacturing Systems (FMS)

Flexible manufacturing systems (FMS) are a logical extension of CAM. They consist of two or more computer-controlled machines linked by automated handling devices such as robots and transport systems. Computers direct the overall sequence of operations and route the workpiece to the appropriate machine, select and load the proper tools, and control the operations performed by the machine. More than one workpiece can be machined simultaneously, and many different parts can be processed in random order.

FMS provide the ability to manufacture small to medium volumes of many different parts economically. The systems therefore have flexibility of a job shop and the high productivity of a production line. FMS can achieve higher machine utilization than stand-alone machines because setup times are reduced, parts are handled more efficiently, and several parts are produced simultaneously. General Electric, for example, modernized its locomotive plant in Erie, Pennsylvania, using FMS. The machining time for engine-frame parts was reduced from 16 days to 16 hours; overall productivity was increased by 240 percent; capacity was increased by 38 percent; and design flexibility was increased as well.

FMS provide high flexibility in coping with engineering and production schedule changes. Manufacturing lead times are reduced because of reduced setup times, enabling a manufacturer to respond more quickly to new products and to changes in demand. As you may recall, that is one of the important issues in manufacturing strategy. Shorter lead times reduce in-process inventory. Finally, since both machining and material handling are under computer control, operators are needed only to perform necessary loading and unloading operations, resulting in a significant cost reduction. All those advantages help to increase profitability and the competitive position of the firm.

FMS, like robots, are not without limitations. They require capital investments that can easily exceed $10 million. Many managers are reluctant to make such an investment, especially since technology advances may make today's FMS obsolete. Further, because FMS must be custom-designed to a company's specific needs, several years may pass before the system is installed and running. In addition, the computer software needed to control a FMS is highly complex and often prone to problems.

Computer-Integrated Manufacturing Systems (CIMS)

Today we are beginning to see the complete integration of CAD/CAE, CAM, and FMS into computer-integrated manufacturing systems (CIMS). Computer-integrated manufacturing (CIM) represent the union of hardware, software, database management, and communications to plan and control production activities from planning and design to manufacturing and distribution.

CIMS are being used for high-volume, highly standardized production where mass-production technology has traditionally been employed. Since they allow for much smaller economically viable batch sizes, a firm is able to match its production efforts to a much wider range of demand and to create competitive advantage through rapid response to market changes and new products.

CIMS also provide all the advantages discussed for CAD/CAE, CAM, and FMS: shorter design cycles, better quality, reduced waste, better management control, and high equipment utilization. According to the National Research Council, companies with CIM experience have been able to

••• Decrease engineering design costs by up to 30 percent.

••• Increase productivity by 40 to 70 percent.

••• Increase equipment utilization by a factor of 2 to 3.

••• Reduce work-in-process and lead times by 30 to 60 percent.

••• Improve quality by a factor of 3 to 4.

Although the cost of developing and implementing a fully operational CIM system can be staggering, and a high degree of management commitment and effort is necessary, many companies are beginning to reap the rewards of carefully planned systems.

Impacts of Automation

To make effective decisions in introducing new technology, managers need to understand the relative advantages and disadvantages of using humans and machines for work. Table 9.6 lists some of the capabilities of people and machines. In general, people can think creatively and adapt to new and unexpected situations much better than machines can. Machines, however, are better suited for complex or repetitive tasks that require precision and speed. The goal of the operations manager is to provide the best synthesis of technology and people.

Automation has many benefits:

••• New products can be introduced with smaller lead times, because CAD/CAE reduces the time required to design and test new ideas.

••• Product life cycles are shorter because of the ability to redesign products faster, and because of the rapid pace of technological improvements in manufacturing.

••• Quality is improved because of CAD/CAE, CAM, FMS, CIM, and improved inspection capabilities such as vision systems.

Table 9.6 Human versus Machine Capabilities

Humans		Machines	
Advantages	*Disadvantages*	*Advantages*	*Disadvantages*
Recognize and use information creatively	Relatively poor short-term memories	Precise, accurate, and fast responses	No creative capability
Improvise and adapt to new situations	Cannot perform many tasks simultaneously	Highly reliable for routine tasks	Decision making limited by programmed instructions
Reason by induction	Slow in response	Can perform tasks beyond human capabilities	Cannot adapt to unexpected situations
Make subjective decisions	Difficulty in maintaining consistency in performance	Fast deductive reasoning	Limited perceptual capability
		Store and process large amounts of information	

••• Work-in-process inventory is reduced because of increased stability in machine operation times.

••• Machine setup and tool change times are reduced and less costly. As a result, smaller lot sizes can be produced, which increases the plant's flexibility.

••• Supervision, energy, and other overhead costs are decreased.

••• With less inventory, materials handling, and labor, smaller facilities can achieve the same production output.

••• Work becomes more challenging and conceptual as automated equipment performs routine and repetitive tasks.

In one sense, such technological developments have enhanced the role of the worker in production systems. On the other hand, increased automation has been a threat to job security. In the future, automation will significantly change the nature of the work force even further. The decrease in jobs for minimally skilled, direct factory workers will be accompanied by a rapid increase in the demand for highly trained specialists. A larger number of technical, professional, and managerial workers will be performing irregular, complex, long-cycle activities. Most of the workers' time will be devoted to mental processes, and much less of it will be spent doing physical work. Of course, the proper balance of human and machine work will vary among industries.

The implications of automation for employment have been a major concern among scholars, legislators, and labor leaders. Certainly, many jobs in direct manufacturing have been lost because of automation. However, the demand for workers to design, operate, maintain, and manage automated systems is increasing. As a result, the trend toward multiple careers and the development of several different skills over a person's working life will become more widespread, and training and retraining will consume a larger portion of working time.

Process Planning and Design

To design a process, several activities must be performed:

1. Identify the individual components of the product and their order of assembly (product analysis).
2. Identify the sequence of production steps required to fabricate each component (process analysis).
3. Select the appropriate technology and equipment to accomplish each processing step (process selection).
4. Design work methods for each processing operation.

Product Analysis

The most common way of defining a product is with a drawing. Figure 9.4 is a drawing of a typical in-line skate on which key components are labeled. Detailed engineering drawings of individual parts, such as the one in Figure 9.5, provide the technical specifications needed by manufacturing personnel and purchasing agents.

Figure 9.4
A Typical In-Line Skate

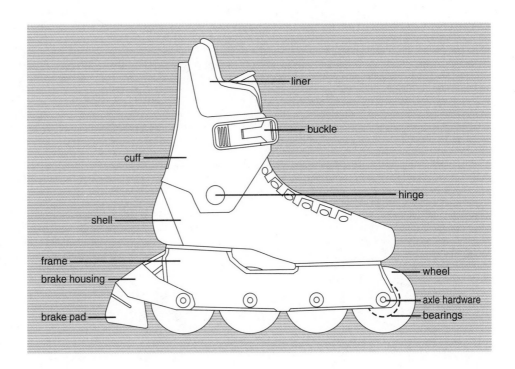

For operations planning and control, additional information is necessary. Product structure is usually expressed in a level-by-level hierarchy showing the logical relationships between parts in an assembly. Figure 9.6 illustrates the product structure for a pair of in-line skates. The first level consists of one left skate and one right skate. The second level defines the parts or subassemblies that make up the "parent items" at the first level. Thus, the left skate consists of one left wheel assembly and one left boot assembly. At the next level, the left wheel assembly, in turn, consists of one frame, four wheels, one set of axle hardware, and four bearings. The items in the product structure, their level of assembly, and the quantity required for each parent item make up the **bill of materials (BOM).** BOMs are used to determine material and part requirements, and for costing out direct material. They are also essential for developing production schedules.

Although the product-structure information describes the logical relationship of parts to one another, it does not specify the sequence of assembly. The assembly sequence is important in determining which operations are to be

Figure 9.5
Detailed Engineering
Drawing

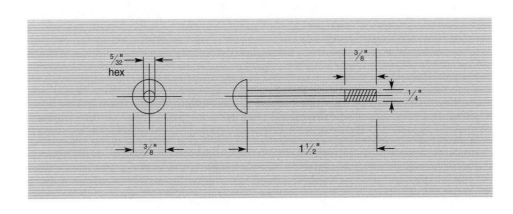

Figure 9.6 Product Structure for In-Line Skates

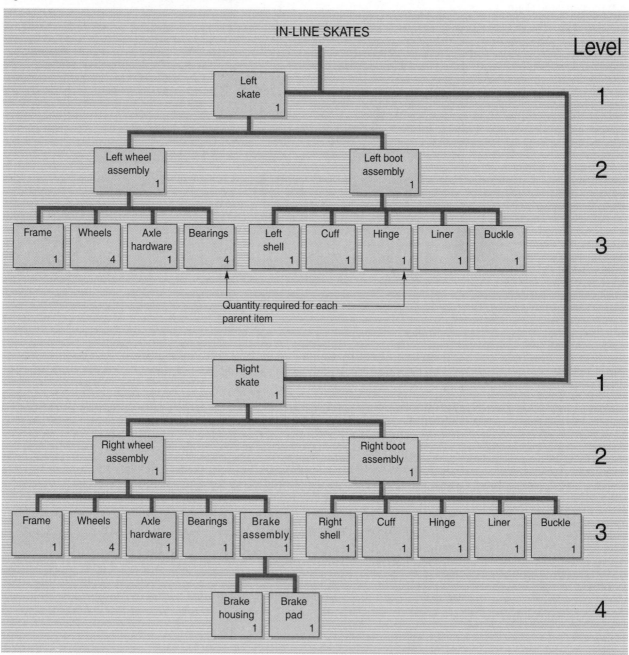

performed by an individual worker and the number of work stations required. An **assembly chart** is a graphical representation of the order of assembly for a product. Figure 9.7 is an assembly chart for the right skate. The circles at the extreme left correspond to the individual parts. As we move to the right, the individual parts are joined together to form subassemblies (denoted by SA-1, SA-2, and so on). Thus, subassembly SA-1 consists of parts 1 through 4. At the extreme right of the figure, subassemblies and individual parts are combined to

Figure 9.7
Right Skate Assembly Chart

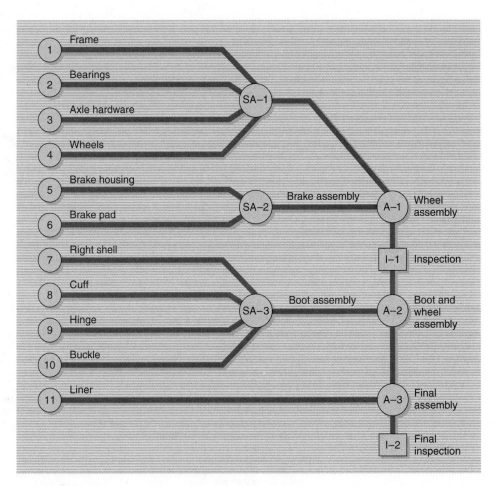

form partial assemblies (A-1, A-2, and so on). The sequence of assembly is from top to bottom of the chart. Inspections often occur between steps as part of quality control.

As a general rule, subassemblies and partial assemblies should contain a small number of parts and be transportable between work stations to allow flexibility in planning the work stations and job assignments. The assembly chart is an important tool in designing layouts for assembly lines, which are discussed in the next chapter. Assembly charts can also be applied to services; Figure 9.8 is an assembly chart for filing a federal income-tax return.

Process Analysis

Process analysis provides a step-by-step description of how products are to be produced. A general description of a process can be illustrated with a flowchart. For instance, Figure 9.9 is a simple flowchart of a printed circuitboard assembly, with each box representing a processing operation. More detailed information about a production process is provided in **flow process charts,** which describe the specific sequence of operations, transportations, inspections, storages, and delays that are the basic elements of any production process. Figure 9.10 is one example. The symbols used are shown in Figure 9.11.

Figure 9.8
Assembly Chart for
Simplified Form 1040
Income-Tax Return

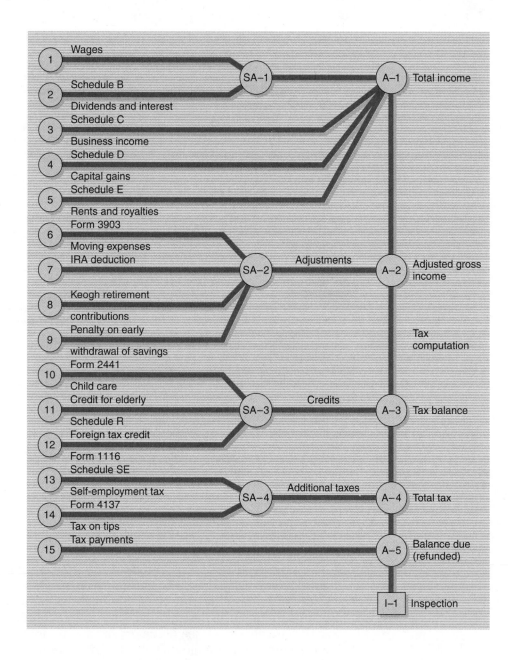

Figure 9.9 Flowchart for Printed Circuitboard Assembly

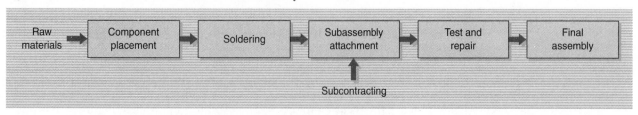

Figure 9.10 Flow-Process Chart

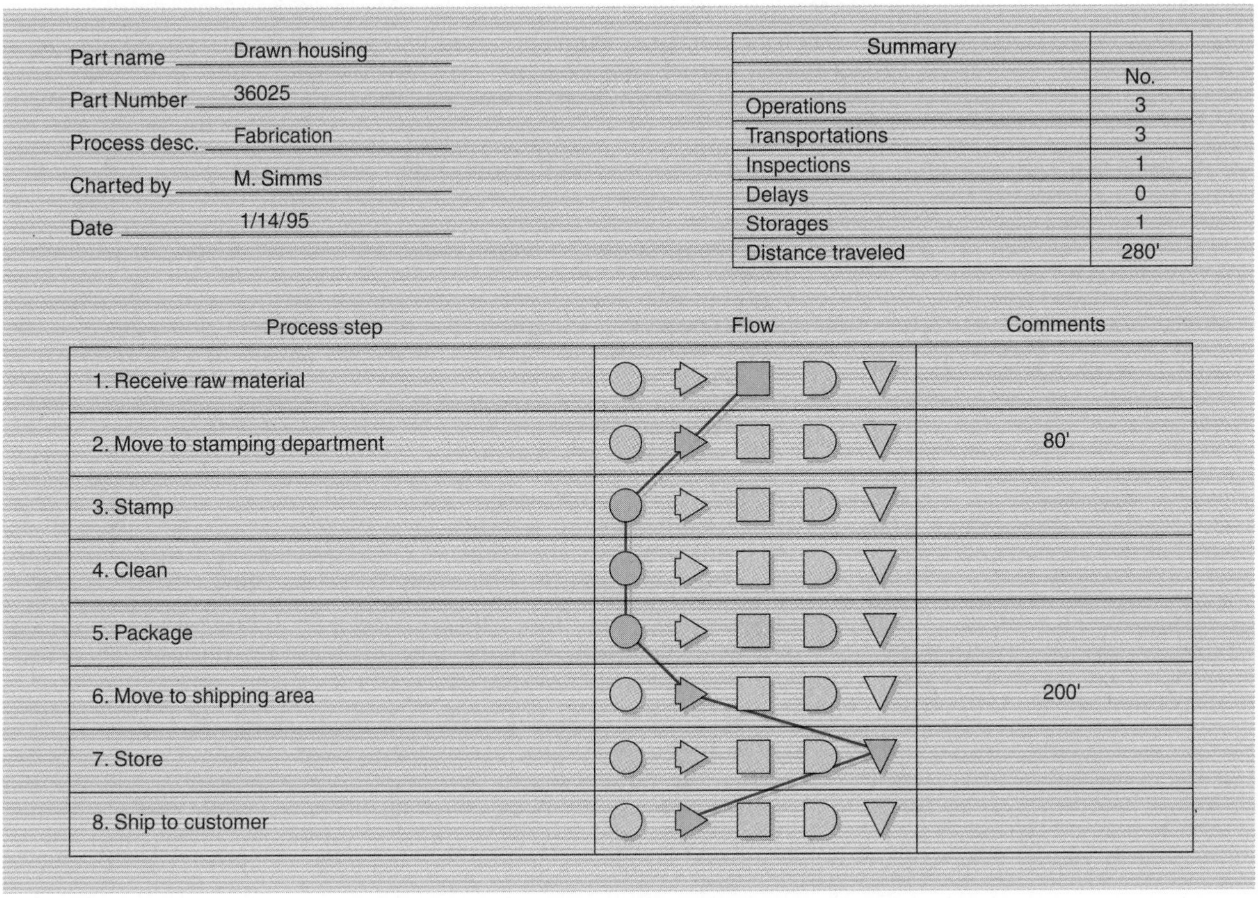

Part name	Drawn housing
Part Number	36025
Process desc.	Fabrication
Charted by	M. Simms
Date	1/14/95

Summary	No.
Operations	3
Transportations	3
Inspections	1
Delays	0
Storages	1
Distance traveled	280'

Process step	Flow	Comments
1. Receive raw material	○ ▷ ■ D ▽	
2. Move to stamping department	○ ▷ □ D ▽	80'
3. Stamp	○ ▷ □ D ▽	
4. Clean	○ ▷ □ D ▽	
5. Package	○ ▷ □ D ▽	
6. Move to shipping area	○ ▷ □ D ▽	200'
7. Store	○ ▷ □ D ▽	
8. Ship to customer	○ ▷ □ D ▽	

Figure 9.11
Flow-Process Chart
Symbols

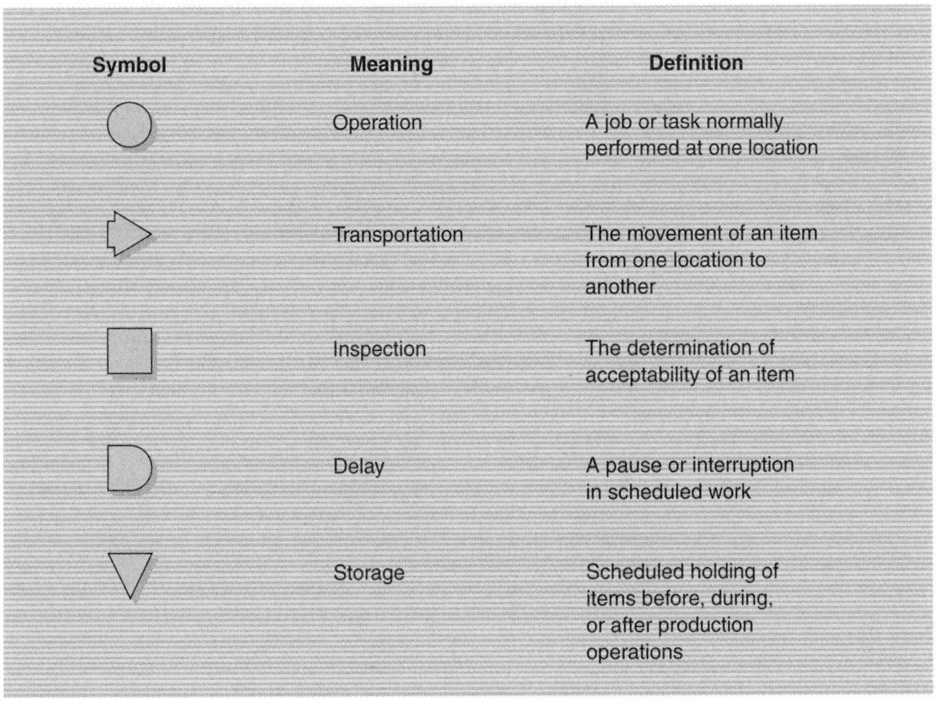

Symbol	Meaning	Definition
○	Operation	A job or task normally performed at one location
▷	Transportation	The movement of an item from one location to another
■	Inspection	The determination of acceptability of an item
D	Delay	A pause or interruption in scheduled work
▽	Storage	Scheduled holding of items before, during, or after production operations

In analyzing a flow-process chart, industrial engineers and operations managers ask questions such as: Can some operations be eliminated or combined? Can transport operations be simplified or eliminated? Why do delays occur? Answers to such questions may lead to changes in work methods, equipment, or even layout and can significantly reduce costs and improve productivity.

Process Selection

After product and process analysis are performed, it is necessary to select the particular technology and equipment to be used. Technology decisions are usually made in product design and R&D groups. At the plant level, specific process and equipment selection become the principal decisions.

Process selection depends on a variety of economic, quantitative, and qualitative factors, much as product design does. To select the best process for producing a given part, the manufacturing engineer must have a thorough understanding of materials and their properties, existing technology, and the desired properties of the final product. For example, cutting speeds depend on the type of material being cut and the cutting tool itself. Typical cutting speeds may be 600 meters per minute for aluminum and 50 meters per minute for titanium alloys; in some cases, speeds may even reach 9,000 meters per minute. The manufacturing engineer needs to know the effects of such speeds on the structural properties of the materials being cut, such as stress properties of aircraft wings. Tool life may also be substantially affected. For example, higher cutting speeds can cause cutting tools to wear out more frequently—and whenever that occurs production must be interrupted to replace them. Thus, financial considerations such as operating costs, labor, and fixed capital expenses weigh heavily in the process-selection decision.

Similar decisions are made in service organizations. Printing can be offset or typeset; hamburgers can be broiled or fried. In a department store, credit verification of bank cards can be done by checking the credit card number against a printed list of bad accounts (manual), by calling a special telephone number for authorization (mechanized), or by using automatic verification equipment at the store itself (automated).

The goal of selecting a specific piece of equipment is to provide the required quantity of output from the production process with appropriate quality at the most economical costs. Constraints on production specifications often limit the available choices. For instance, some products may require a shearing operation, as opposed to a cutting operation. In choosing a computer system for a service organization, memory requirements, speed, and software may limit the feasible alternatives.

Generally, operations personnel have to choose between general-purpose and special-purpose equipment. General-purpose equipment, such as drill presses, lathes, and so on, can be used in a large variety of manufacturing applications. Special-purpose equipment may be limited to only one or two different applications. Thus, the major factors to be considered are the variety of work available, the output rate desired, and the cost.

For plants that produce a large variety of products or produce to customer specifications, general-purpose equipment provides greater flexibility, requires fewer maintenance skills, and allows faster setup times. General-purpose equipment is also less likely to become obsolete as new technology is introduced. Special-purpose equipment, in contrast, generally results in faster production rates because of automated handling or numerical-control features. For manufacturers with only a few product lines and high volume, special-purpose equipment can provide substantial benefits.

A number of economic and noneconomic criteria must be evaluated in selecting a piece of equipment. Economic factors include

1. Rate of return on investment.
2. Budget limitations.
3. Purchase price.
4. Installation cost.
5. Operating expenses.
6. Training costs.
7. Labor savings.
8. Tax implications.
9. Miscellaneous costs (such as computer software for programmable equipment).

Important noneconomic factors include:

1. Installation time.
2. Availability of training.
3. Productivity improvements.
4. Vendor service.
5. Adaptability and flexibility of the equipment.

Example

Making an Equipment-Selection Decision

The Sterling Equipment Corporation is contemplating the purchase of an industrial robot. Equipment from four suppliers has been identified as meeting the basic technical criteria. An economic analysis resulted in the data shown in Table 9.7. In addition, an evaluation of the noneconomic factors resulted in the data shown in Table 9.8.

The plant manager decided to translate the noneconomic factors into numerical scores, with 1 = excellent, 2 = good, 3 = average, 4 = poor. The results of the evaluation are shown in Table 9.9. While Supplier 3 was slightly better than Supplier 1 on the noneconomic criteria (Table 9.9), the fact that the net cost was significantly lower for vendor 1 (Table 9.7) led Sterling to select vendor 1.

The choice of which robot to select in this example was not necessarily straightforward, because it is difficult to assess the relative value of economic and noneconomic criteria. As in product selection and facility location, such decisions must be carefully weighed by the management team.

Table 9.7 Economic Analysis for Equipment Selection

Factor	Supplier			
	1	2	3	4
Purchase cost	$50,000	$70,000	$55,000	$75,000
Installation cost	2,500	1,000	4,500	0
Operating cost	5,000	6,000	7,500	6,500
Training cost	1,000	0	1,000	1,500
Software costs	1,000	1,000	1,500	2,000
Total costs	59,500	78,000	69,500	85,000
Labor savings	30,000	40,000	30,000	45,000
Tax benefits	1,500	2,000	1,000	2,000
Total savings	31,500	42,000	31,000	47,000
Net total cost	$28,000	$36,000	$38,500	$38,000

Table 9.8 Noneconomic Factor Evaluation for Equipment Selection

Factor	Supplier			
	1	2	3	4
Installation lead time	Good	Average	Excellent	Poor
Supplier training	Good	Poor	Good	Average
Productivity improvement	Good	Good	Good	Good
Supplier service	Good	Excellent	Excellent	Good
Flexibility	Excellent	Good	Good	Excellent

Table 9.9 Numerical Scores for Noneconomic Factors in Equipment Selection

Factor	Supplier			
	1	2	3	4
Installation lead time	2	3	1	4
Suppler training	2	4	2	3
Productivity improvement	2	2	2	2
Supplier service	2	1	1	2
Flexibility	1	2	2	1
Total	9	12	8	12

Process Reliability.   We introduced the concept of *product reliability* in Chapter 6. *Process reliability* is an important consideration in process design. The following example shows how the techniques discussed in Chapter 6 can be applied to process design.

Example · **Computing Reliability of Automated Production System**

Figure 9.12 is an example of an automated production system with three operations: turning, milling, and grinding. Individual parts are transformed from the turning center to the milling center, and then to the grinder by a robot; thus, if one machine or the robot fails, the entire production process must stop. The probability that any one component of the system will fail, however, does not depend on any other component of the system.

Conceptually, we can think of the robot and machines in series, as shown in Figure 9.13. The reliability of the system can be computed as

$$R = p_1 p_2 p_3 p_4 \tag{9.1}$$

Thus, in Figure 9.13, if we assume that the reliability of the robot, turning center, milling machine, and grinder are .99, .98, .99, and .96, respectively, then the total reliability is

$$R = (.99)(.98)(.99)(.96) = .92.$$

Figure 9.12 An Automated Manufacturing System

SOURCE: John G. Holmes "Integrating Robots into a Manufacturing System." Reprinted with permission from 1979 Fall Industrial Engineering Conference *Proceedings*. Copyright Institute of Industrial Engineers, 25 Technology Park/Atlanta, Norcross, GA 30092.

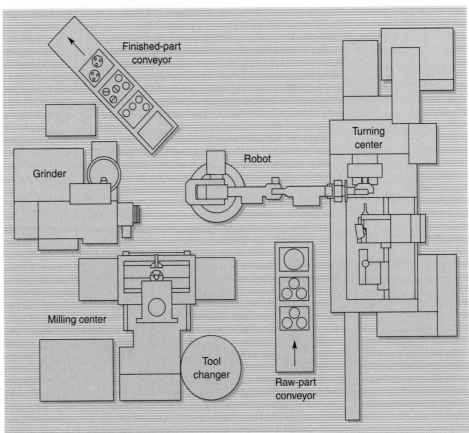

Figure 9.13 A Series Production System

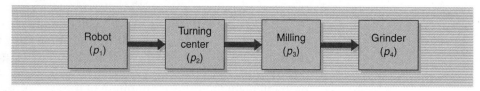

This means there is a .92 probability that the system will be working over a specified period of time. As stated, this calculation assumes that the probability of failure of each component in the system is independent of the others.

Suppose the system is redesigned with two grinders that operate in parallel; if one grinder fails, the other grinder may still work and hence the total system will continue to function. Such a system is illustrated in Figure 9.14. Letting p_{g_1} denote the reliability of grinder 1 and p_{g_2} denote the reliability of grinder 2, the probability that *both grinders will fail* is given by

$$(1 - p_{g_1})(1 - p_{g_2})$$

Since either both grinders will fail, or at least one grinder will not fail, we can compute the probability that at least one grinder will not fail, R_{grinders}, as

$$R_{grinders} = 1 - [(1 - p_{g_1})(1 - p_{g_2})].$$

So, if each grinder has a reliability of 0.96, the reliability of both grinders together is

$$R_{grinders} = 1 - (1 - .96)(1 - .96)$$
$$= 1 - .0016$$
$$= .9984.$$

Notice that the total grinder reliability has increased by adding the extra machine. Now we can use Equation 9.1 to compute the total system reliability, using .9984 as the reliability of the grinders. Essentially, we have replaced the parallel grinders with one grinder whose reliability is .9984. Thus we have

$$R = (.99)(.98)(.99)(.9984) = .96.$$

Figure 9.14 A Series Production System with Parallel Grinders

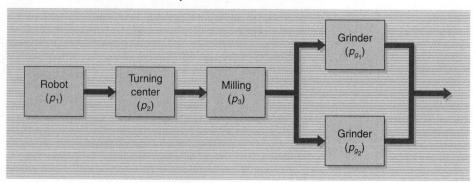

Work-Methods Design

Once equipment is selected, work centers can be defined. A **work center** consists of one or more people and/or machines that can be considered as one unit for the purposes of performing work tasks. For example, a work center can be a single machine or group of machines in one location (such as in Figure 9.12), a group of workers who perform a similar task or closely related set of tasks, such as on an assembly line, or a set of different machines that function together to perform a set of operations on one or more products. In Figure 9.9, for instance, component placement and soldering could be combined into one work center, and test and repair could be split into two distinct work centers. As more work centers are defined, scheduling and control of the production process becomes more difficult, and the data needed for management decision making become more complex. Too few work centers, on the other hand, make it difficult for managers to find bottlenecks and to gather the performance and cost data that are needed for identifying and correcting specific problems. Some of these issues will be discussed further in later chapters.

The final element of process design is specifying work methods at each work center. Two tools that facilitate the design of work methods are operation charts and multiple-activity charts.

Operation Charts. Often used to describe a manual task, an **operation chart** is similar to a flow-process chart in that it uses the same symbols for operation, transportation, inspection, storage, and delay. In the operation chart, however, they apply to individual motions of the left hand and the right hand. For example, an *operation* might consist of grasping a part from a bin; a *transportation* might be the process of moving it to another place; an *inspection* might be holding a part to inspect it; *storage* could represent the process of holding a part in one hand while the other is performing an operation; and *delay* occurs when a hand is idle. Following is an example of the use of an operation chart.

Example

Work-Methods Design Using an Operation Chart

The Freeland Faucet Company manufactures kitchen and bathroom faucets and other plumbing items. One of the workstations at the shop is for the assembly of stems for bathroom faucets. The components of the assembly are shown in Figure 9.15. All items are stored in bins on the workbench. A methods analyst might specify the following procedure. The operator picks up a housing and stem and screws the stem into the housing; next, he or she places a washer into the stem, inserts a screw, and tightens it with a screwdriver. An operation chart for this assembly process is shown in Figure 9.16. In this case, we have not broken down the operation into its fine elements. For example, the process of getting a housing actually consists of reaching for the housing (transport), grasping it (operation), and moving it to the immediate work area (transport). Such detail is the subject of *micromotion study*. Since the left hand is moving throughout most of this process, we have lumped these elements together into one transport operation. Generally, a rough description of the process suffices in methods analysis.

Figure 9.15 Assembly of Faucet-Stem Component

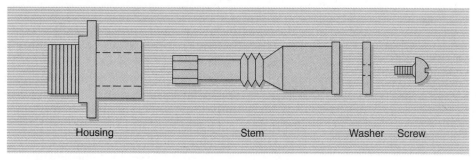

Housing   Stem   Washer   Screw

Figure 9.16 Operation Chart for Faucet-Stem Assembly

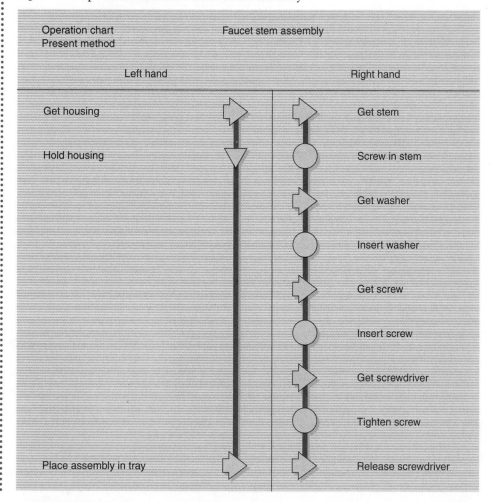

Operation chart   Faucet stem assembly
Present method

Left hand   Right hand

Left hand	Right hand
Get housing	Get stem
Hold housing	Screw in stem
	Get washer
	Insert washer
	Get screw
	Insert screw
	Get screwdriver
	Tighten screw
Place assembly in tray	Release screwdriver

Operation charts are useful in designing the layout of a workplace while simultaneously improving the methods. We will examine that application in the next chapter and revisit this example.

Multiple-Activity Charts. A tool often used to design methods for worker-machine interaction is a **multiple-activity chart.** Here the activities of each component of a system, such as machines and people, are graphically represented along a vertical time scale. Use of this tool is illustrated in the following example.

Work-Methods Design Using a Multiple-Activity Chart

To illustrate the use of a multiple-activity chart, consider the operation of a numerically controlled (NC) drill press. Suppose a worker first inspects and prepares a part for drilling and then positions the part on the machine. After the drilling is completed, the part is removed and inspected. While the machine is running, the part that was previously drilled is assembled to another component and placed on a cart to be moved to the final assembly department. The times for each operation are listed in Table 9.10. Figure 9.17 is a multiple-activity chart for this job. We see that the machine is idle for 5 minutes and that the entire cycle takes 11 minutes. Thus only 5.45 parts can be produced per hour.

Does a better process design exist? If possible, we would like to reduce the idle time and shorten the cycle time. One possibility is to assign an additional worker to the job. The methods analyst, by trial and error, might arrive at the design shown by the multiple-activity chart in Figure 9.18. With that division of work between the operator and the assistant, the total operation time can be

Table 9.10 Activity Times for NC Drill Press Example

Activity	Time (minutes)
Inspect and prepare new part	3
Position part	2
Machine running	3
Remove part	1
Inspect	2
Assemble	3

Figure 9.17 Multiple-Activity Chart for NC Drill Press

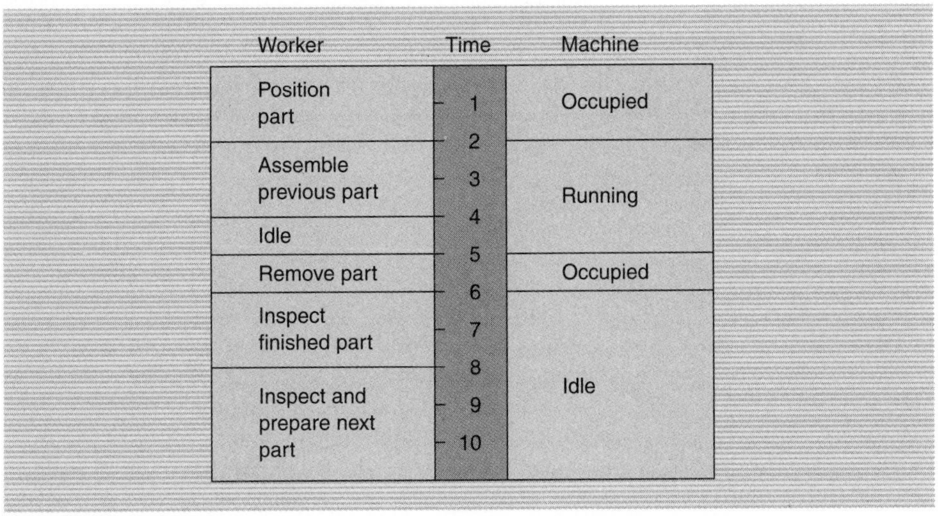

Figure 9.18 Multiple-Activity Chart for Improved Process for NC Drill Press

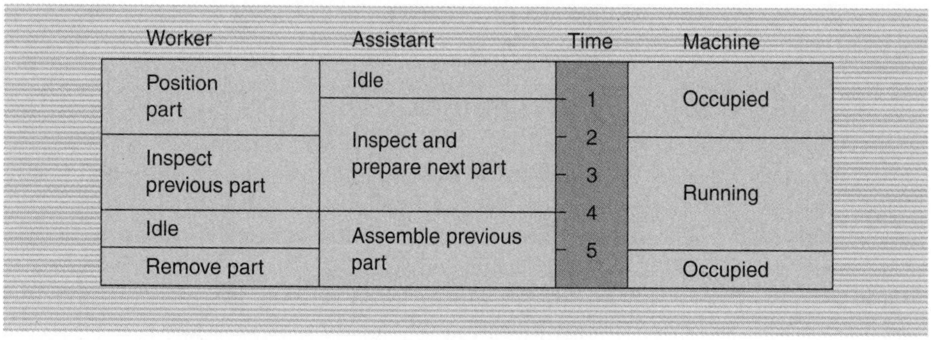

Worker	Assistant	Time	Machine
Position part	Idle	1	Occupied
Inspect previous part	Inspect and prepare next part	2 3	Running
Idle	Assemble previous part	4 5	Running
Remove part	Assemble previous part		Occupied

reduced to 6 minutes, thus increasing production to 10 parts per hour. Idle time on the machine is reduced to zero. Whether the additional production would justify hiring the additional person must then be determined. In that way, multiple-activity charts can be used to design and evaluate alternative methods and work assignments.

Work Measurement

Work measurement is a useful tool for evaluating alternative process designs for labor-intensive work. Its purpose is to develop time standards for the performance of jobs. A **time standard** is generally defined as the amount of time a trained operator working at a normal pace and using a prescribed method takes to perform a task. Some key words in this definition are *trained, normal,* and *method.* To establish usable standards, the operator must be trained to do the job efficiently. Thus, methods analysis and motion study should precede work measurement. By a normal pace, we mean a pace that can be consistently performed by the average worker without undue fatigue.

Work measurement is used in several ways in organizations, namely, for estimating work-force and capacity requirements, determining the cost of production operations for accounting purposes, establishing wage-incentive systems, monitoring worker performance, and scheduling production. In each of those applications, managers are interested in the length of time needed to produce an item or, equivalently, the number of items that can be produced over a certain length of time. Time standards allow easy computation of such measures.

There are several techniques for work measurement. One of the most popular is **time study,** the development of a time standard by observing a task and analyzing it with the use of a stopwatch. The general approach to time study can be described as follows.

1. *Divide the task content into smaller work elements.* This is accomplished by using the techniques of motion study discussed previously.

2. *Measure the time needed to perform each element over a number of cycles.* This is usually done by a trained observer with a stopwatch. Several observations should be taken to account for variability in performance. Assuming that the distribution of element times is normal, the number of cycles that should be observed is determined statistically by the sample size formula:

$$n = \frac{(z_{\alpha/2})^2 \sigma^2}{E^2} \tag{9.2}$$

where $z_{\alpha/2}$ is the value of the standard normal distribution having an area of $\alpha/2$ in the upper tail, σ is an estimate of the standard deviation, and E is the desired sampling error.

3. *Rate the operator's performance of each work element.* A performance rating is a subjective judgment about the pace sustained by the worker. One hundred percent is considered a normal pace; a rating of 115 percent indicates that work is 15 percent above normal. Rating performance accurately requires considerable training.

4. *Use the performance rating to determine the normal element time.* The *normal time* for each element is computed by multiplying the performance rating (expressed as a decimal fraction) by the average element time. The sum of those times is the normal time for the entire operation.

5. *Determine allowances for personal time, fatigue, and unavoidable delays.* Allowances account for time needed to go to the restroom, rest required due to physical activity, and material shortages, equipment malfunctions, and so on.

6. *Determine the standard time.* The *standard time* is determined by adjusting the normal time by the allowance factor:

Standard time = normal time (1 + allowance).

An example of a time study follows.

Example

Determining Standard Time through Time Study

The Freeland Faucet Company can be used to illustrate the time-study procedure. We use the operation chart in Figure 9.16 as the basis for developing the time study, combining several of the smaller work elements for greater accuracy. For instance, "get washer" and "insert washer" are combined. We obtain the following set of work elements:

1. Get housing and stem.
2. Screw in stem.
3. Get and insert washer.
4. Get and insert screw.
5. Tighten screw.
6. Place completed assembly in tray.

To determine the sample size for this example, suppose we desire 90 percent probability that the value of the sample mean provides a sampling error of .01 minute or less. Further assume that σ is estimated from historical experience to be .019. Therefore, $\alpha = .10$, $z_{.05} = 1.645$, and $E = .01$. We then have

$$n = \frac{(1.645)^2(.019)^2}{(.01)^2} = 9.8.$$

Figure 9.19 Spreadsheet for Time-Study Chart—Freeland Faucet Example (TIMESTDY.XLS)

	A	B	C	D	E	F	G	H	I	J	K	L	M	N	O	P
1	Time Study Chart															
2																
3	Faucet Stem Assembly															
4																
5	Work element						Observation									Normal
6			1	2	3	4	5	6	7	8	9	10	Sum	Average	Rating	Time
7	Get housing	Cumulative time	0.03	0.03	0.02	0.03	0.04	0.03	0.04	0.04	0.03	0.03				
8	and stem	Element time	0.03	0.03	0.02	0.03	0.04	0.03	0.04	0.04	0.03	0.03	0.32	0.032	1.00	0.032
9	Screw in stem	Cumulative time	0.13	0.15	0.14	0.16	0.13	0.12	0.14	0.16	0.15	0.13				
10		Element time	0.10	0.12	0.12	0.13	0.09	0.09	0.10	0.12	0.12	0.10	1.09	0.109	1.10	0.120
11	Get and insert	Cumulative time	0.24	0.25	0.26	0.29	0.23	0.21	0.24	0.26	0.27	0.22				
12	washer	Element time	0.11	0.10	0.12	0.13	0.10	0.09	0.10	0.10	0.12	0.09	1.06	0.106	1.00	0.106
13	Get and insert	Cumulative time	0.32	0.33	0.36	0.38	0.33	0.30	0.32	0.33	0.37	0.31				
14	screw	Element time	0.08	0.08	0.10	0.09	0.10	0.09	0.08	0.07	0.10	0.09	0.88	0.088	1.00	0.088
15	Tighten screw	Cumulative time	0.48	0.50	0.54	0.53	0.50	0.45	0.51	0.52	0.58	0.49				
16		Element time	0.16	0.17	0.18	0.15	0.17	0.15	0.19	0.19	0.21	0.18	1.75	0.175	0.97	0.170
17	Place assembly	Cumulative time	0.51	0.53	0.58	0.56	0.54	0.49	0.54	0.55	0.62	0.52				
18	in tray	Element time	0.03	0.03	0.04	0.03	0.04	0.04	0.03	0.03	0.04	0.03	0.34	0.034	1.00	0.034
19															Sum	0.550
20	Allowances															
21	Personal	5%														
22	Fatigue	5%														
23	Delay	10%														
24																
25	Standard Time	0.660														
26																

A sample size of 10 or more will provide the required precision. (Fractional values of n should always be rounded upward to ensure that the precision is at least as good as desired.)

Figure 9.19 illustrates a typical time-study spreadsheet when continuous timing is used. *Continuous timing* involves starting the clock at the beginning of each task and recording the cumulative time at the completion of each work element. The element times are found by subtracting successive cumulative times. These are added and averaged to obtain the mean time for each work element. Performance ratings are given in the next-to-last column. By multiplying the performance rating by the average time, we obtain the normal time for each work element and we add them. We next must determine allowances to compute the standard time. For the faucet-stem assembly, we assume a 5 percent personal allowance, 5 percent fatigue allowance, and 10 percent delay allowance. Therefore the total allowance is 20 percent.

The standard time for the job is then computed as

$$\text{normal time} \times (1 + \text{allowance})$$

where the allowance is expressed as a decimal. For Freeland Faucets, we have

$$\text{standard time} = (.550)(1 + .2) = .660 \text{ minutes per part.}$$

Thus, an assembler of faucet-stem assemblies can be expected to produce at a rate of 1/.660 parts per minute, or about 91 parts per hour.

Work Sampling

Work sampling is a method of randomly observing work over a period of time to obtain a distribution of the activities of an individual or of a group of employees. It can be used to determine the percentage of idle time for people or machines in a job, and also as a means of assessing nonproductive time to determine performance ratings or to establish allowances.

Work sampling is based on the binomial probability distribution, because it is concerned with the proportion of time that a certain activity occurs. The sample size for a work sampling study is found by using the formula:

$$n = \frac{(z_{\alpha/2})^2 p(1 - p)}{E^2} \qquad (9.3)$$

where p is an estimate of the population proportion of the binomial distribution. Obviously, p will never be known exactly, since it is the population parameter we are trying to estimate. We can choose a value for p from past data, a preliminary sample, or a subjective estimate. If p is difficult to determine in those ways, we can select $p = .5$, since it gives us the largest value for $p(1 - p)$ and therefore provides the largest and most conservative sample size.

Work sampling is useful for studying the content of particular jobs as a basis for selecting or justifying new equipment. It is particularly useful when the work is irregular and nonrepetitive, as is often the case with service organizations.

Example

Conducting a Work-Sampling Study

Consider the secretarial staff in a college department office. The secretaries spend their time in various ways, such as

1. Answering the telephone.
2. Typing drafts of technical papers.
3. Revising technical papers.
4. Talking to students.
5. Duplicating class handouts.
6. Other productive activities.
7. Personal time.
8. Idle periods.

Suppose a new word processor that could greatly increase productivity of typing and revising technical papers is being considered. However, the purchase of the word processor is not justified unless it is used a significant percentage of the time. To determine the percentage of time secretaries spend performing the relevant activities, we could observe them at random times and record their activities. If 100 observations are taken, we might get the results in Table 9.11. The percentage of time spent typing or revising is 21 percent + 7 percent = 28 percent.

To determine the needed sample size (that is, the number of observations), suppose we want to estimate the proportion of time spent typing to ±.05, with a 95 percent probability. We use Equation 9.3, with $E = .05$ and $z_{\alpha/2} = 1.96$. Suppose the head secretary estimates that 40 percent of the time is spent typing. This provides a value for p of .4. Then the needed sample size is

$$n = \frac{(1.96)^2(.4)(1 - .4)}{(.05)^2} = 368.79.$$

Table 9.11 Activity Frequency for Work-Sampling Study Example

Activity	Frequency
Answering the telephone	14
Typing drafts	21
Revising papers	7
Talking to students	10
Duplicating	15
Other productive activity	25
Personal	6
Idle	2
	100

Thus, at least 369 observations should be taken. If that is to be done over a one-week (40-hour) period, it represents approximately nine observations per hour (9.225, to be exact). The observations should be taken randomly when work is at a normal level (not during the winter break!).

To take a random sample, we can use the table of random digits in Appendix C. There are several ways to use random digits in deciding when to take observations. For this example, an average of 9.225 observations per hour requires the observations to be spaced, on the average $(60/9.225) = 6.5$ minutes apart. We should not take observations exactly 6.5 minutes apart, however, for then the sample would not be random. Suppose observations are between 3 and 10 minutes apart. If they are random, the average is 6.5 minutes. We can use the random digits as follows. Suppose the first observation is taken at 9:00. We choose numbers from the first row of Appendix C to find how many minutes later we should take the next observation (0 represents 10 minutes, and we discard any 1s or 2s). For instance, the first number is 6; thus we take the next observation at 9:06. The next number is 3, so the third observation is made at 9:09. We discard the 2 and take the next observation 7 minutes later, at 9:16. We see that the time required to take a random sample can be significant; that is one of the disadvantages of random sampling.

The Debate over Work Standards

Work standards have been the subject of much debate since the quality revolution began in the United States. Critics such as W. Edwards Deming have condemned work standards on the basis that they destroy intrinsic motivation in jobs and rob workers of the creativity necessary for continuous improvement. That is certainly true when managers dictate standards in an effort to meet numerical goals set up by their superiors. However, the real culprit in that case is not the standards themselves, but managerial style. The old style of managing reflects Taylor's philosophy: managers and engineers think, and workers do. A TQM-based approach suggests that empowered workers can manage their own processes with help from managers and professional staff.

Experience at NUMMI (see the "Applied P/OM" feature in Chapter 1) has shown that work standards can have very positive results when they are not imposed by dictum, but designed by the workers themselves in a continuous effort to improve productivity, quality, and skills.[13] At the old GM-Fremont plant, industrial engineers performed all methods analysis and work-measurement activities, designing jobs as they saw fit. When the industrial engineers were performing motion studies, workers would naturally slow down and make the work look harder. At NUMMI, team members learned techniques of work analysis and improvement, then timed one another with stopwatches, looking for the safest, most efficient way to do each task at a sustainable pace. They picked the best performance, broke it down to its fundamental elements, and then explored ways to improve the task. The team compared the analyses with ones from other shifts at the same work station, and wrote detailed specifications that became the work standards. Results were excellent. From a TQM perspective, this was simply an approach to reduce variability. In addition, safety and quality improved, job rotation became more effective, and flexibility increased.

P/OM in Practice

Quality Improvement through Process Selection at General Electric[14]

To counteract a declining market share in the automatic dishwasher market in the late 1970s, General Electric resolved to build a better-quality product at less cost by investing heavily in upgrading and automating its production facilities. GE spent $38 million on advanced automation technology and employee retraining programs in its Louisville, Kentucky, plant. The project incorporated advanced automation, point-of-use manufacturing, and standardized product design to reduce production costs while meeting the highest quality standards ever developed for GE dishwashers.

All new tubs and door liners are made from GE-engineered plastic that will not rust, peel, or chip. The special "Permatuf" compound is trucked to Louisville from another plant. The tubs are fabricated by injection-molding machines and delivered immediately via conveyor (an example of point-of-use manufacture) to the tub-structure area, where robots and other automated devices perform a 21-step assembly process. A similar process is used for the door liner. Parts are made only as needed, and each one is quality-checked before entering the

production and assembly process. Simplified, standardized designs further reduce production cost and help ensure consistent quality.

Automation has reduced the number of employees required in some assembly lines from 25 or 30 to two people. GE points out, however, that many of the displaced employees were retrained to perform quality audits and other necessary functions. Thus the automation resulted in upgrading many personnel as well as in improved product quality and productivity.

After the tub structure is completed, overhead conveyors transport it to a nonsynchronous assembly line, where much of the hardware is added by semiautomated equipment such as automatic screwdrivers. In a *nonsynchronous* process, the product stops at each workstation and does not move on until the employee is finished. After the operation is completed, the employee pulls a green handle overhead, which releases the product to join the queue ahead. If the operator cannot complete the job or there is a problem, she or he pulls a yellow handle and the unit is automatically transported to a repair area. If there is a major problem, a red handle can be pulled that shuts down the entire line, alerting supervisory personnel. By providing the operators with such controls, not only is product move-

ment regulated with less chance of human error, but also the quality of work is individually controlled.

Each step of the automated process is monitored by computer. If a part is not assembled properly, the system will not allow the assembly process to be completed; the unit will be sent automatically to a repair area along with a computer printout of specific repair steps needed.

As an added quality-assurance measure, each day 30 units are pulled at random from the final assembly line just before packing and subjected to extensive technical tests. A GE quality technician gives each unit a visual check and tests all operating parts and records against actual performance levels using microprocessors and digital readouts.

As a result of this project, total costs were reduced by more than 10 percent, and 78 percent fewer parts were handled, thus reducing work in process. Most importantly, product quality-improvement goals were exceeded.

Questions for Discussion

1. What was the primary reason General Electric began to update and automate its automatic dishwasher production facilities?

2. What method did GE use to reduce production costs and improve quality?

3. Did automation result in the loss of jobs?

4. Do the workers have more or less control of the production process in their new production facilities? Explain.

5. How does GE verify that the final product is meeting specifications?

Process-Technology Selection for Ohio Edison Company[15]

Ohio Edison Company is an investor-owned electric utility headquartered in northeastern Ohio. Ohio Edison and a Pennsylvania subsidiary provide electrical service to more than 2 million people. Most of the electricity is generated by coal-fired power plants. To meet evolving air-quality standards, Ohio Edison has embarked on a program to replace existing pollution-control equipment on most of its generating plants with more efficient equipment. This program to upgrade air-quality control equipment, combined with the continuing need to construct new generating plants to meet future power requirements, has resulted in a large capital-investment program. Decision analysis was applied to process-technology selection.

The flue gas emitted by coal-fired power plants contains small ash particles and sulfur dioxide (SO_2). Federal and state regulatory agencies have established emission limits for both particulates and sulfur dioxide. Recently, Ohio Edison developed a plan to comply with new air-quality standards at one of its largest power plants. The plant consists of seven coal-fired units and constitutes about one third of the generating capacity of Ohio Edison and the subsidiary company. Most of these units were constructed in the 1960s. Although all the units had initially been constructed

with equipment to control particulate emissions, the equipment was not capable of meeting the new particulate-emission requirements.

A decision had already been made to burn low-sulfur coal in four of the smaller units (units 1 through 4) at the plant to meet SO_2-emission standards. Fabric filters were to be installed on those units to control particulate emissions. Fabric filters, also known as *baghouses,* use thousands of fabric bags to filter out the particulates, functioning in much the same way as a household vacuum cleaner.

It was considered likely, although not certain, that the three larger units (units 5 through 7) at the plant would burn medium- to high-sulfur coal. A method of controlling particulate emissions at those units had not yet been selected. Preliminary studies had narrowed the choice to a decision between fabric filters and electrostatic precipitators (which remove particulates suspended in the flue gas as charged particles by passing the flue gas through a strong electric field). The decision was affected by a number of uncertainties involving

- The way some air-quality laws and regulations would be interpreted. Certain interpretations could require that either low-sulfur coal or high-sulfur Ohio coal (or neither) be burned in units 5 through 7.
- Potential future changes in air-quality laws and regulations.
- An overall plant reliability-improvement program that was underway at the plant. The outcome of the program would affect the operating costs of whichever pollution-control technology was installed in these units.
- Construction costs of the equipment, particularly since limited space at the plant site made it necessary to install the equipment on a massive bridge deck over a four-

lane highway immediately adjacent to the power plant.

- The costs associated with replacing the electrical power required to operate the particulate-control equipment.
- Various miscellaneous factors, such as potential accidents and chronic operating problems that could increase the costs of operating the generating units. The degree to which each of those factors would affect operating costs varied with the choice of technology and with the sulfur content of the coal.

A choice had to be made between two types of particulate-control equipment (fabric filters or electrostatic precipitators) for units 5 through 7. Because of the complexity of the problem, the high degree of uncertainty associated with factors affecting the decision, and the importance of the potential reliability and cost impact on Ohio Edison, decision analysis was used in the selection process.

The measure used to evaluate the outcomes of the particulate technology analysis was the annual revenue requirements for the three large units over their remaining lifetime. Revenue requirements were the monies that would have to be collected from the utility customers to recover costs resulting from the decision. They included direct costs and the costs of capital and return on investment.

A decision tree was constructed to represent the particulate-owned decision, its uncertainties, and costs. A simplified version of the tree is shown in Figure 9.20. The decision and state-of-nature nodes are indicated. Note that to conserve space, a type of shorthand notation is used. The coal-sulfur content state-of-nature node should actually be located at the end of each branch of the capital-cost state-of-nature node, as the dotted lines indicate. Each of the indicated

Figure 9.20 Simplified Particulate-Control Equipment Decision Tree

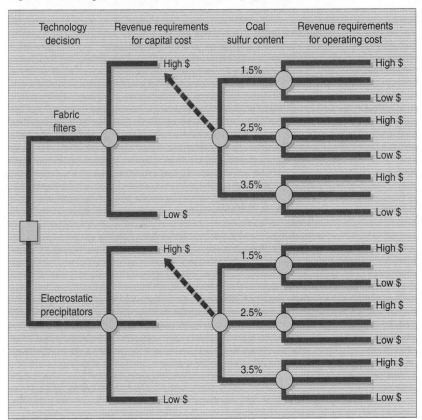

electrostatic precipitator technology than that for the fabric filters.

- ••• The fabric-filter alternative had a higher "upside risk"—that is, a higher probability of high revenue requirements—than did the precipitator alternative.

- ••• The precipitator technology had nearly an 80 percent probability of having lower annual revenue requirements than the fabric filters.

- ••• Although the capital cost of the fabric-filter equipment (the cost of installing the equipment) was lower than that for the precipitator, it was more than offset by the higher operating costs associated with the fabric filter.

These results led Ohio Edison to select the electrostatic-precipitator technology for the generating units in question. Had the decision analysis not been performed, the particulate-control decision might have been based chiefly on capital cost, a decision measure that would have favored the fabric-filter equipment. This application of decision-analysis methodology resulted in a decision that yielded both lower expected revenue requirement and lower risk.

Questions for Discussion

1. Why was decision analysis used for selecting particulate-control equipment for units 5, 6, and 7?

2. List the decision alternatives for the decision-analysis problem developed by Ohio Edison.

3. What were the benefits of using decision analysis in this application?

state-of-nature nodes actually represents several probabilistic cost models or submodels. The total revenue requirements calculated are the sum of the revenue requirements for capital and operating costs. Costs associated with these models were obtained from engineering calculations or estimates. Probabilities were obtained from existing data or the subjective assessments of knowledgeable persons.

A decision tree similar to Figure 9.20 was used to generate cumulative probability distributions for the annual revenue-requirements outcomes calculated for each of the two alternatives. Careful study of these results led to the following conclusions:

- ••• The expected value of annual revenue requirements was approximately $1 million lower for the

Summary of Key Points

••• A firm's process technology affects its ability to manufacture products that meet customer requirements and strategic goals of quality, flexibility, dependability, and cost.

••• A process is specific combination of machines, operators, work methods, materials, tools, and environmental factors that together convert inputs to outputs. Process planning is assisted by assembly drawings, parts lists, and assembly charts.

••• The major types of production processes are continuous-flow, mass (assembly-line), batch (intermittent), job-shop, and project. The types differ in production volume, variety, use of automation, labor-skill needs, machine setup requirements, and unit costs.

••• As a product moves through its life cycle, strategies must adapt. In particular, the process technology used at each stage of the life cycle must support the prevailing volume and flexibility needs.

••• Automation—the use of machines to provide power and control over the production process—is making a significant impact on productivity and quality. Elements of automation include numerically controlled machines, robotics, vision systems, and information technology. When integrated with computers, such technology leads to CAD/CAE, CAM, FMS, and CIM. Automation has also had significant impacts in all areas of the service sector.

••• While automation has improved manufacturing significantly, it has also changed the educational and skill levels required in employees in a way that has been viewed as a threat to job security.

••• Process design consists of product analysis, process analysis, process selection, and work-methods design. Various tools such as flowcharts, route sheets, flow-process charts, operation charts, multiple-activity charts, and work measurement assist process designers in their task.

••• Time study and work sampling help operations managers to estimate resource requirements, determine costs, establish wage-incentive systems, monitor worker performance, and schedule production.

Key Terms

Process
Process technology
Hard technology
Soft technology
Product-process matrix
Automation
Numerically controlled (NC)

Computer numerical control (CNC)
Robot
Machine vision systems
Bar-code technology
Electronic data interchange
Computer-aided design/computer-aided engineering (CAD/CAE)
Computer-assisted manufacturing (CAM)
Flexible manufacturing systems (FMS)
Computer-integrated manufacturing (CIM)
Bill of materials (BOM)
Assembly chart
Flow-process chart
Work center
Operation chart
Multiple-activity chart
Work measurement
Time standard
Time study
Work sampling

Review Questions

1. Define *process technology*.

2. Define a *process*.

3. Discuss the narrow and broad corporate views of process technology as proposed by Hayes and Wheelwright. Why do they advocate the broad view?

4. Distinguish between manual, mechanized, and automated process technology.

5. Explain the difference between make-to-order and make-to-stock production systems. How do operations management activities differ between these types of systems?

6. Explain the differences in continuous-flow, mass-production, batch, job-shop, and project processes.

7. What is the product-process matrix? What implications does it have for operations strategy?

8. Discuss the managerial and technical issues involved in selecting production processes.

9. How does process selection differ from equipment selection?

10. What economic and noneconomic criteria should be evaluated in selecting equipment?

11. Discuss the major factors that have made automation and advanced technology important in manufacturing and service organizations.

12. Explain the basic features of numerical control.

13. Describe a typical industrial robot. What are some common applications of robotics in manufacturing?

14. Discuss applications of vision systems in production.

15. How have automatic identification systems improved productivity and quality?

16. Explain the evolution of and differences among CAD/CAE, CAM, FMS, and CIMS.

17. Discuss the benefits and limitations of flexible manufacturing systems.

18. Explain the relative advantages and disadvantages of humans versus machines and the implications for productivity and quality.

19. Discuss the impacts of automation on the labor force.

20. What information is contained in a bill of materials?

21. What is an assembly chart?

22. What is an operation chart? How can it be used to improve work methods?

23. What information is provided in a multiple-activity chart? How can it be used to improve a process?

24. Define *time standard.* How are time standards used in P/OM?

25. Describe the procedure for developing a time study.

26. Define *work sampling.* Discuss some applications of work sampling in both manufacturing and service organizations.

Discussion Questions

1. Draw a flowchart and discuss the process you follow for
  a. Preparing to go to school or work in the morning.
  b. Studying for an exam.
  c. Shopping at a grocery store.

2. Which process—continuous-flow, mass-production, batch, job-shop, or project—would most likely be used to produce the following?
  a. Telephones
  b. Gasoline
  c. Cigarettes
  d. Air-conditioners
  e. Custom machine tools
  f. Paper
  g. Many flavors of ice cream

3. Develop a product-process matrix for these food services. Justify the location you specify for each.
  a. Fast-food restaurant
  b. Family steak house
  c. Cafeteria
  d. Traditional restaurant
  e. Classic French restaurant

4. Discuss each of these statements. What is wrong with each of them?
  a. "We've thought about computer integration of all our manufacturing functions, but when we looked at it, we realized that the labor savings wouldn't justify the cost."
  b. "We've had these computer-controlled robots on the line for several months now, and they're great! We no longer have to reconfigure the whole line to shift to a different product. I just give the robots new instructions, and they change operations. Just wait until this run is done and I'll show you."

  c. "Each of my manufacturing departments is authorized to invest in whatever technologies are necessary to perform its function more effectively. As a result, we have state-of-the-art equipment throughout our factories—from CAD/CAM to automated materials handling to robots on the line. When we're ready to migrate to a CIM environment, we can just tie all these pieces together."
  d. "I'm glad we finally got that CAD system," the designer said, a computer-generated blueprint in hand. "I was able to draw these plans and make modifications right on the computer screen in a fraction of the time it used to take by hand."
    "They tell me this new computer-aided manufacturing system will do the same for me," the manufacturing engineer replied. "I'll just punch in your specs and find out."

5. List at least one application of automation in each of these service industries:
  a. Financial services
  b. Public and government services
  c. Transportation services
  d. Health-care services
  e. Educational services
  f. Hotel and motel services

6. Find at least three new applications of automation in the service sector that are not discussed in this chapter. What impacts on productivity and quality do you think these applications have had?

7. Write a report discussing the changes resulting from automation in your own college or school of business. What advantages have the faculty and administrators seen as a result?

8. Choose some simple product, such as ball-point pen, a board game, child's toy, and so on. Prepare a bill of materials and assembly chart.

9. Interview a branch manager of a bank to find out what happens to a check written on an account in the bank. On the basis of your interview, construct a route sheet and a flow-process chart for the process.

10. Use your past experiences as a guide to construct a flowchart detailing the sequence of steps involved in each of these service operations.
  a. Cashing a check at a bank
  b. Renewing license plates
  c. Obtaining a new driver's license
  d. Filling a prescription at a pharmacy
Discuss how these operations might be analyzed or improved upon.

11. A bank is trying to decide on the best waiting-line system for its customers. As shown in Figure 9.21, the current method is to have customers wait in individual lines, whereas the proposed method is to have customers wait in one line for the next available teller.
    What operational differences are there between these systems? How might they affect customer perceptions or teller productivity? Can simulation be used to

Figure 9.21
Waiting Line
Configurations for
Discussion Question 11

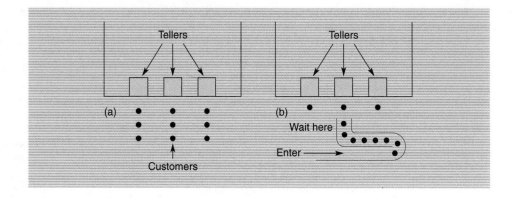

analyze these systems? What data would the bank have to collect? Why might simulation be preferable to actually trying the proposed method?

Notes

1. Michael L. Dertouzos, Richard K. Lester, Robert M. Scloco, and the MIT Commission on Industrial Productivity, *Made in America: Regaining the Productive Edge* (Cambridge, MA: The MIT Press, 1989), pp. 72, 73.

2. Robert H. Hayes and Steven C. Wheelwright, *Restoring Our Competitive Edge: Competing through Manufacturing* (New York: John Wiley & Sons, 1984).

3. Robert H. Hayes and Steven C. Wheelwright, "Link Manufacturing Process and Product Life Cycles," *Harvard Business Review,* January–February 1979, pp. 133–140. Copyright 1979 by the President and Fellows of Harvard College; all rights reserved.

4. Bela Gold, "CAM Sets New Rules for Production," *Harvard Business Review,* November–December 1982, p. 169. Copyright 1982 by the President and Fellows of Harvard College; all rights reserved.

5. Margie J. Russell, "Planning for Flexibility," *Food Engineering,* November 1992.

6. "Where Will Rolls Roll?" *Fortune,* September 6, 1993, p. 66.

7. J. Quinlan, "Those Big, Brainy Eyes," *Material Handling Engineering* 37 No. 7 (1982), pp. 74–81; and J. E. Campbell, "Machine Vision: A Reality for the 1990s," *Quality,* January 1991, pp. 36–37.

8. Stuart F. Brown, "Building Cars with Machines That See," *Popular Science,* October 1985.

9. James B. Treece, "Breaking the Chains of Command," *Business Week/The Information Revolution,* 1994, pp. 112–114.

10. Ibid.

11. Ira Sager, "The Great Equalizer," *Business Week/The Information Revolution,* 1994, pp. 100–107.

12. Bela Gold, "CAM Sets New Rules for Production," *Harvard Business Review,* November–December 1982, pp. 168–174. Copyright 1982 by the President and Fellows of Harvard College; all rights reserved.

13. Paul S. Adler, "Time-and-Motion Regained," *Harvard Business Review,* January–February 1993, pp. 97–108.

14. Adapted from Robert Waterbury, "Automated Quality," *Quality,* November 1983. Reprinted with permission from *Quality,* a Hitchcock publication.

15. The author is indebted to Thomas J. Madden and M. S. Hyrnick of Ohio Edison Company, Akron, Ohio, for providing this application.

Solved Problems

1. A production process consists of three machining operations. A robot is used to transfer parts between machines. The reliabilities of each machine are shown in Figure 9.22. How much will the reliability be improved if a used backup for machine B with a reliability of .85 is purchased?

Figure 9.22
Production Process for
Solved Problem 1

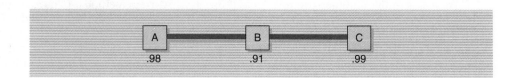

Figure 9.23
Solved Problem 1 Solution

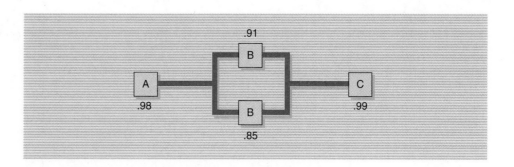

Solution

The reliability of the current system is $R = (.98)(.91)(.99) = .883$. The proposed system is shown in Figure 9.23. The reliability of the parallel system for machine B is $R = 1 - (1 - .91)(1 - .85) = .9865$. Thus, the reliability of the proposed system is $R = (.98)(.9865)(.99) = .957$. This represents an improvement of 8.4 percent.

2. A machine operator operates two machines, each of which requires loading and unloading operations. The time for each operation is given in Table 9.12.

Table 9.12 Data for Solved Problem 2

	Machine 1	**Machine 2**
Loading time	1.33 minutes	2.0 minutes
Operation time	4.00 minutes	3.3 minutes
Unloading time	1.00 minute	1.0 minute

Construct a multiple-activity chart showing the operation of the worker and the machines.

a. What is the utilization level of each machine and the worker?
b. What is the cycle time?
c. What is the output per shift.

Solution

Assume that at time 0, machine 1 is loaded and begins operating while the operator begins loading machine 2 (see Figure 9.24.).

a. Operator utilization = 10.67/13.67 = 78.05 percent.
    Machine 1 utilization = 12.67/13.67 = 92.68 percent.
    Machine 2 utilization = 12.67/13.67 = 92.68 percent.
b. Cycle time = 13.67 minutes for two pieces.
c. Output rate = eight components per hour or 70 pieces per shift from both machines.

3. In a work-sampling study a clerical worker was found to be working 2,700 times in a total of 3,000 observations made over a time span of 240 working hours. The employee's output was 1,800 forms. If a performance rating of 1.05 and an allowance of 15 percent is given, what is the standard output for this task?

Solution

Effective number of hours worked = 2700(240)/3000 = 216.
Output during this period = 1800 forms.
Actual time per form = 216(60)/1800 = 7.2 minutes or 8.33 forms per hour.
Normal time = actual time × performance rating = 7.2(1.05) = 7.56 minutes.
Standard time = 7.56(1.15) = 8.694 minutes.
Standard output = 60/8.694 = 6.9 forms per hour or 55 forms per 8-hour day.

Part Three

Figure 9.24
Solved Problem 2 Solution

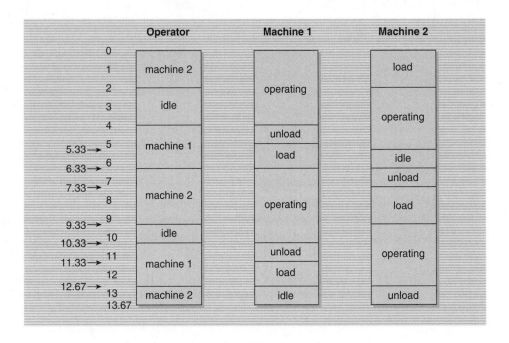

Problems

1. Given the bill of materials for an automobile brake assembly (Figure 9.25), draw an assembly chart. (The bill of materials has been drawn in such a way as to illustrate the sequence of activities in the assembly from left to right.)
2. Given the assembly chart in Figure 9.26, draw the bill of materials diagram.
3. Construct an assembly chart for this recipe (the author's original creation—try it!).

CHICKEN AND MUSHROOM MORNAY

Mornay sauce (*below*)	4 tablespoons butter
4 chicken breasts, boned and skinned	$3/4$ pound fresh mushrooms, sliced
$1/2$ teaspoon salt	pinch of thyme
$1/4$ teaspoon pepper	2 tablespoons dry white wine
flour	$1/2$ cup shredded baby Swiss cheese

Prepare Mornay sauce. While sauce is cooking, melt butter over medium heat in skillet. Salt and pepper chicken and dust lightly with flour. Saute chicken about 15 minutes until tender and lightly browned, turning once. Remove chicken to shallow baking dish and keep warm. In butter remaining in skillet, saute mushrooms with a dash of thyme 5 minutes; add wine and cook 1 minute longer. With slotted spoon, remove mushrooms to baking dish with chicken. Top with mornay sauce and grated cheese. Place under broiler 1–2 minutes until cheese melts and is bubbly. Serve with fresh egg noodles.

Mornay sauce:

1 cup milk	2 tablespoons butter
1 cup chicken broth	2 tablespoons flour
1 tablespoon minced fresh onion	$1/4$ teaspoon salt
1 tablespoon heavy cream	dash pepper
1 bay leaf	3 tablespoons grated Parmesan cheese

Bring milk and broth to a boil with the onion and bay leaf. Let stand 10 minutes. Strain. Melt butter in saucepan. Blend in flour and cook 1 minute, stirring constantly. Whisk in the milk mixture gradually, stirring until boiling. Add salt and pepper and cook 15 minutes, stirring often. Blend in cheese and cream.

4. If your state has a personal income tax, construct an assembly chart for your state income-tax return.

Figure 9.25 Bill of Materials for Problem 1

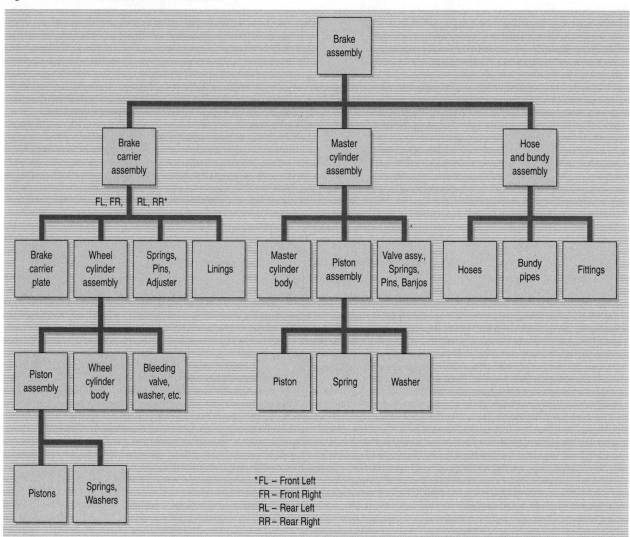

5. Suppose the supplier ratings for the Sterling Equipment Corporation example in the chapter were as shown in Table 9.13.

Table 9.13 Data for Problem 5

Factor	Supplier			
	1	*2*	*3*	*4*
Installation lead time	Poor	Average	Excellent	Good
Supplier training	Good	Poor	Excellent	Average
Productivity improvement	Average	Good	Excellent	Good
Supplier service	Average	Excellent	Good	Good
Flexibility	Good	Good	Excellent	Excellent

Would you still chose supplier 1? Why or why not?

Figure 9.26
Assembly Chart for
Problem 2

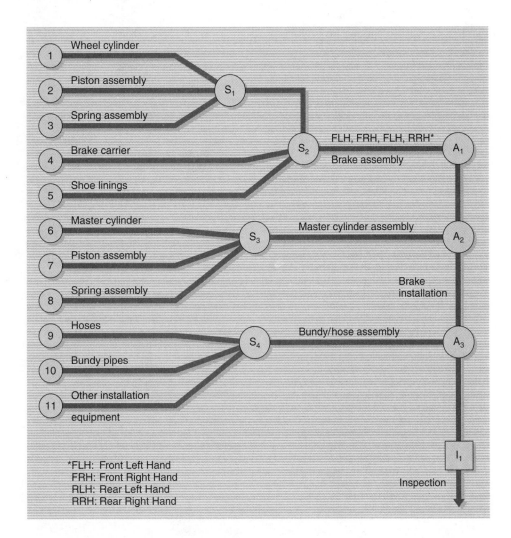

6. Phelps Petroleum Company must decide between two methods of processing oil at a refinery. Method 1 has fixed costs of $12,000 for depreciation, maintenance, and taxes, whereas the fixed costs for Method 2 are $15,000. The variable costs depend on the chemical additives used and the heating requirements. These are $.014 and $.011 per barrel for Methods 1 and 2, respectively. Which method is more economical?

7. In a complex manufacturing process, three operations are performed in series. Because of the nature of the process, machines frequently fall out of adjustment and must be repaired. To keep the system going, two identical machines are used at each operation; thus, if one fails, the other can be used while the first is repaired (see Figure 9.27).

Figure 9.27
Process Diagram for
Problem 7

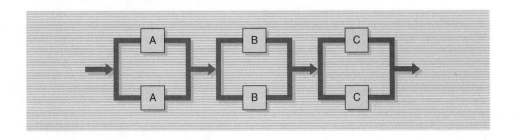

The measured reliabilities of the machines used in each operation are

Operation	A	B	C
Reliability	.60	.75	.70

a. Analyze the system reliability, assuming only one machine at each operation.

b. How much is the reliability improved by having two machines at each operation?

8. Refer to Solved Problem 1. How much would be gained by backing up all three machines? Assume that backup machines A and C have the same reliabilities.

9. You have been asked to (a) make one copy of a 100-page report and (b) copy and collate 50 copies of a four-page memo. Design efficient work methods and construct an operation chart for each task.

10. Observe someone photocopying a large volume of work at your school. Construct a multiple-activity chart for this activity. Can you suggest any methods improvements?

11. Referring to Figure 9.17, suppose the worker runs two machines that produce the same part. Develop a multiple-activity chart for this situation, trying to make the best use of both the worker's time and the machine's time.

12. For the Freeland Faucet example, develop work methods and an operation chart for the case in which the fixture used in the second method is designed to hold six subassemblies.

13. Finger Lakes Wines, Inc., is a small winery in Bluff Point, New York. Because of its relatively small volume, it uses a manual process for applying labels to filled bottles of wine. The label that appears on the front of the bottle has a picture of the winery and information about the type of the wine, its alcohol content, and so on. The label that appears on the back of the bottle describes the history of the winery and briefly describes the type of wine. Both labels must be moistened slightly before they can be applied. Design an efficient work method for applying the labels, and construct an operation chart.

14. Construct a multiple-activity chart for the case of a worker operating two machines that make similar components. The loading and unloading times are both 20 seconds, and the operating time is 45 seconds. Evaluate the utilization of the operator. What is the total output per hour?

15. Construct a multiple-activity chart for a two-machine work center with the data in Table 9.14.

Table 9.14 Data for Problem 15

Activity	Machine A	Machine B
Load	1.3 min.	.5 min.
Operate	4.0 min.	5.0 min.
Unload	.6 min.	.2 min.

One operator oversees both machines. Determine the cycle time, output per hour, and utilization of each machine and the operator.

16. What sample sizes should be used for these time studies?

a. There should be a .95 probability that the value of the sample mean is within two minutes if the standard deviation is four minutes.

b. There should be a 90 percent chance that the sample mean has an error of .10 minute or less when the variance is estimated as .50 minute.

17. Compute the number of observations required in a work-sampling study if the standard deviation is 0.2 minute and there should be a 90 percent chance that the sample mean has an error of

a. 0.15 minute

b. 0.10 minute

c. 0.005 minute

18. In a work-sampling study, what sample size should be used to provide 95 percent probability that the processing time of a single order form has an error of 0.05 minute? There is no estimate of the clerical staff's proportion of productive time.

19. Figure 9.28 shows a partially completed time-study worksheet. Determine the standard time for this operation.

20. Using a rating factor of 1.00, compute the normal time for drilling a hole in a steel plate if these are the observed times (in minutes):

.24	.25	.29	.24	.27
.25	.245	.19	.20	.23

21. Using a fatigue allowance of 20 percent, and given time-study data obtained by continuous time measurement (Table 9.15), compute the standard time.

Table 9.15 Data for Problem 21

Activity	Cycle of Observation					Performance Rating
	1	*2*	*3*	*4*	*5*	
Get casting	0.21	2.31	4.41	6.45	8.59	0.95
Fix into fixture	0.48	2.59	4.66	6.70	8.86	0.90
Drilling operation	1.52	3.65	5.66	7.74	9.90	1.00
Unload	1.73	3.83	5.91	7.96	10.10	0.95
Inspect	1.98	4.09	6.15	8.21	10.30	0.80
Replace	2.10	4.20	6.25	8.34	10.42	1.10

Figure 9.28 Time-Study Worksheet for Problem 19

Work element		Time Study Chart									Sum	Avg	Rating	Normal time
		1	2	3	4	5	6	7	8	9				
A	Cumulative time	.09	.12	.08	.11	.10	.09	.13	.12	.13			1.05	
	Element time													
B	Cumulative time	.23	.28	.21	.20	.24	.22	.26	.25	.25			1.00	
	Element time													
C	Cumulative time	.46	.49	.46	.44	.47	.47	.49	.46	.48			.90	
	Element time													
D	Cumulative time	.61	.66	.62	.59	.69	.67	.67	.66	.70			.85	
	Element time													
E	Cumulative time	.70	.74	.72	.68	.79	.80	.76	.78	.81			1.00	
	Element time													
F	Cumulative time	1.00	1.02	.98	.99	1.07	1.09	1.02	1.06	1.09			1.10	
	Element time													
													Sum	

Allowances: Personal 5%   Standard Time: _____

Fatigue 5%

Delay 5%

22. Provide the data missing from Table 9.16.

Table 9.16 Worksheet for Problem 22

Actual Time	Normal Time	Standard Time	Performance Rating	Fatigue Allowance
10.6			1.06	20%
7.8	7.2			15%
6.5		7.98	1.05	
		6.92	1.10	15%

23. A part-time employee who rolls out dough balls at MamaMia's Pizza was observed over a 40-hour period for a work-sampling study. During that time, she prepared 550 pieces of pizza dough. The analyst made 50 observations and found the employee not working four times. The overall performance rating was 1.10. The allowance for the job is 15 percent. Based on these data, what is the standard time in minutes for preparing a pizza dough?

24. How many observations should be made in a work-sampling study to obtain an estimate of the proportion of time spent changing tools by a production worker within .10 with a 99 percent probability?

25. Figure 9.29 illustrates the actual activity of a typist in the word-processing pool at T. Matthews Law Offices. The senior partner is considering the purchase of new word-processing software to reduce the time spent revising and correcting drafts. Determine the sample size required to estimate the proportion of time spent revising and correcting documents to within 10 percent with 90 percent probability. An initial estimate is that 20 percent of the typist's time is spent on this activity. Perform a work-sampling study using Figure 9.29. How do sample statistics compare with the actual proportion?

Figure 9.29
Activity Chart for
Problem 25

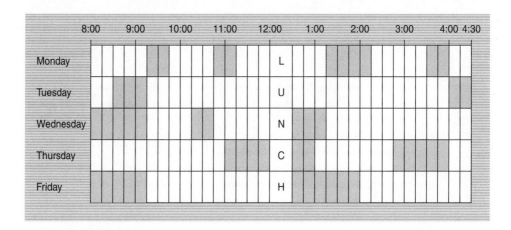

Chapter Ten
Facility Layout and Workplace Design

Chapter Outline

Applied P/OM

P/OM in Practice

The physical design of a facility and its individual workplaces can be an important factor in an organization's ability to be productive and meet its quality objectives. At MamaMia's Pizza, for instance, the kitchen must be designed to maximize the efficiency in preparing pizzas, and packaging those for take-out and delivery, particularly on busy weekend nights. Good facility layout and workplace design will add value to an organization's products and services. Some key objectives of facility-layout studies include reducing costs of handling and carrying work-in-process inventory, minimizing equipment investment, making the best use of space, and improving employee morale and team effectiveness. This chapter addresses specifically

- ••• Principal types of layout patterns that support the different types of production systems introduced in the preceding chapter.
- ••• The importance of materials handling in the design of production facilities.
- ••• Various approaches for designing facility layouts.
- ••• How assembly lines can be balanced to meet operational objectives.
- ••• The design of individual workplaces, with a particular emphasis on human factors that must be considered in promoting a safe and healthful work environment.

Facility Layout

Facility layout refers to the specific arrangement of physical facilities. The purpose of facility layout studies is to minimize delays in materials handling, maintain flexibility, use labor and space effectively, promote high employee morale, and provide for good housekeeping and maintenance. Facility-layout studies are necessary whenever (1) a new facility is constructed, (2) there is a significant change in production or throughput volume, (3) a new product is introduced, or (4) different processes and equipment are installed. They are also useful in service organizations such as libraries, hospitals, restaurants, and banks to minimize customer waiting time, maximize worker productivity, minimize customer travel time, and so on.

Applied P/OM

Sun Microsystems

Sun Microsystems improved productivity and quality through facility design.[1]

Sun Microsystems provides an illustration of the benefits that can be achieved. Founded in 1982, Sun Microsystems produces computer workstation products. Sun's manufacturing facility evolved in stages as the company grew and more capacity was needed. As a result, there was no coordinated process design. Materials, paper, and people were everywhere, often in conflicting flow patterns. Things would always get done, but primarily because of the effectiveness of the workers rather than an effective process flow. Moreover, the product mix was constantly changing. Consequently, managers decided that a new facility was needed. Some of the goals in designing the new facility were to

••• Provide flexibility to meet product changes.

••• Provide high quality through better materials handling and process flow.

••• Provide the ability to track and control materials through computerized systems.

••• Improve employee morale by providing a pleasant work environment.

The new plant increased on-time delivery performance by 50 percent and dramatically improved quality, even with a higher volume of production.

Layout Patterns

Four major layout patterns are commonly used in designing production processes: product layout, process layout, group layout, and fixed position layout.

Product Layout. Continuous-flow, mass-production, and batch-processing production processes are usually physically organized by **product layout.** That is, equipment arrangement is based on the sequence of operations performed in production, and products move in a continuous path from one department to the next. One industry that uses a product-layout pattern is the wine-making industry (see Figure 10.1).

Because all products move in the same direction, product layouts provide a smooth and logical flow of production and enable the use of specialized handling equipment. Other advantages of product layouts include small in-process inventory, short unit-production time, low degree of materials handling, low labor-skill requirements, and simple planning and production-control systems.

However, several disadvantages are associated with product layouts. For instance, a breakdown in one machine can cause an entire production line to shut

Figure 10.1
Product Layout

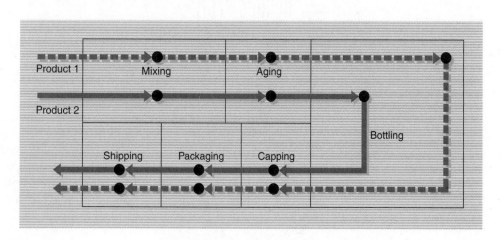

down. In addition, since the layout is determined by the product, a change in product design or the introduction of new products may require major changes in the layout; thus flexibility can be limited. Note also that the capacity of the production line is determined by the bottleneck work center. Finally, and perhaps most important, the jobs in a product-layout facility, such as those on a mass-production line, may provide little job satisfaction. This is primarily because of the high level of division of labor often required, which usually results in monotony.

Process Layout. A **process layout** consists of a functional grouping of machines or activities that do similar work. For example, all drill presses may be grouped together in one department and all milling machines in another. Depending on the processing they require, parts may be moved in different sequences among departments (see Figure 10.2). Job shops are an example of firms that use process layouts to provide flexibility in the products that can be made and the utilization of equipment and labor. Compared to product layouts, process layouts generally require a lower investment in equipment. In addition, the diversity of jobs inherent in a process layout can lead to increased worker satisfaction.

Some of the limitations of process layouts are (1) high handling and transportation costs, primarily because products must be moved frequently between departments; (2) more complicated planning and control systems, because jobs do not always flow in the same direction; (3) longer total production time, because of increased handling between departments; (4) higher in-process inventory, since jobs from several departments may arrive and wait at a particular department; and (5) higher worker-skill requirements, since workers must be able to handle the processing requirements for different orders.

Group Layout. Process layouts, which dominate batch-production facilities, result in a large number of setups for different parts, as well as high materials-handling costs and high work-in-process inventory. Mass-production systems, on the other hand, have few setups and lower handling and work-in-process costs, since all parts go through the same sequence of processes. The idea of **group technology,** or *cellular manufacturing,* is to classify parts into families so that efficient mass-production-type layouts can be designed for the families of parts.

Figure 10.2
Process Layout

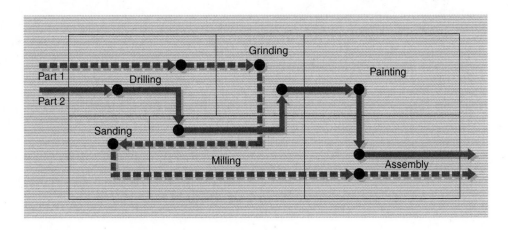

In a **group,** or **cellular, layout,** the design is not according to the functional characteristics of machines, but rather by groups of different machines (called *cells*) needed for producing families of parts. An example of a cell is shown in Figure 10.3. In this figure we see a U-shaped arrangement of machines that is typical of cellular manufacturing. Within this cell, it is easy to see the characteristics of a product layout. Materials move in a straight-line fashion from one machine to the next. Three workers are assigned to this cell. One loads incoming parts on the saw, performs final inspection, and loads the finished part for transportation out of the cell. A second worker operates the two lathes and the grinder, and a third worker operates the three milling machines.

To better understand the group-technology concept, consider a facility that produces two families of parts (Figure 10.4). Parts in the first group are cylindrical and require operations on a lathe, a milling machine, and a drilling machine. Parts in the second group are rectangular and require shearing, milling, and drilling. The traditional process layout shown in Figure 10.5 places shearing machines, lathes, milling machines, and drilling machines in separate departments. As parts from each family pass through milling and drilling departments

Figure 10.3 Schematic of a Cell Using Conventional Machine Tools

SOURCE: J. T. Black, "Cellular Manufacturing Systems Reduce Set Up Time, Make Small-Lot Production Economical." Reprinted from *Industrial Engineering* magazine, November 1983. Copyright Institute of Industrial Engineers, 25 Technology Park/Atlanta, Norcross, GA 30092.

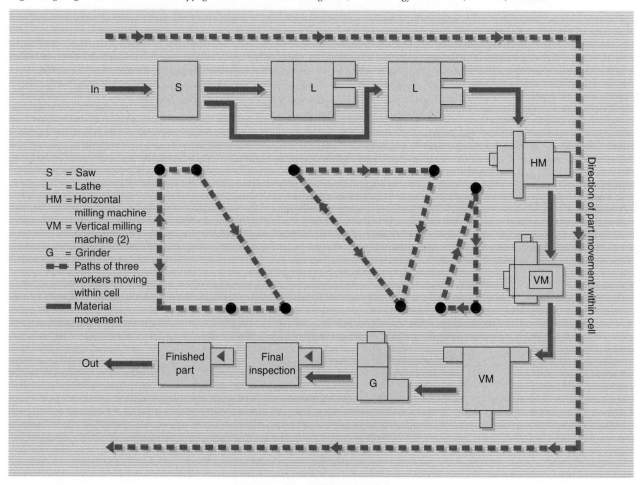

Figure 10.4
Two Part Families

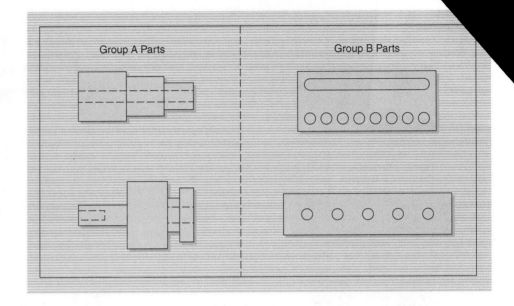

in batches, new setups on the machines must be performed. The group concept establishes a separate machine group consisting of milling and drilling machines for each part family (Figure 10.6). Since part families have similar features, retooling is much easier; hence setup times are reduced, and the system operates in the fashion of a production line. Since the work flow is standardized and centrally located in a group layout, materials-handling requirements are also reduced, enabling workers to concentrate on production rather than on moving parts between machines.

Quicker response to quality problems within cells can improve the overall level of quality. Since machines are closely linked within a cell, additional floor space becomes available for other productive uses. Because workers have greater responsibility in a cellular manufacturing system, they become more aware of their contribution to the final product; this increases their morale and satisfaction and ultimately, quality and productivity. An example at

Figure 10.5
Process Layout

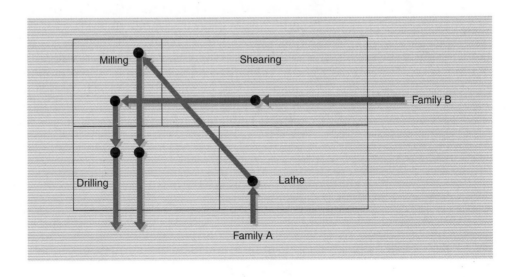

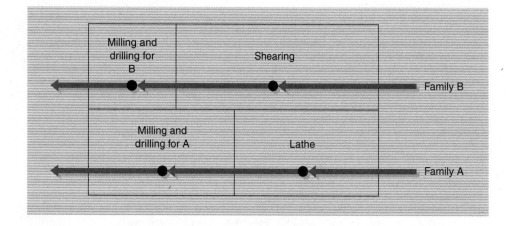

Rockwell's Dallas plant illustrates the improvements that can result from cellular manufacturing.

Applied P/OM

Rockwell International

A cellular design at Rockwell reduced throughput time by almost 90 percent.[2]

Before the cellular approach was implemented at Rockwell's Dallas plant, its job-shop arrangement was that pictured in Figure 10.7. The numbers in the squares indicate the sequence of moves throughout the shop. For example, raw stock went first to the manual mill, then to degrease, deburr, mechanical assembly, and so on. You can observe from this figure that the movement within the factory was very complex. It took a typical part 23 moves and 17.2 weeks to flow through the fabrication shop prior to assembly. This long lead time forced planners to forecast part requirements and thus created large amounts of in-process inventory. By reviewing all part designs, tooling, and fabrication methods through a group-technology part-family analysis, a cell was created that allowed parts to be made with only nine moves in 2.2 weeks; see Figure 10.8. The product movement was simplified considerably.

The impact on cost was substantial, but the major impact was on planning. The planner did not have to predict parts requirements; instead, it was possible to make parts in the fabrication shop fast enough that assembly could be supported without inventory buildup.

Fixed-Position Layout.   The construction of large items, such as heavy machine tools, airplanes, locomotives, and so on, is usually accomplished in one place. Rather than moving the item from one work center to another, tools and components are brought to one place for assembly. This **fixed-position layout**

Figure 10.7 Job-Shop Arrangement at Rockwell's Dallas Plant

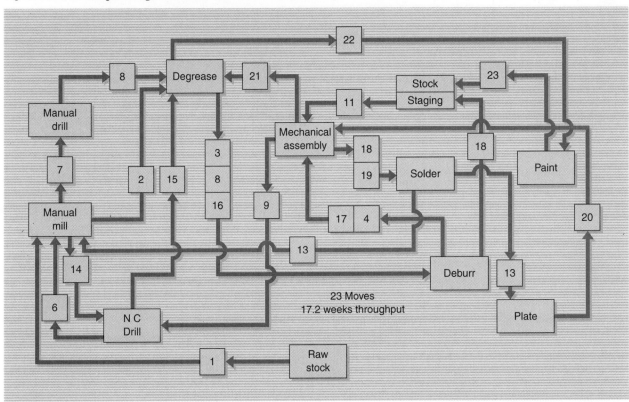

23 Moves
17.2 weeks throughput

Figure 10.8
Cellular Arrangement at
Rockwell's Dallas Plant

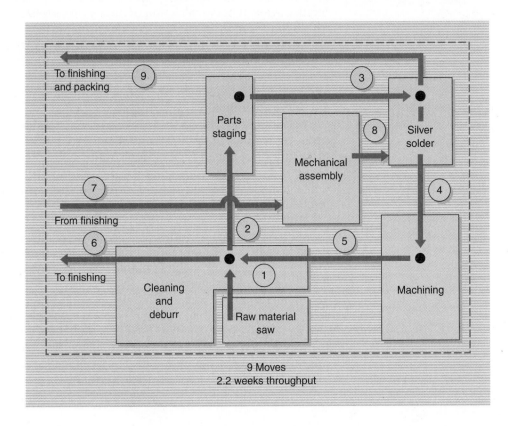

9 Moves
2.2 weeks throughput

Table 10.1 Comparison of Basic Layout Patterns

Factor	Process Layout	Product Layout	Group Layout
Amount of flexibility	High	Low	Moderate
Automation potential	Low	High	Moderate
Type of equipment	General-purpose	Highly specialized	Some specialization
Production volume	Low	High	Moderate
Equipment utilization	Low	High	Moderate
Setup costs and requirements	Low	High	Moderate

is synonymous with the "project" classification of production processes presented in Chapter 9.

Table 10.1 summarizes the relative features of process, product, and group layouts. It is clear that the basic trade-off in selecting among these layout types is flexibility versus productivity. Process layouts offer high flexibility with low productivity, while product layouts have limited flexibility with high productivity. Group layouts are designed to balance the advantages of both types.

Layout Issues in Service Organizations

In service organizations the basic trade-off between product and process layouts concerns the degree of specialization versus flexibility—as well as the productivity that is a concern for both manufacturers and service organizations. Services must consider the volume of demand, range of the types of services offered, degree of personalization of the service, skills of employees, and cost. Those that need the ability to provide a wide variety of services to customers with differing requirements usually use a process layout. For example, libraries place reference materials, serials, and microfilms into separate areas; hospitals group services by function also, such as maternity, oncology, surgery, and X-ray; and insurance companies have office layouts in which claims, underwriting, and filing are individual departments.

Service organizations that provide highly standardized services tend to use product layouts. Figure 10.9 is a product layout for the kitchen at MamaMia's Pizza kitchen. Similarly, course registration at a college or university is probably set up in a product layout, since the registration process is similar for all students. In general, whenever little variety and personalization of services is offered and the volume of demand is high, a product layout is used.

Although group layouts are less common in service organizations than in manufacturing, they are often used in offices of all types. When an office has a typist in each department rather than having a centralized typing pool, it is analogous to a group layout in manufacturing. A typing-pool arrangement exemplifies a process layout.

Some leading hospitals are challenging traditional approaches to layout and are redesigning their operations to have a higher focus on patients while also achieving higher levels of quality and efficiency.[3] Rather than shuffling patients back and forth from one functional department to another (radiology, pharmacy, physical therapy, and so on), cellular service units can be created for high-volume routine services. This "hospital-within-a-hospital" concept is sup-

Figure 10.9
Product Layout for
MamaMia's Pizza Kitchen

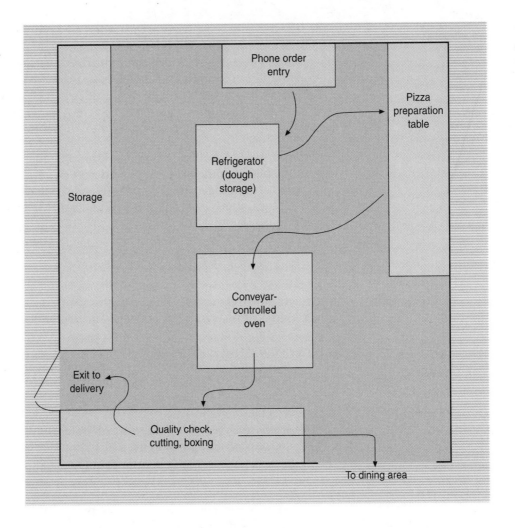

ported by multifunctional teams of healthcare providers who care for patients
during their entire stay, thus providing greater continuity of care as well as reducing scheduling problems and patient transportation requirements. For example, the establishment of a mini-laboratory for frequent, basic tests within a
service unit can produce dramatic decreases in turnaround times.

Materials-Handling Issues

Facility layout is closely linked to **materials handling,** which occurs in all
phases of production and ancillary activities. In the receiving department, materials must be unloaded from trucks and railroad cars and transported to storage or production. During manufacturing itself, materials must be transported
between departments, to and from individual workplaces, and to assembly.
Finally, the finished products must be packaged and stored for shipping. Any
layout, therefore, should support efficient materials flow. Once one knows what
needs to be moved and where it has to go, specific materials-handling equipment can be selected. Because materials-handling costs may range from 20 to
80 percent of the total production cost of a product, it is extremely important

that handling be considered in the design of manufacturing systems. Common types of materials handling-systems are described next.[4]

Industrial trucks such as forklifts are the most commonly used type of materials-handling equipment. Their primary function is maneuvering or transporting goods, and they are generally used when (1) material is moved on an infrequent basis, (2) movement occurs between many different locations, (3) loads are mixed in size and weight, and (4) most of the operations involve physical handling.

Fixed-path *conveyor systems* are more adaptable than industrial trucks to moving a high volume of items. The primary functions of conveyors are transportation and storage, and they are generally used when (1) the route does not vary, (2) continuous movement is required, and (3) automatic sorting, in-process inspection, or in-process storage is required.

Overhead *cranes* are devices fixed by supporting and guiding rails that are used to move or transfer material between points within an area. They are commonly used in operations where (1) the floor-space utilization or the product characteristics render the use of forklift trucks or conveyors undesirable, (2) travel distances and paths are reasonably restricted, and (3) the products are bulky, large, or heavy, such as engines, turbines, machine tools, and many aerospace components.

Automated storage and retrieval systems are high-technology materials-handling or storage configurations that usually involve computer control, unit loads, and digital computer interface/control. They are becoming increasingly popular because of small floor-space requirements, although the capital investment is usually significant.

Tractor-trailer systems pull a train of trailers or load-carrying platforms. They offer the advantages of being able to move large volumes of bulky or heavy material over long distances and not tying up lift trucks, which are primarily used for stacking, loading, and unloading.

Automated guided vehicles (AGVs) are computer-controlled, driverless vehicles guided by wires embedded in the shop floor. Such systems are useful in transporting loads over medium to long distances and are more cost-effective than using forklift trucks with skilled operators.

A variety of materials-handling equipment is used throughout a plant. In the receiving and shipping activities, forklift trucks, cranes, hoists, and portable conveyors are most often used for unloading transport vehicles and moving goods to temporary storage. In storage areas and warehouses, forklift trucks are often used to store and retrieve heavy loads. In more sophisticated, high-volume operations, automated storage and retrieval systems are used. Material movement in assembly-line systems is often accomplished with conveyors. Production lines and facility layout are more effective if materials-handling considerations are integrated into the design. The key is to examine the *total cost* of manufacturing, not simply the costs of the equipment alone.

Design of Product Layouts

Continuous-flow, assembly-line, and many batch-processing production processes are all forms of a **production line,** which can be defined as a fixed sequence of production stages, each consisting of one or more machines or work-

Figure 10.10
Product-Layout Design
Options

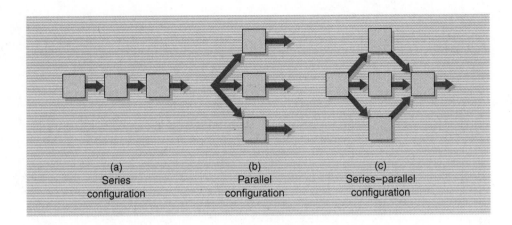

(a)
Series
configuration

(b)
Parallel
configuration

(c)
Series–parallel
configuration

stations. Many alternative configurations are possible for production lines, along with a wide variety of materials-handling equipment. It is a challenge to determine the optimum configurations of operators and *buffers* (queues of work-in-process). Product layouts might have workstations in series, in parallel, or in a combination of both (Figure 10.10). A major design consideration for production lines is to assign operations so that all stages are more or less equally loaded. Consider, for instance, the traditional conveyor-paced production line illustrated in Figure 10.11. In this example, parts move along a conveyor at a rate of one part per minute to three work centers, and each work center performs one of three required operations. The first operation requires 3 minutes per unit; the second, 1 minute; and the third, 2 minutes. The first work center consists of three operators; the second, one operator; and the third, two operators.

The assigned location where a worker performs his or her job is called a *workstation;* it could be a machine or a work bench, for example. In Figure 10.11, a worker removes a part from the conveyor and performs some task at his or her workstation. The completed part is returned to the conveyor and transported to the next work center. The number of workers at each work center was chosen to make the line *balanced.* Since three operators work simultaneously at the first work center, on the average one part will be completed each minute. The same is true for the other work centers. The parts arrive at a rate of one per minute, and parts are completed at that rate.

Conveyor-paced production lines such as this work well when there is a low variance in times required to perform the individual operations. If the operations

Figure 10.11
Traditional Conveyor-Paced
Assembly Line

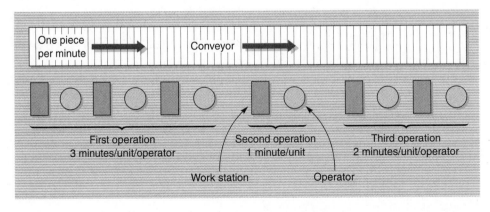

Figure 10.12
Unpaced Assembly Line
with Buffers

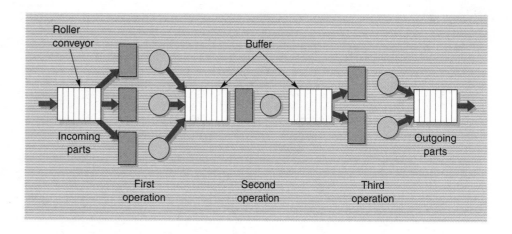

are somewhat complex, which usually results in higher time variance, operators down the line may not be able to keep up with the flow of parts from the preceding work center or may have excessive idle time. In addition, conveyor-paced lines provide no worker control, they are monotonous, and they offer little social interaction. Workers do not identify with the product, and negative behavioral consequences—and quality problems—often result. An alternative is to use unpaced production lines in which work centers are linked by gravity conveyors (which cause parts to simply roll to the end and stop). These act as buffers between the successive operations and eliminate pacing of work tasks. An example is shown in Figure 10.12. These provide more worker autonomy and less feeling of being under "control" of mechanization.

In unpaced production lines, however, there are two sources of delay: flow-blocking delay, and lack-of-work delay. **Flow-blocking delay** occurs when a work center completes a unit but cannot release it because the in-process storage at the next stage is full. The operator must remain idle until storage space becomes available. **Lack-of-work delay** occurs whenever one stage completes work and no units from the previous stage are awaiting processing.

Determining an optimal production-line configuration is a complex task that is often assisted by computer simulation (see Supplementary Chapter A). Queueing, or waiting-line, theory is another tool that is often used to analyze production lines and other systems where arrivals and service rates are random (see Supplementary Chapter C). The following example shows how waiting-line analysis can be used to compare alternative designs.

Example

Waiting-Line Analysis for Service-System Design

A fast-food franchise has a drive-up window. Customers place their orders at an intercom station at the back of the parking lot and then pull up to the service window. Cars arrive at an average rate of 24 per hour. Currently only one employee takes and fills all drive-up orders, and the average service time is 2 minutes. The company is considering two alternatives: hiring a second person in order to reduce the time required to service the customers (average service time can be reduced to 75 seconds), or installing a second drive-up window in paral-

Figure 10.13 Waiting-Line Analysis Results for Single-Channel System with One Employee

	A	B	C	D	E	F	G	H	I
1	Single Channel Queueing Model								
2									
3	Lambda	24							
4	Mu	30							
5									
6	Probability system is empty	0.200							
7	Average number in queue	3.200							
8	Average number in system	4.000							
9	Average time in queue	0.133							
10	Average waiting time in system	0.167							
11	Probability arrival has to wait	0.800							
12									

Figure 10.14 Waiting-Line Analysis for Single-Channel System with Two Employees

	A	B	C	D	E	F	G	H
1	Single Channel Queueing Model							
2								
3	Lambda	24						
4	Mu	48						
5								
6	Probability system is empty	0.500						
7	Average number in queue	0.500						
8	Average number in system	1.000						
9	Average time in queue	0.021						
10	Average waiting time in system	0.042						
11	Probability arrival has to wait	0.500						
12								

lel with the first and stationing a second employee at that window. What improvements would each alternative make in customer service?

If we assume that arrivals are Poisson-distributed and that service times follow an exponential distribution (see Supplementary Chapter C), we can compute the operating characteristics of each system using elementary waiting-line formulas. Using the spreadsheets in Supplementary Chapter C, we obtain the following results.

1. For the current system, consisting of a single channel with a mean arrival rate of 24 cars/hour and a mean service rate of 30 cars/hour, we have the results shown in Figure 10.13.

2. For the two-person system (still a single-channel system, but with a mean service rate of 48 cars/hour), we have the results shown in Figure 10.14.

3. For a multiple–channel system with a single employee in each, we have the results shown in Figure 10.15.

We see that both alternatives significantly reduce the average number of cars in the system and the waiting line as well as the average waiting time. Managers could use this information to perform more-detailed economic analyses of the two alternatives. What would you do next?

Figure 10.15 Waiting-Line Analysis Results for Multiple-Channel System with One Employee

	A	B	C	D	E	F	G	H	I
1	Multiple Server Queueing Model								
2									
3	Lambda	24							
4	Mu	30							
5	Number of servers	2	3	4					
6									
7	Probability system is empty	0.429	0.447	0.449					
8	Average number in queue	0.152	0.019	0.002					
9	Average number in system	0.952	0.819	0.802					
10	Average time in queue	0.006	0.001	0.000					
11	Average waiting time in system	0.040	0.034	0.033					
12	Probability arrival must wait	0.229	0.052	0.010					
13									

Assembly-Line Balancing

Conveyor-paced production lines are commonly used for manual assembly tasks. Because of their importance and widespread use, this subsection discusses the topic of balancing assembly lines. In the example shown in Figure 10.11, workers are allocated to three operations such that the line is perfectly balanced. That is, each work center has the same amount of work per operator per unit of time. In real situations, though, such allocation is seldom possible, and assembly-line balancing can be a complex task.

To begin, we need to know the set of operations to be performed and *precedence relations* among the operations—that is, the sequence in which operations must be performed. This information can be obtained from an assembly chart, which was introduced in Chapter 9. In addition, each operation takes a certain amount of time. For example, consider the simple three-operation assembly line shown in Figure 10.16. Operation A is first, takes .5 minute, and must be completed before operation B can be performed. After operation B, which takes .3 minute, is finished, operation C can be performed; it takes .2 minute. Since all three operations must be performed to complete one part, the total time required to complete one part is .5 + .3 + .2 = 1.0 minute. Thus, in an eight-hour day, if we assume 90 percent efficiency to account for rest breaks and other delays, a production system in which one operator performs all three operations in sequence could produce

(1 part/1 min)(60 minutes per hour)(8 hours per day)(.9 efficiency) = 432 parts/day.

As an alternative to a one-operator production system, suppose three operators work on the line, each performing one of the three operations. The first operator can produce 120 parts per hour, since his or her task time is .5 minute. Thus, a total of

(1 part/.5 min)(60 minutes per hour)(8 hours per day)(.9 efficiency) = 864 parts/day

Figure 10.16
Three-Task Assembly-Line
Balancing Problem

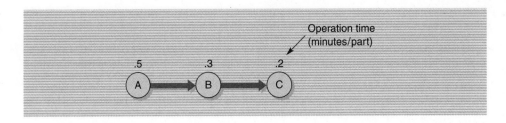

could be sent to operator 2. Since the time operator 2 needs for his or her operation is only .3 minute, he or she could produce

(1 part/.3 min)(60 minutes per hour)(8 hours per day)(.9 efficiency) = 1,440 parts/day.

However, operator 2 cannot do so because the first operator has a lower production rate. This is an example of *lack-of-work delay.* Even though the third operator can produce

(1 part/.2 min)(60 minutes per hour)(8 hours per day)(.9 efficiency) = 2,160 parts/day,

we see that the maximum output of this three-operator assembly line is 864 parts per day.

A third alternative is to use two workstations. The first operator could perform operation A while the second performs operations B and C. Since each operator needs .5 minutes to perform the assigned duties, the line is in perfect balance, and 864 parts per day can be produced. We can achieve the same output rate with two operators as we can with three, thus saving labor costs.

The objective of assembly-line balancing is to assign tasks to individual workstations along the line to minimize the imbalance among workstations while satisfying precedence constraints and achieving the desired output rate. Typically, one either minimizes the number of work centers for a given production rate or maximizes the production rate for a given number of workstations.

An important concept in assembly-line balancing is the **cycle time**—the interval between successive parts coming off the assembly line. In the three-operation example shown in Figure 10.16, if we use only one workstation, the cycle time is 1 minute; that is, one completed assembly is produced every minute. If two workstations are used, as just described, the cycle time is .5 minute. Finally, if three workstations are used, the cycle time is still .5 minute, because task A is the bottleneck, or slowest operation. The line can produce only one assembly every .5 minute.

The cycle time (C) cannot be smaller than the largest operation time, nor can it be larger than the sum of all operation times. Thus,

$$\text{maximum operation time} \leq C \leq \text{sum of operation times}. \qquad (10.1)$$

This provides a range of feasible cycle times. In our example, $.5 \leq C \leq 1.0$.

If H minutes are available per shift, then the minimum and maximum output that can be achieved is computed by

$$\text{minimum output} = H/\text{maximum cycle time} \qquad (10.2)$$

$$\text{maximum output} = H/\text{minimum cycle time.} \qquad (10.3)$$

In our example, suppose we have H = (8 hours) (60 minutes/hour)(.9 efficiency) = 432 productive minutes available per shift. Then,

$$\text{minimum output} = 432/1.0 = 432 \text{ parts/shift}$$

$$\text{maximum output} = 432/.5 = 864 \text{ parts/shift.}$$

In general, if C is the cycle time in minutes and H is the number of productive minutes available per shift, the number of parts that can be produced during the shift is given by

$$\text{output} = H/C. \qquad (10.4)$$

Thus, to produce at least P parts per shift, H/C must be greater than or equal to P. Solving the inequality $H/C \geq P$, we find that to produce at an output rate of P, C must be no greater than H/P, or

$$C \leq H/P. \qquad (10.5)$$

This provides an additional constraint on the feasible cycle time. For example, to produce at least 600 units per shift, the cycle time must be no greater than $432/600 = 0.72$. This means that the one-station assembly line cannot meet the required production; either the two-station or the three-station design must be used.

We may also compute the *minimum number of workstations* that are required using this formula:

$$\text{minimum number of workstations} = P \times (\text{sum of task times})/H. \qquad (10.6)$$

Thus, to produce 600 units per shift in 432 minutes, we need at least

$$\frac{600(1.0)}{432} = 1.38$$

workstations. Obviously, this value must be rounded up to 2.

Suppose we decide to use the three-station configuration in which each task is assigned to a different worker. We see that for each cycle of .5 minute, station A is always busy, but station B is busy only $.3/.5 = .6$, or 60 percent of the time. Similarly, station C is busy only $.2/.5$, or 40 percent of the time. The idle time at each station is equal to the cycle time minus the sum of all the operation times assigned to that station. Thus stations B and C are idle .2 and .3 minute per cycle, respectively. We may compute the *efficiency* of the entire line using this formula:

$$\text{line efficiency} = \frac{\text{sum of all operation times}}{(\text{cycle time})(\text{number of workstations})}. \qquad (10.7)$$

For this example, we have

$$\text{line efficiency} = \frac{1.0}{(.5)(3)} = \frac{1.0}{1.5} = .67 \text{ or } 67 \text{ percent.}$$

This tells us that only 67 percent of the available productive capacity is utilized, or equivalently, that the workers will be idle 33 percent of the time on average because of imbalance of the line. One objective of assembly-line balancing is to maximize the line efficiency.

When the number of possible workstation configurations is very large, these balancing problems are very complex. A procedure is needed for assigning operations to workstations in a systematic manner. One algorithm for assembly-line balancing is:[5]

1. Determine the cycle time required to meet production quotas.
2. Construct a precedence network for the balancing problem.
3. Choose a set of assignable operations consisting of all unassigned operations for which all immediate predecessors have already been assigned.
4. Assign either the operation with the *smallest time first* or the operation with the *largest time first* to a workstation if the cycle time would not be exceeded. Break ties by choosing the lowest operation number. Construct a new set of assignable candidates. If no further operations can be assigned, move on to the next workstation. Continue in this way until all operations have been assigned.

This technique is illustrated with an example.

Example

Balancing an In-Line Skate Assembly Line

Look back at Figure 9.7 in the preceding chapter, the assembly chart for an in-line skate. That figure defines eight operations to be performed during the assembly process:

1. Assemble wheels, bearings, and axle hardware (SA-1).
2. Assemble brake housing and pad (SA-2).
3. Complete wheel assembly (A-1).
4. Inspect wheel assembly.
5. Assemble boot (SA-3).
6. Join boot and wheel subassemblies (A-2).
7. Add liner (A-3).
8. Perform final inspection.

We can represent the precedence relations of these eight operations as prescribed in the assembly chart by the network in Figure 10.17. For example, the network shows that operations 1 and 2 must be completed before operation 3 is performed; similarly, operation 3 must precede operation 4. The numbers next to each operation represent the time needed to complete it.

Figure 10.17 Assembly Line Precedence Network and Feasible Workstation Assignment

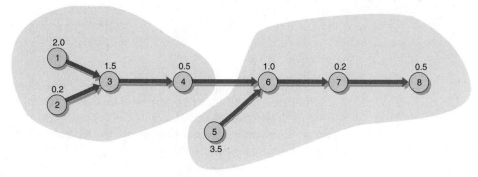

In designing an assembly line for this product, we might assign operations 1, 2, 3, and 4 to one workstation, and operations 5, 6, 7, and 8 to a second as shown in Figure 10.17. However, we could not assign operations 1, 2, 3, 4, and 6 to workstation 1 and operations 5, 7, and 8 to workstation 2, since operation 5 must precede operation 6. If we use only one workstation, the cycle time is 9.4 minutes—the sum of all the processing times. If each operation is assigned to one station, the cycle time is 3.5, the largest operation time. Thus, feasible cycle times must be between 3.5 and 9.4 minutes.

For this example, let us suppose that an output rate of 360 units per week is desired. Operating one shift per day for five days per week amounts to 72 units per shift. Note that at 90 percent efficiency, (.9)(8) = 7.2 productive hours are available; thus, the required cycle time is

$$C = \frac{(7.2 \text{ hours / shift})(60 \text{ minutes / hour})}{72 \text{ units / shift}} = 6.0 \text{ minutes / unit}$$

The problem is to assign operations to workstations without violating precedences or exceeding the cycle time of 6.0. We proceed as follows. Start with station 1 and determine which operations can be assigned. In this case, operations 1, 2, and 5, are candidates, since they have no immediate predecessors. We need some rule for choosing among them. Various rules can be used, and each may result in a different solution. We will arbitrarily assign elements using the rule, *choose the operation with the largest time first.* We therefore assign operation 5 to station 1.

Next, we determine a new set of operations that may be considered for assignment. In general, this set consists of all unassigned operations for which all immediately preceding operations have been assigned. Since operation 4 has not yet been assigned, operation 6 cannot be a candidate. Hence only operations 1 and 2 can be considered at this time. We can assign both operations 1 and 2 to workstation 1 without violating the cycle time restriction. At this point operation 3 becomes the only candidate for assignment. Since the total time for operations 5, 1, and 2 is 5.7 minutes, we cannot assign operation 3 to station 1 without violating the cycle time restriction. In this case, we move on to workstation 2.

At workstation 2, we can assign operations 3, 4, 6, 7, and 8 and still be within the cycle time limit. The final solution is summarized in Table 10.2. We compute the line efficiency as

Table 10.2 Solution to Assembly-Line Balancing Problem

Station	Operations Assigned	Total Operation Time	Idle Time
1	1, 2, 5	5.7	.3
2	3, 4, 6, 7, 8	3.7	2.3
	Totals	9.4 min.	2.6 min.

$$\text{Line efficiency} = \frac{\text{sum of all operation times}}{(\text{cycle time})(\text{number of workstations})}$$

$$= \frac{9.4}{(6.0)(2)} = .78.$$

In the real world, assembly-line balancing is much more complicated.[6] In practice, work-element assignments are often constrained by mechanization or tooling. Fixed equipment such as hard-tooled robot stations cannot be moved without incurring significant expense. In addition, the work is allocated to distribute balance losses over the length of the line, thus providing some balance delay, or "free time," to each worker. In today's industry there is virtually no such thing as a single-model assembly line. In the automotive industry, almost an infinite number of model combinations and work assignments exist. Such mixed-model assembly-line balancing is considerably more difficult to achieve. Good information systems are needed here to ensure that the correct parts are available and that workers know the proper procedures for the specific model being assembled. Some systems provide computer-based workstations that guide workers through the proper steps as different models flow down the line.

Issues in Designing Product Layouts

The choice of paced versus non-paced assembly lines presents some important issues for operations managers. Unpaced lines provide inventory buffers between operations. They can reduce any problems that might be caused by equipment failure or disruptions at workstations; however, they may also increase complacency about quality since a bad part can always be replaced by a good one. In addition, they increase space requirements and costs. Paced lines, in contrast, are extremely vulnerable to breakdowns or poor-quality components being used. However, they can stimulate better quality overall, because a supply of poor-quality components would lead to frequent line stoppages (or a lot of rework or returns). This has been a driving force behind the production systems used by Japanese manufacturers. Recently, however, companies like Toyota have been putting buffers in their systems, primarily because the large numbers of models in their mixed-model lines have made work so complicated that it has become easy to make mistakes.

Paced lines can have a negative behavioral effect on workers, resulting in absenteeism and high turnover. Low job satisfaction often results from monotonous work required by fast cycle times. Although the job-enrichment efforts discussed in Chapter 5 a help ameliorate such problems with paced lines, workers still generally prefer unpaced lines. Automation often provides a better answer than paced lines for assembly operations that require fast cycle times. In situations where that is not possible or desirable, of course, team and participatory (job-enrichment) efforts can significantly improve the human aspects of the jobs. It is wise to empower employees on these assembly lines so that they have the authority to stop the production line if problems arise.

As product designs change, companies must rebalance assembly lines. It is not unusual for Japanese automobile manufacturers to rebalance their lines once per month on average. In the United States, this is done only about three times each year. Rebalancing a line requires redesigning jobs and retraining workers, and may even necessitate a new facilities configuration. Such rebalancing may be necessitated by changes in the desired output rate as customer demand changes. In the short term—to avoid rebalancing—managers might use overtime or extra shifts as options to accommodate changing demand or allow inventory or back orders to accumulate.

Design of Process Layouts

In designing process layouts, we are concerned with the arrangement of departments relative to each other. Materials-handling cost is usually the principal design criterion for new layouts. In general, departments with a large number of moves between them should be located close to one another. To provide a quantitative basis for layout analysis, we need to construct a load matrix. A **load matrix** lists the number of moves from one department to another over some time period, such as one year. That information can be obtained from process routings and planned production schedules.

The handling cost is generally proportional to the distance traveled and the type of equipment used. For example, the cost of transporting materials by forklift truck is higher than that of using a conveyor because of higher capital investment, maintenance, and labor costs. We assume that the movement of all materials takes place by forklift so that cost will simply be proportional to distance. In general, a wide variety of materials-handling equipment can be chosen. The most effective layout-planning methods attempt to integrate the materials-handling selection decision with the layout itself. However, such a discussion is beyond the scope of this book.

Since the distance traveled depends on the layout, we use the following approach:

1. Design a trial layout.
2. Compute the distances between departments.
3. Multiply interdepartmental distances by the volume of flow between departments to create a volume-distance matrix; then compute the total cost.
4. Use the volume-distance matrix created in Step 3 to propose changes in the current layout. Repeat the process (from Step 2) until a satisfactory layout is obtained.

An example of applying this approach follows.

Designing a Process Layout

Consider the situation facing Home Video Equipment, Inc. (HVE), a California company that produces video recording equipment. Increasing sales volume and new product lines have necessitated building a new plant to provide more effective distribution to the eastern United States. HVE must determine how the eight departments needed to produce the video recorders should be laid out. Estimated space needed in each department is as follows:

1. Receiving	1,200 square feet
2. Machining	1,800 square feet
3. Pressing	2,400 square feet
4. Cleaning	600 square feet
5. Plating	1,200 square feet
6. Painting	900 square feet
7. Assembly	2,400 square feet
8. Shipping	1,500 square feet

Table 10.3 shows the annual number of moves between departments. For example, the number of moves from receiving to machining is 200, the number of moves from painting to assembly is 300, and so on. The table indicates that materials move from receiving to either machining or pressing; from machining to plating, painting, or assembly, and so on. From this information, we can draw a flowchart showing the material movement between departments.

Figure 10.18 shows that the general direction of material flow is from receiving to machining and pressing and then to cleaning, plating, and painting, and finally to assembly and shipping. Using this information, we propose the initial layout shown in Figure 10.19. Remember that this layout is just a rough approximation of the relative shapes and sizes of departments. Detailed architectural designs must account for aisles, support pillars, office space, restrooms, and other service facilities. To compute interdepartmental distances, we shall assume that all transportation is between department centers (shown by • in Figure 10.19) and along the coordinate axes. That is, if Departments A and B are centered at coordinates (x_A, y_A) and (x_B, y_B), respectively, the distance between them is

$$d_{AB} = |x_A - x_B| + |y_A - y_B|.$$

Table 10.3 Load Matrix for HVE, Inc.

From	To							
	Receiving	*Machining*	*Pressing*	*Cleaning*	*Plating*	*Painting*	*Assembly*	*Shipping*
Receiving		200	100					
Machining					350	60	20	
Pressing		150		200	100		250	
Cleaning					500		200	
Plating						50	400	
Painting							300	
Assembly								600

Figure 10.18 Material Flow for HVE, Inc.

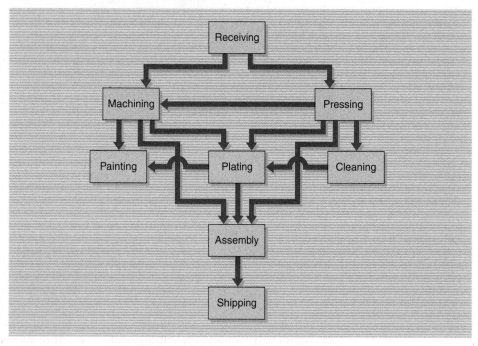

This is most often the case when moving items with trucks along aisles. For this layout, the distance between receiving and storage, whose center is at the point (5.5, 8), and pressing, whose center is at the point (2, 6), is

$$|5.5 - 2| + |8 - 6| = 3.5 + 2 = 5.5.$$

Note that the actual distance is 55 feet because of the scale used. The other interdepartmental distances are computed in a similar fashion. If those distances

Figure 10.19 Initial Layout (Each block represents 10 feet × 10 feet.)

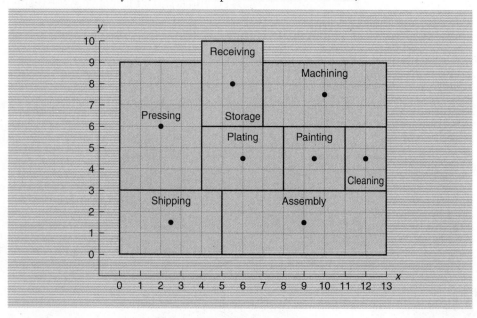

Table 10.4 Volume-Distance Matrix for Initial Layout

From	Receiving	Machining	Pressing	Cleaning	Plating	Painting	Assembly	Shipping
				To				
Receiving		10,000	5,500					
Machining					24,500	1,800	1,400	
Pressing		14,250		23,000	5,500		28,750	
Cleaning					30,000		12,000	
Plating						2,000	24,000	
Painting							12,000	
Assembly								39,000

Significant potential for improvement

Total volume-distance = 251,700

are multiplied by the volume requirements in Table 10.3, we obtain the volume-distance matrix shown in Table 10.4. For example, multiplying the load between receiving and pressing (100) by the distance between the departments (55) yields a volume-distance figure of 5,500, as shown in Table 10.4. Since cost is assumed to be proportional to distance, the volume moved times the distance moved is a surrogate measure of cost.

From this table, we see that the largest costs involve transportation between assembly and shipping, pressing and assembly, and cleaning and plating. The initial layout has other disadvantages. For instance, receiving and shipping are on opposite sides of the building. This can cause a problem if rail is used and might also cause problems in constructing access roads. A second proposal, which places these departments on the same side of the building, is shown in Figure 10.20. You should verify that the total volume-distance for this layout is 214,550, which represents a 15 percent reduction over the initial layout. This was gained by moving cleaning adjacent to plating and pressing closer

Figure 10.20 Second Proposed Layout

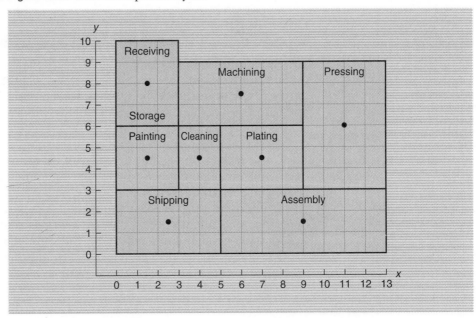

Figure 10.21   Third Proposed Layout

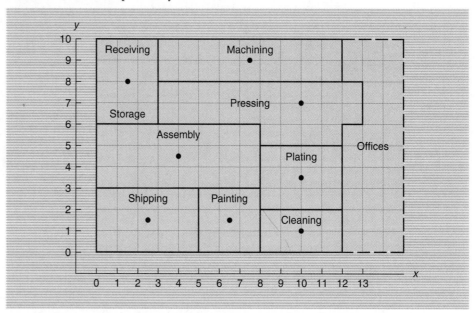

to assembly. However, there is still a high cost involved in moving materials from painting to assembly and from assembly to shipping. In an effort to reduce this cost, a third alternative, shown in Figure 10.21, was proposed.

This layout has a total volume-distance requirement of 183,650. The basic shapes of the machining and pressing departments have been altered considerably. Shape requirements depend on machine sizes and processing requirements to a large extent and must be taken into account prior to a layout analysis. In addition, office space can be provided on the opposite end of the building from shipping and receiving; thus the building can maintain a rectangular shape.

Computerized Layout Planning

The HVE example illustrates that there are a large number of alternative configurations for a process layout. In fact, there are $n!$ possible arrangements of n departments, irrespective of shape. Thus, for the Home Video Equipment example there are $8! = 40,320$ possible arrangements, which makes finding the best possible layout an extremely difficult task. Several computer packages have been written expressly for facility layout.

These packages have the advantage of being able to search among a much larger number of potential layouts than could possibly be done manually. Despite the capabilities of the computer, no layout program will provide optimal solutions for large, realistic problems. Like many practical solution procedures in management science, they are *heuristic;* that is, they can help the user to find a very good, but not necessarily the optimal, solution.

One of the most widely used facility-layout programs is **CRAFT** (Computerized Relative Allocation of Facilities Technique). CRAFT attempts to minimize

Figure 10.22 CRAFT Logic

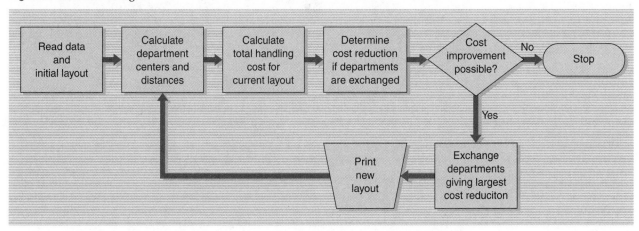

the total materials-handling cost in a manner similar to the approach used in the HVE example. The user must generate an initial layout and provide data on the volume between departments and the materials-handling costs. CRAFT uses the centroid of each department to compute distances and materials-handling costs for a particular layout. In an effort to improve the current solution, CRAFT exchanges two (in later versions, three) departments at a time and determines if the total cost has been reduced. If so, it then uses the new solution as a base for determining new potential improvements. A flowchart describing this procedure is given in Figure 10.22. An example of typical output from CRAFT is plotted with block letters, as shown in Figure 10.23. In this figure, each row or column represents 10 feet, and each letter corresponds to a different department. Thus Department A is 20 × 60, Department B is 30 × 60, and so on.

Other programs that have been used in facilities layout are ALDEP (Automated Layout-DEsign Program) and CORELAP (COmputerized RElationship LAyout Planning). Rather than using materials-handling costs as the primary solution, the user constructs a preference table that specifies how important it is for two departments to be close to one another. These "closeness" ratings follow.

A   Absolutely necessary
B   Especially important
C   Important
D   Ordinary closeness okay
E   Unimportant
F   Undesirable

The programs attempt to optimize the total closeness rating of the layout.

Computer graphics is providing a major advance in layout planning. It allows interactive design of layouts in real time and can eliminate some of the disadvantages, such as irregularly shaped departments, that often result from noninteractive computer packages. Graphics programs also allow more details to be incorporated in the process-layout planning effort. Aisles, obstructions, and individual machine arrangement can be considered in interactive graphics programs.

Figure 10.23
Typical CRAFT Layout

	1	2	3	4	5	6	7	8	9	10	11	12
1	A	A	A	A	A	A	B	B	B	B	B	B
2	A	A	A	A	A	A	B					B
3	C	C	C	C	C	C	B	B	B	B	B	B
4	C					C	E	E	E	D	D	D
5	C					C	E		E	D	D	D
6	C	C	C	C	C	C	E		E	F	F	F
7	H	H	H	H	H	H	E	E	E	F		F
8	H					H	H	H	H	F	F	F
9	H	H	H	H	H	H	H	H	H	G	G	G
10	G	G	G	G	G	G	G	G	G	G	G	G

Design of Group Layouts[7]

The design of group layouts involves three steps: selection of part families, selection of machine groupings or cells, and detailed arrangement of the cells. Selecting part families involves grouping parts whose processing requirements are similar. Several sophisticated methods are used to group parts; only the basic concepts are illustrated in the following example.

Example

Selecting Part Families and Machine Groups in Cellular Manufacturing

Let us consider the collection of parts shown in Figure 10.24. Table 10.5 gives the different processing operations that are required for each part, and indicates that several parts have identical processing requirements. It would be logical to group those into one part family. You should verify that the following part families have identical processing requirements.

Part Family	Parts	Processing Requirements
1	a, f, l	Polish, grind, cut
2	c, e, o	Mill, grind, cut
3	b, d, g	Stamp, grind, cut
4	m, n	Drill, grind, cut
5	h, k	Drill, turn
6	j	Turn, mill
7	i	Drill, turn, mill

These seven part families could be used to define seven cells for a group layout. For example, cell 1 would consist of a polishing machine, grinder, and cutting

Figure 10.24 Group-Technology Parts Example

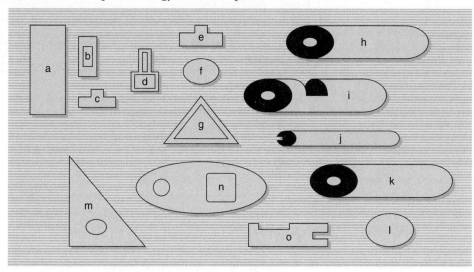

machine. This may not be a good choice if the equipment is expensive or if sufficient equipment is not available (as would be the case if an existing plant is being redesigned). For instance, suppose the plant in this example has only two machines of each type. It would be impossible to create the seven cells defined above without significant capital investment, since four cells require grinding, four require cutting, and so on. In most situations, it is very difficult to define cells on the basis of identical processing requirements; the parts that make up a part family may share many of the same processing steps, but not necessarily all.

One way to resolve this dilemma is to further combine part families. For example, note that if we group milling, cutting, polishing, and grinding into one cell, this cell can process part families 1 and 2. Similarly, part families 3 and 4 can

Table 10.5 Processing Requirements

Part	Drill	Turn	Stamp	Mill	Polish	Grind	Cut
a					x	x	x
b			x			x	x
c				x		x	x
d			x			x	x
e				x		x	x
f					x	x	x
g			x			x	x
h	x	x					
i	x	x		x			
j		x		x			
k	x	x					
l					x	x	x
m	x					x	x
n	x					x	x
o				x		x	x

be processed by a cell that contains drilling, stamping, grinding, and cutting. Finally, part families 5, 6, and 7 can be processed with a cell consisting of drilling, turning, and milling. This would yield the following part families and cells.

Part Family	Parts	Cell	Processes
1	a, f, l	1	Polish, grind,
2	c, e, o		cut, mill
3	b, d, g	2	Stamp, grind,
4	m, n		drill, cut
5	h, k	3	Drill, turn,
6	j		mill
7	i		

In this example, we have attempted to maximize the utilization of existing equipment. Other criteria that can be used in the design of group layouts are

1. Minimizing the number of groups.
2. Consideration of volume of parts through the machine groups.
3. Smoothing the work flow.
4. Consideration of future part design and design changes.
5. Feasibility of particular layout patterns.
6. Consideration of possible process-technology changes.
7. Labor-force skill availability.

The final step in the procedure—designing the detailed layout—is based on considerations similar to those involved in the design of a typical product layout. In general, the number of machines and the bottleneck process will determine the cell capacity; materials-handling requirements should be minimized; and an attempt should be made to balance operator work loads as much as possible. The final design must be evaluated with respect to the planned production rates for the family of parts processed by each cell.

Workplace Design

We can apply the principles of facilities layout on a smaller scale to the design of individual workplaces. Clearly, the workplace should allow for a natural flow of movement as the task is performed. The work-methods analysis discussed in the preceding chapter can provide valuable information for the best physical design of the workplace. The principal questions to be answered are

1. *Who will use the workplace?* Workplace designs often must take into account different physical characteristics of individuals. For example, military personnel have different physical characteristics than the average citizen, and there are differences between men and women.
2. *How will the work be performed?* This includes knowing what items and tools are needed, whether the worker needs to record information, and so on.

3. *What must the worker be able to see?* Workers might need special fixtures for blueprints, test procedures, or other documents.

4. *What must the worker be able to hear?* Workers may need to communicate with others, be able to listen for certain sounds during product testing, or be able to hear warning sounds.

5. *What must the worker be able to reach?* This will affect the location of parts, tools, and other items.

To illustrate some of these issues, let us consider the design of the pizza-preparation table in the kitchen layout for MamaMia's shown in Figure 10.9. Ingredients should be put on the pizzas in the following order: sauce, vegetables (mushrooms, peppers, onions, etc.), cheese, and finally, meat. Since cheese and meat are the highest-cost items and also greatly affect taste and customer satisfaction, the manager requires that those items be weighed to ensure that the proper amounts are included. Figure 10.25 shows a design of this workplace. All items are arranged in the order of assembly within easy reach of the worker and, as the front view illustrates, order tickets are hung at eye level, with the most recent orders on the left to ensure that pizzas are prepared on a first-come-first-served basis.

Methods analysis and operation charts, which we introduced in Chapter 9, are useful tools in workplace design. Recalling the Freeland Faucet example in Chapter 9, note that the operation chart in Figure 9.16 suggests the workstation layout shown in Figure 10.26. From the operation chart, you can see that the left hand of the worker is idle most of the time, holding the housing. A good methods analyst will ask questions such as: Can any motions be eliminated? Can more simultaneous motions be performed? Will a new layout, use of fixtures, or use of different tools improve the operation? The following example shows how methods analysis can lead to an improved layout and higher productivity.

Figure 10.25
Pizza-Preparation
Workplace Design

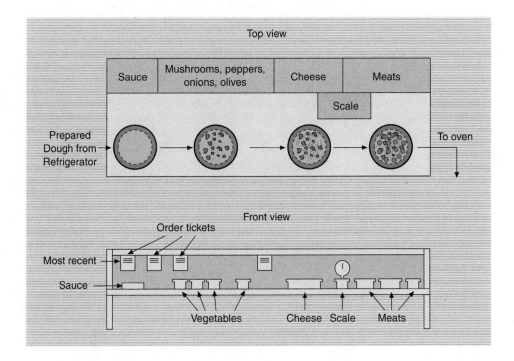

Figure 10.26
Workstation Layout at
Freeland Faucet

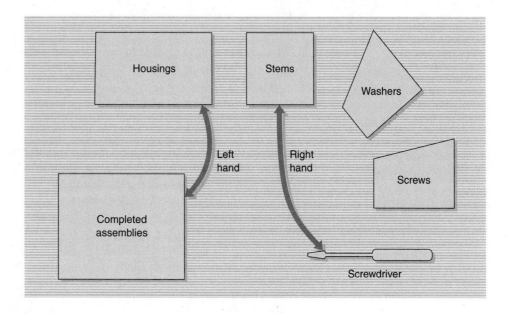

Example

Improving Productivity through Workplace Design and Methods Analysis

After noticing that the employee's right hand does most of the work, the analyst at Freeland Faucet suggested the new layout and operation sequence shown in Figures 10.27 and 10.28. The fixture is used to hold the housing-stem subassembly while the washer and screw are assembled. In addition, a powered screwdriver hanging from above the workplace was suggested. With the assembly in the fixture, the screw head will be pointing up, and the worker need only pull the screwdriver down. This new design frees the left hand because of the fixture,

Figure 10.27 New Workstation Layout for Faucet-Stem Assembly

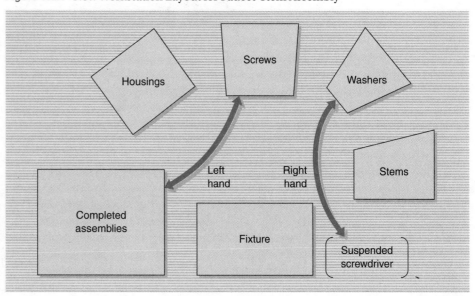

Figure 10.28 Operation Chart for Improved Faucet-Stem Assembly

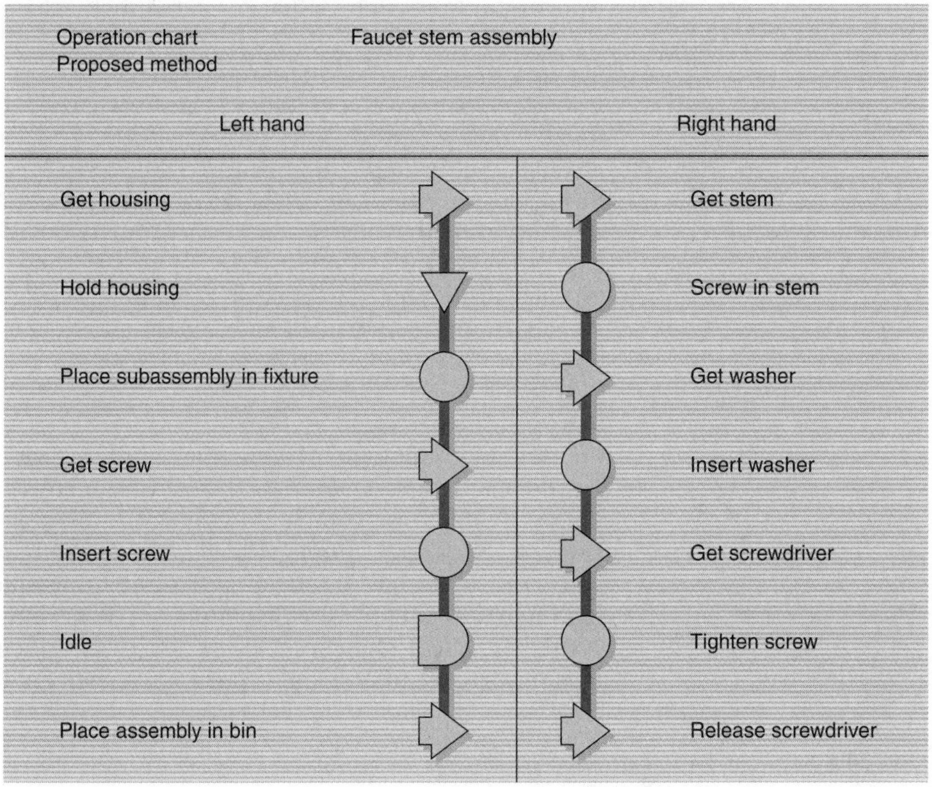

Operation chart Proposed method	Faucet stem assembly	
Left hand		**Right hand**
Get housing		Get stem
Hold housing		Screw in stem
Place subassembly in fixture		Get washer
Get screw		Insert washer
Insert screw		Get screwdriver
Idle		Tighten screw
Place assembly in bin		Release screwdriver

increases symmetry of motions, and reduces transportations. The use of the powered screwdriver also reduces arm fatigue. Can you think of other improvements? How would the method change if the fixture were designed to hold several subassemblies?

The workplace environment is an important consideration for operations management. If not properly designed, it can actually be distracting and result in reduced productivity, or even be dangerous to the employee's health. This is true not only for factory labor, but also for white-collar work, particularly work that is computer-intensive. The field of **ergonomics,** or *human-factors engineering,* is concerned with improving productivity and safety by designing workplaces, tools, instruments, and so on, that take into account the physical capabilities of people. The objectives of a human-factors program are to improve human performance by increasing speed, accuracy, and safety; to reduce energy requirements and fatigue; to reduce the amount and cost of training; to reduce accidents due to human error; and to improve user comfort and acceptance.[8]

Ergonomics

Ergonomics developed as a discipline during World War II, when analysts concluded that the death of many pilots was due to their not having mastered the complicated controls of their airplanes. Ergonomics is evident in a variety of consumer products. Kodak, for example, employs some 40 ergonomists to assist in the design of cameras and copiers as well as in improving work in its own factories. The windshield-level brake light required in 1986 model cars resulted from ergonomic analysis that indicated such lights could reduce rear-end collisions by 50 percent.

Another reason for operations managers to be concerned with ergonomics is the Americans with Disabilities Act (ADA), which became effective in July 1994 for all employers with 15 or more employees. The act prohibits discrimination against qualified individuals with disabilities in "job-application procedures, the hiring, advancement, or discharge of employees, employee compensation, job training, and other terms, conditions, and privileges of employment." As a result, employers sometimes need to modify existing facilities for individuals with physical disabilities—an endeavor that involves ergonomic issues.

Ergonomics draws information from a variety of disciplines, among them physical anthropology and work physiology.

Physical Anthropology. Human beings have a wide range of body characteristics, such as height, arm length, and strength. Physical anthropologists provide important input for workplace design by developing statistical profiles on such characteristics. An example of such *anthropometric data* is given in Table 10.6 for two-handed reach while standing. Typically, these data are presented statistically for different percentiles of the population. For example, the 25th percentile has a depth of reach of 21 inches. This means that 25 percent of the population have a maximum reach of 21 inches or less and 75 percent have a maximum reach of 21

Table 10.6 Standing Two-Arm Reach (inches)

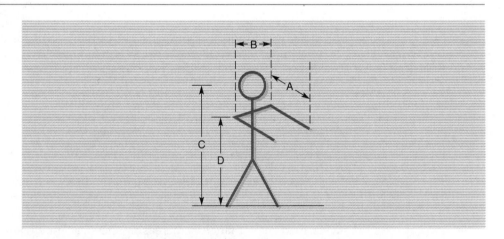

Characteristic		Percentile				
		5th	*25th*	*50th*	*75th*	*95th*
A	Reach	19.25	21.00	22.25	22.75	24.50
B	Shoulder width	15.50	17.00	17.75	18.50	19.50
C	Height to eye level	61.00	63.50	65.25	66.50	69.00
D	Height to shoulder level	52.25	54.75	56.00	57.25	59.00

SOURCE: K. W. Kennedy and B. E. Filler, "Aperture Sizes and Depths of Reach for One- and Two-Handed Tasks," *Report No. AMRL-TR-66-27,* Aerospace Medical Research Labs, Wright Patterson Air Force Base, 1966.

inches or more. Similarly, only 5 percent of the population have a reach of 24.5 inches or more. Anthropometric data assist designers in developing workplaces that are comfortable and functional for the operators intended to use them.

Work Physiology. Work physiology data are usually obtained through experimental observation and measurement. Heart rate and oxygen consumption are monitored and converted into energy use. For example, Table 10.7 illustrates the energy expenditure in kilocalories per minute (a kilocalorie is 1,000 calories and is often called the *large calorie*—the layperson's notion of "calorie") for various jobs studied at Eastman Kodak. How can these data be applied in job design? Jobs with higher energy demands naturally require more rest. A formula for estimating the amount of rest required for a particular job is[9]

$$R = \frac{T(K - S)}{K - 1.5}$$

where R = minutes of rest required.
T = total working time in minutes.
K = energy expenditure.
S = adopted standard of energy expenditure (such as 2–5 kcal/min.).

Thus if $S = 4$ is used as the energy standard, a worker unloading coal cars in a power plant requires

$$R = \frac{60(8 - 4)}{8 - 1.5} \approx 37$$

minutes of rest for each 60-minute period, whereas a worker mixing powdered chemicals requires only

$$R = \frac{60(6 - 4)}{6 - 1.5} \approx 27 \text{ minutes.}$$

Table 10.7 Average Energy Expenditure for Selected Jobs

Job	Energy Expenditure (kilocalories per minute)
Unloading coal cars in power plant	8.0
Handling 38-pound cans of chemicals	6.5
Mixing powdered chemicals	6.0
Loading corrugated cartons of product into boxcars	6.0
Tending cartoning machine	5.2
Cleaning production department	4.9
Handling 46-pound cans of chemicals	4.4
Removing ashes in power plant (94°F)	4.0
Packing on conveyor	3.7
Unloading rolls of film at slitter windup	3.5
Wrapping motion-picture film	3.0
Operating coal displacer	2.1

SOURCE: H. L. Davis, T. W. Faulkner, and C. I. Miller, "Work Physiology," *Human Factors* 11, no. 2 (1969), pp. 157–166. Copyright © 1969 by The Human Factors Society, Inc., and reproduced by permission.

Ergonomics and Cumulative Trauma Disorders

A primary occupational hazard in industry today is musculoskeletal injury involving constriction of nerves, tendons, and ligaments and inflammation of joints, particularly in the lower back, wrists, and elbows. It typically is caused by mismatching human physical abilities and task-performance requirements. Jobs that require heavy lifting, repetition, or the use of improperly designed tools are common culprits. Such injuries, known as **cumulative trauma disorders (CTDs),** include lower back pain, carpal tunnel syndrome, tennis elbow, and other forms of tendinitis. CTDs have become a major focus for ergonomists, particularly since the Bureau of Labor Statistics indicates that their reported incidence has more than tripled between 1984 and 1990. More than half the jobs in the United States today have the potential for CTD. The result may be higher health insurance costs and liability premiums.

Ergonomic studies and proper design of the workplace can reduce or eliminate CTDs. For example, if workpieces or operators have varying heights, an adjustable workbench or floor platform can be used. At Ford Motor Company, a worker who had to assemble a steering column from the outside of the vehicle worked in an extremely bent-over-sideways position that resulted in a lot of pain and lost work days. The solution was to create an eight-inch pit for the worker to stand in. It allowed him to do the same job at a very slight angle, effectively removing the trauma from the job.

Other examples of ergonomic solutions to work-related problems include

- Sure-grip gloves for employees who use hard-to-hold tools.
- Back-support cushions on chairs of employees who work with computers.
- Rubber mats on concrete floors where workers stand for hours.
- Adjustable loading platforms at the end of bottle-filling stations so that employees of all heights can move heavy boxes to pallets without bending or stooping.

Ergonomics is good business. A 1986 study by the U.S. Army Corps of Engineers documented a 20 percent improvement in productivity one year after ergonomic furniture was installed at one site. In 1990 Federal Express instituted new ergonomic initiatives that significantly reduced carpal tunnel syndrome and other stress-related injuries among its employees. Following is an example of good ergonomic design.

Example

Design of Computer Workstations

The design of computer workstations has received much attention by workplace designers as evidence accumulates that computer users are particularly susceptible to job-related health problems. Research suggests the following guidelines for computer workplace design (see Figure 10.29):[10]

- Eyes should be level with the top of the computer.
- The screen should be positioned to eliminate glare, and outside light should be reduced.

Figure 10.29 Human-Factor Guidelines for Computer Workstation Design

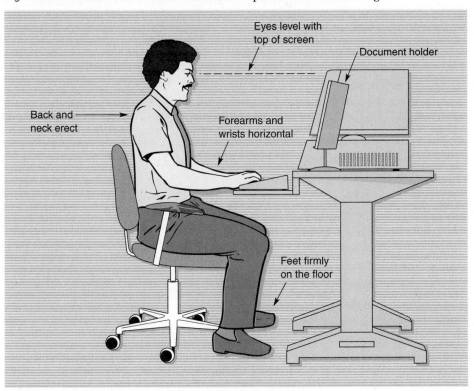

- ••• The back and neck should be erect, and the upper arms should be perpendicular to the floor. The back and thighs should make an angle of slightly more than 90 degrees.
- ••• When typing, forearms and wrists should be as horizontal as possible. Adjustable keyboards may be necessary.
- ••• Air vents should not stir up fibers or dust, which can cause eye and respiratory problems.
- ••• Feet should be firmly on the floor or footrest.
- ••• The workstation should not be close to office machines such as copiers and laser printers that may emit fumes.
- ••• A document holder should be positioned close to the screen and at the same eye level.

Safety and the Work Environment

To provide safe and healthful working conditions and reduce hazards in the work environment, the Occupational Safety and Health Act (OSHA) was passed in 1970. It requires employers to furnish to each of their employees employment and a place of employment free from recognized hazards that are causing or likely to cause death or serious physical harm. As a result of this legislation, the National Institute of Occupational Safety and Health (NIOSH) was formed to enforce standards provided by OSHA. Business and industry must abide by OSHA guidelines or face potential fines and penalties.

Industrial safety is a function of the job, the human operator, and the surrounding environment. The job should be designed so that it will be highly unlikely that a worker can injure himself or herself. This means, for instance, that equipment should be designed so that moving parts are guarded or out of reach. At the same time, the worker must be educated in the proper use of equipment and the methods designed for performing the job. Finally, the surrounding environment must be conducive to safety. This might include nonslip surfaces, warning signs, or buzzers. Three key safety issues are lighting, temperature and humidity, and noise.

Lighting. The type and amount of illumination required depend on the nature of the job. For example, difficult inspection tasks and close assembly work require more light than operating a milling machine or loading crates in a warehouse. The quality characteristics of light vary. Glare, brightness, contrast, and uniformity may contribute to eyestrain and reduce job performance. Those factors should be considered in designing individual workstations as well as offices and factories.

Temperature and Humidity. Temperature and humidity affect a person's comfort and can be a very distracting influence on productivity. A temperature in the low 60s might be ideal for lifting boxes in overalls and gloves but may chill a typist's fingers. Some jobs require extreme temperatures—for example, meatpacking plants and industrial areas where considerable heat is generated by machinery. Among the alternatives for operations managers in such situations are adjusting the humidity (higher temperatures can be tolerated at lower humidity levels); increasing air circulation in high-temperature areas; limiting exposure through rest periods or job rotation; and simply providing adequate protection.

Noise. A third environmental factor that is often a problem is noise. Intense noise over long periods of time can result in impaired hearing. OSHA has set limits on acceptable noise levels and duration. For example, a worker cannot be subject to a 90-decibel noise level for more than nine hours. Noise protection may require controlling the source of noise, absorbing the sound, increasing the distance from the sound, or providing ear protection. Many companies provide background music as a means of blending random noises and providing a pleasant atmosphere.

P/OM in Practice

Design of a University Library Workroom[11]

The workroom in the Southern Technical Institute Library processes about 8,000 new books each year. All new books must pass through the workroom, where they are prepared for shelving in the library's stacks. When the library was built, about 3,000 books were processed each year, and no major additions or remodeling changes have been made since then.

A flow-process chart for the production process of cataloging new books is given in Figure 10.30. Figures 10.31 and 10.32 illustrate the current layout and work flow in the workroom. As you can see from the flow diagram, there is unnecessary movement back and forth across the workroom. In addition, the main storage shelves constitute a barrier to effective flow of materials. A proposed new layout would result in more orderly flow, shorter distance traveled, and more book storage space. By moving the storage shelves out of the center of the room and off to one side, not only can more bookcases be added, but the density of books in a bookcase can be increased by decreasing shelf height from 24 to 12 inches. This corresponds to a 367 percent increase in available shelf space. (Figures 10.33 and 10.34).

In a simple problem such as this, layouts can be designed by visual inspection. However, in more complex industrial situations, handling cost is a major factor. Thus some quantitative analysis would appear to be helpful in process-layout design.

Questions for Discussion

1. What is the primary reason the library workroom needed to be redesigned?
2. What were some of the problems with the original layout?

3. What is the major change in the proposed layout? What benefits are associated with this change?

Productivity Improvement through Ergonomics at Rockwell International[12]

A combined application of group technology and ergonomics in production and materials-handling systems at Rockwell International's Communication Transmission Systems Division resulted in significant productivity improvements in a sheet-fabrication department. The operation was evaluated ergonomically in three areas:

- Material flow between production operations.
- Material and tool handling at each operation.
- Job tasks and workplace design.

The department uses typical metal-working machines, such as numerically controlled punch presses, power brakes, shears, deburring machines, and degreasers, to produce a wide variety of sheet-metal parts for microwave communications equipment.

Problems were being encountered in the department due to a high production volume of parts, large differences in the size of the parts (ranging from 1 inch square to over 6 feet in length), and the large variety of parts produced. The large number of different part numbers resulted in an extremely large number of process routings, machine requirements, and tool setups. Demand was increasing, and this was putting additional strain on production. Managers decided to apply group technology and automation to improve the system.

The department was reorganized into manufacturing cells through group technology. That necessitated determining new methods for material and part transport. The ergonomic

considerations included muscular work requirements, work heights, noise, and vibration. Ten objectives were established:

1. Minimize flow distances and part handling.
2. Route and move parts using operator or handling system.
3. Deliver parts to operator workstations.
4. Provide parts at workbench height.
5. Eliminate lifting of parts.
6. Minimize manual movement of parts.
7. Ensure correct body posture.
8. Reduce static muscular work.
9. Automate where feasible.
10. Minimize noise, vibration, and other potential distractions.

Various materials-transfer methods were evaluated, and three systems were selected. Material carts were selected for adjacent operations to provide a low-cost system that would not require operator lifting and could also be utilized as workbenches. A powered conveyor system was chosen for completed parts because of the longer travel distances. An automatic on-off system was designed using photocells, since operators' hands are both busy when loading the conveyor. In addition, the same-height carts and conveyor would allow operators to slide the parts. Heavy and large parts would be moved with new skid carts.

The second area of improvement was in materials-, tools-, and scrap-handling operations. The ergonomic objective was to minimize the operator effort necessary to prepare for production and to provide work materials at the proper work heights and locations. Setup included the transfer of parts to the workbench, machine setup, disposal of scrap, and machine

Figure 10.30 Flow-Process Chart for Library Workroom

Part name _____	Summary		
Process desc. ___Catalog new book___			No.
Charted by ___P.T.___	Operations		6
Date ___6/21/92___	Transportations		6
	Inspections		1
	Delays		1
	Storages		1
	Present distance traveled		153'
	Proposed distance traveled		90'

Description		Present/proposed
1. Receive books from outside	○ ▷ □ D ▽	
2. Move to check-in area	○ ▷ □ D ▽	33/12 feet
3. Check if duplication of existing book	○ ▷ □ D ▽	
4. Move to catalog research area	○ ▷ □ D ▽	28/8 feet
5. Catalog—Library of Congress Classification	○ ▷ □ D ▽	
5a. If no catalog number, move to storage area	○ ▷ □ D ▽	26/26 feet
5b. Store until number available	○ ▷ □ D ▽	
5c. Move to catalog research area	○ ▷ □ D ▽	20/26 feet
5d. Catalog	○ ▷ □ D ▽	
6. Move to verification area	○ ▷ □ D ▽	28/8 feet
7. Verify	○ ▷ □ D ▽	
8. Move to pocket and call number application area	○ ▷ □ D ▽	18/10 feet
9. Install pocket and date due slip	○ ▷ □ D ▽	
10. Apply call number	○ ▷ □ D ▽	
11. Store until shelving	○ ▷ □ D ▽	

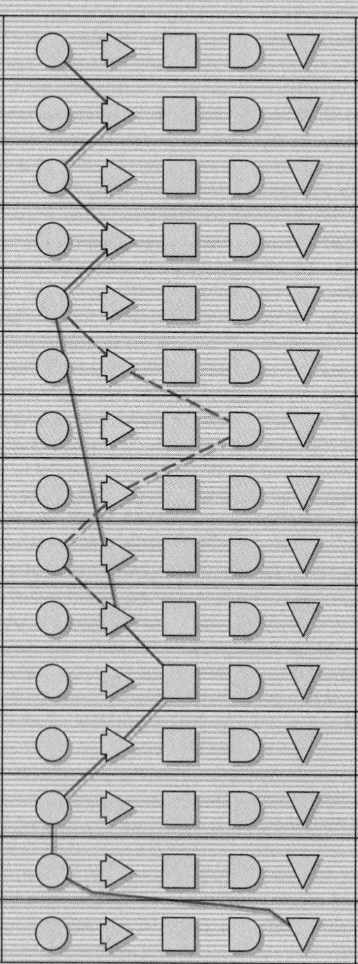

Figure 10.31 Original Layout of Library Workroom

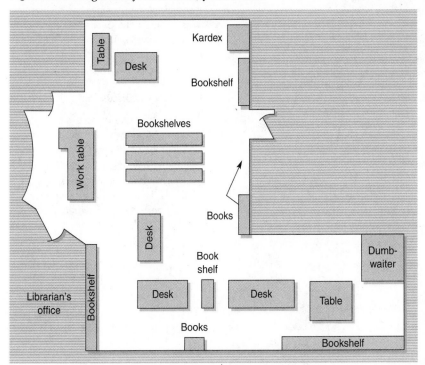

Figure 10.32 Flow Diagram of Original Library Workroom

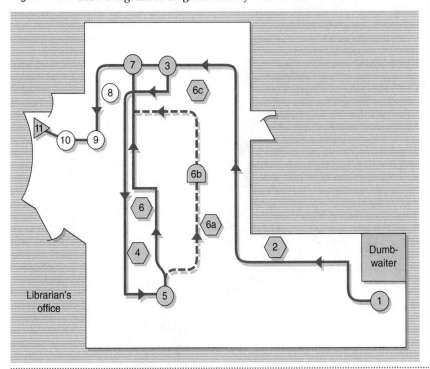

cleanup. Two major improvements were the use of material carts as workbenches and new tool racks that could be placed at the workplace. The material carts could be pushed into place next to the machine tool. Because of this dual use, the carts were specially ordered at a height that would allow the operator to sit or stand at the operation.

The new tool racks were designed to maximize operator efficiency. Design considerations included work heights determined by tool weight, adequate room for grasping tools properly, movement directions in relation to the setup requirements, operator efficiency, and elimination of unnatural body positions.

The last phase of the project was the evaluation of job content and design of the workplace. Operators were given total responsibility for quality control, which included the evaluation of preceding operations and sign-off responsibility. Prior to the change, inspections were performed by an inspection department. Other changes included job flexibility, increased autonomy of the group, development of quality circles, and direct participation in the design of the operation.

The workplaces were designed to enable employees to perform operations sitting or standing, thus allowing posture changes that alternate stress and strain over different muscular groups. Where possible, adjustable benches and chairs were also provided to allow posture flexibility. Several problems were identified for hand tools and machine controls. Where feasible, new tools were purchased or existing tools redesigned, and controls that did not meet normal ergonomic standards were changed where possible.

After six months of implementation, direct manufacturing costs were reduced by 30 percent (a third due to ergonomics changes and the rest to

Figure 10.33 Proposed Layout of Library Workroom. (Note the new location of the bookcases.)

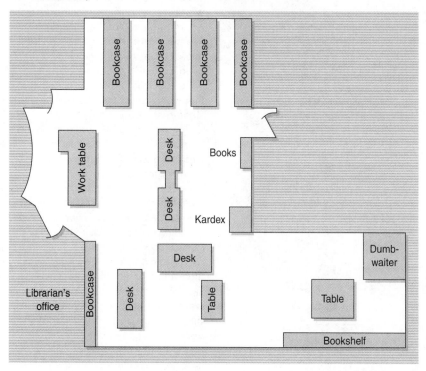

Figure 10.34 Flow Diagram for Proposed Layout of Library Workroom

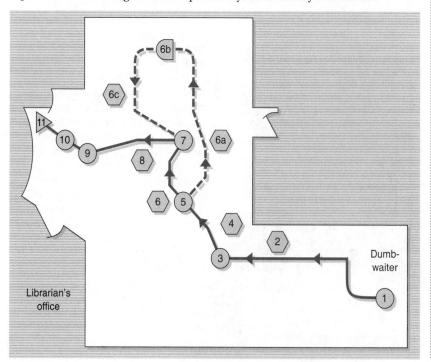

group technology improvements), a throughput improvement of 65 percent was realized (15 percent due to ergonomics and 50 percent due to group technology), and inventory was reduced by $500,000.

Questions for Discussion

1. State how you believe the ergonomics changes in materials-transfer methods caused reductions in direct manufacturing costs.

2. Explain how the changes in work methods described here could have led to a reduction in inventory costs.

Summary of Key Points

••• Effective facilities layout offers the potential to reduce manufacturing cycle times, inventory, space requirements, and materials-handling costs and to improve scheduling, control, quality, and flexibility. Process design is facilitated by flowcharts, route sheets, and flow-process charts.

••• Four types of layout patterns are commonly used: product layout, process layout, group layout, and fixed-position layout. Product layouts are based on the sequence of operations performed, and products move in a continuous path. Process layouts consist of functional groupings of machines or activities that do similar work. Group layouts place machines in cells to produce families of parts. Group layouts can provide significant benefits for improving productivity and flexibility. Fixed-position layouts are used for the construction of large, heavy items.

••• Designing product layouts often involves determining the best configuration of operators and buffers for balancing work. Waiting-line analysis and computer simulation are commonly used in analyzing product layouts. Assembly-line-balancing techniques are used to design paced production lines that will minimize labor costs or achieve a desired output rate.

••• Designing process layout involves determining the best arrangements of departments relative to each other. Usually, the objective is to minimize materials-handling costs. Computerized techniques such as CRAFT are often used to design the process layout.

••• The design of group layouts involves selecting part families, selecting machine groupings, and optimizing the arrangement of the production cells.

••• Ergonomics, or human-factors engineering, is concerned with improving productivity by designing workplaces, tools, instruments, and so one, that are compatible with people's physical capabilities. Ergonomics draws from the disciplines of physical anthropology, work physiology, and biomechanics.

••• Occupational safety is a vital concern in job design. Design of the general work environment, the individual workplace, and work methods must incorporate safety features.

Key Terms

Product layout
Process layout
Group technology
Group (cellular) layout
Fixed-position layout
Materials handling
Production line
Flow-blocking delay
Lack-of-work delay
Cycle time
Load matrix
CRAFT
Ergonomics
Cumulative trauma disorder (CTD)

Review Questions

1. Under what conditions are facility-layout studies conducted?
2. What are the objectives of facility layout?
3. What advantages can be gained from proper attention to facility layout?
4. Describe the major types of layout patterns used in production. What are the advantages and disadvantages of each?
5. Discuss the characteristics of service organizations that affect facility-layout activities.
6. Describe the basic materials-handling systems commonly used in manufacturing.
7. Define *production line.*
8. Distinguish between conveyor-paced and non-conveyor-paced production lines.
9. Distinguish between flow-blocking delay and lack-of-work delay.
10. What are buffers, and why are they necessary?
11. Discuss the issues involved in assembly-line balancing.
12. Describe the approach used in designing process layouts. Will this guarantee an "optimal" solution? Why or why not?
13. How are computers used in layout planning? Explain how CRAFT develops facility layouts.
14. What criteria are used in designing group layouts? Describe the general procedures for forming part families and cells.
15. What questions should be addressed in designing a workplace for an individual worker?
16. What is the role of ergonomics in job design?
17. Explain the contributions of physical anthropology, work physiology, and biomechanics to ergonomics.
18. Explain the importance of ergonomics in reducing cumulative trauma disorders.
19. What environmental factors should be considered in designing jobs? How does OSHA influence these decisions?

Discussion Questions

1. Discuss the type of facilities layout that would be most appropriate for
   a. printing books.

b. performing hospital laboratory tests.

c. manufacturing home furniture.

d. a photography studio.

e. a library.

2. Many company cafeterias are changing from the traditional cafeteria (process) layout to a product layout in which food items are arranged into stations (salads, Italian, cold sandwiches, roast beef and ham, etc.). Discuss the advantages and disadvantages of each type of layout.

3. What type of layout is typically used in a home kitchen? Can you suggest an alternative layout that might have some different advantages?

4. Describe the layout of a typical fast-food franchise such as McDonald's. What type of layout is it? How does it support productivity? Do different franchises (e.g., Burger King or Wendy's) have different types of layouts? Why?

5. List at least five types of production situations (either manufacturing or service) that would have process, product, or group layouts.

6. Discuss the implications of each major layout pattern to the human-resources issues discussed in Chapter 5.

7. Traditional guidelines for materials-handling system design are (a) the best materials handling is no materials handling, (b) the shorter the distance traveled, the better the flow, (c) straight-line materials flow paths are the best, and (d) all loads should be handled in as large a unit load as possible. Discuss why these guidelines may no longer be appropriate in today's manufacturing environment. You might draw upon principles introduced in the preceding chapter.

8. Continuous-flow manufacturing is characterized by the frequent movement of small unit loads. Propose some guidelines for designing materials-handling systems for continuous-flow manufacturing.

9. What ergonomic issues might be appropriate to address in a home kitchen?

10. Describe the ergonomic features in the automobile that you drive most often. If it is an older model, visit a new-car showroom and contrast those features with those found in some newer models.

11. Describe features of your school's physical facilities that support or hinder individuals with physical disabilities.

Notes

1. "Flexibility Helps Company Cope with Rapid Growth," *Modern Materials Handling,* August 1987, pp. 54–56.

2. Dan L. Shunk, "Group Technology Provides Organized Approach to Realizing Benefits of CIMS." *Industrial Engineering,* April 1985. Adapted with permission from Institute of Industrial Engineers, 25 Technology Park/Atlanta, Norcross, GA 30092.

3. R. S. M. Lau and Ronda S. Keenan, "Restructuring for Quality and Efficiency," *Journal for Quality and Participation,* July–August 1994, pp. 38–40.

4. Don T. Phillips and Rodney J. Heisterberg, "Development of a Generalized Manufacturing Simulator (GEMS)," Report No. GEMS-5-77. Prepared for the National Science Foundation, Department of Industrial Engineering, Texas A&M University, December 1, 1977.

5. This procedure is a network adaptation of Hoffman's method in "Assembly Line Balancing with a Precedence Matrix." *Management Science* 9, no. 4 (July 1963).

6. Gene H. Milas, "Assembly Line Balancing: Let's Remove the Mystery," *Industrial Engineering* 22, no. 5 (May 1990), pp. 31–36.

7. Hector H. Guerrero, "Group Technology: I. The Essential Concepts," *Production and Inventory Management* 28, no. 1 (1987), pp. 62–70; and "Group Technology: II. The Implementation Process," *Production and Inventory Management* 28, no. 2 (1987), pp. 1–9. Adapted with permission from The American Production and Inventory Control Society, Inc.

8. R. Dale Huchingson, *New Horizons for Human Factors in Design* (New York: McGraw-Hill, 1981), p. 7.

9. K. F. H. Murrell, *Human Performance in Industry* (New York: Reinhold Publishing Corp., 1965).

10. "The Proper Workplace," *USA Today,* 19 November, 1990, 5D.

11. Lawrence S. Aft, "Work Methods in the Library." Adapted with permission from *Industrial Engineering magazine,* November 1973. Copyright Institute of Industrial Engineers, 25 Technology Park/Atlanta, Norcross, GA 30092.

12. John W. Priest, "Ergonomic Changes in Workplace Can Improve the Productivity of Production Operations," *Industrial Engineering,* July 1985. Adapted with permission from Institute of Industrial Engineers, 25 Technology Park/Atlanta, Norcross, GA 30092.

Solved Problems

1. An assembly operation consists of 10 tasks that must be completed in order from task 1 to task 10. The respective task-completion times in minutes are: .3, .5, .3, .2, .2, .1, .4, .3, .8, and .2. Assume a 40-hour week, a 92 percent efficiency, and a desired production rate of 1,840 units per week.

a. What is the desired cycle time for the assembly line?

b. How many workstations will be required, and what tasks are to be performed at each station?

c. What is the line efficiency for this assembly line?

Solution

a. Desired cycle time is

$$(40 \text{ hrs/week})(60 \text{ min/hr})(.92)/1840 \text{ units} = 1.2 \text{ min/unit.}$$

b. The precedence diagram is

Tasks must be assigned to workstations in numerical order so that the total work time assigned to each station does not exceed 1.2. As Table 10.8 shows, three stations are needed.

Table 10.8 Solved Problem 1 Solution

Workstation	Tasks	Total time
1	1, 2, 3	1.1
2	4, 5, 6, 7, 8	1.2
3	9, 10	1.0
		3.3

c. Line efficiency is

$$3.3/[(1.2)(3)] = .917.$$

2. The departments in the layout shown in Figure 10.35 are all the same size: 50×100 feet. Travel between departments can occur only along the coordinate axes. The number

Figure 10.35
Facility Layout and Monthly Moves for Solved Problem 2

From \ To	A	B	C	D	E	F
A	—	—	50	10	—	90
B	—	—	20	—	—	40
C	15	—	—	—	35	—
D	—	100	—	—	60	—
E	5	—	25	—	—	70
F	—	—	—	5	—	—

of moves per month between departments is shown in the matrix below the layout. Find the total volume-distance of the proposed layout.

Solution
The distances between department centers with positive moves are shown in Figure 10.36. Multiplying the number of moves by the respective distances gives a total volume-distance of 68,500.

Figure 10.36
Solved Problem 2 Solution

From \ To	A	B	C	D	E	F
A	—	—	100	150	—	250
B	—	—	150	—	—	200
C	100	—	—	—	100	—
D	—	100	—	—	150	—
E	200	—	100	—	—	50
F	—	—	—	100	—	—

3. Four departments are to be arranged in a square as shown in Figure 10.37. Material can be moved from any department to another; however, travel can occur only along the co-ordinate axes (not directly across a diagonal). Find the minimum-cost layout for the load matrix in Figure 10.37, assuming that the distance between adjacent departments is 1.

Figure 10.37
Interdepartment Volume
Requirements for Solved
Problem 3

From \ To	A	B	C	D
A	—	10	15	—
B	25	—	5	10
C	15	—	—	20
D	5	10	—	—

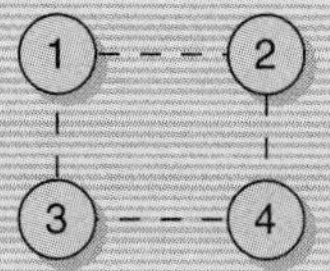

Solution
As Figure 10.38 shows, there are only three unique arrangements for such a configuration.

Problems

1. Peter's Paper Clips uses a three-stage production process: cutting wire to prescribed lengths, inner bending, and outer bending. The cutting process can produce at a rate of 150 pieces per minute; inner bending, 140 pieces per minute, and outer bending, 110 pieces per minute. Determine the hourly capacity of each process and the number of machines needed to meet an output rate of 30,000 units per hour.

Figure 10.38
Solved Problem 3 Solution

Distance matrices:

	A	B	C	D
A	—	1	1	—
B	1	—	2	1
C	1	—	—	1
D	2	1	—	—

	A	B	C	D
A	—	2	1	—
B	2	—	1	1
C	1	—	—	2
D	1	1	—	—

	A	B	C	D
A	—	1	2	—
B	1	—	1	2
C	2	—	—	1
D	1	2	—	—

Total volume distance: 125 (best layout) | 170 | 165

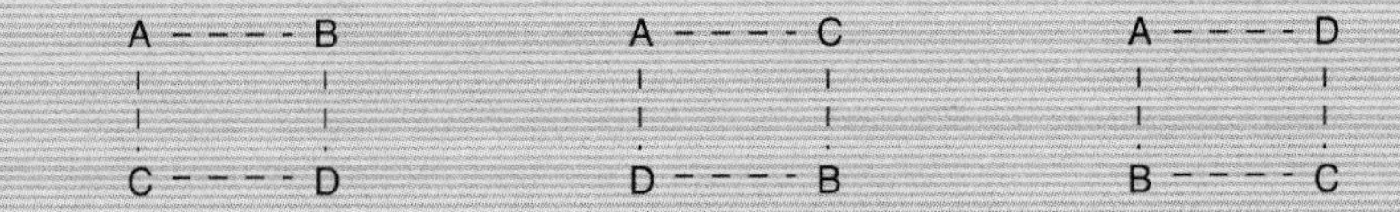

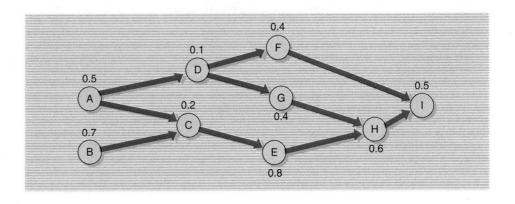

2. A small assembly line for the assembly of power steering pumps needs to be balanced. Figure 10.39 is the precedence diagram. The cycle time is determined to be 1.5 minutes. How would the line be balanced using
a. The shortest time rule?
b. The longest time rule?

Figure 10.39
Precedence Diagram for Problem 2

3. An assembly line with 30 activities is to be balanced. The total amount of time to complete all 30 activities is 42 minutes. The longest activity takes 2.4 minutes and the shortest takes .3 minutes. The line will operate for 450 minutes per day.
a. What are the maximum and minimum cycle times?
b. What output rate will be achieved by each of those cycle times?

4. In Problem 3, suppose the line is balanced using 10 workstations and a finished product can be produced every 4.2 minutes.
a. What is the production rate in units per day?
b. What is the line efficiency?

5. For the in-line skate assembly example in Chapter 9, suppose the times for the individual operations are as given in Table 10.9.

Table 10.9 Data for Problem 5

Operation	Time (sec.)
SA-1	20
SA-2	10
A-1	30
I-1	10
SA-3	30
A-2	20
A-3	10
I-2	20

Assume that inspections cannot be performed by production personnel, but only by persons from quality control. Therefore, assembly operations are separated into three groups for inspection. Design production lines (similar to those of Figure 10.12) to achieve output rates of 120 per hour and 90 per hour. Will those lines have any lack-of-work or flow-blocking delays?

6. A production process consists of four machines in sequence. The production rates of the four machines are 80, 155, 305, and 147 pieces per hour, respectively. A normal working day consists of two eight-hour shifts. The desired daily output is 4,000 pieces.
a. Determine the capacity of each machine.
b. Balance the line, by determining the number of each machine required.
c. What is the utilization of each machine at the desired production level?

7. Determine appropriate part families and machine groupings for the part-process matrix in Table 10.10.

Table 10.10 Data for Problem 7

Part	Turn	Mill 1	Mill 2	Drill	Grind
1	x	x		x	x
2		x		x	x
3	x	x	x	x	x
4	x		x	x	x
5		x			
6	x	x		x	x
7	x	x		x	
8	x		x	x	
9		x			x
10	x		x	x	
11	x	x		x	
12			x	x	x
13	x	x	x	x	x
14	x	x		x	
15			x		x
16	x	x		x	
17	x		x	x	
18	x		x	x	x
19	x		x		
20		x		x	x

8. Repeat Solved Problem 1, increasing the production rate to 2,760 units per week.

9. Solve the assembly-line-balancing problem in Figure 10.40 for cycle times of 10 and 7.

Figure 10.40
Precedence Network for
Problem 9

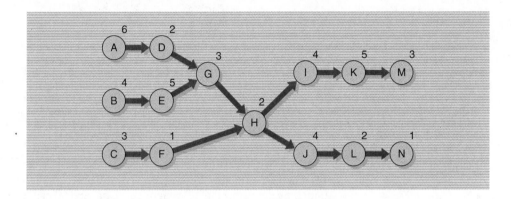

10. We suggested assigning operations to stations on an assembly line by choosing the largest time first among all assignable operations. Solve both the in-line skate assembly problem and Problem 9 using the rule, *choose the assignable operation with the shortest time.* How do these rules compare? Can you think of any other rules or procedures that would achieve a better balance on these problems?

11. Balance the assembly line in Figure 10.41 for (a) a shift output of 80 pieces and (b) a shift output of 30 pieces. Assume an eight-hour shift, and use the rule, *choose the assignable operation with the longest time.* Compute the line efficiency for each case.

Figure 10.41
Precedence Network for
Problem 11

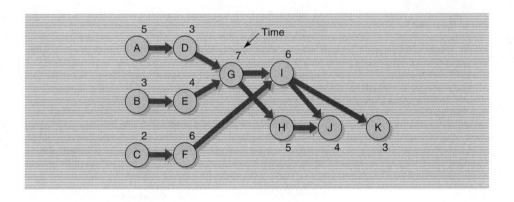

12. Balance the assembly line in Problem 11 using the rule, *choose the assignable operation with the shortest time,* and compare the performance of this rule with the *longest time* rule.

13. For the situation in Problem 11, determine the range of feasible cycle times and the minimum and maximum output that can be achieved.

14. For the activities and precedence relations in Table 10.11:

a. Draw a precedence diagram.

b. Balance the assembly line for an eight-hour-shift output of 30 pieces.

c. Determine maximum and minimum cycle times.

Table 10.11 Data for Problem 14

Activity	Predecessors	Time per Piece (min.)
A	—	7
B	—	2
C	A	6
D	A	10
E	B	3
F	B	2
G	D,E	12
H	C	2
I	F	3
J	H,G,I	9

15. The Raffles Potato Chips manufacturing process consists of (a) chip making, (b) pouching, (c) cartoning, (d) weight checking, and (e) case packing. The rates of each process are given in Table 10.12.

Table 10.12 Data for Problem 15

Process	Rate (per min.)	
Chip making	12,000 chips	
Pouching	1000 pouches	(12 chips per pouch)
Cartoning	220 cartons	(6 pouches per carton)
Weight checking	220 cartons	
Case packing	20 cases	(24 cartons per case)

The production line is to be operated on a one-shift basis (eight hours) with 80 minutes lost time per shift for lunch, breaks, startup, and shutdown. Draw a schematic layout of this system. If 6,000 cases per day are to be produced, analyze the equipment utilization. Where do bottlenecks occur?

16. For Problem 15, determine if additional machines would increase production capacity and better balance the lines.

17. Refer to Figure 10.42. Given the layout of departments, the frequency of movements among them, and the distance between them, determine if less materials handling is achieved by switching departments D and F. Assume diagonal distances to be two units and horizontal/vertical distances between adjacent departments to be one unit.

18. Mantel's Metal Products produces a diversified line of metal goods. An analysis of last year's production orders shows that seven groups of products account for over 95 percent of the total business volume. The production routing for these groups is shown in Table 10.13 and space requirements for each department are

Receiving	1500 square feet
A	2500 square feet
B	1500 square feet
C	2000 square feet
D	1000 square feet
E	500 square feet
Shipping	1500 square feet

a. Prepare a (percent) volume travel chart using the percentages in Table 10.13. (How does this differ from the type discussed in the chapter?)

Figure 10.42
Data for Problem 17

Frequency of Movements
To

From	A	B	C	D	E	F
A	0	10	—	5	5	10
B	5	0	—	5	10	5
C	2	10	0	5	5	1
D	5	10	2	0	5	5
E	10	5	0	0	0	5
F	0	10	5	0	5	0

Present layout   Proposed layout

A	B		A	B
C	D		C	F
E	F		E	D

Table 10.13 Data for Problem 18

Group	Percent Volume by Weight	Department Operation Sequence			
		1	2	3	4
1	20	A	D	E	
2	25	B	C	D	E
3	10	A	D	E	
4	15	C	B	E	
5	10	A	C		
6	8	A	B	D	E
7	8	C	B		

b. By trial and error on graph paper, design a good layout.

19. Using the closeness ratings of A through F described in the discussion of ALDEP and CORELAP, design a layout for the main floor of a new business building from the information given in Table 10.14 and Figure 10.43.

Table 10.14 Data for Problem 19

Function	Space Requirements (sq. ft.)
Main entry	500
Dean's office	450
Student affairs	600
Graduate lounge	400
Auditorium	3000 *(continues)*

Table 10.14 Data for Problem 19 *(continued)*

Function	Space Requirements (sq. ft.)
Large classrooms (5)	1000 each
Computer center	2500
Laboratories (2)	600 each
Undergraduate lounge	600
Reading/study rooms (10)	150 each
Vending area	225

Figure 10.43
Preference Table for
Problem 19

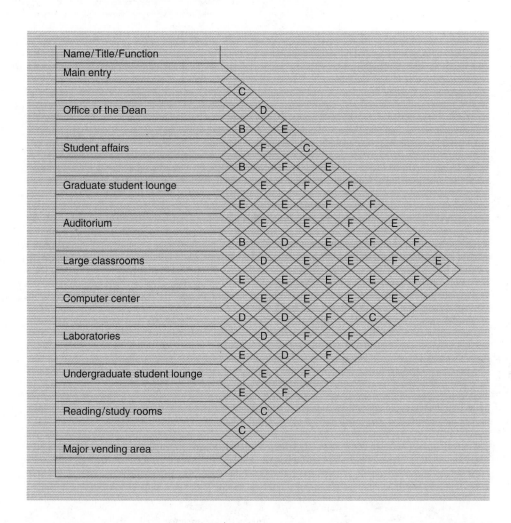

20. A factory uses three types of fork lift trucks operating at a cost of $30, $20, and $10 per hour, respectively. The three types of equipment are housed in separate stations. The frequencies of movement to each department and the distances from each station to the four departments are given in Tables 10.15 and 10.16.

Table 10.15 Equipment Movement Frequencies for Problem 20

Department	Type		
	I	II	III
Turning	10	15	10
Milling	25	15	15
Press shop	30	10	25
Assembly	5	15	30

Table 10.16 Distance Data for Problem 20

From Station	To Department			
	A	B	C	D
1	10	10	5	5
2	5	10	5	10
3	5	5	10	10

The present layout is shown in Figure 10.44.

Figure 10.44
Present Layout for
Problem 20

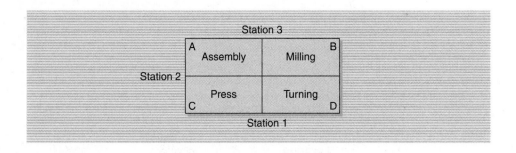

a. What is the present materials-handling cost?
b. Is there any advantage in switching assembly and milling departments?
21. Given the following spatial requirements for six departments and the preference table in Figure 10.45, design a layout.

Department	1	2	3	4	5	6
Area (sq. ft.)	1500	2000	2000	1000	1500	1000

22. Mercy Hospital is renovating an old wing to house four departments: outpatient services, X-ray lab, physical therapy, and orthopedics. Table 10.17 gives the distances in feet between each two existing rooms in the wing. That is, Rooms 1 and 2 are 40 feet apart. Table 10.18 gives the average number of trips per day between each two departments.

Figure 10.45
Preference Table for
Problem 21

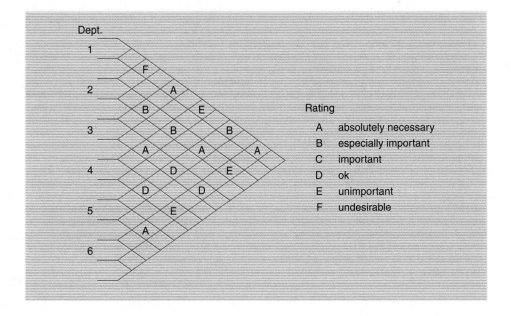

Table 10.17 Interdepartment Distances for Problem 22

Location	1	2	3	4
1	—	40	60	60
2		—	20	30
3			—	15
4				—

Table 10.18 Interdepartment Trips Per Day for Problem 22

Location	Outpatient Service	X-ray Lab	Physical Therapy	Orthopedics
Outpatient service	—	25	42	34
X-ray lab		—	15	55
Physical therapy			—	10
Orthopedics				—

The hospital wants to locate each department in one of the existing four rooms so as to minimize the sum of the trips × distance. What is the best facility design? How many possible ways of locating the departments are there?

23. A company that designs and manufactures interior furnishings for fast-food chains operates a 70,000-square-foot woodworking/assembly area.[†] This area of the plant has

---

[†]John S. Usher, C. A. Ciesielski, and Ralph A. Johanson, "Redesigning an Existing Layout Presents a Major Challenge—and Produces Dramatic Results." Adapted with permission from *Industrial Engineering*, June 1990. Copyright 1990 Institute of industrial Engineers, Norcross, GA.

evolved in a rather ad hoc way over a long period of time. As new machines and processes have been adopted they have not been well integrated into the overall process. As a result, this area of the facility is now hampered with a variety of problems, and at a time of high demand for the company's products. Company managers have decided that the current layout should be studied and possibly redesigned to improve efficiency and increase production with minimum capital investment.

The 10 departments included in this area and their space requirements are

1.	Shipping and receiving	7,000 square feet.
2.	Raw materials storage	4,200 square feet.
3.	Rough cut	7,840 square feet.
4.	Laminate cut	3,520 square feet.
5.	Cabinets	4,800 square feet.
6.	Tables	4,200 square feet.
7.	Woodsleys/solid materials	2,100 square feet.
8.	Walls and decor	6,800 square feet.
9.	Hand finishing and painting	3,500 square feet.
10.	Final assembly and packaging	12,112 square feet.

Figure 10.46 is a from-to chart of unit flows between departments. (Material quantities are expressed in a standard "equivalent" unit.)

Figure 10.46
Unit Flows Between Departments for Problem 23

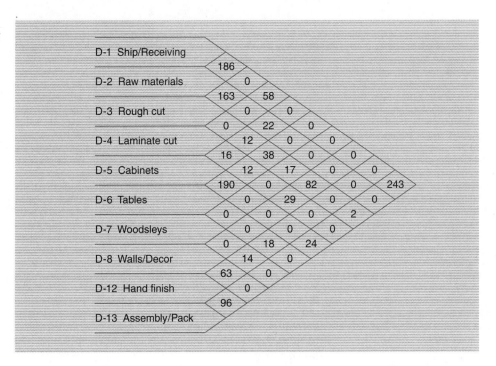

a. Develop a closeness rating for each pair of departments based on the unit flows in Table 10.19.

Table 10.19 Data for Problem 23

Unit Flow	Closeness Rating
≥ 50	A Absolutely necessary
26–50	E Especially important
16–25	I Important
6–15	O Ordinary
0–5	U Unimportant

b. Design a block layout sketch for this facility. Include approximately 2,000 square feet for office, parts, and maintenance. Write a short report explaining the rationale for final design of the facility.

24. Figure 10.47 is a design for a personal-workstation, Discuss the ergonomic features of the design. Should any additional features be included?

Figure 10.47
Workstation Design for
Problem 24

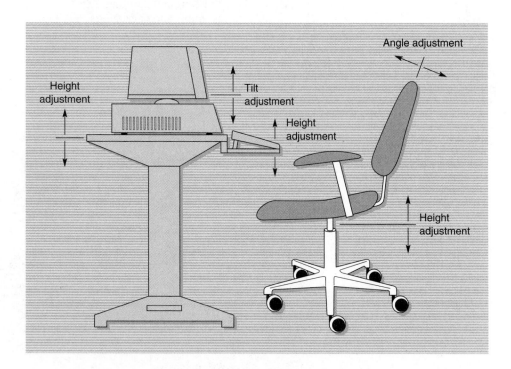

25. An Internal Revenue Service employee responsible for the preliminary check of tax returns must determine if the return was mailed by April 15, if the return is signed, and if the necessary W2 forms are attached to the return. Thus, there are (2)(2)(2) = 8 possible outcomes corresponding to this task; for example, (return on time–signed–W2s attached), (return late–signed–W2s attached), and so on. Design a workstation for this process.

Chapter Outline

Chapter Eleven
Process
Management

Applied P/OM

Spalding
Ritz-Carlton Hotel Company
Eastman Chemical Company
Motorola
AT&T

P/OM in Practice

Process Improvement at Kentucky Fried
Chicken
Applications of Process-Management Tools at
Rotor Clip

The president of Texas Instruments Defense Systems and Electronics Group, a Malcolm Baldrige National Quality Award winner, has a sign in his office that reads, *"Unless you change the process, why would you expect the results to change?"* As we have noted several times in this book, all work is performed by a process. The overwhelming majority of quality and productivity problems are associated with processes; few are caused primarily by workers. Thus, at MamaMia's Pizza, if customers complain about overcooked pizzas or excessively late delivery, it would be fruitless to place blame solely on employees. Rather, it would be managers' responsibility—actually, a shared responsibility with the work force—to improve the processes involved in cooking and delivering the pizzas.

Process management involves (1) **control,** planning and administering the activities necessary to sustain a high level of performance in a process, and (2) **improvement,** identifying opportunities for achieving continuously higher levels of quality in operational performance. The distinction between control and improvement is illustrated in Figure 11.1. Any process-performance measure will fluctuate naturally around some average level. Abnormal conditions will cause an unusual deviation from that pattern. Removing the causes of such abnormal conditions is the essence of control. Improvement, on the other hand, means bringing the performance up to a new level.

Process management is focused on preventing defects and errors, and eliminating such waste as non-value-added processing steps, waiting (delay), and redundancy. Shorter cycle times and faster customer responsiveness are the goals.

Leading businesses devote considerable effort to process-management activities. Usually they begin by identifying the business processes that most affect customer satisfaction—first among the **core processes** that drive the creation of products and services, and then among the **support processes** that are critical to production and delivery. At MamaMia's pizza, for example, the core processes are the production of pizzas and home delivery. Key support processes are order entry, dining-room service, and purchasing.

To apply techniques of process management, processes must be (1) repeatable and (2) measurable. Being repeatable means that the process recurs over time. The cycle may be long, as with product-development processes or patent

Figure 11.1
Control versus Improvement

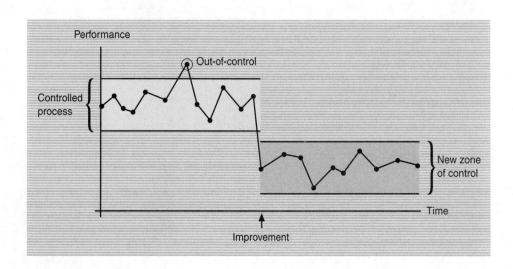

applications, or it may be short, as with an order-entry process or pizza preparation. Repeatability ensures that enough data can be collected to provide useful information, revealing patterns about the process performance that enable managers to detect abnormal conditions and opportunities for improvements, as well as make some predictions about future performance. Obviously, the processes must be measurable for such data to be obtained.

In this chapter we examine strategies for process control and improvement, specifically,

••• The concept of control, and in particular the role of quality control in P/OM.
••• Techniques for preventing defects.
••• The role of maintenance in managing processes and the emerging concept of total productive maintenance.
••• The philosophy of and approaches to continuous improvement.
••• Seven basic tools for process improvement and their applications.

Process Control

Control is the continuing process of evaluating performance and taking corrective action when necessary. Any control system has three components: (1) a standard or goal, (2) a means of measurement of accomplishment, and (3) a means of comparing actual results with the standard, along with feedback to form the basis for corrective action. A simple example of control is checking a finished pizza with the customer's order for correct size and ingredients.

The need for control arises because of the inherent variation in any system or process. Sources of variation in production processes were discussed in Chapter 2 in the context of Deming's philosophy, and the concepts of *common causes* and *special causes* of variation were introduced. Walter Shewhart is credited with recognizing the distinction between common and special causes of variation in the 1920s at Bell Laboratories. A process governed only by common causes is stable despite minor variations and remains essentially constant over time. The variations are predictable and stay within established statistical limits. Controlling a process therefore consists of identifying and removing the special causes of variation. Short-term remedial action for such special causes often can be taken by workers on the shop floor. However, if operators are held accountable for handling problems that are beyond their control, the result is only frustration and eventual game-playing with managers. The vast majority of process-related problems are the result of common-cause variation; these problems are the responsibility of managers.

Quality Control Function

The function of **quality control** is to prevent, detect, and correct product or service nonconformances that would make the product or service unfit for use. Thus, quality control has several objectives:

1. To ensure that purchased materials and components meet predetermined quality standards.

2. To maintain conformance to design specifications throughout the manufacturing process or during the delivery of a service.

3. To achieve the highest possible quality level for the final product or service.

4. To improve productivity by reducing scrap and rework in manufacturing and the number of complaints and returns from customers.

5. To reduce the internal and external failure costs that arise when quality standards are not achieved.

To accomplish these objectives, organizations must develop quality control systems.

Figure 11.2 shows the role of quality control in a production system. To ensure that raw materials and purchased parts meet the stated quality standards, incoming shipments of those goods are often inspected. In this context, *acceptable quality* means meeting the standards developed during the product-design effort.

Traditional practice has been to accept or reject entire lots of materials procured from suppliers, with rejected lots being returned at the supplier's expense. This practice is called **acceptance sampling.** The rationale for acceptance sampling is that suppliers will provide good-quality materials if they know that poor quality lots will be rejected. In practice, though, suppliers give purchasers only the level of quality that was requested, which usually specifies an "acceptable" number of defectives. In addition, the costs of any rejected lots are ultimately passed on to the consumer. Although we briefly discuss acceptance sampling in the next chapter, we emphasize that it is not a preferred method of controlling quality. In a TQM environment, companies should build long-term partnerships based on mutual trust with suppliers, making incoming inspection unnecessary. Instead, supplier quality can be assured through periodic audits either at the supplier's plant or with spot checks.

Because unwanted variation can arise during production—for example, from machines going out of adjustment, worker inattention, or environmental

Figure 11.2 Quality Control in a Production System

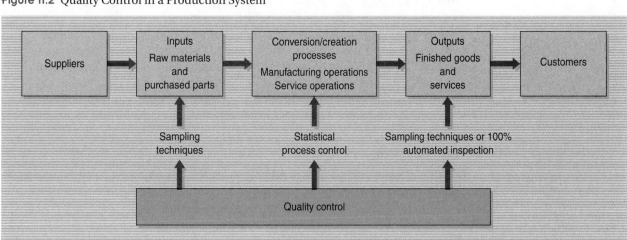

conditions—quality control procedures are needed throughout the production process. Using statistical methods to control quality while a process is operating is called *statistical process control* (SPC). Done properly, SPC can eliminate the need for independent inspection activity by quickly eliminating special causes of variation and making immediate adjustments to stabilize the process. The production operator becomes the inspector, as was the case before the Industrial Revolution. SPC is discussed in depth in the next chapter.

Final inspection is the last point in the manufacturing process where we can verify that the product meets customer requirements and avoid external failure costs. For many consumer products, final inspection consists of functional testing. For instance, a manufacturer of television sets might do a simple test on every unit to make sure it operates properly. However, the company might not test every aspect of the unit, as such characteristics as picture sharpness might have been assured through in-process controls. Computerized test equipment is becoming widespread, allowing for 100 percent inspection to be conducted rapidly and cost effectively.

Quality control also plays an important role in service organizations. Since customer satisfaction is the major goal in the delivery of services, quality control is a vital function. A travel agent, for example, often previews resorts, cruise ships, and so on, before recommending them to clients. While working with a client, the agent might check to see if tickets arrive on time or if any assistance is needed. Finally, the agent might check with the client after his or her return. As another example, a hospital, might use a simple checksheet for inspection of cleanliness. Each item in a patient's room can be checked as either satisfactory or unsatisfactory, with the results being used for measuring efficiency and to identify problems that require correction.

Inspection and Measurement

Designing a quality control system requires determining which quality characteristics are important to monitor, how they should be measured, and what standards will distinguish acceptable quality levels from unacceptable levels. Inspection and measurement form the basis for detecting quality problems and identifying areas for improvement. For example, to determine the quality of a polished chrome faucet, a simple visual inspection may be done; to measure the diameter of a ball bearing, a micrometer or some other measuring device would be used. In a service application, an audit is done to evaluate the quality of an accounting function.

Much controversy has surrounded the role of inspection in quality control. One of Deming's 14 points was originally phrased, "Eliminate mass inspection." In 1990, Deming revised it to, "Understand the purpose of inspection." What Deming was trying to convey in the early version was the need to eliminate quality assurance that was based solely on final inspection, as was common practice in American industry at that time. The task of the inspection department was to seek out defective items in production and remove them to be scrapped or reworked before shipment to customers. Inspection was used as a screening activity for removing nonconforming products from production but did not seek to remove the causes of poor quality. Today's inspector is no longer a policeman, but rather a technical consultant, auditor, and coach. The inspection department is responsible for *assisting* production personnel in developing effective processes, procedures, and practices for controlling and monitoring quality, not for *assuring* quality.

Type of Inspection

The type of inspection performed depends on the characteristic being evaluated or measured. An *attribute* is a characteristic that assumes one of two values; for instance, present or not present, conforming or not conforming, within specification or out of specification, complete or incomplete. An example of an **attribute** measurement is the visual inspection of a pizza to determine whether or not it has enough toppings. Another example is deciding if the diameter of a shaft is within the specified limits of $1.60 \pm .01$ inch (without being concerned about its actual value).

The second type of measurement is **variable** measurement. Here the interest is characteristics that can be measured on a continuous scale; for instance, length or weight. With variable measurement, the concern is with the *degree* of conformance to specifications. Therefore, rather than determining whether or not the diameter of a shaft meets a specification of $1.60 \pm .01$ inch, we are concerned with the actual value of the diameter.

Attribute inspection is usually simpler than variable inspection for several reasons. The inspection itself can be made more quickly and easily, less information needs to be recorded, and administration of the inspection is easier. Statistically, though, attribute inspection is less efficient than variable inspection; it requires a larger sample size than variable inspection to obtain the same amount of statistical information about the quality level of the part, product, or service. The difference can be important when inspection is time-consuming or expensive.

Inspection Quantity

One important decision in inspection planning is the amount of inspection to be performed. Several factors must be considered: the type of product to be inspected, the quality characteristics to be examined, the quality history of the producer, the cost of inspection, and the effect of inspection on the product (for example, destructive testing). The decision is usually to use either 100-percent inspection or some type of sampling procedure.

One-hundred-percent inspection is the inspection of every unit produced. For critical quality characteristics, such inspection is usually required. While it provides the best assurance of conformance to specifications, it is not always perfect because of such problems as human error, faulty measuring equipment, and use of incorrect standards. One-hundred-percent inspection is often not practical because of the time, effort, and costs involved. (And, clearly, it cannot be used when testing is destructive!) With automated inspection techniques, however, 100-percent inspection is becoming more economical and feasible.

Sampling procedures inspect only a portion of a production lot. They are useful in checking large quantities of noncritical quality characteristics. The lower costs of sampling inspection must be weighed against the risk of greater cost incurred by permitting nonconforming products to be accepted. In practice, somewhat surprisingly, sampling procedures have often proved superior to 100-percent inspection because of their ability to overcome systematic forms of human error. Accordingly, sampling procedures are the basis of most quality control procedures used today.

Locating Inspection Activities

In determining where to locate inspection activities, one must consider trade-offs between the explicit costs of detection, repair, and replacement and the implicit costs of unnecessary additional investment in a nonconforming item if inspection is not performed. While the location decision is fundamentally based on economics, it is a complex one, since it is not always easy or possible to quantify the explicit and implicit costs.

Flow-process charts and assembly charts developed during manufacturing planning show the steps performed in manufacturing a product. They are used as a basis for identifying locations to perform inspections. Inspections might be located before or after any or all operations. How does one decide? Some popular rules of thumb are to locate the inspection station

- After operations likely to generate a high proportion of defectives.
- After the finished product is completed.
- Before all processing operations, such as before each machine or assembly operation.
- Before relatively high-cost operations or where significant value is added to the product.
- Before processing operations that may make the detection of defectives difficult or costly, such as operations (like painting) that may mask or obscure faulty attributes.

No one rule fits all situations. Simulation, economic analysis, and other quantitative tools are often used to evaluate a particular design of inspection activities.

In deciding whether or not to inspect an item, one must first ask what the result would be if a nonconforming item were allowed to continue through production or on to the consumer. If the result might be a safety hazard, costly repairs, or some other intolerable condition, then 100-percent inspection must be used. Remember that with sampling, there is always a risk that a small percentage of nonconforming items will be passed. Also, sampling can actually increase costs if performed indiscriminately.

Unless there is destructive testing (in which case, sampling is necessary) or there are critical safety concerns (in which case, 100-percent inspection is warranted), the choice among the three options (the third being no inspection) can be addressed in economic terms. In fact, we can easily show that on a strictly economic basis, the choice is to have either no inspection or 100-percent inspection. That viewpoint was strongly advocated by Deming.

Let C_1 equal the cost of inspection and removal of a nonconforming item, C_2 the cost of repair if a nonconforming item is allowed to continue to the next point in the production process, and p the true fraction of nonconforming items in the lot. The expected cost per item for 100-percent inspection is clearly

C_1; the expected cost per item for no inspection is pC_2. Setting these equal to each other yields the break-even value for p:

$$pC_2 = C_1$$

$$p = \frac{C_1}{C_2}.$$

Thus, if $p > C_1/C_2$, the best decision is to use 100-percent inspection; if $p < C_1/C_2$, it is more economical to do nothing at all.

In practice, however, both the costs C_1 and C_2 and the true fraction of non-conforming items, p, are difficult to determine accurately. The value of C_1 includes the capital cost of equipment used in the inspection process, depreciation, and residual value, and operating costs such as labor, rent, utilities, maintenance, and replacement parts. Included in C_2 are the costs of disassembly and repair, sorting products to find the nonconformances, warranty repair costs if the products are shipped, and cost of lost sales. Many of those costs change over time. In addition, finding p requires sampling inspection in the first place. A useful rule of thumb is to use 100-percent inspection if p is known to be much greater than C_1/C_2, and no inspection it if is much less, but if p is close to C_1/C_2 or is highly variable, sampling should be used for protection and auditing purposes. An example follows.

Example

Using Break-Even Analysis for the Economical Inspection Decision

Let us consider the decision between having 100 percent inspection and no inspection after an intermediate assembly operation for an electronic calculator. To make this decision, we must compare the inspection cost to the penalty cost incurred if a nonconforming item is missed. Suppose it costs an average of 25¢ per unit for the inspector's time, equipment, and overhead. If a nonconforming part is assembled at this stage of production, the calculator will not work properly during final inspection. Rejected calculators must be disassembled and repaired; the work involved averages $8 per unit. The problem is thus to establish a break-even point for the quality level. Figure 11.3 illustrates the costs involved and the break-even point. For a lot size of, for example, 100 items, 100-percent inspection costs 100(.25), or $25. The cost of no inspection depends on the quality level—that is, the proportion nonconforming. If the proportion nonconforming is p, then $100p$ units require rework at a cost of $8 each. Thus the average cost of no inspection is $800p$. The break-even point is found by setting

$$25 = 800p.$$

Thus

$$p = .03125$$

Hence, if the proportion nonconforming is greater than .03125, it is more economical to inspect each assembly.

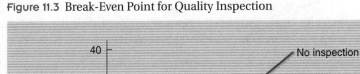

Figure 11.3 Break-Even Point for Quality Inspection

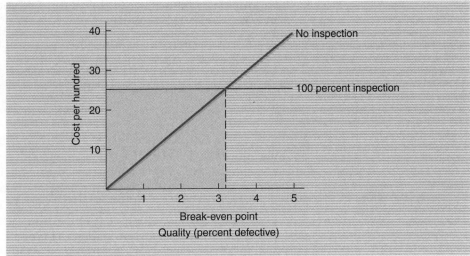

The decision to inspect incoming materials and parts should be based on the quality history of the supplier. If the quality history is very good—as evidenced by good statistical control of the supplier's processes and a low defect rate—there should be no need for inspection. If quality history is poor or there is evidence of lack of statistical control, some form of acceptance sampling should be used.

Human-Factors Issues and Automated Inspection

Because inspection is not an easy task, it is highly subject to human error; error rates of 10 to 50 percent are not uncommon. An experiment that illustrates this point is to ask three people to proofread a lengthy manuscript for typographical errors. Rarely will everyone discover all errors, much less the same ones. The same is true of complicated industrial inspection tasks, especially those involving detailed microelectronics.

Manual human inspection tasks are affected by several factors:[1]

1. *Complexity.* The number of defects identified by an inspector decreases with an increase in the number of parts to be inspected and with less order in their arrangement.
2. *Defect rate.* When the product defect rate is low, inspectors tend to miss more defects than when the defect rate is higher.
3. *Repeated inspections.* Different inspectors miss different defects. Therefore, if an item is inspected by a number of inspectors, a higher percentage of total defects will be caught.
4. *Inspection rate.* The inspector's performance degrades rapidly as the inspection rate increases.

In light of these factors, there are several ways to improve inspection:

••• Minimize the number of quality characteristics considered in an inspection task. Five to six characteristics appear to be the maximum that the human mind can handle well at one time.

••• Minimize disturbing instructions and time pressures.

••• Provide clear, detailed instructions for the inspection task.

••• Design the workspace to facilitate the inspection task and provide good lighting.

Microprocessors and advanced electronics now make automated inspection possible. Automated visual inspection systems can recognize and identify, classify, sort, and inspect objects. For instance, automated visual inspection systems can check snack-food packages for the proper amount of food or check the seals on each package. Such systems are fast; they inspect 2 to 10 objects per second. Robots are also being used for quality inspection. General Electric, for example, uses a robotized X-ray inspection station to manipulate objects in front of an X-ray machine so that human inspectors are not exposed to radiation.[2]

Techniques for Quality Control

One of the more popular approaches to quality control is *statistical process control (SPC)*, which is discussed fully in the next chapter. SPC methods are particularly useful when a company is in the early stages of developing good quality control systems and defect rates are relatively high. In today's near-zero-defect environment in which quality is measured in defects per million opportunities, formal statistical methods are limited. Many manufacturers are eliminating SPC on the production floor, and replacing it with economical 100-percent inspection and other forms of defect prevention. Some of these methods are described here.[3]

A **poka-yoke** is a device that permanently prevents the recurrence of the defect it is designed to eliminate. One example is installing a device on a drill that counts the number of holes drilled in a workpiece; a buzzer sounds if the workpiece is removed before the correct number of holes have been drilled. Similarly, to ensure that critical bolts are tightened on vehicles in a Toyota plant, the wrenches used are kept in a bucket of dye; when a bolt has been missed, it lacks the highly visible color. Poka-yoke epitomizes worker involvement in quality assurance. Because the workers best understand the causes of defects as well as the processes, they are likely to propose the most ingenious solutions.

Successive checking is the design of processes that are physically impossible if preceding processes have produced defective parts. For example, if a part has not been cut to the proper length, it will not fit into the next machine. This approach shortens the time needed for feedback. The worker immediately knows when an error has occurred and can correct the problem before further value-added processing. **Self-checking** uses the same principles, but requires that the worker performing the operation check his or her own output.

Autonomation involves equipping machines with automatic stopping devices and other features that eliminate the possibility that large quantities of defectives will be produced. This concept is not new. It was used at Ford in the early 1950s. A device automatically checked for broken tools after each drilling cycle by sweeping wands by each drill bit. When any one of the wands failed to contact a bit—indicating a broken bit—the station would automatically shut down for repair. Spalding uses this approach in manufacturing golf balls.

Applied P/OM
Spalding

Spalding seeks to make the perfect golf ball.[4]

Spalding has invested $20 million to upgrade its Chicopee, Massachusetts, Top-Flite golf ball factory in an effort to make every one of its annual production of 300 million golf balls perfect. A computer-based quality control system monitors each step of the manufacturing process. Sensors check everything from the ball's cover to the ink stamp. If a problem is detected, sirens blare, red lights flash, and the workstation shuts down until workers correct the problem. Imperfect balls drop into a trash barrel to be sold as factory seconds; the rest roll to final packaging stations.

Quality Control in Services

The most common quality characteristics in services are time (waiting time, service time, delivery time) and number of nonconformances. Both can be measured rather easily. Insurance companies, for example, measure the time to complete different transactions such as new issues, claim payments, and cash surrenders. Hospitals measure the percentage of nosocomial infections and the percentage of unplanned readmissions to the emergency room, intensive care, or operating room within, say, 48 hours. Other quality characteristics are observable rather than measurable. They include errors of wrong kind, wrong quantity, wrong delivery date, and so forth, and behavior—courtesy, promptness, competency, and so on. Hospitals might monitor the completeness of medical charts and the quality of radiology readings, measured by a double-reading process.

It is easy to observe human behavior; it is more difficult, however, to describe and classify the observations. For example, how do you define courteous versus discourteous, or understanding versus indifferent? This is best done by comparing behavior against clear standards. For instance, a standard for "courtesy" might be to address the customer as "mister," "missus," and "miss." "Promptness" might be defined as greeting customers within five seconds of their entering the store, or answering letters within two days of receipt. Observations based on these kinds of standards are easily recorded and counted. The Ritz-Carlton Hotel Company uses such statistical measures of customer service in its quality control efforts.

Applied P/OM

Ritz-Carlton Hotel Company

The Ritz-Carlton relies heavily on data and information in its quality control efforts.[5]

The approach used by The Ritz-Carlton Hotel Company to capture and use customer-satisfaction and quality-related data needs to be real-time and proactive because of the company's intensive personalized service environment. Systems for collecting and using such data are widely deployed throughout the organization. Efforts are centered on various customer segments and product lines.

The systems used enable every employee to collect and utilize quality-related data such as the following on a daily basis.

1. On-line guest-preference information.
2. Quantity of error-free products and services.
3. Opportunities for quality improvement.

An automated property-management system affords on-line access and utilization of guest-preference information at the individual customer level. All employees collect and input the data, and use them as part of their service delivery with individual guests. The quality-production reporting system is a method of aggregating hotel-level data from nearly two dozen sources into a summary format. It serves as an early warning system and facilitates analysis. The processes employees use to identify quality opportunities for improvement are standardized in a textbook, made available throughout the organization.

Today, the goal of the business management system at Ritz-Carlton is to become more integrated, more proactive, and more preventive. Efforts are underway to check work continuously to see if the company is providing what the customer wants most, on time, every time. The test measures are charted statistically to help teams determine where to make improvements. The quality, marketing, and financial results of each hotel are aggregated and integrated to determine what quality factors are driving the financial outcome. These systems enable leaders and teams to better determine goals and justify expenditures.

Total Productive Maintenance

Maintenance costs can contribute significantly to the total cost of sales.[6] Such costs have been increasing two to three times as fast as overall production costs because high-technology machines are replacing direct labor.

Total productive maintenance (TPM) is concerned with keeping equipment functionally available so that it will work when needed, perform to expectations in producing a quality product, and perform reliably with no breakdowns. TPM is based on total quality management (TQM) concepts. Just as inspection has traditionally been the approach to quality control, breakdown repair has been the common approach to maintenance. Improved understanding of failure mechanisms, better design for reliability, and preventive maintenance—particularly with extensive operator involvement—are better approaches. TPM seeks to

••• Maximize overall equipment effectiveness and eliminate unplanned downtime.

••• Create operator "ownership" of the equipment through involving the operator in maintenance activities.

••• Foster continuous efforts to improve equipment operation through employee involvement activities.

TPM can result in improved production rates and thus greater capacity, reduced scrap and rework, smaller inventories, less need for standby equipment, and lower product costs.

Basically, TPM involves workers taking responsibility for the care and maintenance of their equipment and work space, with a focus on prevention rather than correction. Whenever possible, workers perform simple repairs and routine maintenance activities. The maintenance department handles more complex maintenance tasks, trains workers, and keeps spare parts and supplies. The scope of TPM and the benefits associated with its implementation can be seen in its application at Eastman Chemical Company.

Applied P/OM
Eastman Chemical Company

TPM complements a TQM focus on employee involvement and continuous improvement.[7]

TPM began at Eastman Chemical Company in 1987, and within five years more than 120 teams were functioning, comprising over 85 percent of the facility. In its implementation, maintenance personnel work with operators in work zones within the plant with a focus on continuous improvement of processes through improved equipment reliability and maintainability. More than 3,000 tasks have been identified as TPM tasks, 80 percent of which are being performed by equipment operators. These include repairing equipment, changing filters, lubricating, and adjusting. Eastman estimated a six-month payback on its investment in TPM. Prior to TPM, a mixer stoppage would last approximately one hour while maintenance personnel came and reset a tripped motor starter. Now production is restored by an operator in 15 minutes or less. In one instance, after a power plant failure, a team restored production approximately three days sooner than would have been possible under the traditional maintenance organization, saving the company several million dollars. Maintenance cost savings attributable to TPM are estimated to be over $13 million annually.

There are two types of maintenance activities: maintenance needed because of machine failure and preventive maintenance. Maintenance because of machine failure is unavoidable, but can be minimized by a preventive-maintenance program. Such a program helps to achieve better utilization of the maintenance staff through planned scheduling of maintenance work and it can reduce losses due to breakdowns or injury. Determining an appropriate maintenance policy for a piece of equipment should take into account the economic and operational trade-offs involved. The following illustrates how reliability data can be used in this analysis.

Example

Determining a Preventive-Maintenance Policy

A part of a bathroom-tissue production system is a saw/wrapper machine, which cuts long rolls into smaller pieces and packages them prior to placing them into cartons. Historical data on the time between failures is presented in Figure 11.4. From this information, we can calculate the **mean time between failures (MTBF)** by multiplying the midpoint of each cell by its associated probability and adding, as in

$$MTBF = 27.5(.20) + 32.5(.40) + 37.5(.30) + 42.5(.10)$$

$$= 34 \text{ hours.}$$

Assume that in the current system the machine is repaired only when it fails, at an average cost of $50. The company is considering a preventive maintenance program that will cost $30 for each inspection and adjustment. Should this be done, and if so, how often should preventive maintenance occur?

To find the best policy, we must compute and compare average annual costs for both approaches. Consider, for instance, the current policy. Assuming 260 working days per year and one 8-hour shift per day, there are 2,080 hours of available time. If the mean time between failures is 34 hours, we expect 2,080/34 = 61.2 failures per year. Hence the annual cost is (61.2)($50) = $3,060.

Figure 11.4 Histogram of Time between Failures

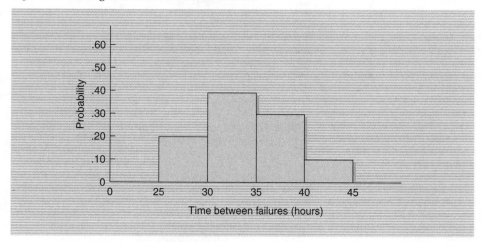

Table 11.1 Maintenance-Cost Computation

(1) Time between Inspections	(2) Number of Inspections per Year	(3) Probability of Failure before Next Inspection	(4) Preventive Maintenance Cost ($)	(5) Failure Cost ($)	Total Cost ($)
25	83.2	0	2,496	0	2,496
30	69.3	.2	2,080	693	2,773
35	59.4	.6	1,782	1,782	3,564
40	52	.9	1,560	2,340	3,900

Now suppose the machine is inspected and adjusted every 25 hours. If we assume that the time until the next failure after adjustment follows the distribution in Figure 11.4, the probability of a failure under this policy is zero. However, inspection every 25 hours would occur $2,080/25 = 83.2$ times per year, resulting in a preventive maintenance cost of $(83.2)(\$30) = \$2,496$.

Next, suppose we inspect the machine every 30 hours. From Figure 11.4, we know the probability of a failure occurring before the next inspection is .20. Thus the total expected annual cost would be the cost of inspection, $(\$30)(2,080/30) = \$2,080$, plus the expected cost of emergency repair, $(\$50)(2,080/30)(.2) = \$693$; hence the total is \$2,773.

We can perform similar calculations for other maintenance intervals, the results are shown in Table 11.1. Thus we see that a maintenance interval of 25 hours results in a minimal cost policy.

In the preceding example we see that as the time between inspections increases, the inspection cost decreases and the failure cost increases. These economic trade-offs are typical of preventive-maintenance problems and generally produce a graph similar to Figure 11.5.

In many large firms, maintenance management is automated and uses a computer. A typical data file might include a description of the equipment, cost

Figure 11.5
Economic Trade-Offs in
Maintenance

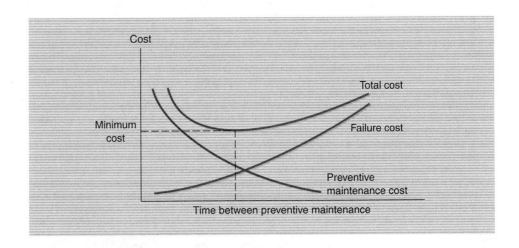

data, warranty information, preventive-maintenance intervals, standard times, and historical data on maintenance time and costs. Reports of scheduled maintenance activities can be generated on a daily or weekly basis, as can reports on backlogs and delays. In addition, such a database can provide productivity reports to managers and cost reports for accounting and budgeting purposes.

Continuous Improvement

Prior to TQM, most U.S. managers concentrated primarily on *maintaining* the quality of products and processes until they could be replaced by new technology. Japanese managers, in contrast, concentrate on continually improving them. The MIT Commission on Industrial Productivity observed this:

> Another area in which U.S. firms have often lagged behind their overseas competitors is in exploiting the potential for continuous improvement in the quality and reliability of their products and processes. The cumulative effect of successive incremental improvements and modifications to established products and processes can be very large and may outpace efforts to achieve technological breakthroughs.[8]

In other words, the commission is saying that improvement should be a proactive task of managers, not simply a reaction to problems and competitive threats.

Many opportunities for improvement exist. Manufacturing defects can be reduced, cycle times shortened, employee morale, satisfaction, and cooperation increased; managerial practices made more effective; product design improved to better meet customers' needs; and manufacturing systems made more efficient. Eliminating unnecessary inventory, transportation, materials handling, worker motions and idle time, and scrap and rework—that is, eliminating any non-value-added step in a process—reduces cycle time along with opportunities for errors or defects.

The concept of continuous improvement was conceived and developed in the United States, yet it is often cited as the most important difference between Japanese and Western management.[9] One of the earliest examples in the United States was at National Cash Register Company (NCR). After a shipment of defective cash registers was returned in 1894, the company's founder discovered unpleasant and unsafe working conditions. He made many changes, including better lighting, new safety devices, ventilation, lounges, and lockers. The company offered extensive evening classes to improve employees' education and skills, and instituted a program for soliciting suggestions from factory workers. Workers received cash prizes and other recognition for their best ideas; by the 1940s the company was receiving an average of 3,000 suggestions each year.

The Lincoln Electric Company, another early pioneer in continuous improvement, designed an "incentive management" system to promote continuous improvement. Workers were rewarded with compensation proportional to output and given increased status and publicity for their contributions. They were not penalized for finding more efficient ways to produce—an inadvertent and unfortunate consequence in some firms when improvements reduce employee hours—but rather were rewarded for their ingenuity and increased productivity. The company profited because fixed overhead could be spread over the increased production. Workers had full responsibility for their workstations and were held accountable for quality. An employee advisory board elected by the work force met regularly with top managers to discuss ideas and to identify problems.

While the experiences at NCR and Lincoln Electric are isolated examples, productivity improvement has always been the focal point of the profession of *industrial engineering* (IE). One productivity improvement program, *work simplification,* was developed by Allan Mogensen on the theory that workers know their jobs better than anyone else. Therefore, if they are trained in the simple steps necessary to analyze the work they are doing, they will be the ones best able to make improvements. Accordingly, work-simplification programs train workers in methods analysis, flowcharting, and diagramming. This concept greatly helped the production effort during World War II.

Another approach, pioneered by Procter & Gamble, is called *planned methods change.* It goes one step further than work simplification, seeking not only to improve, but also to replace or eliminate unnecessary operations. Teams of employees study the operations, establish specific dollar goals as to how much of their cost they will try to eliminate through planned change, and provide positive recognition for success.

As mentioned, a focus on quality improvement in the United States is relatively recent, stimulated by the success of the Japanese. During the rebuilding years after World War II in Japan, many Japanese companies developed continuous improvement programs. Some of the early programs were started by Toshiba in 1946, Matsushita Electric in 1950, and Toyota in 1951. Toyota, in particular, pioneered the just-in-time (JIT) system (see Chapter 15), which showed that making products with virtually zero defects is possible, and reversed the thinking that it is very costly to do so. In fact, JIT proved that making products with extremely low defect levels typically saves money. Most importantly, JIT established a philosophy of improvement, which the Japanese call *kaizen* (ky'zen), discussed next.

Kaizen and the Deming Cycle

Kaizen—a philosophy of continuous improvement—has been called "the single most important concept in Japanese management—the key to Japanese competitive success."[10] In the kaizen philosophy, improvements in all areas of business—cost, meeting delivery schedules, employee safety and skill development, supplier relations, new-product development, and productivity—all enhance the quality of the firm.

Kaizen is different from innovation. Innovation, which is generally the focus of Western management, results in large, short-term, and radical changes in products or processes. Often innovation is the result of substantial investment in equipment or technology with major rebuilding of entire plants. Innovation is dramatic and often championed by a few proponents. Formal economic analyses show large returns on investment. Major innovations such as *material requirements planning* (*MRP*) or *flexible manufacturing systems* (*FMS*) grab the attention of top managers. The American automotive industry, for example, believed that it could cure its quality and competitive problems in the 1970s by the introduction of robots and other types of automated equipment. Managers learned that innovative technologies are not the magic cure.

Kaizen, unlike approaches based solely on innovation, is focused on small, gradual, but frequent improvements over the long term. Financial investment is

Figure 11.6
The Deming Cycle

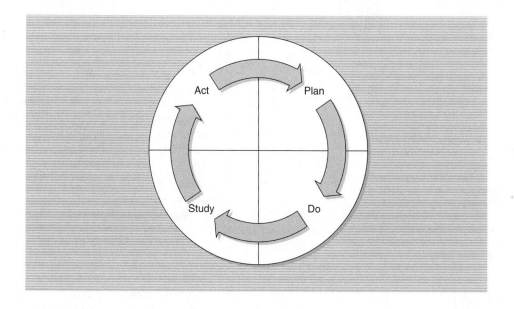

minimal. Everyone, not just top managers, is involved in the process, and many improvements result from the know-how and experience of nonmanagerial workers. People, not technology, are the principal focus. Kaizen is a process-oriented way of thinking rather than the results-oriented approach that is so characteristic of Western management thought. At Nissan Motor, for instance, any suggestion that saves at least 0.6 seconds in a production process is seriously considered by managers. The concept of kaizen is so deeply ingrained in the minds of both managers and workers that they often do not even realize they are thinking in terms of improvement. Innovation is recognized to be an important aspect of kaizen; however, it is emphasized much less in Japan than in the West.

Quality improvement in the kaizen philosophy is first and foremost concerned with the quality of people. The logic is that if the quality of people is improved, the quality of products will follow. This process-oriented approach to improvement encourages constant communication among workers and managers.

The kaizen philosophy is implemented with the **Deming cycle,** shown in Figure 11.6. Deming taught the approach to the Japanese as the "Shewhart cycle"—named for its founder, Walter Shewhart—and the Japanese renamed it in 1950. The Deming cycle consists of four stages: plan, do, study, and act. The *planning* stage consists of analyzing the current situation, gathering data, and planning for improvement. In the *doing* stage, the plan is implemented on a trial basis, such as in a laboratory, pilot production program, or with a small group of customers. The *studying* stage is designed to determine if the trial plan is working correctly and if any further problems or opportunities are apparent. The last stage, *acting,* implements the final plan and ensures that the improvements will be standardized and practiced continuously. This leads back to the *planning* stage for further diagnosis and improvement. As Figure 11.6 illustrates, the cycle never ends; that is, it fosters *continuous improvement.* The improved standards provide the springboard for further improvements.

The essence of kaizen is simple and, upon reflection, just plain common sense. Most companies today train their employees to think in terms of continuous improvement. One example is Motorola.

Applied P/OM

Motorola

The concept of continuous improvement has been embraced by Motorola.

Motorola trains its employees to use a six-step approach for continuous improvement:

1. *Identify the product or service.* What work do I do?
2. *Identify the customer.* For whom is the work being done?
3. *Identify the supplier.* What do I need, and from whom do I get it?
4. *Identify the process.* What steps or tasks are performed? What are the inputs and outputs for each step?
5. *Mistake-proof the process.* How can I eliminate or simplify tasks? What fail-safing devices can I use?
6. *Develop measurements and controls, and improvement goals.* How do I evaluate the process? How can I improve further?

Breakthrough Improvement through Benchmarking and Reengineering

Motorola uses "defects per unit" as a quality measure throughout the company. A "unit" is any output of work, such as a line of computer code, a solder connection, or a page of a document. A "defect" is any failure to meet customer requirements. Motorola developed a concept called "six sigma" quality, which refers to allowing at most 3.4 defects per million units. In 1987 Motorola set the following goal:

> Improve product and services quality ten times by 1989, and at least one-hundred-fold by 1991. Achieve six-sigma capability by 1992. With a deep sense of urgency, spread dedication to quality to every facet of the corporation, and achieve a culture of continuous improvement to assure total customer satisfaction. There is only one ultimate goal: zero defects—in everything we do.

That is certainly an ambitious goal that applies to all areas of the company, including order entry, sales, purchasing, manufacturing, and design. The modern term for such goals is *stretch goals,* or *breakthrough objectives.* Stretch goals force an organization to think in a radically different way, to encourage major improvements as well as incremental ones. When a goal of 10 percent improvement is set, managers or engineers can usually meet it with some minor improvements. However, when the goal is 1,000 percent improvement, employees must be creative. The seemingly impossible is often achieved, yielding dramatic improvements and boosting morale. Two approaches that help companies accomplish such results are benchmarking and reengineering.

Benchmarking. **Benchmarking** can be defined as "measuring your performance against that of best-in-class companies, determining how the best-in-class achieve those performance levels, and using the information as a basis for your own company's targets, strategies, and implementation,"[11] or more simply, "the search of industry best practices that lead to superior performance."[12] Benchmarking helps a company to learn its strengths and weaknesses and those of other industrial leaders and to incorporate the best practices into its own operations.

The concept is not new.[13] In the early 1800s Francis Lowell, a New England industrialist, traveled to England to study manufacturing techniques of the best British mill factories. Henry Ford created the assembly line after taking a tour of a Chicago slaughterhouse and watching carcasses hung on hooks mounted on a monorail move from one workstation to another. Toyota's just-in-time production system was influenced by replenishment practices of U.S. supermarkets. Today's benchmarking was initiated by Xerox, an eventual winner of the Malcolm Baldrige National Quality Award. It has since become a common part of strategy for leading firms.

Three major types of benchmarking have emerged in business. *Performance benchmarking* is used for products and services and might be applied to pricing, technical quality, features, and other quality or performance characteristics. It usually involves direct comparisons or *reverse engineering,* in which competitor's products are taken apart and analyzed. This practice of studying products and processes of competitors in the same industry has been known as *competitive comparison. Process benchmarking* is used for work processes such as billing, order entry, or employee training. This type of benchmarking seeks to identify the most effective practices in companies that perform similar functions, regardless of the industry. For example, the warehousing and distribution practices of L. L. Bean were adapted by Xerox for its spare-parts distribution system. Texas Instruments studied the kitting (order preparation) practices of six companies, including Mary Kay Cosmetics, and designed a process that captured the best practices of each of them, cutting kitting cycle time in half. Granite Rock, a California supplier to the construction industry, benchmarked Domino's Pizza, because concrete, like pizza is perishable and requires rapid delivery to customers. Finally, *strategic benchmarking* examines how companies compete, seeking the winning strategies that have led to competitive advantage and market success. Most companies, like AT&T, have a well-defined and formal benchmarking process.

Applied P/OM
AT&T

AT&T uses a typical benchmarking process.[14]

The benchmarking process at AT&T consists of

1. *Project conception.* Identify the need, and decide to benchmark accordingly.
2. *Planning.* Determine the scope and objectives, and develop a benchmarking plan.
3. *Preliminary data collection.* Collect data on industry companies and similar processes as well as detailed data on your own processes.

4. *Best-in-class selection.* Select companies with best-in-class processes.

5. *Best-in-class collection.* Collect detailed data from companies with best-in-class processes.

6. *Assessment.* Compare your own and best-in-class processes, and develop recommendations.

7. *Implementation planning.* Develop operational improvement plans to attain superior performance.

8. *Implementation.* Enact operational plans, and monitor process improvements.

9. *Recalibaration.* Update benchmark findings, and assess improvements in processes.

Benchmarking has many benefits.[15] Not only does it allow the best practices from any industry to be incorporated creatively into a company's operations, but the very process of benchmarking is motivating to employees. It provides targets that have been achieved by others. Resistance to change may be lessened if ideas for improvement come from other industries. Also, technical breakthroughs from other industries, if duly noted and evaluated, may lead to a breakthrough in the company's own industry.

Benchmarking broadens peoples' experience base and increases knowledge. It is best applied to all facets of a business. For example, Motorola encourages everyone in the organization to ask, "Who is the best person in my own field, and how might I use some of his or her techniques and characteristics to improve my own performance in order to be the best (executive, machine operator, chef, purchasing agent, etc.) in my 'class'?" Used in this fashion, benchmarking becomes a tool for continuous improvement.

Reengineering. **Reengineering** has been defined as "the fundamental rethinking and radical redesign of business processes to achieve dramatic improvements in critical, contemporary measures of performance, such as cost, quality, service, and speed."[16] Reengineering involves asking basic questions about business processes: Why do we do it, and why is it done this way? The answers often uncover obsolete, erroneous, or inappropriate assumptions. Radical redesign involves tossing out existing procedures and reinventing the process, not just incrementally improving it. The focus is on achieving quantum leaps in performance. For example, IBM Credit Corporation cut the process of financing IBM computers, software, and services from seven days to four hours by rethinking the process. The old process had originally been designed to handle difficult applications and required four highly trained specialists and a series of handoffs. The actual work took only about 1.5 hours; the rest of the time was spent in transit or delay. By questioning the assumption that every application was unique and difficult to process, IBM was able to replace the specialists with a single individual supported by a user-friendly computer system that provided access to all the data and tools the specialists would have used.

Successful reengineering requires a fundamental understanding of processes, creative thinking to break away from old traditions and assumptions, and effective use of information technology. Pepsi-Cola has embarked on a program to reengineer all of its key business processes, such as selling and delivery, equipment service and repair, procurement, and financial reporting. In the selling and delivery of its products, for example, customer reps typically stock out of as much as 25 percent of product by the end of the day, resulting in late-day stops not getting full deliveries and the need to return to those accounts. Many other routes return with overstock of other products, increasing handling costs. Redesigning the system to include hand-held computers will enable customer reps to confirm and deliver each day's order and also take a future order for the next delivery to the same customer.[17]

Many authors and consultants suggest that reengineering is completely different from TQM. Many others disagree. The issue is not kaizen versus breakthrough improvement. Incremental and breakthrough improvement are complementary approaches under the TQM umbrella; *both* are necessary to remain competitive. In fact, some experts suggest that reengineering requires TQM support to be successful.[18] Reengineering alone is often driven by upper managers without the full support or understanding of the rest of the organization, and radical innovations may end up as failures. The TQM philosophy encourages participation and systematic study, measurement, and verification of results that can support reengineering efforts.

Process-Improvement Tools

Nearly every leading company has a well-defined methodology for process management. Xerox, for instance, uses a six-step problem-solving process: identifying and selecting the problem, analyzing it, generating potential solutions, Selecting and planning the best solution, implementing the solution, and evaluating the results of the solution. Procter & Gamble uses an eight-step process that consists of issue selection, initial situation analysis, cause analysis, improvement planning, executing the plan, assessing results, standardizing improvements, and making future plans. Individual approaches might be slightly different, but all are focused on identifying the **root cause** of problems, defined aptly by NCR Corporation as "that condition (or interrelated set of conditions) having allowed or caused a defect to occur, which once corrected properly, permanently prevents recurrence of the defect in the same, or subsequent, product or service generated by the process."[19] It is easy to reduce symptoms of problems with temporary measures, but unless the root cause is eliminated, the problems recur.

Various tools are used extensively in problem-solving processes. These tools—as well as some tools developed for systems analysis and creative "brainstorming"—have been compiled and popularized by the Japanese as the "Seven Tools for Quality Control." Actually, that is an unfortunate misnomer, as they are not restricted to quality control applications; they are useful for much broader problem-solving activities in P/OM. Each of the tools is based on visual graphics and is void of complicated mathematics. Thus, they can be learned by any employee, from the CEO to the maintenance person. (Even cocktail waitresses in Japan use them to improve their operations!) These seven tools are flowcharts, checksheets, Pareto diagrams, histograms, cause-and-effect diagrams, scatter diagrams, and run or control charts.

Flowcharts

A **flowchart** is a simple picture of the sequence of steps in a process. Flowcharts help operations managers and the workers who are involved in the process to understand it. Employees can visualize how they fit into the process and who their (internal) suppliers and customers are, which leads to improved communication. When flowcharts are used to train employees in performing their jobs, greater consistency is achieved.

Once a flowchart is constructed, it can be used to identify quality and productivity problems. Questions such as "How does this operation affect the customer?" and "Can we improve or even eliminate this operation?" help to identify opportunities for improvement. A simple example is presented next.

Example | ## A Parking-Garage Operation

Figure 11.7 is a simple flowchart of a parking-garage operation. It illustrates the steps that both the customer and the cashier perform from the time a customer enters the garage until he or she leaves. To improve the operation, we might ask

Figure 11.7 Flowchart for Parking-Garage Operation

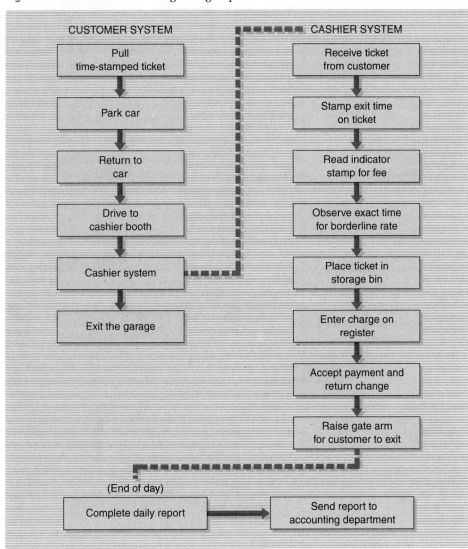

where a customer could become dissatisfied with the service. From the figure we see that customers might become dissatisfied if the ticket machine does not work properly, if they must wait a long time to pay the cashier, or if the cashier makes a mistake. Once such aspects of a process become apparent, the manager can take action. In this case, a need for preventive maintenance of the ticket machine, checking the time clock's accuracy, and continuing personnel training may be indicated.

Checksheets

When investigating P/OM problems, we typically collect data. Nearly any kind of form can be used to collect data. For instance, to collect data on parking charges in the preceding example, the cashier might simply record the amount collected from each customer in a column on a sheet of paper. Clearly, further processing would be required to make sense from such data. **Checksheets** are specialized data-collection forms that facilitate the interpretation of the data. Figure 11.8 is one that might be useful for recording the collection of parking garage charges. From the checksheet, it is easy to visualize the distribution of amounts, to estimate the average value, or to obtain better information about the use of the garage. Other types of checksheets are used to collect helpful information about production processes, such as the frequency of various types of defects or the locations of defects in a product.

Histograms

Histograms are a fundamental tool of descriptive statistics. They are simply graphical representations of frequency distributions. The checksheet in Figure 11.8 is designed to give a histogram of the data. Histograms' importance in production is that they enable managers to better understand the variation in a process in a simple, visual way. They can show when the variation exceeds acceptable performance limits, and they provide a means for tracking improvements in the process over time.

Cause-and-Effect Diagrams[20]

In trying to determine the source of a problem, managers, engineers, and workers often "brainstorm" for possible causes. Often, the causes that are proposed can be categorized into a small number of major classes, such as equipment factors, people factors, work methods, and materials factors. While the brainstorming is going on, however, this order may not be apparent, because the participants are expressing their ideas in a random way. A **cause-and-effect diagram** is a simple graphical tool for organizing a collection of ideas. It is very similar to the written outline you learned to use to help you write a paper or report. A cause-and-effect diagram is also called an *Ishikawa diagram*—after its originator Dr. Kaoru Ishikawa—or a *fishbone diagram*. Figure 11.9 is a generic cause-and-effect diagram. The following example illustrates a practical application of this graphical tool.

Figure 11.8
Checksheet for Parking-
Garage Charges

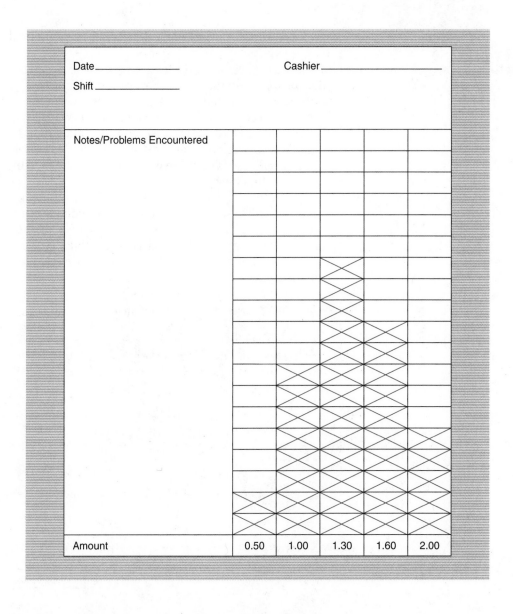

| Date _____ | Cashier _____ | | | | |
| Shift _____ | | | | | |

Notes/Problems Encountered					
			✕		
			✕		
			✕		
		✕	✕		
		✕	✕		
		✕	✕	✕	
		✕	✕	✕	
		✕	✕	✕	
		✕	✕	✕	
	✕	✕	✕	✕	
	✕	✕	✕	✕	✕
Amount	0.50	1.00	1.30	1.60	2.00

Figure 11.9
Generic Cause-and-Effect
Diagram

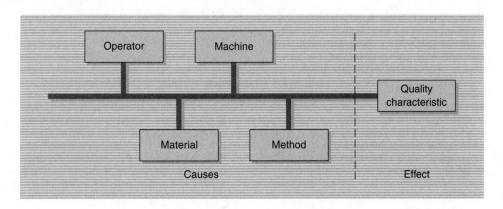

Example

A Cause-and-Effect Diagram for a Soldering Operation

To illustrate a cause-and-effect diagram for a specific problem, consider a soldering operation that occurs in a printed circuitboard manufacturing operation. The quality characteristic monitored in this operation is solder balls. The presence of solder balls can adversely affect the performance of the circuit board. Figure 11.10 is the cause-and-effect diagram. The horizontal line is the main stem of the cause-and-effect diagram. At the right end of this stem we state the *effect* for which we want to determine possible causes. In this case, the effect is solder balls.

From the main stem we have drawn lines that represent the main causes of solder balls. These are the machine, the solder, the flux, the components, and preheat. For each of these main causes, specific causes can be identified; for example, the causes of solder balls attributable to preheat are time and temperature. (You should see now why a cause-and-effect diagram is often called a *fishbone diagram*.)

Figure 11.10 Cause-and-Effect Diagram for Solder Balls

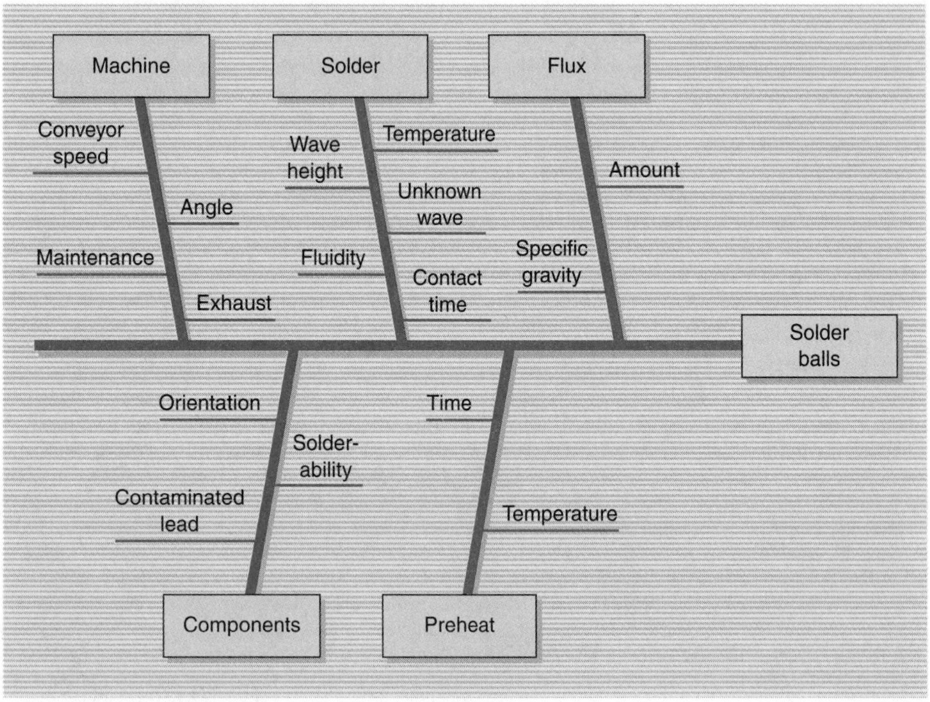

Pareto Diagrams

The *Pareto principle* was named after Italian economist Vilfredo Pareto, who found that about 85 percent of the wealth in Milan was held by about 15 percent of the people. The term was coined by Joseph Juran in 1950 when he observed in many diverse applications that a great proportion of quality problems are caused by a small number of process characteristics (which he termed the *vital few*), whereas a great majority of process characteristics (the *useful many*) account for only a small proportion of the quality problems. For example, three of the 15 weavers in one textile mill were found to account for three-fourths of the defective cloth produced. As another example, 61 percent of the total quality costs at one paper mill were attributable to one category of defect. A **Pareto diagram** is simply a histogram in which frequencies are ordered from largest to smallest. It can very clearly, visually show where the bulk of problems lie and where the greatest opportunities for savings are. An example follows.

Example

Pareto Analysis of Solder Defects

To illustrate how the Pareto diagram can be used to improve quality, the soldering process discussed in the preceding subsection's example can be used. During a week's production, a total of 2,000 printed circuitboards (PCBs) are manufactured. The following solder nonconformities were observed: pinholes, unwetted, blowholes, unsoldered, insufficient solder, and shorts. Studies showed that 800 of the 2,000 PCBs had the following solder nonconformities: 440 had insufficient solder, 120 had blowholes, 80 were unwetted, 64 were unsoldered, 56 had pinholes, and 40 had shorts. Figure 11.11 is the Pareto diagram of these results.

Figure 11.11 Pareto Diagram of Solder Defects before Process Change

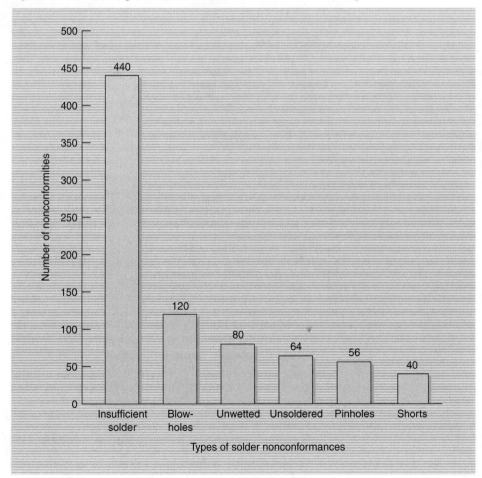

Figure 11.12 Pareto Diagram of Solder Defects after Process Change

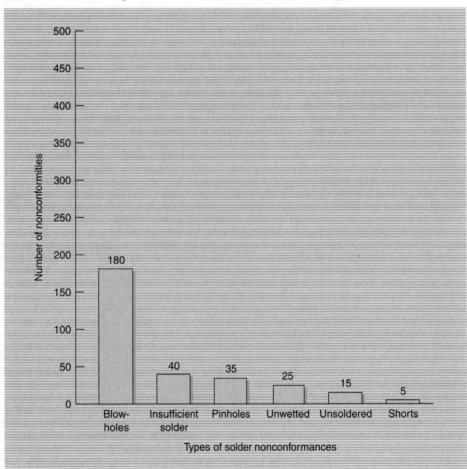

The manufacturing manager used the Pareto diagram to present the results to the engineering personnel responsible for developing the soldering process. It clearly showed that more than half of the soldering nonconformities were due to insufficient solder on the PCB; thus, effort was concentrated there. Figure 11.12 is the Pareto diagram after a process change was implemented on line. As a result of this process change, solder nonconformities dropped from 40 to 15 percent, a quality improvement of 62.5 percent.

Many phenomena in addition to quality factors exhibit the Pareto principle. For example, in inventory analysis, one often finds that a few items account for a large proportion of the total dollar value of the inventory (we shall see this in Chapter 13), and that relatively few items account for the bulk of warehouse space use. Can you think of other applications of the Pareto principle?

Scatter Diagrams

Scatter diagrams (Figure 11.13) are the graphical component of regression analysis. While they do not provide rigorous statistical information, they can

Figure 11.13
An Example of a Scatter
Diagram

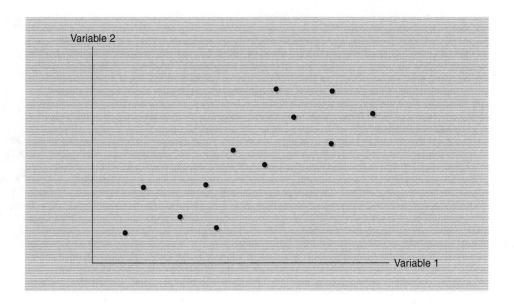

point out important relationships between variables. Typically, the variables be-ing considered represent possible causes and effects obtained from cause-and-effect diagrams. For example, from the cause-and-effect diagram in Figure 11.10, engineers might suspect that the main cause of solder balls is the preheat tem-perature. By designing an experiment in which they vary the preheat tempera-ture, measure the effect on solder balls, and plot the results, the engineers can quickly determine whether their hypothesis is correct.

Run Charts and Control Charts

A **run chart** is a line graph in which data are plotted over time. The vertical axis represents the measurement; the horizontal axis is the time scale. The daily newspaper usually has several examples of run charts, such as the one for the Dow Jones Industrial Average. Run charts show the performance and the varia-tion of a process or some quality or productivity indicator over time. They can be used to track such things as production volume, costs, customer-satisfaction indexes, and so forth. Run charts enable one to summarize data easily in a graphical form that is easy to understand and interpret, identify process changes and trends over time, and show the effects of corrective actions.

The first step in constructing a run chart is to identify the measurement or indicator to be monitored. There are several choices of how to take and report measurements. For *variables data,* we might measure quality characteristics for each individual unit of process output. For low-volume processes, such as chemical production or surgery, this would be appropriate. However, for high-volume production processes or services with large numbers of customers or transactions, it would be impractical. Instead, we take samples of large num-bers on a periodic basis and compute basic statistical measures such as the mean and range or standard deviation. For *attributes data,* we might count the number or proportion of items that do not conform to specifications. We might also be concerned with the number of nonconformances per unit.

Constructing the chart consists of the following steps:

Figure 11.14
Structure of a Control Chart

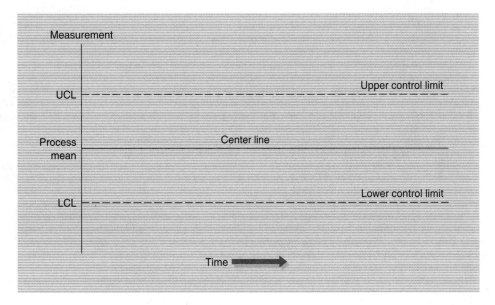

Step 1. Collect the data. If samples are chosen, compute the relevant statistic for each sample, such as the average or proportion.

Step 2. Plot the points on the chart and connect them. You should use graph paper if the chart is constructed by hand or a spreadsheet package if possible.

Step 3. Compute the average of all plotted points and draw it as a horizontal line through the data. This is called the *center line* (*CL*) of the chart.

If the plotted points fluctuate in a stable pattern around the center line, with no large spikes, trends, or shifts, the process would appear to be under control. If unusual patterns are present, the cause for lack of stability should be investigated and corrective action should be taken. Thus, run charts help to identify problems caused by lack of control.

A **control chart** is simply a run chart to which we add two horizontal lines called *control limits:* the *upper control limit* (*UCL*) and *lower control limit* (*LCL*), as illustrated in Figure 11.14. Control limits are chosen statistically so that there is a high probability (generally greater than .99) that points will be between those limits if the process is in control. Control limits make it easier to interpret patterns in a run chart and draw conclusions about the state of control. The details of control charts are discussed in the next chapter.

Example

Monitoring Surgery Infections

Assume that a hospital collects monthly data on the number of infections that arise after surgery (see Figure 11.15). Hospital administrators are concerned that the high percentage of infections in month 12 (1.76 percent) may have

Figure 11.15 Spreadsheet for Surgery Infection Data (SURGERY.XLS)

	A	B	C	D	E	F	G	H	I	J
1	Surgery Infections									
2										
3	Month	Surgeries	Infections	Percent						
4	1	208	1	0.48%						
5	2	225	3	1.33%						
6	3	201	3	1.49%						
7	4	236	1	0.42%						
8	5	220	3	1.36%						
9	6	244	1	0.41%						
10	7	247	1	0.40%						
11	8	245	1	0.41%						
12	9	250	1	0.40%						
13	10	227	0	0.00%						
14	11	234	2	0.85%						
15	12	227	4	1.76%						
16	13	213	2	0.94%						
17	14	212	1	0.47%						
18	15	193	2	1.04%						
19	16	182	0	0.00%						
20	17	140	1	0.71%						
21	18	230	1	0.43%						
22	19	187	1	0.53%						
23	20	252	2	0.79%						
24	21	201	1	0.50%						
25	22	226	0	0.00%						
26	23	222	2	0.90%						
27	24	212	2	0.94%						
28	25	219	1	0.46%						
29	26	223	2	0.90%						
30	27	191	1	0.52%						
31	28	222	0	0.00%						
32	29	231	3	1.30%						
33	30	239	1	0.42%						
34	31	217	2	0.92%						
35	32	241	1	0.41%						
36	33	220	3	1.36%						
37	34	278	1	0.36%						
38	35	255	3	1.18%						
39	36	225	1	0.44%						
40	Totals	7995	55							
41			Average	0.69%						
42										

been caused by some special factor, such as poor surgical procedures or a breakdown in the ventilation system. A run chart constructed from these data by using Microsoft Excel is shown in Figure 11.16. The average percentage of infections is 55/7995 = .688 percent. With formulas that are presented in Chapter 12, the upper and lower control limits are set at 2.35 and 0 percent, respectively, and we see that none of the data points are above the upper control limit. Moreover, there does not appear to be any systematic trend in the data. It is reasonable to conclude that the apparently high rate of infection in period 12 was due to chance.

Figure 11.16 Run Chart for Surgery Infections

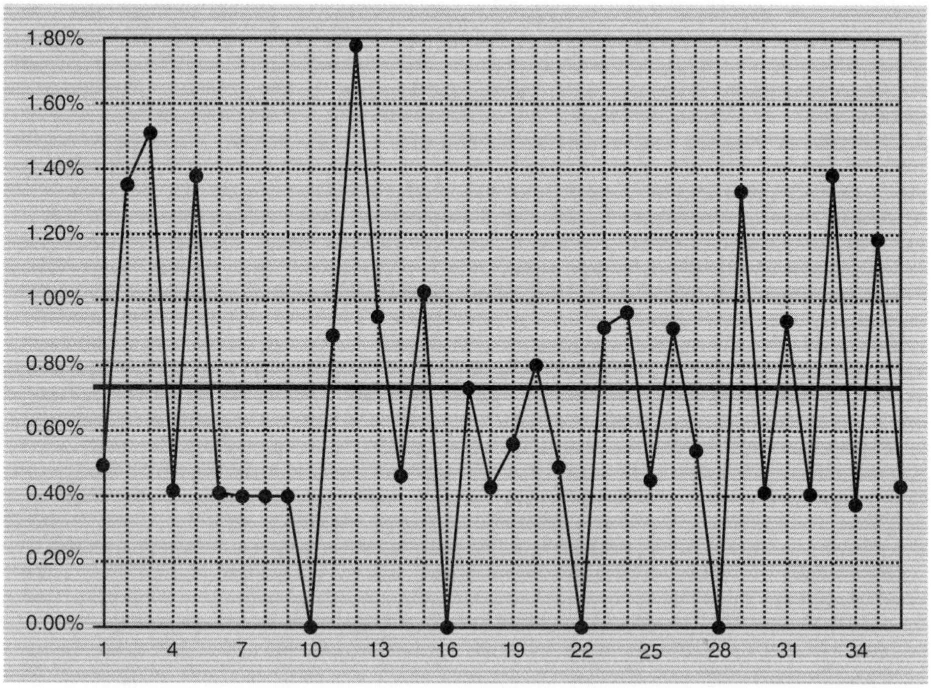

P/OM in Practice

Process Improvement at Kentucky Fried Chicken[21]

Kentucky Fried Chicken (KFC) is a member of the Pepsico family of quick-service restaurants. In an intense competitive environment, such restaurants must offer consistent, high-quality service. Recognizing this fact, KFC became an early adopter of quality management principles in the late 1970s.

In 1989 senior managers in KFC's South Central Division (roughly the Texas and Oklahoma area) discovered that its restaurants were having serious problems. Profit margins had fallen, and KFC was being ranked in the bottom half of the quick-service restaurant industry in speed of service and value for money spent. Slow service in its drive-through window (DTW) operations was a particularly critical problem. KFC set a dramatic improvement in speed of DTW service as its primary goal for restaurants in the division.

Four KFC-owned test sites in Oklahoma city were chosen. They were known for their good operations, motivated managers, and low management turnover. Since the company owned these restaurants, it had control over advertising and promotion and could therefore ensure that any improvements in financial and market performance were the result of improvements in speed of service and other operational changes alone.

After choosing the test restaurants, the DTW test team, all of whom were knowledgeable in quality improvement principles and tools, was formed. On the basis of benchmark data for competitors' service times gathered through market-tracker surveys, the team decided to reduce service time at drive-through windows from over two minutes to 60 seconds at all the test restaurants. Everyone in the division considered that goal unrealistic, but the regional managers believed that only by setting a stretch goal with a shared vision could they inspire people to rise to the occasion and meet or even beat the goal. In addition to setting the goal of dramatically improving DTW time, the team also specified several others:

••• To acknowledge customers within three seconds of their arrival at the speaker.

••• To fill orders within 60 seconds of the customer's arrival at the drive-through window.

••• To serve customers within a total average service time of less than 1.5 minutes.

The test team decided to start the project by developing good baseline information on average service times, as experienced by customers, in all stages of DTW operation. The team needed to measure the time a customer spent at the menu board placing the order, the time a customer took to drive from the menu board to the drive-through window, including waiting time in a queue, if any, and finally the time a customer would "hang" (wait) at the window to get the order, make payment, and drive away. Computerized timers were purchased to acquire that information.

Armed with service-time information, the team met again to prepare and analyze a Pareto chart of the components of total service time, which showed that about 58 percent of total service time in the DTW operation was due to window hang-time. Thus, then, was where the team's greatest challenge and opportunity to improve speed of service lay. Brainstorming to generate ideas for reducing hang-time, and using process-improvement methods, the team developed several general rules for eliminating unnecessary motion and thereby reducing hang-time:

••• Take no more than two steps to get what is needed to fill a customer's order.

••• Do not bend over to get anything needed to fill a customer's order.

••• Do not lift anything up that is needed to fill a customer's order.

••• Reach up and pull things down that are needed to fill a customer's order.

The team also decided to form in each restaurant a team of experienced DTW employees (called the Restaurant Team), who were responsible for generating process-improve-

ment ideas and for implementing them in individual restaurants.

The test team decided to introduce a *blocker log* in which DTW employees could record "blockers," that is, underlying causes of delays. The log was a simple $2 spiral binder with a pen attached. Whenever they could not fill a customer order within the target window hang-time, a buzzer on the timer would go off, signaling DTW employees to identify the blocker and write it down in the blocker log. In many cases the blocker was obvious, but in others DTW employees held impromptu discussions to figure it out.

Every two weeks, the team systematically analyzed the reasons recorded in the blocker logs. Pareto charts and Ishikawa diagrams helped them identify the most frequent and important blockers. Then the team challenged and encouraged DTW employees to generate solutions for eliminating or reducing the frequency of important blockers. The managers implemented selected solutions—and the whole procedure was repeated.

In one of the early meetings, the team developed a fishbone diagram (Figure 11.17) identifying three key causes of slow service: problems with headsets, out-of-product condition, and poor equipment layout. With the help of Restaurant Teams and DTW employees, the team members developed and implemented plans for solving each of those problems in each of the four restaurants. For example, they solved the headset problem by instituting a procedure for testing all headsets regularly to ensure that they worked properly, and by ordering and stocking adequate supplies of frequently needed batteries and replacement belts.

The four restaurants repeated this process for about 10 months until they achieved the major goal of 60-seconds window hang-time. Some of the lessons learned in the test and the ma-

jor changes made to operational procedures and facilities follow.

1. *Rationalize process flow, and improve equipment layout to eliminate wasted motion and reduce service time.* The employees of each restaurant totally reorganized their drive-through areas, putting products, condiments, bags, boxes, cups, and salads in more convenient locations. They positioned each item along the pack line according to its demand level. High-demand products were made easily accessible to the packers and were also placed in the display packing system to be more visible to the cooks and the DTW leaders so that they could replenish them "just in time."

2. *Change product mix and specifications.* The restaurant streamlined their menus to eliminate a number of slow-moving items. The team tested "even-dollar pricing" for the big-pack items on the menu board. For example, they priced a 10-piece (chicken) meal at $11.18 so that inclusive of tax it totaled $12.00. Both the customer and the cashier saved a lot of effort and time counting change. The even-dollar items averaged 15 to 20 seconds less at the window.

3. *Since many small process improvements ultimately add up to a large improvement, implement as many process-improvement ideas as possible.* Each idea may have had only a tiny effect on service time. Collectively, however, the ideas had a large impact. For example, the restaurants eliminated redundant packaging boxes so that packers needed only one or two standard boxes to pack any order. Consequently, packers could focus on packing orders in the shortest possible time without worrying about whether they were using the proper box.

4. *Use headsets to create customer focus and to convert serial activities into parallel ones.* The use of headsets

Figure 11.17 KFC Cause-and-Effect Diagram

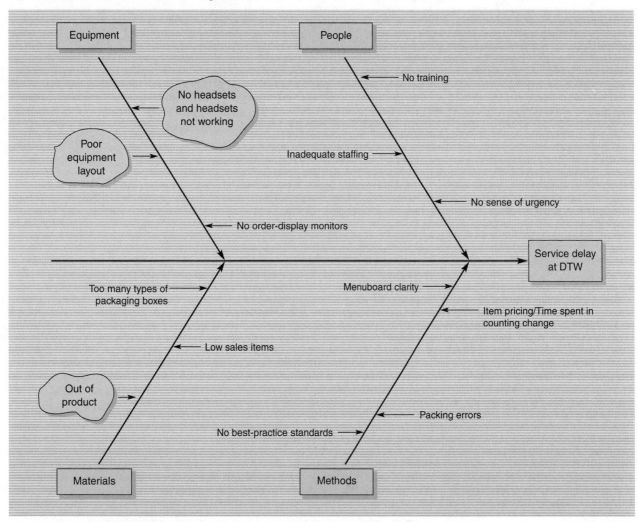

by all DTW employees enabled them to perform their jobs while simultaneously listening to customer orders. It also helped improve order accuracy. Converting serial activities into parallel ones in that way proved very useful in reducing the window hang-time.

5. *Because the customer participates in the service process, give the customer clear instructions on what he or she is supposed to do.* One simple idea was to install clear signs, such as an order-here sign at the drive-through menu board speaker. The sign reduced customer confusion and thereby the time spent at the menu board. Another idea was to rearrange the menu board to improve its clarity so that customers could place orders faster and more easily.

6. *Use the timer as a focal point for motivating team members.* The DTW timer was perhaps the single most important tool in improving the speed of service. The timer served as a constant reminder to the DTW employees that the customers were waiting. Once each customer departed, the timer displayed both the window hang-time for that customer and the average window hang-time since the beginning of that day. Serving as a scorecard and as a focal point for motivation, the timer helped each restaurant's DTW leader set a pace during rush periods.

7. *Create an environment conducive to problem-solving, establish simple procedures so that employees can suggest improvements, and act immediately on suggestions.* One of the important rules the team followed was to act immediately on employee suggestions—that is, to decide quickly whether it would implement a suggestion and, if so, to implement it immediately. The result was an unprecedented level of excitement and enthusiasm among DTW employees.

8. *Use rigorous training and motivating techniques through individual or team incentives as keys to process improvement.* Prior to the test, employees were simply assigned to DTW without receiving any special training in how to work effectively and efficiently in that area. When the team instituted specific DTW training, productivity and camaraderie improved noticeably. Some restaurants used games and awards to get all their employees involved in the DTW test. For example, if the DTW employees hit the target window hang-time, all the restaurant employees, and not just the DTW employees, were rewarded for their performance.

9. *Make process improvement a way of life for managers.* The compensation of restaurant general managers is tied to the performance of their individual restaurants. As the test progressed, operational performance began to improve noticeably, and the general managers became increasingly committed to the idea of continuous improvement.

10. *Always keep an eye on the competition.* Through the use of market-tracker surveys, the team regularly conducted service-time studies on immediate competitors within the test area.

Over a period of 42 weeks, the team was able to reduce average window hang-time from the initial 125 seconds to the goal of 60 seconds

(Figure 11.18). With a total improvement of 65 seconds, the window hang-time was cut by more than half! Simultaneously, labor productivity, cost performance, profit margins, and customer satisfaction showed substantial improvement.

After successfully concluding the test, KFC managers decided to gradually roll out the speed-of-service program to other KFC-owned restaurants in the division. Within two years, managers and employees at all 2,000 KFC-owned restaurants had been trained to improve speed of service at both the drive-through window and the front counter. Senior managers at KFC monitor the program, and all restaurant managers are tracking speed-of-service performance on a real-time basis, taking corrective actions immediately as necessary.

Questions for Discussion

1. How were some of the process-design principles discussed in the preceding chapter applied in this improvement process?

2. Explain the role of tools and methodologies discussed in this chapter in KFC's process improvement initiative.

3. One may ask whether this was simply a Hawthorne effect. How do you think KFC managers would respond to that question?

Applications of Process-Management Tools at Rotor Clip[24]

Rotor Clip Company, Inc., of Somerset, New Jersey, is a major manufacturer of retaining rings and self-tightening hose clamps and a firm believer in the use of simple graphical analysis tools for improving quality. Several years ago one of its clamps was failing stress testing during final inspections. No reason was apparent, so managers and supervisors decided to develop a cause-and-effect diagram in their search for a solution. Every employee involved with the part was called to a meeting to discuss the problem. The group was encouraged to brainstorm possible reasons for the problem, and the fishbone diagram in Figure 11.19 resulted.

After considering all possible causes, they concluded that the salt temperature of the quenching tank (a heat-treating step) was too close to the martensite line. This factor was selected for study, but tests established

Figure 11.18 Run Chart of Service-Time Improvement

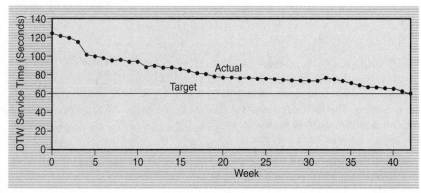

Figure 11.19 Fishbone Diagram for Rotor Clip Clamp Problem

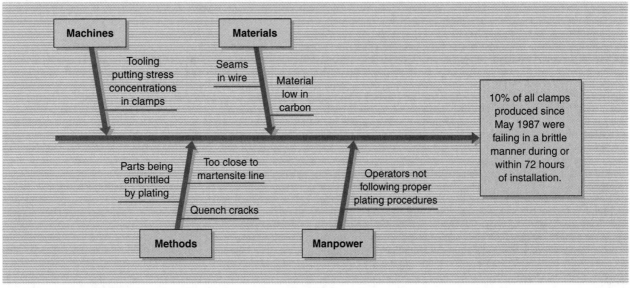

Source: Bruce Rudin, "Simple Tools Solve Complex Problems," *Quality*, April 1990, pp. 50–51.

that raising the salt temperature did not alleviate the problem. The group met again and agreed to investigate a second possibility, inadequate seams in one wire, as a possible cause. Wire samples that failed inspection were examined metallographically, and the seams were confirmed as the major cause of the defective parts. The material was returned to the supplier, and the new material yielded parts that passed the final inspection.

Another application of graphical analysis was the use of a Pareto diagram to study rising premium freight charges for shipping retaining rings. After three months of collecting data, a study group was able to draw conclusions. Their Pareto diagram is shown in Figure 11.20. The results were startling. The most common reasons for premium delivery-service use was customer requests. It was decided

Figure 11.20 Pareto Diagram of Customer Calls

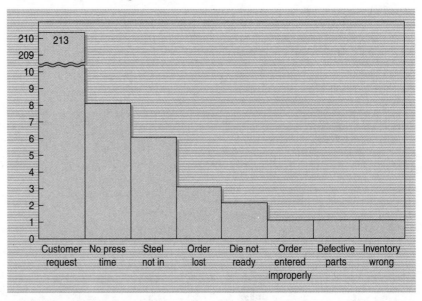

Source: Bruce Rudin, "Simple Tools Solve Complex Problems." Reprinted with permission from *Quality* (April 1990), a publication of Hitchcock Publishing, a Capital Cites/ABC, Inc., Company.

Figure 11.21 Scatter Diagram of New Customers versus Advertising Dollars

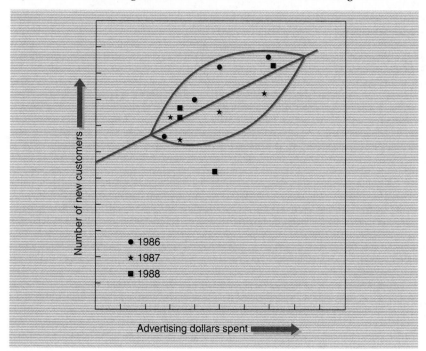

1986
1987
1988

Number of new customers

Advertising dollars spent

Source: Bruce Rudin, "Simple Tools Solve Complex Problems." Reprinted with permission from *Quality* (April 1990), a publication of Hitchcock Publishing, a Capital Cities/ABC, Inc., Company.

cult to determine the effect of advertising expenditures on the bottom line. Managers wanted to learn if the amount of money spent on advertising correlates with the number of new customers. Each quarter's advertising dollars spent were plotted against the number of each quarter's new customers for three consecutive years (see Figure 11.21). A strong positive correlation was found. The results were fairly consistent from year to year except for the second quarter of 1988, an "outlier." Checking the media schedule, the advertising department discovered that experimental image ads had dominated that period's advertising thrust. This knowledge prompted the advertising department to eliminate image ads from its schedule.

Questions for Discussion

1. Once the seam problem in the clamps was understood, what controls needed to be instituted to prevent the problem from occurring again?

2. In the freight-charge example, what steps do you think the company should take with customers who consistently request expedited shipments?

3. How might the advertising department continue to use scatter diagrams in the future? How might top managers use the results in setting budget priorities?

to continue the study to identify the customers that consistently requested expedited shipments and to work closely with them to find ways to reduce costs. The second-largest contributor to the problem was the lack of available machine time. Once a die is installed in a stamping press, it is run until the maximum number of parts (usually a million) is produced before

it is removed for routine maintenance. Although this policy results in efficient utilization of tooling, it ties up the press and ultimately accounts for some rush shipments. The policy was revised to limit die runs in order to fill orders more efficiently.

A third application was the use of a scatter diagram by the advertising department. In the past it has been diffi-

Summary of Key Points

••• Process management involves control—maintaining acceptable levels of process performance—and improvement—continuously achieving higher levels of quality and operational performance. Both a company's core processes and its support processes are involved. They must be repeatable and measurable.

••• A control system consists of a standard or goal, a means of measuring accomplishment, and comparison of results to the standard or goal, with feedback supplied for corrective action.

••• Quality control systems are directed toward preventing, detecting, and correcting product or service nonconformances. Quality control typically takes place at the receipt of purchase materials, during production processes, and upon completion of production. Quality control is often more difficult in services than in manufacturing since the important behavioral characteristics in services are often difficult to control.

••• Inspection and measurement form the basis for quality control activity. Key issues that must be considered are what to inspect, where to inspect, and how much to inspect. Inspection quantity is generally an economic decision, based on the risk of allowing a nonconforming item to continue to the next stage of production. Human limitations make inspection difficult, but automated equipment is now making reliable, 100-percent inspection economical in many cases.

••• Techniques for preventing defects in production processes include poka-yoke, successive checking and self-checking, and autonomation.

••• Total productive maintenance (TPM) requires that workers take responsibility for their equipment and workspace, with a focus on prevention rather than correction. TPM fits well within the TQM philosophy by fostering teamwork and a spirit of continuous improvement.

••• Continuous improvement takes many forms: gradual improvement strategies (kaizen) supported by the plan-do-study-act process (Deming cycle), benchmarking (the search for best practices), and reengineering (the radical redesign of business processes).

••• Process improvement consists of identifying problems, analyzing them, generating solutions, and implementing the results. Seven easy-to-use tools—flowcharts, checksheets, Pareto diagrams, histograms, cause-and-effect diagrams, scatter diagrams, and run charts and control charts—support process-improvement efforts.

Key Terms

Process management
Control
Improvement
Core processes
Support processes
Quality control
Acceptance sampling
Attribute
Variable
One-hundred-percent inspection
Sampling procedures
Poka-yoke
Successive checking
Self-checking
Autonomation
Total productive maintenance (TPM)
Mean time between failures (MTBF)
Kaizen
Deming cycle
Benchmarking
Reengineering
Root cause
Flowchart
Checksheet
Histogram
Cause-and-effect diagram
Pareto diagram
Scatter diagram
Run chart
Control chart

Review Questions

1. Define *process management*. Why is it important to any business?
2. Explain the difference between a core process and a support process. Provide some examples.
3. Describe the components of any control system.
4. List the objectives of the quality control function.
5. Why has inspection been a controversial subject?
6. Explain the difference between attribute measurements and variable measurements. Provide some examples.
7. Describe approaches used to locate inspection activities in manufacturing.
8. Explain the economic trade-offs in determining whether to inspect all (100-percent inspection) or nothing.
9. What are the challenges of visual inspection? How can human-factor impediments to visual inspection be reduced?

10. Describe the key methods for defect prevention in manufacturing. How might they be applied in services?

11. How does the quality control function in services differ from that in manufacturing?

12. Define *total productive maintenance*.

13. Explain the difference between innovation and continuous improvement. Why are both necessary to achieve competitive advantage?

14. Define *work simplification* and *planned-methods change*. How do they differ from one another?

15. Define the Japanese concept of *kaizen*. How does it differ from traditional Western approaches to improvement?

16. Define *stretch goal*. How can such goals help an organization?

17. Define *benchmarking*. What are its benefits?

18. Define *reengineering*. How does it relate to TQM?

19. Describe the Deming cycle. How does it relate to continuous improvement?

20. Explain and provide examples of the seven basic process-improvement tools. What role does each play in process improvement?

21. Explain the difference between a run chart and a control chart.

Discussion Questions

1. Why is it necessary for a process to be repeatable and measurable in order to come under the purview of process management? Provide some examples of processes that have these characteristics and some that do not.

2. List some of the common processes you perform as a student. How might you go about controlling and improving them?

3. Are classroom examinations a means of control or improvement? Which should they be?

4. Provide examples of common and special causes of variation in the following:
   a. Taking a college examination
   b. Grilling a hamburger
   c. Meeting a scheduled appointment

5. Identify some quality problems that you face in your work or school activities and some poka-yokes that might prevent them.

6. How might kaizen be applied in a class?

7. Interview some faculty members as to whether they benchmark other educational programs. Ask what types of information they might seek to improve curriculum and course content.

8. Identify some of the major processes a student encounters in a college or university. What types of noneducational institutions perform similar processes and might be candidates for benchmarking?

9. Write down your process for preparing for an exam. How might you reengineer that process to shorten it or make it more effective?

10. State at least three possible applications of the Deming cycle in your personal life.

11. Provide two examples of each of the seven quality control tools (different from those in the chapter) based on your own experience or research, such as in your personal life, school activities, or work.

12. Develop a flowchart of your daily routine, from getting up in the morning to going to school or work. How might you improve that routine?

13. Design a checksheet to help a high school student who is getting poor grades on a math quiz determine the source of his or her difficulty.

14. Develop cause-and-effect diagrams for the following problems:
   a. Poor exam grade
   b. No job offers
   c. Too many speeding tickets
   d. Late for work or school

15. A new MamaMia's franchise uses the following process.*

   a. Customer telephones the restaurant to place an order.

   b. Employee answers telephone, writes down order, and hands order to chef in the kitchen.

   c. Chef assembles pizza by hand.

   d. Chef bakes pizza in one of the four ovens.

   e. Assistant verifies the heated pizza matches the order and places it in a cardboard box and then in an insulated carrier.

   f. Driver picks up pizza, gets small bills for change, checks map in store, gets in car, and drives to customer's location.

   g. Driver gives pizza to customer, collects cash (no credit), and gives change to customer.

   The manager wants to be able to deliver pizza to any customer in the city and keep investment in new technology no more than 1.2 times current yearly profits. He has set some stretch goals:

   (i) Deliver pizza in half the time of competitors—customers want to have pizza delivered within approximately 10 minutes.

   (ii) Deliver pizza that wins taste tests against both other delivered pizzas and restaurant pizzas.

   (iii) Provide the extras typically found in restaurants, such as grated cheese, garlic, and hot peppers.

   In a team of students, propose some reengineering ideas to meet these stretch goals.

16. Refer to the flowchart of the car rental process in Figure 11.22.

   a. Discuss the types of inspections and measurements the company might use to manage this process.

   b. Discuss how process-improvement methodologies might be applied to this process.

Figure 11.22
Flowchart for Discussion
Question 16

SOURCE: W. Earl Sasser, R. Paul
Olsen, and D. Daryl Wyckoff,
*Management of Service Operations;
Text, Cases, and Readings*
(Needham Heights, MA: Allyn and
Bacon, Inc., 1978), p. 74. Copyright
© 1978 by Allyn and Bacon.
Reprinted with permission.

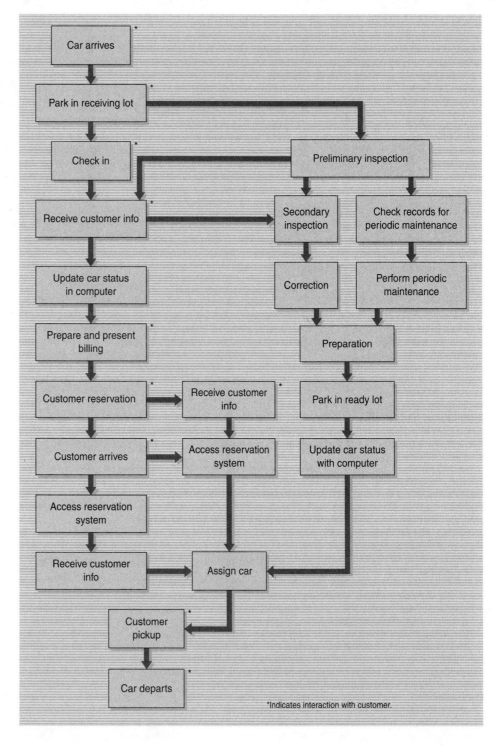

*Indicates interaction with customer.

c. Starting from a "clean sheet," propose some reengineering solutions to redesign this process.

Notes

1. Douglas H. Harris and Frederick B. Chaney, *Human Factors in Quality Assurance* (New York: John Wiley & Sons, 1969).

2. "Inspection: A New Role for Robots," *Quality Progress,* August 1982, p. 50.

3. The following discussion is adapted from Alan G. Robinson and Dean M. Schroeder, "The Limited Role of Statistical Quality Control in a Zero-Defect Environment," *Production and Inventory Management,* third quarter 1990, pp. 60–65.

4. Rhonda Richards, "Top-Flite Puts New Spin on Golf-Ball War," *USA Today,* November 20, 1992, pp. B1, B2.

5. Adapted from The Ritz-Carlton Hotel Company Application Summary, 1992 Winner, Malcolm Baldrige National Quality Award. © 1994, The Ritz Carlton Hotel Company. All rights reserved.

6. "Total Productive Maintenance," *Manufacturing Insights,* December 1989 (Coopers & Lybrand Cincinnati Management Consulting Services).

7. Bill N. Maggard and David M. Rhyne, "Total Productive Maintenance: A Timely Integration of Production and Maintenance," *Production and Inventory Management Journal* 33, no. 4 (fourth Quarter 1992), pp. 6–10.

8. M. L. Dertouzos, R. K. Lester, R. M. Solow, and the MIT Commission on Industrial Productivity, *Made in America* (Cambridge, MA: MIT Press, 1989), p. 74.

9. Dean M. Schroeder and Alan G. Robinson, "America's Most Successful Export to Japan: Continuous Improvement Programs," *Sloan Management Review* 32, no. 2, (Spring 1991), pp. 67–81.

10. Imai Masaaki, *KAIZEN—The Key to Japan's Competitive Success* (New York: McGraw-Hill, 1986).

11. Lawrence S. Pryor, "Benchmarking: A Self-Improvement Strategy," *Journal of Business Strategy,* November–December 1989, pp. 28–32.

12. Robert C. Camp, *Benchmarking: The Search for Industry Best Practices That Lead to Superior Performance* (Milwaukee, WI: ASQC Quality Press and UNIPUB/Quality Resources, 1989).

13. Christopher E. Bogan and Michael J. English, "Benchmarking for Best Practices: Winning through Innovative Adaptation," *Quality Digest,* August 1994, pp. 52–62.

14. AT&T Consumer Communication Services, Summary of 1994 Application for the Malcolm Baldrige National Quality Award.

15. Camp, op. cit.

16. Michael Hammer and James Champy, *Reengineering the Corporation* (New York: HarperCollins, 1993), p. 32.

17. P. Kay Coleman, "Reengineering Pepsi's Road to the 'Right Side Up' Company," *Insights Quarterly* 5, no. 3 (Winter 1993), pp. 18–35.

18. Gerhard Plenert, "Process Re-Engineering: The Latest Fad Toward Failure," *APICS—The Performance Advantage* 4, no. 6 (June 1994), pp. 22–24.

19. "NCR Corporation" in *Profiles in Quality* (Needham Heights, MA: Allyn and Bacon, 1991).

20. The next two subsections are adapted from Williams S Messina, *Statistical Quality Control for Manufacturing Managers* (New York: John Wiley & Sons, 1987), pp. 10–13. Permission granted through the American Society of Quality Control.

21. Reprinted by permission of Uday M. Apte and Charles C. Reynolds, "Quality Management at Kentucky Fried Chicken," *Interfaces* 25, no. 3 (May-June, 1995), pp. 6-21. Copyright 1995, Institute for Operations Research and the Management Sciences, 290 Westminster Street, Providence, Rhode Island 02903 USA.

24. Adapted from Bruce Rudin, "Simple Tools Solve Complex Problems," *Quality,* April 1990, pp. 50–51.

---

*Adapted from AT&T Quality Steering Committee, *Reengineering Handbook,* AT&T Bell Laboratories, 1991.

Solved Problems

1. A watch manufacturer has the option of inspecting each crystal. If a bad crystal is assembled, the cost of disassembly and replacement after the final test and inspection is $1.40. Each crystal can be tested for 8 cents. Perform a break-even analysis to determine the percent nonconforming for which 100-percent inspection is better than no inspection at all.

Solution

$$C_1 = \$.08$$
$$C_2 = \$1.40$$

$$C_1/C_2 = .057$$

Therefore, if the actual error rate is greater than .057, 100-percent inspection is best; otherwise, no inspection is warranted.

2. The MTBF (mean time between failures) for a computer's central processing unit is normally distributed with a mean of 14 days and a standard deviation of three days. Each failure costs the company $500 in lost computing time and repair costs. A shutdown for preventive maintenance can be scheduled during nonpeak times and will cost only $100. As the manager in charge of computer operations, you are to determine whether a preventive-maintenance program is worthwhile. What is your recommendation?

Solution

The spreadsheet in Figure 11.23 shows the analysis. Failure probabilities are computed by using the Excel function NORMDIST. The optimal maintenance interval is nine days.

3. An analysis of customer complaints at a large mail-order house revealed the following data.

Billing errors	867
Shipping errors	1,960
Unclear charges	9,650
Long delay	6,672
Delivery errors	452

Figure 11.23
Spreadsheet for Solved
Problem 2 Solution

	A	B	C	D	E	F	G
1	Preventive Maintenance						
2							
3	Days between	Number per	Prob. of failure	Inspection	Failure	Total	
4	inspection	year	before next inspection	cost	cost	cost	
5	5	52.0	0.0013	$5,200.00	$35.10	$5,235.10	
6	6	43.3	0.0038	$4,333.33	$82.99	$4,416.33	
7	7	37.1	0.0098	$3,714.29	$182.28	$3,896.57	
8	8	32.5	0.0228	$3,250.00	$369.69	$3,619.69	
9	9	28.9	0.0478	$2,888.89	$690.30	$3,579.19	
10	10	26.0	0.0912	$2,600.00	$1,185.75	$3,785.75	
11	11	23.6	0.1587	$2,363.64	$1,875.02	$4,238.65	
12	12	21.7	0.2525	$2,166.67	$2,735.34	$4,902.00	
13	13	20.0	0.3694	$2,000.00	$3,694.41	$5,694.41	
14	14	18.6	0.5000	$1,857.14	$4,642.86	$6,500.00	
15	15	17.3	0.6306	$1,733.33	$5,464.84	$7,198.17	
16	16	16.3	0.7475	$1,625.00	$6,073.50	$7,698.50	
17	17	15.3	0.8413	$1,529.41	$6,433.81	$7,963.22	
18	18	14.4	0.9088	$1,444.44	$6,563.47	$8,007.92	
19							
20							

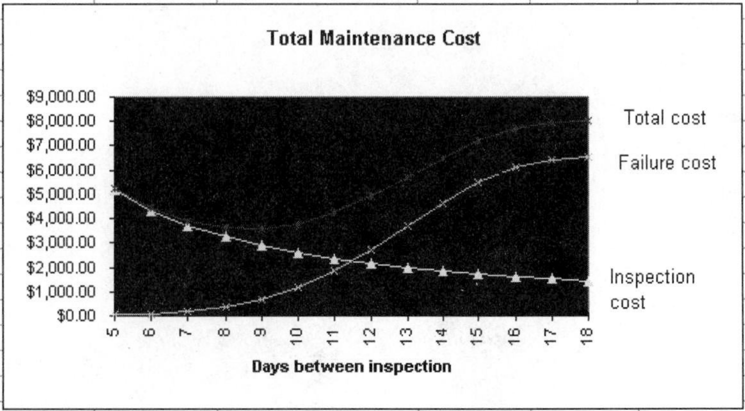

Construct a Pareto diagram for these data. What conclusions can you draw?

Solution
Total errors are 19,601 (percentages rounded to whole numbers). Table 11.2 gives the data for each complaint category.

Table 11.2 Data for Solved Problem 3

Complaint	Number	Percent	Cumulative Percent
Unclear charges	9,650	49	49
Long delays	6,672	34	83
Shipping errors	1,960	10	93
Billing errors	867	4	97
Delivery errors	452	2	99

Almost half the errors are due to unclear charges, and over 80 percent are attributable to the first two categories. These are the ones to which managers should direct their attention. Figure 11.24 is the Pareto diagram.

Figure 11.24
Pareto Diagram for Solved
Problem 3 Solution

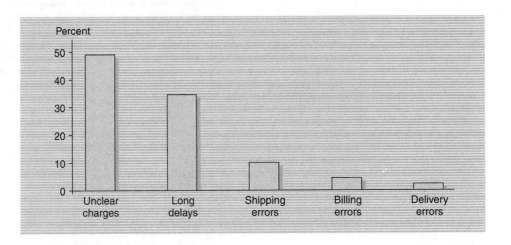

Problems

1. The cost to inspect a credit card statement in a bank is 25 cents, while correction of a mistake later amounts to $500. What is the break-even point in errors per thousand transactions for which 100-percent inspection is no more economical than no inspection?

2. For a particular piece of equipment, the probability of failure during a given week is as follows.

Week of Operation	1	2	3	4	5	6
Probability of Failure	.20	.10	.10	.15	.20	.25

Managers are considering a preventive-maintenance program that would be implemented at the end of a given week of production. The production loss and downtime cost associated with an equipment failure is estimated to be $1,500 per failure. If it costs $100 to perform the preventive maintenance, when should the firm implement the program? What is the total maintenance and failure cost associated with your recommendation, and how many failures can be expected each year? Assume 52 weeks of operation per year.

3. Let t denote the number of days of operation before preventive maintenance is necessary for a particular piece of equipment. Analysis of historical operating data shows that the annual cost of preventive maintenance is $32,000/t$ and the annual cost of failure is $320t$.

a. Develop an equation that will show the total annual preventive-maintenance and failure cost as a function of the time before preventive maintenance, t.

b. Use your answer to part a to compute the total cost for a preventive-maintenance period of five days.

c. Use trial and error to evaluate the total cost for a variety of values of t. What preventive-maintenance period appears to provide the lowest total cost?

d. Assuming 260 working days per year, what is the cost of each preventive maintenance performed?

4. The probabilities of breakdown of a particular machine versus the number of hours since previous maintenance are given in Table 11.3.

Table 11.3 Data for Problem 4

Number of Hours after Previous Maintenance	Probability
10	0.01
20	0.05
30	0.15
40	0.15
50	0.15
60	0.15
70	0.20
80	0.14

The number of working days in a year is 250 on a two-shift basis. A breakdown costs $350 to repair, and preventive maintenance costs $150.

a. What is the MTBF?

b. What is the maintenance cost if no preventive maintenance is followed?

c. What is the cost of a preventive-maintenance policy carried out once every 10 hours?

d. Decrease the frequency of preventive maintenance in steps of 10 hours, and evaluate total costs. Find the best maintenance policy.

5. Refer to Figure 11.4, the histogram of the time between failures in the equipment-maintenance example. What preventive-maintenance period would you recommend if the preventive-maintenance cost were $50 and the average cost for an equipment failure were $30? How many breakdowns a year should you expect under your preventive-maintenance program?

6. Bill Barry, president of Pacific Plastics, Inc. (PPI), has become concerned about reports that downtime for PPI's plastic injection-molding machines has been increasing. The downtime for a machine includes the time the machine must wait for a repair service technician to arrive after a breakdown plus the actual repair time. Currently PPI has three plastic injection-molding machines, which are repaired by one service technician. However, because of an increase in business, PPI is considering the purchase of three additional machines. Bill is concerned that with the additional machines the downtime problem will increase.

An analysis of historical data shows that the probability of each machine breaking down during one hour of operation is .10. In addition, the distribution of the repair time for a machine that breaks down is as

Repair Time (hours)	1	2	3	4	5
Probability	.20	.35	.25	.15	.05

The loss in revenue associated with a machine being down for one hour is $100. PPI pays its service technician $22 per hour, and it is believed that additional service technicians can be hired at the same wage rate.

In reviewing the breakdown problem, Bill decided that the best way to learn about the machine-repair operation would be to simulate the performance of the system. The simulation would have to deal with the two conflicting sources of cost: the cost of the service technician(s) and the cost of machine downtime. PPI could minimize the first cost by employing only one service technician, or it could minimize the second by hiring so many service technicians that a machine could be serviced immediately after a breakdown.

In developing the simulation model, you can assume that any breakdowns will be treated as occurring at the beginning of the hour of operation. Thus, if a machine were to break down in hour 4, it would be considered to break down at the beginning of the hour. If one hour is spent waiting for a service technician and the length of time required to service the machine is two hours, the machine would be down during hours 4, 5, and 6, then be ready for operation at the beginning of hour 7. You can also assume that the probability of any machine breakdown is independent of the breakdown of any other machine, and that the service times are also independent of other service times.

Prepare a report that discusses the general development of the simulation model, the conclusions you plan to draw by using the model, and any recommendations you have about the best decision for PPI. Include the following:

a. List the information the simulation model should generate so that the decision can be made about the desired number of service technicians.

b. Set up a flowchart of the machine-repair operation for one machine and one service technician.

c. Use a random-number table and hand computations to demonstrate the simulation of the machine-repair operation with three machines and one service technician. Use a table similar to Table A.5 (in Supplementary Chapter A) to summarize 10 hours of simulation results.

d. Develop a simulation model for the machine-repair operation when PPI expands to six machines. Use your simulation results to make a recommendation about the number of service technicians PPI should employ.

7. The following list gives the number of seconds customers have waited for a telephone service representative today. Construct a histogram, and discuss any conclusions you might reach.

5	7	7	15	3
21	15	22	10	8
10	6	8	18	4
14	5	7	8	10

8. The most recent record of the numbers of hours a machine has operated until failure follows. Construct a histogram, and discuss any conclusions you might reach.

10.5	5.0	15.3	16.8	9.2
4.2	12.6	7.8	11.5	12.6
20.2	27.5	8.9	12.2	18.2
14.5	14.0	5.5	15.5	8.9

9. The manager at MamaMia's Pizza has logged customer complaints over the past three months. From the data given in Table 11.4 construct a Pareto diagram. What should the manager do?

Table 11.4 Data for Problem 9

Type of complaint	Frequency
Wrong order	3
Late delivery	17
Note enough toppings	1
Not hot enough	8
Excessive wait in dining room	12

10. Seventeen batches of a raw material were tested for the percentage of a particular chemical (x). It is believed that the amount of this chemical influences an important quality characteristic of the final product (y). The test data are given in Table 11.5. Construct a scatter diagram of the data, and discuss any conclusions you might reach.

Table 11.5 Data for Problem 10

x	y
3.5	7.0
3.2	8.0
4.5	8.4
5.0	7.6
3.8	10.5
5.4	9.2
5.3	11.7
6.0	8.8
6.1	10.1
6.1	11.0
6.9	10.7
7.0	11.9
7.4	9.6
7.5	8.2
8.5	9.1
8.2	11.1
9.0	13.0

11. The following list gives the number of defects found in 30 samples of 100 electronic assemblies taken on a daily basis over one month. Plot these data on a run chart, computing the average value (center line). How do you interpret the chart?

1	6	5	5	4	3	2	2	4	6
2	1	3	1	4	5	4	1	6	15
12	6	3	4	3	3	2	5	7	4

12. A catalog order-filling process for personalized printed products can be described as follows.* Telephone orders are taken over a 12-hour period each day. Orders are collected from each order clerk at the end of the day and checked for errors by the supervisor, usually the next morning. Because of the supervisor's heavy work load, this one-day batch of orders usually does not get to the data-processing department until after 1:00 P.M. Orders are invoiced by the data-processing department in the one-day batches and then printed and "matched back" with the original orders. (At this point, if the order is for a new customer, it is returned to the person who did the new-customer verification and set up the new account for that customer, both of which must be done before an order from a new customer can be invoiced.) The next step is order verification and proofreading. The orders, with invoices attached, are given to a person who verifies that all required information is present and correct. If there is a question, it is checked by computer or by calling the customer. Finally, the completed orders are sent to the typesetting department of the printshop.

a. Develop a flowchart for this process.

b. Discuss opportunities for improving the productivity and the quality of service in this situation.

13. An independent outplacement service helps unemployed executives find jobs. One of the major activities of the service is preparing resumes. Three word processors work at the service and type resumes and cover letters. They are assigned to individual clients, currently about 120. Turnaround time for typing is expected to be 24 hours. The word-processing operation begins with clients placing work in the assigned word processor's bin. When the word processor picks up the work (in batches), it is logged in by use of a clock time stamp, and the work is typed and printed. After the batch is completed, the word processor puts the documents in the clients' bins, logs in the time delivered, and picks up new work. A supervisor tries to balance the work load for the three word processors. Lately, many of the clients have been complaining about errors in their documents—misspellings, missing lines, wrong formatting, and so on. The supervisor has told the word processors to be more careful, but the errors persist.

a. Develop a cause-and-effect diagram that might help to identify the source of errors.

b. How might the supervisor study ways to reduce the amount of errors? What tools might the supervisor use to do so, and how might they be applied?

14. Welz Business Machines sells and services a variety of copiers, computers, and other office equipment.† The company receives many calls daily for service, sales, accounting, and other departments. All calls are handled centrally through customer-service representatives and routed to other individuals as appropriate. A number of customers have complained about long waits when calling for service. A market-research study found that customers become irritated if the call is not answered within five rings. Scott Welz, the company president, authorized the customer-service department manager, Tim, to study this problem and find a method to shorten the call-waiting time for its customers.

Tim met with the service representatives to attempt to determine the reasons for long waiting times. The following conversation ensued:

Tim: "This is a serious problem; how a customer phone inquiry is answered is the first impression the customer receives from us. As you know, this company was founded on efficient and friendly service to all our customers. It's obvious why customers have to

*Adapted from Ronald G. Conant, "JIT in a Mail Order Operation Reduces Processing Time from Four Days to Four Hours," *Industrial Engineering* 20, no. 9 (September 1988), pp. 34–37.

†This problem was developed from a classic example published in "The Quest for Higher Quality: The Deming Prize and Quality Control," by RICOH of America, Inc.

wait: you're on the phone with another customer. Can you think of any reasons that might keep you on the phone for an unnecessarily long time?"

Robin: "I've noticed that quite often that the party I need to route the call to is not present. It takes time to transfer the call and then wait to see if it is answered. If the party is not there, I end up apologizing and have to transfer the call to another extension."

Tim: "You're right, Robin. Sales personnel often are out of the office for sales calls, absent on trips to preview new products, or not at their desks for a variety of reasons. What else might cause this problem?"

Ravi: "I get irritated at some customers who spend a great deal of time complaining about a problem that I cannot do anything about except refer to someone else. Of course, I listen and sympathize with them, but this eats up a lot of time."

LaMarr: "Some customers call so often, they think we're long-lost friends and strike up a personal conversation."

Tim: "That's not always a bad thing, you realize."

LaMarr: "Sure, but it delays my answering other calls."

Nancy: "It's not always the customer's fault. During lunch times, we're not all available to answer the phone."

Ravi: "Right after we open at 9:00 A.M., we get a rush of calls. I think that many of the delays are caused by these peak periods."

Robin: "I've noticed the same thing between 4 and 5 P.M."

Tim: "I've had a few comments from department managers that they received routed calls that didn't fall in their areas of responsibility and had to be transferred again."

Mark: "But that doesn't cause delays at our end."

Nancy: "That's right, Mark, but I just realized that sometimes I simply don't understand what the customer's problem really is. I spend a lot of time trying to get him or her to explain it better. Often, I have to route it to *someone* because other calls are waiting."

Ravi: "Perhaps we need to have more knowledge of our products."

Tim: "Well, I think we've covered most of the major reasons as to why many customers have to wait. It seems to me that we have four major reasons: the phones are short-staffed, the receiving party is not present, the customer dominates the conversation, and you may not understand the customer's problem. We need to collect some information next about these possible causes. I will set up a data-collection sheet that you can use to track some of these things. Mark, would you help me on this?"

Over the next two weeks, the staff collected data on the frequency of reasons why some callers had to wait (Table 11.6).

Table 11.6 Data for Problem 14

Reason	Total number
A. Operators short-staffed	172
B. Receiving party not present	73
C. Customer dominates conversation	19
D. Lack of operator understanding	61
E. Other reasons	10

a. From the conversation between Tim and his staff, draw a cause-and-effect diagram.
b. Perform a Pareto analysis of the data collected.
c. What actions might the company take to improve the situation?

Chapter Outline

Applied P/OM

P/OM in Practice

Chapter Twelve
Statistical Quality Control

The task of quality control is to ensure that the product reaching the consumer conforms to specifications and is fit for use. An important aspect of quality control is identifying and removing unwanted variation (from special as opposed to common causes) in production and service processes and continually seeking to reduce common causes of variation. Companies such as McDonald's have achieved competitive success by doing just that—providing products and services of consistent quality day in and day out.

If the output of a production process is subject only to common causes of variation, we say that the process is *in statistical control* (or simply *in control*), and no changes or adjustments are necessary. When assignable (special) causes are present, the process is said to be *out of control* and needs correction. Production personnel need to be able to determine when a process is in or out of control to maintain adequate levels of productivity and quality.

Workers often make two basic mistakes: adjusting a process that is already in control or failing to correct a process that is out of control (see Table 12.1). While it is clear that a truly out-of-control process must be corrected, many production workers mistakenly believe that whenever process output is off target, some adjustment must be made. Actually, overadjusting a process that is in control will increase the variation in the output. Thus, workers must know when to leave a process alone to keep variation at a minimum.

Traditionally, process-control decisions have been based on a policy of detection—that is, after-the-fact product inspection by quality control personnel not associated with production. The problem with this approach is that a large quantity of nonconforming products might have already been made by the time inspection is performed. Unnecessary costs will be incurred to correct large quantities of nonconforming product. Additionally, the quality control inspector does not know if the nonconformance was due to assignable causes or if the process is simply not capable of producing to specifications. This situation can easily create conflict between manufacturing and quality personnel and depress employee morale. An alternative is ongoing control over the process by the person who knows it best—the operator. This approach of focusing on the process, rather than the product, is a prevention-oriented strategy of inspection best accomplished by statistical process control, the subject of this chapter. Specifically addressed in this chapter are

••• The control charts commonly used in statistical process control.

••• Applications of those control charts in manufacturing and service.

••• Basic terminology and statistical calculations for acceptance-sampling plans that are still used in many companies as a part of their quality control efforts.

Table 12.1 Decisions and Risks in Process Control

	Process State	
Decision	*In Control*	*Out of Control*
Adjust process	Mistake	Correct decision
Leave process alone	Correct decision	Mistake

Statistical Process Control (SPC)

Statistical process control (SPC) is a methodology for monitoring quality of conformance and eliminating assignable (special) causes of variation in a process. It uses **control charts**—graphical tools that indicate when a process is in control or out of control—to do this. To see why SPC is desirable, consider Table 12.2, which shows 150 measurements of a quality characteristic from a manufacturing process. Each row corresponds to a sample of size 5 taken every 15 minutes. The mean of each sample is also given. Figure 12.1 is a histogram of these data. Note that the data form a relatively symmetrical distribution around the overall mean of 10.7616. From the histogram alone, what might you conclude about the state of control for this process? Bear in mind that a histogram cannot distinguish between common and assignable causes of variation. The

Table 12.2 Quality Characteristic Measurements

Sample Number	Observations					Mean
1	10.682	10.689	10.776	10.798	10.714	10.7318
2	10.787	10.860	10.601	10.746	10.779	10.7546
3	10.780	10.667	10.838	10.785	10.723	10.7586
4	10.591	10.727	10.812	10.775	10.730	10.7270
5	10.693	10.708	10.790	10.758	10.671	10.7240
6	10.749	10.714	10.738	10.719	10.606	10.7052
7	10.791	10.713	10.689	10.877	10.603	10.7346
8	10.744	10.779	10.660	10.737	10.822	10.7484
9	10.769	10.773	10.641	10.644	10.725	10.7104
10	10.718	10.671	10.708	10.850	10.712	10.7318
11	10.787	10.821	10.764	10.658	10.708	10.7476
12	10.622	10.802	10.818	10.872	10.727	10.7682
13	10.657	10.822	10.893	10.544	10.750	10.7332
14	10.806	10.749	10.859	10.801	10.701	10.7832
15	10.660	10.681	10.644	10.747	10.728	10.6920
16	10.816	10.817	10.768	10.716	10.649	10.7532
17	10.826	10.777	10.721	10.770	10.809	10.7806
18	10.828	10.829	10.865	10.778	10.872	10.8344
19	10.805	10.719	10.612	10.938	10.807	10.7762
20	10.802	10.756	10.786	10.815	10.801	10.7920
21	10.876	10.803	10.701	10.789	10.672	10.7682
22	10.855	10.783	10.722	10.856	10.751	10.7934
23	10.762	10.705	10.804	10.805	10.809	10.7770
24	10.703	10.837	10.759	10.975	10.732	10.8012
25	10.737	10.723	10.776	10.748	10.732	10.7432
26	10.748	10.686	10.856	10.811	10.838	10.7878
27	10.826	10.803	10.764	10.823	10.886	10.8204
28	10.728	10.721	10.820	10.772	10.639	10.7360
29	10.803	10.892	10.741	10.816	10.770	10.8044
30	10.774	10.837	10.872	10.849	10.818	10.8300

Figure 12.1
Histogram of Quality
Measurements

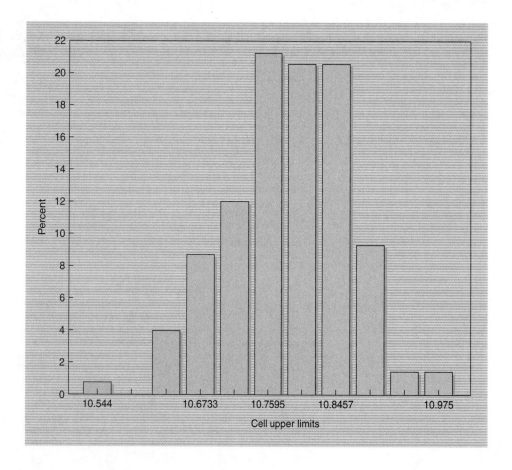

problem is that the dimension of *time* is not considered in a histogram, and assignable causes occur sporadically over time. For example, tools wear out after some period of use, materials from different shipments may vary, and substitute operators run processes when the regular operators are absent.

Since the time increments between samples are equal, the sample number is an appropriate surrogate for time. Let us plot the mean of each sample against the time at which the sample was taken. This is shown in the run chart in Figure 12.2. We clearly see that the mean shifted upward at about sample 17. It is likely that some assignable cause led to this shift and that some adjustment is necessary to bring the process back on target. The histogram does not indicate this.

Control charts were introduced in the previous chapter (see Figure 11.14). The horizontal axis is centered on the process mean and represents time; the vertical axis represents the value of the statistic computed for the attribute or variable. UCL and LCL denote the upper control limit and the lower control limit, respectively. These limits are chosen so that there is a high probability (generally greater than .99) that sample values will fall randomly between these limits *if the process is in control.*

The natural variability of process output is often described by the normal distribution. From statistics, we know that 99.7 percent of normally distributed values are within three standard deviations (σ) of the mean (μ). This is illustrated in Figure 12.3. Thus if a process is in control, we expect about .3 percent

Figure 12.2
Graph of Sample Means
versus Time

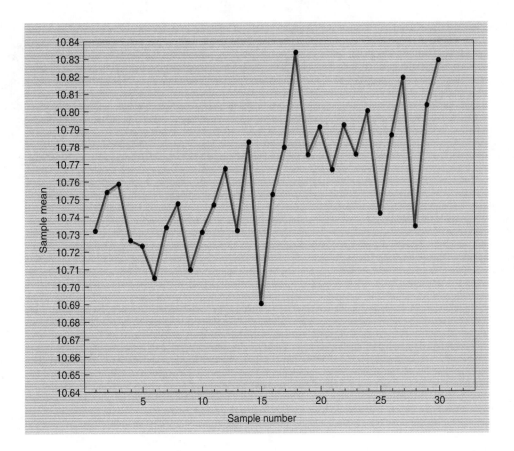

of the output to be outside the 6-σ range. For large samples ($n \geq 30$), the *central-limit theorem* states that the distribution of the sample mean, *x*, is approximately normal, with mean μ and standard deviation $\sigma_x = \sigma / \sqrt{n}$. This holds true even if the process output itself is not normally distributed (see Figure 12.4). If the process output is normally distributed, however, the sampling distribution of *x* will be normally distributed for any sample size. Therefore, if a process is in control, 99.7 percent of the *sample means* lie within $3\sigma_x$ of the true process mean. Hence, in using a control chart to monitor sample means, upper and lower control limits are usually chosen to be $\mu + 3\sigma_x$ and $\mu - 3\sigma_x$, respectively.

Figure 12.3
Six-σ Range for Normally
Distributed Process Output

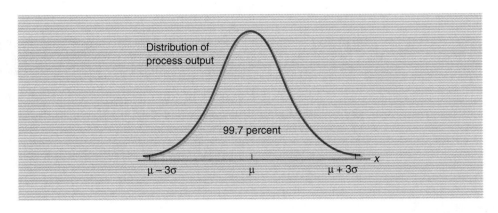

Figure 12.4
Distribution of Sample
Means of Process Output

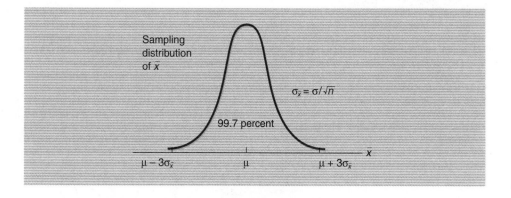

The benefits of using control charts can be summarized as follows:

••• Control charts are simple, effective tools for achieving statistical control. They can be maintained at the workstation by the operator, thus giving the people closest to the operation reliable information on when action should be taken and when it should not.

••• When a process is in statistical control, its performance to specification is predictable. Both producer and customer can rely on consistent quality levels, and both can rely on stable costs for achieving that quality level.

••• After a process is in statistical control, its performance can be further improved to reduce variation.

••• Control charts provide a common language for communication between the people on different shifts operating a process; between line production (operator, supervisor) and support activities (maintenance, material control, process engineering, quality control); between different stations in the process; between supplier and user; and between the manufacturing/assembly plant and the design-engineering activity.

••• By distinguishing assignable from common causes of variation, control charts give a good indication of whether problems are correctable locally or require management action. This minimizes the confusion, frustration, and cost of misdirected problem-solving efforts.

Constructing Control Charts

Many different types of control charts exist. All are similar in structure, but the specific formulas used to compute control limits for them differ. Moreover, different types of charts are used for different types of measurements, that is, for variable versus attribute data. *Variable data,* which are measured along a continuous scale, usually require x- ("x-bar") and R-charts. *Attribute data,* which are expressed as either conforming or nonconforming, usually require p-, c-, or u-charts.

Table 12.3 Factors Used in Quality Control Calculations

Sample Size, n	D_3	D_4	A_2	d_2
2	0	3.27	1.88	1.128
3	0	2.57	1.02	1.693
4	0	2.28	.73	2.059
5	0	2.11	.58	2.326
6	0	2.00	.48	2.534
7	.08	1.92	.42	2.704
8	.14	1.86	.37	2.847
9	.18	1.82	.34	2.970
10	.22	1.78	.31	3.078

Constructing x̄- and R-Charts

To construct a control chart for variable data, we first take M samples of n observations and compute the mean, x_i, and range, R_i, for the ith sample. Next, we compute the average sample mean,

$$\bar{\bar{x}} = \frac{\bar{x}_1 + \bar{x}_2 + \cdots \bar{x}_M}{M}$$

and overall range

$$\bar{R} = \frac{R_1 + R_2 + \cdots + R_M}{M}.$$

An x-chart will be constructed to depict the variation in the centering of the samples, and an R-chart to depict the variation in the ranges of the samples. The range is often used instead of the standard deviation because it is much easier to compute—it is simply the difference between the largest and smallest values in a sample. The R-chart is constructed first, since the control limits for the x-chart depend on the average range. If the R-chart is out of control, the x-chart may not provide good information.

To compute control limits for the R-chart, we use factors D_3 and D_4 from Table 12.3; those factors depend on the size of the sample. Such tables are widely available and make it easy to compute limits using R.* The control limits are

$$UCL = D_4\bar{R}$$

$$LCL = D_3\bar{R}.$$

To compute the control limits for the x-chart, we use the factor A_2 in Table 12.3. Then, assuming that the R-chart is in control, control limits for the x-chart are calculated as

$$UCL = \bar{\bar{x}} + A_2\bar{R}$$

$$LCL = \bar{\bar{x}} - A_2\bar{R}.$$

---

*Complete tables can be found in most books on quality control—for example, James R. Evans and William M. Lindsay, *The Management and Control of Quality*, 3d ed. (St. Paul: West, 1996).

Example

Constructing an x̄-Chart and R-Chart

The Goodman Tire and Rubber Company periodically tests its tires for tread wear under simulated road conditions. To study and control its manufacturing processes, the company uses x- and R-charts. Twenty samples, each containing three radial tires, were chosen from different shifts over several days of operation. Figure 12.5 is a spreadsheet that provides the data, sample averages and ranges, and control limits. Since $n = 3$, the control-limit factors for the R-chart are $D_3 = 0$ and $D_4 = 2.57$. The control limits as computed in the spreadsheet are

$$\text{UCL} = D_4\bar{R} = 2.57(11.4) = 29.3$$
$$\text{LCL} = D_3\bar{R} = 0(11.4) = 0$$

For the x-chart, $A_2 = 1.02$; thus the control limits are

$$\text{UCL} = 29.17 + 1.02(11.4) = 40.79$$
$$\text{LCL} = 29.17 - 1.02(11.4) = 17.54$$

The R- and x-charts for the sample data, charted with Microsoft Excel, are shown in Figures 12.6 and 12.7, respectively. The process appears to be in statistical control.

Figure 12.5 Spreadsheet for x- and R-Charts (GOODMAN.XLS)

	A	B	C	D	E	F	G	H	I	J	K	L	M	N
1	Goodman Tire and Rubber Company													
2														
3	Sample	Tread Wear				Average	LCL	UCL		Range	LCL	UCL		
4	1	31	42	28		33.67	17.54	40.79		14	0.00	29.30		
5	2	26	18	35		26.33	17.54	40.79		17	0.00	29.30		
6	3	25	30	34		29.67	17.54	40.79		9	0.00	29.30		
7	4	17	25	21		21.00	17.54	40.79		8	0.00	29.30		
8	5	38	29	35		34.00	17.54	40.79		9	0.00	29.30		
9	6	41	42	36		39.67	17.54	40.79		6	0.00	29.30		
10	7	21	17	29		22.33	17.54	40.79		12	0.00	29.30		
11	8	32	26	28		28.67	17.54	40.79		6	0.00	29.30		
12	9	41	34	33		36.00	17.54	40.79		8	0.00	29.30		
13	10	29	17	30		25.33	17.54	40.79		13	0.00	29.30		
14	11	26	31	40		32.33	17.54	40.79		14	0.00	29.30		
15	12	23	19	25		22.33	17.54	40.79		6	0.00	29.30		
16	13	17	24	32		24.33	17.54	40.79		15	0.00	29.30		
17	14	43	35	17		31.67	17.54	40.79		26	0.00	29.30		
18	15	18	25	29		24.00	17.54	40.79		11	0.00	29.30		
19	16	30	42	31		34.33	17.54	40.79		12	0.00	29.30		
20	17	28	36	32		32.00	17.54	40.79		8	0.00	29.30		
21	18	40	29	31		33.33	17.54	40.79		11	0.00	29.30		
22	19	18	29	28		25.00	17.54	40.79		11	0.00	29.30		
23	20	22	34	26		27.33	17.54	40.79		12	0.00	29.30		
24		Grand averages:				29.17				11.40				
25														

Constructing p-Charts

Recall that attribute data assume only two values, such as good or bad, pass or fail, and so on. Although attributes cannot be measured, they can be counted,

Figure 12.6 *R*-Chart for Goodman Tires

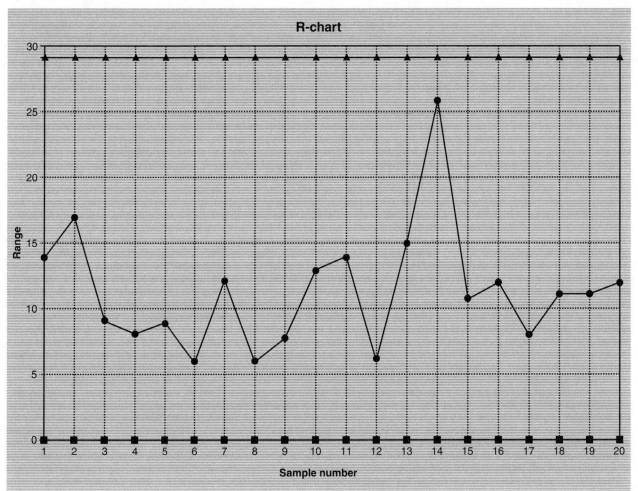

and they are useful in many situations, particularly in service organizations. A drawback in using attribute data is that large samples (of size 100 or greater) are necessary to obtain valid statistical results.

For attribute measurements, we are often concerned with monitoring and controlling the *proportion of nonconforming items*. The control chart used is called a *p*-chart, with *p* the proportion found in a sample. If we take, for example, *M* samples of *n* pieces of output over a long period of time during which the process is known to be in control, we can calculate the proportion nonconforming in each sample as y/n, where *y* is the number of nonconforming items in the particular sample. If we let p_i be the proportion nonconforming in the *i*th sample, the average proportion nonconforming for the *M* samples, $\bar{p}$, is

$$\bar{p} = \frac{p_1 + p_2 + \cdots + p_M}{M}.$$

From the central-limit theorem, we expect a high percentage of samples to have a proportion nonconforming within three standard deviations of $\bar{p}$. Since an estimate of the *standard deviation* of the proportions nonconforming, $s_{\bar{p}}$, is

Figure 12.7 $\bar{x}$-Chart for Goodman Tires

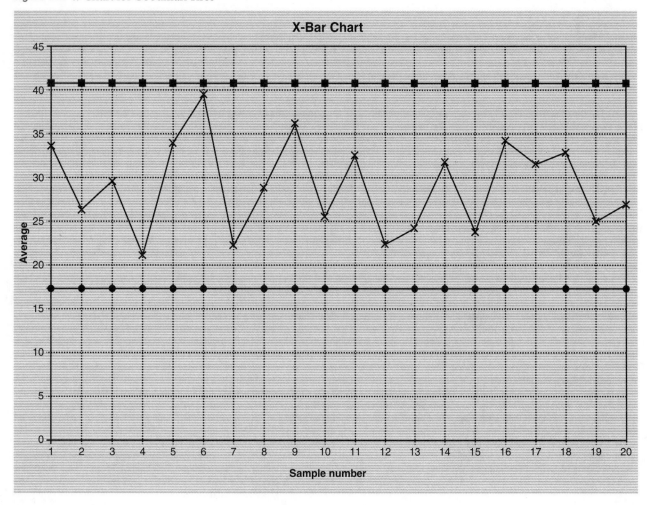

we set control limits to be

$$s_{\bar{p}} = \sqrt{\frac{\bar{p}(1 - \bar{p})}{n}}$$

$$\text{UCL} = \bar{p} + 3s_{\bar{p}}$$

and

$$\text{LCL} = \bar{p} - 3s_{\bar{p}}.$$

If LCL is less than zero, a value of zero is used. The following example illustrates the construction of a p-chart.

Example ⋮ ## Constructing a p-Chart

The operators of automated sorting machines in a post office must read the ZIP code on letters and divert the letters to the proper carrier routes. Over a month's

Figure 12.8 Spreadsheet for Postal Sorting Errors (POSTAL.XLS)

	A	B	C	D	E	F	G	H	I	J	
1	Postal Sorting Errors										
2											
3		Sample		Proportion							
4	Sample	size	Errors	defective	LCL	UCL					
5	1	100	3	0.03	0	0.066					
6	2	100	1	0.01	0	0.066					
7	3	100	0	0.00	0	0.066					
8	4	100	0	0.00	0	0.066					
9	5	100	2	0.02	0	0.066					
10	6	100	5	0.05	0	0.066					
11	7	100	3	0.03	0	0.066					
12	8	100	6	0.06	0	0.066					
13	9	100	1	0.01	0	0.066					
14	10	100	4	0.04	0	0.066					
15	11	100	0	0.00	0	0.066					
16	12	100	2	0.02	0	0.066					
17	13	100	1	0.01	0	0.066					
18	14	100	3	0.03	0	0.066					
19	15	100	4	0.04	0	0.066					
20	16	100	1	0.01	0	0.066					
21	17	100	1	0.01	0	0.066					
22	18	100	2	0.02	0	0.066					
23	19	100	5	0.05	0	0.066					
24	20	100	2	0.02	0	0.066					
25	21	100	3	0.03	0	0.066					
26	22	100	4	0.04	0	0.066					
27	23	100	1	0.01	0	0.066					
28	24	100	0	0.00	0	0.066					
29	25	100	1	0.01	0	0.066					
30			Total	0.55							
31			p-bar	0.022							
32			std.dev.	0.01467							
33											

time, 25 samples of 100 letters were chosen, and the number of errors was recorded. Figure 12.8 is a spreadsheet summarizing the data and control chart calculations. The proportion defective in each sample is simply the number of errors divided by 100. Adding the proportions defective and dividing by 25 yields $\bar{p} = .55/25 = .022$. The standard deviation is computed as

$$s_{\bar{p}} = \sqrt{\frac{.022(1 - .022)}{100}} = .01467.$$

Thus UCL = $.022 + 3(.01467) = .066$, and LCL = $.022 - 3(.01467) = -.022$. Since the LCL is negative and the actual proportion nonconforming cannot be less than zero, the LCL is set equal to zero (using the Excel function MAX in column E). Figure 12.9 is the control chart. Although no values above the UCL or below the LCL were observed in this example, the occurrence of such values might indicate operator fatigue or the need for more experience or training.

Constructing c- and u-Charts

A p-chart monitors the proportion of nonconforming items, but a nonconforming item may have more than one nonconformance. For instance, a circuit-board may have several solder defects, or an invoice may have multiple errors.

Part Three

Figure 12.9 *p*-Chart for Postal Sorting Errors

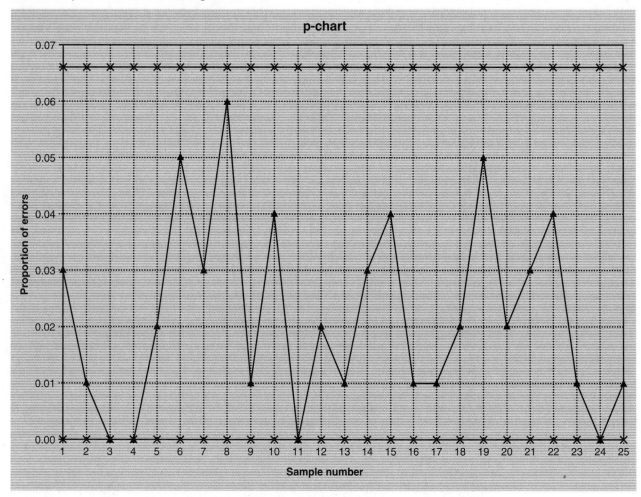

To monitor the number of nonconformances per item, we use a *c*-chart or a *u*-chart. The *c*-chart is used to control the total number of nonconformances per unit when the size of the sampling unit is constant. If sampling unit sizes are variable, a *u*-chart is used to control the average number of nonconformances per unit.

The *c*-chart is based on the *Poisson probability distribution.* To construct a *c*-chart, we must first estimate the average number of nonconformances per unit, $\bar{c}$. This is done by taking at least 25 samples of equal size, counting the number of nonconformances per sample, and finding the average. Since the standard deviation of the Poisson distribution is the square root of the mean, we have

$$s_c = \sqrt{\bar{c}}.$$

Thus, control limits are given by

$$UCL_c = \bar{c} + 3\sqrt{\bar{c}}$$
$$LCL_c = \bar{c} - 3\sqrt{\bar{c}}.$$

Example

Constructing a c-Chart

Figure 12.10 shows the number of machine failures over a 25-day period. The total number of failures is 45; therefore, the average number of failures per day is

$$\bar{c} = 45/25 = 1.8.$$

Hence, control limits for a c-chart are given by

$$UCL_c = 1.8 + 3\sqrt{1.8} = 5.82$$

and

$$LCL_c = 1.8 - 3\sqrt{1.8} = -2.22$$

or zero.

Figure 12.10 Spreadsheet for c-Chart of Machine Failures (MACHFAIL.XLS)

	A	B	C	D	E	F	G	H	I	J	
1	Machine Failures										
2											
3		Number of									
4	Day	failures	LCL	UCL							
5	1	2	0	5.82							
6	2	3	0	5.82							
7	3	0	0	5.82							
8	4	1	0	5.82							
9	5	3	0	5.82							
10	6	5	0	5.82							
11	7	3	0	5.82							
12	8	1	0	5.82							
13	9	2	0	5.82							
14	10	2	0	5.82							
15	11	0	0	5.82							
16	12	1	0	5.82							
17	13	0	0	5.82							
18	14	3	0	5.82							
19	15	0	0	5.82							
20	16	2	0	5.82							
21	17	4	0	5.82							
22	18	1	0	5.82							
23	19	2	0	5.82							
24	20	0	0	5.82							
25	21	3	0	5.82							
26	22	2	0	5.82							
27	23	1	0	5.82							
28	24	4	0	5.82							
29	25	0	0	5.82							
30	Total	45									
31	c-bar	1.8									
32											

Part Three

Figure 12.11 *c*-Chart for Daily Machine Failures

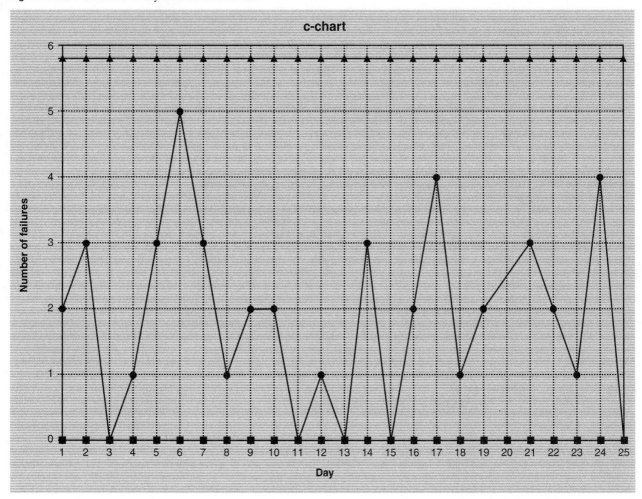

The chart shown in Figure 12.11 and appears to be in control. Such a chart can be used for continued control or for monitoring the effectiveness of a quality improvement program.

As long as the subgroup size is constant, a *c*-chart is appropriate. In many cases, however, the subgroup size is not constant or the production process does not yield discrete, measurable units. For example, suppose that in an auto assembly plant, several different models are produced that vary in surface area. The number of nonconformances will not then be a valid comparison among different models. In other applications, such as the production of textiles, photographic film, or paper, there is no convenient set of items to measure. In such cases, a standard unit of measurement is used, such as nonconformances per square foot or defects per square inch. The control chart used in these situations is called a u-chart.

The variable u represents the average number of nonconformances per unit of measurement, that is, $u = c/n$, where n is the size of the subgroup (such as square feet). We compute the center line u for M samples each of size n_i as follows.

$$\bar{u} = \frac{c_1 + c_2 + \cdots + c_M}{n_1 + n_2 + \cdots + n_M}$$

The standard deviation of the ith sample is estimated by

$$s_u = \sqrt{\bar{u}/n_i}.$$

The control limits, based on three standard deviations for the ith sample, are then

$$\mathrm{UCL}_u = \bar{u} + 3\sqrt{\bar{u}/n_i}$$

and

$$\mathrm{LCL}_u = \bar{u} - 3\sqrt{\bar{u}/n_i}.$$

Note that if the size of the subgroups varies, so will the control limits.

Example : Constructing a u-Chart

A catalog distributor ships a variety of orders each day. The packing slips often contain errors such as wrong purchase order numbers, wrong quantities, or incorrect sizes. Figure 12.12 shows the data collected during August. Since the sample size varies each day, a u-chart is appropriate.

To construct the chart, we first compute the average number of errors per slip, u, as shown in column C of Figure 12.12, by dividing the total number of errors (213) by the total number of packing slips (2,565):

$$u = 213/2,565 = .083.$$

The standard deviation for a particular sample size, n_i, is therefore

$$s_u = \sqrt{.083/n_i}.$$

With this statistic, the control limits are computed in the last two columns of Figure 12.12. As with a p-chart with variable sample sizes, we substitute the sample size in the formula for the standard deviation to find individual control limits. Figure 12.13 is the control chart generated from the spreadsheet. One point (number 2) appears to be out of control. Note that the control limits vary because of different sample sizes.

Figure 12.12 Spreadsheet for *u*-Chart of Packing Slip Data (PACKING.XLS)

	A	B	C	D	E	F	G	H	I	J	
1	Packing Slip Errors										
2											
3		Number	Number								
4	Day	of slips	of errors	Errors/slip	LCL	UCL					
5	1	92	8	0.087	0	0.173					
6	2	69	13	0.188	0	0.187	◄── Out of control				
7	3	86	6	0.070	0	0.176					
8	4	85	13	0.153	0	0.177					
9	5	101	5	0.050	0	0.169					
10	6	87	5	0.057	0	0.176					
11	7	71	3	0.042	0	0.186					
12	8	83	8	0.096	0	0.178					
13	9	103	4	0.039	0	0.168					
14	10	82	6	0.073	0	0.179					
15	11	90	7	0.078	0	0.174					
16	12	80	4	0.050	0	0.180					
17	13	70	4	0.057	0	0.186					
18	14	73	11	0.151	0	0.184					
19	15	89	13	0.146	0	0.175					
20	16	91	6	0.066	0	0.174					
21	17	78	6	0.077	0	0.181					
22	18	88	6	0.068	0	0.175					
23	19	76	8	0.105	0	0.182					
24	20	101	9	0.089	0	0.169					
25	21	92	8	0.087	0	0.173					
26	22	70	2	0.029	0	0.186					
27	23	72	11	0.153	0	0.185					
28	24	83	5	0.060	0	0.178					
29	25	69	6	0.087	0	0.187					
30	26	79	3	0.038	0	0.180					
31	27	79	8	0.101	0	0.180					
32	28	76	6	0.079	0	0.182					
33	29	92	7	0.076	0	0.173					
34	30	80	4	0.050	0	0.180					
35	31	78	8	0.103	0	0.181					
36	Totals	2565	213								
37		u-bar	0.083								
38											

Choosing between c- and u-Charts. Since the *c*- and *u*-charts apply to situations in which the quality characteristics inspected do not necessarily come from discrete units, confusion may arise as to which chart is appropriate. The key issue to consider is *whether the sampling unit is constant.* For example, suppose an electronics manufacturer produces circuitboards. The boards may contain various defects, such as faulty components, missing connections, and so on. The sampling unit is the circuitboard. If it is constant (all boards are the same), a *c*-chart is appropriate. If the process produces boards of varying sizes with different numbers of components and connections, a *u*-chart would apply.

As another example, consider a telemarketing firm that wants to track the number of calls needed to make one sale. In this case there is no physical sampling unit. However, think of an analogy with the circuitboards. The sale may correspond to the circuitboard, and the number of calls to the number of defects. In both examples, the number of occurrences of something as related to a constant entity is being measured. Thus, a *c*-chart is appropriate.

Figure 12.13 *u*-Chart for Packing Slip Errors

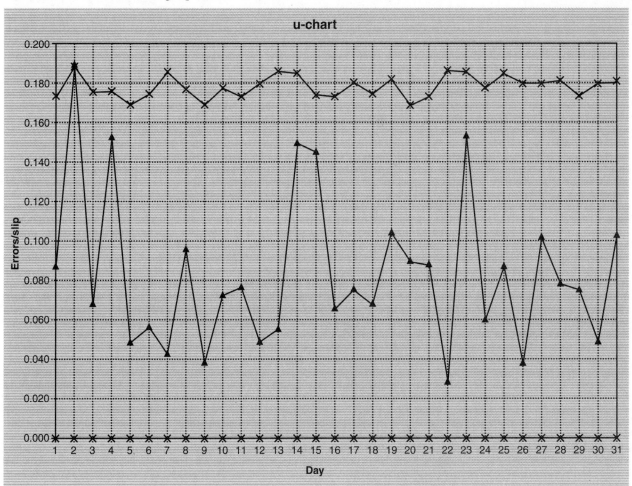

Interpreting Control Charts

The location of points and the patterns of points in a control chart enable one to determine, with only a small chance of error, whether or not a process is in statistical control. The first indication that a process may be out of control is a point that is outside the control limits. If such a point is found, the operator or supervisor should first check for the possibility that the control limits were miscalculated or that the point was plotted incorrectly. If neither is the case, there is strong evidence that the process mean has shifted, that the variability of the process has changed, or that the measurement system has changed. A second indication that the process may be out of control is the presence of a large number of points above or below the center line. This can indicate an equipment problem, a change in materials, new operators, or a change in measurement technique or tools. Eight points in a row above or below the center line, 10 of 11, or 12 of 14 signals the need for an investigation. If this occurs *below* the center line on the range chart, it indicates a potential improvement in the process—which likewise warrants a careful investigation to determine if indeed a change for the better has occurred and why.

In general, about two-thirds of the points should lie within the middle third of the region between the upper and lower control limits. If this is not the case, the samples may have been drawn from two or more different sources. For instance, a mix of two different materials might have been used, or the samples may have been from a machine having two spindles. Two rules of thumb used to detect such out-of-control states are (1) two of three consecutive points in the outer one-third region between the center line and one of the control limits and (2) four of five consecutive points in the outer two-thirds region. Examples of these guidelines are illustrated in Figure 12.14.

A third thing to look for in a control chart is any pattern or trend. A common pattern is an increasing or decreasing trend. As tools wear down, for example, the diameter of a machined part will gradually become larger. Changes in temperature or humidity, general equipment deterioration, dirt buildup on fixtures, or operator fatigue may cause such a trend. About six or seven consecutive points that increase or decrease in value should be regarded as out of con-

Figure 12.14
Interpretation of Control
Charts

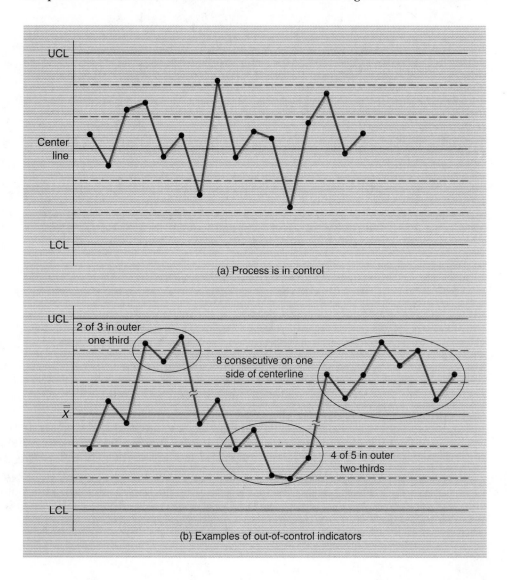

trol. A wave or cycle pattern is also unusual and should be suspect. It might be a result of seasonal effects of material deliveries, temperature swings, maintenance cycles, or periodic rotation of operators. Again, if an out-of-control condition is indicated, one should first check for errors in constructing the control chart. Although the numbers of samples are limited, the control charts for both examples in this section appear to be in control.

Applications of Control Charts

Control charts have three basic applications: (1) to establish a state of statistical control, (2) as monitoring devices to signal the existence of assignable causes in order to maintain a state of statistical control, and (3) to determine process capability.

The Goodman Tire and post office examples illustrated how to construct control charts for determining whether a process is in a state of statistical control. If any variations due to assignable causes are found when initially constructing a control chart, managers and quality-assurance personnel must identify the underlying causes and eliminate them. Only after a process has been brought into control can its ability to consistently produce output that conforms to specifications be determined.

After a process is determined to be in control, the control charts should be used daily to monitor production, identify any variations due to assignable causes that might arise, and make corrections as necessary. More importantly, control charts indicate when to leave a process alone. Unnecessary adjustments to a process result in nonproductive labor, reduced production, and increased variability of output.

SPC is more productive if the operators themselves take the samples and chart the data. In this way, they can make adjustments as needed, without delay. Many companies conduct in-house training programs to teach operators and supervisors elementary methods of SPC. Such training has the added benefit of increasing their quality consciousness.

It is not uncommon for improvements in conformance to follow the introduction of control charts on the shop floor, particularly when the process is labor-intensive. Apparently, broadening the job responsibilities of the operators often produces positive behavioral modifications (as first demonstrated in the Hawthorne studies). Under such circumstances, it is advisable to revise control limits periodically as improvements occur.

Process Capability

Process capability refers to the total variation due to common causes. If we assume that process output is normally distributed, we can estimate the process standard deviation, σ (not the standard deviation of the *sample* mean, $\sigma_{\bar{x}}$), by the sample standard deviation, s. We compute s by dividing the average range by a constant, d_2, which can be found in Table 12.3. That is,

$$s = \frac{\bar{R}}{d_2}.$$

Figure 12.15
Process Capability versus
Design Specifications

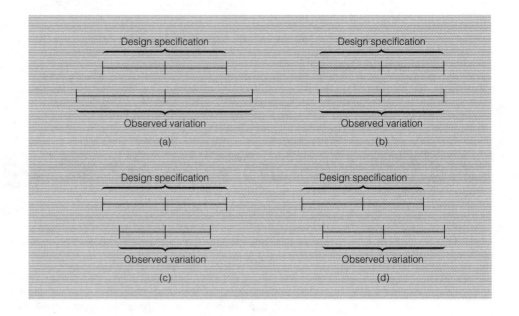

The process capability is then given by $\bar{\bar{x}} \pm 3s$.

In the Goodman Tire example, $R = 11.4$, and the sample size is 3. From Table 12.3 we find that $d_2 = 1.693$, so an estimate of the process standard deviation for those data is

$$s = 11.4/1.693 = 6.73.$$

The process capability is determined to be $29.17 \pm 3(6.73)$ or 8.98 to 49.36. This means that as long as the process remains in control, the tread wear for individual tires can be expected to vary between 8.98 and 49.36 hundredths of an inch when evaluated under the same simulated road conditions.

The process capability is usually compared to the design specifications to indicate the ability of the process to meet the specifications. Figure 12.15 illustrates four possible situations that can arise when the observed variability of a process is compared to design specifications. In part a, the range of process variation is larger than the design specification; thus it will be impossible for the process to meet specifications a large percentage of the time. Managers can either scrap or rework nonconforming parts (100-percent inspection is necessary), invest in a better process with less variation, or change the design specifications. In part b, the process is able to produce according to specification, although it will require close monitoring to assure that it remains in that position. In part c, the observed variation is tighter than the specifications; this is the ideal situation from a quality control viewpoint, since little inspection or control is necessary. Finally, in part d, the observed variation is the same as the design specification, but the process is off-center; thus some nonconforming product can be expected.

For example, in the Goodman Tire situation, suppose the specifications are such that tread wear should be held to a maximum of 40 hundredths of an inch during the road test. Using the estimated standard deviation of 6.73 and the normal probability distribution, we can calculate the percentage of tires that

Figure 12.16
Normal Probability for
Goodman Tire's Process
Capability

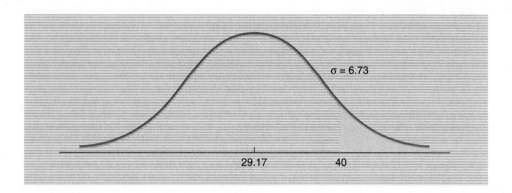

normal probability distribution, we can calculate the percentage of tires that can be expected to exceed this specification.

The shaded area under the normal curve in Figure 12.16 represents the proportion of tires that exceed the specifications. Since the standard normal value corresponding to 40 is

$$z = \frac{40 - 29.17}{6.73} = 1.61,$$

from Appendix B we see that the shaded area is $.5 - .4452 = .0548$. Thus, about 5.5 percent of the tires would exceed the specification.

Process capability is important both to product designers and to manufacturing-process engineers. If product specifications are too tight, the product will be difficult to manufacture. Production personnel will be under pressure and will have to spend a lot of time adjusting the process and inspecting output. Process engineers must also understand the implications of process capability. For example, if a design specification requires a length of metal tubing to be cut to within .1 inch, and the process consists of a worker using a ruler and a hacksaw, a large percentage of nonconforming parts will probably result because of the worker's inability to provide the desired precision. Hence product-design and process-selection decisions must be integrated.

Service Organizations

In preceding chapters, we noted differences between manufacturing and service organizations. We observed that service organizations share features that differ from those of manufacturing, including direct contact with the customer, large volumes of transactions and processing, and in many cases large amounts of paperwork. It is easy to see that there are considerable sources of error in recording transactions and in processing. It is not unusual to see a newspaper report of a billing error amounting to thousands or hundreds of thousands of dollars.

Although control charts were first developed and used in a manufacturing context, they are easily applied to service organizations. The major difference is the quality characteristic that is controlled. Many of the standards used in service industries form the basis for quality-control charts. Some examples of using SPC to improve service operations were reported at IBM in Kingston, New York.

Applied P/OM:

IBM Corporation

IBM used control charts successfully in improving preemployment physical examination and purchase-order-processing systems.[1]

At one IBM branch, preemployment physical examinations took too long and taxed the medical staff assigned to conduct them. Such examinations are vital for assuring that employees can perform certain jobs without excess stress and that they pose no health threat to other employees. Therefore, the challenge IBM faced was to maintain the quality of the exam while reducing the time needed to perform it by identifying and eliminating waiting periods between the various parts of it.

Preliminary control charts revealed that the average time required for the examination was 74 minutes, but the range varied greatly. New equipment and additional training of the medical staff were suggested as means of shortening the average time. Initial charts indicated that the process was out of control, but continued monitoring and process improvements lowered the average time to 40 minutes, and both the average and range were brought into statistical control with the help of x- and R-charts.

Another problem involved purchase orders. The steps in processing purchase orders are fairly routine. The person requesting an item or service fills out a requisition and forwards it to a buyer who translates it into an order. The buyer selects a vendor, usually after a number of bids. But at this IBM branch, time and money were being lost by human error in the purchase-order-processing system, and both requesters and buyers were contributing to the problem. Of great concern were nonconforming documents originated by the purchasing department itself. The department started to count them. Data on weekly purchase orders and orders in error were monitored, and a p-chart was constructed that showed an average error rate of 5.9 percent. After the buyers reviewed the data, they found that the process had actually changed during the data collection period, resulting in a shift in the mean to 3.7 percent. The use of the chart also showed out-of-control conditions resulting from vacations. Substitute buyers created a high percentage of rework because of the work load and their unfamiliarity with particular aspects of the process. Preventive measures were created for peak vacation periods to provide sufficient coverage and ensure that backup personnel understand the process better.

The key to using control charts effectively lies in defining the appropriate quality measures to be monitored. Once this is done and agreed upon by managers, the use of control charts becomes routine. Table 12.4 lists a few potential applications of control charts for services.

Implementing Statistical Process Control

Implementing the use of control charts on the factory floor requires much work and commitment. People experienced in using SPC have found that five factors are necessary for successful implementation.

Table 12.4 Control-Chart Applications in Service Organizations

Organization	Quality Measure
Hospital	Lab-test accuracy
	Insurance-claim accuracy
	On-time delivery of meals and medication
Bank	Check-processing accuracy
Insurance company	Claims-processing response time
	Billing accuracy
Post office	Sorting accuracy
	Time of delivery
	Percentage of express mail delivered on time
Ambulance	Response time
Police department	Incidence of crime in a precinct
	Number of traffic citations
Hotel	Proportion of rooms satisfactorily cleaned
	Checkout time
	Number of complaints received
Transportation	Proportion of freight cars correctly routed
	Dollar amount of damage per claim
Auto service	Percentage of time work completed as promised
	Number of complaints

1. *Top-management commitment is essential.* This includes financial resources for measurement instruments, calculators or computers and software, and training in the mechanics of SPC for workers. Managers must demonstrate that SPC is not a fad that will disappear in a few months, but an ongoing commitment to improve quality.

2. *Projects need a champion.* That is, some individual in the company who has both the responsibility and the authority to make the SPC program work must take a leadership position.

3. *Only one problem should be addressed at a time.* Mistakes will be made at the beginning, and the company will learn from them. In choosing an initial project, managers should select one that stands to benefit most from SPC and that has high visibility both to top managers and other workers. One good success story will encourage others to try SPC, so good communication and publicity are needed within the company.

4. *Education and training of all employees is essential.* Everyone needs to understand why SPC is being used and what it can do to improve quality and help the workers do a better job. Workers must understand that SPC will benefit them, and that it is not a management scheme to place blame on them.

5. *All instruments used for quality measurements must be properly calibrated and maintained in good working order.* Calibration means ensuring that measuring instruments measure true values with required levels of precision. It requires additional resources and a high level of commitment from both managers and the workforce.

Control charts sometimes fail in organizations for a number of reasons. Operators sometimes do not trust a new tool. Old methods, such as correcting a process only if production is out of specification or adjusting machines after every batch, are difficult habits to break. Also, in some cases operators do not receive enough training or practice, or do not fully understand the benefits of control charts. Another reason for failure is the lack of a plan for corrective action. The concept of control requires that assignable causes be identified and corrected. Failure to act on control-chart signals increases variability, reduces the importance of the chart, and undermines the entire quality program.

One must also be sure to use the appropriate chart. Attribute charts are easier to use, but sometimes variable charts are more appropriate. Moreover, managers must show commitment, not simply lip service, to SPC. Their commitment will be evident in their decisions when the use of control charts means that taking a needed corrective action will delay a shipment, or when the nonconformance level rises in the rush to meet an order. (Operators may quickly see that they are wasting their time and stop using SPC.) In addition, control charts require maintenance. Control limits must be updated periodically as elements of the process change and as assignable causes are eliminated. An outdated chart is useless.

Acceptance Sampling

Acceptance sampling is used to make a decision about whether to accept or reject a group of items on the basis of specified quality characteristics. The group of items in question is usually called a *lot*. The general acceptance-sampling procedure is shown in Figure 12.17. A lot is received from a supplier or from final assembly. Items from the lot are inspected for quality characteristics, and the re-

Figure 12.17
Acceptance-Sampling
Procedure

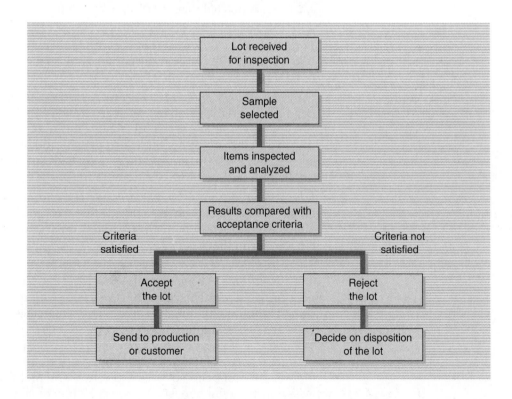

sults are compared with acceptance criteria. If those criteria are satisfied, the lot is accepted and sent to production or shipped to customers; otherwise, the lot is rejected. The determination of whether to accept or reject a lot is often called *lot sentencing.* We emphasize that this is the true purpose of acceptance sampling; it is not appropriate to use acceptance sampling to determine the average value of a quality characteristic or the percentage of the lot that does not conform to standards. Other statistical sampling techniques should be used in those cases.

In any sampling procedure, there is risk of making an incorrect decision. That is, based on a sample of the items in a lot, a lot of poor quality might be accepted or a lot of good quality might be rejected. In quality control terminology, the probability of rejecting a lot of good quality is commonly referred to as the **producer's risk.** These errors create a risk for the producer (supplier), because a customer may erroneously reject a lot of good quality on the basis of a small sample and return it to the producer. The probability of accepting a lot of poor quality is called the **consumer's risk.** In a similar way, a consumer may test a lot and erroneously accept it as good. Later, when the product is put into the production process, it is discovered to be of poor quality.

Acceptance sampling is implemented with a **sampling plan.** A *sampling plan* for attribute inspection is a decision rule that can be used to determine whether to reject the lot on the basis of the number of nonconforming items in a sample of items from the lot. To make this decision we must specify a sample size (n) and an acceptance number (c). Then, if the number of nonconforming items in the sample is less than or equal to c, we accept the lot. If the number of nonconforming items is greater than c, we reject the lot. This type of sampling plan is called a *single-sampling plan* and is illustrated in Figure 12.18.

Various other sampling plans are used. For instance, in a *double-sampling plan,* illustrated in Figure 12.19, two sample sizes, n_1 and n_2, and two acceptance numbers, c_1 and c_2 with $c_1 < c_2$, are specified. First, a sample of n_1 items is

Figure 12.18
Single-Sampling-Plan Logic

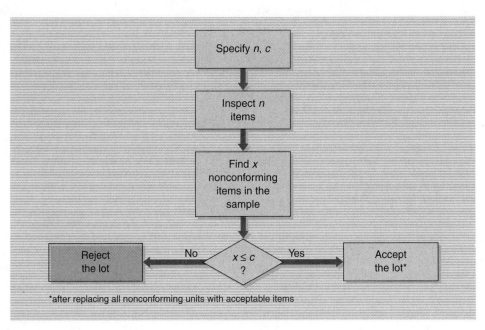

Figure 12.19 Double-Sampling-Plan Logic

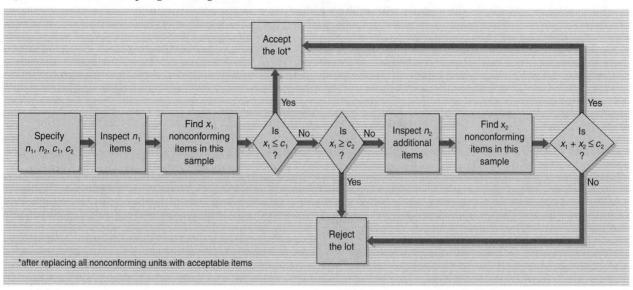

*after replacing all nonconforming units with acceptable items

taken. If the number of nonconforming items, x_1, is less than or equal to c_1, the lot is accepted. If the number nonconforming is greater than c_2, the lot is rejected. If $c_1 < x_1 \le c_2$, a second sample of n_2 items is taken. If the total number of nonconforming items in both samples ($x_1 + x_2$) exceeds c_2, the lot is rejected; otherwise it is accepted.

Acceptance sampling has been widely used for several reasons. Since it is based on statistical principles, it provides for risk assessment in the decision. In addition, it is relatively inexpensive and particularly well suited to destructive testing situations. It takes less time than 100-percent inspection. It also requires less handling, which decreases the chance of damage. Finally, acceptance sampling generally does not lead to inspector fatigue as does 100-percent inspection. Acceptance sampling is a very flexible method; the amount of inspection can be varied depending on the quality history of the items being inspected. Since entire lots are rejected, it places economic and psychological pressure on vendors to improve quality rather than simply replace the nonconforming items.

Despite its widespread use, acceptance sampling has been condemned as an inspection practice because it is not compatible with the philosophy of prevention and improvement. Acceptance sampling is based on a policy of *detection*— that is, after-the-fact product inspection by quality control personnel not associated with production. The problem with the approach is the risk that a large quantity of nonconforming products might have already been made, in which case unnecessary costs will be incurred to correct the mistakes. Additionally, the inspector does not know if nonconformance is caused by special (assignable) causes or because the controlled process is simply not capable of producing to specifications. This can easily result in (1) conflict among manufacturing, engineering, purchasing, and quality personnel; (2) low employee morale; and (3) customer dissatisfaction. An alternative is to maintain ongoing control over the process by the person who knows it best—the operator—using SPC.

As a temporary measure for quality control, however, acceptance sampling can serve a critical role.[2] A key factor is whether or not the process in question is in statistical control. As we have said, when a process is in statistical control, the only variations in it are caused by random variations—common causes. Since the only difference between "good" lots and "bad" lots is random product variation, the likelihood of another bad lot occurring is no greater after a bad one than after a good one. Thus, there is nothing to gain by accepting or rejecting lots that are in reality statistically indistinguishable. This is one of Deming's principal criticisms of acceptance inspection.

When a process is not in statistical control, variation in lots is due to some assignable (special) cause, and the likelihood of consecutive bad lots is much greater. Thus it is reasonable to inspect the lots surrounding a bad lot more carefully. Sampling inspection makes sense only if there is something to be learned from it.

P/OM in Practice

Using SQC for Process Improvement at Dow Chemical Company[3]

The magnesium department of the Dow Chemical Company plant in Freeport, Texas, has produced magnesium, a silvery light metal, for more than 70 years. It was the first major group in Texas Operations to train all of its technical people and managers in the use of statistical quality control (SQC) techniques, following the example set by the automobile industry.

Some of the earliest successful applications of SQC were in chemical-process areas. Figures 12.20 and 12.21 show the improvement in the dryer analysis after SQC and retraining were implemented. In addition to the fact that the process control required significant improvement, differences between operators existed. The dark circles in Figure 12.20 represent one operator in question; the open circles represent the other operators. On examination, it was found that the operator had not been properly trained in the use of SQC, even though the operator had been performing the

Figure 12.20 Before-and-After $\overline{x}$-Charts on Dryer Analysis

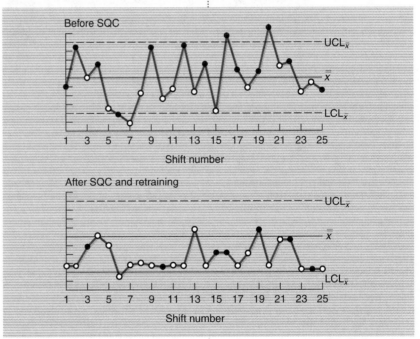

analysis for two years. There was immediate improvement in the consistency of the operators' analyses after retraining.

The use of control charts in the control room made the operators realize that their attempts to fine-tune the process introduced a great deal of

Figure 12.21 Before-and-After *R*-Charts on Dryer Analysis

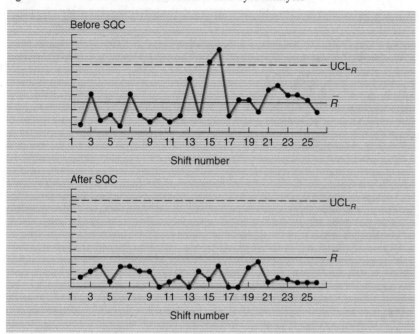

2. Briefly describe how Dow Chemical used SQC techniques in the casting operations.

Process Control Management at Corning Incorporated[4]

Corning Incorporated has adapted statistical quality control in a unique fashion at several of its electronic plants in the United States and in Europe. In its approach, called *process control management (PCM)*, the burden of continuous checking is placed on the operators, and processes that continually produce excellent-quality products are seldom checked by personnel. Data obtained from several operations are fed into the system and tabulated to produce a picture of current operations. These data are available to production, quality control, and engineering for analysis and evaluation. Quality control may then increase its monitoring of processes that are questionable, while reducing involvement with those running with consistent excellence. Annual savings have been estimated at more than $200,000 in direct labor and $300,000 in yield improvement.

Analysis is based on past experience, historical data, process-capability studies, and other statistical methods. Each machine in a process is categorized as one of four quality levels identified by color codes. *Level I* denotes a problem-free, excellent machine or process and is identified by the color blue. Most of the machines of a process should enter this category. The manufacturing costs are low, and requirements for the next operation or for final release to the customer are satisfied. Under level 1, it is necessary only to verify that changes have not occurred. Full trust is given to production personnel at this level, and it is assumed that the process will continue in full control and produce excellent-quality parts under constant oper-

unwanted variation. The before-and-after range charts (*R*-charts) show the improvement; see Figure 12.21.

As with many chemical and manufacturing operations, when the variability of the feedstock to one operation is reduced, it is possible to reduce the variability of the basic operation. With tighter control over the concentration of magnesium hydroxide from the filter plant, Dow was able to exert much tighter control on the subsequent neutralization operation. As seen in Figure 12.22, the differences are substantial. The upper control limit (UCL) on the second range chart is about where the center line is on the first. A similar situation exists on the $\bar{x}$-charts. These improvements resulted without any additional instrumentation or operators.

Another application involved the casting operation. On primary magnesium, for example, Dow calculated a process-capability index—the ratio of the specified tolerance to the six-sigma natural variation—of meeting

minimum magnesium content of 99.8 percent purity and found it to be over 10, based on more than 10,000 samples. Thus, there had been little incentive to use control charts in this operation because of the comfortable level of compliance. However, ingots are also graded according to their surface quality. Using control charts, Dow found that although the process was in control, the number of rejects was much higher than desired. After several months of analysis and modifications, the process was improved.

Dow has had success everywhere it has used SQC in the magnesium process. Savings of several hundred thousand dollars per year have been realized, and new applications are continually being discovered.

Questions for Discussion

1. Briefly describe how SQC techniques were used to make improvements in the dryer analysis.

Figure 12.22 The $\bar{x}$- and R-Charts on Neutralizer Excess Alkalinity before and after SQC

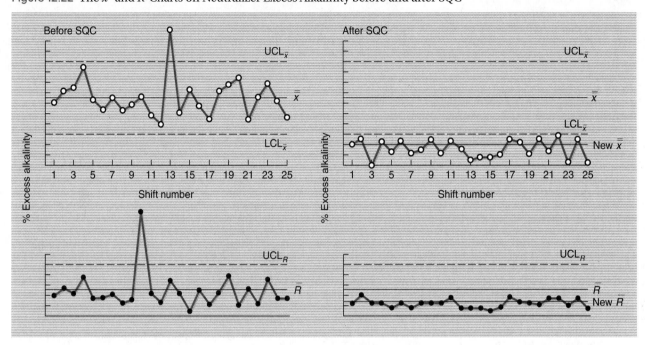

Figure 12.23 Example of Quality-Level Settings

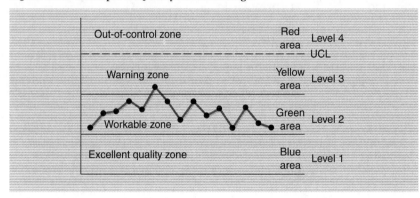

ator verification. Quality control personnel make only occasional random checks on these processes.

In *level 2,* the machine or process is classified as workable and is identified by the color green. This level requires that the process inspector be directed to the same machine more often than required by level 1. The machine chosen and the frequency of visits by quality control (QC) personnel is higher. Production personnel still exercise full control, but QC monitors the processes more closely to detect any deterioration and trend toward a level-3 classification.

Level 3 denotes borderline operations, and the identifying color is yellow. The inspectors are directed to step up the monitoring of these machines. Very tight control is required, and every effort is expended to bring the offending machines back into the relative safety of level 2.

In *level 4,* machines designated out of control (color red) are immediately shut down and repaired. Parts produced for evaluation after the machine is repaired are segregated into lots for special consideration by QC. Maximum support is provided by QC whenever machines reach this level.

Conventional control charts and process-capability studies are used to designate the levels. Figure 12.23 is an example of a *p*-chart and the color codes. It enables operators to immediately detect changes in the process and alert QC personnel. QC support is directed from the process-control monitor console, which may be operated manually or be computer-supported or fully computerized. This support provides continuously adjusted levels of machines and processes and directs QC personnel to the next machine to be checked.

Corning has found that the system maintains and improves quality by motivating production-department personnel and by charging them with the responsibility for making acceptable products without sacrificing yield. It also has improved interdepartmental communications by developing a feeling of teamwork. Each plant has its own adaptation of PCM to fit its specific needs.

Questions for Discussion

1. What does Corning call its approach to statistical quality control?

What benefits have been achieved by using this process?

2. Explain the method for categorizing machines.

3. What type of control chart is shown in Figure 12.23? Briefly explain how this chart is used.

Summary of Key Points

••• Statistical process control (SPC) uses control charts to identify assignable causes of variation in a process and to help operators maintain a state of statistical control. Control charts can be used to establish a state of statistical control, to provide ongoing monitoring of a process, and to evaluate process capability.

••• Process capability is the total variation attributable to common causes. Typically measured by a six-sigma (standard deviation) spread, it is compared to design specifications to assess the ability of a process to meet specifications.

••• Successful implementation of SPC requires top-management commitment, a champion, focused effort, education and training, and properly calibrated and maintained measuring instruments.

••• Acceptance sampling is an inspection method in which the decision about whether to accept or reject a lot is made by comparing the number of defects in a sample with a specified acceptance number. The method involves establishing the statistical risks of making incorrect decisions. "Producer's risk" is the probability of rejecting a good-quality lot; "consumer's risk" is the probability of accepting a poor-quality lot. Although acceptance sampling has been widely used, it does not prevent poor quality or promote improvement. As a temporary measure, however, it can be useful.

Key Terms

Statistical process control (SPC)
Control chart
Process capability
Producer's risk
Consumer's risk
Sampling plan

Review Questions

1. What do we mean when we say that a process is *in statistical control*?
2. What is statistical process control, and what benefits can be gained from using it?
3. Explain why histograms do not provide sufficient information to determine the state of statistical control.
4. Describe the various types of control charts and their applications.
5. What benefits can control charts provide?
6. Discuss how to interpret control charts. What types of patterns indicate a lack of control?
7. What is the purpose of a process-capability study?
8. Describe the key factors in successful implementation of statistical process control in an organization.
9. List some applications of control charts in service organizations.
10. What is the purpose of acceptance sampling?
11. Describe the general acceptance-sampling procedure.

Discussion Questions

1. Provide some examples in business or daily life in which a controlled process is erroneously adjusted and an out-of-control process is ignored.
2. Discuss some situations for which control charts might not be very useful.
3. How might control charts help to improve customer-supplier relationships?

4. Develop a "personal-quality checklist" on which you tally nonconformances in your personal life (such as being late for work or school, not completing homework on time, not getting enough exercise, and so on). What type of chart would you use to monitor your performance?

5. Provide several applications of each type of control chart that are different from those discussed in this chapter.

6. Interview a manager at a nearby company who is using SPC. Report on the challenges the company faced in training its workers and in using SPC effectively. How has SPC helped it become more competitive?

7. What would Deming have said about SPC? About acceptance sampling? What are the fundamental differences between these two approaches?

Notes

1. W. J. McCabe, "Improving Quality and Cutting Costs in a Service Organization," *Quality Progress,* June 1985, pp. 85–89.

2. Dan K. Fitzsimmons, "Gaining Acceptance for Acceptance Sampling," *Quality Progress,* April 1989, pp. 46–48.

3. Adapted from Clifford B. Wilson, "SQC + Mg: A Positive Reaction," *Quality Progress,* April 1988, pp. 47–49.

4. Adapted from Basile A. Denissoff, "Process Control Management," *Quality Progress* 13, no. 6 (June 1980), pp. 14–16. © 1980 American Society for Quality Control. Reprinted by permission.

Solved Problems

1. A production process, sampled 30 times with a sample size of 8, gave these $\bar{\bar{x}}$ and $\bar{R}$ values: $\bar{\bar{x}} = 28.5$, $\bar{R} = 1.6$

a. Construct R- and $\bar{x}$-charts for this process.

b. At a later stage, six samples produced these results for $\bar{x}$: 28.001, 28.25, 29.13, 28.72, 28.9, 28.3. Is the process in control?

c. Does this set of sample results for the $\bar{x}$-chart indicate that the process is out of control: 28.3, 28.7, 28.1, 28.9, 28.01, 29.01? Why or why not?

Solution

From Table 12.3, $n = 8$, we have $A_2 = .37$, $D_3 = .14$, and $D_4 = 1.86$.

a. The $\bar{x}$-chart:

$$\text{UCL} = 28.5 + .37(1.6) = 29.092$$
$$\text{LCL} = 28.5 - .37(1.6) = 27.908$$

The R-chart:

$$\text{UCL} = 1.86(1.6) = 2.976$$
$$\text{LCL} = .14(1.6) = 0.224$$

b. The sample 29.13 is above the UCL, signifying an out-of-control condition.

c. While all points are within the control limits, Figure 12.24 shows that an unusual pattern is beginning to emerge—the points are alternately drifting toward the control limits.

2. Over several weeks, 20 samples of 50 packages of synthetic-gut tennis strings were tested for breaking strength; 38 packages failed to conform to the manufacturer's specifications. Compute control limits for a p-chart.

Solution

$$\bar{p} = 38/1000 = .038$$
$$\text{Standard deviation} = \sqrt{(.038)(.962) / 50} = .027$$

Figure 12.24
$\bar{x}$-Chart for Solved
Problem 1 Solution

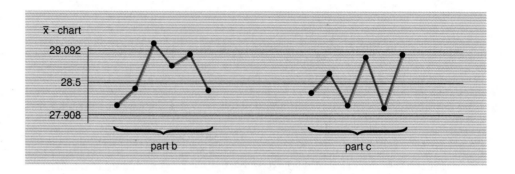

Control limits:

$$UCL = .038 + 3(0.27) = .119$$

$$LCL = .038 - 3(.027) = -.043$$

so set LCL = 0.

3. A controlled process exhibits $\bar{\bar{x}} = 2.50$ and $\bar{R} = 0.42$. Samples of size 4 were used to construct the control charts. What is the process capability? If specifications are 2.60 ± 0.25, how well can this process meet them?

Solution
From Table 12.3, $d_2 = 2.059$. Thus, $s = \bar{R}/d_2 = 0.42/2.059 = 0.20$. The process capability is $\bar{\bar{x}} \pm 3s = 2.50 \pm 3(0.20)$, or 1.90 to 3.10. Because the specification range is 2.35 to 2.85 with nominal 2.60, we may conclude that the true natural variation exceeds the specifications by a large amount. In addition, the process is off-center.

Problems

1. Thirty samples of size 3 resulted in $\bar{\bar{x}} = 16.51$ and $\bar{R} = 1.30$. Compute control limits for $\bar{x}$- and R-charts.

2. Twenty-five samples of size 5 resulted in $\bar{\bar{x}} = 5.42$ and $\bar{R} = 2.0$. Compute control limits for $\bar{x}$- and R-charts, and estimate the standard deviation of the process.

3. Use the sample data in Table 12.5 to construct $\bar{x}$- and R-charts. Assume that the sample size is 5:

Table 12.5 Data for Problem 3

Sample	$\bar{x}$	R	Sample	$\bar{x}$	R
1	95.72	1.0	11	95.80	.6
2	95.24	.9	12	95.22	.2
3	95.18	.8	13	95.56	1.3
4	95.44	.4	14	95.22	.5
5	95.46	.5	15	95.04	.8
6	95.32	1.1	16	95.72	1.1
7	95.40	.9	17	94.82	.6
8	95.44	.3	18	95.46	.5
9	95.08	.2	19	95.60	.4
10	95.50	.6	20	95.74	.6

4. Develop $\bar{x}$- and R-charts for the data in Table 12.6.

Table 12.6 Data for Problem 4

Sample	\multicolumn{5}{c}{Observations}				
	1	*2*	*3*	*4*	*5*
1	3.05	3.08	3.07	3.11	3.11
2	3.13	3.07	3.05	3.10	3.10
3	3.06	3.04	3.12	3.11	3.10
4	3.09	3.08	3.09	3.09	3.07
5	3.10	3.06	3.06	3.07	3.08
6	3.08	3.10	3.13	3.03	3.06
7	3.06	3.06	3.08	3.10	3.08
8	3.11	3.08	3.07	3.07	3.07
9	3.09	3.09	3.08	3.07	3.09
10	3.06	3.11	3.07	3.09	3.07

5. Thirty samples of size 3, listed in Table 12.7, were taken from a machining process over a 15-hour period.
a. Compute the mean and standard deviation of the data, and plot a histogram.
b. Compute the mean and range of each sample, and plot them on control charts. Does the process appear to be in statistical control? Why or why not?

Table 12.7 Data for Problem 5

Sample	\multicolumn{3}{c}{Observations}		
1	3.55	3.64	4.37
2	3.61	3.42	4.07
3	3.61	3.36	4.34
4	4.13	3.50	3.61
5	4.06	3.28	3.07
6	4.48	4.32	3.71
7	3.25	3.58	3.51
8	4.25	3.38	3.00
9	4.35	3.64	3.20
10	3.62	3.61	3.43
11	3.09	3.28	3.12
12	3.38	3.15	3.09
13	2.85	3.44	4.06
14	3.59	3.61	3.34
15	3.60	2.83	2.84
16	2.69	3.57	3.28
17	3.07	3.18	3.11
18	2.86	3.69	3.05
19	3.68	3.59	3.93
20	2.90	3.41	3.37
21	3.57	3.63	2.72
22	2.82	3.55	3.56
23	3.82	2.91	3.80

(continues)

Table 12.7 Data for Problem 5 (continued)

Sample	Observations		
24	3.14	3.83	3.80
25	3.97	3.34	3.65
26	3.77	3.60	3.81
27	4.12	3.38	3.37
28	3.92	3.60	3.54
29	3.50	4.08	4.09
30	4.23	3.62	3.00

6. In testing the resistance of a component used in a microcomputer, these data in Table 12.8 were obtained:

Table 12.8 Data for Problem 6

Sample	Observations		
1	414	388	402
2	408	382	406
3	396	402	392
4	390	398	362
5	398	442	436
6	400	400	414
7	444	390	410
8	430	372	362
9	376	398	382
10	342	400	402
11	400	402	384
12	408	414	388
13	382	430	400
14	402	409	400
15	399	424	413
16	460	375	445
17	404	420	437
18	375	380	410
19	391	392	414
20	394	399	380
21	396	416	400
22	370	411	403
23	418	450	451
24	398	398	415
25	428	406	390

Construct $\bar{x}$- and R-charts for these data. Determine if the process is in control. If it is not, eliminate any assignable causes and compute revised limits.

7. Twenty-five samples of 100 items each were inspected, and 68 were found to be defective. Compute control limits for a p-chart.

8. At Mama Mia's, a 20-week study of 30 pizzas per week found a total of 18 pizzas made improperly. Construct a p-chart to monitor this process.

9. The proportions nonconforming for an automotive piston are given in Table 12.9 for 20 samples. Two hundred units are inspected each day. Construct a p-chart and interpret the results.

Table 12.9 Data for Problem 9

Sample	Proportion Nonconforming	Sample	Proportion Nonconforming
1	.04	11	.07
2	.05	12	.09
3	.03	13	.05
4	.02	14	.04
5	.02	15	.03
6	.04	16	.04
7	.04	17	.03
8	.06	18	.05
9	.04	19	.02
10	.08	20	.04

10. One hundred insurance claim forms are inspected daily for 25 working days, and the number of forms with errors are recorded as in Table 12.10. Construct a p-chart. If any points are outside the control limits, assume that assignable (special) causes have been determined. Then construct a revised chart.

Table 12.10 Data for Problem 10

Day	Number Nonconforming	Day	Number Nonconforming
1	2	14	2
2	1	15	1
3	2	16	3
4	3	17	4
5	0	18	0
6	2	19	0
7	0	20	1
8	2	21	0
9	7	22	2
10	1	23	8
11	3	24	2
12	0	25	1
13	0		

11. Find control limits for a c-chart with $\bar{c} = 9$.

12. Consider the following data showing the number of calls a stockbroker needed to make to successfully complete a sale. Construct a c-chart and interpret the results.

Sale Number	1	2	3	4	5	6	7	8	9	10
Number of Calls	4	15	13	20	17	22	26	17	20	22

13. Find control limits for a u-chart with $\bar{c} = 9$ and $n = 4$; also with $n = 5$ and $n = 6$.

14. A trucking company is studying its billing process. Over a 15-day period, it obtained the results in Table 12.11.

Table 12.11 Data for Problem 14

Day	No. of Bills	No. of Errors
1	54	6
2	76	8
3	67	8
4	89	20
5	76	13
6	84	11
7	61	11
8	73	10
9	90	14
10	98	10
11	82	13
12	64	13
13	72	10
14	88	11
15	86	12

Construct a u-chart for errors per bill. Is the process in control? Is the process satisfactory?

15. Discuss the interpretation of each of the control charts presented in Figure 12.25.

16. For Problem 4, estimate the process capability by first computing the sample standard deviation and then computing $\bar{R}/d_2$. Why is there a difference?

17. Determine the process capability for the data in Problem 6. Suppose the specifications for the resistance are 400 ± 40. What would you conclude?

18. Gotfryd Hydraulics, Inc., manufactures hydraulic machine tools. It has had a history of leakage trouble resulting from a certain critical fitting. Twenty-five samples of machined parts were selected, one per shift, and the diameter of the fitting was measured. The results are given in Table 12.12.

a. Construct control charts for the data in the table.

b. It was discovered that the regular machine operator was absent when samples 4, 8, 14, 22 were taken. How will this affect the results in part a?

c. Table 12.13 presents measurements taken during the next 10 shifts. What information does this provide to the quality-control manager?

Table 12.12 Data for Problem 18, Part a

| Sample | Diameter Measurement (cm) Observation | | | |
	1	*2*	*3*	*4*
1	10.94	10.64	10.88	10.70
2	10.66	10.66	10.68	10.68
3	10.68	10.68	10.62	10.68
4	10.03	10.42	10.48	11.06
5	10.70	10.46	10.76	10.80
6	10.38	10.74	10.62	10.54

(continues)

Figure 12.25
Control Charts for
Problem 15.

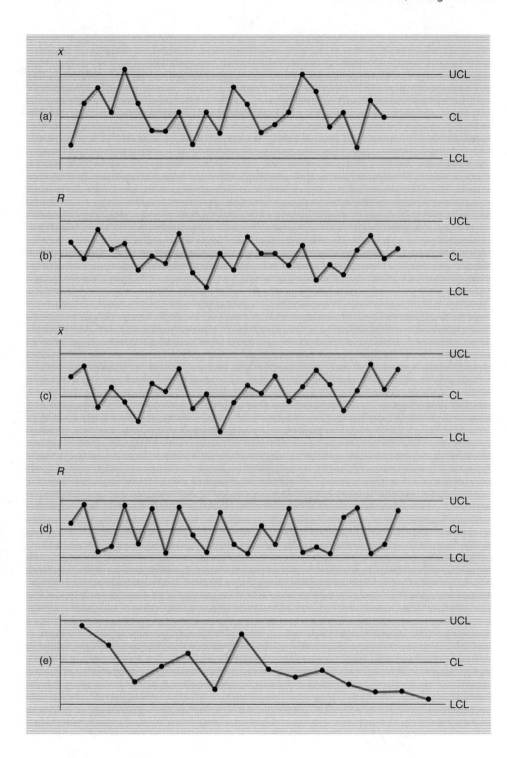

Table 12.12 Data for Problem 18, Part a (continued)

Sample	Diameter Measurement (cm) Observation			
	1	*2*	*3*	*4*
7	10.46	10.90	10.52	10.74
8	10.66	10.04	10.58	11.04
9	10.50	10.44	10.74	10.66
10	10.58	10.64	10.60	10.26
11	10.80	10.36	10.60	10.22
12	10.42	10.36	10.72	10.68
13	10.52	10.70	10.62	10.58
14	11.04	10.58	10.42	10.36
15	10.52	10.40	10.60	10.40
16	10.38	10.02	10.60	10.60
17	10.56	10.68	10.78	10.34
18	10.58	10.50	10.48	10.60
19	10.42	10.74	10.64	10.50
20	10.48	10.44	10.32	10.70
21	10.56	10.78	10.46	10.42
22	10.82	10.64	11.00	10.01
23	10.28	10.46	10.82	10.84
24	10.64	10.56	10.92	10.54
25	10.84	10.68	10.44	10.68

Table 12.13 Data for Problem 18, Part b

Additional Sample	Observation			
	1	*2*	*3*	*4*
1	10.40	10.76	10.54	10.64
2	10.60	10.28	10.74	10.86
3	10.56	10.58	10.64	10.70
4	10.70	10.60	10.74	10.52
5	11.02	10.36	10.90	11.02
6	10.68	10.38	10.22	10.32
7	10.64	10.56	10.82	10.80
8	10.28	10.62	10.40	10.70
9	10.50	10.88	10.58	10.54
10	10.36	10.44	10.40	10.66

Effective operation of a production process depends on proper management of materials, from purchasing through final assembly. Materials management decisions are *tactical* decisions, because they involve relatively short time horizons and support strategic goals and objectives.

Chapter 13 discusses the management of inventory for production and describes some basic inventory management systems. Chapter 14 presents a variety of quantitative models that support inventory management decisions.

In recent years, efforts to reduce manufacturing inventories have driven tactical planning. Two of the most important techniques for reducing inventory as well as for improving quality are just-in-time and synchronous manufacturing, the subjects of Chapter 15. Those techniques are the basis for *lean production* - an approach to streamlining operations for unprecedented levels of productivity, quality, and customer service.

Part IV
Managing Materials

Chapter Thirteen
Materials and Inventory Management

aterials and inventory management is one of the most important functions of P/OM. **Materials management** involves planning, coordinating, and controlling the acquisition, storage, handling, and movement of raw materials, purchased parts, semifinished goods, supplies, tools, and other materials that are needed in the production process. Any idle goods or materials that are held for future use are called **inventory.** MamaMia's Pizza, for instance, must maintain inventories of dough, toppings, sauce, and cheese, as well as supplies such as boxes, napkins, and so on. For many organizations, the expenses associated with financing and maintaining inventories are a substantial part of the cost of doing business. In large firms, especially those with many or expensive products, these costs can run into millions of dollars.

Materials and inventory managers, then, are faced with the dual challenges of maintaining sufficient inventories to meet demand while at the same time incurring the lowest possible cost. For example, MamaMia's manager must determine how many fresh dough balls to order. Since dough is perishable (lasting about three and a half days), ordering too many may result in waste, while ordering too few may put the business in the catastrophic position of not being able to fill a customer's order.

This is the first of three chapters on inventory-management issues. It examines the traditional role of materials and inventory management and presents some economic models for inventory analysis. Understanding the traditional approach is important as a basis for understanding modern viewpoints. In Chapter 14, we present several quantitative decision models and analysis methods that apply to special inventory-management situations. Finally, in Chapter 15 we show why the traditional models are at odds with contemporary wisdom and introduce the "just-in-time" concept of materials management. This chapter specifically addresses

••• The importance of inventory in meeting strategic customer-service and financial objectives.

••• The scope of materials-management activities.

••• The nature and characteristics of inventory problems.

••• Methods for analyzing and controlling inventory systems.

••• Simple models for inventory decisions.

The Strategic Importance of Inventory

From the operational perspective, inventory is an important aspect of production operations. Inventory affords *economies of scale* in purchasing and production whereby the purchase of large lots of raw materials and components typically accrues savings through quantity discounts and truckload-discount transportation rates—even when the entire quantity is not needed all at once. Such inventory is called **lot-size inventory.** In production, lot-size inventories help spread fixed setup costs over more items and balance setup cost with inventory investment. **Work-in-process (WIP) inventories** have traditionally been used to increase manufacturing efficiency. They act as buffers between work centers or departments to enable the production system to continue operating when machines break down, when supplier shipments are late, or when a large proportion of parts is defective. In service organizations, physical products are not made, but inventories of supplies—such as forms in an insurance company or drugs in a hospital—are essential to the successful operation of the organization.

Finished-goods inventories minimize the effects of varying demand for finished goods and provide better customer service. It is rarely possible to predict sales levels accurately, and a firm runs the risk of losing many customers if it runs out of stock. **Fluctuation inventory** or **safety stock** is maintained in case of such an event. Another reason for having inventory is that many items have high seasonal demand. It might be impossible to produce enough during a short selling season because of limited production capacity. **Anticipation inventory** is therefore built up during the off-season to meet future estimated demand.

Despite their obvious value, inventories present some operational limitations and financial concerns. High levels of WIP inventories, for example, can make it more difficult to change product lines, since they must be phased out when that occurs. Hence, their very existence can limit a key strategic variable of the firm: its flexibility to produce a wide variety of products to meet customers' needs. In addition, a firm should not tolerate unreliable machines, late supplier shipments, or defective parts, but maintaining large WIP inventories simply hides such problems and makes them acceptable.

Inventory represents a major financial investment for any company when costs of transportation, warehousing, and capital are considered. Better control of inventory can reduce operating expenses. If the "right" inventory is carried, profits can be increased through additional sales revenues. From a top-management perspective, therefore, inventories have significant impact on a company's balance sheet and income statement.

A further complication is that nearly every department in an organization views inventory objectives differently. The marketing department prefers high inventory levels to provide the best possible customer service. Purchasing agents tend to buy in large quantities to take advantage of quantity discounts and lower freight rates. Similarly, production managers want high inventories to prevent production delays. But, as we have discussed, financial personnel seek to minimize inventory investment and warehousing costs.

A TQM focus helps to put the different objectives in perspective. Inventory should be managed to support strategic customer-satisfaction and operational goals such as availability, quick response, or manufacturing flexibility. When managers understand the true purpose of inventory, conflicts between organizational units in this regard should not occur.

Materials Management

Figure 13.1 depicts the essential materials-management activities of a production system. There are three components: the management of raw materials and purchased parts (purchasing, receiving, storage, and retrieval), the management of finished goods (packaging and shipping, storage and retrieval in warehouses, and distribution to the customer), and the management of materials during the conversion process (handling and storage of work-in-process inventories). All these activities involve inventory in some form.

Figure 13.1
Materials-Management
Activities

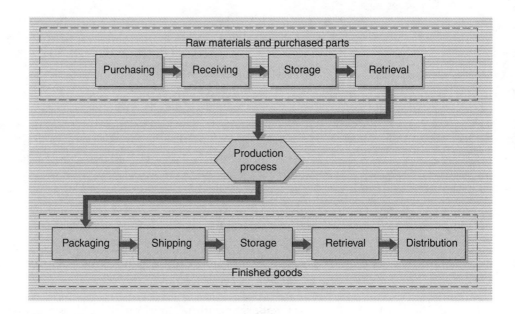

Purchasing

The **purchasing** or **procurement** function is responsible for acquiring raw materials, component parts, tools, and other items required from outside suppliers. The purchasing department in any organization acts as an interface between suppliers and the production function. Since materials are one of the largest sources of cash outlay in any manufacturing firm, their acquisition requires careful management.

The principal goal of purchasing is to support its key internal customer: manufacturing. Thus, purchasing must do much more than simply buying according to the quoted line-item purchase price. Purchasing must ensure quality, delivery performance, and technical support. Moreover, purchasing must continually seek new suppliers and products and be able to evaluate their potential to the company. The responsibilities of a purchasing department include learning the material needs of the organization, selecting suppliers and negotiating price, ensuring delivery, and monitoring cost, quality, and delivery performance. Accordingly, purchasing agents must maintain good relations and communication with other departments, such as accounting and finance, where budgets are prepared; product design and engineering, where material specifications are set; production, where timely delivery is essential; and the legal department, where contracts are reviewed.

Though purchasing activities are varied, the principal ones can be summarized as follows.

1. *Receive purchase requisitions.* These are documents generated by production or inventory control that authorize material purchases.

2. *Review and evaluate requisitions.* The purpose here is to determine if less costly items can be substituted or if an item can be eliminated entirely. This activity is called *value analysis.*

3. *Select qualified suppliers.* Suppliers should be able to provide goods that meet the firm's quality specifications, to deliver them on time at an acceptable price, and to cooperate with the purchasing department when special situations arise, such as changes in specifications or volume and service problems.

4. *Aggregate and place orders.* Aggregating orders can result in quantity discounts and reduced transportation rates.

5. *Follow up and expedite.* Purchasing must monitor deliveries and production schedules and expedite deliveries and schedules when necessary. Entire production lines have been shut down because of delays in obtaining a part worth only a few cents.

6. *Authorize payments.* Purchasing must work closely with receiving and accounting to ensure that all ordered goods are delivered before payment is authorized.

7. *Keep records.* With thousands of products and materials, dozens or hundreds of suppliers, and numerous requisitions, an accurate information system is essential.

In most organizations, there are three classes of purchased items. One consists of large items that are either purchased on a one-time basis or very infrequently—for example, machine tools, computing equipment, and transportation vehicles. A second consists of items purchased in small quantities, or infrequently purchased, or low in cost, such as printer ribbons and other office supplies and small tools. A third consists of high-volume-use items such as sheet metal or bulk raw materials.

Purchasing procedures may vary with the type of item purchased. For instance, items involving large capital expenditures often require competitive bids based on detailed technical specifications and legal contracts, whereas small items can be ordered by departmental secretaries through catalogs or purchased outright without any formal procedure. In the latter case, payments are usually made from petty-cash funds or small-supplies budgets, thus eliminating unnecessary paperwork and time. High-volume purchases, however, are often handled by **blanket contracts** wherein a large quantity is contracted for delivery over a long period of time and delivery dates are not specified. Instead, as material is needed, release orders are sent out for delivery, perhaps on a monthly or weekly basis. The buyer can take advantage of quantity discounts and be assured of supply in this way.

Receiving, Packaging, Shipping, and Warehousing

Receiving functions are to unload inbound goods from their transportation vehicles, to verify that proper quantities are received in good condition and of adequate quality, and to prepare the goods for storage or production. **Packaging** and **shipping** departments are responsible for ensuring that finished goods are packaged properly to prevent damage, are labeled correctly, and are loaded onto the right transportation vehicles.

Warehousing coordinates receiving and shipping, and physically maintains inventory. Warehousing is very labor-intensive. With the increase in product variety, shorter product life cycles, higher customer demands for service, information technology, and a global marketplace, there is a great opportunity to improve productivity and quality in warehouse operations through better employee training and information technology.

Physical Distribution

Physical distribution is responsible for selecting transportation carriers, managing company-owned fleets of vehicles, and controlling interplant movement of materials and goods. As such, this function plays a key role in satisfying customers. An efficient distribution system can enable the company to operate with lower inventory levels, thus reducing costs.

The term **traffic** is often used to refer to the daily operations of managing the transportation function. Specifically, the role of traffic is to

1. Purchase transportation services.
2. Select appropriate modes of shipment and specific carriers.
3. Negotiate transportation rates and contracts.
4. Trace shipments in transit and expedite them when necessary.
5. File claims for damaged goods.
6. Audit freight bills.

Traffic personnel are also involved in special studies, such as warehouse location and fleet-routing problems.

The purchase of transportation services is a complex decision, since varied services are available—rail, motor carrier, air, water, and pipeline. *Pipelines* have limited use and accessibility and are used primarily for such products as oil and natural gas. Similarly, *water transportation* is generally limited to transporting large quantities of bulky items, for instance, raw materials such as coal and other ores.

The critical factors in transportation decisions are speed, accessibility, cost, and capability. Weight restrictions and loading and unloading facilities would sometimes be included in these considerations. A comparison of three modes of transportation illustrates their differences on those factors (Table 13.1). *Rail transit* is generally slow and is used primarily for shipping large volumes of relatively low-value items over long distances. However, rail cars often encounter long delays and are less dependable than other forms of transportation. *Motor carriers* have high availability and can ship nearly anywhere. Transportation costs are higher with this mode, and it is used most often for short distances and smaller shipments. Weight and size constraints limit the capability of trucks

Table 13.1 Comparison of Transportation Modes

Characteristic	Rail	Truck	Air
Speed	3	2	1
Accessibility	2	1	3
Cost	1	2	3
Load capability	1	2	3
Note: The best ranking is 1.			

for carrying certain loads, but their scheduled service is more dependable than that of rail. *Air transportation* is highly dependable and very fast, although it is less accessible than the other modes. Costs are higher, but this mode of transport may be cheaper overall than surface transportation because of reduced packaging needs. Clearly, air cargo carriers cannot handle very large loads.

Carriers within a particular mode differ. The traffic manager is responsible for selecting the carrier that not only gives a good rate, but also has proven customer-service policies for delivery, damage rates, claims handling, and so on.

Supplier Management and Partnership

The quality of outputs from a production system can be no better than the quality of inputs. Thus it is unwise to treat suppliers as adversaries, as many companies have done in the past. In the 1980s many U.S. firms changed their adversarial supplier relationships to secure improved quality by establishing productive partnerships. Where suppliers' quality substantially improved as a result, companies were also able to eliminate or substantially reduce inventories and incoming inspection and testing.

Supplier partnerships proved to have many other benefits as well. When close relationships are developed, the total number of suppliers can be reduced, since there is no need for competition among suppliers for the same products. The older practice of having many suppliers bid on each order—with the lowest price accepted—is losing favor except on standard items. With larger contracts, suppliers benefit from economies of scale and customers benefit from volume discounts. Moreover, with long-term contracts, suppliers are more willing to invest in process and system improvements. Many customers even provide assistance in making such improvements. In return, they receive better products and service. Also, suppliers' experts can be brought in at the early design stages to take advantage of their specialized knowledge. Most suppliers welcome the opportunity to help their customers. It is not unusual to find supplier representatives working with product-design teams. GTE Directories has taken this concept a step further with its "employee-exchange" program.

Applied P/OM

GTE Directories

Partnerships provide a basis for supplier management at GTE Directories.[1]

GTE Directories, a leading Yellow Pages publisher, establishes unique partnerships with its suppliers. One example is an employee-exchange program with paper suppliers. To help paper manufacturers understand GTE's business so that they can better meet its needs, and to help employees understand the paper business so they can better articulate their needs, GTE sends press operators to work in suppliers' mills while suppliers send paper-makers to work in GTE printing plants. Not only has this approach strengthened GTE's relationship with suppliers, it has increased both parties' awareness of the effects of poor quality on productivity.

Many companies are now requiring suppliers to provide evidence, such as quality control charts or test results, showing that their manufacturing processes are under tight control. The evidence is then used in eliminating or reducing incoming inspection so that items can go directly to production areas for immediate use. A side benefit is the reduction of inventories and associated problems of outdated stocks, deterioration, and scrap or rework if design changes are made. **Supplier-certification programs,** such as Florida Power and Light's program, evaluate suppliers according to various criteria such as quality, cost, and delivery.

Applied P/OM

Florida Power and Light

Quality assurance and improvement are the focus of FPL's supplier-certification program.[2]

Florida Power and Light (FPL) has a three-tiered supplier-certification program to identify "Quality Vendors," "Certified Vendors," and "Excellent Vendors." To become a Quality Vendor, a supplier's products or services must meet basic requirements on quality, cost, delivery, and safety. In addition, the supplier must have a quality-improvement process in place and must demonstrate that it has achieved significant improvements. It must also have an audit system for certifying the process and the results. To become a Certified Vendor, the supplier must additionally demonstrate the use of statistical process control and prove that its processes can meet FPL's specification requirements. It must be able to document its capability and have a plan for continuous quality improvement. To achieve Excellent Vendor status, a supplier must demonstrate its ability to exceed FPL's specification requirements, employ reliability-assurance techniques, and show that quality improvement is a central part of its management system.

Information Technology in Materials Management

Some important needs in materials management include having accurate receipt information, reducing the time spent in staging (between receipt and storage), accurately identifying loads that have been received, selecting storage locations, updating inventory records, routing customer orders for picking, generating bills of lading, and providing various managerial reports. A control system is needed to effectively manage warehouse operations by identifying and coordinating the work that needs to be done, directing the accomplishment of the work so as to maximize performance, and reporting the status of work. Materials-management operations have benefited greatly from information technology, particularly bar coding and radio frequency (RF) communications.[3]

Nearly every product today has a **bar-code** label. Bar-code scanners read the symbols on the label by measuring the width of the bars and spaces and differentiating between symbols by the amount of light reflected. Bar coding reduces labor intensity by eliminating the need to key-in information. It also greatly improves data accuracy and reduces human error. In retail store operations, for example, the use of bar codes streamlines the ordering and inventory control efforts. When a consumer purchases a product, the checkout scanner records the sale from the bar code. The information is processed by the in-store computer, which automatically triggers an order when the stock level drops to a critical threshold. This enables the store to order smaller lot sizes more frequently, thus reducing the need for inventory space. It also enables the manufacturer to match production to demand, lessening the need for costly warehouse storage and providing faster response. Such systems eliminate paper processing, saving managers' time and reducing errors.

Radio frequency (RF) communications hardware consists of either hand-held or truck-mounted units that allow information to be sent to workers electronically from a central computer. Such devices help to provide real-time updates of receipts and orders, reduce labor idle time by eliminating the need for workers to return to a central location to receive new work instructions, and improve tracking of materials. Better and faster information provides faster customer response.

The integration of bar coding and RF technology provides the basis for modern materials control systems, which reduce operating costs, improve productivity, and improve customer service. It also forms the basis of an "intelligent warehouse," which integrates computer systems, material handling equipment, storage equipment, and workers. In a typical system, a receiving operator will select the purchase order from an RF terminal and scan the bar code from the incoming delivery. The product is available immediately for cross-docking, shipping, or storage. A putaway operator will scan the item, and a system-generated storage location will be displayed on an RF terminal. If multiple items are to be stored, the system will route the operator in the most efficient manner. Orders are sent to operators' RF terminals along with routing instructions. When items are picked, bar codes are scanned to update the records and verify the correct pick. A shipping report is printed and, by means of electronic data interchange, the customer can be notified of the order status.

A computer-intelligent warehouse can achieve zero information errors through bar-code verification of every material movement, rapid response through electronic communication, high labor productivity through computer-directed task instructions, and improved space utilization through greater inventory and storage location accuracy. Henry Ford Hospital is one of the many service organizations that benefits from bar coding.

Applied P/OM

Henry Ford Hospital

Bar coding keeps track of inventory in Henry Ford Hospital.[4]

The Henry Ford Hospital in Detroit is a 1,000-bed-general medical and surgical teaching institution that serves more than 1.5 million patients per year. The hospital previously used a manual system for tracking, billing, and restocking pharmaceuticals. Although the job was getting done, the paperwork became extremely difficult to maintain. The manual keyboard entry of records was both time-consuming and prone to error. The tracking of controlled substances and floor-stock replacement of bulk items

ing of controlled substances and floor-stock replacement of bulk items were other major problems.

Drugs are stored in the pharmacy's main stockroom and are distributed upon request to various satellite pharmacies and to clinics throughout the community. The 2,500 different drugs are arranged alphabetically by generic name, and the stockroom shelves use bar-code labels to identify the drug item number.

When the stockroom receives a requisition, the clerk responsible for filling the order goes to the stockroom floor with a portable bar-code-transaction manager and a hand-held laser scanner. Each requesting department has a bar-coded cost-center number and drug-quantity number on a preprinted menu that is used for tracking costs. The clerk scans the cost-center number at the beginning of the requisition cycle and then the item number from the shelf and the quantity-issued number. When all requisitions are filled, the clerk uploads the data from the portable scanning unit to an IBM personal computer. The PC creates a file and prints a copy of the data scanned to verify what was actually pulled from the shelf.

At the end of the day, a variety of reports can be created to monitor the work load and the inventory control. All transactions are uploaded to the hospital's mainframe computer, which automatically generates a report telling the pharmacy when a particular item needs to be reordered.

The pharmacy replaces floor-stock items in each nursing unit on a daily basis. Each nursing unit has a bar-code menu that includes the unit's cost-center number and list of floor-stock drugs. When a stockroom clerk visiting each nursing unit's medication storage area sees the minimum acceptable quantity of an item, the clerk scans the menu for the cost-center number, drug item label, and the number label, which conveys the type and quantity of item needed and the station to which it should be charged. Back in the stockroom, the data are uploaded into the PC, which produces a pick list of items for distribution to all stations.

Classifying Inventory Problems

A large variety of inventory problems is possible.[5] For instance, a self-serve gasoline station maintains an inventory of only a few grades of gasoline, whereas a large appliance store may carry several hundred different items and brands. Demand for gasoline is relatively constant, while the demand for air-conditioners is highly seasonal and variable. If a gasoline station runs out of gas, a customer will go elsewhere. However, if an appliance store does not have a particular item in stock, the customer may be willing to order the item and wait for delivery. Since the inventory characteristics of the gasoline station and appliance store differ significantly, the proper control of inventories requires different approaches.

One of the first steps in analyzing an inventory problem should be to describe the essential characteristics of the environment and inventory system. Although it is impossible to consider all characteristics here, we address the more important ones. Table 13.2 summarizes inventory problems.

Table 13.2 Classification Scheme for Inventory Problems

Characteristic	Attributes
Number of items	One or many
Nature of demand	Independent or dependent; deterministic or stochastic; static or dynamic
Number of time periods in planning horizon	One or many
Lead time	Deterministic or stochastic
Stockouts	Back orders or lost sales

Number of Items

Many inventory control models determine the inventory policy for only one item at a time. For organizations with hundreds or thousands of distinct items, applying such models might prove difficult. In such cases, items are often aggregated, or partitioned, into groups with similar characteristics or dollar value. It is easier to design effective inventory systems for controlling a smaller number of groups of items.

With multiple items, there may be various constraints such as warehouse or budget limitations that affect inventory policy. Other interactions among products also must be considered. For example, certain groups of products tend to be demanded together, such as motor oil and oil filters, certain chemicals, or food items.

Nature of Demand

Demand can be classified as either independent or dependent, deterministic or stochastic, and dynamic or static. By *independent demand,* we mean demand that is not influenced by operations, but rather by the market. Inventories of finished goods have independent demand characteristics. Items are said to have *dependent demand* if their demand is related to that of another item. For example, a chandelier may consist of a frame and six light-bulb sockets. The demand for chandeliers is independent, while the demand for sockets is dependent on the demand for chandeliers.

In many situations, demand is reasonably stable and thus can be accurately forecast. In such cases, demand can be assumed to be known with certainty. We call this *deterministic demand.* In other cases, demand is highly variable and can be specified only by a probability distribution. In this case, we refer to it as *stochastic demand.* Accurate forecasting is more difficult here. Such is often the case with one-time sales or seasonal items.

Demand may also fluctuate over time or be stable throughout the year. For instance, such food items as bread and milk exhibit relatively stable demand, while the demand for such items as pumpkins and fruitcakes varies significantly over the year. Stable demand is usually called *static demand,* and demand that varies over time is referred to as *dynamic demand.*

Number of Time Periods

In some cases, the selling season is relatively short, and any leftover items cannot be physically or economically stored until the next season. For example, Christmas trees that have been cut cannot be stored until the following year, and other items, such as seasonal fashions, are sold at a loss simply because there is no storage space or it is uneconomical to keep them for the next year. This "single-period" inventory problem requires a different analysis than problems in which inventory is held from one time period to the next.

Lead Time

Lead time is the amount of time between the placement of an order and its receipt. Lead time may be relatively constant or stochastic (in which case it may be described by some probability distribution). It is affected by transportation carriers. Rail, truck, and air transportation have different characteristics. For example, the lead time for products shipped by air may be less variable than that for products shipped by rail. Also included in lead time is the time the supplier needs to process the order or to produce it if it is not readily available.

Stockouts

When no stock is available (*stockout*) to satisfy the demand for an item, it is either back-ordered or a sale is lost. A *back order* occurs when a customer is willing to wait for the item; a *lost sale* occurs when the customer is unwilling to wait and purchases the item elsewhere. Back orders result in additional costs for transportation, expediting, or perhaps buying from another supplier at a higher price. A lost sale has an associated opportunity cost, which may include loss of goodwill and potential future revenue.

From a customer-service viewpoint, firms never want to incur a stockout; indeed, in situations such as blood inventories, stockouts can be tragic. However, in many situations back orders may be economically justified. For instance, with high-value items such as commercial jet planes, no inventory is carried and a back-order state always exists. Back orders may also be planned to smooth demand on the work force. When unplanned back orders occur, one of several reasons can usually be identified, including forecast inaccuracies on usage or lead time, unreliable supplier delivery, clerical errors, quality problems, insufficient safety stock, and transportation accidents.

Inventory Costs

Inventory costs fit into four major categories: cost of the items themselves, order-preparation costs, inventory-holding costs, and shortage costs. The cost of maintaining inventory is the principal criterion for determining inventory policy—how much inventory to carry and the frequency of ordering.

The *cost of items* is an important consideration when quantity discounts are offered; it may be more economical to purchase large quantities at a lower unit cost. In most cases, however, the cost of the item is constant.

Ordering costs are incurred because of the work involved in placing purchase orders with suppliers and organizing the ordered items for production within a plant. For purchased items, this can include such activities as order processing, filling out forms, selecting suppliers, fixed handling costs, processing receiving documents, and inspecting goods when they arrive. If a manufactured lot is ordered within a plant, the ordering costs (generally called *setup costs*) include paperwork, machine setup, and startup scrap. Ordering costs do not depend on the number of items purchased or manufactured, but rather on the number of orders that are placed.

Inventory-holding or **inventory-carrying costs** include all expenses incurred because inventory is carried. In this category are such items as rent, electricity, heat, insurance, taxes, spoilage, obsolescence, and the cost of capital. Rent, utilities, and so on, are fixed costs associated with maintaining the storage facilities and are relatively easy to measure from accounting data. Spoilage and obsolescence costs apply to food and drug items, which may have only a limited shelf life, or to novelty and seasonal items such as large toy stocks or Christmas trees. The **cost of capital** invested in inventory normally accounts for the largest component of inventory-holding costs. Cost of capital is the product of the value of a unit of inventory, the length of time held, and an interest rate associated with a dollar tied up in inventory. The interest rate can be highly volatile and depends on the prime interest rate, the risk environment of the firm, and management goals for rates of return on investment.[6] Since many of these factors are difficult to determine, holding charges are often based on managers' judgment, rather than on strict accounting principles.

Back orders incur additional costs for shipping, invoicing, and labor involved in handling the paperwork, receiving the goods, and notifying customers. Lost sales result in lost profit opportunities and in possible future loss of revenues, which are referred to as **goodwill costs.**

From this discussion, you may wonder how inventory models can ever be used effectively, since the important inventory costs are difficult to measure. Fortunately, inventory models are generally quite *robust*. That is, even if the cost figures used are merely good approximations, there is generally little variation in the resulting solution recommended by the model. Consequently, even the simplest models have been used successfully in reducing inventory costs in many companies.

Three primary decisions must be made in relation to inventory: (1) how to monitor inventory, (2) how much should be ordered, and (3) when orders should be placed. Each has an important impact on cost. The greater the control placed on monitoring inventory levels, the higher the cost of clerical work and data processing. On the other hand, better control may result in fewer stockouts and improved customer service. The quantity and frequency of ordering also affect inventory costs. If large lots are ordered, more inventory is carried on the average. This means that fewer orders are placed and ordering costs are low, but that holding costs are high. On the other hand, if frequent small orders are placed, ordering costs are high, but holding costs are low. These costs must be balanced to achieve a minimum-cost inventory policy.

Inventory-Management Systems

Inventory-management systems define the operating practices that allow for the timely ordering and delivery of the correct materials to support production or customer-service objectives. As we have seen, there is a large variety of inventory problems—multiple items, dependent or independent demand, and so on. Therefore, one type of management system may not be applicable for all inventory problems. Effective inventory control may require a combination of several systems. This chapter introduces common approaches for controlling and managing inventory for *independent demand.* The control of *dependent-demand* inventory is primarily a scheduling issue and is discussed in Chapter 17.

ABC Inventory Analysis

One useful method for defining inventory-management needs is *ABC analysis.* It is an application of the Pareto principle and consists of categorizing inventory items into three groups, called the **ABC classification,** according to their total annual dollar usage.

1. *A items* account for a large dollar value but a relatively small percentage of total items.
2. *C items* account for a small dollar value but a large percentage of total items.
3. *B items* are between A and C.

Typically, A items comprise 70 to 80 percent of the total dollar usage but only 15 to 30 percent of the items, whereas C items account for 5 to 15 percent of the total dollar value and about 50 percent of the items. There is no specific rule on where to make the division between A and B items or between B and C items; the percentages used here simply serve as a guideline. An example of using ABC analysis follows.

Example

Finding an ABC Inventory Classification

Consider the data for 20 inventoried items of a small company shown in the spreadsheet in Figure 13.2. The last column gives the projected annual dollar usage of each item, which is found by multiplying the annual projected usage based on forecasts (in units) by the unit cost. We can sort these data easily in Microsoft Excel as shown in Figure 13.3. Here, we have also listed the cumulative percentage of items, cumulative dollar usage, and cumulative percent of total dollar usage. Analysis of Figure 13.3 indicates that about 70 percent of the total dollar usage is accounted for by the first five items, that is, only 25 percent of the items. In addition, the lowest 50 percent of the items account for only about 5 percent of the total dollar usage.

Figure 13.2 Usage-Cost Data for 20 Inventoried Items (ABCINV.XLS, page 1)

	A	B	C	D	E	F	G	H	I
1	ABC Inventory Analysis								
2									
3		Projected		Projected					
4	Item	Annual		Annual					
5	Number	Usage	Unit Cost	Dollar Usage					
6	1	15,000	$5.00	$75,000					
7	2	6,450	$20.00	$129,000					
8	3	5,000	$45.00	$225,000					
9	4	200	$12.50	$2,500					
10	5	20,000	$35.00	$700,000					
11	6	84	$250.00	$21,000					
12	7	800	$80.00	$64,000					
13	8	300	$5.00	$1,500					
14	9	10,000	$35.00	$350,000					
15	10	2,000	$65.00	$130,000					
16	11	5,000	$25.00	$125,000					
17	12	3,250	$125.00	$406,250					
18	13	9,000	$0.50	$4,500					
19	14	2,900	$10.00	$29,000					
20	15	800	$15.00	$12,000					
21	16	675	$200.00	$135,000					
22	17	1,470	$100.00	$147,000					
23	18	8,200	$15.00	$123,000					
24	19	1,250	$0.16	$200					
25	20	2,500	$0.20	$500					

Figure 13.3 ABC Analysis Calculations (ABCINV.XLS, page 2)

	A	B	C	D	E	F	G	H	I
28			Projected		Projected	Cumulative	Cumulative	Cumulative	
29		Number	Usage	Unit Cost	Dollar Usage	Dollar	Percent	Percent	
30	Rank	Item	Annual		Annual	Usage	of Total	of Items	
31	1	5	20,000	$35.00	$700,000	$700,000	26.12%	5%	
32	2	12	3,250	$125.00	$406,250	$1,106,250	41.27%	10%	
33	3	9	10,000	$35.00	$350,000	$1,456,250	54.33%	15%	
34	4	3	5,000	$45.00	$225,000	$1,681,250	62.72%	20%	
35	5	17	1,470	$100.00	$147,000	$1,828,250	68.21%	25%	
36	6	16	675	$200.00	$135,000	$1,963,250	73.24%	30%	
37	7	10	2,000	$65.00	$130,000	$2,093,250	78.09%	35%	
38	8	2	6,450	$20.00	$129,000	$2,222,250	82.91%	40%	
39	9	11	5,000	$25.00	$125,000	$2,347,250	87.57%	45%	
40	10	18	8,200	$15.00	$123,000	$2,470,250	92.16%	50%	
41	11	1	15,000	$5.00	$75,000	$2,545,250	94.96%	55%	
42	12	7	800	$80.00	$64,000	$2,609,250	97.34%	60%	
43	13	14	2,900	$10.00	$29,000	$2,638,250	98.43%	65%	
44	14	6	84	$250.00	$21,000	$2,659,250	99.21%	70%	
45	15	15	800	$15.00	$12,000	$2,671,250	99.66%	75%	
46	16	13	9,000	$0.50	$4,500	$2,675,750	99.82%	80%	
47	17	4	200	$12.50	$2,500	$2,678,250	99.92%	85%	
48	18	8	300	$5.00	$1,500	$2,679,750	99.97%	90%	
49	19	20	2,500	$0.20	$500	$2,680,250	99.99%	95%	
50	20	19	1,250	$0.16	$200	$2,680,450	100.00%	100%	
51									

ABC analysis gives managers useful information. Class A items represent a substantial inventory investment and typically have limited availability. In many cases they are single-sourced and thus need close control to reduce uncertainties in supply. This involves complete, accurate record keeping, continuous monitoring of inventory levels, frequent accuracy counts, and maximum attention to order sizes and frequency of ordering. Because of these items' large cost, small lot sizes and frequent deliveries from suppliers are common and result in very short lead times, which require close cooperation between the buyer and supplier and a high level of quality.

Class C items need not be as closely controlled. Large quantities of these items might be ordered to take advantage of quantity or transportation discounts, and inventory levels might simply be checked periodically without maintaining any formal records. Easy to procure from multiple suppliers, they have short lead times.

Class B items are in the middle. In many cases, these items are ordered very infrequently and consist mainly of service parts for older products still in use. Their availability may be limited, and thus long lead times can be expected. Orders are usually handled individually, which necessitates more control than is needed for C items, but they are not as critical as those for A items.

Control Systems for Independent Demand

There are two basic types of inventory-control systems: continuous-review systems and periodic-review systems.

In a **continuous-review system,** the inventory position is continuously monitored. **Inventory position** is defined as the amount on hand *plus* any amount on order but not yet received *minus* back orders. Whenever the inventory position falls at or below a level *r*, called the **reorder point,** an order for *Q* units is placed (see Figure 13.4). Values for *Q* and *r* are determined in advance. If

Figure 13.4
Operation of a Continuous-Review Inventory System

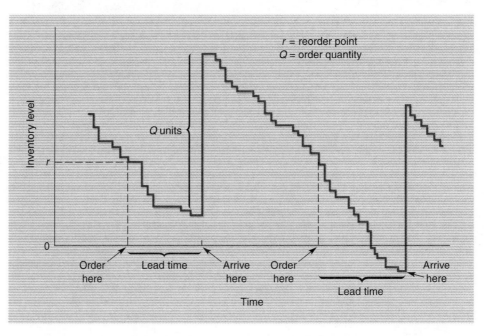

the reorder decision is based solely on the on-hand inventory level, orders would be placed continuously as the stock falls below r. This would clearly be incorrect; that is why inventory position is used to trigger orders.

Most retail department stores have computerized cash registers that are tied into a continuous-review system. When the clerk enters the item code number, the computer automatically reduces the inventory level for that unit by one and checks to see if the reorder point has been reached. If so, it signals that a purchase order should be initiated to replenish the stock. If computers are not used in such systems, some form of manual system is necessary for monitoring daily usage and checking to see if the reorder point has been reached. This requires substantial clerical effort and commitment by the users to fill out the proper forms when items are used, and is often a source of errors.

One version of a continuous-review system that eliminates the need for daily reporting and is often used for small parts is called the *two-bin system*. Consider a supply of small parts kept in a bin with a second (full) bin in reserve. When the first bin is empty, a resupply order is placed and the second bin is used. The second bin contains at least enough material to last during the lead time. This system is easily implemented by placing a card at the bottom of the bin, which is turned in when the last item is taken. A variation of this system is often used in bookstores. The next-to-last copy of a book in stock contains a card with appropriate reorder information; the cashier removes the card when the book is sold.

In **periodic-review systems** the inventory position is checked only at fixed intervals of time. If the inventory position is at or below the reorder point, r, when checked, an order is placed for sufficient stock to bring the inventory position *up to R*, called the *reorder level* (see Figure 13.5). Such systems usually involve stock clerks making the rounds and physically checking the inventory levels. Notice that if the lead time is always shorter than the time between reviews,

Figure 13.5
Operation of a Periodic-Review Inventory System

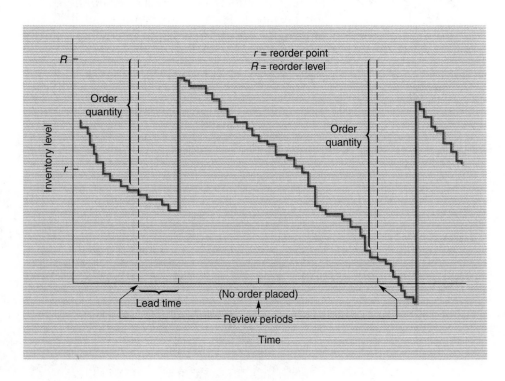

the reorder point can be based on inventory level rather than inventory position, since there will never be an order outstanding. This makes implementation easier. The reorder point for each item can be identified by a tag on the shelf, and the stock clerk needs only to compare it to the number of items remaining.

The choice of which system to use depends on a variety of factors. Continuous-review systems require that accurate records of inventory positions be maintained. With today's computer systems, this is usually easy to do; however, in some situations it is not economical to monitor inventory continuously when manual records must be updated. Continuous-review systems offer tighter control of inventoried items, since orders can be placed to ensure that stockout risks are minimized. Thus, high-value (A) items are usually controlled with continuous-review systems. Periodic-review systems are useful when a large number of items is ordered from the same supplier, since individual orders will be placed at the same time. Thus, shipments can be consolidated, resulting in lower freight rates. This type of system is the one most often used in controlling C items.

Cycle Counting

A sophisticated, computerized inventory system is worthless if it is inaccurate. And inventory systems tend to accumulate errors over time due to errors in counting and recording the amount of goods received, misidentification of the goods, theft, and so on. These errors arise from poor design of forms, untrained personnel, carelessness, theft, or poor document control. Therefore, some method of checking the actual physical inventory is necessary. One approach is to shut down the plant or warehouse periodically and count the inventory. The disadvantages of this method are that productive time is lost, and overtime premiums are usually required to accomplish the task during off hours.

An alternative to closing for inventory is **cycle counting,** a system for continuous physical counting of inventory throughout the year. It allows scheduling of physical counts to ensure that all parts are counted and that higher-value parts (A items) are counted more frequently than lower-value parts (B and C items). With cycle counting, inventory is counted when orders are placed and received, when the inventory record shows a zero or negative (obviously an error) balance, when the last item is removed from stock, or on a fixed-interval periodic basis.

There are several benefits to cycle counting. Errors can be detected on a more timely basis, and causes can be investigated and corrected. Annual physical inventory counts are eliminated, and the loss of productive time is minimized. A high level of inventory accuracy can be achieved on a continuous basis, and the firm can have a correct statement of assets throughout the year. Also, the specialized teams of cycle counters that are usually established for this become efficient in obtaining good counts, reconciling differences, and finding solutions to system errors.

The ABC classification is usually used to determine the frequency of cycle counting. Clearly, errors are more critical for A items, since their values are higher. It is recommended that an accuracy of ± 0.2 percent be maintained for A items, ± 1 percent for B items, and ± 5 percent for C items. FMC Corporation uses cycle counting this way.

Applied P/OM

FMC Corporation

Cycle counting at FMC Corporation is based on ABC analysis.[7]

An ABC analysis at FMC Corporation resulted in the following breakdown.

Class	Number of Items	Percent	Value	Percent
A	2,973	8	$41,704,252	87
B	4,155	12	4,292,290	9
C	28,687	80	1,853,364	4

The A items were subdivided into two classes: regular A items and super A items, those items having unit costs of $1,000 or greater. Management policy stated that super A items be counted every month, regular A items every 2 months, B items every 4 months, and C items once a year. The following schedule was established.

Class	Number of Items	Counts per Year	Work Days between Counts	Days Available	Average Daily Counts
Super A	1,173	12	20	15	*
A	1,800	6	40	30	60
B	4,155	3	80	60	70
C	28,687	1	240	180	160

*See explanation in text.

Super A items are each counted once per month, resulting in (1173)(12) = 14,076 counts per year. Average daily counts for the other classes of items are computed by dividing the number of items by the days available for counting (based on a 20-day work month). This all amounts to a total of 66,276 annual counts, or an average of 5,500 per month. The FMC warehouse in Bowling Green, Kentucky, where this approach is used, has achieved an inventory accuracy of 99 percent due to the cycle counting program.

Measuring Inventory-System Performance

Measurements of inventory performance can be a powerful tool for targeting opportunities for inventory reduction and improved profitability, identifying items that require special emphasis, supporting increased customer service levels, and pinpointing potential obsolescence.[8] Inventory performance should be measured in order to improve replenishment policies, practice, and systems, evaluate the effectiveness of materials-management activities, determine the viability of product lines, support decisions to dispose of surplus items, and assist in financial inventory valuation.

A practical approach for measuring inventory-management performance is to classify inventory into five categories:[9]

1. *Operating inventory*—any inventory less than or equal to the maximum allowable level
2. *Surplus inventory*—any inventory exceeding the operating-inventory maximum, but less than a specified amount that defines "excess" inventory. Most companies have a policy defining excess inventories based on financial policies.
3. *Excess inventory*—inventory beyond surplus as defined by financial policy
4. *Obsolete inventory*—inventory classified as obsolete because of discontinuation, expiration of shelf life, and so forth.
5. *New-product inventory*—a classification suggested because demand for new products is slow in the early stages of the product life cycle.

This classification system can be applied to finished goods, raw materials, work in process, or any other categories that a company may define. The existence of surplus inventory should be viewed as an indication of a control problem requiring attention. A manager might compare the total excess and obsolete inventory to the reserve provided in the balance sheet and bring any discrepancies to financial management. The classification also helps to evaluate whether any overall problems appear to exist in the inventory-management process and provide the basis for corrective action and process modifications.

Modeling Inventory Decisions

This section introduces a "classical" economic model for inventory management that has formed the basis for the study of inventory throughout the twentieth century. Despite its limitations, it provides important insights into the economics of inventory and a foundation for the discussion of current issues.

Economic Order Quantity (EOQ) Model

The best-known and most fundamental inventory model is the **economic order quantity (EOQ)** model, which was developed in the early 1900s. Several important assumptions are made in using the EOQ model:

••• Only a single item under continuous review is considered,
••• The entire quantity ordered arrives in the inventory at one time,
••• The demand for the item has a constant, or nearly constant, rate.

The condition of **constant-demand rate** simply means that the same number of units are taken from inventory each period of time—such as five units every day, 25 units every week, 100 units every four-week period, and so on. We also assume that the lead time is constant and that no stockouts are allowed. Further, the EOQ model is concerned with two basic decisions: how much to order, and when to place an order.

Figure 13.6
Sketch of the Inventory
Level

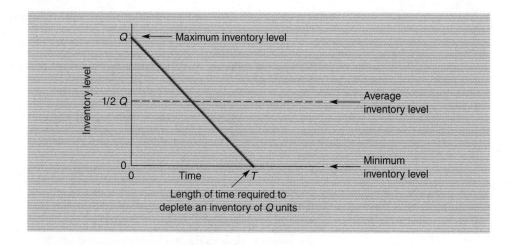

The How-Much-To-Order Decision. The how-much-to-order decision involves selecting an order quantity that is a compromise between (1) keeping small inventories and ordering frequently and (2) keeping large inventories and ordering infrequently. The first alternative would probably result in undesirably high ordering costs, while the second alternative would probably result in undesirably high inventory-holding costs. The EOQ model minimizes the total cost equal to the sum of the inventory-holding cost and the ordering cost.*

We begin by defining Q to be the size of the order. The inventory level has a maximum value of Q units when the order of size Q is received from the manufacturer. The inventory is depleted, at which time another shipment of Q units will be received. With the assumption of a constant demand rate, a sketch of the inventory level from the time that Q units are received until the inventory is depleted is shown in Figure 13.6. Note that the sketch indicates that the average inventory level for the period in question is $1/2Q$. This should appear reasonable, since the maximum inventory level is Q, the minimum is 0, and the inventory level declines at a constant rate over the period.

Figure 13.6 shows the inventory pattern during one order-cycle period, T. As time goes on, this pattern will repeat. The complete inventory pattern is shown in Figure 13.7. If the average inventory during each cycle is $1/2Q$, the average inventory level over any number of cycles is also $1/2Q$. So as long as the time period involved contains an integral number of order cycles, the average inventory for the period will be $1/2Q$.

The inventory-holding cost can be calculated by multiplying the average inventory by the cost of carrying one unit in inventory for the stated period. The period of time selected for the model is up to the user; it can be one week, one month, one year, or more. However, since the inventory-carrying costs for many industries and businesses are expressed as an annual percentage or rate, most inventory models are developed on an annual cost basis. Let

---

*While management scientists typically refer to "total cost" models for inventory systems, many of these models describe only the total *variable,* or *relevant,* costs for the decision being considered. Costs not affected by the how-much-to-order decision are considered to be fixed, or constant, and are not included in the model.

Figure 13.7
Inventory Pattern for the
EOQ Inventory-Decision
Model

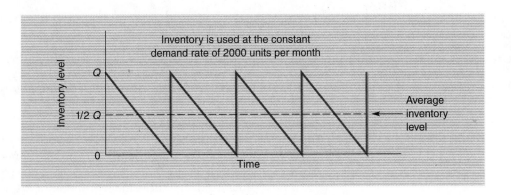

I = annual inventory-carrying charge.

C = unit cost of the inventory item.

The cost of storing one unit in inventory for the year, denoted by C_h, is given by $C_h = IC$. Thus, the general equation for annual inventory-holding cost is

$$\begin{matrix}\text{annual inventory-} \\ \text{holding cost}\end{matrix} = \begin{pmatrix}\text{average} \\ \text{inventory}\end{pmatrix}\begin{pmatrix}\text{annual holding} \\ \text{cost} \\ \text{per unit}\end{pmatrix} = \frac{1}{2}QC_h \quad \textbf{(13.1)}$$

To complete the total-cost model, we must now include the ordering cost. The goal is to express this cost in terms of the order quantity, Q. Since the inventory-holding cost is expressed on an annual basis, we need to express ordering costs as an annual cost. Letting D denote the annual demand for the product, we know that by ordering Q units each time we order, we have to place D/Q orders per year. If C_o is the cost of placing one order, the general expression for the annual ordering cost is

$$\begin{matrix}\text{annual ordering} \\ \text{cost}\end{matrix} = \begin{pmatrix}\text{number of} \\ \text{orders} \\ \text{per year}\end{pmatrix}\begin{pmatrix}\text{cost} \\ \text{per} \\ \text{order}\end{pmatrix} = \left(\frac{D}{Q}\right)C_o. \quad \textbf{(13.2)}$$

Thus the total annual cost—inventory-holding cost given by equation 13.1 plus ordering cost given by equation 13.2—can be expressed as

$$TC = \frac{1}{2}QC_h + \frac{D}{Q}C_o. \quad \textbf{(13.3)}$$

The development of this total-cost model has gone a long way toward helping solve the inventory problem. We now are able to express the total annual cost as a function of one of the decisions, *how much* should be ordered. Equation 13.3 is the general total-cost equation for inventory situations in which the assumptions of the EOQ model are valid.

The next step is to find the order quantity, Q, that does, in fact, minimize the total cost as stated in equation 13.3. By using differential calculus, we can show that the quantity that minimizes the total cost, denoted by Q^*, is given by the formula

$$Q^* = \sqrt{\frac{2DC_o}{C_h}}. \qquad (13.4)$$

This formula is referred to as the *economic order quantity (EOQ) formula.*

The When-To-Order Decision.   Now that we know how much to order, we want to answer the second question of when to order, expressed most often in terms of the reorder point. For inventory systems using the constant-demand rate assumption and a fixed lead time, the reorder point is the same as the *lead-time demand*—that is, the demand that occurs between the time the order is placed and when it is received. The general expression for the reorder point is

$$r = dm$$

where r = reorder point,   (13.5)
d = demand per day, and
m = lead time for a new order in days.

The question of how frequently the order should be placed can now be answered. This period between orders is referred to as the *cycle time.* Previously (see equation 13.2), we defined D/Q as the number of orders placed in a year. The general expression for a cycle time of T days is given by

$$T = \frac{N}{D/Q^*} = \frac{NQ^*}{D} \qquad (13.6)$$

where N = number of days of operation for the year.
An example of how to determine EOQ follows.

Example : ## Determining the Economic Order Quantity (EOQ)

To illustrate the use of the EOQ model, let us consider the situation faced by the Holton Drug Company, which operates a chain of 142 drugstores in Minnesota and northern Wisconsin. From a main warehouse in St. Paul, Holton supplies the individual drugstores with nearly 1,000 products. The company's historical inventory policy has involved monthly orders placed directly with the manufacturers of the various products and held at its main warehouse. As its product line has grown, Holton's top managers have expressed concern about the sizable inventory levels and the associated high inventory costs.

As a result, Holton's inventory manager has been asked to make a detailed cost analysis of the items carried in inventory to see if a better inventory policy can be established. The inventory manager has selected one of Holton's top-selling products, All-Bright toothpaste, for an initial study.

The demand for All-Bright toothpaste over the past six months has been as follows:

Month	Demand (cases)
1	2,025
2	1,950
3	2,100
4	2,050
5	1,975
6	1,900
Total cases	12,000
Average cases per month	2,000

Strictly speaking, these monthly demand figures do not show a constant demand rate. However, given the relatively low variability exhibited by the monthly demands, inventory planning with a constant rate of 2,000 cases per month appears to be acceptable. Currently, Holton's cost for All-Bright toothpaste is $12.00 per case.

Holton estimates its cost of capital at a rate of 12 percent. Insurance, taxes, breakage, pilferage, and warehouse overhead are estimated to be approximately 6 percent of the value of the inventory. Thus the annual inventory-holding costs are estimated to be 18 percent of the value of the inventory. Since the cost of one case of All-Bright toothpaste is $12.00, the cost of holding, or carrying, one case of All-Bright in inventory for one year is .18($12.00) = $2.16.

The next step in the inventory analysis is to determine the cost of placing an order for All-Bright toothpaste. The cost includes the salaries of the purchasing agents and clerical support staff, transportation costs, and miscellaneous costs such as paper, postage, and telephone costs, which are estimated to be $38.00 regardless of the quantity requested in the order.

From this information, we have

$$D = 24{,}000 \text{ cases per year.}$$

$$C_o = \$38 \text{ per order.}$$

$$I = 18 \text{ percent.}$$

$$C = \$12.00 \text{ per case.}$$

$$C_h = IC = \$2.16.$$

Using the All-Bright toothpaste data, the total-cost model becomes

$$TC = \frac{1}{2}Q(\$2.16) + \frac{24{,}000}{Q}(\$38.00)$$

$$= 1.08Q + \frac{912{,}000}{Q}.$$

(13.7)

Thus, the minimum-cost order quantity as given by equation 13.4 is

$$Q^* = \sqrt{\frac{2(24{,}000)(38)}{2.16}} = 919 \text{ cases (rounded to a whole number).}$$

Using this order quantity in equation 13.7 shows that the inventory for All-Bright toothpaste can be handled with a total annual cost of

$$TC = 1.08(919) + 912,000/919 = \$1,984.90.$$

We can compare this value with the current purchasing policy for All-Bright, which called for monthly orders of the amount $Q = 2,000$. The total annual cost is

$$TC = 1.08(2,000) + \frac{912,000}{2,000} = \$2,616.00.$$

Thus, the EOQ analysis has resulted in a $\$2,616.00 - \$1,984.90 = \$631.10$, or 24.1 percent, cost reduction. Notice also that the total ordering costs ($992.52) are equal to the total holding costs ($992.38), with the small difference due to rounding. In general, this will always be true for the EOQ model.

The manufacturer of All-Bright toothpaste guarantees a three-day delivery on any order placed by Holton. Considering weekends and holidays, Holton operates 250 days per year. So, on a daily basis, the annual demand of 24,000 cases corresponds to a demand of $24,000/250 = 96$ cases. Thus we anticipate

$$(3 \text{ days})(96 \text{ cases per day}) = 288$$

cases of All-Bright to be sold during the three days it takes a new order to reach the Holton warehouse. Since the three-day delivery period is the lead time for a new order, the 288 cases of demand during this period is the lead-time demand. Therefore, Holton should order a new shipment of All-Bright toothpaste from the manufacturer when the inventory position reaches a reorder level of 288 cases.

Finally, we note that Holton will place $24,000/919 = 26.12$, or approximately 26 orders per year for All-Bright toothpaste. With 250 working, or operating, days per year, Holton should be placing an order every $250/26 = 9.6$ days. Thus, the cycle time is computed as 9.6 days.

Sensitivity Analysis for EOQ Model. Even though substantial time has been spent in arriving at the inventory-carrying charge (18 percent) and ordering cost ($38.00), we should realize that those figures are, at best, good estimates. Therefore, we may want to consider how much the order-size recommendation would differ if the estimated ordering and holding costs had been different. To determine this, we can calculate the recommended order quantity under several different cost conditions, as shown in the spreadsheet in Figure 13.8. The spreadsheet also provides a variety of information from the EOQ model. As you can see from the sensitivity table, the value of Q^* appears relatively stable, even with some variations in the cost estimates. Based on these results, it appears that the best order quantity for All-Bright toothpaste is somewhere around 850 to 1,000 cases and definitely not near the current order quantity of 2,000 cases. In addition, the projected total costs using Q^* and $Q = 919$, as shown in Figure 13.8, indicate that there is very little risk associated with implementing the calculated order quantity of 919 cases. For the worst situations shown in Figure 13.8, the total cost using the 919-case order quantity is only $7 more expensive than the minimum total cost in the *"Using Optimal EOQ*"* column.

Figure 13.8
Spreadsheet for EOQ Model
and Sensitivity Analysis
(EOQMODEL.XLS)

	A	B	C	D	E	
1	Economic Order Quantity Model					
2						
3	Model Inputs			Model Outputs		
4						
5	Annual Demand, D	24,000		Optimal Order Quantity	918.94	
6	Ordering Cost, Co	$38.00		Annual Holding Cost	$ 992.45	
7	Unit Cost, C	$12.00		Annual Ordering Cost	$ 992.45	
8	Carrying Charge, I	18%		Total Annual Cost	$ 1,984.90	
9	Lead Time (Days)	3		Maximum Inventory Level	918.94	
10	Operating Days/Year	250		Average Inventory Level	459.47	
11				Reorder Point	288	
12				Number of Orders/Year	26.12	
13				Cycle Time (Days)	9.57	
14						
15	Sensitivity Analysis of Assumptions					
16						
17			Optimal Order	Projected Total Cost		
18	Carrying Charge	Order Cost	Quantity	Using Optimal EOQ	Using Q = 919	
19	16%	$ 36	948.68	$ 1,821.47	$ 1,822.39	
20	16%	$ 40	1000.00	$ 1,920.00	$ 1,926.85	
21	20%	$ 36	848.53	$ 2,036.47	$ 2,042.95	
22	20%	$ 40	894.43	$ 2,146.63	$ 2,147.41	
23						

From this analysis we can say that this EOQ model is insensitive to small variation or errors in the cost estimates. This is a property of EOQ models in general, which indicates that if we have at least reasonable estimates of ordering and inventory-holding costs, we should obtain a good approximation of the true minimum-cost order quantity.

This is evident in Figure 13.9, a graph of the holding, ordering, and total cost for various order quantities. You can see that the total-cost curve is relatively flat close to the optimal value, Q^*. So we can conclude that small variations in the actual order quantity used will have little effect on the total cost.

Using the EOQ Model. The inventory model and analysis has led to a recommended order quantity of 919 units. Of course, the decision maker should feel free to modify the final order-quantity recommendation to meet the unique circumstances of a given inventory situation.

In the case of All-Bright toothpaste, the order quantity of 919 resulted in a cycle time of 9.6 days. The inventory manager felt that there would be some benefits of establishing a 10-day, or two-week, cycle time for the item. In particular, the manager was interested in keeping open the possibility that other items could be placed on the two-week order cycle so that multiple products ordered from the same manufacturer could be handled in one shipment. This way, in addition to inventory-cost savings, there is the possibility of transportation cost savings. The adjustment to the 10-day, or two-week, cycle time increased the recommended order quantity to

$$(10 \text{ days})(96 \text{ cases per day}) = 960 \text{ cases.}$$

Using equation 13.7 and $Q = 960$ units results in a total cost of $1,987. Thus, the recommended policy has a $2,616 - $1,987 = $629, or 24 percent, savings over the current inventory policy. If similar savings can be made on a large number

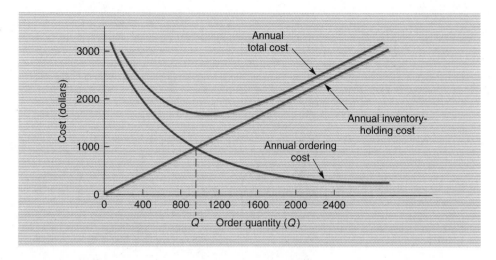

Figure 13.9
Graph of Annual Inventory-Holding, Ordering, and Total Cost for All-Bright Toothpaste

of items Holton carries in inventory, the use of the inventory decision model can provide significant benefits to the company.

The new policy will also lead to a reduction in warehouse space requirements. Under the current ordering policy, with an order quantity of 2,000 cases, the average inventory level should be $Q/2 = 1,000$ cases. Under the new policy, the 960-case order quantity results in an average inventory level of $960/2 = 480$ cases. Therefore, we anticipate a decrease of $1,000 - 480 = 520$ cases, or a 52 percent decrease in warehouse space needs.

Service Levels and Uncertainty in Demand

One of the critical assumptions of the EOQ model is that demand is constant. In many cases, though, demand is *relatively* constant but still fluctuates around an average value. This fluctuation can often be described by a *probability distribution*. The decision models used to analyze these inventory systems are referred to as *stochastic-demand models*. Since the level of mathematical sophistication required for an exact formulation of order quantity-reorder point inventory models with stochastic demand is beyond the scope of this book, we restrict our discussion of these inventory-decision problems to a heuristic procedure that should provide good, workable solutions without relying on advanced mathematical techniques. Although this solution procedure can be expected to provide only approximations to the optimal inventory decisions, it has been found to yield very good decisions in many practical situations.

Let us consider the case of Southern Office Supplies, Inc., in Atlanta, Georgia. Southern distributes a wide variety of office supplies and equipment to customers in Atlanta and northern Georgia. Suppose we consider the inventory problem associated with a laser printer paper product. The paper is purchased in reams from a firm in Portland, Oregon. Southern wants to recommendation on how much it should order and when it should place orders so that a low-cost inventory operation can be realized. Ordering costs are $45.00 per order, one ream of paper costs $3.80, and Southern uses a 20 percent annual inventory-carrying cost rate for its inventory. The inventory-holding cost is $C_h = .20(\$3.80) = \$.76$. With its numerous customers, Southern experiences an uncertain, or stochastic, demand in that the number of orders varies considerably from day to day and from week to week. Demand is not specifically known, but historical sales data indicate that an annual demand of 15,000 reams, while not exact, is a good estimate of the anticipated annual volume.

As an approximation of the best order quantity, we can apply the EOQ model with the expected annual volume substituted for the annual demand, D. In Southern's case, we have

$$Q^* = \sqrt{\frac{2DC_o}{C_h}} = \sqrt{\frac{2(15,000)(45)}{0.76}} = 1,333 \text{ reams.}$$

When we studied the sensitivity of the EOQ models, we learned that the total cost of operating an inventory system is relatively insensitive to order quantities that are in the neighborhood of Q^*. Using this knowledge, we expect 1,333 reams per order to be a good approximation of the optimal order quantity. Even if annual demand were as low as 13,000 or as high as perhaps 17,000 units, 1,333 reams should be a relatively good, low-cost order size. Thus, given our best estimate of annual demand at 15,000 reams, we use $Q^* = 1,333$. Using that order quantity, Southern can anticipate placing $D/Q^* = 15,000/1,333$, or approximately 11 orders per year, slightly more than a month apart.

We now want to establish the reorder point that will trigger the ordering process. Further pertinent data indicate that it usually takes two weeks for Southern to receive a new supply of paper from the manufacturer. With a two-week demand of (15,000 reams/52 weeks) $\times$ 2 = 577 reams, we might first suggest a 577-unit reorder point. However, it now becomes extremely important to consider the probabilities of the various demands. If 577 reams is the *average* two-week demand, and if the demands are symmetrically distributed about 577, then demand will be greater than 577 reams roughly 50 percent of the time. This means Southern would show a stockout before an incoming shipment arrived about 50 percent of the time. This shortage rate would probably be viewed as unacceptably high. To reduce the chances of a stockout, *safety stock* can be carried. The amount of safety stock is related to the reorder point, which in turn determines the probability of a stockout. Let us see how these factors are related and how an appropriate level of safety stock can be determined.

To determine a reorder point for which there is a low likelihood of a stockout, it is necessary to establish a probability distribution for the lead-time demand, called the **lead-time-demand distribution,** and analyze stockout probabilities. Usually, the lead-time-demand distribution is assumed to be normal, although any demand probability distribution is acceptable. By collecting historical data on actual demands during the lead-time period, an analyst should be able to determine if the normal distribution or some other probability distribution is the most realistic picture of the lead-time-demand distribution.

Given the lead-time-demand probability distribution, we can now determine how the reorder point, r, affects the probability of running out of the item. Since stockouts occur whenever the lead-time demand exceeds the reorder point, we can find the probability of stockout by using the lead-time-demand distribution to compute the probability of demand exceeding r.

We can now approach the when-to-order problem by defining a cost per stockout and then attempting to include that cost in a total-cost equation. A more practical approach may be to ask managers to establish an acceptable **service level,** an expression of the desired probability that the company will not have a stockout during a lead-time period. For example, a .95 service level exists when there is a 95 percent chance the inventory will be able to satisfy all demand occurring before the next shipment arrives. In other words, there is a .05 probability the firm will have a stockout during the lead-time period.

If demand for a product is stochastic, a manager who says he or she will never tolerate a stockout is being somewhat unrealistic, because attempting to avoid stockouts completely requires high reorder points, high inventory levels, and the associated high inventory-holding cost.

When a normal probability distribution provides a good approximation of lead-time demand, the general expression for reorder point is

$$r = \mu + z\sigma \qquad\qquad (13.8)$$

where z = the number of standard deviations necessary to achieve the acceptable service level,
   μ = expected lead-time demand, and
   σ = standard deviation of lead-time demand.

Let us return to the Southern Office Supplies situation for a specific example.

Example

Determining Safety-Stock Levels

Using historical data and some judgment, we can assume that the lead-time-demand distribution for Southern's paper product is a normal distribution with a mean of 577 reams and a standard deviation of 100 reams. This distribution is shown in Figure 13.10.

Suppose Southern's managers desire a service level of .95; that is, a 5 percent probability of a stockout during a given lead time period is tolerable. With 11 orders anticipated per year, the 5 percent level of stockouts means Southern should have a stockout for this product roughly once every two years. Let us consider how we could find the reorder point, r, that provides this level of service. This situation is shown graphically in Figure 13.11.

Figure 13.10 Distribution of Demand during Lead Time for Southern Office Supplies, Inc.

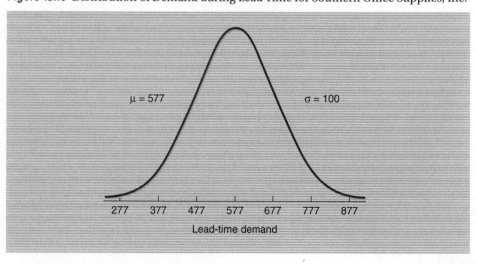

μ = 577   σ = 100

277   377   477   577   677   777   877

Lead-time demand

From the normal distribution tables in Appendix B, we see that an r-value that is 1.645 standard deviations above the mean will allow stockouts 5 percent of the time. Therefore, for the assumed normal distribution for lead-time demand with $\mu = 577$ and $\sigma = 100$, the reorder point, r, is determined by

$$r = 577 + 1.645(100) \approx 577 + 165 = 742 \text{ reams.}$$

In these computations, we see that the reorder point is based on the expected lead-time demand, plus a safety stock of 165 reams.

Thus, the inventory decision is to order 1,333 reams whenever the inventory position reaches the reorder point of 742. This policy should work to minimize inventory costs and simultaneously to satisfy demand with a 5 percent probability of stockout during a lead-time period. The anticipated annual cost for this system is as follows:

Ordering cost	$\left(\dfrac{D}{Q}\right)C_o = \left(\dfrac{15{,}000}{1{,}333}\right)45 =$	\$506
Holding cost, normal inventory	$\left(\dfrac{Q}{2}\right)C_h = \left(\dfrac{1{,}333}{2}\right)(.76) =$	\$507
Holding cost, safety stock	$(165)C_h = (165)(.76) \quad\quad =$	\$125
Total cost		\$1,138

If Southern can assume that a known, constant demand rate of 15,000 reams per year exists for the paper product, then $Q^* = 1{,}333$, $r = 577$, and a total annual cost of $\$506 + \$507 = \$1{,}013$ can be expected. When demand is uncertain and can be expressed only in probabilistic terms, a larger total cost can be expected. The larger cost occurs in the form of larger inventory-holding costs due to the fact that more inventory must be maintained to prevent frequent stockouts. For Southern this additional inventory, or safety stock, is 165 units, with an additional cost of \$125 per year.

Figure 13.11 Reorder Point That Allows 5 Percent Chance of Stockout for Southern Office Supplies, Inc.

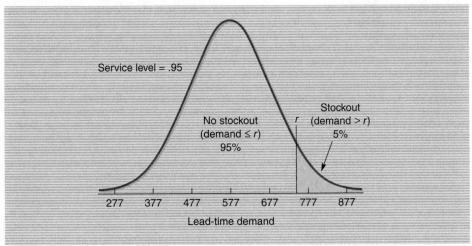

Figure 13.12
Spreadsheet for Safety
Stock Analysis
(SOUTHERN.XLS)

	A	B	C	D	E	F
1	Southern Office Supplies					
2						
3	Model Inputs			Model Outputs		
4						
5	Annual Demand	15,000		Optimal Order Quantity	1332.78	
6	Ordering Cost	$ 45.00		Annual Holding Cost	$ 506.46	
7	Unit Cost	$ 3.80		Annual Ordering Cost	$ 506.46	
8	Carrying Charge	20%		Total Annual Cost	$1,012.92	
9						
10	Lead Time Demand					
11	Mean	577				
12	Standard dev.	100				
13						
14						
15	Safety Stock Analysis					
16						
17	Service	Probability	Normal probability	Reorder	Safety	Additional
18	Level	of Stockout	z-value	Point	Stock	Cost
19	0.99	0.01	2.326	810	233	$ 176.80
20	0.95	0.05	1.645	741	164	$ 125.01
21	0.90	0.10	1.282	705	128	$ 97.40
22	0.85	0.15	1.036	681	104	$ 78.77
23	0.80	0.20	0.842	661	84	$ 63.96
24						

Figure 13.12 is a spreadsheet for computing the costs associated with normal inventory levels using the EOQ model as well as additional costs incurred for various safety stock levels. (The z-values are found by using the Microsoft Excel function NORMINV). We see that decreasing the service level permits a lower safety stock, although it increases the probability of a stockout. Thus, the manager must make a trade-off between inventory costs and customer service.

P/OM in Practice

Application of ABC Inventory Analysis in Hospital Inventory Management[10]

In recent years, cost-containment activities have become particularly important to hospital operations managers, stimulated by major revisions in health-care reimbursement policies and significant growth in marketing activities by private-sector health care organizations. Recognizing that poor inventory control policies reflect ineffective use of organizational assets, many hospital managers have sought to institute more systematic approaches to the control of supply inventories.

The ABC classification method was applied to a group of 47 disposable *stock-keeping units (SKUs)*, a common term used for inventoried items, in a hospital-based respiratory therapy unit.

Table 13.3 displays the data elements and resulting computed values for the problem, created on a personal computer with a spreadsheet program. The classification listing of SKUs was rank-ordered by annual dollar usage.

A natural break in the sequential decrease of SKU annual dollar usage is apparent between the tenth SKU (pleural drainage bottles—$2407.50) and the eleventh SKU (croupette canopy—$1075.20). This discontinuity provides a logical basis for distin-

guishing class A items from those in class B. Thus, the first 10 SKUs in Table 1 were designated as class A items. They represent 21.3 percent of all SKUs and account for $38,013.70 of annual usage, or 73.5 percent of the total usage value for all supply items.

The next 13 SKUs, numbers 11 through 23, were assigned to the second category: class B. A visual inspection of the tabular listing shows slight discontinuities in the annual dollar usage values between items 19 and 20 and again between items 28 and 29. However, informed judgment reflecting the importance of various SKUs in achieving departmental goals was used to identify SKUs 20 through 23 as members of the class B grouping,

Table 13.3 ABC Classification of Disposable SKUs for Respiratory Therapy Department

Sequential SKU Number	Cumulative % of All SKUs	Total Annual Usage	Average Unit Cost	Annual Dollar Usage	Cumulative Annual Dollar Usage	Cumulative Annual Percent Usage	ABC Inventory Class
1	2.1	117	$ 49.92	$5,840.64	$ 5,840.64	11.3	A
2	4.3	27	210.00	5,670.00	11,510.64	22.3	A
3	6.4	212	23.76	5,037.12	16,547.76	32.0	A
4	8.5	172	27.73	4,769.56	21,317.32	41.2	A
5	10.6	60	57.98	3,478.80	24,796.12	48.0	A
6	12.8	94	31.24	2,936.56	27,732.68	53.7	A
7	14.9	100	28.20	2,820.00	30,552.68	59.1	A
8	17.0	48	55.00	2,640.00	33,192.68	64.2	A
9	19.1	33	73.44	2,423.52	35,616.20	68.9	A
10	21.3	15	160.50	2,407.50	38,023.70	73.6	A
11	23.4	210	5.12	1,075.20	39,098.90	75.6	B
12	25.5	50	20.87	1,043.50	40,142.40	77.7	B
13	27.7	12	86.50	1,038.00	41,180.40	79.7	B
14	29.8	8	110.40	883.20	42,063.60	81.4	B
15	31.9	12	71.20	854.40	42,918.00	83.0	B
16	34.0	18	45.00	810.00	43,728.00	84.6	B
17	36.2	48	14.66	703.68	44,431.68	86.0	B
18	38.3	12	49.50	594.00	45,025.68	87.1	B
19	40.4	12	47.50	570.00	45,595.68	88.2	B
20	42.6	8	58.45	467.60	46,063.28	89.1	B
21	44.7	19	24.40	463.60	46,526.88	90.0	B
22	46.8	7	65.00	455.00	46,981.88	90.9	B
23	48.9	5	86.50	432.50	47,414.38	91.7	B
24	51.1	12	33.20	398.40	47,812.78	92.5	C
25	53.2	10	37.05	370.50	48,183.28	93.2	C
26	55.3	10	33.84	338.40	48,521.68	93.9	C
27	57.4	4	84.03	336.12	48,857.80	94.5	C
28	59.6	4	78.40	313.60	49,171.40	95.1	C
29	61.7	2	134.34	268.68	49,440.08	95.6	C
30	63.8	4	56.00	224.00	49,664.08	96.1	C
31	66.0	3	72.00	216.00	49,880.08	96.5	C
32	68.1	4	53.02	212.08	50,092.16	96.9	C
33	70.2	4	49.48	197.92	50,290.08	97.3	C
34	72.3	27	7.07	190.89	50,480.97	97.7	C
35	74.5	3	60.60	181.80	50,662.77	98.0	C
36	76.6	4	40.82	163.28	50,826.05	98.3	C
37	78.7	5	30.00	150.00	50,976.05	98.6	C
38	80.9	2	67.40	134.80	51,110.85	98.9	C
39	83.0	2	59.60	119.20	51,230.05	99.1	C
40	85.1	2	51.68	103.36	51,333.41	99.3	C
41	87.2	4	19.80	79.20	51,412.61	99.5	C
42	89.4	2	37.70	75.40	51,488.01	99.6	C
43	91.5	2	29.89	59.78	51,547.79	99.7	C
44	93.6	1	48.30	48.30	51,596.09	99.8	C
45	95.7	1	34.40	34.40	51,630.49	99.9	C
46	97.9	1	28.80	28.80	51,659.29	99.9	C
47	100.00	3	8.46	25.38	51,684.67	100.0	C

with SKUs 24 through 28 then being labeled, along with the last 20 SKUs, as class C items. Although class C contains over one-half of all inventory items, their total annual usage value amounts to only 8.3 percent of the total expenditures for all disposable supplies during the year. These results are summarized for each of the designated inventory classes in Table 13.4.

With the ABC classification, three distinct control policies were designed to manage the items.

Policy for Class A Items

In practice, usage for the 10 class A items was monitored closely, and forecasts were updated monthly. Stock replenishment occurred weekly, or more frequently if the reorder point was encountered. Minimum stock levels were established relative to the (1) expected product lead times, (2) availability of substitute SKUs, and (3) SKU criticality. Twice per year these reorder points were reviewed as necessary and revised. A physical inventory was performed weekly to verify recorded stock levels for these SKUs. If several suppliers were available or alternative acceptable products were being distributed, a competitive bidding process was employed.

Policy for Class B Items

The 13 class B inventory items in the respiratory therapy unit were replenished on a biweekly basis. Some emphasis was placed on negotiating price discounts through blanket-order commitments with major suppliers. A reevaluation of safety-stock levels for the class B items produced some reductions when explicit computations of the trade-offs between stockout risk and additional carrying cost were assessed.

Policy for Class C Items

The ordering of the 24 SKUs in class C was automated. These SKUs were counted and replenished to a preestablished maximum value every two to three months, as time permitted. The two-bin concept was often used to trigger the purchase of an economic order quantity between replenishment points. Limited storage capacity ruled out ordering large quantities of C-class items. Coordination of purchases for these SKUs occurred when class A and B items were being ordered from two major suppliers.

As competition among nonprofit service organizations (such as hospitals) increases, operations managers will need to utilize more cost-minimizing approaches (similar to the ABC method) to aid in policy formulation. Significant cost savings can accrue if managers will allocate appropriate resources to control the important inventory items. Real benefits are available for a reasonable investment of managerial time and energy, especially in designing control procedures for class A and B items.

Questions for Discussion

1. Describe the differences in the inventory policies for the three classes of inventory items.
2. Discuss the value and advantages of using an ABC system to improve materials and inventory management.

Inventory-Control System for Quick-Copy Center[11]

At the Colorado School of Mines, demand patterns in the copy-center environment had been highly seasonal, following a similar pattern during each school year, and had exhibited an increasing trend from year to year. Requests for low-demand items (odd colors of paper, for example) were very erratic, while use of high-demand items (such as $8 \frac{1}{2} \times 11$ white three-hole paper) was predictably seasonal. Unacceptably high stock levels of low-demand items were being maintained, and emergency orders on high-demand items were frequent. Data records were sparse and had been kept with little consistency, often consisting of monthly orders with no record of beginning or ending inventories or increased inventory with no ordering. Several of the 75 stockkeeping units (SKUs) were obtained via discount cost schedules, and one source had a $150 minimum-order requirement. Lead times generally had minor variances, with means of one to 10 working days. Storage space was insufficient to accommodate a one-week supply during peak demand and was partitioned into product families. Stockout penalties were very high, and orders were placed by managers at the verbal request of the workers.

Table 13.4 Summary Parameter Values for ABC Classification

ABC Inventory Class	Number of SKU Members	% of Total SKUs	Annual Dollar Usage	% of Annual Dollar Usage
A	10	21.3%	$38,023.70	73.6%
B	13	27.6	9,390.68	18.1
C	24	51.1	4,270.29	8.3
Totals	47	100.0%	$51,684.67	100.0%

The workers were well-seasoned, experienced, and highly proficient in the intuitive management of the copy center. Daily work schedules were highly erratic; hence, time available to maintain an inventory-control system would be very irregular. Polite political tensions existed between managers and workers, resulting from a history of poor communication, lack of resources available to assist in controlling the inventory, lack of accountability for inventory decisions, and a previous failure to implement a manual inventory-control system. The workers were resistant to management control, and managers were not satisfied with the way inventory was being managed. It was evident that an inventory system was needed to achieve a balance between the workers' need for flexibility to adapt to uncertain and highly varying demand and managers' desire that the inventory be managed efficiently.

The problem solution therefore required that the workers operate an inventory-control system yet be unable to manipulate the system into practical ineffectiveness. The operators would have to be given sufficient historical demand data to allow for intelligent deviation from a suggested ordering pattern, and the freedom to fine-tune the ordering patterns when those patterns began to violate the constraints of limited inventory space and high stockout penalties. System integrity would have to be beyond compromise, and any deviations from a suggested order pattern would be flagged to prevent accidental, duplicate, or oversized orders.

A system consisting of a set of computer programs linked by batch files and a spreadsheet was developed. The spreadsheet was designed to handle systematic inventory maintenance. It calculated inventory adjustments and brought new orders to the attention of the operator with immediate

and visible results as the inventory was being updated and orders were being generated. It contained appropriate demand patterns from previous periods and made forecasts immediately available to the operator during inventory maintenance. This allowed the operator to program intuition into the order pattern intelligently as it was generated, giving him or her a sense of ownership and control over the system while retaining the system's integrity. To accomplish this, inventory parameters were partitioned appropriately between managers and workers. The workers were given direct control over parameters that directly affected the inventory, while managers were given direct control over all remaining parameters and the ability to closely monitor any variations in the inventory parameters controlled by the workers. Managers were able to survey, but not modify, all inventory parameters through the user interface and require that they be modified by the workers if appropriate. This improved communication between managers and workers and produced an accountability for parameter settings. It also ensured that the workers were given enough control over the system so that they would actually use it.

The workers were given direct control over the product names, stock numbers, SKUs, weeks of safety stock, and maximum and minimum inventory levels. Safety-stock and maximum-inventory levels were therefore tightly controlled by the operators to prevent shortages and overstocking, which allowed the limited storage space to be used efficiently. Control of product stock numbers enabled workers to group products into families in the user interface and to place high-demand groups near the top of the list for easy access. Historical and forecasted demand patterns were also made conveniently available to the workers so that deviations from the

suggested ordering pattern could be made intelligently.

Managers could view all of these inventory-parameter values and had direct control over the ordering process itself and all global parameters (i.e., current interest rate and ordering cost, sensitivity coefficients for forecasting and lead time, etc.), indirectly controlling the inventory levels through the workers.

Seasonal-demand patterns suggested the use of time units for safety stock instead of the typical product units. The basic idea was to establish a time period over which the safety stock would be able to supply demand in the event that lead time was longer than expected or when demand was unusually heavy. The number of item units in the safety stock was derived from the demand forecast for the time duration chosen. This allowed the safety stock to grow in periods of high demand and shrink during periods of low demand. The frequent occurrence of zero-demand periods for low-demand products generated the potential for zero safety stock and "planned" stockouts, but this was easily overcome by the use of a minimum stock level in conjunction with the time units. That approach allowed for a lower holding cost and a higher service level in environments where demand was seasonal, and it also was useful under conditions where warehouse capacity was constraining for products whose peak demand seasons were offset from one another.

The system was designed to maintain a one-year history of demand patterns and react to environmental changes by updating seasonality and trend coefficients, corresponding to a 52-week season, to generate an appropriate weekly forecast for each SKU. New weekly forecasts of product demand are then used to find a current order point for each product from the forecasted demand for the required weeks of safety stock and lead time.

Lot sizes are determined from the forecast by one of several heuristics chosen by managers, and are bounded by minimum and maximum stock levels to accommodate limited inventory storage space. All of the lot-sizing techniques included have been designed to incorporate discount cost schedules when determining ordering patterns.

Both managers and workers were involved in the gathering and refining of data for system initialization. Managers compiled sparse and scattered data records into convenient forms and made them available for analysis. Records that were largely incomplete for the necessary application were adjusted subjectively with the advice and consideration of the copy-center supervisor. Records that showed an inexplicable rise in inventory levels were "doctored" by the

workers from subjective recollections of product history, and monthly ordering patterns were smoothed out and placed in weekly time intervals in such a way that the data appeared feasible to the copy-center supervisor. Some item records appeared to be duplicated and were therefore compiled into one-product histories, and seasonality coefficients were derived for all products from their appropriate histories and cleared with the supervisor for feasibility. This process was based primarily on the subjective "feel" of the copy-center supervisor, product by product, until the resulting forecasts made by the system were in agreement with worker intuition.

Success has been difficult to measure quantitatively since precise records prior to solution acceptance are sparse, yet several results are apparent. In the first year of use, only one brief stockout occurred, there was no flooding of storage space, and

overordering was eliminated. Political tensions have been eased significantly, and job-related stresses have been greatly reduced by improved communication, accountability for copy-center operation, and regular computerized maintenance of inventory records. A reduction in total inventory costs is apparent, while high service levels are being maintained.

Questions for Discussion

1. Explain how behavioral and political concerns affected the design of the inventory-control system. How were those concerns addressed?
2. Why were "time units" used for safety stock rather than product units? What advantages do you think this had?
3. Discuss some of the issues involved in designing the computer support for this inventory control system.

Summary of Key Points

••• Materials management involves planning, coordinating, and controlling the acquisition, storage, handling, and movement of raw materials, purchased parts, semifinished goods, supplies, tools, and other materials that are required in production. Materials-management activities include purchasing, receiving, storage, packaging, shipping, and physical distribution.

••• Inventory consists of idle goods held for future use. In manufacturing, inventory includes raw materials, work-in-process, and finished goods. Inventory is important to production operations, yet presents some operational limitations and financial concerns. Inventory should support strategic customer-satisfaction and operational-performance goals.

••• Many companies are now focusing efforts on developing better relations with suppliers to improve quality and eliminate or reduce inventories and incoming inspection. Companies use supplier certification programs to qualify suppliers who can meet cost, quality, and delivery standards.

••• Information technology, especially bar-coding and radio-frequency communications, provides a means of improving the quality and productivity of materials-management activities.

••• Inventory problems can be classified according to the number of items, the nature of demand, the number of time periods, lead time, and stockouts. The principal costs in inventory modeling are ordering costs, carrying costs, and shortage costs.

••• ABC analysis is useful for measuring inventory performance, defining appropriate methods of controlling different types of inventory, and targeting needed improvements.

••• Two types of control systems are used for independent-demand inventory situations: continuous-review systems and periodic-review systems. Cycle counting is a system for continuous physical counting of inventory throughout the year.

••• Classical decision models such as the economic order quantity (EOQ) model provide important insights into the economics of inventory and are applicable in many situations.

••• When demand is probabilistic, safety stock is usually carried to reduce the risk of shortages. The optimal safety-stock level can be determined by specifying a desired service level—the probability of having no shortages during the lead-time demand period.

Key Terms

Materials management
Inventory
Lot-size inventory
Work-in-process (WIP) inventories
Fluctuation inventory
Safety-stock
Anticipation inventory
Purchasing
Procurement
Blanket contract
Receiving
Packaging
Shipping
Warehousing
Physical distribution
Traffic
Supplier-certification program
Bar code
Radio frequency (RF) communication
Lead time
Ordering costs
Inventory-holding (or inventory-carrying) costs
Cost of capital
Goodwill costs
ABC classification
Inventory position
Continuous-review system
Reorder point
Periodic-review system
Cycle counting
Economic order quantity (EOQ)
Constant-demand rate
Lead-time-demand distribution
Service level

Review Questions

1. Define *materials management.*
2. Define *inventory.* Name the five major types of inventory.
3. Explain the importance of inventory in production operations.
4. How does inventory affect traditional financial measures in a firm?
5. List the major activities of materials management.

6. List the principal objectives and activities in a purchasing department.
7. Discuss the major responsibilities of receiving, packaging, shipping, and warehousing.
8. Discuss the role of physical distribution in materials management. What are the critical factors in selecting a mode of transportation?
9. What are the relative advantages and disadvantages of rail, truck, and air for transporting goods?
10. Explain the importance of supplier partnerships.
11. What is a supplier-certification program?
12. Discuss the applications of bar coding and radio-frequency communications in materials management.
13. Why did Henry Ford Hospital automate its materials-management system?
14. What are the major factors used in classifying inventory problems?
15. Explain the difference between back orders and lost sales.
16. What are the major costs associated with inventory? How can these costs be determined in practice?
17. Explain the ABC classification for inventory. Of what value is ABC analysis?
18. Discuss how ABC analysis can be used in situations that do not involve inventory.
19. Describe the operation of a continuous-review inventory system.
20. Describe the operation of a periodic-review inventory system.
21. What is cycle counting? How can it best be implemented?
22. Why is it important to measure inventory-system performance? Discuss how inventory-profile reports assist in evaluating inventory systems.
23. List the assumptions behind the EOQ model.
24. Define *constant-demand rate.*
25. How is the annual inventory-holding cost expressed in the EOQ model?
26. Discuss the EOQ model's sensitivity to changes in the model parameters.
27. Discuss some practical aspects of inventory decision making that the EOQ model does not take into account.
28. Define *service level.* Why is it not necessarily desirable to attempt to attain a 100-percent service level?

Discussion Questions

1. Discuss some of the issues that MamaMia's Pizza might face in inventory management, purchasing, and supplier partnerships.
2. How might the classification scheme in Table 13.2 be applied to MamaMia's inventory problems?
3. List some products in your personal or family "inventory." How do you manage them? (For instance, do

you constantly run to the store for milk after it is gone?) How might the ideas in this chapter change your way of managing?

4. Interview a manager at a local business about its inventory and materials-management system, and prepare a report summarizing its approaches. Does it use any formal models? Why or why not? How does it determine inventory-related costs?

5. Develop a scoring model to select an appropriate transportation mode (see Table 13.1).

6. Try to develop some novel uses of bar-coding and radio-frequency communications to improve productivity and quality.

7. List the common inventory items that you might find at a business like MamaMia's Pizza. What would be a likely ABC classification?

8. Would MamaMia's Pizza use a continuous- or periodic-review system for fresh dough (purchased from a bakery on contract)? What would be the advantages and disadvantages of each in this situation?

9. How would a business realistically determine an acceptable service level for the uncertain-demand-inventory situation?

10. Discuss how you might use simulation (see Supplementary Chapter A) to address inventory problems with uncertain demand that cannot be assumed to follow a normal probability distribution?

Notes

1. GTE Directories, 1994 Application Summary for the Malcolm Baldrige National Quality Award.

2. John J. Hudiburg, *Winning with Quality: The FPL Story* (White Plains, NY: Quality Resources, 1991).

3. "Warehouse Control Technologies," Print Series M0001, Tompkins Associates Incorporated, Raleigh, NC.

4. Adapted from Geoffrey Abdian, "Bar-Code Tracking Cuts Data Entry at Henry Ford Hospital," *Industrial Engineering* 20, no. 10 (1988), pp. 43-45. Copyright Institute of Industrial Engineers, 25 Technology Park/Atlanta, Norcross, GA 30092.

5. A more complete technical classification and survey of inventory problems is given in E. A. Silver, "Operations Research in Inventory Management," *Operations Research* 29 (1981), pp. 628-645.

6. Everette S. Gardner, "Inventory Theory and the Gods of Olympus," *Interfaces* 10, no. 4 (1980), pp. 42-45.

7. Jim Cantwell, "The How and Why of Cycle Counting: The ABC Method," *Production and Inventory Management* 26, no. 2 (1985), pp. 50-54. Reprinted with permission, The American Production and Inventory Control Society, Inc.

8. "Measuring Inventory Performance to Improve Profitability," *Manufacturing Insights,* November 1990 (Coopers & Lybrand Cincinnati Management Consulting Services).

9. James A. G. Krupp, "Measuring Inventory Management Performance," *Production and Inventory Management Journal* 35, no. 4 (fourth quarter 1994), pp. 1–6.

10. Adapted from Richard A. Reid, "The ABC Method in Hospital Inventory Management: A Practical Approach," *Production and Inventory Management* 28, no. 4 (1987), pp. 67-70. Reprinted with permission, The American Production and Inventory Control Society, Inc.

11. Adapted from Timothy R. Hayes, "An Inventory Control System for The Colorado School of Mines Quick Copy Center, *Production and Inventory Management Journal* 35, no. 4, (fourth quarter 1994), pp. 50–53. Reprinted with permission of APICS, Inc.

Solved Problems

1. Perform an ABC analysis for the items in Table 13.5.

Table 13.5 Data for Solved Problem 1

Item	Annual Usage	Unit Value	Item	Annual Usage	Unit Value
1	8,800	68.12	7	112,000	7.59
2	9,800	58.25	8	198,000	3.19
3	23,600	75.25	9	210,000	2.98
4	40,000	53.14	10	168,000	4.27
5	60,000	26.33	11	100,000	9.00
6	165,000	4.52	12	7,000	13.57

Solution
Sorting the items in the descending order to total value we get the data in Table 13.6.

Table 13.6 Data for Solved Problem 1 Solution

Item	Annual Usage	Unit Value	Total Value	Cum. Number	% Items	Cum. Dollars	% Value
4	40,000	53.14	2,125,600	40,000	3.43	2,125,600	17.61
3	23,600	75.25	1,775,900	63,600	5.46	3,901,500	32.32
5	60,000	26.33	1,579,800	123,600	10.61	5,481,300	45.40
12	70,000	13.57	949,900	193,600	16.62	6,431,200	53.27
11	100,000	9.00	900,000	293,600	25.20	7,331,200	60.73
7	112,000	7.59	850,080	405,600	34.81	8,181,280	67.77
6	165,000	4.52	745,800	570,600	48.97	8,927,080	73.95
10	168,000	4.27	717,360	738,600	63.39	9,644,440	79.89
8	198,000	3.19	631,620	936,600	80.38	10,276,060	85.12
9	210,000	2.98	625,800	1,146,600	98.40	10,901,860	90.31
1	8,800	68.12	599,456	1,155,400	99.16	11,501,316	95.27
2	9,800	58.25	570,850	1,165,200	100	12,072,166	100.00

There is no "correct" breakdown into A, B, and C categories. The first four items account for 53 percent of dollar value, while the last three items account for about 10 percent. Thus, the following classification would be reasonable.

Class	Items
A	4, 3, 5, 12
B	11, 7, 6, 10, 8
C	9, 1, 2

2. Suppose R&B Beverage Company distributes a soft-drink product that has a constant annual demand rate of 3,600 cases. A case of the soft drink costs R&B $5. Ordering costs are $20 per order, and inventory-holding costs are charged at 25 percent of the cost per unit. There are 250 working days per year, and the lead time is four days. Identify these aspects of the inventory policy:
a. Economic order quantity.
b. Reorder point.
c. Cycle time.
d. Total annual cost.

Solution
a. $Q^* = \sqrt{2DC_0 / C_h} = \sqrt{2(3600)(20) / [.25(5)]} = 339.41$.

b. $r = dm = 3600(4)/250 = 57.6$.

c. $T = 250Q^*/D = 250(339.41)/3,600 = 23.57$ days.

d. $TC = (1/2)Q_h + (D/Q)C_0 = (.5)(339.41)(.25)(5) + 3,600(20)/339.41 = 424.27$.

3. Cress Electronics Products manufactures components used in the automotive industry. Cress purchases parts from a variety of suppliers. One supplier provides a part where the assumptions of the EOQ model are realistic. The annual demand is 5,000 units. Ordering costs are $80 per order, and inventory-carrying costs are figured at an annual rate of 25 percent.

a. If the cost of the part is $20 per unit, what is the economic order quantity?

b. Assume 250 days of operation per year. If the lead time for an order is 12 days, what is the reorder point?

c. If the lead time for the part is seven weeks (35 days), what is the reorder point?

d. What is the reorder point for part c if the reorder point is expressed in terms of inventory on hand rather than inventory position?

Solution

a.
$$Q^* = \sqrt{\frac{2DC_o}{C_h}} = \sqrt{\frac{2(5000)(80)}{(.25)(20)}} = 400$$

b.
$$r = dm = \frac{5,000}{250}(12) = 240$$

c.
$$r = dm = \frac{5,000}{250}(35) = 700 \text{ (inventory position)}$$

d. Since $r = 700$ and $Q^* = 400$, one order will be outstanding when the reorder point is reached. Thus the inventory on hand at the time of reorder will be $700 - 400 = 300$.

4. Floyd Distributors, Inc., provides a variety of auto parts to small local garages. It purchases parts from manufacturers according to the EOQ model and then ships the parts from a regional warehouse directly to its customers. For a particular type of muffler, Floyd's EOQ analysis recommends orders with $Q^* = 25$ to satisfy an annual demand of 200 mufflers. There are 250 working days per year, and the lead time averages 15 days.

a. What is the reorder point if Floyd assumes a constant demand rate?

b. Suppose an analysis of Floyd's muffler demand shows that the lead-time demand follows a normal distribution, with $\mu = 12$ and $\sigma = 2.5$. If Floyd's managers can tolerate one stockout per year, what is the revised reorder point?

c. What is the safety stock for part b? If $C_h = \$5/\text{unit/year}$, what is the extra cost due to the uncertainty of demand?

Solution

a.
$$r = dm = (200/250)15 = 12$$

b.
$$\frac{D}{Q} = \frac{200}{25} = 8 \text{ orders/year}$$

The limit of one stockout per year means that

$$P(\text{stockout/cycle}) = \tfrac{1}{8} = .125.$$

Area in tail (see figure below) $= .125$, $z = 1.15$. That is,

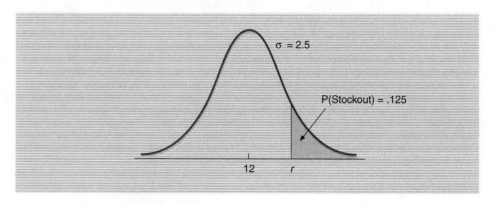

$$z = \frac{r - 12}{2.5} = 1.15$$

or

$$r = 12 + 1.15(2.5) = 14.875 \approx 15.$$

c. Safety Stock is 3 units. Added cost is 3($5) = $15/year.

Problems

1. The Welsh Corporation uses 10 key components in one of its manufacturing plants. Perform an ABC analysis from the data in Table 13.7.

Table 13.7 Data for Problem 1

SKU	Unit Cost	Annual Demand
WC219	.10	12,000
WC008	1.20	22,500
WC916	3.20	700
WC887	.41	6,200
WC397	5.00	17,300
WC654	2.10	350
WC007	.90	225
WC419	.45	8,500
WC971	7.50	2,950
WC713	10.50	1,000

2. Develop an ABC curve for the data in Table 13.8.

Table 13.8 Data for Problem 2

Item	Annual Usage	Unit Cost	Item	Annual Usage	Unit Cost
1	2400	$19.51	11	500	$ 40.50
2	6200	32.60	12	2000	15.40
3	8500	10.20	13	2400	14.60
4	3200	6.80	14	6300	35.80
5	6000	4.50	15	4750	17.30
6	750	55.70	16	2700	51.75
7	8200	3.60	17	1600	42.90
8	9000	44.90	18	1350	25.30
9	5800	35.62	19	5000	67.00
10	820	82.60	20	1000	125.00

3. A&M Industrial Products purchases a variety of parts used in small industrial tools. Inventory has not been tightly controlled, and managers think that costs can be substantially reduced. The items in Table 13.9 comprise the inventory of one product line. Perform an ABC analysis of this inventory situation.

Table 13.9 Data for Problem 3

Part Number	Annual Demand	Unit Cost	Part Number	Annual Demand	Unit Cost
A367	700	.04	P157	13	3.10
A490	3,850	.70	P232	600	.12
B710	400	.29	R825	15,200	.12
C615	600	.24	S324	20	30.15
C712	7,200	2.60	S404	400	.12
D008	680	51.00	S692	75	12.10
G140	45	100.00	T001	20,000	.005
G147	68,000	.0002	X007	225	.15
K619	2,800	5.25	Y345	8,000	.16
L312	500	1.45	Z958	455	2.56
M582	8,000	.002	Z960	2,000	.001
M813	2,800	.0012			

4. Given the weekly demand data in Table 13.10 illustrate the operation of a continuous-review inventory system with a reorder point of 75, an order quantity of 100, and a beginning inventory of 125. Lead time is one week. All orders are placed at the end of the week. What is the average inventory and number of stockouts?

Table 13.10 Data for Problem 4

Week	Demand	Week	Demand
1	25	7	50
2	30	8	35
3	20	9	30
4	40	10	40
5	40	11	20
6	25	12	25

5. For the situation described in Problem 4, illustrate the operation of a periodic-review system with a two-week review period (end of every alternate week), a reorder point of 75, and a reorder level of 150. Initial inventory is 125. What is the average inventory and number of stockouts?

6. Table 13.11 gives the daily demand of a certain oil filter at an auto supply store. Illustrate the operation of a continuous-review inventory system by graphing the inventory level versus time if $Q = 40$, $r = 15$, and the lead time is three days. Assume that orders are placed at the end of the day and that they arrive at the beginning of the day. Thus if an order is placed at the end of day 5, it will arrive at the beginning of day 9. Assume that 30 units are on hand at the start of day 1.

Table 13.11 Data for Problem 6

Day	Demand	Day	Demand
1	6	5	5
2	8	6	6
3	5	7	1
4	4	8	1
			(continues)

Table 13.11 Data for Problem 6 (continued)

Day	Demand	Day	Demand
9	3	18	3
10	8	19	5
11	8	20	9
12	6	21	3
13	7	22	6
14	0	23	1
15	2	24	9
16	4	25	1
17	7		

7. For the data given in Problem 6, illustrate the operation of a periodic-review inventory system with a reorder level of 40, a reorder point of 15, and a review period of five days.

8. MamaMia's Pizza purchases its pizza delivery boxes from a printing supplier. MamaMia's delivers on average 200 pizzas each month. Boxes cost 20 cents each, and each order costs $10 to process. Because of limited storage space, the manager wants to charge inventory holding at 30 percent of the cost. The lead time is one week, and the restaurant is open 360 days per year. Determine the economic order quantity, reorder point, number of orders per year, and total annual cost. If the supplier raises the cost of each box to 25 cents, how would these results change?

9. Refer to the situation in Problem 8. Suppose the manager of MamaMia's wants to order 200 boxes each month. How much more than the optimal cost will be necessary to implement this policy?

10. A general property of the EOQ inventory model is that total inventory-holding and total ordering costs are equal or balanced at the optimal solution. Use the data in Solved Problem 2 to show that this result is observed. Use equations 13.1, 13.2, and 13.4 to show in general that total inventory-holding costs and total ordering costs are equal whenever Q^* is used.

11. The reorder point (see equation 13.5) is defined as the lead-time demand for the item. In cases of long lead times, the lead-time demand and thus the reorder point may exceed the economic order quantity, Q^*. In such cases the inventory position will not equal the inventory on hand when an order is placed, and the reorder point may be expressed in terms of either inventory position or inventory on hand. Consider the EOQ model with $D = 5,000$, $C_o = \$32$, $C_h = \$2$, and 250 working days per year. Identify the reorder point in terms of inventory position and in terms of inventory on hand for each of these lead times.

a. 5 days.
b. 15 days.
c. 25 days.
d. 45 days.

12. The XYZ Company purchases a component used in the manufacture of automobile generators directly from the supplier. XYZ's generator production, which is operated at a constant rate, will require 1,200 components per month throughout the year. Assume ordering costs are $25 per order, unit cost is $2.00 per component, and annual inventory holding costs are charged at 20 percent. The company operates 250 days per year, and the lead time is five days.

a. Compute the EOQ, total annual inventory-holding and ordering costs, and the reorder point.

b. Suppose XYZ's managers like the operational efficiency of ordering in quantities of 1,200 units and ordering once each month. How much more expensive would this policy be than your EOQ recommendation? Would you recommend in favor of the 1,200-unit order quantity? Explain. What would the reorder point be if the 1,200-unit quantity were acceptable?

13. Tele-Reco is a new specialty store that sells television sets, videotape recorders, video games, and other television-related products. A new Japanese-manufactured videotape recorder costs Tele-Reco $600 per unit. Tele-Reco's inventory-carrying cost is figured at an annual rate of 22 percent. Ordering costs are estimated to be $70 per order.

a. If demand for the new videotape recorder is expected to be constant at a rate of 20 units per month, what is the recommended order quantity for the videotape recorder?

b. What are the estimated annual inventory-holding and ordering costs associated with this product?

c. How many orders will be placed per year?

d. With 250 working days per year, what is the cycle time for this product?

14. Develop a spreadsheet similar to EOQMODEL.XLS (Figure 13.8) to examine the sensitivity of the constant demand assumption for the Holton Drug Co. example. Prepare graphs showing total cost as demand varies for both Q^* and well as for $Q = 919$.

15. Nation-Wide Bus Lines is proud of the six-week driver-training program it conducts for all new Nation-Wide drivers. The program costs Nation-Wide $22,000 for instructors, equipment, and so on, and is independent of the number of new drivers in the class as long as the class size remains less than or equal to 35. The program must provide the company with approximately five new fully trained drivers per month. After completing the training program, new drivers are paid $1,800 per month but do not work until a full-time driver position is open. Nation-Wide views the $1,800 as a holding cost necessary to maintain a supply of newly trained drivers available for immediate service. Viewing new drivers as inventory units, how large should the training classes be in order to minimize Nation-Wide's total annual training and new-driver idle-time costs? How many training classes should the company hold each year? What is the total annual cost of your recommendation?

16. For Floyd Distributors in Solved Problem 4, we were given $Q^* = 25$, $D = 200$, $C_h = \$5$, and a normal lead-time demand distribution, with $\mu = 12$ and $\sigma = 2.5$.

a. What is Floyd's reorder point if the firm is willing to tolerate two stockouts during the year?

b. What is Floyd's reorder point if the firm wants to restrict the probability of a stockout on any one cycle to at most 1 percent?

c. What are the safety-stock levels and the annual safety-stock costs for the reorder points found in parts a and b?

17. Brauch's Pharmacy has an expected annual demand for a leading pain reliever of 800 boxes, which sell for for $6.50 each. Each order costs $6.00, and the inventory carrying charge is 20 cents. The expected demand during the lead time is normal, with a mean of 25 and a standard deviation of 3. Assuming 52 weeks per year, what reorder point provides a 95-percent service level? How much safety stock will be carried? If the carrying charge were 25 cents instead, what would be the total annual inventory-related cost?

18. A product with an annual demand of 1,000 units has $C_0 = \$30$ and $C_h = \$8$. The demand exhibits some variability such that the lead-time demand follows a normal distribution, with $\mu = 25$ and $\sigma = 5$.

a. What is the recommended order quantity?

b. What are the reorder point and safety-stock level if the firm desires at most a 2-percent probability of a stockout on any given order cycle?

c. If the manager sets the reorder point at 30, what is the probability of a stockout on any given order cycle? How many times would you expect to stockout during the year if this reorder point were used?

19. The B&S Novelty and Craft Shop in Bennington, Vermont, sells a variety of quality handmade items to tourists. It will sell 300 handcarved miniature replicas of a Colonial soldier each year, but the demand pattern during the year is uncertain. The replicas sell for $20 each, and B&S uses a 15-percent annual inventory-holding cost rate. Ordering costs are $5 per order, and demand during the lead time follows a normal distribution, with $\mu = 15$ and $\sigma = 6$.

a. What is the recommended order quantity?

b. If B&S is willing to accept a stockout roughly twice a year, what reorder point would you recommend? What is the probability that B&S will have a stockout in any one order cycle?

c. What are the safety-stock level and annual safety-stock costs for this product?

 20. Modify the SOUTHERN.XLS spreadsheet (Figure 13.12) to examine the implications of various service levels in Problems 17, 18, and 19. What decisions would you recommend?

Chapter 14
Decision Models for Inventory Management

hapter 13 discussed two quantitative decision models for inventory management: the economic order quantity (EOQ) and stochastic-demand models. This chapter presents several other such models and approaches for inventory analysis. We emphasize again that a quantitative model does not
necessarily give operations managers the *best* decision. Intangible factors such
as quality, risk, and service must be considered in evaluating the solution provided by a quantitative model. Nevertheless, models like the ones described in
this chapter have helped many businesses to improve their decision making.

An Inventory Model with Planned Shortages

As noted in Chapter 13, there are cases in which it may be desirable—from an
economic point of view—to plan for and allow shortages. This situation is most
common when the value per unit of the inventory is very high, and hence the
inventory-holding cost is high. An example is a new-car dealer's inventory. It is
not uncommon for a dealer not to have the specific car you want in stock.
However, if you are willing to wait several weeks, the dealer will order the car for
you. This is a back-order situation.

Using the back-order assumption for shortages, we now present an extension to the EOQ model presented in Chapter 13. The EOQ-model assumptions
of the goods arriving in inventory all at one time and a constant demand rate
for the product will be used.

If we let S indicate the amount of the shortage or the number of back orders
that have accumulated when a new shipment of size Q is received, the inventory system for the back-order case has these characteristics:

1. With S back orders existing when a new shipment of size Q arrives, the S back
   orders will be shipped to the appropriate customers immediately, and the remaining $(Q - S)$ units will be placed in inventory.
2. $Q - S$ will be the maximum inventory level.
3. The inventory cycle of T days will be divided into two distinct phases: t_1 days
   when inventory is on hand and orders are filled as they occur and t_2 days
   when there is a stockout and all orders are placed on back order.

The inventory pattern for this model, where negative inventory represents the
number of back orders, is shown in Figure 14.1.

To develop an expression of total cost for the inventory model with back orders, we encounter the usual inventory-holding costs and ordering costs. In addition, we incur a back-ordering cost in terms of labor and special-delivery
costs directly associated with the handling of back orders. Another portion of
the back-order cost can be expressed as a loss of goodwill with customers due
to their having to wait for their orders. Since the *goodwill cost* depends on how
long the customer has to wait, it is customary to adopt the convention of expressing all back-order costs in terms of how much it costs to have a unit on
back order for a stated period of time. This method of computing cost is similar
to the method we used to compute the inventory-holding cost. We can compute
a total annual cost of back orders once the average back-order level and the
back-order cost per unit per unit time are known. As you recall, this is the same
type of information that is needed to calculate inventory-holding costs.

Figure 14.1
Inventory Pattern for an
Inventory Model with Back
Orders

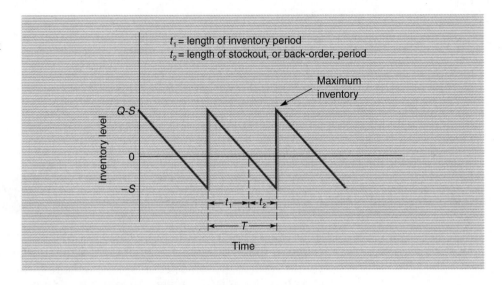

Admittedly, the back-order cost rate (especially the goodwill cost) is difficult to determine in practice. However, noting that EOQ models are rather insensitive to the cost estimates, we should feel confident that reasonable estimates of the back-order cost will lead to a good approximation of the overall minimum-cost inventory decision.

Letting C_b be the cost to maintain one unit on back order for one year, the three sources of cost in this planned-shortage inventory model can be expressed as in the following equations.

$$\text{inventory-holding cost} = \frac{(Q - S)^2}{2Q} C_h \qquad (14.1)$$

$$\text{ordering cost} = \frac{D}{Q} C_o \qquad (14.2)$$

$$\text{back-ordering cost} = \frac{S^2}{2Q} C_b \qquad (14.3)$$

Thus our total-annual-cost expression (TC) becomes

$$TC = \frac{(Q - S)^2}{2Q} C_h + \frac{D}{Q} C_o + \frac{S^2}{2Q} C_b. \qquad (14.4)$$

Given the cost estimates C_h, C_o, and C_b, and the annual demand, D, we can begin to determine the minimum-cost values for our inventory decisions, Q and S. With two decision components, a trial-and-error approach, though valid, becomes cumbersome. Using calculus, analysts have established the following minimum-cost formulas for the order quantity, Q^*, and the planned back orders, S^*.

$$Q^* = \sqrt{\frac{2DC_o}{C_h}\left(\frac{C_h + C_b}{C_b}\right)} \qquad (14.5)$$

and

$$S^* = Q^*\left(\frac{C_h}{C_h + C_b}\right)$$ (14.6)

An example follows.

Example

Determining the Optimal Order Quantity with Back Orders

RCB Electronics Company is concerned about an expensive part used in television repair. The cost of the part is $125, and RCB's inventory-holding rate is 20 percent. The cost to place an order is estimated to be $40. The annual demand, which occurs at a constant rate throughout the year, is 800 parts. Because of the cost of the item, RCB's inventory manager continually seeks ways to reduce the amount of inventory carried for the part. Currently, the inventory policy is based on the EOQ model, with

$$Q^* = \sqrt{\frac{2DC_o}{C_h}} = \sqrt{\frac{2(800)(40)}{.20(125)}} = 51 \text{ parts.}$$

The total annual cost of inventory-holding and ordering has been

$$TC = \frac{1}{2}QC_h + \frac{D}{Q}C_o = \frac{1}{2}(51)(.20)(125) + \left(\frac{800}{51}\right)(40)$$

$$= \$637.50 + 627.50 = \$1,265.$$

With an average inventory of $Q/2 = 51/2 = 25.5$ parts evaluated at $125 each, RCB's inventory manager has expressed a willingness to allow back ordering if it will help reduce the $(25.5)(\$125) = \$3,187.50$ average inventory investment for the part.

In attempting to develop a cost estimate for a back order, the manager felt a one-week cost in the neighborhood of $1.00 to $1.25 per unit would be a reasonable assumption. On an annual basis, a unit back-order cost of $60 was assigned. Let us use the inventory-decision model with planned shortages to see what the effect of back ordering would be on RCB's inventory policy.

Using equations 14.5 and 14.6, the optimal order quantity, Q^*, and the optimal number of back orders, S^*, become

$$Q^* = \sqrt{\frac{2(800)(40)}{.20(125)}\left(\frac{.20(125) + 60}{60}\right)} = 60 \text{ parts}$$

and

$$S^* = 60\left(\frac{.20(125)}{.20(125) + 60}\right) = 18 \text{ parts.}$$

Both Q^* and S^* have been rounded to whole numbers to simplify the remaining calculations. Using equations 14.1, 14.2, and 14.3, we find the following costs associated with the inventory policy.

$$\text{inventory-holding cost} = \frac{(Q - S)^2}{2Q}C_h$$

$$= \frac{(60 - 18)^2}{2(60)}(.20)(125) = \$367.50.$$

$$\text{ordering cost} = \frac{D}{Q}C_o = \frac{800}{600}(40) = \$533.33$$

$$\text{back-ordering cost} = \frac{S^2}{2Q}C_b = \frac{(18)^2}{2(60)}(60) = \$162.00$$

The total cost is $367.50 + $533.33 + $162.00 = $1,062.83, and hence the back-ordering policy provides a $1,265 − $1,062.83 = $202.17, or 16 percent, cost reduction when compared to the EOQ model.

Let us look more closely to see how this savings has come about. From the above inventory-holding cost calculation, we see that there will be an average of 14.7 units in inventory and that the inventory-holding cost has been reduced from $637.50 to $367.50, a savings of $270. The inventory investment for the 14.7 units is (14.7)($125) = $1,837.50, which is $1,350 less than the $3,187.50 required by the EOQ model. Thus we see that allowing shortages in the form of back orders enables us to make significant cost reductions in the amount of inventory carried. However, this savings is offset somewhat by the cost associated with the back orders, which is $162.00. An additional savings comes from a reduction in the number of orders placed, which in this example results in a cost reduction of $627.50 − $533.33 = $94.17. The net effect of these cost adjustments is that the back ordering does in fact reduce the total cost of the RCB inventory operation.

As a final observation, note that the daily demand for the part is (800 parts)/(250 days) = 3.2 parts per day. Since the maximum number of back orders is 18, we see that the length of the back-order period will be 18/3.2 = 5.6 days. This tells RCB's inventory manager that a person experiencing an out-of-stock situation will have to wait at most five to six working days (approximately a week) to obtain a part.

Economic Production Lot-Size Model

Another inventory-decision model, the **production lot-size model,** is similar to the EOQ model in that we are attempting to determine *how much* we should order or produce and *when* the order should be placed. Again, we make the assumption of a constant demand rate. However, instead of the goods arriving at the warehouse in a shipment of size Q^* as assumed in the EOQ model, we assume that units are supplied to inventory at a constant rate over several days or several weeks. The assumption of a *constant supply rate* implies that the same number of units is supplied to inventory each period of time—for example, 10 units every day, 50 units every week, and so on. This model is designed for production situations in which once an order is placed, production begins and a constant number of units are added to inventory each day until the production

Figure 14.2
Inventory Pattern for
Production Lot-Size
Inventory Model

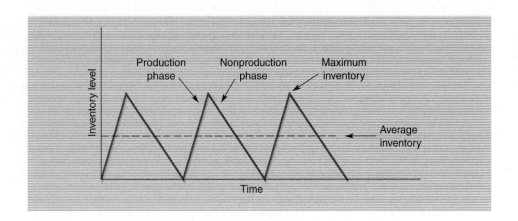

run has been completed. To satisfy demand and avoid back orders, the production rate must be greater than the demand rate. This ensures a gradual buildup of inventory during the production period. When the production run is completed, the inventory shows a gradual decline until a new production run is started. The inventory pattern for this system is shown in Figure 14.2.

If we have a production system that produces 50 units per day, and we decide to schedule 10 days of production each time we want additional units, we have a 50(10) = 500-unit production run size. Alternative terminology may refer to the 500 units as the *production lot size* or the *lot quantity*. We denote the production lot size by Q and build a model that minimizes total annual cost.

As in the EOQ model, we are now dealing with two costs, the inventory-holding cost and the ordering cost. While the inventory-holding cost is identical to our definition in the EOQ model, the ordering cost may be more correctly referred to as *production-setup cost*. This cost, which includes labor hours, material, and lost production costs incurred while preparing the production system for operation, is a fixed cost that occurs for every production run, regardless of the production quantity.

Let us begin building our model by attempting to write the inventory-holding cost in terms of our production quantity, Q. Again, our approach is to develop an expression for average inventory and then establish the holding costs associated with the average inventory level. We use a one-year time period and an annual cost for our model.

We saw in the EOQ model that the average inventory was simply one-half the maximum inventory, or $Q/2$. Since Figure 14.2 shows a constant inventory-buildup rate during the production run and a constant inventory-depletion rate during the nonproduction period, the average inventory for the production lot-size model will also be half of the maximum inventory level. However, in this inventory system the production quantity, Q, does not go into inventory at one time, and thus the inventory level never reaches a level of Q units.

To compute the maximum inventory level, define the following symbols:

d = daily demand rate for the product.

p = daily production rate for the product.

t = number of days for a production run.

Since we are assuming p is larger than d, the excess production each day is $p - d$, which is the daily rate of inventory buildup. If we run production for t days and place $p - d$ units in inventory each day, the inventory level at the end of the production run will be $(p - d)t$. From Figure 14.2 we can see that the inventory level at the end of the production run is also the maximum inventory level. Thus we can write

$$\text{maximum inventory} = (p - d)t. \tag{14.7}$$

If we know we are producing a production quantity of Q units at a daily production rate of p units, then $Q = pt$, and we can compute the length of the production run t to be

$$t = \frac{Q}{p} \text{ days.} \tag{14.8}$$

Therefore,

$$\text{maximum inventory} = (p - d)t = (p - d)\left(\frac{Q}{p}\right) \tag{14.9}$$

$$= \left(1 - \frac{d}{p}\right)Q.$$

The average inventory, which is half of the maximum inventory, is given by

$$\frac{1}{2}\left(1 - \frac{d}{p}\right)Q. \tag{14.10}$$

With an annual inventory holding cost of C_h per unit, the general equation for annual inventory-holding cost is

$$\binom{\text{average}}{\text{inventory}}\begin{pmatrix}\text{annual holding}\\ \text{cost}\\ \text{per unit}\end{pmatrix} = \frac{1}{2}\left(1 - \frac{d}{p}\right)QC_h. \tag{14.11}$$

If D is the annual demand for the product and C_o is the setup cost for a production run, then the total annual setup cost, which takes the place of the total annual ordering costs of the EOQ model, is

$$\binom{\text{number of production}}{\text{runs per year}}\binom{\text{setup cost}}{\text{per run}} = \left(\frac{D}{Q}\right)C_o. \tag{14.12}$$

Thus, the total annual cost (TC) model is

$$TC = \frac{1}{2}\left(1 - \frac{d}{p}\right)QC_h + \frac{D}{Q}C_o. \tag{14.13}$$

In this total-cost model, we use the ratio of daily demand to daily production, d/p. Actually this ratio of demand to production is the same regardless of the period of time considered. In terms of an annual demand, D, and an annual production capacity, P, the ratio $D/P = d/p$. Substituting D/P for d/p in equation 14.13 provides this total-annual-cost model:

$$TC = \frac{1}{2}\left(1 - \frac{D}{P}\right)QC_h + \frac{D}{Q}C_o. \qquad (14.14)$$

Equations 14.13 and 14.14 are equivalent. However equation 14.14 may be used more frequently, since an *annual cost* model tends to make the analyst think in terms of collecting *annual* demand (D) and *annual* production (P) data rather than daily-rate data.

Given the estimates of the inventory-holding cost, C_h, setup cost, C_o, annual demand rate, D, and annual production rate, P, we can use a trial-and-error approach to compute the total annual cost for various lot sizes, Q. However, we can also use the minimum-cost formula for Q^*, which has been developed by using differential calculus. The formula is

$$Q^* = \sqrt{\frac{2DC_o}{(1 - D/P)C_h}}. \qquad (14.15)$$

An example follows.

Example

Determining the Optimal Production Lot Size

Forum Shoes, Inc., produces a basic dress shoe for men, which sells throughout the year at a constant demand rate. Total annual demand for the shoe is 21,000 pairs. Forum's production costs are $22 per pair, with annual inventory-holding cost figured at a 16-percent rate. The setup of the production line operation, including cleaning, preparation, and changeover from the previous production operation requires several hours of work, at a cost of $200. On an annual basis, the production capacity for the dress shoes is 50,000 pairs. Given this demand, production rate, and cost information, what is the recommended production lot size that will minimize the total inventory-holding cost and production-setup cost? Using Equation 14.15, we have

$$Q^* = \sqrt{\frac{2(21,000)(200)}{(1 - 21,000/50,000)(.16)(22)}}$$

$$= \sqrt{\frac{8,400,000}{2.0416}} = 2,028 \text{ pairs.}$$

Thus production runs, or lot sizes, of 2,028 pairs of shoes are recommended for the Forum dress shoes. With 250 days of operation per year, the daily production capacity is 50,000/250 days = 200 shoes. The length of a production run, then, should be scheduled for 2,028/200 = 10.14 days. After seeing these results, Forum's inventory manager reduced the production lot size to 2,000 pairs because this figure would help scheduling, as the production runs would be for the more convenient 10-day, or two-week, periods.

Equation 14.14 shows that the production lot size of 2,000 pairs enables the system to operate with an annual cost of

$$TC = \frac{1}{2}\left(1 - \frac{21,000}{50,000}\right)(2,000)(.16)(22) + \frac{21,000}{2,000}(200)$$

$$= 2042 + 2100 = \$4,142.$$

Other relevant data include the fact that a five-working-day lead time is required to schedule and set up a production run. With daily demand $d = 21,000/250 = 84$ pairs, the reorder point becomes $r = 5(84) = 420$ pairs.

On an annual basis, $D/Q = 21,000/200 = 10.5$ shows that 10 or 11 production runs should be scheduled during the year. The cycle time, or the time between production runs, is $T = 250(2,000)/21,000 = 24$ working days.

Summary of EOQ Models

Table 14.1 summarizes the cost components and optimal order quantities for the EOQ, production lot-size, and planned-shortage models. These models are quite similar. For instance, the only difference between the production lot-size and EOQ models is the fact that in the former, an order is produced over a finite period of time and not delivered all at once. One way of delivering the product all at once is to have an extremely large production rate. If P grows indefinitely, it is easy to see that the term D/P in the formulas for the holding cost and Q^* becomes insignificant, and the formulas lead to the EOQ. Similarly, the assumption of not allowing stockouts is equivalent to having an extremely high stockout cost. If C_b gets very large, the term $C_h/(C_h + C_b)$ gets very small, forcing S^* to become zero. Also, the term $(C_h + C_b)/C_b = C_h/C_b + 1$ in the formula for Q^* will become 1 as C_b grows infinitely large, because the term C_h/C_b will drop out. These again lead to the EOQ formulas. Using quantitative models is much easier if they make sense!

Quantity Discounts for EOQ Model

In Chapter 13 we stated that the cost of items is an important consideration in many inventory decisions. Letting the purchase cost per unit be denoted by C, the total purchase cost for an annual demand, D, is CD. In the EOQ model, we assumed that the demand, D, and the purchase cost, C, were both constant. Therefore, this portion of the total cost would not be affected by the order-quantity decision.

We now consider inventory policies for situations where the purchase cost of the item depends on the quantity ordered and should be included in the total-cost model. We are talking here about **quantity discounts**—lower unit costs offered by suppliers as an incentive for large purchase quantities.

Typically, a company offers several discount categories. For example, for every item ordered up to 1,000, a base unit price applies; if the order is for 1,001 to 2,000 items, a discounted unit price (of, perhaps, 2 percent) applies; for every additional item ordered beyond 2,000, a larger discount (say, 4 percent) applies. To compute the optimal order quantity, a three-step procedure is used.

Table 14.1 Summary of EOQ Models

Model	Holding Cost	Order Cost	Stockout Cost	Q*
EOQ	$\frac{1}{2}QC_h$	$\frac{D}{Q}C_o$	—	$\sqrt{\dfrac{2DC_0}{C_h}}$
Economic Production Lot Size	$\frac{1}{2}\left(1-\dfrac{D}{P}\right)QC_h$	$\frac{D}{Q}C_o$	—	$\sqrt{\dfrac{2DC_0}{\left(1-\dfrac{D}{P}\right)C_h}}$
EOQ with Planned Shortages	$\dfrac{(Q-S)^2}{2Q}C_h$	$\frac{D}{Q}C_o$	$\dfrac{S^2}{2Q}C_b$	$\sqrt{\dfrac{2DC_0}{C_h}\left(\dfrac{C_h+C_b}{C_b}\right)}$ and $S^* = Q^*\left(\dfrac{C_h}{C_h+C_b}\right)$

Step 1. Compute Q^* using the EOQ formula for the unit cost associated with each discount category.

Step 2. For Q^*s that are too small to qualify for the assumed discount price, adjust the order quantity upward to the nearest order quantity that will allow the product to be purchased at the assumed price.

If a calculated Q^* for a given price is larger than the *highest* order quantity that provides the particular discount price, that discount price need not be considered further, since it cannot lead to an optimal solution. While this may not be obvious, it does turn out to be a property of the EOQ quantity-discount model.

When quantity discounts are considered, the annual purchase cost (annual demand, D, times the unit cost, C) is included in the total-cost model:

$$TC = \frac{Q}{2}C_h + \frac{D}{Q}C_o + DC. \qquad (14.16)$$

Using this total-cost formula, we can determine the optimal order quantity for the EOQ discount model in step 3.

Step 3. For each of the order quantities resulting from steps 1 and 2, compute the total annual cost using the unit price from the appropriate discount category and equation 14.16. The order quantity yielding the minimum total annual cost is the optimal order quantity.

We illustrate this procedure with an example.

Example : ## Determining the Optimal Order Quantity with Quantity Discounts

Let us return to the Holton Drug Company example introduced in Chapter 13. Holton used the EOQ model to conclude that it should order All-Bright toothpaste in quantities of 919 cases per order. The EOQ recommendation was based on this information:

Annual demand	24,000 cases
Cost per case	$12.00
Inventory-holding charge	18%
Order cost	$38.00

Now let us assume that the manufacturer of All-Bright toothpaste has offered its customers this quantity-discount schedule:

Discount Category	Order Size	Discount	Unit Cost
1	0–3,999	0	$12.00
2	4,000–11,999	3%	11.64
3	12,000 and over	5%	11.40

The 5-percent discount looks attractive; however, the 12,000-case order quantity is substantially more than the current recommendation of 919 cases. Since the larger order quantities require higher inventory-carrying costs, we should prepare a thorough cost analysis before making a final inventory-policy decision.

The Excel spreadsheet in Figure 14.3 performs the necessary calculations. In column F we place the larger of the EOQ and the minimum order size for each discount category. For example, the EOQ for discount category 2 is

$$Q_2^* = \sqrt{2DC_o/C_h} = \sqrt{\frac{2(24,000)(38)}{(.18)(11.64)}} = 933.$$

However, since this is below the minimum required order size, we adjust the order quantity up to 4,000. Similarly, the EOQ for discount category 3 is 943, so we set the order quantity to 12,000. The cost calculations appear in columns G through J.

As you can see, a decision to order 4,000 units at the 3-percent discount rate yields the minimum-cost solution. While the 12,000-unit order quantity would

Figure 14.3 Spreadsheet for Quantity Discount Model (DISCOUNT.XLS)

	A	B	C	D	E	F	G	H	I	J	
1	Quantity Discount Inventory Model										
2											
3	Annual demand		24,000								
4	Cost per unit		$ 12.00								
5	Carrying charge		18%								
6	Order cost		$ 38.00								
7											
8		Min.			Unit		Annual	Annual	Annual	Total	
9	Discount	Order		Unit	Holding	Order	Holding	Ordering	Purchase	Annual	
10	Category	Size	Discount	Cost	Cost	Quantity	Cost	Cost	Cost	Cost	
11	1	-	0%	$12.00	$ 2.16	918.94	$ 992	$ 992	$ 288,000	$ 289,985	
12	2	4,000	3%	$11.64	$ 2.10	4000	$ 4,190	$ 228	$ 279,360	$ 283,778	
13	3	12,000	5%	$11.40	$ 2.05	12000	$ 12,312	$ 76	$ 273,600	$ 285,988	
14											
15	Note: All costs are rounded to nearest dollar										
16											

result in a 5-percent discount, its excessive inventory-holding cost prevents it from being the best decision.

Note that the sum of the inventory and ordering costs with $Q^* = 4,000$ is $4,190.40 + 228.00 = $4,418.40$. This portion of the total cost is substantially more than the $1,984.90 cost associated with the 919-unit order size. In effect, the quantity-discount savings of 3 percent per unit is so great that we are willing to operate the inventory system with a substantially higher inventory level and substantially higher inventory-holding cost. Provided space is available to handle larger inventories, purchasing in larger quantities to obtain discounts is economically sound.

An Alternate Solution Method

An alternate, more direct procedure for finding the optimal solution to quantity-discount models was suggested by Professor S. K. Goyal of Concordia University.[1] It can be described as follows. Let C_k be the unit cost and Q_k be the minimum order quantity for discount category k, for $k = 1, 2, \ldots n$.
Step 1. Compute

$$C^* = \frac{1}{D}\left[\frac{Q_n}{2}iC_n + \frac{D}{Q_n}C_o + DC_n - \sqrt{2DC_oiC_n}\right] \quad (14.17)$$

Step 2. For each purchase price C_k less than C^* compute the total annual cost using equation 14.16 at order quantities given by the larger of

$$Q_k$$

and

$$\sqrt{\frac{2DC_o}{iC_k}}$$

Step 3. Compare all the total annual costs obtained in step 2. The order quantity that provides the lowest total annual cost is the optimal order quantity.

An example using Goyal's method follows.

Example

Determining the Optimal Order Quantity with Goyal's Method

We will solve the Holton Drug Company example by using this approach. First compute C^* using equation 14.17:

$$C^* = \frac{1}{24,000}\left[\frac{12,000}{2}(.18)(11.40) + \frac{24,000}{12,000}(38) + 24,000(11.40)\right.$$

$$\left. - \sqrt{2(24,000)(38)(.18)(11.40)}\right] = \$11.83.$$

Next, consider all prices less than $11.83. Note that we need not consider discount category 1 since $12.00 is greater than $11.83. For category $k=2$, we use Q = larger of 4,000 and

$$\sqrt{\frac{2(24,000)(38)}{.18(11.64)}} = 933,$$

or 4,000. Total cost is

$$\frac{4,000}{2}(.18)(11.64) + \frac{24,000}{4000}(38) + 24,000(11.64) = \$283,778.40.$$

For category $k=3$, we use $Q = $ larger of 12,000 and

$$\sqrt{\frac{2(24,000)(38)}{.18(11.40)}} = 943,$$

or 12,000. Total cost is

$$\frac{12,000}{2}(.18)(11.40) + \frac{24,000}{12,000}(38) + 24,000(11.40) = \$285,988.00.$$

The smallest total annual cost occurs for $k = 2$, the 4,000-unit order quantity.

Lot Sizing for Dynamic Demand

A fundamental assumption behind the EOQ model is that demand is constant over time. In many situations, such as when demand is seasonal or when orders are placed intermittently, that assumption is unrealistic. In this section we introduce some techniques for dealing with dynamic (changing) demand. Usually demand is given in discrete time periods, such as in weeks. The goal of lot sizing is to determine a schedule (i.e., how much and when to order) that will minimize total cost.

Suppose the ordering cost for a particular item is $150 and that it costs $1 per unit per week to store the item in inventory, charged at the end of the week. The forecast of demand follows.

Week	1	2	3	4	5	6	7	8	9	10	11	12
Requirement	20	20	30	40	140	360	500	540	460	80	0	20

We can use the economic order quantity to establish an ordering schedule. The average weekly demand is $(20 + 20 + 30 + \ldots + 0 + 20)/12 = 184.2$. Hence the EOQ is

$$Q^* = \sqrt{2DC_o / C_h} = \sqrt{\frac{2(184.2)(150)}{1}} = 235.$$

We order 235 units to be available in week 1; this will satisfy demand through week 4 but not through week 5. Continuing in this fashion we arrive at the following schedule.

Week	1	2	3	4	5	6	7	8	9	10	11	12
Demand	20	20	30	40	140	360	500	540	460	80	0	20
Orders	235				235	235	405	540	460	235		
Ending inventory	215	195	165	125	220	95	0	0	0	155	155	135

Note that the order quantity must be increased when demand plus the previous week's inventory exceeds the lot size (as occurs in week 7). Of course, additional orders of 235 could be placed earlier to cover this demand, but that would only increase the ordering and holding costs.

Seven orders are placed over this 12-week horizon, and the total end-of-week inventory is $(215 + 195 + \ldots + 135) = 1{,}460$ units. Thus, the total cost of this policy is

$$
\begin{array}{rl}
\text{7 orders at \$150 per order} = & \$1{,}050 \\
\text{1,460 units at \$1/week} = & \underline{1{,}460} \\
& \$2{,}510
\end{array}
$$

Larger inventory-carrying costs than necessary are incurred because of the mismatch between the order quantity and the demand, causing excess inventory to be carried week to week. We now present three alternate methods that overcome some of the difficulties associated with the EOQ approach.

Periodic-Order Quantity

The **periodic-order-quantity method** is very simple. The economic order quantity is divided by the average demand to yield an *economic time interval* between orders. Orders are placed at these intervals for all known future demands. Since the economic order quantity is 235, the economic time interval is $235/184.2 = 1.3$, or every one to two weeks. With 2-week intervals, orders would be planned as follows:

Week	1	2	3	4	5	6	7	8	9	10	11	12
Demand	20	20	30	40	140	360	500	540	460	80	0	20
Orders	40		70		500		1040		540			20
Ending inventory	20	0	40	0	360	0	540	0	80	0	0	0

Essentially, we would order to satisfy the next two weeks' demand. The total ordering cost is $900 (6 orders × $150), and holding cost is $1,040, for a total cost of $1,940 over the 12-week horizon. This is a $570 improvement over the EOQ-based policy. Check for yourself to see that the total cost of a one-week periodic-order-quantity policy would be $1,650.

Part-Period Balancing

Recall that for the EOQ model, the total ordering cost equals the total holding cost for Q^*. The **part-period-balancing method** uses this fact in attempting to balance these costs for dynamic demand. Using the data just given, let us determine how much to order at the beginning of the time horizon. We assume that all orders are multiples of weekly requirements. Thus initially we can order 20 units, 40 units (first two weeks' demand), 70 units (first three weeks' demand), and so on. Since each order costs $150, we try to order the amount for which holding costs come closest to $150. Suppose we order 20 units, the first week's demand. Since there would be no ending inventory, the holding cost would be zero.

Next, consider ordering 40 units (two weeks' demand). The ending inventory in week 1 would be 20. At a carrying cost of $1 per unit per week, the total holding cost would be $20. Similarly, ordering 70 units would result in ending inventories of 50 and 30 in weeks 1 and 2, respectively, and a holding cost of $50(1) + 30(1) = \$80$. We still have not matched the ordering cost of $150, so we consider the first four weeks of demand. If we order 110 units, the holding cost would be $90(1) + 70(1) + 40(1) = \$200$. This is the closest value to the ordering cost of $150; thus we order 110 units initially. This covers the first four weeks. To determine the scheduled receipts in week 5 we repeat this procedure, beginning with the demand for week 5, weeks 5 and 6, and so on. You should verify that part-period balancing yields this solution with a total cost of $1,240:

Week	1	2	3	4	5	6	7	8	9	10	11	12
Demand	20	20	30	40	140	360	500	540	460	80	0	20
Orders	110				140	360	500	540	560			
Ending inventory	90	70	40	0	0	0	0	0	100	20	20	0

Silver-Meal Heuristic

A method that is both computationally efficient and effective in terms of providing very good solutions with dynamic demand was developed by Edward Silver and Harlan Meal.[2] The **Silver-Meal method** is similar to part-period balancing in that we consider ordering one period's demand, then two period's demand, and so on, stopping when the *average cost* per period exceeds that of the previous period. This is best illustrated by using the same problem with which we have been working.

First, consider ordering only enough to satisfy demand in the first week. There is no holding cost, so the total cost is simply the ordering cost, $150. If we order for the first two weeks, the total cost is computed by adding any holding costs to the ordering cost. The ordering cost is $150, and we must carry the second week's demand of 20 units for one period at a cost of $1 per unit per week, or $20. Thus the total cost is $170. The *average cost per week* is $170/2 = \$85$. This is *less* than the average cost incurred if we order only one week's demand, which is $150. Therefore we continue, considering ordering for the first three weeks.

The total cost for ordering three weeks' demand, or 70 units, is $150 + 50(1)$ $+ 30(1) = \$230$. Thus the average cost per week is $\$230/3 = \$76.67$, which is less than that of the previous week, $85. Again we continue. If we order 110 units, or four weeks' demand, the average cost is

$$\frac{150 + 90(1) + 70(1) + 40(1)}{4} = \$87.50.$$

This now is *greater* than the average cost for the first three weeks, so we stop and order 70 units, or three weeks' demand. Notice that once we find that the average cost for ordering a given number of weeks' demand exceeds that of the previous week, we order enough to fill the demand up to the *previous* week, not to the week currently under consideration.

Next, we move the time horizon to week 4 and begin the procedure again. If we order only to fill the demand for week 4, the cost is $150. If we consider the demand for weeks 4 and 5, the average cost per week is

$$\frac{150 + 140(1)}{2} = \$145$$

which is less than $150, so we continue. Ordering for weeks 4, 5, and 6 gives an average cost of $336.67, which is greater than $145. Therefore, in week 4 we order the demand for weeks 4 and 5, or 180 units.

The complete solution to the example problem using the Silver-Meal heuristic is given in the table that follows. You should verify this solution for weeks 6 through 12. The total cost is $1,260.

Week	1	2	3	4	5	6	7	8	9	10	11	12
Demand	20	20	30	40	140	360	500	540	460	80	0	20
Orders	70			180		360	500	540	560			
Ending inventory	50	30	0	140	0	0	0	0	100	20	20	0

Many other lot-sizing methods have been developed. One method that gives the true minimum total cost is the **Wagner-Whitin algorithm,** which implicitly evaluates all possible ways of ordering to meet the demand at minimum total cost. However, it is somewhat more complicated than the other methods we have discussed and is rather time-consuming to perform by hand, though extremely easy to implement on a computer.[3] The optimal solution to the example problem found by the Wagner-Whitin algorithm turns out to be the same one that was found by the part-period-balancing procedure. This is merely a coincidence; in general, part-period balancing will not produce the minimum-cost solution.

A study by the author and others compared EOQ, part-period balancing, and Silver-Meal heuristics with the Wagner-Whitin algorithm. The results showed that EOQ was more than 30 percent higher than the minimum-cost schedule; part-period balancing, about 7 percent higher; and Silver-Meal, only about 2 percent higher. In addition, the Silver-Meal heuristic was the fastest in terms of computer time.

Single-Period Inventory Model

In our previous treatment of inventory problems we assumed that the inventory system operates continuously and that there are many repeating cycles, or periods. Furthermore, we assumed that the inventory may be carried for one or more repeat periods and that we will place repeat orders for the product in the future. The **single-period inventory model,** on the other hand, applies to inventory situations in which *one* order is placed for the product. At the end of the period the product has either sold out, or there is a surplus of unsold items to sell for a salvage value. Single-period models are used in situations involving seasonal or perishable items that cannot be carried in inventory and sold in future periods. One example would be ordering pizza dough for Mama Mia's, which stays fresh for only three and one-half days. Other examples include seasonal clothing such as bathing suits and winter coats and daily newspapers. In such a single-period inventory situation, the only inventory decision is *how much* of the product to order at the start of the period. Because newspaper sales is an excellent example of the single-period situation, the single-period inventory problem is sometimes referred to as the *newsboy problem.*

Obviously, if the demand were known for a single period, the solution would be easy: we would simply order the amount we knew would be demanded. However, in most single-period cases the exact demand is not known and may vary widely. If we are going to analyze this type of inventory-decision problem quantitatively, we will need information about the probabilities of the various demand possibilities. So the single-period model is another type of stochastic demand model.

Let us show how *marginal analysis* can be used to determine the optimal order quantity for a single-period inventory situation. Marginal analysis addresses the how-much-to-order question by comparing the cost or loss of ordering one additional unit with the cost or loss of not ordering one additional unit. The costs involved are defined as

c_o = the cost per unit of *overestimating* demand; this cost represents the loss of ordering one additional unit and finding that it cannot be sold.

c_u = the cost per unit of *underestimating* demand; this cost represents the opportunity loss of not ordering one additional unit and finding that it could have been sold.

The following example shows that the optimal order quantity (Q^*) satisfies the expression:

$$P(\text{demand} \leq Q^*) = \frac{c_u}{c_u + c_o}. \tag{14.18}$$

Example

Determining the Optimal Single-Period Order Quantity

Let us consider a single-period inventory model that could be used to make an ordering decision for the Johnson Shoe Company. The buyer for the company has decided to order a summer-weight casual shoe for men that has just been

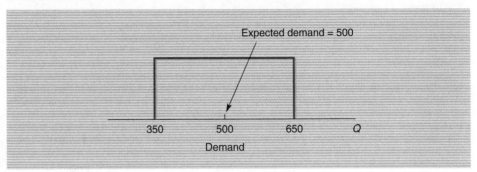

Figure 14.4 Uniform Probability Distribution of Demand for Johnson Shoe Company Size 10D Shoes

shown at a buyers' show in New York City. Johnson plans to hold a special August clearance sale in an attempt to sell all shoes that have not been sold by July 31. The shoes cost $40 per pair and retail for $60 per pair. At the sale price of $30 per pair, it is expected that all surplus shoes can be sold during the August sale. Let us suppose that the uniform probability distribution shown in Figure 14.4 describes the demand for the size 10D shoes. Note that the range of demand is from 350 to 650 pairs of shoes and that the average or expected demand is 500 pairs.

The Johnson Shoe Company will incur the cost of overestimating demand whenever it orders too much and has to sell the extra shoes during the August sale. Thus the cost per unit of overestimating demand is equal to the purchase cost per unit minus the August sale price per unit; that is, $c_o = \$40 - \$30 = \$10$. In other words, Johnson will lose $10 for each pair of shoes that it orders over the quantity demanded. The cost of underestimating demand is the lost profit (opportunity loss) due to the fact that a pair of shoes that could have been sold was not available in inventory. Thus the per-unit cost of underestimating demand is the difference between the regular selling price per unit and the purchase cost per unit; that is, $c_u = \$60 - \$40 = \$20$. Equation 14.18 shows that the optimal order size for Johnson shoes must satisfy this condition:

$$P(\text{demand} \le Q^*) = \frac{c_u}{c_u + c_o} = \frac{20}{20 + 10} = \frac{20}{30} = \frac{2}{3}.$$

We can find the optimal order quantity, Q^*, by referring to the assumed probability distribution in Figure 14.4 and finding the value of Q that will provide $P(\text{demand} \le Q^*) = {}^2/_3$. To do this, we note that in the uniform distribution the probability is evenly distributed over the range from 350 to 650 pairs of shoes. Thus we can satisfy the expression for Q^* by moving two-thirds of the way from 350 to 650. Since this is a range of $650 - 350 = 300$, we move 200 units from 350 toward 650. Doing so provides the optimal order quantity of 550 pairs of size 10D shoes.

We note that in Equation 14.18 the value of $c_u/(c_u + c_o)$ will be equal to 0.50 whenever $c_u = c_o$; in this case we select an order quantity corresponding to the median of the probability distribution of demand. With this choice it is just as likely to have a stockout as a surplus. This makes sense, since the costs are

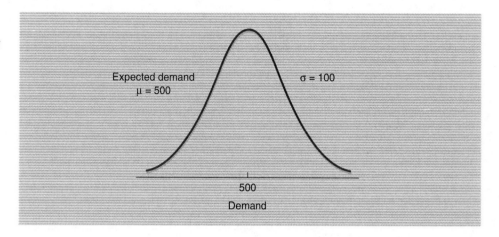

equal. Whenever $c_u < c_o$, Equation 14.18 leads to the choice of an order quantity more likely to be less than demand; hence a higher risk of a stockout is present. However, for the Johnson Shoe example, $c_u > c_o$, and the optimal order quantity leads to a higher risk of a surplus. This can be seen from the fact that the order quantity is 50 pairs of shoes over the expected demand of 500 pairs of shoes. Thus the optimal order quantity for Johnson has a probability of a stockout of one-third and a probability of a surplus of two-thirds. This is what we should have expected, since $c_u = 20$ is greater than $c_o = 10$.

In the Johnson Shoe Company example a uniform probability distribution was used to describe the demand for the size 10D shoes. However, any probability distribution of demand can be used for the single-period inventory model. Using the cost of overestimation and underestimation, Equation 14.18 can be used to find the location of Q^* in any appropriate demand probability distribution. For example, suppose a normal probability distribution with a mean of 500 and a standard deviation of 100 had been a better description of the demand distribution for the size 10D shoes. This probability distribution is shown in Figure 14.5. With $c_u = \$20$ and $c_o = \$10$ as previously computed, equation 14.18 still shows that the optimal order quantity, Q^*, must satisfy the requirement that $P(\text{demand} \leq Q^*) = {}^2/_3$. We simply use the table of areas under the normal curve to find the Q^* where this condition is satisfied.

Figure 14.6
Probability Distribution of
Demand for Johnson Shoe
Company Showing
Location of Optimal Order
Quantity, Q^*

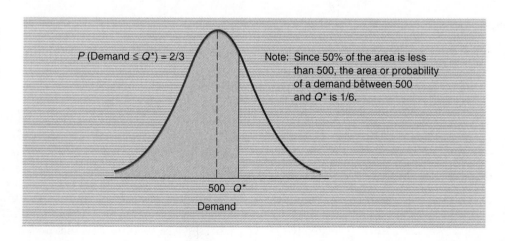

Referring to Figure 14.6, $P(\text{demand} \leq Q^*) = {}^2/_3$ requires a 0.1667 area, or probability, between the mean demand of 500 and the optimal order quantity, Q^*. From Appendix B we see that the 0.1667 area under the normal curve occurs at $z = 0.43$ standard deviation above the mean. With the mean, or expected demand, given by $\mu = 500$ and the standard deviation given by $\sigma = 100$, we have

$$Q^* = \mu + .1667\sigma = 500 + .43(100) = 543.$$

Thus, with the assumed normal probability of demand, Johnson should order 543 pairs of the size 10D shoes in anticipation of customer orders.

Simulation Models for Inventory Analysis

So far in this chapter, we have concentrated on analytical inventory-decision models. But what should you do when the characteristics of an inventory system do not appear to agree with the assumptions of any inventory decision model? In this case, there are two alternatives: (1) attempt to develop and use a specially designed decision model that correctly reflects the characteristics of the system of (2) attempt to develop and experiment with a computer simulation model that will indicate the impact of various decision alternatives on the cost of operating the system. Computer simulation (reviewed in Supplementary Chapter A) is an important decision-analysis tool because it has the flexibility to model unique features of the system that are difficult to represent in purely mathematical terms. In this section we demonstrate the use of simulation in making inventory-policy decisions.

Sound Systems, Inc., is a retail firm that carries high-quality audio equipment, including a well-known stereo radio system for automobiles. Demand for the stereos is subject to variability, and it has been very difficult to anticipate when and how much the demand for the product will be. On approximately half the days when the store is open no one orders a stereo system. However, about one day per month, three or even four orders may occur. If variable demand were the only source of uncertainty, the order quantity and reorder-point decision could be based on a single-period inventory model like the one presented earlier in the chapter. However, the auto stereo system inventory problem is further complicated by the fact that the lead time varies between one and five days. These lead times have caused the store to run out of inventory on several occasions, which has resulted in back orders.

After an analysis of delivery charges and other costs associated with each order, the store manager estimated an order cost of $40 per order. An analysis of interest, insurance, and other costs of carrying inventory led to an estimate for the holding cost of $.20 per unit per day. Finally, the shortage cost was estimated to be $100 per unit. The total cost of the system is given by the sum of the ordering cost, the holding cost, and the shortage cost. The objective is to find the combination of order quantity and reorder point that will result in the lowest possible total cost.

A first step in the simulation approach to this inventory problem is to develop a model that can be used to simulate the total cost corresponding to a specific order size and reorder point. Then, using this model, the two decision variables can be varied systematically to determine what appears to be the low-est-cost combination. Let us see what is involved in developing such a model to carry out a one-day simulation of the inventory process.

One-Day Simulation. This is a continuous-review inventory system with back orders as described in Chapter 13. Assume that a specific reorder point and order quantity have been selected. We must begin each day of the simulation by checking whether any ordered inventory has arrived. If so, the current inventory on hand must be increased by the quantity of goods received. Note that this assumes that orders are received and inventory on hand is updated at the start of each day. If this assumption is not appropriate, a different model, perhaps calling for goods to be received at the end of the day, would have to be developed.

Next, our simulator must generate a value for the daily demand from the appropriate probability distribution. If there is sufficient inventory on hand to meet the daily demand, the stock level will be decreased by the amount of the daily demand. In addition, the inventory position (inventory on hand plus on order minus back orders) is also decreased by the daily demand. If, however, inventory on hand is not sufficient to satisfy all the demand, we will satisfy as much of the demand as possible. Any unsatisfied demand will result in a back order, for which we compute a shortage cost.

After the daily order has been processed by the simulator, the next step is to determine if the inventory position has reached the reorder point and a new order should be placed. If an order is placed, the company incurs an ordering cost and a lead time must be randomly generated to reflect the time between the order placement and the receipt of the goods.

Finally, an inventory-holding cost—20 cents for each unit in the daily ending inventory—is computed. The sum of the shortage costs, ordering costs, and inventory-holding costs becomes the total daily cost for the simulation. Performing the above sequence of operations would complete one day of the simulation. Figure 14.7 depicts this daily simulation process for the auto stereo system operation.

The daily simulation process should be repeated for as many days as necessary to obtain meaningful results. The output from the simulation will show the total cost involved in using one particular order quantity and reorder point combination.

Suppose the store has a complete set of records showing the demand for the auto stereos for the past year (300 days). Furthermore, suppose the records also show the number of days between placement and receipt of each order over the same period. Table 14.2 shows the frequency and relative frequency distributions for the store's demand and lead-time data.

To carry out the simulation steps depicted in Figure 14.7, we must develop a procedure for generating values from the demand and lead-time distributions. As described in Supplementary Chapter A, we associate with each value of the random variable an interval of pseudorandom numbers such that the probability of generating a pseudorandom number in that interval is the same as the relative frequency of the associated demand and lead time. The intervals of pseudorandom numbers are shown in columns A through D of the spreadsheet in Figure 14.8.

Spreadsheet Simulation. Columns F through T in Figure 14.8 show the remainder of an Excel implementation for this inventory simulation. It generally fol-

Figure 14.7
Flowchart of Simulation of
One Day's Operation for the
Sound Systems Stereo
Inventory

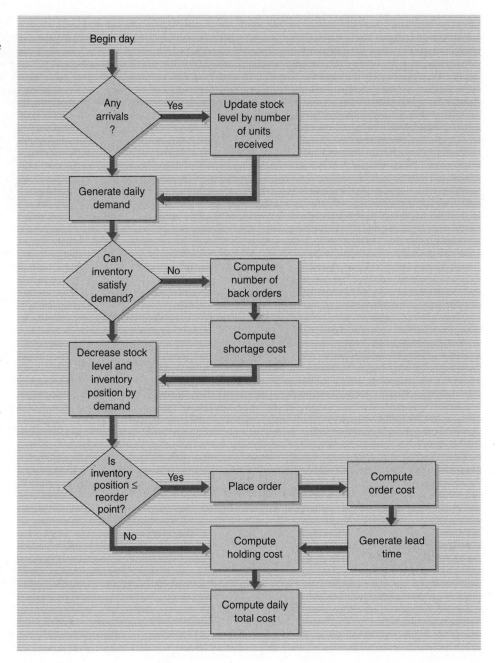

lows the flowchart in Figure 14.7. Initial values of the order quantity, reorder point,
initial inventory, and cost data are provided in the first four rows of columns E
through M. Cell R4 computes the average daily cost over the 20 days of the simulation. To understand how it works, we will step through a few days of the process.

At the start of day 1, five units are in inventory and no orders arrive (thus,
the inventory position is also five). A pseudorandom number, 0.812, is generated by using the RAND function; this corresponds to a daily demand of two
units and an ending inventory and inventory position of three. Since the inventory position is equal to the reorder point, an order is placed. The inventory position now increases by the amount of the order. A pseudorandom number is

Table 14.2 Frequency and Relative Frequency Distributions for Demand and Lead Time in Sound Systems Problem

| | Demand | | | | Lead Time | | |
	Units	Relative Frequency	Frequency	Days	Relative Frequency	Frequency
	0	150	.50	1	6	.20
	1	75	.25	2	3	.10
	2	45	.15	3	12	.40
	3	15	.05	4	6	.20
	4	15	.05	5	3	.10
		300	1.00		30	1.00

generated for the lead time, indicating that an order will arrive the following day. Total daily cost consists of holding three units at a unit cost of $0.20 and a $40 order cost. At the start of the second day, an order of five units is received and demand is found to be four. Thus the ending inventory is $3 + 5 - 4 = 4$ units. Since this is greater than the reorder point, no new order is placed. Costs consist only of the holding cost.

Next, skip to day 9. The demand of four units depletes the inventory on hand. An order is placed, due to arrive two days later. The inventory position is equal to the stock level (zero) plus on order (five) minus back orders (zero). On day 10, a demand of two results in two units back ordered. The inventory position is decreased by two $(5 - 2 = 3)$ and now equals the reorder point. Another order is placed (the one on day 9 has not yet arrived), and will also arrive on day

Figure 14.8 Spreadsheet Implementation of Sound Systems Inventory Simulation (INVSIM.XLS)

	A	B	C	D	E	F	G	H	I	J	K	L	M	N	O	P	Q	R	S	T
1	Sound Systems Inventory Simulation																			
2					Order Quantity			5		Order Cost			$ 40							
3	Demand Distribution				Reorder Point			3		Holding Cost			$ 0.20							
4					Initial Inventory			5		Back Order Cost			$ 100		Average cost/day			$ 27.65		
5	Random Number Range		Demand																	
6	0.00	0.50	0																	
7	0.50	0.75	1			Beg	Order	Units			End	Back	Order	Inv		Lead	Hold	Order	Short	Total
8	0.75	0.90	2		Day	Inv	Rec'd	Rec'd	R.N.	Dmd	Inv	Order	Placed?	Pos	R.N.	time	Cost	Cost	Cost	Cost
9	0.90	0.95	3		1	5		0	0.812	2	3	0	YES	8	0.057	1	$ 0.60	$ 40.00	$ -	$ 40.60
10	0.95	1.00	4		2	3	YES	5	0.977	4	4	0	NO	4			$ 0.80	$ -	$ -	$ 0.80
11					3	4		0	0.618	1	3	0	YES	8	0.828	4	$ 0.60	$ 40.00	$ -	$ 40.60
12	Lead Time Distribution				4	3		0	0.266	0	3	0	NO	8			$ 0.60	$ -	$ -	$ 0.60
13					5	3		0	0.348	0	3	0	NO	8			$ 0.60	$ -	$ -	$ 0.60
14	Random Number Range		Lead Time		6	3		0	0.410	0	3	0	NO	8			$ 0.60	$ -	$ -	$ 0.60
15	0.00	0.20	1		7	3	YES	5	0.913	3	5	0	NO	5			$ 1.00	$ -	$ -	$ 1.00
16	0.20	0.30	2		8	5		0	0.614	1	4	0	NO	4			$ 0.80	$ -	$ -	$ 0.80
17	0.30	0.70	3		9	4		0	0.953	4	0	0	YES	5	0.266	2	$ -	$ 40.00	$ -	$ 40.00
18	0.70	0.90	4		10	0		0	0.762	2	-2	2	YES	8	0.156	1	$ -	$ 40.00	$ 200.00	$ 240.00
19	0.90	1.00	5		11	-2	YES	10	0.080	0	8	0	NO	8			$ 1.60	$ -	$ -	$ 1.60
20					12	8		0	0.106	0	8	0	NO	8			$ 1.60	$ -	$ -	$ 1.60
21					13	8		0	0.628	1	7	0	NO	7			$ 1.40	$ -	$ -	$ 1.40
22					14	7		0	0.901	3	4	0	NO	4			$ 0.80	$ -	$ -	$ 0.80
23					15	4		0	0.990	4	0	0	YES	5	0.459	3	$ -	$ 40.00	$ -	$ 40.00
24					16	0		0	0.597	1	-1	1	NO	4			$ -	$ -	$ 100.00	$ 100.00
25					17	-1		0	0.496	0	-1	0	NO	4			$ -	$ -	$ -	$ -
26					18	-1	YES	5	0.176	0	4	0	NO	4			$ 0.80	$ -	$ -	$ 0.80
27					19	4		0	0.609	1	3	0	YES	8	0.642	3	$ 0.60	$ 40.00	$ -	$ 40.60
28					20	3		0	0.300	0	3	0	NO	8			$ 0.60	$ -	$ -	$ 0.60
29																				

Table 14.3 Simulated Average Daily Costs for Sound Systems

Reorder Point	Reorder Quantity			
	5	*15*	*25*	*35*
3	16.30	8.45	5.50	5.98
5	11.44	5.90	5.63	5.61
7	9.57	5.16	5.15	5.73
10	9.51	5.62	5.75	6.21

11. This brings the inventory position back up to eight units. On day 11, both orders arrive (10 units) and no units are demanded. After satisfying the two accumulated back orders, the ending inventory is eight. At this point, the inventory position is the stock level (eight) plus on order (zero, since the orders have arrived) minus back orders (zero, since they have been satisfied), or eight units. From this discussion, you should be able to follow the remaining logic and calculations in the spreadsheet.

In designing the spreadsheet, the daily demand in column J is determined by using the random number generated in column I and the VLOOKUP function over the range A6 through D10 in Figure 14.8. Note that the inventory level (column K) is allowed to go negative, denoting the accumulated number of back orders. The process by which orders are received after the proper lead time is best understood by studying the cell formulas in the spreadsheet itself, which your instructor can provide, because it depends on using combinations of logical IF, AND, and OR functions in Excel.

Prior to drawing any conclusions based on these limited simulation results, we should run the simulation for many more days, and test other order quantity–reorder point combinations.

The spreadsheet in Figure 14.8 was expanded to simulate the inventory system for 500 days. Table 14.3 shows the average of five independent runs of this 500-day simulation for various combinations of the order quantity and reorder point. We see that the results indicate that low-cost values are in the range of a reorder point of seven and reorder quantity of about 15 to 25. To pinpoint a better solution, we might explore a finer grid of combinations around these values, for instance, reorder points of six, seven, and eight and reorder quantities between 10 and 30. We leave this to you as a problem at the end of this chapter. Simulation cannot guarantee an optimal solution, but can help to identify near-optimal solutions for similar inventory management problems.

P/OM in Practice

Applications of Inventory Models at Pfizer Pharmaceuticals[4]

Pfizer Pharmaceuticals is a vertically integrated company that manufactures many chemicals used in its finished products. The company operates in 65 countries in five major fields: agriculture, specialty chemicals, materials science, consumer products, and health care (whose pharmaceutical segment accounts for more than 50 percent of the company's sales). In the early 1980s, the combination of high interest rates, rapid growth of the pharmaceutical business, and historically high inventories dictated a more focused approach to managing inventory. Divisional management embarked on a program to (1) control and improve inventory turnover, (2) understand and manage the forces behind the swings in inventory levels, and (3) improve the accuracy of dollar inventory forecasts and thus improve cash-flow projections.

The initial step in the program was a comprehensive analysis of the inventory-management function as it presently existed. It revealed these problems and opportunities:

1. The lack of an accurate and adequately detailed database to support the analysis and monitoring of inventory performance was confusing the management process.

2. Responsibility for inventory management was assigned to several organizations. Raw materials and work-in-process (WIP) inventories were managed at the local plant level, while finished-goods inventories were managed and planned by the headquarters production-planning and inventory-control (PPIC) function.

3. Inventories were not part of the performance evaluation objectives at the plant level.

4. Inventory data were highly aggregated and did not allow meaningful trend analysis or an understanding of how management intervention affected inventories.

5. Methods for inventory management were not consistent among the different plants.

6. The methods used in inventory management were not "state-of-the-art."

7. Inventory forecasting was manual, time-consuming, inaccurate, and not routine.

8. The impact of the operating differences between the dosage and organic-synthesis phases of production on inventory management was not clearly understood.

9. Inconsistent definition of the different classes of inventories among plants (what belongs in finished goods, WIP, raw materials, and so forth) prevented meaningful interplant comparisons.

10. The quantitative impact of capacity constraints, degree of vertical integration, and product mix on inventory was not fully understood, which resulted in inaccurate and counterproductive comparisons between plants and divisions within the company.

The second phase was to develop a plan of action to propose to senior managers. This plan was summarized as follows:

1. A centralized function for divisional inventory management was needed to assure that appropriate, up-to-date management techniques were developed and applied consistently across the divisional locations.

2. Major inventory categories (such as finished goods, WIP, purchased materials, and so forth) needed to be defined accurately, and inventory data reported consistently throughout the divisions. This required changes in the divisional inventory accounting and reporting systems.

3. Management-science models specifically tailored to the operational needs of dosage and synthesis plants needed to be created.

4. Inventories would become part of the objectives in overall performance evaluation at the plant level. This would require a functional reporting system and the definition of quantitative targets against which performance could be measured. These objectives would be set using the output of the models.

5. A computer-based inventory-forecasting system would be designed and implemented to improve the speed and accuracy of all inventory forecasts.

The third phase of the project was to develop detailed inventory models to use in the system. Inventory models had to meet several criteria:

1. Output from the models would become the quantitative objective of a performance-measurement system.

2. Since local managers would have to agree to the objectives, the models needed to be intuitively understandable.

3. Since the new methods were to be phased in over a short period of time, they had to be easy to implement, especially in data processing and programming.

4. All models had to be cost-effective; that is, the expected cost savings

in inventory investment had to be greater than the cost of model design and implementation.

Detailed models and techniques were designed and introduced for these applications:

- Finished-goods lot sizes and safety stocks
- Target WIP inventories in the dosage plants
- Organic-synthesis "campaign sizes" (run quantities) in the chemical plants
- Organic-synthesis safety stocks
- Inventory forecasting
- Purchased-materials inventory strategies

The full implementation of the new inventory-management program depended on organizational changes and top-management support.

1. The PPIC organization was restructured to emphasize the increased focus on inventories. The position of inventory manager was created to provide centralized expertise and to develop state-of-the-art management techniques.
2. A control system was designed that used the output of the models as control parameters. In addition, a reporting system was instituted to track inventory performance, to maintain program visibility, and to identify opportunities for reducing inventory.
3. Routine communication of performance and standards of performance was crucial to successful implementation of the program. Individual targets for each of the major inventory categories at each plant were agreed upon in advance with local managers, ensur-

ing that all principals in the organization understood and accepted the objectives. Acceptance of the inventory program was not immediate, particularly because of its innovative nature and the initial concern about headquarters becoming more involved in plant matters. As with all such programs, strong commitment from senior managers was a must. During development, the PPIC group used this commitment and numerous formal presentations to keep the program visible and to encourage local organizations as progress was made. With this approach, the inventory-management program became a cooperative venture between headquarters and plant managers. This ensured a broad base of support, sustained commitment, and ultimately a successful program.

The full design and implementation took only 1.5 worker-years over a period of three calendar years. Several student interns programmed the models, and the full expense for the program totaled less than $100,000.

The main impact was in inventory reductions in the following areas: finished-goods lot sizes, $2.9 million; finished-goods safety stocks, $5.9 million; purchased materials, $5.8 million; organic-synthesis safety stocks, $5.1 million; organic-synthesis campaign sizes, $2.1 million; and dosage WIP, $2.1 million; for a total of $23.9 million in inventory reductions.

The positive cash-flow benefit of $23.9 million results in a permanent savings in interest and insurance expenses of $3.6 million per year, estimated at an average, conservative carrying cost of 15 percent. The drop in inventory levels alone resulted in a significant increase in the return on investment for the U.S. pharmaceutical

group. Further opportunities for reduction of $7.9 million were formally included in the 1984 pharmaceutical operating plan.

The increased emphasis on inventory management was extended to other PPIC areas, which led to some unexpected positive results in customer service, particularly a dramatic decrease in weekly national back orders, from an average of $778,000 in 1980 to $31,000 in 1983. In 1983 customer service jumped to an unprecedented 99.98 percent, a record high for the division and at the leading edge of performance within the U.S. pharmaceutical industry as reported in surveys issued by the industry's trade association. Although the positive impact of decreased back orders was difficult to quantify, it was estimated internally that 10 percent of back orders resulted in lost sales. By comparing the difference in weekly back orders between 1980 and 1983 and assuming a 10 percent lost-sales rate, the company estimated increases in sales at $3.8 million per year.

The introduction of the finished-goods model triggered a series of schedule policy changes for high-volume products. They came to be campaigned under an optimal policy that reduced total setup costs and increased equipment efficiency and productivity. The impact of these policy changes was a reduction in annual setup costs of $250,000.

Finally, as a result of the improved product supplies, total freight costs were reduced by $280,000 per year: air shipments, formerly needed to avoid stockouts in branch warehouses, were needed to a lesser extent. These savings were estimated by comparing direct freight billings and were not adjusted to reflect the fact that shipping volumes doubled over a period of three years.

The total annual savings directly attributable to the inventory-management program were as follows.

Inventory-carrying costs	$3,600,000
Increased sales	3,800,000

Savings in setup costs	250,000
Reduced freight costs	280,000
	$7,930,000

Questions for Discussion

1. What were some of the problems and difficulties of Pfizer that led to consideration of using inventory models?

2. List some of the benefits resulting from the use of inventory models.

Summary of Key Points

••• In many inventory situations a shortage, or stockout, may be desirable economically, particularly when the inventory-holding cost is high. In a back-order situation, customers will wait for items that are out of stock. An extension of the EOQ model can be developed to find the optimal order quantity and back-order level for minimizing total costs.

••• The economic production lot size is an extension of the EOQ model in which the order quantity is produced gradually over a period of time instead of being delivered all at once.

••• Quantity discounts are offered by suppliers to provide an incentive for large purchase quantities. The optimal order quantity can be calculated by using a simple procedure involving the economic order quantity (EOQ).

••• In situations in which demand varies over discrete time periods, the assumptions of the EOQ model are violated. Alternative methods for determining an ordering schedule include the periodic-order quantity, part-period balancing, and the Silver-Meal heuristic.

••• Single-period inventory models apply to situations in which only one order is placed for an item. At the end of the period, either the product has sold out or there is a surplus of unsold items that must be sold for a salvage value. Seasonal items usually are in this category. The optimal order quantity is found through marginal analysis, which attempts to balance the cost of overestimating demand with the cost of underestimating demand.

••• Simulation models are useful for analyzing inventory systems with probabilistic demand. They allow operations managers to study the effects of changing assumptions in the model and to search for near-optimal solutions.

Key Terms

Production lot-size model
Quantity discount
Periodic-order-quantity method
Part-period-balancing method
Silver-Meal method
Wagner-Whitin algorithm
Single-period inventory model

Review Questions

1. What types of costs are associated with back orders?
2. How does the economic production lot-size model differ from the EOQ model?
3. Describe the general procedure for finding optimal order quantities using the quantity-discount inventory model.
4. What are some of the problems associated with using EOQ for determining lot sizes with dynamic demand?
5. Describe the periodic-order-quantity approach to lot sizing.
6. Describe the method of part-period balancing.
7. Describe the Silver-Meal approach to dynamic lot sizing.
8. Explain the approach used to solve the newsboy problem.
9. Explain how simulation can be used to analyze inventory problems.

Discussion Questions

1. Give some examples, different from those in the text, of when planned shortages might be beneficial.
2. How should a company balance economic and customer-service objectives when using the planned-shortage model?

3. Discuss how C_b might be estimated in practice. Is it an accounting value or a judgmental value?

4. Discuss some disadvantages that a firm might face when applying the quantity-discount model.

5. Describe several real situations in which dynamic demand is more appropriate than constant demand.

6. How does the philosophy behind part-period balancing relate to the EOQ model?

7. Give some examples, different from those in the text, of when the single-period model would apply.

Notes

1. Private communication.

2. E. A. Silver and H. C. Meal, "A Heuristic for Selecting Lot Size Quantities for the Case of a Deterministic Time-Varying Demand Rate and Discrete Opportunities for Replenishment," *Production and Inventory Management* 14 (1973), pp. 64–74.

3. James R. Evans, "An Efficient Implementation of the Wagner-Whitin Algorithm for Dynamic Lot Sizing," *Journal of Operations Management* 5, no. 2 (1985), pp. 229–236.

4. Reprinted by permission of P. P. Kleuthgen and J. C. McGee, "Development and Implementation of an Integrated Inventory Management Program at Pfizer Pharmaceuticals," *Interfaces* 15, no. 1 (January–February 1985), pp. 69–87. Copyright 1985 The Institute of Management Sciences, 290 Westminster Street, Providence, RI 02903, USA.

Solved Problems

1. The pro shop at Perfect Skate Ice Arena specializes in custom fitting of boots and blades and draws skaters from as far away as 250 miles. The annual demand for one of the top figure-skating blades is 60. The blades cost $280, and the shop figures its holding-cost rate at 25 percent. The cost of ordering from the manufacturer is $30. The manager of the pro shop would like to maintain a high level of customer service by always having the blades in stock, but is getting pressure from the owner to reduce costs and is considering allowing back orders. She estimates that the back-order cost would be $200 per year. What should she do?

Solution

$$D = 60$$

$$C = \$280$$

$$i = .25$$

$$C_o = \$30$$

$$c_b = \$200$$

The EOQ model *without* back orders specifies

$$Q^* = \sqrt{\frac{2DC_o}{C_h}} = \sqrt{\frac{2(60)(30)}{.25(280)}} = 7.17 \text{ or } 7.$$

The total annual inventory cost using an EOQ of 7 is

$$TC = \frac{1}{2}QC_h + \frac{D}{Q}C_o = \frac{1}{2}(7)(.25)(280) + \left(\frac{60}{7}\right)(30) = \$245 + \$257.14 = \$502.14.$$

Using equations 14.5 and 14.6, we find the following the optimal order-quantity and back-order levels.

$$Q^* = \sqrt{\frac{2DC_o}{C_h}\left(\frac{C_h + C_b}{C_b}\right)} = \sqrt{\frac{2(60)(30)}{(.25)(280)}\left(\frac{70 + 200}{200}\right)} = 8.33 \text{ or } 8$$

$$S^* = Q^* \left(\frac{C_h}{C_h + C_b} \right) = (8) \left(\frac{70}{10 + 200} \right) = 2.07 \text{ or } 2$$

From equation 14.4, we get

$$TC = \frac{(Q - S)^2}{2Q} C_h + \frac{D}{Q} C_o + \frac{S^2}{2Q} C_b$$

$$= \frac{(8 - 2)^2}{2(8)} (70) + \frac{60}{8} (30) + \frac{(2)^2}{2(8)} (200)$$

$$= \$157.50 + \$225 + \$50 = \$423.50.$$

The pro shop manager can save approximately $70 per year by allowing back orders. However, the estimated back-order cost should be scrutinized carefully, and she must consider long-term impacts on customer satisfaction. The savings may not be worth the potential effects of customer dissatisfaction.

2. All-Star Bat Manufacturing, Inc. supplies baseball bats to major- and minor-league baseball teams. After an initial order in January, demand over the six-month baseball season is approximately constant at 1,000 bats per month. Assuming that the production process can produce up to 4,000 bats per month, the setup costs are $200 per setup, the production cost is $10 per bat, and that All-Star uses a 2-percent monthly inventory-holding cost, what production lot size would you recommend for meeting the demand during the baseball season? If All-Star operates 20 days per month, how often will the production process operate, and what is the length of a production run?

Solution
This is a production lot-size model. However, the operation is only six months rather than a full year. The basis for analysis may be for periods of one month, six months, or a full year. The inventory policy will be the same. In the following analysis we use a monthly basis.

$$Q^* = \sqrt{2DC_o / [(1 - D / P)C_h]} = \sqrt{2(1,000)(200) / [(1 - 1,000 / 4,000)(.02)(10)]} = 1,633$$

$$T = 20Q/D = 20(1,633)/1,000 = 32.66$$

$$\text{Production run length} = Q/(P/20) = 1,633/(4,000/20) = 8.165 \text{ days.}$$

3. Assume the quantity-discount schedule in Table 14.4 is appropriate.

Table 14.4 Data for Solved Problem 3

Order Size	Discount	Unit Cost
0 to 49	0%	$30.00
50 to 99	5	28.50
100 or more	10	27.00

If annual demand is 150 units, ordering cost is $20 per order, and annual inventory-carrying cost is 25 percent, what order quantity would you recommend?

Solution

$$Q_1 = \sqrt{2(150)(20)/[.25(30)]} = 28.28; \text{use } Q_1 = 28$$

$$Q_2 = \sqrt{2(150)(20)/[.25(28.5)]} = 29.02; \text{use } Q_2 = 50 \text{ for a 5\% discount}$$

$$Q_3 = \sqrt{2(150)(20)/[.25(27)]} = 29.81; \text{use } Q_3 = 100 \text{ for a 10\% discount}$$

Table 14.5 Solved Problem 3 Solution

Category	Unit Cost	Order Quantity	Inventory Cost	Order Cost	Purchase Cost	Total Cost
1	$30.00	28	$105.00	$107	$4,500	$4,712.00
2	28.50	50	178.13	60	4,275	4,335.00
3	27.00	100	337.50	30	4,050	4,417.50

$Q = 50$ to obtain the lowest total cost. The 5 percent discount is worthwhile.

4. Production of a seasonal product is planned over a six-month horizon. One lot can be produced each month. The unit cost is $5 and the carrying charge is 50 cents per month. The fixed cost of setting up production is $100. Monthly demand from November through April is 40, 60, 100, 80, 70, and 30. What is the best production lot-size decision using the Silver-Meal heuristic?

Solution
November: See Table 14.6.

Table 14.6 Solved Problem 4 Solution for November

Production Horizon	Q	Setup Cost	Holding Cost	Total Cost	Average Monthly Cost
One month	40	$100	$ 0	$100	$100
Two months	100	100	30	130	65
Three months	200	100	130	230	76.67

First decision: Produce 100 units in November.
January: See Table 14.7.

Table 14.7 Solved Problem 4 Solution for January

Production Horizon	Q	Setup Cost	Holding Cost	Total Cost	Average Monthly Cost
One month	100	$100	$ 0	$100	$100
Two months	180	100	40	140	70
Three months	250	100	110	210	70
Four months	280	100	155	255	63.75

Second decision: Produce 280 units in January.

$$Order\ cost = \$200.$$
$$Holding\ cost = \$185.$$
$$Total\ cost = \$385.$$

5. Grateful Fred sells souvenir T-shirts at rock concerts. The shirts are specially ordered with the city and date of the concert, so he cannot take them to another city after the concert. He buys the shirts for $15 each and sells them for $35 before and during the concert. He sells any remaining shirts outside the concert grounds for $10 after the concert ends, and can usually dispose of all of them. For a typical concert, demand is normally distributed, with a mean of 2,500 and standard deviation of 200. How many shirts should Fred order?

Solution

$$C_o = \$15 - \$10 = \$5$$
$$C_u = \$35 - 15 = \$20$$

$$P(\text{demand} \le Q^*) = \frac{C_u}{C_u + C_o} = \frac{20}{20 + 5} = .80$$

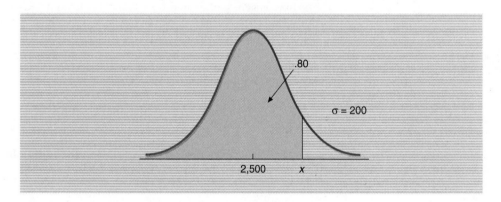

From Appendix B, $z = .84$. Thus,

$$Q^* = \mu + .84\sigma = 2,500 + .84(200) = 2,668\ \text{shirts}.$$

Problems

1. The manager of an inventory system believes that inventory models are important decision-making aids. Although the manager often uses an EOQ policy, he has never considered a back-order model because of his assumption that back orders are "bad" and should be avoided. However, with upper managers' continued pressure for cost reduction, *you* have been asked to analyze the economics of a back-ordering policy for some products. For a specific product with $D = 800$ units per year, $C_o = \$150$, $C_h = \$3$, and $C_b = \$20$, what is the economic difference in the EOQ and the back-order model? If the manager adds constraints that no more than 25 percent of the units may be back-ordered and that no customer will have to wait more than 15 days for an order, should the back-order inventory policy be adopted? Assume 250 working days per year.

2. If the lead time for new orders is 25 days for the inventory system discussed in Problem 1, find the reorder point for both the EOQ and the back-order models.

3. The A&M Hobby Shop carries a line of radio-controlled model racing cars. Demand for the cars is assumed to be constant at a rate of 30 cars per month. The cars cost $70 each, and ordering costs are approximately $15 per order regardless of the order size. Inventory-carrying costs are 20 percent annually.

a. Determine the economic order quantity and total annual cost under the assumption that no back orders are permitted.

b. Using a $45 per unit per year back-order cost, determine the minimum-cost inventory policy and total annual cost for the model racing cars.

c. What is the maximum number of days a customer would have to wait for a back order under the policy in part b? Assume that the Hobby Shop is open for business 300 days per year.

d. Would you recommend an inventory policy that allows back orders for this product? Explain.

e. If the lead time is 8 days, what is the reorder point for both a no-back-order and a back-order inventory policy?

4. Marilyn's Interiors sells silk floral arrangements in addition to other home furnishings. Because space is limited and she does not want to tie up a lot of money in inventory, Marilyn uses a back-order policy for most items. A popular silk arrangement costs $40, and Marilyn sells an average of 15 per month. Ordering costs are $30, and she values her inventory holding cost at 25 percent. Marilyn figures the back-order cost to be $40 annually. What is the optimal order quantity and planned back-order level? What if customer cancellations and other loss of goodwill increase the back-order cost to $100 annually?

 5. Modify the EOQMODEL.XLS spreadsheet from Chapter 13 for a back-order situation and apply it to the RCB Electronics example.

6. Assume that a production line operates such that the production lot-size model is applicable. Give $D = 8000$ units per year, $C_o = \$100$, and $C_h = \$2$ per unit per year, compute the minimum-cost production lot size for each of these production rates:

a. 7,000 units per year

b. 14,000 units per year

c. 28,000 units per year

d. 100,000 units per year

Compute the EOQ-recommended lot size using Equation 14.15. What two observations can you make about the relationship between the EOQ model and the production lot-size model?

7. Wilson Publishing Company produces books for the retail market. Demand for a current book is expected to occur at a constant annual rate of 7,200 copies. The cost of one copy of the book is $14.50. Inventory-holding costs are based on an 18 percent annual rate, and production setup costs are $150 per setup. The equipment the book is produced on has an annual production volume of 25,000 copies. There are 250 working days per year, and the lead time for a production run is 15 days. Use the production lot-size model to compute these values:

a. Minimum-cost production lot size

b. Number of production runs per year

c. Cycle time

d. Length of a production run

e. Maximum inventory level

f. Total annual cost

g. Reorder point

8. A well-known manufacturer of several brands of toothpaste uses the production lot-size model to determine production quantities for its various products. The product known as Extra White is currently being produced in production lot sizes of 5,000 units. The length of the production run for this quantity is 10 days. Because of a recent shortage of a particular raw material, the supplier of the material has announced a cost increase that will be passed along to the manufacturer of Extra White. Current estimates are that the new raw material cost will increase the manufacturing cost of the toothpaste products by 23 percent per unit. What will be the effect of this price increase on the production lot sizes for Extra White?

9. AutoMart produces and distributes its own line of automotive parts. The annual demand for a certain brake component is 25,000. The manufacturing facility can produce at a rate of 85,000 per month. The unit manufacturing cost is $28, and setup costs amount to $3,500. The carrying charge is 20 percent. What is the economic production lot size for this component?

 10. Modify the EOQMODEL.XLS spreadsheet from Chapter 13 for the production-lot size situation and apply it to the Forum Shoes example.

11. Using the RCB Electronics example from this chapter, show that as C_b increases, the optimal solution to the back-order model approaches the EOQ solution. Use the following sequence of values for C_b: 90, 120, 180, and 600.

12. Using the Forum Shoes example from the book, show that as P increases from 50,000 to 250,000 in increments of 50,000, the optimal solution begins to approach that specified by the EOQ model.

13. Apply Goyal's method for quantity discounts to Solved Problem 3, and show that the results are the same.

14. Apply the EOQ model to the quantity-discount situation shown in Table 14.8.

Table 14.8 Data for Problem 14

Discount Category	Order Size	Discount	Unit Cost
1	0 to 99	0%	$10.00
2	100 or more	3	9.70

Assume that $D = 500$ units per year, $C_o = \$40$, and the annual inventory-holding cost is 20 percent. What order quantity do you recommend?

15. Keith Shoe Stores carries a basic black dress shoe for men that sells at an approximate constant rate of 500 pairs of shoes every three months. Keith's current buying policy is to order 500 pairs each time an order is placed. It costs Keith $30 to place an order. Inventory-carrying costs have an annual rate of 20 percent. With the order quantity of 500, Keith obtains the shoes at the lowest possible unit cost of $28 per pair. Other quantity discounts offered by the manufacturer are listed in Table 14.9.

Table 14.9 Data for Problem 15

Order Quantity	Price per Pair
0–99	$36
100–199	32
200–299	30
300 or more	28

What is the minimum-cost order quantity for the shoes? What are the annual savings of your inventory policy over the policy currently being used by Keith?

16. In discussing the EOQ model with quantity discounts, we stated that if the Q^* for a price category is larger than necessary to qualify for the category price, the category cannot be optimal. Use the two discount categories in Problem 14 to show that this is true. That is, plot the total-cost curves for the two categories and show that if the category-2 minimum cost, Q, is an acceptable solution, we do not have to consider category 1.

17. Apply the periodic-order-quantity and part-period-balancing methods to Solved Problem 4. How do your results compare with the Silver-Meal heuristic?

18. The demand for a particular product over the next 12-week period will be as follows: 500, 400, 300, 190, 80, 0, 0, 80, 190, 300, 400, and 500 units. The cost per order is $500, and the inventory-holding cost is $2 per unit per week.

a. What is the average weekly demand?

b. Using your answer to part a, assume the EOQ constant-demand-rate assumption holds, and compute the EOQ. What is the total cost under this policy, assuming the inventory-holding cost is charged on the basis of the inventory carried at the end of each weekly period?

c. Reduce inventory-carrying cost to zero by ordering each week exactly what is demanded for the week. What is the cost of this inventory policy?

19. For the situation described in Problem 18, determine the lot-sizing policy using periodic-order quantity, part-period balancing, and the Silver-Meal heuristic.

20. The demand for cases of chlorine pellets for swimming pools at Von Tibel's Hardware is

May	15
June	40
July	130
August	85
September	20

The cost to place an order from the manufacturer is $20, and the carrying cost per case per month is 75 cents. Determine the best lot-sizing policy using part-period balancing and the Silver-Meal heuristic.

21. The J&B Card Shop sells calendars featuring a different Colonial picture for each month. The once-a-year order for each year's calendar arrives in September. From past experience the September-to-July demand for the calendars can be approximated by a normal distribution with $\mu = 500$ and $\sigma = 120$. The calendars cost $3.50 each, and J&B sells them for $7 each.

a. If J&B throws out all unsold calendars at the end of July (that is, salvage value is zero), how many calendars should be ordered?

b. If J&B reduces the calendar price to $1 at the end of July and can sell all surplus calendars at this price, how many calendars should be ordered?

22. The Gilbert Air-Conditioning Company is considering the purchase of a special shipment of portable air-conditioners manufactured in Japan. Each unit will cost Gilbert $80 and it will be sold for $125. Gilbert does not want to carry surplus air-conditioners over until the following year. Thus all supplies will be sold to a wholesaler, who has agreed to take all surplus units for $50 per unit. Assume that the air-conditioner demand has a normal distribution with $\mu = 20$ and $\sigma = 6$.

a. What is the recommended order quantity?

b. What is the probability that Gilbert will sell all units it orders?

23. A popular newsstand in a large metropolitan area is attempting to determine how many copies of the Sunday paper it should purchase each week. Demand for the newspaper on Sundays can be approximated by a normal distribution with $\mu = 700$ and $\sigma = 100$. The newspaper costs the newsstand 40 cents a copy and sells for 75 cents. The newsstand does not receive any value from surplus papers and thus absorbs a 100 percent loss on all unsold papers.

a. How many copies of the Sunday paper should be purchased each week?

b. What is the probability that the newsstand will have a stockout?

c. The manager of the newsstand is concerned about the newsstand's image if the probability of stockout is high. Customers often purchase other items after coming to the newsstand for the Sunday paper, and frequent stockouts would cause customers to go to another newsstand. The manager agrees that a $1 loss of goodwill cost should be assigned to any stockout. What are the new recommended order quantity and the new probability of a stockout?

24. A perishable dairy product is ordered daily at a particular supermarket. The product, which costs $1.19 per unit, sells for $1.65 per unit. If units are unsold at the end of the day, the supplier takes them back at a rebate of $1 per unit. Assume that daily demand is approximately normally distributed with $\mu = 150$ and $\sigma = 30$.

a. What is your recommended daily order quantity for the supermarket?

b. What is the probability that the supermarket will sell all the units it orders?

c. In problems such as these, why would the supplier offer a rebate as high as $1? For example, why not offer a nominal rebate of, say, 25 cents per unit? What happens to the supermarket order quantity as the rebate is reduced?

25. Bushnell's Sand and Gravel (BSG) is a small firm that supplies sand, gravel, and top-soil to contractors and landscape firms. BSG maintains an inventory of high-quality, screened topsoil, which is used to supply the weekly orders for two companies: Bath Landscaping Service and Pittsford Lawn Care, Inc. The problem for BSG is to determine how many cubic yards of screened topsoil to have in inventory at the beginning of each week to satisfy the needs of both its customers. BSG would like to select the lowest possible inventory level that would have a .95 probability of satisfying the combined weekly orders from both customers. The demand distributions for the two customers are given in Table 14.10.

Table 14.10 Data for Problem 25

	Weekly Demand	Relative Frequency
Bath Landscaping	10	.20
	15	.35
	20	.30
	25	.10
	30	.05
Pittsford Lawn Care	30	.20
	40	.40
	50	.30
	60	.10

Simulate 20 weeks of operation for beginning inventories of 70 and of 80 cubic yards. Based on your limited simulation results, how many cubic yards should BSG maintain in inventory? Discuss what you would want to do in a full-scale simulation of this problem.

26. Domoy Cycles, Inc., purchases a certain model of motorcycle for $5,778. To finance the purchase of this model, Domoy must pay an 18-percent annual interest rate on borrowed capital. This interest rate amounts to approximately $20 per cycle per week. Orders for additional units can be placed each week, but a minimum order size of five is required on any given order. It currently takes three weeks to receive a new shipment after the order is placed. The cost of placing an order is $50. If Domoy runs out of motorcycles in inventory, a shortage cost of $300 per unit is incurred. Currently Domoy has 20 units of this model in inventory. Historical data showing the weekly demand are given in Table 14.11. Assuming an order quantity of 15 and a reorder point of 10, perform a 12-week simulation of Domoy's operation. Use the first 12 two-digit random numbers from row x of Appendix C where x is the fourth digit of your Social Security number. Show your simulation results in a table.

Table 14.11 Data for Problem 26

Number of Sales	Number of Weeks
0	2
1	5
2	8
3	22
4	10
5	3
	Total 50

27. Use the INVSIM.XLS spreadsheet to determine the best order quantity-reorder point combination in the range $6 \leq R \leq 8$ and $10 \leq Q \leq 30$. You will have to expand the spreadsheet to simulate 500 days.

28. Wagner Fabricating Company is reviewing the economic feasibility of manufacturing a part that it currently purchases from a supplier. Forecasted annual demand for the part is 3,200 units. Wagner operates 250 days per year. Wagner's financial analysts have established a cost of capital of 14 percent on the use of funds for investments within the company. In addition, over the past year $600,000 has been the average investment in the company's inventory. Accounting information shows that a total of $24,000 was spent on taxes and insurance related to the company's inventory. In addition, it has been estimated that $9,000 was lost due to inventory shrinkage, which included damaged goods as well as pilferage. A remaining $15,000 was spent on warehouse overhead, including utility expenses for heating and lighting.

An analysis of the purchasing operation shows that approximately two hours are required to process and coordinate an order for the part regardless of the quantity ordered. Purchasing salaries average $28 per hour, including employee benefits. In addition, a detailed analysis of 125 orders showed that $2,375 was spent on telephone, paper, and postage directly related to the ordering process.

A five-day lead time is required to obtain the part from the supplier. An analysis of demand during the lead time shows that lead-time demand is approximately normally distributed with a mean of 64 units and a standard deviation of 10 units. Service-level guidelines indicate that one stockout per year is acceptable.

Currently the company has a contract to purchase the part from a supplier at a cost of $18 per unit. However, over the past few months, the company's production capacity has been expanded. As a result, excess capacity is now available in certain production departments, and the company is considering the alternative of producing the parts itself.

Forecasted utilization of equipment shows that production capacity will be available for the part being considered. The production capacity is available at the rate of 1,000 units per month, with up to five months of production time available. It is felt that with a two-week lead time, schedules can be arranged so that the part can be produced whenever needed. The demand during the two-week lead time is approximately normally distributed with a mean of 128 units and a standard deviation of 20 units. Production costs are expected to be $17 per part.

A concern of managers is that setup costs will be significant. The total cost of labor and lost production time is estimated to be $50 per hour, and it will take a full eight-hour shift to set up the equipment for producing the part.

Develop a report for managers of Wagner Fabricating that will address the question of whether the company should continue to purchase the part from the supplier or

Develop a report for managers of Wagner Fabricating that will address the question of whether the company should continue to purchase the part from the supplier or should begin to produce the part itself. Include the following factors in your report:

a. An analysis of the inventory-holding cost, including the appropriate annual inventory-holding cost rate.

b. An analysis of ordering costs, including the appropriate cost per order from the supplier.

c. An analysis of setup costs for the production operation.

d. A development of the inventory policy for these two alternatives:
   i. ordering a fixed quantity, Q, from the supplier
   ii. ordering a fixed quantity, Q, from in-plant production

e. Include the following in the policies of part d.
   • Quantity Q.
   • Number of order or production runs per year.
   • Cycle time.
   • Reorder point.
   • Amount of safety stock.
   • Expected maximum inventory level.
   • Average inventory level.
   • Total annual inventory-holding cost.
   • Total annual ordering cost.
   • Total annual cost of the units purchased or manufactured.
   • Total annual cost of the purchase policy.
   • Total annual cost of the production policy.

f. Make a recommendation as to whether the company should purchase or manufacture the part. What is the saving associated with your recommendation as compared with the other alternative?

Chapter Outline

Chapter Fifteen
Lean Production and Synchronous Manufacturing

Applied P/OM

P/OM in Practice

Try to imagine the following scenario for MamaMia's Pizza. The kitchen is crammed with indirect workers on their way to relieve one or another of the pizza preparers. Inspectors are checking every step of the pizza-making process. Housekeepers are cleaning up discarded pieces of dough and excess toppings from the floor. Other workers are bringing dough from the refrigerator to the food-preparation table. Next to each workstation are piles of unfinished pizzas waiting for the addition of sauce, toppings, or cheese—each of which is the responsibility of a different individual. Some workers are rushing about madly while others stand by idly, reading the daily newspaper. Between the oven and the packaging table are piles of pizzas that have been set aside because they were made incorrectly. In one corner of the kitchen are stacked boxes of dough, meats, and cheeses from suppliers, none of which have been checked or properly stored.

Now picture a much different situation. Indirect workers, who add no value to the product, are nowhere to be seen; all workers are adding value to the pizzas. The space between production operations is small, allowing little room to store excess inventory and fostering close communication among workers. Pizzas flow smoothly from one preparation step to the next. When an incorrect order is discovered, all work stops and the team works together to uncover the reason and prevent it from occurring again. Every pizza coming out of the oven is correct and immediately boxed for delivery to the customer. There are no large supplies of dough and other ingredients; they are delivered fresh daily by the restaurant's suppliers.

The first scenario may be a bit difficult to imagine for a small pizza business. However, it describes the classic mass-production environment typical of U.S. automobile plants a couple of decades ago. The second scenario is more typical of a Japanese automobile plant at the same time. The elimination of waste, reduced inventories, improvement of quality, and development of human resources featured therein are characterized today as **lean production.** The concept was developed at Toyota Motor Company.[1]

Toyota recognized the limitations of Western automobile production, which relied on massive and expensive stamping press lines to produce car panels. The dies in the presses weighed many tons and specialists needed up to a full day to switch them for a new part. To compensate for long setup times, large lot sizes were produced so that machines could be kept busy while others were being set up. This resulted in large work-in-process inventories remaining idle between successive steps of the process and high levels of indirect labor and overhead being necessary to account for inventory and materials transportation and handling, both of which increased cost and decreased productivity.

Initially, Toyota produced at most a few thousand cars each year. In addition, Toyota's budget was so small that the company could afford only a few press lines to stamp the many different parts required in an automobile. A Japanese engineer, Taiichi Ohno, was thus inspired to develop simple die-changing techniques that enabled him to change dies frequently—every two or three hours instead of two or three months. He also thought to have production workers change the dies themselves instead of sitting idle while specialists did the work. This required a highly skilled and motivated work force, but by the late 1950s the time for changing dies had been reduced from a day to three minutes. In the process, it was discovered that it actually cost less per part to make small batches than to make huge production runs. The savings resulted from the elimination of massive inventories and the fact that making small batches of parts caused errors and defects to be known immediately and hence corrected. Large work-in-process and lot-size inventories hide poor quality. If a part is defective, another is present to replace it. The higher the rate of defectives, the larger the amount of inventory required to cover for it. There is no incentive to find the causes of poor quality and correct them.

The "Toyota production system" changed the nature of manufacturing worldwide. Lean production has become the norm for world-class companies competing in today's global market. It depends on **synchronous manufacturing,** which is any systematic method of moving material quickly and smoothly through the productive resources of a manufacturing facility in response to market demand.

One approach to synchronous manufacturing is **just-in-time (JIT)** materials management, the objective of which is to eliminate all sources of waste, including unnecessary inventory and scrap. Although the modern JIT production concept was developed by the Toyota Motor Company of Japan and then adopted by other Japanese companies, the principles of JIT were actually promoted by Henry Ford as early as 1930. Today many American firms are employing JIT procedures.

A second approach to synchronous manufacturing, **constraint management,** is based on the idea of effectively exploiting a company's limited resources. This chapter specifically addresses

- Elements of the JIT philosophy and organizational changes needed to make it work effectively.
- Applications of JIT in service organizations.
- The theory of constraints.

Just-in-Time (JIT) Concept

The concept of JIT has evolved from a narrow perspective of an ideal production system to a broad-based philosophy. An early definition of JIT was "the idea of producing the necessary units in the necessary quantities at the necessary time."[2] Today the JIT philosophy is aimed at eliminating all forms of waste (anything that does not add value to the product), plus improving quality and productivity.

To understand how JIT evolved, we need to examine some of the characteristics of Japan and its people. Japan is approximately the size of California, and 80 percent of the land is mountainous. Since Japan's population is much larger than California's, it is easy to understand the space limitations in that country. In addition, since Japan has few natural resources, the Japanese people tend to avoid waste as much as possible in every aspect of their lives. And waste takes many forms. In manufacturing, for example, inventory is considered waste, since there is little land available for large plants or warehouses to store inventory. Also classified as waste are scrap resulting from poor quality; minutes spent in unnecessary inspection; extra labor and time required by inefficient production operations, schedules, and manufacturing procedures; overproduction resulting from a desire to avoid manufacturing costs such as additional setups; delays caused by unnecessary movement of materials from one fixture to another or from the production floor to inventory and back; and inefficient materials flow because of poor layout of machines. Thus, Japanese production systems have evolved around the characteristically Japanese principle of reducing waste.

Figure 15.1 is a framework for JIT. The top portion of the figure shows the linkages between JIT and many elements of operations management discussed throughout this book: top management support (leadership), human resources management, quality management, manufacturing stategy, and technology management. All are linked by a companywide focus on continuous improvement and employee participation, two of the key elements of total quality management. The core elements of JIT are classified into six categories:

1. Production-floor management.
2. Scheduling.
3. Process and product design.
4. Work-force management.
5. Supplier management.
6. Information systems.

All of them are discussed in general terms in this book; however, the uniqueness of JIT lies in the specific practices in each of those categories and their relationship with one another, leading to improved manufacturing performance and, ultimately, competitive advantage. (Some issues relating to the last category, information systems, will be discussed in Chapters 17 and 18.)

Production-Floor Management

JIT management of the flow of materials on the production floor entails reducing setup times, using small lot sizes, and employing preventive maintenance, pull production, and *Kanban*.

Setup-Time Reduction.   Long setup times waste manufacturing resources. Moreover, short setup times enable a manufacturer to make short production runs and frequent changeovers, thus achieving high flexibility and product variety—important strategic objectives. As we discussed in relation to Toyota, Japanese manufacturers have reported remarkable reductions in setup times. Yammar Diesel reduced a machining-line tool setting from 9.3 hours to nine minutes, and Toyo Kogyo reduced a ring-gear cutter tool setting from more than six hours to 10 minutes. Similar results have been achieved in the United States. A chain-saw manufacturer reduced setup time on a punch press from more than two hours to three minutes, and a Midwestern manufacturer was able to cut equipment setup time on a 60-ton press from 45 minutes to one minute. This was accomplished through process improvements such as storing the required tools next to the machine, using conveyors to move the tools in and out of the machine, and improving the labeling and identification. Previously, the setup tools were poorly identified, poorly organized, and stored far from the machine, requiring a forklift to transport them. The new changeovers or setups can be performed by the machine operator with no indirect assistance. Harley-Davidson also reduced its setup time, both by process and product-part changes.

Figure 15.1 Just-in-Time Manufacturing Framework

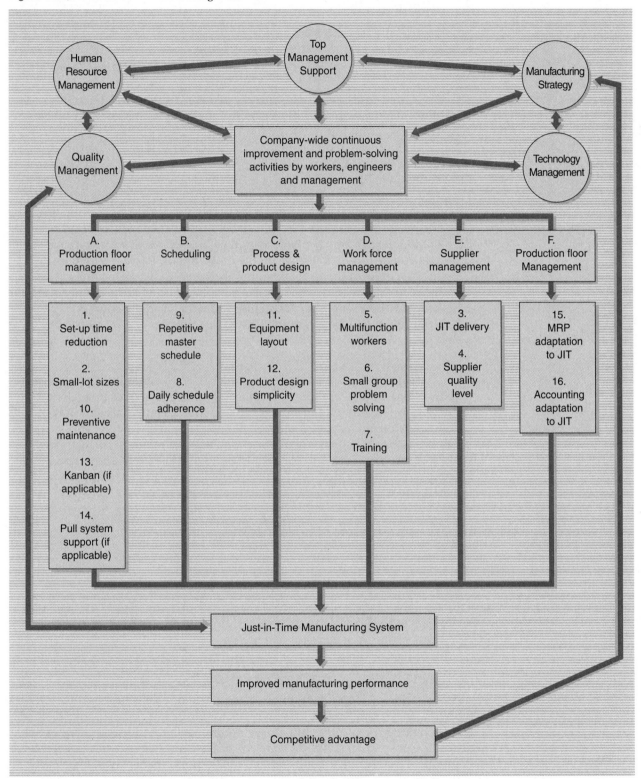

SOURCE: Sadao Sakakibara, Barbara B. Flynn, and Roger G. Schroeder, "A Framework and Measurement Instrument for Just-In-Time Manufacturing," *Production and Operations Management* 2, no. 3 (Summer 1993), pp. 177–194.

Applied P/OM

Harley-Davidson

Simple design changes helped reduce setup time at Harley-Davidson.[3]

After Harley-Davidson's market share fell from a near monopoly to less than 30 percent in the early 1980s, the company embarked on an aggressive strategy for improving quality and manufacturing efficiency. Lean production was an important part of that effort. Simple design changes, in both products and processes, helped it achieve dramatic reductions in setup time. For example, using "C"-shaped spacing washers instead of "O" types enabled operators to loosen nuts and slide in the "C" washers from the side to reposition a machine instead of taking the nuts off and lifting the machine to replace the "O" washers. Another change involved two crankpins that were similar except for a hole drilled at a 45-degree angle in one and at a 48-degree angle in the other. It took two hours to reposition the machine for the new operation. Engineers designed a common hole angle in the two parts, and changeovers could be made by simply inserting or removing a set of spacers on the fixture that held the crankpin for drilling. Setup time was reduced to three minutes.

Small Lot Sizes.   A continuous flow of small lot sizes minimizes unnecessary inventory investment. For example, small lots of engine parts can go directly to the assembly line rather than storage. This eliminates materials handling as well as reducing inventory space requirements.

Setup costs are usually highly correlated with setup times, since most of the costs of setup are incurred by long setup times and lost production time. Small lot sizes are economical if setup costs are small. This can be seen by examining the EOQ and economic lot-size models presented in Chapters 13 and 14.

$$\text{EOQ:} \quad Q^* = \sqrt{\frac{2DC_o}{C_h}}$$

$$\text{ELS:} \quad Q^* = \sqrt{\frac{2DC_o}{(1 - D/P)C_h}}$$

As the order or setup cost, C_o, decreases, Q^* clearly decreases, as does the total cost.

For purchased materials, establishing long-term relationships with single-source suppliers provides an environment conducive to small, frequent deliveries. Long-term contracts encourage supplier loyalty and reduce the risk of interrupted supplies. A major component of the ordering cost is the cost of receiving, inspecting, and storing material for future use. Small lot sizes can be delivered directly to production, thus eliminating many costly receiving activities. In the past, when suppliers were considered adversaries, safety stock was maintained as insurance against poor supplier performance. Working closely with suppliers on improving quality and establishing a relationship of mutual trust can eliminate the need for inspection, further reducing ordering costs and delays in the production cycle.

Preventive Maintenance.   Since excess work-in-process inventory is not available to compensate for equipment breakdowns, production equipment must have high reliability. This means good preventive maintenance. When machines break down, the root causes must be found and permanent solutions implemented to prevent further breakdowns. Furthermore, preventive maintenance should seek not only to avoid breakdowns, but also to improve the overall capability of processes. Total productive maintenance, described in Chapter 11, involves the operators themselves in maintenance activities, thereby reducing idle time because operators do not have to wait for maintenance specialists.

Pull Production and Kanban.   A primary challenge in JIT production is the coordination of successive production activities. An automobile, for instance, consists of thousands of parts. It is extremely difficult to coordinate the transfer of materials and components between production operations to realize the JIT concept of having materials and assemblies arrive at precisely the right time. Most factories use a system of *push production* in which they make parts and then send them to subsequent operations or to storage. Of course, a breakdown of some process or demand fluctuations will consequently create an imbalance of inventory between processes.

At Toyota, the process is reversed. Employees at a given operation go to the source of required parts, such as machining or subassembly, and withdraw the units as they need them. Then just enough new parts are manufactured or procured to replace those withdrawn. Thus, if inventories are needed at all, they are minimized. As the process from which parts were withdrawn replenishes the items it transferred out, it draws on the output of its preceding process, and so on. This **pull production** system, in which items are delivered or produced only when they are required, begins at final assembly and works backward through all workstations in the production process, continuing even to subcontractors and suppliers. The objective is to create a smooth, rapid flow of all products from the time materials and purchased parts are received until the time the final product is shipped to the customer.

A key element of just-in-time production as developed in Japan is an information system called **Kanban,** the Japanese word for "card." The type and number of units required by a process are written on Kanbans and used to initiate withdrawal and production of items through the production process. Figure 15.2 shows how the withdrawal Kanbans and production-ordering Kanbans operate. The carrier of process B goes to the store of process A (step 1) with the withdrawal Kanbans and empty pallets after a sufficient number have accumulated. When the necessary number of parts are withdrawn, the worker detaches the production-ordering Kanbans that were attached to the inventory and places them at the Kanban receiving post, leaving the empty pallets (step 2). For each production-ordering Kanban detached, a withdrawal Kanban is put in its place (step 3). When these units are used, the withdrawal Kanban is placed in the withdrawal Kanban post (step 4). In process A, the production-ordering Kanbans are collected and placed in the production-ordering Kanban post (step 5). These Kanbans provide the authority to produce the parts (step 6), and the Kanbans move physically with the parts throughout the operations in process A (step 7). The completed parts are placed in inventory, along with their production-ordering Kanbans (step 8). In this way, many individual processes are interconnected. Production orders and withdrawal quantities under Kanban are approximately

Figure 15.2 Steps Involved in Using the Two Kanbans

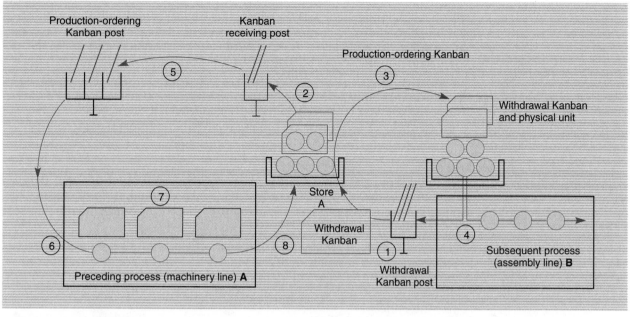

SOURCE: Reprinted with permission from *Industrial Engineering* magazine, May 1981. Copyright Institute of Industrial Engineers, 25 Technology Park/Atlanta, Norcross, GA 30092.

10 percent of the daily demand. With such small lot sizes, it is unnecessary to warehouse in-process (WIP) inventory, thus minimizing holding costs.

The amount of WIP inventory is equal to the number of Kanban cards issued times the size of the standard container used. The following equation is used to calculate the initial number of Kanban cards required.

$$\frac{D(T_w + T_p)(1 + \alpha)}{C}$$

where D = the average daily production rate as determined from the master production schedule.

T_w = the waiting time of Kanban cards in decimal fractions of a day (that is, the waiting time of a part).

T_p = the processing time per part, in decimal fractions of a day.

C = the capacity of a standard container.

α = a policy variable determined by the efficiency of work centers using the part.

For example, suppose that D = 50 parts/day, T_w = .20, T_p = .10, C = 5, and α = 1. Then the number of Kanban cards is calculated as

$$\frac{50(.20 + .10)(1 + 1)}{5} = 6.$$

Once the system is running, supervisors can pull Kanban cards from the system as they observe that certain work centers can function with less WIP. As D changes from month to month, the number of cards is increased or reduced appropriately. Since the number of cards is directly proportional to the amount of WIP inventory, both managers and production workers strive to reduce the number of cards in the system through reduced lead time ($T_w + T_p$) or through other improvements.

Note that Kanban is simply a way of pulling parts from the preceding workstation, beginning at final assembly so that the entire manufacturing operation is synchronized to the final-assembly schedule. JIT production prohibits the source of production from pushing inventory forward only to wait idle if it is not needed.

Although the dual-card Kanban system just described is used by Toyota in producing automobiles, a more common approach, especially in the West, is the single-card Kanban system that signals requirements from the preceding production stage, often by a simple visual system. Schonberger cites some examples:[4]

- In General Electric's lamp division, which consists of multiple plants in the state of Ohio, truck drivers from component plants collect Kanban cards and empty containers when they unload. The card signals which components are to be delivered on the next trip.
- At a Hewlett-Packard plant, the signal for a subassembly shop that makes computer-system modules to send another plastic tub of parts forward is removal of the present plastic tub of parts from a sensing platform.
- At another Hewlett-Packard facility, an empty "Kanban square" outlined in yellow tape is the visual signal for the preceding workstation to forward another disk-drive unit.

Scheduling

In Chapter 9, we described several types of manufacturing processes. One of the most common types is *mass production,* sometimes called *repetitive manufacturing.* Automobiles, appliances, and many other products are made in this way, with the same or similar operations repeated over and over and an uninterrupted flow of materials going through the sequence of operations. Repetitive manufacturing keeps inventories and lead times lower than batch or job-shop production, thus leading to increased productivity and lower cost. However, it takes careful design and commitment by both managers and workers for repetitive manufacturing to be effective. The Japanese have recognized this potential in developing the JIT system, which requires a repetitive master schedule that must be rigorously met.

Repetitive Master Schedule.   To operate smoothly, a JIT system must minimize fluctuation in production demand. This is accomplished by making finished-product lot sizes as small as possible, ideally one, and having a **level master schedule** whereby small lot sizes of each product are made every day and even every hour.

For example, suppose the production schedule for the next month calls for 600 units of product A, 1,000 units of product B, and 400 units of product C. A typical mass-production plan would be to produce all of product A, then change over to B, and finally to C. During the month, warehouses would be overstocked with product A and have none of product C until the end of the month. A level schedule smooths production of all products over the month. Assuming that 20 working days are available, the daily production would be 30 units of A, 50 units of B, and 20 units of C. In a JIT environment, this product mix might be smoothed out even further. If 480 minutes are available during the day, the average cycle time per unit would be

$$(480 \text{ minutes})/(100 \text{ units}) = 4.8 \text{ minutes/unit}$$

The cycle time for each product is calculated as follows.

$$\text{Product A} = (4.8)(100/30) = 16 \text{ minutes/unit}$$
$$\text{Product B} = (4.8)(100/50) = 9.6 \text{ minutes/unit}$$
$$\text{Product C} = (4.8)(100/20) = 24 \text{ minutes/unit}$$

Production might occur in the following order: B-A-B-C-B-A-B-C-B-A. Such a smooth flow requires rapid changeover and workers who know how to switch from one product to another. A level production schedule also helps smooth demand for tooling, supplies, maintenance, and other activities.

Because the pull production that is entailed in a JIT system requires a high degree of repetitiveness and fixed routings, JIT production is not universally applicable. Nearly all types of production have some degree of repetitiveness, however. In some cases, a small number of products or product families represent a large proportion of production volume. The JIT approach can be effectively applied to these "vital few" products, while the remaining products can be controlled by traditional methods.

Product and Process Design

For a JIT system to function effectively, traditional product and process design activities usually have to be modified.

Equipment Layout. Poor equipment layout is one of the major causes of inefficiency in manufacturing. In a typical U.S. manufacturing environment, material is transported from a supplier's truck to a warehouse, then later transported from the warehouse to the plant, and finally stored in a holding area or even restocked in another warehouse. In a common process layout, material is often transferred between departments during the manufacturing operations. Consequently, unnecessary costs are incurred in the form of inventory, materials handling, production delays, and so forth.

JIT production requires a smooth flow in which materials introduced at one end of the process move without delay to finished product. Thus, the layout should be in a straight line or U-shaped cells involving the group technology discussed in Chapter 9.

As you will recall, group technology combines several machines that perform different tasks into a single work center so that the tasks can be performed without moving large lots of in-process inventories. For example, the pieces of equipment can be placed close together and connected by short roller conveyors. As a result, materials or parts can flow one piece at a time from machine to machine. Inventory is reduced to minimal levels, and operators can move one piece at a time without the need for forklifts or other bulk-materials-handling equipment. In addition, a group layout enables workers to work on more than one machine at a time, thus increasing efficiency. This means workers must be trained to operate several different machines in a JIT environment. Automation, such as robots, is often used for routine operations in work cells, freeing workers to attend to multiple machines while robots transfer or load parts. Omark provides an example of the type of layout changes that are necessary to support a JIT system.

Applied P/OM

Omark

Omark uses improved layout to support its JIT concept.[5]

The benefits of improved layout can be seen at Omark's Guelph, Ontario, plant, which makes chain saws. Originally, the distance the product had to travel within the plant was 2,620 feet and flow time was 21 days. Within two years, the distance was reduced to 173 feet and the time to three days by moving metal-forming machines together and eliminating much of the work-in-process (WIP) inventory. Omark's ultimate marketing strategy is to fill orders from the factory and eliminate finished-goods warehouses altogether.

Product-Design Simplicity. Chapter 6 discussed many aspects of product design that support lean production and JIT. The Applied P/OM feature for Harley-Davidson further exemplified this point. Simplicity of design and standardization within multiple products can result in faster changeovers and require less complex skills of workers in a level-production-schedule environment.

Work-Force Management

People are a critical aspect of total quality control in a JIT environment, in which all employees are regarded as valuable resources who can provide many solutions to problems and ideas for improving performance. As a result, the JIT concept demands that employees be empowered to make important decisions such as stopping production when a problem is identified. The Japanese call this concept *yo-i-don.* In their companies, if a problem is discovered by an operator, the operator can signal for assistance by activating an *andon,* or yellow warning light. If the problem is not corrected within, say, one minute, a red light will automatically come on, a siren will sound, and the entire production line will stop. Managers and workers will immediately rush to the scene and try to locate the source of the problem and correct it.

As JIT systems in the West apply their versions of this *yo-i-don* concept, management-employee relationships are being forced to change. Managers must respond to criticism from workers—engage in participative management—if they truly support the JIT approach. Employee motivation depends on an atmosphere of mutual trust and cooperation among managers and nonmanagers. Three key JIT practices based on this type of management-employee relationship are use of multifunction workers, small-group problem solving, and training.

Multifunction Workers. In a traditional Western manufacturing facility, there is a high subdivision of labor and strict adherence to union job classifications. For example, union contracts may prohibit a milling machine operator from being assigned to operate a drill press. But to obtain a smooth work flow, workers in group-technology cells must be able to switch from one machine to the next and to perform their own setups, maintenance, and inspection. Such *multifunction workers* help to eliminate inventory between processes, reduce the number of workers required, and create in employees a greater sense of involvement and participation in the total production process. However, labor unions often balk at the concept. Many companies form union-management committees to seek union cooperation.

Small-Group Problem Solving. Process improvement, as discussed in Chapter 11, depends on the creativity of employees, particularly working in teams. *Small-group problem solving* attempts to tap this creativity by encouraging workers to bring production-related problems as well as ideas for improvement opportunities to team problem-solving sessions on a regular basis.

Training. The JIT philosophy requires that managers invest heavily in training. The Japanese concept of "lifetime training" enables them to take full advantage of the JIT environment. Training is focused on how to perform a job more efficiently and with better quality, use of various problem-solving techniques such as statistical process control, and new skills that increase worker flexibility. In the United States JIT training has also been aimed at eliminating bad habits formed in traditional American manufacturing environments, such as the tendency to assume only limited responsibility and to produce the minimum work possible.

Supplier Management

Because of the importance of suppliers to the effective operation of JIT, the role of purchasing in JIT is dramatically different from conventional practice. Suppliers must be able to deliver small lot sizes on a continuous basis and have high quality levels.

JIT Delivery. Table 15.1 contrasts JIT purchasing with conventional purchasing practices. Instead of sending one large shipment that must be counted, inspected, and stored before issuance to the production floor, suppliers in a JIT system make smaller deliveries on a daily basis or more frequently to accommodate that day's production schedule. For that reason, a JIT system functions best when suppliers are located in close geographic proximity to the manufac-

Table 15.1 JIT Purchasing versus Conventional Purchasing

Conventional Purchasing	Just-in-Time Purchasing
1. Large delivery lot sizes, typically covering several weeks' requirements. Infrequent deliveries.	Small delivery lot sizes based on the immediate needs for production usage. Very frequent deliveries; e.g., several times per day.
2. Deliveries timed according to buyer's request date.	Deliveries synchronized with buyer's production schedule.
3. Several suppliers used for each part. Multiple sourcing used to maintain adequate quality and competitive pricing.	Few suppliers used for each part. Often parts are single-sourced.
4. Inventories typically maintained for parts.	Little inventory required because deliveries are expected to be made frequently, on time, and with high-quality parts.
5. Short-term purchasing agreements. Suppliers pressured by threat of withdrawing business.	Long-term purchasing agreements. Suppliers pressured by obligation to perform.
6. Products designed with few constraints on number of different purchased components used.	Products designed with great effort to use only currently purchased parts. Objective is to maximize the commonality of parts.
7. Minimal exchange of information between supplier and buyer.	Extensive exchange of information about production schedules, production processes, etc.
8. Purchasing agent as primary focus of communication with supplier.	Purchasing agent as facilitator of many points of communication between design engineers, production engineers, etc.
9. Prices established by suppliers.	Buyer works with supplier to reduce supplier's costs and thereby reduce prices.
10. Geographic proximity of supplier not important for supplier-selection decision.	Geographic proximity considered very important.

Source: James R. Freeland, "A Survey of Just-in-Time Purchasing Practices in the United States," DSWP-89-23, The Darden School, University of Virginia, July 1989. Reprinted with permission, The American Production and Inventory Control Society, Falls Church, VA.

turer. In North America, where industry is frequently geographically dispersed, transportation delays often make it difficult to achieve this type of vendor support. Saturn Corporation, however, proves it can be done.

Applied P/OM

Saturn Corporation

Supplier management is central to Saturn's effectiveness.[6]

Saturn's automobile plant in Spring Hill, Tennessee, manages its supplier so well that in four years it had to stop its production line just once—and for only 18 minutes—because the right part was not delivered at the right time. Saturn maintains virtually no inventory. A central computer directs trucks to deliver preinspected and presorted parts at precise times to the factory's 56 receiving docks, 21 hours a day, six days a week. Of Saturn's more than 300 suppliers, most are not even located near the plant, but are in 39 states and an average of 550 miles away from Spring Hill. Ryder System, the Miami transportation services company, manages the Saturn network. Tractors pulling trailers that are 90 percent full on average arrive daily at a site two miles from Saturn's factory. The drivers uncouple the trailers, which contain bar-coded, reusable plastic containers full of parts, and shuttle tractors deliver them to the plant. Saturn is linked electronically with all its suppliers and reorders parts each time a car comes off the assembly line, an example of a pull production system in action.

In a true JIT environment, shipments are received in standardized containers, each containing standardized quantities, so that there is no reason to unpack and count all incoming goods. This practice also eliminates the potential for damage through handling and saves space.

Supplier Quality.   JIT purchasing requires that the manufacturer trust the supplier to deliver on time and with zero defects. To build such trusting relationships requires a reduction in the number of suppliers used. All U.S. companies that have implemented JIT systems have reduced the number of suppliers to five or fewer—even to one—for a given part. This way the manufacturer can work more closely with the supplier or suppliers, thus improving design and product quality and reducing costs.

In return for the extra effort suppliers make to accommodate JIT manufacturers with more frequent deliveries, standardized shipments, and better quality, suppliers are rewarded with long-term contracts. Hewlett-Packard, for instance, has given its JIT suppliers 18- to 36-month contracts with the potential for renegotiation every six to 13 months in exchange for quality improvement or cost reduction.

Accounting-Information Systems[7]

Several traditional cost-accounting practices contribute to the kind of waste that JIT systems are designed to eliminate: tracking and reporting direct labor for purposes of overhead allocation, tracking and reporting machine utilization, using full-absorption costing to determine costs for in-process inventory, and variance reporting.[8] In a JIT environment, small and numerous batches make tracking and reporting direct labor against each production order as in a job-costing system impractical. In addition, increased automation associated with JIT has dramatically reduced direct labor, making it inappropriate to distribute overhead. Machine-utilization tracking encourages managers to produce beyond demand requirements, thus building inventories, which is contrary to JIT goals of inventory reduction. In JIT environments, lead times are much shorter than in traditional manufacturing systems. Hence there is little incentive to allocate costs to inventory at any level other than that of finished products. Finally, variance reports are generally not available until the following working day in a traditional manufacturing environment, so any action initiated as a result takes place long after problems have occurred. Such traditional accounting practices have hindered JIT implementation in many companies. Therefore, changes to the accounting system are necessary for effective application of JIT.

JIT Linkages to Management Practices

As can be seen from the preceding discussion, JIT production requires many internal and external changes for an organization. Reconfiguring the physical layout of the manufacturing process, changing production-control methods and building new supplier relationships cannot be done overnight. Toyota took 20 to 30 years to develop and refine its efficient production system. With today's knowledge and the experiences of others, however, a company should be able to implement a JIT system within two years with a clear set of objectives and a carefully designed implementation plan—and with the commitment and involvement of all employees, from top managers to the line operators. Because of the close relationship between the JIT concept and TQM, companies that subscribe to a TQM philosophy have better success in implementing JIT production.

Top Management Support

Prior to implementation, top managers should have a basic understanding of the JIT concept to take full advantage of the firm's resources, both physical and human. Some difficult questions must be addressed: How will performance be measured? Who will perform equipment setup? Who is responsible for quality control? Managers must be willing to sacrifice short-term profits for significantly larger long-term gains. That is contrary to the bottom-line emphasis of Western management, but is essential for a successful JIT system.

Human Resource Management

A survey of JIT implementation in the United States found that, according to 83 percent of respondents, the single most important factor in success was the cellular layout of the plant.[9] Layout changes resulted in reductions in space requirements, throughput times, and WIP, and improvements in quality due to early detection of defects. Seventy-one percent of respondents indicated that simplification in materials handling was important, but only 9 percent felt that automated materials handling provided a significant advantage. However, the survey indicated that automated materials handling is important when done in conjunction with flexible manufacturing systems. In addition, 92 percent of respondents felt that employees are a positive force for change in the implementation of JIT—implying the importance of education and training.

A survey of firms that have implemented JIT found that most organizations use training and development programs as a principal means of securing worker cooperation and commitment to JIT.[10] The survey indicated that the number of job classifications dropped significantly as a result of cross-training programs. However, increased worker involvement and empowerment are often a major problem for middle managers. Many traditional managers are uncomfortable sharing responsibilities that they view as primarily managerial roles. This problem can be overcome by allowing middle managers to become more involved with the planning and coordination of JIT activities. Somewhat surprisingly, the survey did not find any major problems in negotiating with unions. In fact, several organizations succeeded in obtaining union consessions on worker utilization simply by adding job-security provisions to their labor agreements.

Quality Management

JIT cannot function properly if production has a high rate of defective items. Thus, it requires painstakingly careful attention to quality, both in purchasing and in production. Since lot sizes are small, and there is no safety stock to back up nonconforming items, any quality problem disrupts the flow of materials throughout the plant. In fact, one advantage of small lot sizes is that they reveal quality problems that would have been hidden by large inventories. Another advantage is that machines are not overworked and can be properly maintained when lot sizes are small. Breakdowns are therefore less likely, and better-conditioned machines improve product quality.

Japanese production workers are their own quality inspectors; knowing that a problem can stop the entire system provides the incentive to produce good-quality parts consistently. Purchased items are not inspected; they are expected to be defect-free when they are received. Japanese manufacturers take great pains to ensure that supplier quality is perfect, even to the extent of helping suppliers solve their own quality problems.

The group-technology layouts discussed earlier help promote higher quality as well as efficiency. With one-piece production flow, inspection methods must be incorporated as part of the operator's responsibilities, and production defects must be identified immediately and corrected. To ensure that no defective parts are allowed to flow in the system, the Japanese use *poka-yoke* methods (see Chapter 11) involving the use of automatic devices to stop machines if quality deteriorates. For example, during a milling process, holes may be drilled into the tooling plate, allowing a small amount of compressed air to pass through. If the work piece does not rest properly on the tooling plate because of the presence of a chip, the flow of compressed air will not be stopped and the machine will be shut off automatically.

The impact of quality in JIT extends down to the housekeeping of the workplace. Cleanliness, simplification, and proper organization promote a safer environment and reduce wasted time, motion, and resources.

Benefits of JIT Production

The most obvious benefit from using JIT is the cost benefit resulting from a reduction in WIP inventory. Besides the lower inventory investment, lower expenditures for facilities, equipment, and labor also accrue. Moreover, there is less need for sophisticated inventory-control systems and WIP tracking, making production control highly simplified. Another major benefit is the improved quality that results from participation of the work force in problem solving. Better quality, in turn, results in less wasted material, fewer labor hours on rework, and fast feedback on defects. Thus costs are further reduced and productivity is increased by quality improvements. Figure 15.3 illustrates this cause-and-effect chain.

Figure 15.3
Effects of JIT Production
Management

SOURCE: Richard J. Schonberger, "Some Observations on the Advantages and Implementation Issues of Just-in-Time Production Systems," *Journal of Operations Management* 1, no. 1 (1982). Reprinted with permission, Journal of the American Production and Inventory Control Society, Inc.

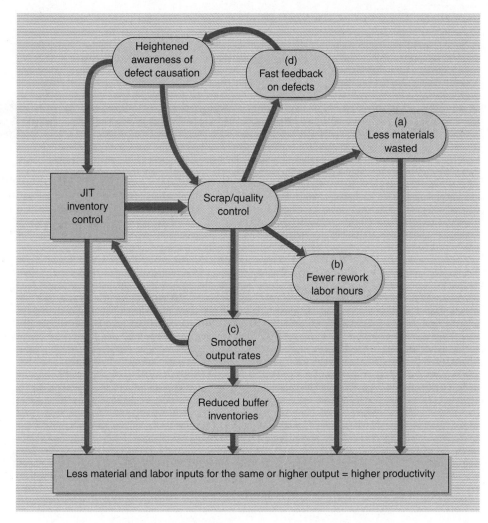

Using the principles of JIT, Toyota reduced its production time from 15 days to one day. Toyota also found that every time the WIP inventory level halved relative to production volume, labor productivity increased. Over a 10-year period labor productivity increased about 40 percent. Other Japanese manufacturers of automobiles, motorcycles, and electronic products have reported similar results. In the United States, a motor-control manufacturer reduced production time from eight weeks to one week, halved its inventory level, halved its required floor space, and reduced indirect labor costs significantly. Examples of other specific benefits reported are[11]

- Punch press setup time reduced from one hour to one minute.
- Inventory turns increased from 16 to 30.
- Scrap reduced from 2.5 percent to 0.9 percent.
- Warehouse and/or stockroom eliminated.
- Lead times reduced from 15 days to 1.5 days.
- Die change time reduced from 56 minutes to 1.5 minutes.

- WIP inventory cut from 22 days to one day.
- Number of forklifts cut from 50 to six.
- Worker productivity increased 38 percent.

Applications of JIT in Service Organizations

JIT has had its biggest impact in manufacturing, but service organizations are increasingly finding applications for it. The JIT philosophy supports the reduction of cycle time, which many organizations—manufacturing and nonmanufacturing alike—now regard as a key element of their corporate strategies. From this viewpoint, JIT may even have a greater potential impact in services than in manufacturing.

One overnight package-delivery service saw its inventory investment climb from $16 million to $34 million with conventional inventory-management techniques.[12] Implementing JIT reduced its inventory investment, but the company's major objective was to increase profits by providing a 99.9 percent level of service to its customers. Before JIT implementation its service level—computed by dividing the number of items filled weekly by the number of items requested—was 79 percent. After JIT the level was 99 percent, and the firm looked forward to meeting its goal. Baxter International is another service company that has experienced the benefits of a JIT system.

Applied P/OM
Baxter International

Baxter International fills hospital orders on a just-in-time basis.[13]

St. Luke's Episcopal Hospital in Houston has applied JIT to its dispensing of hospital supply products. Most hospitals maintain a large inventory of supplies in a central storeroom and replenish the supplies needed in the various areas of the hospital on a regular basis. St. Luke's adopted a radical strategy; it closed its warehouse and sold its inventory to Baxter International, a major hospital supplier. Baxter has become a partner with the hospital in managing, ordering, and delivering supplies. Baxter fills orders in exact, sometimes small, quantities and delivers them directly to the hospital departments, including operating rooms and nursing floors. The hospital is now saving $350,000 annually due to staff reductions and $162,500 by eliminating its inventory. Its storeroom has been converted to patient care and other productive uses.

The fundamental purpose of JIT is the elimination of waste and continuous improvement. We saw that in manufacturing, sources of waste include storing, moving, expediting, scheduling, and inspection. Many service activities—for example, administrative operations such as ordering and billing—have analogous sources of waste: filing, mailing, "rush" orders, prioritizing, and proofing. Flowcharting (see Chapter 11) is a good way to identify these sources of waste. A flowchart identifies the internal customers of any activity and the activities that do not add value to the process, making it easy to see where improvements are possible and to incorporate JIT techniques such as standardization, multifunctional workers, and group technology. At the Nashua Corporation, for example, a JIT-oriented study of administrative operations reduced order-cycle time from three days to one hour, office space requirements by 40 percent, and errors by 95 percent, and increased productivity by 20 percent.[14] More importantly, attitudes were changed; everyone now works to improve the process continually and provide better service to the customer.

An example of JIT implementation in a mail-order operation is presented as a "P/OM in Practice" case later in this chapter.

Constraint Management[15]

A popular approach to synchronous manufacturing is called constraint management, or the **theory of constraints (TOC).** Its principal objective is to establish a process of continuous improvement through synchronous manufacturing, and it is based on the premise that constraints determine the performance of any system. A *constraint* is any resource lack that prevents the system from achieving continuously higher levels of performance. Limited capacity at work centers, inflexible work rules, inadequate labor skills, and an ineffective management philosophy are all forms of constraints. Constraint resources determine the throughput of the facility, because they limit a plant's production level to their own capacity; the excess capacity of nonconstraint resources cannot be used. Since the number of such constraints is typically small, TOC focuses on identifying them, managing them carefully, linking them to the market to ensure an appropriate product mix, and scheduling the nonconstraint resources to enhance the competitiveness of the production process. In addition to improving throughput, constraint management can help to reduce inventories, lower operating costs, and improve responsiveness.

Constraint management contrasts sharply with JIT, which uses the *Kanban* pull system, in its focus on resources rather than finished product as a basis for scheduling all operations. Like JIT, however, TOC assumes that material flows in small batches, called *transfer batches,* consisting of the required number of units that need to be processed before the next operation is done. Unlike JIT, TOC *process batches,* the number of units processed with one setup, may be larger than transfer batches. Although this would seem to be inefficient, the rationale is that nonconstraints may be inefficient. Once material is released, it will flow quickly to the constraints. Nonconstraint resources will not tend to accumulate inventory since they operate solely to feed the constraints. Therefore, it is not necessary to try to optimize every resource, but only the critical ones.

Figure 15.4 summarizes the steps in synchronizing the manufacturing process in constraint management. The initial step is to identify the firm's constraint resources. Next, *time buffers* are placed at key points in the process to protect throughput. Three of these points are of particular importance:

Figure 15.4 Steps in Synchronizing the Manufacturing Process

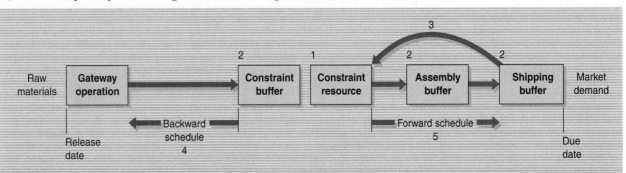

1. Identify the constraint resources.
   • Identify work centers where inventory accumulates.
   • Look for a late-expedite pattern in parts produced at constraint resources.
   • Identify consistently late orders.

2. Place time buffers in critical locations to protect throughput.
   • Use buffers in front of constraint resources to keep them running.
   • Use buffers at assembly points of convergence to ensure timely output.
   • Use buffers at end of the production process to meet specific customer orders.

3. Determine the production schedule for the constraint resource.
   • Link the constraint resource to market demand, looking at the order lead times between the constraint resource and the shipping buffer.
   • Trade off the constraint resources' limited capacity between process and setup times.

4. Control release of materials to the production floor to feed constraint resources.
   • Backward-schedule from the constraint resource to gateway operations.
   • Establish priority rules to determine the sequence in which jobs are to be processed when conflicts arise.

5. Move material processed on the constraint resource quickly and smoothly through the remaining operations.
   • Forward-schedule work stations that follow the constraint resource.
   • Allow transfer and process batches to vary to ensure a smooth materials flow.

• In front of the constraint resource.
• At assembly points where parts that have been processed on the constraint resource converge.
• At the finished goods/shipping area.

The three remaining steps in the synchronization process all serve to link the system's resources so that the constraint resources can operate continually and all materials can flow smoothly through the facility. The schedule for a constraint resource is based on that resource's limited capacity, market demand, and the lead times from the constraint resource to the shipping buffer. Then, workstations that precede a constraint resource are backward-scheduled from the time buffer to the gateway operation. Thus, the gateway operation is scheduled to release materials in a way that supports the constraint resource. Similarly, workstations that follow a constraint resource are scheduled forward from the constraint resource (Chapter 18 discusses this scheduling process further).

When this approach is used, the method of establishing lot sizes is different. Rather than using the costs of setups at nonconstraint resources to establish batch sizes, trade-offs among throughput, lead times, and setups at the constraint resource determine the batch size. Further, process and transfer batches of the nonconstraint resources are allowed to vary to maintain flow, avoid timing constraints, and reduce lead times.

Constraint management goes beyond the scheduling function, however. Once the constraint resources are identified, the nature of key management decisions—product costing, performance measurement, product and process design, and so on—change. Through these changes, constraint management helps a firm to achieve the desired global or plantwide coordination of its manufacturing resources.

Binney and Smith, maker of Crayola crayons, and Procter & Gamble both use TOC in their distribution efforts. Binney and Smith had high inventory levels yet poor customer service. By using TOC to better position its distribution inventories, it was able to reduce inventories and improve service. Procter & Gamble reported $600 million in savings through inventory reduction and elimination of capital improvement through TOC.

The concept of synchronization using TOC applies not only to manufacturing, but also to administrative functions, as Stanley Furniture has shown.

Applied P/OM
Stanley Furniture

Stanley Furniture applied synchronous manufacturing concepts to its order-entry process.[16]

Stanley Furniture in Stanleytown, Virginia, had implemented synchronous manufacturing concepts in its assembly line, but soon discovered that order entry was a key constraint in the administrative process, which accounted for nearly half of the customer lead time. Order entry was a batch manufacturing process using a first-come, first-served scheduling rule. Key process steps were to receive orders, enter orders into a sales-order system, approval credit, notify master production scheduling (MPS), modify the MPS, modify the final assembly schedule, and consolidate orders for shipping. Waiting before each of those steps lengthened lead times. In analyzing this process, a team found that credit approval was the constraining activity. After streamlining the credit-approval process, the company was able to establish new procedures that better integrated order entry and inventory management, having eliminated credit approval as a system constraint. This led the team to tackle problems in the shipping function. Once this constraint was broken through several improvements, they identified the assembly line as the constraining resource. As a result, over 60 percent of orders are now shipped within seven days of receipt, and 95 percent are shipped within 15 days of receipt, a substantial improvement from the original 45-day lead time.

P/OM in Practice

Implementing JIT in a U.S. Toyota Motor Facility[17]

The Toyota Motor Manufacturing (TMM) plant in Long Beach, California, a wholly owned subsidiary of Toyota, is an excellent example of JIT implementation in the United States. Begun in 1972, TMM fabricates, assembles, and paints four models of truck beds for Toyota light trucks. Annual production exceeds 150,000 units, and the plant employs about 375 people in a 300,000-square-foot production area in 14 buildings.

JIT was gradually introduced in the plant. Implementation started in the assembly area and gradually expanded to other manufacturing functions as well as a selected number of suppliers over a two-year period. A group of managers, each of them assigned to a specific JIT responsibility, started a pilot project and planned the detailed JIT implementation.

There were many initial problems, including an immediate loss in manufacturing volume. As one problem was solved, many others surfaced. Fortunately, Toyota understood that problems would occur in the short run but that time spent in solving them would translate into significant long-term benefits and cost savings.

Kanban is used at the Toyota Long Beach plant to control the flow of material and production operations. It is understood that Kanban, by itself, is only a small piece of the total JIT planning and control system. The environment created by the Kanban attention and JIT philosophy is mostly responsible for continuous improvements in manufacturing and for reducing the WIP inventory.

Kanban is the primary method of shop-floor control. The Kanbans in this plant are traveling paper tickets containing detailed information that provides control requirements and even

satisfies accounting and IRS needs. This is in contrast to many Japanese plants, where Kanbans are simple (usually triangular) pieces of metal with limited information.

In one instance, Kanbans are combined with bar coding to obtain rapid access to inventory-level information and to facilitate WIP cycle counting. Many types of Kanbans are used to trigger different operations or to order raw material. The Kanbans are placed on hooks on a board beside the entrance to each area. The hook board is the staging area for the Kanbans, which circulate between the suppliers and the warehouse, the warehouse and the press department, and so on.

TMM cycles 4,000 to 5,000 Kanbans per day, which requires an immense amount of manual sorting and placing on the proper hooks each day. The company uses a single-Kanban method of recirculation, whereby the Kanban represents both the authority to produce and also the move and identification ticket. The hook board is color-coded, as are the Kanbans, to indicate raw material or other stages of manufacturing. The motto, of course, is "no Kanban—no production."

An attempt is made to decrease the number of Kanbans each month to constantly drive down the in-process inventory and increase the inventory cycles. The objective is to reduce the lot sizes to one and the WIP inventory to zero.

However, the schedule is not as rigid as in many other plants. A small safety stock is considered acceptable to allow for some flexibility in shifting the sequence of the operations or the mixture of the products. It also enables the plant to meet the schedule without exhausting the supply and interrupting the line. In the paint and stamping operations, the nature of manufacturing calls for a certain quantity per production run. In this

case, a number of Kanbans accumulate before they trigger the production of the preceding operation.

The master schedule is used to calculate the number of Kanbans. The calculations are simple and mostly manual. The products are made to order, which is anticipatory due to the difficulty of coordination with Japan in terms of the precise timing and destination of the orders. Additional flexibility is built in to allow for changing priorities. Ideally, the truck should arrive in time for the bed to be assembled and then shipped to the dealers and delivered to the customers. Study teams are constantly working to coincide the orders without sacrificing the flexibility and the ability to deliver the trucks to the customers.

Kanban is an example of the Toyota philosophy of managing by sight or visual control everywhere possible. This is done through color, light boards, hook boards, charts, and graphs at any opportunity. The visual controls facilitate immediate identification of problems such as shortage or excess of parts as well as any other unusual occurrence.

Visual controls are also extended to testing and shipping areas. They are easy to understand and inexpensive and they allow for immediate detection. There is a control chart for each critical operation, graphing the performance of that operation versus the acceptable level. A buzzer is used to indicate a problem or a failure in a function. An unusually long buzz notifies the supervisor that the machine is out of sequence and additional help should be dispatched.

A computerized board in the assembly area contains many colored lights indicating the status of machines and orders. Another board provides information on the scheduled versus the actual production as well as the reason for the variance. It provides workers with immediate feedback and general awareness to assist them in taking corrective action when needed.

Toyota attributes its success to the simultaneous materialization of the JIT system and respect for human beings. The workers are made aware that the purpose of process-improvement activities is not to eliminate their jobs, but to utilize them more effectively and thus help guarantee their jobs. The sole purpose of reducing costs by means of JIT is to obtain a better market competitive edge and thereby maintain the need for production—and thus workers' jobs—in the long run.

AT TMM, many workers voluntarily belong to "quality circles," which meet weekly in paid overtime. The company initially established a circle in the press area and then in the paint and the maintenance areas. The overall trend has been a rapid growth in the number of quality circles, the number of suggestions made, and the quality and complexity of suggestions. These circles were a great source of problem solving in preparation for JIT implementation.

The quality circles are particularly useful in implementing changes that workers tend to oppose. A JIT system requires many drastic changes in manufacturing. Quality circles may be used to educate workers as to the benefits of JIT and convince them that making the necessary changes is worthwhile. Quality circles may also be used to implement and support the required changes very quickly. They usually solve a number of smaller problems while they are working on the main problem. Employee suggestions are well recognized by TMM managers and rewarded, though not necessarily financially.

The company has firmly maintained the policy of retaining any worker whose job is eliminated in the productivity-improvement process by transferring his or her employment to another area.

Prior to the JIT system, the amount of raw-material and WIP inventories and also of finished goods in the shipping area was of great concern to managers. Another concern was hidden problems in quality and material-handling procedures. A worker could produce several hours' worth of defective units before they were discovered.

The immediate improvement from the implementation of JIT was the reduction of inventories, which resulted in a major reduction in carrying and handling costs. The average WIP inventory was lowered by about 45 percent and the raw-material inventory by approximately 24 percent in one year.

The warehousing cost of material was reduced by about 30 percent; the carrying and control costs were lowered accordingly. The policy was clear: Don't buy, don't move, and don't produce unless there is an immediate need. The suppliers were initially concerned, but were soon encouraged to rely on a continuous JIT order and to deliver accordingly.

As the inventory was drained, the overloaded buildings were emptied, and many hidden problems in handling and moving the material surfaced. The warehouse was reorganized, and the additional space was utilized for other productive purposes. Improvements in handling procedures resulted in shorter movement distances and fewer needs for equipment.

The material was delivered directly to the point of use. About 30 percent of the forklifts were eliminated as the average movement time and distance were reduced. In the production area, the number of presses was reduced by 30 percent. The same operations were performed with approximately 20 percent reduction in labor, and the production volume per shift was increased by 40 percent in less than two years. Some of these improvements were direct results of JIT production, but many were simply due to

changes made by the workers, inspired by the JIT atmosphere.

The most noticeable improvements are in worker attitudes and awareness. The JIT environment offers continuous challenge in the sense that there is no reserved inventory to comfort production. As a problem arises in the sequence, the line comes to a halt immediately. Thus, the workers are constantly stimulated to discover problems and fix them.

Absentee rate and nonproduction time are substantially reduced. Labor turnover and interdepartmental conflicts are diminished. The effects are translated into the process and result in productivity improvements. The outgoing product quality is improved and therefore the warranty costs and replacement parts are reduced substantially. The plant was recently given a safety award (only four awards were granted in five years) as the number of internal problems and accidents was reduced.

Costs are down, productivity and quality are up, employee morale is high, and TMM is in a strong international competitive position, all thanks primarily to JIT.

Questions for Discussion

1. How was JIT introduced in the Long Beach Toyota plant? Why do you think it was done in this way?
2. How was the Toyota philosophy of providing management by sight or visual control implemented in this plant? What advantages does this have?
3. What benefits were derived from implementing JIT?

An Application of JIT in Mail-Order Processing[18]

Semantodontics is a direct marketing company that sells nationally by catalog to dentists. One of its major product lines is personalized printed products. This product line was creating a larger than normal number of customer complaints, resulting in an increasing number of calls to the customer-service department. A study of the reasons for customer-service calls indicated that 64 percent of them involved two questions: "What is this charge on my statement?" and "Where is my order?"

After some investigation, both of these questions were found to be related to the long lead times required to produce personalized printed products. Customers often waited three or more weeks, and some statements mailed at the end of the month showed charges for orders invoiced but not yet printed. Therefore, the company began to study the process involved in meeting customer orders.

Figure 15.5 is a flowchart of the order-filling process. In the first step, telephone orders were taken over a 12-hour period each day. They were collected at the end of the day and checked for errors by the supervisor of the phone department, usually the following morning. Depending on how busy the supervisor was, the one-day batch of print orders would often not get to the data-processing department until after 1:00 P.M.

In the data-processing step, the telephone orders were invoiced, still in one-day batches. Then the invoices were printed and matched back to the original orders. This step usually took most of the next day to complete. At this point in the process, if the order was for a new customer, it was sent to the person who did customer verification and set up new customer accounts on the computer. Setting up a new account would often delay an order by a day or more.

The next step was order verification and proofreading. Once invoicing

Figure 15.5 Flowchart of Order-Filling Process

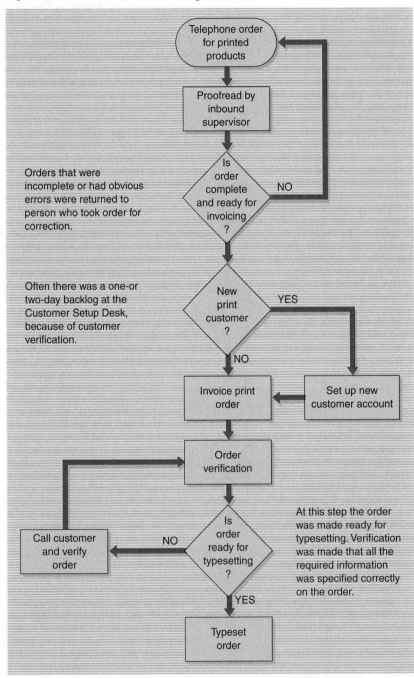

was completed, the orders with invoices attached were given to a person who verified that all the required information was present and correct to permit typesetting. If there was a question at this time, the order was checked by computer or by calling the customer. It was common for this step to have a two-day backlog of orders waiting for verification.

Finally, the completed orders were sent to the typesetting department of the printshop. Using current methods, an order for an existing customer took at least four days to flow from the order taker to typesetting. Often a new customer's order took a day or two longer. In addition, there was often more than a one-day backlog of orders at each step in the process.

This operation provided a classic opportunity to apply the JIT philosophy that lot sizes should be reduced as much as possible. In the telephone department, a system was developed to make the order batches smaller. Under this new system, the daily telephone orders are divided into three batches. The telephone supervisor reviews these smaller batches promptly

and sends them to the data-processing department three times daily, at 9:00 A.M., noon, and 3:00 P.M.

In the data-processing department, each batch of orders is invoiced. The smaller invoice batch size improved productivity of the matching operation by making it easier to match an invoice to its original order. It was also determined that the new-customer setup procedure was the bottleneck for about 20 percent of the orders. Customer verification required looking up the customer in various directories or checking with the customer by telephone. This often took a day or more to complete. A careful review showed that verification of each customer was an unnecessary step in the process for telephone orders because the person taking the order had already talked with the customer. By removing this step of the setup procedure, new customer setup time was dramatically reduced to only a few minutes.

The third step of the process, print-order verification, had always been thought to be the bottleneck. Even with smaller batch sizes, delays were still expected. However, the person in

this position began working faster to complete each batch before the next one arrived. Getting smaller batches (rather than having a two-day backlog and always being behind) resulted in increased job satisfaction as well as increased productivity.

After implementation of the JIT principles, the average order arrived at the typesetting department less than four hours after it was taken. This resulted in a significant reduction in the typesetting and printshop backlog. A large percentage of print orders is now being processed, printed, and shipped in less than four days. The customer receives the finished order in less than two weeks. After the first month of using the new system, Semantodontics observed a 20 percent reduction in customer service calls.

Questions for Discussion

1. Why did Semantodontics study the customer-order process?
2. How were JIT principles applied to the order-processing function? What benefits were realized?

Summary of Key Points

- Lean production is dedicated to improving production effectiveness through the elimination of waste, reduction of inventories, improvement of quality, and the development of human resources. Synchronous manufacturing is any systematic method of moving material quickly and smoothly through a manufacturing facility. Two approaches to synchronous manufacturing are just-in-time (JIT) and constraint management.

- JIT is a philosophy for materials management and control whose objective is to eliminate all sources of waste, including unnecessary inventory and scrap in production, and thus improve quality and productivity.

- JIT is based on six key components: production-floor management, scheduling, process and product design, work-force management, supplier management, and information systems. It must be linked to higher-level elements of a company's management organization. Figure 15.1 summarizes the important elements of JIT.

- Kanban (Japanese for "card") is a card-driven information system often used in JIT to initiate withdrawal and production of items throughout a production process.

- JIT depends on high quality because of small lot sizes. Employees are empowered to identify and correct problems at the source. Suppliers support JIT by delivering frequently in standardized containers so as to eliminate intermediate storage.

- JIT results in reduced work-in-process inventories, lower facility costs, simplified production control, work-force participation, improved quality, higher productivity, and increased profits.
- Constraint management, or the theory of constraints (TOC), is based on the concept of identifying and managing the vital few constraints in a production system and viewing them as drivers of production. Like JIT, TOC can improve throughput, reduce inventories, lower costs, and improve responsiveness.

Key Terms

Lean production
Synchronous manufacturing
Just-in-time (JIT)
Constraint management
Pull production
Kanban
Level master schedule
Theory of constraints (TOC)

Review Questions

1. Explain the characteristics of lean production.
2. Explain the underlying philosophy of JIT.
3. What cultural and geographic characteristics in Japan led to the development of JIT?
4. List and briefly describe the six core elements of JIT.
5. Explain the importance of short setup times and small lot sizes in a JIT environment.
6. What is pull production? Why is JIT most applicable to repetitive manufacturing situations?
7. Explain how a Kanban system operates.
8. Of what value is a level master schedule? What organizational changes are needed to operate under a level schedule?
9. What aspects of facility layout and production methods support the JIT philosophy?
10. Why are workers critical to success in JIT systems? What traditional management practices must be changed to reflect this new philosophy?
11. What is the role of suppliers in JIT systems?
12. How does JIT purchasing differ from conventional purchasing practices?
13. What does the Japanese term *yo-i-don* mean?
14. What are some of the problems that traditional accounting systems cause in a JIT environment?
15. Discuss the importance of total quality management to successful JIT operation.
16. Discuss the benefits of JIT. How does JIT lead to higher productivity?
17. Explain how the JIT concept can be adapted to service organizations.
18. Define *constraint*.
19. Explain the process of synchronizing a manufacturing process in the theory of constraints (TOC) philosophy.

Discussion Questions

1. What impediments to JIT might a typical U.S. company face?
2. Interview a manager at a nearby company that uses JIT. Report on how it is implemented and the benefits the company has realized.
3. What types of "setups" do you perform in your work or school activities? How might you reduce the setup times?
4. Explain how Kanban might be used in your school's registration process to improve service.
5. Discuss how JIT might be applied in a fast-food restaurant. Draw a flowchart of the operation.
6. Identify some constraints in your work or school processes. Discuss how you might exploit them to improve performance.

Notes

1. James P. Womack, Daniel T. Jones, and Daniel Roos, *The Machine That Changed the World* (New York: HarperPerennial, 1990).
2. Y. Monden, "What Makes the Toyota Production System Really Tick," *Industrial Engineering,* January 1981, pp. 36–46.
3. Jon Van, "Leaks No Longer Stain Harley-Davidson Name," *Chicago Tribune,* November 4, 1991.
4. Richard J. Schonberger, "Just-in-Time Production Systems: Replacing Complexity with Simplicity in Manufacturing Management," *Industrial Engineering* 16, no. 10 (October 1984), pp. 52–63.
5. Ibid.
6. Ronald Henkoff, "Delivering the Goods," *Fortune,* November 28, 1994, pp. 64–78.
7. Much of this information has been drawn from Scott R. Hedin and Gregory R. Russell, "JIT Implementation: Interaction Between the Production and Cost-Accounting Functions," *Production and Inventory Management Journal* 33, no. 3 (third quarter 1992), pp. 68–73.
8. B. Maskell, "Management Accounting and Just-in-Time," *Management Accounting* 68, no. 3 (1986), pp. 32–34.
9. Thomas J. Billesbach, "A Study of the Implementation of Just-in-Time in the United States," *Production and Inventory Management Journal* 32, no. 3 (1991), pp. 1–4.

10. Jin H. Im, Sandra J. Hartman, and Philip J. Bondi, "How Do JIT Systems Affect Human Resource Management?" *Production and Inventory Management Journal* 35, no. 1 (first quarter 1994), pp. 1–4.

11. Mehran Sepehri, *Just-in-Time, Not Just in Japan* (Falls Church, VA: American Production and Inventory Control Society, 1986); and R. J. Schonberger, *World-Class Manufacturing* (New York: The Free Press, 1986).

12. R. Inman and S. Mehra, "JIT Implementation within a Service Industry: A Case Study," *International Journal of Service Industry Management* 1, no. 3 (1990). See also R. Inman and S. Mehra, "JIT Applications for Service Environments," *Production and Inventory Management Journal* 32, no. 3 (1991), pp. 16–21.

13. Milt Freudenheim, "Removing the Warehouse from Cost-Conscious Hospitals," *The New York Times,* Sunday, March 3, 1991, p. F5.

14. Paul E. Dickinson, Earl C. Dodge, and Charles S. Marshall, "Administrative Functions in a Just-in-Time Setting," *Target,* Fall 1988, pp. 12–17.

15. Portions of this discussion were adapted from Stanley E. Fawcett and John N. Pearson, "Understanding and Applying Constraint Management in Today's Manufacturing Environments," *Production and Inventory Management Journal* 32, no. 3 (third quarter 1991). Reprinted with permission, The American Production and Inventory Control Society, Falls Church, VA. See also Stanley C. Gardiner, John H. Blackstone, Jr. and Lorraine R. Gardiner, "The Evolution of the Theory of Constraints," *Industrial Management* 36, no. 3 (1994), pp. 13–16.

16. Michael S. Spencer and Samuel Wathen, "Applying the Theory of Constraints' Process Management Technique to an Administrative Function at Stanley Furniture," *National Productivity Review* 13, no. 3 (Summer 1994), pp. 379–385.

17. Adapted from Mehran Sepehri, "How Kanban System Is Used in an American Toyota Motor Facility," *Industrial Engineering* 17, no. 2 (1985). Copyright Institute of Industrial Engineers, 25 Technology Park/Atlanta, Norcross, GA 30092.

18. Adapted from Ronald G. Conant, "JIT in a Mail-Order Operation Reduces Processing Time from Four Days to Four Hours," *Industrial Engineering* 20, no. 9 (1988), pp. 34–37. Copyright Institute of Industrial Engineers, 25 Technology Park/Atlanta, Norcross, GA 30092.

Part V
Planning and
Scheduling

This part pertains to managing work flow in production operations. In Chapter 16, aggregate planning and master scheduling are introduced. Those tools are used to anticipate and plan for production over an intermediate time horizon. The plans must be translated into detailed schedules for either making or purchasing the components of the goods that are to be produced. Such material requirements planning is discussed in Chapter 17.

Techniques for short-term scheduling in manufacturing and service operations are presented in Chapter 18, with a special emphasis on scheduling within the firm's capacity constraints. Chapter 19 covers the scheduling and control of complex projects, describing the use of project management techniques to ensure that projects stay within time and budget constraints.

Chapter Outline

Chapter Sixteen
Aggregate Production Planning and Master Scheduling

Applied P/OM

P/OM in Practice

Production planning and master scheduling involve determining future production levels over a time horizon of several months to one year. Whereas the production plan establishes an intermediate-range goal for the company's products and capacity utilization in total, the master schedule provides the input for detailed scheduling and control at the operational level.

Top management involvement in production planning is essential, especially in establishing manufacturing, marketing, and financial plans. From a manufacturing perspective, for instance, the production plan assists in determining the required intermediate capacity and the needed capacity adjustments. From marketing's perspective, the production plan determines the amount of product that will be available to meet demand. Finally, from the viewpoint of finance, the production plan identifies funding needs and establishes the basis for budgeting decisions.

Poor production planning can lead to excessive inventory levels and increased carrying costs or back orders and reduced customer service. For a business like MamaMia's, which produces in response to customers' orders rather than building inventory in anticipation of future demand, these activities may not seem as critical as they would be for traditional manufacturing firms. However, MamaMia's must plan its food purchases and adjust its production capacity (such as number of food preparers and drivers) in anticipation of seasonal demand changes and special holiday peak demands. Thus, in companies of all sizes, good production planning is necessary to achieve productivity and customer-service goals.

This chapter covers the fundamental concepts and techniques used in production planning and master scheduling, specifically,

••• The key planning strategies for meeting fluctuating demand.

••• Quantitative approaches to developing low-cost production plans.

••• The role of master scheduling and rough-cut capacity planning in the production-planning process.

••• Short-term capacity-planning strategies often used in service organizations.

Production-Planning Process

Figure 16.1 illustrates the essential elements of the production-planning and scheduling process. The elements examined in this chapter are aggregate production planning, master production scheduling, rough-cut capacity planning, and final-assembly scheduling. The nonshaded areas in the figure—materials requirements planning (MRP), short-range scheduling, and related capacity issues—are discussed in subsequent chapters.

Accurate demand estimation is a necessary input to production planning. It should include not only forecasts of future product demand but also actual orders for which commitments have been made, service and spare-part requirements, warehouse inventory requirements, and inventory level adjustments as determined by the strategic business plan. More accurate forecasts can be made for aggregate groups of items, particularly over long time horizons. Since production plans are made for up to one year's time, demand and production/inventory levels are usually expressed by aggregate measures of capacity such as dollars, tons, gallons, machine hours, or units of product groups.

Figure 16.1
Production-Planning and
Scheduling Process

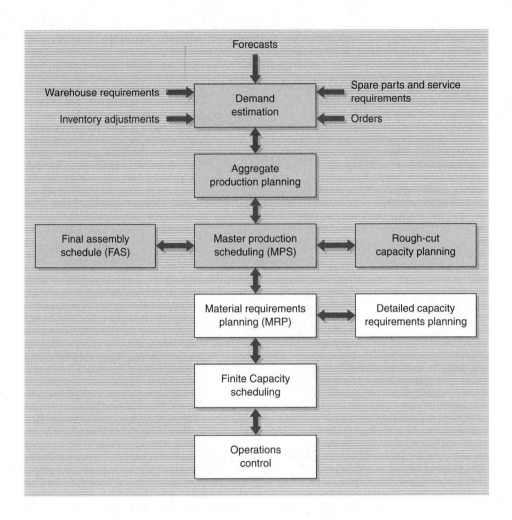

Aggregate production planning is the development of monthly or quarterly production requirements for product groups or families that will meet the estimates of demand. Manufacturing, marketing, and financial managers are responsible for developing the production plan. Gross capacity considerations must be taken into account during production planning. If production to satisfy demand cannot be achieved within existing resource limitations, managers may have to make intermediate-range capacity adjustments. If long-term trends are evident, managers may also want to consider strategic resource changes.

Once an aggregate production plan is made, it must be broken apart—disaggregated—into time-phased requirements for individual products. The time-phased plan is called the **master production schedule (MPS).** The MPS usually provides weekly product requirements over a 6- to 12-month time horizon. It is not a forecast, but rather a schedule of when production should be completed in order to satisfy demand. The MPS is used by operating personnel in making detailed plans for procuring materials, producing components, and the final assembly of the finished goods.

Rough-cut capacity planning involves analysis of the MPS to determine whether sufficient capacity is available at critical points in the production process. Specific operations such as final assembly, painting, or finishing are examined to predict where bottlenecks will occur. This provides a rapid determination of the feasibility of the MPS. Often adjustments to the MPS are made as a result of this analysis. Rough-cut capacity planning generally covers a three-month time horizon.

The **final assembly schedule (FAS)** is a statement of the final products that are to be assembled from MPS items. The FAS is usually not prepared as far in advance as the MPS. In some firms, the MPS and FAS are identical; in others they are distinct schedules. For example, final products may differ only in labeling, packaging, painting, or finish. In such cases the MPS is concerned only with the basic items, while the FAS distinguishes among the final products.

Note the hierarchical nature of the planning process in Figure 16.1. Plans are developed and passed down the hierarchy to the next level, leading to the ultimate goal of production on the shop floor. Plans made at each level must be consistent with those developed at the next-higher level. Thus the MPS must be consistent with the aggregate production plan; the materials requirements plan must be consistent with the MPS; and short-range schedules must be consistent with the materials requirements plan.

Production planning is an important component of manufacturing strategy, since both are concerned with how capacity is managed. The capacity question is particularly important when demand is highly seasonal. Managers must ask: To what extent will inventory serve as a buffer against uncertain demand? Will customer demand be managed through planned back orders? Will the labor force fluctuate through planned layoffs and rehiring as demand fluctuates, or will excess capacity be carried during periods of low demand? Decisions in these areas must address profitability, customer service, and the flexibility to introduce new products and change the product mix.

Aggregate Production and Capacity Planning

The first step in the production-planning process is to translate demand forecasts into planned monthly production levels. Aggregate planning focuses on overall capacity, because it is concerned with product groups as opposed to individual products. Aggregate-capacity measures—barrels per month, units per month, labor hours per month, and so on—are used in specifying the plan. For instance, a sport-shoe manufacturer might consider broad product lines such as tennis shoes, cross-training shoes, and hightop basketball shoes in developing an aggregate production plan. Individual styles, colors, and sizes are not considered at this level. Another example is provided by Rowntree MacKintosh Canada, Ltd., a food-export company.

Applied P/OM

Rowntree MacKintosh Canada, Ltd. (Part a)

Aggregate plans at Rowntree MacKintosh Canada are focused on quality, personnel, capital, and customer-service objectives.[1]

Rowntree MacKintosh Canada, Ltd., exports confectionery and grocery products (e.g., candy bars, boxed chocolates, cookies, and peanut butter) to over 120 countries. The Canadian factory in Toronto manufactures 16 major brand items which generate 75 distinct product lines.

One of the major brand items that has a highly seasonal demand is boxed chocolates. Boxed chocolates are produced in three types, with a total of nine distinct end items: Black Magic, in 2-lb., $1\frac{1}{2}$-lb., 1-lb., and $\frac{1}{2}$-lb. boxes; Rendezvous, in 14-oz. boxes; and Dairy Box, in the same four sizes as Black Magic.

Forecasting is accomplished by dividing the year into 13 periods of four weeks each. Sales planning provides an end-item forecast, by period, for the full 13 periods. This estimate is updated every four weeks, reflecting the latest information on available inventories and estimated sales for the next 13 periods.

Aggregate planning is performed by first converting all end items to a poundage figure. The planning task is to calculate levels of production that will best meet the quality, personnel, capital, and customer service restrictions. These restrictions are summarized as:

1. *Quality.* An important quality consideration is the age of the product when it reaches the consumer. It is essential that products reach the consumer within well-defined, acceptable time periods to ensure freshness.

2. *Personnel.* It is stated company policy and practice to maintain a stable work force. Short-term capacity can be increased with overtime and/or with part-time employees.

3. *Capital restrictions.* The amount of inventory investment has become a major concern, and inventory levels must be kept low to meet restrictions on capital investment.

4. *Customer-service levels.* The nature of the industry makes it necessary to strive for 100 percent customer service. The desire to minimize inventory investment often conflicts with this goal.

If demand is relatively constant, developing a production plan is not difficult. First, we must determine a time horizon, commonly one year, and obtain a sales forecast over that period. Next, minimum inventory levels must be established to provide desired levels of customer service. The desirable inventory levels at the beginning and at the end of the planning horizon must be determined. The total production required over the planning horizon is the total sales forecast plus or minus any desired change in inventory. The required monthly or weekly production rates are then easily determined. For example, suppose an automotive parts company has a current inventory of air filters of 80,000 and wants to reduce the level to 50,000 over the next year. The demand forecast calls for sales of 500,000 filters. The total production required is then 500,000 less 30,000 (the net change in inventory level), or 470,000. Thus an average of about 39,167 (470,000 divided by 12) filters per month need to be manufactured. Producing a constant amount each month is an acceptable strategy *provided that* demand is also relatively constant. When demand is seasonal or fluctuates significantly over the planning period, production must be planned more carefully lest shortages and/or high inventory levels result.

Strategies for Meeting Fluctuating Demand

A variety of strategies address fluctuating demand by altering intermediate-range capacity. There are four major types of aggregate-planning strategies: production-rate changes, work-force changes, inventory smoothing, and demand shifting. The choice of strategy depends on corporate policies, practical limitations, and cost factors. The strategies and their relevant costs are summarized in Table 16.1.

Production-Rate Changes. One of the most common means of increasing the production rate without changing existing resources is through planned overtime. Generally, this requires wage premiums to be paid. Alternatively, hours can be reduced during slow periods. However, reduced pay can seriously affect employee morale.

The production rate may also be altered by subcontracting during periods of peak demand. This would probably not be a feasible alternative for some companies, but it is effective in industries that manufacture a large portion of their own parts, such as the machine-tool industry. When business is brisk, components can be subcontracted; when business is slow, the firm may act as a subcontractor to other industries that may be working at capacity. In that way, a stable work force is maintained.

Work-Force Changes. Changing the size of the work force is usually accomplished through hiring and layoffs. Both have disadvantages. Hiring additional labor usually results in higher costs for the personnel department and for training. Layoffs result in severance pay and additional unemployment insurance costs, as well as low employee morale. Also, seniority "bumping" practices can change the skills mix of the work force and result in inefficient production. A stable work force may be obtained by staffing the plant for peak production levels, but then many workers may be idle during low-demand periods.

In many industries changing work-force levels is not a feasible alternative. In firms that consist primarily of assembly operations with low skill requirements, however, it may be cost-effective. The toy industry is a good example.

Table 16.1 Aggregate-Planning Strategies and Cost Factors

Strategy	Cost Factors
Production-rate changes	
Overtime	Wage premiums
Undertime	Opportunity losses
Subcontracting	Additional overhead
Work-force changes	
Hiring and laying off	Training costs and separation pay
Inventory smoothing	
Build inventories	Carrying costs
Allow shortages	Back-order and lost-sales costs
Demand shifting	
Pricing strategies	Lower profit margins
Advertising promotions	Administrative costs

Accurate forecasts for the winter holiday season cannot be made until whole-sale buyers have placed orders, usually around midyear. Toy companies maintain a minimal number of employees until production is increased for the holidays. Then they hire a large number of part-time workers in order to operate at maximum capacity. As another example, the U.S. Postal Service hires extra mail carriers during the holiday season to increase its capacity. In general, service facilities must meet demand through work-force changes, because other alternatives are simply not feasible. Rowntree MacKintosh Canada, Ltd., uses both work-force and production-rate changes to meet fluctuating demand.

≡ Applied P/OM

Rowntree MacKintosh Canada, Ltd. (Part b)

Rowntree MacKintosh Canada's strategy for meeting fluctuating demands has two components.[2]

At Rowntree MacKintosh Canada, the daily production rate with one regular shift is 9,000 pounds. Table 16.2 gives the production alternatives for one period (20 days' production). Table 16.3 illustrates a typical aggregate production plan. Notice that production is substantially increased in

Table 16.2 Production Alternatives at Rowntree MacKintosh Canada

Hours Worked	Output per Day	Output per Period	Work Force
8	9,000	180,000	regular shift
12	13,500	270,000	regular + part time
13	14,900	298,000	regular + part time
14	16,300	326,000	regular + part time
15	17,600	352,000	regular + part time
16	19,000	380,000	two full shifts

Table 16.3 Aggregate Production Plan for Rowntree MacKintosh Canada

Period	Estimated Stock	Estimated Production	Estimated Sales
1	145,201	180,000	155,310
2	169,891	180,000	101,190
3	248,701	90,000	120,630
4	218,071	90,000	135,825
5	172,246	247,000	102,750
6	316,496	380,000	61,140
7	635,356	361,000	62,550
8	933,806	95,000	34,440
9	994,366	361,000	107,790
10	1,247,576	380,000	462,600
11	1,164,976	321,000	1,034,610
12	451,366	180,000	337,260
13	294,106	90,000	238,905
		2,955,000	2,955,000

period 5 and decreased in period 12 to account for the seasonality of demand. (The low production in period 8 is the result of a vacation shutdown.) Minimum acceptable inventory levels are maintained for customer service. Inventory levels in the plan are controlled to meet the quality standards. Thus, the two components of work-force capacity and production rate are adjusted in Rowntree's strategic plan.

Inventory Smoothing.   Inventory is often built up during slack periods and held for peak periods, though this increases inventory-carrying costs and necessitates sufficient warehouse space. For some products, such as perishable commodities, this alternative cannot be considered. A related strategy is to carry back orders or to tolerate lost sales during peak demand periods. But this may be unacceptable if profit margins are low and competition is high.

Another typical strategy for smoothing inventory is to make products whose seasonal peaks are opposite. Companies that produce home-heating equipment are usually in the air-conditioning business as well. Thus marketing and product mix have a direct impact on the decisions involved in aggregate planning.

Demand Shifting.   Various marketing strategies can be employed to influence demand. For example, higher prices can be charged to reduce peak demand, whereas low prices, coupons, and increased advertising can be used to reduce inventories and increase demand during slack times (such as the winter months for lawn mowers and garden items).

Cost Considerations

The major costs associated with implementing a production plan include the costs of production, inventory holding and stockout, and capacity change. Production costs typically have a fixed cost for setup and a variable cost per unit produced. (See, for instance, the development of the production lot-size model in Chapter 14.) Inventory-holding and stockout costs are usually directly proportional to the amount of inventory and stockouts. Capacity-change costs take different forms. There may be a fixed cost associated with, for example, hiring an additional employee, as well as a variable cost for wages paid. If overtime is used, then only variable costs may be appropriate.

Example

Planning for Seasonal Demand

Let us consider the situation faced by Golden Breweries, a producer of Golden Brew and Golden Delight beers. The spreadsheet in Figure 16.2 shows a monthly aggregate demand forecast for the next year. Note that the demand forecast fluctuates quite a bit over the year, with seasonal peaks in the summer and winter holiday season.

How should Golden Breweries plan production for the next 12 months in the face of fluctuating demand? Let us suppose the company has a normal production capacity of 2,200 barrels per month and a current inventory of 1,000 barrels. If it produces at normal capacity each month, we have the

Figure 16.2 Spreadsheet for Golden Breweries Production Plan (GOLDEN.XLS)

	A	B	C	D	E	F	G	H
1	Golden Breweries Production Plan							
2								
3	Production cost ($/bbl)			$ 70.00				
4	Inventory holding cost ($/bbl)			$ 1.40				
5	Lost sales cost ($/bbl)			$ 90.00				
6	Overtime cost ($/bbl)			$ 6.50				
7	Undertime cost ($/bbl)			$ 3.00				
8	Rate change cost ($/bbl)			$ 5.00				
9	Normal production rate			2,200				
10								
11					Cumulative			
12			Cumulative		Product	Ending	Lost	
13	Month	Demand	Demand	Production	Availability	Inventory	Sales	
14						1,000		
15	January	1,500	1,500	2,200	3,200	1,700	0	
16	February	1,000	2,500	2,200	5,400	2,900	0	
17	March	1,900	4,400	2,200	7,600	3,200	0	
18	April	2,600	7,000	2,200	9,800	2,800	0	
19	May	2,800	9,800	2,200	12,000	2,200	0	
20	June	3,100	12,900	2,200	14,200	1,300	0	
21	July	3,200	16,100	2,200	16,400	300	0	
22	August	3,000	19,100	2,200	18,600	0	500	
23	September	2,000	21,100	2,200	21,300	200	0	
24	October	1,000	22,100	2,200	23,500	1,400	0	
25	November	1,800	23,900	2,200	25,700	1,800	0	
26	December	2,200	26,100	2,200	27,900	1,800	0	
27								
28		Production	Inventory	Lost Sales	Overtime	Undertime	Rate Change	
29	Month	Cost	Cost	Cost	Cost	Cost	Cost	
30								
31	January	$ 154,000	$ 2,380	$ -	$ -	$ -	$ -	
32	February	$ 154,000	$ 4,060	$ -	$ -	$ -	$ -	
33	March	$ 154,000	$ 4,480	$ -	$ -	$ -	$ -	
34	April	$ 154,000	$ 3,920	$ -	$ -	$ -	$ -	
35	May	$ 154,000	$ 3,080	$ -	$ -	$ -	$ -	
36	June	$ 154,000	$ 1,820	$ -	$ -	$ -	$ -	
37	July	$ 154,000	$ 420	$ -	$ -	$ -	$ -	
38	August	$ 154,000	$ -	$ 45,000	$ -	$ -	$ -	
39	September	$ 154,000	$ 280	$ -	$ -	$ -	$ -	
40	October	$ 154,000	$ 1,960	$ -	$ -	$ -	$ -	
41	November	$ 154,000	$ 2,520	$ -	$ -	$ -	$ -	
42	December	$ 154,000	$ 2,520	$ -	$ -	$ -	$ -	
43		$1,848,000	$ 27,440	$ 45,000	$ -	$ -	$ -	
44								
45	Total cost	$1,920,440						

production/inventory schedule given in Figure 16.2. To calculate the ending inventory level each month, note that

$$\text{beginning inventory} + \text{production} - \text{demand} = \text{ending inventory} \quad (16.1)$$

For example, in February we have

$$1,700 + 2,200 - 1,000 = 2,900.$$

At this constant production rate, Golden Breweries will build up an inventory of 3,200 barrels in March and suffer lost sales of 500 barrels in August, one of the peak demand months for beer. Incurring shortages and carrying high inventories may not be a good business policy. Another possible difficulty with this schedule is the availability of sufficient storage space for inventories as large as 3,200 barrels.

A production plan is often illustrated graphically. Figure 16.3 is a graph of cumulative demand and cumulative production obtained from columns C and E in the spreadsheet. Note that the cumulative product availabilities for September through December are adjusted for lost sales. Since there are no back orders, the inventory level cannot become negative. Thus in September, we essentially begin anew with zero inventory. We must add the lost sales to the cumulative production to maintain the correct relationship: cumulative production less cumulative demand equals current inventory level. If back orders are allowed, inventory values would be negative and we would not have to make any adjustments.

We see that a shortage occurs when the cumulative production curve falls *below* the cumulative demand curve. Also note that the distance between the curves represents the accumulated inventory each month or the amount of lost sales. To avoid shortages, the cumulative production curve must always lie above the cumulative demand curve. This type of graphical method is often used to construct alternative production plans.

Figure 16.3 Full-Capacity Aggregate Production Plan

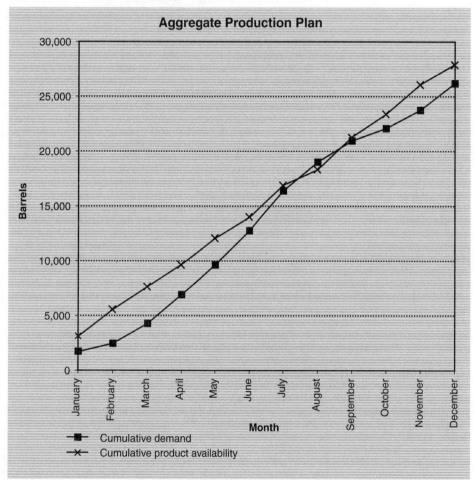

Next, the costs are considered. Assume that the production cost is $70 per barrel, inventory-holding costs amount to $1.40 per barrel per month of ending inventory, lost sales have an opportunity cost of $90 per barrel, overtime costs $6.50 additional per barrel, and there is a $5 per barrel charge to change the production rate. Cost of undertime (production below full capacity) is $3 per barrel. The lower portion of the spreadsheet in Figure 16.2 computes the cost of the production plan.

Companies use various strategies for long-term production planning. As the following discussion of "Industry Practice" shows, these strategies depend on whether demand increases or decreases.

Applied P/OM

Industry Practice

Production-planning options depend on the direction of demand shifts.[3]

A survey of industry practice in production planning showed that the likelihood of using various production planning strategies depends on the type of demand shift. In response to an increase in demand, companies tend to add shifts, add capacity, increase overtime, and reduce inventory. However, if demand decreases, the more likely options are to lay off workers, reduce the number of shifts worked, increase sales efforts, and decrease production lead times. In assessing these strategies, companies place the highest importance on overtime, shortage, hiring, and holding costs, and place less importance on layoff, idle time, and subcontracting costs.

Quantitative Approaches to Aggregate Planning

The Golden Breweries example in the preceding section illustrated the analysis of a **level production strategy;** that is, production is the same in each period. Such a strategy avoids rate changes but, as is evident in Figure 16.2, can result in excessive inventories and possibly lost sales.

The antithesis of a level production strategy is to set production equal to the forecasted demand; this is called a **chase-demand strategy.** While inventories will be reduced and lost sales will be eliminated, many rate changes will occur. Figure 16.4 shows a spreadsheet for a chase-demand strategy in which the initial inventory of 1,000 is maintained as safety stock. We see that this strategy reduces the total cost somewhat to $1,913,850. A major portion of the cost of this strategy is due to rate changes.

Needless to say, countless numbers of alternate strategies could be employed. Since many costs change simultaneously, it is difficult to assess the impact of the overall cost effects. Quantitative methods to assist the decision maker in evaluating alternate strategies and finding the best production plan can be extremely valuable.

Figure 16.4
Evaluation of a Chase-
Demand Strategy Using the
Excel Spreadsheet
(GOLDEN.XLS)

	A	B	C	D	E	F	G	H
1	Golden Breweries Production Plan							
2								
3	Production cost ($/bbl)			$ 70.00				
4	Inventory holding cost ($/bbl)			$ 1.40				
5	Lost sales cost ($/bbl)			$ 90.00				
6	Overtime cost ($/bbl)			$ 6.50				
7	Undertime cost ($/bbl)			$ 3.00				
8	Rate change cost ($/bbl)			$ 5.00				
9	Normal production rate			2,200				
10								
11					Cumulative			
12			Cumulative		Product	Ending	Lost	
13	Month	Demand	Demand	Production	Availability	Inventory	Sales	
14						1,000		
15	January	1,500	1,500	1,500	2,500	1,000	0	
16	February	1,000	2,500	1,000	3,500	1,000	0	
17	March	1,900	4,400	1,900	5,400	1,000	0	
18	April	2,600	7,000	2,600	8,000	1,000	0	
19	May	2,800	9,800	2,800	10,800	1,000	0	
20	June	3,100	12,900	3,100	13,900	1,000	0	
21	July	3,200	16,100	3,200	17,100	1,000	0	
22	August	3,000	19,100	3,000	20,100	1,000	0	
23	September	2,000	21,100	2,000	22,100	1,000	0	
24	October	1,000	22,100	1,000	23,100	1,000	0	
25	November	1,800	23,900	1,800	24,900	1,000	0	
26	December	2,200	26,100	2,200	27,100	1,000	0	
27								
28		Production	Inventory	Lost Sales	Overtime	Undertime	Rate Change	
29	Month	Cost	Cost	Cost	Cost	Cost	Cost	
30								
31	January	$ 105,000	$ 1,400	$ -	$ -	$ 2,100	$ 3,500	
32	February	$ 70,000	$ 1,400	$ -	$ -	$ 3,600	$ 2,500	
33	March	$ 133,000	$ 1,400	$ -	$ -	$ 900	$ 4,500	
34	April	$ 182,000	$ 1,400	$ -	$ 2,600	$ -	$ 3,500	
35	May	$ 196,000	$ 1,400	$ -	$ 3,900	$ -	$ 1,000	
36	June	$ 217,000	$ 1,400	$ -	$ 5,850	$ -	$ 1,500	
37	July	$ 224,000	$ 1,400	$ -	$ 6,500	$ -	$ 500	
38	August	$ 210,000	$ 1,400	$ -	$ 5,200	$ -	$ 1,000	
39	September	$ 140,000	$ 1,400	$ -	$ -	$ 600	$ 5,000	
40	October	$ 70,000	$ 1,400	$ -	$ -	$ 3,600	$ 5,000	
41	November	$ 126,000	$ 1,400	$ -	$ -	$ 1,200	$ 4,000	
42	December	$ 154,000	$ 1,400	$ -	$ -	$ -	$ 2,000	
43		$1,827,000	$ 16,800	$ -	$ 24,050	$ 12,000	$ 34,000	
44								
45	Total cost	$1,913,850						
46								

Heuristic Approach

With a spreadsheet, it is easy to perform "what if?" analyses of alternative aggregate planning strategies. A recommended heuristic approach is to begin with a level production strategy.[4] Then, through trial and error, the solution can be improved. Graphs of the cumulative demand and product availability often assist in identifying improved solutions. Also, examining individual cost categories can highlight areas where costs can be reduced. For example, if examination of costs indicates that inventory cost is relatively high and back-order cost is relatively low, one might search for periods where the ending inventory is high and adjust the production level for those periods. Good solutions generally can be found quickly by such an interactive approach.

Figure 16.5
An Alternate Production
Plan Evaluation

	A	B	C	D	E	F	G	H
1	Golden Breweries Production Plan							
2								
3	Production cost ($/bbl)			$ 70.00				
4	Inventory holding cost ($/bbl)			$ 1.40				
5	Lost sales cost ($/bbl)			$ 90.00				
6	Overtime cost ($/bbl)			$ 6.50				
7	Undertime cost ($/bbl)			$ 3.00				
8	Rate change cost ($/bbl)			$ 5.00				
9	Normal production rate			2,200				
10								
11					Cumulative			
12			Cumulative		Product	Ending	Lost	
13	Month	Demand	Demand	Production	Availability	Inventory	Sales	
14						1,000		
15	January	1,500	1,500	1,500	2,500	1,000	0	
16	February	1,000	2,500	1,500	4,000	1,500	0	
17	March	1,900	4,400	1,500	5,500	1,100	0	
18	April	2,600	7,000	2,600	8,100	1,100	0	
19	May	2,800	9,800	2,600	10,700	900	0	
20	June	3,100	12,900	2,600	13,300	400	0	
21	July	3,200	16,100	2,900	16,200	100	0	
22	August	3,000	19,100	2,900	19,100	0	0	
23	September	2,000	21,100	2,000	21,100	0	0	
24	October	1,000	22,100	2,000	23,100	1,000	0	
25	November	1,800	23,900	2,000	25,100	1,200	0	
26	December	2,200	26,100	2,000	27,100	1,000	0	
27								
28		Production	Inventory	Lost Sales	Overtime	Undertime	Rate Change	
29	Month	Cost	Cost	Cost	Cost	Cost	Cost	
30								
31	January	$ 105,000	$ 1,400	$ -	$ -	$ 2,100	$ 3,500	
32	February	$ 105,000	$ 2,100	$ -	$ -	$ 2,100	$ -	
33	March	$ 105,000	$ 1,540	$ -	$ -	$ 2,100	$ -	
34	April	$ 182,000	$ 1,540	$ -	$ 2,600	$ -	$ 5,500	
35	May	$ 182,000	$ 1,260	$ -	$ 2,600	$ -	$ -	
36	June	$ 182,000	$ 560	$ -	$ 2,600	$ -	$ -	
37	July	$ 203,000	$ 140	$ -	$ 4,550	$ -	$ 1,500	
38	August	$ 203,000	$ -	$ -	$ 4,550	$ -	$ -	
39	September	$ 140,000	$ -	$ -	$ -	$ 600	$ 4,500	
40	October	$ 140,000	$ 1,400	$ -	$ -	$ 600	$ -	
41	November	$ 140,000	$ 1,680	$ -	$ -	$ 600	$ -	
42	December	$ 140,000	$ 1,400	$ -	$ -	$ 600	$ -	
43		$ 1,827,000	$ 13,020	$ -	$ 16,900	$ 8,700	$ 15,000	
44								
45	Total cost	$ 1,880,620						
46								

For example, Figure 16.5 shows another production plan that reduces the frequent rate changes and eliminates lost sales. For this plan, the total cost is $1,880,620. The zero ending inventories in periods 8 and 9 might be a concern. They can be avoided by increasing production in periods 7 and 8 by some amount.

Linear Programming Approach

Although a trial-and-error approach will probably find a relatively low-cost solution, it is not likely to find the minimum-cost solution. *Linear programming* (see Supplementary Chapter D) is one technique for finding the minimum-cost solution, and many large corporations use it for production-planning problems.

A linear programming formulation for the Golden Breweries example is somewhat complicated to describe and such models are discussed in more advanced books. However, using linear programming, the minimum total cost for the Golden Breweries problem is $1,796,670. A problem at the end of this chapter will ask you to use the spreadsheet heuristic to find a production plan that achieves this cost.

For certain production-planning assumptions, a special type of linear program—the transportation problem—can be used to find minimum-cost production plans quite easily. That approach is discussed in the next section.

A Transportation Model

A transportation model will find a minimum-cost production plan when various sources of production are available (for example, regular time, overtime, and subcontracting), when production and inventory costs are linear, and when there is a limited capacity for each production source in each time period. In such situations, the solution process is very simple. This approach is illustrated in the following example.

Example

A Transportation Model for Aggregate Planning

The Snow Sporting Goods Company is a producer of a variety of recreational equipment. The demand forecast for one product, all-terrain skis, over the five winter months is 5,000, 12,000, 11,000, 7,500, and 5,000 units (a set of skis). Suppose the production cost is $50 per unit made on regular time and $54 per unit produced on overtime. The skis can also be subcontracted at a cost of $57 per unit. Inventory-holding costs are $6 per unit each month and no back orders are allowed. In each month, 9,000 units can be produced on regular time, 1,800 units on overtime, and up to 2,500 units can be subcontracted.

The transportation tableau in Figure 16.6 shows the structure of the problem. Each row corresponds to a source of production in a particular month. The numbers in the right margin are the capacities. For example, row 1 shows that up to 9,000 units can be produced on regular time in period 1; row 2 shows that up to 1,800 units can be produced on overtime in period 1; row 3 shows that up to 2,500 units can be produced by a subcontractor in period 1; and so on for periods 2, 3, 4, and 5. The columns correspond to the periods in which the production can be used. The numbers at the bottom of each column represent the demand for that period. Several cells have been crossed out. This is because production in one period cannot be used to satisfy demand in an earlier period (for instance, demand in period 2 cannot be satisfied by production in period 4) under the assumption of no back orders. Costs shown in the upper-right corner of each cell are calculated as follows: If a unit is produced in period t and held until period k, then the cost is the sum of production in period t plus holding costs for period $t, t + 1, ..., k - 1$. For instance, the cost of producing in regular time in period 1 and holding until period 4 is $50 + 6 + 6 + 6 = 68$.

The problem now can be easily solved. Starting in period 1, we attempt to satisfy demand by using the cheapest cost alternative available, as long as capacity is available. The cheapest source in column 1 is regular-time production in period 1. Since a capacity of 9,000 units is available and demand is 5,000, we

Figure 16.6 Transportation Tableau for Snow Sporting Goods Aggregate-Planning Problem

This indicates production in period 1 (overtime) and holding until period 2

Production period		Demand period 1		2		3		4		5		capacity
1	Regular time		50		56		62		68		74	9000
	Overtime		54		60		66		72		78	1800
	Subcontract		57		63		69		75		81	2500
2	Regular time				50		56		62		68	9000
	Overtime				54		60		66		72	1800
	Sucontract				57		63		69		75	2500
3	Regular time						50		56		62	9000
	Overtime						54		60		66	1800
	Sucontract						57		63		69	2500
4	Regular time								50		56	9000
	Overtime								54		60	1800
	Sucontract								57		63	2500
5	Regular time										50	9000
	Overtime										54	1800
	Sucontract										57	2500
Demand		5000		12,000		11,000		7500		5000		

Figure 16.7 Solution to Snow Sporting Goods Aggregate-Planning Problem

Production period		Demand period 1		2		3		4		5		capacity
1	Regular time	5000	50	1200	56		62		68		74	9000
	Overtime		54		60		66		72		78	1800
	Subcontract		57		63		69		75		81	2500
2	Regular time			9000	50		56		62		68	9000
	Overtime			1800	54		60		66		72	1800
	Sucontract				57		63		69		75	2500
3	Regular time					9000	50		56		62	9000
	Overtime					1800	54		60		66	1800
	Sucontract					200	57		63		69	2500
4	Regular time							7500	50		56	9000
	Overtime								54		60	1800
	Sucontract								57		63	2500
5	Regular time									5000	50	9000
	Overtime										54	1800
	Sucontract										57	2500
Demand		5000		12,000		11,000		7500		5000		

Table 16.4   Summary of Solution to Snow Sporting Goods Problem Shown in Figure 16.7

Period	Demand	Regular-Time Production	Cost	Overtime Production	Cost	Sub-Contract	Cost	End-of-Period Inventory	Cost
1	5,000	6,200	$ 310,000	0	$ 0	0	$ 0	1,200	$7,200
2	12,000	9,000	450,000	1,800	97,200	0	0	0	0
3	11,000	9,000	450,000	1,800	97,200	200	11,400	0	0
4	7,500	7,500	375,000	0	0	0	0	0	0
5	5,000	5,000	250,000	0	0	0	0	0	0
			$1,835,000		$194,400		$11,400		$7,200

Total cost = $2,048,000

produce 5,000 units. Once the demand in a period is satisfied, we move on to the next period. In period 2, the cheapest source is regular-time production in period 2. However, the demand is 12,000 units and only 9,000 units can be produced without exceeding capacity. Thus we produce 9,000 and then must find the *next* cheapest alternative with available capacity for the remaining 3,000 units. This is to produce 1,800 by using overtime in period 2 and the remaining 1,200 units using regular time in period 1. Next, we move on to period 3, and so on until all demand is satisfied. The final solution is given in Figure 16.7 and summarized in Table 16.4. The numbers in each cell show the amount of production to be scheduled for each source in each period.

Master Scheduling and Rough-Cut Capacity Planning

The aggregate production plan represents a firm's aggregate measure of manufacturing output. Implementing it requires a disaggregation of the plan into individual products. The *master production schedule* (MPS) is the final statement of how many finished items are to be produced and when they are to be produced. It is a commitment to a production plan, not a sales plan. The master schedule must consider the total demand on a factory's resources and the capacity of the plant and its suppliers to meet those demands. All planning for materials, labor, and equipment is derived from the MPS. Typically, the master schedule is developed for weekly time periods over a 6- to 12-month horizon. An example of a partial MPS is shown in Figure 16.8.

The purpose of the master schedule is to translate the aggregate plan into a separate plan for individual items. It also provides a means for evaluating alternative schedules in terms of capacity requirements, provides input to the *material requirements planning* (MRP) system, and helps managers generate priorities for scheduling by setting due dates for the production of individual items.

Developing the MPS can be a very complicated task, especially for products with a large number of operations. For example, at Dow Corning, there are 12 master schedulers, responsible for scheduling 4,000 packaged products over a 26-week time horizon.[5] In process industries with only a few different operations, master production scheduling is somewhat easier.

Figure 16.8
Portion of an MPS

	Week							
	1	2	3	4	5	6	7	8
A		200		200		350		
B	150	100		190			120	
.	.	.	.	.	.	.	.	.
.	.	.	.	.	.	.	.	.
.	.	.	.	.	.	.	.	.
X			75		75	75		60

Totals
(Aggregate production plan)

500	800	350	600	280	750	420	300

The MPS is developed somewhat differently depending on the type of industry (make-to-stock versus make-to-order) and the number of items produced (few or many). For *make-to-stock* industries, a net demand forecast (that is, after on-hand inventory is subtracted) is used. If only a few final products are produced, the MPS is a statement of the individual product requirements. If many items are produced—for instance, more than 500—it is impractical to develop an MPS on an individual-product basis. In such cases, individual products are usually grouped into product families, and some method of proportionately decomposing the plan into a schedule for individual items is employed. A common approach is to apportion by using historical percentage of sales.

For *make-to-order* industries, order backlogs provide the needed customer-demand information; thus the known customer orders determine the MPS. In industries where a few basic components are assembled in many different combinations to produce a large variety of end products, the MPS is usually developed for the basic components and not for the end products. An example is automobiles, in which basic components are engines, transmissions, body components, and so forth. The *final assembly schedule* (FAS) is used for the actual finished products. To illustrate the basic concepts of master production scheduling, we will use another Golden Breweries example.

Example

Developing a Master Production Schedule

Suppose Golden's managers have decided to use the production plan in Figure 16.5. Since the company produces two products, Golden Brew and Golden Delight, the master scheduler must translate the aggregate production plan into a weekly schedule for each product. Golden's beer is produced in cases of 24 16-ounce cans (three gallons). Each barrel holds 32 gallons; the product mix, as determined by historical sales data, is relatively constant, a 70–30 percent split between Golden Brew and Golden Delight. With this information, we can project the monthly production for each product for the first seven months as shown in Table 16.5.

To simplify our calculations, we assume there are four weeks in each month. Then the average weekly production required is as shown in Table 16.6. At Golden's plant, only one product can be produced at a time since they share common facilities such as mixing equipment, bottling, capping, and case packing. Using a master schedule as determined by Table 16.6 would probably not be economical, as there would be frequent changeovers of products and thus high setup costs. One method of reducing the number of product changeovers is to produce in large batch sizes. Table 16.7 shows a possible master schedule in which products are alternated on a weekly basis.

Table 16.5 Monthly Production Projections for Golden Breweries

Month	Aggregate Production		Product Mix	
	Barrels	*Cases*	*Golden Brew (cases)*	*Golden Delight (cases)*
January	1,500	16,000	11,200	4,800
February	1,500	16,000	11,200	4,800
March	1,500	16,000	11,200	4,800
April	2,600	27,733	19,413	8,320
May	2,600	27,733	19,413	8,320
June	2,600	27,733	19,413	8,320
July	2,900	27,733	19,413	8,320

Table 16.6 Average Weekly Production Requirements for Golden Breweries

Product	Week												
	1	*2*	*3*	*4*	*5*	*6*	*7*	*8*	*9*	*10*	*11*	*12*	*13*
Golden Brew	2,800	2,800	2,800	2,800	2,800	2,800	2,800	2,800	2,800	2,800	2,800	2,800	4,853
Golden Delight	1,200	1,200	1,200	1,200	1,200	1,200	1,200	1,200	1,200	1,200	1,200	1,200	2,080

Product	Week												
	14	*15*	*16*	*17*	*18*	*19*	*20*	*21*	*22*	*23*	*24*	*25*	*26*
Golden Brew	4,853	4,853	4,853	4,853	4,853	4,853	4,853	4,853	4,853	4,853	4,853	4,853	4,853
Golden Delight	2,080	2,080	2,080	2,080	2,080	2,080	2,080	2,080	2,080	2,080	2,080	2,080	2,080

Table 16.7 Master Schedule for Golden Breweries

Product	Week												
	1	*2*	*3*	*4*	*5*	*6*	*7*	*8*	*9*	*10*	*11*	*12*	*13*
Golden Brew	5,600	0	5,600	0	5,600	0	5,600	0	5,600	0	5,600	0	9,706
Golden Delight	0	2,400	0	2,400	0	2,400	0	2,400	0	2,400	0	2,400	0

Product	Week												
	14	*15*	*16*	*17*	*18*	*19*	*20*	*21*	*22*	*23*	*24*	*25*	*26*
Golden Brew	0	9,706	0	9,706	0	9,706	0	9,706	0	9,706	0	9,706	0
Golden Delight	4,160	0	4,160	0	4,160	0	4,160	0	4,160	0	4,160	0	4,160

Uniform Plant Loading[6]

For most manufacturers, production requirements vary from period to period. The greater the variability, the greater the opportunity to create waste in the organization. Typically, products are produced in long production runs, which results in excessive inventories and fluctuating resource requirements. Capacities are set to peak work demands rather than average rates. The concept of **uniform plant loading (UPL)** is to smooth the variability of demand on a firm's resources. For example, suppose three products (A, B, and C) have monthly demands of 20,000, 10,000, and 10,000 units per month, respectively. Assuming 20 work days each month, the daily uniform load would be 1,000 units of A, 500 units of B, and 500 units of C. Extending this concept to cycle times and assuming a 480-minute shift, each unit of A requires 480/1,000, or .48 minutes, to be produced, and each unit of B and C requires 480/500, or .96 minutes. Knowing this, managers can allocate the equipment and labor resources needed to support the required capacity.

UPL is a key component of just-in-time production (see Chapter 15) and has been practiced extensively in Japan. Japanese manufacturers attempt to produce the same quantity of each end item each day. This allows a smooth flow of parts through the factory and minimizes expediting, rework, and other delays. In addition, employees become used to the same schedule, which makes disruptions less likely. To accomplish this, no changes in the MPS are permitted within a specified period, typically ranging from one week to one month.

Rough-Cut Capacity Planning

In the Golden Breweries example, we have not determined whether there is sufficient capacity available on a short-term basis to be able to achieve the MPS. As previously stated, under normal conditions the plant has a capacity of 2,200 barrels per month, or 5,867 cases per week. With overtime, capacity can be increased to 2,800 barrels per month, or 7,467 cases per week. These restrictions are due to the physical limitations of the production equipment. From Table 16.7 we see that up to week 12, we are able to produce within capacity. Beyond that point, the planned schedule for Golden Brew cannot be achieved within the limitation of 7,467 cases per week. We would therefore say that the master schedule is *not feasible*. This is the essence of rough-cut capacity planning—namely, converting the MPS into capacity needs for key resources and then determining whether the master schedule is feasible with respect to capacity limitations. If it is not feasible, the master scheduler must revise the MPS to stay within capacity constraints. In some cases, it may even be necessary to revise the aggregate production plan. Table 16.8 shows a feasible master schedule developed by trial and error that meets the capacity limitations each week. Note that as in Table 16.7, two product changeovers each month must be made. For example, in weeks 14 and 15 Golden Delight will be produced, and early in week 15 a changeover will be made to Golden Brew. This will be produced until week 18, when a changeover to Golden Delight will be made, and so on. Rough-cut capacity planning is an iterative process in conjunction with master production scheduling, as shown in Figure 16.9. Often, several iterations are necessary before a realistic master schedule is produced.

Part Five

Table 16.8 A Feasible MPS for Golden Breweries

	Week												
Product	*1*	*2*	*3*	*4*	*5*	*6*	*7*	*8*	*9*	*10*	*11*	*12*	*13*
Golden Brew	5,600	0	5,600	0	5,600	0	5,600	0	5,600	0	5,600	0	7,467
Golden Delight	0	2,400	0	2,400	0	2,400	0	2,400	0	2,400	0	2,400	0

	Week												
Product	*14*	*15*	*16*	*17*	*18*	*19*	*20*	*21*	*22*	*23*	*24*	*25*	*26*
Golden Brew	0	4,478	7,467	7,467	0	4,478	7,467	7,467	0	4,478	7,467	7,467	0
Golden Delight	7,467	853	0	0	7,467	853	0	0	7,467	853	0	0	7,467

Figure 16.9
Rough-Cut Capacity
Planning and Master
Scheduling

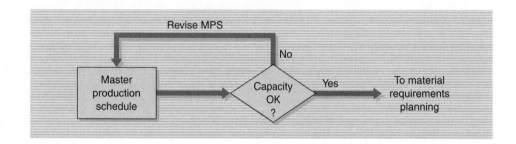

Capacity profiles are usually developed by department or work center. One method of rough-cut capacity planning is called *capacity planning using overall factors*. This technique allocates capacity requirements to individual departments or work centers on the basis of historical data on work loads. An example follows.

Example

Capacity Planning Using Overall Factors[7]

Consider the MPS for two end products, A and B, as shown in Table 16.9. Suppose product A requires .95 labor-hours per unit and B requires 1.85 labor-hours per unit. Then, in period 1, the total capacity requirement (expressed in labor-hours) is calculated as

(33 units of A)(.95 hours/unit) + (17 units of B)(1.85 hours/unit) = 62.8 hours.

Now suppose these items are manufactured in three work centers. Table 16.10 gives historical data on the number of labor-hours worked in each work center during the past year. These data show that 60.3 percent, 30.4 percent, and 9.3 percent of total labor-hours were reported at work centers 1, 2, and 3, respectively. Applying these percentages to the total-capacity-requirement estimates (such as 62.8 hours for period 1), we obtain an estimate of the labor capacity required in each work center. These results are shown in Table 16.11.

Table 16.9 MPS for Products A and B

	Time Period												
Product	1	2	3	4	5	6	7	8	9	10	11	12	13
A	33	33	33	40	40	40	30	30	30	37	37	37	37
B	17	17	17	13	13	13	25	25	25	27	27	27	27

Table 16.10 Historical Data on Labor Use for Products A and B

Work Center	1st Quarter	2nd Quarter	3rd Quarter	4th Quarter	Total	% of Total Labor Hours
1	125	90	150	140	505	60.3%
2	55	60	80	60	255	30.4%
3	18	15	20	25	78	9.3%
					838	

Table 16.11 Rough-Cut Capacity Requirements for Products A and B

Work Center	Historical Work Center Percentage	Time Period						
		1	2	3	4	5	6	7
1	60.3%	37.87	37.87	37.87	37.41	37.41	37.41	45.07
2	30.4%	19.09	19.09	19.09	18.86	18.86	18.86	22.72
3	9.3%	5.84	5.84	5.84	5.78	5.78	5.78	6.96
Total plant capacity		62.80	62.80	62.80	62.05	62.05	62.05	74.75

Work Center	Historical Work Center Percentage	Time Period						Total Hours
		8	9	10	11	12	13	
1	60.3%	45.07	45.07	51.32	51.32	51.32	51.32	566.33
2	30.4%	22.72	22.72	25.87	25.87	25.87	25.87	285.49
3	9.3%	6.96	6.96	7.91	7.91	7.91	7.91	87.38
Total plant capacity		74.75	74.75	85.10	85.10	85.10	85.10	939.20

Capacity planning using overall factors requires only a minimal amount of data and is used in a number of manufacturing firms. However, because it does not use detailed product and process data such as bills of materials, it provides only approximations of actual capacity requirements at individual work centers. Other techniques, beyond the scope of this book, can be used to obtain more accurate capacity estimates.

It is a good idea to check planned inventory levels in relation to an MPS. We can use equation 16.1 on a weekly basis to do this. Using the projected demand

Table 16.12 Inventory Analysis for Golden Breweries MPS

Week	Golden Brew			Golden Delight		
	Demand	*Production*	*Inventory**	*Demand*	*Production*	*Inventory**
1	2,800	5,600	10,267	1,200	0	2,000
2	2,800	0	7,467	1,200	2,400	3,200
3	2,800	5,600	10,267	1,200	0	2,000
4	2,800	0	7,467	1,200	2,400	3,200
5	1,867	5,600	11,200	800	0	2,400
6	1,867	0	9,333	800	2,400	4,000
7	1,867	5,600	13,066	800	0	3,200
8	1,867	0	11,199	800	2,400	4,800
9	3,547	5,600	13,252	1,520	0	3,280
10	3,547	0	9,705	1,520	2,400	4,160
11	3,547	5,600	11,758	1,520	0	2,640
12	3,547	0	8,211	1,520	2,400	3,520
13	4,853	7,467	10,825	2,080	0	1,440
14	4,853	0	5,972	2,080	7,467	6,827
15	4,853	4,478	5,597	2,080	853	5,600
16	4,853	7,467	8,211	2,080	0	3,520
17	5,227	7,467	10,451	2,240	0	1,280
18	5,227	0	5,224	2,240	7,467	6,507
19	5,227	4,478	4,475	2,240	853	5,120
20	5,227	7,467	6,715	2,240	0	2,880
21	5,787	7,467	8,395	2,480	0	400
22	5,787	0	2,608	2,480	7,467	5,387
23	5,787	4,478	1,299	2,480	853	3,760
24	5,787	7,467	2,979	2,480	0	1,280
25	5,973	7,467	4,473	2,560	0	(1,280)†
26	5,973	0	(1,500)†	2,560	7,467	3,627

*Initial inventory = 1,000 barrels (7,467 cases of Golden Brew and 3,200 cases of Golden Delight).
†Assumed lost sales.

from Figure 16.2 and translating this into cases per week, we arrive at Table 16.12, which shows the projected short-term fluctuations in inventory for both products and can thus be used in assessing the feasibility of the master schedule from the viewpoint of safety stock. We see that lost sales are incurred in weeks 25 and 26. An adjustment to the MPS would be necessary to prevent this.

Using the Master Schedule

It is clear from the Golden Breweries example that master production scheduling can be a complicated process. Let us summarize some of the observations we made through the example. First, the MPS should relate to the aggregate production plan; that is, the planned monthly schedule should equal the aggregate plan when totaled over all products. Second, rough-cut capacity planning assists the master production scheduler in developing a feasible schedule by identifying potential production bottlenecks. Often, the MPS must be revised several times to make it feasible. Third, other ways of evaluating an MPS include investigating the number and cost of setups or product changeovers and short-term inventory fluctuations.

The MPS is important, since it forms the basis for future production-planning activities. Therefore, it must be adaptive to changes in the environment. Seldom will forecasted demands be realized or production plans be adhered to perfectly. As each week passes, operations managers must compare scheduled production with actual results and make changes as necessary. Master production scheduling is a full-time job! Too many changes, however, indicate that the scheduling is not being performed correctly, in which case there is a risk of poor productivity and low levels of customer service. In the next chapter, we examine how the MPS is used in the planning of component production.

In addition to its use in resource planning and as an input to materials control, the MPS has other important applications. First, the MPS simplifies the task of customer delivery by specifying what is to be produced and when it is to be produced. Through proper coordination between marketing and manufacturing, customer-delivery performance can be improved. Second, the MPS can be used for budgeting purposes by financial personnel, since it indicates changes in inventories of finished goods and, indirectly, of materials and components. Since requirements are known by time period, budgets for labor and supplies can be developed through capacity-planning data.

Final Assembly Schedule

As noted previously in the chapter, the *final assembly schedule* (FAS) is a schedule of the assembly of the individual end products from MPS items. The MPS is used to produce orders for component parts; the FAS must guarantee that those components are available when they are needed. The development of an FAS is constrained by the availability of items scheduled on the MPS, inventory, lead-time requirements, and the capacity of the assembly process. The FAS represents the final commitment for production, and its authorization is usually held back until the latest possible time to allow flexibility and better customer service.

Short-Term Capacity Planning in Service Organizations

In terms of capacity planning, the main way services differ from goods is that services are produced and consumed simultaneously. Consequently, service inventories cannot be built during periods of slack demand in the same way as in manufacturing. Capacity is necessarily short term. Strategies for short-term capacity can be grouped into two categories: controlling supply and altering demand.

Controlling Supply

The use of part-time or seasonal employees to *control supply* is quite common in service organizations. For example, fast-food restaurants employ large numbers of part-time employees with varying work schedules to match capacity to demand. Retailers use part-time workers during the winter holiday season.

Amusement parks and resort hotels use full-time seasonal employees during their peak seasons.

Similar to using part-time employees is adjusting short-term work schedules. Hospitals, restaurants, banks, and many other service organizations schedule employees on variable shifts to match fluctuating demands over a day or week. This topic is discussed further in Chapter 18.

Another method of adjusting service capacity is to shift work to slack periods. For example, hotel clerks prepare bills and perform other paperwork at night, when check-in and check-out activity is light. This leaves them more time to service customers during the daytime hours.

Cross-training employees to perform different tasks creates the flexibility required to meet peak demands. Thus, in supermarkets, it is common for personnel to work as cashiers during busy periods and to assist with stocking during slow periods. A "P/OM in Practice" case at the end of this chapter illustrates the development of a short-term forecasting model used precisely for this purpose.

Increasing customer participation in the service process also increases capacity while reducing demands on the physical resources of an organization. Examples of this strategy include self-service gasoline pumps, "bag-your-own" policies in supermarkets, and self-service salad bars in restaurants.

A final method of capacity planning by controlling supply is capacity sharing. Fire stations in neighboring townships or villages do this routinely. Hospitals also employ this strategy. Every hospital, for example, need not purchase every expensive, specialized piece of equipment. A consortium of several hospitals might be set up in which each hospital focuses on a particular specialty and shares services. A blood bank is another example of capacity sharing.

Altering Demand

Another means of meeting fluctuating demand in service organizations is to *alter demand* by influencing consumer behavior. For example, the demand at health clinics is often heaviest early in the week. Demand may be smoothed by offering appointments later in the week.

Differential pricing schemes that serve to increase demand during normally non-peak hours are common. For example, bars and restaurants offer "happy hours," telephone rates are reduced during evenings and weekends to stimulate demand, movie theaters offer special matinee prices, and so on. New service packages are often developed to utilize idle capacity during off-peak times. For instance, many fast-food restaurants have introduced breakfast service, and many hotels offer special weekend packages.

Like manufacturing, service organizations must manage capacity and "plan production." Although the approaches differ in many ways, the goal is the same: to maintain a level of service that meets the strategic goals of the organization at a low cost.

P/OM in Practice

Production Planning for American Olean Tile Company[8]

The American Olean Tile Company (AO) manufactures a wide variety of ceramic tile products ranging from indoor and outdoor tile for walls and tile for residential and heavy commercial floors to tiles for elaborate mural designs. The company operates eight factories throughout the United States that supply approximately 120 sales distribution points (SDPs), which are combinations of marketing sales territories and company-owned warehouses. AO produces three basic lines of tile products: glazed tile, ceramic mosaics, and quarry tile. The production process begins with crushing and milling and leads to firing of the tile in large kilns.

Expansion and growth of the distribution network prompted AO's managers to develop new production-planning approaches. A hierarchical production-planning system was developed to improve integration of the annual plan, short-range scheduling, and inventory control. The quarry tile division was the first to be addressed. The product line was grouped into 10 product families, each comprising several hundred items. Figure 16.10 shows AO's production-planning and scheduling framework for the quarry tile division.

The planning process began with an annual subjective sales forecast for total quarry-division sales expressed in terms of square feet of tile. The director of market planning, in consultation with other top managers, generated this sales projection based on a combination of economic trends and specific market developments. The forecast was allocated to each product family and apportioned to the SDPs on the basis of the ratio of their annual total sales to the total of all quarry-tile sales during the previous year. Some adjustments were then made by the planning and marketing staffs.

A monthly production plan was developed by plant-level production personnel on the basis of these assignments and on seasonal inventory targets and demand patterns. The monthly production plan, scheduled orders received from large customers, and short-range-demand forecasts generated at each SDP were combined into a master production schedule (MPS) by product family at each plant. The planning horizon for the MPS was the upcoming quarter, and the length of the planning period was typically one to two weeks.

Process industries tend to schedule capacity first and then materials, whereas fabrication and assembly industries schedule material use first. AO uses a short-range-scheduling model, which first determines the assignment of production lines by planning period to meet the master schedule while minimizing the total variable manufacturing, setup, and inventory costs. Then a short-range-production schedule and associated material requirements for each plant are established.

The use of this hierarchical planning and scheduling system has helped to improve coordination and communication between departments and has substantially reduced production and distribution costs, saving between $400,000 and $750,000 per year. As a whole, the system significantly enhances American Olean's ability to position itself competitively in the marketplace. The system suggested significant changes in product family mixes and uncovered comparative cost advantages in terms of delivered cost from each plant. The process of developing the system stimulated closer coordination between the marketing and

Figure 16.10 Hierarchical Production Planning and Scheduling Framework for American Olean Quarry Tile Division

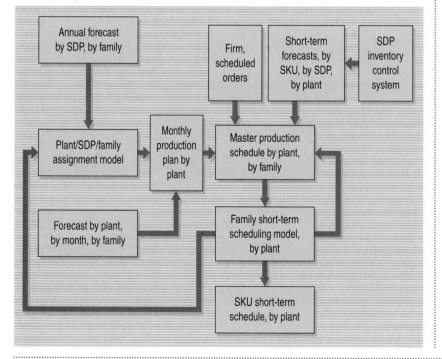

manufacturing departments in meeting the needs of sales territories.

In summary, the hierarchical production-planning system is an approach that integrates decision making and communication across corporate and plant-level organizations.

Questions for Discussion

1. Explain how the forecast is used in planning. Is it an aggregate forecast?
2. What were the inputs and outputs of the monthly production plan developed by plant-level personnel?

A Forecasting Model for Supermarket Checkout Services[9]

Customer service is a critical aspect in the management of grocery stores. Because of highly variable demand, store managers must make frequent short-term decisions about staffing checkout counters. The number of checkers at any time can be adjusted by the store manager to control the length of the waiting lines and hence customer waiting time. It is usually possible to assign an employee who is working in another part of the store—the produce department, for example—to work temporarily at a checkout counter during periods of high demand.

One large grocery chain was investigating the use of a laser-based scanner at the doors of the store to count arriving and departing customers. Company managers wanted to use this information to forecast demand at the checkout counters about 30 minutes in the future to make staffing adjustments before long lines developed.

Figure 16.11 is a schematic diagram of the system operation. Customers enter the store, shop, wait in line at one of several checkout counters, and then leave the store. The uncertainty in arrival rates at the checkout counters is due to not know-

ing how long customers will shop. Clearly, if the store arrival time and shopping time were known, the time at which a customer will arrive at the checkout counter could be computed.

A forecasting model was developed on the assumption that the demand for checkout services is related closely to the number of shoppers in the store; the larger the population of

Figure 16.11 Grocery-Store Customer Flow

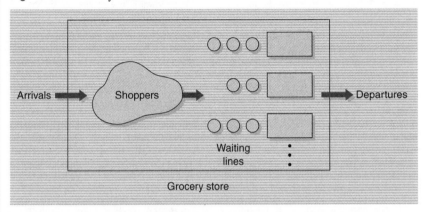

Figure 16.12 Customer Demand Distribution During a Day

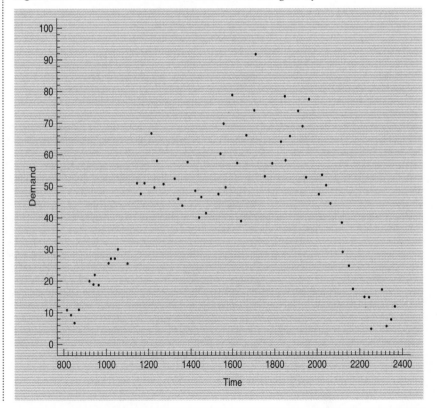

shoppers, the larger will be the demand for checkout services. If the probability distribution of shopping times is relatively stable, the number of customers demanding checkout service will be proportional to the number of customers in the store. Over a one-week period, data on store arrivals, departures, lengths of checkout lines, and the number of cashiers working at the end of fixed time intervals were collected. In effect, these provided "snapshots" of the state of the store over time. By keeping a running total of arrivals less departures, the store could calculate the number of customers in the store at any time.

From the arrival and departure data, a variable representing checkout service demand in any given period was created as follows. Let

y = number of customers demanding checkout service during a time period,

Q = number of customers in line at the end of the period,

C = number of checkers working at the end of the period, and

d = number of departures during a time period.

An estimate of the demand during a given period is then given by

$$y = d + Q + C.$$

The rationale for this equation is that the demand is equal to the number of departures (people who actually obtained service), plus the number waiting to be served (current demand), plus the number of checkers (assuming that all are busy).

The first analysis conducted was an investigation of demand fluctuation over time. Figure 16.12 is an example of data collected during one day. In general, demand follows a bimodal distribution with peaks at roughly noon and 6 P.M. each day. The next

step was to identify quantities that would effectively predict demand for future time periods. Intuition would dictate that the number of customers in the store in earlier periods would be of importance. Likewise, the arrival rate of customers would be a significant variable. Figure 16.13 shows demand as a function of the number of arrivals to the store three time periods earlier. (Each period was 15 minutes, so this provides demand data for 30 to 45 minutes in the future.) From this figure, we see that as the number of arriving customers increases, so does demand for checkout services. This relationship was not surprising. What was surprising was the highly linear relationship found for many of the days. This indicated that regression models might work extremely well.

The choice of prediction variables was determined by intuition, the strong relationships suggested by the data, and by extensive analysis of certain statistical measures of model adequacy. The model that was ultimately developed used $y(t + 3)$—that is, the demand three time periods into the future—as the dependent variable, with the following independent variables:

$N(t)$ = number of customers in the store in Period t.

$N(t - 1)$ = number of customers in the store in Period t - 1.

$a(t)$ = number of customers arriving in Period t.

Thus, if t is the time period of 2:15 to 2:30, the model includes the number of customers in the store at 1:30 to

Figure 16.13 Projected Customer Demand Three Time Periods in the Future

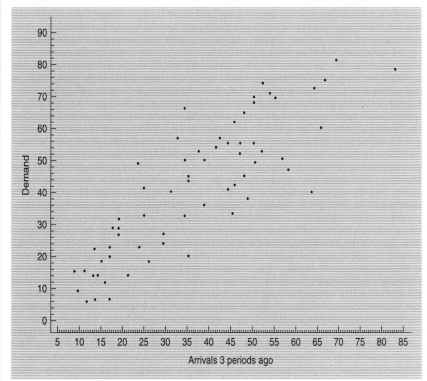

1:45 and at 1:15 to 1:30 and the number of arrivals during the period of 1:30 to 1:45. Therefore, a forecast for the period of 2:15 to 2:30 can be made at 1:45. An example of the actual model for one day is

$$y(t + 3) = .34431 - .12760\ N(t)$$
$$+ .31627\ N(t - 1)$$
$$+ .90634\ a(t).$$

The coefficient of determination, R^2, was .80, which indicated that a high percentage of the variation in demand was explained by the variables chosen.

Questions for Discussion

1. How did the grocery store determine the number of customers in the store at any one time?
2. What were the independent variables in the regression model?
3. Do you think an exponential smoothing model (see Appendix to Chapter 7) might do a better job of predicting demand for checkout services? Why or why not?
4. How much lead time does the store manager have to get the appropriate number of checkers to the checkout counter? Do you think the lead time is sufficient?

Summary of Key Points

••• Production planning and master scheduling involve determining future production levels over a time horizon of several months to one year. The production plan establishes an intermediate-range goal, and the master schedule provides input for detailed scheduling policies.

••• Production planning begins with demand estimation. Aggregate planning is the development of monthly or quarterly production requirements for product groups. Master production scheduling involves disaggregating the aggregate plan into time-phased requirements for individual products. Rough-cut capacity planning involves analyzing the master production schedule (MPS) to determine whether sufficient capacity is available. Finally, final assembly scheduling (FAS) establishes the schedule for the assembly of the final products.

••• With fluctuating demand, aggregate planning strategies include production rate changes, work-force changes, inventory smoothing, and demand shifting. Typically, one attempts to balance the associated costs in developing a minimum- or low-cost strategy. Spreadsheets, linear programming models, and the transportation model can assist in the aggregate-planning effort.

••• Uniform plant loading (UPL) is the concept of producing the same quantity of each end item every day. This concept supports just-in-time production and results in a lower level of resource requirements.

••• In service organizations, short-term capacity planning may control supply by use of part-time employees, variable work shifts, cross-training, increased customer participation, or capacity sharing and may alter demand by use of reservation systems, differential pricing, or idle capacity during off-peak times.

Key Terms

Aggregate production planning
Master production schedule (MPS)
Rough-cut capacity planning
Final assembly schedule (FAS)
Level production strategy
Chase-demand strategy
Uniform plant loading (UPL)

Review Questions

1. Describe the essential elements of the production-planning and scheduling process.
2. What is aggregate production planning? How does it differ from master production scheduling?
3. Discuss the role of inventory in aggregate production planning.
4. What costs need to be considered in aggregate production planning? Why?
5. What factors should be considered in choosing a planning horizon?
6. How frequently should the aggregate production plan be updated?
7. Why is aggregate production planning much more difficult when demand is seasonal?

8. Explain the various strategies available for meeting fluctuating demand. What costs are involved with each?

9. Explain how spreadsheets, linear programming models, and the transportation model can be used to assist in aggregate planning.

10. What is a master production schedule? Why is it important?

11. Explain how a master production schedule is constructed. For what does a master scheduler look?

12. What is the purpose of rough-cut capacity planning?

13. Explain how capacity planning by overall factors is performed.

14. How does capacity planning in service organizations differ from capacity planning in manufacturing organizations?

15. Explain the strategies for controlling supply and altering demand for short-term capacity planning in service organizations. Provide examples of each strategy.

Discussion Questions

1. Discuss the advantages and disadvantages of the various strategies for aggregate planning in terms of cost to the firm, operational performance, responsiveness to customers, and employee morale. How might a company balance those issues in choosing a strategy?

2. Explain why industry practice for production planning (see "Applied P/OM: Industry Practice") varies with increases and decreases in demand. Are the reported practices consistent with the relative emphasis placed on costs?

3. Interview a production manager at a nearby company to determine how the company plans its production for fluctuating demand. What approaches do they use? Are they consistent with the Applied P/OM survey results reported in the chapter?

4. Draw analogies between production planning and course/faculty planning at your college or university. Determine how such planning is performed. Are there analogies with rough-cut capacity planning, master scheduling, and final assembly scheduling?

5. How might a college or university apply the short-term capacity planning strategies for controlling supply or altering demand discussed in this chapter?

Notes

1. Adapted from Martin S. Visagie, "Production Control in a Flow Production Plant," *APICS 1975 Conference Proceedings*, pp. 161–166. Reprinted with permission, The American Production and Inventory Control Society, Inc.

2. Ibid.

3. Frank L. DuBois and Michael D. Oliff, "Aggregate Production Planning in Practice," *Production and Inventory Management Journal* 32, no. 3 (third quarter 1991).

4. Scott M. Shafer, "A Spreadsheet Approach to Aggregate Planning," *Production and Inventory Management Journal* 32, no. 4 (Fourth Quarter 1991), pp. 4–10.

5. W. L. Berry, T. E. Vollmann, and D. Clay Whybark, *Master Production Scheduling: Principles and Practice* (Falls Church, VA: American Production and Inventory Control Society, Inc., 1979).

6. "Uniform Plant Loading: The Critical Foundation for Just-in-Time," *Manufacturing Insights,* July 1989 (Coopers & Lybrand Cincinnati Management Consulting Services).

7. William L. Berry, Thomas G. Schmitt, and Thomas E. Vollmann, "Capacity Planning Techniques for Manufacturing Control Systems: Information Requirements and Operational Features," *Journal of Operations Management* 3, no. 1 (1982), pp. 13–24. Adapted with permission from The American Production and Inventory Control Society, Inc.

8. Matthew J. Liberatore and Tan Miller, "A Hierarchical Production Planning System," *Interfaces* 15, no. 4 (July-August 1985), pp. 1–11. Copyright 1985. Adapted with permission from The Institute of Management Sciences, 290 Westminster Street, Providence, RI 02903, USA.

9. This case is based on a project in which the author was involved.

Solved Problems

1. A manufacturer of stamped metal parts has the following sales forecast for the next five weeks for a particular part.

Week	1	2	3	4	5
Forecast	2,000	2,500	3,000	3,000	3,500

Beginning inventory equals 13,000 units, and the firm wants to maintain this level at the end of the planning period.

a. What weekly production rate is necessary?
b. What is the ending inventory level over time (using your answer to part a)?
c. Suppose the company wants to reduce its inventory level to 10,000 units. How would the production plan change?

Solution
a. The average demand per week is

$$(2,000 + 2,500 + 3,000 + 3,000 + 3,500)/5 = 2,800 \text{ units/week.}$$

b. The ending inventories are given in Table 16.13.

Table 16.13 Solved Problem 1 Solution

	Week				
	1	*2*	*3*	*4*	*5*
Beginning inventory	13,000	13,800	14,100	13,900	13,700
+ *Production*	2,800	2,800	2,800	2,800	2,800
− *Demand*	2,000	2,500	3,000	3,000	3,500
= *Ending inventory*	13,800	14,100	13,900	13,700	13,000

c. Since 3,000/5 = 600 = average reduction/week required, production should be reduced by 600 to 2,200 units per week. Ending inventory will then be 10,000 units.
2. Given the following demand pattern and unit production cost of $1.20, overtime costs of $1.30 per unit, and undertime costs of $1.40 per unit, compute the cost of a level production strategy.

Month	1	2	3	4	5	6	7	8	9	10	11	12
Demand (1000s)	24	22	26	20	20	20	22	23	24	26	28	28

The inventory-holding cost is 20 cents per unit per month. In the case of level production strategy, assume a desired ending inventory of 24,000. The beginning inventory for both cases is 20,000 units. The capacity for regular production is 24,000 units, and there is an overtime capacity of 4,000 units.

Solution
Beginning inventory is 20,000; ending inventory is 24,000. Total demand is 283,000; thus, average production level is 23,917. Total cost is $408,504. See Table 16.14.

Table 16.14 Solved Problem 2 Solution

Month	Demand	Production	Inventory	Production Costs	Inventory Costs	Overtime Costs	Shortage Costs	Total Costs
1	24,000	23,917	19,917	$28,700	$3,983	$0	$0	$32,683
2	22,000	23,917	21,834	28,700	4,367	0	0	33,067
3	26,000	23,917	19,751	28,700	3,950	0	0	32,650
4	20,000	23,917	23,668	28,700	4,734	0	0	33,434
5	20,000	23,917	27,585	28,700	5,517	0	0	34,217
6	20,000	23,917	31,502	28,700	6,300	0	0	35,000
								(*continues*)

Table 16.14 Solved Problem 2 Solution (continued)

Month	Demand	Production	Inventory	Production Costs	Inventory Costs	Overtime Costs	Shortage Costs	Total Costs
7	22,000	23,917	33,419	28,700	6,684	0	0	35,384
8	23,000	23,917	34,336	28,700	6,867	0	0	35,567
9	24,000	23,917	34,253	28,700	6,851	0	0	35,551
10	26,000	23,917	32,170	28,700	6,434	0	0	35,134
11	28,000	23,917	28,087	28,700	5,617	0	0	34,317
12	28,000	23,917	24,004	28,700	4,800	0	0	33,500

3. Microdevices makes a memory expansion board for microcomputers. The company has the following orders over the next six months.

Month 1:	2,000	Month 4:	4,500
Month 2:	5,000	Month 5:	2,000
Month 3:	8,000	Month 6:	8,000

Monthly production capacities are 5,000 units on regular time and 1,000 units on overtime, and up to 2,000 can be subcontracted each month. Production costs are $20 per unit on regular time and $25 per unit on overtime; the cost per unit for the components subcontracted is $28. Inventory-holding costs are charged at the rate of $1 per unit per month. Use the transportation model to develop a production schedule for Microdevices for the next six months.

Solution
Figure 16.14 is the six-month production schedule for Microdevices.
4. The CammShaft Company subcontracts production for major automotive manufacturers. Three standard end items are produced, and a six-month master production schedule is given in Table 16.15.

Table 16.15 Data for Solved Problem 4

			Month			
	1	*2*	*3*	*4*	*5*	*6*
Product A	140	180	200	150	120	100
Product B	100	100	150	150	100	100
Product C	200	250	250	250	300	300

Products A, B, and C require .60, 1.20, and 1.00 labor-hours per unit, respectively. Over the past year, the fabrication department reported 1,950 labor-hours, whereas the assembly department reported 1,050 labor-hours. Determine the rough-cut capacity requirements for each department and for the total plant for the next six months.

Solution
For each time period, multiply the hours/unit times the demand to obtain the total capacity requirements. The fabrication department used 1,950/3000 = 65 percent of the capacity over the last year; assembly used 1,050/3,000 = 35 percent of the capacity. Allocate the total according to these percentages. Monthly capacity requirements are given in Table 16.16.

Figure 16.14
Solved Problem 3 Solution

PRODUCTION PERIOD	1	2	3	4	5	6	CAPACITY
1 REG. TIME	20 **2000**	21	22 **3000**	23	24	25	5000
OVERTIME	25	26	27	28	29	30	1000
SUBCONTR.	28	29	30	31	32	33	2000
2 REG. TIME		20 **5000**	21	22	23	24	5000
OVERTIME		25	26	27	28	29	1000
SUBCONTR.		28	29	30	31	32	2000
3 REG. TIME			20 **5000**	21	22	23	5000
OVERTIME			25	26	27	28	1000
SUBCONTR.			28	29	30	31	2000
4 REG. TIME				20 **4500**	21	22	5000
OVERTIME				25	26	27	1000
SUBCONTR.				28	29	30	2000
5 REG. TIME					20 **2000**	21 **3000**	5000
OVERTIME					25	26	1000
SUBCONTR.					28	29	2000
6 REG. TIME						20 **5000**	5000
OVERTIME						25	1000
SUBCONTR.						28	2000
DEMAND	2000	5000	8000	4500	2000	8000	

Table 16.16 Data for Solved Problem 4 Solution

	Month					
	1	*2*	*3*	*4*	*5*	*6*
Total	404	478	550	520	492	480
Fabrication	262.6	310.7	357.5	338	319.8	312
Assembly	141.4	167.3	192.5	182	172.2	168

Problems

1. Consider the following six-month demand forecast.

Month	Jul	Aug	Sept	Oct	Nov	Dec
Demand Forecast	800	900	1,000	700	600	550

a. Compute the cumulative demand for each month and the average demand per month.

b. If the production for each month is set equal to the average demand, compute the net ending inventory for each month, assuming that the ending inventory for June is 150 units and that all shortages are back-ordered.

c. Draw a graph of cumulative production and cumulative demand.

2. A six-month forecast of microwave ovens follows.

Month	1	2	3	4	5	6
Forecast	600	800	500	1,000	700	1,200

An initial inventory of 2,000 is available, and the company wants to maintain a 500-unit safety stock at the end of the six-month planning horizon. What monthly production rate is necessary?

3. The projected aggregate demand of a certain product is given for the next 12 months. What is the minimum level of constant production necessary to meet demand and incur no stockouts? Assume an initial inventory of 150. Show your results on a graph.

Month	1	2	3	4	5	6	7	8	9	10	11	12
Demand	480	530	500	480	470	520	450	480	500	530	570	600

4. Chapman Pharmaceuticals, a large manufacturer of drugs, has this aggregate demand forecast for a liquid cold medicine.

Month	J	F	M	A	M	J	J	A	S	O	N	D
Liters (1000s)	180	120	75	60	20	15	15	15	30	70	90	150

a. Given that the firm has a capacity of 80,000 liters per month and that the initial inventory is 190,000 liters, show by means of a graph the sales level, the production level, and the inventory level over the next 12 months.

b. What is the minimum level of production necessary to maintain a nonnegative inventory?

c. Develop a plan that includes overtime for which inventory levels are held to at least 100,000 liters each month.

5. For Chapman Pharmaceuticals in Problem 4, suppose inventory-holding costs are $25 per 1,000 liters per month, regular-time production costs are $350 per 1,000 liters, and overtime premiums add an additional 20 percent. Compute the cost of the production plans developed in parts a and c in Problem 4.

6. Refer to Chapman Pharmaceuticals in Problems 4 and 5. Suppose normal capacity is 80,000 liters per month and a maximum of 20,000 liters can be produced in overtime. Given that the initial inventory in January is 150,000 liters and there are no other inventory restrictions, construct a linear programming model for this situation.

7. Refer to Solved Problem 2. Compute the cost of a chase-demand strategy. How does this strategy compare with the level production strategy in terms of cost? What about customer-service considerations?

 8. Use the GOLDEN.XLS spreadsheet to attempt to find a production plan with the minimum total cost of $1,796,670.

9. The Westerbeck Company manufactures several models of automatic washers and dryers. The projected requirements over the next year for their washers follow.

Month	Jan	Feb	Mar	Apr	May	June	Jul	Aug	Sep	Oct	Nov	Dec
Requirement	800	1030	810	900	950	1340	1100	1210	600	580	890	1000

Current inventory is 100 units. Current capacity is 960 units per month. The average salary of production workers is $1,300 per month. Overtime is paid at time and a half up to 20 percent additional time. Each production worker accounts for 30 units per month. Additional labor can be hired for a training cost of $250, and current workers can be laid off at a cost of $500. Any increase or decrease in the production rate costs $5,000 for tooling, setup, and line changes. This does not apply, however, to overtime. Inventory-holding costs are $25 per unit per month. Lost sales are valued at $75 per unit. Determine at least two different production plans, trying to minimize the cost of meeting the next year's requirements.

10. Refer to Solved Problem 3. Set up a linear programming model to develop a production schedule for Microdevices over the next six months and find the optimal solution. Is it the same as the transportation solution?

11. Refer to Solved Problem 3. At the end of month 2, Microdevices received a new order for 1,800 additional components in month 4 and 1,000 additional units in month 5. Develop a revised production schedule for Microdevices for months 3 through 6.

12. The demand for a certain manufactured product during the next four months is expected to be 175, 235, 270, and 220 units, respectively. The cost of manufacturing with regular, overtime, and subcontract options and the capacities are given in Table 16.17. The inventory-holding cost is $5 per month. Use a transportation model to determine the least-cost production plan.

Table 16.17 Data for Problem 12

Options	Cost of Manufacturing	Capacity per Week
Regular production	75	50
Overtime production	85	12.5
Subcontract operations	100	25

13. The demand for a certain product over a six-month period is given as follows.

Month	1	2	3	4	5	6
Demand	1,475	1,300	1,325	1,150	1,500	1,275

The firm has the option of regular production at a cost of $12 per unit, subcontracting at a cost of $18 per unit, and overtime production at a cost of $16 per unit. The holding cost is $2.40 per month. The capacities over the six-month period are shown in Table 16.18.

Table 16.18 Data for Problem 13

Period	Regular Production	Overtime Production	Subcontracting
1	800	150	150
2	850	200	150
3	900	200	150
4	900	200	200
5	950	250	200
6	950	250	200

The beginning inventory is 575 units, and the desired ending inventory at the end of six months is 200 units. Find the least-cost production plan using a transportation model. Also, compute the total cost of this production plan.

14. Hartmann Company is trying to determine how much of each of two products should be produced over the coming planning period. The only serious constraints involve labor availability in three departments. Labor availability, labor utilization, and product profitability are indicated in Table 16.19.

Table 16.19 Data for Problem 14

	Product 1	Product 2	Hours of Labor Available
Profit unit	$30.00	$15.00	—
Dept. A hours/unit	1.00	0.35	100
Dept. B hours/unit	0.30	0.20	36
Dept. C hours/unit	0.20	0.50	50

a. Develop a linear programming model of the Hartmann Company's problem. Solve it to determine the optimal production quantities of products 1 and 2.

b. Suppose that 10, 6, and 8 hours of overtime may be scheduled in departments A, B, and C, respectively. The cost per hour of overtime is $18 in department A, $22.50 in department B, and $12 in department C. Formulate a linear programming model that can be used to determine optimal production quantities if overtime is made available. What are the optimal production quantities, and what is the revised profit? How much overtime do you recommend using in each department? What is the increase in profit if overtime is used?

15. The Silver Star Bicycle Company will be manufacturing men's and women's models of its Easy-Pedal 10-speed bicycle during the next two months, and the company would like a production schedule indicating how many bicycles of each model should be produced in each month. Current demand forecasts call for 150 men's and 125 women's models to be shipped during the first month and 200 men's and 150 women's models to be shipped during the second month. Additional data are shown in Table 16.20.

Table 16.20 Data for Problem 15

Model	Production Costs	Labor Required for Manufacturing (hours)	Labor Required for Assembly (hours)	Current Inventory
Men's	$40	10	3	20
Women's	$30	8	2	30

Last month Silver Star used a total of 4,000 hours of labor. Its labor relations policy will not allow the combined total hours of labor (manufacturing plus assembly) to increase or decrease by more than 500 hours from month to month. In addition, the company charges monthly inventory at the rate of 2 percent of the production cost based on the inventory levels at the end of the month. Silver Star would like to have at least 25 units of each model in inventory at the end of the two months.

    a. Establish a production schedule that minimizes production and inventory costs and satisfies the labor-smoothing, demand, and inventory requirements. What inventories will be maintained, and what are the monthly labor requirements?

    b. If the company changed the constraints so that monthly labor increases and decreases could not exceed 250 hours, what would happen to the production schedule? How much would the cost increase? What would you recommend?

16. An electronics firm produces two types of printed circuitboards for computer assembly. Based on current and anticipated orders, the projected demand over the next eight weeks is as shown in Table 16.21.

Table 16.21 Data for Problem 16

	Week							
	1	*2*	*3*	*4*	*5*	*6*	*7*	*8*
Type A	15	20	30	30	20	20	10	20
Type B	10	5	0	0	10	20	20	20

Circuitboard A is produced in lots of 50, and B in lots of 30. Current inventories of each type are 20 and 10, respectively. Safety stocks of 10 and 5 are carried for boards A and B. Develop a master schedule based upon this information.

17. For the Golden Breweries example, consider this seven-month aggregate plan in Table 16.22.

Table 16.22 Data for Problem 17

Month	**Barrels**
January	1500
February	1500
March	1500
April	2800
May	2800
June	2800
July	2800

Assuming the same product profile (24 16-ounce cans per case and a 70–30 percent split between Golden Brew and Golden Delight), show that an alternating master schedule like the one in Table 16.7 is *infeasible,* and construct a feasible master schedule.

18. A firm that manufactures three types of hydraulic cylinders has this aggregate production plan over the next three months:

January:	1500 cylinders
February:	1475 cylinders
March:	1450 cylinders

The product mix is usually of the ratio 25:30:45 percent among wheel, master, and slave cylinders, respectively. The production capacity is 380 cylinders per week. Formulate a feasible master production schedule with weekly time periods. The initial inventories are 50, 60, and 90 units, respectively, and are also the safety stocks for the three types of cylinders.

19. A firm that makes three products has developed the three-month aggregate production plan shown in Table 16.23. Also shown are marketing estimates of the monthly product mix because of seasonal fluctuations. Initially there are 300 units of product A, 100 units of product B, and 75 units of product C in inventory. The weekly capacity of the plant is 220 units. Develop a feasible master production schedule for this situation, providing for a safety stock of 25 units for each product.

Table 16.23 Data for Problem 19

Month	Projected Requirements	Planned Production Level	Product Mix		
			A	B	C
July	650	850	.40	.25	.35
August	975	850	.40	.35	.25
September	1000	850	.30	.50	.20

20. A leather-goods manufacturer produces wallets, purses, and belts. A four-month master production schedule is shown in Table 16.24.

Table 16.24 Data for Problem 20

	Month			
	1	2	3	4
Wallets	1,500	2,000	2,000	1,500
Purses	900	1,200	1,200	600
Belts	2,500	2,000	2,000	1,500

Wallets, purses, and belts require 15, 40, and 10 minutes of labor, respectively. Over the past six months, the stitching department accounted for 80 percent of production capacity and assembly used the rest. Determine rough-cut capacity requirements for each department and for the plant overall for the next four months.

21. A small manufacturer of marine radios has quarterly sales data for the past seven years, as shown in Table 16.25.

Table 16.25 Data for Problem 21

	Quarter				
Year	1	2	3	4	Total Sales
1	60	150	100	40	350
2	100	180	150	70	500
3	140	260	230	120	750

(Continues)

Table 16.25 Data for Problem 21 *(continued)*

Year	Quarter				Total Sales
	1	*2*	*3*	*4*	
4	190	280	250	180	900
5	220	340	280	210	1050
6	240	360	300	200	1100
7	280	400	350	270	1300

a. Sketch a graph of this time series. If a linear trend appears to be present, determine the trend equation.

b. Show the four-quarter, moving-average values for this time series. Plot this along with the original time series. Using the moving average, compute seasonal factors for the four quarters.

c. Develop a quarterly forecast for next year using the techniques discussed in the Appendix to Chapter 7.

d. The plant has capacity to manufacture 130 radios per month. Develop three alternate monthly production plans for the next year, assuming there are 80 radios currently in inventory. Show your results graphically and in tabular form. Include a discussion of safety stock, overtime, rate changes, and so on. What if forecasts are 10 percent too low? Which of your plans would appear to be best?

e. For what long-range capacity requirements should the company be preparing?

Chapter Outline

Chapter Seventeen
Material Requirements Planning

Applied P/OM

P/OM in Practice

nventories that support the production process are called *manufacturing inventories.* Since manufacturing inventories serve a different purpose than finished-goods inventories, different management techniques are required for them. **Material requirements planning (MRP)** is a technique used to plan for and control manufacturing inventories. Though the name is somewhat recent, the concept is an old one that has become practical because of the ability of computers to carry out the necessary calculations fast and efficiently.

Figure 17.1 is a flowchart of the production-planning and scheduling process introduced in the previous chapter. The *master production schedule* (MPS) lists the finished products that must be produced to meet anticipated demand. Many of these products consist of individual parts or subassemblies that must be manufactured or purchased. The data that show the makeup of each product are given in the *bill of materials,* which was discussed in Chapter 9. Using these data, MRP determines the requirements and schedule for (1) manufacturing the components and subassemblies, and/or (2) purchasing the materials needed for meeting the requirements of the MPS. Essentially, MRP uses the MPS to project the requirements for the individual parts or subassemblies. Those requirements are compared with on-hand inventory levels and scheduled receipts on a time-phased basis so that lots can be scheduled to be produced or received as needed. The purpose of MRP is to ensure that materials and all the

Figure 17.1
Production-Planning and
Scheduling Process

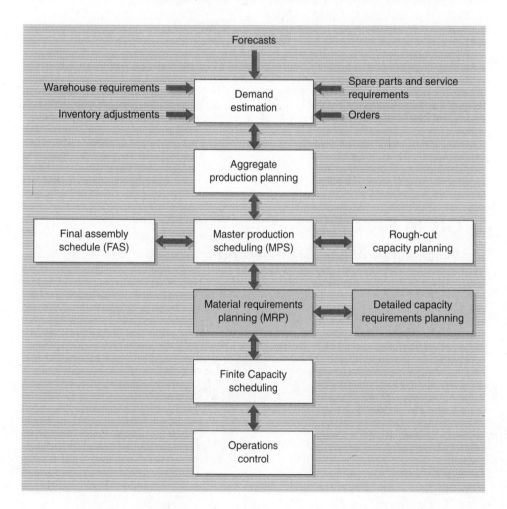

individual parts and subassemblies are available in the right quantities and at the right time so that finished products can be completed according to the MPS.

The key inputs to an MRP system, then, are the MPS, inventory records, and bill of materials for each product that is manufactured. The primary output of an MRP system is a report that gives (1) the purchasing department a schedule for obtaining raw materials and purchased parts and (2) the production managers a detailed schedule for manufacturing the product and controlling manufacturing inventories. An *MRP system* has three major functions: control of inventory levels, assignment of priorities for components, and determination of capacity requirements at a more detailed level than the process of rough-cut capacity planning. This chapter describes those functions, with specific attention to

••• The philosophy, mechanics, and applications of MRP.

••• How MRP forms the basis for comprehensive manufacturing resource-planning systems.

••• The limitations of MRP and the need for integrating capacity considerations into material-scheduling decisions.

Dependent Demand and the MRP Concept

In Chapter 13 we discussed inventory management for *independent-demand* items such as finished goods. This chapter focuses on the *dependent-demand* items—raw materials, components, and subassemblies—that are used in the *production* of finished goods. The demand for such items is dependent on the number of finished goods that are scheduled to be produced, and this number can be derived from the MPS. (In contrast, demand for finished goods must be forecast.)

To illustrate dependent demand and the MRP concept, consider the Finger Lakes Celebration Doll Co. The company purchases unpainted ceramic dolls to be carefully hand-painted in its upstate New York factory. Suppose product demand for one of Finger Lake's popular Birthday Celebration Dolls consists of independent demand from many customers. Since this independent demand occurs somewhat randomly, the total demand rate is often fairly constant, and the assumptions needed to support the use of the production lot-size model are reasonable. (See Chapter 14.)

The finished-product inventory level is shown at the top of Figure 17.2. When production (that is, painting) of the finished doll is initiated (point A on the time axis), the unpainted dolls are withdrawn from inventory. The inventory level for unpainted dolls is shown at the bottom of the figure. When the unpainted-doll inventory level falls below its reorder point, an order is placed with the supplier. The shipment is received at point B, and the inventory is replenished. However, note that the unpainted doll is not needed again until the next production run for the finished product, which is scheduled to occur at point C. Clearly, the investment in the unpainted doll inventory between points B and C is unnecessary. We can eliminate this unnecessary component inventory by "backing up" from point C according to the purchase lead time so that the unpainted dolls will arrive just at time C. This situation is illustrated in Figure 17.3. Note that the unpainted-doll inventory level and corresponding inventory investment is less in Figure 17.3 than it is in Figure 17.2.

Figure 17.2
Inventory Levels of
Finished Products and
Purchased Parts without an
MRP System

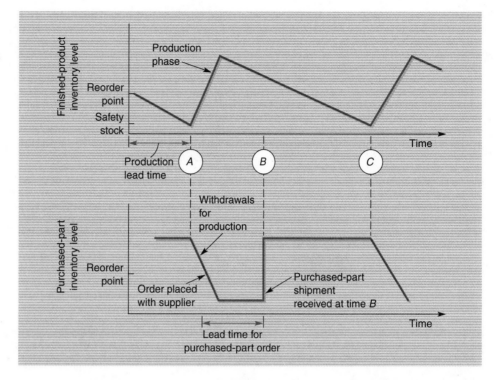

Figure 17.3
Inventory Levels of
Finished Products and
Purchased Parts with an
MRP System

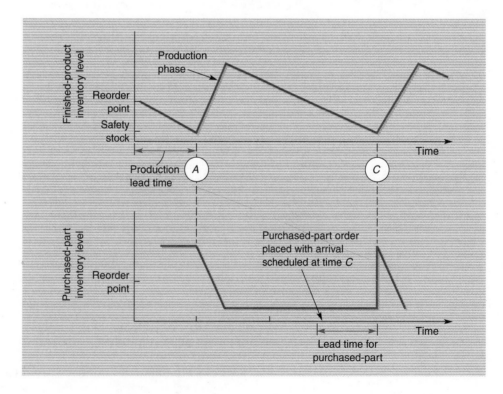

What makes this process difficult to implement is that many products consist of dozens or hundreds of components, many of which are successively dependent on others. Therefore, there must be accurate data and a reliable computer system to perform the many calculations that are required. The reduction of computer costs and development of software have made MRP an important part of many production systems. Indeed, it is being used in all types of industries, though it is especially predominant in the machine-tool, electronics, and transportation-equipment industries. These are characterized by a combination of make-to-order and make-to-stock products and assembly/fabrication manufacturing.

MRP Information Systems

Because a large amount of data must be stored and processed in an MRP system, a computerized information system is essential. It must include the data in the MPS and the bill of materials (BOM) and be able to produce the reports needed by production and purchasing. MRP software is available from many manufacturers of computer equipment as well as from independent software developers. Usually, the MRP software is just one module of a total manufacturing package that includes forecasting, order entry, BOM and inventory-file maintenance, and shop-floor control modules.

Recall that the MPS provides a statement of the number of finished products to produce in each time period, generally weekly. Consider, for example, the MPS for the Spiecker Manufacturing Company, a major producer of outdoor home power equipment. A portion of its MPS is given in Figure 17.4. For an example, let us focus on the 1,250 14-inch snowblowers scheduled to be made during week 15.

Recall from Chapter 9 that the bill of materials (BOM) shows the hierarchical relationship of the finished product to its various components. Figure 17.5 shows the BOM for Spiecker's 14-inch snowblower. The finished product is at the top of the hierarchy (level 0). It consists of one main housing assembly, one wheel assembly, one engine assembly, and one handle assembly. The components at each level of the BOM hierarchy are "parent items" for those at the next level. Thus, for example, the wheel assembly (level 1) is the parent item for the

Figure 17.4
Portion of MPS for Spiecker Manufacturing

Item . . .	End of week					
	11	12	13	14	15	16 . . .
.						
.						
.						
12-inch snowblower	0	250	750	250	250	0
14-inch snowblower	1000	0	500	1500	1250	250
.						
.						
.						

Figure 17.5
Portion of BOM for 14-inch
Snowblower

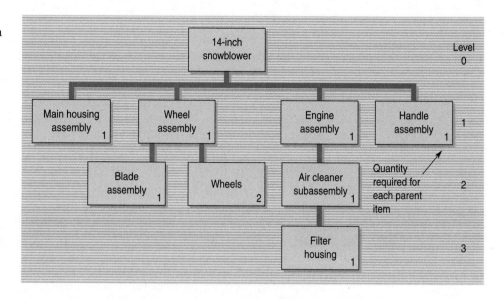

level-2 components, blade assembly and wheels. From the BOM, we can determine exactly how many components are needed to produce the quantity of finished products stated in the MPS.

Figure 17.5, of course, is greatly simplified. The actual BOM is exploded so that each individual part is identified in its assembly hierarchy. In an MRP system, the file containing the BOM is sometimes called the *product-structure file*.

Inventory status information must be maintained on each item in the BOM. Typical data elements are part number, on-hand quantity, on-order quantity, cost data, and procurement lead time. This file must be linked to production and purchasing to update orders, receipts, and issues from stock.

A schematic diagram of an MRP information system is given in Figure 17.6. The BOM, inventory files, and MPS are the primary inputs to the MRP com-

Figure 17.6
An MRP Information
System

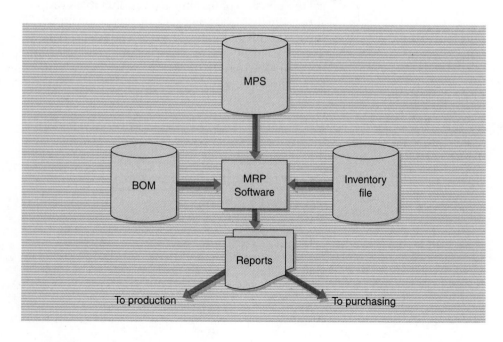

puter software. The output from MRP calculations is the determination of the amount of each BOM item required and the dates they are needed. This information is used to plan order releases for purchased parts and for in-house production of components. Planned order releases are generated automatically by the MRP information system, along with orders that should be rescheduled, modified, or canceled. In this way, MRP becomes a tool for operational planning by production managers.

MRP Calculations

In MRP terminology, time periods, which are called **buckets,** are usually one week in length. Although small buckets such as one week are good for scheduling production over a short time horizon, they may be too precise for long-range planning. Thus, larger buckets are often used as the planning horizon gets larger. For the Spiecker Manufacturing problem, we assume that all buckets are one week in length.

The MPS in Figure 17.4 calls for the final assembly of 1,250 units of the 14-inch snowblower during week 15 of the current planning period. We shall use this to illustrate the MRP calculations. Similar calculations must be performed for *every* end item and week on the MPS. In the following example, we first consider the question of when to schedule production or purchase orders for assemblies or components to meet this MPS.

Example

Time-Phasing Calculations in MRP

Suppose the time required to assemble the four main assemblies of the snowblower is one week. (This is called the *final-assembly lead time.*) Then 1,250 units each of the main-housing assembly, wheel assembly, engine assembly, and handle assembly must be completed no later than the end of week 14. Table 17.1 gives the production lead times and on-hand inventory levels for the remaining components and assemblies:

Figure 17.7 shows when the production of each component or assembly must be carried out in order to complete the final assembly by week 15. This figure was developed by "backing up" from the time the component or assembly is

Table 17.1 Production Lead Times

Component or Assembly	Lead Time (weeks)	Inventory
Main housing assembly	3	400
Wheel assembly	1	200
Blade assembly	2	800
Wheels	1	2,300
Engine assembly	4	450
Air cleaner subassembly	1	250
Filter housing	2	500
Handle assembly	1	400

Figure 17.7 Time-Phased Assembly Schedule

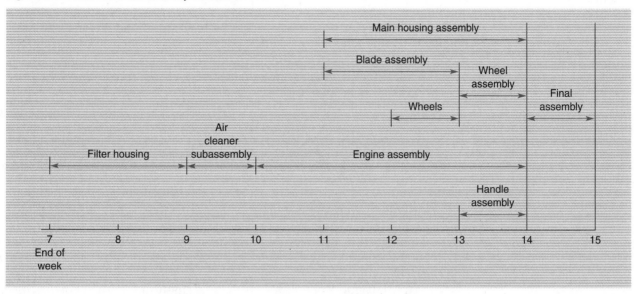

Table 17.2 Time-Phasing Calculations

	End of Week
Complete order for engine assemblies	14
Minus lead time for engine assemblies	−4
Place an order for engine assemblies	10 ←Order engine assemblies.
Complete order for air cleaner subassemblies	10
Minus lead time of air cleaner subassemblies	−1
Place an order for air cleaner subassemblies	9 ←Order air cleaner subassemblies.
Complete order for filter housings	9
Minus lead time of filter housings	−2
Place an order for filter housings	7 ←Order filter housings.

required by the amount of that item's lead time—a process called **time phasing.** For instance, to have the main housing assembly ready by the end of week 14, production must be started by the end of week 11, since its lead time is three weeks. Time-phasing calculations for the engine assembly, which consists of three BOM levels of components, are shown in Table 17.2.

The next question we consider is how many components or assemblies to produce. First we compute the *gross requirements* of each component or assembly using the BOM. This is the quantity of the component needed to support production at the next-higher level of assembly. For example, the gross-component requirement for the filter housing is the number of filter housings required to meet the number of air cleaner subassemblies needed; the gross-component requirement for the air cleaner subassembly is the number of air cleaners needed to meet the requirement for the engine assembly; and so on.

Gross requirements, however, must be adjusted by the number of units in inventory and the scheduled receipts. *Scheduled receipts* are orders that have already been placed and are due to be delivered. (In our illustration we assume, for simplicity, that all scheduled receipts are zero.)

The formula for computing the net requirements is

$$\frac{\text{net-component}}{\text{requirement}} = \frac{\text{gross-component}}{\text{requirement}} - \frac{\text{scheduled}}{\text{receipts}} - \frac{\text{on-hand}}{\text{inventory}}$$

Example

Computing Net-Component Requirements

The net requirements for each component or assembly are computed as follows.

Quantity of snowblowers to be produced	1,250	(Level 0)
Gross requirements, main housing assembly	1,250	(Level 1)
Less main housing assemblies in inventory	− 400	
Net requirements, main housing assembly	850	
Gross requirements, wheel assembly	1,250	(Level 1)
Less wheel assemblies in inventory	− 200	
Net requirements, wheel assemblies	1,050	
Gross requirements, blade assembly	1,050	(Level 2)
Less blade assemblies in inventory	− 800	
Net requirements, blade assembly	250	
Gross requirements, wheels	2,100	(Level 2)
Less wheels in inventory	−2,300	
Net requirements, wheels	(200)	←(0 required)
Gross requirements, engine assembly	1,250	(Level 1)
Less engine assemblies in inventory	− 450	
Net requirements, engine assembly	800	
Gross requirements, air cleaner subassembly	800	(Level 2)
Less air cleaner subassemblies in inventory	− 250	
Net requirements, air cleaner subassembly	550	
Gross requirements, filter housing	550	(Level 3)
Less filter housings in inventory	− 500	
Net requirements, filter housing	50	
Gross requirements, handle assembly	1,250	(Level 1)
Less handle assemblies in inventory	− 400	
Net requirements, handle assembly	850	

Note that, although the net requirement for the engine assembly is 800, MRP uses the dependent-demand information to show that only 550 air cleaners and 50 filter housings are needed.

We can organize the calculations shown and the time-phasing information into a table called an *item record,* as shown in Figure 17.8. The time-phased net requirements generate orders that are usually scheduled to be received when the net requirements are needed (*planned order receipts*). Lot-sizing techniques, such as the ones introduced in Chapter 14, are usually used to group *planned order releases* into production lots to reduce setups. If the BOM is exploded into

Part Five

Figure 17.8 MRP Item Record Illustrating Time Phasing

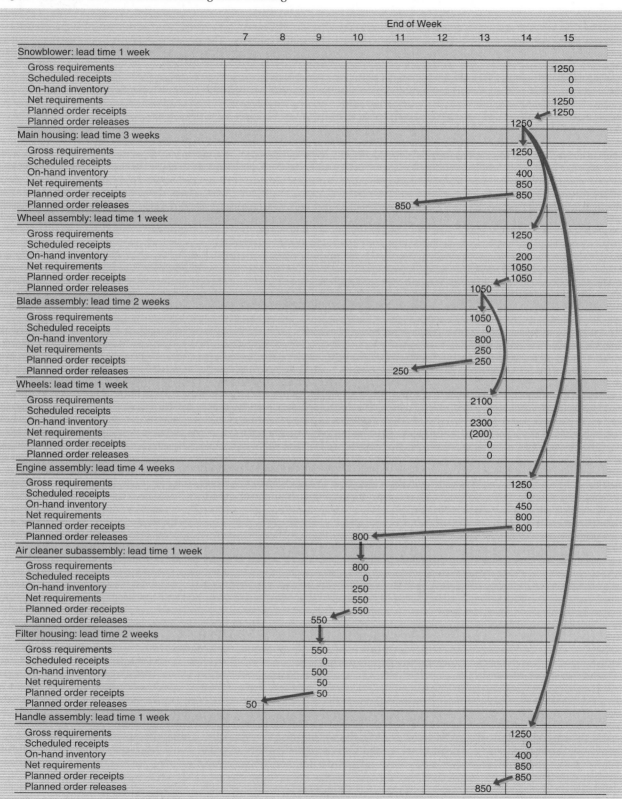

	End of Week								
	7	8	9	10	11	12	13	14	15
Snowblower: lead time 1 week									
Gross requirements									1250
Scheduled receipts									0
On-hand inventory									0
Net requirements									1250
Planned order receipts									1250
Planned order releases								1250	
Main housing: lead time 3 weeks									
Gross requirements								1250	
Scheduled receipts								0	
On-hand inventory								400	
Net requirements								850	
Planned order receipts								850	
Planned order releases					850				
Wheel assembly: lead time 1 week									
Gross requirements								1250	
Scheduled receipts								0	
On-hand inventory								200	
Net requirements								1050	
Planned order receipts								1050	
Planned order releases							1050		
Blade assembly: lead time 2 weeks									
Gross requirements							1050		
Scheduled receipts							0		
On-hand inventory							800		
Net requirements							250		
Planned order receipts							250		
Planned order releases				250					
Wheels: lead time 1 week									
Gross requirements							2100		
Scheduled receipts							0		
On-hand inventory							2300		
Net requirements							(200)		
Planned order receipts							0		
Planned order releases							0		
Engine assembly: lead time 4 weeks									
Gross requirements								1250	
Scheduled receipts								0	
On-hand inventory								450	
Net requirements								800	
Planned order receipts								800	
Planned order releases			800						
Air cleaner subassembly: lead time 1 week									
Gross requirements				800					
Scheduled receipts				0					
On-hand inventory				250					
Net requirements				550					
Planned order receipts				550					
Planned order releases			550						
Filter housing: lead time 2 weeks									
Gross requirements			550						
Scheduled receipts			0						
On-hand inventory			500						
Net requirements			50						
Planned order receipts			50						
Planned order releases	50								
Handle assembly: lead time 1 week									
Gross requirements								1250	
Scheduled receipts								0	
On-hand inventory								400	
Net requirements								850	
Planned order receipts								850	
Planned order releases							850		

detailed part requirements, a complete schedule for shop orders and purchase requisitions is available.

The calculations shown are only for *one week* of the MPS. Clearly, the total number of calculations is enormous, making a computer is essential. Fortunately, because of modern computer technology, we find that what was an unmanageable problem for earlier manual approaches is now routinely handled by an MRP system.

Regeneration versus Net-Change Systems

MRP systems must be capable of adapting to changes in forecasts, lead times, product structures, and so on. There are two fundamental approaches for updating net requirements in response to such changes. In the **regeneration approach,** the entire materials plan is recalculated periodically—for instance, each week—based on current information. This method usually consumes a large amount of computer time. In the **net-change approach,** the MRP system recalculates requirements *whenever necessary* but only for those components affected by a change. Both approaches are effective; however regeneration is easier to implement because the recalculations are done periodically. On the other hand, regeneration is less responsive; information is current only at the time the calculations are done. Although net change is more difficult to implement, it is highly responsive to changes in requirements and provides more timely information. Table 17.3 contrasts the two approaches.

Table 17.3 Regeneration versus Net-Change Systems

Key System Characteristics	Regeneration	Net-Change Approach
Frequency of replanning	Limited: weekly or less	High: daily or continuous
Planning trigger	The entire master schedule on a regular basis	Changes in the status of the master schedule or specific parts
Extent of explosion	Every item in the master schedule	Only items with status changes
Processing mode	Batch	On-line or batch
Validity of requirements data over time	Deteriorates between batch processes	No deterioration because of continuous file updating
Data-processing efficiency	Highly efficient	Relatively inefficient
Response time to change	Limited by infrequency of replanning	Quick because of frequent replanning or on-line updating
Ability to purge inaccurate requirements planning	Yes	No
Files that can be updated	Inventory data only	Inventory data and requirements data
Number of operating phases	Two: periodic requirements planning and intraperiod file updating	One: combined updating and requirements planning

Source: Gene J. D'Ovidio and Richard L. Behling, "Material Requirements Planning," in Gavriel Salvendy, ed., *Handbook of Industrial Engineering* (New York: John Wiley & Sons, 1982), 11.6.13. Copyright © 1982 by John Wiley & Sons. Reprinted by permission of John Wiley & Sons, Inc.

Uses and Benefits of MRP

The outputs available from an MRP information system provide timely and useful information to production and inventory managers. The three principal uses of MRP are for planning and controlling inventory, detailed capacity planning, and priority planning on the shop floor.

Inventory Planning and Control

The calculations performed by MRP yield planned order releases for purchased parts and manufactured components. In this fashion, MRP assists operations managers in planning and controlling inventories by answering the basic questions of what to order, how much to order, when to order, and when delivery should be scheduled.

Although the Spiecker Manufacturing example did not illustrate it, MRP usually applies some lot-sizing technique (for example, part-period balancing or periodic-order quantity) to combine the net requirements for several periods into realistic, planned order releases. This is necessary when the net requirements for an individual item are spread out over many time periods. Lot sizing is usually performed by MRP prior to determining the planned order releases by backing up, or offsetting, the lead time.

Capacity Requirements Planning

In Chapter 16 we discussed how rough-cut capacity-planning techniques are used to determine the feasibility of an MPS. MRP is insensitive to capacity limitations. It simply determines what materials and components are required in order to meet the MPS. **Capacity requirements planning (CRP)** is the process of determining the amount of labor and machine resources required to accomplish the tasks of production on a more detailed level, taking into account all component parts and end items in the materials plan. CRP requires detailed input information for all components and assemblies such as MRP-planned order releases, on-hand quantities, current status of shop orders, routing data, and time standards.

The process of CRP is similar to that of rough-cut capacity planning. The difference is that the MRP system establishes the exact order quantities and timing for each component part, whereas the MPS simply states the schedule of end items. In addition, rough-cut capacity planning examines key equipment or work centers—that is, bottlenecks. CRP examines many more work centers, and thus provides more detailed information.

Capacity requirements are computed by multiplying the number of units scheduled for production at a work center by the unit-resource requirements and then adding in the setup time. These requirements are then summarized by time period and work center. To illustrate CRP calculations, suppose the planned order releases for a component are as follows.

Time Period	1	2	3	4
Planned Order Release	20	0	25	25

Assume the component requires 1.10 hours of labor per unit in a particular work center and 1.5 hours of setup time; the capacity requirement in period 1 is

$$(20 \text{ units})(1.10 \text{ hours/unit}) + 1.5 \text{ hours} = 23.5 \text{ hours.}$$

Similarly, in periods 3 and 4, we have

$$(25 \text{ units})(1.10 \text{ hours/unit}) + 1.5 \text{ hours} = 29 \text{ hours.}$$

Such information is usually provided in a *load report,* as illustrated in Figure 17.9. If sufficient capacity is not available, decisions must be made about overtime, transfer of personnel between departments, subcontracting, and so on. The master production schedule may also have to be revised to meet available capacity. This requires that the MRP program be run again. The integration of capacity requirements, master scheduling, and MRP is often called a *closed-loop MRP system;* see Figure 17.10. In this way, capacity requirements planning provides a feedback between master scheduling and MRP.

Figure 17.9
A Sample Load Report

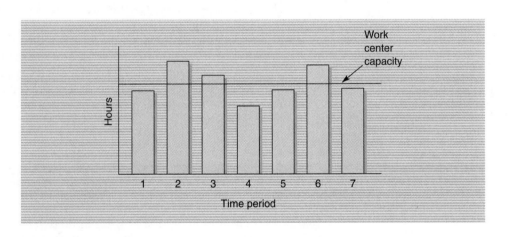

Figure 17.10 Closed-Loop MRP System

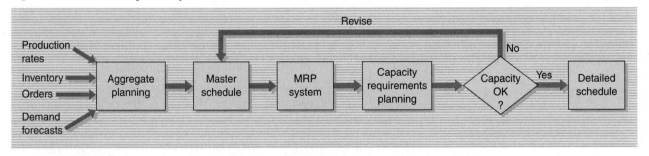

Priority Planning

Each order in a plant is prioritized by assigning a due date to it. Once the priorities of *orders* are established, individual operation schedules can be derived. This is discussed in the next chapter. The role of MRP in priority planning is to establish valid order priorities when orders are released to the shop and to keep them up-to-date.

For instance, in the Spiecker Manufacturing problem, assume that during the manufacture of the filter-housing component, a machine breakdown occurs that will delay production of the housings for one week. Managers must analyze the potential effects of a one-week delay in the production of the filter housings. Because an MRP system maintains information on all items in inventory, this information is available. For example, the MRP system would examine the bill of materials to determine the impact of a week's delay in the filter housing on the production schedule for all other components. In addition, if managers elect to delay production by a week, all components affected by the change would then be updated by the MRP system to reflect new production schedules.

In that way, MRP assists operations managers in making decisions about rescheduling orders and canceling or suspending orders on the MPS as priorities change. In a factory with many hundreds of orders, this is nearly impossible to do manually, but it is routine for computerized MRP systems. In addition, the MRP information system enables managers to obtain reports on projected inventory levels, vendor delivery performance and lead times, and exceptions such as late orders, high scrap, and so on.

MRP also provides benefits in other areas of the firm. For example, purchasing can achieve improved vendor relations and better utilization of time. Receiving can reduce labor requirements through improved scheduling of work by knowing when shipments will arrive. Marketing can achieve better customer relations through more reliable delivery, and finance can improve planning and control.

Planning and Implementing MRP

A significant amount of preplanning is required in order to apply MRP. A comprehensive review of a company's manufacturing system should include examinations of

1. *Operating policies*—organization and staffing, customer-service objectives.
2. *Materials-management systems*—master scheduling, capacity planning, production control, inventory control.
3. *Customer demand*—forecast accuracy, variability.
4. *Purchasing and manufacturing operations*—volumes, lead times, performance to schedule.

Such an examination will help to identify areas that must be improved before MRP can be implemented.

Because MRP necessitates a comprehensive change in a firm's approach to manufacturing, it requires a high level of discipline throughout the organization. Many MRP systems have been successful, but others have failed. Failures can usually be attributed to one of two causes: lack of accuracy and realism in data and information or inadequate planning and implementation.

Accuracy and Realism

The old computer adage "garbage in, garbage out" is especially true for MRP systems. Inaccuracies in inventory records, bills of materials, and master schedules can be disastrous for MRP.

Errors in inventory records will lead to inaccuracies in the MRP calculations of net requirements. Thus, managers are continually responding to crises caused by parts shortages and other inconsistencies, and in the end the integrity of the MRP system is lost. Inaccurate inventory records are most often caused by a lack of formal receiving procedures, unlocked storerooms, inappropriate forms or ineffective materials-information systems, and a lack of audit procedures.

Errors in bills of materials (BOMs) can cause the MRP system to signal a need for materials that are not actually required, or not to signal a need for required items. Usually such inaccuracies are the result of missing BOMs for some items and/or of a lack of control and communication about design changes.

Quigley suggests three sampling tests for checking accuracy:[1]

1. Take a finished product that is boxed and ready to ship. Disassemble it and verify the bill of materials for that product. This must be 100 percent correct.

2. Sample three parts from inventory. Check the on-hand level against inventory records. These should be within 1 to 2 percent of each other.

3. Obtain a status report from production control on current production, current targets, and next month's plan. Ask for the same information from materials control and assembly. These reports should be in agreement.

Looking back at Figure 17.6, we see that tests 1 and 2 are used to verify accuracy of the BOM and inventory files to the MRP system. Test 3 is performed to ensure that proper coordination between departments at the front and back ends of production is taking place. Such checks should be made periodically if an MRP system is to operate successfully. Good physical inventory control, such as cycle counting (described in Chapter 13), is one method for ensuring inventory accuracy.

Since the MPS drives the MRP system, it too must be accurate and realistic. Schedules that call for production of quantities that exceed the capacity of the plant or those that do not include all items that are actually produced will obviously lead to problems. An unrealistic MPS is often reflected in large numbers of overdue orders, excessively high amounts of indirect labor performed by direct-labor employees, or too many late jobs that must be expedited. Such problems can be minimized by careful attention to aggregate planning and the use of capacity requirements in a closed-loop system. We will consider issues of translating material requirements plans into feasible, realistic, short-term schedules in the next chapter.

MRP in Service Organizations

Many service organizations have features analogous to those of manufacturing firms. For example, in a restaurant, meals can be thought of as end items. The service required to assemble an order can be defined in terms of BOMs and lead times. For labor-intensive services, the analogy to the BOM would be a "bill of labor." However, because of the greater customization and uncertainty of needs in many service organizations, not all possible end items can be defined. For service organizations that offer more structured services, the concepts of MRP can be useful.

For example, the MRP concept can be applied to planning capacity requirements in colleges and universities. In determining how many sections of a course to schedule, a university needs to know the number of students who need to take the course. In this illustration, the end items are graduates in the respective major. The number of graduates can be forecasted on a short-range basis from current demands, projections of high school graduates, employment trends, and so on. From this information, an MPS can be constructed.

The curriculum, described for each major, constitutes the bill of materials. The prerequisite structure of courses defines the product structure in the BOM. This can then be exploded by semester or quarter to give a schedule of time-phased course requirements for each department. Department heads and deans can use this information to plan capacity in terms of faculty, teaching assistants, classrooms, computer facility requirements, and the like.

In one of the P/OM in Practice cases, we show how requirement-planning-systems concepts can be used to improve the management of an expensive surgical inventory.

Manufacturing Resource Planning (MRP II)

After the development of formalized MRP systems, it became evident that the MRP concept had potential for more than just planning of materials. Managers began to expand the concept to include other manufacturing resources allocated to production, particularly financial resources, since production is often measured in terms of dollars. The use of an MRP-based system to plan all the resources of a manufacturing company is called **manufacturing resource planning (MRP II).** As a tool for managing, predicting, and controlling a company's resources and operating investments, MRP II, in essence, converts a marketing statement of demand into a workable production plan. It involves the broader functions of purchasing, capacity planning, and master scheduling in addition to inventory, production, and strategic financial planning. Because of the competitive pressures to increase quality and shorten lead times, MRP II is viewed today as an important element of computer-integrated manufacturing, which was introduced in Chapter 9. An example of how MRP II can help bring together diverse business functions is the experience of the Marley Cooling Tower Company.

Applied P/OM:

Marley Cooling Tower Company

MRP II helped break down barriers between departments at Marley Cooling Tower Company.[2]

Implementing MRP II altered the company culture of Marley Cooling Tower Company, and affected how people perceived their jobs there and their roles in the company's success. For instance, engineers had long thought of the company as an engineering firm, but marketing had a different view of the company, and sales had still another view. MRP II helped everyone realize that the company is a *manufacturing firm.* Engineers began to appreciate the strong relationship between how they designed components and the ease of manufacturing them. They also came to see a direct link between the number of engineering change orders generated and the amount of excess and obsolete inventory the company had to absorb. Production came to appreciate the difference between making month-end quotas and making the right thing at the right time because a customer needs it. Accounting came to see that in order to get a true picture of costs and profitability, it needed to work from a common bill of material, rather than from its own version. Implementation of MRP II fostered the sharing of information among departments and led to the recognition that all departments are interdependent in a successful company.

The principal attributes of MRP II are as follows:[3]

1. It is a *top-down system,* beginning with the formulation of strategic business plans that are formalized and restated as functional strategies.

2. It uses a *common database* to evaluate alternative policies. Manufacturing data can be converted into financial data, and formal procedures are followed to maintain accuracy and introduce changes in the data.

3. *What-if* simulation capabilities are routinely used to evaluate alternative plans. The system is capable of generating detailed resource requirements for evaluation purposes.

4. It is a *total company system,* in which functional groups interact commonly and formally and make joint decisions.

5. It is *user-transparent.* Users at all levels understand and accept the logic and realism of the system and need not work outside the formal system.

A typical MRP II System is shown in Figure 17.11. It includes the vertical dimension of production planning, MPS, MRP, and shop-floor control. The system also includes inventory control, purchasing, and other planning considerations. Exxon Office System's use of MRP II illustrates the value of such a system.

Figure 17.11
Structure of MRP II System

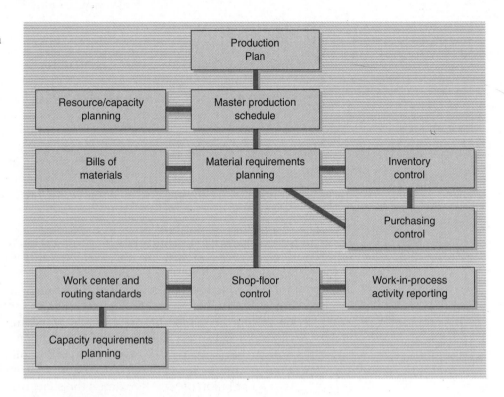

Applied P/OM

Exxon Office Systems

Exxon Office Systems realized many intangible and financial benefits through MRP II.[4]

The Qyx Division of Exxon Office Systems is a manufacturer of electronic typewriters located in Lionville, Pennsylvania. Qyx managers recognized early that future growth would strain its manufacturing operations and that a more effective control system was needed. The Qyx typewriter consists of hundreds of parts, the majority of which are purchased. There is also a heavy concentration in product improvements and value engineering. Thus it is critical that the shop be provided with the right parts, in the right quantities, and at the right time.

Qyx was a new company and had no formal manufacturing-control system. A team representing various functional areas of the company was created to develop a plan for a closed-loop MRP system. Three important identified objectives were to minimize inventory investment, maximize customer service, and optimize plant efficiency. For each of these objectives, the appropriate roles of material management, manufacturing, engineering, accounting, and data processing were studied. From this study a list of specifications that were required in a total system was developed.

The key to implementing the MRP II system, as with all projects in operations management, was commitment and teamwork at all levels of the organization. Within seven months after the project was initiated, the system was fully implemented. In the first six months after implementation, many intangible and financial benefits were noted. Among them were

••• Reduction of inventories by 30 percent.

••• Improvement in inventory accuracy from under 50 percent to 95 percent.

••• Higher accuracy in bills of materials.

••• Reduction in outstanding purchasing commitments.

••• Reduction in overdue purchase orders.

••• Improvement in on-time deliveries.

••• Reduction in inbound freight charges.

••• Reduction in overtime.

In addition to the tangible, financial benefits, the company was provided with more timely and accurate information with which to work and plan. This increased morale and productivity in the company.

MRP II systems accrue the benefits of ordinary MRP systems, including reduced manufacturing inventories, fewer stockouts, and improved delivery. As a strategic planning system, however, MRP II has demonstrated other unique benefits.[5] One firm, whose business objectives included level employment, used MRP II to convince marketing personnel that it was necessary to smooth the sales plan so that manufacturing could level its labor requirements. Another firm used the simulation capability to formulate contingency plans for minimizing the adverse effects of strikes on the firm's operation. Using MRP II to identify strike-induced capacity shortages and to schedule vendors to make up the projected capacity shortfalls, the firm was able to meet all of its commitments and deliveries during a 13-week strike. In a third firm, the use of MRP II enabled the lead times for new-product development and introduction to be reduced. The system linked the material-planning and product-engineering groups during the development process and was able to achieve better coordination.

MRP II in a TQM Environment

MRP II has benefited many manufacturing companies with improved customer service and with enhanced operational performance in the form of reduced inventories, lower production costs, and greater flexibility. But the benefits are even greater in companies that focus on total quality management (TQM). Here, continuous-improvement efforts result in a simplification of MRP II planning techniques. For example, when companies take a process view of production, complex routings are eliminated and the number of items in a bill of material is frequently reduced. With fewer items for which to plan, the planning process itself becomes more straightforward.

Experts predict that MRP II will evolve into an integrated management process that extends horizontally across the company, including product development, sales, marketing, manufacturing, and finance.[6] It also will extend vertically throughout a company's supply chain to include suppliers and customers. Eastman Kodak, for instance, has already begun to use MRP II to manage its worldwide supply chain. This evolution grows naturally from the fundamental purpose of MRP II: to link projected demand plans to supply plans so that the resources of manufacturers, their suppliers, and their customers are used in the most efficient and cost-effective way. The key to achieving this purpose is interaction and communication between planning and execution and between suppliers and customers. The ability to use MRP II as an integrated management process requires a high level of operational excellence—one of the key focal points of TQM.

Contrasting Production-Planning Philosophies[7]

JIT, MRP, and synchronous manufacturing all have similar objectives: to reduce inventory investment and to improve productivity and customer service. However, the approaches differ in their rationale, appropriate application, and implications for materials management and operational control. JIT seeks to eliminate all sources of waste in production activities by providing the right part at the right place at the right time. The JIT philosophy emphasizes waste reduction throughout the organization by reducing inventories and scrap, and by encouraging greater employee involvement in the production process. It is particularly well-suited for repetitive manufacturing environments. With MRP, all production activities are derived from the MPS. The emphasis is on constructing a valid MPS and then executing according to that plan, using computers and sophisiticated information processing. MRP is best-suited for job shops or other environments that require great production flexibility. Such flexibility comes at a cost—namely, higher inventories and greater waste than in a JIT system. Synchronous manfacturing is focused on moving material quickly through the productive resources of a manufacturing facility in response to market demand. The goal is to identify constraint resources and achieve synchronization by improving the management of those resources by scheduling to keep them busy.

Table 17.4 summarizes the key differences among the approaches. It is important for managers of production operations to understand these differences and develop the appropriate infrastructure to support their chosen approach.

Table 17.4 Contrasts among JIT, MRP, and Synchronous Manufacturing

	JIT	MRP	Synchronous Manufacturing
Goal	Ensure production meets customer demand.	Ensure production meets customer demand.	Ensure production meets customer demand.
Underlying Philosophy	Eliminate *all* kinds of waste.	All production activities are derived from MPS.	Identify and manage constraints (theory of constraints).
Where Used	Repetitive manufacturing.	Job shop; custom shop.	Appropriate for all manufacturing environments.
MPS Focus	Level/constant production flow.	Highly variable production flow.	Keep constraint resources busy; seek steady flow through synchronizing the constraint resources and through inventories (buffers) at specified production stages.
Scheduling	Demand driven; pull.	MPS driven; push/pull.	Constraint-resource driven.
Lot Sizes	Small.	Select lot size to balance setup costs with carrying costs.	May vary throughout production process (keep constraint resources busy).
Inventory	Very low (to expose problems).	High (allows costly flexibility).	Reasonably low; limited to buffers.
Suppliers	Few (treated as part of team).	Many (in cost competition).	Cooperative relationship.
Lead Time	Short.	Longer.	Sufficient to keep constraint resources busy.
Manufacturing: Cycle Time	Very short.	Longer.	Short.
Labor Skills	Multiskilled; focus on teamwork.	Specialized-skill.	Somewhat specialized; focus on teamwork; employees are an integral part of the whole system.
Quality Control	Quality at source; worker is responsible for quality; goal is zero defects/scrap.	Haphazardly applied; some inspection stations; scrap/waste tolerated.	Emphasis is on improving quality through reduction of inventories and better synchronization of production processes.

P/OM in Practice

Implementing an MRP II System in Mexico[8]

TREMEC (Transmisiones y Equipos Mecanicos, S.A. de C.V.), a subsidiary of Clark Equipment Company, is a manufacturing facility located in Querétaro, Mexico. TREMEC produces manual transmissions for automobiles, buses, and small trucks, employing about 6,000 people. In the late 1980s, the company's managers, composed of U.S. citizens and Mexican citizens trained or educated in the United States, faced numerous problems:

- An unskilled work force, many of whom had difficulty filling out their own time sheets.
- Unskilled middle managers, driven by nepotism or bribes.
- Poor relations between top managers and the heavily unionized labor force. The average worker did not consider himself a part of the company, to the extent that he often did not show up for work for several days after receiving a paycheck.
- Machinery that was either old or technologically too new for the work force. Equipment repair was often performed by cannibalizing other machines for parts.
- Unreliable power supplies. Power surges and brownouts were frequent.
- Communications difficulties.
- Poor or meaningless production standards. Employees did not understand the purpose of production data or the procedures for recording them correctly.
- A crisis-management mentality. Planned schedules were often changed by expeditors trying to push rush jobs through the plant.
- High inventories due to sporadic deliveries of raw materials and delays at border crossings.

The company decided to implement an MRP II system to improve production standards, provide managers with better information, improve employee-manager relations, reduce inventories, and route materials more accurately. It was felt that automated data collection would reduce the number of errors and force more discipline on managers and shop-floor supervisors.

Some of the unconventional problems in the organization required unconventional solutions. Implementation was performed much more slowly than would have been necessary in a U.S. plant. Computer screens had to be converted to Mexican Spanish. Surge protection and power backup systems were installed. Special personnel were hired to fill out job cards for the factory workers. This allowed TREMEC to hire more workers—a national goal encouraged by tax incentives to companies.

The MRP II system did help to resolve various manufacturing problems. Because the work force was unskilled, many input documents were simplified or eliminated. This improved the accuracy of the input data, as there was less reliance on the writing ability of the average worker. Middle managers were trained intensively in MRP concepts. The system helped the various levels of managers to understand the methodology behind the development of production schedules, and it helped to ease tensions between employees and managers by providing a scapegoat on which managers could blame production problems. MRP II also allowed maintenance to be scheduled, which made repair and replacement of old machinery easier.

By providing improved data-collection techniques, the new system dramatically improved production standards. Better data and access to the resulting information helped to reduce the number of crises. In implementing the system, however, it was difficult to get upper managers to take advantage of the system, because they were so busy "fighting fires" that they had little time to learn about the system. Work-in-process inventories were reduced, but not to the extent anticipated, because the work force had little experience with the system and did not trust it.

The problems in implementing MRP II were based largely on cultural differences. The U.S. managers selected a system with which they were comfortable without recognizing the differences in management requirements in Mexico. Accurate data were difficult to collect in the Mexican environment. Whereas MRP II is focused on achieving high efficiency, the Mexican national goal is full employment. Training that is effective for Mexican workers cannot be accomplished with a U.S. timetable; it took more than seven years for users to become comfortable with the system. Similar systems have been implemented in the United States in two years.

Questions for Discussion

1. What problems did TREMEC face that hindered the implementation of the MRP II system? How do they differ from those of typical U.S. manufacturing facilities?

2. What lessons can U.S. managers learn from TREMEC's experience about implementing new technological systems internationally, particularly in underdeveloped countries?

An MRP System for Houston's Park Plaza Hospital[9]

Park Plaza Hospital is a privately owned 374-bed facility with a surgical suite of nine operating rooms. These operating rooms are reserved at least a week in advance by physicians with surgery privileges at the hospital. Thus, at any time, the schedule of planned operations for the next seven days is known with some certainty. Anything beyond that horizon is far less certain. After an operation has been entered on the surgical schedule, it must be confirmed on two other occasions: 72 hours before and 48 hours before the operation. This scheduling process allows the assignment of staff (nursing, orderlies, etc.) and the preparation of the necessary supplies and equipment for the specific procedure. The patient is generally admitted to the hospital about 12 hours before the operation.

Most surgery is performed during normal working hours (7 A.M. to 5 P.M.), Monday through Friday and some Saturdays. The operations themselves average about 45 minutes. Obviously, however, different operations take different amounts of time; there is no set time for any procedure, and they differ from case to case and physician to physician. This lack of predictability is further complicated by evidence that physicians perceive that they work more quickly than they actually do.

As a result, the surgical schedule for any given operating room on any given day (and hence, for the seven-day planning horizon) is not entirely fixed. The schedule includes such information as: date, operating room number, scheduled time, patient name, patient room number, operation, physician, estimated time, and planned anesthesia.

Supplies for any operation fit into three general categories:

1. Disposable items that can be used only once.
2. Reusable instruments that are recycled and used again; i.e., they are cleaned, sterilized, and placed back into inventory (for example, pickups, clamps, etc.).

3. A limited number of high-technology instruments—the limitation is due to their high costs (for example, a CAT-scan, heart-lung machine, etc.).

In addition, the stock required for any operation depends on the particular procedure and physician—each having his or her preference as to the instruments and disposable supplies needed for a given procedure. Supplies and instruments are drawn from inventory according to a Physician's Preference Sheet that lists these requirements by procedure and by physician. The goal of the MRP system for Park Plaza is to ensure that these required supplies arrive at the proper place (the correct operating room) at the proper time, correctly assigned by surgical procedure and physician, and that appropriate and accurate inventory levels are maintained.

To demonstrate the application of requirements planning to the surgical suite, a nomenclature that relates to the hospital environment is required. Table 17.5 shows the nomenclature and compares it to the terminology employed in manufacturing applications. We next define each system component in the context of the surgical suite and describe the role of each in the system.

The first component of the system is the seven-day-horizon surgical schedule, the analog of an MPS. In this case, however, each product is de-

fined as a specific physician performing a specific procedure. This definition is necessary, as has been explained, because the physicians have different preferences. Thus, if we have k physicians, each performing n procedures, we can identify as many as $k \times n$ separate products.

Whereas in the conventional MPS the end items are physical products, here the end items represent procedures performed by a specific physician, and each end item has a quantity of only one. However, in both cases, the end item remains the target of the material flow and the output of the process.

The surgical requirements file—the analog of the BOM—contains the materials and supplies needed for the various procedures (or level-0 end items). In the traditional MRP system, the BOM file defines the final product in terms of its components; in the surgical suite such components are the supplies required for a particular surgical procedure in accordance with physician preference. Thus, the items on the Physician's Preference Sheet are defined as level-1 components that must be ready for use (sterilized if appropriate) in the procedure.

Extending this concept further, all items that require sterilization are considered level-2 subassemblies with lead times equal to their required sterilization time (which ranges from five minutes to 16 hours) and recycling. Although this means that inventory records must be kept on two levels,

Table 17.5 MRP Application Terminology

Manufacturing	Health Care
Master production schedule	Surgical schedule
Bill of materials	Surgical requirements file
Inventory	Inventory item file

such a scheme provides an effective method for handling items that must be sterilized. Sterilization units can be viewed as machine centers with limited capacity. Outputs of the system are a projected load for sterilization and a schedule for release of sterilized items to projected inventory.

The procedure for systems operation is shown in Figure 17.12. The system operation begins with an inquiry to the surgical schedule. If capacity is available in the surgical schedule, the procedure is to update the schedule by inserting the surgery in the appropriate spot. The schedule is then exploded through the surgical requirements file to generate gross requirements for all necessary materials and supplies. Note that a specific identified product (a particular physician performing a specific procedure) is traceable to a single Physician's Preference Sheet. The gross requirements thus generated are netted against the projected on-hand inventory for all items required. A sample record for a reusable component is shown in Table 17.6.

The key database elements of the system are the Surgical Schedule File, Inventory Item File, and Surgical Requirements File. The *Surgical Schedule File* should contain all posted surgeries for a specific day and their anticipated needed times for each operating room. It includes such data as

- Operation number.
- Scheduled date and time.
- Operating room number.
- Patient room number.
- Patient name.
- Procedure(s).
- Anesthesia.
- Physician name.

The *Inventory Item File* is a time-phased inventory record of surgical supplies and instruments required by one or more procedures. Particular care must be taken in this file to distinguish between disposable and reusable items. Data in this file include

- Unique item number.
- Description of the item.
- Level.
- Gross requirements.
- Quantity on hand (current, allocated, projected available).
- Scheduled receipts.
- Planned order releases.
- Standard inventory ordering data (lot size, order point, lead time, vendor information).
- Recycling time (if applicable).

The *Surgical Requirements File* is the functional equivalent of a single-item BOM for a particular procedure.* This file identifies quantities of each item needed for each procedure as well as the specific size and/or brand of the item. The file is divided into two parts: common items and preference items. The common items are those materials used by *all* physicians when performing the procedure; the preference items reflect physician differences in surgical material requirements. Collectively, these items

Figure 17.12 System Logic

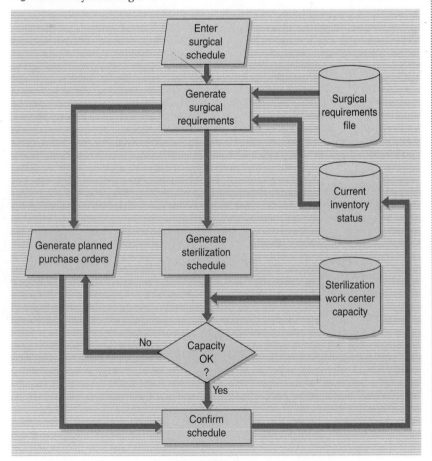

Table 17.6 Item Record for Reusable Part

ITEM: Blade, #10	Sterilization lead time: 2 periods; Procurement lead time: 1 period												
							Period						
	0	1	2	3	4	5	6	7	8	9	10	11	12
Gross requirements		5	5	10	10	10	15			5	10		
Scheduled receipts													
Projected sterilized				5	5	10	10	10	10	5		5	10
Projected on-hand	15	10	5	0	0	0	0	10	20	20	10	15	25
Net requirements					5		5						
Planned order receipts					5		5						
Planned order release				5		5							

establish the inventory requirements for each procedure in this manner:

- Level-0 element number (procedure identifier).
- Lower-level element numbers of common items.
- Lower-level element numbers of preference items (for each physician associated with level-0 element number).

Table 17.7 illustrates the surgical requirements file for a bronchoscopy. Observe that the upper portion lists the inventory items used by all physicians; the lower portion lists the additional inventory items requested by specific physicians.

In the environment for which the system was developed, the chief nurse of the surgical suite functions as the medical analog to the materials manager. He or she is in charge of all surgical-scheduling and equipment-sterilization activities and is responsible for inventory management of all required medical supplies for the surgical suite—all tools, instruments, and equipment (not medications) required for all procedures.

The storeroom, sterilization facilities, and operating rooms themselves are lo-cated in one contiguous area under the chief surgical nurse's control. In this area, an inventory of the more than 2,000 items used in the various surgical procedures is maintained. Inventory balances are updated by an on-line transaction-driven, batch-processing system that provides a complete inventory status report for all items each week. In addition, a query-driven system provides access to the current level of inventory on hand for each item.

The entire system is designed to be operated by nursing personnel. Its success and acceptance stem from two factors:

1. *Reliability of operation.* It generates reliable schedules and ensures adequate supplies. The reduction of problems in this area has led to greater physician satisfaction and a more harmonious relationship with nursing personnel.
2. *Simplicity of operation.* Its outputs include a daily schedule of surgical procedures, a list of items to be drawn from the storeroom, a list of items to be purchased, and a sterilization schedule.

The application of requirements planning to the surgical suite demonstrates

Table 17.7 Surgical Requirements for a Bronchoscopy

Common items
   Bronchoscopy set, rigid
   Suction tubing
   Telescope, right angle
   Telescope, forward oblique
   Glass slides
   Fixative
   Specimen trap
   Table cover
   Towels
Preference items
Dr. *****
   Flexible bronchoscope
   Gloves, size 6 1/2 brown
Dr. *****
   Gloves, size 7 1/2
   Local set

how job-shop techniques can be employed in a nonmanufacturing environment where there are resource and time constraints but not a physical final product. It gives hospital adminis-

*The data recorded in the file assume that all items have been prepared for surgery. Therefore, the distinction between component levels is not important.

trators a better vehicle to understand and control the investment in material and supplies in this rapidly increasing cost area. Furthermore, the use of MRP-based technology ensures that materials are available when needed, protects against the overcapitalization of inventory, and aids in formulating and adjusting reordering policies.

Questions for Discussion

1. In a surgical context, what is the counterpart of a "product" in a traditional manufacturing environment? Briefly explain how this term is defined.

2. In a surgical context, what is the analog of the BOM, and how is it defined?

3. What person in the surgical suite is the analog to the materials manager in a traditional manufacturing environment? Briefly describe this person's duties.

4. What are the primary factors that determine the success and acceptance of MRP in the surgical suite?

Summary of Key Points

••• Material requirements planning (MRP) is a technique used to plan for and control manufacturing inventories. The key inputs are the master production schedule (MPS), inventory records, and bills of materials. The outputs are schedules for obtaining raw materials and purchased parts and a detailed schedule for manufacturing and inventory control. The three principal applications of MRP are for planning and controlling inventory, detailed capacity planning, and shop-floor priority planning.

••• The demand for materials and manufactured components is determined by the commitments for finished goods reflected in the master production schedule. By "backing-up" from the time that finished goods are required using the lead times for production or purchasing components and assemblies, unnecessary inventories can be reduced.

••• MRP requires a computerized information system and software to perform the calculations. This requires accurate inventory records and a realistic MPS. Employee education and training are essential for successful implementation.

••• MRP II is a tool for managing, predicting, and controlling a company's resources and operating investments. It incorporates the functions of purchasing, capacity planning, and master scheduling as well as inventory and production planning. MRP II can help a company to achieve increased cooperation among functional units by focusing them on common strategic goals.

••• Although MRP is similar to JIT and synchronous manufacturing in that it seeks to reduce inventory investment and improve productivity and customer service, many differences exist, as summarized in Table 17.4.

Key Terms

Material requirements planning (MRP)
Bucket
Time phasing
Regeneration approach
Net-change approach
Capacity requirements planning (CRP)
Manufacturing resource planning (MRP II)

Review Questions

1. What is the role of MRP in the production-planning and scheduling process?
2. What are the major functions of an MRP system?
3. Distinguish between independent and dependent demand.
4. How can the use of MRP reduce unnecessary inventory holding?
5. What are the components of an MRP information system?
6. What is the function of the bill of materials in an MRP system?
7. Explain how net-component requirements are calculated.
8. Explain the concept of time phasing.
9. Distinguish between the regeneration approach and the net-change approach in MRP.
10. What is capacity requirements planning? How does it interface with MRP?
11. Of what value is MRP in areas of a firm other than production?
12. Discuss the importance of accuracy and realism in implementing MRP.
13. How can the MRP concept be applied in a service organization?
14. What is manufacturing resource planning? How does it differ from MRP?

15. What are the benefits of MRP II?

16. How does MRP differ from JIT and synchronous manufacturing?

Discussion Questions

1. Construct a bill of materials for your college curriculum, thinking of core courses, electives, and so on as components of the "end item." How might MRP concepts apply?

2. Interview a production manager at a nearby company that uses MRP. What benefits does the manager feel MRP offers? What problems are encountered in its use?

3. Describe some situations in which a regeneration approach would be preferable to a net-change approach, and vice versa.

4. Provide some examples, different from those given in the text, of when MRP might be applied in a service organization.

5. Can MRP concepts be applied in a quick-service restaurant like McDonald's? Explain.

Notes

1. Philip E. Quigley, "Pre-MRP Planning: Make These Three Tests before Implementing," *Industrial Engineering* 12, no. 2 (February 1980), pp. 36–37.

2. Joe Trino, "MRP II Implementations Reap Strategic and Tactical Benefits," *Industrial Engineering* 23, no. 3 (March 1991), pp. 46–48.

3. S. A. Melnyk, R. F. Gonzalez, and S. J. Anderson, "Manufacturing Resource Planning: Insights into a New Corporate Way of Life," *APICS Research Report 82-8,* March 1983 (American Production and Inventory Control Society).

4. "Controlling Growing Manufacturing Ops with CINCOM's MRPS," *Production & Inventory Management Review,* July 1981. Copyright 1981 by T. D. A. Publications, Inc. Adapted with permission.

5. S. A. Melnyk, and R. F. Gonzalez, "MRP II: The Early Returns Are In," *Production and Inventory Management* 26, no. 1 (1985), pp. 124–137.

6. Walter Goddard and James Correll, "MRP in the Year 2000," *APICS—The Performance Advantage* 4, no. 3 (March 1994), pp. 38–42.

7. The author is grateful to Professor Richard A. Reid of the University of New Mexico for suggesting this discussion and providing Table 17.5.

8. Gerhard Plenert, "Developing a Production System in Mexico," *Interfaces* 20, no. 3 (May–June 1990), pp. 14–23. Adapted with permission. Copyright 1990 by Operations Research Society of America and The Institute of Management Sciences, 290 Westminster Street, Providence, RI 02903 USA.

9. E. Steinberg, B. Khumawala, and R. Scamell, "Requirements Planning Systems in the Health Care Environment," *Journal of Operations Management* 2, no. 4 (1982), pp. 251–259. Adapted with permission from *Journal of the American Production and Inventory Control Society, Inc.*

Solved Problems

1. An electrical appliance, A, consists of three major subassemblies: B, C, and D. One unit of A consists of two units of B, one unit of C, and three units of D. Subassembly B consists of two units of D, one unit of E, and one unit of F. Subassembly C consists of two units of E. Subassembly D consists of one unit of E and one unit of F. A second major appliance, G, consists of three units of D and four units of F.

a. Draw the bill of materials for products A and G.

b. If 50 units of A and 25 units of G are required for the month of May, compute the requirements for all components and subassemblies.

Solution

a. Figure 17.13 is the bill of materials.

b. Requirements for May

A	50
G	25
B	50(2) = 100
C	50(1) = 50
D	50(3) + 25(3) + 100(2) = 425

Figure 17.13
Solved Problem 1 Solution

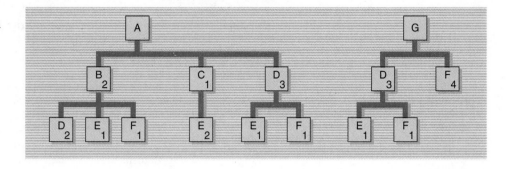

E	$100(1) + 50(2) + 425 = 625$
F	$100(1) + 425 + 25(4) = 625$

2. Table 17.8 is the MRP table pertaining to a low-level purchased item. Complete the table, assuming a lead time of two weeks.

Table 17.8 Data for Solved Problem 2

	Week								
	10	*11*	*12*	*13*	*14*	*15*	*16*	*17*	*18*
Gross requirements	150	0	175	0	150	0	175	0	150
Scheduled receipts	125	0	150	0	175	0	125	0	0
On hand	75								
Net requirements									
Planned order receipts									
Planned order release									

Solution
Table 17.9 is the completed MRP table.

Table 17.9 Solved Problem 2 Solution

	Week								
	10	*11*	*12*	*13*	*14*	*15*	*16*	*17*	*18*
Gross requirements	150	0	175	0	150	0	175	0	150
Scheduled receipts	125	0	150	0	175	0	125	0	0
On-hand	75	50	25	25	50	50	0	0	(150)
Net requirements									150
Planned order receipts									150
Planned order release								150	

Problems

1. For the Spiecker Manufacturing example discussed in this chapter, determine the net requirements for the engine assembly, the air cleaner subassembly, and the filter housing if the number of units in inventory are 500, 375, and 250, respectively. Assume that 1,250 units of the 14-inch snowblower are still required in week 15.

2. For the Spiecker example, determine the effect on time phasing if lead times are 5 for the engine assembly, 2 for the air cleaner subassembly, and 3 for the filter housing.

3. Given the following parts list, draw the bill of materials:

End-Item components	A(2), B(1), C(3)
Part A components	D(1), E(1)
Part B components	F(2), G(1)
Part D components	C(2)
Part F components	C(1), H(2)

4. In Solved Problem 1, suppose 100 units of A and 50 units of G are required for the month of June and that at the end of May, this is the stock on hand:

Item	A	G	B	C	D	E	F
Stock on Hand	50	25	50	20	350	0	175

Calculate the requirements for all components and subassemblies.

5. C&D Lawn Products manufactures a rotary spreader for applying fertilizer. A portion of the BOM is shown in Figure 17.14. Assuming 3,000 lawn spreaders are needed to satisfy a customer's order, determine the net requirements for the base assembly, wheel subassembly, and tires. Assume that 1,000, 1,500, and 800 of each component, respectively, are currently in inventory.

Figure 17.14
BOM for Problem 5

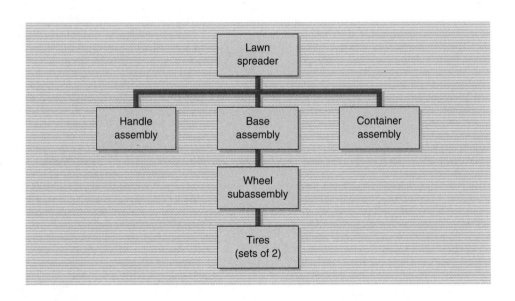

6. In Problem 5, assume that the lead times for the base assembly, wheel subassembly, and tires are 2, 4, and 5 weeks, respectively. If all components must be completed no later than week 15 of the current production period, when must orders be placed to meet the production schedule?

7. The parts used in manufacturing a yo-yo are shown in Figure 17.15. One thousand yo-yos are needed by week 10. Current inventory levels and lead times are shown in Table 17.10.

Figure 17.15
BOM for Problem 7

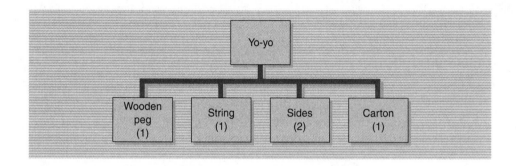

Table 17.10 Data for Problem 7

Part	Inventory (units)	Lead time (weeks)
Wooden peg	100	1
String	500	1
Sides	200	5
Cartons	—	3

It is known that 200 sides have already been ordered and will arrive at week 6. When all the parts are available, it takes one week to assemble 1,000 yo-yos.

a. Determine the net requirements for all components.

b. Use time phasing to determine an overall schedule.

8. The parts used in the manufacturing of a toy car are shown in Figure 17.16. Five hundred toy cars are needed by week 12. Current inventory levels and lead times are given in Table 17.11.

Figure 17.16
BOM for Problem 8

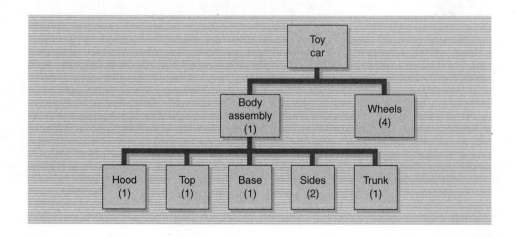

Table 17.11 Data for Problem 8

Item	Inventory (units)	Lead time (weeks)
Toy car	100	2
Body assembly	125	5
Hood	—	3
Top	100	2
Base	175	4
Side	200	3
Trunk	300	2
Wheels	800	3

a. Determine the net requirements for all components.

b. Use time phasing to determine an overall schedule.

9. Given the product structure and gross requirements schedules for final assemblies A and G shown in Figure 17.17, complete Table 17.12 for item F. The lead time for F is two weeks. Assume that the scheduled receipts, on hand, and lead times for B and D are all zero.

Figure 17.17
BOM for Problem 9

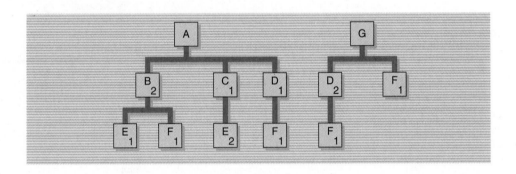

					Week			
Gross Requirements	4	5	6	7	8	9	10	11
A	100	0	100	0	100	0	100	0
G	0	50	0	50	0	50	0	50

Table 17.12 Data for Problem 9 (Item F)

Week	4	5	6	7	8	9	10	11
Gross requirements								
Scheduled receipts	200	100	400	100	175	100	150	150
On hand	100							
Net requirements								
Planned order receipts								
Planned order release								

10. The BOM for a pair of in-line skates is shown in Figure 17.18. Given the information in Table 17.13, determine net requirements for all components and an ordering schedule. Assume that 500 pairs of skates are needed by week 10.

Figure 17.18
BOM for Problem 10

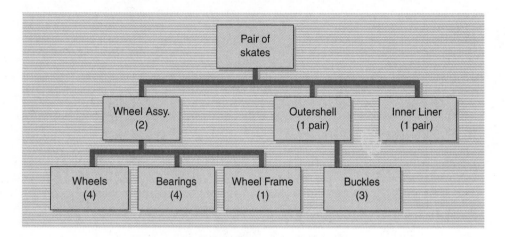

Table 17.13 Data for Problem 10

Item	Inventory	Lead time
Pair skates	50	1
Wheel assembly	100	2
Outer shell	25 pairs	3
Inner liner	0 pairs	3
Wheels	1500	1
Bearings	3000	1
Wheel frame	600	2
Buckles	5000	1

11. A plant stand consists of these parts:
Four long legs.
Four short legs.
Eight crossbars.
Four middle glass retainers.
Four top glass retainers.
Two glass shelves.
Sixteen screws (to fasten crossbars).
Four leg caps.
 The stand and assembly chart are given in Figure 17.19.
a. Construct a structured BOM for this product.
b. Develop a time-phased MRP for all components to meet the needs of an MPS that calls for 300 units on day 5, 400 units on day 10, 300 units on day 15, and 300 units on day 20. Current on-hand inventories and lead times (days) are shown in Table 17.14.

Figure 17.19
Problem 11

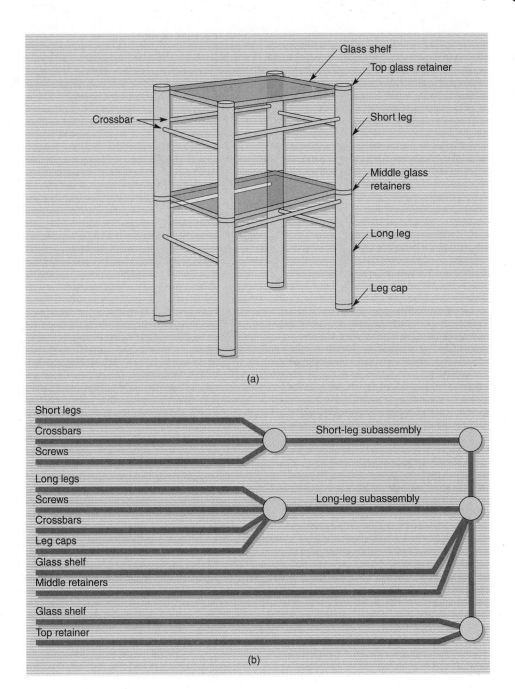

(a)

(b)

Table 17.14 Data for Problem 11

Component	On-Hand Inventory	Lead Time (days)
Finished stand	200	3
Short-leg subassembly	200	5
Long-leg subassembly	150	5
Long leg	1,800	6
Short leg	1,800	6
Crossbar	6,000	5
Middle retainer	500	2
Top retainer	400	2
Glass shelves	250	6
Screws	5,000	1
Leg caps	6,000	2

Chapter Outline

Chapter Eighteen
Operations Scheduling and Production-Activity Control

Applied P/OM

Tibor Machine Products

P/OM in Practice

Western Electric's Semiconductor Production-Control System

Computer-Assisted Dispatching of Tank Trucks for Mobil Oil Corporation

Scheduling refers to the assignment of priorities to manufacturing orders and allocation of work to specific work centers. A schedule specifies the timing and sequence of production and the amount of work to be completed at any work center during any time period. **Production-activity control** provides data and information to production supervisors—work-in-process, manufacturing-order status, actual output, and measures of efficiency, utilization and productivity—to enable them to ensure that materials and tools are available when needed, track progress against planned requirements, and make short-term adjustments when necessary.

Figure 18.1 illustrates the relationship of scheduling (specifically, finite capacity scheduling, which will be defined shortly) and production-activity control to the overall scope of production planning and scheduling. The output from *material requirements planning* (MRP) provides a plan for producing components, assemblies, and end products. On the shop floor, however, first-line supervisors face the problem of detailed day-to-day scheduling and control of production in response to higher-level planning. They must address such questions as: How can I complete orders on time? What can I produce this week or today? What is a good schedule to optimize machine utilization or other criteria? Their goals are to *meet customer-service objectives* by completing orders on time, *minimize production costs* by reducing work-in-process (WIP) inventory

Figure 18.1
The Production-Planning and Scheduling Process

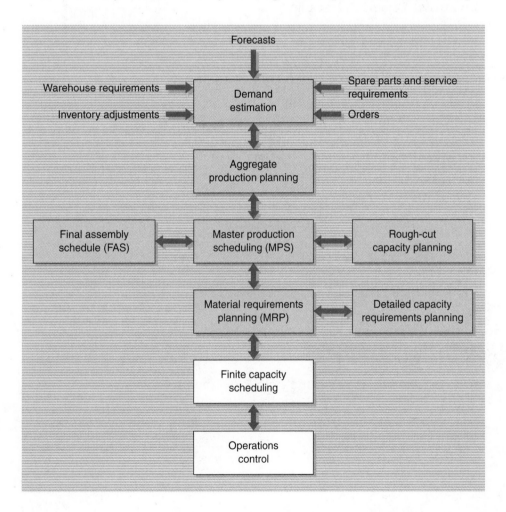

and unnecessary machine setups, and *maximize resource utilization* by minimizing idle time and reducing in-plant congestion. These goals often conflict, and when they do, operations managers must determine the appropriate balance. Quality, however, should never be sacrificed to meet any of these goals. And since quality requires a long-term commitment, these goals present a dilemma to managers who are evaluated on short-term results.

Service organizations also face important scheduling decisions. For example, customer demand for pizzas varies during a typical week and even over different hours of the day at MamaMia's Pizza, and the manager must schedule employees accordingly. Beverage suppliers, who deliver to MamaMia's and many other businesses, must schedule their delivery vehicles to ensure on-time delivery and use their fleet of delivery vehicles efficiently.

This chapter will address, specifically,

••• Key issues in operations scheduling and production-activity control.
••• The scope of finite capacity scheduling and common approaches for developing good schedules.
••• Special scheduling techniques in manufacturing and service organizations.

Finite Capacity Scheduling

Scheduling approaches such as MPS (master production scheduling) and MRP (material requirements planning) assume infinite capacity and ignore important resource constraints. The resulting schedule may be impossible to accomplish on the factory floor. In contrast, **finite capacity scheduling (FCS)** is based on given resource levels that cannot be changed in the short planning horizon that the scheduler faces. FCS matches the work to be done against the available resources. The result is a schedule that never exceeds available capacity and is always feasible to implement on the factory floor. Once the schedule is implemented, of course, managers and supervisors must control progress and may need to make adjustments for machine breakdowns or other problems.

The complexity of FCS generally requires sophisticated computer software to integrate and process the variety of data needed to produce a useful schedule. Key inputs into any scheduling system include the types of jobs that can be processed by different resources; specific process routings; processing, setup, and changeover times; due dates or shipping dates; resource availability, such as the number of shifts; and downtime and planned maintenance. As some scheduling approaches depend on precise information from the factory floor, data accuracy is vital to success. Many computer-based scheduling systems exist that perform schedule evaluation, schedule generation, and automated scheduling.[1] In *schedule evaluation*, the schedules are manually generated and then assessed by the computer to determine feasibility and to estimate performance measures. In *schedule generation*, the computer produces the schedules, which are then reviewed manually. The human scheduler uses his or her judgment and experience to improve the schedule. At the highest level of sophistication—*automated scheduling*—the computer can generate a schedule, identify problems, and create new schedules. Many benefits can accrue from the right system, as Tibor Machine Products, a small company in the Chicago area, discovered.

Applied P/OM

Tibor Machine Products

Finite scheduling software provides numerous benefits at Tibor Machine Products.[2]

As Tibor Machine Products changed its marketing strategy to develop new customers and new markets, it discovered some difficult challenges in its manufacturing scheduling process. The unique requirements of new customers resulted in longer and more complex product routings and more variation in ordering patterns. Tibor was using an MRP system that did not contain FCS. In its new environment, it needed to generate schedules quickly in an easy-to-understand format, make what-if analyses, and quickly regenerate a schedule. An FCS software package helped the company meet those needs and provided many other long-term benefits, including a large reduction in lot sizes, identification of production bottlenecks, better overtime planning, and even better equipment acquisition.

In selecting a specific approach for FCS, a manager must first consider the criteria on which to evaluate schedules. These criteria are often classified into three categories: shop-performance, due-date, and cost-based criteria. The applicability of the various criteria depends on the availability of data.

Shop-performance criteria pertain only to information about the start and end times of jobs and focus on shop performance such as machine utilization and WIP inventory. Two common measures are **makespan,** the time needed to process a given set of jobs, and **flowtime,** the amount of time a job spends in the shop. A short makespan aims to achieve high equipment utilization and resources by getting all jobs out of the shop quickly. Low flowtimes reduce WIP inventory.

Due-date criteria pertain to customers' required **due dates,** or internally determined shipping dates. Two common measures are **tardiness,** the amount of time by which the completion time exceeds the due date (tardiness is defined as zero if the job is completed before the due date), and **lateness,** the difference between the completion time and the due date (either positive or negative). Another common measure is the number of tardy or late jobs. In contrast to shop-performance criteria, these measures focus externally on customer satisfaction. Table 18.1 summarizes shop performance and due-date criteria.

Table 18.1 Common Scheduling Criteria

Criterion	Definition	Objective
Makespan	Time to process a set of jobs	Minimize makespan
Flowtime	Time a job spends in the shop	Minimize average flowtime
Tardiness*	The amount by which completion time exceeds the job's due date	Minimize number of tardy jobs or the maximum tardiness
Lateness	The difference between completion time and due date	Minimize average lateness or the maximum lateness

*If a job is completed before its due date, then tardiness is zero.

Cost-based criteria, might seem to be the most obvious criteria, but it is often difficult to identify the relevant cost components and obtain accurate estimates of their values. In most cases, costs are considered implicitly in shop-performance and due-date criteria.

Several approaches can be used for finite capacity scheduling.[3] They include optimization-based approaches, dispatching rules and simulation-driven approaches, and constraint-based scheduling. The following sections describe and illustrate these approaches.

Optimization-Based Scheduling

Optimization approaches seek to develop an "optimal" schedule to minimize or maximize some scheduling criterion. Many optimization approaches are based on complex linear or integer programming models. An advantage of these approaches is that the scheduling criteria and resource capacity can be considered explicitly in the optimization model. Disadvantages are that objectives must be precisely quantified and a considerable amount of computer processing may be necessary to find a solution. Complex optimization models are not discussed in this book. Rather, we will illustrate how several simple scheduling problems can be solved in an optimal fashion.

Job-Shop Scheduling

In a pure job shop, several jobs are processed, each of which may have a unique routing among departments or machines in the shop. The two important decisions an operations manager must make involve scheduling and sequencing the jobs. Technically speaking, *scheduling* is the process of assigning start and completion times to particular jobs. **Sequencing** refers to determining the order in which jobs are processed. In practice, however, this distinction is seldom made, and the term *scheduling* generally denotes both the timing and sequencing of jobs.

In general, job-shop scheduling is very difficult, but some special cases lend themselves to simple solutions. Although they are not common, these special cases provide understanding and insight into the more difficult practical problems. The special cases considered in this chapter are

1. *Scheduling on a single processor.* Several jobs must be scheduled at one work center.
2. *Scheduling in a flowshop.* Several jobs may require many processing steps, but they all require the same sequence.

Sequencing on a Single Processor

The simplest scheduling problem is that of processing *n* jobs on a single processor, and it arises in many situations. For example, in a serial production system, the bottleneck machine or work center controls the output of the entire system. Thus, it is critical to schedule the bottleneck machine efficiently. In other cases, such as in a chemical plant, the entire plant may be viewed as a single processor. Another reason for studying the single-processor scheduling problem is that it is a component of more complex systems and thus provides insight about more complex problems. For the single-processor sequencing problem, a very simple rule finds a minimal average flowtime sequence: *Process the jobs in order of shortest processing time first.* This is called the **shortest processing time,** or **SPT** rule. An example of its use follows.

Example

Sequencing by Shortest Processing Time

Consider a shop that has one maintenance mechanic to repair failed machines. We can think of the mechanic as the processor and the machines awaiting repair as the jobs. Let us assume that six machines are down, with estimated repair times given here, and that no new jobs arrive.

Job	1	2	3	4	5	6
Processing Time (hours)	8	4	7	3	6	5

No matter which sequence is chosen, the makespan is the same, since the time to process all the jobs is the sum of the processing times. Therefore, we use average flowtime as the criterion to minimize. Applying the SPT rule, we use the sequence 4–2–6–5–3–1. Then the flowtimes for the jobs are as follows.

Job	Flowtime
4	3
2	$3 + 4 = 7$
6	$7 + 5 = 12$
5	$12 + 6 = 18$
3	$18 + 7 = 25$
1	$25 + 8 = 33$

Thus the average flowtime for these six jobs is $(3 + 7 + 12 + 18 + 25 + 33)/6 = 16.33$. This means that the average time a machine will wait to be repaired is about 16 hours.

Scheduling with Due Dates

It has been proven that SPT gives the smallest average flowtime and smallest average lateness of all scheduling rules that might be chosen. A disadvantage of the SPT rule becomes apparent in a heavily loaded shop, however. If new jobs arrive frequently, those with long processing times are continually pushed back and may remain in the shop a long time. Thus it is advantageous to consider sequencing rules that take into account the due dates of jobs.

A popular and effective rule for scheduling on a single processor is the *earliest-due-date rule,* which dictates sequencing jobs in order of earliest due date first. This rule minimizes the maximum job tardiness and job lateness. It does not minimize the average flowtime or average lateness, as SPT does, however. An example of how the earliest due-date rule is used follows.

Example

Sequencing by Earliest Due Date

Suppose five jobs have these processing times and due dates.

Job	Processing Time	Due Date
1	4	15
2	7	16
3	2	8
4	6	21
5	3	9

If the jobs are sequenced in the order 1–2–3–4–5, then the flowtime, tardiness, and lateness for each job are calculated as follows.

Job	Flowtime	Due Date	Tardiness	Lateness
1	4	15	0	−11
2	4 + 7 = 11	16	0	−5
3	11 + 2 = 13	8	5	5
4	13 + 6 = 19	21	0	−2
5	19 + 3 = 22	9	13	13
Average	13.8		3.6	0

If we use the shortest-processing-time rule to schedule the jobs, we obtain the sequence 3–5–1–4–2. The flowtime, tardiness, and lateness are then as given in the following table.

Job	Flowtime	Due Date	Tardiness	Lateness
3	2	8	0	−6
5	2 + 3 = 5	9	0	−4
1	5 + 4 = 9	15	0	−6
4	9 + 6 = 15	21	0	−6
2	15 + 7 = 22	16	6	6
Average	10.6		1.2	−3.2

Note that the maximum tardiness and the maximum lateness are both 6. Using the earliest-due-date rule, we obtain the sequence 3–5–1–2–4. The flowtime, tardiness, and lateness for this sequence are given in the following table.

Job	Flowtime	Due Date	Tardiness	Lateness
3	2	8	0	−6
5	2 + 3 = 5	9	0	−4
1	5 + 4 = 9	15	0	−6
2	9 + 7 = 16	16	0	0
4	16 + 6 = 22	21	1 ← Maximum	1 ← Maximum
Average	10.8		0.2	−3.0

The maximum time that any job is tardy or late is one day; however, the average lateness is worse than with the SPT rule.

The procedures we have presented for sequencing jobs are based on scheduling *forward* from the current date. With these procedures the actual completion dates cannot be known until the schedule is finished. If due dates are to be met and tardiness cannot be tolerated, time phasing is often done *backward*. For instance, for the five-job problem we have been discussing, each job must be started by the time indicated in this table in order to meet the required due dates.

Job	Due Date	Latest Start
1	15	11
2	16	9
3	8	6
4	21	15
5	9	6

Meeting such deadlines might require overtime or subcontracting if sufficient capacity is unavailable. Backward scheduling is typical in the aircraft industry (when due dates are established by government contracts) and in MRP systems.

Two-Machine Flowshop Problem

A **flowshop** is a job shop in which all jobs have the same routing. In this section, we consider a simple flowshop with only two operations. We assume that each job must be processed first on machine 1 and then on machine 2. Processing times for each job on each machine are known. In contrast to sequencing jobs on a single processor, the makespan can vary for each different sequence. Therefore for the two-machine flowshop problem, it makes sense to try to find a sequence with the smallest makespan.

S. M. Johnson developed the following algorithm in 1954 for finding a minimum makespan schedule:[4]

1. List the jobs and their processing times on machines 1 and 2.
2. Find the job with the shortest processing time (on either machine).
3. If this time corresponds to machine 1, sequence the job *first;* if it corresponds to machine 2, sequence the job *last.*
4. Repeat Steps 2 and 3, using the next-shortest processing time and working *inward* from both ends of the sequence until all jobs have been scheduled.

An example of the application of Johnson's rule follows.

Example

Sequencing with Johnson's Rule

Hirsch Products is a small manufacturer that produces certain custom parts that first require a shearing operation and then a punch-press operation. Hirsch currently has orders for five jobs, which have processing times (days) estimated as follows.

Job	Shear	Punch
1	4	5
2	4	1
3	10	4
4	6	10
5	2	3

The jobs can be sequenced in any order but they must be sheared first. Therefore, we have a flowshop situation.

Suppose the jobs are sequenced in the order 1–2–3–4–5. This schedule can be represented by a simple *bar chart* showing the schedule of each job on each machine along a horizontal time axis (Figure 18.2). This shows, for instance, that job 1 is scheduled on the shear for the first four days, job 2 for the next four days, and so on. We construct a bar chart for a given sequence by scheduling the first job as early as possible on the first machine (shear). Then, as soon as the job is completed, it can be scheduled on the punch press, provided that no other job is currently in progress. First, note that all jobs follow each other on the shearing machine. Because of variations in processing times, however, the punch press is often idle while awaiting the next job. The makespan is 37 days, and the flowtimes for the jobs follow.

Job	1	2	3	4	5
Flowtime	9	10	22	34	37

Thus the average flowtime is $(9 + 10 + 22 + 34 + 37)/5 = 22.4$ days.

Applying Johnson's rule, we find that the shortest processing time is for job 2 on the punch press.

Job	Shear	Punch
1	4	5
2	4	①
3	10	4
4	6	10
5	2	3

Figure 18.2 Bar Chart for Sequence 1–2–3–4–5 in Hirsch Products Example

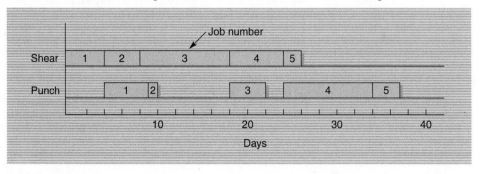

Figure 18.3 Bar Chart for Sequence 5-1-4-3-2 in Hirsch Products Example

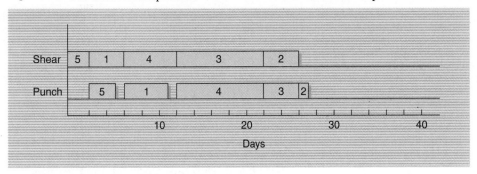

Since the minimum time on either machine is on the second machine, job 2 is scheduled last.

———— ———— ———— ———— __2__

Next, we find the second-shortest processing time. It is 2, for job 5 on machine 1. Therefore, job 5 is scheduled first.

__5__ ———— ———— ———— __2__

In the next step, we have a tie between job 1 on the shear and job 3 on the punch press. When a tie occurs, either job can be chosen. If we pick job 1, we have the following sequence.

__5__ __1__ ———— ———— __2__

Continuing with Johnson's rule, the last two steps yield the complete sequence.

__5__ __1__ ———— __3__ __2__

__5__ __1__ __4__ __3__ __2__

The bar chart for this sequence is shown in Figure 18.3. The makespan is reduced to 27 days, and the average flowtime is also improved from the original schedule, having a value of 18.2 days.

Dispatching Rules and Simulation-Based Approaches

One of the major difficulties of optimization-based approaches is that most real-life problems are too large and complex for them to handle effectively. In the most general job-shop situation, we must sequence n jobs on m machines, and each job may have a unique routing. If so, there are up to $(n!)^m$ possible schedules. For example, when $n = 5$ and $m = 4$, there are more than 200 million schedules! These problems are too difficult to solve optimally, and heuristic methods must be used.

Another problem with optimization-based approaches is they assume a *static* situation in which all jobs are available at the same time and no new jobs are created during processing. In real manufacturing environments, scheduling is dynamic—jobs are continually being created, eliminated, and changed, and unforeseen events such as machine breakdowns occur that invalidate previously developed schedules. Hence, scheduling decisions must be made over time. Simulation-based approaches apply one or more **dispatching rules** to rank the order of jobs waiting to be processed at a machine in order to use available capacity effectively. Simulation modeling enables a manager to experiment with a model of the production system to choose the best dispatching rule for a particular set of criteria and shop conditions.

Priority Dispatching Rules

Dispatching rules used in dynamic job-shop situations are usually based on either the attributes of the job—such as processing time or number of operations—or on the characteristics of the shop itself at the particular time. The former class of rules are described as *static* rules, since job priorities can be calculated before any production activity begins. The latter class of rules are described as *dynamic,* since job priorities change over time, depending on the progress of a job in relation to others.* Dynamic priorities must be calculated each time a machine-loading decision is made. Some priority dispatching rules that have been suggested are listed in Table 18.2.

Since jobs arrive intermittently over time, we must usually resort to simulation (see Supplementary Chapter A) to evaluate a dispatching rule. We illustrate how to do this with a small example. The example also illustrates how such rules are used in practice.

Table 18.2 Priority Dispatching Rules for Job Shops

Rule	Description
Static Priorities	
1. Earliest release date	Time job is released to the shop
2. Shortest processing time	Processing time of operation for which job is waiting
3. Total work	Sum of all processing times
4. Earliest due date	Due date of job
5. Least work remaining	Sum of processing times for all operations not yet performed
6. Fewest operations remaining	Number of operations yet to be performed
Dynamic Priorities	
7. Work in next queue	Amount of work awaiting the next machine in a job's processing sequence
8. Slack time	Time remaining until due date *minus* remaining processing time
9. Slack/remaining operations	Slack time *divided by* the number of operations remaining
10. Critical ratio	Time remaining until due date *divided* by days required to complete job

---

*Do not be confused by the use of the terms *static* and *dynamic.* In the preceding section the terms referred to how jobs arrive at a shop. Here they refer to the type of dispatching rule used.

Simulation of Dispatching Rules

Lynwood Manufacturing is a small job shop with a lathe, drill press, milling machine, and grinder. Jobs arrive as customers place orders. For simulation purposes, the job arrivals must be specified. This is usually done through analysis of historical data. Let us assume that four jobs will arrive in the near future. Their characteristics are given in Table 18.3.

Table 18.3 Job Data for Lynwood Job Shop

Job	Arrival Time	Processing Sequence (Processing Time)*
1	0	$L(10)$, $D(20)$, $G(35)$
2	0	$D(25)$, $L(20)$, $G(30)$, $M(15)$
3	20	$D(10)$, $M(10)$
4	30	$L(15)$, $G(10)$, $M(20)$

*For example, job 1 must be processed first by lathe, second by drill press, and third by the grinder with times 10, 20, and 35, respectively.
L = Lathe; D = Drill; G = Grinder; M = Mill

We also need a method of depicting the status of the shop at any point in time. We can do this with the type of illustration shown in Figure 18.4. Note in this illustration that each machine is represented by a box; jobs being processed and waiting are denoted by circles in and above the box. Beneath each box is listed the completion time of any job that is being processed by that machine.

Figure 18.4 Status of Lynwood Job Shop at Any Point in Time

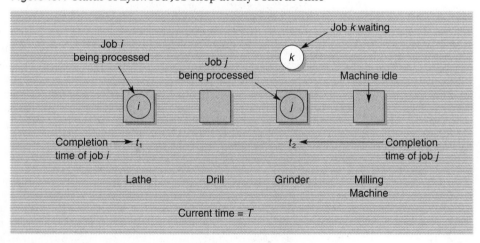

Figure 18.5 is a flowchart of the simulation process. In simulating the behavior of the Lynwood Manufacturing job shop over time, we increment time by five units, because the processing times (in Table 18.3) are in multiples of 5. Further, we assume that the time needed to move jobs between machines is negligible.

We begin the simulation at time $T = 0$ and use the *least-work-remaining* rule (number 5 in Table 18.2) to schedule jobs. At time 0, jobs 1 and 2 arrive. Job

Figure 18.5 Flowchart for Simulating Lynwood Manufacturing Job Shop

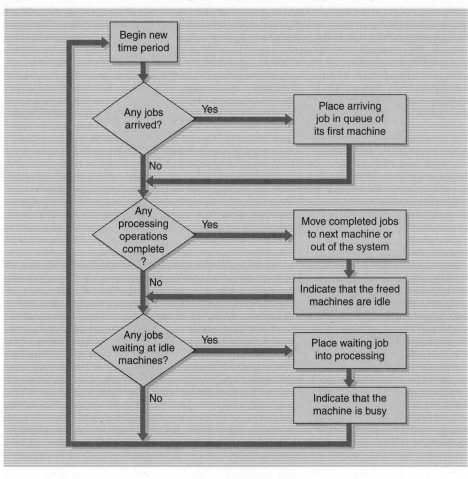

1 is immediately scheduled on the lathe, and job 2 is assigned to the drill press. The status of the shop at time 0 is as shown in Figure 18.6.

Figure 18.6 Status of Lynwood Job Shop at Time 0

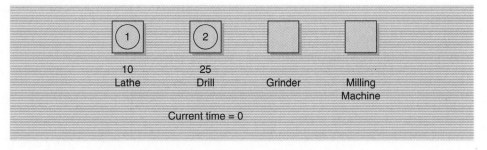

Within a particular time interval only two possible events can occur: either a new job arrives or the processing of some job is completed. If nothing occurs during a time interval, we simply move on to the next interval. In this example, nothing occurs at time 5, but job 1 is finished on the lathe at time 10. Since job 2 is still on the drill press at time 10, job 1 must wait. The status of the shop then is as shown in Figure 18.7.

Figure 18.7 Status of Lynwood Job Shop at Time 10

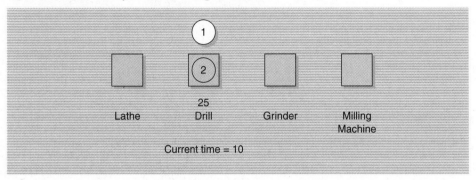

Nothing happens at time 15. At time 20, job 3 arrives and joins the queue at the drill press, as shown in Figure 18.8.

Figure 18.8 Status of Lynwood Job Shop at Time 20

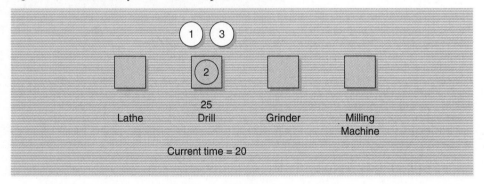

At time 25, job 2 is completed on the drill press. A decision must be made whether to schedule job 1 or job 3 next. The work remaining for job 1 is $20 + 35 = 55$, and for job 3 the total remaining processing time is $10 + 10 = 20$. Thus job 3 is scheduled next, and job 2 moves to the lathe, as shown in Figure 18.9. Continuing in this way, we trace the status of the shop over time, as shown in Figure 18.10, until all four jobs are completed.

Figure 18.9 Status of Lynwood Job Shop at Time 25

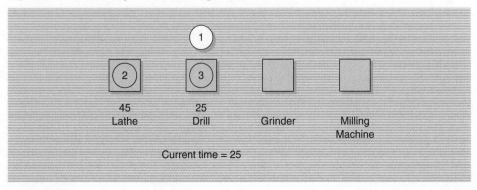

Figure 18.10 Simulation of Lynwood Job Shop Status over Time

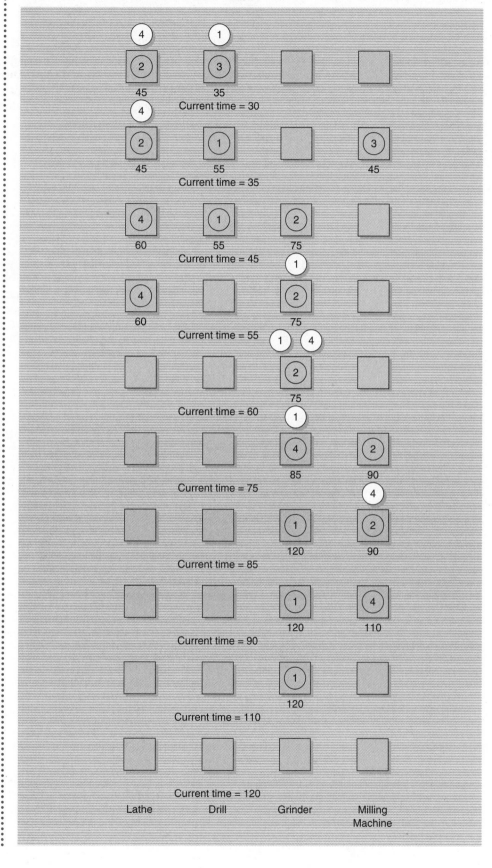

Current time = 30

Current time = 35

Current time = 45

Current time = 55

Current time = 60

Current time = 75

Current time = 85

Current time = 90

Current time = 110

Current time = 120

Lathe   Drill   Grinder   Milling
                                              Machine

We can construct a bar chart of the result of this scheduling process, as shown in Figure 18.11. Statistics on machine utilization and job-waiting times and completion times can now be computed easily and used as measures for comparing various dispatching rules. A summary is provided in Table 18.4. Simulations such as these also give the manager an idea of where bottlenecks might occur or where more capacity is needed.

Figure 18.11 Bar Chart for Lynwood Job Shop

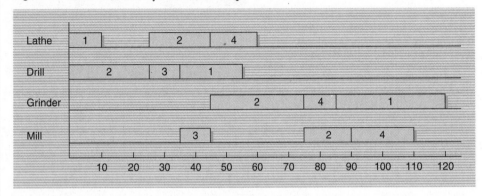

Table 18.4 Simulation Results Using Least-Work-Remaining Rule for Lynwood Job Shop

Job	Waiting Time	Completion Time	Machine	Idle Time*
1	55	120	Lathe	75
2	0	90	Drill	65
3	25	45	Grinder	45
4	65	110	Mill	75

*Makespan minus processing time

Selecting a Dispatching Rule

Obviously, to obtain useful results about the performance of dispatching rules, simulations must be conducted over sufficiently long periods of time and for reasonably realistic shop configurations. Extensive studies have been conducted to analyze these rules.[5] There is no single best dispatching rule to use for job-shop scheduling, since these rules are very dependent on the shop configuration and the sequence of job arrivals. However, the simulation studies have shown that the shortest processing time (SPT) rule (number 2 in Table 18.2), though very simplistic, is one of the best rules. In general, SPT results in fewer jobs waiting in queues than many of the other rules. However, jobs that do wait (those with longer processing times) usually wait a long time. This can be avoided by modifying the rule to place higher priorities on jobs that have been waiting an extensive amount of time. The slack-time and slack-remaining-operations rules (numbers 8 and 9 in Table 18.2) are among the best dynamic rules.

When due dates are important, the critical-ratio rule (number 10 in Table 18.2) is very useful. The *critical ratio* is the ratio of the demand time of a job to the supply time. For instance, if it takes eight days to make an order and the order is needed in 10 days, the critical ratio is $10/8 = 1.25$. If this index is greater than 1, the job is ahead of schedule; if it is equal to 1, the job is on time; and if it is less than 1, the job is behind schedule. The use of this index enables managers to see easily the status of all jobs and to place priorities accordingly. The earliest-due-date rule has also been shown to be effective.

One factor that determines whether a static or a dynamic rule should be selected is the amount of information gathering required. With a static rule, priorities can be placed on the route card when it is issued. Dynamic rules require constant feedback from the shop floor and recalculation of priorities, which often requires a computer system for efficient data processing. The cost of implementing such a system may indeed outweigh the benefits derived from using a dynamic scheduling rule.

Constraint-Based Scheduling

Constraint-based scheduling arises from principles of synchronous manufacturing and the theory of constraints discussed in Chapter 15. This approach was introduced to the United States in 1979 by Creative Output, Inc., (COI) of Milford, Connecticut, under the name **OPT (Optimized Production Technology).**

The OPT software provides a detailed description of the production system in a *product network* that reflects the reality of the manufacturing process. (A problem at the end of the chapter illustrates a product network.) The network shows exactly how a product is made, using information commonly found in a company's BOM (bill of materials) and routing files. Each operation is defined by specifying the resources used, setup times, and run times. In addition, the model allows for specification of desired stock levels at each operation, maximum stock limits, minimum batch quantities, scheduled delays, order quantities, and due dates. Resource descriptions must also be specified; these include the relative efficiency of various resources, available overtime, and additional resources required for setting up the operation.

OPT works by sequentially considering, at fixed intervals of time, how production resources should be used to meet requirements.[6] The time intervals are based on the minimum amount of work that managers feel should be scheduled at a time. This minimum time interval is converted into a minimum transfer-batch quantity of each product (oftentimes one unit) at each operation. Making decisions at the end of these equal intervals of time synchronizes the system with these modular batches being processed and transferred every period. Operations are defined in terms of a particular product with a specific set of common available resources. At each interval of time, the operation could be idle, start from an idle state, continue processing, or shut down. These decisions must be made at each interval of time. OPT prioritizes the products by using a weighted function that may include the desired product mix, due date, safety stock level, and use of bottleneck resources. Resources are allocated according to the priorities assigned to each product, with the objective of continuing or starting up production of the highest-priority products subject to available resources. Using this strategy, the program sequentially constructs a schedule.

Figure 18.12
Drum-Buffer-Rope
Relationships

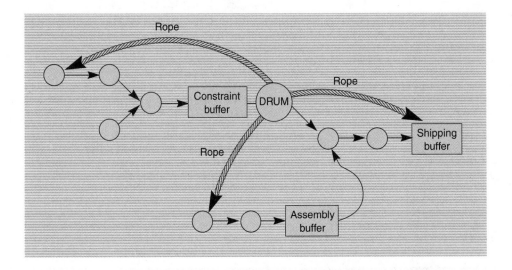

The schedule development is termed **drum-buffer-rope,** and is based on the following analogies.[7] The *drum* is a system constraint or other critical resource that sets the pace or "beat" that drives the rest of the schedule. The *ropes* are schedules or other signaling methods that tie the release of raw materials and customer promise dates to the production at the drum. *Buffers* are extra materials on the shop floor that result from work being released earlier than the minimum time required to complete all production steps. Figure 18.12 illustrates the relationships between these three components.

Although very little WIP inventory is maintained, the buffer inventories help to compensate for unavoidable variations in flowtime. The constraint buffer ensures that the drum is always busy; the assembly buffer ensures that parts completed at the drum are not delayed at assembly; and the shipping buffer ensures that customer promise dates can be met. The key idea to pace all production activities by the production of the drum.

Drum-buffer-rope scheduling consists of

1. Identifying the constraint.
2. Sequencing jobs on the constraint.
3. Deciding on the size of the constraint buffers.
4. Deciding on the size of the shipping buffers (which forward scheduled material from the constraint to shipping and fix the due date to the customer).

In effect, this reduces to a single-machine scheduling problem at the constraint. A simple example of drum-buffer-rope scheduling follows.

Example

Scheduling Pictures for a Junior High School Yearbook[8]

The basic process for taking yearbook pictures consists of the following steps.

1. All students associated with an organization are assembled and seated in rows.
2. The photographer frames the picture, says "Smile!", and takes the pictures.
3. Student names must be associated with the pictures.

Under the old system, all students reported to the gymnasium at the same time, resulting in a confusing process of sorting them into groups and deciding which group to photograph next. Identifying students after pictures were developed involved many lost student-classroom hours and was prone to error.

A new process divided the bleachers on the side of the gym into three major sections, A, B, and C, which served as staging areas for specific student groups. A list of student organizations was prepared in advance. Students in the first three organizations were called to the gym over the public-address system. As they arrived, they lined up on the empty section of the bleachers reserved for their group. When all members had arrived, a clipboard was passed down each row for the students to sign. When this was done, the photographer took the group picture, the students returned to class, and the next group was called to the gym. The photographer cycled among each of the three staging areas, and very little time was lost in this changeover activity.

The drum, or critical resource, was the photographer. The ropes, which control the release of material, were not schedules, but rather students who were released to the system by calling the office secretary on a walkie-talkie. The constraint buffer was the assembled students waiting to be photographed. This ensured that the photographer was seldom idle due to lack of readiness of a group. Shipping and assembly buffers were not relevant in this situation.

Twenty organizations were photographed in two hours, about half the time needed with previous methods. There was a minimum loss of class time and a lower error rate in recording names associated with the pictures. In other words, the new system provided lower work-in-process rates, faster flowtimes, higher throughput, better quality, and higher productivity than the old method.

Constraint-based scheduling can be summarized by a set of rules used by the OPT software to guide the creation of a schedule. Developed by Creative Output, Inc. (COI), these rules are

1. *Balance flow, not capacity.* That is, we should not attempt to keep all the resources busy, but should focus on maintaining a smooth flow of material.

2. *The level of utilization of a nonconstraining resource is not determined by its own potential, but by some constraint in the system.* Nonconstraining resources should be scheduled and operated in a manner consistent with constraints such as bottlenecks in the system. Nonbottleneck operations should not produce more than the bottleneck operations can absorb.

3. *Utilization and activation of a resource are not synonymous.* This is an intuitive rule if we consider utilization as the degree to which we *should* use a resource (to reach the strategic goal of profitability) and activation as the degree to which we *can* use a resource.

4. *An hour lost at a bottleneck is an hour lost for the entire system.* The OPT philosophy stresses the importance of maintaining 100 percent utilization of constraining resources to maximize output.

5. *An hour saved at a nonbottleneck is just a mirage.* Since the capacity of a system is limited by the constraining resources, saving time at a nonbottleneck does not affect the throughput of the system.

6. *Bottlenecks govern both throughput and inventory in the system.* COI argues that work-in-process inventories are a function of the amount of work

required to keep the bottlenecks busy; inventories can be controlled by where the bottlenecks are.

7. *The transfer batch may not, and many times should not, be equal to the process batch.* The OPT philosophy is that flexibility in batch processing is essential to speeding the flow of product from raw material to finished goods.

8. *The process batch should be variable, not fixed.* When different numbers of parts are manufactured on different equipment, the process batch needs to be varied to maintain a smooth, rapid flow of materials to customers.

9. *Schedules should be determined by looking at all constraints simultaneously. Lead times are the result of a schedule and cannot be predetermined.* Although MRP assumes predetermined lead times, OPT suggests that lead times are not fixed but variable.

Concerning the last rule, consider the production of two parts needed for an assembly. Part A requires processing on machines X and Y, with times of 20 hours and 5 hours, respectively. Part B requires processing on machines X and Z, with times of 6 hours and 15 hours, respectively. Whereas the lead times of parts A and B appear to be 25 and 21, note that since both require processing on machine X first, if part A is initially released to the shop, its actual lead time will be 25 hours, whereas B's will be 41. If part B is released first, its actual lead time will be 21 hours, whereas A's will be 31. Hence, the lead time is a function of the schedule.

A number of corporations have reported significant benefits from using OPT.[9] For example, one company was able to eliminate several million dollars of planned equipment purchases, reduce the plant staffing by 50 percent, and cut planned cycle time by 25 percent. Another firm used OPT scheduling to reduce its manufacturing lead time and finished-goods inventory by 50 percent, even though its number of manufactured end items increased by 35 percent.

Special Scheduling Problems in Manufacturing and Service Organizations

Batch-Production Scheduling

Many make-to-stock manufacturers produce different products on common facilities. For example, a soft-drink manufacturer may produce several flavors at one facility, and a soap company may package several sizes on the same packaging lines. In these situations, products are generally produced in batches. The decisions faced by managers of such production systems are how much to produce in each batch and the sequence, or order, in which the batches are to be produced.

The batch quantity (which can be equivalently characterized as the length of time for a production run) and the frequency of production affect inventory levels and setup costs. A setup cost is incurred each time a changeover for a new product is required. With longer production runs, more inventory is carried and fewer setups are incurred. The optimal batch quantity can be computed by using the economic production lot-size model discussed in Chapter 14. When several products share common facilities, however, batch sizes must be modified, because product sequencing also affects cost. For instance, setup costs may vary with the sequence of product changeovers, as in changing a packaging line from small to medium size versus small to large size, or going from cola to lemon-lime versus cola to diet cola.

Discussion in this section is limited to inventory considerations. A technique that is often used in batch-processing situations is *scheduling by runout time*. This technique can be illustrated with an example.

Example

Scheduling by Runout Time

Suppose a consumer-products company produces five sizes of a laundry soap at one plant. Lot sizes and demand data are given in Table 18.5. The first question to ask is whether capacity is sufficient to meet the demand for all product sizes. To produce the weekly demand for the small size requires $150/833 = .18$ week. The medium size requires $250/1,000 = .25$ week; the large size, $150/750 = .20$ week; the jumbo size, $100/900 = .11$ week; and the giant size, $100/600 = .17$ week. Thus, meeting the total weekly demand requires $.18 + .25 + .20 + .11 + .17 = .91$ week of production time. This leaves machinery idle 9 percent of the time. The idle time can be used for setup and maintenance. When capacity is not sufficient, shortages will occur. This means that the aggregate plan is inconsistent with the capacity available.

Suppose the company adopts a "cyclic" schedule of producing the economic lot size for each product size in rotation. From Table 18.5 we see that it would take a total of $1.2 + .8 + 2.0 + 2.0 + 1.0 = 7$ weeks to produce the economic lot sizes of all products. Let us see what would happen during that time. For the small size, we begin with an inventory of 800 units. If we produce 1,000 units, we will have a total of 1,800 units available to satisfy the demand during the seven weeks until we produce the small size again. Since seven weeks' demand is $7(150) = 1050$ units, we see that we will be able to cover the demand and have some inventory remaining when the next production cycle begins.

Now consider the medium size. With an initial inventory of 600, producing 800 units will make 1,400 units available for satisfying the seven weeks' demand. However, seven weeks' demand is $7(250) = 1,750$ units; the cyclic economic-lot-size schedule will lead to shortages. An alternative is to use runout time as a scheduling rule. The **runout time** (R) for a product is defined as

$$R = \frac{\text{inventory level}}{\text{demand rate}}$$

Table 18.5 Lot Size and Demand Data for Five Product Sizes

Product Size	Economic Lot Size	Production Time (weeks)	Production Rate (units/week)	Demand (units/week)	Current Inventory
Small	1,000	1.2	833	150	800
Medium	800	0.8	1,000	250	600
Large	1,500	2.0	750	150	2,000
Jumbo	1,800	2.0	900	100	2,500
Giant	600	1.0	600	100	525

That is, the runout time is the length of time inventory will be available to satisfy demand.

If runout times are calculated for each product size, we can schedule the product with the smallest runout time first. The runout times in weeks for each product size are calculated as shown in Table 18.6. Thus, we would schedule the medium size first. From Table 18.5, we see that the lot size of 800 will take .8 of a week to produce. At the end of .8 week, the updated inventory levels are found by subtracting .8 week's demand from the current levels, as shown in Table 18.7. Next, we use these updated inventory levels to compute new runout times as shown in Table 18.8, and then we select the next product size to run, which would be the giant size.

Notice that in using the smallest runout time, we are not scheduling all products in a rotating sequence. Instead, we schedule them one at a time in response to current inventory levels and anticipated demand. This is, then, a dynamic approach. It does not consider inventory-holding costs, stockout costs, or setup costs. Even with this rule, shortages may occur. (More sophisticated mathematical models exist, but they are beyond the scope of this book.) Managers should carefully examine projected inventory levels for all products to see if they are being depleted too fast or building up to unnecessarily high levels. Production schedules can be adjusted, if necessary, by aggregate planning approaches such as overtime, undertime, or other capacity-change strategies.

Table 18.6 Runout Times for Five Product Sizes

Size	Runout Time
Small	$800/150 = 5.33$
Medium	$600/250 = 2.40$
Large	$2,000/150 = 13.33$
Jumbo	$2,500/100 = 25.00$
Giant	$525/100 = 5.25$

Table 18.7 Updated Inventory for Five Product Sizes

Size	Inventory
Small	$800 - 150(.8) = 680$
Medium	$600 - 250(.8) + 800 = 1,200$
Large	$2,000 - 150(.8) = 1,880$
Jumbo	$2,500 - 100(.8) = 2,420$
Giant	$525 - 100(.8) = 445$

Table 18.8 New Runout Times Based on Updated Inventory

Size	Runout Time
Small	$680/150 = 4.53$
Medium	$1,200/250 = 4.80$
Large	$1,880/150 = 12.53$
Jumbo	$2,420/100 = 24.20$
Giant	$445/100 = 4.45$

Personnel Scheduling

Personnel scheduling problems are prevalent in service organizations. Examples include scheduling telephone operators, turnpike toll-booth operators, airline reservation clerks, hospital nursing staff, police officers, fast-food outlet employees, and many others. In a typical fast-food restaurant, personnel scheduling is extremely complex. Since sales volume fluctuates over each day, employee requirements vary dramatically. For instance, whereas only one person may be required in the grill and counter areas during slow periods, eight or more may be needed during peak periods. Shifts vary from three to eight hours, and employees differ in their availability for work each day of the week because of school or family schedules. Finally, the skills and performance levels required for the various work areas differ. A typical operation might have three work areas, 150 employees, and 30 work shifts. This represents more than 100,000 possible scheduling assignments!

Personnel scheduling attempts to match available personnel with the needs of the organization by

1. Determining the quantity of work to be done.
2. Determining the staffing required to perform the work.
3. Determining the personnel available.
4. Matching available personnel to staffing requirements, and developing a work schedule.

The first step, determining the quantity of work to be done, is often facilitated by graphing the demand over time. If service demands are relatively level over time, it is usually easy to schedule personnel on standard weekly work shifts. If the work load varies within a shift, as is the case for telephone operators or fast-food outlet employees, the problem becomes one of scheduling shifts to meet the varying demand.

Determining the staffing required must take into account worker-productivity factors, personal allowances, sickness, vacations, and so on. Personnel availability is a function of employee time off for sickness and vacation and of the use of part-time and temporary employees and other sources of labor.

The matching of personnel to staffing requirements is the most difficult step. Different approaches are required for different situations because of the nature of constraints. Let us examine a relatively simple problem of scheduling personnel with consecutive days off in the face of fluctuating requirements.

Example

Scheduling Consecutive Days Off[10]

The Sam Brent Bridge has nine manual toll booths in addition to several automatic toll collectors. From traffic-flow data, the following minimum personnel requirements for the week were determined.

Day	Mon	Tue	Wed	Thur	Fri	Sat	Sun
Minimum Personnel	8	6	6	6	9	5	3

We want to schedule the employees so that each employee has two consecutive days off and all labor requirements are met. We proceed as follows. First, we locate the set of at least two consecutive days with smallest requirements. That is, we find the day with the smallest demand, the next-smallest, and so on, until there are at least two consecutive days. We then circle the requirements for those two consecutive days. We choose Sunday first and then Saturday. We stop here, since these days are consecutive. Thus we have the following, for employee 1.

Day	Mon	Tue	Wed	Thur	Fri	Sat	Sun
Requirements	8	6	6	6	9	⑤	③

We assign employee 1 to work on all days that are *not* circled, that is, Monday through Friday. Then we subtract 1 from the requirement for each day that employee will work. This gives us the following for employee 2.

Day	Mon	Tue	Wed	Thur	Fri	Sat	Sun
Requirements	7	5	5	5	8	5	3

The procedure is repeated with this new set of requirements for employee 2.

Day	Mon	Tue	Wed	Thur	Fri	Sat	Sun
Requirements	7	⑤	⑤	⑤	8	⑤	③

When there are several alternatives, as in this case, we do one of two things. First, we try to choose a *pair* of days with the lowest requirement. If there are still ties, we are to choose the *first* available pair. In this case, however, we again use Saturday and Sunday as days off for employee 2, since this pair has the smallest requirement. We subtract 1 from each working day's requirement.

Day	Mon	Tue	Wed	Thur	Fri	Sat	Sun
Requirements	6	4	4	4	7	5	3

Circling the smallest requirements until we obtain at least two consecutive days yields the following for employee 3.

Day	Mon	Tue	Wed	Thur	Fri	Sat	Sun
Requirements	6	④	④	④	7	5	③

The only pairs from which we can choose are Tue–Wed and Wed–Thur, so we choose Tue–Wed by the tie-breaking rule. The result follows.

Day	Mon	Tue	Wed	Thur	Fri	Sat	Sun
Requirements	5	4	4	3	6	4	2

Continuing with this procedure, we obtain the sequence of requirements shown in Table 18.9 (with circled numbers representing the lowest-requirement pair selected). The employee schedule is shown in Table 18.10. Even though some requirements are exceeded, the solution minimizes the number of workers required. A more difficult problem that we do not address is that of determining a schedule of rotating shifts so that employees do not always have the same two days off. This is a more practical situation.

Table 18.9 Sequence of Requirements for Employee Schedule for Toll Bridge

Employee Number	Mon	Tue	Wed	Thur	Fri	Sat	Sun
4	5	4	4	3	6	④	②
5	4	3	③	②	5	4	2
6	3	2	3	2	4	③	①
7	②	①	2	1	3	3	1
8	2	1	①	⓪	2	2	0
9	①	⓪	1	0	1	1	0
10	1	⓪	⓪	0	0	0	0

Table 18.10 Employee Schedule for Toll Bridge

Employee Number	Mon	Tue	Wed	Thur	Fri	Sat	Sun
1	X	X	X	X	X		
2	X	X	X	X	X		
3	X			X	X	X	X
4	X	X	X	X	X		
5	X	X			X	X	X
6	X	X	X	X	X		
7			X	X	X	X	X
8	X	X			X	X	X
9			X	X	X	X	X
10	X			X	X	X	X
Total	8	6	6	8	10	6	6

Progress Control

Murphy's law states that if something can go wrong it will, and this is especially true with schedules. Thus it is important that progress be monitored on a continuing basis. Production controllers must know the status of orders that are ahead of schedule or behind schedule due to shortages of material, work centers that are backlogged, changes in inventory, labor turnover, and sales commitments. Schedules must be changed when these things occur.

Figure 18.13
Bar Chart for Monitoring
Schedule Progress

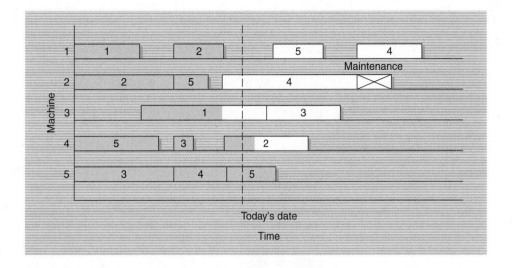

Short-term capacity fluctuations also necessitate changes in schedules. Factors affecting short-term capacity include absenteeism, labor performance, machine failures, tooling problems, and material shortages. They are inevitable and unavoidable. Some alternatives available to operations managers for coping with capacity shortages are overtime, short-term subcontracting, alternate production routing, and reallocations of the work force.

Bar charts are useful tools for monitoring production, and an example is shown in Figure 18.13. The shaded areas indicate completed work. This chart shows, for example, that job 4 has not yet started on machine 2, job 1 is currently behind schedule on machine 3, and jobs 2 and 5 are ahead of schedule. Perhaps needed material has not yet been delivered for job 4, or perhaps machine 3 has had a breakdown. In any event, it is up to production-control personnel to revise the schedule or to expedite jobs that are behind schedule. Many other types of graphical aids are useful and commercially available.

Computerized Production-Control Systems

Computerized information systems are used extensively for production control in large plants. It is not uncommon for a manufacturing facility to consist of hundreds of work centers or machines and to process thousands of different parts. The sheer complexity of scheduling in such firms requires a computerized approach. A typical information system is illustrated in Figure 18.14. Three primary inputs to a production control system are the route file, work-center file, and shop-order file. The *route file* contains the routing information for each customer's order, including part numbers, operations performed, standards, and so on. The *work-center file* includes capacity information, and the *shop-order file* contains the data on each customer's order. Typical outputs include load reports, shop schedules, and order-status reports. Updates may occur daily or even every few hours. They involve a lot of data collection and processing, and maintenance of accuracy is vitally important. Automatic identification systems are being used more frequently to accomplish this. Many systems have on-line query capabilities, whereby a salesperson can check the status of a customer's

Figure 18.14
Information System for
Production Scheduling and
Control

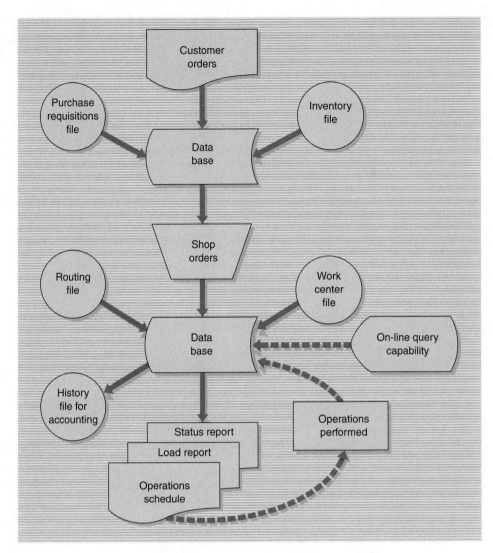

query capabilities, whereby a salesperson can check the status of a customer's order or project a delivery date.

For a computerized control system to work efficiently, it needs accurate information and the support of managers. Also, the users of the system need to be trained and educated. The "P/OM in Practice" case study involving Western Electric's Semiconductor Production-Control System illustrates some of the problems, solutions, and behavioral implications in the design and implementation of a computerized production-control system.

P/OM in Practice

Western Electric's Semiconductor Production-Control System[11]

In the manufacture of semiconductors, it is difficult to achieve consistent electrical and mechanical characteristics. Because of the nature of semiconductor processing, the percentage of good parts produced, referred to as *manufacturing yields,* may vary from one group of materials to another. Consequently, there is constant uncertainty as to the amount of in-process inventories required for machine loading and delivery estimates.

A second problem arises because materials' electrical properties can be significantly changed with no corresponding changes in their physical appearance. Thus it is difficult to keep track of various products during processing. Western Electric's Reading Works makes several hundred types of semiconductors. In view of these problems, Reading developed a computerized production-control system to replace an inadequate manual system.

The system designers recognized that computerization is often misunderstood or resented by both shop employees and shop managers. Accordingly, users' feelings were considered in implementation along with solution requirements, data collection, and accuracy. For instance, Reading's system calculates current production yields from raw data provided by the shop, and this information is used by shop managers to plan future production. Although the planning function can also be computerized, this was *not* done, so that shop supervisors would feel their experience and judgment were valued.

Many production-control systems have failed because of a lack of coordination between efforts of the designers and the users. In the Reading project, users saw the need for providing fast, accurate data collection, while the designers saw the need for providing flexibility for changing needs and greater sophistication as the system matured. User involvement was assured by including first- and second-level shop supervisors, production-control managers, information systems specialists, and industrial engineers on the development team.

In the old system, there was no need for real-time response. This was unsatisfactory for the new system, however. It was found that shop training and system modifications could be better coordinated by one person, and that was already being done informally under the current system. This concept led to the establishment of a special terminal operator in each area, whose duties were to collect production records and enter them into the computer.

To provide the desired accuracy of data, several steps were taken. The hardware and software used were selected to provide error-detection capability. Terminal operators were responsible for prescreening of data, and a checklist of the previous day's entries was provided for post-entry screening. Also, shop supervisors were responsible for their employees' accuracy in data recording and entry.

The production data collected are used to update three major system files and to produce shop reports. These files contain the operations for each manufactured part, the location of all in-process inventories, and summarized production data for specific time periods. Responsibility for file maintenance was given to the production-control department. The information the system provides includes

1. *Daily inventory status*—tracking and expediting of specific products.
2. *Yield calculations*—shop planning and production scheduling.
3. *Calculation of potential good product.*
4. *Production status*—current customer orders and expected future shipments.
5. *Labor efficiency*—individual and department.
6. *Absence reporting.*

Daily reports are distributed to first-line supervisors and selected shop personnel, whereas summaries are prepared for higher-level managers on a daily, weekly, or monthly basis for tactical planning purposes.

The new system has helped to alleviate some of the problems associated with semiconductor manufacturing and has also reduced clerical effort required for effective production control. It is worthwhile to point out that this system provides information, not decisions. The production-control department uses the information to make better decisions.

Questions for Discussion

1. Discuss why Western Electric decided to computerize its production-control system.
2. Explain the role of user involvement in successful systems development.
3. What steps were taken to ensure quality?

Computer-Assisted Dispatching of Tank Trucks for Mobil Oil Corporation[12]

In the spring of 1985 a nationwide system for dispatching and processing customer orders for gasoline and distillates began full operation at Mobil Oil Corporation. It is a completely integrated, highly automated system that controls the flow of $4 billion annual sales from initial order entry to final delivery, confirmation, and billing. Although the entire process is overseen by a handful of people in a small office in Valley Forge, Pennsylvania, it operates more efficiently than the old system in all respects: it provides better customer service; greatly improved credit, inventory, and operating cost control; and significantly reduced distribution costs. Central to this new system is CAD (computer-assisted dispatch), designed to assist human dispatchers in real-time as they determine the means by which ordered product will be safely and efficiently delivered to customers.

Under the best of conditions, dispatching is hard work. The dispatcher must attend to myriad details of customer, vehicle fleet, and product status. Dispatching petroleum tank trucks involves following intricate rules governing safe and efficient operation. The costs of distribution are very sensitive to dispatching decisions, and even small errors in judgment can severely disrupt daily operations.

When considering the dispatching problem, one must account for several factors, as illustrated in Figure 18.15.

An area may have several terminals (sources of product). Each terminal may have different products available, and a product may have a different cost at each terminal. Although over 20 products may be distributed, three grades of motor gasoline constitute most of the volume.

The trucks available include Mobil's own trucks and hired trucks. The trucks have different capacities, different numbers and sizes of separate bulk cargo compartments, and different cost structures. Assigning orders to trucks may require adjusting the ordered quantities of products so that they will fit into the truck compartments. Further, equipment compatibility must be considered, and the routes must reflect the various weight jurisdictions through which the trucks pass, as well as the cost of road and bridge tolls.

The objectives of the dispatching process are to minimize the cost of delivered product, to balance the work

load among the company trucks, and to load the maximum weight on a truck while adhering to all laws and proper loading rules. These conflicting objectives must be met within the constraints of maintaining customer-service levels. Decisions pertain to

1. Assigning orders to terminals.
2. Assigning orders to delivery trucks.
3. Adjusting order quantities to fit truck compartments.
4. Loading trucks to their maximum legal weight.
5. Routing trucks and sequencing deliveries.

These decisions must take into account truck cost; product cost, availability, specific gravity, and temperature; equipment compatibility; weight jurisdiction; and delivery policy. Because of the complexity of the decisions and the interaction among them, human

Figure 18.15 Small-Area Dispatch

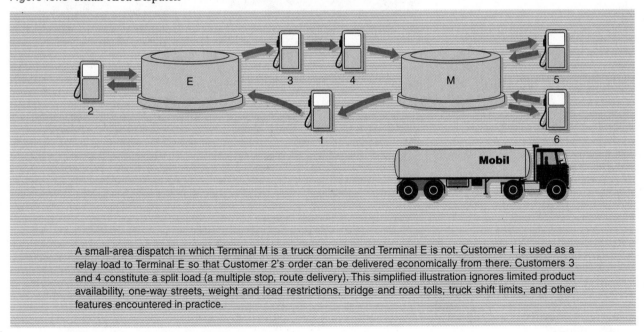

A small-area dispatch in which Terminal M is a truck domicile and Terminal E is not. Customer 1 is used as a relay load to Terminal E so that Customer 2's order can be delivered economically from there. Customers 3 and 4 constitute a split load (a multiple stop, route delivery). This simplified illustration ignores limited product availability, one-way streets, weight and load restrictions, bridge and road tolls, truck shift limits, and other features encountered in practice.

dispatchers usually seek "acceptable" solutions rather than striving for ideal ones. They may be guided by simple decision rules that perform reasonably well on the average but poorly in specific situations. In such an environment, dispatchers cannot be expected to look for lowest-cost solutions. In fact, they are not even aware of all the data needed for optimal solutions.

The CAD system developed to automate the dispatching process makes major business decisions involving (1) own versus hired transportation, (2) sourcing, (3) vehicle loading, and (4) routing. The overall objectives of the system are to minimize all costs, maintain service levels, and remain safe and legal.

CAD cannot completely replace the human dispatcher, because many crucial aspects of the dispatching process are not quantifiable. However, relieving human dispatchers of the routine dispatching tasks allows them to concentrate on the qualitative aspects of the specific dispatching situation and to quickly see the economic impact of manually overriding CAD's recommended solutions.

The CAD system was fully implemented during the first half of 1985. With its implementation, Mobil completed the consolidation of three manual centers into one automated center dispatching about 50,000 orders for light products per month. By 1987 the productivity of dispatching personnel had more than doubled, on the basis of the number of orders delivered per person. The costs of communications and computer operation were higher

than originally forecasted, but so were the savings. Annual net cost savings for product distribution of well over $2 million were realized. Even greater benefits were expected as dispatchers became better acquainted with their new tools.

Questions for Discussion

1. To gain further insight into the difficulties associated with tank-truck loading, consider this simplified example. Examine Figure 18.16. The truck's compartments are to be filled, and different products cannot be mixed in the same compartment. You are allowed to adjust the volume of each product loaded if necessary to fit it within the compartment capacities. In no case, however, may you adjust the total volume by more than (plus or minus) 400 gallons.

Three orders are given in Table 18.11. In each case, the total volume and truck capacity is 11,800 gallons. Show how each order can be loaded on the truck. Why is order 3 much harder to load?

2. Explain the benefits of the CAD system for Mobil Oil Corporation. Why can it not completely replace the human decision maker?

Figure 18.16 Tank-Truck Loading

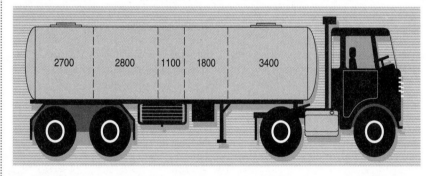

Table 18.11 Orders for Tank-Truck Loading

Product	Order 1 (Easy to Fit)	Order 2 (Not So Easy)	Order 3 (Hard)
Super	2900	3500	2900
Regular	3400	1100	4000
Unleaded	5500	7200	4900

Summary of Key Points

••• Scheduling and production-activity control is focused on meeting customer-service objectives, minimizing production costs, and maximizing resource utilization.

••• Finite capacity scheduling (FCS) matches work against available resources to ensure a feasible schedule. Three major approaches are optimization, dispatching rules and simulation, and constraint-based scheduling. Four principal criteria for evaluating schedules are makespan, flowtime, tardiness, and lateness.

••• For sequencing on a single processor, applying the shortest processing time (SPT) rule minimizes the average flowtime. For situations involving due dates, the earliest-due-date rule minimizes the maximum job tardiness and maximum job lateness. Johnson's rule provides a means of determining the minimum makespan schedule for a two-machine flowshop problem. Although these simple situations are not frequently encountered in practice, analyzing them provides general insights that can be applied to complex job-scheduling problems.

••• The general job-scheduling problem is usually approached by using priority dispatching rules, which can be studied and evaluated by using computer simulation. The choice of a rule depends on the shop configuration and the sequence of job arrivals. Among the best rules for this is the SPT rule.

••• The objective of constraint-based scheduling to achieve synchronization by managing constraint resources such as bottlenecks closely and scheduling all operations off of them. The theory of constraints is implemented through the computerized tool of optimized production technology (OPT).

••• Batch-production scheduling applies to make-to-stock manufacturers that produce different products on common facilities. With variable demands and production rates, batch scheduling typically focuses on maintaining sufficient inventories to meet demand. Runout-time scheduling is a heuristic method for accomplishing this objective.

••• Service organizations have some unique and difficult scheduling problems. The scheduling of personnel is typically approached with several efficient heuristic procedures that provide good, workable solutions.

••• Progress control is necessary for monitoring schedules on a timely basis to make needed corrections. Most production-control systems are computerized and integrated with other manufacturing information systems.

Key Terms

Scheduling
Production-activity control
Finite capacity scheduling (FCS)
Makespan
Flowtime
Due date
Tardiness
Lateness
Sequencing
Shortest processing time (SPT)
Flowshop
Dispatching rules
OPT (optimized production technology)
Drum-buffer-rope
Runout time

Review Questions

1. What are the goals of scheduling and production-activity control?
2. Define *finite-capacity scheduling*.
3. List and define the criteria commonly used to evaluate schedules.
4. Distinguish between scheduling and sequencing.
5. Compare the effectiveness of the shortest processing time (SPT) and earliest-due-date rules with respect to the scheduling criteria in Table 18.1 for a single-machine scheduling problem.
6. Explain why the schedule chosen in a single-machine scheduling problem will not affect makespan.
7. Distinguish between a flowshop and a job shop.
8. Why is the general (n machine) job-shop scheduling problem so difficult to solve?
9. Distinguish between static and dynamic dispatching rules.
10. List several dispatching rules. How can one evaluate the effectiveness of a rule?
11. How is drum-buffer-rope scheduling performed?
12. Why is a bottleneck operation critical to the OPT philosophy?
13. List some of the advantages and disadvantages of OPT.
14. Explain how runout time is used to schedule batch-production processes. What are the limitations of using a cyclic schedule for this problem?
15. What are the general steps in solving personnel-scheduling problems?
16. What is the purpose of progress control?
17. Explain the need for expediting. Can it ever be avoided?
18. Discuss the structure and use of computerized production-control systems.

Discussion Questions

1. Discuss how you decide to schedule your school assignments. Do your informal scheduling rules correspond to any of those in this chapter?
2. Interview an operations manager at a nearby manufacturing or service company to find out about scheduling problems the company faces and how they are addressed.
3. Can you think of other important criteria on which to evaluate schedules?

4. How might a manager decide which type of scheduling criteria to use?

5. Discuss some advantages and disadvantages of the various dispatching rules in Table 18.2.

6. In the discussion of OPT, this statement is made: "An hour lost at a bottleneck is an hour lost for the total system." Explain its meaning.

7. Describe some situations, different from those in the chapter, in which batch-production scheduling might be used.

8. What types of scheduling or sequencing issues arise in professional and amateur sports? What criteria might be important in evaluating the schedules?

9. Discuss scheduling and sequencing issues in municipal services such as garbage collection, school-bus routing, or snowplowing. What types of criteria and approaches might be used?

10. List some examples of personnel scheduling in service organizations.

Notes

1. A. Alan B. Pritsker and Kent Snyder, "Simulation for Planning and Scheduling," *APICS—The Performance Advantage* 4, no. 8 (August 1994), pp. 36–41.

2. Joseph Corso, "Challenging Old Assumptions with Finite Capacity Scheduling," *APICS—The Performance Advantage* 3, no. 11 (November 1993), pp. 50–53.

3. Scott P. Baird and Ali S. Kiran, "Finite Capacity Scheduling: A Guided Tour," *American Production and Inventory Control Society 37th Annual Conference Proceedings,* 1994, pp. 14–19; and Bill Kirchmier, "Finite Capacity Scheduling," *American Production and Inventory Control Society 37th Annual Conference Proceedings,* 1994, pp. 20–22.

4. S. M. Johnson, "Optimal Two- and Three-Stage Production Schedules with Setup Times Included," *Naval Research Logistics Quarterly* 1, no. 1 (March 1954).

5. A survey of results can be found in J. H. Blackstone, D. T. Phillips, and G. L. Hogg, "A State-of-the-Art Survey of Dispatching Rules for Manufacturing Job Shop Operations," *International Journal of Production Research* 20 (1982), pp. 27–45.

6. F. Robert Jacobs, "The OPT Scheduling System: A Review of a New Production Scheduling System," *Production and Inventory Management* 24, no. 3 (third quarter 1983), pp. 47–51; and Donald W. Fogarty, John H. Blackstone, Jr., and Thomas R. Hoffmann, *Production & Inventory Management,* 2d ed. (Cincinnati, OH: South-Western Publishing Co., 1991), pp. 662–663.

7. Reprinted with the permission of APICS, Inc., "Drum-Buffer-Rope Scheduling and Pictures for the Yearbook," *Production and Inventory Management Journal* 35, no. 3, W. Steven Demmy and Barbara Sue Demmy (third quarter 1994), pp. 45–47.

8. Ibid.

9. Adapted from Creative Output, Inc., *OPT Management System* (Milford, CT: Creative Output, Inc.).

10. This approach is suggested in R. Tibrewala, D. Phillippe, and J. Browne, "Optimal Scheduling of Two Consecutive Idle Periods," *Management Science* 19, no. 1 (September 1972), pp. 71–75.

11. E. H. Heilman, R. W. Loy, and W. F. Byers, "Production Control System for Semiconductors," *Industrial Engineering,* August 1976. Copyright © Institute of Industrial Engineers, Inc., 25 Technology Park/Atlanta, Norcross, GA 30092. Adapted with permission.

12. Gerald G. Brown, Carol J. Ellis, Glenn W. Graves, and David Ronen, "Real-Time, Wide-Area Dispatch of Mobil Tank Trucks," *Interfaces* 17, no. 1 (1987), pp. 107–120. Copyright 1987. Adapted with permission from The Institute of Management Sciences, 290 Westminster Street, Providence, RI 02903, USA.

Solved Problems

1. Five jobs are waiting to be processed on a single machine (Table 18.12). Use the shortest processing time (SPT) rule to sequence the jobs. Compute the flowtime, tardiness, and lateness for each job. Also compute the average flowtime, average tardiness, and average lateness for all jobs.

Table 18.12 Data for Solved Problem 1

Job	Processing Time	Due Date
1	7	21
2	3	7
3	5	8
4	2	5
5	6	17

Solution

As shown in Table 18.13, the SPT sequence is 4–2–3–5–1.

Table 18.13 Solved Problem 1 Solution

Job	Flowtime	Due Date	Tardiness	Lateness
4	2	5	0	−3
2	5	7	0	−2
3	10	8	2	2
5	16	17	0	−1
1	23	21	2	2
Average	11.2		0.8	−0.4

2. A simple manufacturing process involving machined components consists of two operations done on two different machines. The status of the queue the beginning of a particular week is shown in Table 18.14.

Table 18.14 Data for Solved Problem 2

Job Number	Number of Components	Scheduled Time on Machine 1 (min. per piece)	Schedule Time on Machine 2 (min. per piece)
101	200	2.5	2.5
176	150	1.5	0.5
184	250	1.0	2.0
185	125	2.5	1.0
201	100	1.2	2.4
213	100	1.2	2.2

The processing on machine 2 must follow processing on machine 1. Schedule these jobs to minimize the makespan. Illustrate the schedule you arrive at with a bar chart.

Solution

Because this is a two-machine flowshop problem, Johnson's rule is applicable. Total time on each machine is the product of the number of components and the unit times as shown in Table 18.15.

Table 18.15 Solved Problem 2 Solution

Job	Machine 1	Machine 2
101	500	500
176	225	75
184	250	500
185	312.5	125
201	120	240
213	120	220

The sequence specified by Johnson's rule is 201–213–184–101–185–176. The schedules are shown on the following Gantt charts.

Machine 1:

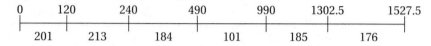

Machine 2:

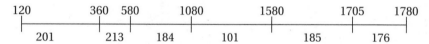

3. A detergent manufacturer uses a single facility for filling and packaging all four of its products. The inventory at the beginning of a particular week, the average demand, the production rate, and lot size are given in Table 18.16 (in ounces). If runout time is used for scheduling this activity, how would the activity be scheduled during the first two weeks?

Table 18.16 Data for Solved Problem 3

Product	Inventory	Weekly Demand	Production Rate/Week	Lot Size
Brand A, Size A	10,000	5,000	20,000	10,000
Brand A, Size B	12,000	4,000	5,000	5,000
Brand B, Size A	15,000	3,000	12,000	6,000
Brand C, Size A	6,000	1,000	2,000	1,000

Solution
Table 18.17 represents the initial status.

Table 18.17 Solved Problem 3 Solution, Step 1

Product	Inventory	Demand	Runout Time
1	10,000	5,000	2.0 Schedule first
2	12,000	4,000	3.0
3	15,000	3,000	5.0
4	6,000	1,000	6.0

Since the economic lot size for item 1 (brand A, size A) is 10,000, that is, half of one week's run, the next decision arises after one-half week. Table 18.18 represents time = 0.5 week.

Table 18.18 Solved Problem 3 Solution, Step 2

Product	Inventory	Demand	Runout Time
1	17,500	5,000	3.5
2	10,000	4,000	2.5
3	13,500	3,000	4.5
4	5,500	1,000	5.5

Schedule product 2, which takes one week. Note that the inventory for product 1, 17,500, is found by

$$10,000 - .5(5000) + 10,000$$

Table 18.19 represents time = 1.5 weeks.

Table 18.19 Solved Problem 3 Solution, Step 3

Product	Inventory	Demand	Runout Time
1	12,500	5,000	2.5
2	11,000	4,000	2.75
3	10,500	3,000	3.5
4	4,500	1,000	4.5

Schedule product 1, which takes 0.5 week. This takes us through the first two weeks.
4. MamaMia's Pizza forecasts these minimal requirements for drivers on a daily basis.

Day	Mon	Tue	Wed	Thur	Fri	Sat	Sun
Minimum Personnel	2	1	1	3	4	5	2

Each driver should have two consecutive days off. How many drivers are required?

Solution
Table 18.20 gives one of several alternate solutions possible.

Table 18.20 Solved Problem 4 Solution

Step	Mon	Tue	Wed	Thur	Fri	Sat	Sun
1	2	①	①	3	4	5	2
2	①	①	1	2	3	4	1
3	1	1	⓪	①	2	3	0
4	⓪	0	0	1	1	2	⓪
5	0	0	0	⓪	⓪	1	0

(continues)

Table 18.20 Solved Problem 4 Solution *(Continued)*

Employee	Work Schedule
1	Mon, Thur, Fri, Sat, Sun
2	Wed, Thur, Fri, Sat, Sun
3	Mon, Tue, Fri, Sat
4	Thur, Fri, Sat
5	Sat

With part-time student help, some "employee" schedules might be covered by two or more different drivers. For example, employee 1's schedule might be covered by one driver working Monday, Thursday, and Saturday, and another on Friday and Sunday. Another alternative is to smooth the schedule by combining these solutions. For example, employee 5 might cover Monday and Thursday in employee 1's schedule. This would provide more even employment for all drivers.

Problems

1. These six jobs are to be scheduled on a single machine:

Job	1	2	3	4	5	6
Processing Time (min.)	240	130	210	90	170	165

    a. Suppose the jobs are processed in numerical order. Compute the average flow-time after each job is completed.

    b. In what order would the jobs be processed using the SPT rule? Compute the average flowtime after each job is completed. Compare this answer with your answer to part a.

    c. In what sense does SPT minimize the average flowtime? Why would this rule be preferable to any other approach?

2. A machine shop has five jobs awaiting processing as shown in Table 18.21.

Table 18.21 Data for Problem 2

Job	Processing Time	Due Date
A	15	26
B	25	32
C	20	35
D	10	30
E	12	20

Compute the average flowtime, tardiness, and lateness for the following sequences:

    a. SPT sequence.

    b. Earliest due-date sequence.

    c. B–A–E–C–D.

3. Schedule the jobs in Solved Problem 1 using the earliest-due-date rule. How do the performance measures compare with those produced by the SPT rule?

4. Tony's Income Tax Service personnel can estimate the time required to complete customers' tax returns by using the time standards shown in Table 18.22.

Table 18.22 Data for Problem 4

Form	Standard Time (min.)
1040 short	10
1040 long	15
Schedule A	15
Schedule B	5
Schedule G	10
Schedule C	15
Schedule SE	5
Form 2106	10

One morning, five customers are waiting, needing the forms shown in Table 18.23.

Table 18.23 Customer Data for Problem 4

Customer	Forms
A	1040 long, schedules A and B
B	1040 long, schedules A, B, SE, and 2106
C	1040 short
D	1040 long, schedules A, B, and G
E	1040 long, schedules A, B, C, and 2106

a. If these customers are processed on a first-come, first-served basis, what is the flow-time for each and the average flowtime?
b. If SPT is used, how will the flowtimes differ?

5. Mike Reynolds has four assignments due in class tomorrow, and his class times are as shown in Table 18.24.

Table 18.24 Data for Problem 5

Class	Time
Finance 216	8 A.M.
P/OM 385	10 A.M.
Marketing 304	12 Noon
Psychology 200	4 P.M.

Each class lasts one hour, and Mike has no other classes. It is now midnight, and Mike estimates that the finance, P/OM, marketing, and psychology assignments will take him four, five, three, and six hours, respectively. How should he schedule the work? Can he complete all of it?

6. A copy business operates with a single Xerox copier. At the beginning of a particular day the jobs listed in Table 18.25 were awaiting processing.

Table 18.25 Data for Problem 6

Job	Job Content
1	500 forms regular size
	250 forms large size
2	100 forms regular size
	400 forms large size
3	1,000 forms regular size
4	1,500 forms large size
5	1,200 forms regular size
	300 forms large size

Regular forms take an average of 10 seconds to complete, while the larger ones take 12 seconds. If processing is always by job, calculate the flowtime of each job and the average flowtime for the
a. first-come, first-served rule.
b. SPT rule.
What is the makespan in both cases?

7. A small consulting group of a computer systems department has seven projects to complete. How should the projects be scheduled? The time in days and project deadlines are given in Table 18.26.

Table 18.26 Data for Problem 7

	Project						
	1	2	3	4	5	6	7
Time	4	9	12	16	9	15	8
Deadline	12	24	60	28	24	36	48

8. Monday morning Baxter Industries has the jobs shown in Table 18.27 awaiting processing in two departments, mill and drill.

Table 18.27 Data for Problem 8

	Time Required (hours)	
Job	Mill	Drill
216	8	4
327	6	10
462	10	5
519	5	6
258	3	8
617	6	2

a. Develop a minimum makespan schedule using Johnson's rule. Graph the results on a bar chart.
b. Assuming an eight-hour workday, suppose two new jobs arrive Wednesday morning as shown in Table 18.28.

Table 18.28 Additional Data for Problem 8

Job	Mill	Drill
842	4	7
843	10	8

How should the schedule be changed?

9. Dan's Auto Detailing business performs two major activities: exterior cleanup, and interior detailing. Based on the size of car and condition, time estimates for six cars on Monday morning are as shown in the accompanying table.

	Car					
	1	*2*	*3*	*4*	*5*	*6*
Exterior	60	75	90	45	65	80
Interior	30	40	20	30	15	45

Sequence the cars so that all exterior detailing is done first and total completion time is minimized.

10. Compute the number of possible schedules for a general job shop with n jobs and m machines for each of these cases:
   a. $n = 3, m = 2$
   b. $n = 2, m = 3$
   c. $n = 3, m = 3$
   d. $n = 4, m = 4$

11. For the Lynwood Manufacturing job-shop data in Table 18.3, simulate the first-come, first-served, SPT, and total-work dispatching rules. Draw a bar-chart schedule for each simulation and critically compare these rules with the least-work-remaining rule simulated in the chapter.

12. Seven jobs with different due dates arrive at a two-machine flowshop in the sequence shown in Table 18.29.

Table 18.29 Data for Problem 12

Job	Arrival Date	Due Date	Processing Time Machine 1	Machine 2
1	0	6	1	3
2	1	6	4	1
3	2	12	5	4
4	4	8	3	1
5	6	15	1	3
6	8	16	4	2
7	10	20	1	5

a. Apply the slack-time dispatching rule to schedule these jobs. What is the critical ratio of all jobs when each job arrives?

b. Construct a bar chart for the schedule. How much idle time is there for each machine? What is the lateness of all jobs?

13. Six jobs with different due dates and processing times on two sequential machines arrive during the first 10 days of August as shown in Table 18.30. Schedule the jobs using the slack-time dispatching rule. Compute the waiting times and completion times, machine utilization, etc. (Illustrate the process.) Also compute the critical ratio for when each job arrives.

Table 18.30 Data for Problem 13

			Processing Time	
Job	Arrival Date	Due Date	*Machine 1*	*Machine 2*
1	July 31	Aug. 10	5	3
2	Aug. 1	Aug. 27	2	7
3	Aug. 3	Aug. 15	4	5
4	Aug. 4	Aug. 20	3	6
5	Aug. 5	Aug. 30	8	7
6	Aug. 9	Nov. 15	6	9

14. Refer to Solved Problem 3. Continue scheduling products through week 4.

15. Referring to the example of batch-scheduling laundry-soap product sizes in the chapter, suppose that the demands for the five products are 250, 300, 500, 800, and 300 units per week, respectively. Show that
    a. Demand greatly exceeds available capacity.
    b. Using the runout-time method will eventually result in shortages.

16. A soft-drink manufacturer bottles six flavors on a single machine. Relevant data are given in Table 18.31.

Table 18.31 Data for Problem 16

Flavor	Economic Lot Size (gallons)	Bottling Time (hours)	Demand (gallons/ day)	Current Inventory
Cola	7,500	32	3,000	5,000
Orange	4,000	17	1,000	3,000
Diet cola	5,000	21	2,000	4,500
Lemon-lime	2,000	8	800	1,500
Ginger ale	3,000	13	700	2,000
Club soda	3,500	15	1,200	2,100

Using the smallest-runout-time rule, which flavor should be produced first? What inventory levels will result? Assume three shifts per day.

17. A hospital emergency room needs the following numbers of nurses.

Day	M	T	W	T	F	S	S
Min. number	4	3	2	5	7	8	3

Each nurse should have two consecutive days off. How many full-time nurses are required?

18. A supermarket has the following minimum personnel requirements during the week. Each employee is required to have two consecutive days off. How many regular employees are required?

Day	Mon	Tue	Wed	Thur	Fri	Sat	Sun
Minimum Personnel	4	4	5	6	6	5	4

19. Your business manufactures and sells one assembly. The assembly is made from four different parts, each of which requires three to five manufacturing operations on three common machining centers (see Figure 18.17). There is a 60-minute setup for each operation for each part. Each part has a WIP inventory value of $100 the moment it is started at the first operation. Assembly and shipment occur instantaneously when a matched set of parts is available. Demand for your assembly is unlimited, as is the raw material supply. When you start, no WIP inventory exists in the system, and the three machines are not set up.

Figure 18.17
Product Routing for
Problem 19

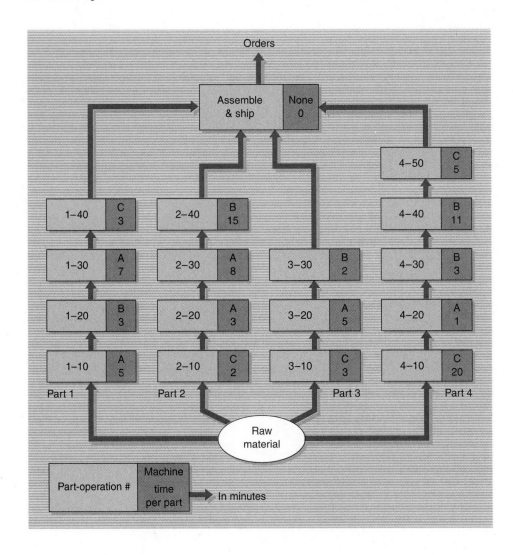

The objective is to produce as much as possible. The best schedule is the one that generates the most throughput without violating any of these constraints:

1. The schedules must be realistic. (For instance, you cannot run two parts on the same machine simultaneously.)
2. Inventory must never exceed $50,000 (500 parts).
3. At least 140 assemblies must be shipped each week.
4. At least 680 assemblies must have been shipped by the end of the first four weeks.
5. Only 40 days (eight weeks) of production time are available, and you may work 24 hours a day.

Develop a schedule that meets these constraints, showing the results with a bar chart.[†]

[†]"The OPT Quiz." Reproduced with permission of Creative Output, Inc.

Chapter Outline

P/OM in Practice

Chapter Nineteen
Project Planning, Scheduling, and Control

I t is certainly not unusual for a small business like MamaMia's Pizza to consider expanding as its popularity and financial strength increase. Some of the major tasks in planning for expansion are hiring architects, designing the new restaurant or restaurants, hiring contractors, building the restaurant(s), purchasing and installing equipment, and hiring and training employees. Each of these major tasks consists of numerous subtasks that must be performed in a particular sequence, on time, and on budget. Taken together, these activities constitute a **project.** Other examples of projects include the development of new products and processes, implementing an MRP II system, or preparing a corporate annual report. **Project management** involves all activities associated with planning, scheduling, and controlling projects. This chapter addresses

••• The scope of project management and specific approaches to project planning, scheduling, and control.

••• Quantitative techniques for scheduling project activities with and without limited resources, including the variability of time estimates.

••• Time/cost trade-off approaches that focus on reducing project time at minimum cost.

Scope of Project Planning and Management

All project-management decisions involve three factors: time, resources, and cost. Managers need to know how much *time* a project should take and when specific activities should be started and completed so that deadlines can be established and progress of the project monitored. Managers must also determine the *resources,* such as people and equipment, available for the project and how they should be allocated among the various activities. Finally, the *cost* of the project must be determined and then controlled. Managers seek ways to minimize costs without jeopardizing deadlines.

Although project-management activities are often carried on by functional managers, organizations also may have specific people designated as *project managers.* They lead the project activities, plan and track progress of the work, and provide direction to project personnel. Typically, project managers are found in technical areas such as research and development, engineering design, and installation of computer systems. However, the methods used in project management can be successfully applied by functional managers in many of their normal activities.

Project managers are usually generalists who have wide backgrounds and experience. In addition to managing the project, they must manage the relationships among the project team, the parent organization, and the client. In this regard, the project manager's ability to *facilitate* is more important than his or her ability to supervise. The project manager must also have sufficient technical expertise to resolve disputes among functional specialists. In general, successful project managers have four key skills: a bias toward task completion, technical and administrative credibility, interpersonal and political sensitivity, and leadership ability.

Two of the more useful tools that have been developed to assist project managers in their scheduling efforts are PERT (*p*roject *e*valuation and *r*eview *t*echnique) and CPM (*c*ritical-*p*ath *m*ethod). Although these tools have the same general purpose and use much of the same terminology, they were developed independently. PERT was introduced in the late 1950s specifically for planning, scheduling, and controlling the Polaris missile project. Since many activities associated with that project had never been attempted previously, it was difficult to predict the time needed to complete the various tasks. PERT was developed as a means of handling the uncertainties in activity completion times.

CPM, on the other hand, was developed primarily for scheduling and controlling industrial projects where job or activity times were known. CPM offered the option of reducing activity times by adding more workers and/or resources, usually with increased costs. Thus CPM allowed time and cost trade-offs for the various activities in projects.

Today the distinction between PERT and CPM as two separate techniques has largely disappeared. Modern project management software combines the features of PERT and CPM so that a distinction between the two techniques is no longer necessary.

Project-Planning Process

The project-planning process involves determining the set of activities that must be performed and when they should be completed to meet the organization's goals. The project-planning process consists of the following steps:

1. *Project definition.* Determine the activities that must be completed and the sequence required to perform them.
2. *Resource planning.* For each activity, determine the resource needs: personnel, time, money, equipment, materials, and so on.
3. *Project scheduling.* Specify a time schedule for each activity.
4. *Project control.* Establish the proper controls for determining progress. Develop alternative plans in anticipation of problems in meeting the planned schedule.

When projects are late, it is often because of failure to perform these four tasks adequately.

Let us consider a specific example to illustrate the process of project planning. The R. C. Coleman Company distributes a variety of food products to grocery stores and supermarkets. In the company's current warehouse operation, order-picking personnel fill each order, and the goods move to the warehouse shipping area. Because of the high labor cost and relatively low productivity of hand order-picking, the company has decided to install a computer-controlled order-picking system. R. C. Coleman's director of material management, John White, has been named the project manager in charge of coordinating the selection and installation of the automated system. In the following sections, we address the various tasks of project definition, resource planning, project scheduling, and project control that he will face in his role as project manager.

Project Definition

The first step in the project-planning process is to define the project's individual activities and the sequence in which they must be performed. To do this effectively, we need to distinguish between an activity and an event. **Activities** are tasks that *consume* time; **events** are *points* in time that represent the start or completion of a set of activities. Projects can be defined completely in terms of activities, but most managers think in terms of both activities and events. Events can be regarded as milestones by which to measure the progress of a project. Thus it is often convenient to specify events and then define the activities necessary to accomplish the events. In any case, it is necessary to have a complete set of project activities in order to proceed with the planning process. An example of how this is done follows.

Example

Identifying Activities and Events

After consulting with members of the engineering staff and warehouse management personnel, John White compiled this initial list of activities (tasks that consume time) and events (points in time) associated with the project:

- Begin project (event).
- Determine equipment needs (activity).
- Obtain vendor proposals (activity).
- Select vendor (activity).
- Design new warehouse layout (activity).
- Design computer interface (activity).
- Order system (activity).
- Warehouse layout complete (event).
- Interface computer (activity).
- Installation complete (event).
- Train system operators (activity).
- Test system (activity).
- Automated system ready for operation (event).

This list was reviewed and discussed several times to be sure that no activities were omitted from the project definition. In particular, the "warehouse layout complete" event implied that the "lay out warehouse" activity needed to be added to the activity list. Similarly, the event "installation complete" signaled the additional activity of "install system." After several trials, John developed the final list of activities shown in Table 19.1.

Note that associated with the project activities in Table 19.1 is a set of activities in the column labeled **immediate predecessors,** the one or more activities that *must be completed before* an activity is started. For instance, activities A and B can be started anytime, since they do not depend on the completion of prior activities. However, activity C cannot be started until both activities A and B

Table 19.1 Activities for R. C. Coleman Warehouse Automation Project

Activity	Description	Immediate Predecessors
A	Determine equipment needs	—
B	Obtain vendor proposals	—
C	Select vendor	A, B
D	Order system	C
E	Design new warehouse layout	C
F	Lay out warehouse	E
G	Design computer interface	C
H	Interface computer	D, F, G
I	Install system	D, F
J	Train system operators	H
K	Test system	I, J

have been completed. The immediate-predecessor information determines the sequence in which the activities must be performed.

Once all activities and immediate predecessors have been identified, we can construct a graphical representation of the project called a **project network,** or **PERT/CPM network.** A project network consists of numbered circles connected by arrows. The circles represent events and are called **nodes.** The straight and curved arrows connecting the nodes, called **branches** or **arcs,** correspond to activities. Each arc starts at a node and ends at a node, and thus a project network portrays the predecessor relationships among the activities. An example of the construction of a project network follows.

Example

Constructing a Project Network

Let us construct a project network for the R. C. Coleman project activities and events as listed in Table 19.1. Figure 19.1 shows the completed network. We begin with a node corresponding to "begin project." The activities that follow this node are those that have no immediate predecessors; that is, activities A and B. Thus the beginning of the network appears as

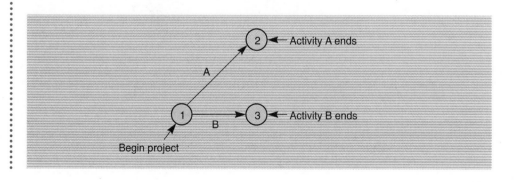

Figure 19.1 PERT/CPM Network for the R. C. Coleman Project

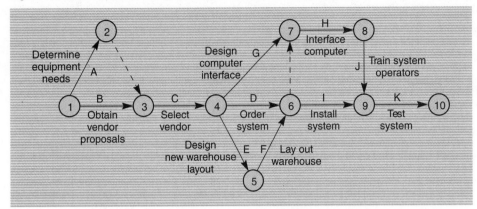

Node 2 represents the event "activity A ends," and node 3 represents the event "activity B ends."

Next, we see that activity C must follow the completion of both activities A and B. Clearly activity C cannot start at both nodes 2 and 3. To show this, we use an arc that does not correspond to an actual activity in the project but simply indicates a predecessor relationship. This is a dashed line portraying a **dummy activity.** We draw this portion of the network like this:

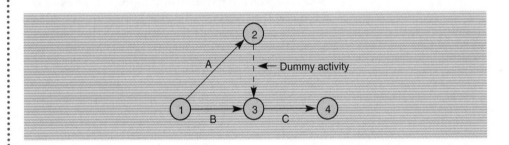

Next, we see that activity C is the immediate predecessor of activities D, E, and G. Adding them makes the network look like this:

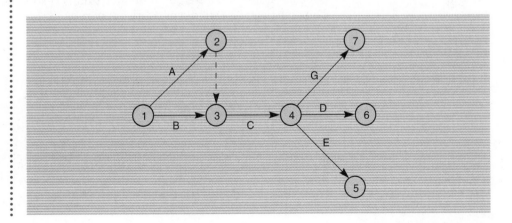

We continue to add activities, making sure to maintain the proper predecessor relationships as shown in Figure 19.1. Notice that we have a second dummy-activity arc from node 6 to node 7. Using the dummy activity from node 6 to node 7 maintains D, F, and G as the immediate predecessors for activity H, while ensuring that *only* D and F are the immediate predecessors of activity I.

When constructing project networks, you should ensure that at most one activity joins any two nodes. Computer procedures for analyzing PERT/CPM networks often require activities to be uniquely defined by two node numbers. This was the reason the dummy activity from node 2 to 3 was added in Figure 19.1, thus making activity A uniquely defined by nodes 1 to 2 and activity B uniquely defined by nodes 1 to 3.

We should also point out that project networks can be drawn in which *nodes* correspond to *activities* and arcs are used only to represent precedence relationships. These networks are called *activity-on-node networks.* Figure 19.2 shows one for the R. C. Coleman project. Activity-on-node networks have the advantage that dummy arcs are never necessary, which tends to make them easier to conceptualize. Their major disadvantage, however, is that events do not have an explicit graphical representation as they do in activity-on-arc networks.

Now that the definition phase of the R. C. Coleman warehouse automation project has been completed (see Table 19.1 and Figure 19.1), the next task is to define the resources that will be required for each activity.

Resource Planning

Once a network for the project has been established, information is needed about the resources that are required for completing each activity. For scheduling purposes, the most important resource requirement is *time*. In many situations, activity times can be estimated accurately. For example, in projects such as construction or maintenance, a manager may have sufficient experience or historical data to provide fairly accurate activity time estimates. In addition, the nature of these activities may have low variability, and thus times would be

Figure 19.2
Activity-on-Node
Representation of R. C.
Coleman Project

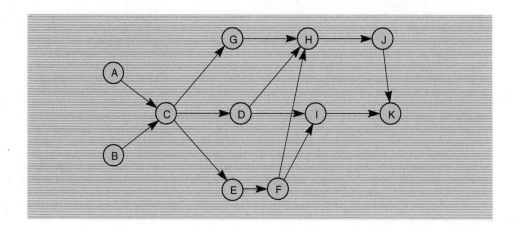

relatively constant. In other cases though, activity times are uncertain and perhaps best described by a range of possible values. In these instances the uncertain activity times are treated as random variables with associated probability distributions. Usually three time estimates are obtained for each activity:

1. **Optimistic time** (*a*)—the activity time if everything progresses in an ideal manner.
2. **Most probable time** (*m*)—the most likely activity time under normal conditions.
3. **Pessimistic time** (*b*)—the activity time if significant breakdowns and/or delays occur.

Example

Computing Mean and Variance of Activity Times

John White gathered information from warehouse personnel, industrial engineers, and other sources and developed the time estimates listed in the first three columns of Table 19.2. To schedule these activities we determine the **average** or **expected time** (*t*), for each activity using the following formula.

$$t = \frac{a + 4m + b}{6}$$

(19.1)

Thus, for activity A, we compute the expected time to be

$$t = \frac{2 + 4(3) + 4}{6} = \frac{18}{6} = 3 \text{ weeks.}$$

Similarly, the expected time for activity B is 5 weeks. Figure 19.3 shows the probability distribution for activity B. Note that different values of *a*, *b*, and *m* will result in different shapes for the activity time distribution. This provides considerable flexibility in modeling project times. For uncertain activity times, we compute the variance of activity times with the following formula.

Table 19.2 Activity Time Estimates and Calculations for R. C. Coleman project (in weeks)

Activity	Optimistic Time (*a*)	Most Probable Time (*m*)	Pessimistic Time (*b*)	Expected Time (weeks)	Variance σ^2
A	2	3	4	3	.11
B	3	4	11	5	1.78
C	1	2	3	2	.11
D	4	5	12	6	1.78
E	3	5	7	5	.44
F	2	3	4	3	.11
G	2	3	10	4	1.78
H	2	3	4	3	.11
I	2	3	10	4	1.78
J	1	2	3	2	.11
K	1	2	3	2	.11

Figure 19.3 Activity Time Distribution for Activity B of R. C. Coleman Project

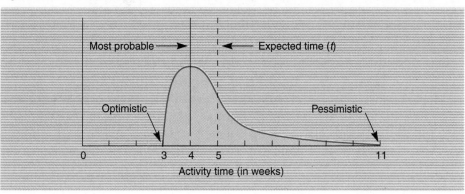

$$\text{variance of activity time*} = \left(\frac{b - a}{6}\right)^2 \tag{19.2}$$

As you can see, the difference between the pessimistic (b) and optimistic (a) time estimates greatly affects the value of the variance. With large differences in these two values, managers have a high degree of uncertainty in the activity time. Accordingly, the variance given by equation 19.2 will be large.

For activity A, the variance, denoted by σ_A^2, is

$$\sigma_A^2 = \left(\frac{4 - 2}{6}\right)^2 = \left(\frac{2}{6}\right)^2 = .11.$$

Activity B, on the other hand, has a greater uncertainty in completion time than activity A. The variance measure for activity B is

$$\sigma_B^2 = \left(\frac{11 - 3}{6}\right)^2 = \left(\frac{8}{6}\right)^2 = 1.78.$$

The remaining expected times and variances are summarized in Table 19.2.

---

*The variance equation is based on the notion that a standard deviation is approximately one-sixth of the difference between the extreme values of the distribution: $(b - a)/6$. The variance is simply the square of the standard deviation.

Besides time, a variety of other resources may be required for project activities. They might include

••• Executives, managers, and supervisors.

••• Professional and technical personnel.

••• Capital.

••• Materials.

••• Equipment and tools.

••• Clerical services.

The project manager must determine how many of these resources are required, if they are available, and where in the organization they can be obtained. Then she or he must bring these resources together at the proper times to perform the activities of the project.

Cost Estimating and Budgeting

Resource planning requires budgeting, and budgeting requires cost estimating. For project activities performed on a routine basis, such as in home construction, experienced cost estimators can predict costs very accurately by using historical data, supplier pricing, and so on. For other activities, costs can only be estimated judgmentally.

The components of a project that generate costs may not correspond to specific project activities, as the activities may be too detailed for conveniently controlling costs. In such cases, related activities under the control of one department or manager are often grouped together to form what are referred to as **work packages.** For small projects, a work package may consist of only one activity. We will assume that each activity is a work package to keep our discussion simple.

Two common budgeting practices are top-down and bottom-up budgeting. *Top-down budgeting* is a hierarchical approach that begins with senior and mid-level managers using their judgment and available data to estimate costs of major project activities. These estimates are passed down to lower-level managers, who are responsible for breaking them down into more estimates for smaller subtasks. *Bottom-up budgeting* starts with the lowest-level tasks, converting labor and material estimates into dollar figures and aggregating them into higher-level activities until a total project budget is developed. This approach is typically more accurate because individuals close to the work tasks have better knowledge of costs. However, it is common for lower-level managers to pad their estimates to ensure that they will not overrun their budgets. A hybrid approach is to negotiate plans and budgets through the management hierarchy. In that way, all levels of managers participate in the process, leading to more realistic and mutually agreed upon budgets.

Table 19.3 gives cost estimates and budgeted costs per month for the R. C. Coleman project activities. At this point, we are unable to develop a specific budget over time because we do not know when specific activities are to be scheduled.

Project Scheduling

The determination of when activities are to be performed is called *scheduling*, and it is the next task in the project planning process. A schedule enables a manager to assign resources effectively and to monitor progress and take corrective action when necessary. A very useful tool for graphically depicting a schedule is a **Gantt chart,** named after Henry L. Gantt, a pioneer of scientific management. Gantt charts enable the operations manager to know exactly what activities should be performed at a given time and, more importantly, to monitor daily progress of a project so that corrective action can be taken when necessary. An example of how such a chart is constructed follows.

Table 19.3 Cost Estimates for R. C. Coleman Project

Activity	Expected Time (weeks)	Cost Estimate	Budgeted Cost per Week
A	3	$1,200	$400
B	5	2,500	500
C	2	500	250
D	6	300	50
E	5	6,000	1,200
F	3	9,000	3,000
G	4	4,400	1,100
H	3	3,000	1,000
I	4	4,000	1,000
J	2	3,200	1,600
K	2	1,800	900
	Total project costs	$35,900	

Example

Constructing a Gantt Chart

To construct a Gantt chart, we list the activities on a vertical axis and use a horizontal axis to represent time. The symbols used in a Gantt chart are defined in Table 19.4.

The PERT/CPM network (Figure 19.1) and the estimated times in Table 19.2 assist us in constructing a Gantt chart. We assume that each activity will be scheduled as early as possible. The resulting schedule will be an "early start" schedule. For instance, activities A and B can begin at time 0. For these activities, we place Gantt chart symbol number 1 at time 0 and symbol number 2 at the completion times of 3 and 5, respectively. The top portions of these symbols are joined by a lighter line to indicate the duration of the activity. Activity C cannot begin until A is completed; thus this activity is scheduled to begin at time 5. After activity C is completed at time 7, activities G, D, and E can be scheduled. Continuing in this way, we construct the Gantt chart shown in Figure 19.4.

From Figure 19.4 we see that the entire project is scheduled to be completed in 22 weeks. What happens if an activity is delayed? Suppose, for example, that activity E takes six weeks instead of five weeks. Because E is a predecessor of F and the starting time of F is the same as the completion time of E, F is forced to begin one week later. This forces a delay in activity H, which in turn delays activities J and K. In addition, activity I is also delayed one week. The Gantt chart for this new schedule is shown in Figure 19.5.

Table 19.4 Gantt Chart Symbols

Symbol Number	Symbol	Description
1	⌐	Scheduled starting time for activity
2	⌐	Scheduled completion time for activity
3	▬	Completed work for an activity
4	⋈	Scheduled delay or maintenance
5	∨	Current date for progress review

Figure 19.4 Early-Start Schedule for R. C. Coleman Project

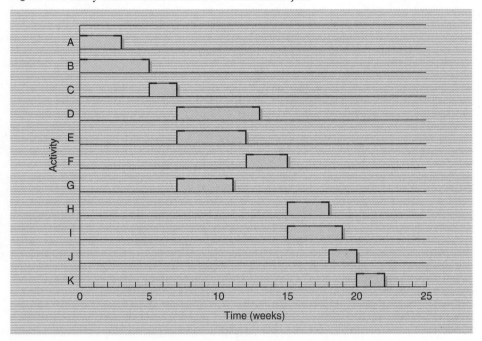

Figure 19.5 Early-Start Schedule with Activity E Delayed One Week

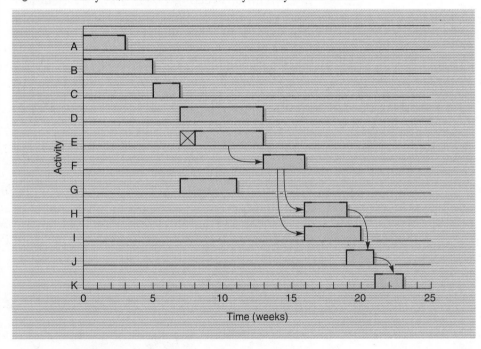

The effect that delays in one activity have on other activities can be seen better by referring to the project network in Figure 19.1. A *path* in the network is a sequence of activities, performed *in order,* that starts at the beginning node (node 1 in the R. C. Coleman network) and ends with the completion node (node 10 in the R. C. Coleman network). In Figure 19.1, one path consists of activities B, C, D, I, and K; another consists of activities B, C, G, H, J, and K.

Whenever the scheduled completion time for some activity is the same as the scheduled start time for a successor activity along a path, any delay in the activity will force a delay in the successor activity. If this holds true for *all* activities on some path from the start of the project to the end, the activities on the path are called **critical activities** and the path is referred to as a **critical path.** Critical activities are those for which any delay will push back the completion date of the entire project. For the R. C. Coleman project, the critical activities are B, C, E, F, H, J, and K and the dummy activity from node 6 to node 7.

The following example shows how to calculate the critical path directly from the network and also how to obtain some other important scheduling information.

Example

Finding a Critical Path

Figure 19.6 shows the R. C. Coleman project network with expected activity times labeled on the arcs. Note that dummy activities have an expected activity time of zero. This example applies a step-by-step procedure for finding the critical path.

Starting at the network's origin (node 1) and using a starting time of 0, we will compute an *earliest start* and *earliest finish* time for each activity in the network.

Let

ES = earliest start time for a particular activity.

EF = earliest finish time for a particular activity.

t = expected activity time for the activity.

This expression yields the earliest finish time for a given activity.

Figure 19.6 Expected Activity Times for R. C. Coleman Project

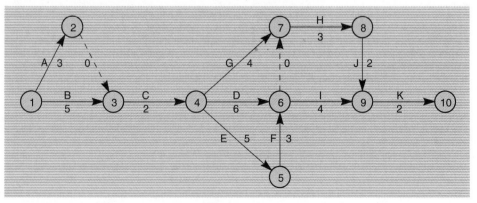

Figure 19.7 Nodes 1, 2, 3, and 4 in R. C. Coleman Network

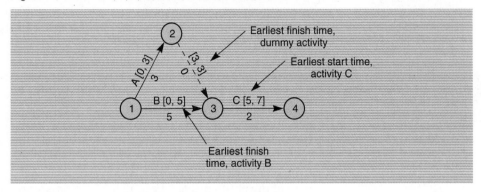

$$EF = ES + t \qquad\qquad (19.3)$$

For example, for activity A, $ES = 0$ and $t = 3$; thus its earliest finish time is $EF = 0 + 3 = 3$. We write the earliest start and earliest finish times directly on the network diagram in brackets next to the letter of the activity.

The **earliest start time** for an activity leaving a particular node is equal to the *largest* value of the earliest finish times for all activities entering the node. Applying this rule to the portion of the network involving nodes 1, 2, 3, and 4, we obtain what is shown in Figure 19.7. Note that applying the earliest start-time rule at node 3 results in the earliest start time for activity C being the larger value of the earliest finish times for the two entering activities, B and the dummy activity.

Proceeding in a *forward pass* through the network, we can establish an earliest start time and an earliest finish time for each activity. The R. C. Coleman network with *ES* and *EF* values is shown in Figure 19.8. Note that the earliest finish time for activity K, the last activity, is 22 weeks. Thus the earliest completion time for the entire project is 22 weeks.

It is relatively easy to identify the critical path from the early start/early finish schedule. Simply work backward from the terminal node, beginning with the activity with the largest early finish time (if multiple activities end at the terminal node). Then, continuing backward through the network, identify activities for which the early finish time of an activity entering a node equals the early start

Figure 19.8 Earliest Start and Finish Times for R. C. Coleman Project

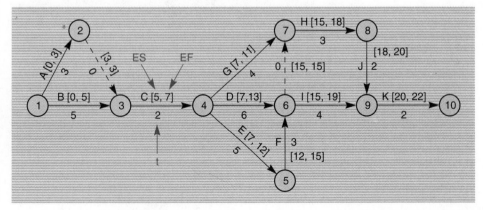

time of an activity leaving the node. This is best illustrated with an example. In Figure 19.8, activity K is on the critical path because it is the only activity ending at the terminal node. At node 9, either activity I or J must be on the critical path. The early finish time for activity J is equal to the early start time for activity K (which is not true for activity I). Thus, activity J is on the critical path. From node 8, we see that H must be on the critical path. Applying the rule at node 7, the dummy activity from node 6 to node 7 is on the critical path. At node 6, we find that activity F is on the critical path, since its early finish time is equal to the early start time of the dummy activity. Continuing, we see that activities E, C, and B comprise the remainder of the critical path. Thus, the entire critical path is B–C–E–F–(6,7) dummy–H–J–K. The sum of the individual activity times is 22.

We can identify the critical path in an alternate way and compute additional information for scheduling purposes by making a *backward-pass* calculation. Starting at the completion point (node 10) and using a latest finish time of 22 weeks for activity K, we trace back through the network computing a *latest start* and *latest finish* time for each activity. We use a latest finish time of 22 weeks for activity K, because we want to finish the project as quickly as possible. This is not necessary, and we might use a later target date for project completion in performing the subsequent calculations.

Let

$$LS = \text{latest start time for a particular activity.}$$

$$LF = \text{latest finish time for a particular activity.}$$

This expression yields the latest start time for a given activity.

$$LS = LF - t \qquad \qquad (19.4)$$

Given that $LF = 22$ and $t = 2$ for activity K, the latest start time for this activity is $LS = 22 - 2 = 20$.

The **latest finish time** for an activity entering a particular node is equal to the *smallest* value of the latest starting times for all activities leaving the node. Logically, then, the latest time an activity can be finished is equal to the earliest (smallest) value for the latest start time of following activities. The complete network with the LS and LF backward-pass calculations is shown in Figure 19.9.

Figure 19.9 Latest Start and Finish Times (in Parentheses under Earliest Times) for R. C. Coleman Project

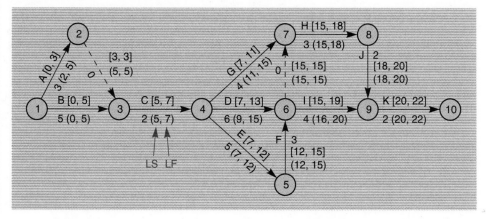

The latest start and latest finish times for the activities are written in parentheses directly below the earliest start and earliest finish times.

Note the application of the latest-finish-time rule at node 4. The latest finish time for activity C ($LF = 7$) is the smallest value of the latest-start times for the activities that leave node 4; that is, the smallest LS value for activities G ($LS = 11$), D ($LS = 9$), and E ($LS = 7$), which is 7.

After obtaining the start and finish activity times as summarized in Figure 19.9, we can find the amount of slack, or free time, associated with each of the activities. **Slack** is defined as the length of time an activity can be delayed without affecting the completion date for the project. The amount of slack for each activity is computed as follows.

$$\text{Slack} = LS - ES = LF - EF \qquad (19.5)$$

For example, we see that the slack associated with activity A is $LS - ES = 2 - 0 = 2$ weeks. This means that activity A could be delayed up to two weeks (could start anywhere between weeks 0 and 2) and the entire project could still be completed in 22 weeks. This activity therefore is not a critical activity and is not part of the critical path. Using equation 19.5 again, we see that the slack associated with activity C is $LS - ES = 5 - 5 = 0$. Since this activity has no slack time, it is a critical activity and is on the critical path. In general, critical-path activities have zero slack.

The start and finish times shown on the network in Figure 19.9 provide a detailed schedule for all activities. Putting this information into tabular form gives us Table 19.5. Note that activities B, C, E, F, H, J, and K have zero slack and thus form the critical path in the R. C. Coleman network. Table 19.5 also shows the slack, or delay, that can be tolerated for each of the noncritical activities before they will cause a project delay. The Gantt chart schedule that we constructed earlier gives the same earliest start/earliest finish schedule as in this table. The critical-path calculations provide additional information to the project manager about latest start, latest finish, and slack times.

Table 19.5 Activity Schedule for R. C. Coleman Project (in weeks)

Activity	Earliest Start	Earliest Finish	Latest Start	Latest Finish	Slack ($LS - ES$)	Critical Path
A	0	3	2	5	2	
B	0	5	0	5	0	✓
C	5	7	5	7	0	✓
D	7	13	9	15	2	
E	7	12	7	12	0	✓
F	12	15	12	15	0	✓
G	7	11	11	15	4	
H	15	18	15	18	0	✓
I	15	19	16	20	1	
J	18	20	18	20	0	✓
K	20	22	20	22	0	✓

Variability in Project-Completion Date

While we treated the activity times as fixed at their expected values during the critical-path calculations, we are now ready to consider the effect of uncertainty, or variability, of activity times on the project-complete date. Obviously, any variation in these critical-path activities can cause variation in the project-completion date. Also, if a noncritical activity is delayed long enough to expend all of its slack time, that activity will become part of a new critical path, and further delays there will extend the project-completion date. The PERT procedure uses the variance in the critical-path activities to determine the variance in the project-completion date, as the following example shows.

Example

Probability Calculations for Project-Completion Times

If we let T denote the R. C. Coleman project duration—determined by the critical path of B–C–E–F–H–J–K then

$$T = t_B + t_C + t_E + t_F + t_H + t_J + t_K$$
$$= 5 + 2 + 5 + 3 + 3 + 2 + 2 = 22 \text{ weeks.}$$

Therefore, the variance (σ^2) in project duration is given by the sum of the variances of the critical-path activities:

$$\sigma^2 = \sigma_B^2 + \sigma_C^2 + \sigma_E^2 + \sigma_F^2 + \sigma_H^2 + \sigma_J^2 + \sigma_K^2$$
$$= 1.78 + .11 + .44 + .11 + .11 + .11 + .11 = 2.77.$$

This formula is based on the assumption that all the activity times are independent. If two or more activities are dependent, the formula provides only an approximation to the variance of the project completion time.

Since we know that the standard deviation is the square root of the variance, we can compute the standard deviation, σ, for the project completion time as:

$$\sigma = \sqrt{\sigma^2} = \sqrt{2.77} = 1.66.$$

We assume that the distribution of the project-completion time, T, follows a normal probability distribution* as shown in Figure 19.10. With this assumption we can compute the probability of meeting a specified completion date. For example, suppose R. C. Coleman managers have allotted 25 weeks for the project. Although they expect completion in 22 weeks, they want to know the probability that they will meet the 25-week deadline. This probability is shown graphically as the shaded area in Figure 19.11. The z-value for the normal distribution at $T = 25$ is given by

$$z = \frac{25 - 22}{1.66} = 1.81.$$

Figure 19.10 Normal Distribution of Project-Completion Time Variation for R. C. Coleman Project

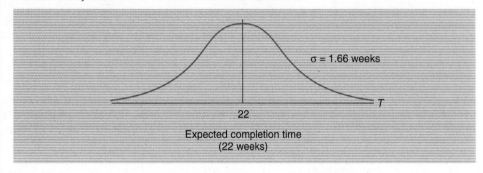

Figure 19.11 Probability of Completing R. C. Coleman Project within 25 Weeks

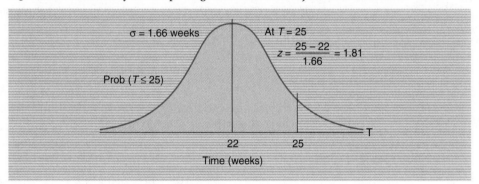

Using $z = 1.81$ and the tables for the standard normal distribution (see Appendix B), we see that the probability of the project meeting the 25-week deadline is $.4649 + .5000 = .9649$. Thus, while variability in the activity time may cause the project to exceed the 22-week expected duration, there is an excellent chance that the project will be completed before the 25-week deadline.

---

*The use of the normal probability distribution as an approximation is based on the *central limit theorem,* which states that the sum of independent activity times follows a normal distribution as the number of activities becomes large.

The procedure described is only approximate, since we have *assumed* that the distribution of *T* is normal. Moreover, this method assumes that only one critical path exists; if there are two or more critical paths, this method tends to underestimate the project-completion time. Also, when several noncritical paths are close (in terms of time) to the critical path, caution must be exercised in interpreting the results, since randomness in activity times may cause one of the other paths to be critical. Simulation is often used in such situations to gain a clearer perspective on project-completion times and critical activities.

Figure 19.12
Typical Progress Report

SOURCE: *Improving Management Skills: A Workbook.* Copyright © S. J. Mantel, J. M. McKinney, and R. Riley 1977. Used by permission.

Project name: _____
     Date: _____

PERIODIC PROGRESS REPORT

1. What results have we attained so for?
2. ☐ Are we ahead of schedule?   ☐ On schedule?   ☐ Behind schedule?
3. Has the objective changed or been modified?
4. Has the situation changed or been modified?
5. What unanticipated problems are we now facing?

6. What changes need to be made? _____

7. Whose approval is needed for these changes? _____

8. Action steps for me to take.

9. What additional problems are anticipated? _____

Progress Control

Because of the uncertainty of task times, unavoidable delays, or other problems, projects rarely, if ever, progress on schedule. Managers must therefore monitor performance of the project and take corrective action when needed. A typical progress report is shown in Figure 19.12. Schedules should be revised periodically on the basis of such reports. An example of how progress reports are produced and used follows.

Example

Using a Gantt Chart for Progress Control

Let us return to the R. C. Coleman project. Figure 19.13 is a Gantt progress chart for the project at week 9. Note that Gantt symbol number 3 (the color block) is used to denote the actual progress of activities at a given point in time. We see that activities A, B, and C have already been completed, activity D is ahead of schedule, activity E has not yet begun, and activity G is right on schedule. A progress chart such as this allows the manager to see the status of a project quickly. It also provides the information required to revise the schedule. For instance, since E is a critical activity and it is currently late, the project will be delayed unless the times for future activities can be shortened. This might be done by adding more resources to certain activities, working overtime, and so on. These are the decisions that a project manager must make on an ongoing basis to control a project.

Figure 19.13 Progress Chart for the R. C. Coleman Project at Week 9

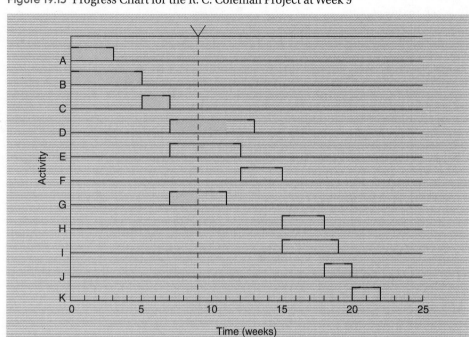

Budget Control

After a schedule is developed, a budget can be developed showing when costs are likely to be incurred and what they are likely to be during the project duration. First let us assume that all activities begin at their earliest possible starting date. Using the weekly activity cost rates shown in Table 19.3 and the earliest start times, we can prepare a weekly cost forecast as shown in Table 19.6. By summing the costs in each column, we obtain the total cost anticipated for each month of the project. Finally, by accumulating the monthly costs, we can show the budgeted total cost schedule provided all activities are started at the *earliest* starting times. We could also develop a budget based on all activities being started at their *latest* starting times (see Problem 16).

An effective budgetary control system monitors costs throughout the project's duration, comparing actual costs for all completed and in-process activities to the appropriate budgeted costs. It gives the project manager up-to-date information on the cost status of each activity. If actual costs exceed budgeted costs, a cost overrun has occurred. If actual costs are less than budgeted costs, we have a cost underrun. This information enables the project manager to take corrective action when necessary. An example of how cost overruns and underruns are detected follows.

Table 19.6 Weekly Cost Forecast for R. C. Coleman Project

Week Activity	1	2	3	4	5	6	7	8	9	10	11	12	13	14	15	16	17	18	19	20	21	22
A	400	400	400																			
B	500	500	500																			
C				500	500																	
D						250	250															
E								50	50	50	50	50	50									
F								1,200	1,200	1,200	1,200	1,200										
G													3,000	3,000	3,000							
H								1,100	1,100	1,100	1,100											
I																1,000	1,000	1,000				
J																1,000	1,000	1,000	1,000			
K																			1,600	1,600	900	900
Weekly cost	900	900	900	500	500	250	250	2,350	2,350	2,350	2,350	1,250	3,050	3,000	3,000	2,000	2,000	2,000	2,600	1,600	900	900
Cumulative cost	900	1800	2700	3200	3700	3950	4200	6550	8900	11250	13600	14850	17900	20900	23900	25900	27900	29900	32500	34100	35000	35900

Example | Determining Cost Overruns and Underruns

Table 19.7 shows the cost and completion status for the R. C. Coleman project as of week 10. The "% completion" column indicates what proportion of each activity has been completed. By multiplying this percentage by the budgeted cost shown in Table 19.7, we determine the budgeted cost in the next column based on the actual amount of work completed.

By subtracting the budgeted cost from the actual cost, we can determine any cost overruns or underruns. We see that activities A and G are below budget, although costs for activities C and E are exceeding their budgets. The total project is $90 over budget at this point.

Table 19.7 Activity Cost and Completion Status at End of Week 10 for R. C. Coleman Project

Activity	Actual Cost	% Completion	Budgeted Cost	Difference
A	$1,050	100%	$1,200	$(150)
B	2,500	100	2,500	0
C	600	100	500	100
D	150	50	150	0
E	2,000	20	1,200	800
F	0	0	0	0
G	3,300	90	3,960	(660)
H	0	0	0	0
I	0	0	0	0
J	0	0	0	0
K	0	0	0	0
	$9,600		$9,510	$ 90

Planning and Scheduling with Limited Resources

The early-start schedule we developed in Figure 19.4 gives no consideration to resources. It simply assumes that sufficient resources are available for all activities scheduled at the same time. Usually, however, resources such as labor and equipment that must be shared among the activities are limited. Determining how to allocate limited resources is often a very challenging puzzle. A common objective is to minimize the project duration within the resource constraints.

Let us look at an example of this.

Example | Minimizing Project Duration within Resource Limitations

To illustrate how project manager John White can make decisions that will minimize project time when resource limitations occur, let us consider activity F in the R. C. Coleman project. This activity, "lay out warehouse," includes such subtasks as moving stock to a temporary storage area, removing existing storage racks, shifting the office location, painting new aisle and safety markers, and so on. A network that provides the detailed information for the specific subtasks is

Figure 19.14 Network for Warehouse-Layout Subtasks for R. C. Coleman Project

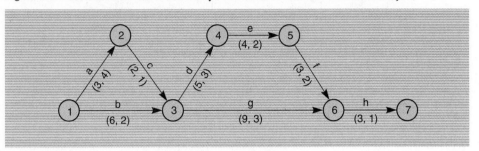

shown in Figure 19.14. The number of days required to complete each subtask activity and the number of people needed are shown in parentheses on the network's arcs. For example, the numbers 3, 4 in parentheses below the arc corresponding to activity a indicates that activity a requires three days with four people working together. Thus the critical path defined by activities b, d, e, f, and h provides the expected completion time of 21 days, or three weeks.

Figure 19.15 shows a Gantt-chart schedule based on the earliest-start times. Using this chart, we can now construct a *resource-loading chart* that will show the amount of resource—that is, the number of people—required at any time by that particular schedule. This is done by adding the number of people required for all activities at each point in time. The resource-loading chart for the schedule in Figure 19.15 is shown in Figure 19.16. The maximum value of 6 tells us that six people are needed to complete the project within its scheduled time of 21 days.

Suppose, however, that only five employees are available. The only way to accommodate this constraint is to delay certain activities; if the activities are

Figure 19.15 Gantt Chart for Early-Start Schedule for R. C. Coleman Warehouse-Layout Subtasks

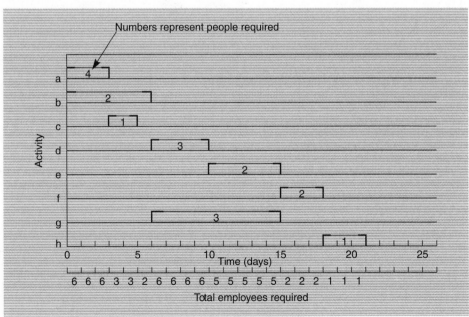

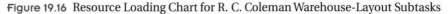

Figure 19.16 Resource Loading Chart for R. C. Coleman Warehouse-Layout Subtasks

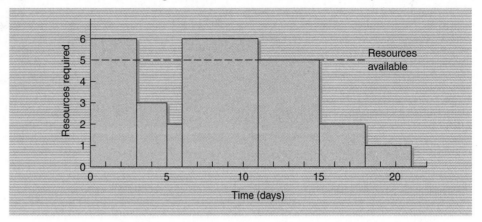

critical, the project duration will be extended. Finding the minimum project time that will meet this constraint is a very difficult problem. Although a number of quantitative techniques can be used to find the optimal solution, they are beyond the scope of this book.

A variety of heuristic rules ("rules of thumb") can be applied here, three of which are

1. Schedule the task with the shortest time first.
2. Schedule the task with the longest time first.
3. Schedule tasks with the least variability in time first.

Let us illustrate rule 1 for the R. C. Coleman example. At the start of the project, activities a and b cannot be scheduled simultaneously because only five employees are available. Using heuristic 1, we would schedule activity a first because it has the shortest time. Because of the resource constraint; activity b cannot be scheduled at the same time as activity a; therefore, we schedule activity b immediately after activity a. The Gantt chart at this point looks like this.

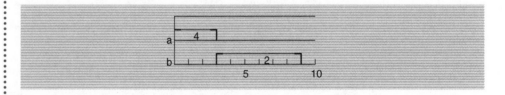

Now activity c is the only activity that can be scheduled next. Because it must follow activity a and requires only one person, it can be scheduled to start at the same time as b.

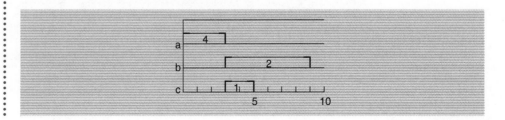

Figure 19.17 Revised Schedule with Resource Limit for R. C. Coleman Project

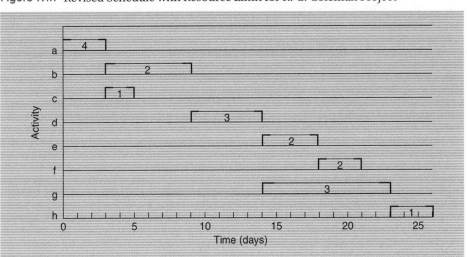

Next, we must choose to schedule either activity d or activity g. Again, because their combined resource requirements exceed 5, we choose to schedule activity d first because of its shorter time. Continuing in this manner, we arrive at the schedule in Figure 19.17. The other rules can be applied in a similar manner, although we cannot tell in advance which will give the best results. Observe that the time needed to lay out the warehouse was lengthened to 26 days due to the resource limitation. Since the warehouse-layout activity is critical, lengthening the time for laying out the warehouse will lengthen the duration of the entire project.

Time/Cost Trade-offs

We now consider an approach to project scheduling that enables the project manager to add resources to selected activities in order to reduce activity times, and thus project-completion times. Since adding resources, such as more workers, overtime, and so on, generally increases project costs, the decision to reduce activity times must take into account these added costs. In effect, the project manager's decision must weigh the benefits of decreased activity time against increased project cost.

In order to illustrate this aspect of project management, let us reconsider the warehouse-layout activity for the R. C. Coleman project (activity F in Table 19.1). The network diagram of the activity's subtasks is shown in Figure 19.14. Recall that the critical path of the network consists of subtasks b, d, e, f, and h and that 21 days will be required to complete the warehouse layout.

Now suppose that R. C. Coleman's warehouse automation project is behind schedule and that it has become imperative for the layout activity to be completed within 18 working days instead of 21. Thus, the project manager must shorten selected activity times, which is usually done by adding resources such as labor and/or overtime in a procedure called **crashing.** Since the added resources associated with crashing usually result in added project costs, the manager will want to identify the least-cost ways to crash and then crash only the amount necessary for meeting the specified completion date. He or she therefore needs the following information on each activity:

1. Estimated activity cost under the normal or expected activity time.
2. Activity completion time under maximum crashing (that is, shortest possible activity time).
3. Estimated activity cost under maximum crashing.

Let

$$\tau_n = \text{normal activity time,}$$

$$\tau_c = \text{crashed activity time (with maximum crashing),}$$

$$C_n = \text{normal activity cost, and}$$

$$C_c = \text{crashed activity cost (with maximum crashing).}$$

We can compute the *maximum* possible activity time reduction, *M,* due to crashing with this formula.

$$M = \tau_n - \tau_c \qquad (19.6)$$

On a per-unit-time basis (for example, per day), the crashing cost, *K,* for each activity is given by

$$K = \frac{C_c - C_n}{M}. \qquad (19.7)$$

For example, if activity a in Figure 19.14 has a normal activity time of three days at a cost of $500, we have $\tau_n = 3$ and $C_n = 500$. Suppose maximum crashing of this activity indicates that for a cost of $800 the activity could be completed in one day. This information provides $\tau_c = 1$ with $C_c = 800$. Thus, using equations 19.6 and 19.7, we see that activity a can be crashed a maximum of $M_c = 3 - 1 = 2$ days at a crashing cost of

$$K_a = \frac{800 - 500}{2} = \frac{300}{2} = \$150 \text{ per day.}$$

We make the assumption that any portion of the activity crash time can be achieved for a corresponding portion of the activity crashing cost. For example, if we decided to crash activity a by only one day, we assume that this would cost $150, and result in a total activity cost of $500 + $150 = $650. The complete normal and crash data for the warehouse-layout activity are given in Table 19.8.

Crashing Activities at Minimum Cost

Now, the question is *which* activities should be crashed and *how much* these activities should be crashed in order to meet the 18-day completion deadline with a minimum added cost. Your first reaction might be to consider crashing the critical-path activities b, d, e, f, and h. Table 19.8 shows us that activities f and h cannot be crashed. However, activity b can be crashed up to a maximum of three days at a cost of $50 per day. This crashing decision would reduce the

Table 19.8 Normal and Crash Data for R. C. Coleman Warehouse-Layout Activity

Activity Subtask	Normal Time τ_n	Crash Time τ_c	Normal Cost C_n	Crash Cost C_c	Maximum Crash Days $(M = \tau_n - \tau_c)$	Crash Cost per Day $K = \dfrac{C_c - C_n}{M}$
a	3	1	$ 500	$ 800	2	$150
b	6	3	800	950	3	50
c	2	1	900	1,100	1	200
d	5	3	500	800	2	150
e	4	3	400	500	1	100
f	3	*	600	—	—	—
g	9	5	1,000	1,320	4	80
h	3	*	300	—	—	—

*These activities cannot be crashed.

b–d–e–f–h path to the desired 18-day completion; the total added cost would be $150. While this looks like a good decision, it is important to realize that crashing some activities may cause other activities to form a new critical path. For example, if b is crashed from six to three days, a–c–d–e–f–h will become the new critical path, with a completion time of 20 days, which would not meet the 18-day completion time. Thus care must be taken in making crashing decisions.

Let us reconsider the crashing decision for the warehouse-layout network shown in Figure 19.18. If we crash b by more than one day ($50 per day), we must also crash a and/or c. Since the cost of crashing a and c is relatively high, let us try to crash other activities on the current critical path. Because the cost to crash activity d is $150 per day and the cost to crash activity e is $100 per day, suppose we decide to crash the less expensive activity e.

Since activity e can be crashed for a maximum of one day, the final day of crashing then comes from activity d ($150). Checking other paths in the network, we find that crashing activities b, d, and e by one day each ($50 + $150 + $100) enables us to meet the 18-day completion time with a total added cost of $300.

In reaching these crashing decisions, we took a trial-and-error approach, testing the desirability of each crashing decision by inspecting the network to determine how it would affect other activities in the project. Although this approach can be effective with rather small networks, it is less so with larger networks. Another approach for determining optimal crashing uses a linear programming model of the problem.

Figure 19.18
Warehouse-Layout Network
for R. C. Coleman Project

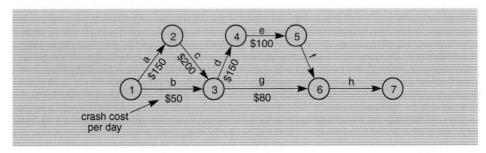

Linear Programming Model for Crashing Decisions

To construct a linear programming model for the crashing decision, we define the following decision variables.

$$x_i = \text{time of occurrence of Event i}$$

$$y_j = \text{amount of crash time used for Activity j}$$

Note that the normal-time project cost of $5,000 (obtained by summing the column of normal costs in Table 19.8) does not depend on what crashing decisions we will make. As a result, we can minimize the total project cost (normal costs plus crashing costs) by minimizing the crashing costs. Thus, the linear programming objective function becomes

$$\min 150\,y_a + 50\,y_b + 200\,y_c + 150\,y_d + 100\,y_e + 80\,y_g.$$

The linear programming constraints that must be developed include those that describe the network, limit the activity crash times, and result in meeting the desired project-completion time. Of these, the constraints used to describe the network are perhaps the most difficult, being based on the conditions that

1. The time of occurrence of event i (x_i) must be greater than or equal to the activity-completion times for all activities leading into that event.
2. An activity start time is equal to the occurrence time of its preceding event.
3. An activity time is equal to its normal time less the length of time it is crashed.

Using an event-occurrence time of zero at node 1 ($x_1 = 0$), we can create this set of network-description constraints:

Event 2:   Event 2 must occur no earlier than the time it takes to complete activity a ($3 - y_a$), plus the start time for activity a ($x_1 = 0$). Thus,

$$x_2 \geq 3 - y_a + 0 \qquad \text{or} \qquad x_2 + y_a \geq 3$$

Since two activities lead to event (node) 3, we have these two constraints.
Event 3:

$$x_3 \geq 6 - y_b + 0 \qquad\qquad x_3 + y_b \geq 6$$
$$\text{or}$$
$$x_3 \geq 2 - y_c + x_2 \qquad\qquad x_3 + y_c - x_2 \geq 2$$

Event 4:

$$x_4 \geq 5 - y_d + x_3 \qquad \text{or} \qquad x_4 + y_d - x_3 \geq 5$$

Event 5:

$$x_5 \geq 4 - y_e + x_4 \qquad \text{or} \qquad x_5 + y_e - x_4 \geq 4$$

Event 6: (Note that activity f cannot be crashed, so y_f does not appear here.)

$$x_6 \geq 3 + x_5 \qquad\qquad x_6 - x_5 \geq 3$$
$$\text{or}$$
$$x_6 \geq 9 - y_g + x_3 \qquad\qquad x_6 + y_g - x_3 \geq 9$$

Event 7:

$$x_7 \geq 3 + x_6 \qquad\qquad \text{or} \qquad\qquad x_7 - x_6 \geq 3$$

The maximum allowable crash-time constraints follow.

$$y_a \leq 2$$
$$y_b \leq 3$$
$$y_c \leq 1$$
$$y_d \leq 2$$
$$y_e \leq 1$$
$$y_g \leq 4$$

To account for the desired project completion time of 18 days, we add the constraint

$$x_7 \leq 18.$$

Adding the nonnegativity restrictions and solving this linear programming model (see Supplementary Chapter D), we obtain the following solution.

$$
\begin{array}{ll}
x_2 = 3 & y_a = 0 \\
x_3 = 5 & y_b = 1 \\
x_4 = 9 & y_c = 0 \\
x_5 = 12 & y_d = 1 \\
x_6 = 15 & y_e = 1 \\
x_7 = 18 & y_g = 0
\end{array}
$$

The objective function is $300.

Note that this is the same solution we obtained by using the heuristic procedure. This is a coincidence. Generally the heuristic procedure does not provide the optimal solution.

P/OM in Practice

Relocating St. Vincent's Hospital[1]

St. Vincent's Hospital and Medical Center moved from a 373-bed hillside facility in Portland, Oregon, to a new 403-bed facility five miles away in a suburban area. Due to construction delays, much of the new equipment ordered for installation in the new hospital was delivered to the old hospital and put into use. Thus, when construction of the new facility was completed, a large volume of equipment had to be moved from the old facility to the new one.

A huge variety of planning considerations had to be taken into account. Army vehicles and private ambulances were to be used to move patients; local merchants would be affected by the move; police assistance would be required; and so on. To coordinate these and other activities, a project network was constructed and used as the basic planning tool for activities that began eight months before the move. A portion of this network is shown in Figure 19.19. The entire network contained dozens of activities and events.

The network was developed by first establishing major *milestones* (events) that had to be reached. Activities necessary to accomplish these events were added until the final project definition was complete. Close cooperation with hospital department heads early in the planning process was essential for determining individual moving needs and opening channels of communication. Critical activities

were determined by using a computer program. Lists of activities, scheduled times, and graphical bar charts were automatically provided by the computer program. The input times were updated during the move to show progress and to determine any needs for reallocation of resources.

Although many modifications to plans were made during the process, the basic planning document, the project network, remained unchanged. According to the user, "It remained the constant framework on which all plans were based and developed. The time spent in the early development of sound plans proved to be a wise investment."

It is important to realize that the activities shown in Figure 19.19 were

Figure 19.19 Portion of St. Vincent's Hospital Project Network (heavy arrows denote critical activities).

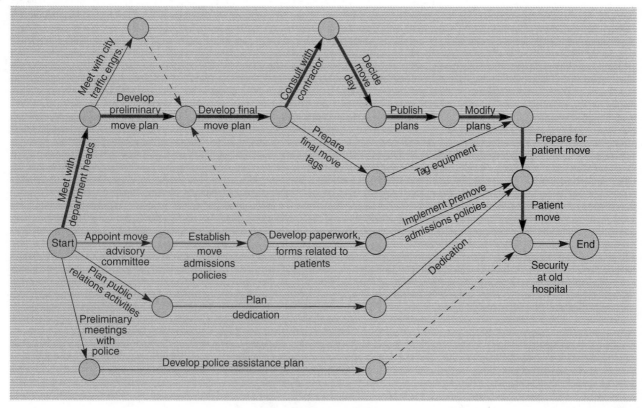

broken down into more detail for actual implementation. For example, for the activity "patient move," managers had to determine which patients to move first (for example, intensive care), the equipment that would have to be in place to support each class of patient, and so on. Again, this illustrates the hierarchical nature of planning and decision making. A network diagram such as this can provide an overall planning structure, but each activity must be implemented by managers at lower levels of the organization.

Questions for Discussion

1. Develop a list of activities and immediate predecessors using the network shown in Figure 19.19.

2. Is there sufficient detail in Figure 19.19 to actually implement the project? Explain.

Project Control for Bechtel Power Corporation[2]

In the Bechtel Power Corporation, project-control activities begin as soon as company managers and the client define the job requirements, the scope of work, overall schedules, and the project's magnitude. Important control documents are prepared and are used to monitor the project during its planning and implementation phases. These include

- *Scope of Services Manual,* which establishes a baseline for identifying changes in services and a definition of engineering, home-office support, and field nonmanual services that will be performed by the company.
- *Division of Responsibility Document,* which describes the responsibilities of the company, the client, and the major suppliers.
- *Project Procedures Manual,* which defines the procedures involved in interface activities among the com-

pany, the client, and the major suppliers with respect to engineering, procurement, construction, preoperational services, quality assurance, quality control, project control, and communication.

- *Technical Scope Document,* which describes the project's physical plant, establishes the design basis, and provides input to the civil/structural, architectural, plant design, mechanical, electrical, and control systems disciplines.
- *Project Activity Control Guide,* which aids in the administration of project activities by identifying and time-phasing the development and execution of project plans, programs, procedures, controls, and other significant activities required for effective operation of the project.

After the project has been defined and the preliminary control documents prepared, the project manager and his team develop the project-control system that will be used throughout the project. The main objectives of the project-control system are to develop a monitorable plan that reflects expected performance of the contract work and to establish a work-control system that provides the information necessary for the team, the company managers, and the client to identify problem areas and initiate corrective action.

The control system includes

- A project plan covering expected scope, schedule, and cost performance.
- A continuous monitoring system that measures the performance against the project plan through the use of modular monitoring tools.
- A reporting system that identifies deviations from the project plan by means of trends and forecasts.

- Timely actions to take advantage of beneficial trends or to correct deviations.

The first activity in project control is the development of a well-conceived project plan that adequately defines the project scope, schedule, and cost. This plan is developed in four stages as the project evolves. It begins with a *proposal schedule* and *cost estimate* based on the scope obtained from the client showing type, size, location, and required services. Following project award, a front-end schedule is implemented to identify activities for the first 12 to 18 months. The process plant layout, major equipment, and key operating parameters are developed during this period.

The *trend base schedule* and *estimate* are established as the second-stage plan. It is used to establish early project budgets (such as engineering and home office costs) for reporting and control.

A trend program, based on this plan, is implemented to provide a mechanism for identifying changes in project technical scope, scope of services, and the current plan of engineering, procurement, and construction. A monthly trend report is developed for the project team, company managers, and client managers. The trend program also identifies scope changes for potential contract changes. It extends through the life of the project.

In the third stage, the *preliminary plan* is developed on the basis of a project technical scope document containing actual project data. It updates the trend base schedule and estimate and ensures that the current plan is consistent with the scope of work.

The more comprehensive *project plan* is the fourth stage. Based on established minimum criteria, it forms the basis for all detailed cost and schedule budgets; therefore, it is necessary that the company and the client concur that the defined scope accurately reflects what will be built. This plan is usually the basis for contractual cost and schedule goals.

Each plan has as its basis for cost, schedule, and material control a definition of the technical scope of the project and the scope of services to be provided. Also identified are milestone dates to be achieved and project procedures to be followed by the client, the company, and major suppliers.

The project plan is scheduled in a hierarchical and sequential manner. The *milestone summary schedule,* comprising about 50 lines of major project milestones, is the basic schedule. It is expanded into engineering, construction and startup *summary schedules* of approximately 500 activities each. Intermediate and detail schedules follow. The *intermediate schedule* contains about 3,000 activities. As each plan develops, the elements of scope, schedule, and cost are integrated by a standard numbering system and are displayed in budgets that are used as a frame of reference for continuous monitoring.

Manual or computerized continuous monitoring tools are used to moni-

tor project progress and identify potential deviations from established budgets. These tools monitor engineering and home-office labor-hours and cost, quantities, schedules, commitments, and the cost of project materials as well as contracts/subcontracts and construction performance.

Work-process flowcharts and quantity takeoffs are used to monitor the design, procurement, and installation of commodities; to identify commodity status; and to identify responsibilities for work functions. These flowcharts depict the information flow from conceptual design through construction and startup. Deviations from the project plan are identified and reported to managers for corrective action. This continuous monitoring of quantities is called *quantity tracking* and is generally computerized.

After the project plan has been prepared, forecasts are made semiannually that reflect the current scope, schedule, and cost of the project. They are the bases for planning the remaining work and updating the schedule. They provide an up-to-date evaluation of project costs and a cur-

rent basis for project monitoring and control.

The project plan, budgets, continuous-monitoring tools, trending/change control, and forecasting produce the information needed by managers to evaluate the current situation and take appropriate action. Client management reports, prepared periodically, include project status, an executive summary, a production summary, and detailed reports about cost, commitments, subcontracts, and work progress.

Project planning and monitoring identify beneficial trends and detrimental deviations. Nonetheless, the action taken by the company-client team is the most critical aspect of the control cycle.

Questions for Discussion

1. What control documents are prepared in order to monitor the project during planning and implementation?
2. What is the purpose of the project control system? What components make up the system?
3. Briefly describe the four stages of the project plan.

Summary of Key Points

••• Project management involves planning, scheduling, and controlling complex projects. Management decisions must take into account time, resources, and cost. Project managers lead project activities, plan and track work progress, and provide direction.

••• The project-planning process consists of project definition, resource planning, project scheduling, and project control.

••• Defining a project involves identifying its activities and events. These are usually graphically represented by a project-network diagram.

••• The most critical resource in project management is time. Activity times are often described by three estimates to allow for uncertainty. Other resources, such

as personnel, capital, and materials, also influence project-management decisions.

••• Project scheduling is aided by Gantt charts and the techniques of PERT and CPM. These methods enable project managers to determine start and completion times for project activities and to determine which activities are critical for meeting established time constraints. Gantt charts are also useful for controlling the progress of projects.

••• With limited resources, project managers must determine appropriate allocations to project activities. Typically, the objective is to minimize the project duration or to smooth the resources over time.

••• Budgetary control is important to ensure that projects are completed within resource limitations. By comparing actual with projected costs at various points in time, managers can determine whether cost overruns or underruns have occured and can make appropriate decisions.

••• Sometimes crashing is necessary, that is, the shortening of completion time by devoting additional resources to certain project activities. Optimal crashing solutions can be found by using a linear programming model.

Key Terms

Project
Project management
Activity
Event
Immediate predecessor
Project network
PERT/CPM network
Node
Branch
Arc
Dummy activity
Optimistic time
Most probable time
Pessimistic time
Average time
Expected time
Work package
Gantt chart
Critical activity
Critical path
Earliest start time
Latest finish time
Slack
Crashing

Review Questions

1. Discuss the three major factors that influence project-management decisions.
2. Describe the role of the project manager. What skills should he or she possess?
3. Discuss the key elements of the project-planning process.
4. Distinguish between an event and an activity.
5. Why are network diagrams used in project management?
6. Explain the use of dummy activities in a project network.
7. Explain what optimistic time, most probable time, and pessimistic time estimates are. How would you estimate these times for a specific activity?

8. Explain the usefulness of Gantt charts to a manager.
9. Define *critical path*. Describe, in your own words, the procedure for finding a critical path.
10. What is the effect of uncertainty of activity times on the total project completion time?
11. Discuss the importance of project control.
12. Explain the processes for budgeting projects and controlling budgets as projects are performed.
13. What is a resource-loading chart, and how is it used?
14. Describe the procedure used for resource leveling.
15. Explain the concept of crashing in project management.
16. Discuss the advantages and disadvantages of using (a) the trial-and-error approach and (b) the linear programming model for crashing decisions.

Discussion Questions

1. Prepare a job profile for a want ad for a project manager.
2. The local chapter of the Operations Management Association is planning a dinner meeting with a nationally known speaker, and you are responsible for organizing it. How could the methodology discussed in this chapter help you?
3. Find an application of project management in your own life (for example, in your home, fraternity, or business organization). List the activities and events that comprise the project, and draw the precedence network. What problems did you encounter in doing this?
4. Discuss how the procedures for finding critical paths would change if activity-on-node networks were used.
5. What are the practical problems in attempting to estimate uncertain activity times?
6. Prepare a report on current available project management software by reviewing some trade publications or talking with practicing project managers.
7. Discuss the rationale for each of the three heuristics proposed for resource allocation in project networks. Under what conditions might each one be preferable?

Notes

1. R. S. Hanson, "Moving the Hospital to a New Location," *Industrial Engineering,* November 1972. Copyright, Institute of Industrial Engineers, 25 Technology Park/Atlanta, Norcross, GA 30092. Adapted with permission.
2. F. A. Hollenbach, "Project Control in Bechtel Power Corporation" in David I. Cleland and William R. King, eds., *Project Management Handbook* (New York: Van Nostrand Reinhold, 1983). Adapted with permission.

Solved Problems

1. Construct a project network for a project with the activities shown in Table 19.9.

Table 19.9 Data for Solved Problem 1

Activity	Immediate Predecessors
A	—
B	—
C	A
D	A
E	C, B
F	C, B
G	D, E

The project is completed when activities F and G are both completed.

Solution
Figure 19.20 is the project network.

Figure 19.20
Solved Problem 1 Solution

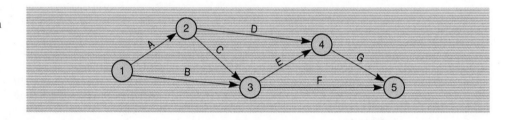

2. Consider the project network in Figure 19.21 (times shown in weeks).

Figure 19.21
Network for Solved
Problem 2

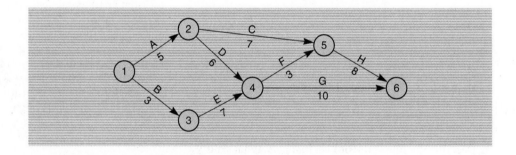

a. Identify the critical path.
b. How long will it take to complete the project?
c. Can activity D be delayed without delaying the entire project? If so, how many weeks?
d. Can activity C be delayed without delaying the entire project? If so, how many weeks?
e. What is the schedule for activity E (that is, start and finish times)?

Solution
a. The critical path is A–D–F–H, as shown in Figure 19.22.

Figure 19.22
Solved Problem 2 Solution

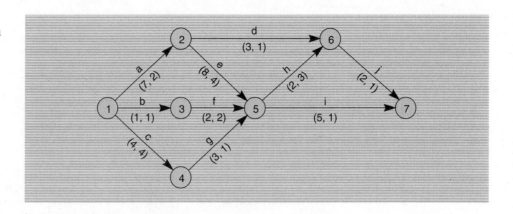

b. 22 weeks.
c. No, it is a critical activity.
d. Yes, 2 weeks (the slack on activity C)
e. Schedule for activity E:

Earliest start	3
Latest start	4
Earliest finish	10
Latest finish	11

3. MamaMia's Pizza is reconfiguring its kitchen to accommodate a new oven and order-entry system. Figure 19.23 is the project network, with expected times (in days) and variances.

Figure 19.23
Project Network for Solved
Problem 3

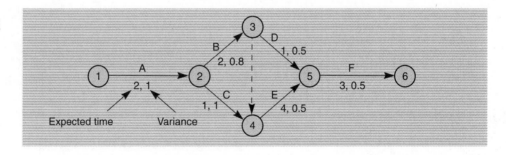

a. What is the expected completion time and variance for the project?
b. What is the probability that the project will meet an eight-day deadline?

Solution
a. The critical path is easy to identify by inspection: A–C–E–F, with an expected completion time of $2 + 1 + 4 + 3 = 10$. The variance of the project time is the sum of the variances on the critical path: $1 + 1 + .5 + .5 = 3.0$.

b.
$$z = \frac{8 - 10}{\sqrt{3.0}} = -1.15$$

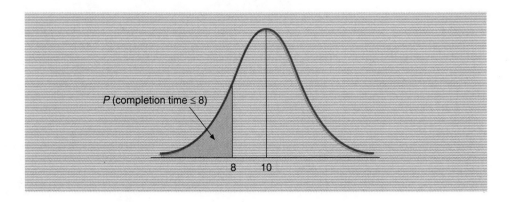

From Appendix B, we see the probability from 0 to z is .3749. Therefore,

$$P \text{ (completion time} \le 8) = .5000 - .3749 = .1251.$$

4. Referring to Solved Problem 2, apply the data given in Table 19.10.

Table 19.10 Data for Solved Problem 4

Activity	Normal Time	Crash Time	Normal Cost	Crash Cost
A	5	4	$ 600	$ 700
B	3	2	1,200	2,000
C	7	4	1,500	3,000
D	6	4	500	1,100
E	7	5	400	600
F	3	2	150	250
G	10	6	800	2,400
H	8	6	1,600	2,600

Formulate a linear programming model for the optimal crashing decision to meet a 19-week deadline.

Solution

Activity	$M = \tau_n - \tau_c$	$K = \dfrac{C_c - C_n}{M}$
A	1	100
B	1	800
C	3	500
D	2	300
E	2	100
F	1	100
G	4	400
H	2	500

$$\min 100y_A + 800y_B + 500y_C + 300\,y_D + 100y_E + 100y_F + 400y_G + 500y_H$$

$$x_1 = 0$$

$$x_2 \geq 5 - y_A$$

$$x_3 \geq 3 - y_B$$

$$x_4 \geq 6 - y_D + x_2$$

$$x_4 \geq 7 - y_E + x_3$$

$$x_5 \geq 7 - y_C + x_2$$

$$x_5 \geq 3 - y_F + x_4$$

$$x_6 \geq 8 - y_H + x_5$$

$$x_6 \geq 10 - y_G + x_4$$

$$y_A \leq 1$$

$$y_B \leq 1$$

$$y_C \leq 3$$

$$y_D \leq 2$$

$$y_E \leq 2$$

$$y_F \leq 1$$

$$y_G \leq 4$$

$$y_H \leq 2$$

$$x_6 \leq 19$$

Problems

1. The Mohawk Discount Store chain is designing a management-training program for individuals at its corporate headquarters. The company would like to design the program so that the trainees can complete it as quickly as possible. There are important precedence relationships that must be maintained between assignments or activities in the program. For example, a trainee cannot serve as an assistant store manager until after she or he has had experience in the credit department and at least one sales department. Table 19.11 shows the activity assignments that must be completed by each trainee:

Table 19.11 Data for Problem 1

Activity	Immediate Predecessors
A	—
B	—
C	A
D	A, B
E	A, B
F	C
G	D, F
H	E, G

Construct a project network for this problem. Do not attempt to perform any further analysis.

2. Consider the project network in Figure 19.24.

Figure 19.24
Network for Problem 2

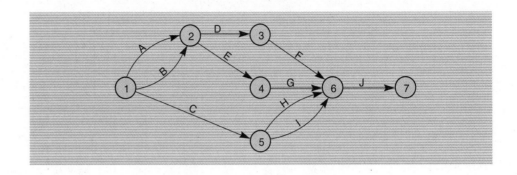

a. Add dummy activities to eliminate the problem of activities having the same starting and ending nodes.

b. Add dummy activities that will satisfy these immediate predecessor requirements:

Activity	Immediate Predecessors
H	B, C
I	B, C
G	D, E

3. Construct a project network for the activities listed in Table 19.12.

Table 19.12 Data for Problem 3

Activity	Immediate Predecessor
A	—
B	—
C	A
D	A, B
E	C, D
F	C, D
G	E
H	F

4. Give the estimates in Table 19.13 of activity times (days) for a small project, compute the expected activity-completion times and the variance for each activity.

Table 19.13 Data for Problem 4

Activity	Optimistic Time	Most Probable Time	Pessimistic Time
A	4	5	7
B	8	9	12
C	7	7.5	11
D	7	9	10
E	4	7	9
F	5	6	7

5. Construct an early-start schedule using a Gantt chart for the project network in Figure 19.25.

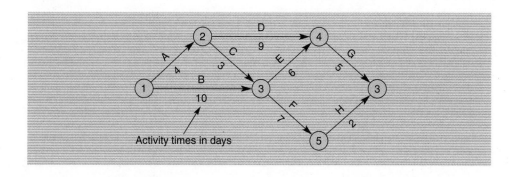

6. Construct an early-start schedule using a Gantt chart for the project network in Figure 19.26.

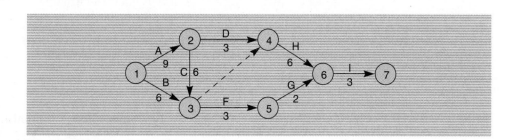

7. Consider the project network in Figure 19.27.

Figure 19.27
Network for Problem 7

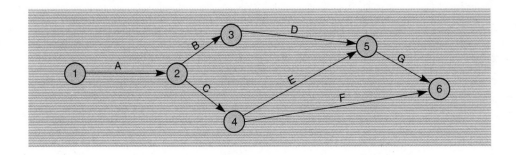

The appropriate managers have made the estimates shown in Table 19.14 for the optimistic, most probable, and pessimistic times (in days) for completion of the activities.

Table 19.14 Data for Problem 7

Activity	Optimistic Time	Most Probable Time	Pessimistic Time
A	1	4	7
B	2	3	10
C	4	4	10
D	3	5	7
E	1	7	7
F	2	9	10
G	2	3	4

a. Compute the expected activity times and the variances.
b. Construct an early-start Gantt chart.
c. Which activities are critical?
8. Suppose you are in charge of planning and coordinating next spring's sales-management training program. The activity information for this project is listed in Table 19.15.
a. Draw the project network for the problem.
b. Compute expected activity times.
c. Construct an early-start Gantt chart.

Table 19.15 Data for Problem 8

Activity	Description	Immediate Predecessors	Optimistic Time	Most Probable Time	Pessimistic Time
A	Plan topic	—	1.5	2	2.5
B	Obtain speakers	A	2	2.5	6
C	List meeting locations	—	1	2	3
D	Select location	C	1.5	2	2.5
E	Speaker travel plans	B, D	0.5	1	1.5
F	Final check with speakers	E	1	2	3
G	Prepare and mail brochure	B, D	3	3.5	7
H	Take reservations	G	3	4	5
I	Last-minute details	F, H	1.5	2	2.5

9. Maffei Manufacturing Co. is planning to install a new flexible manufacturing system. The activities that must be performed, their immediate predecessors, and estimated activity times are shown in Table 19.16. Draw the project network and find the critical path.

Table 19.16 Data for Problem 9

Activity	Description	Immediate Predecessors	Estimated Activity Time (days)
A	Analyze current performance	—	3
B	Identify goals	A	1
C	Conduct study of existing operation	A	6
D	Define new system capabilities	B	7
E	Study existing technologies	—	2
F	Determine specifications	D	9
G	Conduct equipment analyses	C, F	10
H	Identify implementation activities	C	3
I	Determine organizational impacts	H	4
J	Prepare report	E, G, I	2
K	Establish audit procedure	H	1

10. Colonial State College is considering building a new athletic complex on campus. The complex would provide a new gymnasium for intercollegiate basketball games, expanded office space, classrooms, and intramural facilities. The activities that would have to be completed before beginning construction are listed in Table 19.17.

Table 19.17 Data for Problem 10

Activity	Description	Immediate Predecessors	Time (weeks)
A	Survey building site	—	6
B	Develop initial design	—	8
C	Obtain board approval	A, B	12
D	Select architect	C	4
E	Establish budget	C	6
F	Finalize design	D, E	15
G	Obtain financing	E	12
H	Hire contractor	F, G	8

a. Develop a project network for this project.
b. Identify the critical path.
c. Develop a detailed schedule for all activities in the project.
d. Does it appear reasonable that construction could begin one year after the decision to begin the project? What is the project-completion time?

11. Suppose the estimates of activity times (weeks) were as shown in Table 19.18 for the network shown in Solved Problem 2.

Table 19.18 Data for Problem 11

Activity	Optimistic Time	Most Probable Time	Pessimistic Time
A	4	5	6
B	2.5	3	3.5
C	6	7	8
D	5	5.5	9
E	5	7	9
F	2	3	4
G	8	10	12
H	6	7	14

What is the probability that the project will be completed within
a. 20 weeks?
b. 22 weeks?
c. 24 weeks?
12. Consider the project network in Figure 19.28.

Figure 19.28
Network for Problem 12

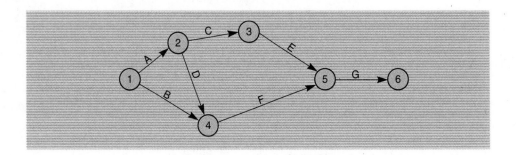

In Table 19.19 the appropriate managers have made estimates of the optimistic, most probable, and pessimistic times (in days) for completion of the activities.

Table 19.19 Data for Problem 12

Activity	Optimistic Time	Most Probable Time	Pessimistic Time
A	5	6	7
B	5	12	13
C	6	8	10
D	4	10	10
E	5	6	13
F	7	7	10
G	4	7	10

a. Find the critical path.
b. How much slack time, if any, is there for activity C?
c. Determine the expected project-completion time and the variance.
d. Find the probability that the project will be completed in 30 days or less.

13. A competitor of Kozar International, Inc., has begun marketing a new instant-developing film project. Kozar has had a similar product under study in its R&D department but has not yet been able to begin production. Because of the competitor's action, top managers have asked for a speedup of R&D activities so that Kozar can produce and market instant film at the earliest possible date. The network for the project and the activity time estimates in months are shown in Figure 19.29 and Table 19.20.

Figure 19.29
Network for Problem 13

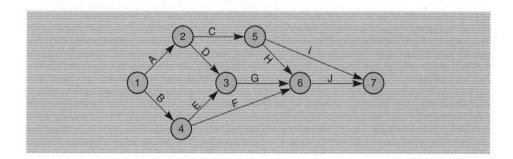

Table 19.20 Data for Problem 13

Activity	Optimistic Time	Most Probable Time	Pessimistic Time
A	1	1.5	5
B	3	4	5
C	1	2	3
D	3.5	5	6.5
E	4	5	12
F	6.5	7.5	11.5
G	5	9	13
H	3	4	5
I	2	3	4
J	2	2.5	6

a. Develop an activity schedule for this project, and define the critical activities.
b. What is the probability the project will be completed in time for Kozar to begin marketing the new product within one and a half years? within two years?

14. The product-development group at Landon Corporation has been working on a new computer software product that has the potential to capture a large market share. Through outside sources, Landon's managers have learned that a competitor is working to bring a similar product to market. As a result, Landon's top managers have increased pressure on the product-development group. The group's leader has turned to PERT/CPM as an aid in scheduling the activities remaining before the new product can be brought to the market. The project network she developed and her activity time estimates in weeks are shown in Figure 19.30 and Table 19.21.

Figure 19.30
Network for Problem 14

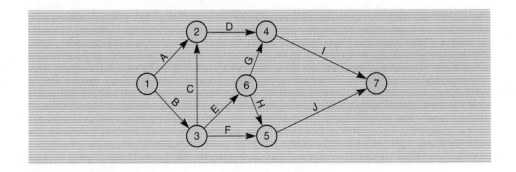

Table 19.21 Data for Problem 14

Activity	Optimistic Time	Most Probable Time	Pessimistic Time
A	3	4	5
B	3	3.5	7
C	4	5	6
D	2	3	4
E	6	10	14
F	7.5	8.5	12.5
G	4.5	6	7.5
H	5	6	13
I	2	2.5	6
J	4	5	6

a. Develop an activity schedule for this project, and identify the critical-path activities.
b. What is the probability that the project will be completed so that Landon Corporation can introduce the new product within 25 weeks? Within 30 weeks?
15. For the R. C. Coleman project, suppose that managers had originally started with the schedule given in Figure 19.4. After 13 weeks, the project's status is as follows:

Activity A was completed in six weeks.
Activity B was completed in four weeks.
Activity C was completed in two weeks.
Activity D was delayed four weeks.
Activity H is anticipating a one-week delay.

What is the status of the remainder of the project, and what revised schedule should be followed?
16. Develop a budget for the R. C. Coleman project, assuming that all activities are begun at their *latest* starting times.

17. Consider the project network in Figure 19.31 with the expected activity costs in Table 19.22.

Figure 19.31
Network for Problem 17

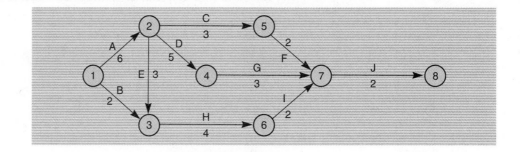

Table 19.22 Data for Problem 17

Activity	Expected Cost (Thousands of $)
A	$ 90
B	16
C	3
D	100
E	6
F	2
G	60
H	20
I	4
J	2

Develop a total-cost budget based on both an earliest-start and a latest-start schedule.
18. Consider the project network in Figure 19.32 and the activity time and cost data in Table 19.23.

Figure 19.32
Network for Problem 18

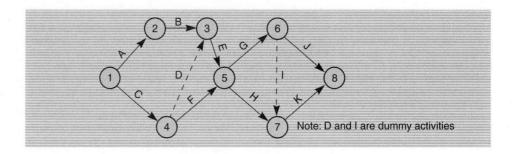

Note: D and I are dummy activities

Table 19.23 Data for Problem 18

Activity	Expected Time (weeks)	Variance	Budgeted Cost
A	3	.3	$ 6,000
B	2	.5	4,000
C	8	2.0	16,000
D	0	.0	0
E	6	1.0	18,000
F	4	.2	20,000
G	5	.4	15,000
H	1	.1	2,000
I	0	.0	0
J	5	1.0	5,000
K	6	.6	12,000

a. Develop an activity schedule for the project.
   i. What is the critical path?
   ii. What is the expected completion date?
   iii. What is the probability of meeting a desired six-month (26-week) completion date?
b. Develop a budget for total project costs over the project's duration. What should the range be for expenditures after 12 weeks of the project?

19. Referring to the network in Problem 18, suppose that after 12 weeks of operation the data shown in Table 19.24 are available on all completed and in-process activities.

Table 19.24 Data for Problem 19

Activity	Actual Cost	% Completion
A	$ 5,000	100
B	4,000	100
C	18,000	100
E	9,000	50
F	18,000	75

Is the project in control based on both time and cost considerations? What corrective action, if any, is desirable?

20. Two astronauts for the next space shuttle flight are performing a variety of scientific experiments, many of which depend on the results of previous experiments. Some experiments require both astronauts working together; others can be performed by either one. Figure 19.33 gives the sequence of experiments along with the time required and number of astronauts needed. Use both the shortest-time-first rule and longest-time-first rule to schedule these experiments. Compare your results.

Figure 19.33
Network for Problem 20

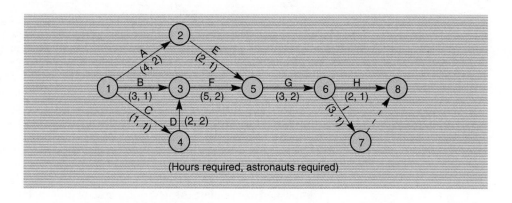

(Hours required, astronauts required)

21. Consider Figure 19.34, a network with activity times shown in days, and the crash data for the project from Table 19.25.

Figure 19.34
Network for Problem 21

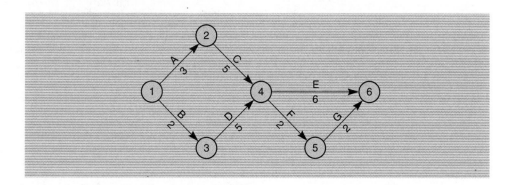

Table 19.25 Data for Problem 21

Activity	Normal Time	Crash Time	Normal Cost	Crash Cost
A	3	2	$ 800	$1,400
B	2	1	1,200	1,900
C	5	3	2,000	2,800
D	5	3	1,500	2,300
E	6	4	1,800	2,800
F	2	1	600	1,000
G	2	1	500	1,000

a. Find the critical path and the expected project duration.
b. What is the total project cost using the normal times?

c. If a project must be crashed, a logical, or commonsense, approach is to crash the least expensive critical activity. Assuming managers desire a 12-day project completion, which critical-path activity would be crashed using the least-expensive-critical-activity philosophy?

d. As the critical-path activities are crashed, other paths may become critical, requiring further crashing decisions. For the crashing decision you made in part c, compute the new critical path and crash additionally as necessary to meet the 12-day project-completion date. What is the activity schedule and total project cost required to meet the 12-day completion date?

22. Office Automation, Inc., has developed a proposal for introducing a new computerized office system that will improve word processing and interoffice communications for a particular company. Contained in the proposal is a list of activities that must be accomplished to complete the new office-system project. Information about the activities is shown in Table 19.26.

Table 19.26 Data for Problem 22

Activity	Description	Immediate Predecessors	Normal Time	Crash Time	Normal Cost	Crash Cost
A	Plan needs	—	10	8	$ 30	$ 70
B	Order equipment	A	8	6	120	150
C	Install equipment	B	10	7	100	160
D	Set up training lab	A	7	6	40	50
E	Training course	D	10	8	50	75
F	Test system	C, E	3	—	60	—

Times are in weeks and costs are in thousands of dollars.

a. Show the network for the project.

b. Develop an activity schedule for the project using normal times.

c. What are the critical-path activities, and what is the expected project-completion time?

d. Assume the company wants to complete the project in 26 weeks. What crashing decisions would you recommend for meeting the completion date at the least possible cost? Work through the network, and attempt to make the crashing decisions by inspection.

e. Develop an activity schedule for the crashed project.

f. What is the added project cost to meet the 26-week completion time?

23. Consider the project network in Figure 19.35 and the activity costs in Table 19.27.

Figure 19.35
Network for Problem 23

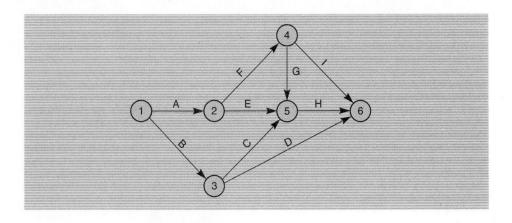

Table 19.27 Data for Problem 23

Activity	Normal Time	Crash Time	Normal Cost	Crash Cost
A	3	2	$ 8,000	$ 9,000
B	8	6	600	1,000
C	6	4	10,000	12,000
D	5	2	4,000	10,000
E	13	10	3,000	9,000
F	4	4	5,000	5,000
G	2	1	1,200	1,400
H	6	4	3,500	4,500
I	2	1	700	800

a. Find the critical path and the minimum project-duration time.

b. If a deadline of 17 time periods is imposed, what activities should be crashed, what is the crashing cost, and what are the critical activities of the crashed network?

24. Refer to Problem 21. Assume that managers desire a 12-day project-completion time.

a. Formulate a linear programming model that can be used to assist with the crashing decisions.

b. What activities should be crashed?

c. What is the total project cost for the 12-day completion time?

25. A computer-system installation project consists of eight activities. The immediate predecessors and activity times in weeks are given in Table 19.28.

Table 19.28 Data for Problem 25

Activity	Immediate Predecessor	Time
A	—	3
B	—	6
C	A	2
D	B, C	5
E	D	4
F	E	3
G	B, C	9
H	F, G	3

a. Draw the project network for this project.

b. What are the critical-path activities?

c. What is the project completion time?

d. Assume that the project must be completed in 16 weeks. Crashing of the project is necessary. Relevant information is shown in Table 19.29. Formulate a linear programming model that can be used to make the crashing decisions for this network.

e. Solve the linear programming model and make the minimum-cost crashing decisions. What is the added cost of meeting the 16-week completion time?

f. Develop a complete activity schedule using the crashed activity times.

Table 19.29 Additional Data for Problem 25

Activity	Normal Time	Crash Time	Normal Cost	Crash Cost
A	3	1	$ 900	$1,700
B	6	3	2,000	4,000
C	2	1	500	1,000
D	5	3	1,800	2,400
E	4	3	1,500	1,850
F	3	1	3,000	3,900
G	9	4	8,000	9,800
H	3	2	1,000	2,000

26. The R. A. Hamilton Company has manufactured home workshop tools for a number of years. Recently, a member of the company's new-product research team submitted a report suggesting the company consider manufacturing a heavy-duty cordless electric drill that could be powered by a special rechargeable battery. Because no other manufacturer currently has such a product, management hopes that the product can be manufactured at a reasonable cost and that its portability will make it extremely attractive.

   Hamilton's top managers have initiated a project to study the feasibility of this idea. The end result of the feasibility project will be a report recommending the action to be taken for this new product. The project manager has identified a list of activities and a range of times necessary to complete each activity. This information is given in Table 19.30.

Table 19.30 Data for Problem 26

Activity	Description	Immediate Predecessors	Times (weeks) a	m	b
A	R&D product design	—	3	7	11
B	Plan market research	—	2	2.5	6
C	Manufacturing process study	A	2	3	4
D	Build prototype model	A	6	7	14
E	Prepare market questionnaire	A	2	3	4
F	Develop cost estimates	C	2.5	3	3.5
G	Preliminary product testing	D	2.5	4	5.5
H	Market survey	B, E	4.5	5.5	9.5
I	Pricing and forecast report	H	1	2	3
J	Final report	F, G, I	1	2	3

a.   Develop a complete PERT/CPM analysis for this project. Include the project network, a calculation of expected times and variances, the critical activities, and the earliest possible project-completion date. In addition, construct an early-start Gantt chart and compute probabilities for completing the project by weeks 18, 20, 22, and 24. Discuss how this information can be used by the R. A. Hamilton project manager.

b.   The costs for each activity are given in Table 19.31. Develop a total-cost budget based on both an earliest-start and a latest-start schedule. Also, prepare an analysis for each of the three points in time shown in Table 19.32. For each case, show the percentage overrun or underrun for the project to date, and indicate any corrective action that should be undertaken. Why is this information important to the project manager? (Note: If an activity is not listed, assume that it has not been started.)

Table 19.31 Cost Data for Problem 26

Activity	Expected Cost (Thousands of $)
A	$ 90
B	16
C	3
D	100
E	6
F	2
G	60
H	20
I	4
J	2

Table 19.32 Problem 26

Activity	Actual Cost (Thousands of $)	% Completion
At the end of fifth week		
A	$ 62	80%
B	6	50
At end of tenth week		
A	$ 85	100%
B	16	100
C	1	33
D	$100	80
E	4	100
H	10	25
At end of fifteenth week		
A	$ 85	
B	16	
C	3	
D	105	
E	4	100%
F	3	
G	55	
H	25	
I	4	

Supplementary Chapter A Computer Simulation

Chapter Outline

Computer simulation techniques are used to describe the behavior of real-world systems over time. A *system* is usually described by a logical flowchart detailing the sequence of steps performed. A computer program is written that simulates—mimics—the detailed actions that occur in the system. For example, in simulating a manufacturing facility, the program would track each job as it moves from machine to machine and maintain statistics on how long the job may have waited for processing and the total time taken to complete the job. Other factors such as machine breakdowns can be included in the simulation to add realism and complexity to the model.

Computer simulation is an important tool in P/OM because it can be used to model and analyze an extremely wide variety of practical situations that cannot be approached by other types of statistical or management-science models. Many practical problems are so complex that it is impossible to determine exact relationships among decision variables. Other practical problems have high levels of uncertainty that preclude the use of traditional methods of analysis. Simulation modeling can overcome these difficulties. In general, as the number of probabilistic components of a system increases, the more likely it is that simulation will be the best approach.

There are other advantages in using computer simulation. One is that the simulation model provides a convenient experimental laboratory. Once the computer program has been developed, it is usually relatively easy to experiment with the model. An analyst can perform "what if" studies—that is, change the design characteristics or operating rules to determine their impact without changing the actual system. For instance, the number of jobs entering a manufacturing facility can be changed to learn the effect of greater demand on waiting times.

Simulation models have proven useful at all levels of decision making, including strategic business planning. They are also used extensively to analyze and design manufacturing processes, to determine inventory and capacity policies, and to model production-control and material-management systems.

Because of its many advantages, simulation is perhaps the most often used tool in management science today. In this supplementary chapter we introduce the basic concepts of computer simulation by discussing its use in waiting-line situations. The use of simulation in inventory analysis is described in Chapter 14.

Lincoln Savings Bank Drive-in Window Problem

Lincoln Savings Bank has been having difficulty in servicing customers at its Forest Park branch drive-in window during the peak Saturday-morning period. Long waiting lines during this period have resulted in customer complaints. The branch manager has suggested that a study be conducted to investigate alternatives for improving service.

Figure A.1 describes the logic of the system's operation. Drivers enter the system and approach the drive-in window. If cars are already at the window, the new arrival must wait in line until the drivers ahead have been serviced. Otherwise, the driver proceeds to the window, processes his or her transactions, and leaves.

In modeling this system, we count the number of arrivals and determine whether or not a customer is being serviced during each one-minute interval. Then we consider what happens during the next one-minute interval, and so forth. A simulation model that increments time in fixed intervals like this is referred to as a **fixed-time simulation model.** Simulation models that increment time by the occurrence of the next event (time of next arrival, time of next service, and so on) are referred to as *next-event simulation models* (introduced later in the chapter). During this process, we keep track of such information as the number of cars waiting, the number of arrivals, and the number of cars serviced by the drive-in window during each minute. These statistics form the basis for the simulation results, which will be analyzed by the branch manager.

Preliminary Data Analysis

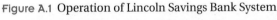

From a study of traffic flow, the bank estimated the probability distribution of customer arrivals as shown in Table A.1 for the peak business period on Saturday morning. As the data show, there is a .55 probability of no customer arriving during a given one-minute period, a .25 probability of one customer arriving, and so on.

Historical data also show that the time to service a customer ranges from one to four minutes. Using these data, the bank estimated the probability distribution of service time, also shown in Table A.1.

Figure A.1 Operation of Lincoln Savings Bank System

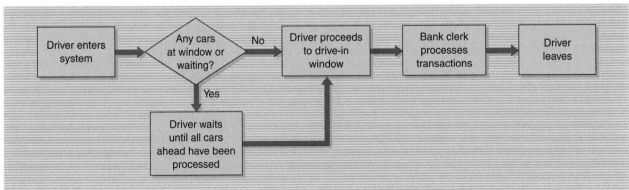

Table A.1 Probability Distribution for Arrivals and Service Times

Number of Customers Arriving	Probability	Service Time (minutes)	Probability
0	.55	1	.50
1	.25	2	.30
2	.10	3	.15
3	.10	4	.05
	1.00		1.00

Simulation of Customer Arrivals

Before developing the complete simulation model, we concentrate on simulating the number of customers arriving during any one-minute period. Our example of Lincoln Savings Bank shows how the probabilistic component of a real-world process or system is modeled.

The technique used to simulate customer arrivals is based on the use of random numbers, a familiar part of basic statistics.[1] A table of random numbers is found in Appendix C of this book. Twenty random numbers from the first line of this table follow.

63271   59986   71744   51102

The specific digit appearing in a given position is a random selection of the digits 0, 1, 2, . . ., 9, with each digit having an equal chance of selection. The grouping of the numbers in sets of five is simply for the convenience of making the table easier to read.

Suppose we select random numbers from the table in sets of two digits. There are 100 two-digit random numbers from 00 to 99, with each two-digit random number having a $1/100 = .01$ chance of occurring. While we could select two-digit random numbers from any part of the random number table, suppose we start by using the first row of Appendix C. The first 10 of the two-digit random numbers are the following.

63   27   15   99   86   71   74   45   11   02

Now let us see how we can simulate the number of customers arriving in a one-minute period by associating a given number of arrivals with each of these two-digit random numbers. For example, let us consider the possibility of no customers arriving during that interval. The probability distribution in Table A.1 shows this event to have a .55 probability for each minute. Since each of the two-digit random numbers has a .01 probability of occurrence, we can let 55 of the 100 possible two-digit random numbers correspond to no customers arriving. Any 55 numbers from 00 to 99 will do, but for convenience we associate the arrival of zero customers with the first 55 two-digit numbers: 00, 01, 02, 03, . . ., 54. Thus any time one of these two-digit numbers is observed in a random selection, we will say that no customers arrived during that period. Because the numbers 00 to 54 include 55 percent of the possible two-digit random numbers, we expect the arrival of no customers for any given one-minute interval to have a probability of .55.

Table A.2 Random-Number Assignments for Customers Arriving at Drive-in Window During One-Minute Period

Interval	Simulated Arrivals	Probability
00–54	0	.55
55–79	1	.25
80–89	2	.10
90–99	3	.10
		1.00

Table A.3 Simulated Customer Arrivals at Drive-in Window During 10 One-Minute Periods

Period	Random Number	Simulated Customer Arrivals
1	63	1
2	27	0
3	15	0
4	99	3
5	86	2
6	71	1
7	74	1
8	45	0
9	11	0
10	02	0
Total arrivals (10 minutes)		8

Now consider the possibility of one customer arriving during a one-minute period, an event with a .25 probability of occurring (see Table A.1). Letting 25 of the 100 two-digit numbers (such as 55, 56, 57, 58, . . ., 79) correspond to a simulated arrival of one customer will provide a .25 probability for one customer arriving. Continuing to assign the number of customers arriving to sets of two-digit numbers according to the probability distribution shown in Table A.1 results in the number and customer-arrival assignments shown in Table A.2.

Using Table A.2 and the two-digit random numbers in the first row of Appendix C (63, 27, 15, 99, 86, . . .), we can simulate the number of customers arriving during each one-minute period of the three minutes. The results for 10 such one-minute periods are shown in Table A.3. Note, for example, that the first two-digit random number, 63, is in the interval 55–79; thus, according to Table A.2 this corresponds to one customer arriving during the first one-minute period.

By selecting a two-digit random number for each one-minute period, we can simulate the number of customer arrivals during that period. This number is the same as the probability distribution given in Table A.1. Thus, the simulation of customer arrivals has the same characteristics as the specified distribution of customer arrivals.

For any simulation model it is relatively easy to apply this random-number procedure to simulate values of a random variable. First develop a table similar

Table A.4 Random-Number Assignments for Customer Service Times at the Bank Drive-in Window

Interval	Service Time	Probability
00–49	1 minute	.50
50–79	2 minutes	.30
80–94	3 minutes	.15
95–99	4 minutes	.05
		1.00

to Table A.2 by associating an interval of random numbers with each possible value of the random variable. In doing so, be sure the probability of selecting a random number from each interval is the same as the actual probability associated with the value of the random variable. Then each time a value of the random variable is needed, simply select a new random number and use the corresponding interval of random numbers to find the value of the random variable. Using a similar procedure, we see that the random-number intervals given in Table A.4 can be used to simulate service times for customers at the Lincoln Savings Bank drive-in window.

Simulation Model for Lincoln Savings Bank Drive-in Window

Now that we know how to simulate the number of customers arriving and the service times, let us proceed with the development of the logic for the Lincoln Bank simulation model.

Whenever we need to generate a value for the number of customers arriving and/or the service time, we use the random numbers from row 10 of Appendix C. Tables A.2 and A.4 are used to determine the corresponding number of customer arrivals and the service times. For convenience, the first five two-digit random numbers from row 10 are reproduced here.

81   62   83   61   00

In developing the logic and mathematical relationships for the simulation model, we follow the logic and relationships of the actual operation as closely as possible. To demonstrate the simulation process, we begin with an idle, or empty, system and simulate what happens for each of the first three periods (Figures A.2 through A.4). Try to follow the logic of the model and see if you agree with the statements in the "Things That Happen" columns.

The flowchart of the simulation model we have been using is shown in Figure A.5. Continue to use the random numbers from row 10 of Appendix C and see if you can conduct the simulation calculations for the first 10 periods of operation. Your simulation results should agree with those in Table A.5.

At this point we have succeeded in simulating 10 periods, or a total of 10 minutes of operation. Although the results in Table A.5 do not show evidence of long waiting lines, a 10-minute simulation period is too short a time frame for

Figure A.2
Status of System for First
One-Minute Simulation
Period

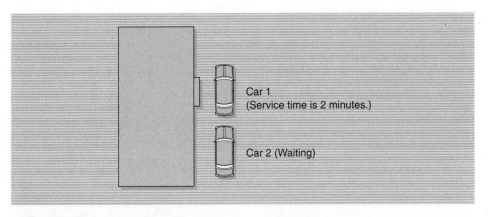

Random Number	Things That Happen
81	Two cars arrive for service; the first car, identified as car 1, gets immediate service.
62	The service time for car 1 is 2 minutes, so this car will not be finished until the end of period 2.

Figure A.3
Status of System for Second
One-Minute Simulation
Period

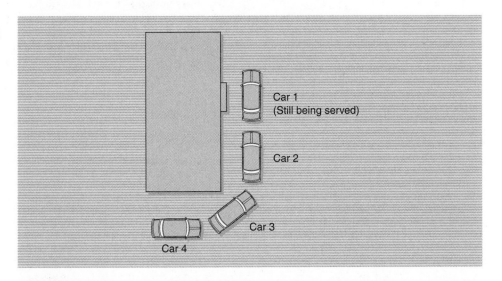

Random Number	Things That Happen
83	Two more cars, identified as cars 3 and 4, arrive for service. The drive-in window is still busy serving the customer from period 1; thus a total of three cars (one waiting plus two new customers) are waiting for service this period.

Figure A.4
Status of System for Third
One-Minute Simulation
Period

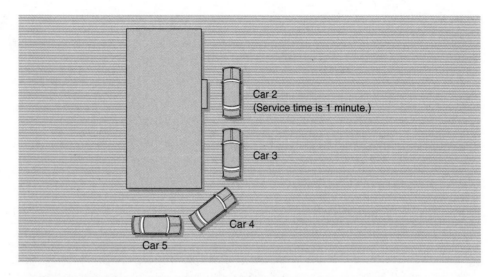

Random Number	Things That Happen
61	One more car, identified as car 5, arrives for service. This service area is free at the beginning of this period, since the customer from period 1 (car 1) has completed service and left the bank. One car from the waiting line (car 2) begins service, leaving three cars still awaiting service.
00	The service time for the customer in car 2 is 1 minute, and thus car 2 will finish service at the end of this period.

Figure A.5 Flowchart of Lincoln Savings Bank Simulation Model

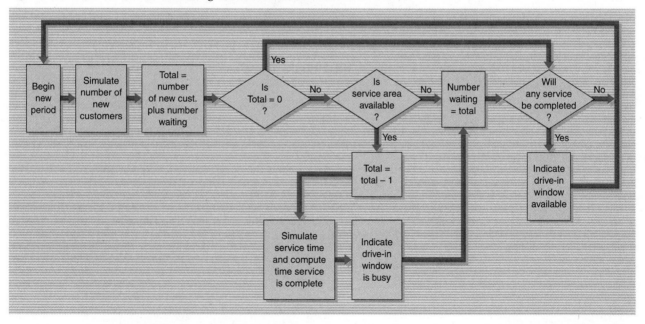

Table A.5 Simulation Results from 10 One-Minute Periods at Lincoln Bank Drive-in Window

Period	Random Number	Number of New Customers	Is Service Area Available?	Random Number	Service Time	Number Waiting	Was Service Completed This Period?
1	81	2	Yes	62	2	1	No
2	83	2	No	—	—	3	Yes
3	61	1	Yes	00	1	3	Yes
4	39	0	Yes	25	1	2	Yes
5	45	0	Yes	68	2	1	No
6	35	0	No	—	—	1	Yes
7	37	0	Yes	63	2	0	No
8	60	1	No	—	—	1	Yes
9	24	0	Yes	21	1	0	Yes
10	98	3	Yes	06	1	2	Yes

drawing general conclusions about the operation of the drive-in system. To take full advantage of the simulation procedure, we must continue to simulate the system's operation for many more time periods. But even for this relatively small simulation problem, continuing the hand simulation computations as we have been doing is obviously impractical, if not impossible. Thus we look to the computer for the necessary assistance.

Computer Simulation: Generating Pseudorandom Numbers

Spreadsheet programs have the capability of generating numbers which, for all practical purposes, have the same properties as the numbers selected from random-number tables. These numbers are called **pseudorandom numbers.** In computer simulations pseudorandom numbers are used in exactly the same way as we used the random numbers selected from random-number tables.

Most mathematical formulas designed to generate pseudorandom numbers produce numbers from 0 up to, but not including, 1. Thus we must now associate an interval of pseudorandom numbers with each number of arrivals so that the probability of generating a pseudorandom number in the interval will be equal to the probability of the corresponding number of arrivals. Table A.6 shows how this can be done for the number of cars arriving at the Lincoln Savings Bank drive-in window. Note that Table A.6 shows that a pseudorandom

Table A.6 Pseudorandom-Number Intervals and Associated Number of Customer Arrivals

Interval of Pseudorandom Numbers	Simulated Customer Arrivals	Probability
.00 but less than .55	0	.55
.55 but less than .80	1	.25
.80 but less than .90	2	.10
.90 but less than 1.00	3	.10
		1.00

Table A.7 Pseudorandom-Number Intervals and Associated Service Times for Customers

Interval of Pseudorandom Numbers	Service Time (minutes)	Probability
.00 but less than .50	1	.50
.50 but less than .80	2	.30
.80 but less than .95	3	.15
.95 but less than 1.00	4	.05
		1.00

number less than .55 corresponds to no arrivals, that a pseudorandom number greater than or equal to .55 but less than .80 corresponds to one arrival, and so on. Table A.7 provides the pseudorandom-number intervals that can be used to simulate the service times for customers.

Spreadsheet Simulation for Lincoln Savings Bank Problem

Figure A.6 is an Excel spreadsheet implementation of the Lincoln Savings Bank problem. The logic of the cell formulas is best understood by studying them, as they depend on various IF, AND, and OR logic operations. The VLOOKUP function is used to select outcomes from the arrival and service time distributions. Observe that the results differ from those in Table A.5 because different random numbers were used to generate customer arrivals and service times. You must therefore be cautious in interpreting simulation results. To obtain useful results, a simulation program should be run several times with different sets of random numbers so that variations in the results can be assessed.

Figure A.7 shows the number waiting from the simulation for 100 minutes of operation. As you can see, conclusions about the system drawn from this simulation would certainly differ from those drawn on the basis of the 10-minute simulations; the number of customers waiting grows significantly. Recall that a primary objective of simulation is to describe the behavior of a real system. Do these results agree with what the bank manager would actually observe? Of course not. In the actual system, a customer will either park the car and transact business inside the bank or leave and return at another time if the line is too long. An important step in any simulation study is the **validation** of the simulation model—that is, showing that it accurately represents the real-world system it is designed to simulate.

For the Lincoln Savings Bank, the branch manager has observed that there are seldom more than four or five cars waiting at the drive-in window. Thus it appears that drivers will not join the waiting line (technically, this is called *balking*) if four or more cars are already waiting. The computer program could be modified to reflect this behavior. (How would the flowchart in Figure A.5 change?) By finding how many customers balk, the branch manager would have a better measure of customer dissatisfaction.

Since the simulation results indicate that a single drive-in window cannot handle the amount of business anticipated during peak periods on Saturday mornings, the manager might investigate the effect of adding a second drive-in

Figure A.6 Spreadsheet
Implementation of Lincoln
Savings Bank Problem
(LINCOLN.XLS)

	A	B	C	D	E	F	G	H	I
1	Lincoln Savings Bank Simulation								
2									
3	Arrival Distribution				Service Time Distribution				
4	Random Number		Number of		Random Number		Number of		
5	Interval		Arrivals		Interval		Arrivals		
6	0.00	0.55	0		0.00	0.50	1		
7	0.55	0.80	1		0.50	0.80	2		
8	0.80	0.90	2		0.80	0.95	3		
9	0.90	1.00	3		0.95	1.00	4		
10									
11		Random	Number of	Server	Random	Service	Number	Service	
12	Time Period	Number	Arrivals	Available?	Number	Time	Waiting	Completion?	
13							0		
14	1	0.811	2	YES	0.421	1	1	YES	
15	2	0.487	0	YES	0.830	3	0	NO	
16	3	0.779	1	NO			1		
17	4	0.313	0	NO			1	YES	
18	5	0.269	0	YES	0.839	3	0	NO	
19	6	0.325	0	NO			0	NO	
20	7	0.937	3	NO			3	YES	
21	8	0.145	0	YES	0.118	1	2	YES	
22	9	0.165	0	YES	0.888	3	1	NO	
23	10	0.505	0	NO			1	NO	
24									

Figure A.7 Number Waiting During 100 Minutes of Operation

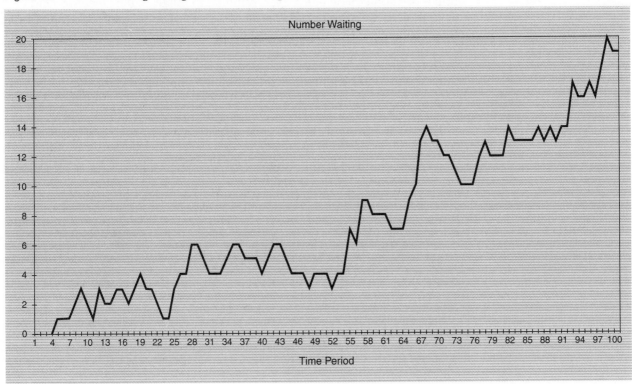

window. Simulation would be an ideal way to study this alternative, since the expense of actually constructing the second window need not be incurred.

Next-Event Simulation Models

With a fixed-time simulation model, information is lost. For example, suppose two customers arrive in the first minute. Since we do not know their actual times of arrival, calculations of statistics such as waiting time will not be very accurate. In addition, we may run through many simulation cycles where nothing happens in the system under consideration. This wastes computer time, particularly for large simulations.

Next-event simulation models increment time on the basis of the next event that will occur instead of using fixed-time intervals. An **event** is an action that changes the system. For example, there are two types of events in the Lincoln Savings Bank problem: arrivals and service completions. When a customer arrives, the number of customers in the system is increased; when a service completion occurs, the number of customers in the system is decreased. At any other time, the system does not change. The simulation time clock is updated whenever an event occurs.

Next-event models are used more commonly in practice than fixed-time simulation models. For a next-event simulation model of the Lincoln Savings Bank problem, we need to know the actual times of customer arrivals and the actual length of service times. Table A.8 shows the arrival times and service times for 10 customers. We see that the first customer arrives at time 0.12 and uses 1.46 minutes of service time. Since the window is available, this customer begins service at time 0.12 (incurring no waiting time) and completes service at time $0.12 + 1.46 = 1.58$. The second customer does not arrive until time 2.21, so the second event is the service completion of the first customer at 1.58.

The second customer arrives at time 2.21 (the third event) and immediately begins service. Since this customer's service time is 3.50, the service completion event occurs at time $2.08 + 3.50 = 5.71$. However, the fourth event is the arrival

Table A.8 Arrival and Service Times for 10 Customers

Customer	Arrival Time	Service Time
1	0.12	1.46
2	2.21	3.50
3	3.22	.20
4	5.06	.44
5	5.61	.65
6	5.64	1.62
7	5.98	4.54
8	7.95	.13
9	12.13	3.13
10	14.14	1.45

of customer 3 at time 3.22. The window is busy when customer 3 arrives and this customer must wait until the second customer departs at time 5.71.

Figure A.8 summarizes the logic for this next-event simulation. Whenever the next event occurs, we update the simulation clock to the current time of the event. If the event is a new arrival, we check to see if the service area is available. If it is, we compute the time of the service-completion event and record that the service area is no longer available. If it is not available, the customer must wait. If the event is a service completion, we check to see if any customers are waiting. If there are, we compute the service-completion time for the next customer. If not, then we record that the service area is now available. We then return to the beginning and select the next event to occur. Table A.9 shows the results of a next-event simulation of the Lincoln Savings Bank problem.

Figure A.8 Next-Event Simulation Logic for Lincoln Savings Bank

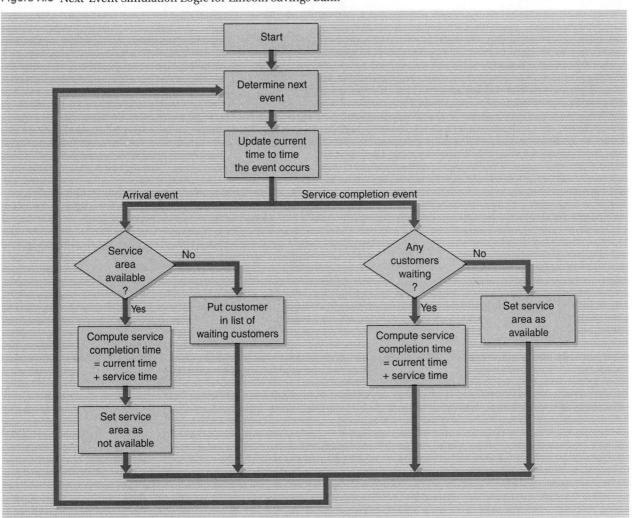

Table A.9 Next-Event Simulation Results for Lincoln Savings Bank

Event Time	Customer	Event Type	Number Waiting	Service Area Available?
0	—	Start	0	yes
0.12	1	Arrival	0	no
1.58	1	Service completion	0	yes
2.21	2	Arrival	0	no
3.22	3	Arrival	1	no
5.06	4	Arrival	2	no
5.61	5	Arrival	3	no
5.64	6	Arrival	4	no
5.71	2	Service completion	3	no
5.91	3	Service completion	2	no
5.98	7	Arrival	3	no
6.35	4	Service completion	2	no
7.00	5	Service completion	1	no
7.95	8	Arrival	2	no
8.62	6	Service completion	1	no
12.13	9	Arrival	2	no
13.16	7	Service completion	1	no
13.29	8	Service completion	0	no
14.14	10	Arrival	1	no
16.42	9	Service completion	0	no
17.87	10	Service completion	0	yes

Key Terms

Fixed-time simulation model
Pseudorandom numbers
Validation
Next-event simulation model
Event

Review Questions

1. Discuss the role of flowcharts in computer simulation modeling.
2. Describe how random numbers are used to simulate uncertain events in simulation models.
3. Define *validation* in the context of simulation. Why is validation important?
4. Explain the difference between fixed-time and next-event simulation models.
5. What advantages do next-event simulation models have over fixed-time models?

Note

1. See, for example, Rand Corporation, *A Million Random Digits with 100,000 Normal Deviates* (New York: The Free Press, 1955, 1983).

Solved Problems

1. A retail store has had the daily demand shown in Table A.10 for a particular product.

Table A.10 Data for Solved Problem 1

Sales (units)	Frequency (days)
0	4
1	6
2	14
3	12
4	7
5	5
6	2
Total	50

a. Develop a relative frequency distribution for the given data.
b. Use the random numbers from row 4 of Appendix C to simulate daily sales for a 10-day period.

Solution
a. The relative frequency distribution is shown in Table A.11.

Table A.11 Solved Problem 1 Solution

Sales	Relative Frequency	Random numbers
0	.08	00–07
1	.12	08–19
2	.28	20–47
3	.24	48–71
4	.14	72–85
5	.10	86–95
6	.04	96–99

b. Using the first 10 random numbers from row 4 of Appendix C, we obtain the daily sales for 10 days of simulated operation shown in Table A.12.

Table A.12 Solved Problem 1 Solution

Day	Random number	Sales
1	46	2
2	27	2
3	68	3
4	74	4
5	53	3
6	44	2
7	79	4
8	06	0
9	71	3
10	22	2

2. A New York City corner newsstand orders 250 copies of the *New York Times* daily. Primarily because of weather conditions, the demand for newspapers varies from day to day. The probability distribution of the demand for newspapers follows.

Number of Newspapers	150	175	200	225	250
Probability	0.10	0.30	0.30	0.20	0.10

The newsstand makes 15 cents profit on every paper sold, but it loses 10 cents on every paper unsold by the end of the day. Use 10 days of simulated results to determine the average daily profit if 250 newspapers are ordered.

Solution
To simulate demand, the following random number intervals can be used

Interval	Demand
00–09	150
10–39	175
40–69	200
70–89	225
90–99	250

Using row 2 in Appendix C, we obtain the results shown in Table A.13.

Table A.13 Solved Problem 2 Solution

Day	R.N.	Demand	Number Sold	Number Unsold	Profit
1	88	225	225	25	$225(.15) - 25(.10) = \$31.25$
2	54	200	200	50	$200(.15) - 50(.10) = 25.00$
3	70	225	225	25	$225(.15) - 25(.10) = 31.25$
4	98	250	250	0	$250(.15) = 37.50$
5	96	250	250	0	$250(.15) = 37.50$
6	95	250	250	0	$250(.15) = 37.50$
7	43	200	200	50	$200(.25) - 50(.10) = 25.00$
8	67	200	200	50	$200(.15) - 50(.10) = 25.00$
9	91	250	250	0	$250(.15) = 37.50$
10	15	175	175	75	$175(.15) - 75(.10) = 18.75$
					Average profit/day $= \$30.63$

Problems

Most of the problems in this section are designed to enable you to perform simulations with hand calculations. To keep the calculations reasonable, we ask you to consider only a few decision alternatives and relatively short periods of simulation. Although this should give you a good understanding of the simulation process, the results will not be sufficient for you to make final conclusions or decisions about the problem. If you have access to a computer, we suggest that you develop a computer simulation model for some of the problems. By using the model to test several decision alternatives over a much longer simulated period of time, you will be able to obtain sufficient information for making decisions.

1. Table A.14 gives data on the number of visitors to King's Palace amusement park on a summer day (rounded to the nearest 1,000) during the last season was.

Table A.14 Data for Problem 1

Number of Visitors	Frequency
25,000	5
26,000	7
27,000	6
28,000	9
29,000	23
30,000	30
31,000	18
35,000	3

a. Develop a relative frequency distribution for these data.

b. Using the random numbers in row 7 of Appendix C, simulate attendance for a 15-day period. What is the average attendance?

2. A study was conducted in order to investigate the number of cars arriving at the drive-in window of Community Savings Bank. The data shown in Table A.15 were collected for 100 randomly selected five-minute intervals.

Table A.15 Data for Problem 2

Arrivals	Frequency (intervals)
0	12
1	24
2	37
3	19
4	8
Total	100

a. Develop a relative frequency distribution for the given data.

b. Use random numbers to simulate the number of customer arrivals between 9:00 A.M. and 9:15 A.M. on a given day.

3. Decca Industries has experienced the weekly absenteeism frequency given in Table A.16 in the past 20 weeks.

Table A.16 Data for Problem 3

Employees Absent	Frequency (weeks)
1	2
2	4
3	7
4	3
5	2
6	2
Total	20

a. Develop a relative frequency distribution for the given data.

a. Develop a relative frequency distribution for the given data.

b. Use random numbers to simulate weekly absenteeism for a 15-week period.

4. Charlestown Electric Company is building a new generator for its Mt. Washington plant. Even with good maintenance procedures, the generator will periodically fail or break down. Historical figures for similar generators indicate the following relative frequency of failures during a year.

Number of Failures	0	1	2	3
Relative Frequency	.80	.15	.04	.01

Assume the useful lifetime of the generator is 25 years. Use simulation to estimate the number of breakdowns that will occur in the 25 years of operation. Is it common to have five or more consecutive years of operation without a failure?

5. Use row 15 of Appendix C to simulate 15 minutes of operation for the Lincoln Savings Bank application presented in this chapter. Show your simulation results in the format of Table A.5.

6. A service technician for a major photocopier company is trained to service two models of copier: the X100 and the Y200. Approximately 60 percent of the technician's service calls are for the X100, and 40 percent are for the Y200. The service time distributions for the two models is shown in Table A.17.

Table A.17 Data for Problem 6

X100		Y200	
Time (minutes)	Relative Frequency	Time (minutes)	Relative Frequency
25	0.50	20	0.40
30	0.25	25	0.40
35	0.15	30	0.10
40	0.10	35	0.10

a. Show the random-number intervals that can be used to simulate the type of machine to be serviced and the length of the service time.

b. Simulate 20 service calls. What is the total service time the technician spends on the 20 calls?

7. Given here are 50 weeks of breakdowns-per-week data for a production line. A simulation of breakdowns will help the production manager better understand production delays and costs resulting from the breakdowns.

Number of Breakdowns	0	1	2	3	4	5
Number of Weeks	2	5	8	22	10	3

a. Develop the relative frequency distribution for the data.

b. Use random numbers to simulate the production breakdowns for a 12-week period.

8. Bushnell's Sand and Gravel (BSG) is a small firm that supplies sand, gravel, and top-soil to contractors and landscaping firms. BSG maintains an inventory of high-quality, screened topsoil for supplying the weekly orders for two companies: Bath Landscaping Service and Pittsford Lawn Care, Inc. BSG wants to determine how many cubic yards of screened topsoil to have in inventory at the beginning of each week to satisfy the needs of both its customers. The objective is to establish the lowest possible inventory level that would have a 0.95 probability of satisfying the combined weekly orders from both customers. The demand distributions for the two customers are shown in Table A.18.

Table A.18 Data for Problem 8

	Weekly Demand	Relative Frequency
Bath Landscaping	10	0.20
	15	0.35
	20	0.30
	25	0.10
	30	0.05
Pittsford Lawn Care	30	0.20
	40	0.40
	50	0.30
	60	0.10

Simulate 20 weeks of operation for beginning inventories of 70 and of 80 cubic yards. Based on your limited simulation results, how many cubic yards should BSG maintain in inventory? Discuss what you do in a full-scale simulation of this problem.

9. A project has four activities (A, B, C, and D) that must be completed sequentially in order to complete the project. The probability distribution for the time required to complete each of the activities is shown in Table A.19.

Table A.19 Data for Problem 9

Activity	Activity Time (weeks)	Probability
A	5	0.25
	6	0.30
	7	0.30
	8	0.15
B	3	0.20
	5	0.55
	7	0.25
C	10	0.10
	12	0.25
	14	0.40
	16	0.20
	18	0.05
D	8	0.60
	10	0.40

a. Use a random number procedure to simulate the completion time for each activity. Sum the activity times to establish a completion time for the entire project.

b. Use the simulation procedure developed in part a to simulate 20 completions of this project. Show the distribution of completion times and estimates the probability that the project can be completed in 35 weeks or less.

10. Repeat the simulation in Solved Problem 2 using order quantities of 175, 200, and 250. What order quantity would your recommend?

11. Bristol Bikes, Inc. wants to develop an order-quantity and reorder-point policy that would minimize the total costs associated with its inventory of exercise bikes. The relative frequency distribution for retail demand on a weekly basis follows.

Demand	0	1	2	3	4	5
Probability	0.20	0.50	0.10	0.10	0.05	0.05

The relative frequency distribution for lead time follows.

Lead Time (weeks)	1	2	3	4
Relative Frequency	0.10	0.25	0.60	0.05

The inventory-holding costs are $1 per unit per week, the ordering cost is $20 per order, the shortage cost is $25 per unit, and the beginning inventory is seven units. Using an order quantity of 12 and a reorder point of 5, simulate 10 weeks of operation of this inventory system.

12. Production requirements at the Karlin Krafts Company have fluctuated over the past few months. The product manager has authorized a simulation study to obtain an estimate of potential daily production requirements to better schedule production activities. Historical data on production requirements are given in Table A.20.

Table A.20 Data for Problem 12

Daily Production Requirement	Frequency
0	2
100	4
200	7
300	12
400	14
500	5
600	6
	50

a. Determine a relative frequency distribution for this information.
b. Use these random numbers to simulate sales for a 6-day period.

21   77   80   20   85   27

13. Paula Williams is currently completing the design for a drive-in movie theater in Big Flats, New York. She has purchased the land and is now attempting to determine the number of automobiles to accommodate. Each automobile location requires installing a speaker system at a total cost of $250 per location. From her experience with five other drive-ins she has been operating for eight years, Paula estimates that the nightly attendance will range from 100 to 500 automobiles with the relative frequencies given in Table A.21.

Table A.21 Data for Problem 13

Approximate Number of Automobiles	Relative Frequency
100	0.10
200	0.25
300	0.40
400	0.15
500	0.10

a. Simulate 20 days of attendance for capacities of 300, 400, and 500.

b. In the 20 days of simulated operations, how many daily demands of 300 would you have expected? Did you observe this many in your simulation? Should you have? Explain.

c. After personnel and other operating costs, Paula's average profit is $1 per car. Using your 20 days of simulated data, what is the average nightly profit for the capacities of 300, 400, and 500? How many days of operation will it take Paula to recover the speaker installation cost if all profits are allocated to this cost?

14. A firm with a national chain of hotels and motels is interested in learning where individuals prefer to stay when on business trips. Three competing hotel and motel chains are included in the study: Marimont Inns, Harrison Inns, and Hinton Hotels. The study found that where an individual stays on one trip is a good predictor of where she or he will stay on the next trip. However, the study also showed that individuals tend to switch from one chain to another. The probabilities of staying at each chain are shown in Table A.22. For example, if an individual stays at a Marimont Inn on one trip, there is a .70 probability that he or she will stay at a Marimont Inn on the next trip, a .10 probability of staying at a Harrison Inn the next trip, and a .20 probability of staying at a Hinton Hotel the next trip. Similar probability values are shown for individuals staying at Harrison Inns and Hinton Hotels on particular trips.

Table A.22 Data for Problem 14

Stayed at	Probability for Next Stay		
	Marimont	*Harrison*	*Hinton*
Marimont	.70	.10	.20
Harrison	.20	.60	.20
Hinton	.15	.05	.80

a. Show the random-number assignments that can be used to simulate the next visit for an individual staying at the Marimont, Harrison, and Hinton chains.

b. Develop a flowchart that describes the process for simulating where an individual will stay during a series of business trips.

c. Assume an individual most recently stayed at a Marimont Inn. Simulate where he or she will stay on the next 50 business trips. What percentage of the time will the person select each chain? Which appears to be the most popular chain?

d. Repeat the simulation in part c, starting with an individual most recently staying at a Harrison Inn. Repeat part c again with the individual most recently staying at a Hinton Hotel. Which chain is most popular based on these simulation results?

15. Mt. Washington Garage sells regular and unleaded gasoline. Pump 1 is a self-service pump. Pump 2, a full-service pump, is used by customers who are willing to pay a higher cost per gallon to have an attendant pump the gas, check the oil, and so on. Both pumps can service one car at a time. On the basis of past data, the owner of the garage estimates that 70 percent of the customers select the self-service pump and 30 percent want full service. The arrival rate of cars for each minute of operation is given by the probability distribution in Table A.23.

Table A.23 Arrival Data for Problem 15

Number of Arrivals in One Minute of Operation	Probability
0	.10
1	.20
2	.35
3	.30
4	.05
	1.00

The time needed to service a car, which depends on whether the self-service or full-service pump is used, is given by the probability distribution in Table A.24.

Table A.24 Service Time Data for Problem 15

Self-Service Pump		Full-Service Pump	
Service Time (min.)	*Probability*	*Service Time (min.)*	*Probability*
2	.10	3	.20
3	.20	4	.30
4	.60	5	.35
5	.10	6	.10
	1.00	7	.05
			1.00

Study the operation of the system with a 10-minute simulation. As part of your analysis, consider these types of questions. What is the average number of cars waiting for service per minute at both pumps? What is the average time a car must wait for service? Prepare a brief report for Mt. Washington Garage that describes your analysis and any conclusions you are able to draw.

16. Conduct a next-event simulation of the Lincoln Savings Bank using the arrival and service times given in Table A.25.

Table A.25 Data for Problem 16

Customer	Arrival Time	Service Time
1	3.37	.03
2	3.51	.53
3	4.32	.53
4	5.12	.91
5	6.21	.47
6	6.65	2.47
7	6.67	1.22
8	9.07	.23
9	11.33	1.47
10	11.82	.47

17. Refer to Problem 15. Suppose the *time between arrivals* (in minutes) follows the probability distribution shown in Table A.26.

Table A.26 Data for Problem 17

Time between Arrivals	Probability
.25	.05
.35	.30
.50	.35
1.00	.20
2.00	.10

a. Show the random-number assignments that can be used to simulate the time between arrivals.

b. Simulate the time between arrivals for 10 customers, and compute their arrival times.

c. Using the same distribution of service times as in Problem 15, conduct a next-event simulation for the 10 customers in part b.

 18. Modify the spreadsheet LINCOLN.XLS to model balking behavior if four or more cars are waiting.

Supplementary Chapter B Decision Analysis

Chapter Outline

Decision analysis is a methodology for determining the best of several decision alternatives under conditions of uncertainty about future events. For example, the manufacturer of a new style or line of seasonal clothing would like to manufacture large quantities of the product if consumer acceptance and, consequently, demand for the product are going to be high. Unfortunately, the seasonal clothing items require the manufacturer to make a production-quantity decision before the actual demand is known. Future events, which are not within the control of the decision maker and are unknown at the time of the decision, are called *states of nature*. In the example, states of nature might be designated as "high demand," "medium demand," and "low demand." Alternatively, they might be quantified as "demand estimated as 15,000 units," "demand estimated as 10,000 units," and "demand estimated as 5,000 units." For each combination of production-volume decision and subsequent state of nature, a *payoff* can be computed. For instance, if the manufacturer decides to produce 10,000 units, but demand is low, the manufacturer will incur the cost of producing the 10,000 units but will receive revenue for sales of only 5,000; the remaining units will have to be disposed of at a loss. On the other hand, if sales are medium or high, all 10,000 units will be sold, and the net profit can be computed. The payoff would be the net profit.

Decision analysis has many applications in product selection, plant capacity expansion, location decisions, inventory analysis, and other areas of P/OM. Various techniques are available for determining optimal decision strategies under different scenarios, such as when no knowledge of the likelihood of states of nature is available, or when probability estimates of states of nature are known. In this supplementary chapter we introduce the basic concepts and procedures of decision analysis, using a capacity-expansion problem to illustrate the methodology.

Edmund Chemicals Company Capacity-Expansion Problem

To illustrate decision analysis, let us consider the problem facing the Edmund Chemicals Company, a medium-size producer of industrial chemical products. The company has recently developed a new synthetic industrial lubricant that will increase tool life for machining operations in metal-fabrication industries. A new plant would be necessary to produce the lubricant on a large scale, but expanding the existing facilities would allow production on a smaller scale. Managers are uncertain which decision to choose. Clearly, the best decision depends on future demand. If the demand for the product is high, the expansion alternative will not provide enough capacity to meet all the demand and profits will be lost. If demand is low, and a new plant is built, the excess capacity will substantially reduce the return on investment. With an unstable economy, it is difficult to predict actual demand for the product.

Formulating the Decision Problem

The two *states of nature* for Edmund Chemicals correspond to low and high product acceptance. It is assumed that states of nature include everything that can possibly happen and that they do not overlap; that is, the states of nature are defined so that one and only one of them will occur.

Let

d_1 = decision to expand the existing plant.

d_2 = decision to build a new plant.

s_1 = state of nature corresponding to low product demand.

s_2 = state of nature corresponding to high product demand.

To determine which alternative to choose, we need information on the profit associated with each combination of a decision alternative and a state of nature.

Using the best information available, the managers of Edmund Chemicals have estimated the *payoffs,* or profits, for the Edmund Chemicals' capacity-planning problem shown in Table B.1. A table of this form is referred to as a **payoff table.** In general, entries in a payoff table can be stated in terms of profits, costs, or any other measure of output that may be appropriate for the particular situation being analyzed. The notation we use for the entries in the payoff table

Table B.1 Payoff Table for Edmund Chemicals Problem

Decision Alternative	State of Nature	
	Low Product Demand (s_1)	*High Product Demand (s_2)*
Expand existing plant (d_1)	$200,000	$300,000
Build new plant (d_2)	$100,000	$400,000

is $V(d_i, s_j)$, which denotes the payoff, V, associated with decision alternative d_i and state of nature s_j. Using this notation, we see that $V(d_2, s_1) = \$100,000$.

Decision Making without Probabilities

Sometimes decision makers have little confidence in their ability to assess the probabilities of the various states of nature, or perhaps they want to consider only the best- and worst-case analyses. Different criteria can be used to reflect different attitudes toward risk, and they may result in different decision recommendations.

For a problem in which the output measure is profit, as it is in the Edmund Chemicals problem, three common criteria are

1. **Maximax**—the decision that will *maximize* the *maximum* possible profit among all states of nature. This is an optimistic, or risk-taking, approach.
2. **Maximin**—the decision that will *maximize* the *minimum* possible profit among all states of nature. This is a conservative, or risk-averse, approach.
3. **Minimax regret**—the decision that will *minimize* the *maximum* opportunity loss (the cost of lost opportunity) associated with the states of nature. This approach is neither purely optimistic nor conservative.

We will apply these criteria for the Edmund Chemicals problem. For the maximax criterion, we see that if d_1 is selected, the maximum payoff is $300,000, and it occurs for s_2. If d_2 is selected, the maximum payoff is $400,000, also for s_2. The decision maker should choose d_2, since it results in the largest possible payoff.

For the maximin criterion, we see that if d_1 is chosen, the minimum payoff is $200,000, whereas if d_2 is selected, the minimum payoff is $100,000. Thus, to maximize the minimum payoff, the decision maker should choose d_1.

To apply the minimax-regret criterion, we must first construct a **regret** or **opportunity-loss matrix.** The opportunity loss associated with a particular decision, d_i, and state of nature, s_j, is the *difference* between the *best* payoff that the decision maker can receive by making the *optimal* decision d^* corresponding to s_j, $V(d^*, s_j)$, and the payoff for choosing any arbitrary decision d_i and having s_j occur, $V(d_i, s_j)$. For example, if we *know* that s_1 will occur, the best decision is to choose $d^* = d_1$ and receive a payoff of $200,000: the opportunity loss will be zero. If we choose d_2, we will receive only $100,000 and will lose the opportunity to receive $200,000 − $100,000 = $100,000. Similarly, if we know that s_2 will occur, the best decision is $d^* = d_2$; an opportunity loss of $400,000 − $300,000 = $100,000 will occur if we choose d_1. Table B.2 is the complete regret matrix for this event.

Table B.2 Regret Matrix for Edmund Chemicals Problem

Decision	State of Nature		Maximum Regret
	s_1	s_2	
d_1	0	100,000	100,000
d_2	100,000	0	100,000

The maximum regret associated with each decision is shown to the right of the matrix. Thus, the decision maker is indifferent between choosing d_1 and d_2. Had the maximum-regret values differed, the decision maker would have made the decision that would lead to the lesser maximum-regret value.

For problems in which the output measure is cost, the optimistic decision is *minimin,* the decision that minimizes the minimum possible payoff over all states of nature. The conservative decision is *minimax,* the decision that minimizes the maximum possible payoff over all states of nature. Finally, the minimax-regret criterion does not differ, since regret is *always* a cost. Care is needed in computing the opportunity loss correctly. It is still the difference between the best possible payoff (received by making the optimal decision) and the payoff of any other decision. The only difference when the output measure is cost is that the "best" payoff is the lowest cost, not the highest profit. The difference must be viewed as an absolute value—that is, the *savings* in cost—since it does not make sense for opportunity losses to be negative.

Criterion of Expected Monetary Value

In many situations, good probability estimates can be developed for the states of nature. The *expected monetary value* (EMV) criterion is an approach that uses probability estimates for the state of nature. The EMV criterion requires the analyst to compute the expected value for each decision alternative and to then select the alternative yielding the best expected value. Let

$$P(s_j) = \text{probability of occurrence for state of nature } s_j.$$

$$N = \text{number of possible states of nature.}$$

Since one and only one of the N states of nature can occur, the associated probabilities must satisfy these two conditions.

$$P(s_j) \geq 0 \qquad \text{for all states of nature } j$$

$$\sum_{j=1}^{N} P(s_j) = P(s_1) + P(s_2) + \cdots + P(s_N) = 1$$

The EMV for decision alternative d_i is given by

$$\text{EMV}(d_i) = \sum_{j=1}^{N} P(s_j) V(d_i, s_j). \qquad \text{(B.1)}$$

Let us now return to the Edmund Chemicals problem to see how the EMV criterion can be applied. Suppose managers believe the probability that market demand will be low is .4 and the probability that market demand will be high is .6. Thus $P(s_1) = .4$ and $P(s_2) = .6$. Using the payoff values $V(d_i, s_j)$ shown in Table B.1 and Equation B.1, we can calculate expected monetary values for the two decision alternatives by

$$\text{EMV } (d_1) = .4 \, (200{,}000) + .6 \, (300{,}000) = \$260{,}000.$$

$$\text{EMV } (d_2) = .4 \, (100{,}000) + .6 \, (400{,}000) = \$280{,}000.$$

Thus, according to the EMV criterion, the decision to build a new plant, d_2, with an EMV of \$280,000 is the recommended capacity alternative.

Decision Trees

Decision problems can be depicted graphically with a **decision tree.** Figure B.1 is a decision tree of the Edmund Chemicals capacity-planning problem. Note that the tree shows the natural, or logical, progression of the decision-making process. First, the firm must make its decision (d_1 or d_2); then, once the decision is implemented, the state of nature (s_1 or s_2) occurs. The number at each end point of the tree represents the payoff associated with a particular chain of events. For example, the topmost payoff of 200,000 arises when managers make the decision to expand the existing plant (d_1) and product acceptance turns out to be low (s_1). The next-lower terminal point of 300,000 is reached when managers make the decision to expand the existing plant (d_1) and the true state of nature turns out to be s_2, high product acceptance.

In the terminology associated with decision trees, we refer to the intersections, or junction points, of the tree as **nodes** and the arcs, or connectors, between the nodes, as **branches.** Figure B.2 shows the Edmund Chemicals decision tree with the nodes numbered 1 to 3 and the branches labeled as decision or state-of-nature branches. When the branches *leaving* a given node are decision branches, we refer to the node as a *decision node*. Decision nodes are denoted by squares. Similarly, when the branches leaving a given node are state-of-nature branches, we refer to the node as a *state-of-nature node*. These are denoted by circles. Thus it is clear in the figure that node 1 is a decision node, whereas nodes 2 and 3 are state-of-nature nodes.

At decision nodes, the decision maker selects the particular decision branch (d_1 or d_2) that will be taken. Selecting the best branch is equivalent to making the best decision. However, the state-of-nature branches are not controlled by the decision maker; thus the specific branch followed from a state-of-nature node depends on the probabilities assigned to the branches. Using $P(s_1) = .4$ and $P(s_2) = .6$, Figure B.3 is the Edmund Chemicals decision tree with state-of-nature branch probabilities.

Figure B.1
Decision Tree for the
Edmund Chemicals
Problem

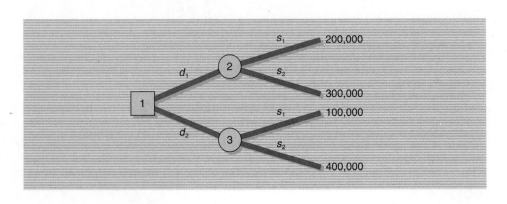

Figure B.2
Decision Tree for Edmund
Chemicals Problem with
Node and Branch Labels

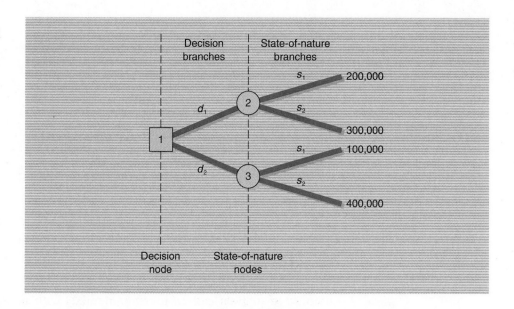

Figure B.3
Decision Tree for Edmund
Chemicals Problem with
State-of-Nature Branch
Probabilities

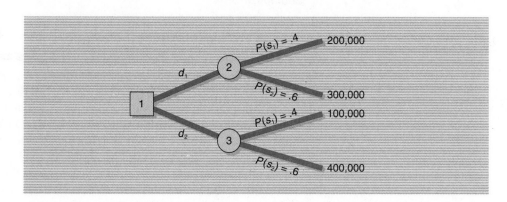

Determining an Optimal Decision Strategy

We now use the branch probabilities and the criterion of expected monetary value to arrive at the optimal decision for Edmund Chemicals. Working *backward* through the decision tree, we first compute the expected monetary value of each state-of-nature node. That is, at each state-of-nature node, we weight the possible payoffs by their chances of occurrence. The expected monetary values for nodes 2 and 3 are computed by

$$\text{EMV (node 2)} = .4 \, (200{,}000) + .6 \, (300{,}000)$$
$$= 260{,}000.$$

$$\text{EMV (node 3)} = .4 \, (100{,}000) + .6 \, (400{,}000)$$
$$= 280{,}000.$$

Figure B.4
Decision Node 1 in
Edmund Chemicals
Problem

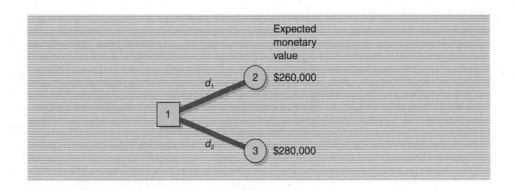

We now continue backward through the tree to the decision node. Since the expected monetary values for nodes 2 and 3 are known, the decision maker can view decision node 1 as shown in Figure B.4. Since the decision maker controls the branch leaving a decision node and since we are trying to maximize expected monetary value, the best decision branch at node 1 is d_2. Thus the decision-tree analysis leads us to recommend d_2, with an expected monetary value of $280,000.

Expected Value of Perfect Information

Suppose Edmund Chemicals was able to conduct a market research study that would determine which of the two states of nature is more likely. Such studies are not without cost, however, so the company would need to weigh the expected improvement in payoff against the cost of having such information.

Suppose the company could determine *with certainty* which state of nature would occur. We see that if s_1 is known to occur, the best decision would be to choose d_1 and receive a profit of $200,000. However, if s_2 is known to occur, the best decision would be to choose d_2 and receive a profit of $400,000.

However, since $P(s_1) = .4$ and $P(s_2) = .6$, the expected monetary value of this decision strategy with perfect information is

$$(0.4)(200,000) + (0.6)(400,000) = \$320,000.$$

Recall that without the perfect information, the decision maker would choose d_2, which has an expected monetary value of $280,000. By having perfect information, we see that the value of the expected payoff is increased by

$$\$320,000 - 280,000 = \$40,000.$$

This difference is called the *expected value of perfect information* (EVPI), and it represents the maximum amount the company should be willing to pay for *any* information about the states of nature, no matter how good it is.

Extensions

Decision trees are useful for structuring complex decision processes. For example, Edmund Chemicals' initial decision might be whether or not to conduct a

Figure B.5 Extended Decision Tree for Edmund Chemicals Problem

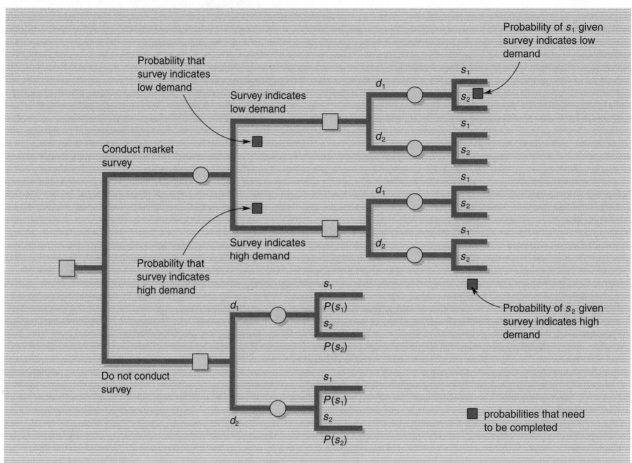

market survey. If the survey is taken, a new set of states of nature will be introduced. The company will not know the results of the market survey until after it
is completed; the survey will probably indicate whether product demand will be
high or low. Figure B.5 is the decision tree corresponding to these sequential decisions. Notice that the probabilities of the states of nature would depend on
the survey results. For example, if the survey indicated that product demand is
low, we would expect the probability of s_1, given this knowledge to be smaller
than 0.4. Similarly, if the survey indicated high product demand, we would expect the probability of s_2, given this knowledge to be greater than 0.6. These
probabilities, as well as the probabilities of what the survey will indicate, can be
computed by using a technique known as *Bayesian analysis*. The mathematics
of this method is beyond the scope of this book. A textbook on management
science will provide further details.

Key Terms

Payoff table
Maximax
Maximin
Minimax regret
Regret
Opportunity-loss matrix
Decision tree
Nodes
Branches

Review Questions

1. Define the three major components of a decision problem.

2. What information is provided in a payoff table?
3. Describe how the following criteria are applied to a decision problem in which the objective is to maximize profit.
    a. maximax
    b. maximin
    c. minimax regret
4. How do the criteria in question 3 change if the objective is to minimize cost?
5. Explain the concept of *regret* in decision analysis.
6. In what situations would the expected monetary value criterion be useful? In what situations would it not be useful?
7. Explain the structure and purpose of a decision tree.
8. What does the expected value of perfect information provide to a decision maker?

Solved Problems

1. Maling Manufacturing needs to purchase a new piece of machining equipment. The two choices are a conventional (labor-intensive) machine and an automated (computer-controlled) machine. Profitability will depend on demand volume. Table B.3 presents an estimate of profits over the next three years.

Table B.3 Data for Solved Problem 1

	Demand volume	
Decision	*Low*	*High*
Conventional machine	$15,000	$21,000
Automated machine	$ 9,000	$35,000

What decisions would be indicated by maximax, maximin, and minimax-regret criteria?

Solution

Decision	**Maximum profit**	**Minimum profit**
Conventional (D_1)	$21,000	$15,000 ←
Automated (D_2)	$35,000 ←	$ 9,000
	maximax decision = D_2	maximin decision = D_1

Regret matrix:

Decision	**Low**	**High**	**Maximum**
Conventional (D_1)	0	$14,000	$14,000
Automated (D_2)	$6,000	0	$ 6,000 ←
			minimax regret decision = D_2

Figure B.6
Solved Problem 2 Solution

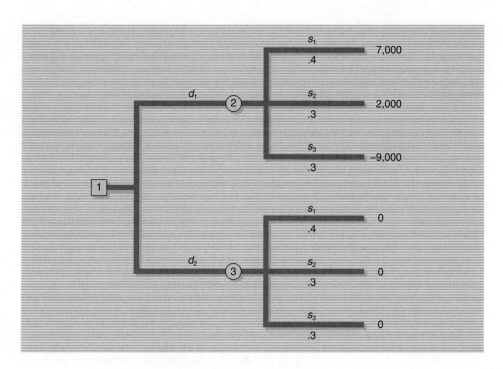

2. Martin's Service Station is consideraing investing in a heavy-duty snowplow this fall. Martin has analyzed the situation carefully and feels that this would be a very profitable investment if the snowfall is heavy, somewhat profitable if the snowfall is moderate, and would result in a loss if the snowfall is light. Specifically, Martin forecasts a profit of $7,000 if snowfall is heavy and $2,000 if it is moderate, and a $9,000 loss if it is light. From the Weather Bureau's long-range forecast, Martin estimates that P(heavy snowfall) = 0.4, P(moderate snowfall) = 0.3, and P(light snowfall) = 0.3.
a. Prepare a decision tree for Martin's problem.
b. Using the EMV criterion, would you recommend that Martin invest in the snowplow?

Solution
a. Figure B.6 is the decision tree.

$$d_1 = \text{invest.}$$

$$d_2 = \text{do not invest.}$$

$$s_1 = \text{heavy.}$$

$$s_2 = \text{moderate.}$$

$$s_3 = \text{light.}$$

$$P(s_1) = .4$$

$$P(s_2) = .3$$

$$P(s_3) = .3$$

b. Recommended decision: d_1 (invest)

$$\text{EMV } (d_1) = .4(7,000) + .3(2,000) + .3(-9,000) = \$700$$

$$\text{EMV } (d_2) = 0$$

Problems

1. Suppose a decision maker faced with four decision alternatives and four states of nature develops the profit-payoff table shown in Table B.4..

Table B.4 Data for Problem 1

	State of Nature			
Decision	s_1	s_2	s_3	s_4
d_1	14	9	10	5
d_2	11	10	8	7
d_3	9	10	10	11
d_4	8	10	11	13

a. If the decision maker knows nothing about the chances or probability of occurrence of the four states of nature, what decision would be indicated by the maximax, maximin, and minimax-regret criteria?

b. Which decision criterion do you prefer? Explain. Should the decision maker establish the most appropriate decision criterion before analyzing the problem? Explain.

c. Assume the payoff table provides *cost*, rather than profit, payoffs. What is the recommended decision using the optimistic, conservative, and minimax-regret decision criteria?

2. Suppose the decision maker in Problem 1 obtains information that enables these probability estimates to be made: $P(s_1) = 0.5$, $P(s_2) = 0.2$, $P(s_3) = 0.2$, $P(s_4) = 0.1$.

a. Use the expected monetary value (EMV) criterion to determine the optimal decision.

b. Now assume the entries in the payoff table are costs, and use the EMV criterion to determine the minimum-cost solution.

3. Southland Corporation's decision to produce a new line of recreational products has resulted in the need to construct either a small plant or a large plant. The decision as to which size to select depends on the marketplace reaction to the new product line. To conduct an analysis, marketing managers have decided to view the possible long-run demand as low, medium, or high. The payoff table shown in Table B.5 gives the projected profits in millions of dollars.

Table B.5 Data for Problem 3

	Long-Run Demand		
Decision	*Low*	*Medium*	*High*
Small plant	150	200	200
Large plant	50	200	500

a. Construct a decision tree for this problem and determine the best decisions using the maximax, maximin, and minimax-regret decision criteria.

b. Assume that the best estimate of the probability of low long-run demand is 0.20, of medium long-run demand is 0.15, and of high long-run demand is 0.65. What is the best decision using the EMV criterion?

4. Milford Trucking, located in Chicago, has requests to haul two shipments, one to St. Louis and one to Detroit. Because of a scheduling problem, Milford will be able to accept only one of these assignments. The St. Louis customer has guaranteed a return shipment, and the Detroit customer has not. Thus if Milford accepts the Detroit shipment and cannot find a Detroit-to-Chicago return shipment, the truck will return to Chicago empty. The payoff table for profit is shown in Table B.6.

Table B.6 Data for Problem 4

Destination	Return Shipment from Detroit (s_1)	No Return Shipment from Detroit (s_2)
St. Louis (d_1)	2,000	2,000
Detroit (d_2)	2,500	1,000

If the probability of a Detroit return shipment is 0.4, what should Milford do?

5. McHuffter Condominiums, Inc., of Pensacola, Florida, recently purchased land near the Gulf of Mexico and is attempting to determine the size of the condominium development it should build there. Three sizes of developments are being considered: small d_1, medium, d_2, and large, d_3. At the same time an uncertain economy makes it difficult to ascertain the demand for the new condominiums. McHuffter's managers realize that a large development followed by a low demand could be very costly to the company. However, if McHuffter makes a conservative, small-development decision and then finds high demand, the firm's profits will be lower than they might have been. With the three levels of demand—low, medium, and high—McHuffter's managers prepared the payoff table shown in Table B.7.

Table B.7 Data for Problem 5

Decision	Demand (in Thousands of Dollars)		
	Low	*Medium*	*High*
Small	$400	$400	$400
Medium	100	600	600
Large	−300	300	900

If P(low) = 0.20, P(medium) = 0.35, and P(high) = 0.45, what decision is recommended by the EMV critierion?

6. Construct a decision tree for the McHuffter Condominiums problem (Problem 5). What is the expected value at each state-of-nature node? What is the optimal decision?

7. Construct a decision tree for Solved Problem 1. Suppose the probabilities of low and high demand volume are estimated to be 0.7 and 0.3, respectively. What decision would you recommend?

8. Refer again to the investment problem faced by Martin's Service Station (Solved Problem 2). Martin can purchase a blade to attach to his service truck that can be used to plow driveways and parking lots. Since this truck would also need to be available to start cars, etc., Martin would not be able to generate as much revenue plowing snow if he elects this alternative, but he would keep his loss smaller if there is light snowfall. Under this alternative Martin forecasts a profit of $3,500 if snowfall is heavy, $1,000 if it is moderate, and a $1,500 loss if snowfall is light.

a. Prepare a new decision tree showing all three alternatives.

b. Using the EMV approach, what is the optimal decision?

9. The Gorman Manufacturing Company must decide whether to purchase a component part from a supplier or to manufacture the component at its own plant. If demand is high, it would be to Gorman's advantage to manufacture the component. If demand is low, however, Gorman's unit manufacturing cost will be high because of underutilization of equipment. The projected profit in thousands of dollars for Gorman's make-or-buy decision is shown in Table B.8.

Table B.8 Data for Problem 9

	Demand		
Decision	*Low*	*Medium*	*High*
Manufacture component	−20	40	100
Purchase component	10	45	70

The states of nature have these probabilities: P(low demand) = 0.35, P(medium demand) = 0.35, and P(high demand) = 0.30. Use a decision tree to recommend a decision.

10. A firm produces a perishable food product at the cost of $10 per case. The product sells for $15 per case. For planning purposes, the company is considering possible demands of 100, 200, and 300 cases. If the demand is less than production, the excess production is discarded. If demand is more than production, the firm—in an attempt to maintain a good service image—will satisfy the excess demand with a special production run at a cost of $18 per case. The product, however, always sell at $15 per case.

a. Set up the payoff table for this problem.

b. If $P(100)$ = 0.2, $P(200)$ = 0.2, and $P(300)$ = 0.6, should the company produce 100, 200, or 300 cases?

11. Sealcoat, Inc., has a contract with one of its customers to supply a unique liquid chemical product used in the manufacture of a lubricant for airplane engines. Because of the chemical process Sealcoat uses, batch sizes for the product must be 1,000 pounds. The customer has agreed to adjust manufacturing to the full-batch quantities and will order either one, two, or three batches every three months. Since production includes a one-month aging process, Sealcoat must make its production (how much to make) decision before the customer places an order. Thus the product demand alternatives are 1,000, 2,000, and 3,000 pounds, but the exact demand is unknown.

Sealcoat's manufacturing costs are $150 per pound, and the product sells at the fixed contract price of $200 per pound. If the customer orders more than Sealcoat has produced, Sealcoat has agreed to absorb the added cost of filling the order by purchasing a higher-quality substitute product from another chemical firm. The substitute product, including transportation expenses, will cost Sealcoat $240 per pound. Since the product cannot be stored more than two months without spoilage, Sealcoat cannot inventory excess production until the customer's next three-month order. Therefore, if the customer's current order is less than Sealcoat has produced, the excess production will be reprocessed and will then be valued at $50 per pound.

The decision in this problem is: How much should Sealcoat produce given the costs and the possible demands of 1,000, 2,000, and 3,000 pounds? From historical data and analysis of the customer's future demands, Sealcoat has developed the probability distribution for demand shown in the Table B.9.

Table B.9 Data for Problem 11

Demand	**Probability**
1,000	0.3
2,000	0.5
3,000	0.2

a. Develop a payoff table for the problem.

b. How many batches should Sealcoat produce every three months?

12. A quality-control procedure involves 100-percent inspection of parts received from a supplier. Historical records show the observed defect rates given in Table B.10.

Table B.10 Defect Rates for Problem 12

Percent Defective	Probability
0	0.15
1	0.25
2	0.40
3	0.20

The cost to inspect the 100 percent of the parts received is $250 for each shipment of 500 parts. If the shipment is not 100 percent inspected, defective parts will cause rework problems later in the production process. The rework cost is $25 per each defective part.
a. Complete the payoff table shown here, in which entries represent the total cost of inspection and reworking.

	Percent Defective			
Decision	*0*	*1*	*2*	*3*
100% inspection	$250	$250	$250	$250
No inspection				

b. The plant manager is considering eliminating the inspection process to save the $250 inspection cost per shipment. Do you support this action? Use EMV to justify your answer.
c. Show the decision tree for this problem.
13. The R&D manager of the Beck Company is trying to decide whether or not to fund a project to develop a new lubricant. It is assumed that the project will be a major technical success, a minor technical success, or a failure. The company estimates the value of a major technical success as $150,000, since the lubricant could be used in a number of products the company is making. If the project is a minor technical success, its value is estimated as $10,000, since Beck feels the knowledge gained will benefit some other ongoing projects. If the project is a failure, it will cost the company $100,000.

Based on the opinion of the scientists involved and the manager's own subjective assessment, the following probabilities are assigned.

$$P(\text{major success}) = 0.15$$

$$P(\text{minor success}) = 0.45$$

$$P(\text{failure}) = 0.40$$

a. According to the EMV criterion, should the project be funded?
b. Suppose a group of expert scientists from a research institute could be hired as consultants to study the project and make a recommendation. If this study would cost $30,000, should the Beck Company hire the consultants?
14. Consider again the problem faced by the Beck Company R&D manager (Problem 13). Suppose an experiment can be conducted to shed some light on the technical feasibility of the project. There are three possible outcomes of the experiment:

I_1 = prototype lubricant works well at all temperatures.

I_2 = prototype lubricant works well only at temperatures above 10°F.

I_3 = prototype lubricant does not work well at any temperature.

How would the decision tree be modified to include this information?

15. Explain how decision analysis techniques can be implemented on spreadsheets. Design spreadsheets for the examples in this chapter.

Everyone has experienced waiting in line at the supermarket, the post office, the bank, and any number of other places. In these and many other situations, waiting time is undesirable for all parties concerned. Yet, the solution, added service capability, is costly. Managers must weigh the potential benefit of shorter customer waiting times against the potential costs.

Waiting line models have been applied to many different problems, including finding optimum staffing schedules at toll plazas, determining the best number of clerks at tool cribs, balancing costs and customer service at banks through teller staffing, and configuring hospital service facilities. Quantitative models have been developed for this purpose, based on *queueing theory*, the study of waiting lines (**queues**).

Queueing analysis can be performed with analytical models or simulation models. Analytical models are much simpler to use but are based on restricted assumptions that limit their use except as approximations to the real system. Simulation models are better equipped to capture the dynamic behavior of a waiting-line system over time. Often analytical and simulation models are used in combination; an analytical model is used to get a ball-park estimate, and then simulation provides detailed analysis.

For a given waiting-line system, queueing models may be used to identify various performance measures, called *operating characteristics,* such as

1. Percentage of time or probability that the service facilities are idle.
2. Probability of a specific number of units (customers) in the system (the *system* includes the waiting line plus the service facility).
3. Average number of units in the waiting line.
4. Average number of units in the system.
5. Average time a unit spends in the waiting line.
6. Average time a unit spends in the system.
7. Probability that an arriving unit must wait for service.

Managers who are provided with this information are better equipped to make decisions that balance desirable service levels with service costs.

Supplementary Chapter C
Waiting-Line Models

Chapter Outline

Waiting-Line Analysis of Airport Security Screening
  Arrival Distribution
  Service-Time Distribution
  Queue Discipline
Single-Channel Waiting-Line Model with Poisson Arrivals and Exponential Service Times
Multiple-Channel Waiting-Line Model with Poisson Arrivals and Exponential Service Times
Economic Analysis of Waiting-Lines

Many analytical waiting-line models exist, each based on unique assumptions about the nature of arrivals, service times, and other aspects of the system. Some of the common models are:

1. Single- or multiple-channel with Poisson arrivals and exponential service times. (This is the most elementary situation.)
2. Single-channel with Poisson arrivals and arbitrary service times. (Service times may follow any probability distribution, and only the average and the standard deviation need to be known.)
3. Single-channel with Poisson arrivals and deterministic service times. (Service times are assumed to be constant.)
4. Single- or multiple-channels with Poisson arrivals, arbitrary service times, no waiting line. (Waiting is not permitted. If the server is busy when a unit arrives, the unit must leave the system but may try to reenter at a later time.)
5. Single- or multiple-channels with Poisson arrivals, exponential service times, and a finite calling population. (A finite population of units is permitted to arrive for service.)

In this supplement, we focus only on the first model; other textbooks devoted exclusively to management science develop the other models.

Waiting-Line Analysis of Airport Security Screening

We illustrate the development of the basic waiting-line model for the problem of designing an airport security-screening system. Process design and facility-layout activities are currently being conducted for a new terminal at a major airport. One particular concern is the design and layout of the passenger-security-screening system. A waiting-line analysis of the screening system will help to determine if the screening systems to be located at the entrance to each concourse will provide adequate service to the airport passengers.

To develop a waiting-line model for the security-screening system, we must identify some important characteristics of the system: (1) the arrival distribution of the passengers, (2) the service-time distribution for the screening operation, and (3) the waiting-line, or queue, discipline for the passengers.

Arrival Distribution

Defining the arrival distribution for a waiting line consists of determining how many units arrive for service in given periods of time, for example, the number of passengers arriving at the screening facility during each one-minute period. Since the number of passengers arriving each minute is not a constant, we need to define a probability distribution that will describe the passenger arrivals.

For many waiting lines, the arrivals occurring in a given period of time appear to have a *random pattern*—that is, although we may have a good estimate of the total number of expected arrivals, each arrival is independent of other arrivals, and we cannot predict when it will occur. In such cases, a good description of the arrival pattern is obtained from the **Poisson probability distribution:**

$$P(x) = \frac{\lambda^x e^{-\lambda}}{x!} \quad \text{for } x = 0, 1, 2, \ldots \qquad \text{(C.1)}$$

where, in waiting-line applications,

x = number of arrivals in a specific period of time,

λ = average, or expected, number of arrivals for the specific period of time, and

$e \approx 2.71828$.

For the passenger-screening process, the wide variety of flight schedules and the variation in passenger arrivals for the various flights cause the number of passengers requiring screening to vary substantially. For example, data collected from the actual operation of similar screening facilities show that in some instances, 20 to 25 passengers arrive during a one-minute period. At other times, however, passenger arrivals drop to three or fewer passengers during a one-minute period. Since passenger arrivals cannot be controlled and appear to occur in an unpredictable fashion, a random arrival pattern appears to exist. Thus the Poisson probability distribution should provide a good description of the passenger-arrival pattern. Airport planners have projected passenger volume through the year 2010 and estimate that passengers will arrive at an average rate of nine passengers per minute during the peak activity periods. Using this average, or **mean arrival rate** (λ = 9), we can use the Poisson distribution to compute the probability of x passenger arrivals in a one-minute period.*

$$P(x) = \frac{9^x e^{-9}}{x!} \qquad \text{(C.2)}$$

Sample calculations for x = 0, 5, and 10 passenger arrivals during a one-minute period follow.†

$$P(0) = \frac{9^0 e^{-9}}{0!} = .0001$$

$$P(5) = \frac{9^5 e^{-9}}{5!} = .0607$$

$$P(10) = \frac{9^{10} e^{-10}}{10!} = .1186$$

Using the Poisson probability distribution, we expect it to be very rare to have a one-minute period in which no passengers (x = 0) arrive for screening, since $P(0) = .0001$. Five passenger arrivals occur with a probability $P(5) = .0607$, and 10 with a probability of $P(10) = .1186$. The probabilities for other numbers of passenger arrivals can also be computed. Figure C.1 shows the arrival distribution for passengers based on the Poisson distribution. In practice you would want to record the actual number of arrivals per time period for several days or

---

*Appendix A provides a table for computing $e^{-\lambda}$.
†In computing the values of factorals, ($x!$), $x! = x(x - 1)(x - 2) \ldots (2)(1)$. For example, 5! = 5(4)(3)(2)(1) = 120. Note that 0! is defined to be 1.

Figure C.1
Poisson Distribution of
Passenger Arrivals

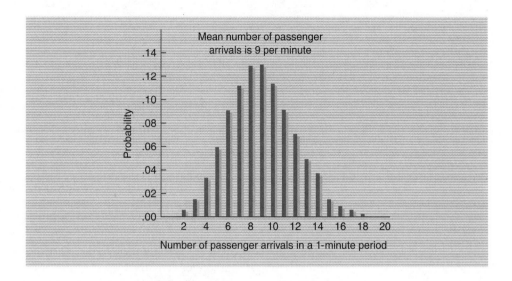

weeks and then compare the frequency distribution of the observed number of arrivals to the Poisson distribution to see if the Poisson distribution is a good approximation of the arrival distribution.

Service-Time Distribution

A service-time probability distribution is needed to describe how long it takes to process a passenger through the screening operation. This length of time is referred to as the *service time* for the passenger. Although many passengers will complete the screening process in a relatively short time, others will take a long time because they must repeat the walk-through screening when the system detects a metal object such as keys. Thus we expect service times to vary from passenger to passenger. In the development of waiting-line models, operations researchers have found that the exponential probability distribution can often be used to describe the service-time distribution. The **exponential probability distribution** is defined by the expression

$$f(x) = \mu e^{-\mu x} \qquad \text{for } x \geq 0. \tag{C.3}$$

In waiting-line applications,

   x = service time.

   μ = average or expected number of units that the service facility can handle in a specific period of time.

   $e \approx 2.71828$.

If we use an exponential service-time distribution, *the probability of a service being completed within a specific period of time*, t, *is given by*

$$P(\text{service time} \leq t) = 1 - e^{-\mu t}. \tag{C.4}$$

Figure C.2
Probability That a
Passenger Will Be Serviced
in *t* Minutes

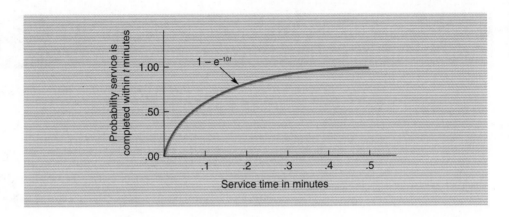

By collecting data on service times for similar screening systems in operation at other airports, we find that the system can handle an average of 10 passengers per minute. Using a **mean service rate** of $\mu = 10$ in equation C.4, we find that the probability of a screening service being completed within t minutes is

$$P(\text{service time} \le t) = 1 - e^{-10t}.$$

Now we can compute the probability that a passenger completes the screening process (that is, is serviced) within any specified time, t. For example,

$$P(\text{service time} \le .1 \text{ minutes}) = 1 - e^{-10(.1)} = 1 - e^{-1} \approx .6321.$$
$$P(\text{service time} \le .25 \text{ minutes}) = 1 - e^{-10(.25)} = 1 - e^{-2.5} \approx .9179.$$

Thus, using the exponential distribution, we would expect 63.21 percent of the passengers to be serviced in six seconds or less ($t = .1$ minute or less) and 91.79 percent in 15 seconds or less ($t = .25$ minute or less). Using the 15-second time period, we see that relatively few passengers (8.21 percent) require more than 15 seconds to go through the screening operation. Figure C.2 shows graphically the probability that t minutes or less will be required to service a passenger.

In the analysis of a specific waiting line, we want to collect data on actual service times to see if the exponential distribution assumption is appropriate. If you find other service time patterns (such as a normal service-time distribution or a constant service-time distribution), the exponential distribution should not be used.

Queue Discipline

In describing a waiting line we must define the manner in which the waiting units are ordered for service. For the airport problem, and in general for most customer-oriented waiting lines, the waiting units are ordered on a *first-come, first-served* basis—referred to as a *FCFS* queue discipline. When people wait in line for an elevator, it is usually the last one in line who is the first one serviced (that is, first to leave the elevator). Other types of queue disciplines assign priorities to the waiting units and service the unit with the highest priority first. We will restrict our attention to waiting lines with a FCFS queue discipline.

Single-Channel Waiting-Line Model with Poisson Arrivals and Exponential Service Times

The waiting-line model presented in this section can be applied to waiting lines that meet these assumptions or conditions:

1. The waiting line has a single channel.
2. The pattern of arrivals follows a Poisson probability distribution.
3. The service times follow an exponential probability distribution.
4. The queue discipline is first-come, first served (FCFS).

Since we have assumed that these conditions are applicable to the airport problem, we can show how this waiting-line model can be used to analyze the security screening operation.

Let us begin by reviewing the notation,

λ = expected number of arrivals per time period (mean arrival rate).

μ = expected number of services possible per time period (mean service rate).

For the airport passenger-screening problem we have already concluded that λ = 9 passengers per hour and that μ = 10 passengers per hour.

Using the assumptions of Poisson arrivals and exponential service times, quantitative analysts have developed the following expressions to define the operating characteristics of a **single-channel waiting line.**[*]

1. The probability that the service facility is idle (that is, the probability of 0 units in the system):

$$P_0 = \left(1 - \frac{\lambda}{\mu}\right)$$

(C.5)

2. The probability of n units in the system:

$$P_n = \left(\frac{\lambda}{\mu}\right)^n P_0$$

(C.6)

3. The average number of units waiting for service:

$$L_q = \frac{\lambda^2}{\mu(\mu - \lambda)}$$

(C.7)

4. The average number of units in the system:

$$L = L_q + \frac{\lambda}{\mu}$$

(C.8)

5. The average time a unit spends waiting for service:

$$W_q = \frac{L_q}{\lambda} \qquad \text{(C.9)}$$

6. The average time a unit spends in the system (waiting time plus service time):

$$W = W_q + \frac{1}{\mu} \qquad \text{(C.10)}$$

7. The probability that an arriving unit has to wait for service:

$$P_w = \frac{\lambda}{\mu} \qquad \text{(C.11)}$$

The values of the mean arrival rate, λ, and the mean service rate, μ, are clearly important components in these formulas. From equation C.11, we see that the ratio of these two values, λ/μ, is simply the probability that an arriving unit must wait because the server is busy. This λ/μ is often referred to as the **utilization factor** for the waiting line.

The formulas for determining the operating characteristics of a single-channel waiting line presented in equations C.5 through C.11 are applicable only when the utilization factor, λ/μ, is less than 1. This condition occurs when the mean service rate, μ, is greater than the mean arrival rate, λ, and hence when the service rate is sufficient to process or service all arrivals.

Returning to the airport passenger-screening problem, we see that with $\lambda = 9$ and $\mu = 10$, we can use equations C.5 through C.11 to determine the operating characteristics of the screening operation. This is done as follows.

$$P_0 = \left(1 - \frac{\lambda}{\mu}\right) = \left(1 - \frac{9}{10}\right) = .10$$

$$L_q = \frac{\lambda^2}{\mu(\mu - \lambda)} = \frac{9^2}{10(10 - 9)} = \frac{81}{10} = 8.1 \text{ passengers}$$

$$L = L_q + \frac{\lambda}{\mu} = 8.1 + \frac{9}{10} = 9.0 \text{ passengers}$$

$$W_q = \frac{L_q}{\lambda} = \frac{8.1}{9} = .9 \text{ minute per passenger}$$

$$W = W_q + \frac{1}{\mu} = .9 + \frac{1}{10} = 1.0 \text{ minute per passenger}$$

$$P_w = \frac{\lambda}{\mu} = \frac{9}{10} = .90$$

Using this information, we can learn several important things about the airport passenger-screening operation. In particular, we see that passengers wait an average of .90 minutes (54 seconds) before starting the screening process. With this as the average, many passengers wait even longer than 54 seconds. In airport operations with passengers rushing to meet plane connections, this waiting time was judged to be undesirably high. In addition, the facts that the average waiting line is 8.1 passengers and that 90 percent of the arriving passengers must wait for screening indicate that something should be done to improve the efficiency of the airport passenger-screening operation.

These operating characteristics are based on the assumption of an arrival rate of 9 per minute and a service rate of 10 per minute. As the figures are based on airport planners' estimates, they are subject to forecasting errors. It is easy to examine the effects of a variety of assumptions about arrival and service rates on the operating characteristics by using a spreadsheet such as the one in Figure C.3. In this spreadsheet, we compute the operating characteristics for the baseline assumptions and also examine the effect of changes in the mean arrival rate from 7 to 10 passengers per minute.

What do the data in this figure tell us about the design of the airport passenger-screening process? They tell us that if the mean arrival rate is seven passengers per minute, the system functions acceptably. On the average, only 1.63 passengers are waiting and the average waiting time of .23 minutes (approximately 14 seconds) appears acceptable. However, we see that the mean arrival rate of nine passengers provides undesirable waiting characteristics, and if the rate increases to 10 passengers per minute, the screening system as proposed is completely inadequate. When $\lambda = \mu$, the operating characteristics are not defined (as indicated by #DIV/0!), meaning that these times and numbers of passengers grow infinitely large. These results show that airport planners need to consider layout and/or design modifications that will improve the efficiency of the passenger-screening process.

If a new screening facility or process can be designed that will improve the passenger-service rate equations C.5 through C.11 can be used to predict operating characteristics under any revised mean service rate, μ. Developing a spreadsheet with alternative mean service rates provides the information to determine which, if any, of the screening facility designs can handle the passenger volume acceptably. A problem will ask you to do this.

Figure C.3
Spreadsheet for Single Channel Queueing Model (SCQUEUE.XLS)

	A	B	C	D	E	F	G	H	I
1	Single Channel Queueing Model								
2									
3	Lambda	7	8	9	10				
4	Mu	10.00	10.00	10.00	10.00				
5									
6	Probability system is empty	0.30	0.20	0.10	0.00				
7	Average number in queue	1.63	3.20	8.10	#DIV/0!				
8	Average number in system	2.33	4.00	9.00	#DIV/0!				
9	Average time in queue	0.23	0.40	0.90	#DIV/0!				
10	Average waiting time in system	0.33	0.50	1.00	#DIV/0!				
11	Probability arrival has to wait	0.70	0.80	0.90	1.00				
12									

Given the information in Figure C.3, we want to evaluate the alternative of expanding the screening process to a two-channel system. We discuss this model next.

Multiple-Channel Waiting-Line Model with Poisson Arrivals and Exponential Service Times

A logical extension of the single-channel waiting line is the **multiple-channel waiting line.** Here, although customers wait in a single line, they move to one of two or more channels to be serviced. The airport passenger-screening example involved a single channel. However, a multiple-channel waiting-line model could be applied if an additional screening facility is built so that two passengers can be serviced simultaneously. Arriving passengers would form a single waiting line and wait for either of the two service areas to become available. Figure C.4 is a diagram of this system.

In this section we present formulas that can be used to compute various operating characteristics for a multiple-channel waiting line. The model we will use can be applied to situations that meet these assumptions:

1. The waiting line has two or more identical channels.
2. The arrivals follow a Poisson probability distribution with a *mean arrival rate* of λ.
3. The service times have an exponential distribution.
4. The *mean service rate*, μ, is the same for each channel.
5. The arrivals wait in a single line and then move to the first open channel for service.
6. The queue discipline is first-come, first-served (FCFS).

Figure C.4
A Two-Channel Airport
Screening Facility

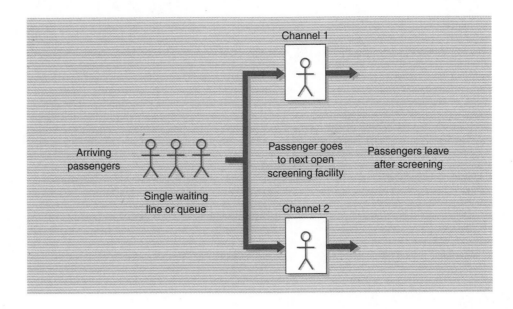

Using these assumptions, operations researchers have developed formulas for determining the operating characteristics of the multiple-channel waiting line.

Let

k = number of channels,

λ = mean arrival rate for the system, and

μ = mean service rate for *each* channel.

The following equations apply to multiple-channel waiting lines for which the overall mean service rate, $k\mu$, is greater than the mean arrival rate, λ. In such cases, the service rate is sufficient to process all arrivals.

1. The probability that all k service channels are idle (that is, the probability of zero units in the system):

$$P_0 = \frac{1}{\left[\sum_{n=0}^{k-1} \frac{(\lambda/\mu)^n}{n!}\right] + \frac{(\lambda/\mu)^k}{(k-1)!}\frac{\mu}{k\mu - \lambda}} \tag{C.12}$$

2. The probability of n units in the system:

$$P_n = \frac{(\lambda/\mu)^n}{k!\, k^{n-k}} P_0 \quad \text{for } n > k \tag{C.13}$$

$$P_n = \frac{(\lambda/\mu)^n}{n!} P_0 \quad \text{for } 0 \le n \le k \tag{C.14}$$

3. The average number of units waiting for service:

$$L_q = \frac{(\lambda/\mu)^k \lambda\mu}{(k-1)!(k\mu - \lambda)^2} P_0 \tag{C.15}$$

4. The average number of units in the system.

$$L = L_q + \frac{\lambda}{\mu} \tag{C.16}$$

5. The average time a unit spends waiting for service:

$$W_q = \frac{L_q}{\lambda} \tag{C.17}$$

6. The average time a unit spends in the system (waiting time + service time):

$$W = W_q + \frac{1}{\mu} \tag{C.18}$$

7. The probability that an arriving unit must wait for service:

$$P_w = \frac{1}{k!}\left(\frac{\lambda}{\mu}\right)^k \frac{k\mu}{k\mu - \lambda} P_0 \qquad\qquad \textbf{(C.19)}$$

Although the equations describing the operating characteristics of a multiple-channel waiting line with Poisson arrivals and exponential service times are somewhat more complex than the single-channel equations, they provide the same information and are used exactly as we used the results from the single-channel model. To simplify the use of equations C.12 through C.19, Table C.1 shows values of P_0 for selected values of λ/μ. Note that the values provided correspond to cases for which $k\mu > \lambda$; hence the service rate is sufficient to service all arrivals.

For an application of the multiple-channel waiting-line model, we return to the airport passenger-screening problem and consider the desirability of expanding the screening facility to provide two screening locations at the entry to each concourse. How does this design compare to the single-channel alternative?

We answer this question by applying equations C.12 through C.19 specifically for the two-channel ($k = 2$) waiting line. Using $\lambda = 9$ passengers per minute and $\mu = 10$ passengers per minute for each of the screening facilities, we have these operating characteristics.

$$P_0 = .3793 \text{ (from Table C.1 for } \lambda/\mu = .9 \text{ and } k = 2)$$

$$L_q = \frac{(9/10)^2(9)(10)}{(2 - 1)!\,(20 - 9)^2}\,(.3793) = .23 \text{ passengers}$$

$$L = .23 + \frac{9}{10} = 1.13 \text{ passengers}$$

$$W_q = \frac{.23}{9} = .026 \text{ minutes}$$

$$W = .026 + \frac{1}{10} = .126 \text{ minutes}$$

$$P_w = \frac{1}{2!}\left(\frac{9}{10}\right)^2 \left(\frac{20}{20 - 9}\right)(.3793) = .279$$

These operating characteristics suggest that the two-channel operation would handle the volume of passengers extremely well. Specifically, note that the total time in the system is an average of .126 minute (approximately 8 seconds), which is excellent. The percentage waiting is 27.9 percent, which is acceptable, especially in light of the short average waiting time.

Figure C.5 is a spreadsheet designed to compute operating characteristics for up to eight servers in the multiple-server queueing model using the arrival and service rates for the security-screening example. (The Microsoft Excel function HLOOKUP is used to compute the summation and the term $(\lambda/\mu)^n/n!$ in

Table C.1 Values of P_0 for Multiple-Channel Waiting Lines with Poisson Arrivals and Exponential Service Times

Ratio λ/μ	Number of Channels (k)			
	2	3	4	5
0.15	0.8605	0.8607	0.8607	0.8607
0.20	0.8182	0.8187	0.8187	0.8187
0.25	0.7778	0.7788	0.7788	0.7788
0.30	0.7391	0.7407	0.7408	0.7408
0.35	0.7021	0.7046	0.7047	0.7047
0.40	0.6667	0.6701	0.6703	0.6703
0.45	0.6327	0.6373	0.6376	0.6376
0.50	0.6000	0.6061	0.6065	0.6065
0.55	0.5686	0.5763	0.5769	0.5769
0.60	0.5385	0.5479	0.5487	0.5488
0.65	0.5094	0.5209	0.5219	0.5220
0.70	0.4815	0.4952	0.4965	0.4966
0.75	0.4545	0.4706	0.4722	0.4724
0.80	0.4286	0.4472	0.4491	0.4493
0.85	0.4035	0.4248	0.4271	0.4274
0.90	0.3793	0.4035	0.4062	0.4065
0.95	0.3559	0.3831	0.3863	0.3867
1.00	0.3333	0.3636	0.3673	0.3678
1.20	0.2500	0.2941	0.3002	0.3011
1.40	0.1765	0.2360	0.2449	0.2463
1.60	0.1111	0.1872	0.1993	0.2014
1.80	0.0526	0.1460	0.1616	0.1646
2.00		0.1111	0.1304	0.1343
2.20		0.0815	0.1046	0.1094
2.40		0.0562	0.0831	0.0889
2.60		0.0345	0.0651	0.0721
2.80		0.0160	0.0521	0.0581
3.00			0.0377	0.0466
3.20			0.0273	0.0372
3.40			0.0186	0.0293
3.60			0.0113	0.0228
3.80			0.0051	0.0174
4.00				0.0130
4.20				0.0093
4.40				0.0063
4.60				0.0038
4.80				0.0017

the denominator of P_0. The function FACT computes factorials.) With three servers, we see a significant improvement over two servers in the operating characteristics; beyond this, the improvement is negligible. In addition, we can use the spreadsheet to show that even if the mean arrival rate for passengers exceeds the estimated nine passengers per minute, the two-channel system should operate nicely.

Figure C.5
Spreadsheet for Multiple
Server Queueing Model
(MULTIQUE.XLS)

	A	B	C	D	E	F	G	H	I	J
1	Multiple Server Queueing Model									
2										
3	Lambda	9								
4	Mu	10								
5	Number of servers	2	3	4	5	6	7	8		
6										
7	Probability system is empty	0.379	0.403	0.406	0.407	0.407	0.407	0.407		
8	Average number in queue	0.229	0.030	0.004	0.001	0.000	0.000	0.000		
9	Average number in system	1.129	0.930	0.904	0.901	0.900	0.900	0.900		
10	Average time in queue	0.025	0.003	0.000	0.000	0.000	0.000	0.000		
11	Average waiting time in system	0.125	0.103	0.100	0.100	0.100	0.100	0.100		
12	Probability arrival must wait	0.279	0.070	0.014	0.002	0.000	0.000	0.000		
13										
14										
15										
16	Lookup table	0	1	2	3	4	5	6	7	8
17		1.000	0.900	0.405	0.122	0.027	0.005	0.001	0.000	0.000
18				1.900	2.305	2.427	2.454	2.459	2.459	2.460
19				0.405	0.122	0.027	0.005	0.001	0.000	0.000
20										

Economic Analysis of Waiting-Lines

As we have shown, waiting-line models can be used to determine operating characteristics of a waiting-line system. In the economic analysis of waiting lines we will seek to use the information provided by the waiting-line model to develop a cost model for the waiting line under study. Then we can use the model to help the manager balance the cost of customers having to wait for service against the cost of providing the service.

In developing a cost model for the airport security-screening problem, we will consider the cost of passenger time, both waiting time and servicing time, and the cost of operating the system. Let C_W = the waiting cost per minute per passenger and C_S = the cost of operating each channel per minute. Clearly, the passenger waiting-time cost cannot be accurately determined; managers must estimate a reasonable value that might reflect the potential loss of future revenue should a passenger switch to another airport or airline because of perceived unreasonable delays. This is called the *imputed cost* of waiting. Suppose C_W is estimated to be $50 per hour, or $.83 per minute. The cost of operating each channel is more easily determined, as it consists of the wages of the security personnel and the cost of equipment. Let us assume that C_S = $40 per hour, or $.67 per minute.

Therefore, the total cost per minute is

$$C_W L + C_S k = .83L + .67k$$

Table C.2 Costs per Minute of Airport Screening Alternatives

System	k	System Cost	L	Passenger Cost	Total Cost
Single-channel	1	.67(1) = .67	9	.83(9) = 7.47	$8.14
Two-channel	2	.67(2) = 1.34	1.13	.83(1.13) = .94	$2.28

where L = average number of passengers in the system and k = number of channels. Table C.2 summarizes the cost for the one- and two-channel scenarios. We see that the cost per minute for the single-channel system is nearly four times the cost of the two-channel system.

Because the imputed costs of waiting are difficult to determine, decisions about waiting-line systems are often based on desired service goals rather than an economic model. However, when the expenses of waiting and service operation are borne by the service provider, an economic model makes sense. Such would be the case in determining the number of repair-persons to have in a factory, for example. In this case, managers can more readily assign a cost to a machine being out of service and waiting for repair.

Key Terms

Queue
Poisson probability distribution
Mean arrival rate
Exponential probability distribution
Mean service rate
Single-channel waiting line
Utilization factor
Multiple-channel waiting line

Review Questions

1. Define *operating characteristics.*

2. Describe some of the common analytical waiting line models.
3. What information is necessary to analyze a waiting line?
4. List the assumptions underlying the basic single-channel waiting-line model.
5. What are the assumptions of the multiple-channel waiting-line model?
6. Explain the process of economic analysis of waiting lines.
7. How are analytical waiting-line models similar to simulation models? How are they different?

Solved Problems

1. The reference desk of a large library receives requests for assistance at a mean rate of 10 requests per hour, and it is assumed that the desk has a mean service rate of 12 requests per hour.
a. What is the probability that the reference desk is idle?
b. What is the average number of requests that will be waiting for service?
c. What is the average waiting time plus service time for a request for assistance?
d. What is the utilization factor?

Solution

a.
$$P_0 = 1 - \frac{\lambda}{\mu} = 1 - \frac{10}{12} = .1667$$

b.
$$L_q = \frac{\lambda^2}{\mu(\mu - \lambda)} = \frac{10^2}{12(12 - 10)} = 4.1667$$

c.
$$W_q = \frac{L_q}{\lambda} = .4167 \text{ hours}$$

$$W = W_q + \frac{1}{\mu} = .5 \text{ hours (30 minutes)}$$

d.
$$P_w = \frac{\lambda}{\mu} = \frac{10}{12} = .8333$$

2. A fast-food franchise operates a drive-up window. Orders are placed at an intercom station at the back of the parking lot. After placing an order, the customer pulls up and waits in line at the drive-up window until the cars in front have been served. By hiring a second person to help take and fill orders, the manager hopes to improve service. With one person filling orders, the average service time for a drive-up customer is two minutes; with a second person working, the average service time can be reduced to 1 minute, 15 seconds. Note that the drive-up window operation with two people is still a single-channel waiting line. However, with the addition of the second person, the averaging service time can be decreased. Cars arrive at the rate of 24 per hour.
a. Determine the average waiting time when one person is working the drive-up window.
b. With one person working the drive-up window, what percentage of time will that person not be occupied serving customers?
c. Determine the average waiting time when two people are working at the drive-up window.
d. With two persons working the drive-up window, what percentage of time will no one be occupied serving drive-up customers?
e. Would you recommend hiring a second person to work the drive-up window? Justify your answer.

Solution
a.
$$\lambda = 24 \qquad \mu = \frac{60}{2} = 30$$

$$L_q = \frac{\lambda^2}{\mu(\mu - \lambda)} = \frac{24^2}{30(30 - 24)} = 3.2$$

$$W_q = \frac{L_q}{\lambda} = .1333 \text{ hours (8 minutes)}$$

b.
$$P_0 = 1 - \frac{\lambda}{\mu} = 1 - \frac{24}{30} = .20$$

c.
$$\lambda = 24 \qquad \mu = \frac{60}{1.25} = 48$$

$$L_q = \frac{\lambda^2}{\mu(\mu - \lambda)} = \frac{24^2}{48(48 - 24)} = .5$$

$$W_q = \frac{L_q}{\lambda} = .0208 \text{ hours (1.25 minutes)}$$

d.
$$P_0 = 1 - \frac{\lambda}{\mu} = 1 - \frac{24}{48} = .50$$

e. Yes, waiting time is reduced from $W_q = 8$ to $W_q = 1.25$.

Problems

The following waiting-line problems are all based on the assumptions of Poisson arrivals and exponential service times.

1. Arrivals to a single channel queue occur at an average rate of 3 per minute. Develop the probability distribution for the number of arrivals for $x = 0$ through 10.

2. Trucks using a single-channel loading dock have a mean arrival rate of 12 per day. The loading/unloading rate is 18 per day.

a. What is the probability that the truck dock will be idle?

b. What is the average number of trucks waiting for service?

c. What is the average time a truck waits for the loading or unloading service?

d. What is the probability that a new arrival will have to wait?

3. A mail-order nursery specializes in European beech trees. New orders, which are processed by a single shipping clerk, have a mean arrival rate of six per day and a mean service rate of eight per day.

a. What is the average time an order spends in the queue waiting for the clerk to begin service?

b. What is the average time an order spends in the system?

4. Assume trucks arriving for loading/unloading at a truck dock from a single-channel waiting line. The mean arrival rate is four trucks per hour and the mean service rate is five trucks per hour.

a. What is the probability that the truck dock will be idle?

b. What is the average number of trucks in the queue?

c. What is the average number of trucks in the system?

d. What is the average time a truck spends in the queue waiting for service?

e. What is the average time a truck spends in the system?

f. What is the probability that an arriving truck will have to wait?

5. Marty's Barber Shop has one barber. Customers arrive at a rate of 2.2 per hour, and haircuts are given at an average rate of five customers per hour.

a. What is the probability that the barber is idle?

b. What is the probability that one customer is receiving a haircut and no one is waiting?

c. What is the probability that one customer is receiving a haircut and one customer is waiting?

d. What is the probability that one customer is receiving a haircut and two customers are waiting?

e. What is the probability that more than two customers are waiting?

f. What is the average time a customer waits for service?

6. Trosper Tire Company has decided to hire a new mechanic to handle all tire changes for customers ordering new tires. Two mechanics are available for the job. One mechanic has limited experience and can be hired for $7 per hour. It is expected that this mechanic can service an average of three customers per hour. A mechanic with several years of experience is also being considered for the job. This mechanic can service an average of four customers per hour, but must be paid $10 per hour. Assume that customers arrive at the Trosper garage at the rate of two per hour.

a. Compute waiting-line operating characteristics for each mechanic.

b. If the company assigns a customer-waiting cost of $15 per hour, which mechanic provides the lower operating cost?

7. Agan Interior Design provides home and office decorating assistance. In normal operation an average of 2.5 customers arrive per hour. One design consultant is available to answer customer questions and make product recommendations. The consultant averages 10 minutes with each customer.

a. Compute operating characteristics for the customer waiting line.

b. Service goals dictate that an arriving customer should not wait for service more than an average of five minutes. Is this goal being met? What action do you recommend?

c. If the consultant can reduce the average time spent with customers to eight minutes, will the service goal be met?

8. Pete's Market is a small local grocery store with one checkout counter. Shoppers arrive at the checkout lane at an average rate of 15 customers per hour and the average order takes three minutes to ring up and bag. What information would you develop to help Pete analyze the current operation? If Pete does not want the average time waiting for service to exceed five minutes, what would you tell him about the current system?

9. Refer to Problem 7. After reviewing the analysis, Pete felt it would be desirable to hire a full-time person to assist in the checkout operation. Pete believed that if this employee assisted the cashier, average service time could be reduced to two minutes. However, Pete was also considering installing a second checkout lane, which could be operated by the new person. This would provide a two-channel system with the average service time of three minutes for each customer. Should Pete use the new employee to assist on the current checkout counter or to operate a second counter? Justify your recommendation.

10. Keuka Park Savings and Loan currently has one drive-in teller window. Cars arrive at a mean rate of 10 per hour. The mean service rate is 12 cars per hour.

a. What is the probability that the service facility will be idle?

b. If you were to drive up to the facility, how many cars would you expect to see waiting and being serviced?

c. What is the average time waiting for service?

d. What is the probability an arriving car will have to wait?

e. As a potential customer of the system, would you be satisfied with these waiting-line characteristics? How do you think managers could go about assessing its customers' feelings about the current system?

11. To improve its customer service, Keuka Park Savings and Loan (Problem 10) wants to investigate the effect of a second drive-in teller window. Assume a mean arrival rate of 10 cars per hour. In addition, assume a mean service rate of 12 cars per hour for each window. What effect would adding a new teller window have on the system? Does this system appear acceptable?

12. Fore and Aft Marina is a new marina planned for a location on the Ohio River near Madison, Indiana. Assume that Fore and Aft decides to build one docking facility and expects a mean arrival rate of five boats per hour and a mean service rate of 10 boats per hour.

a. What is the probability that the boat dock will be idle?

b. What is the average number of boats that will be waiting for service?

c. What is the average time a boat will wait for service?

d. What is the average time a boat will spend at the dock?

e. If you were the owner, would you be satisfied with this level of service?

13. The owner of the Fore and Aft Marina in Problem 12 is investigating the possibility of adding a second dock. Assume a mean arrival rate of five boats per hour for the marina and a mean service rate of 10 boats per hour for each channel.

a. What is the probability that the boat dock will be idle?

b. What is the average number of boats that will be waiting for service?

c. What is the average time a boat will wait for service?

d. What is the average time a boat will spend at the dock?

e. If you were the owner, would you be satisfied with this level of service?

14. The City Beverage Drive-Thru is considering a two-channel system. Cars arrive at the store at the mean rate of six per hour. The service rate for each channel is 10 per hour.

a. What is the probability that both channels are idle?

b. What is the average number of cars waiting for service?

c. What is the average time waiting for service?

d. What is the average time in the system?

e. What is the probability of having to wait for service?

15. Consider a two-channel waiting line with a mean arrival rate of 50 per hour and a mean service rate of 75 per hour for each channel.

a. What is the probability that both channels are idle?

b. What is the average number of cars waiting for service?

c. What is the average time waiting for service?

d. What is the average time in the system?

e. What is the probability of having to wait for service?

16. For a two-channel waiting line with a mean arrival rate of 14 per hour and a mean service rate of 10 per hour per channel, determine the probability that an arrival must wait. What is the probability of waiting if the system is expanded to three channels?

17. Big Al's Quickie Car Wash has two wash bays. Each bay can wash 15 cars per hour. Cars arrive at the carwash at the rate of 15 cars per hour on the average, join the waiting line, and move to the next open bay when it becomes available.

a. What is the average time waiting for a bay?

b. What is the probability that a customer will have to wait?

c. As a customer of Big Al's, do you think the system favors the customer? If you were Al, what would be your attitude toward this service level?

18. Refer to the Agan Interior Design situation in problem 7. Agan is evaluating two alternatives:

1. Use one consultant with an average service time of eight minutes per customer.

2. Expand to two consultants, each of whom has an average service time of 10 minutes per customer.

If the consultants are paid $16 per hour and the customer waiting time is valued at $25 per hour, should Agan expand to the two-consultant system? Explain.

19. Refer to Solved Problem 2. Space is available to install a second drive-up window adjacent to the first. The manager is considering adding such a window. One person will be assigned to service customers at each window.

a. Determine the average customer waiting time for this two-channel system.

b. What percentage of the time will both windows be idle?

c. What design would you recommend: one attendant at one window, two attendants at one window, or two attendants and two windows with one attendant at each window?

20. Design a spreadsheet similar to Figure C.3 to study changes in the mean service rate from 10 to 15 for $\lambda = 9$ passengers per minute.

 21. Using the spreadsheet MULTIQUE.XLS, determine the effect of increasing passenger arrival rates of 10, 12, 14, 16 and 18 on the operating characteristics of the airport security screening example.

Linear programming procedures are among the most widely used models in management science, especially in production, and especially in aggregate production planning and distribution planning. The methodology is used to determine the optimal allocation of limited resources among competing alternatives. For example, a manufacturer might use linear programming to develop a production schedule and an inventory policy that will satisfy sales demand in future periods while minimizing production and inventory costs. Or a company that has warehouses located throughout the United States may use it to determine *which warehouse* should ship *how much product* to *which customers* so that the total distribution costs are minimized.

These two applications have some common features. In both cases, the concern is to minimize some quantity. In the first example, the desire is to minimize production and inventory costs; in the second, the desire is to minimize distribution costs. All linear programming problems have as their *objective* the minimization or maximization of some quantity.

Another characteristic of all linear programming problems is that there are restrictions, or *constraints,* that limit the extent to which the objective can be pursued. In the aggregate-planning problem, the manufacturer is restricted by the constraints that product demand must be satisfied and that production capacities are limited. In the distribution problem, the minimum-cost shipping schedule is constrained by the product available at each warehouse and the requirement that demand must be satisfied.

In this supplementary chapter, we discuss the process of developing linear programming models and explain basic properties and solution methods. These principles will enable you to solve larger and more practical problems efficiently by using computer packages like Microsoft Excel. We begin by developing a small production-planning model for a chemical firm.

Supplementary Chapter D Linear Programming

Chapter Outline

Softwater, Inc., Product-Mix Problem
Mathematical Statement of Softwater, Inc., Problem

P/OM Applications of Linear Programming
Production Scheduling

A Blending Problem

Graphical Solution of Linear Programs
Summary of Graphical Solution Procedure for Maximization Problems

Extreme Points and Optimal Solution

Finding Exact Locations of Extreme Points

Solving Linear Programs with Microsoft Excel
Interpreting the Solution

Simplex Method
Setting Up Linear Programs for Simplex Method

Simplex Solution Procedure

Minimization Problems

Softwater, Inc., Product-Mix Problem

Softwater, Inc., manufactures and sells a variety of chemical products used in purifying and softening water. One of its products is a pellet that is produced and sold in 40- and 80-pound bags. A common production line packages both products, although the fill rate is slower for 80-pound bags. Softwater is currently planning its production schedule and wants to develop a linear programming model that will assist in its production-planning effort.

The company has orders for 20,000 pounds over the next week. Currently, it has 4,000 pounds in inventory. Thus it should plan on an aggregate production of at least 16,000 pounds. Softwater has a sufficient supply of pellets to meet this demand but has limited amounts of packaging materials available, as well as a limited amount of time on the packaging line. The problem is to determine how many 40- and 80-pound bags to produce in order to maximize profit, given limited materials and time on the packaging line. To develop a linear programming formulation of this problem, we start by defining the objective function.

Every linear programming problem has a specific objective. For Softwater, Inc., the objective is to maximize profit. To express this mathematically let

x_1 = the number of 40-pound bags produced.

x_2 = the number of 80-pound bags produced.

If the company makes $2 for every 40-pound bag produced, it will make $2x_1$ dollars if it produces x_1 40-pound bags. And if it makes $4 for every 80-pound bag produced, it will make $4x_2$ dollars if it produces x_2 80-pound bags. Denoting total profit by the symbol z, and dropping the dollar signs for convenience, we have

$$z = 2x_1 + 4x_2. \qquad \text{(D.1)}$$

Softwater, Inc., must determine the values for the variables x_1 and x_2 that will yield the highest possible value of z. In linear programming terminology we refer to x_1 and x_2 as the *decision variables*. Since the objective—to maximize total profit—is a *function* of these decision variables, we refer to $2x_1 + 4x_2$ as the **objective function.** Using *max* as an abbreviation for *maximize*, the objective is written as

$$\max z = 2x_1 + 4x_2.$$

Suppose Softwater decided to produce 200 40-pound bags and 300 80-pound bags. With Equation D.1, the profit would be

$$z = 2(200) + 4(300)$$
$$= 400 + 1,200$$
$$= 1,600 \text{ dollars.}$$

What if Softwater decided on a different production schedule, such as 400 40-pound bags and 400 80-pound bags? In that case, the profit would be

$$z = 2(400) + 4(400)$$

$$= 800 + 1,600$$

$$= 2,400 \text{ dollars.}$$

Certainly the latter production schedule is preferable in terms of the stated objective of maximizing profit. However, it may not be possible for Softwater to produce that many bags. For instance, there might not be enough materials or enough time available on the packaging line to produce those quantities.

In this problem, any particular combination of 40- and 80-pound bags is referred to as a **solution** to the problem. However, only these solutions that satisfy *all* the constraints are referred to as **feasible solutions.** The particular feasible production combination, or feasible solution, that results in the largest profit will be referred to as the **optimal solution.** At this point, however, we have no idea what the optimal solution is because we have not developed a procedure for identifying feasible solutions. This requires us to first identify all the constraints of the problem in a mathematical expression.

Every 40- and 80-pound bag produced must go through the packaging line. In a normal workweek, this line operates 1,500 minutes. The 40-pound bags, for which the line was designed, each require 1.2 minutes of packaging time; the 80-pound bags require 3 minutes per bag. The total packaging time required to produce x_1 40-pound bags is $1.2x_1$, and the time required to produce x_2 80-pound bags is $3x_2$. Thus the total packaging time required for the production of x_1 40-pound bags and x_2 80-pound bags is given by

$$1.2x_1 + 3x_2.$$

Since only 1,500 minutes of packaging time are available, it follows that the production combination we select must satisfy the constraint

$$1.2x_1 + 3x_2 \leq 1,500. \qquad \textbf{(D.2)}$$

This constraint mathematically denotes the requirement that the total packaging time used cannot exceed the amount available.

Softwater has 6,000 square feet of packaging materials available; each 40-pound bag requires 6 square feet and each 80-pound bag requires 10 square feet of these materials. Since the amount of packaging materials used cannot exceed what is available, we obtain a second constraint for the linear programming problem:

$$6x_1 + 10x_2 \leq 6,000. \qquad \textbf{(D.3)}$$

The aggregate production requirement is for the production of 16,000 pounds of softening pellets per week. Since the small bags contain 40 pounds of pellets and the large bags contain 80 pounds, we must impose this aggregate-demand constraint:

$$40x_1 + 80x_2 \geq 16,000. \qquad \textbf{(D.4)}$$

Finally, we must prevent the decision variables x_1 and x_2 from having negative values. Thus, the two constraints

$$x_1 \geq 0 \qquad \text{and} \qquad x_2 \geq 0 \qquad \textbf{(D.5)}$$

must be added. These constraints are referred to as the **nonnegativity constraints.** Nonnegativity constraints are a general feature of all linear programming problems and are written in this abbreviated form:

$$x_1, x_2 \geq 0.$$

Mathematical Statement of Softwater, Inc., Problem

The mathematical statement, or *formulation*, of the Softwater problem is now complete. The complete mathematical model for the Softwater problem follows:

$$\max z = 2x_1 + 4x_2 \quad \text{(profit)}$$

subject to

$$
\begin{aligned}
1.2x_1 + 3x_2 &\leq 1{,}500 && \text{(packaging line)} \\
6x_1 + 10x_2 &\leq 6{,}000 && \text{(materials availability)} \\
40x_1 + 80x_2 &\geq 16{,}000 && \text{(aggregate production)} \\
x_1, x_2 &\geq \phantom{16{,}00}0 && \text{(nonnegativity)}
\end{aligned}
$$

Our job now is to find the *product mix* (that is, the combination of x_1 and x_2) that satisfies all the constraints and, at the same time, yields a value for the objective function that is greater than or equal to the value given by any other feasible solution. Once this is done, we will have found the optimal solution to the problem.

This mathematical model of the Softwater problem is a **linear program.** The problem has an objective and constraints, which characterize all linear programs, but in addition, it has another special feature that makes it a linear program. This feature is that the objective function *and* all **constraint functions** (the left sides of the constraint inequalities) are *linear* functions of the decision variables.

Mathematically speaking, a function in which each variable appears in a separate term and is raised to the first power is called a **linear function.** The objective function, $(2x_1 + 4x_2)$, is linear, since each decision variable appears in a separate term and has an exponent of 1. If the objective function were $2x^2_1 + 4\sqrt{x_2}$, it would not be a linear function, and we would not have a linear program. The amount of packaging time required is also a linear function of the decision variables for the same reasons. Similarly, the functions on the left side of all the constraint inequalities (the constraint functions) are linear functions.

P/OM Applications of Linear Programming

The possible applications of linear programming in P/OM are endless. In this section we present two examples of modeling complexities not dealt with in the Softwater, Inc., problem.

Production Scheduling

One of the most important applications of linear programming is for multi-period planning, such as production scheduling. Let us consider the case of the Bollinger Electronics Company, which produces two electronic components for an airplane-engine manufacturer. The engine manufacturer notifies the Bollinger sales office each quarter as to its monthly requirements for components during each of the next three months. The order shown in Table D.1 has just been received for the next three-month period.

One feasible schedule would be to produce at a constant rate for all three months. This would set monthly production quotas at 3,000 units per month for component 322A and 1,500 units per month for component 802B. Although this schedule would be appealing to the production department, it may be undesirable from a total-cost point of view because it ignores inventory costs. For instance, producing 3,000 units of component 322A in April will result in an end-of-month inventory level of 2,000 units for both April and May.

A policy of producing the amount demanded each month would eliminate the inventory-holding-cost problem; however, the wide monthly fluctuations in production levels might cause some serious production problems and costs. For example, production capacity would have to be available to meet the total 8,000-unit peak demand in June. This might require substantial labor adjustments, which in turn could lead to increased employee turnover and training problems. Thus it appears that the best production schedule will be one that is a compromise between the two alternatives.

The production manager must identify and consider costs for production, storage, and production-rate changes. In the remainder of this section we show how a linear programming model of the Bollinger Electronics production and inventory process can be formulated to account for these costs in order to minimize the total cost.

We will use a double-subscript notation for the decision variables in the problem. We let the first subscript indicate the product number and the second subscript the month. Thus in general, x_{im} denotes the production volume in units for product i in month m. Here $i = 1, 2$, and $m = 1, 2, 3$; $i = 1$ refers to component 322A, $i = 2$ to component 802B, $m = 1$ to April, $m = 2$ to May, and $m = 3$ to June.

If component 322A costs \$20 per unit to produce and component 802B costs \$10 per unit to produce, the production-cost part of the objective function is

$$20x_{11} + 20x_{12} + 20x_{13} + 10x_{21} + 10x_{22} + 10x_{23}$$

Note that in this problem the production cost per unit is the same each month, and thus we need not include production costs in the objective function;

Table D.1 Three-Month Demand Schedule for Bollinger Electronics Company

	April	May	June
Component 322A	1,000	3,000	5,000
Component 802B	1,000	500	3,000

that is, no matter what production schedule is selected, the total production costs will remain the same. In cases where the cost per unit may change each month, the variable production costs per unit per month must be included in the objective function. We have elected to include them so that the value of the objective function will include all the costs associated with the problem.

To incorporate the relevant inventory costs into the model, we let I_{im} denote the inventory level for product i at the end of month m. Bollinger has determined that on a monthly basis, inventory-holding costs are 1.5 percent of the cost of the product—that is, $0.015 \times \$20 = \$0.30$ per unit for component 322A, and $0.015 \times \$10 = \$0.15$ per unit for component 802B. We assume that monthly ending inventories are acceptable approximations of the average inventory levels throughout the month. Given this assumption, the inventory-holding cost portion of the objective function can be written as

$$0.30I_{11} + 0.30I_{12} + 0.30I_{13} + 0.15I_{21} + 0.15I_{22} + 0.15I_{23}.$$

To incorporate the costs due to fluctuations in production levels from month to month, we need to define these additional decision variables:

R_m = increase in the total production level during month m compared with month $m - 1$.

D_m = decrease in the total production level during month m compared with month $m - 1$.

After estimating the effects of employee layoffs, turnovers, reassignment-training costs, and other costs associated with fluctuating production levels, Bollinger estimates that the cost associated with increasing the production level for any given month is $0.50 per unit increase. A similar cost associated with decreasing the production level for any given month is $0.20 per unit. Thus the third portion of the objective function, for production-fluctuation costs, can be written as

$$0.50R_1 + 0.50R_2 + 0.50R_3 + 0.20D_1 + 0.20D_2 + 0.20D_3.$$

By combining all three costs, we obtain the complete objective function.

$$20x_{11} + 20x_{12} + 20x_{13} + 10x_{21} + 10x_{22} + 10x_{23} + 0.30I_{11}$$
$$+ 0.30I_{12} + 0.30I_{13} + 0.15I_{21} + 0.15I_{22} + 0.15I_{23}$$
$$+ 0.50R_1 + 0.50R_2 + 0.50R_3 + 0.20D_1 + 0.20D_2 + 0.20D_3$$

Now let us consider the constraints. First we must guarantee that the schedule meets customer demand. Since the units shipped can come from the current month's production or from inventory carried over from previous periods, we have these basic requirements.

$$\begin{pmatrix} \text{ending} \\ \text{inventory} \\ \text{from previous} \\ \text{month} \end{pmatrix} + \begin{pmatrix} \text{current} \\ \text{production} \end{pmatrix} \geq \begin{pmatrix} \text{this month's} \\ \text{demand} \end{pmatrix}$$

The difference between the left side and the right side of the equation will be the amount of ending inventory at the end of this month. Thus the demand requirement takes the following form.

$$\begin{pmatrix} \text{ending} \\ \text{inventory} \\ \text{from previous} \\ \text{month} \end{pmatrix} + \begin{pmatrix} \text{current} \\ \text{production} \end{pmatrix} - \begin{pmatrix} \text{ending} \\ \text{inventory} \\ \text{for this} \\ \text{month} \end{pmatrix} = \begin{pmatrix} \text{this} \\ \text{month's} \\ \text{demand} \end{pmatrix}$$

Suppose the inventories at the beginning of the three-month scheduling period were 500 units for component 322A and 200 units for component 802B. Recalling that the demand for both products in the first month (April) was 1,000 units, we see that the constraints for meeting demand in the first month become

$$500 + x_{11} - I_{11} = 1,000$$

and

$$200 + x_{21} - I_{21} = 1,000.$$

Moving the constants to the right side of the equation, we have

$$x_{11} - I_{11} = 500$$

and

$$x_{21} - I_{21} = 800.$$

Similarly, we need demand constraints for both products in the second and third months. These can be written as follows.

Month 2:
$$I_{11} + x_{12} - I_{12} = 3,000$$
$$I_{21} + x_{22} - I_{22} = 500$$

Month 3:
$$I_{12} + x_{13} - I_{13} = 5,000$$
$$I_{22} + x_{23} - I_{23} = 3,000$$

If the company specifies a minimum inventory level at the end of the three-month period of at least 400 units of Component 322A and at least 200 units of Component 802B, we can add the constraints

$$I_{13} \geq 400 \quad \text{and} \quad I_{23} \geq 200.$$

Let us suppose we have the additional information available on production, labor, and storage capacity given in Table D.2. Machine, labor, and storage space requirements are given in Table D.3. To reflect these limitations, the following constraints are necessary.

••• Machine capacity:

$$0.10x_{11} + 0.08x_{21} \leq 400 \quad \text{(Month 1)}$$
$$0.10x_{12} + 0.08x_{22} \leq 500 \quad \text{(Month 2)}$$
$$0.10x_{13} + 0.08x_{23} \leq 600 \quad \text{(Month 3)}$$

Table D.2 Machine, Labor, and Storage Capacities

	Machine Capacity (hours)	Labor Capacity (hours)	Storage Capacity (square feet)
April	400	300	10,000
May	500	300	10,000
June	600	300	10,000

Table D.3 Machine, Labor, and Storage Requirements for Components 322A and 802B

	Machine (hours/unit)	Labor (hours/unit)	Storage (sq. ft./unit)
Component 322A	0.10	0.05	2
Component 802B	0.08	0.07	3

••• Labor capacity:

$$0.05x_{11} + 0.07x_{21} \le 300 \qquad \text{(Month 1)}$$

$$0.05x_{12} + 0.07x_{22} \le 300 \qquad \text{(Month 2)}$$

$$0.05x_{13} + 0.07x_{23} \le 300 \qquad \text{(Month 3)}$$

••• Storage capacity:

$$2I_{11} + 3I_{21} \le 10,000 \qquad \text{(Month 1)}$$

$$2I_{12} + 3I_{22} \le 10,000 \qquad \text{(Month 2)}$$

$$2I_{13} + 3I_{23} \le 10,000 \qquad \text{(Month 3)}$$

We must also guarantee that R_m and D_m will reflect the increase or decrease in the total production level for month m. Suppose the production levels for March, the month before the start of the current scheduling period, were 1,500 units of component 322A and 1,000 units of component 802B for a total production level of $1,500 + 1000 = 2,500$ units. We can find the amount of the change in production for April from the relationship

$$\text{April production} - \text{March production} = \text{change.}$$

Using the April production decision variables, x_{11} and x_{21}, and the March production of 2,500 units, we can rewrite this relationship as

$$x_{11} + x_{21} - 2,500 = \text{change.}$$

Note that the change can be positive or negative, reflecting an increase or decrease in the total production level. With this rewritten relationship, we can use the increase in production variable for April, R_1, and the decrease in production variable for April, D_1, to specify the constraint for the change in total production for the month of April.

$$x_{11} + x_{21} - 2{,}500 = R_1 - D_1$$

Of course, we cannot have an increase in production and a decrease in production during the same one-month period; thus either R_1 or D_1 will be zero. If April requires 3,000 units of production, we will have $R_1 = 500$ and $D_1 = 0$. If April requires 2,200 units of production, we will have $R_1 = 0$ and $D_1 = 300$. This way of denoting the change in production level as the difference between two nonnegative variables, R_1 and D_1, permits both positive and negative changes in the total production level. If a single variable, say c_m, had been used to represent the change in production level, only positive changes would be permitted—because of the nonnegativity requirement.

Using the same approach in May and June (always subtracting the previous month's total production from the current month's total production) yields these constraints for the second and third months of the scheduling period.

$$(x_{12} + x_{22}) - (x_{11} + x_{21}) = R_2 - D_2$$
$$(x_{13} + x_{23}) - (x_{12} + x_{22}) = R_3 - D_3$$

Placing the variables on the left side and the constants on the right side, we have the complete set of what are commonly referred to as *production-smoothing constraints*.

$$
\begin{aligned}
x_{11} + x_{21} \qquad\qquad\qquad\qquad\qquad -R_1 + D_1 &= 2{,}500 \\
-x_{11} - x_{21} + x_{12} + x_{22} \qquad\qquad\quad - R_2 + D_2 &= 0 \\
-x_{12} - x_{22} + x_{13} + x_{23} - R_3 + D_3 &= 0
\end{aligned}
$$

The initially rather small, two-product, three-month scheduling problem has now developed into an 18-variable, 20-constraint linear programming problem. Note that this problem has involved only one machine process, one type of labor, and one storage area. Actual production scheduling problems typically involve several machine types, several labor grades, and/or several storage areas. A typical application might involve developing a production schedule for 100 products over a 12-month horizon—representing a problem that could have more than 1,000 variables and constraints.

A Blending Problem

Blending problems arise whenever a manager must decide how to combine two or more resources in order to produce one or more products.

These types of problems occur frequently in the petroleum industry (such as blending crude oil to produce different-octane gasolines) and the chemical industry (such as blending chemicals to produce fertilizers, weed killers, and so on). In these applications, managers must decide how much of each resource to purchase in order to satisfy product specifications and product demands at minimum cost.

To illustrate a blending problem, consider the Grand Strand Oil Company that produces regular-grade and premium-grade gasoline products by blending three petroleum components. The gasolines are sold at different prices, and the petroleum components have different costs. The firm wants to determine how

Table D.4 Petroleum Component Cost and Supply

Petroleum Component	Cost/Gallon	Amount Available
Component 1	$0.50	5,000 gallons
Component 2	$0.60	10,000 gallons
Component 3	$0.82	10,000 gallons

to blend the three components into the two products in such a way as to maximize profits.

Data available show that the regular-grade gasoline can be sold for $1.20 per gallon and the premium grade gasoline for $1.40 per gallon. For the current production-planning period, Grand Strand can obtain the three components at the costs and in the quantities shown in Table D.4.

The product specifications for the regular and premium gasolines, shown in Table D.5, restrict the amounts of each component that can be used in each gasoline product. Current commitments to distributors require Grand Strand to produce at least 10,000 gallons of regular-grade gasoline.

The Grand Strand blending problem is to determine how many gallons of each component should be used in the regular blend and in the premium blend. The optimal solution should maximize the firm's profit, subject to the constraints on the available petroleum supplies shown in Table D.4, the product specifications shown in Table D.5, and the requirement for at least 10,000 gallons of regular-grade gasoline.

We can use double-subscript notation to denote the decision variables for the problem. Let

$$x_{ij} = \text{gallons of component } i \text{ used in gasoline } j$$

where i = 1, 2, or 3 for component 1, 2, or 3 and

              j = r if regular or

               = p if premium.

The six decision variables become

     x_{1r} = gallons of Component 1 in regular gasoline.

     x_{2r} = gallons of Component 2 in regular gasoline.

Table D.5 Specifications for Grand Strand's Products

Product	Specifications
Regular gasoline	At most 30% Component 1 At least 40% Component 2 At most 20% Component 3
Premium gasoline	At least 25% Component 1 At most 40% Component 2 At least 30% Component 3

x_{3r} = gallons of Component 3 in regular gasoline.

x_{1p} = gallons of Component 1 in premium gasoline.

x_{2p} = gallons of Component 2 in premium gasoline.

x_{3p} = gallons of Component 3 in premium gasoline.

With the notation for the six decision variables just defined, the total *gallons of each type of gasoline produced* can be expressed as the sum of the gallons of the blended components.

$$regular\ gasoline = x_{1r} + x_{2r} + x_{3r}$$

$$premium\ gasoline = x_{1p} + x_{2p} + x_{3p}$$

Similarly, the total *gallons of each component used* can be expressed as these sums.

$$Component\ 1 = x_{1r} + x_{1p}$$

$$Component\ 2 = x_{2r} + x_{2p}$$

$$Component\ 3 = x_{3r} + x_{3p}$$

The objective function of maximizing the profit contribution can be developed by identifying the difference between the total revenue from the two products and the total cost of the three components. By multiplying the $0.50 per gallon price by the total gallons of regular gasoline, the $0.54 per gallon price by the total gallons of premium gasoline, and the component cost per gallon figures in Table D.4 by the total gallons of each component used, we find the objective function to be

$$max\ 1.20(x_{1r} + x_{2r} + x_{3r}) + 1.40(x_{1p} + x_{2p} + x_{3p}) - 0.50(x_{1r} + x_{1p})$$
$$- 0.60(x_{2r} + x_{2p}) - .82(x_{3r} + x_{3p}).$$

By combining terms, we can then write the objective function as:

$$max\ 0.70x_{1r} + 0.60x_{2r} + 0.38x_{3r} + 0.90x_{1p} + 0.80x_{2p} + 0.58x_{3p}.$$

Limitations on the availability of the three components can be expressed by these three constraints.

$$x_{1r} + x_{1p} \le 5,000 \quad (Component\ 1)$$
$$x_{2r} + x_{2p} \le 10,000 \quad (Component\ 2)$$
$$x_{3r} + x_{3p} \le 10,000 \quad (Component\ 3)$$

Six constraints are now required to meet the product specifications stated in Table D.5. The first specification states that component 1 must account for at most 30 percent of the total gallons of regular gasoline produced. That is,

$$\frac{x_{1r}}{x_{1r} + x_{2r} + x_{3r}} \le 0.30$$

or

$$x_{1r} \leq 0.30(x_{1r} + x_{2r} + x_{3r}).$$

When this constraint is rewritten with the variables on the left side of the equation and a constant on the right side, the first product-specification constraint becomes

$$0.70x_{1r} - 0.30x_{2r} - 0.30x_{3r} \leq 0.$$

The second product specification listed in Table D.5 can be written as

$$\frac{x_{2r}}{x_{1r} + x_{2r} + x_{3r}} \geq 0.40$$

or

$$x_{2r} \geq 0.40\,(x_{1r} + x_{2r} + x_{3r})$$

and thus

$$-0.40x_{1r} + 0.60x_{2r} - 0.40x_{3r} \geq 0.$$

Similarly, the four additional blending specifications shown in Table D.5 can be written as follows.

$$-0.20x_{1r} - 0.20x_{2r} + 0.80x_{3r} \leq 0$$

$$0.75x_{1p} - 0.25x_{2p} - 0.25x_{3p} \geq 0$$

$$-0.40x_{1p} + 0.60x_{2p} - 0.40x_{3p} \leq 0$$

$$-0.30x_{1p} - 0.30x_{2p} + 0.70x_{3p} \geq 0$$

The constraint for at least 10,000 gallons of the regular-grade gasoline is written

$$x_{1r} + x_{2r} + x_{3r} \geq 10{,}000.$$

Thus the complete linear programming model with six decision variables and 10 constraints can be written as follows.

$$\max\ 0.70x_{1r} + 0.60x_{2r} + 0.38x_{3r} + 0.90x_{1p} + 0.80x_{2p} + 0.58x_{3p}$$

subject to

$$x_{1r} + x_{1p} \leq 5{,}000$$

$$x_{2r} + x_{2p} \leq 10{,}000$$

$$x_{3r} + x_{3p} \leq 10{,}000$$

$$0.70x_{1r} - 0.30x_{2r} - 0.30x_{3r} \leq 0$$

$$-0.40x_{1r} + 0.60x_{2r} - 0.40x_{3r} \geq 0$$

$$-0.20x_{1r} - 0.20x_{2r} + 0.80x_{3r} \leq 0$$

$$0.75x_{1p} - 0.25x_{2p} - 0.25x_{3p} \geq 0$$

$$-0.40x_{1p} + 0.60x_{2p} - 0.40x_{3p} \leq 0$$

$$-0.30x_{1p} - 0.30x_{2p} + 0.70x_{3p} \geq 0$$

$$x_{1r} + x_{2r} + x_{3r} \geq 10{,}000$$

$$x_{1r}, x_{2r}, x_{3r}, x_{1p}, x_{2p}, x_{3p} \geq 0$$

Next, we illustrate how to represent and solve two-variable problems graphically by using the Softwater, Inc., example.

Graphical Solution of Linear Programs

Let us begin the graphical solution procedure by developing a graph that can be used to display the possible solutions (x_1- and x_2-values) for the Softwater problem. The graph in Figure D.1 has values of x_1 on the horizontal axis and values of x_2 on the vertical axis. Any point on the graph can be identified by the x_1- and x_2-values, which indicate the position of the point along the x_1- and x_2-axes, respectively. Since every point (x_1, x_2) corresponds to a possible solution, every point on the graph is called a *solution point*. The solution point where $x_1 = 0$ and $x_2 = 0$ is referred to as the *origin*.

The next step is to show which of the possible combinations of x_1 and x_2—that is, solution points—correspond to feasible solutions for the linear program. Since both x_1 and x_2 must be nonnegative, we need only consider points where $x_1 \geq 0$ and $x_2 \geq 0$. This is indicated in Figure D.2 by arrows pointing in the direction of production combinations that will satisfy the nonnegativity constraints—namely, points in the first quadrant.

Earlier we saw that the inequality representing the packaging-line constraint was of the form

$$1.2x_1 + 3x_2 \leq 1{,}500.$$

Figure D.1
Graph of Solution Points for
Two-Variable Softwater,
Inc., Problem

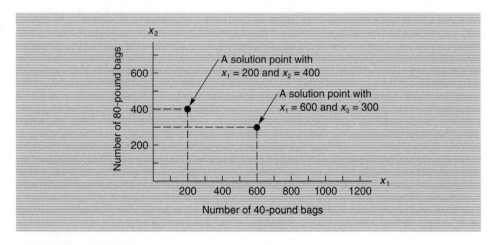

Figure D.2
Nonnegativity Constraints

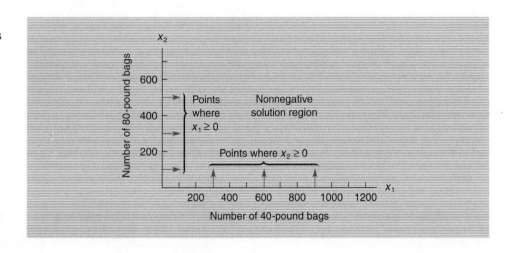

To show all solution points that satisfy this relationship, we start by graphing the line corresponding to the *equation*

$$1.2x_1 + 3x_2 = 1{,}500.$$

The graph of this equation is found by identifying two points that lie on the line and then drawing a line through the points. Setting $x_1 = 0$ and solving for x_2, we see that the point $x_1 = 0$, $x_2 = 500$ satisfies the above equation. To find a second point that satisfies the equation, we set $x_2 = 0$ and solve for x_1. Doing this, we obtain $1.2x_1 + 3(0) = 1{,}500$; hence, $x_1 = 1{,}250$. Thus a second point satisfying the equation is $x_1 = 1{,}250$, $x_2 = 0$. Given these two points, we can now graph the line corresponding to the equation

$$1.2x_1 + 3x_2 = 1{,}500.$$

This line, which will be called the *packaging-line constraint (PL)*, is shown in Figure D.3.

Recall that the inequality representing the packaging-line constraint is

$$1.2x_1 + 3x_2 \le 1{,}500.$$

Figure D.3
Packaging-Line (*PL*)
Constraint

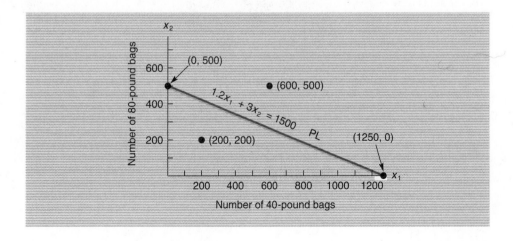

Can you identify all the solution points that satisfy this constraint? Since we have the line where $1.2x_1 + 3x_2 = 1,500$, we know that any point on this line must satisfy the constraint. But where are the solution points that satisfy $1.2x_1 + 3x_2 < 1,500$? Consider two solution points, $x_1 = 200$, $x_2 = 200$ and $x_1 = 600$, $x_2 = 500$. You can see from Figure D.3 that the first solution point is below the constraint line and the second is above the constraint line. Which of these solutions will satisfy the packaging-line constraint? For the point $x_1 = 200$, $x_2 = 200$, we see that

$$1.2x_1 + 3x_2 = 1.2(200) + 3(200)$$
$$= 240 + 600 = 840.$$

Since the 840 minutes is less than the 1,500 minutes available, the $x_1 = 200$, $x_2 = 200$ production combination, or solution point, satisfies the constraint. For $x_1 = 600$, $x_2 = 500$, we have

$$1.2x_1 + 3x_2 = 1.2(600) + 3(500)$$
$$= 720 + 1,500 = 2,220.$$

Since the 2,220 minutes is greater than the 1,500 minutes available, the $x_1 = 600$, $x_2 = 500$ solution point does not satisfy the constraint and is thus an unacceptable production alternative.

This suggests that any point *below* the *PL* line satisfies the constraint. You may want to satisfy yourself by selecting additional solution points above and below the constraint line and checking to see if the solutions satisfy the constraints. You will see that only solution points on or below the constraint line satisfy the constraint. The region of the graph corresponding to the solution points that satisfy the packaging-line constraint are shaded in Figure D.4.

Next let us identify all solution points that satisfy the packaging-materials, or materials-availability, constraint (M).

$$6x_1 + 10x_2 \leq 6,000.$$

We start by drawing the constraint line corresponding to the equation

$$6x_1 + 10x_2 = 6,000.$$

Figure D.4
Feasible Region for
Packaging-Line (*PL*)
Constraint

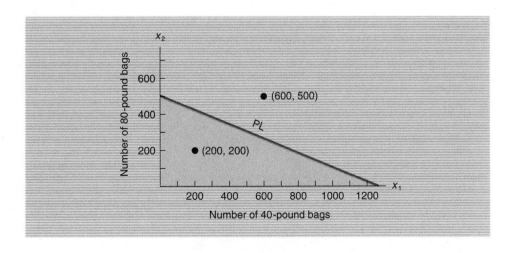

As before, the graphing of a line is most easily done by finding two points on the line and then connecting them. Thus we first set x_1 equal to zero and solve for x_2, which yields the point $x_1 = 0$, $x_2 = 600$. Next we set x_2 equal to zero and solve for x_1, which gives the second point, $x_1 = 1,000$, $x_2 = 0$. In Figure D.5 we have drawn the line corresponding to the materials constraint (M). Using the same approach as for the packaging-line constraint, we realize that only points on or below the line satisfy the materials-availability constraint. The shaded region in Figure D.5 corresponds to all feasible production combinations or feasible solution points for packaging-materials availability.

In a similar manner, we determine the set of all feasible production combinations for the aggregate-production constraint (AP). This constraint is $40x_1 + 80x_2 \geq 16,000$. If we graph the equation

$$40x_1 + 80x_2 = 16,000$$

by first setting x_1 equal to zero and solving for x_2, we obtain the point $x_1 = 0$, $x_2 = 200$. Next, setting x_2 equal to zero and solving for x_1, we obtain the point $x_1 = 400$, $x_2 = 0$. Note that this constraint contains the symbol for greater than or equal to. If we choose a point on either side of the line, such as (100, 100) and (400, 200), we find that

$$40(100) + 80(100) = 12,000$$

and

$$40(400) + 80(200) = 32,000.$$

The point (100, 100) does *not* satisfy the constraint $40x_1 + 80x_2 \geq 16,000$; however, the point (400, 200) does satisfy it. Therefore, the feasible region for this constraint is given by the shaded region in Figure D.6. Note that this extends without bound in the first quadrant above the constraint line.

We now have three separate graphs showing the feasible solution points for each of the three constraints. In a linear programming problem, we need to identify the solution points that satisfy all the constraints simultaneously. To find these solution points, we draw the three constraints on one graph and observe the region containing the points that do in fact satisfy all the constraints

Figure D.5
Feasible Region for
Materials Constraint (M)

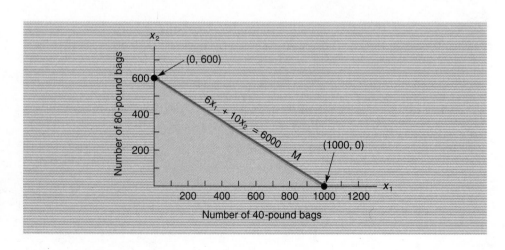

Figure D.6
Feasible Region for
Aggregate-Production
Constraint (*AP*)

Figure D.6
Feasible Region for
Aggregate-Production
Constraint (*AP*)

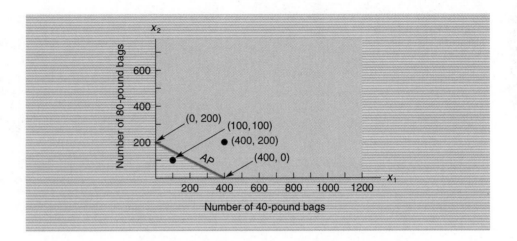

simultaneously. This combined-constraint graph is shown in Figure D.7. The shaded region in this figure includes every solution point that satisfies all the constraints. Since solutions that satisfy all the constraints are called *feasible solutions,* the shaded region is called the *feasible solution region,* or simply the *feasible region.* Any point on the boundary of the feasible region or within the feasible region is a *feasible solution point.*

Recall that the optimal solution for any linear programming problem is the feasible solution that provides the best possible value of the objective function. We could arbitrarily select feasible solution points (x_1, x_2) and compute their associated profits as $2x_1 + 4x_2$. However, the difficulty with this is that there are too many feasible solutions (actually an infinite number) to evaluate. Thus, we would like to have a systematic way of identifying the feasible solution that does in fact maximize the profit for Softwater, Inc.

Let us start this final step of the graphical solution procedure by drawing the feasible region on a separate graph. This is shown in Figure D.8. Rather than selecting an arbitrary feasible solution and computing the associated profit, let us select an arbitrary profit and identify all the feasible solution points (x_1, x_2) that will yield it. For example, what feasible solution points provide a profit of $1,200? That is, what value of x_1 and x_2 in the feasible region will make the objective function $2x_1 + 4x_2$ equal 1,200?

Figure D.7
Feasible Region in
Combined-Constraint
Graph

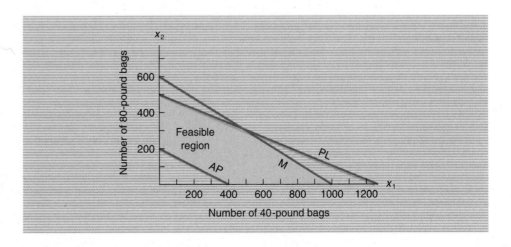

Figure D.8
Feasible Region for
Softwater, Inc.

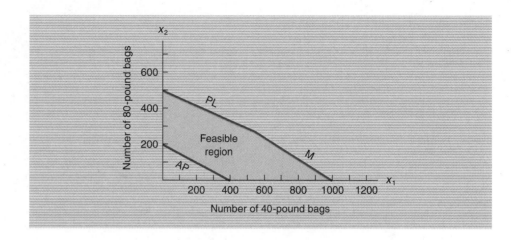

The expression $2x_1 + 4x_2 = 1{,}200$ is simply the equation of a line. Thus all feasible solution points (x_1, x_2) yielding a profit of $1,200 must be on the line. The procedure for graphing the profit or objective-function line is the same as graphing a constraint line. Letting x_1 equal zero, we see that x_2 must be 300, and thus the solution point $x_1 = 0$, $x_2 = 300$ is on the line. Similarly, by letting x_2 equal zero, we see that the solution point $x_1 = 600$, $x_2 = 0$ is also on the line. Drawing the line through these two solution points identifies all the solution points that have a profit of $1,200. A graph of this profit line is presented in Figure D.9. From this graph, you can see that there are an infinite number of feasible production combinations that will provide a $1,200 profit.

Since the objective is to find a feasible solution point that has the highest profit, let us proceed by selecting higher profit values—for example, $1500 and $2100—and finding the feasible solution points that yield them. We must find the x_1 and x_2 values on the lines for

$$2x_1 + 4x_2 = 1{,}500$$

and

$$2x_1 + 4x_2 = 2{,}100.$$

Figure D.9
$1,200 Profit Line

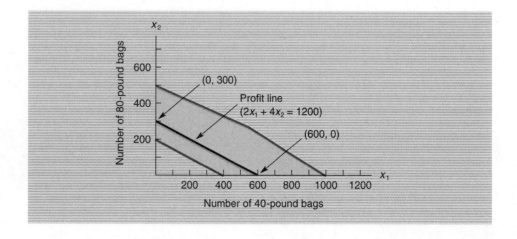

Figure D.10
Selected Profit Lines

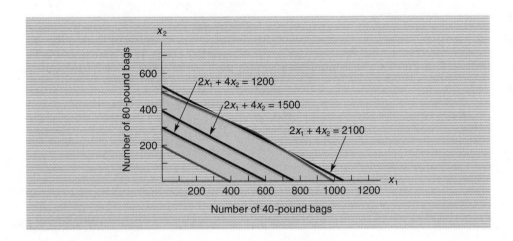

Using the previous procedure for graphing profit and constraint lines, we have drawn the $1,500 and $2,100 profit lines on the graph in Figure D.10. Although not all solution points on the $2,100 profit line are in the feasible region, at least some points on the line are, and thus it is possible to obtain a feasible production combination that provides a $2,100 profit.

Can we find a solution that yields even higher profits? From Figure D.10 you should notice that (1) the profit lines are parallel to each other and (2) higher profit lines occur as we move farther from the origin. These properties can now be used to determine the optimal solution to the problem. By continuing to move the profit line farther from the origin so that it remains parallel to the other profit lines, we can obtain solution points that yield higher and higher values for the objective function. However, at some point, we will find that any further outward movement will place the profit line outside the feasible region. Since points outside the feasible region are unacceptable, a point in the feasible region that lies on the highest profit line is an optimal solution to our linear program.

You should now be able to identify the optimal solution point for the Softwater, Inc., problem. Use a ruler or the edge of a piece of paper to help you move the profit line as far from the origin as you can. The optimal solution is shown graphically in Figure D.11.

Figure D.11
Optimal Solution for
Softwater, Inc., Problem

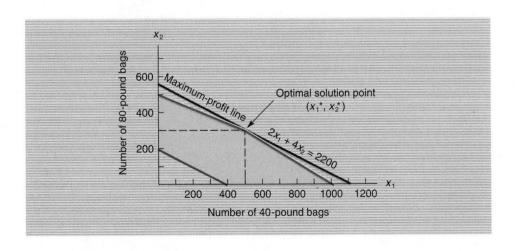

The optimal values of the decision variables x_1 and x_2 (denoted with asterisks) are the x_1 and x_2 values at the optimal solution point. Depending on the accuracy of your graph, you may or may not be able to read the *exact* x_1 and x_2 values from the graph. The best we can do with respect to the optimal solution point in Figure D.11 is to conclude that the optimal production combination consists of approximately 500 40-pound bags and 300 80-pound bags. As you will see later, the actual x_1 and x_2 values at the optimal solution point are indeed $x_1 = 500$ and $x_2 = 300$. In a later subsection you will learn how to compute exact optimal solution values.

Summary of Graphical Solution Procedure for Maximization Problems

The steps of the graphical solution procedure for a *maximization* problem follow.

1. Prepare a graph of the feasible solution points for each constraint.
2. Determine the feasible solution region by identifying the solution points that satisfy all the constraints simultaneously.
3. Draw a profit line showing all values of the variables x_1 and x_2 that yield a specified value of the objective function.
4. Move parallel profit lines toward higher profits (usually away from the origin) until further movement would take the profit line completely outside the feasible region.
5. Any feasible solution point that is touched by the highest possible profit line is the optimal solution.
6. Determine, at least approximately, the optimal values of the decision variables by reading the x_1 and x_2 values at an optimal solution point directly from the graph.

Solving a minimization problem graphically requires modification of steps 4 and 5. In step 4 the objective-function lines are moved parallel to each other toward lower values. In step 5 any feasible solution point that is touched by the lowest possible objective function line is an optimal solution.

Extreme Points and Optimal Solution

Suppose the profit on the Softwater, Inc., 40-pound bag is reduced from $2 to $1 per bag, while the profit on the 80-pound bag and all the constraint conditions remain unchanged. The complete linear programming model of this new problem is identical to the previous mathematical model, except for the revised objective function:

$$\max z = x_1 + 4x_2.$$

Figure D.12 shows the graphical solution of the Softwater, Inc., problem with the revised objective function. Note that since the constraints have not changed, the feasible solution region has not changed. However, the profit lines are altered.

Figure D.12
Optimal Solution for
Softwater, Inc., Problem
with Objective Function of
$x_1 + 4x_2$

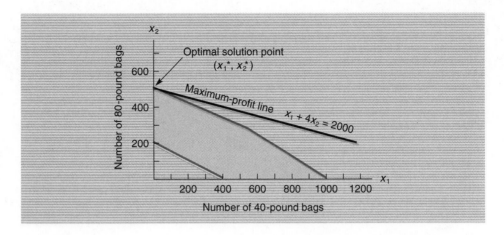

By moving the profit line in a parallel manner away from the origin, we find the optimal solution point shown in Figure D.12. The exact values of the decision variables at this point are $x_1 = 0$ and $x_2 = 500$. Thus the reduced profit for the 40-pound bags has caused a change in the optimal solution. In fact, as you may have suspected, this calls for cutting back the production of the lower-profit, 40-pound bags and increasing the production of the higher-profit, 80-pound bags.

Looking closely at the graphical solutions in Figures D.11 and D.12 you should notice that the optimal solutions occur at the vertices, or "corners," of the feasible region. In linear programming terminology, these vertices are referred to as the *extreme points* of the feasible region. Thus the feasible region of the Softwater, Inc., problem has five vertices, or five extreme points; see Figure D.13. In general

> An optimal solution to a linear programming problem can be found at an extreme point of the feasible solution region for the problem.

This is a very important property of all linear programming problems because it means that you do not have to evaluate *all* feasible solution points. In fact, you need to consider only the feasible solutions that occur at the extreme points of

Figure D.13
Five Extreme Points of
Feasible Region for
Softwater, Inc., Problem

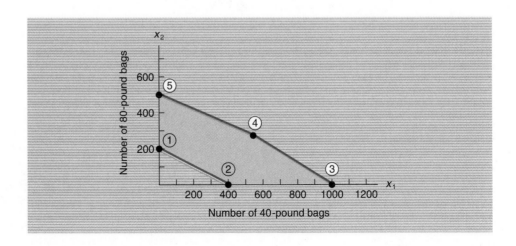

Figure D.14
Optimal Solution Points for
Softwater, Inc., Problem
with Objective Function of
$2.4x_1 + 6x_2$

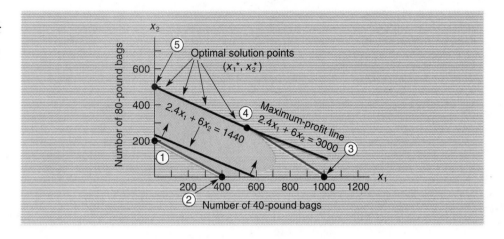

the feasible region. This is very important for efficient computer solution of linear programs.

What happens if the highest profit line coincides with one of the constraint lines on the boundary of the feasible region? This case is shown for the objective function $2.4x_1 + 6x_2$ in Figure D.14. Does an optimal solution still occur at an extreme point? The answer is yes. In fact, for this case the optimal solution occurs at extreme points 4 and 5, and any solution point on the line joining these two points. This is the special case of *alternate optimal solutions.*

Finding Exact Locations of Extreme Points

Let us consider extreme point 4 of the Softwater problem, as shown in Figure D.15. In the graphical solution procedure, extreme point 4 was identified as the optimal solution. However, we had difficulty reading the exact values of x_1 and x_2 directly from the graph. Actually, the best we could do was to approximate the values of the decision variables.

Referring to Figure D.15, note the constraint lines that determine the exact location of extreme point 4. The *PL* constraint line and the *M* constraint line combine to determine this extreme point. That is, extreme point 4 is on both the *PL* line,

Figure D.15
Feasible Region for
Softwater, Inc., Problem

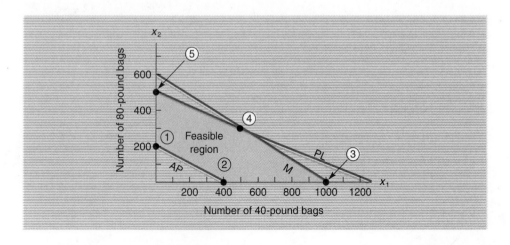

$$1.2x_1 + 3x_2 = 1{,}500, \tag{D.6}$$

and the M line,

$$6x_1 + 10x_2 = 6{,}000. \tag{D.7}$$

Thus the values of the decision variables x_1 and x_2 at extreme point 4 must satisfy both equations D.6 and D.7. Using equation D.6 and solving for x_1 gives

$$1.2x_1 = 1{,}500 - 3x_2$$

or

$$x_1 = 1{,}250 - \frac{5}{2}x_2. \tag{D.8}$$

Substituting this expression of x_1 into equation D.7 and solving for x_2 provides

$$6\left[1{,}250 - \frac{5}{2}x_2\right] + 10x_2 = 6{,}000$$

$$7{,}500 - 15x_2 + 10x_2 = 6{,}000$$

$$-5x_2 = -1{,}500$$

$$x_2 = 300.$$

Using $x_2 = 300$ in equation D.8 and solving for x_1 provides

$$x_1 = 1{,}250 - \frac{5}{2}(300)$$

$$= 1{,}250 - 750$$

$$= 500.$$

Thus the exact location of extreme point 4 is $x_1 = 500$ and $x_2 = 300$. This is, of course, what we had identified earlier by reading the approximate values on the graph.

Solving Linear Programs with Microsoft Excel

Although a graphical solution method can be used for solving linear programs with two variables, more complex problems require computer solution. Microsoft Excel provides the capability for solving linear programs. The first step is to construct a spreadsheet model for the problem, such as the one shown in Figure D.16 for the Softwater, Inc., example. The problem data are given in the range of cells A4:E8 in the same way that we write the mathematical model. Cells B12 and C12 provide the values of the decision variables. Formulas for the left side of each constraint are given in cells B15 through B17. For example, the formula for the left side of the packaging constraint in cell B15 is =B6*B12+C6*C12. The value of the objective function, =B5*B12+C5*C12, is entered in cell B19.

To solve the problem, select the Solver option from the Tools menu in the Excel control panel. The Solver dialog box, also shown in Figure D.16, will appear.

Supplementary Chapter D

Figure D.16
Spreadsheet Model for
Softwater, Inc.
(SOFTWATR.XLS)

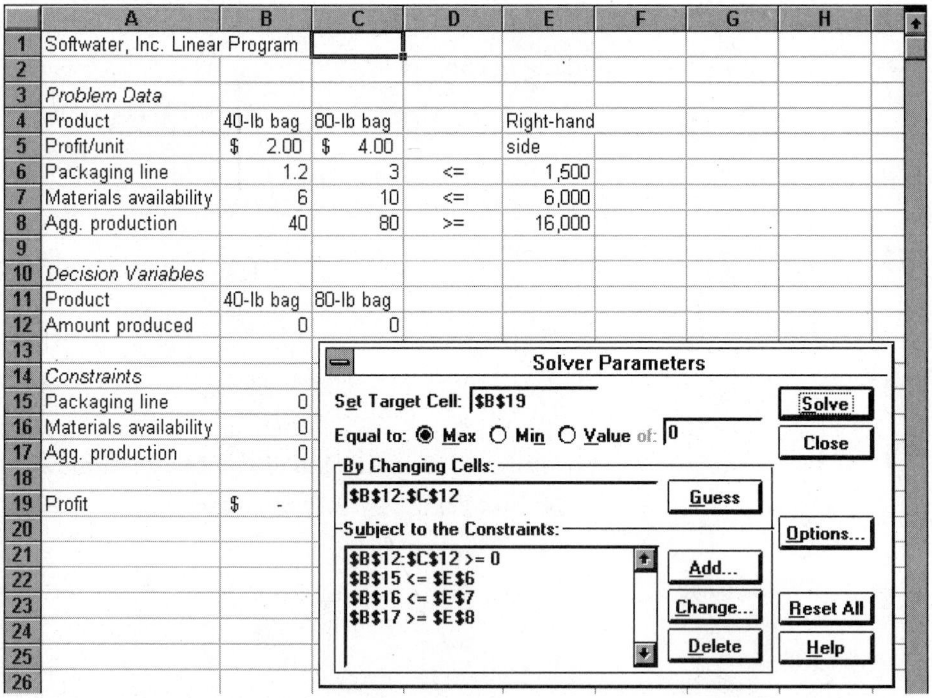

The target cell is the one that contains the objective function value. Changing cells are those that hold the decision variables. Constraints are constructed in the constraint box or edited by using the Add, Change, or Delete buttons. Excel does *not* assume nonnegativity; thus, this must be explicitly added to the constraint box by setting the range of decision variables ($B$12:$C$12) greater than or equal to zero. You should also select the Options button and choose "Assume linear model" from the options menu. Then click on Solve in the dialog box, and Excel will find the optimal solution as shown in Figure D.17.

Figure D.17
Optimal Solution to
Softwater, Inc., Example
from Microsoft Excel Solver

Figure D.18
Solver Results Dialog Box

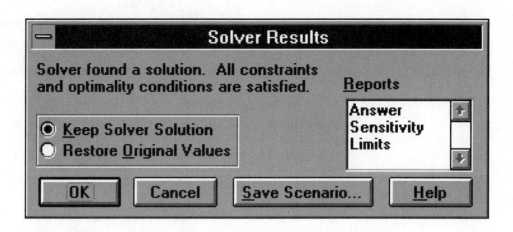

Interpreting the Solution

After a solution is found, Solver allows you to generate three reports—an Answer Report, a Sensitivity Report, and a Limits Report—from the solution dialog box as shown in Figure D.18. These reports are placed in separate sheets in the spreadsheet file. The Answer Report (Figure D.19) provides basic information about the solution. The Constraints section requires further explanation. "Cell Value" refers to the left side of the constraint if we substitute the optimal values of the decision variables:

Figure D.19
Solver Answer Report

Microsoft Excel 5.0 Answer Report
Worksheet: [SOFTWATR.XLS]Sheet1
Report Created: 3/3/96 13:27

Target Cell (Max)

Cell	Name	Original Value	Final Value
$B$19	Profit 40-lb bag	$ -	$ 2,200.00

Adjustable Cells

Cell	Name	Original Value	Final Value
$B$12	Amount produced 40-lb bag	0	500
$C$12	Amount produced 80-lb bag	0	300

Constraints

Cell	Name	Cell Value	Formula	Status	Slack
$B$15	Packaging line 40-lb bag	1500	$B$15<=$E$6	Binding	0
$B$16	Materials availability 40-lb bag	6000	$B$16<=$E$7	Binding	0
$B$17	Agg. production 40-lb bag	44000	$B$17>=$E$8	Not Binding	28000
$B$12	Amount produced 40-lb bag	500	$B$12>=0	Not Binding	500
$C$12	Amount produced 80-lb bag	300	$C$12>=0	Not Binding	300

Packaging line: 1.2(500) + 3(300) = 1,500 minutes.

Materials: 6(500) + 10(300) = 6,000 square feet.

Production: 40(500) + 80(300) = 44,000 pounds.

We see that the amount of time used on the packaging line and the amount of materials used are at their limits. We call such constraints *binding*. However, the aggregate production has exceeded its requirement by 44,000 − 16,000 = 28,000 pounds. This difference is referred to as the *slack* in the constraint. In general, slack is the absolute difference between the left and right sides of a constraint. The last two constraints in this report are nonnegativity and can be ignored.

The top portion of the Sensitivity Report (Figure D.20) tells us the ranges for which the objective-function coefficients can vary without changing the optimal values of the decision variables. They are given in the "Allowable Increase" and "Allowable Decrease" columns. Thus, the profit coefficient on 40-pound bags may vary between 1.6 and 2.4 without changing the optimal product mix. If the coefficient is changed beyond these ranges, the problem must be solved anew. The lower portion provides information about changes in the right side values of the constraints. The shadow price is the change in the objective function value as the right side of a constraint is increased by one unit. Thus, for the packaging line constraint, an extra minute of line availability will improve profit by 67 cents. Similarly, a reduction in line availability will reduce profit by 67 cents. This will hold for increases or decreases within the allowable ranges in the last two columns.

Finally, the Limits Report (Figure D.21) shows the feasible lower and upper limits on each individual decision variable if everything else is fixed. Thus, if the number of 80-pound bags is fixed at 300, the number of 40-pound bags can go as low as zero or as high as 500 and maintain a feasible solution. If it drops to zero, the objective function (target result) will be $1,200.

Figure D.20
Solver Sensitivity Report

Microsoft Excel 5.0 Sensitivity Report
Worksheet: [SOFTWATR.XLS]Sheet1
Report Created: 3/3/96 13:27

Changing Cells

Cell	Name	Final Value	Reduced Cost	Objective Coefficient	Allowable Increase	Allowable Decrease
$B$12	Amount produced 40-lb bag	500	0	2	0.4	0.4
$C$12	Amount produced 80-lb bag	300	0	4	1	0.666666667

Constraints

Cell	Name	Final Value	Shadow Price	Constraint R.H. Side	Allowable Increase	Allowable Decrease
$B$15	Packaging line 40-lb bag	1500	0.666666667	1500	300	300
$B$16	Materials availability 40-lb bag	6000	0.2	6000	1500	1000
$B$17	Agg. production 40-lb bag	44000	0	16000	28000	1E+30

Figure D.21
Solver Limits Report

Microsoft Excel 5.0 Limits Report
Worksheet: [SOFTWATR.XLS]Sheet1
Report Created: 3/3/96 13:27

	Target		
Cell	Name	Value
$B$19	Profit 40-lb bag	$2,200.00

	Adjustable		Lower Target		Upper Target	
Cell	Name	Value	Limit	Result	Limit	Result
$B$12	Amount produced 40-lb bag	500	0	1200	500	2200
$C$12	Amount produced 80-lb bag	300	0	1000	300	2200

Simplex Method

Most computer solvers are based on the **simplex method**—an algorithm that systematically searches among corner points until it identifies an optimal solution or determines that none exist. We will illustrate the basic mechanics of the simplex method to help you understand how this approach works. We will restrict our discussion to problems with *only* less-than-or-equal-to constraints, using a simplified version of the Softwater, Inc., problem by ignoring the aggregate production constraint:

$$\max z = 2x_1 + 4x_2$$

$$1.2x_1 + 3x_2 \le 1,500 \quad \text{(packaging line)}$$

$$6x_1 + 10x_2 \le 6,000 \quad \text{(materials availability)}$$

$$x_1, x_2 \ge 0.$$

Setting Up Linear Programs for Simplex Method

The simplex method requires that all constraints be expressed as *equations*. We may convert any less-than-or-equal-to constraint to an equation by adding a **slack variable.** For example, the first constraint,

$$1.2x_1 + 3x_2 \le 1,500$$

specifies that

$$(\text{total packaging time used}) \le (\text{packaging time available}).$$

Then, obviously,

$$\begin{pmatrix}\text{total packaging} \\ \text{time used}\end{pmatrix} + \begin{pmatrix}\text{packaging} \\ \text{time not used}\end{pmatrix} = \begin{pmatrix}\text{packaging} \\ \text{time available}\end{pmatrix}.$$

Letting s_1 represent the packaging time not used (slack), we have

$$1.2x_1 + 3x_2 + s_1 = 1{,}500.$$

Thus, a slack variable simply represents the difference between the right side and left side of a less-than-or-equal-to constraint. We can convert the materials-availability constraint (M) into an equation in a similar manner by adding a different slack variable, s_2.

$$6x_1 + 10x_2 + s_2 = 6{,}000.$$

Here, s_2 represents unused material. Note that both s_1 and s_2 must be nonnegative for the constraints to be feasible.

The linear program can now be stated as follows.

$$\max z = \quad 2x_1 + \quad 4x_2 + 0s_1 + 0s_2$$
$$1.2x_1 + \quad 3x_2 + \quad s_1 \qquad\quad = 1{,}500$$
$$6x_1 + 10x_2 \qquad\quad + \quad s_2 = 6{,}000$$
$$x_1,\, x_2,\, s_1,\, s_2 \geq 0$$

You can readily observe that if $x_1 = x_2 = 0$, then we have a solution, $s_1 = 1{,}500$, $s_2 = 6{,}000$, and $z = 0$. In the terminology of the simplex method, this is a *basic feasible solution*. The variables set to zero (x_1 and x_2) are called *nonbasic variables*, while the remaining variables (s_1 and s_2) are called *basic variables*.

Simplex Solution Procedure

The simplex method seeks to replace one basic variable with a nonbasic variable if it results in a better solution. The main steps of the simplex method follow.

1. Determine if increasing any nonbasic variable from zero will improve the current solution. If not, then the current solution is optimal.
2   Determine which basic variable to replace.
3. Perform the "switch" by manipulating the equations so that the new basic variable has a 1 in the row of the variable it replaced, and zeros everywhere else. (We will see how this can be done quite easily in a tabular fashion.)

Figure D.22 is the **simplex tableau**—a representation of the problem in tabular form—for the initial solution. At the top of each column corresponding to a variable we list the objective-function coefficient (which we call "C_j"). These are the profit contributions per unit of each variable. The C_js corresponding to basic variables are written at the left of the tableau. The numbers in the "Z_j" row are computed by multiplying the C_js in the leftmost column (corresponding to

Figure D.22
Simplex Tableau

c_j		2	4	0	0	
	Basic Variables	x_1	x_2	s_1	s_2	Right-hand-side (RHS)
0	s_1	1.2	3	1	0	1,500
0	s_2	6	10	0	1	6,000
	z_j	0	0	0	0	0
	$c_j - z_j$	2	4	0	0	objective-function value

basic variables) by the corresponding values in every other column and summing. For example, under x_1, we have

$$(0)(1.2) + (0)(6) = 0.$$

The Z_j value in the "RHS" column represents the value of the objective function for this basic feasible solution. By subtracting Z_j from C_j for each variable, we obtain the last row, "$C_j - Z_j$."

The $C_j - Z_j$ values for nonbasic variables represent the unit contribution to the objective function by *increasing* the value of this variable ($C_j - Z_j = 0$ for all basic variables). Thus, a positive value means that the objective function will increase; a negative value indicates a decrease.

The $C_j - Z_j$ values form the basis for step 1 of the simplex method. For a maximization problem, a positive $C_j - Z_j$ indicates that an increase in the nonbasic variable will improve the solution. If all $C_j - Z_j$ values are zero or less, the solution is optimal.

We select the nonbasic variable having the largest $C_j - Z_j$ to become basic because it has the highest rate of contribution to profit. This designates the *pivot column*. In this example, we see that the pivot column corresponds to x_2. In step 2, we determine which basic variable to replace. To do this, we divide the right-hand-side (RHS) value by the tableau value in the pivot column *as long as the valve in the pivot column is positive,* and select the minimum.

Figure D.23 shows this calculation. The row in which the minimum occurs is called the *pivot row*. Row 1, corresponding to s_1, is the pivot row. The intersection of the pivot column and pivot row is called the *pivot number* shown circled in Figure D.23.

Step 3 of the simplex method—finding the new basic feasible solution—is accomplished as follows.

Figure D.23
Finding Pivot Row in Simplex Tableau

		2	4	0	0		
	Basic Variables	x_1	x_2	s_1	s_2	RHS	minimum
0	s_1	1.2	③	1	0	1,500	1500/3 = 500 ←
0	s_2	6	10	0	1	6,000	6000/10 = 600
	z_j	0	0	0	0	0	
	$c_j - z_j$	2	4	0	0		

Pivot column

3a. Divide the pivot row by the pivot number (see Figure D.24).

3b. For every row that is not a pivot row, first identify the number in the *pivot column*. Then multiply every element in the *pivot row* by this number, and subtract the result from the corresponding element in that row (see Figure D.25). *Do not change* the pivot row in the tableau, however. This results in a 1 where the pivot number was, and zeros everywhere else in the pivot column.

3c. Complete the new tableau by changing the basic variables and corresponding C_js, and computing new Z_j and $C_j - Z_j$ values as shown in Figure D.26.

Figure D.24
Step 3a in Simplex Method

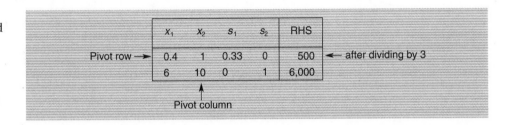

Figure D.25
Step 3b in Simplex Method

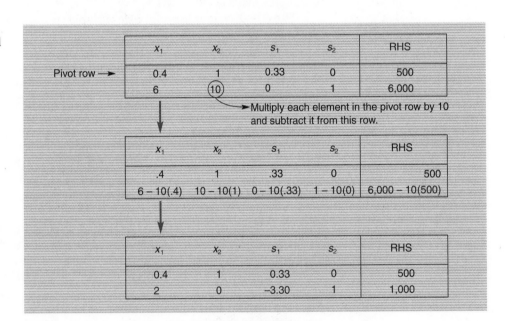

Figure D.26
New Simplex Tableau

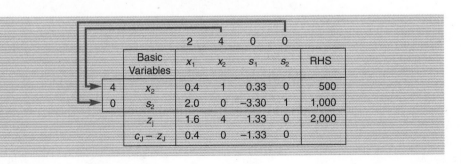

Figure D.27
Final Simplex Tableau

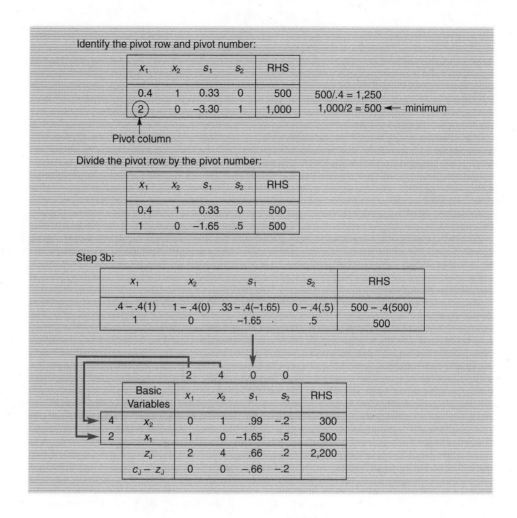

From Figure D.26, we see that the new basic solution is $x_1 = 0$, $x_2 = 500$, $s_1 = 0$, $s_2 = 1,000$, and $z = 2,000$. To determine if this solution is optimal, we check the $C_j - Z_j$ row. The value of 0.4 for x_1 indicates that the objective function can be improved further by making x_1 basic. Therefore, we repeat the steps of the simplex method, using x_1 as the pivot column. Figure D.27 shows the remaining steps. Because no $C_j - Z_j$ is positive in the final tableau, we have the optimal solution.

Minimization Problems

There are two ways to handle minimization problems. First, we could change the rule for selecting the pivot column. Instead of choosing the largest positive $C_j - Z_j$, we choose the most negative $C_j - Z_j$. If all are positive or zero, we have the optimal solution.

The second approach is to multiply the objective function by -1 and treat it as a maximization, remembering to multiply the final objective-function value by -1 when finished.

Key Terms

Objective function
Solution
Feasible solution
Optimal solution
Nonnegativity constraints
Linear program
Constraint function
Linear function
Simplex method
Slack variable
Simplex tableau

Review/Discussion Questions

1. List the components of every linear programming problem.

2. Discuss the meaning of the term *linear* in linear programming.
3. Describe some applications of linear programming in P/OM.
4. List the major types of constraints in production-scheduling problems.
5. Can you think of other applications of blending problems?
6. Describe verbally the graphical solution procedure for linear programs.
7. Define *feasible region*.
8. Explain the importance of extreme points in solving linear programs.
9. Define *shadow price*.
10. Explain the interpretation of "RIGHT-HAND SIDE RANGES" and "OBJECTIVE COEFFICIENT RANGES" in the linear programming computer output.

Solved Problems

1. Par, Inc., is a small manufacturer of golf equipment and supplies. Par has been convinced by its distributor that a market exists for both a medium-priced golf bag, referred to as a *standard* model, and a high-priced golf bag, referred to as a *deluxe* model. The distributor is so confident of the market that if Par can produce the bags at a competitive price, the distributor has agreed to purchase all the bags that Par can manufacture over the next three months. A careful analysis of the manufacturing requirements resulted in Table D.6.

The director of manufacturing estimates that 630 hours of cutting and dyeing time, 600 hours of sewing time, 708 hours of finishing time, and 135 hours of inspection and packaging time will be available for the production of golf bags during the next three months.

Table D.6 Data for Solved Problem 1

Product	Production Time (hours per bag)				Profit per Bag
	Cutting/ Dyeing	Sewing	Finishing	Inspection/ Packaging	
Standard	$7/10$	$1/2$	1	$1/10$	$10
Deluxe	1	$5/6$	$2/3$	$1/4$	$ 9

a. Assuming that Par wants to maximize profit, how many bags of each model should it manufacture?
b. What profit can Par earn with the production quantities arrived at in part a?
c. How many hours of production time should be scheduled for each operation?
d. What is the slack time in each operation?

Solution
a. Let x_1 = number of standard bags, and x_2 = number of deluxe bags to produce. The model is

$$\max 10x_1 + 9x_2$$

$$\tfrac{7}{10}x_1 + 1x_2 \leq 630$$

$$\tfrac{1}{2}x_1 + \tfrac{5}{6}x_2 \leq 600$$

$$1x_1 + \tfrac{2}{3}x_2 \leq 708$$

$$\tfrac{1}{10}x_1 + \tfrac{1}{4}x_2 \leq 135$$

$$x_1, x_2 \geq 0$$

As shown in Figure D.28, the optimal solution is 540 standard bags and 252 deluxe bags.

Figure D.28
Solved Problem 1 Solution

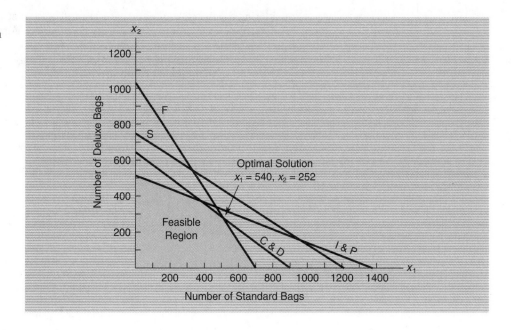

b. Profit is $7,668.
c. & d. The production time and slack time for each operation are given in Table D.7.

Table D.7 Solved Problem 1 Constraint Values

Operation	Production Time	Slack
Cutting and Dyeing	630	0
Sewing	480	120
Finishing	708	0
Inspection and Packaging	117	18

2. *Make or buy.* The Carson Stapler Manufacturing Company forecasts a 5,000-unit demand for its Sure-Hold model during the next quarter. This stapler is assembled from three major components: base, staple cartridge, and handle. Until now Carson has manufactured all three components. However, the forecast of 5,000 units is a new high in sales volume, and the firm doubts that it will have sufficient production capacity to make all the components. It is considering contracting a local firm to produce at least some of the components. The production-time requirements per unit are given in Table D.8.

Table D.8 Data for Solved Problem 2

| Department | Production Time (hours) | | | Total Department Time Available (hours) |
	Base	Cartridge	Handle	
A	0.03	0.02	0.05	400
B	0.04	0.02	0.04	400
C	0.02	0.03	0.01	400

After considering the firm's overhead, material, and labor costs, the accounting department has determined the unit manufacturing cost for each component. These data, along with the purchase price quotations by the contracting firm are given in Table D.9. Formulate a linear programming model for the make-or-buy decision for Carson that will meet the 5,000-unit demand at a minimum total cost.

Table D.9 Additional Data for Solved Problem 2

Component	Manufacturing Cost($)	Purchase Cost ($)
Base	$0.75	$0.95
Cartridge	0.40	0.55
Handle	1.10	1.40

Solution

Let

x_1 = number of units of the base manufactured.

x_2 = number of units the cartridge manufactured.

x_3 = number of units of the handle manufactured.

x_4 = number of units of the base purchased.

x_5 = number of units of the cartridge purchased.

x_6 = number of units of the handle purchased.

$$\min .75x_1 + .40x_2 + 1.10x_3 + .95x_4 + .55x_5 + 1.40x_6$$

s.t.

$$.03x_1 + .02x_2 + .05x_3 \leq 400 \quad \text{(Dept. A)}$$
$$.04x_1 + .02x_2 + .04x_3 \leq 400 \quad \text{(Dept. B)}$$
$$.02x_1 + .03x_2 + .01x_3 \leq 400 \quad \text{(Dept. C)}$$
$$x_1 \qquad\qquad + x_4 \qquad\qquad = 5{,}000$$
$$x_2 \qquad\qquad + x_5 \qquad = 5{,}000$$
$$x_3 \qquad\qquad + x_6 = 5{,}000$$
$$x_1, x_2, x_3, x_4, x_5, x_6 \geq 0$$

Problems

1. Graphing constraint lines is an essential step in the graphical method. Show a separate graph of the constraint lines and feasible solutions for each of these constraints.
a. $3x_1 + 2x_2 \leq 18$
b. $12x_1 + 8x_2 \geq 480$
c. $5x_1 + 10x_2 = 200$

2. Show a separate graph of the constraint lines and feasible solutions for each of these constraints.
a. $3x_1 - 4x_2 \geq 60$
b. $-6x_1 + 5x_2 \leq 60$
c. $5x_1 - 2x_2 \leq 0$

3. Solve this linear program.

$$\max 5x_1 + 5x_2$$
$$1x_1 \qquad \leq 100$$
$$1x_2 \leq 80$$
$$2x_1 + 4x_2 \leq 400$$
$$x_1, x_2 \quad \geq \quad 0$$

4. Consider this linear programming problem.

$$\max 2x_1 + 3x_2$$
$$1x_1 + 2x_2 \leq 6$$
$$5x_1 + 3x_2 \leq 15$$
$$x_1, x_2 \quad \geq \quad 0$$

Find the optimal solution. What is the value of the objective function at the optimal solution?

5. For this linear programming problem:

$$\max 3x_1 + 3x_2$$
$$2x_1 + 4x_2 \leq 12$$
$$6x_1 + 4x_2 \leq 24$$
$$x_1, x_2 \quad \geq \quad 0$$

a. Find the optimal solution.
b. If the objective function were changed to $2x_1 + 6x_2$, what would the optimal solution be?
c. How many extreme points are there? What are the values of x_1 and x_2 at each extreme point?

6. Refer to Solved Problem 1. Suppose the selling price for the Par, Inc., standard bag must be reduced by $7 due to competitive pressures. No other costs or prices are affected.
a. What are the optimal production quantities?
b. What constraint lines combine to form the optimal extreme point?

7. Suppose the managers of Par, Inc. (Solved Problem 1), encounter each of these situations:

a. The accounting department revises its estimate of profit on the deluxe bag to $18 per bag.
b. A newer, low-cost material is available for the standard bag, and the profit contribution per standard bag can be increased to $20 per bag. (Assume that the profit contribution of the deluxe bag is the original $9 value.)

c. New sewing equipment is available that would increase the sewing-operation capacity to 750 hours. (Assume that $10x_1 + 9x_2$ is the appropriate objective function.)
If each of the above conditions is encountered separately, what are the optimal solution and profit contribution in each situation?

8. The Erlanger Manufacturing Company makes two products. The profit estimates are $25 for each unit of product 1 sold and $30 for each unit of product 2 sold. The labor-hour requirements for the products in the three production departments are shown in Table D.10.

Table D.10 Data for Problem 8

Department	Product 1	Product 2
A	1.50	3.00
B	2.00	1.00
C	.25	.25

The departments' production supervisors estimate that the following number of labor-hours will be available during the next month: 450 hours in department A, 350 hours in department B, and 50 hours in department C. Assuming that the company wants to maximize profits,

a. What is the linear programming model?
b. Find the optimal solution. How much of each product should be produced, and what is the projected profit?
c. What is the scheduled production time and slack time in each department?

9. M&D Chemicals produces two products sold as raw materials to companies manufacturing bath soaps, laundry detergents, and other soap products. Based on an analysis of current inventory levels and potential demand for the coming month, M&D's managers have specified that the total production of products 1 and 2 combined must be at least 350 gallons. Also, a major customer's order for 125 gallons of product 1 must be satisfied. Product 1 requires two hours of processing time per gallon, and product 2 requires one hour; 600 hours of processing time are available in the coming month. Production costs are $2 per gallon for product 1 and $3 per gallon for product 2.

a. Determine the production quantities that will satisfy the specified requirements at minimum cost.
b. What is the total product cost?
c. Identify the amount of any surplus production.

10. Refer to the M&D Chemicals situation in Problem 9. Suppose, because of the use of some new equipment, the production cost for product 2 is reduced to $1.50 per gallon.

a. What are the optimal production quantities?
b. What constraint lines combined to form the optimal extreme point?

11. Car Phones, Inc., sells two models of car telephones, model x and model y. Records show that three hours of sales time are used for each model x phone sold, and five hours for each model y phone. A total of 600 hours of sales time is available for the next four-week period, and management-planning policies call for minimum sales goals of 25 units for both model x and model y.

a. Show the feasible region for the problem.
b. Assuming the company makes $40 profit on each model x sold and a $50 profit on each model y sold, what is the optimal sales goal for the company for the next four-week period?
c. Develop a constraint, and show the feasible region if management adds the restriction that Car Phones must sell at least as many model-y phones as model-x phones.

d. What is the new optimal solution if the constraint in part c is added to the problem?

12. Photo Chemicals produces two types of photograph-developing fluids. Both products cost Photo Chemicals $1 per gallon to produce. Based on an analysis of current inventory levels and outstanding orders for the next month, Photo Chemicals managers have specified that at least 30 gallons of product 1 and at least 20 gallons of product 2 must be produced during the next two weeks. They have also stated that an existing inventory of highly perishable raw material required in the production of both fluids must be used within the next two weeks. The current inventory of the perishable raw material is 80 pounds. Although more of this raw material can be ordered if necessary, any of the current inventory that is not used within the next two weeks will spoil; hence the management requirement that at least 80 pounds be used in the next two weeks. Furthermore, it is known that product 1 requires 1 pound of this perishable raw material per gallon and product 2 requires 2 pounds per gallon. Since the firm's objective is to keep its production costs at the minimum possible level, the managers are looking for a minimum-cost production plan that uses all the 80 pounds of perishable raw material and provides at least 30 gallons of product 1 and at least 20 gallons of product 2. What is the minimum-cost solution?

13. Reconsider the Par, Inc., situation in Solved Problem 1. Suppose the managers add the requirements that at least 500 standard bags and at least 360 deluxe bags must be produced.

a. Graph the constraints for this revised problem. What happens to the feasible region? Explain.

b. If there are no feasible solutions, explain what is needed to produce 500 standard bags and 360 deluxe bags.

14. Managers of High Tech Services (HTS) would like to develop a model that will help allocate technicians' time between service calls to regular-contract customers and new customers. A maximum of 80 hours of technician time is available over the two-week planning period. To satisfy cash-flow requirements, at least $800 in revenue (per technician) must be generated during the two-week period. Technician time for regular customers generates $25 per hour. However, technician time for new customers generates an average of only $8 per hour because in many cases a new-customer contact does not provide billable services. To ensure that new-customer contacts are being maintained, the time technicians spend on new-customer contacts must be at least 60 percent of the time technicians spend on regular-customer contacts. Given these revenue and policy requirements, HTS would like to determine how to allocate technicians' time between regular customers and new customers so that the total number of customers contacted during the two-week period will be maximized. Technicians require an average of 50 minutes for each regular-customer contact and one hour for each new-customer contact.

a. Develop a linear programming model that will enable HTS to determine how to allocate technicians' time between regular customers and new customers.

b. Graph the feasible region.

c. Solve the appropriate simultaneous linear equations to determine the values of x_1 and x_2 at each extreme point of the feasible region.

d. Find the optimal solution.

Note to Student: The following problems have been designed to give you an understanding and appreciation of the broad range of problems in P/OM that can be formulated as linear programs. They are more challenging than the preceding problems, because most of them require more than two decision variables to formulate the problem correctly. However, you will need access to a linear programming computer package to develop the solution and make the requested interpretations.

15. *Product mix.* Better Products, Inc., is a small manufacturer of three products it produces on two machines. In a typical week, 40 hours of time are available on each machine. Profit contribution and production time in hours per unit are given in Table D.11.

Table D.11 Data for Problem 15

	Product		
	1	2	3
Profit/unit	$30	$50	$20
Machine 1 time/unit	0.5	2.0	0.75
Machine 2 time/unit	1.0	1.0	0.5

Two operators are required for machine 1. Thus two hours of labor must be scheduled for each hour of machine-1 time. Only one operator is required for machine 2. A maximum of 100 labor-hours is available for assignment to the machines during the coming week. Other production requirements are that product 1 cannot account for more than 50 percent of the units produced and that product 3 must account for at least 20 percent of the units produced.

a. How many units of each product should be produced to maximize the profit contribution? What is the projected weekly profit associated with your solution?

b. How many hours of production time will be scheduled on each machine?

16. *Quality assurance.* Hilltop Coffee manufactures a coffee product by blending three types of coffee beans. The cost per pound and the available pounds of each bean are given in Table D.12.

Table D.12 Data for Problem 16

Bean	Cost/ Pound	Available Pounds
1	$0.50	500
2	0.70	600
3	0.45	400

Consumer tests with coffee products were used to provide quality ratings on a 0-to-100 scale, with higher ratings indicating higher quality. Product-quality standards for the blended coffee require a consumer rating for aroma to be at least 75 and a consumer rating for taste to be at least 80. The aroma and taste ratings for coffee made from 100 percent of each bean are given in Table D.13.

Table D.13 Consumer Ratings for Problem 16

Bean	Aroma Rating	Taste Rating
1	75	86
2	85	88
3	60	75

It is assumed that the aroma and taste attributes of the coffee blend will be a weighted average of the attributes of the beans used in the blend.

a. What is the minimum-cost blend of the three beans that will meet the quality standards and provide 1,000 pounds of the blended coffee product?

b. What is the bean cost per pound of the coffee blend?

17. *Blending problem.* Ajax Fuels, Inc., is developing a new additive for airplane fuels. The additive is a mixture of three liquid ingredients: A, B, and C. For proper performance, the total amount of additive (amount of A + amount of B + amount of C) must be at least 10 ounces per gallon of fuel. For safety reasons, however, the amount of additive must not exceed 15 ounces per gallon of fuel. The mix or blend of the three ingredients is critical. At least one ounce of ingredient A must be used for every ounce of ingredient B. The amount of ingredient C must be greater than one-half the amount of ingredient A. If the cost per ounce for ingredients A, B, and C is $0.10, $0.03, and $0.09, respectively, find the minimum-cost mixture of A, B, and C for each gallon of airplane fuel.

18. *Production routing.* Lurix Electronics manufactures two products that can be produced on two different production lines. Both products have their lowest production costs when produced on the more modern of the two production lines. However, the modern production line does not have the capacity to handle the total production. As a result, some production must be routed to the older production line. Table D.14 shows the data for total production requirements, production-line capacities, and production costs.

Table D.14 Data for Problem 18

	Production Cost/Unit		Minimum Production Requirement
	Modern Line	*Old Line*	
Product 1	$3.00	$5.00	500 units
Product 2	$2.50	$4.00	700 units
Production-line capacity	800	600	

Formulate a linear programming model that can be used to make the production routing decision. What are the recommended decision and the total cost? (Use notation of the form x_{11} = units of product 1 produced on line 1.)

19. *Equipment acquisition.* The Two-Rivers Oil Company near Pittsburgh transports gasoline to its distributors by trucks. The company has recently received a contract to begin supplying gasoline distributors in southern Ohio and has $600,000 available to spend on the necessary expansion of its fleet of gasoline tank trucks. Three models of trucks are available as shown in Table D.15.

Table D.15 Data for Problem 19

	Capacity (gallons)	Purchase Cost ($)	Monthly Operating Costs* ($)
Super Tanker	5,000	$67,000	$550
Regular Line	2,500	55,000	425
Econo-Tanker	1,000	46,000	350

*Includes depreciation

The company estimates that the monthly demand for the region will be 550,000 gallons of gasoline. Due to the size and speed differences of the truck models, they vary in the number of possible deliveries or round trips per month; trip capacities are estimated at 15 per month for the Super Tanker, 20 per month for the Regular Line, and 25 per month for the Econo-Tanker. Based on maintenance and driver availability, the firm does not want to add more than 15 new vehicles to its fleet. In addition, the company wants to purchase at least three of the new Econo-Tankers to use on the short-run, low-demand routes. As a final constraint, the company does not want more than half of its purchases to be Super Tankers.

a. If the company wants to satisfy the gasoline demand with minimal monthly operating expense, how many models of each truck should it purchase?

b. If the company did not require at least three Econo-Tankers and allowed as many Super Tankers as needed, what would the optimal strategy be?

20. *Labor balancing.* The Williams Calculator Company manufactures two models of calculators, the TW100 and the TW200. The assembly process requires three people, and the assembly times are given in Table D.16.

Table D.16 Data for Problem 20

	Assembler		
	1	*2*	*3*
TW100	4 min	2 min	3.5 min
TW200	3 min	4 min	3 min

Company policy is to balance work loads on all assembly jobs. In fact, managers want to schedule work so that no assembler will have more than 30 minutes more work per day than other assemblers. This means that in a regular 8-hour shift, all assemblers will be assigned at least 7.5 hours of work. If the firm makes a $2.50 profit for each TW100 and a $3.50 profit for each TW200, how many units of each calculator should be produced per day? How much time will each assembler be assigned per day?

The **transportation problem** is a special type of linear program that arises in planning the distribution of goods and services from several supply points to several demand locations. Usually the quantity of goods available at each supply location (origin) is limited, and a specified quantity of goods is needed at each demand location (destination). With a variety of shipping routes and differing transportation costs for the routes, the objective is to determine how many units should be shipped from each origin to each destination so that all destination demands are satisfied with a minimum total transportation cost.

The transportation problem in relation to location and distribution planning was discussed in Chapter 8. This supplementary chapter shows how to model various transportation problems and solve them by using Microsoft Excel.

Supplementary Chapter E
The Transportation Problem

Chapter Outline

Modeling the Transportation Problem
Modeling and Solving the Transportation Problem on a Spreadsheet
Understanding the Solution
Modeling Special Situations

Modeling the Transportation Problem

Let us consider the problem faced by Foster Generators, Inc. Currently Foster has two plants: one in Cleveland, Ohio, and one in Bedford, Indiana. Generators produced at the plants (origins) are shipped to distribution centers (destinations) in Boston, Chicago, St. Louis, and Lexington, Kentucky. Recently, an increase in demand has caused Foster to consider adding a new plant to provide expanded production capacity. After some study, the location alternatives for the new plant have been narrowed to York, Pennsylvania, and Clarksville, Tennessee.

To help them decide between the two locations, managers have asked for a comparison of the projected operating costs for the two locations. As a start, they want to know the minimum shipping costs from three origins (Cleveland, Bedford, and York) to the four distribution centers if the plant is located in York. Then, finding the minimum shipping cost from the three origins including Clarksville instead of York to the four distribution centers will provide a comparison of transportation costs; this will help them determine the better location.

We will illustrate how this shipping-cost information can be obtained by solving the transportation problem with the York location alternative. (Problem 6 at the end of the chapter asks you to solve a transportation problem using the Clarksville location alternative.) Using a typical one-month planning period, the production capacities at the three plants are shown in Table E.1. Forecasts of monthly demand at the four distribution centers are shown in Table E.2. The transportation cost per unit for each route is shown in Table E.3.

A convenient way of summarizing the transportation-problem data is with a **transportation tableau** such as the one for the Foster Generators problem in Table E.4. Note that the 12 **cells** in the tableau correspond to the 12 possible shipping routes from the three origins to the four destinations. We denote the

Table E.1 Production Capacities for Foster Generators

Origin	Plant	Production Capacity (units)
1	Cleveland	5,000
2	Bedford	6,000
3	York	2,500
	Total	13,500

Table E.2 Forecasted Monthly Demand for Foster Generators

Destination	Distribution Center	Demand Forecast (units)
1	Boston	6,000
2	Chicago	4,000
3	St. Louis	2,000
4	Lexington	1,500
	Total	13,500

amount shipped from origin i to destination j by the variable x_{ij}. The entries in the column at the right of the tableau represent the supply available at each plant, and the entries at the bottom represent the demand at each distribution center. Note that total supply equals total demand. The entry in the upper right corner of each cell represents the per-unit cost of shipping over the corresponding route.

Looking across the first row of this tableau, we see that the amount shipped from Cleveland to all destinations must equal 5,000, or

$$x_{11} + x_{12} + x_{13} + x_{14} = 5,000$$

Similarly, the amount shipped from Bedford to all destinations must be 6,000.

$$x_{21} + x_{22} + x_{23} + x_{24} = 6,000$$

Finally, the amount shipped from York to all destinations must total 2,500.

$$x_{31} + x_{32} + x_{33} + x_{34} = 2,500$$

Table E.3 Transportation Cost per Unit for Foster Generators Problem

	Destination			
Origin	Boston	Chicago	St. Louis	Lexington
Cleveland	$3	$2	$7	$6
Bedford	7	5	2	3
York	2	5	4	5

Table E.4 Transportation Tableau for Foster Generators Problem

Cell corresponding to shipments from Bedford to Boston

Total supply and total demand

We also must ensure that each destination receives the required demand. Thus, the amount shipped *from* all origins to Boston must equal 6,000.

$$x_{11} + x_{21} + x_{31} = 6{,}000$$

For Chicago, St. Louis, and Lexington, we have similar constraints.

Chicago: $\quad x_{12} + x_{22} + x_{32} = 4{,}000$

St. Louis: $\quad x_{13} + x_{23} + x_{33} = 2{,}000$

Lexington: $\quad x_{14} + x_{24} + x_{34} = 1{,}500$

If we ship x_{11} units from Cleveland to Boston, we incur a total shipping cost of $3x_{11}$. By summing the costs associated with each shipping route, we have the total cost expression that we want to minimize.

$$\text{Total cost} = 3x_{11} + 2x_{12} + 7x_{13} + 6x_{14} + 7x_{21} + 5x_{22} + 2x_{23} + 3x_{24} + 2x_{31} + 5x_{32} + 4x_{33} + 5x_{34}.$$

By including nonnegativity restrictions, $x_{ij} \geq 0$ for all variables, we have modeled the transportation problem as a linear program.

Because the transportation problem is a linear program, several methods can be used to solve it. Many management science textbooks discuss an iterative solution method that is performed directly on the tableau. In this book, however, discussion is restricted to use of Microsoft Excel. Examining the spreadsheet solution in the tableau provides some insight as to why the solution is optimal.

Modeling and Solving the Transportation Problem on a Spreadsheet

As described in Supplementary Chapter D, the Solver option in the Microsoft Excel Tools menu provides the capability of solving linear programs. Figure E.1 is a spreadsheet model of the Foster Generators transportation problem along with the Solver Parameters dialog box from Excel. Cells in the range A3:F8 provide the model data in a form similar to the transportation tableau. Solver works best when all the data have approximately the same magnitude. Hence, we have scaled the supplies and demands by expressing them in thousands of units so that they are similar to the unit costs.

In Figure E.1, the range B13:E15 corresponds to the output variables (amount shipped) in the problem. In Solver, these are referred to as *changing cells*. They must be specified in the dialog box. The constraints are constructed in the dialog box by using the Add, Delete, and Change buttons. In the constraint section of the dialog box, note that the first constraint specifies nonnegativity of the range of output variables. Solver does not assume nonnegativity! The supply and demand constraints are modeled in cells B19:C25. They guarantee that the amount shipped into a city must equal the amount shipped out. For the origins (Cleveland, Bedford, and York), the amount shipped in represents the supply

Figure E.1
Spreadsheet Model and
Solver Dialog Box for the
Foster Generators Problem
(FOSTER.XLS)

	A	B	C	D	E	F
1	Foster Generators					
3		Boston	Chicago	St. Louis	Lexington	Supply (000)
4	Cleveland	3	2	7	6	5
5	Bedford	7	5	2	3	6
6	York	2	5	4	5	2.5
8	Demand (000)	6	4	2	1.5	
10	Decision variables					
12		Boston	Chicago	St. Louis	Lexington	
13	Cleveland	0	0	0	0	
14	Bedford	0	0	0	0	
15	York	0	0	0	0	
17	Constraints					
18		In	Out			
19	Cleveland	5	0			
20	Bedford	6	0			
21	York	2.5	0			
22	Boston	0	6			
23	Chicago	0	4			
24	St. Louis	0	2			
25	Lexington	0	1.5			
27	Total cost($000)	0				

Solver Parameters

Set Target Cell: $B$27
Equal to: ○ Max ● Min ○ Value of: 0
By Changing Cells:
$B$13:$E$15
Subject to the Constraints:
$B$13:$E$15 >= 0
$B$19:$B$25 = $C$19:$C$25

Solve
Close
Guess
Options...
Add...
Change...
Reset All
Delete
Help

(cells F4:F6). The amount shipped out is the sum of the changing cells for that origin. Thus, the formula for cell C19 is =B13+C13+D13+E13. For destinations (Boston, Chicago, St. Louis, and Lexington), the amount shipped out is the demand (cells B8:E8). The amount shipped in is the sum of the changing cells for that destination. Thus, the formula for cell B22 is =B13+B14+B15. In the dialog box, the second constraint states that all values in the range B19 through B25 must equal the corresponding values in cells C19 through C25. These are precisely the constraints we developed in the linear programming model.

The target cell is the one that contains the objective function. This is cell B27 and is defined by multiplying the unit costs in the range B4:E6 by the values of the changing cells in the range B13:E15 and summing. Note that the target cell is to be minimized. To solve the model, you should first select the Options button and click on Assume Linear Model. When you return to the Solver dialog box, click on Solve. The optimal values of the changing cells will appear in the spreadsheet as shown in Figure E.2. The solution to the Foster Generators transportation problem is summarized in Table E.5.

Understanding the Solution

Table E.6 shows the solution to the Foster Generators transportation problem in the transportation tableau. How can we tell that this solution is indeed optimal? Suppose we ship one unit to any other route, for instance, York–Chicago. To ensure that only 2,500 units are shipped from York, we must reduce the shipment

Figure E.2
Optmial Solution to the
Foster Generators Problem

	A	B	C	D	E	F	G	H	I	J
1	Foster Generators									
2										
3		Boston	Chicago	St. Louis	Lexington	Supply (000)				
4	Cleveland	3	2	7	6	5				
5	Bedford	7	5	2	3	6				
6	York	2	5	4	5	2.5				
7										
8	Demand (000)	6	4	2	1.5					
9										
10	Decision variables									
11										
12		Boston	Chicago	St. Louis	Lexington					
13	Cleveland	3.5	1.5	0	0					
14	Bedford	0	2.5	2	1.5					
15	York	2.5	0	0	0					
16										
17	Constraints									
18		In	Out							
19	Cleveland	5	5							
20	Bedford	6	6							
21	York	2.5	2.5							
22	Boston	6	6							
23	Chicago	4	4							
24	St. Louis	2	2							
25	Lexington	1.5	1.5							
26										
27	Total cost($000)	39.5								
28										

Table E.5 Optimal Solution to Foster Generators Problem

Route		Units Shipped	Unit Cost ($)	Total Cost ($)
From	To			
Cleveland	Boston	3,500	3	10,500
Cleveland	Chicago	1,500	2	3,000
Bedford	Chicago	2,500	5	12,500
Bedford	St. Louis	2,000	2	4,000
Bedford	Lexington	1,500	3	4,500
York	Boston	2,500	2	5,000
				39,500

from York to Boston by one unit. But then we would have to increase the amount shipped from Cleveland to Boston to ensure that Boston shipments remain at 6,000 units. This necessitates a reduction in the Cleveland–Chicago allocation by one unit. Notice that this also maintains the 4,000-unit requirement to Chicago. Table E.7 summarizes these series of adjustments.

What is the effect of these adjustments on the total cost? This is summarized below.

Table E.6 Optimal Tableau for the Foster Generators Transportation Problem

| Origin | Destination | | | | Origin Supply |
	Boston	Chicago	St. Louis	Lexington	
Cleveland	3 / 3,500	2 / 1,500	7	6	5,000
Bedford	7	5 / 2,500	2 / 2,000	3 / 1,500	6,000
York	2 / 2,500	5	4	5	2,500
Destination Demand	6,000	4,000	2,000	1,500	

Table E.7 Increasing Shipments from York to Chicago

| Origin | Destination | | | | Origin Supply |
	Boston	Chicago	St. Louis	Lexington	
Cleveland	3 / 3,501 / ~~3,500~~	2 / 1,499 / ~~1,500~~	7	6	5,000
Bedford	7	5 / 2,500	2 / 2,000	3 / 1,500	6,000
York	2 / 2,499 / ~~2,500~~	5 / 1	4	5	2,500
Destination Demand	6,000	4,000	2,000	1,500	

Changes	Effect on Cost
Add one unit to York-Chicago	+5
Subtract one unit from York-Boston	−2
Add one unit from Cleveland-Boston	+3
Subtract one unit from Cleveland-Chicago	−2
Net effect	+4

This shows that the total cost will *increase* by $4 for every additional unit allocated between York and Chicago. Clearly, this solution would not be optimal. You may verify that allocating additional units along any other empty shipment route will also increase total cost by using similar logic. This approach also forms the basis for solving transportation problems by identifying profitable routes and allocating as many units as possible. Complete descriptions of this approach may be found in many management science texts.

Modeling Special Situations

Let us see how the following special situations are handled with the solution procedure:

1. Total supply not equal to total demand.
2. Maximization objective.
3. Unacceptable transportation routes.

When the total supply is not equal to the total demand we must first introduce a dummy origin or dummy destination. If total supply is greater than total demand, we introduce a **dummy destination** with demand exactly equal to the excess of supply over demand. Similarly, if total demand is greater than total supply, we introduce a **dummy origin** with supply exactly equal to the excess of demand over supply. In either case, we assign cost coefficients of zero to every route into a dummy destination and every route out of a dummy origin. The reason for doing this is that no shipments will actually be made from a dummy origin or to a dummy destination when the solution is implemented.

To handle unacceptable transportation routes, we assign unacceptable routes an extremely high cost, denoted M, to keep them out of the solution. Thus if we have a transportation route from an origin to a destination that for some reason cannot be used, we simply assign that route a per unit cost of M, and the route will not enter the solution. Unacceptable routes would be assigned a per unit value of $-M$ in a maximization problem.

Let us now consider an example to show how special situations can be handled. In the process we will also show how production costs can be taken into account in a transportation problem. Suppose we have three plants (origins) with the production capacities shown in Table E.8. We also have demand for the product at three retail outlets (destinations). The demand forecasts for the current planning period are shown in Table E.9. The production costs at the plants

Table E.8. Production Capacities for Three Plants

Plant	Production Capacity
P_1	50
P_2	40
P_3	30
Total	120

differ, and the sales prices at the retail outlets vary. Taking prices, production costs, and shipping costs into consideration, the profits for producing one unit at plant i, shipping it to retail outlet j, and selling it at retail outlet j are presented in Table E.10.

Table E.9. Demand Forecasts for Three Retail Outlets

Retail Outlet	Forecasted Demand
R_1	45
R_2	15
R_3	30
Total	90

Table E.10. Profit per Unit for Producing at Plant P_i and Selling at Retail Outlet R_j

Plant	Retail Outlet		
	R_1	R_2	R_3
P_1	2	8	10
P_2	6	11	6
P_3	12	7	9

Figure E.3
Excel Spreadsheet for
Transportation Example
(TRANSP.XLS)

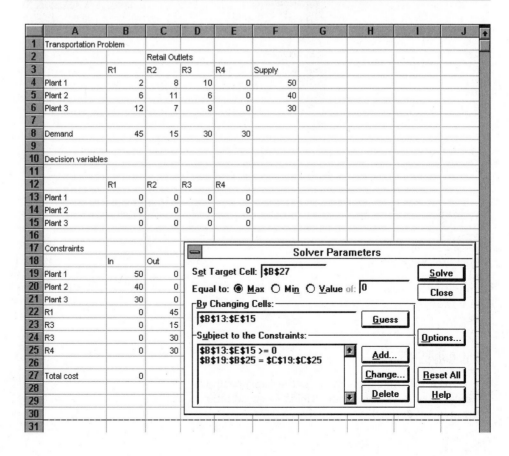

We note first that the total production capacity exceeds the total demand at the retail outlets. Thus we must introduce a dummy retail outlet with demand exactly equal to the excess production capacity. We therefore add retail outlet R_4 with a demand of 30 units. The per unit profit for shipping from each plant to retail outlet R_4 is set to zero, since these units will not actually be shipped. Figure E.3 is an Excel spreadsheet for this problem. The only difference from the Foster Generations problem is that the target cell is set equal to a maximization instead of a minimization. The optimal solution is shown in Figure E.4.

Figure E.4
Optimal Solution to
Transportation Problem
Example

	A	B	C	D	E	F	G	H	I	J
1	Transportation Problem									
2			Retail Outlets							
3		R1	R2	R3	R4	Supply				
4	Plant 1	2	8	10	0	50				
5	Plant 2	6	11	6	0	40				
6	Plant 3	12	7	9	0	30				
7										
8	Demand	45	15	30	30					
9										
10	Decision variables									
11										
12		R1	R2	R3	R4					
13	Plant 1	0	0	30	20					
14	Plant 2	15	15	0	10					
15	Plant 3	30	0	0	0					
16										
17	Constraints									
18		In	Out							
19	Plant 1	50	50							
20	Plant 2	40	40							
21	Plant 3	30	30							
22	R1	45	45							
23	R3	15	15							
24	R3	30	30							
25	R4	30	30							
26										
27	Total cost	915								
28										

Key Terms

Transportation problem
Transportation tableau
Cell
Dummy destination
Dummy origin

Review Questions

1. Describe different applications of the transportation problem. That is, to what might origins and destinations correspond in different situations?

2. Explain how to model and solve transportation problems with Microsoft Excel.
3. Describe how to handle the following special situations in the transportation problem:
   a. Unequal supply and demand.
   b. Maximization objective.
   c. Unacceptable transportation routes.

Solved Problem

1. Consider the transportation problem shown in Figure E.5 and its costs per unit as given below.

Figure E.5 Transportation Network for Solved Problem 1

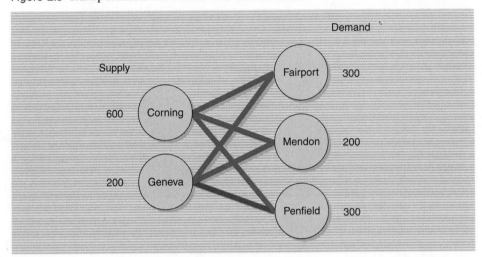

	Cost		
	Fairport	*Mendon*	*Penfield*
Corning	16	10	14
Geneva	12	12	20

a. Develop a linear program for this problem.
b. Show that the following solution is optimal.

	Fairport	Mendon	Penfield
	16	10	14
Corning	100	200	300
	12	12	20
Geneva	200		

Solution

a. Min $16x_{11} + 10x_{12} + 14x_{13} + 12x_{14} + 12x_{15} + 20x_{16}$ subject to

$$\text{Corning:} \quad x_{11} + x_{12} + x_{13} = 600$$

$$\text{Geneva:} \quad x_{21} + x_{22} + x_{23} = 200$$

Fairport: $x_{11} + x_{21} = 300$

Mendon: $x_{21} + x_{22} = 200$

Penfield: $x_{31} + x_{32} = 300$

$x_{ij} \geq 0$

b.

Net effect on cost:
$12 - 10 + 16 - 12 = +6$

Net effect on cost:
$20 - 14 + 16 - 12 = +10$

Problems

1. An appliance store owns two warehouses and has three major regional stores. Supply, demand, and transportation costs for refrigerators are provided below.

		Store		
Warehouse	*A*	*B*	*C*	**Supply**
1	6	8	5	80
2	12	3	7	40
Demand	20	50	50	

a. Set up the transportation tableau.
b. Find an optimal solution using Excel.

2. A product is produced at three plants and shipped to three warehouses, with transportation costs per unit as shown in Table E.11. Find the optimal solution.

Table E.11 Data for Problem 2

Plant	Warehouse			Plant Capacity
	W_1	W_2	W_3	
P_1	20	16	24	300
P_2	10	10	8	500
P_3	12	18	10	100
Warehouse demand	200	400	300	

3. Consider the minimum-cost transportation problem in Table E.12.
a. Construct the linear program.

Table E.12 Data for Problem 3

Origin	Destination			Origin Supply
	Los Angeles	San Francisco	San Diego	
San Jose	4	10	6	100
Las Vegas	8	16	6	300
Tucson	14	18	10	300
Destination Demand	200	300	200	700

b. Find an optimal solution.
c. How would the optimal solution differ if we must ship 100 units on the Tucson–San Diego route?
d. Because of road construction, the Las Vegas–San Diego route is now unacceptable. Resolve the initial problem with this change.
4. Find the optimal solution to the transportation problem shown in Table E.13.

Table E.13 Data for Problem 4

Origin	Destination D_1	D_2	D_3	Origin Supply
O_1	6	8	8	250
O_2	18	12	14	150
O_3	8	12	10	100
Destination Demand	150	200	150	

5. Solve the minimum-cost transportation problem shown in Table E.14.

Table E.14 Data for Problem 5

Origin	Destination D_1	D_2	D_3	Supply
O_1	1	3	4	200
O_2	2	6	8	500
O_3	2	5	7	300
Demand	200	100	400	

Since total supply (1,000 units) exceeds total demand (700 units), which origins may consider alternate uses for their excess supply and still maintain a minimum total transportation cost solution?

6. Reconsider the Foster Generators transportation and facilities-location problem. Assume that the York plant location alternative is replaced with the Clarksville, Tennessee, location. Using the 2,500-unit capacity for the Clarksville plant and the unit transportation costs shown in Table E.15, determine the minimum-cost transportation-problem solution if the new plant is located in Clarksville.

Table E.15 Data for Problem 6

Shipping from Clarksville to	Unit Cost
Boston	9
Chicago	6
St. Louis	3
Lexington	3

Compare the total transportation costs of the York and Clarksville plant locations. Which location provides for lower-cost transportation?

7. Forbelt Corporation has a one-year contract to supply motors for all refrigerators produced by the Ice Age Corporation. Ice Age manufactures the refrigerators at four locations around the country: Boston, Dallas, Los Angeles, and St. Paul. Plans call for these numbers (in thousands) of refrigerators to be produced at the four locations.

Boston	50
Dallas	70
Los Angeles	60
St. Paul	80

Forbelt has three plants that are capable of producing the motors. The plants and their production capacities (in thousands) follow.

Denver	100
Atlanta	100
Chicago	150

Because of varying production and transportation costs, the profit Forbelt earns on each lot of 1,000 units depends on which plant produced it and to which destination it was shipped. Table E.16 gives the accounting department estimates of the profit per unit (Shipments are made in lots of 1,000 units.):

Table E.16 Data for Problem 7

	Shipped to			
Produced at	Boston	Dallas	Los Angeles	St. Paul
Denver	7	11	8	13
Atlanta	20	17	12	10
Chicago	8	18	13	16

Given profit maximization as a criterion, Forbelt would like to determine how many motors should be produced at each plant and how many should be shipped from each plant to each destination.

8. Arnoff Enterprises manufactures the central processing unit (CPU) for a line of personal computers. The CPUs are manufactured in Seattle, Columbus, and New York and shipped to warehouses in Pittsburgh, Mobile, Denver, Los Angeles, and Washington, DC, for further distribution. The transportation tableau in Table E.17 shows the number of CPUs available at each plant and the number of CPUs required by each warehouse. The shipping costs (dollars per unit) are also shown.

Table E.17 Data for Problem 8

Plant	Warehouse					Supply
	Pittsburgh	Mobile	Denver	Los Angeles	Washington	
Seattle	10	20	5	9	10	9,000
Columbus	2	10	8	30	6	4,000
New York	1	20	7	10	4	8,000
Demand	3000	5000	4000	6000	3000	21,000

a. Determine the number of CPUs that should be shipped from each plant to each warehouse to minimize the total transportation cost.

b. The Pittsburgh warehouse has just increased its order by 1,000 units, and Arnoff has authorized the Columbus plant to increase its production by 1,000 units. Do you expect this development to lead to an increase or a decrease in the total transportation cost? Solve for the new optimal solution.

9. Show that the solution to the Foster Generators Problem is optimal by verifying that allocations along all other routes have a positive net effect on cost.

10. Show that the solution to the transportation problem in Figure E.4 is optimal by examining the effect of allocating shipments along each of the remaining routes.

Appendixes

Appendix A: Values of e^{-iN} To find $e^{-1.5}$, for example, choose $N = 15$ and $i = 0.10$.

						i						
N	*.01*	*.02*	*.03*	*.04*	*.05*	*.06*	*.07*	*.08*	*.09*	*.10*	*.11*	*.12*
1	0.990	0.980	0.970	0.961	0.951	0.942	0.932	0.923	0.914	0.905	0.896	0.887
2	0.980	0.961	0.942	0.923	0.905	0.887	0.869	0.852	0.835	0.819	0.803	0.787
3	0.970	0.942	0.914	0.887	0.861	0.835	0.811	0.787	0.763	0.741	0.719	0.698
4	0.961	0.923	0.887	0.852	0.819	0.787	0.756	0.726	0.698	0.670	0.644	0.619
5	0.951	0.905	0.861	0.819	0.779	0.741	0.705	0.670	0.638	0.607	0.577	0.549
6	0.942	0.887	0.835	0.787	0.741	0.698	0.657	0.619	0.583	0.549	0.517	0.487
7	0.932	0.869	0.811	0.756	0.705	0.657	0.613	0.571	0.533	0.497	0.463	0.432
8	0.923	0.852	0.787	0.726	0.670	0.619	0.571	0.527	0.487	0.449	0.415	0.383
9	0.914	0.835	0.763	0.698	0.638	0.583	0.533	0.487	0.445	0.407	0.372	0.340
10	0.905	0.819	0.741	0.670	0.607	0.549	0.497	0.449	0.407	0.368	0.333	0.301
11	0.896	0.803	0.719	0.644	0.577	0.517	0.463	0.415	0.372	0.333	0.298	0.267
12	0.887	0.787	0.698	0.619	0.549	0.487	0.432	0.383	0.340	0.301	0.267	0.237
13	0.878	0.771	0.677	0.595	0.522	0.458	0.403	0.353	0.310	0.273	0.239	0.210
14	0.869	0.756	0.657	0.571	0.497	0.432	0.375	0.326	0.284	0.247	0.214	0.186
15	0.861	0.741	0.638	0.549	0.472	0.407	0.350	0.301	0.259	0.223	0.192	0.165
16	0.852	0.726	0.619	0.527	0.449	0.383	0.326	0.278	0.237	0.202	0.172	0.147
17	0.844	0.712	0.600	0.507	0.427	0.361	0.304	0.257	0.217	0.183	0.154	0.130
18	0.835	0.698	0.583	0.487	0.407	0.340	0.284	0.237	0.198	0.165	0.138	0.115
19	0.827	0.684	0.566	0.468	0.387	0.320	0.264	0.219	0.181	0.150	0.124	0.102
20	0.819	0.670	0.549	0.449	0.368	0.301	0.247	0.202	0.165	0.135	0.111	0.091
21	0.811	0.657	0.533	0.432	0.350	0.284	0.230	0.186	0.151	0.122	0.099	0.080
22	0.803	0.644	0.517	0.415	0.333	0.267	0.214	0.172	0.138	0.111	0.089	0.071
23	0.795	0.631	0.502	0.399	0.317	0.252	0.200	0.159	0.126	0.100	0.080	0.063
24	0.787	0.619	0.487	0.383	0.301	0.237	0.186	0.147	0.115	0.091	0.071	0.056
25	0.779	0.607	0.472	0.368	0.287	0.223	0.174	0.135	0.105	0.082	0.064	0.050
26	0.771	0.595	0.458	0.353	0.273	0.210	0.162	0.125	0.096	0.074	0.057	0.044
27	0.763	0.583	0.445	0.340	0.259	0.198	0.151	0.115	0.088	0.067	0.051	0.039
28	0.756	0.571	0.432	0.326	0.247	0.186	0.141	0.106	0.080	0.061	0.046	0.035
29	0.748	0.560	0.419	0.313	0.235	0.176	0.131	0.098	0.074	0.055	0.041	0.031
30	0.741	0.549	0.407	0.301	0.223	0.165	0.122	0.091	0.067	0.050	0.037	0.027

						i						
N	.13	.14	.15	.16	.17	.18	.19	.20	.21	.22	.23	.24
1	0.878	0.869	0.861	0.852	0.844	0.835	0.827	0.819	0.811	0.803	0.795	0.787
2	0.771	0.756	0.741	0.726	0.712	0.698	0.684	0.670	0.657	0.644	0.631	0.619
3	0.677	0.657	0.638	0.619	0.600	0.583	0.566	0.549	0.533	0.517	0.502	0.487
4	0.595	0.571	0.549	0.527	0.507	0.487	0.468	0.499	0.432	0.415	0.399	0.383
5	0.522	0.497	0.472	0.449	0.427	0.407	0.387	0.368	0.350	0.333	0.317	0.301
6	0.458	0.432	0.407	0.383	0.361	0.340	0.320	0.301	0.284	0.267	0.252	0.237
7	0.403	0.375	0.350	0.326	0.304	0.284	0.264	0.247	0.230	0.214	0.200	0.186
8	0.353	0.326	0.301	0.278	0.257	0.237	0.219	0.202	0.186	0.172	0.159	0.147
9	0.310	0.284	0.259	0.237	0.217	0.198	0.181	0.165	0.151	0.138	0.126	0.115
10	0.273	0.247	0.223	0.202	0.183	0.165	0.150	0.135	0.122	0.111	0.100	0.091
11	0.239	0.214	0.192	0.172	0.154	0.138	0.124	0.111	0.099	0.089	0.080	0.071
12	0.210	0.186	0.165	0.147	0.130	0.115	0.102	0.091	0.080	0.071	0.063	0.056
13	0.185	0.162	0.142	0.125	0.110	0.096	0.085	0.074	0.065	0.057	0.050	0.044
14	0.162	0.141	0.122	0.106	0.093	0.080	0.070	0.061	0.053	0.046	0.040	0.035
15	0.142	0.122	0.105	0.091	0.078	0.067	0.058	0.050	0.043	0.037	0.032	0.027
16	0.125	0.106	0.091	0.077	0.066	0.056	0.048	0.041	0.035	0.030	0.025	0.021
17	0.110	0.093	0.078	0.066	0.056	0.047	0.040	0.033	0.028	0.024	0.020	0.017
18	0.096	0.080	0.067	0.056	0.047	0.039	0.033	0.027	0.023	0.019	0.016	0.013
19	0.085	0.070	0.058	0.048	0.040	0.033	0.027	0.022	0.018	0.015	0.013	0.010
20	0.074	0.061	0.050	0.041	0.033	0.027	0.022	0.018	0.015	0.012	0.010	0.008
21	0.065	0.053	0.043	0.035	0.028	0.023	0.018	0.015	0.012	0.010	0.008	0.006
22	0.057	0.046	0.037	0.030	0.024	0.019	0.015	0.012	0.010	0.008	0.006	0.005
23	0.050	0.040	0.032	0.025	0.020	0.016	0.013	0.010	0.008	0.006	0.005	0.004
24	0.044	0.035	0.027	0.021	0.017	0.013	0.010	0.008	0.006	0.005	0.004	0.003
25	0.039	0.030	0.024	0.018	0.014	0.011	0.009	0.007	0.005	0.004	0.003	0.002
26	0.034	0.026	0.020	0.016	0.012	0.009	0.007	0.006	0.004	0.003	0.003	0.002
27	0.030	0.023	0.017	0.013	0.010	0.008	0.006	0.005	0.003	0.003	0.002	0.002
28	0.026	0.020	0.015	0.011	0.009	0.006	0.005	0.004	0.003	0.002	0.002	0.001
29	0.023	0.017	0.013	0.010	0.007	0.005	0.004	0.003	0.002	0.002	0.001	0.001
30	0.020	0.015	0.011	0.008	0.006	0.005	0.003	0.002	0.002	0.001	0.001	0.001

Appendix B: Areas of the Standard Normal Distribution

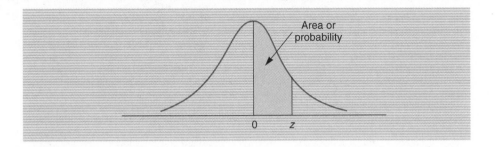

Entries in the table give the area under the curve between the mean and z standard deviations above the mean. For example, for $z = 1.25$, the area under the curve between the mean and z is 0.3944.

z	0.00	0.01	0.02	0.03	0.04	0.05	0.06	0.07	0.08	0.09
0.0	0.0000	0.0040	0.0080	0.0120	0.0160	0.0199	0.0239	0.0279	0.0319	0.0359
0.1	0.0398	0.0438	0.0478	0.0517	0.0557	0.0596	0.0636	0.0675	0.0714	0.0753
0.2	0.0793	0.0832	0.0871	0.0910	0.0948	0.0987	0.1026	0.1064	0.1103	0.1141
0.3	0.1179	0.1217	0.1255	0.1293	0.1331	0.1368	0.1406	0.1443	0.1480	0.1517
0.4	0.1554	0.1591	0.1628	0.1664	0.1700	0.1736	0.1772	0.1808	0.1844	0.1879
0.5	0.1915	0.1950	0.1985	0.2019	0.2054	0.2088	0.2123	0.2157	0.2190	0.2224
0.6	0.2257	0.2291	0.2324	0.2357	0.2389	0.2422	0.2454	0.2486	0.2518	0.2549
0.7	0.2580	0.2612	0.2642	0.2673	0.2704	0.2734	0.2764	0.2794	0.2823	0.2852
0.8	0.2881	0.2910	0.2939	0.2967	0.2995	0.3023	0.3051	0.3078	0.3106	0.3133
0.9	0.3159	0.3186	0.3212	0.3238	0.3264	0.3289	0.3315	0.3340	0.3365	0.3389
1.0	0.3413	0.3438	0.3461	0.3485	0.3508	0.3531	0.3554	0.3577	0.3599	0.3621
1.1	0.3643	0.3665	0.3686	0.3708	0.3729	0.3749	0.3770	0.3790	0.3810	0.3830
1.2	0.3849	0.3869	0.3888	0.3907	0.3925	0.3944	0.3962	0.3980	0.3997	0.4015
1.3	0.4032	0.4049	0.4066	0.4082	0.4099	0.4115	0.4131	0.4147	0.4162	0.4177
1.4	0.4192	0.4207	0.4222	0.4236	0.4251	0.4265	0.4279	0.4292	0.4306	0.4319
1.5	0.4332	0.4345	0.4357	0.4370	0.4382	0.4394	0.4406	0.4418	0.4429	0.4441
1.6	0.4452	0.4463	0.4474	0.4484	0.4495	0.4505	0.4515	0.4525	0.4535	0.4545
1.7	0.4554	0.4564	0.4573	0.4582	0.4591	0.4599	0.4608	0.4616	0.4625	0.4633
1.8	0.4641	0.4649	0.4656	0.4664	0.4671	0.4578	0.4686	0.4693	0.4699	0.4706
1.9	0.4713	0.4719	0.4726	0.4732	0.4738	0.4744	0.4750	0.4756	0.4761	0.4767
2.0	0.4772	0.4778	0.4783	0.4788	0.4793	0.4798	0.4803	0.4808	0.4812	0.4817
2.1	0.4821	0.4826	0.4830	0.4834	0.4838	0.4842	0.4846	0.4850	0.4854	0.4857
2.2	0.4861	0.4864	0.4868	0.4871	0.4875	0.4878	0.4881	0.4884	0.4887	0.4890
2.3	0.4893	0.4896	0.4898	0.4901	0.4904	0.4906	0.4909	0.4911	0.4913	0.4916
2.4	0.4918	0.4920	0.4922	0.4925	0.4927	0.4929	0.4931	0.4932	0.4934	0.4936
2.5	0.4938	0.4940	0.4941	0.4943	0.4945	0.4946	0.4948	0.4949	0.4951	0.4952
2.6	0.4953	0.4955	0.4956	0.4957	0.4959	0.4960	0.4961	0.4962	0.4963	0.4964
2.7	0.4965	0.4966	0.4967	0.4968	0.4969	0.4970	0.4972	0.4972	0.4973	0.4974
2.8	0.4974	0.4975	0.4976	0.4977	0.4977	0.4978	0.4979	0.4979	0.4980	0.4981
2.9	0.4981	0.4982	0.4982	0.4984	0.4984	0.4984	0.4985	0.4985	0.4986	0.4986
3.0	0.4986	0.4987	0.4987	0.4988	0.4988	0.4989	0.4989	0.4989	0.4990	0.4990

Appendix C: Random Digits

63271	59986	71744	51102	15141	80714	58683	93108	13554	79945
88547	09896	95436	79115	08303	01041	20030	63754	08459	28364
55957	57243	83865	09911	19761	66535	40102	26646	60147	15702
46276	87453	44790	67122	45573	84358	21625	16999	13385	22782
55363	07449	34835	15290	76616	67191	12777	21861	68689	03263
69393	92785	49902	58447	42048	30378	87618	26933	40640	16281
13186	29431	88190	04588	38733	81290	89541	70290	40113	08243
17726	28652	56836	78351	47327	18518	92222	55201	27340	10493
36520	64465	05550	30157	82242	29520	69753	72602	23756	54935
81628	36100	39254	56835	37636	02421	98063	89641	64953	99337
84649	48968	75215	75498	49539	74240	03466	49292	36401	45525
63291	11618	12613	75055	43915	26488	41116	64531	56827	30825
70502	53225	03655	05915	37140	57051	48393	91322	25653	06543
06426	24771	59935	49801	11082	66762	94477	02494	88215	27191
20711	55609	29430	70165	45406	78484	31639	52009	18873	96927
41990	70538	77191	25860	55204	73417	83920	69468	74972	38712
72452	36618	76298	26678	89334	33938	95567	29380	75906	91807
37042	40318	57099	10528	09925	89773	41335	96244	29002	46453
53766	52875	15987	46962	67342	77592	57651	95508	80033	69828
90585	58955	53122	16025	84299	53310	67380	84249	25348	04332
32001	96293	37203	64516	51530	37069	40261	61374	05815	06714
62606	64324	46354	72157	67248	20135	49804	09226	64419	29457
10078	28073	85389	50324	14500	15562	64165	06125	71353	77669
91561	46145	24177	15294	10061	98124	75732	00815	83452	97355
13091	98112	53959	79607	52244	63303	10413	63839	74762	50289
73864	83014	72457	22682	03033	61714	88173	90835	00634	85169
66668	25467	48894	51043	02365	91726	09365	63167	95264	45643
84745	41042	29493	01836	09044	51926	43630	63470	76508	14194
48068	26805	94595	47907	13357	38412	33318	26098	82782	42851
54310	96175	97594	88616	42035	38093	36745	56702	40644	83514
14877	33095	10924	58013	61439	21882	42059	24177	58739	60170
78295	23179	02771	43464	59061	71411	05697	67194	30495	21157
67524	02865	39593	54278	04237	92441	26602	63835	38032	94770
58268	57219	68124	73455	83236	08710	04284	55005	84171	42596
97158	28672	50685	01181	24262	19427	52106	34308	73685	74246
04230	16831	69085	30802	65559	09205	71829	06489	85650	38707
94879	56606	30401	02602	57658	70091	54986	41394	60437	03195
71446	15232	66715	26385	91518	70566	02888	79941	39684	54315
32886	05644	79316	09819	00813	88407	17461	73925	53037	91904
62048	33711	25290	21526	02223	75947	66466	06232	10913	75336

Appendix D: Binomial Probabilities

Entries in the table give the probability of x successes in n trials of a binomial experiment, where p is the probability of a success on one trial. For example, with six trials and $p = .40$, the probability of two successes is .3110.

						p					
n	x	.05	.10	.15	.20	.25	.30	.35	.40	.45	.50
1	0	.9500	.9000	.8500	.8000	.7500	.7000	.6500	.6000	.5500	.5000
	1	.0500	.1000	.1500	.2000	.2500	.3000	.3500	.4000	.4500	.5000
2	0	.9025	.8100	.7225	.6400	.5625	.4900	.4225	.3600	.3025	.2500
	1	.0950	.1800	.2550	.3200	.3750	.4200	.4550	.4800	.4950	.5000
	2	.0025	.0100	.0225	.0400	.0625	.0900	.1225	.1600	.2025	.2500
3	0	.8574	.7290	.6141	.5120	.4219	.3430	.2746	.2160	.1664	.1250
	1	.1354	.2430	.3251	.3840	.4219	.4410	.4436	.4320	.4084	.3750
	2	.0071	.0270	.0574	.0960	.1406	.1890	.2389	.2880	.3341	.3750
	3	.0001	.0010	.0034	.0080	.0156	.0270	.0429	.0640	.0911	.1250
4	0	.8145	.6561	.5220	.4096	.3164	.2401	.1785	.1296	.0915	.0625
	1	.1715	.2916	.3685	.4096	.4219	.4116	.3845	.3456	.2995	.2500
	2	.0135	.0486	.0975	.1536	.2109	.2646	.3105	.3456	.3675	.3750
	3	.0005	.0036	.0115	.0256	.0469	.0756	.1115	.1536	.2005	.2500
	4	.0000	.0001	.0005	.0016	.0039	.0081	.0150	.0256	.0410	.0625
5	0	.7738	.5905	.4437	.3277	.2373	.1681	.1160	.0778	.0503	.0312
	1	.2036	.3280	.3915	.4096	.3955	.3602	.3124	.2592	.2059	.1562
	2	.0214	.0729	.1382	.2048	.2637	.3087	.3364	.3456	.3369	.3125
	3	.0011	.0081	.0244	.0512	.0879	.1323	.1811	.2304	.2757	.3125
	4	.0000	.0004	.0022	.0064	.0146	.0284	.0488	.0768	.1128	.1562
	5	.0000	.0000	.0001	.0003	.0010	.0024	.0053	.0102	.0185	.0312
6	0	.7351	.5314	.3771	.2621	.1780	.1176	.0754	.0467	.0277	.0156
	1	.2321	.3543	.3993	.3932	.3560	.3025	.2437	.1866	.1359	.0938
	2	.0305	.0984	.1762	.2458	.2966	.3241	.3280	.3110	.2780	.2344
	3	.0021	.0146	.0415	.0819	.1318	.1852	.2355	.2765	.3032	.3125
	4	.0001	.0012	.0055	.0154	.0330	.0595	.0951	.1382	.1861	.2344
	5	.0000	.0001	.0004	.0015	.0044	.0102	.0205	.0369	.0609	.0938
	6	.0000	.0000	.0000	.0001	.0002	.0007	.0018	.0041	.0083	.0156
7	0	.6983	.4783	.3206	.2097	.1335	.0824	.0490	.0280	.0152	.0078
	1	.2573	.3720	.3960	.3670	.3115	.2471	.1848	.1306	.0872	.0547
	2	.0406	.1240	.2097	.2753	.3115	.3177	.2985	.2613	.2140	.1641
	3	.0036	.0230	.0617	.1147	.1730	.2269	.2679	.2903	.2918	.2734
	4	.0002	.0026	.0109	.0287	.0577	.0972	.1442	.1935	.2388	.2734
	5	.0000	.0002	.0012	.0043	.0115	.0250	.0466	.0774	.1172	.1641
	6	.0000	.0000	.0001	.0004	.0013	.0036	.0084	.0172	.0320	.0547
	7	.0000	.0000	.0000	.0000	.0001	.0002	.0006	.0016	.0037	.0078
8	0	.6634	.4305	.2725	.1678	.1001	.0576	.0319	.0168	.0084	.0039
	1	.2793	.3826	.3847	.3355	.2670	.1977	.1373	.0896	.0548	.0312
	2	.0515	.1488	.2376	.2936	.3115	.2965	.2587	.2090	.1569	.1094
	3	.0054	.0331	.0839	.1468	.2076	.2541	.2786	.2787	.2568	.2188
	4	.0004	.0046	.0185	.0459	.0865	.1361	.1875	.2322	.2627	.2734

						p					
n	x	.05	.10	.15	.20	.25	.30	.35	.40	.45	.50
8	5	.0000	.0004	.0026	.0092	.0231	.0467	.0808	.1239	.1719	.2188
	6	.0000	.0000	.0002	.0011	.0038	.0100	.0217	.0413	.0703	.1094
	7	.0000	.0000	.0000	.0001	.0004	.0012	.0033	.0079	.0164	.0312
	8	.0000	.0000	.0000	.0000	.0000	.0001	.0002	.0007	.0017	.0039
9	0	.6302	.3874	.2316	.1342	.0751	.0404	.0207	.0101	.0046	.0020
	1	.2985	.3874	.3679	.3020	.2253	.1556	.1004	.0605	.0339	.0176
	2	.0629	.1722	.2597	.3020	.3003	.2668	.2162	.1612	.1110	.0703
	3	.0077	.0446	.1069	.1762	.2336	.2668	.2716	.2508	.2119	.1641
	4	.0006	.0074	.0283	.0661	.1168	.1715	.2194	.2508	.2600	.2461
	5	.0000	.0008	.0050	.0165	.0389	.0735	.1181	.1672	.2128	.2461
	6	.0000	.0001	.0006	.0028	.0087	.0210	.0424	.0743	.1160	.1641
	7	.0000	.0000	.0000	.0003	.0012	.0039	.0098	.0212	.0407	.0703
	8	.0000	.0000	.0000	.0000	.0001	.0004	.0013	.0035	.0083	.0176
	9	.0000	.0000	.0000	.0000	.0000	.0000	.0001	.0003	.0008	.0020
10	0	.5987	.3487	.1969	.1074	.0563	.0282	.0135	.0060	.0025	.0010
	1	.3151	.3874	.3474	.2684	.1877	.1211	.0725	.0403	.0207	.0098
	2	.0746	.1937	.2759	.3020	.2816	.2335	.1757	.1209	.0763	.0439
	3	.0105	.0574	.1298	.2013	.2503	.2668	.2522	.2150	.1665	.1172
	4	.0010	.0112	.0401	.0881	.1460	.2001	.2377	.2508	.2384	.2051
	5	.0001	.0015	.0085	.0264	.0584	.1029	.1536	.2007	.2340	.2461
	6	.0000	.0001	.0012	.0055	.0162	.0368	.0689	.1115	.1596	.2051
	7	.0000	.0000	.0001	.0008	.0031	.0090	.0212	.0425	.0746	.1172
	8	.0000	.0000	.0000	.0001	.0004	.0014	.0043	.0106	.0229	.0439
	9	.0000	.0000	.0000	.0000	.0000	.0001	.0005	.0016	.0042	.0098
	10	.0000	.0000	.0000	.0000	.0000	.0000	.0000	.0001	.0003	.0010
11	0	.5688	.3138	.1673	.0859	.0422	.0198	.0088	.0036	.0014	.0005
	1	.3293	.3835	.3248	.2362	.1549	.0932	.0518	.0266	.0125	.0054
	2	.0867	.2131	.2866	.2953	.2581	.1998	.1395	.0887	.0513	.0269
	3	.0137	.0710	.1517	.2215	.2581	.2568	.2254	.1774	.1259	.0806
	4	.0014	.0158	.0536	.1107	.1721	.2201	.2428	.2365	.2060	.1611
	5	.0001	.0025	.0132	.0388	.0803	.1321	.1830	.2207	.2360	.2256
	6	.0000	.0003	.0023	.0097	.0268	.0566	.0985	.1471	.1931	.2256
	7	.0000	.0000	.0003	.0017	.0064	.0173	.0379	.0701	.1128	.1611
	8	.0000	.0000	.0000	.0002	.0011	.0037	.0102	.0234	.0462	.0806
	9	.0000	.0000	.0000	.0000	.0001	.0005	.0018	.0052	.0126	.0269
	10	.0000	.0000	.0000	.0000	.0000	.0000	.0002	.0007	.0021	.0054
	11	.0000	.0000	.0000	.0000	.0000	.0000	.0000	.0000	.0002	.0005
12	0	.5404	.2824	.1422	.0687	.0317	.0138	.0057	.0022	.0008	.0002
	1	.3413	.3766	.3012	.2062	.1267	.0712	.0368	.0174	.0075	.0029
	2	.0988	.2301	.2924	.2835	.2323	.1678	.1088	.0639	.0339	.0161
	3	.0173	.0853	.1720	.2362	.2581	.2397	.1954	.1419	.0923	.0537
	4	.0021	.0213	.0683	.1329	.1936	.2311	.2367	.2128	.1700	.1208

n	x	.05	.10	.15	.20	p .25	.30	.35	.40	.45	.50
12	5	.0002	.0038	.0193	.0532	.1032	.1585	.2039	.2270	.2225	.1934
	6	.0000	.0005	.0040	.0155	.0401	.0792	.1281	.1766	.2124	.2256
	7	.0000	.0000	.0006	.0033	.0115	.0291	.0591	.1009	.1489	.1934
	8	.0000	.0000	.0001	.0005	.0024	.0078	.0199	.0420	.0762	.1208
	9	.0000	.0000	.0000	.0001	.0004	.0015	.0048	.0125	.0277	.0537
	10	.0000	.0000	.0000	.0000	.0000	.0002	.0008	.0025	.0068	.0161
	11	.0000	.0000	.0000	.0000	.0000	.0000	.0001	.0003	.0010	.0029
	12	.0000	.0000	.0000	.0000	.0000	.0000	.0000	.0000	.0001	.0002
13	0	.5133	.2542	.1209	.0550	.0238	.0097	.0037	.0013	.0004	.0001
	1	.3512	.3672	.2774	.1787	.1029	.0540	.0259	.0113	.0045	.0016
	2	.1109	.2448	.2937	.2680	.2059	.1388	.0836	.0453	.0220	.0095
	3	.0214	.0997	.1900	.2457	.2517	.2181	.1651	.1107	.0660	.0349
	4	.0028	.0277	.0838	.1535	.2097	.2337	.2222	.1845	.1350	.0873
	5	.0003	.0055	.0266	.0691	.1258	.1803	.2154	.2214	.1989	.1571
	6	.0000	.0008	.0063	.0230	.0559	.1030	.1546	.1968	.2169	.2095
	7	.0000	.0001	.0011	.0058	.0186	.0442	.0833	.1312	.1775	.2095
	8	.0000	.0000	.0001	.0011	.0047	.0142	.0336	.0656	.1089	.1571
	9	.0000	.0000	.0000	.0001	.0009	.0034	.0101	.0243	.0495	.0873
	10	.0000	.0000	.0000	.0000	.0001	.0006	.0022	.0065	.0162	.0349
	11	.0000	.0000	.0000	.0000	.0000	.0001	.0003	.0012	.0036	.0095
	12	.0000	.0000	.0000	.0000	.0000	.0000	.0000	.0001	.0005	.0016
	13	.0000	.0000	.0000	.0000	.0000	.0000	.0000	.0000	.0000	.0001
14	0	.4877	.2288	.1028	.0440	.0178	.0068	.0024	.0008	.0002	.0001
	1	.3593	.3559	.2539	.1539	.0832	.0407	.0181	.0073	.0027	.0009
	2	.1229	.2570	.2912	.2501	.1802	.1134	.0634	.0317	.0141	.0056
	3	.0259	.1142	.2056	.2501	.2402	.1943	.1366	.0845	.0462	.0222
	4	.0037	.0349	.0998	.1720	.2202	.2290	.2022	.1549	.1040	.0611
	5	.0004	.0078	.0352	.0860	.1468	.1963	.2178	.2066	.1701	.1222
	6	.0000	.0013	.0093	.0322	.0734	.1262	.1759	.2066	.2088	.1833
	7	.0000	.0002	.0019	.0092	.0280	.0618	.1082	.1574	.1952	.2095
	8	.0000	.0000	.0003	.0020	.0082	.0232	.0510	.0918	.1398	.1833
	9	.0000	.0000	.0000	.0003	.0018	.0066	.0183	.0408	.0762	.1222
	10	.0000	.0000	.0000	.0000	.0003	.0014	.0049	.0136	.0312	.0611
	11	.0000	.0000	.0000	.0000	.0000	.0002	.0010	.0033	.0093	.0222
	12	.0000	.0000	.0000	.0000	.0000	.0000	.0001	.0005	.0019	.0056
	13	.0000	.0000	.0000	.0000	.0000	.0000	.0000	.0001	.0002	.0009
	14	.0000	.0000	.0000	.0000	.0000	.0000	.0000	.0000	.0000	.0001
15	0	.4633	.2059	.0874	.0352	.0134	.0047	.0016	.0005	.0001	.0000
	1	.3658	.3432	.2312	.1319	.0668	.0305	.0126	.0047	.0016	.0005
	2	.1348	.2669	.2856	.2309	.1559	.0916	.0476	.0219	.0090	.0032
	3	.0307	.1285	.2184	.2501	.2252	.1700	.1110	.0634	.0318	.0139
	4	.0049	.0428	.1156	.1876	.2252	.2186	.1792	.1268	.0780	.0417

n	x	.05	.10	.15	.20	.25	.30	.35	.40	.45	.50
						p					
15	5	.0006	.0105	.0449	.1032	.1651	.2061	.2123	.1859	.1404	.0916
	6	.0000	.0019	.0132	.0430	.0917	.1472	.1906	.2066	.1914	.1527
	7	.0000	.0003	.0030	.0138	.0393	.0811	.1319	.1771	.2013	.1964
	8	.0000	.0000	.0005	.0035	.0131	.0348	.0710	.1181	.1647	.1964
	9	.0000	.0000	.0001	.0007	.0034	.0116	.0298	.0612	.1048	.1527
	10	.0000	.0000	.0000	.0001	.0007	.0030	.0096	.0245	.0515	.0916
	11	.0000	.0000	.0000	.0000	.0001	.0006	.0024	.0074	.0191	.0417
	12	.0000	.0000	.0000	.0000	.0000	.0001	.0004	.0016	.0052	.0139
	13	.0000	.0000	.0000	.0000	.0000	.0000	.0001	.0003	.0010	.0032
	14	.0000	.0000	.0000	.0000	.0000	.0000	.0000	.0000	.0001	.0005
	15	.0000	.0000	.0000	.0000	.0000	.0000	.0000	.0000	.0000	.0000
16	0	.4401	.1853	.0743	.0281	.0100	.0033	.0010	.0003	.0001	.0000
	1	.3706	.3294	.2097	.1126	.0535	.0228	.0087	.0030	.0009	.0002
	2	.1463	.2745	.2775	.2111	.1336	.0732	.0353	.0150	.0056	.0018
	3	.0359	.1423	.2285	.2463	.2079	.1465	.0888	.0468	.0215	.0085
	4	.0061	.0514	.1311	.2001	.2252	.2040	.1553	.1014	.0572	.0278
	5	.0008	.0137	.0555	.1201	.1802	.2099	.2008	.1623	.1123	.0667
	6	.0001	.0028	.0180	.0550	.1101	.1649	.1982	.1983	.1684	.1222
	7	.0000	.0004	.0045	.0197	.0524	.1010	.1524	.1889	.1969	.1746
	8	.0000	.0001	.0009	.0055	.0197	.0487	.0923	.1417	.1812	.1964
	9	.0000	.0000	.0001	.0012	.0058	.0185	.0442	.0840	.1318	.1746
	10	.0000	.0000	.0000	.0002	.0014	.0056	.0167	.0392	.0755	.1222
	11	.0000	.0000	.0000	.0000	.0002	.0013	.0049	.0142	.0337	.0667
	12	.0000	.0000	.0000	.0000	.0000	.0002	.0011	.0040	.0115	.0278
	13	.0000	.0000	.0000	.0000	.0000	.0000	.0002	.0008	.0029	.0085
	14	.0000	.0000	.0000	.0000	.0000	.0000	.0000	.0001	.0005	.0018
	15	.0000	.0000	.0000	.0000	.0000	.0000	.0000	.0000	.0001	.0002
	16	.0000	.0000	.0000	.0000	.0000	.0000	.0000	.0000	.0000	.0000
17	0	.4181	.1668	.0631	.0225	.0075	.0023	.0007	.0002	.0000	.0000
	1	.3741	.3150	.1893	.0957	.0426	.0169	.0060	.0019	.0005	.0001
	2	.1575	.2800	.2673	.1914	.1136	.0581	.0260	.0102	.0035	.0010
	3	.0415	.1556	.2359	.2393	.1893	.1245	.0701	.0341	.0144	.0052
	4	.0076	.0605	.1457	.2093	.2209	.1868	.1320	.0796	.0411	.0182
	5	.0010	.0175	.0668	.1361	.1914	.2081	.1849	.1379	.0875	.0472
	6	.0001	.0039	.0236	.0680	.1276	.1784	.1991	.1839	.1432	.0944
	7	.0000	.0007	.0065	.0267	.0668	.1201	.1685	.1927	.1841	.1484
	8	.0000	.0001	.0014	.0084	.0279	.0644	.1134	.1606	.1883	.1855
	9	.0000	.0000	.0003	.0021	.0093	.0276	.0611	.1070	.1540	.1855
	10	.0000	.0000	.0000	.0004	.0025	.0095	.0263	.0571	.1008	.1484
	11	.0000	.0000	.0000	.0001	.0005	.0026	.0090	.0242	.0525	.0944
	12	.0000	.0000	.0000	.0000	.0001	.0006	.0024	.0081	.0215	.0472
	13	.0000	.0000	.0000	.0000	.0000	.0001	.0005	.0021	.0068	.0182
	14	.0000	.0000	.0000	.0000	.0000	.0000	.0001	.0004	.0016	.0052

n	x	.05	.10	.15	.20	.25	.30	.35	.40	.45	.50
							p				
	15	.0000	.0000	.0000	.0000	.0000	.0000	.0000	.0001	.0003	.0010
	16	.0000	.0000	.0000	.0000	.0000	.0000	.0000	.0000	.0000	.0001
	17	.0000	.0000	.0000	.0000	.0000	.0000	.0000	.0000	.0000	.0000
18	0	.3972	.1501	.0536	.0180	.0056	.0016	.0004	.0001	.0000	.0000
	1	.3763	.3002	.1704	.0811	.0338	.0126	.0042	.0012	.0003	.0001
	2	.1683	.2835	.2556	.1723	.0958	.0458	.0190	.0069	.0022	.0006
	3	.0473	.1680	.2406	.2297	.1704	.1046	.0547	.0246	.0095	.0031
	4	.0093	.0700	.1592	.2153	.2130	.1681	.1104	.0614	.0291	.0117
	5	.0014	.0218	.0787	.1507	.1988	.2017	.1664	.1146	.0666	.0327
	6	.0002	.0052	.0301	.0816	.1436	.1873	.1941	.1655	.1181	.0708
	7	.0000	.0010	.0091	.0350	.0820	.1376	.1792	.1892	.1657	.1214
	8	.0000	.0002	.0022	.0120	.0376	.0811	.1327	.1734	.1864	.1669
	9	.0000	.0000	.0004	.0033	.0139	.0386	.0794	.1284	.1694	.1855
	10	.0000	.0000	.0001	.0008	.0042	.0149	.0385	.0771	.1248	.1669
	11	.0000	.0000	.0000	.0001	.0010	.0046	.0151	.0374	.0742	.1214
	12	.0000	.0000	.0000	.0000	.0002	.0012	.0047	.0145	.0354	.0708
	13	.0000	.0000	.0000	.0000	.0000	.0002	.0012	.0045	.0134	.0327
	14	.0000	.0000	.0000	.0000	.0000	.0000	.0002	.0011	.0039	.0117
	15	.0000	.0000	.0000	.0000	.0000	.0000	.0000	.0002	.0009	.0031
	16	.0000	.0000	.0000	.0000	.0000	.0000	.0000	.0000	.0001	.0006
	17	.0000	.0000	.0000	.0000	.0000	.0000	.0000	.0000	.0000	.0001
	18	.0000	.0000	.0000	.0000	.0000	.0000	.0000	.0000	.0000	.0000
19	0	.3774	.1351	.0456	.0144	.0042	.0011	.0003	.0001	.0002	.0000
	1	.3774	.2852	.1529	.0685	.0268	.0093	.0029	.0008	.0002	.0000
	2	.1787	.2852	.2428	.1540	.0803	.0358	.0138	.0046	.0013	.0003
	3	.0533	.1796	.2428	.2182	.1517	.0869	.0422	.0175	.0062	.0018
	4	.0112	.0798	.1714	.2182	.2023	.1491	.0909	.0467	.0203	.0074
	5	.0018	.0266	.0907	.1636	.2023	.1916	.1468	.0933	.0497	.0222
	6	.0002	.0069	.0374	.0955	.1574	.1916	.1844	.1451	.0949	.0518
	7	.0000	.0014	.0122	.0443	.0974	.1525	.1844	.1797	.1443	.0961
	8	.0000	.0002	.0032	.0166	.0487	.0981	.1489	.1797	.1771	.1442
	9	.0000	.0000	.0007	.0051	.0198	.0514	.0980	.1464	.1771	.1762
	10	.0000	.0000	.0001	.0013	.0066	.0220	.0528	.0976	.1449	.1762
	11	.0000	.0000	.0000	.0003	.0018	.0077	.0233	.0532	.0970	.1442
	12	.0000	.0000	.0000	.0000	.0004	.0022	.0083	.0237	.0529	.0961
	13	.0000	.0000	.0000	.0000	.0001	.0005	.0024	.0085	.0233	.0518
	14	.0000	.0000	.0000	.0000	.0000	.0001	.0006	.0024	.0082	.0222
	15	.0000	.0000	.0000	.0000	.0000	.0000	.0001	.0005	.0022	.0074
	16	.0000	.0000	.0000	.0000	.0000	.0000	.0000	.0001	.0005	.0018
	17	.0000	.0000	.0000	.0000	.0000	.0000	.0000	.0000	.0001	.0003
	18	.0000	.0000	.0000	.0000	.0000	.0000	.0000	.0000	.0000	.0000
	19	.0000	.0000	.0000	.0000	.0000	.0000	.0000	.0000	.0000	.0000

n	x	.05	.10	.15	.20	.25	.30	.35	.40	.45	.50
						p					
20	0	.3585	.1216	.0388	.0115	.0032	.0008	.0002	.0000	.0000	.0000
	1	.3774	.2702	.1368	.0576	.0211	.0068	.0020	.0005	.0001	.0000
	2	.1887	.2852	.2293	.1369	.0669	.0278	.0100	.0031	.0008	.0002
	3	.0596	.1901	.2428	.2054	.1339	.0716	.0323	.0123	.0040	.0011
	4	.0133	.0898	.1821	.2182	.1897	.1304	.0738	.0350	.0139	.0046
	5	.0022	.0319	.1028	.1746	.2023	.1789	.1272	.0746	.0365	.0148
	6	.0003	.0089	.0454	.1091	.1686	.1916	.1712	.1244	.0746	.0370
	7	.0000	.0020	.0160	.0545	.1124	.1643	.1844	.1659	.1221	.0739
	8	.0000	.0004	.0046	.0222	.0609	.1144	.1614	.1797	.1623	.1201
	9	.0000	.0001	.0011	.0074	.0271	.0654	.1158	.1597	.1771	.1602
	10	.0000	.0000	.0002	.0020	.0099	.0308	.0686	.1171	.1593	.1762
	11	.0000	.0000	.0000	.0005	.0030	.0120	.0336	.0710	.1185	.1602
	12	.0000	.0000	.0000	.0001	.0008	.0039	.0136	.0355	.0727	.1201
	13	.0000	.0000	.0000	.0000	.0002	.0010	.0045	.0146	.0366	.0739
	14	.0000	.0000	.0000	.0000	.0000	.0002	.0012	.0049	.0150	.0370
	15	.0000	.0000	.0000	.0000	.0000	.0000	.0003	.0013	.0049	.0148
	16	.0000	.0000	.0000	.0000	.0000	.0000	.0000	.0003	.0013	.0046
	17	.0000	.0000	.0000	.0000	.0000	.0000	.0000	.0000	.0002	.0011
	18	.0000	.0000	.0000	.0000	.0000	.0000	.0000	.0000	.0000	.0002
	19	.0000	.0000	.0000	.0000	.0000	.0000	.0000	.0000	.0000	.0000
	20	.0000	.0000	.0000	.0000	.0000	.0000	.0000	.0000	.0000	.0000

Answers to Selected Problems*

Chapter 4

4. Productivity indexes
   February—0.97
   March—1.02
   April—1.03
   May—0.89
   June—0.86

6.

	Year 1	Year 2	Year 3
total sales/total inputs	1.1224	1.0932	1.1376
total sales/labor dollars	3.9286	3.9091	4.4286

8. a. 268.97 units of output/dollar input
   b. 433.33 units of output/dollar input
11. 200 sq. ft. additional floor space required; total annual costs = $1,200.00; productivity must increase by 0.006.

Chapter 6

2. a. Alternative A: X = 40,000
      Alternative B: X = 24,000
   b. Recommend alternative B
   c. Breakeven = 50,667 units
6. Product C has the highest score.
7. a. .7608
   b. .7763

Chapter 7

1. 540 passengers/hour = maximum capacity
5. a. 101,908 bolts
   c. one additional machine
8. 16 machines, 19 or 20 operators
12. 12 loan officers
15. For x = 2, y = 3.00 hours
    For x = 3, y = 2.54 hours
17. 23.60 hours
19. Build large

Appendix to Chapter 7

4. $T = 20746.67 - 351.429t$
7. a. Yes
   b. $Y_t = 22.857 + 15.536t$
   c. $Y_8 = 147.15$
11. a.

Quarter	Seasonal Index	Adjusted
1	1.239	1.271
2	0.597	0.613
3	0.485	0.498
4	1.578	1.619

14. a.

Week	5-Week Moving Average Forecast
6	19.60
7	19.40
8	19.20
9	19.00
10	18.80
11	19.20
12	19.00

20. MSE = 5660.36
    $F_{11} = 292.71$
24. a. MAD = 2.655
    b. Yes
25. For 3-period forecasts, MAD = 1.93
    For 4-period forecasts, MAD = 2.09

Chapter 8

2. Location 1.
3. Prefer locations in order 1, 4, 2, 3
8. a. $C_x = 8.65$, $C_y = 6.55$
   b. $C_x = 8.87$, $C_y = 9.82$
13. Total profit = $297,000. Customer 2 demand is 1000 short. Customer 3 demand is 3000 short.
19. a. Site B.
    b. Site C.
21. Zone 3

Chapter 9

7. a. .315
   b. .717
14. a. Operator utilization = 94%
    b. 84.7 pieces/hour
18. $n = 385$ (conservative estimate with $p = .5$)
20. 0.2405
25. $n = 44$ observations

Chapter 10

1. 4 cutting machines; 4 inner bending machines; 5 outer bending machines
3. a. minimum cycle time = 2.4 min
      maximum cycle time = 42 min
   b. 187.5 and 10.7 units/day
9. a. C = 10
      Station 1: A, B
      Station 2: C, D, E
      Station 3: F, G, H, I
      Station 4: J, K
      Station 5: L, M, N
      Efficiency = 0.90
13. $7 \leq C \leq 48$
    Minimum output = 10
    Maximum output = 68
15. Bottleneck is chip-maker and poucher
    Time/shift = 400 min.
    Output required = 10,368,000 chips

*Most of these are only the final answer. Complete worked-out solutions can be found in the *Instructor's Manual.*

17. Current layout: 256
    Proposed layout: 262
20. a. Total cost = 29,250
    b. Total cost = 29,250

Chapter 11

3. b. $8000
   c. t = 10
   d. $123
4. a. 53.3 hours
   b. $26,266.00
   c. Total costs = $61,400.00
   d. About every 60 hours
7. Most customers wait between 6 and 10 seconds; however, 15 percent must wait more than 20 seconds
11. Samples 21 and 22 appear suspect.

Chapter 12

1. $LCL_x = 15.184$
   $UCL_x = 17.836$
   $LCL_R = 0$
   $UCL_R = 3.341$
4. $\bar{\bar{x}} = 3.078, \bar{R} = .053$
   $\bar{x}$-chart:
      UCL = 3.109
      LCL = 3.047
   R-chart:
      UCL = .112
      LCL = 0
7. p = .0272
   s = .0163
   LCL = 0
   UCL = .0761
11. LCL = 0
    UCL = 18
16. σ estimate = .0228
    Process capability = (3.0096, 3.164)
    Actual σ = .0047
    Process capability = (3.064, 3.092)
18. a. $LCL_R = 0$
       $UCL_R = .977$
       $LCL_x = 10.272$
       $UCL_x = 10.898$

Chapter 13

4. a. Average weekly inventory = 69.8
   b. No stockouts
6. Place orders on days 3, 11, 15, and 20
10. Total inventory cost = $328.64
12. a. TC = $536.66
    b. For Q = 1200, TC = 540, Cost increase is only $3.34
16. a. r = 14
    b. r = 18
    c. 2, $10 and 6, $30
18. a. $Q^* = 86.6$
    b. Safety stock = 10
    c. P (stockout) = .1587

Chapter 14

2. EOQ model, r = 80
   Back-order model, r = 40.44
4. $Q^* = 36.74$
   $S^* = 7.35$ for $C_b = \$40$.
7. a. 1078.12
   b. 6.68
   c. 37.43
   d. 10.78
   e. 767.62
   f. $1001.74
   g. 432
15. Reduce Q to 300 pairs/order. Annual savings is $480.00.
18. a. Average demand = 245
    b. $Q^* = 350$
21. a. $P(D \le Q^*) = .5$
       order 500
    b. $P(D \le Q^*) = .58$
       order 524
24. a. $P(D \le Q^*) = .7077$
       order 167
    b. .2923
    c. order quantity increases

Chapter 16

5. Production cost = $336,000
   Inventory cost = $66,500
   Total cost = $402,500
7. Total cost = $389,200
14. X1 = 77.89, X2 = 63.16, profit = $3,284.21
21. a. $b_1 = 155.357$
    c.

Quarter	Forecast
1	332.4
2	516.5
3	437.2
4	248.6

Chapter 17

1. Order 1,250 snowblowers in week 14.
   Order 750 engines in week 10.
   Order 375 air cleaners in week 9.
   Order 125 filter housings in week 7.
7. a.

Item	Net Requirements
Wooden pegs	900
Strings	500
Sides	1600
Cartons	1000

   b. Order 1000 yo-yos in week 9.
      Order 900 wooden pegs in week 8.
      Order 500 strings in week 8.
      Order 1600 sides in week 4.
      Order 1000 cartons in week 6.

Chapter 18

1. b. 4-2-6-5-3-1
3. Average flowtime = 11.6
   Average tardiness = 1.0
   Average lateness = 0.40
5. Finance, P/OM, marketing, psychology
7. 1-2-5-4-6-7-3
12. Jobs 3–7 are late
15. a. 2.66 weeks
    b. Schedule giant, medium, jumbo in order.
18. Six employees are needed.

Chapter 19

4.

Activity	Expected Time	Variance
A	5.17	.25
B	9.33	.44
C	8.00	.44
D	8.66	.25
E	6.83	.69
F	6.00	.11

7. c. A-C-E-G
10. b. B-C-E-F-H
    d. Yes, completion time = 49 weeks
12. a. A-D-F-G
    b. Slack on C is 1.5 days
    c. σ^2 = 2.36
       E(T) = 29.5 days
    d. P(30 days) = .6293
15. Delay on H is irrelevant; project is delayed 2 weeks.
19. E is behind schedule; F is ahead of schedule
22. c. A-B-C-F critical; time = 31 weeks
    d. Crash A 2 weeks, B 2 weeks, C 1 week, D 1 week, E 1 week, Cost = $112.5
24. b. Crash C 1 day, Crash E 1 day
    c. Crash cost = $900.00. Total cost = $9,300.00.
26. Critical path is A-D-G-J

Supplementary Chapter A

2.

Arrivals	Random Numbers
0	00–11
1	12–35
2	36–72
3	73–91
4	92–99

6.

Service Call	R.N.
X-100	00–59
Y-200	60–99

Time(X-100)	R.N.
25	00–49
30	50–74
35	75–89
40	90–99

Time(Y-200)	R.N.
20	00–39
25	40–79
30	80–89
35	90–99

Supplementary Chapter B

1. a. maximax – d_1
      maximin – d_3
      minimax regret – d_3
   c. optimistic – d_1
      conservative – d_2 or d_3
3. Choose d_2; EV = 365
5. Choose d_2; EV = 500
9. Choose d_2; EV = 40.25
13. a. Do not fund
    b. Do not hire the consultants

Supplementary Chapter C

3. a. .375 days
   b. .5 days
5. a. .56
   b. .2464
   c. .1084
   d. .0477
   e. .0375
   f. .157 hours
9. a. L_q = .5, W_q = .0333 hours
   b. L_q = .1227, W_q = .0082 hours
   c. Use one counter with 2 people.
12. a. .50
    b. .50
    c. .1 hour
    d. .2 hour
    e. Yes, unless W_q = 6 is considered too long.
15. a. P_0 = .3333
    b. L_q = 1.3333
    c. L = 2
    d. W_q = .0267 hour
    e. W = .04 hour
18. Use one consultant.

Supplementary Chapter D

3. x_1 = 100, x_2 = 50, objective function = 750
6. a. x_1 = 0, x_2 = 540, profit = 4860
   b. Inspection and Packaging and the nonnegativity con-

straint on x_1

8. b. $x_1 = 100$, $x_2 = 100$, $z = 5500$
10. a. $x_1 = 125$, $x_2 = 225$
    b. First and second constraints
12. $x_1 = 30$, $x_2 = 25$, cost $= 55$

Supplementary Chapter E

2. P_1 to W_2 : 300
   P_2 to W_1 : 100
   P_2 to W_2 : 100
   P_2 to W_3 : 300
   P_3 to W_1 : 100
4. One solution:

From origin	To destination	Amount
1	1	150
1	2	50
1	3	50
2	2	150
3	3	100

Cost = 4500
6. Total cost = $51,500.00.
   York plant provides a $12,000.00 per month savings.

Glossary

ABC classification A grouping of inventoried items into three classes: items accounting for a large dollar value but a relatively small percentage of all items, items accounting for a small dollar value but a large percentage of all items, and items intermediate between those two classes.

Acceptance sampling Accepting or rejecting entire lots of materials on the basis of a sample.

Activity A specific job or task that is a component of a project.

Aggregate production planning The establishment of aggregate production and inventory levels over a medium-range time horizon.

Anticipation inventory Inventory built up during the off season to meet peak demand.

Appraisal costs Expenditures for measuring and analyzing quality-related data.

Arcs Another term for **branches.**

Assembly chart A graphical representation of a product's order of assembly.

Assurance A term in service quality referring to employees' knowledge and courtesy and their ability to inspire trust and confidence in customers.

Attribute A (quality) characteristic that assumes only one of two possible values.

Automation The use of machines to provide power and control over a production process.

Autonomation The equipping of machines with automatic stopping devices that reduce the possibility of producing defects.

Average time In PERT/CPM, computed as $(a + 4m + b)/6$.

Bakayake The use of automatic stopping devices on machines to prevent poor quality.

Bar code technology The use of bar code symbols to store and retrieve information by means of computer-based scanners.

Bar coding The process of identifying items by using bar code symbols.

Benchmarking The identification of industry best practices that lead to superior performance.

Bill of materials (BOM) A structured parts list showing the hierarchical relationship of components and the number required in an assembly.

Branch In PERT/CPM, a line that connects nodes and represents activities in the network. In decision analysis, a branch represents a decision or state of nature.

Break-even point The point at which total cost equals total revenue.

Bucket A term denoting a time period used in the master schedule.

Business logistics The management of materials and goods from the point of origin to the point of consumption.

Capacity The capability of a system to produce a quantity of output in a particular time period.

Capacity requirements planning (CRP) A system for determining whether a planned production schedule can be met with available capacity and, if not, making adjustments as necessary.

Cause-and-effect diagram A graphical tool that organizes a collection of ideas by showing the possible causes of some effect.

Cell In a **transportation tableau,** a particular shipping route between an origin and a destination.

Center-of-gravity method A quantitative approach to locating a facility that minimizes the distance or cost of transportation weighted by the volume of goods moved.

Chase demand strategy A production planning strategy in which production is equal to forecasted demand.

Checksheet A data-collection form that facilitates interpretation of the data.

Competitive advantage A firm's ability to achieve market superiority over its competitors.

Computer-aided design/computer-aided engineering (CAD/CAE) The use of a computer to develop and test product ideas without actually building prototypes.

Computer-assisted manufacturing (CAM) Computer control of the manufacturing process.

Computer-integrated manufacturing (CIM) The union of hardware, software, database management, and communications to plan and control production activities.

Computer numerical control (CNC) Control of a machine by a computer.

Concurrent engineering The process of continuously involving all major functions necessary for getting a product to market in the product's development, from ideation through sales.

Consolidation Bringing the orders of several customers together at a warehouse rather than shipping directly from several factories.

Constant demand rate An assumption of many inventory decision models that the same number of units is taken from inventory in each time period.

Constraint An equation or inequality that rules out certain combinations of variables as feasible solutions.

Constraint function The left side of a constraint relationship (that is, the part of the constraint containing the variables).

Constraint management A process of continuous improvement through synchronous manufacturing.

Consumers The ultimate purchasers of goods and services.

Consumer's risk The probability of accepting a bad lot.

Continuous-review system An inventory system in which the inventory level is monitored continuously and an order is placed when the level drops below the reorder point.

Control The process of comparing results with goals and taking corrective action when needed.

Control chart A graphical means of depicting sample characteristics over time, used for process control. Control charts are usually constructed for proportion defective, means, and ranges.

Conversion process A process that changes the inputs of a production system into outputs or products.

Core processes The processes that drive the creation of products and services.

Corporate strategy Definition of the businesses in which a corporation will participate and the plans for acquiring and allocating resources among those businesses.

Cost of capital The cost a firm incurs, usually as interest payments on borrowed funds or dividend payments on stock, to obtain capital for investment. The cost of capital, which may be stated as an annual percentage rate, is part of the holding cost associated with maintaining inventory levels.

Cost of quality Cost associated with avoiding poor quality or incurred as a result of poor quality.

CRAFT Computerized Relative Allocation of Facilities Technique, a computer-based system for facility layout.

Crashing The process of reducing an activity time by adding resources and hence usually cost.

Critical activity An activity whose delay will delay the entire project; a critical-path activity.

Critical path The longest sequence of activities or path in a project management (PERT/CPM) network. The time needed to traverse this path is the estimated project duration.

Cross-docking A process by which products are unloaded from plants and immediately sorted and reloaded for shipment to customers without intermediate storage.

Cumulative trauma disorder (CTD) Injury due to repetitive motion.

Customer contact The simultaneous physical presence of the customer and the service provider in a service system.

Cycle counting The process of taking a physical count of each item once during its replenishment cycle.

Cycle time (1) The length of time between the placing of two consecutive or-

ders. (2) The time required to produce one item on an assembly line.

Cyclical component The component of a time-series model that results in periodic above-trend and below-trend behavior of the time series lasting more than one year.

Decision tree A graphical representation of a sequence of decisions and states of nature.

Defect A failure to meet a specification or requirement in a product or service.

Deming cycle An approach for continuously improving products and services; its components are plan, do, study, and act.

Demonstrated capacity A system's proven capacity calculated from actual output performance data.

Deseasonalized time series A time series from which the effect of season has been removed by dividing each original time-series observation by a corresponding seasonal factor.

Design for manufacture (DFM) An approach to product design that attempts to ensure that products can be manufactured efficiently.

Design review A formal process of studying a product design to identify potential problems and to suggest new ideas and solutions before production begins.

Diseconomies of scale Inefficiencies in production arising from large facilities.

Dispatching rules Rules that assign priorities to jobs for processing.

Distinctive competencies Strengths unique to an organization.

Drum-buffer-rope A scheduling approach based on tying the release of materials to critical resources.

Due date A promised delivery date.

Dummy activity A fictitious activity with zero activity time used to represent precedence or whenever two or more activities have the same starting and ending nodes.

Dummy destination A destination added to make total supply equal to demand in a transportation problem. The demand assigned to the dummy destination is the excess of the actual supply over the actual demand.

Dummy origin An origin added to make total supply equal to total demand in a transportation problem. The supply assigned to the dummy origin is the excess of the actual demand over the actual supply.

Earliest start time The earliest time at which an activity can begin.

Economic order quantity (EOQ) The order quantity that minimizes the total inventory costs in the most fundamental inventory-decision model.

Economies of scale Efficiencies in production whereby per-unit manufacturing costs increase at a slower rate than production volume.

Electronic data interchange (EDI) Technology that allows information to be transmitted and shared electronically.

Empathy Caring, individualized attention provided to customers.

Empowerment Giving employees authority to make decisions and gain greater control over their work.

Ergonomics A field of study relating the physical capabilities of human beings to the design of tools, instruments, and workplaces.

Event In PERT/CPM, an event occurs when all the activities leading into a node have been completed. In simulation, an action that changes the system.

Expected time The average activity time.

Exponential probability distribution A probability distribution used to describe the pattern of service times for some waiting lines.

Exponential smoothing A forecasting technique that uses a weighted average of past time-series values to arrive at smoothed time-series values that can be used as forecasts.

External customers Intermediate customers between a producer and the end consumer.

External failure costs Costs incurred after poor quality products reach the customer.

Failure mode and effects analysis (FMEA) A technique for anticipating possible failures in products and suggesting corrective design actions.

Feasible solution A solution that satisfies all the constraints.

Final assembly schedule (FAS) A statement of the final products that are to be assembled from MPS items.

Finite capacity scheduling Matching work against available resources to produce a feasible schedule.

Fixed-position layout A layout in which the construction of a large product is accomplished in one place.

Fixed-time simulation model A simulation approach that increments time in fixed intervals.

Flexibility The capacity of a production system to adapt successfully to changing environmental conditions and process requirements.

Flexible manufacturing system (FMS) Two or more computer-controlled machines linked by handling devices.

Flow-blocking delay Delay incurred when a production stage completes a unit but cannot release it to the next stage.

Flow-process chart A description of the sequence of activities in a production process, generally operations, inspection, movement, storage, and delay.

Flowchart A step-by-step picture of a process.

Flowshop A job shop in which all jobs have the same routing.

Flowtime The time a particular job spends in the shop.

Fluctuation inventory Inventory maintained to reduce the number of stockouts resulting from fluctuations in demand or lead time.

Forecast error The difference between a time-series value and its corresponding forecast.

Forecasting The process of estimating future demand or requirements.

Functional failure A failure early in the life of a product due to manufacturing or material defects.

Gainsharing A program of sharing a firm's financial gains from improved productivity and profitability with the workers responsible for them.

Gantt chart A graphical representation of a schedule used to plan and monitor progress.

Global integration The coordination and balancing of the global resources of a firm.

Goodwill cost A cost associated with a back order, a lost sale, or any form of stockout or unsatisfied demand. It can be used to reflect the loss of future profits due to a customer's demand being unsatisfied.

Group (cellular) layout A layout in which machine groups are arranged to process families of parts with similar characteristics.

Group technology A concept for identifying and classifying part families so that efficient mass-production layouts can be designed for items traditionally manufactured in a process layout.

Guiding principles Attitudes and policies to be followed by all employees to realize a company's vision.

Hard technology Technology involving the application of computers, sensors, robots, and other mechanical and electronic aids.

Hidden factory The part of a plant used to rework parts, replace products, or retest and reinspect rejected items.

High performance work systems Job and organizational designs that lead to high performance, greater flexibility, and rapid response to changing customer requirements.

Histogram A graphical interpretation of a frequency distribution.

House of Quality A planning matrix in quality function deployment relating the voice of the customer and technical features.

Immediate predecessor An activity that must immediately precede a given activity.

Improvement Identifying opportunities for achieving higher levels of quality and performance.

Interlinking Quantitative modeling of cause and effect relationships between external and internal performance criteria.

Internal customers The recipients of goods and services from internal suppliers.

Internal failure costs Costs due to unsatisfactory quality discovered before delivery of a product to customers.

Inventory Any idle resource that is waiting to be used.

Inventory-holding or inventory-carrying costs All costs associated with maintaining an inventory investment: cost of the capital investment in the inventory, insurance, taxes, warehouse overhead, and so on. It can be stated as a percentage of the inventory investment or as a cost per unit.

Inventory position The amount of inventory in stock plus any amount on order but not yet received minus back orders.

Irregular component In a time-series model, the component that reflects the random variation of the actual time series values beyond what can be explained by the trend, cyclical, and seasonal components.

Job The set of tasks an individual worker performs.

Job design The determination of specific job tasks and responsibilities, the work environment, and work methods.

Job enlargement Horizontal expansion of job duties to give workers more variety.

Job enrichment Vertical expansion of job duties to give workers more responsibility.

Just in time (JIT) An approach to materials management and control designed to produce or deliver parts and materials when they are required in production.

Kaizen The Japanese term for "continuous improvement."

Kanban Japanese for "card"; an information system for implementing JIT.

Key business factors Elements of a business that affect strategic planning, design, quality, and human resource development and management. They include markets, customers, employees, facilities, technology, and suppliers.

Lack-of-work delay Delay incurred when a production stage completes a unit and no units are waiting to be processed.

Lateness The difference (positive or negative) between a job's completion time and its due date.

Latest finish time The latest time at which an activity can be completed without delaying the project.

Leadership The right to exercise authority and the ability to achieve results from people and systems.

Lead time The time between the placing of an order and its receipt in the inventory system.

Lead-time demand distribution In probabilistic inventory models, the distribution of demand that occurs during the lead-time period.

Lean production An approach to production employing multiskilled workers, cross-functional teams, integrated communications, supplier partnerships, and highly flexible automated machines to produce a wide variety of products.

Learning curve A curve that describes the relationship between the production time per unit and the number of units produced.

Level master schedule A schedule in which small lots of each product are produced each day or even each hour.

Level production strategy A production planning strategy in which production remains the same in each period.

Life-cycle curve A graph of sales volume over time for a product.

Linear function A mathematical expression in which the variables appear in separate terms and are raised to the first power.

Linear program A mathematical model with a linear objective function, a set of linear constraints, and non-negative variables.

Load matrix A matrix used in the design of process layouts that shows the number of movements between departments during some time period.

Lot-size inventory Inventory purchased or manufactured in lots to take advantage of economies of scale.

Machine vision systems Optical devices for noncontact sensing of information for controlling machines.

Makespan The time required to complete a set of jobs.

Management science The application of scientific methodology to managerial decision making.

Manufacturing resource planning (MRPII) A comprehensive system that coordinates MRP with shop-floor control, inventory, and other aspects of material management.

Manufacturing strategy (1) The operations strategy in a manufacturing organization. (2) The set of goals and policies that guide manufacturing decisions.

Master production schedule (MPS) A time-phased statement of how many individual items are to be produced, obtained by disaggregating the aggregate production plan.

Material requirements planning (MRP) A computerized data-processing system for scheduling production and controlling the level of inventory for components with dependent demand.

Materials handling The handling and transportation of materials during production.

Materials management The area of P/OM concerned with the acquisition, storage, handling, and movement of materials and finished goods from procurement to distribution to customers.

Maximax An optimistic decision criterion that maximizes the maximum payoff among all states of nature.

Maximin A conservative decision criterion that maximizes the minimum payoff among all states of nature.

Mean absolute deviation (MAD) A measure of forecast accuracy. MAD is the average of the absolute values of the forecast errors.

Mean arrival rate The expected number of customers or units arriving or entering a system in a given period of time.

Mean service rate The expected number of customers or units that can be serviced by one server in a given period of time.

Mean square error (MSE) An approach to measuring the accuracy of a forecasting model; the average of the squared differences between the forecast values and the actual time-series values.

Mean time between failures The average time between failures of a repairable item.

Measurement reliability How well a measurement instrument consistently measures the true value.

Minimax regret A decision criterion that minimizes the maximum opportunity loss associated with the states of nature.

Mission The reason for a firm's existence.

Model A representation of a real object or situation.

Modular design The design of components for assembly in a variety of ways to meet individual consumer needs.

Most probable time The most likely time estimate for an activity.

Moving averages A method of forecasting or smoothing a time series by averaging successive groups of data points; can be used to identify the combined trend/cyclical component of the time series.

Multifactor productivity The ratio of total output to a subset of inputs.

Multiple-activity chart A graphical representation of simultaneous activities of machines and/or people.

Multiple-channel waiting line A waiting line with two or more parallel, identical servers.

Net change approach In MRP, a method in which outputs are updated only for components that have changes.

Next-event simulation model A simulation model in which time is incremented according to when successive events occur.

Node An intersection or junction point in a network or decision tree.

Nominal specifications Target values for product design characteristics.

Nonconformity Another term for **defect**.

Non-negativity constraints A set of constraints that requires all variables to be positive.

Numerically controlled (NC) system An early example of automation in which a computer program provided instructions on paper tape for controlling tool movement on a machine.

Objective function All linear programs have a linear objective function that is to be either maximized or minimized. In most linear programming problems, the objective function is used to measure the profit or cost of a particular solution.

One-hundred percent inspection Inspection of every unit produced.

Operation chart A chart used to describe simultaneous motions of hands in performing a task.

Operations The set of all activities associated with producing goods and services.

Operations research A problem-solving approach usually based on the application of mathematical models.

Operations strategy A firm's manufacturing/service strategy defined by its focus on product technology, capacity, facilities and location, process technology, human resources, operating decisions, supplier integration, and quality.

Opportunity loss matrix A matrix showing the difference between the best possible payoff and any other payoff for each state of nature.

OPT (optimized production technology) A planning and scheduling tool based on a set of rules for scheduling bottleneck operations in a product network.

Optimal solution A feasible solution that maximizes or minimizes the value of the objective function.

Optimistic time Time estimate based on the assumption that the activity will progress in an ideal manner.

Ordering cost The fixed cost (salaries, paper, transportation, and so on) of placing an order.

Packaging The department responsible for preparing material for shipment.

Pareto analysis Ordering the frequencies of occurrence of something from highest to lowest.

Pareto diagram A histogram in which frequencies are ordered from highest to lowest.

Part-period balancing method Lot-sizing method that attempts to balance ordering and holding costs.

Partial factor productivity The ratio of total output to a single input.

Payoff table A table that shows the payoffs resulting from particular decisions and particular states of nature.

Periodic order quantity method Lot-sizing method based on calculation of an economic time interval between orders.

Periodic-review system An inventory system in which the inventory level is reviewed at fixed time intervals. If the inventory level is below the reorder point at the time of review, an order is placed for enough stock to raise the inventory position to a given level.

PERT/CPM network See **project network**.

Pessimistic time Time estimate based on the assumption that the most unfavorable conditions will prevail.

Physical distribution Movement of materials by transportation carriers, company-owned fleets, and interplant means.

Poisson probability distribution A probability distribution used to describe the random arrival pattern for some waiting lines.

Poka-yoke A device that permanently prevents the recurrence of a defect.

Prevention costs Costs incurred to prevent nonconforming products from being made.

Process A sequence of activities intended to produce a result for a customer.

Process capability The range over which the natural variation of a process occurs.

Process layout A layout in which machines or activities are arranged by function.

Process management The activities of controlling and improving production processes.

Process technology The methods and equipment used to manufacture a product or deliver a service.

Procurement The acquisition of goods and services, including purchasing, stores, traffic, receiving, and inspection.

Producer's risk The probability of rejecting a good quality lot.

Product-development process Idea generation, concept development, product/process development, full-scale production, product introduction, and market evaluation.

Product layout A layout in which equipment is arranged in the sequence of operations performed on a product or group of products.

Product lead time Total time needed to deliver a finished product.

Product-process matrix A framework for analyzing the relationship between process technology and product structure.

Product simplification The process of simplifying product designs and assembly to reduce manufacturing lead times and improve productivity, quality, flexibility, and customer response.

Production The process of converting or transforming resources into goods and services.

Production activity control The process of ensuring that materials and tools are available when needed, tracking progress against plans, and making any necessary adjustments to a schedule.

Production line A fixed sequence of production stages.

Production lot-size model Similar to the EOQ model, but assumes orders are received gradually over time instead of instantaneously.

Production/operations management (P/OM) Management of the operations involved in producing goods and services and of the interface with supporting functions in the organization.

Production system The collection of inputs, conversion/creation processes, outputs, feedback mechanisms, and managers involved in production.

Productivity A measure of the effectiveness with which an organization uses its resources in transforming inputs to outputs; in other words, the ratio of the output of a production system to the input.

Productivity index The ratio of productivity in some time period to the productivity of a base period.

Project A set of activities that must be performed in a particular sequence, on time, and on budget.

Project management All activities associated with planning, scheduling, and controlling projects.

Project network A graphical representation of a project's activities and events.

Pseudorandom numbers Computer-generated numbers that have the properties of random numbers; they are developed from mathematical expressions.

Pull production Delivering or producing items only when they are required; the basis of just-in-time production.

Purchasing The function of economically acquiring the raw materials and supplies needed for production.

Quality circle A group of workers who work closely together to identify and solve problems related to quality and productivity.

Quality control The use of a series of planned measurements to determine whether quality standards are being met.

Quality council A steering committee of senior managers who are responsible for incorporating quality issues into an organization's strategic planning process and who coordinate the overall effort.

Quality engineering The concept of designing quality products and processes and predicting potential problems before production begins.

Quality function deployment A method for ensuring that customers' requirements are met in the design process; includes the design of production systems.

Quality trilogy Joseph Juran's model of quality: quality planning, quality control, and quality improvement.

Quantity discount Discount or lower unit cost offered by a manufacturer when a customer purchases a larger quantity of the product.

Queue A waiting line.

Queuing theory The theory of the behavior of waiting lines.

Radio frequency (RF) communication Communication of information, usually within a factory, by means of hand-held communication devices.

Receiving The function of controlling and accepting inbound shipments of materials.

Redundancy The use of multiple components performing the same function so that the entire system will fail only if all components fail.

Reengineering The fundamental rethinking and radical redesign of business processes to achieve dramatic improvements.

Regeneration approach A method by which MRP outputs are updated periodically for all components.

Regret The cost of lost opportunity.

Reliability (1) The probability that a process or system will perform satisfactorily over a specified period of time. (2) The probability that a product or process will perform satisfactorily over a period of time under specified operating conditions. (3) In services, the ability to perform a service dependably and accurately.

Reliability engineering The design, manufacture, and ensurance of highly reliable products.

Reliability failure A failure after some period of use.

Reliability management The process of ensuring reliability throughout the production process, from defining customer requirements to analyzing field failure data.

Reorder point The inventory level at which a new order should be placed.

Research and development (R&D) The development and application of new technology to meet customers' emerging needs.

Robot A programmable machine designed to handle materials or tools in performing a variety of tasks.

Robust Being insensitive to external sources of variation.

Root cause The underlying reason for a problem.

Rough-cut capacity planning Analysis of the master production schedule to determine its feasibility with respect to capacity limitations.

Run chart A line graph in which data are plotted over time.

Runout time The ratio of an item's current inventory level to its demand rate.

Safety stock See **fluctuation inventory**.

Sampling plan The specification of a sample size and an acceptance number for sampling from a lot.

Sampling procedures Approaches used to inspect a portion of a production lot.

Scatter diagram A graphical representation of the relationship in the behavior of two variables.

Scheduling The process of establishing starting times and completion times for jobs.

Scoring model A procedure for quantitatively evaluating several criteria by assigning numerical values to attributes of the criteria.

Seasonal component The component of the time-series model that shows a periodic pattern over one year or less.

Self-checking The practice of workers checking their own output for defects.

Self-managed team A group of six to 18 highly trained employees that is responsible for turning out a well-defined segment of work.

Sequencing Determining the order in which a set of jobs is to be performed.

Service A social act that takes place by direct contact between the customer and representatives of the service company.

Service level The probability of no stockouts during the lead time.

Shipping The department responsible for loading material onto transport vehicles.

Shortest processing time (SPT) The scheduling rule that jobs will be performed in order of shortest processing time first.

Silver-Meal method A lot-sizing heuristic based on analysis of the average cost per period.

Simplex method An algorithm for solving linear programming problems by systematically searching corner points.

Simplex tableau A representation of a linear program in tabular form for use with the simplex method.

Simulation A technique for describing the behavior of a real-world system over time, most often employing a computer program to perform the simulation computations.

Simultaneous engineering Another term for **concurrent engineering**.

Single-channel waiting line A waiting line with only one server.

Single-period inventory model An inventory model that assumes only one order is placed for the product, and at the end of the period, the item has either sold out or a surplus of unsold items will be sold for salvage value.

Slack In a project network, the length of time an activity can be delayed without affecting the project completion date.

Slack variable Used to convert a less-than-or-equal-to constraint to an equality constraint in linear programming.

Smoothing constant A parameter of the exponential smoothing model that provides the weight to be given to the most recent time-series value in calculating the forecast value.

Socio-technical approach Seeking job designs that provide high levels of performance and a satisfying job and work environment.

Soft technology Technology for applying computer software and other techniques to support managers of manufacturing and service organizations.

Solution A set of values for the variables in a problem.

Specifications Design characteristics defined by targets and tolerances.

Statistical process control A method of using control charts to identify and eliminate assignable causes of variation and to monitor quality.

Strategic business units (SBUs) Families of products having similar characteristics or methods of production.

Strategic capacity planning The process of determining the types and amounts of resources required for implementing an organization's strategic plan.

Strategic planning The determination of long-term goals, policies, and plans for an organization.

Strategic service vision The definition of a service strategy, including identification of target markets, development of a service concept, design of the operating strategy, and design of the service delivery system.

Successive checking The design of subsequent processes that cannot operate on defective parts.

Suggestion system A means of encouraging employee participation in reducing costs or improving quality.

Supplier certification program A program that evaluates suppliers' quality, cost, and delivery to establish their ability to meet the purchaser's standards.

Suppliers Providers of goods and services.

Support processes Processes that are critical to production and delivery but do not drive the creation of products and services.

Synchronous manufacturing Systematic, efficient movement of material through a manufacturing facility to meet market demand.

Tangibles Physical facilities, equipment, or appearance of employees that contribute to the perception of service quality.

Tardiness The amount by which completion time exceeds the due date.

Team A small number of people committeed to a common purpose.

Theoretical capacity A system's maximum output capability, with no adjustments for scheduled maintenance, unplanned downtime, shutdowns, or other interruptions.

Theory of constraints (TOC) The basis for **constraint management**.

Time phasing Adding the dimension of time to inventory-status data.

Time series A set of observations measured at successive points in time or over successive periods of time.

Time-series models Statistical forecasting models based on extrapolation of historical data.

Time standard The amount of time needed to perform a task by a trained operator working at a normal pace and by the prescribed method.

Time study The development of time standards through stopwatch observation.

Tolerances Product specifications that define the precision required to achieve performance.

Total cycle time The time needed to meet a customer's requirements.

Total productive maintenance A process that keeps equipment functional and reliable through continuous employee involvement in improving equipment operation.

Total productivity The ratio of total output to total input.

Total quality management (TQM) An integrative management concept of continuously improving the quality of delivered goods and services through the participation of all levels and functions of the organization.

Traffic The daily management of transportation.

Transportation problem The problem of determining how much to ship from each origin to each destination to minimize total distribution costs.

Transportation tableau A table showing origins, destinations, routes, costs, supplies, and demands in a transportation problem; it facilitates the solution algorithm calculations.

Trend A long-run shift or movement in a time series that is observable over several periods.

Uniform plant loading A method of smoothing variable demand on a firm's resources.

Utilization factor Probability that a server is busy.

Validation In simulation, the process of determining that a simulation model accurately represents the real-world system it is designed to simulate.

Value Quality related to price.

Value analysis (1) The process of trying to reduce product costs by substituting less expensive materials, redesigning nonessential parts, and so on. (2) The review of product costs to evaluate their contribution to product value.

Value engineering The process of trying to minimize product costs during the product design phase by ensuring that each element serves its intended function.

Variable A physical quantity or any characteristic to which continuous values are assigned.

Variety A wide range of products and options.

Vendors See **suppliers**.

Vision A concept of where an organization is headed and what it intends to be in the future.

Voice of the customer Customers' requirements expressed in their own language.

Wagner-Whitin algorithm A method for finding optimal solutions to lot-sizing problems.

Warehousing The process of physically maintaining inventory.

Work center A uniquely defined group of workers or machines.

Work-in-process (WIP) inventory Inventory on the production floor at various stages of processing, between operations, or awaiting final assembly.

Work sampling A method of randomly observing work over a period of time to determine the types and frequencies of activities performed.

Work measurement Methods for developing time standards for work tasks.

Work package A set of activities under the control of one department or manager.

Work sampling A method of randomly observing work over a period of time to obtain a distribution of activities.

World class Characterization of a company that can meet customer demands in price, quality, and time at low cost and that has achieved a high degree of excellence in its products, processes, and business support systems.

Index